Digital Literacy:
Skills & Strategies

Digital Literacy:
Skills & Strategies

Editors

Laura Nicosia, PhD
James F. Nicosia, PhD

Salem Press
A Division of EBSCO Information Services, Inc.
Ipswich, Massachusetts

GREY HOUSE PUBLISHING

Publisher's Cataloging-In-Publication Data
(Prepared by The Donohue Group, Inc.)

Names: Nicosia, Laura M., editor. | Nicosia, James F., editor.
Title: Digital literacy : skills & strategies / editors, Laura Nicosia & James F. Nicosia, Montclair State University, New Jersey.
Description: Ipswich, Massachusetts : Salem Press, a division of EBSCO Information Services, Inc. ; Amenia, NY : Grey House Publishing, [2022] | Includes bibliographical references and index.
Identifiers: ISBN 9781637003923
Subjects: LCSH: Computer literacy. | Information technology. | Digital media.
Classification: LCC QA76.9.C64 D54 2022 | DDC 004–dc23

FIRST PRINTING
PRINTED IN THE UNITED STATES OF AMERICA

TABLE OF CONTENTS

PUBLISHER'S NOTE

Salem Press is pleased to announce our *Digital Literacy: Skills & Strategies* volume, a carefully curated selection of essays aimed at increasing awareness and understanding of the changing digital landscape in education and in society at large.

Digital technology is creating a progressively borderless world, one in which ideas and information can be shared in a decentralized manner. Along with this democratization, however, has come misinformation (unwitting or deliberate), data privacy issues, and all manner of cybercrime. Digital literacy—broadly defined as understanding and being able to use digital devices and technologies such as internet platforms and social media—has become an essential component to living, working, and taking part in education in modern society. Critical thinking skills and science and data literacy are paramount to maneuvering the digital information environment with confidence.

This new volume explores a wide range of topics for those wishing to augment their technological skills and comprehension. Making sense of how devices, software, and digital platforms operate can help in navigating many of the technologies that have become part of daily life. Taking a look back at how computers and later technologies developed sheds light on how profound an effect digital technology has had on humanity, with developments such as artificial intelligence raising questions about what it even means to be human. Access to digital technology plays an important role in determining individual opportunity, and several efforts are underway to lessen the digital divide.

Digital Literacy: Skills & Strategies begins with a comprehensive introduction written by volume editors Laura Nicosia and James F. Nicosia that clarifies the scope of the volume in relation to the ever-evolving nature of technology. This is followed by 174 entries written by technological, educational, and legal experts. Topics include assessing digital literacy, coding in the curriculum, data management, the Freedom of Information Act, game-based learning, identity theft, online safety, open source, social impacts of cybercrime, and virtual reality, to name a few. Categories begin with a brief introduction, followed by a background on the topic, and end with a list of reference sources for readers to explore.

This work also contains helpful appendices, including:

- Charts and graphs from federal and other sources;
- Glossary;
- Timeline;
- Websites and Organizations;
- Bibliography;
- Subject Index

Salem Press extends appreciation to all involved in the development and production of this work. Names and affiliations of contributors follow the Editor' Introduction.

Digital Literacy: Skills & Strategies, as well as all Salem Press reference books, is available in print and as an e-book. Please visit www.salempress.com for more information.

INTRODUCTION

Digital Literacy: Consuming, Creating, Collaborating, and Communicating in the Electronic Age

Depending on the context and the field of inquiry, the concept of digital literacy can be applied very rigidly or very liberally. Indeed, etymologically, the first word in the term, "digital," refers to the manipulation of one's fingers, but that is certainly not a definition that would apply today. Most readers selecting this book are likely to bring with them a preconceived notion of just what digital literacy entails and may find entries listed within it to be too narrow, too broad, or, alternatingly, both. The word "digital" presents itself in the average reader's mind as, most probably, in opposition to the word "analog," in the technological sense. That is, technology of a computerized nature, wherein any task is accomplished by a series of computer chips interacting with each other via binary coding, is what they may consider "digital." As such, loosely considered, this is the foundation from which we proceed.

Technologically, the information age owes almost all its advances to the computer chip. Little occurs in our everyday world, and little occurs in the minutiae of almost all professional fields, without the use of a computer. In that sense, the discussion of all things twenty-first century defines digital literacy. That being said, a volume encompassing "all things twenty-first century" would be a large volume, indeed.

This book aims to introduce users to explanations of cutting-edge, as well as everyday, technology—explaining these technologies and their primary elements through clear prose informed by expert analysis. The terms in this book may serve to augment the understanding of those who are unfamiliar with today's digital tools, those with strong foundations of the postmodern world's technological conceptions, and those who will benefit from defining technologies that even a decade ago might not have existed. This is a timely volume that, by definition, must also begin an immediate descent into obsolescence as time accrues.

Johannes Gutenberg's printing press (1440) revolutionized how we see, understand, and define our places within this universe. The printed word began a democratization of knowledge, fostered the groundwork for a modern, knowledge-based economy, and in some ways ushered in modernity itself. Information became both a product and a tool that required societies to reframe their understanding of what is assumed to be true and what is deemed useful. As a result, there was a dramatic shift in the epistemology of the age.

Digital technologies and ubiquitous data on the internet have transformed our lives and our civilization yet again. Immediate access to information, rapid marketing and deployment of new technologies, shifting definitions of public versus private lives, and emergent participatory media have prompted us to revisit and reconsider our personal, intellectual, emotional, social, and political epistemologies and literacies.

Like any technology before it (how notebooks and pencils changed education in the nineteenth century!), digital technology has changed the way we teach and learn, communicate and listen, work and play. The new ways we may interact—along with the merely improved and "different-but-perhaps-not-improved" methodologies—bring with them possibilities and problems from varied social, political, economic, recreational, and educational perspectives.

Early versions of this collection considered—and entries within here occasionally do use—terms like "twenty-first century technology" and "computer literacy" as synonyms for digital literacy. Indeed, the technological landscape of the twenty-first century inevitably incorporates computers so frequently that referring specifically to them becomes redundant. But one thing remains certain: those who want to remain productive members of society must acquire, and then retain, digital literacy. This includes, but is not limited to, the technical, social, and critical thinking skills that allow us to participate in the twenty-first century in meaningful ways.

The digital world, a term that itself will eventually become outmoded as it expands profoundly, and literate members of the global society—which, invariably, the world has become—must keep pace with the technological additions to everyday living, working, and communicating. This volume thus includes forays into the social, technical, and critical thinking skills that empower users to be collaboratively, linguistically, analytically, and creatively proficient across a breadth of educational, economic, professional, technological, and communication landscapes.

Overview

The title of this volume, *Digital Literacy: Skills & Strategies*, presupposes that readers will understand that—while there is still a deep dependency on the original use of reading and writing as the cornerstones of literacy—*digital* literacy is an evolving and dynamic skillset. Achieving digital literacy thus requires a high level of comfort and familiarity with many things internet and all things computer related.

As with all technology-enhanced activities, becoming digitally literate involves the acquisition of new competencies. These skillsets help users to learn how to *use* digital tools and to understand the end product of what one is producing, retrieving, synthesizing, sharing, or collaborating on, while *using* those tools. Digital literacy is both an ability and a product.

Digital literacies evolve as new technologies emerge, and as shopworn tools (technologies that become obsolete or dated) diminish in use. Consequently, digital literacy is an ongoing process that will never end. Besides being a life-long endeavor, the continual pursuit of digital literacy involves using a set of tools across various discourses and modes. Within the realm of these evolving literacies, users interact, produce, share, and engage with others to create a more participatory culture of digitally literate, worldly citizens who navigate their lives beyond print literacy. Ultimately, digital literacy allows users to participate in online lives while fostering the democratization of data, products, and facts.

Thinking about Critical Thinking

Critical thinking regarding the authority of data and textual authorship is an urgent facet of digital literacy. In other words, we must repeatedly ask ourselves questions such as, "How do we know something to be true and accurate?" and "How do we develop this state of thinking as we are learning about digital facts and big data?" The answers to such questions point to the import of this collection.

The more we understand the vocabulary and facts *about* digital content and activities, the more judicious users can be. Once secure in what one is doing while culling data and participating in online activities, users can become *content creators* (producers of knowledge, products, and digital artifacts) rather than consumers of others' contents—and can do so safely and with familiarity rather than fear.

Identity Theft and Other Dangers

As a correlative to being a digital creator, users must be made aware of the dangers of online activities. As in any arena where large groups meet, the internet has its fair share of users with questionable intent—criminals who seek to steal users' personal and financial information, for instance. Identity theft is at an all-time high, and much of that is the result of users divulging information that is sensitive on sites that are dubious or not secure. Statistics vary depending on sources, but it is agreed that there is an identity theft nearly every 14 seconds with upwards of fifty percent of Americans having their online identities jeopardized between 2020 and 2022. A great deal of the rise in these cases can be attributed to the Covid pandemic, when much of our personal and professional lives shifted from brick-and-mortar buildings to online activities. This collection has numerous essays that discuss internet safety, identity theft, computer viruses, fraud, and so on.

Along with reading the essays in this volume, users should consider the role of critical thinking before venturing onto sites that ask for sensitive information: passwords, birthdates, addresses, phone numbers, and so on. One of the most overlooked yet essential foundations for safety in the digital age is as follows: to be critical thinkers regarding digital literacy, users must first be strong in print literacy (for there is much reading, and much interpretation of that reading, done online). One must be able to ascertain the differences between *good* and *bad* data, misinformation, "alternate facts," and even information that is purposely planted to distract users from the truth (malinformation).

In this sense, digital and information literacy are closely connected with education itself (both formal and informal). Just as readers often question the information in printed tabloids or pamphlets, users should grow comfortable raising questions about who is producing an online site or app. While the internet is often considered the great democratizer, it is also made up of sites and products that have advertisers and financial backers. Fancy websites with all the "bells and whistles" are often the products of those with the most money, power, and access. One must not equate simple, clean sites with low-brow status. Users must get comfortable questioning who gets to produce and valorize various modes of information, whose ideas, apps, and sites get circulated and discussed, and whose get marginalized or pushed down on search results.

Because we must recognize these kinds of inequities that exist on the internet, we must also acknowledge the gaps that exist between those who engage with and participate in online endeavors and those who do not. There are people for whom access to reliable and reasonably priced internet is difficult, if not impossible. There are people who do not engage with anything online and even shy away from smart phones or smart devices entirely. This disconnect or gap is called the "digital divide." If in some small way this volume bridges that gap, we are more than delighted to have taken part in its creation.

Laura Nicosia

James F. Nicosia

Montclair State University

CONTRIBUTORS

Michael Adams
CUNY Graduate Center

Michael Auerbach
Marblehead, MA

Ashley Baker
Pernod Ricard

Craig Belanger
Journal of Advancing Technology

Raymond D. Benge
Tarrant County College

Kermin Bhot
Humber College

Tyler Biscontini
Independent Scholar

Jennifer Bouchard
Western Connecticut State University

Jill Bronfman
University of California at Hastings

Joseph I. Brownstein
Johns Hopkins University

Cait Caffrey
Northeast Editing

Shaunté Chácon
Independent Scholar

Marjee Chmiel
University of Maryland

Nancy W. Comstock
College Misericordia

Kathryn Cook
University of North Carolina at Chapel Hill

Patrick G. Cooper
Salem State University

Kehley Coviello
Independent Scholar

Joy Crelin
Independent Scholar

Trevor Cunnington
Independent Scholar

Joseph Dewey
University of Pittsburgh

Myra Din
Brooklyn Law School

Donald R. Dixon
California State University, Sacramento

Matt Donnelly
Loyola Marymount University

Bethany Groff Dorau
Historic New England

Sally Driscoll
Fairfield University

Mark Dziak
Northeast Editing

Maya Eagleton
Pima Community College

Patricia S. Edens
Medical Writer

Marlanda English
Capella University

Andrew Farrell
Independent Scholar

Andrew M. Forman
Hofstra University

Justin D. García
Indiana University, Bloomington

Ian Gill
Independent Scholar

Melissa A. Gill
David A Clarke School of Law

Kristen P. Goessling
Pennsylvania State University

Ursula Gorham
University of Maryland

Sage L. Graham
Independent Scholar

Jim Greene
University of Tennessee

Glenda Griffin
Sam Houston State University

Adam Groff
Newburyport, MA

Allison Hahn
St. Norbert College

Stuart A. Hargreaves
Chinese University of Hong Kong

Angela Harmon
Independent Scholar

Katharina Hering
Georgetown Law

Micah L. Issitt
Independent Scholar

Karen A. Kallio
University of Massachusetts Amherst

Jane E. Kirtley
Northwestern University

Rebecca Kivak
Skirts and Scuffs

Gayla Koerting
University of South Dakota

Jennifer Kretchmar
University of North Carolina at Chapel Hill

Bill Kte'pi
Independent Scholar

Jack Lasky
Northeast Editing

M. Lee
Independent Scholar

Charles E. MacLean
Indiana Tech Law School

J. N. Manuel
Independent Scholar

Michael Mazzei
Independent Scholar

Douglas B. McKechnie
United States Air Force Academy

Roman Meinhold
Assumption University

Daniel J. Metcalfe
DoJ Office of Information and Privacy

Elizabeth Mohn
Northeast Editing

Jake D. Nicosia
Stevens Institute of Technology

James F. Nicosia
Montclair State University

Laura Nicosia
Montclair State University

Gretchen Nobahar
Washington Area Metropolitan Transit Authority

R. Craig Philips
Michigan State University

Luca Prono
Bologna, Italy

Elizabeth Rholetter Purdy
Georgia State University

Richard M. Renneboog
Independent Scholar

Wylene Rholetter
Auburn University

Mari Rich
NYU Tandon School of Engineering

Scott Russell
Indiana University

Ana Santos Rutschman
Uppsala University

John Richard Schrock
Independent Scholar

Richard Sheposh
Northeast Editing

Elaine Sherman
Independent Scholar

Noëlle Sinclair
Independent Scholar

Kerry Skemp
Enprecis, Inc.

Rich Stein
Independent Scholar

Alexander Stingl
University of Warwick

Robert E. Stoffels
Independent Scholar

John Teehan
Independent Scholar

Jennifer A. Vadeboncoeur
University of British Columbia

Maura Valentino
Central Washington University

Noelle Vance
Colorado State University

Joseph C. Viola
Independent Scholar

Linda Volonino
Canisius College

Kathy Warnes
University of Toledo

Donald A. Watt
Middletown, Idaho

Nathan A. B. Watt
Independent Scholar

Bethany White
Mississippi College

George M. Whitson
University of Texas at Tyler

Ruth A. Wienclaw
University of Memphis

Max Winter
University of Iowa

Robin L. Wulffson
*American College of Obstetrics and
Gynecology*

Scott Zimmer
Alliant International University

3D PRINTING

Introduction

Three-dimensional (3D) printing, also known as "additive manufacturing" (AM), comprises several automated processes for building 3D objects from layers of plastic, paper, glass, or metal. 3D printing creates strong, light 3D objects quickly and efficiently. It builds 3D objects by adding successive layers of material onto a platform. This process differs from traditional, or subtractive, manufacturing, also called "machining." In machining, material is removed from a starting sample until the desired structure remains. Most AM processes use less raw material and are therefore less wasteful than machining.

Background

The first AM process was developed in the 1980s, using liquid resin hardened by ultraviolet (UV) light. By the 2000s, several different AM processes had been developed. Most of those processes use liquid, powder, or extrusion techniques. Combined with complex computer modeling and robotics, AM could launch a new era in manufacturing in which even complex mechanical objects could be created by AM.

The earliest AM technique was stereolithography (SLA), patented in 1986 by Chuck Hull. SLA uses liquid resin or polymer hardened by UV light to create a 3D object. A basic SLA printer consists of an elevator platform suspended in a tank filled with light-sensitive liquid polymer. A UV laser hardens a thin layer of resin. The platform is lowered, and the laser hardens the next layer, fusing it to the first. This process is repeated until the object is complete. The object is then cleaned and cured by UV. This technique is also called "vat photopolymerization" because it takes place within a vat of liquid resin. Various types of SLA printing processes have been given alternate names, such as "photofabrication" and "photosolidification."

Also in the 1980s, engineers at the University of Texas created an alternate process that uses powdered solids instead of liquid. Selective layer sintering (SLS), or powder bed fusion, heats powdered glass, metal, ceramic, or plastic in a powder bed until the material is "sintered." To sinter something is to

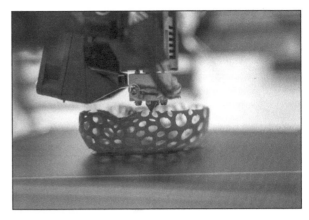

3-D printing machine in action. Photo via iStock/kynny. [Used under license.]

cause its particles to fuse through heat or pressure without liquefying it. A laser is used to sinter thin layers of the powder selectively, with the unfused powder underneath giving structural support. The platform is lowered and the powder compacted as the laser passes over the object again.

Software and Modeling

3D printing begins with a computer-aided design (CAD) drawing or 3D scan of an object. Those drawings or scans are usually saved in a digital file format known as STL, originally short for "stereolithography" but since given other meanings, such as "surface tessellation language." STL files "tessellate" the object—that is, cover its surface in a repeated pattern of shapes. Though any shape can be used, STL files use a series of nonoverlapping triangles to model the curves and angles of a 3D object. Errors in the file may need repair. "Slices" of the STL file determine the number and thickness of the layers of material needed.

Extrusion Printing

Material extrusion printing heats plastic or polymer filament and extrudes it through nozzles to deposit a layer of material on a platform. One example of this process is called "fused deposition modeling" (FDM). As the material cools, the platform is lowered, and another layer is added atop the last layer. Creating extruded models often requires the use of a structural support to prevent the object from collapsing. Extrusion printing is the most affordable and commonly available 3D printing process.

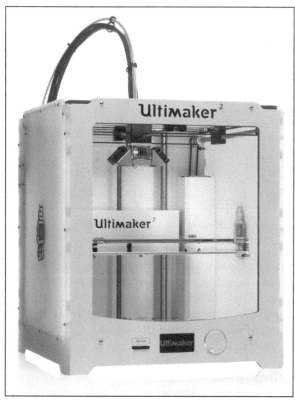

3-D printing machine. Photo by Guy Sie, via Wikimedia Commons.

Emerging and Alternative Methods

Several other 3D printing methods are also emerging. In material jetting, an inkjet printer head deposits liquefied plastic or other light-sensitive material onto a surface, which is then hardened with UV light. Another inkjet printing technique is binder jetting, which uses an inkjet printer head to deposit drops of glue-like liquid into a powdered medium. The liquid then soaks into and solidifies the medium. In directed energy deposition (DED), metal wire or powder is deposited in thin layers over a support before being melted with a laser or other heat source. Sheet lamination fuses together thin sheets of paper, metal, or plastic with adhesive. The resulting object is then cut with a laser or other cutting tool to refine the shape. This method is less costly but also less accurate than others.

The Future of 3D Printing

While AM techniques have been in use since the 1980s, engineers believe that the technology has not yet reached its full potential. Its primary use has been in rapid prototyping, in which a 3D printer is used to quickly create a 3D model that can be used to guide production. In many cases, 3D printing can create objects that are stronger, lighter, and more customizable than objects made through machining. Printed parts are already being used for planes, race cars, medical implants, and dental crowns, among other items. Because AM wastes far less material than subtractive manufacturing, it is of interest for conservation, waste management, and cost reduction. The technology could also democratize manufacturing, as small-scale 3D printers allow individuals and small businesses to create products that traditionally required industrial manufacturing facilities. However, intellectual property disputes could also occur more often as 3D printing becomes more widespread.

—*Micah L. Issitt*

References

Hutchinson, Lee. "Home 3D Printers Take Us on a Maddening Journey into Another Dimension." *Ars Technica*, 27 Aug. 2013, arstechnica.com/gadgets/2013/08/home-3d-printers-take-us-on-a-maddening-journey-into-another-dimension/.

Matulka, Rebecca, and Matty Greene. "How 3D Printers Work." *Energy.gov*, 19 June 2014, www.energy.gov/articles/how-3d-printers-work.

"The Printed World." *Economist*, 10 Feb. 2011, www.economist.com/briefing/2011/02/10/the-printed-world.

A

ACCESS TO COMMUNICATIONS TECHNOLOGY

Introduction

Early proponents of digital communications technology believed that it would be a powerful tool for disseminating knowledge and advancing civilization. While there is little dispute that the internet has changed society radically in a relatively short period of time, there are many still unable to take advantage of the benefits it confers because of a lack of access. Whether the lack is due to economic, geographic, or demographic factors, this "digital divide" has serious societal repercussions, particularly as most aspects of life in the twenty-first century, including banking, health care, and education, are increasingly conducted online.

In its simplest terms, the digital divide refers to the gap between people who have easy, reliable access to the internet and those who do not. In the United States, that divide occurs in varying contexts. The Federal Communications Commission (FCC) reports that in urban areas, 97 percent of Americans have access to high-speed broadband service. However, only 65 percent of Americans living in rural areas have access to that service. In all, according to the FCC, some 30 million Americans cannot access the benefits of the digital age because of deficiencies in the broadband infrastructure.

Even in regions with good connectivity, there are differences in which households have access to computers and the internet because of socioeconomic factors. A study conducted by the Pew Research Center in 2019 found that 46 percent of US adults with household incomes below $30,000 per year did not have a computer at home, while 44 percent did not have broadband internet at home. Race and ethnicity are also significant factors in the United States' digital divide: the Pew Research Center reported in 2019 that 42 percent of African American adults and 43 percent of Hispanic adults did not have a desktop or laptop computer at home, compared to only 18 percent of Caucasian adults. Individuals without home computers must instead use smartphones or public facilities such as libraries—which restrict how long a patron can remain online—severely limiting their ability to fill out job applications and complete homework effectively.

There is also a marked divide between digital access in highly developed nations and that which is available in other parts of the world. Globally, the International Telecommunication Union (ITU), a specialized agency within the United Nations that deals with information and communication technologies (ICTs), estimates that as many as 3 billion people living in developing countries may still be unconnected by 2023.

Background

The ITU, which had been founded in 1865 to manage the first international telegraph networks, began publishing the ICT Development Index (IDI) in 2009 and continued to do so on an annual basis through 2017. The ITU did not publish the IDI in 2018 or 2019.

The IDI combines eleven key indicators into one benchmark measure that can be used to monitor and compare advancements in ICT (information and communications technology) between countries, and over time. The index is aimed at first tracking individual nations' ICT readiness: the level of networked infrastructure and access to ICTs as measured by number of fixed-telephone subscriptions, mobile-cellular telephone subscriptions, international internet bandwidth per internet user, households with a computer, and households with internet access.

Next, ICT intensity (the level of use of ICTs in the country) is examined by surveying how many individuals use the internet, how many have fixed broadband subscriptions, and how many have mobile-broadband subscriptions. Finally, a snapshot of ICT impact (the concrete outcomes of more efficient and effective ICT use) is taken by looking at mean years of schooling, gross secondary enrollment, and gross tertiary enrollment. Those factors serve as proxy indicators of overall skills and abilities.

In 2017, the United States ranked at number sixteen in the IDI. The top five spots were taken by Iceland, South Korea, Switzerland, Denmark, and the United Kingdom.

Accessibility for People with Physical Disabilities

People with physical disabilities are also sometimes subject to a digital divide—a state of affairs that is easily overlooked by those who can effortlessly manipulate a mouse, hear output from speakers, and clearly see whatever appears on a screen. True accessibility means, however, that everyone can use the same technology as anyone else, regardless of their level of vision, hearing, or manual dexterity.

In the United States, the Americans with Disabilities Act (ADA) sets forth guidelines for digital accessibility, although compliance has not always been widespread. To address that issue, user experience designers are increasingly ensuring that technology can be employed successfully by people with a wide range of functional abilities. Users of desktop computers, for example, can now input information in multiple ways, including via mouse, keyboard, or speech-recognition software.

Why It Matters

A constantly growing number of essential services are conducted digitally. Thus, those on the wrong side of the digital divide miss out on the long-term benefits of innovative technology. In addition, their day-to-day lives become exponentially harder, as information vital to their health, safety, and financial stability is provided online. Consider, for example, the contrast between clicking a few links on a Department of Motor Vehicles website and waiting for hours to get in-person help at a local Department of Motor Vehicles (DMV) office. Most important, the digital divide perpetuates economic inequality and impedes social mobility given how often school coursework, even for the very youngest students, involves computer use. Additionally, many well-paying jobs rely on employees being at least somewhat computer literate.

There are strong indications that a citizenry with unimpeded access to the internet can more easily engage civically, leading to healthier democracies and participatory decision-making. Consider the case of North Korea, whose regime has greatly limited global internet access for its citizens. Growing a more robust information infrastructure can also be a pathway to economic growth for less developed nations, since ICTs tend to be associated with marked improvements in productivity. There are, in short, clear benefits to closing the digital divide—and myriad ramifications to allowing people to remain members of what has been called an "analog underclass."

—*Mari Rich*

References

Anderson, Monica, and Madhumitha Kumar. "Digital Divide Persists Even as Lower-Income Americans Make Gains in Tech Adoption." *Pew Research Center*, 7 May 2019, www.pewresearch.org/fact-tank/2019/05/07/digital-divide-persists-even-as-lower-income-americans-make-gains-in-tech-adoption/.

"Bridging the Digital Divide for All Americans." *Federal Communications Commission*, www.fcc.gov/about-fcc/fcc-initiatives/bridging-digital-divide-all-americans.

"Digital Accessibility." *Partnership on Employment & Accessible Technology*, www.peatworks.org/futureofwork/a11y.

"The ICT Development Index (IDI): Conceptual Framework and Methodology." *International Telecommunication Union*, www.itu.int/en/ITU-D/Statistics/Pages/publications/mis/methodology.aspx.

James, Jeffrey. "The ICT Development Index and the Digital Divide: How Are They Related?" *Technological Forecasting and Social Change*, vol. 79, no. 3, 2012, 587–94, doi.org/10.1016/j.techfore.2011.08.010.

Li, Austen, and Jacqueline Sussman. "Bridging the Digital Divide." *Wharton School of the University of Pennsylvania Public Policy Initiative*, 10 Apr. 2018, publicpolicy.wharton.upenn.edu/live/news/2420-bridging-the-digital-divide/for-students/blog/news.

Perrin, Andrew, and Erica Turner. "Smartphones Help Blacks, Hispanics Bridge Some—But Not All—Digital Gaps with Whites." *Pew Research Center*, 20 Aug. 2019, www.pewresearch.org/fact-tank/2019/08/20/smartphones-help-blacks-hispanics-bridge-some-but-not-all-digital-gaps-with-whites/.

"Time to Close the Digital Divide." *Financial Times*, 22 May 2020, www.ft.com/content/df6d1cd2-9b6e-11ea-adb1-529f96d8a00b.

ALGORITHMS

Introduction

An algorithm is a set of steps to be followed in order to solve a particular type of problem. Having originated within the field of mathematics, algorithms make it easier for mathematicians to think of better ways to solve certain types of problems, because looking at the steps needed to reach a solution sometimes helps them to see where an algorithm can be made more efficient by eliminating redundant steps or using different methods of calculation. Algorithms are also key to computer science and enable the automation of various processes, including the generation and manipulation of curves in computer-aided design (CAD) programs.

Background

The word *algorithm* originally came from the name of a Persian mathematician, Al-Khwarizmi, who lived in the ninth century CE and wrote a book about the ideas of an earlier mathematician from India, Brahmagupta. At first the word simply referred to the author's description of how to solve equations using Brahmagupta's number system, but as time passed it took on a more general meaning.

First it was used to refer to the steps required to solve any mathematical problem, and later it broadened still further to include almost any kind of method for handling a particular situation. The concept has been analogized to a recipe for baking a cake; just as the recipe describes a method for accomplishing a goal (baking the cake) by listing each step that must be taken throughout the process, an algorithm is an explanation of how to solve a problem that describes each step necessary.

Algorithms in Mathematics

Algorithms are often used in mathematical instruction because they provide students with concrete steps to follow, even before the underlying operations are fully comprehended. There are algorithms for most mathematical operations, including subtraction, addition, multiplication, and division. For example, a well-known algorithm for performing subtraction is known as the "left-to-right algorithm." As its name suggests, this algorithm requires one to first line up the two numbers one wishes to find the difference between so that the units digits are in one column, the tens digits in another column, and so forth.

Next, one begins in the leftmost column and subtracts the lower number from the upper, writing the result below. This step is then repeated for the next column to the right, until the values in the units column have been subtracted from one another. At this point the results from the subtraction of each column, when read left to right, constitute the answer to the problem.

By following these steps, it is possible for a subtraction problem to be solved even by someone still in the process of learning the basics of subtraction. This demonstrates the power of algorithms both for performing calculations and for use as a source of instructional support.

Algorithms in Computer-Aided Design (CAD)

Algorithms are also important within the field of computer science. For example, without algorithms, a computer would have to be programmed with the exact answer to every set of numbers that an equation could accept in order to solve an equation—an impossible task. By programming the computer with the appropriate algorithm, the computer can follow the instructions needed to solve the problem, regardless of which values are used as inputs.

Algorithms are crucial to a wide range of computer technologies, facilitating the sorting and analysis of data, the use of automated decision-making processes, and other key functions. In CAD

Ada Lovelace's diagram from "note G," the first published computer algorithm. Photo via Wikimedia Commons. [Public domain.]

programs, algorithms are particularly useful in automating the drawing of shapes that would otherwise require time-consuming calculations. For example, CAD programs use algorithms to generate curves and to enable designers to manipulate those curves in accordance with their needs.

—*Scott Zimmer*

References

Cormen, Thomas H. *Algorithms Unlocked.* MIT Press, 2013.

Ferguson, R. Stuart. *Practical Algorithms for 3D Computer Graphics.* 2nd ed., AK Peters/CRC Press, 2013.

Fitter, Hetal N., Akash B. Pandey, Divyang D. Patel, and Jitendra M. Mistry. "A Review on Approaches for Handling Bezier Curves in CAD for Manufacturing." *Procedia Engineering*, vol. 97, 2014, pp. 1155–66.

MacCormick, John. *Nine Algorithms That Changed the Future: The Ingenious Ideas That Drive Today's Computers.* Princeton UP, 2012.

O'Leary, Timothy, Linda O'Leary, and Daniel O'Leary. *Computing Essentials 2021.* McGraw-Hill, 2020.

Parker, Matt. *Things to Make and Do in the Fourth Dimension: A Mathematician's Journey through Narcissistic Numbers, Optimal Dating Algorithms, at Least Two Kinds of Infinity, and More.* Farrar, 2014.

Sarkar, Jayanta. *Computer Aided Design: A Conceptual Approach.* CRC Press, 2017.

Schapire, Robert E., and Yoav Freund. *Boosting: Foundations and Algorithms.* MIT Press, 2012.

Steiner, Christopher. *Automate This: How Algorithms Came to Rule Our World.* Penguin, 2012.

Valiant, Leslie. *Probably Approximately Correct: Nature's Algorithms for Learning and Prospering in a Complex World.* Basic, 2013.

ANCHORED INSTRUCTION

Introduction

Anchored instruction is a technology-based problem-solving teaching method. The method engages students in a problem-solving process that is tied, or anchored, to a realistic technology-based video presentation. Technology is used to present the story or anchor because it is a vehicle to engage students in the higher-order thinking skills they will need to solve the problems. Anchored instruction falls within the social constructivist paradigm, and is closely associated with situated learning. Anchored instruction is more relevant for middle school students, since the problems are difficult but not as complex as true problem-based learning (PBL).

Background

Anchored instruction engages students in a problem-solving process that is tied or anchored to a realistic technology-based presentation. The instruction is anchored to a story, not to a lecture, and video clips provide students with relevant details to help solve the problem. The stories, or anchors, are designed to "motivate students and help them learn to think and reason about important, complex problems" (CTGV, 1992a). In addition, video technology is used to present the story because it is a vehicle to engage students in the higher-order thinking skills they will need to solve the problems. Also, video

results in superior memory because information is dual-coded as both verbal and nonverbal representations.

Dr. John D. Bransford is credited with developing the anchored instruction theory while working at the Cognition and Technology Group at Vanderbilt. From 1984 to 1999, Dr. Bransford was the director of the Learning Technology Center at Vanderbilt, and under his leadership the CTGV grew from seven people the first year to more than 100 in 1999. Some of the technology-based programs developed during that time include the Jasper Woodbury Problem Solving Series in Mathematics, the Scientists in Action Series, and the Little Planet Literacy Series. Many of the programs are being used in schools around the globe.

Roots in Social Constructivism

Anchored instruction falls within the social constructivist paradigm, and it is closely associated with situated learning. Constructivism is a broad framework and philosophy of education where learning is an active process of knowledge construction. Constructivism is often contrasted with objectivist or behaviorist models. In behaviorism, learning is a process of conditioning and the mind is an empty vessel that the teacher passively fills—it is a teacher-centered approach. On the other hand, constructivist approaches are often described as learner-centered because the learner has control over the learning process, and students actively construct knowledge

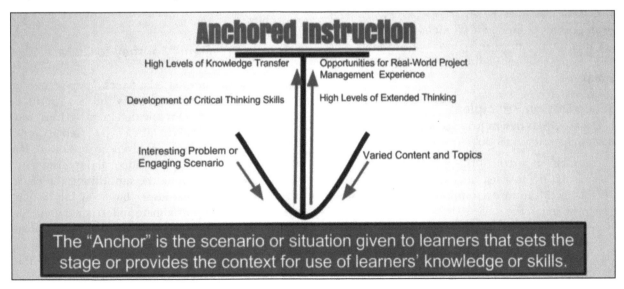

Image by Evan Glazer, via Wikimedia Commons.

and are encouraged to develop metacognitive processes. Learner control is a critical aspect of the anchored instruction model. Furthermore, in anchored instruction, students actively engage in critical thinking to solve the problems presented in the story anchor.

Macro Contexts

Anchored instruction is more relevant for middle school students, since the problems are difficult but not as complex as true PBL. However, anchored instruction sets the stage for PBL at the secondary and postsecondary levels. The anchored environments are sometimes referred to as macro contexts because students must work out a solution to a complex set of connected problems. It is important when selecting and designing the macro context that students, who are novices, can use some of their available knowledge just like experts. Experts can learn to adjust their thinking to solve a problem.

In a 2011 study of high school students, data showed a highly significant difference between students who studied using the anchored instruction and the teacher-centered. Students said the anchored instruction video made their class interesting and interactive, enabled them to study involving realistic situation, motivated them to learn on their own, promoted collaboration, allowed them to learn about environment aside from statistics, provided them episodic memory cues, and changed their perception of statistics. The students also said that they liked the new approach in learning compared to their usual classwork. Finally, cooperative learning is an important component of anchored instruction, but it is important to recognize that teachers may need to provide scaffolding to avoid the pitfalls of group work.

Seven Design Principles

There are seven design principles used with the anchored instruction model:

1. Anchored instruction is a generative learning format because learners are motivated to construct or produce a solution to the open-ended problem in the story;
2. Anchored instruction is a video-based presentation that enhances textbook learning with audio, animation, graphics, simulation, color, and realism;

3. The narrative format of anchored instruction makes it more authentic and the realistic storyline enriches the context of the characters and events;
4. The complexity of the problem demands the learner's full attention and stimulates their curiosity to solve the problem;
5. Data are embedded in the story so that learners must explore the content; students must also learn how to identify pertinent data because not all data in the story are necessary to solve the problem;
6. Learners are given opportunities to transfer knowledge from one subject area, such as algebra, to other settings in the same subject area;
7. There are links to other areas of study within the storyline so that learning can occur across the curriculum.

Applications

A frequently mentioned anchored instruction program is the Jasper Woodbury Series, developed by CTGV in 1992. The video-based segments in the Jasper Series are approximately fifteen to twenty minutes in length, and designed to pose problems that grade 5+ students must solve through reasoning and effective communication. The students must solve the problems on their own before they can see how the characters in the video solved the problem. The problems are like traditional word problems in mathematics instruction, but are not as structured or explicit.

A Simple Problem: "Journey to Cedar Creek"

In the story "Journey to Cedar Creek," Jasper eagerly reads his newspaper and scours the ads for used boats. He finds a boat for sale that interests him, and he begins making plans to take a trip to Cedar Creek to see the boat. Students are given various bits of information throughout the video about distances, weather conditions, when the sun will set, the price of gas, how much cash Jasper has, how big his gas tank is, and the approximate miles per gallon his outboard motor will get. During the video, small problems come up that change the parameters of the trip planning. For example, along the way the shear pin in Jasper's outboard motor breaks, and he must have it repaired for a modest price at Dixon's Boat Repair. Even though Mr. Dixon did not charge a lot of money, Jasper now has a potential cash flow problem and wonders whether he has enough money for gas to get to Cedar Creek and back again. He also wonders if he has time to complete his trip before the sun sets.

After the students have finished watching the video, they are asked two questions: when should Jasper leave for home, and can he make it without running out of fuel? Since there is only one route Jasper can take, one mode of transportation, and a set budget, this is a relatively simple problem for the students to solve and involves approximately fifteen steps. In addition to the main problem, CTGV provides analogous and extension problems so that the teacher can focus more of the students' attention on the mathematics in the Jasper story. For example, analogous problems focus on the time and fuel sub-problems in the context of the original story where one to three factors have been changed. The "Journey to Cedar Creek" story is an example of a complex trip-planning problem.

A Complex Problem: "Rescue at Boone's Meadow"

A more difficult trip-planning problem is called "Rescue at Boone's Meadow." This video begins with Larry teaching Emily some basic facts about his ultralight airplane. A few weeks later, Emily takes her first solo flight in Larry's airplane, and Larry, Emily, and Jasper go out to supper to celebrate at Hilda's restaurant and service station. During their meal, Jasper tells his friends about a fishing trip he is planning to take in Boone's Meadow, which is a five-hour hike from Hilda's. While fishing, Jasper hears a gunshot and discovers a wounded eagle; he uses a two-way radio to call Hilda for help. Hilda tells Emily about Jasper's call, and Emily drives to the nearest veterinarian to ask for advice. Meanwhile, throughout the various scenes, clues are dropped about gas prices, speed limits, rates of fuel consumption, the ultralight plane's payload capacity, weather conditions, distances, and runway length requirements. Emily's challenge is to decide the quickest way to get the wounded eagle to the veterinarian, and how long the rescue will take. This problem is more complex because there is more than one route to take, two modes of transportation available, two speeds of travel, and two potential drivers. In other

words, there is no single right answer, and students are asked to justify any assumptions they make. Extension problems for this anchor include the addition of headwind and tailwind effects.

Classroom Applications

As can be seen from the story descriptions, students are engaged in Jasper's adventures because the context is realistic and they must find a solution to the characters' problems. Because students are generating their own ideas, they have a sense of ownership in the learning activity.

Teaching Enhanced Anchored Mathematics

An example of an anchored instruction video was developed by B. A. Bottge and his Teaching Enhanced Anchored Mathematics (TEAM) associates at the University of Wisconsin's Center for Education Research. The TEAM website contains a streamed online video of an anchored instruction story called "Fraction of the Cost." In this video, three students go on a quest to figure out if they can build a ramp for their skateboards. Teachers are encouraged to let students build a model of the skateboard ramp with Popsicle sticks. There is no log-in required to watch the online streamed video, and teachers can also request a free copy on compact disc/read-only memory (CD-ROM) by sending a written request to TEAM using their school's letterhead. In addition, teachers are encouraged to take advantage of the teacher training options provided by TEAM.

Case Technologies to Enhance Literacy Learning

Another collaboration on anchored instruction is the Case Technologies to Enhance Literacy Learning. According to the CTELL website, the goal of the project is "to improve children's reading achievement by re-conceptualizing teacher education through case-based, anchored instruction with multimedia cases delivered over the Internet." Each CTELL anchor video is approximately one hour in length, and the interface allows users to interact with the video segments in a random-access fashion.

Other Resources

Although there are few current videos developed specifically for anchored instruction, like the Jasper

Woodbury Series, there are several educational video producers whose material can be adapted to anchored instruction. Scholastic's Read 180 program is designed to help schools meet No Child Left Behind (NCLB) requirements, especially for struggling readers. Read 180 uses collaborative learning in small groups with video segments that are described as anchor DVDs on the company's website. Unitedstreaming is a service sold by Discovery Education, a division of Discovery Communications, and claims that more than half of all schools in the United States subscribe. BrainPop offers standards-based educational videos for K-8 schools. Although the BrainPop and united streaming websites do not specifically mention anchored instruction, many of the movies could be adapted for anchored instruction.

Further Insights

Bottge et al. have published many research reports about the effects of anchored instruction on academic achievement. His findings are encouraging, and students in several studies who participated in video-based instruction performed significantly better than students who solved traditional word problems. In addition, Bottge et al. found that students taught using anchored instruction were better able to maintain and transfer what they learned several weeks later when compared with students taught with traditional word problems. Other researchers also found that students were better able to transfer knowledge to an analogous task after exposure to anchored instruction. Furthermore, Langone, Malone, and Clinton found that students in an anchored instruction group outperformed students in the non-anchored group in an eight-week follow-up test, which provides further evidence that students exposed to anchored instruction retain more of what they learned. Finally, Glaser et al. studied the interactions between teachers and students, and found that student-teacher interactions more than doubled following an anchored instruction intervention, indicating more engagement by students in the learning process.

However, Bottge identifies several disadvantages of anchored instruction, especially when using this approach for students with disabilities. First, the difficulty level of anchored instruction problems is high and may be too hard for students with limited memory. Scaffolds must be in place to help students

handle the cognitive demands of the problem. Foster also points out that the video anchors have no mechanism to help students who are stuck or unmotivated. Second, there is a lack of detail about the skills and concepts measured in anchored instruction research, and there is a need for more specifics about what assessments are measured. Finally, teacher training is an important component of anchored instruction, and teachers need to make sure student groups are working cooperatively. For example, if the group process breaks down, weaker students may end up simply copying work done by stronger students.

Kurz and Batarelo conducted a study to determine if preservice teachers, who have not been given a presentation about the benefits of anchored instruction, are able to appreciate the significance of anchored instruction for their students, and to assess how they view their students' learning using anchored instruction. The study examined the reactions of four preservice teachers to "Rescue at Boone's Meadow" from the Jasper Woodbury Series. All four teachers found significance when using anchored instruction with their students, but the researchers believe this positive result at least partly came about because of opportunities the preservice teachers had to collaborate with each other and a knowledgeable mentor. The preservice teachers could see the benefits of a realistic problem-solving environment on their own, and the authors concluded that giving preservice teachers hands-on experience in the classroom was more beneficial than lectures about the advantages of anchored instruction. Furthermore, Kariuki and Duran found that anchored instruction was an effective way for preservice teachers to learn about and teach with technology tools.

AI for Students with Disabilities

Many authors have studied the use of anchored instruction with disabled students. Reith et al. examined the effect anchored instruction had on the length and level of teachers' responses to students' questions, the length and level of students' answers, and students' participation in the classroom activities. The results of the study supported the use of anchored instruction for students with disabilities. Reith et al. found that as teachers increased the length and level of their responses to students' questions, students reciprocated with longer and higher-level answers. In addition, school attendance improved and students seemed to be more actively engaged in the classroom activities.

Crews et al. followed up on the need for scaffolding with anchored instruction, and developed the Adventure Player, Anchored Interactive Learning Environment (AILE). The Adventure Player is a computer-based program that gives learners tools to solve the problem, but also helps them make the concepts associated with the problem explicit. In other words, the Adventure Player's tools "are designed with built-in scaffolds to assist students in bridging gaps in their knowledge of complex aspects of the problem-solving process" (Crews et al.). The Adventure Player was structured to provide scaffolds for "Rescue at Boone's Meadow" from the Jasper Woodbury Series. When students enter a plan of action, the program tells them if the action is valid, invalid, or incomplete. For example, walking to Boone's Meadow is a valid action, even though it may not be an ideal solution, but driving to Boone's Meadow is not valid because there is no road access. An incomplete action is flying the ultra-light plane to Boone's Meadow because a pilot is needed to use this option. Research results found that 79 percent of students using the Adventure Player system generated complete plans, compared to only 8 percent of students using just the video.

—Kathryn Cook

References

The Adventure of Jasper Woodbury. Peabody.vanderbilt. edu.

Bottge, B. A., M. Heinrichs, Z. Mehta, et al. "Teaching Mathematical Problem Solving to Middle School Students in Math, Technology Education, and Special Education Classrooms." *Research in Middle Level Education*, vol. 27, 2004, p. 17.

Bottge, B. A., E. Rueda, P. T. Laroque, et al. "Integrating Reform-Oriented Math Instruction in Special Education Settings." *Learning Disabilities Research and Practice*, vol. 22, 2007, pp. 96–109.

Cena, M. E., and J. P. Mitchell. "Anchored Instruction: A Model for Integrating the Language Arts Through Content Area Study." *Journal of Adolescent and Adult Literacy*, vol. 41, 1998, p. 559.

Chen, I. *Technology and Learning Environment: An Electronic Textbook.* Viking.coe.uh.edu.

Crews, T., G. Biswas, S. Goldman, and J. Bransford. "Anchored Interactive Learning Environments." *International Journal of AI in Education*, vol. 8, 1997, pp. 142–78.

CTELL—Case Technologies to Enhance Literacy Learning. Ctell.uconn.edu.

CTGV. "Anchored Instruction and Its Relationship to Situated Cognition." *Educational Researcher*, vol. 19, 1990, pp. 2–10.

___. "The Jasper Series as an Example of Anchored Instruction: Theory, Program Description, and Assessment Data." *Educational Psychologist*, vol. 27, 1992, pp. 291–315.

___. *Anchored Instruction in Science and Mathematics: Theoretical Basis, Developmental Projects, and Initial Research Findings.* SUNY P, 1992.

Faculty Spotlight: John Bransford. Depts.washington. edu/coe/news/facand#x005f;spotlight/brans-ford.html.

Foster, C. "Anchored Instruction. (Hoffman, B.)" *Encyclopaedia of Educational Technology.* Coe.sdsu. edu.

Glaser, C. W., H. J. Rieth, C. K. Kinzer, et al. "A Description of the Impact of Multimedia Anchored Instruction on Classroom Interactions." *Journal of Special Education Technology*, vol. 14, 1999, pp. 27–43.

Kariuki, M., and M. Duran. "Using Anchored Instruction to Teach Preservice Teachers to Integrate Technology in the Curriculum." *Journal of Technology and Teacher Education*, vol. 12, 2004, pp. 431–45.

Kim, A. "DVDs Poised to Become Future Teaching Tool." *T H E Journal*, vol. 30, 2002, pp. 2–3.

Klein, A. "As NCLB Waivers Take Hold, Revision of Law Remains Up in Air." *Education Week*, vol. 32, 2013, p. 25.

Kurz, T. L., and I. Batarelo. "Using Anchored Instruction to Evaluate Mathematical Growth and Understanding." *Journal of Educational Technology Systems*, vol. 33, 2004, pp. 421–36.

Langone, J., D. M. Malone, and G. N. Clinton. "The Effects of Technology-Enhanced Anchored Instruction on the Knowledge of Preservice Special Educators." *Teacher Education and Special Education*, vol. 22, 1999, pp. 85–96.

Lee, M. *Anchored Instruction in a Situated Learning Environment.* Association for the Advancement of Computing in Education (AACE), 2002. (ERIC Document Reproduction Service No. ED477052).

Love, M. S. "Multimodality of Learning Through Anchored Instruction." *Journal of Adolescent and Adult Literacy,* vol. 48, 2004, pp. 300–310.

Prado, M. M., and R. S. Gravoso. "Improving High School Students' Statistical Reasoning Skills: A Case of Applying Anchored Instruction." *Asia-Pacific Education Researcher (De La Salle University Manila),* vol. 20, 2011, pp. 61–72.

"A Research Synthesis of the Literature on Multimedia Anchored Instruction in Preservice Teacher Education." *Journal of Special Education Technology,* vol. 26, 2011, pp. 1–22.

Rieth, H. J., D. P. Bryant, C. K. Kinzer, et al. "An Analysis of the Impact of Anchored Instruction on Teaching and Learning Activities in Two Ninth-Grade Language Arts Classes." *Remedial and Special Education,* vol. 24, 2003, p. 173.

Serafino, K., and T. Cicchelli. "Cognitive Theories, Prior Knowledge, and Anchored Instruction on Mathematical Problem Solving and Transfer." *Education and Urban Society,* vol. 36, 2003, pp. 79–93.

Shyu, H.-Y. "Effects of Media Attributes in Anchored Instruction." *Journal of Educational Computing Research,* vol. 21, 199, pp. 119–39.

"TEAM—Advancing the Math Skills of Low-Achieving Adolescents in Technology-Rich Learning Environments." 2007, wcer.wisc.edu.

"Using Technology to Support Education Reform—September 1993." 2001, ed.gov.

Zydney, J., B. A. Mannheimer, and T. Hasselbring. "Finding the Optimal Guidance for Enhancing Anchored Instruction." *Interactive Learning Environments,* vol. 22, no. 5, 2014.

ANDROID OS

Introduction

Introduced to consumers by the technology company Google, the Android operating system (OS) debuted on the mobile-device market with the release of the T-Mobile G1 (or HTC Dream)

smartphone in 2008. The OS quickly became a major competitor in that market and by 2020 was one of the dominant mobile operating systems both in the United States and worldwide.

Mobile computing is the fastest-growing segment of the tech market. As pricing has become more affordable, developing nations, particularly in Africa, are the largest growing market for smartphones. With smartphones, users shop, gather information, connect via social media such as Twitter and Facebook, and communicate—one of the uses more traditionally associated with phones.

Since its launch in 2008, Android has become one of the most ubiquitous operating systems running on mobile phones. By 2019, 2.5 billion Android devices were active worldwide.

Background

Android came about amid a transformative moment in mobile technology. Prior to 2007, slide-out keyboards mimicked the typing experience of desktop personal computers (PCs). In June of that year, Apple released its first iPhone, forever altering the landscape of mobile phones. Apple focused on multitouch gestures and touch-screen technology. Nearly concurrent with this, Google's Android released its first application program interface (API).

The original API of Google's new OS first appeared in October 2008. The Android OS was first installed on the T-Mobile G1, also known as the HTC Dream. This prototype had a very small set of preinstalled applications (apps), and as it had a slide-out QWERTY keyboard, there were no touch-screen capabilities. It did have native multitasking, which Apple's iOS did not yet have. Still, to compete with Apple, Google was forced to replace physical

The Android robot logo. Image via Wikimedia Commons. [Public domain.]

keyboards and access buttons with virtual onscreen controls. The next iteration of Android shipped with the HTC Magic and was accompanied by a virtual keyboard and a more robust app marketplace. Among the other early features that have stood the test of time are the pull-down notification list, home-screen widgets, and strong integration with Google's Gmail service.

One later feature, the full-screen immersive mode, became quite popular as it reduces distractions. First released with Android 4.4, "KitKat," in 2013, it hides the navigation and status bars while certain apps are in use. It was retained for the release of Android 5.0, "Lollipop," in 2015, as well as for subsequent releases.

Android Changes and Grows

Both of Google's operating systems—Android and its cloud-based desktop OS, Chrome—are based on the free open-source OS Linux, created by engineer Linus Torvalds and first released in 1991. Open-source software is created using publicly available source code. The open-source development of Android has allowed manufacturers to produce robust, affordable products that contribute to its widespread popularity in emerging and developing markets. This may be one reason why Android has captured many more new users than its closest rival, Apple's iPhone operating system (iOS). This strategy has kept costs down and has also helped build Android's app marketplace, the Google Play Store, which offers about 3 million apps, many free of charge. By 2020 Android made up more than 70 percent of the global mobile operating system market.

This open-source development of Android has had one adverse effect: the phenomenon known as forking, which occurs primarily in China. Forking is when a private company takes the OS and creates their own products apart from native Google services such as email. Google seeks to prevent this loss of control (and revenue) by not supporting these companies or including their apps in its marketplace.

Google's business model has always focused on a "rapid iteration, web-style update cycle." By contrast, rivals such as Microsoft and Apple have had a more deliberate pace due to hardware issues. One benefit of Google's faster approach is the ability to address issues and problems in a timely manner. A drawback

is the phenomenon known as cloud rot. As the cloud-based OS grows older, servers that were once devoted to earlier versions are repurposed. Since changes to the OS initially came every few months, apps that worked a month prior would suddenly lose functionality or become completely unusable. Later Android updates have been released on a timescale of six months or more.

Throughout many of Android's first years of existence, new versions of the OS were known by both version numbers and dessert-themed code names, such as Cupcake (version 1.5), Ice Cream Sandwich (version 4.0), and Oreo (versions 8.0 and 8.1). Following the release of Pie (version 9), however, Google moved away from that naming scheme with Android version 10, released in 2019. Android version 11, released as a public beta in June of 2020, was likewise referred to by its version number rather than by a themed nickname.

Android's Future

One of the biggest concerns about Android's future is the issue of forking. Making the code available to developers at no cost has made Android a desirable and cost-effective alternative to higher-end makers such as Microsoft and Apple, but it has also made Google a target of competitors. Another consideration for Android's future is its link to the Chrome OS, also a Google product. Google plans to keep the two separate. Further, Google executives have made it clear that Chromebooks (laptops that run Chrome) and Android devices have distinct purposes. Android's focus has been on touch-screen technology, multitouch gesturing, and screen resolution, making it a purely mobile OS for phones, tablets, wearable devices, and televisions. Meanwhile, Chrome has developed tools that are more useful in the PC and laptop environment, such as keyboard shortcuts. However, an effort to unify the appearance and functionality of Google's different platforms and devices called Material Design was introduced in 2014. Further, Google has ensured that Android apps can be executed on Chrome and has made the Google Play Store available on Chromebooks. Such implementations suggest a slow merging of the Android and Chrome user experiences.

—Andrew Farrell

References

Amadeo, Ron. "The (Updated) History of Android." *Ars Technica*, 31 Oct. 2016, arstechnica.com/gadgets/2016/10/building-android-a-40000-word-history-of-googles-mobile-os/.

Bajarin, Tim. "Google Is at a Major Crossroads with Android and Chrome OS." *PCMag*, 21 Dec. 2015, www.pcmag.com/opinions/google-is-at-a-major-crossroads-with-android-and-chrome-os.

Brandom, Russell. "There Are Now 2.5 Billion Active Android Devices." *Verge*, 7 May 2019, www.theverge.com/2019/5/7/18528297/google-io-2019-android-devices-play-store-total-number-statistic-keynote.

Clement, J. "Google Play: Number of Available Apps 2009-2020." *Statista*, 17 June 2020, www.statista.com/statistics/266210/number-of-available-applications-in-the-google-play-store/.

Edwards, Jim. "Proof That Android Really Is for the Poor." *Business Insider*, 27 June 2014, www.businessinsider.in/Proof-That-Android-Really-Is-For-The-Poor/articleshow/37328668.cms.

"Mobile Operating System Market Share Worldwide." *Statcounter*, May 2020, gs.statcounter.com/os-market-share/mobile/worldwide.

Newman, Jared. "Android Laptops: The $200 Price Is Right, but the OS May Not Be." *PCWorld*, 26 Apr. 2013, www.pcworld.com/article/2036451/android-laptops-the-200-price-is-right-but-the-os-may-not-be.html.

___. "With Android Lollipop, Mobile Multitasking Takes a Great Leap Forward." *Fast Company*, 6 Nov. 2014, www.fastcompany.com/3038213/with-android-lollipop-mobile-multitasking-takes-a-great-leap-forward.

Raphael, J. R. "Android Versions: A Living History from 1.0 to 11." *Computerworld*, 26 June 2020, www.computerworld.com/article/3235946/android-versions-a-living-history-from-1-0-to-today.html.

ANONYMITY AND ANONYMIZERS

Introduction

Anonymity and anonymizers are concepts that have taken on a new significance in the digital age. While anonymous communication is protected by the First Amendment of the US Constitution, complete anonymity, particularly when communicating on the internet, is difficult to achieve for the average person. Anonymizers can be used to accomplish nearly complete anonymity in digital communication.

Background

In *Talley v. California*, 362 U.S. 60 (1960), the US Supreme Court determined that the First Amendment's free speech clause protects anonymous speech. Long before digital communication existed, a City of Los Angeles ordinance prohibited the distribution of a leaflet or handbill unless it identified the name and address of its publisher. A leafleteer was arrested for failing to comply with the ordinance and argued that the requirement that he identify himself by name and address violated his constitutional right to freedom of speech. The Court agreed.

The Court reasoned that anonymous communication has historically played an important part in the development of society and social change. For example, the Court pointed to various instances in US history where colonists who supported the revolution and the Founding Fathers themselves engaged in anonymous speech. The Court determined that prohibiting anonymous speech would have a chilling effect on speech and, in particular, would lessen the distribution of literature critical of government. The Court has affirmed this protection of anonymous speech in cases such as *McIntyre v. Ohio Elections Commission*, 514 U.S. 334 (1995).

Appearances versus Reality

The internet has provided the appearance of facilitating anonymous communication. Users are able to access digital communication platforms and contribute to the discussion of ideas without revealing much, if any, information about themselves. Whether through social networks, email, blogs, or chatrooms, users can create fabricated persona, or no persona at all, and engage in an exchange of ideas without revealing their true identity—thus retaining anonymity. Many scholars argue that this anonymity provided by the internet democratizes communication and thus increases the exchange of ideas that the First Amendment was intended to protect. Others argue that anonymous communication through the internet results in more caustic, hurtful speech and disconnects speakers from the emotional injury they may cause. Anonymous speech may simply provide protection for people who engage in illegal threats and intimidation.

Many people access the internet through an entity, such as a private company, that acts as an internet service provider. The internet service provider connects its users to the internet and thus often has access to its customers' information. While most internet service providers allow their customers to engage others on the internet anonymously, the internet service provider nevertheless retains the customer's name and other personally identifiable information. As a result, when users have anonymously communicated via the internet and the communication is the basis for legal action, courts have been asked to order internet service providers to reveal the identity of the anonymous user. Because of the constitutional commitment to protect anonymous speech, courts have struggled to articulate the proper standard for when to require internet service providers to reveal their users' identities. Moreover, the US government has allegedly accessed users' identity and data through internet service providers' records regardless of users' attempts to remain anonymous.

Because a user may not want his or her internet use to be traceable, he or she may use an anonymizer to try to accomplish complete anonymity. Anonymizers are tools that protect a user's personally identifiable information by masking his or her internet protocol address— the way a computer and its user is identified on an internet service provider's network. Masking the internet protocol address makes it difficult to trace a user's internet usage, thus ensuring his or her privacy.

There are two basic forms of anonymizers: networked anonymizers and single-point anonymizers. Networked anonymizers transfer the user's communication or other internet traffic through a network of internet server computers before it arrives at its destination website. The destination website then routes its information back to the user through the same network. The path the information takes between the original sources is thus obscured and difficult to map, and the user's internet protocol address is not associated with having visited a particular website, where he or she may have shared information or communicated. These sorts of anonymizers are generally considered more secure because of the multiple connections through which the information must travel. A single-point anonymizer is a website through which a user can surf the web. The anonymizer website communicates on behalf of the user and sends a request to the destination website for the user. The destination website then sends information back to the anonymizer website, which then encrypts the communication and provides it to the user seeking anonymity. As with any technology, anonymizers are used by people with both good and ill intentions. They can be used to engage in debate and criticism without the threat of being exposed and retaliated against for one's beliefs. At the same time, however, anonymizers can be used by people with nefarious goals, such as internet-related crime.

Anonymity has long been recognized as a valuable tool for communicating fringe, minority, or unpopular views without the threat of retaliation. Online anonymity has extended that benefit to millions of people while at the same time providing protection for those that might abuse it. Although true online anonymity is difficult to achieve, technology such as anonymizers allow those who seek anonymity to protect their identity from those who may want to reveal it.

—*Douglas B. McKechnie*

References

Barrett Lidsky, Lyrissa. "Silencing John Doe: Defamation and Discourse in Cyberspace." *Duke Law Journal*, vol. 49, no. 4, 2000, pp. 855–946.

Kizza, Joseph Migga. *Ethical and Social Issues in the Information Age*. 4th ed., Springer, 2010.

Payton, Theresa, and Theodore Claypoole. *Privacy in the Age of Big Data: Recognizing Threats, Defending Your Rights, and Protecting Your Family*. Rowman & Littlefield, 2014.

APPLE

Introduction

From its inception, Apple occupied a unique place among technology companies by typically both manufacturing the hardware and programming the software for its devices. This contrasted with companies such as Microsoft, which developed the Windows operating system and licensed it for use on personal computers (PCs) manufactured by other companies. Although Apple experienced difficulties in the 1990s as the result of failed partnerships and product launches, the return of cofounder Steve Jobs in 1997 was widely credited with getting the company back on track for dramatic success.

Beginning with the redesigned iMac desktop computer in 1998, Apple went on to develop a series of popular consumer products that helped transform the nature of personal computing and media consumption. In August 2018, it became the first-ever publicly traded company to be worth $1 trillion. While Apple's cultural impact and financial success were extraordinary, it also faced ongoing criticisms on a variety of issues, ranging from labor practices to data privacy.

Background

Apple Computer was founded on April 1, 1976, by twenty-one-year-old Steven Jobs and twenty-six-year-old Stephen Wozniak. Their initial idea was that they would assemble computers for their friends. They did not realize the potential their ideas had to revolutionize the personal computer industry. Ultimately, their goal became making computer technology widely accessible to the mass population. These entrepreneurs recognized that most consumers at that time saw computers as too expensive and too complex to use. Jobs envisioned the firm offering products that would contribute to human efficiency as much as the electric typewriter, the calculator, and the photocopy machine had done.

Jobs and Wozniak, both graduates of Homestead High School in Santa Clara, California, began collaborating in 1976 at the Homebrew Computer Club in Palo Alto, California. Wozniak was a superior product engineer and designer, and Jobs had a grasp on the demands of the marketplace. They designed their first machine in Jobs's bedroom and used $1,300 from the sale of Jobs's Volkswagen and

Overhead view of Apple Park, the company's headquarters in Cupertino, California. Photo by Arne Müseler, via Wikimedia Commons.

Wozniak's scientific calculator to assemble their first working model in Jobs's parents' garage. They chose Apple as the name for their venture because they thought it conveyed a nonthreatening yet high-technology image. Their original plan was to limit production to circuit boards, but after Jobs's first sales call yielded an order for fifty units, they rethought their strategy and decided to offer fully assembled microcomputers.

Their first model, the Apple I, was introduced and sold without a monitor, keyboard, or casing, at a price of $666. It was the first single-board computer with onboard read-only memory (ROM), which told the machine how to load other programs from an external source, and with a built-in video interface. Orders for their "personal computer," mainly from hobbyists, soon reached six hundred units.

Jobs and Wozniak then faced the problem of improving the original model without sacrificing its key selling features, its simplicity and compactness. Their efforts resulted in the introduction in 1977 of the Apple II, the first fully assembled, programmable microcomputer that did not require users to know how to solder, wire, or program. The Apple II had a keyboard, a color monitor, and expansion capabilities for peripheral devices. These features gave the new model considerable flexibility and inspired numerous independent firms to develop third-party add-on devices and software programs. The resulting software library soon included more than ten thousand programs ranging from games to sophisticated business applications.

Demand soon outstripped the founders' ability to produce the machine. They turned to Mike Markkula, who had been a marketing manager at Intel

Corporation, a fast-growing manufacturer of integrated circuits. Markkula contributed at least $91,000 to the company (by some estimates, as much as $250,000), secured a line of credit with Bank of America, and raised more than $500,000 from venture capitalists; he was named chairman of the company in May, 1977. One month later, Michael Scott was placed in the position of president of the firm.

Markkula wrote Apple's first business plan. Its objectives included capturing a market share at least twice that of the nearest competitor, realizing at least 20 percent pretax profit, and growing to $500 million in annual sales within ten years by continuing to make significant contributions to the home computer industry. In addition, the plan called for the establishment and maintenance of a corporate culture that would be conducive to personal growth and development for the firm's employees. The plan also called for an "easy exit" for its founders within five years, should they wish to disassociate themselves from the enterprise.

Apple II was a huge commercial success, and in 1980 the company became a publicly traded company. However, the next few products released by Apple were not nearly as successful. Also, other manufacturers of personal computers, including International Business Machines (IBM), had appeared on the scene and provided stiff competition. Four years later, in 1984, Apple released the Macintosh. The Mac changed the way people used home computers. It was smaller, better looking, and easier to use than other personal computers then available.

Introduced in 1984, the Apple MacIntosh was the first widely sold home computer to feature a graphical user interface (GUI). This model, dubbed the computer "for the rest of us," incorporated a GUI inspired by Xerox's Alto Computer. Apple decided to use GUI on its upcoming business computer, Lisa. Programming whiz Bill Atkinson devised the routines, later called QuickDraw, that created Lisa's graphics. He added many refinements: a menu bar at the top of the screen; pull-down menus; instant redraw of hidden windows; and unprecedented user interaction with screen objects, including draggable windows, file icons and folders, and a trash can for deleting items. Also, Apple refined the mouse when testing revealed that a single button was less confusing.

Jobs had a decisive influence on Mac aesthetics. Its unusual shape became as iconic as the Volkswagen Beetle. The Mac, with a very sharp and stable monitor, had square pixels for better graphics and font rendering. It also included many proportional, multiple-sized fonts with descenders, designed by artist Susan Kare, for "what you see is what you get" (WYSIWYG) documents. This was unprecedented in personal computing. The fonts included accents and special characters for European languages. Its GUI sported other refinements, such as the graying of unavailable choices in pull-down menus and elegant round-cornered rectangles used for dialogue box buttons. Kare gave the Mac its distinctive personality with her often whimsical icons: the "happy Mac" that greeted users when it was booting normally, the wristwatch when the computer was busy, and the round, fused bomb when the Mac hung up. She also created its playful Cairo font, composed entirely of pictures.

Although the MacIntosh was an innovative product, the business continued to decline, and Jobs was fired from Apple in 1985. Jobs started a new company called NeXT, Inc., devoted to creating hardware and software. Jobs then bought an animation company and called it Pixar Animation Studios. This studio has made many successful films such as the Toy Story series, *Finding Nemo, WALL-E, The Incredibles,* and *Cars.*

In 1996 Apple bought NeXT from Jobs for $427 million. Apple, in serious financial trouble, brought Jobs on board as the chief executive officer (CEO) to turn things around. Jobs began to remake Apple by focusing on new and innovative products beyond personal computers. Apple released the very popular iPod music player and iTunes music system in 2001. The iPod led to the iPhone in 2007, the first successful smartphone. The iPhone lead, in turn, to the iPad. Jobs's skill was creating unique products that developed new technologies, and these innovations made Apple very successful all over the world.

Macintosh was developed for the business (focusing on productivity and desktop publishing) and education markets. Its compact design and ease of use caught the attention of the market, although the original models were criticized for lacking the computing power required for some business applications. After a series of modifications and upgrades, the Macintosh gained widespread acceptance.

Mac OS X

Mac OS X, the tenth version of the Macintosh operating system, was released on March 24, 2001. It combined a stable UNIX-based platform with a visually appealing user interface called Aqua. For software developers, OS X introduced the Carbon application programming interface (API) and the X-code integrated development environment (IDE) for writing code. OS X was a key step in making Macs a central focus of consumer computing culture. Cat-themed names for OS X releases were popular with enthusiasts and eventually became marketing devices. OS X versions progressed from Cheetah (version 10.0) and Puma (10.1) in 2001 to Jaguar (10.2) in 2002, Panther (10.3) in 2003, Tiger (10.4) in 2005, Leopard (10.5) in 2007, Snow Leopard (10.6) in 2009, Lion (10.7) in 2011, and Mountain Lion (10.8) in 2012. Beginning with Mavericks (10.9) in 2013, the company moved away from the cat-themed names to names associated with California, subsequently introducing Yosemite (10.10) in 2014 and El Capitan (10.11) in 2015. In 2016, macOS Sierra was released, representing Apple's attempt to bring some consistency to the naming of operating systems for all of its products, such as iOS and watch OS. MacOS High Sierra followed in 2017 and macOS Mojave followed in 2018. Each update has brought new features, including chat programs, customizable widgets (such as a calculator or dictionary), a file and application search, or a simple backup system.

Goodbye PowerPC, Hello Intel

In 2006, Apple replaced PowerPC microprocessors with Intel microprocessors in all of its computers. This shift was accompanied by name changes: the PowerMac desktop, iBook, and PowerBook laptops became the Mac Pro, MacBook (discontinued for general consumers in 2012 and revived in 2015 with a new, redesigned line featuring a Retina display), MacBook Pro, and MacBook Air, respectively, while the iMac desktop kept its name. Black MacBooks marked the first time Mac laptops were made available in black, an option that continued until 2008. In 2017, a new generation of MacBook, MacBook Pro, and MacBook Air models was launched.

The original Apple logo. Image via Wikimedia Commons. [Public domain.]

The iMac desktop computer evolved from its signature egg shape to a more modern monitor-based appearance, including a transition from colored plastic to white plastic and then aluminum. Thanks in part to designer Jonathan Ive's aesthetic, Mac computers were generally perceived as aesthetically appealing as well as easy to use, and were popular choices for purposes such as graphic design. Critics alleged limited processing power for resource-intensive activities, particularly games; bemoaned Apple's tight control over all components of the hardware and software; and found the computers overpriced—even though some direct comparisons found Apple computers to be faster and less expensive than PCs.

Goodbye Intel, Hello M1

In 2018, Apple stunned the computing world with the announcement that they would be phasing out Intel chips in all their computing machines. Intel had been until that time the industry standard, but developers at Apple had secretly been designing an all-on-one-motherboard processor that would vastly improve the communication process between individual chip elements. Designed specifically for the future Apple products (as opposed to previous chips, which had a more generic application), the Apple chip, dubbed M1, would be native to Apple products. In 2022, the next generation of chips, somewhat clumsily named M1 Max and M1 Ultra, were featured in their latest professional-level home computer, the Mac Studio. The Max featured a 10-core central processing unit (CPU) with 8 performance cores and 2 efficiency cores, a 24-core GPU, a 16-core Neural Engine, and 400GB/s memory bandwidth. The Ultra, essentially two Max chips piggybacked upon each other, doubled the speed of those numbers.

iPod

The iPod is a portable media player designed by Apple for the storage and playback of audio files. Although digital audio players (usually called MP3 players) had existed before the iPod, they generally had little memory, confusing controls, limited features, and a clunky appearance. MP3 players were not regarded as a serious substitute for a portable cassette or compact disc (CD) player. When Steve Jobs introduced the iPod in 2001, he gave the world an MP3 player that was both elegant and functional.

The key to the development of the iPod was a tiny hard drive manufactured by Toshiba that, despite its 1.8-inch size, held 5 gigabytes of data, capable of storing up to one thousand songs. With the addition of the newly developed high-speed FireWire technology, the iPod prototype finally took shape. The device would be small enough to fit in a pocket, have enough space to hold up to a thousand songs, and have the ability to interface with iTunes to load a large number of songs quickly and conveniently. The iPod was developed in less than six months, faster than any major product in the company's history.

The iPod used a laptop hard drive rather than flash memory as most early MP3 players used. This feature enabled the iPod to provide much more capacity, although at the cost of some battery life and ruggedness. However, carefully designed software allowed songs to be loaded from the hard drive into a buffer. This feature simultaneously reduced battery drain and decreased the chance that a sudden shock could crash the hard drive.

The interface by which the user controlled the iPod was also given careful thought. The menu system was based to some degree on that of the Apple Macintosh operating system. The touch wheel and its successor, the click wheel, enabled the user to move smoothly from one menu to the other, controlling multiple playlists with ease.

The iPod evolved rapidly, with many new iterations: the iPod photo, which could display images; the iPod Mini (later iPod Nano) and iPod Shuffle, smaller versions of the iPod available in multiple colors; and the iPod Touch, a wireless-enabled touch-screen device. Beginning with fifth-generation (late 2005) iPods and third-generation (2007) iPod Nanos, the devices supported video content. The seventh-generation Nano was released in 2012 and the sixth-generation Touch was released in 2015.

iTunes Store

Launched in 2003, the iTunes Store created a marketplace for consumers to legally purchase music online and transfer it to an iPod or other media player. Files were initially available in advanced audio coding (AAC) format and used digital rights management (DRM) restrictions to prevent distribution of copyrighted content, although DRM-free content would become available in 2007 and DRM would be eliminated from music files by 2009. Single songs were typically sold for $0.99 and full albums for

The Macintosh, released in 1984, was the first mass-market personal computer to feature an integral graphical user interface and mouse. Photo by Marcin Wichary from San Francisco, U.S.A., via Wikimedia Commons.

$9.99. A version of iTunes for Windows was also released in 2003 to help Windows users enjoy iTunes Store offerings.

Due to international laws and consumer preferences, each country has its own iTunes Store, typically with a different selection of content. The first international iTunes Stores (for the United Kingdom, France, and Germany) launched in June 2004, and 119 countries had stores by the end of 2012. In addition to purchased content, the iTunes Store offered free subscriptions to user-submitted audio or video podcast recordings.

The American iTunes Store went on to sell audiobooks (through a partnership with Audible.com), video content in 2005, and games in 2006. Apple TV, a device for streaming media content from the iTunes Store and other sources such as Netflix and YouTube to a traditional television, was released in March 2007; the fourth generation was released in 2015. In 2012, iTunes U made educational content from major institutions available through the iTunes Store.

The iTunes Store was a hit with consumers, selling more than 1 million songs in its first five days, 70 million songs in its first year, and 35 billion songs by 2014. The store also boosted iPod sales: while fewer than four hundred thousand devices were sold in 2001, that number rose to 20 million iPods worldwide in 2005, and more than 50 million were sold per year from 2007 to 2010, at which time the iPhone surpassed the iPod in popularity. In 2019, only the iPod Touch (7th generation) remained in production.

iPhone

The iPhone, a revolutionary touch-screen smartphone, was released in 2007. The day after the initial announcement, Apple stock hit a then-record high of $97.80 per share, a preview of later peaks that reached $700 in 2012 (the stock was split in 2014). Before the introduction of the iPhone, smartphone penetration seemed largely relegated to the corporate market, with more than 80 percent of the market using Blackberry, Windows, and Palm devices in 2006. After the introduction of the iPhone, general smartphone adoption grew more quickly, reaching nearly 60 percent in 2014 (from 8 percent in 2007). By 2015, the iPhone represented 40 percent of the market share for smartphones.

A sleek style and aluminum casing made the iPhone visually distinctive. Initially available with 4 GB or 8 GB of storage, later versions would run to 16 GB and even 64 GB. Subsequent iterations were the iPhone 3G (2008), followed by the 3GS (2009); the 4 (2010) and 4S (2011); the 5 (2012), 5C (2013), and 5S (2013); the 6 and 6 Plus (both 2014); the 6S and 6S Plus (2015); the SE (2016); the 7 and 7 Plus (2016); and the 8, 8 Plus, and X (2017). The iPhone X, released in November 2017, was named to mark the tenth anniversary of the first iPhone.

The iPhone uses the iOS platform, a version of the core Mac OS X operating system. The iPhone interface features icons that open up different applications such as messaging, calendar, email, camera, photos, video, maps, music, and weather. The iPhone did not support Adobe Flash videos, a conscious decision made by Apple to promote the development of mobile-friendly HTML5 video solutions. Apple was one of the first smartphone vendors to popularize the "pinch-to-zoom" gesture.

The iPhone has been marketed as a user-friendly way to access the internet and all types of media, and the iOS platform made it possible to do so in unprecedented ways. Just as anyone could record and submit a podcast for free distribution through the iTunes Store, anyone could develop and submit an iPhone application for inclusion in the App Store. Apple's success with the iPhone was, in part, because the device was more a computer than a phone, and it changed consumer expectations regarding how they interacted with the web. However, after several generations of the phone criticism grew that Apple was resting on its laurels and that competitors' devices were offering more features and lower prices. Some observers raised concerns with planned obsolescence as well.

iPad

The iPad, Apple's version of the tablet computer, was initially released in 2010. With a touch screen, the iPad allows users to browse the internet, take photographs and video, and engage in myriad other activities, with hundreds of thousands of apps available for download. While generally considered less groundbreaking than the iPhone, the iPad proved to be another popular success for Apple, selling hundreds of millions of units and helping to bring tablet computers into the mainstream. The first iPad

Steve Jobs shows off the iPhone 4 at the 2010 Worldwide Developers Conference. Photo by Matthew Yohe, via Wikimedia Commons.

featured a 9.7-inch screen, which has remained a standard feature of the full-size device. Apple has released several generations of the iPad. The updated line that debuted in 2012 featured storage capacities ranging from 16 to 128 GB, with 1080p high-definition photo and video cameras. 2017 saw another update of the basic iPad model.

A smaller version of the iPad, the iPad Mini, was also released in 2012, with a second generation out the following year, a third generation released in 2014, and a fourth generation produced in 2015. The device has all of the features of the larger version, but in a 7.9-inch display screen. Additionally, in 2013, the iPad Air hit the market, boasting a Retina display and a thinner but more powerful design; a second version was subsequently released the following year. A 12.9-inch iPad Pro, with more powerful specifications than the base models, was announced in 2015, and a smaller version with the traditional 9.7-inch screen was released in 2016. The second-generation iPad Pro was launched in 2017, with the smaller version increasing to a 10.5-inch screen.

Apple Watch

In 2015, Apple CEO Tim Cook announced that Apple would be releasing its first iteration of a wearable technological device, the Apple Watch. With a focus on blending convenient access to customizable applications and information with the promotion of daily activity and health monitoring, the Apple Watch allows users to sync to their iPhones to read e-mails, answer calls, and send messages while also using a global positioning system (GPS), heart-rate monitor, and accelerometer functions to manage physical activity. The original version came in several different faces and band combinations. In 2016, a second generation was released that included Apple Watch Series 1 and Series 2. The Apple Watch Series 3 followed in September 2017 and introduced long-term evolution (LTE) cellular connectivity.

Retail Stores and Events

The first retail Apple Stores opened in 2001, creating another channel for Apple to attract customers. The retail stores, which numbered more than four hundred worldwide in 2015, are typically located in malls or areas with heavy foot traffic. Apple products prominently displayed at the front of the stores allow consumers to conduct hands-on trials. Apple exercises careful control over the layout and appearance of each store.

To further the image of Apple as a consumer-friendly company, Apple Stores feature Genius Bars—tables staffed with dedicated technical support. Consumers can drop in unscheduled to receive free support and repairs for Apple products under warranty. Apple Stores also host classes to help consumers learn to use their new Apple products. This customer-focused, brand-driven approach was initially distinctive in a world where computer support had often been provided by independent vendors, not necessarily the computer manufacturers themselves. In 2006, Apple Stores phased out traditional point-of-sale cash registers in favor of small mobile payment devices carried by staff members, increasing the high-tech feel of being in an Apple Store. iPads were used for transactions.

The stores have been widely credited for building a base of popular support for Apple products, and have also been financially successful. When new stores open or new Apple products are released, many consumers wait in long lines to be the first to enter or get the product. The popularity of product launches echoed the popularity of events such as Apple's Worldwide Developers Conference

(WWDC) and Macworld Expo, where major product announcements and releases often take place. Jobs was particularly known for his understated but emotional presentation style at such events, as well as for his tendency to wear denim pants and black turtlenecks. (Cook took over for Jobs as CEO in August 2011; Jobs died in October of that year.)

The Apple Store concept was emulated by other companies, including Sony and Microsoft, which opened stores with similar visual details such as glass storefronts, long tables displaying products, and enthusiastic employees in colorful T-shirts.

Criticism and Lawsuits

Criticism has been leveled at Apple, including complaints about tight controls over applications (specifically restrictions on the use of Adobe Flash) and unexplained app rejections; reports of labor abuses by Chinese Apple suppliers; and allegations of monopolizing content distribution. A tightly controlled and somewhat secretive company, Apple rarely responds directly to criticism, but it did launch investigations of working conditions at suppliers and began publishing annual labor reports in 2008.

Impact

Apple's unique approach to personal computing altered the manner in which computer manufacturers competed. Apple pioneered the concept of integrating hardware and software to offer new possibilities. For example, integration of high-resolution displays with scalable fonts (alphanumeric characters that can be printed in a variety of sizes) and graphics capabilities allowed people to create sophisticated documents on their personal computers. Through the integration of a microphone and a compact disc/read-only memory (CD-ROM) drive with specialized software, users could now work with sound, video, and animation.

Most other computer manufacturers could not integrate hardware and software as expediently because they did not manage the software development for their systems. Most, instead, licensed the same system software (MS-DOS) from one company (Microsoft). As a result, many of their products were indistinguishable, and companies often competed solely on the basis of price. Manufacturers of "clones" of IBM computers set off price wars in the hardware arena. Although Apple lowered prices to remain competitive, much of its sales growth came through product innovation.

By 1986, with the introduction of the Mac Plus and the LaserWriter printer, Apple began to make significant inroads into the business market. The company also embarked on a program to reduce both costs and prices, allowing it to sell aggressively to large businesses, a historically weak market for Apple. Combining traditional computer applications such as word processing and spreadsheets with pioneering concepts such as desktop publishing, three-dimensional (3D) computer-assisted design, and interactive multimedia tools (with text, animation, and sound) carried the Apple tradition for innovation forward.

Apple Computer rose from its modest origins in a garage to become the second-largest manufacturer of personal computers, behind IBM. The company's Macintosh line became widely known for its user-friendliness and superior graphics capabilities. As a result of planning and the vision of Jobs and Wozniak in Apple's early years, personal computing became accessible to the general population. Apple successfully changed how general users view personal computing, and some of the company's significant product features were soon mimicked by competing firms. Through its continual emphasis on product innovations, Apple redefined how people process and transmit information.

—Kerry Skemp, Andrew M. Forman, Elaine Sherman,
R. Craig Philips, and Kermin Bhot

References

Carlton, Jim. *Apple: The Inside Story of Intrigue, Egomania, and Business Blunders.* HarperBusiness, 1998.

Dormehl, Luke. *The Apple Revolution: Steve Jobs, the Counterculture and How the Crazy Ones Took Over the World.* Virgin Books, 2012.

Drucker, Jesse, and Simon Bowers. "After a Tax Crackdown, Apple Found a New Shelter for Its Profits." *The New York Times,* 6 Nov. 2017, www.nytimes.com/2017/11/06/world/apple-taxes-jersey.html.

Isaacson, Walter. *Steve Jobs.* Simon & Schuster, 2011.

Kane, Yukari Iwatani. *Haunted Empire: Apple after Steve Jobs.* HarperBusiness, 2014.

Lashinsky, Adam. *Inside Apple: How America's Most Admired—and Secretive—Company Really Works.* Business Plus, 2012.

Levy, Steven. "Apple Is Defying History with Its Pricey iPhone X." *Wired*, 12 Sept. 2017, www. wired.com/story/ apple-is-defying-history-with-its-pricey-iphone-x/.

Linzmayer, Owen W. *Apple Confidential 2.0: The Definitive History of the World's Most Colorful Company*. Rev. 2nd ed., No Starch Press, 2004.

Nicas Jack. "Apple Is Worth $1,000,000,000: Two Decades Ago, It Was Almost Bankrupt." *The New York Times*, 2 Aug. 2018, www.nytimes. com/2018/08/02/technology/apple-stock-1-trillion-market-cap.html.

Sander, Peter J. *What Would Steve Jobs Do? How the Steve Jobs Way Can Inspire Anyone to Think Differently and Win*. McGraw-Hill, 2012.

Segall, Ken. *Insanely Simple: The Obsession That Drives Apple's Success*. Portfolio/Penguin, 2012.

APPS/APPLICATIONS

Introduction

Apps, or applications, are collections of code or software designed to run on a particular device. Common usage includes mobile apps that are formulated to be downloaded and run on mobile devices or to be used exclusively for a particular type or brand of mobile device. Apps are also being developed for wearable devices, unmanned aerial vehicles (UAVs), and biometric devices. Software platforms for app development use similar tools, called application programming interfaces (APIs), within the platform to design and run the apps.

One of the unique features of apps versus computer software, in general, is that apps are focused on the individual user, a specific function, or both. There are apps that offer simple services or provide the user with a stream of unanalyzed information (e.g., streams regarding sports statistics, current weather, stock market ups and downs, directions, and traffic updates).

At the other end of the complexity spectrum, some apps, such as gaming or social media apps, offer a complete experience within the app. Between these two types, a variety of apps, such as calendaring and communication functions, offer services that accept some input from the user but maintain the essence of their programmed structure. Most users access these apps from a mobile device, whether the apps come preloaded when the user purchases the device or are individually selected and downloaded from an app store. Generally, the term "app" is used for applications that run on mobile devices, whereas the term "application" is used for desktop computer applications. Here the term "app" is used without distinction.

Background

Apps have provided a broader platform than conventional computer software for nontechnical designers to approach the market and develop innovations. Several app-creation languages offer simpler functionality than traditional software languages, allowing an individual to translate a business idea into an app design. Usually, apps are brought to market much more rapidly than are new computer programs. An app store, or the marketplace for apps on any given device, is broken down into two primary platforms: one for Apple devices and one for devices that run on the Android platform. Other app markets include those operated by Amazon, Facebook, Google, Hewlett-Packard, Microsoft, and Research In Motion. The introduction of the Apple iPhone in 2007 marked a transition from app provision by carriers to app provision by device manufacturers. When the Apple app store opened in 2008, just a few hundred apps were available, with a significant percentage of free apps offered. In more recent years, Apple and Android app stores have each offered more than a million apps. Apple strictly controls access to its market, and it is considered more difficult to enter than the Android market.

The user experience in operating apps is considered one of the main factors that drives the success or failure of any given app. Mobile app designers pay particular attention to the appearance—or graphical user interface (GUI)—of the app as well as the app's actual function. Components of the user experience include ease of download, cost, sensitivity of data input, look and feel of the screens shown to the user, number of screens or clicks required to complete transactions, accuracy of information provided, and number of push or automated notifications. The next front in the development of new apps is to move from high-touch, separate functionalities, such as entering an event into a calendar, to lower-impact background functionalities such as passive check-ins for location and display of card format information.

Apps and Privacy

The Federal Trade Commission (FTC) generally issues privacy regulations governing app design and information collection. Apps that utilize healthcare data are also regulated under the Health Insurance Portability and Accountability Act of 1996 (HIPAA), 110 Stat. 1936 (1996). The payment card industry (PCI) governs apps that involve financial transactions using credit cards. Generally, the app's promises to protect privacy appear in the app's privacy policy statement, but they may appear elsewhere in the marketing materials or security assurances. The FTC and other regulatory advice encourage privacy by design. Under this principle, privacy may be considered during the design phase, or at the onset of app programming, rather than after the new app is released to and used by consumers.

Because the US government is concerned about the amount and type of data collected from children under the age of thirteen, Congress enacted the Children's Online Privacy Protection Act (COPPA) in 1998, 112 Stat. 2681 (1998). COPPA's restriction on data about children applies to apps, and a large number of children interact with mobile devices and tablets in the highly accessible app format. Once an app is downloaded, often the only barrier to children's access is that they must touch or click on it to open it, and it is not necessary for them to log in to start the app. Thus, children can access apps easily, and many apps are designed and marketed with children as the primary target, such as educational and gaming apps.

Apps are also different from other methods of electronic collection of personal data because they frequently continue running and collecting data even when the user is not actively engaged with the app. Also, apps may gather data that does not directly relate to the primary function of the app, such as apps that note the user's physical location, peruse photos, or mine personal contacts on the mobile device even if these activities are not strictly necessary for the app's operation. In one example, an app that converted the light-emitting diode (LED) flash from a phone's camera operation into a consistent flashlight function also happened to collect location data when the app was running. Following the collection

of the user's personal data, apps can process it, sell it, or upload it to the internet.

The collection and sale of personal data from apps has become a significant market. One of the best ways to ascertain whether an app is collecting personal data for use beyond the functioning of the app is to look at the price for downloading the app. If the app is free to the user, there's a good chance that the app will capture user data for sale to third-party advertisers. Otherwise, the app could not turn a profit. Even if the app has a fee associated with a download, there's a possibility that the app could capture data from users that is not required for the app to function as promised.

Often, it is much more difficult for mobile app users to determine whether they are being tracked by an app than whether they are being tracked by a website in a traditional online environment. Apps track their users by identification codes such as the device's serial number; the Unique Device Identifier (UDID); or the carrier's identification number for that phone's customer of record, the International Mobile Station Equipment Identity (IMEI). Unlike cookies, which are used to track an individual's use of web pages online, these unique identifiers cannot be controlled by the individual user. However, mobile device operating systems usually have a settings menu that includes a privacy setting for apps, which allows the user to adjust the collection and location tracking settings for individual apps or for all apps on that device.

A notice on personal data collection by mobile apps may be issued on the carrier, device, or platform level, but ultimately it is the responsibility of the app company itself to notify its customers. The app may offer broad notices in its privacy policy about the type of data it collects and how it uses this data, which ideally should be related to the provision of the stated services and not for ancillary revenue. The app could also provide just-in-time notices informing the app user that a certain point of data, such as automatic location tracking, is about to be collected either affirmatively from user input or behind the scenes without additional action on the part of the user. The app, in addition to offering notice, must also obtain customer consent before proceeding with the data collection.

The collection of users' personal data by apps is particularly problematic given questions surrounding mobile app security. While this security is enhanced by the closed nature of mobile systems vis-à-vis internet systems, apps nevertheless remain vulnerable to hacks and viruses. As app markets mature, multiple points of access mean multiple points of entry for security threats. Also, as individual users allow more and more of their personal data to be housed on mobile devices, this big data becomes extremely valuable to a hacker's intent on accessing this information to commit fraud or identity theft, or introduce malware to control the device remotely.

—*Jill Bronfman*

References

BinDhim, Nasser F., and Lyndal Trevena. "Health-Related Smartphone Apps: Regulations, Safety, Privacy and Quality." *BMJ Innovations* 1, no. 2, 2015, pp. 43–45.

"Consumer Watchdog Calls California 'Apps' Privacy Agreement a Step Forward, but Says Do Not Track Legislation Is Necessary to Protect Consumers." *Marketing Weekly News*, 10 Mar. 2012.

Engdahl, Sylvia. *Mobile Apps*. Greenhaven Press, 2014.

"FTC Report Raises Privacy Concerns on Mobile Apps for Children." *Entertainment Close-Up*, 26 Feb. 2012.

Martínez-Pérez, Borja, Isabel De La Torre-Díez, and Miguel López-Coronado. "Privacy and Security in Mobile Health Apps: A Review and Recommendations." *Journal of Medical Systems* 39, no. 1, 2014, p. 181.

Melson, Brent. "Protecting Privacy and Security in Software and Mobile Apps: How to Take Precautions to Keep Your Data Secure." *Wireless Design & Development*, 1 July 2015.

Mohapatra, Manas, Andrew Hasty, et al. "Mobile Apps for Kids Current Privacy Disclosures Are Disappointing." *Federal Trade Commission*, 1 Feb. 2012.

Shema, Mike. "Browser & Privacy Attacks." *Hacking Web Apps: Detecting and Preventing Web Application Security Problems*. Syngress, 2012.

Sweatt, Brian, Sharon Paradesi, Ilaria Liccardi, Lalana Kagal, and Alex Pentland. "Building Privacy-Preserving Location-Based Apps." *2014 Twelfth Annual International Conference on Privacy, Security and Trust, Toronto, Ontario, Canada, July 23–24, 2014*. IEEE/Wiley, 2014.

ARTIFICIAL INTELLIGENCE

Introduction

Artificial intelligence (AI) is the design, implementation, and use of programs, machines, and systems that exhibit human intelligence, with its most important activities being knowledge representation, reasoning, and learning. Artificial intelligence encompasses a number of important subareas, including voice recognition, image identification, natural language processing, expert systems, neural networks, planning, robotics, and intelligent agents. Several important programming techniques have been enhanced by AI researchers, including classical search, probabilistic search, and logic programming.

Artificial intelligence is a broad field of study, and definitions of the field vary by discipline. For computer scientists, AI refers to the development of programs that exhibit intelligent behavior. The programs can engage in intelligent planning (timing traffic lights), translate natural languages (converting a Chinese website into English), act like an expert (selecting the best wine for dinner), or perform many other tasks. For engineers, AI refers to building machines that perform actions often done by humans. The machines can be simple, like a computer vision system embedded in an ATM (automated teller machine); more complex, like a robotic rover sent to Mars; or very complex, like an automated factory that builds an exercise machine with little human intervention. For cognitive scientists, AI refers to building models of human intelligence to better understand human behavior.

Background

In the early days of AI, most models of human intelligence were symbolic and closely related to cognitive psychology and philosophy, the basic idea being that regions of the brain perform complex reasoning by processing symbols. Later, many models of human cognition were developed to mirror the operation of the brain as an electrochemical computer, starting with the simple Perceptron, an artificial neural network described by Marvin Minsky in 1969, graduating to the backpropagation algorithm described by David E. Rumelhart and James L. McClelland in 1986, and culminating in a large number of supervised and unsupervised learning algorithms.

When defining AI, it is important to remember that the programs, machines, and models developed by computer scientists, engineers, and cognitive scientists do not actually have human intelligence; they only exhibit intelligent behavior. This can be difficult to remember because artificially intelligent systems often contain large numbers of facts, such as weather information for New York City; complex reasoning patterns, such as the reasoning needed to prove a geometric theorem from axioms; complex knowledge, such as an understanding of all the rules required to build an automobile; and the ability to learn, such as a neural network learning to recognize cancer cells. Scientists continue to look for better models of the brain and human intelligence.

The History of AI

Although the concept of AI probably has existed since antiquity, the term was first used by American scientist John McCarthy at a conference held at Dartmouth College in 1956. In 1955–56, the first AI program, Logic Theorist, had been written in information processing language (IPL), a programming language, and in 1958, McCarthy invented Lisp, a programming language that improved on IPL. *Syntactic Structures* (1957), a book about the structure of natural language by American linguist Noam Chomsky, made natural language processing into an area of study within AI. In the next few years, numerous researchers began to study AI, laying the foundation for many later applications, such as general problem solvers, intelligent machines, and expert systems.

In the 1960s, Edward Feigenbaum and other scientists at Stanford University built two early expert systems: DENDRAL, which classified chemicals, and MYCIN, which identified diseases. These early expert systems were cumbersome to modify because they had hard-coded rules. By 1970, the OPS expert system shell, with variable rule sets, had been released by Digital Equipment Corporation as the first commercial expert system shell. In addition to expert systems, neural networks became an important area of AI in the 1970s and 1980s. Frank Rosenblatt introduced the Perceptron in 1957, but it was *Perceptrons: An Introduction to Computational Geometry* (1969), by Minsky and Seymour Papert, and the two-volume *Parallel Distributed Processing: Explorations in the Microstructure of Cognition* (1986), by Rumelhart, McClelland, and the PDP Research Group, that

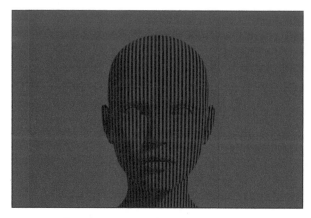

Image via iStock/akinbostanci. [Used under license.]

really defined the field of neural networks. Development of AI has continued, with game theory, speech recognition, robotics, and autonomous agents being some of the best-known examples.

How It Works

The first activity of AI is to understand how multiple facts interconnect to form knowledge and to represent that knowledge in a machine-understandable form. The next task is to understand and document a reasoning process for arriving at a conclusion. The final component of AI is to add, whenever possible, a learning process that enhances the knowledge of a system.

Knowledge Representation

Facts are simple pieces of information that can be seen as either true or false, although in fuzzy logic, there are levels of truth. When facts are organized, they become information, and when information is well understood, over time, it becomes knowledge. To use knowledge in AI, especially when writing programs, it has to be represented in some concrete fashion. Initially, most of those developing AI programs saw knowledge as represented symbolically, and their early knowledge representations were symbolic. Semantic nets, directed graphs of facts with added semantic content, were highly successful representations used in many of the early AI programs. Later, the nodes of the semantic nets were expanded to contain more information, and the resulting knowledge representation was referred to as frames. Frame representation of knowledge was very similar to object-oriented data representation, including a theory of inheritance.

Another popular way to represent knowledge in AI is as logical expressions. English mathematician George Boole represented knowledge as a Boolean expression in the 1800s. English mathematicians Bertrand Russell and Alfred Whitehead expanded this to quantified expressions in 1910, and French computer scientist Alain Colmerauer incorporated it into logic programming, with the programming language Prolog, in the 1970s. The knowledge of a rule-based expert system is embedded in the if-then rules of the system, and because each if-then rule has a Boolean representation, it can be seen as a form of relational knowledge representation.

Neural networks model the human neural system and use this model to represent knowledge. The brain is an electrochemical system that stores its knowledge in synapses. As electrochemical signals pass through a synapse, they modify it, resulting in the acquisition of knowledge. In the neural network model, synapses are represented by the weights of a weight matrix, and knowledge is added to the system by modifying the weights.

Reasoning

Reasoning is the process of determining new information from known information. Artificial intelligence systems add reasoning soon after they have developed a method of knowledge representation. If knowledge is represented in semantic nets, then most reasoning involves some type of tree search. One popular reasoning technique is to traverse a decision tree, in which the reasoning is represented by a path taken through the tree. Tree searches of general semantic nets can be very time-consuming and have led to many advancements in tree-search algorithms, such as placing bounds on the depth of search and backtracking.

Reasoning in logic programming usually follows an inference technique embodied in first-order predicate calculus. Some inference engines, such as that of Prolog, use a back-chaining technique to reason from a result, such as a geometry theorem, to its antecedents, the axioms, and also show how the reasoning process led to the conclusion. Other inference engines, such as that of the expert system shell CLIPS, use a forward-chaining inference engine to see what facts can be derived from a set of known facts.

Neural networks, such as backpropagation, have an especially simple reasoning algorithm. The knowledge of the neural network is represented as a matrix of synaptic connections, possibly quite sparse. The information to be evaluated by the neural network is represented as an input vector of the appropriate size, and the reasoning process is to multiply the connection matrix by the input vector to obtain the conclusion as an output vector.

Learning

Learning in an AI system involves modifying or adding to its knowledge. For both semantic net and logic programming systems, learning is accomplished by adding or modifying the semantic nets or logic rules, respectively. Although much effort has gone into developing learning algorithms for these systems, all of them, to date, have used ad hoc methods and experienced limited success. Neural networks, on the other hand, have been very successful at developing learning algorithms. Back-propagation has a robust supervised learning algorithm in which the system learns from a set of training pairs, using gradient-descent optimization, and numerous unsupervised learning algorithms learn by studying the clustering of the input vectors.

Applications and Products

There are many important applications of AI, ranging from computer games to programs designed to prove theorems in mathematics. This section contains a sample of both theoretical and practical applications.

One of the most successful areas of AI is expert systems. Literally thousands of expert systems are being used to help both experts and novices make decisions. There are several categories of expert systems, but by far the most popular are the rule-based expert systems. Most rule-based expert systems are created with an expert system shell. The first successful rule-based expert system shell was the OPS 5 of Digital Equipment Corporation (DEC), and the most popular modern systems are CLIPS, developed by the National Aeronautics and Space Administration (NASA) in 1985, and its Java clone, Jess, developed at Sandia National Laboratories in 1995. All rule-based expert systems have a similar architecture, and the shells make it fairly easy to create an expert system as soon as a knowledge engineer gathers the knowledge from a domain expert.

The most important component of a rule-based expert system is its knowledge base of rules. Each rule consists of an if-then statement with multiple antecedents, multiple consequences, and possibly a rule certainty factor. The antecedents of a rule are statements that can be true or false and that depend on facts that are either introduced into the system by a user or derived as the result of a rule being fired. For example, a fact could be red-wine and a simple rule could be if (red-wine) then (it-tastes-good). The expert system also has an inference engine that can apply multiple rules in an orderly fashion so that the expert system can draw conclusions by applying its rules to a set of facts introduced by a user. Although it is not absolutely required, most rule-based expert systems have a user-friendly interface and an explanation facility to justify its reasoning.

Most theorems in mathematics can be expressed in first-order predicate calculus. For any particular area, such as synthetic geometry or group theory, all provable theorems can be derived from a set of axioms. Mathematicians have written programs to automatically prove theorems since the 1950s. These theorem provers either start with the axioms and apply an inference technique, or start with the theorem and work backward to see how it can be derived from axioms. Resolution, developed in Prolog, is a well-known automated technique that can be used to prove theorems, but there are many others. For Resolution, the user starts with the theorem, converts it to a normal form, and then mechanically builds reverse decision trees to prove the theorem. If a reverse decision tree whose leaf nodes are all axioms is found, then a proof of the theorem has been discovered.

Gödel's Incompleteness Theorem (proved by Austrian-born American mathematician Kurt Gödel) shows that it may not be possible to automatically prove an arbitrary theorem in systems as complex as the natural numbers. For simpler systems, such as group theory, automated theorem proving works if the user's computer can generate all reverse trees or a suitable subset of trees that can yield a proof in a reasonable amount of time. Efforts have been made to develop theorem provers for higher-order logics than first-order predicate calculus, but these have not been very successful.

Computer scientists have spent considerable time trying to develop an automated technique for proving the correctness of programs, that is showing that any valid input to a program produces a valid output. This is generally done by producing a consistent model and mapping the program to the model. The first example of this was given by English mathematician Alan Turing in 1931, by using a simple model now called a "Turing machine." A formal system that is rich enough to serve as a model for a typical programming language, such as C++, must support higher-order logic to capture the arguments and parameters of subprograms. Lambda calculus, denotational semantics, von Neuman geometries, finite state machines, and other systems can provide a model onto which all programs of a language can be mapped. Some of these do capture many programs, but devising a practical automated method of verifying the correctness of programs has proven difficult.

Intelligent Tutor Systems

Almost every field of study has many intelligent tutor systems available to assist students in learning. Sometimes the tutor system is integrated into a package. For example, in some versions of Microsoft Office developed during the late 1990s and early 2000s, an embedded intelligent helper provided popup help boxes to a user when it detected the need for assistance and full-length tutorials if it detected more help was needed. In addition to the intelligent tutors embedded in programs as part of context-sensitive help systems, there are a vast number of stand-alone tutoring systems in use.

The first stand-alone intelligent tutor was SCHOLAR, developed by J. R. Carbonell in 1970. It used semantic nets to represent knowledge about South American geography, provided a user interface to support asking questions, and was successful enough to demonstrate that it was possible for a computer program to tutor students. At about the same time, the University of Illinois developed its PLATO computer-aided instruction system, which provided a general language for developing intelligent tutors with touch-sensitive screens, one of the most famous of which was a biology tutorial on evolution. Of the thousands of later intelligent tutors, SHERLOCK, a training environment for electronic

Feature detection (pictured: edge detection) helps AI compose informative abstract structures out of raw data. Photo by JonMcLoone at English Wikipedia, via Wikimedia Commons.

troubleshooting, and PUMP, a system designed to help learn algebra, are typical.

Electronic Games

Electronic games have been played since the invention of the cathode-ray tube for television. In the 1980s, games such as *Solitaire*, *Pac-Man*, and *Pong* for personal computers became almost as popular as the stand-alone game platforms. By the 2020s, multiuser internet games were enjoyed by young and old alike, and game playing on mobile devices had become an important application. In all of these electronic games, the user competes with one or more intelligent agents embedded in the game, and the creation of these intelligent agents uses considerable AI. When creating an intelligent agent that will compete with a user or, as in *Solitaire*, just react to the user, a programmer has to embed the game knowledge into the program.

For example, in chess, the programmer would need to capture all possible configurations of a chess board. The programmer also would need to add reasoning procedures to the game; for example, there would have to be procedures to move each individual chess piece on the board. Finally, and most important for game programming, the programmer would need to add one or more strategic decision modules to the program to provide the intelligent agent with a strategy for winning. In many cases, the strategy for winning a game would be driven by probability; for example, the next move might be a pawn, one space forward, because that yields the best probability of winning, but a heuristic strategy is also

possible; for example, the next move is a rook because it may trick the opponent into a bad series of moves.

Careers and Coursework

A major in computer science is the most common way to prepare for a career in AI. One needs substantial coursework in mathematics, philosophy, and psychology as a background for this degree. For many of the more interesting jobs in AI, one needs a master's or doctoral degree. Most universities teach courses in AI, neural networks, or expert systems, and many have courses in all three. Although AI is usually taught in computer science, it is also taught in mathematics, philosophy, psychology, and electrical engineering. Taking a strong minor in any field is advisable for someone seeking a career in AI because the discipline is often applied to another field.

Those seeking careers in AI generally take a position as a systems analyst or programmer. They work for a wide range of companies, including those developing business, mathematics, medical, and voice recognition applications. Those obtaining an advanced degree often take jobs in industrial, government, or university laboratories developing new areas of AI.

Social Context, Ethics, and Future Prospects

After AI was defined by McCarthy in 1956, it has had a number of ups and downs as a discipline, but the future of AI looks good. Almost every commercial program has a help system, and increasingly these help systems have a major AI component. Health care is another area that is poised to make major use of AI to improve the quality and reliability of the care provided, as well as to reduce its cost by providing expert advice on best practices in health care. Smartphones and other digital devices employ AI for an array of applications, syncing the activities and requirements of their users.

Ethical questions have been raised about trying to build a machine that exhibits human intelligence. Many of the early researchers in AI were interested in cognitive psychology and built symbolic models of intelligence that were considered unethical by some. Later, many AI researchers developed neural models of intelligence that were not always deemed ethical. The social and ethical issues of AI are nicely represented by HAL, the Heuristically programmed Algorithmic computer, in Stanley Kubrick's 1968 film *2001: A Space Odyssey*, which first works well with humans, then acts violently toward them, and is in the end deactivated.

Another important ethical question posed by AI is the appropriateness of developing programs to collect information about users of a program. Intelligent agents are often embedded in websites to collect information about those using the site, generally without the permission of those using the website, and many question whether this should be done.

In the mid-to-late 2010s, fully autonomous self-driving cars were developed and tested in the United States. In 2018, an Uber self-driving car hit and killed a pedestrian in Tempe, Arizona. There was a safety driver at the wheel of the car, which was in self-driving mode at the time of the accident. Even before the accident occurred, ethicists raised questions regarding collision-avoidance programming and moral and legal responsibility, among others. The accident led Uber to suspend its driverless-car testing program for several months. However, Uber resumed testing its self-driving cars in select cities following the incident, and companies such as Waymo and Tesla likewise continued their work within the field of semiautonomous or fully autonomous vehicles.

As more complex AI is created and imbued with general, humanlike intelligence (instead of concentrated intelligence in a single area, such as Deep Blue and chess), it will run into moral requirements as humans do. According to researchers Nick Bostrom and Eliezer Yudkowsky, if an AI is given "cognitive work" to do that has a social aspect, the AI inherits the social requirements of these interactions. The AI then needs to be imbued with a sense of morality to interact in these situations. If an AI has humanlike intelligence and agency, the Bostrom has also theorized that AI will need to also be considered both persons and moral entities. There is also the potential for the development of superhuman intelligence in AI, which would breed superhuman morality. The questions of intelligence and morality and who is given personhood are some of the most significant issues to be considered contextually as AI advance.

—*George M. Whitson*

References

Alpaydin, Ethem. *Introduction to Machine Learning.* 4th ed., MIT Press, 2020.

Basl, John. "The Ethics of Creating Artificial Consciousness." *American Philosophical Association Newsletters: Philosophy and Computers*, vol. 13., no. 1, 2013, pp. 25–30.

Berlatsky, Noah. *Artificial Intelligence.* Greenhaven Press, 2011.

Bostrom, Nick. "Ethical Issues in Advanced Artificial Intelligence." *NickBostrom.com*, 2003, nickbostrom.com/ethics/ai.html.

Bostrom, Nick, and Eliezer Yudkowsky. "The Ethics of Artificial Intelligence." *The Cambridge Handbook of Artificial Intelligence*, edited by Keith Frankish and William M. Ramsay, Cambridge UP, 2014, pp. 316–34.

Hawkins, Andrew J. "Uber Has Resumed Testing Its Self-Driving Cars in San Francisco." *Verge*, 10 Mar. 2020, www.theverge.com/2020/3/10/21172213/uber-self-driving-car-resume-testing-san-francisco-crash.

Kendal, Simon, and Malcolm Creen. *An Introduction to Knowledge Engineering.* Springer-Verlag, 2007.

Laalaoui, Yacine, and Nizar Bouguila, editors. *Artificial Intelligence Applications in Information and Communication Technologies.* Springer International, 2015.

Minsky, Marvin, and Seymour A. Papert. *Perceptrons: An Introduction to Computational Geometry.* Reissue ed., MIT Press, 2017.

Nyholm, Sven, and Jilles Smids. "The Ethics of Accident-Algorithms for Self-Driving Cars: An

Applied Trolley Problem?" *Ethical Theory & Moral Practice*, vol. 19, no. 5, 2016, pp. 1275–89.

Rumelhart, David E., James L. McClelland, and the PDP Research Group. *Parallel Distributed Processing: Explorations in the Microstructure of Cognition.* 2 vols. 1986. MIT Press, 1989.

Russell, Stuart, and Peter Norvig. *Artificial Intelligence: A Modern Approach.* 4th ed., Pearson, 2020.

ASSESSING DIGITAL LITERACY

Introduction

Digital literacy is defined as the ability to function in the modern world of interconnected computer networks by accessing information, understanding it and synthesizing it, and then communicating that information to others across the network. Because there are a wide range of skill levels at which various individuals can perform these functions, and a vast array of devices, technologies, and applications that may be used for these purposes, it is important to develop mechanisms in ways that have broad applicability across different contexts.

Background

Technology changes very rapidly, so it has been challenging to develop a reliable set of standards to measure how adept students and others are at using it. It is not uncommon for an assessment to be developed around questions that were more relevant when the project began than they are as it is being completed. For this reason, the more widely adopted forms of digital literacy assessment tend to focus not on specific technologies but on skill sets that exist at a higher level of abstraction.

One such set of standards has been developed by the International Society for Technology in Education (ISTE). The ISTE has different sets of standards for different groups, including teachers, administrators, students, coaches (educators who assist with technology, rather than athletics), and computer science teachers. The ISTE standards for students address six different areas: creativity, collaboration, research, critical thinking, citizenship, and operation of technology.

The availability of standards such as those of ISTE is only one piece of the puzzle, however; there must also be a system for comparing the standards with the performance of a group to determine how they perform. An example of such an assessment system is the one developed by the Northstar Digital Literacy Project in Minnesota. Northstar is a project that was initiated by a cooperative effort among several public libraries and nonprofits in Minnesota after the recession which began in 2008, with the purpose of helping those who were unemployed or underemployed to acquire skills related to technology and to obtain verification that they possessed such skills. Users of the Northstar training completed online training modules and were then able to complete online assessments of the skills they acquired through the training. Those who successfully complete the assessments can print certificates that they can include with their job application materials.

Libraries and Digital Literacy

Libraries have for many years played a leading role in providing instruction in digital literacy skills and in assessing the effectiveness of such instruction. One of the main services provided by libraries has always been to help people learn how to locate information, how to organize it and analyze it and then synthesize it to apply it to real world problems. Traditionally this was done using books and paper-based card catalogs, but with the computer revolution and the arrival of the internet, libraries have adapted their traditional forms of instruction to accommodate the new tools now available to them.

Libraries are now on the front lines of assisting people in learning how to use computers, how to connect to the internet and find information, and how to communicate with others online. At the same time, most libraries must engage in an ongoing struggle for funding support from their parent agencies, whether a city government, university administration, or school principal. This is because there is often skepticism that libraries are being used to a significant degree, and even if they are, whether they do an adequate job of meeting people's information needs. For this reason, libraries tend to be quite rigorous about collecting assessment data about all their activities, to use this information to demonstrate to their funding agencies the nature and effectiveness of their activities. This explains why so many digital literacy assessment initiatives can be traced to libraries.

Assessing Digital Literacy: Hard and Soft Skills

The assessment of digital literacy tends to fall into two broad categories. The first of these includes assessments that measure skills related to technology. These can be related to computer hardware or to computer software, and indicate the degree to which people are able to utilize equipment such as printers, keyboards, mice, storage media like flash drives and optical disks, as well as network technology such as routers, switches, modems, and cables. These types of skills lend themselves to straightforward assessment procedures, as the abilities being measured are either possessed or are not possessed.

The second category of assessments is less clear cut, as it concentrates on assessing the behaviors of users. These behaviors include perceptions and attitudes toward many aspects of life online: piracy and copyright, privacy and the disclosure of personal information on both a voluntary and involuntary basis, and what is commonly referred to as one's digital footprint, which can be described as the trail one leaves online in the form of internet browser history entries, postings in online forums and on social media, and similar details.

There is a third category of skill to consider regarding digital literacy, but it has thus far proven difficult to describe, much less evaluate: sometimes referred to as generativity, it involves one's ability to produce something altogether new after having drawn upon others' ideas. The goal of digital literacy is to assist people in reaching the stage of generativity, but up until the present this often seems to happen of its own accord, after a large amount of trial and error and persistence on the part of the user, rather than in response to any pedagogical strategy.

The results of most digital literacy assessments share some features. Most students score well at measures of technical capability, that is, being able to operate a computer, and of digital citizenship, most likely because many of the skills required for mastery of digital citizenship are also necessary in order safeguard one's privacy and finances from intrusion or potential misuse. Scores on other areas, however, tend to be much lower, particularly those pertaining to the ability to search for and locate information, and to use critical thinking and decision-making skills to evaluate that information. These results have been interpreted as indications of a frequent misconception which arises in the context of digital literacy assessment, namely, the conflation of exposure to technology with the capability of using that technology in meaningful ways. For example, it is frequently assumed that young people who have grown up with regular access to the internet and are comfortable using all sorts of gadgets and applications must also be adept at applying their critical thinking skills to evaluate the information that their devices help them to obtain.

Assessing Digital Literacy: Digital Literacy in Schools

These are the types of tasks for which people tend to score lowest in digital literacy tests. Reviews of such results have prompted many educators to make renewed calls for focusing instruction less on the technological tools that are available at a given point in time—because this set of tools changes so rapidly—and more on developing students' ability to discern which tool is appropriate to use in different situations. Thus, assessments of digital literacy are having real impacts on the types and modes of instruction in schools.

Many programs have begun to experiment with approaches where students are asked to perform a task, such as to develop a presentation explaining a task, but the students are given the freedom to choose what types of information sources they will draw upon and what technological tools they believe will be best adapted to presenting the results of their work. One group might do its research in the library, reading books and articles, while another might conduct interviews and surveys using social media; similarly, one group's results might be presented as a brief video, while another could develop a traditional presentation.

A "Common Core" Approach

Several researchers have suggested that the most effective approach to developing digital literacy is different from most of the attempts that have been made. These efforts have tended to treat digital literacy as a set of skills and behaviors that exists separately from other fields, much like the subject of electrical engineering exists separately from, for example, meteorology. This has led to digital literacy assessment efforts that happen outside of the regular curriculum, often taking place as part of a general (and typically brief) library instruction session or lecture series. Students thus begin to think of digital literacy as something that only pertains to library research, when a more accurate and useful understanding might place digital literacy inside the curriculum of other subjects, making it a skill more central to all aspects of education, rather than just in one or two fields.

This approach would require either a more comprehensive effort at assisting instructors in teaching digital literacy effectively, or collaboration in developing a curriculum between subject matter experts and experts in digital literacy. In either case, the result could be a curriculum for biology or literature or fine arts that includes assignments and assessments designed to build the student's digital literacy within the course's subject scope. For example, instead of learning about biology in biology class and digital literacy in a library session, a library expert in digital literacy could work with the biology faculty to build a course syllabus that includes assignments designed to promote digital literacy, such as finding scholarly articles about an assigned topic in biology, evaluating these sources for credibility and bias, and then producing a summary of findings. This approach would make digital literacy a common thread running throughout the curricula of all classes, potentially allowing the gains realized in one subject area to translate over to other subject areas, as digital literacy skills used in one subject are applied elsewhere with similar success.

Viewpoints

For a digital literacy assessment tool to effectively measure a population's performance, there is general agreement that it must have some basic characteristics. These may include, but are not limited to, verification of validity and reliability of the sort any assessment tool requires, multiple observers and observations, consistency, usefulness, an implementation that is feasible to accomplish, fairness so that all participants have an equal chance to demonstrate their abilities, and alignment between the context and the assessment instrument. All these factors may not be present at optimal levels in an assessment, but when they are the information obtained tends to be of higher quality. Some of the more difficult evaluations to carry out in an objective manner are those

that deal not with measurable competencies with specific technologies, nor with strictly behavioral components, but with the ability to assess an information source's credibility.

The nature of the difficulty of accurately assessing this competency is because a person's perceived success at this function can vary somewhat according to the ideological position of the observer. It can be all too easy for the evaluator to conclude that the student's critical thinking ability is lacking, when in fact the student and the reviewer simply disagree about which sources are credible and which are not. An example of this would be an instructor who believes that the local newspaper prints nothing but lies, and a student who has great faith in the same paper and reads it regularly. The student might have arrived at his or her opinion about the paper in a perfectly rational, sound way, but the instructor will at the very least suffer a fleeting temptation to conclude that no one who finds value in the publication can possibly be using his or her rational faculties.

Thus, a major pitfall in the assessment of digital literacy can be reviewer bias. This has caused some to suggest that the proper context for the promotion of digital literacy and its systematic assessment is the home rather than the school or the library. The idea behind this suggestion is that parents who want their children to be digitally literate most often also want this digital literacy to be compatible with the family's beliefs and attitudes, so digital literacy initiatives undertaken in the home will have the advantage of incorporating the family judgments about digital literacy and credibility. One potential challenge to this suggestion is that there is a basic lack of expertise throughout much of the world concerning digital literacy, so shifting responsibility for digital literacy to the family would be a de facto means of shutting down all progress in fostering digital citizenship. Librarians have resisted this type of suggestion—considering the digital divide and emphasizing their mission to empower members of their communities to obtain and find the information they need—whether it is in conflict with others in those communities or even within their families.

—Scott Zimmer

References

Brooks-Young, S., and International Society for Technology in Education. *Digital-Age Literacy for Teachers: Applying Technology Standards to Everyday Practice.* International Society for Technology in Education, 2007.

Cartelli, A. *Current Trends and Future Practices for Digital Literacy and Competence.* Information Science Reference, 2012.

Cohen, D. J., and T. Scheinfeldt. *Hacking the Academy: New Approaches to Scholarship and Teaching from Digital Humanities.* U of Michigan P, 2013.

Coiro, J. *Handbook of Research on New Literacies.* Lawrence Erlbaum Associates/Taylor and Francis, 2008.

Eisenberg, M., C. A. Lowe, K. L. Spitzer, et al. *Information literacy: Essential Skills for the Information Age.* Libraries Unlimited, 2004.

Goldman, S. R., K. Lawless, J. Pellegrino, et al. "A Technology for Assessing Multiple Source Comprehension: An Essential Skill of the 21st Century." *Technology-based Assessments for 21st Century Skills: Theoretical and Practical Implications from Modern Research,* edited by M. C. Mayrath, J. Clarke-Midura, D. H. Robinson, G. Schraw, Information Age Publishing, 2012, pp. 173–209.

Greenstein, L. *Assessing 21st Century Skills: A Guide to Evaluating Mastery and Authentic Learning.* Corwin, 2012

Mackey, T. P., and T. Jacobson. *Using Technology to Teach Information Literacy.* Neal-Schuman, 2008.

Martin, A. M., and K. R. Roberts. "Digital Native ≠ Digital Literacy." *Principal,* vol. 94, no. 3, 2015, pp. 18–21.

Neal, M. R. *Writing Assessment and the Revolution in Digital Texts and Technologies.* Teachers College Press, 2011.

Neumann, C. "Teaching Digital Natives: Promoting Information Literacy and Addressing Instructional Challenges." *Reading Improvement,* vol. 53, no. 3, 2016, pp. 101–6.

Smith, J. K., L. I. Given, H. Julien, et al. "Information Literacy Proficiency: Assessing the Gap in High School Students' Readiness for Undergraduate Academic Work." *Library and Information Science Research,* vol. 35, no. 2, 2013, pp. 88–96.

Stergioulas, L., and H. Drenoyianni. *Pursuing Digital Literacy in Compulsory Education.* Peter Lang, 2011.

Thomson, S., B. L. J. De, and Australian Council for Educational Research. *Preparing Australian Students for the Digital World: Results from the PISA 2009 Digital Reading Literacy Assessment.* ACER Press, 2012.

Watson, J. A., and L. L. Pecchioni. "Digital Natives and Digital Media in the College Classroom: Assignment Design and Impacts on Student Learning." *Educational Media International,* vol. 48, no. 4, 2011, pp. 307–20.

Wiesinger, S., and R. Beliveau. *Digital Literacy: A Primer on Media, Identity, and the Evolution of Technology.* Peter Lang, 2016.

ASSISTIVE AND ADAPTIVE TECHNOLOGY

Introduction

Assistive and adaptive technology comprises specialized equipment and applications that are used to enable people with disabilities and those with age-related functional decline to function effectively in the world. Assistive products, which allow easier completion of tasks and more independence, are sometimes custom designed or modified to serve a particular individual's needs. Examples include mobility devices, such as walkers, wheelchairs, and prostheses. Assistive technology includes screen-reading software, speech synthesizers, and eye-gaze and head-pointing software, among many others. Adaptive devices enable people to work on standard computers or other devices by altering existing equipment. For example, using an alternate keyboard, magnifying a screen, adding more visible colors, or using gesture controls are considered adaptive technologies.

Background

Until the latter part of the twentieth century, individuals with disabilities were mostly invisible. Often kept at home, sometimes institutionalized, children and adults were routinely excluded from education and employment opportunities, and most public buildings were inaccessible. However, in 1973, Section 504 of the Rehabilitation Act established that individuals with physical or mental impairments must be protected from discrimination. The law required employers to make reasonable accommodations for workers with physical disabilities and other disorders. The Americans with Disabilities Act, modeled after the Civil Rights Act of 1964, followed in 1990. It mandated accommodations such as wheelchair access to most buildings to ensure access to government programs and services and participation in ordinary daily activities. Once personal computers came into widespread use, they became a vehicle for further inclusion, and technicians developed specialized assistive technology for people with blindness, deafness, and physical disabilities.

With the advent of computers and access to the internet, the worlds of communication, education, services, and activities opened up for people with disabilities. Those who previously could not read because of impaired vision or learning disabilities, who could not write because of paralysis or missing limbs, who could not speak because of injury or muscle degeneration, rapidly gained access to programs and equipment that could help them. However, most technology still required a certain level of physical dexterity and usually the ability to see. The limitations particularly affected those who were blind or who could not manipulate a mouse or type on a keyboard. Technicians and occupational therapists took an interest in adapting computer technology and designed alternate keyboards and adaptive controls to replace standard equipment. Sound clues, joysticks, trackballs, and electronic pointing devices became available, and specialized software provided additional assistance.

Technology for Those with Low Vision

Blind people have long used human or canine helpers, Braille text, and recorded books, but they possessed little independence. Increasingly high-tech devices, including text-to-speech programs, began to provide better communication for those with impaired vision. By the twenty-first century, smartphones had taken assistive technology a giant leap forward. Mobile users could access the personal assistant, which responded to verbal instructions and answered the same way, while podcasts, audiobooks, news, and other information are accessible through voice commands. Equipped with built-in screen readers, global positioning system (GPS) mapping and directions, and applications such as text recognition, color and light readers, and

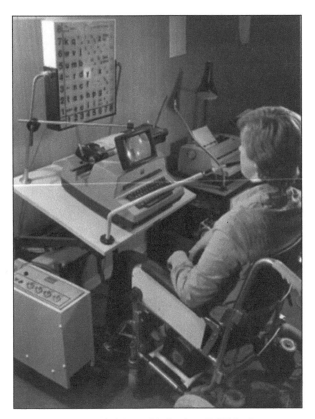

The Patient Operated Selector Mechanism (POSM), first developed in the early 1960s, is an assistive technology used to send signals to a device using air pressure by "sipping" (inhaling) or "puffing" (exhaling) on a straw, tube or "wand." It is primarily used by people who do not have the use of their hands. Photo via Wikimedia Commons. [Public domain.]

universal product code (UPC) and quick response (QR) code scanners, the technology released blind and low-vision people from constant dependence on others. VizWiz and oMoby apps recognized images and could transmit photos with questions to be answered in real time by volunteers; Aira, a similar app, transmits a live video feed and GPS tracking from the user's smartglasses to a personal assistant, who describes the location to the user and helps them navigate. As of 2018, indoor-mapping and 3D-sensing software capabilities were in development, as was the driverless car, all of which would provide greater independence for many people.

Assistive Technology for Deafness and Hearing Loss

People with impaired hearing waited a long time for assistive technology to meet their needs, according to the National Association of the Deaf. Routine use of closed captioning on television and movies did not become widely available until the late 1990s.

This is one reason people who are deaf or hard of hearing eagerly embraced pagers, videophones, and text messaging when they became available. While teletypewriters (TTY) and other telecommunications devices for the deaf (TDDs) allowed deaf or hard of hearing people to communicate by telephone, widely available relay services later allowed the user to speak to the recipient while incoming messages were read by the person who could not hear. Video phones enabled the use of American Sign Language (ASL), and Skype and Facetime, videoconferencing and instant-messaging web applications, are also useful for people with hearing loss.

Additional software solutions were developed specifically to address the needs of deaf and hard of hearing users. Much like the text-to-speech readers designed for low-vision individuals, the KinTrans program converts ASL recorded via three-dimensional (3D) camera to text or voice, and vice versa, improving communication with non-signers. Similarly, the Hearing AI app allows users to visualize, and thus follow, conversational speech and to receive vibration alerts for audible alarms.

Technology for People with Physical Disabilities

The Americans with Disabilities Act opened doors for people with physical disabilities, and the demand for assistive technology grew. People affected by cerebral palsy, spinal cord injuries, degenerative diseases, or injuries enjoyed increased independence through technological innovations. Electric wheelchairs and mobility scooters, along with vans equipped with lifts, helped people get around, while the assistive devices added to computers greatly extended access to communication, education, and employment. Instruments including switches, joysticks, and pointing tools were operated by a single finger or were strapped to the head or chin to move the cursor or press keys. Alternate keyboards and touch screens permitted additional access. Advances in sensors have led to devices such as a stabilizing utensil handle and a biofeedback rehabilitation belt that help people with tremors to eat and walk more steadily.

The prominent physicist Dr. Stephen Hawking was disabled by amyotrophic lateral sclerosis (ALS),

also known as Lou Gehrig's disease. As his muscles gradually atrophied as a result of the disease, Hawking lost mobility and the ability to speak; yet assistive technology enabled him to continue his research, travel, and writing. Hawking operated his computer using switches controlled by one thumb or by blinking his eyes. He had a sophisticated electric wheelchair and communicated and delivered speeches using a voice synthesizer. Remembered most for his scientific contributions, Hawking also brought such technologies and devices into the mainstream and demonstrating that those with disabilities need not be confined by them.

—*Nancy W. Comstock*

References

"Assistive Technology, Accommodations, and the Americans with Disabilities Act." *Assistive Technology Partners*. Assistive Technology Partners, U of Colorado, 2011, www.ucdenver.edu/academics/colleges/medicalschool/programs/atp/Documents/ATAccommodationsandtheAmericanwithDisabilitiesAct.pdf.

Davis, Amanda. "Three Life-Changing Technologies at the 2017 Assistive Technology Conference." *The Institute*. IEEE, 10 Mar. 2017, theinstitute.ieee.org/ieee-roundup/blogs/blog/three-lifechanging-technologies-at-the-2017-assistive-technology-conference.

Dormehl, Luke. "Assistive Tech Is Progressing Faster Than Ever, and These 7 Devices Prove It." *Digital Trends*, 6 Apr. 2018, www.digitaltrends.com/cool-tech/assistive-tech-examples.

"Dr. Stephen Hawking: A Case Study on Using Technology to Communicate with the World." *DO-IT Knowledge Base*, U of Washington, 2013. www.washington.edu/doit/articles?370.

"Google Unveils Smartphone with 3D Sensors." *BBC News: Technology*. BBC, 20 Feb. 2014. wn.com/computer_accessibility/bbc.

Greenemeier, Larry. "5 Mobile Technologies Help Level the Playing Field for People with Disabilities." *Scientific American*, 5 Aug. 2015, www.scientificamerican.com/article/5-mobile-technologies-help-level-the-playing-field-for-people-with-disabilities-video.

"Information and Technical Assistance on the Americans with Disabilities Act." *ADA.gov*. US Department of Justice, Civil Rights Division, www.ada.gov/ada_intro.htm.

"Making Communication and Information Accessible." *National Association of the Deaf.* National Association of the Deaf, 2014, nad.org/issues/technology.

Rose, Damon. "Smartphone Cameras Bring Independence to Blind People." *BBC News: Technology.* BBC, 12 July 2012.

"Top 10 iPhone Apps for People Who Are Deaf or Hard of Hearing." *Accessible Technology Coalition.* AT Coalition, 2014, atcoalition.org/news/top-10-iphone-apps-people-who-are-deaf-or-hard-hearing.

"Your Rights under Section 504 of the Rehabilitation Act." *Fact Sheet.* US Department of Health and Human Services Office for Civil Rights, 2006, www.hhs.gov/ocr/civilrights/resources/factsheets/504.pdf.

ASSISTIVE TECHNOLOGY IN EDUCATION

Introduction

Assistive technology (AT) refers to devices that assist special needs students with physical or intellectual impairments in adapting to a standard classroom environment. These devices include alternate keyboards, Braille displays, voice recognition software, reading comprehension programs, and speech synthesizers. Such devices are but the latest in a series of advances—encouraged financially and legislatively by states and the federal government—to harness the power of technology to enrich the lives of the disabled. By using AT, students who would previously have been unable to go to school, or to do so with great difficulty, have been able to learn along with the rest of their peers. The removal of these barriers to learning is considered one of the most rewarding uses of technology. The Assistive Technology Act of 2004 contains the rules and regulations that schools are required to follow when dealing with special education students requiring AT. By law, all students with special needs, whether they use AT or not, are required to be given a Free Appropriate Public Education (FAPE) from kindergarten through grade 12.

Background

The US government has been a supporter of AT measures since the 19th century. In 1879, the US Congress gave $10,000 to the American Printing House for the Blind to produce Braille materials. Later, in 1958, they funded efforts to close-caption films for the deaf. In the 1960s, as the field of special education coalesced, the federal government again entered the picture by funding two Special Education Materials Centers to help discover the best ways to distribute AT materials to special education teachers. According to data provided by the National Assistive Technology Technical Assistance Partnership, "The Assistive Technology Act of 1998, as amended (P.L. 108-364), provides funding to support grants to states throughout the United States and its territories for AT programs. The mission of the state AT programs is to get technology into the hands of those who need it so they can be more independent and improve functional capabilities to reach educational, life, and employment goals" (State Assistive Technology Programs, 2011).

As the congressional authors of the reauthorized Technology-Related Assistance for Individuals with Disabilities Act of 1994 noted, AT in its broadest sense is about the empowerment of all disabled people—young and old—using technology:

> Substantial progress has been made in the development of AT devices, including adaptations to existing devices that facilitate activities of daily living that significantly benefit individuals with disabilities of all ages. These devices, including adaptations, increase involvement in, and reduce expenditures associated with, programs and activities that facilitate communication, ensure independent functioning, enable early childhood development, support educational achievement, provide and enhance employment options, and enable full participation in community living for individuals with disabilities. Access to such devices can also reduce expenditures associated with early childhood intervention, education, residential living, independent living, recreation opportunities, and other aspects of daily living. (Technology-Related Assistance)

The Technology-Related Assistance for Individuals with Disabilities Act goes on to define an AT device as "any item, piece of equipment, or product system, whether acquired commercially off the shelf, modified, or customized, that is used to increase, maintain, or improve functional capabilities of individuals with disabilities" (Technology-Related Assistance).

Types of Assistive Technologies

According to Blackhurst & Edyburn, AT for students with disabilities can be subdivided into the seven general problem areas they address:

- Existence problems are associated with the functions needed to sustain life, such as eating, grooming, dressing, elimination, and hygiene. Solutions may include adapted utensils, dressing aids, adapted toilet seats, toilet training, and occupational therapy services;
- Communication problems are associated with the functions needed to receive, internalize, and express information, such as oral and written expression, visual and auditory reception, and social interaction. Solutions may include hearing amplifiers, captioned video, speech aids, sign language training, magnifiers, picture boards, writing and drawing aids, pointers, alternative input and output devices for computers, augmentative communication services, social skills training, and speech/language pathology services;
- Body support, protection, and positioning problems are associated with the functions needed to stabilize, support, or protect a portion of the body, such as standing, sitting, alignment, stabilizing, and preventing injury from falls. Solutions may include prone standers, furniture adaptation, support harnesses, stabilizers, slings, head gear, and physical therapy services;
- Travel and mobility problems are associated with the functions needed to move horizontally or vertically, such as crawling, walking, using stairs, lateral and vertical transfers, and navigating in the environment. Solutions may include wheelchairs, scooters, hoists, cycles, ambulators, walkers, crutches, canes, and orientation and mobility services;
- Environmental interaction problems are associated with the functions needed to perform activities across environments, such as operating equipment and accessing facilities. Solutions may include the use of switches to control equipment, remote control devices, adapted, ramps, automatic door openers, modified furniture, driving aids, and rehabilitation engineering services;
- Education and transition problems are associated with the functions needed to participate in learning activities and to prepare for new school settings or post-school settings such as assessment, learning, access to the general education curriculum, creative and performing arts, using instructional materials, and preparing for new environments. Solutions may include adapted instructional materials, educational software, computer adaptations, community-based instruction, creative arts therapy, AT, and other related services;
- Sports, fitness, and recreation problems are associated with the functions needed to participate in individual or group sports, play, hobby and craft activities such as individual and group play, leisure activities, sports, exercise, games, and hobbies. Solutions may include modified rules and equipment, Special Olympics, adapted aquatics, switch-activated cameras, Braille playing cards, and adapted physical education services.

Barriers to Implementation

Despite much progress, many researchers maintain that there are significant barriers to be overcome before AT can deliver benefits for all students who need it. Alper and Raharinirina list four major impediments to AT access:

- Despite the existing educational technology, accessible technology is unavailable to many students with disabilities and their families. For example, Norman observed that not all groups have equal access, primarily due to limited financial resources;
- The high costs of equipment and lack of funding to access devices or services, as well as lack of information regarding AT for families of individuals with disabilities, are often primary barriers;
- Professionals' lack of knowledge about technology can be a major obstacle. For example, few training programs for special education

teachers include courses or class sessions on AT applications and issues; and

- Lack of ongoing support can constitute a main problem. Eligibility issues are often important obstacles, and have led to the underutilization of AT by individuals with disabilities.

These realities make research showing the value of AT for special needs students even more poignant. For example, one study of secondary school students showed that "four assistive software tools (speech synthesis, spellchecker, homophone tool, and dictionary)" yielded "a significant assistive value … across several domains of literacy" (Lange et al.).

As more of these students are being educated in inclusive classrooms, where they are expected to perform grade-level work but not always given specialized support, teachers are searching for ways to educate students with disabilities more effectively. Yet too many teachers are unaware of the potential of assistive technologies to empower students struggling to work independently at their grade level.

The results of a 2011 study by Jost and Mosley revealed a moderate awareness and low level of working knowledge among general education teachers regarding ATs in the classroom. However, these teachers, who are increasingly expected to develop capacities to use such technologies to connect individual learners to the curriculum, also express a high degree of interest in and openness to AT, suggesting the need for more AT classes for teachers as part of the curriculum on instructional technology.

According to Bouck, Flanagan, Miller, and Bassette, the potential category of ATs has grown to include a wide range of commercially available products, many of which are transportable, easy to use, low cost, and socially acceptable, such as MP3 players, smartphones, and tablets. The stigmatization of those who require AT can be greatly reduced by providing access to devices that are readily available, broadly advertised to the public, and desired by one's peers.

Assistive Technology Services

Assistive technology services are how AT gets into the hands of students and others who make use of it. According to the 2004 amendments to the Assistive Technology Act of 1998, AT services include:

- "The evaluation of the assistive technology needs of an individual with a disability";

- "…purchasing, leasing, or otherwise providing for the acquisition of assistive technology devices by individuals with disabilities";
- "…selecting, designing, fitting, customizing, adapting, applying, maintaining, repairing, replacing, or donating assistive technology devices";
- "coordination and use of necessary therapies, interventions, or services with assistive technology devices";
- "training or technical assistance for an individual with a disability or, where appropriate, the family members, guardians, advocates, or authorized representatives of such an individual";
- "training or technical assistance for professionals (including individuals providing education and rehabilitation services and entities that manufacture or sell assistive technology devices), employers, providers of employment and training services, or other individuals who provide services to, employ, or are otherwise substantially involved in the major life functions of individuals with disabilities";
- "…expanding the availability of access to technology, including electronic and information technology, to individuals with disabilities."

This process is crucial in matching students' needs with the AT that best fits their educational objectives and developmental abilities. Parents, school administrators and teachers must work together to ensure that students are being properly evaluated through AT services, set up with AT as needed and then tracked through an Individualized Education Program (IEP) that can adjust to their evolving educational needs and progress.

The Assistive Technology Act of 2004

The federal government has taken a proactive role in requiring the use of AT in US public school classrooms. The Assistive Technology Act of 2004 contains the rules and regulations that schools are required to follow when dealing with students requiring AT. The act itself begins by outlining state and federal government involvement in AT from the 1980s to the present. It then attempts to build on past success by creating a grant program to equip states with the financial resources they need to help citizens—the disabled and their caregivers—with a wide range of AT support, including the use of AT in the K-12 public school classroom. These include access to:

- **Alternate keyboards:** Computer keyboards designed to mitigate or eliminate repetitive stress injury by improving the user's posture when typing. Examples include split or tented keyboards.
- **Assistive technology services:** An umbrella term used to refer to the processes by which AT products are discussed, purchased, maintained, and monitored.
- **Braille displays:** A device made up of a row of special "soft" cells that "display" on-screen information in a tactile manner.
- **Reading comprehension programs:** Computer software designed to help students improve reading comprehension through interactive activities.
- **Speech synthesizers:** Software that reads aloud the text appearing on a computer screen.
- **Voice recognition software:** Computer software that converts spoken language into words on a computer display.

More directly relevant to students with disabilities are special education laws that come alongside the Assistive Technology Act of 2004. Public Law 94-142, The Education for all Handicapped Children Act of 1975 has ultimately transformed into the Individuals with Disabilities Education Act of 2004 (IDEA). IDEA guarantees the right of all children with disabilities to a free and appropriate public education (FAPE) in the "least restrictive environment."

Individualized Family Service Plans and Individualized Education Programs

The Individuals with Disabilities Education Act of 2004 (IDEA) is one of the most granular special education laws on the books. It focuses on how the individual students' needs are identified before they are addressed using means such as AT. The identification of needs comes through a federal mandate the legislators call an Individual Education Plan (IEP). The IEP is developed by a team of professionals, parents, and the sometimes the student. The IEP team reports on the student's strengths and weaknesses and defines short- and long-term goals with specific objectives for the student to reach. As part of such

planning processes, all parties involved are required to consider the technologies that may be helpful in meeting the objectives in the IEP.

The New Jersey Department of Education has created model IEP forms "to assist [New Jersey public school] districts in ensuring that all required components of the IEP are included." Granting some state-to-state variation, these forms are a useful guide for thinking through the IEP process. The "US Department of Education" has also published its own model IEP forms, as required by IDEA.

—Matt Donnelly

References

Alnahdi, G. "Assistive Technology in Special Education and the Universal Design for Learning." *Turkish Online Journal of Educational Technology*, vol. 13, 2014, pp. 18–23.

Alper, S., and S. Raharinirina. "Assistive Technology for Individuals with Disabilities: A Review and Synthesis of the Literature." *Journal of Special Education Technology*, vol. 21, 2006, pp. 47–64.

Assistive Technology Act of 2004. Public Law 108-364. Frwebgate.access.gpo.gov.

Bauer, S., L. J. Elsaesser, M. Scherer, et al. "Promoting a Standard for Assistive Technology Service Delivery." *Technology and Disability*, vol. 26, 2014, pp. 39–48.

Behrmann, M., and J. Schaff. "Assisting Educators with Assistive Technology: Enabling Children to Achieve Independence in Living and Learning." *Children and Families*, vol. 42, 2001, pp. 24–28.

Blackhurst, A. E., and D. L. Edyburn. "A Brief History of Special Education Technology." *Special Education Technology Practice*, vol. 2, 2000, pp. 21–36.

Bishop, J. "The Internet for Educating Individuals with Social Impairments." *Journal of Computer Assisted Learning vol. 19*, 2013, pp. 546–56.

Bouck, E. C. "A National Snapshot of Assistive Technology for Students with Disabilities." *Journal of Special Education Technology*, vol. 31, no. 1, 2016, pp. 4–13.

___. *Assistive Technology.* SAGE Publications, 2017.

Bouck, E. C., S. Flanagan, B. Miller, et al. "Rethinking Everyday Technology as Assistive Technology to Meet Students' IEP Goals." *Journal of Special Education Technology*, vol. 27, 2012, pp. 47–57.

Cook, A. M., and S. Hussey. *Assistive Technologies: Principles and Practice.* 2nd ed., Elsevier/Mosby, 2001.

Green, Joan L. *Assistive Technology in Special Education: Resources for Education, Intervention, and Rehabilitation.* Prufrock Press, 2014.

Jones, V. L., and L. J. Hinesmon-Matthews. "Effective Assistive Technology Consideration and Implications for Diverse Students." *Computers in the Schools,* vol. 31, 2014, pp. 220–32.

Jost, M. B., and B. F. Mosley. "Where IT's AT? Teachers, Assistive Technology, and Instructional Technology." *Journal of Technology Integration in the Classroom,* vol. 3, 2011, pp. 5–16.

Lange, A., M. McPhillips, G. Mulhern, et al. "Assistive Software Tools for Secondary-Level Students with Literacy Difficulties." *Journal of Special Education Technology,* vol. 21, 2006, pp. 13–22.

"State Assistive Technology Programs." *Exceptional Parent,* vol. 41, 2011, pp. 46–48.

Technology-Related Assistance for Individuals with Disabilities Act of 1994. Public Laws 100-407 and 103-218. Resna.org.

AUDIO STREAMING

Introduction

Music streaming services offer vast libraries of songs and albums and allow subscribers to listen to anything in the collection by way of an internet connection. Many of the services also allow a limited level of access at no charge, as a means of encouraging potential customers to try out the service before signing up as paid subscribers. Music streaming services are able to offer access to songs and albums through licensing agreements they make with the record labels that own the rights to those songs and albums. The music streaming services are permitted to share access to music with their subscribers, in exchange for monetary compensation paid to the music owners. Understanding how the music industry came to allow this sort of arrangement requires a review of how the industry has evolved since the late twentieth century.

Background

Up until the late 1980s and early 1990s, the music industry was firmly under the control of record labels, most of which were large corporations or divisions of companies with other interests. Record labels would find and recruit musicians, record their music, and then market that music to consumers, who would purchase it on some type of physical medium, such as vinyl record albums, eight-track tapes, audiocassettes, or compact discs. Those who purchased music were licensed to listen to it themselves or to sell the physical album, tape, or disc to others, but not to make copies. Despite these limitations on consumers' rights, it was common for people to copy music onto blank media, either to make it more portable, or to share it with friends. While such actions technically infringed the record labels' copyright, it would have been virtually impossible to stop, so little was done by record companies to prevent or prosecute individuals from this type of small-scale sharing.

The music landscape began to change in the 1990s due to the emergence of the internet in a form that was usable even by people without advanced knowledge of computers and to advances made in digital compression technology. When compact discs became common in the marketplace, this caused a shift from analog music storage (i.e., vinyl records and audiotapes) toward digital music storage (e.g., compact discs and audio files). With analog storage media, recording media captured music as ranges of sound going up and down in wavelike patterns. Copying music to and from analog media was

Photo via iStock/MixMedia. [Used under license.]

of limited utility, because each time a copy was made, there was some physical wearing of the original physical medium, resulting in a deterioration in sound quality over the life of the master recording. Commercial copies of the master were slightly degraded reproductions of the original master, the quality of which depended on the limitations of the storage medium, which also deteriorated with use, introducing noise. Copying a commercial copy, usually onto magnetic tape in the form of audiocassettes, further degraded sound quality and added background noise. Compact discs changed this, because they stored information digitally, as a series of ones and zeroes. This meant that each time a compact disc was copied, the copy was flawless—one could listen to the original compact disc and the copy and there would be no way to distinguish the two. This made unauthorized sharing of music a much greater potential source of trouble for record labels, because if people could obtain perfect copies of music from friends, there would be no need to buy music themselves.

These issues were compounded tenfold by the rise of the internet, a digital platform. With music available in digital form and the internet available as a means of transmitting digital information, record labels would have faced a nightmare scenario, but for one factor—file size. The average compact disc could store about seven hundred megabytes of information, and a typical album would take up at least half of that space. Since internet speeds at the time were a small fraction of what they came to be, sharing several hundred megabytes of information online was almost impossible and would take days or weeks even if it could be done. To the record companies' chagrin, however, this quickly changed. File compression software takes a digital file as input and transforms it according to compression algorithms so that it takes up less computer storage space. It does this by looking for patterns in the digital file and then coming up with what are essentially abbreviations for each pattern.

Thus, if the pattern 0101001101101 is found to occur frequently in a file, then the compression software might translate this string of thirteen characters as Am9, for example, thus reducing the amount of storage space needed from thirteen to three. The best-known compression software for audio files that emerged around this time is still in use: mp3. Mp3 software can reduce file sizes by factors of ten or

more. This, coupled with ever-increasing internet speeds, made online music sharing a reality that the music industry at last had to face.

Piracy

Music piracy almost instantly became commonplace, once file compression and moderately fast internet access became the norm. A wide variety of programs and protocols for sharing files emerged, and the music industry responded to each one by using legal action, or the threat thereof, to discourage people from sharing. Many of the early file-sharing applications, such as Napster, Kazaa, and others, were also significant security risks for users, because they functioned by opening the part of the user's computer where music was stored, so that it could be browsed by other users of the file-sharing application. Even this limited, restricted form of access was sometimes enough for a determined hacker to take control of another person's computer, with devastating consequences.

Still, there were many users who felt that this could not happen to them because they were too sophisticated in their knowledge of computer security. It was the mindset of this group that was the target of the music industry's legal action. The industry worked with internet service providers (ISPs) to identify people who were using file-sharing software, and then filed lawsuits against these individuals. Often, the music industry would have designated employees use the file-sharing networks, posing as ordinary users, to gather information about which users were sharing and what files were being shared.

Music industry lawsuits frequently alleged damages in the tens of thousands of dollars, even for sharing a single song, because they estimated the cost of producing and releasing the song, and then also estimated the lost revenue incurred because of all the people who downloaded the song instead of purchasing it legitimately. At first these lawsuits saw some success, and cases were widely reported in

Spotify logo. Image via Wikimedia Commons. [Public domain.]

which a parent was suddenly liable for hundreds of thousands of dollars in damages because their child illegally downloaded music with the family computer. Gradually, however, courts became more skeptical of the record companies' claims about their financial losses, as well as the technologically questionable methods they used to connect an ISP customer's identity with a user account on a file-sharing platform.

What was needed was a commitment by record labels to modernize their distribution methods and channels, so that their customers would not continue to flock to file-sharing applications in order to obtain the music they wanted to hear, without the restrictions on usage that record companies had traditionally required through their use of digital rights management (DRM) software incorporated into the music they sold. People wanted to be able to buy individual songs instead of having to purchase an entire album only to listen to one song on the record. They also wanted to be able to buy a song once and listen to it on different computers and devices, without having to pay again and without having to go through complicated steps necessitated by DRM. However, this did not happen.

The music industry was too fearful that taking steps to adapt its offerings to customers' evolving expectations would open up the floodgates for music pirates and file sharers all over the world, leading to bankruptcy for record companies. This created a void in the music marketplace, an empty space that was unfilled by a product that consumers actually desired.

New Players in the Market

Into this empty space stepped technology giants such as Apple and Google. These companies attempted to provide consumers with a means of interacting with their music in the way they wanted to. Both companies began offering what amounted to online storage options for legitimately acquired music. Users would import their music collections into these services and would then be able to access the music from any device that Google or Apple (or another such company) recognized. These services solved some issues that had long plagued music lovers—online storage and management, access from multiple devices—but not others. Music remained relatively expensive despite the huge technological advances that have made its production

Soundcloud logo. Image via Wikimedia Commons. [Public domain.]

and distribution less resource-intensive. People wanted to listen to music anywhere and anytime, but who did not possess their own digital collection and did not have the resources to acquire one. This was a relatively large percentage of the music buying public, and it represented a demographic that continued to have significant incentives to engage in file sharing and piracy in order to obtain their music.

In response to this persistent need, streaming music services emerged. These were launched by companies that arranged licensing and royalties with most major record labels and charged users subscription fees to have access to all of the music they wanted, all of the time. Streaming services collect the subscription fees from users and then makes payments to record companies based on how many times each company's music was streamed by users. While some free accounts are available, they have limited functionality or require users to listen to advertisements between songs, as a way of paying for the service.

Streaming services do not have every piece of music ever recorded, but their collections tend to be so large that for the average user, the selection is fairly comprehensive. This allows users to avoid having to spend time and money collecting music from their favorite artists, and simply start listening. If at any time they wish to cancel their subscription, they can do so. Rates are modest, usually adding up to less than twenty dollars per month.

Issues

Music streaming does not solve every problem, although it does what it is intended to do quite well. One issue is fairly obvious: music streaming services are only as good as one's internet connection, so in rural areas where mobile phone signals are weak or nonexistent, or in places where buildings, terrain, or other features interfere with signals, it can be difficult or impossible to use them. Some services compensate for this by allowing a limited amount of content to be downloaded to a mobile device, but in general this is discouraged since permitting too much downloaded content might encourage piracy

Amazon Music logo. Image via Wikimedia Commons. [Public domain.]

or violate the licensing agreements between the streaming service and the record labels. Another disadvantage is that for those who come to rely on streaming music subscription services, if they find it necessary to stop paying their subscription, they will instantly lose access to their music, regardless of how long they have subscribed to the service. There is no feature that allows users to build up equity in the service so that they acquire perpetual rights to some content; it is an all-or-nothing proposition.

On the more positive side, streaming music services have some social interaction features that provide their users with benefits not available elsewhere. Most have options to play random music, and to allow users to either listen to each track or to skip over the ones they do not care for. Each time a user listens or skips, the streaming service remembers that preference and builds a profile for the user, which it can use in order to recommend new music that is likely to suit the user's taste. In this way, users can discover new music that they otherwise might not have ever encountered.

Some services also make it possible for users to share songs and playlists with one another. Playlists, collections of songs that are assembled by users according to their tastes or for a particular purpose, such as a birthday party or wedding, serve much the same purpose as old-fashioned "mix-tapes," from the audiocassette era, and like mix-tapes, playlists and music sharing encourage people within the service's user community to listen to still more streaming content. To a lesser extent, some streaming services allow users to share their musical tastes on social media, although this tends to be limited to sharing lists of song titles rather than recordings of entire songs, for copyright reasons.

—*Scott Zimmer*

References

Borja, K., and S. Dieringer. "Streaming or Stealing? The Complementary Features between Music Streaming and Music Piracy." *Journal of Retailing & Consumer Services*, vol. 32, 2016, pp. 86–95, doi:10.1016/j.jretconser.2016.06.007.

Borja, K., S. Dieringer, and J. Daw. "The Effect of Music Streaming Services on Music Piracy among College Students." *Computers in Human Behavior*, vol. 45, 2015, pp. 69–76, doi:10.1016/j.chb.2014.11.088.

Hagen, A. N. "The Metaphors We Stream By: Making Sense of Music Streaming." *First Monday*, vol. 21, no. 3, 2016, p. 8, doi:10.5210/fm.v21i3.6005.

———. "The Playlist Experience: Personal Playlists in Music Streaming Services." *Popular Music & Society*, vol. 38, no. 5, 2015, pp. 625–45, doi:10.1080/03007766.2015.1021174.

Hampton-Sosa, W. "The Impact of Creativity and Community Facilitation on Music Streaming Adoption and Digital Piracy." *Computers in Human Behavior*, vol. 69, 2017, pp. 444–53, doi:10.1016/j.chb.2016.11.055.

Kim, J., C. Nam, and M. H. Ryu. "What Do Consumers Prefer for Music Streaming Services?: A Comparative Study between Korea and US." *Telecommunications Policy*, vol. 41, no. 4, 2017, pp. 263–72, doi:10.1016/j.telpol.2017.01.008.

Lee, W., C. Chen, J. Huang, and J. Liang. "A Smartphone-based Activity-aware System for Music Streaming Recommendation." *Knowledge-Based Systems*, vol. 131, 2017, pp. 70–82, doi:10.1016/j.knosys.2017.06.002.

Pongnumkul, S., and K. Motohashi. "A Bipartite Fitness Model for Online Music Streaming Services." *Physica A*, vol. 490, 2018, pp. 1125–37, doi:10.1016/j.physa.2017.08.108.

Sinclair, G., and J. Tinson. "Psychological Ownership and Music Streaming Consumption." *Journal of Business Research*, vol. 71, 2017, pp. 1–9, doi:10.1016/j.jbusres.2016.10.002.

Werner, A. "Moving Forward: A Feminist Analysis of Mobile Music Streaming." *Culture Unbound: Journal of Current Cultural Research*, vol. 7, 2015, pp. 197–213.

AUGMENTED REALITY

Introduction

Augmented reality (AR) refers to any technology that inserts digital interfaces into the real world. For the most part, the technology has included headsets and glasses that people wear to project interfaces onto the physical world, but it can also include cell phones and other devices. In time, AR technology could be used in contact lenses and other small wearable devices.

Augmented reality is related to, but separate from, virtual reality. Virtual reality attempts to create an entirely different reality that is separate from real life. Augmented reality, however, adds to the real world and does not create a unique world. Users of AR will recognize their surroundings and use the AR technology to enhance what they are experiencing. Both augmented and virtual realities have become better as technology has improved. A number of companies (including large tech companies such as Google) have made investments in augmented reality in the hopes that it will be a major part of the future of technology and will change the way people interact with technology.

In the past, AR was seen primarily as a technology to enhance entertainment (e.g., gaming, communicating, etc.); however, AR has the potential to revolutionize many aspects of life. For example, AR technology could provide medical students with a model of a human heart. It could also help people locate their cars in parking lots. AR technology has already been used in cell phones to help people locate nearby facilities (e.g., banks and restaurants), and future AR technology could inform people about nearby locations, events, and the people they meet and interact with.

Background

The term "augmented reality" was developed in the 1990s, but the fundamental idea for augmented reality was established in the early days of computing. Technology for AR developed in the early twenty-first century, but at that time AR was used mostly for gaming technology.

In the early 2010s, technology made it possible for AR headsets to shrink and for graphics used in AR to improve. Google Glass (2012) was one of the first AR devices geared toward the public that was not meant for gaming. Google Glass, created by the large tech company Google, was designed to give users a digital interface they could interact with in ways that were somewhat similar to the way people interacted with smartphones (e.g., taking pictures, looking up directions, etc.). Although Google Glass was not a success, Google and other companies developing similar products believed that eventually wearable technology would become a normal part of everyday life.

During this time, other companies were also interested in revolutionizing AR technology. Patent information released from the AR company Magic Leap (which also received funding from Google) indicated some of the technology the company was working on. One technology reportedly will beam images directly into a wearer's retinas. This design is meant to fool the brain so it cannot tell the difference between light from the outside world and the light coming from an AR device. If this technology works as intended, it could change the way people see the world.

Microsoft's AR company, HoloLens, had plans for technology that was similar to Magic Leap's, though the final products would likely have many differences. HoloLens was working to include spatial sound so that the visual images would be accompanied by sounds that seem to be closer or farther away, corresponding with the visuals. For example, a person could see an animal running toward them on

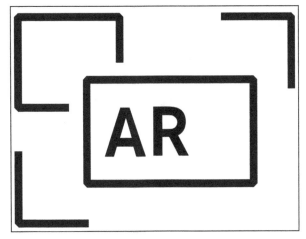

The AR-Icon can be used as a marker on print as well as on online media. It signals the viewer that digital content is behind it. The content can be viewed with a smartphone or tablet. Image by Schwarz Gruppe Design, via Wikimedia Commons.

the HoloLens glasses, and they would hear corresponding sounds that got louder as the animal got closer.

Other AR companies, such as Leap Motion, have designed AR products to be used in conjunction with technology people already rely on. This company developed AR technology that worked with computers to change the type of display people used. Leap Motion's design allowed people to wear a headset to see the computer display in front of them. They could then use their hands to move the parts of the display seemingly through the air in front of them (though people not wearing the headset would not see the images from the display). Other companies also worked on making AR technology more accessible through mobile phones and other devices that people use frequently.

The Future of AR

Although companies such as Magic Leap and HoloLens have plans for the future of AR, the field still faces many obstacles. Developing wearable technology that is small enough, light enough, and powerful enough to provide users with the feeling of reality is one of the biggest obstacles. AR companies are developing new technologies to make AR performance better, but many experts agree that successfully releasing this technology to the public could take years.

Another hurdle for AR technology companies is affordability. The technology they sell has to be priced so that people will purchase it. Since companies are investing so much money in the

10.000 Moving Cities*, by Marc Lee. Augmented Reality Multiplayer Game/Art Installation.* Photo by Marc Lee, via Wikimedia Commons.

development of high-tech AR technology, they might not be able to offer affordable AR devices for a number of years. Another problem that AR developers have to manage is the speed and agility of the visual display. Since any slowing of the image or delay in the process could ruin the experience for the AR user, companies have to make sure the technology is incredibly fast and reliable.

In the future, AR devices could be shrunk to even small sizes and people could experience AR technology through contact lenses or even bionic eyes. In 2022, AR can be used by devices such as AR capable cell phones. Yet, AR technology still has many challenges to overcome before advanced AR devices become popular and mainstream. Technology experts agree that AR technology will likely play an important role in everyday life in the future. Experts agree that the AR market will attain a staggering $198 billion by 2025.

Predictions for AR technologies tend to focus on the following uses and markets: mobile augmented environments; indoor and outdoor navigation for trucking, deliveries, and transportation; healthcare and medical schools; shopping services; and remote assistance and customer service.

—Elizabeth Mohn and Laura Nicosia

References

Altavilla, Dave. "Apple Further Legitimizes Augmented Reality Tech with Acquisition of Metaio." *Forbes.* Forbes.com, LLC, 30 May 2015, www. forbes.com/sites/davealtavilla/2015/05/30/apple-further-legitimizes-augmented-reality-tech-with-acquistion-of-metaio/.

Man wearing smartglasses, wearable computer glasses that add information alongside or to what the wearer sees. Photo by Kai Kowalewski, via Wikimedia Commons.

"Augmented Reality." *Webopedia.* Quinstreet Enter-
    prise, 13 Aug. 2015, www.webopedia.com/
    TERM/A/Augmented_Reality.html.
Farber, Dan. "The Next Big Thing in Tech: Aug-
    mented Reality." *CNET.* CBS Interactive Inc., 7
    June 2013, www.cnet.com/news/
    the-next-big-thing-in-tech-augmented-reality/.
Folger, Tim. "Revealed World." *National Geographic.*
    National Geographic Society, ngm.nationalgeo-
    graphic.com/big-idea/14/augmented-reality.
Kofman, Ava. "Dueling Realities." *The Atlantic.* The
    Atlantic Monthly Group, 9 June 2015, www.
    theatlantic.com/technology/archive/2015/06/
    dueling-realities/395126/.
Makarov, Andrew. "10 Augmented Reality Trends of
    2022: A Vision of the Future." *MobiDev,* 1 Jan.
    2022, mobidev.biz/blog/
    augmented-reality-trends-future-ar-technologies.
McKalin, Vamien. "Augmented Reality vs. Virtual
    Reality: What Are the Differences and Similari-
    ties?" *TechTimes.com.* TechTimes.com, 6 Apr.
    2014, techtimes.com/articles/5078/20140406/
    augmented-reality-vs-virtual-reality-what-are-the-
    differences-and-similarities.htm.
Vanhemert, Kyle. "Leap Motion's Augmented-Re-
    ality Computing Looks Stupid Cool." *Wired.*
    Condé Nast, 7 July 2015, www.wired.
    com/2015/07/
    leap-motion-glimpse-at-the-augmented-reality-
    desktop-of-the-future/.

AVATARS AND SIMULATION

Introduction

Avatars and simulation are elements of virtual reality (VR), which attempts to create immersive worlds for computer users to enter. Simulation is the method by which the real world is imitated or approximated by the images and sounds of a computer. An avatar is the personal manifestation of a particular person. Simulation and VR are used for many applications, from entertainment to business.

Background

Computer simulation and VR have existed since the early 1960s. While simulation has been used in

Avatar in the virtual world Second Life. Image via Wikimedia Commons. [Public domain.]

manufacturing since the 1980s, avatars and virtual worlds have yet to be widely embraced outside gaming and entertainment. VR uses computerized sounds, images, and even vibrations to model some or all of the sensory input that human beings constantly receive from their surroundings every day. Users can define the rules of how a VR world works in ways that are not possible in everyday life. In the real world, people cannot fly, drink fire, or punch through walls. In VR, however, all of these things are possible, because the rules are defined by human coders, and they can be changed or even deleted. This is why users' avatars can appear in these virtual worlds as almost anything one can imagine—a loaf of bread, a sports car, or a penguin, for example. Many users of virtual worlds are drawn to them because of this type of freedom.

Because a VR simulation does not occur in physical space, people can "meet" regardless of how far apart they are in the real world. Thus, in a company that uses a simulated world for conducting its meetings, staff from Hong Kong and New York can both occupy the same VR room via their avatars. Such virtual meeting spaces allow users to convey nonverbal cues as well as speech. This allows for a greater degree of authenticity than in telephone conferencing.

Mechanics of Animation

The animation of avatars in computer simulations often requires more computing power than a single workstation can provide. Studios that produce animated films use render farms to create the smooth and sophisticated effects audiences expect. Before the rendering stage, a great deal of effort goes into designing how an animated character or avatar will look, how it will move, and how its textures will behave during that movement.

For example, a fur-covered avatar that moves swiftly outdoors in the wind should have a furry or hairy texture, with fibers that appear to blow in the wind. All of this must be designed and coordinated by computer animators. Typically, one of the first steps is keyframing, in which animators decide what the starting and ending positions and appearance of the animated object will be. Then they design the movements between the beginning and end by assigning animation variables (avars) to different points on the object. This stage is referred to as in-betweening, or tweening. Once avars are assigned, a computer algorithm can automatically change the avar values in coordination with one another.

Alternatively, an animator can change "in-between" graphics by hand. When the program is run, the visual representation of the changing avars will appear as an animation.

In general, the more avars specified, the more detailed and realistic that animation will be in its movements. In an animated film, the main characters often have hundreds of avars associated with them. For instance, the 1995 film *Toy Story* used 712 avars for the cowboy Woody. This ensures that the characters' actions are lifelike, since the audience will focus attention on them most of the time. Coding standards for normal expressions and motions have been developed based on muscle movements. The moving picture experts group (MPEG)-4 international standard includes 86 face parameters and 196 body parameters for animating human and humanoid movements. These parameters are encoded into an animation file and can affect the bit rate (data encoded per second) or size of the file.

Educational Applications

Simulation has long been a useful method of training in various occupations. Pilots are trained in flight simulators, and driving simulators are used to prepare for licensing exams. Newer applications have included training teachers for the classroom and improving counseling in the military. VR holds the promise of making such vocational simulations much more realistic. As more computing power is added, simulated environments can include stimuli

An avatar used by an automated online assistant providing customer service on a web page. Image courtesy of Bemidji State University, via Wikimedia Commons.

that better approximate the many distractions and detailed surroundings of the typical driving or flying situation, for instance.

VR in 3D

Most instances of VR that people have experienced so far have been two-dimensional (2D), occurring on a computer or movie screen. While entertaining, such experiences do not really capture the concept of VR. Three-dimensional (3D) VR headsets such as the Oculus Rift may one day facilitate more lifelike business meetings and product planning. They may also offer richer vocational simulations for military and emergency personnel, among others.

—*Scott Zimmer*

References

Chan, Melanie. *Virtual Reality: Representations in Contemporary Media.* Bloomsbury, 2014.

Gee, James Paul. *Unified Discourse Analysis: Language, Reality, Virtual Worlds, and Video Games.* Routledge, 2015.

Griffiths, Devin C. *Virtual Ascendance: Video Games and the Remaking of Reality.* Rowman, 2013.

Hart, Archibald D., and Sylvia Hart Frejd. *The Digital Invasion: How Technology Is Shaping You and Your Relationships.* Baker, 2013.

Kizza, Joseph Migga. *Ethical and Social Issues in the Information Age.* 5th ed., Springer, 2013.

Lien, Tracey. "Virtual Reality Isn't Just for Video Games." *Los Angeles Times,* 8 Jan. 2015.

Parisi, Tony. *Learning Virtual Reality: Developing Immersive Experiences and Applications for Desktop, Web, and Mobile.* O'Reilly, 2015.

B

BANDCAMP

Introduction

The commercial music industry has followed a certain mode of operation since time immemorial. Composers, who also tended to be performers with a particular instrumental expertise, would record their compositions on score sheets using standard musical notation. Even in the time of Mozart and other classical composers, the composer was managed by an agent who would arrange for performances for paying audiences. The income from performances provided the livelihood for both the composer and the agent, and the musical scores themselves were jealously guarded properties such that only the actual composer would be able to present the music in the manner it was intended to be presented. With copyright laws, musical scores became a commercial commodity and ownership of music was no longer the province only of composers.

Agents, patrons, and others could buy or otherwise acquire ownership of the copyright to a particular piece of music, giving them the sole right to say who could perform the copyrighted works, typically for a fee. Fast forward to the much more recent development of the recording industry and recorded music. In this industry, with a music production company, or recording label the company owns the copyright for the compositions it produces and delivers royalties to the label artists for their performance to the composer or writer of the particular work (the songwriter), as well as others involved in the production who are listed on the physical label of the recording medium distribution (e.g., 45-rpm singles, long-playing (LP) albums, extended play (EP) short albums, compact disc (CD), digital video disc (DVD) and Blu-ray discs). Others, such as background singers, studio musicians, and graphic artists, are generally paid a flat rate for their work on a particular production.

Those costs are recovered by the producers from commercial sales and licensing deals such as theme songs for TV shows and movies, and for use in advertisements. Promotion of the artists and commercial recordings is a very significant cost to the recording label, and that aspect is generally handled by agents, with costs being recovered from ticket sales as well. Taken altogether, the return to the artists and composers is historically low unless they become phenomenally successful commercially, perhaps forming their own recording labels and managing other artists. The Beatles, for example, began their commercial career with manager Brian Epstein under the Decca and Capitol record labels before forming their own Apple Records label with its familiar Granny Smith green apple label art. Many other contemporary artists, however, never achieve the level of success that would allow such a transition and remain instead as part of the recording industry establishment throughout their careers.

Background

Overlooked by the industry are those artists and composers who either weren't afforded the opportunity to sign with an established label, or who chose not to work in that milieu while creating their own songs. These are the independents, the musical equivalent of authors who choose to self-publish their books rather than accept small returns while the publisher garners the lion's share of the proceeds. For independent musicians and songwriters, this is where Bandcamp comes in. Bandcamp is a non-label music storage and streaming service that can be used by independent artists and established recording artists. Bandcamp refers to itself as an online record store and music community where fans, discover, connect with, and directly support the artists they like. Users of Bandcamp are able to purchase musical recordings offered for sale as digital albums, which represents about 60 percent of Bandcamp's sales; individual music tracks or songs; vinyl record disks; CDs and cassettes. T-shirts are also sold through Bandcamp. Of those sales, fully 82 percent of the proceeds is delivered directly to the artists rather than passing through the many hands reaching for a piece in a label company. Bandcamp directly retains about 10 percent of the proceeds from sales to support its operation, with the rest being used to pay various fees associated with licensed labeled pieces that are made available.

Bandcamp is the quintessential win-win-win situation for artists, users and recording companies. For artists, the return on sales is immediate and substantial, especially for independent artists who have only to produce a quality recording of their work and upload it to Bandcamp for sale, with none of the ancillary costs associated with the traditional recording industry. For users, Bandcamp offers a vast amount of music that is simply not available from the traditional industry. This allows them to explore and find new music and artists that appeal to their tastes, whether as single songs or as album collections. For recording companies, Bandcamp provides a means to test market an artist's potential for success before offering to sign them on with the label and investing in the risks that come with promotion bringing great success.

An independent artist who performs well on Bandcamp may, after all, be worth being offered a recording contract, though the artists may also choose to remain independent, in which case the recording company invests nothing and loses nothing. Recording companies are also able to provide the recordings they control through Bandcamp music sales, though this may seem somewhat counterintuitive.

It has always been argued, and has resulted in numerous cases being brought before the courts, that the artists and songwriters should receive the major share of the proceeds from the sale of their music recordings. It has also always been argued that the artists and songwriters should be able to retain ownership of the copyright for their works. In many cases, a label company has ended its contracts with an artist, yet retained ownership of copyright for that artist's works. Two of the most high-profile cases of an artist's loss of copyright, and the ability to

perform their own existing music portfolio, involved Paul McCartney of the aforementioned Beatles. The entire portfolio of Lennon-McCartney songs written for the Beatles was purchased by Michael Jackson, and forced McCartney to buy it back from Jackson's estate. More recently, Taylor Swift's portfolio was retained by her former record label company, leaving her unable to perform the songs she had written and forcing her to rewrite the compositions in different arrangements in order to avoid copyright violation. Bandcamp eliminates the possibility of such scenarios, and everybody wins.

—*Richard M. Renneboog*

References

Arditi, David. *Streaming Culture: Subscription Services and the Unending Consumption of Culture.* Emerald Group, 2021.

Gordon, Steve. *The Future of the Music Business: How to Succeed with the New Digital Technologies.* Hal Leonard, 2011.

Oswald, Vanessa. *Indie Rock: Finding an Independent Voice.* Greenhaven Publishing LLC, 2018.

Riselvato, John. *Bandcamp for Artists and Music Labels: Marketing Tips to Sell More Music and Merch.* Amazon Digital Services LLC, 2020.

Rolston, Clyde Philip, Amy Macy, Tom Hutchison and Paul Allen. *Record Label Marketing: How Music Companies Brand and Market Artists in the Digital Era.* CRC Press, 2015.

Zager, Michael. *Music Production: A Manual for Producers, Composers, Arrangers, and Students.* Rowman & Littlefield, 2021.

BINARY HEXADECIMAL REPRESENTATIONS

Introduction

The binary number system is a base-2 number system, used by digital devices to store data and perform mathematical operations. The hexadecimal number system is a base-16 number system. It enables humans to work efficiently with large numbers stored as binary data.

Digital computers process and store all data in binary. Image via iStock/mycola. [Used under license.]

Background

A mathematical number system is a way of representing numbers using a defined set of symbols. Number systems take their names from the number of symbols the system uses to represent numbers. For example, the most common mathematical number system is the decimal system, or base-10 system. *Deci-* means "ten." It uses the ten digits 0 through 9 as symbols for numbers. Number systems can be based on any number of unique symbols, however. For example, the number system based on the use of two-digit symbols (0 and 1) is called the "binary" or "base-2" system.

Both the decimal and binary number systems use the relative position of digits in a similar way when representing numbers. The value in the rightmost, or first, position is multiplied by the number of digits used in the system to the zero power. For the decimal system, this value is 10^0. For the binary system, this value is 2^0. Both 10^0 and 2^0 are equal to 1. Any number x raised to the zero power is equal to 1. The power used increases by one for the second position and so on.

The Importance of the Binary Number System

The binary number system is used to store numbers and perform mathematical operations in computers systems. Such devices store data using transistors, electronic parts that can each be switched between two states. One state represents the binary digit 0 and the other, the binary digit 1. These binary digits are bits, the smallest units of data that can be stored and manipulated. A single bit can be used to store the value 0 or 1. To store values larger than 1, groups of bits are used. A group of four bits is a nibble (also referred to as nyble or nybble). A group of eight bits is a byte.

Using Hexadecimal to Simplify Binary Numbers

The hexadecimal number system is a base-16 system. It uses the digits 0 through 9 and the letters A through F to represent numbers. The hexadecimal digit, or hex digit, A has a decimal value of 10. Hex digit B equals 11, C equals 12, D equals 13, E equals 14, and F equals 15. In hexadecimal, the value 10 is equal to 16 in the decimal system. Using hexadecimal, a binary nibble can be represented by a single symbol. For example, the hex digit F can be used instead of the binary nibble 1111 for the decimal value 15. Sixteen different combinations of bits are possible in a binary nibble. The hexadecimal system, with sixteen different symbols, is therefore ideal for working with nibbles. Computers can quickly and easily work with large numbers in binary, which makes them the unique "users" of binary. Humans, on the other hand, have a harder time using binary to work with large numbers. Binary uses many more digits than hexadecimal does to represent large numbers. Hex digits are therefore easier for humans to use to write, read, and process than binary.

—*Maura Valentino*

References

"Binary Representation and Computer Arithmetic." *Australian National University,* courses.cecs.anu. edu.au/courses/ENGN3213/Documents/ PROJECT_READING_MATERIAL/Binary%20 Representation%20and%20Computer%20 Arithmetic.pdf.

Cheever, Erik. "Representation of Numbers." *Swarthmore College,* www.swarthmore.edu/NatSci/ echeeve1/Ref/BinaryMath/NumSys.html.

Glaser, Anton. *History of Binary and Other Nondecimal Numeration.* Rev. ed., Tomash, 1981.

Govindjee, S. "Internal Representation of Numbers." *University of California Berkeley,* 2013, faculty. ce.berkeley.edu/sanjay/e7/numbers.pdf.

Harris, Patricia. *What Are Binary and Hexadecimal Numbers?* Rosen Publishing Group, 2018.

Lande, Daniel R. "Development of the Binary Number System and the Foundations of Computer Science." *Mathematics Enthusiast,* 2014, pp. 513–40.

"A Tutorial on Data Representation: Integers, Floating-Point Numbers, and Characters." *Nanyang Technological University Singapore,* Jan. 2014, www3.ntu.edu.sg/home/ehchua/programming/java/datarepresentation.html.

BLENDED LEARNING

Introduction

Blended learning refers to an educational experience that is not entirely conducted through in-person class meetings, nor through purely online interactions, but uses a combination of these strategies. Students meet in person from time to time, but between these meetings they also interact with one another and with their instructors online, using streaming video, email, chat, and other forms of computer mediated communication.

Background

Attempts at blended learning began almost as soon as the earliest incarnation of the internet came on the scene, in the 1960s. Educators immediately realized the potential benefits that could be realized by incorporating technology into the delivery of instruction, the economies of scale that could be achieved with a single instructor able to reach far more students that just those who could fit into a traditional classroom (synchronous learning). At first the main obstacles to blended learning were technological limitations and the expense required to overcome them; computers were slow and network bandwidth was in extremely short supply, so delivery of streaming video over a network was simply impossible.

Some early forms of blended learning circumvented such issues by distributing course content on compact disc/read-only memory (CD-ROM) media or by using cable connections to transmit course content as a video feed. These limitations have been largely transcended by the advent of the internet and the drastic increases in available bandwidth throughout the 1980s and 1990s. It is now possible for instructors to teach in front of a webcam and broadcast their lectures live to an unlimited number of users who are located all over the world—anywhere that has internet connectivity, including cloud computing. In addition to being available via this sort of livestreaming, the lecture can also be recorded as it happens for later viewing by those who were not able to tune in as the instruction was delivered. This type of time-shifting of content delivery is known as asynchronous learning, because the instructor and the student do not have to be engaged with one another at the same time—the lecture can be given and posted online, and the student can access it hours, days, or weeks later.

The convenience of asynchronous learning is clear from this example, and is a major reason for the expanding popularity of blended learning. More and more students are choosing to pursue their education later in life, and must balance the demands of their coursework against other demands on their time from work and childcare. A blended learning model gives these students more flexibility as they strive to maintain this balance. Instead of having to be in class every Wednesday evening from six until ten, a student can log on to her course's learning management system at any time of the day or night and watch that week's lecture. This means that students can structure their education around their lives, rather than having to do the opposite. What's more, competency-based learning (CBL), an approach to asynchronous learning, relies on the demonstrated acquisition of relevant skills by students as a means of evaluating progress, rather than the accumulation of hours of instruction time. CBL is lauded for its flexible approach to education, which allows students to learn in their own ways and demonstrate that learning in their own ways as well.

Forms of Blended Learning

Blended learning can take a wide variety of forms, depending on what technologies are being used (instant messaging, chat, video streaming, audio streaming, video chat, etc.) and how the instructor chooses to formulate the blend. Some instructors use technology as a minor support to their face-to-face lectures; an example of this would be distributing syllabi and other course materials by email or online, and accepting online submission of assignments, but otherwise delivering most instruction in person. This type of blended learning is the closest to traditional instruction, because the face-to-face component is still what drives the course.

At the other end of the continuum, one finds classes in which everything happens online, from instruction to class discussion and collaboration on assignments. The only face-to-face meetings that occur in this type of scenario are those requested by the student or instructor for some special purpose. Between these two extremes there are several more balanced approaches; one of these is rotation, where class meetings alternate between in person and online. This style of blended learning can be especially useful for students who are not yet used to the possibilities that educational technology has to offer, because it lets them test out the new features while still relying on regular meetings in person. As students become accustomed to working online, they may choose to move toward what is known as a flex model, in which most of the coursework happens online but in person meetings can be arranged if needed.

Another popular approach is for students to organize themselves into lab groups, in which members meet at a designated location to work online at regular times. This lab format can be especially helpful for students who prefer online coursework but have a hard time staying focused or are easily distracted—the lab gives them a place that they must be at a certain time, so they feel more accountable for getting their work done. One feature that all blended learning approaches have in common is that they give the student more responsibility for taking charge of their own learning and more power over when and how that learning will happen.

The Future of Blended Learning

Blended learning is often assumed to be an all or nothing approach, but in fact it can be implemented in smaller steps and at specific levels of institutional engagement. The most basic and limited form of blended learning occurs at the level of individual activities within a course. For example, a traditional face-to-face course might incorporate an assignment that requires students to email their papers to one another for an informal peer review, and then return the papers with comments and recommendations for the author. Often this approach is used by instructors as they are first experimenting with blended learning.

If all goes well, their likely next step will be to expand the blended component so that it pervades the entire course. This course-level blending will then require that most, if not all, segments of the class, so that all major, graded components include both online and in person elements. The transition from activity level blending to class level blending often is the most jarring for new students and for instructors unaccustomed to modern technology. The next level of blending occurs at the program level, when a significant number of instructors in a department or program have successfully adopted a blended course model; at this point the program itself can be described as blended. Many such programs have begun to advertise this achievement in their marketing literature, proclaiming themselves as innovative or hybrid-course approaches to education.

Finally, it is possible for an entire institution to adopt a blended approach to learning, although it is still somewhat rare. Those organizations that have achieved this level of blending tend to be corporations with locations all over the world, a configuration that demands training that is available from anywhere. There are also a moderate number of colleges and universities that employ institution-level blended models, with the most notable examples tending to be for-profit, online universities. Because this fully implemented blended approach is still the exception rather than the rule, society tends to view such organizations as either extremely modern and formidable (corporate training programs are seen this way) or as decidedly suspicious and unorthodox (in the case of blended and online universities). In the near future, these impressions are likely to evolve, as people become more accustomed to moving back and forth between the online and the in-person realms.

Issues

One drawback to blended learning has long been the level of comfort with technology that participants must possess to experience its benefits. Because many of the technologies that blended learning is built upon are relatively new, there are many people who are unfamiliar with them. This can be a source of anxiety, particularly for older students who are returning to school after a long absence or who deferred their own education until after they had raised their children. These older students tend to be less comfortable with new technologies, and many of them are already anxious about whether they will be able to succeed academically when many of their classmates are decades younger than they are.

The prospect of having to learn how to use new learning tools such as video chat and instant messaging, while one is adjusting to being in a classroom, can push some students over the edge and cause them to give up on the idea of completing their course of study. Some programs are constructed with an awareness of these potential forms of anxiety, and often these programs will try to ease students into the blended learning environment by structuring beginning classes to have a significant face-to-face component. Then, later in the program, after students have had time to adjust, additional forms of blended learning may be introduced.

Occasionally blended learning has encountered opposition when school officials seek to introduce it to their campuses. This tends to happen more often when it is used at middle school and high school levels than in colleges or universities. The most common objection arises amid concern that the hidden purpose for adopting blended learning is not to take advantage of the benefits of the latest technology, nor to make it easier for students with busy lives to balance their many obligations, but instead to operate the institution more efficiently in the hope of eventually being able to reduce the number of teaching staff by replacing some teachers with computers. Most research suggests that in the unusual circumstances when this is truly the goal, it is a goal that is not likely to be realized.

Blended learning tends to allow education to proceed more efficiently in the sense that participants can communicate with one another over great distances and at varying times, but this efficiency does not often translate into a need for fewer instructors and support staff. Staff and instructors' duties are certainly changed by the introduction of blended learning, but those duties are rarely diminished. For example, instead of instructional support staff spending an hour printing, collating, and stapling the syllabus an instructor plans to distribute in a face-to-face class, they may spend the time organizing an email distribution list which contains the email addresses of all class participants so that the syllabus can be sent to them electronically.

Some observers have expressed concerns that blended learning, if not implemented properly, may exacerbate the so-called digital divide. The digital divide is a concept that describes the unequal access to technology that exists because of the stratification of society into different economic classes. Many families are unable to afford their own computers, tablets, smartphones, and similar gadgetry, and even when some of these devices are available (e.g., most libraries have computers for public use) not everyone has the time or the educational background to be able to make use of them. This means that for a large segment of society, the potential benefits of blended learning either may be unavailable or may come at too high a price to be realistic options.

This raises the question of proper implementation of blended learning, because if those responsible for launching a blended learning program apply sufficient forethought, there are frequently alternatives that can make the program available to participants regardless of their financial status. These can take the form of grants, scholarships, or the use of a lab-type blended learning environment as described above, where students use a shared computer lab facility to perform the online portion of their work. The benefits of establishing an equitable form of blended learning are many; not only does it promote the interests of fairness and justice, but it also enriches the instructional environment through the inclusion of the perspectives of those of lower socioeconomic status.

—*Scott Zimmer*

References

Al-Busaidi, K. A., and H. Al-Shihi. "Key Factors to Instructors' Satisfaction of Learning Management Systems in Blended Learning." *Journal of Computing in Higher Education,* vol. 24, no. 1, 2012, pp. 18–39.

Demirer, V., and I. Sahin. "Effect of Blended Learning Environment on Transfer of Learning: An Experimental Study." *Journal of Computer Assisted Learning,* vol. 29, no. 6, 2013, pp. 518–29.

Garrison, D. R., and N.D. Vaughan. *Blended Learning in Higher Education: Framework, Principles, and Guidelines.* Jossey-Bass, 2018.

Gecer, A. "Lecturer-Student Communication in Blended Learning Environments." *Educational Sciences: Theory and Practice,* vol. 13, no. 1, 2013, pp. 362–67.

Geçer, A., and F. Da . "A Blended Learning Experience." *Educational Sciences: Theory and Practice*,
vol. 12, no. 1, 2012, pp. 438–42.

Glazer, F. S. *Blended Learning: Across the Disciplines,
Across the Academy.* Stylus, 2012.

Golden, T. P., and A. Karpur. "Translating Knowledge Through Blended Learning: A Comparative Analysis of Face-To-Face and Blended
Learning Methods." *Rehabilitation Research, Policy,
and Education*, vol. 26, no. 4, 2012, pp. 305–14.

Gruba, P., and D. Hinkleman. *Blending Technologies
in Second Language Classrooms.* Palgrave Macmillan, 2012.

Keamy, R. "Of Waves and Storms: Supporting
Colleagues Adopting Blended Approaches in
Their Teaching." *Transformative Dialogues:
Teaching and Learning Journal*, vol. 10, no. 3, 2017.

Nicolson, M., L. Murphy, and M. Southgate.
Language Teaching in Blended Contexts. Dunedin
Academic P, 2011.

Oliver, K. M., and D. T. Stallings. "Preparing
Teachers for Emerging Blended Learning
Environments." *Journal of Technology and Teacher
Education*, vol. 22, no. 1, 2014, pp. 57–81.

Shand, K., and S. Farrelly. "Using Blended Teaching
to Teach Blended Learning: Lessons Learned
from Pre-Service Teachers in an Instructional
Methods Course." *Journal of Online Learning
Research*, vol. 3, no. 1, 2017.

Snart, J. A. *Hybrid Learning: The Perils and Promise of
Blending Online and Face-To-Face Instruction in
Higher Education.* Praeger, 2010.

Stevens, M. "Space for All: Middle Level Students in
Blended Learning Environments." *Voices from the
Middle*, vol. 24, no. 2, 2016, pp. 50–55.

Torrisi-Steele, G., and S. Drew. "The Literature
Landscape of Blended Learning in Higher
Education: The Need for Better Understanding
of Academic Blended Practice." *International
Journal for Academic Development*, vol. 18, no. 4,
2018, pp. 371–83.

Tucker, C. R., T. Wycoff, T., and J. T. Green. *Blended
Learning in Action: A Practical Guide Toward
Sustainable Change.* Corwin, 2017.

Wankel, C., and P. Blessinger. *Increasing Student
Engagement and Retention in E-Learning Environ-
ments: Web 2.0 and Blended Learning Technologies.*
Emerald, 2013.

BLOOM'S TAXONOMY

Introduction

Bloom's Taxonomy of Educational Objectives was
developed in the late 1940s by a group of university
examiners—one of whom was Benjamin Bloom of
the University of Chicago—for the purpose of facilitating the sharing of test materials. Although developed for a select audience, the Taxonomy became a
worldwide phenomenon and was soon part of the
everyday vocabulary of educators worldwide. The
Taxonomy itself is a hierarchy of behaviorally defined educational outcomes; the six objectives are
knowledge, comprehension, application, analysis,
synthesis, and evaluation. Despite its popularity,
there are many who argue the Taxonomy is philo-
sophically and empirically unsound. Still others suggest it hasn't made a substantial impact on what
teachers do in the classroom.

Background

Descriptions of Bloom's taxonomy of educational
objectives (Taxonomy) usually begin with superla-
tives. Indeed, forty years after its original publication, *The Taxonomy of Educational Objectives* has sold
more than 1 million copies and has been translated
into more than twenty different languages. It is discussed in nearly every education textbook and has
become one of the most frequently cited sources in
educational research.

Many point out that frequent reference to a
piece of work is an insufficient standard by which to
measure its impact as an effective tool. In other
words, although the Taxonomy has become part of
the vocabulary of educators, it may be a less central
component of their practice. With regard to curriculum development, for example, Sosniak argues the
Taxonomy has become a mere footnote. But a discussion of how the Taxonomy might fall short is premature without first understanding what it was intended to do.

The idea for an educational taxonomy was first
discussed at an informal meeting of university examiners at the 1948 annual conference of the American
Psychological Association. The group's original intention was to create a common framework of educational objectives that would facilitate the exchange
of test items and materials among university examiners, and stimulate research on the relationship

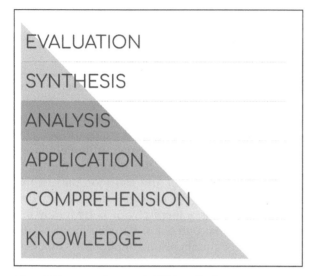

EVALUATION

SYNTHESIS

ANALYSIS

APPLICATION

COMPREHENSION

KNOWLEDGE

Bloom's Taxonomy. Image via Wikimedia Commons.
[Public domain.]

between education and evaluation. The Taxonomy was intended to be "a small volume" for a select audience, but instead turned into a "basic reference for all educators worldwide" (Bloom). The phenomenal popularity of the Taxonomy can only be explained, Bloom himself argues, "by the fact that it filled a void; it met a previously unmet need for basic, fundamental planning in education. For the first time, educators were able to evaluate the learning of students systematically."

In addition, larger cultural shifts, and changing ideas about the purpose of schooling, helped create an environment receptive to the development of clearly defined educational outcomes. In the 1960s, President Lyndon Johnson declared a war on poverty, a significant part of which was the investment of federal funds into educational programs for students from disadvantaged backgrounds. Along with the funding, however, came an increased emphasis on accountability, "with each program having to be evaluated in terms of students' achievement of the program's objectives" (Airasian). Federally funded programs such as Head Start also signaled a seismic shift in beliefs about teaching and learning, from the notion that students were limited by innate ability to the idea that it is the environment that affects learning most. "Once the notion that most students could learn was accepted, emphasis in testing shifted away from sorting individuals and toward finding ways to enhance and certify student learning" (Airasian). Objectives gave educators a tool to

demonstrate student learning and the effectiveness of federally funded programs.

Although the Taxonomy has become known as "Bloom's Taxonomy," Benjamin Bloom—then an examiner at the University of Chicago—was just one of many who contributed to the project.

The authors of the Taxonomy approached the task of defining and classifying educational outcomes in much the same way that biologists classified living things into the categories we refer to as: phylum, class, order, family, genus, and species. The group made it clear that *what* they intended to classify was the change produced in an individual as a result of participating in an educational experience. In Bloom's own words, "What we are classifying is the intended behavior of students—the ways in which individuals are to act, think, or feel as a result of participating in some unit of instruction." The outcomes, they believed, reflected changes in behavior that could be observed across different content areas, so that "a single set of classifications should be applicable in all...instances" (Anderson and Sosniak). The group aimed to develop taxonomies in three different domains—the cognitive, affective, and psychomotor domains—but only completed the first two. What follows is a description of the Taxonomy of educational objectives of the cognitive domain.

Description of the Taxonomy

The Taxonomy was developed with several guiding principles in mind, the first of which is reflected in the intention to classify educational objectives as changes in *behavior*. The authors noticed that teachers spoke about learning in nebulous terms, referring to student outcomes as "understanding," "comprehension," and "grasping the core or essence" of something. They wanted to give teachers a tool to speak about outcomes with greater precision, and thus proposed that "virtually all educational objectives...have their counterparts in student behavior" (Bloom).

Although the authors recognized that by defining learning in behavioral terms, they were making a value judgment, they strove for impartiality and objectivity to the greatest extent possible. They believed the classification should be "a purely descriptive scheme in which every type of educational goal can be represented in a relatively neutral fashion" (Bloom). In other words, the Taxonomy was not intended to suggest that certain outcomes were better than others, or exclude certain types of outcomes from the Taxonomy altogether.

As the group began to brainstorm lists of educational objectives, they quickly realized that complex behaviors included simpler behaviors. In order to incorporate this relationship into the Taxonomy, they organized their educational objectives as a hierarchy. "Thus, our classifications may be said to be in the form where behaviors of type A form one class, behaviors of type AB form another class, while behaviors of type ABC form still another class" (Bloom). The educational process, they concluded, was one of building upon simpler behaviors to form more complex behaviors.

The following six categories form the hierarchy of Bloom's Taxonomy:

- Knowledge
- Comprehension
- Application
- Analysis
- Synthesis
- Evaluation

Before defining each category in greater detail, a fourth guiding principle should be brought to light. Specifically, Bloom and the authors made a distinction between knowledge and the other five objectives of the Taxonomy—which they referred to collectively as *skills and abilities*. They regarded knowledge—the remembering of information—as a necessary but not sufficient outcome of learning. In other words, knowledge is a prerequisite for other types of outcomes, and not the sole aim of education. "What is needed is some evidence that students can do something with their knowledge, that is, that they can apply the information to new situations and problems" (Anderson and Sosniak). Given the rapidly changing culture of the twentieth century, they argued, skills and abilities would help students adapt to new situations more readily than the mere acquisition of information.

Knowledge

The first educational objective—knowledge—is defined as "those behaviors and test situations which emphasize remembering, either by recognition or recall, of ideas, material, or phenomena. The behavior expected of a student in the recall situation is very similar to the behavior he was expected to have during the original learning situation" (Bloom). The authors then make a distinction between concrete types of knowledge and more abstract forms of knowledge, which they organize into three separate categories: knowledge of specifics, knowledge of ways and means of dealing with specifics, and knowledge of universals and abstractions in a field. Remembering the exact date of an event is an example of knowledge of specifics, understanding how culture has changed over time is an example of knowledge of ways and means of dealing with specifics, and familiarity with theoretical approaches to education is an example of knowledge of universals and abstractions in a field.

Comprehension

Comprehension, what the authors argue is the largest class of the five skills and abilities, occupies the second rung of the hierarchy. Although the largest, it is also perhaps the least intuitive, since most think of comprehension either in terms of reading comprehension or as complete understanding of a message. Instead, the authors of the Taxonomy define it as "those objectives, behaviors, or responses which represent an understanding of the literal message contained in a communication" (Bloom). Understanding of the literal message is communicated in three ways—the ability to *translate* the original communication into other terms, the ability to *interpret* what was said (e.g., understanding the relative importance or interrelationships between ideas expressed), and the ability to *extrapolate* the information by making inferences or judgments.

Application

Application is relative to comprehension; it requires the skills and abilities of lower classifications, but goes beyond them as well. A student who applies a principle when prompted to do so demonstrates comprehension, but a student who applies a principle in a new situation in which a solution has not been specified is demonstrating application. In other words, application is about transfer of training. The authors argue that developing good problem-solving skills, as opposed to learning how to apply specific facts in specific situations, encourages transfer. Being able to discuss current events in relation to principles of civil liberties and civil rights is an example of application.

Analysis

Analysis, requiring even more complex skills than those required in comprehension and application, "emphasizes the breakdown of the material into its constituent parts and the detection of the relationships of the parts and of the way they are organized" (Bloom). When teachers ask students to identify supporting statements and conclusions, for example, or to distinguish fact from opinion, they are asking students to engage in analysis. They further organize this objective into analysis of elements, analysis of relationships, and analysis of organizational principles. The ability to identify a hypothesis is an example of analysis of elements, the ability to detect logical errors in an argument is an example of analysis of relationships, and the ability to infer an author's point of view an example of analysis of organizational principles.

Synthesis

The fifth level of the hierarchy is defined as "the putting together of elements and parts so as to form a whole. This is a process of working with elements, parts, etc., and combining them in such a way as to constitute a pattern or structure not clearly there before" (Bloom). The authors identify synthesis as the educational objective most closely related to creativity, and further delineate it according to three different *products* of synthesis: a unique communication, a plan or proposed set of operations, or a set of abstract relations. The ability to speak extemporaneously is an illustration of the first product. The ability to develop a lesson plan for an instructional unit is example of the second product, while the ability to develop a theory of learning is an example of the third.

Evaluation

Evaluation sits at the top of the hierarchy because the authors believe it includes behaviors defined in each of the other five categories. In addition to those behaviors, however, it also includes an element of judgment. "Evaluation is defined as the making of judgments about the value, for some purpose, of ideas, works, solutions, methods, material, etc." (Bloom). Even though evaluation is last in the Taxonomy, the authors argue that it shouldn't be viewed as the last step in thinking; "It is quite possible that the evaluative process will in some cases be the prelude to the acquisition of new knowledge" (Bloom).

Bloom distinguishes between judgments made in terms of internal evidence—as when a student evaluates whether an author's ideas flow logically from one to the other—or in terms of external criteria—such as when a student evaluates a piece of artwork according to external standards of that style or period of art.

Further Insights

As Bloom himself recognized, "a final criterion is that the taxonomy must be accepted and used by the workers in the field if it is to be regarded as a useful and effective tool. Whether or not it meets this criterion can be determined only after a sufficient amount of time has elapsed" (Bloom). One of the more immediate applications was made by teachers, who quickly recognized that as much as 90 percent of their instructional time was spent teaching to the lowest level of the Taxonomy, "with very little time spent on the higher mental processes that would enable students to apply their knowledge creatively" (Bloom). Given the test of time however, the Taxonomy might not fare so well. Although widely *known*, it may be less widely *used*. The following discusses the impact of the Taxonomy on testing, curriculum development, research, and teacher education.

According to Airasian, "objectives per se have been very influential in the testing and evaluation movement over the past quarter century, but not objectives stated in the form advocated in the Taxonomy." The authors of the Taxonomy intended for their objectives to be tailored to the needs of local teachers and administrators; therefore, the objectives themselves, what Airasian calls "behavioral" objectives, were specific and concrete, but broad enough that they still required teachers to further specify them for their own uses. Since that time, testing has become more centralized and standardized; as a result, the "external testing programs [have] served to reduce the incentive for and reliance on locally stated educational objectives" (Airasian).

As stated earlier, the original intention of the Taxonomy was to facilitate the exchange of test materials among university examiners. What it was intended to do beyond this is less clear. Sosniak argues that its attention to curriculum development was merely an afterthought, and one without much substance. She writes, "the Taxonomy was developed first; attention to curriculum was inserted later." Although the language was changed, it was changed "without considerable rethinking or rewriting of the volume" (Sosniak). As a result, the Taxonomy has not informed the practice of curriculum development to the extent its popularity suggests. In addition, Sosniak speculates, the trend toward increased specificity and detail in educational objectives has made it burdensome for teachers to incorporate them into lesson plans. Finally, disagreement about the nature of objectives—specifically, whether behavioral-based objectives represent all kinds of learning—limited their use in the classroom.

Moreover, the way the educational community talks about student learning goals has changed over time. "The same forces that have moved the field away from the term *behavioral objectives* may also be moving the field away from *instructional objectives*," Marken and Morrison write. "If there has been a shift over the last several decades from a focus on training and instruction to a focus on education and learning, then it is perhaps not surprising to see a reduction in the terms *instructional* and *behavioral objectives* and a rise in the use of *educational* and *learning objectives*."

Anderson corroborates the limited impact of the Taxonomy on teachers, despite the heavy emphasis teacher education programs place on the use of the Taxonomy in the classroom. Thus, even though teachers learn how to use the Taxonomy to plan lessons, prepare tests, ask questions, and assign classroom tasks, research suggests teachers no longer rely on the Taxonomy once they begin teaching on their own. Studies show most teachers develop lesson plans in terms of what they want students to do (e.g., activities) as opposed to what they want students to learn (e.g., outcomes). In addition, teachers continue to focus their instruction and evaluation on lower-order thinking; a recent review of over 9,000 test items revealed that over 80 percent were written at the lowest level of the Taxonomy.

Marzano, in an effort to support the application of the Taxonomy to instructor lesson-planning, published five recommendations for educators seeking to clearly delineate what they want students to learn and know. They are:

1. Create an internally consistent system.
2. Start with objectives that focus on a single unit of instruction.
3. Break the objective into a learning progression.
4. Use the learning progression to establish daily targets.
5. Translate daily targets into student-friendly language.

Although limited in terms of its impact in the classroom, the Taxonomy has made tremendous contributions to educational research. With regard to teaching methods, for example, significant empirical evidence has been found to support the notion that methods utilizing one-way communication (e.g., lecture) help students achieve lower-order objectives, while methods requiring two-way communication (e.g., group activities) foster higher-order objectives. Similarly, research has shown that real-world experiences facilitate the attainment of higher-order objectives to a greater extent than classroom activities. Within the classroom, descriptive studies reveal that teacher questioning focuses on lower-order objectives, with only 20 percent of questions actually requiring students to think (Anderson). This finding is consistent across age, subject matter and ability level.

Viewpoints

While some may quibble about whether the Taxonomy is a useful tool for classroom teachers, others take issue with the Taxonomy itself. The following section will briefly outline some of the philosophical and empirical arguments against the guiding principles and content of the Taxonomy, and end with a word about how the Taxonomy has evolved in response to such criticism.

Furst summarizes the arguments of many of the critics, taking aim first at the author's claim of impartiality and neutrality. A taxonomy of educational objectives that excludes any and all objectives that cannot be behaviorally specified, he argues, is inherently partial. Secondly, he outlines philosophical arguments against the separation of content from process. Referencing the philosophy of Wittgenstein, who insisted on the study of particulars as opposed to the development of general categories, Furst stresses the artificiality of such a separation. The process of remembering, for example, cannot be separated from the remembering of some *thing*. The separation of the cognitive domain from the affective domain has also garnered critical attention, for parceling out "the world of knowledge from the world of values" (Furst).

In addition to philosophical criticisms of the Taxonomy, others have taken issue with the hierarchical relationship between the objectives. As Bloom explained, the structure of the taxonomy should reflect "real" relationships, thus researchers should expect to find empirical validation in support of such structure. Kreitzer and Madaus summarize two types of empirical investigations—those that investigate the reliability of classifications of test items according to taxonomic level and those that investigate the cumulative/hierarchical nature of the taxonomy. In sum, studies show reliability varies according to the level of training, and that despite increasingly sophisticated statistical techniques, no one has been able to validate the hierarchical structure. At the same time, "no one has been able to demonstrate that [the structure] does not exist" (Kreitzer and Madaus). In the end, Kreizter and Madaus suggest that empirical validation may be unnecessary, especially given that the Taxonomy—validated or not—helped educators "make sense of their world."

A discussion of Bloom's Taxonomy wouldn't be complete without mention of the ways in which it continues to evolve. Just as it has been translated into multiple languages, the Taxonomy has been shaped and reshaped by educators in response to criticisms and the changing educational environment. Anderson and Krathwohl, two of the contributing authors to the original Taxonomy, have developed a revised Taxonomy; the new Taxonomy further delineates knowledge as factual, conceptual, procedural, and metacognitive, partially in response to criticisms of the separation of process from content. In the end, it is the adaptability and evolution of the Taxonomy that may be the greatest measure of its contribution to teaching and learning, rather than the impact of the Taxonomy as it was conceived over fifty years ago.

—Jennifer Kretchmar

References

Airasian, P. "The Impact of the Taxonomy on Testing and Evaluation." *Bloom's Taxonomy: A Forty-Year Retrospective*, edited by L. W. Anderson and L. A. Sosniak, U of Chicago P, 1994, pp. 1–8.

Anderson, L. W. "Research on Teaching and Teacher Education." *Bloom's Taxonomy: A Forty-Year Retrospective*, edited by L. W. Anderson and L. A. Sosniak, U of Chicago P, 1994, pp. 9–19.

Anderson, L. W., and L. A. Sosniak, editors. *Bloom's Taxonomy: A Forty-Year Retrospective*. U of Chicago P, 1994.

Bloom, B. S. "Reflections on the Development and Use of the Taxonomy." *Bloom's Taxonomy: A Forty-Year Retrospective*, edited by L. W. Anderson and L. A. Sosniak, U of Chicago P, 1994, pp. 1–8.

Bloom, B.S., M. D. Englelhart, E. J. Furst, et al. *Taxonomy of Educational Objectives: The Classification of Educational Goals. Handbook I: Cognitive Domain.* Longman, 1954.

Furst, E. J. "Bloom's Taxonomy: Philosophical and Educational Issues." *Bloom's Taxonomy: A Forty-Year Retrospective*, edited by L. W. Anderson and L. A. Sosniak, U of Chicago P, 1994, pp. 28–40.

Krathwohl, D. R. "A Revision of Bloom's Taxonomy: An Overview." *Theory into Practice,* 2002, pp. 212–18.

Kreitzer, A. E., and G. F. Madaus. "Empirical Investigations of the Hierarchical Structure of the Taxonomy." *Bloom's Taxonomy: A Forty-Year Retrospective*, edited by L. W. Anderson and L. A. Sosniak, U of Chicago P, 1994, pp. 28–40.

Marken, J., and G. Morrison. "Objectives Over Time: A Look at Four Decades of Objectives in the Educational Research Literature." *Contemporary Educational Technology,* vol. 4, 2013, pp. 1–14.

Marzano, R. J. "Targets, Objectives, Standards: How Do They Fit?" *Educational Leadership,* vol. 70, 2013, pp. 82–83.

Rohwer, W. D., and K. Sloane. "Psychological Perspectives." *Bloom's Taxonomy: A Forty-Year Retrospective*, edited by L. W. Anderson and L. A. Sosniak, U of Chicago P, 1994, pp. 41–63.

Sosniak, L. A. "The Taxonomy, Curriculum, and Their Relations." *Bloom's Taxonomy: A Forty-Year Retrospective*, edited by L. W. Anderson and L. A. Sosniak, U of Chicago P, 1994, pp. 41–63.

Weisburg, H. K. "Knowledge in Bloom." *School Librarian's Workshop,* vol. 33, 2012, p. 19.

BOTS

Introduction

The term bot refers to any autonomous software application that runs automated tasks over a network, often the internet. Typically performed at a much faster rate than that which would be possible for a human, the tasks are simple and repetitive.

By some estimates, bots make up more than half the traffic on the internet. Bots fit broadly into four categories: social, commercial, malicious, and helpful—which can at times overlap. Most scholars also include automated personal assistants like Amazon's Alexa, Apple's Siri, and Google Assistant in discussions of bots.

Background

Some scholars trace the origin of bots to Alan Turing and the Turing Test. In 1964 Joseph Weizenbaum at the Massachusetts Institute of Technology (MIT) Artificial Intelligence Laboratory created the ELIZA, a social or chat bot programmed to respond to a number of keywords. Though incapable of "learning" through interaction alone, ELIZA caused several participants in the experiment to become emotionally attached to it during their "conversations." As Weizenbaum noted at the time, "extremely short exposures to a relatively simple computer program could induce powerful delusional thinking in quite normal people."

Modern chat bots are far more adaptive than ELIZA and employ natural language processing systems to relate keywords and patterns from a database and formulate their responses. Companies will often employ chatbots as a first layer of customer service on a website. Chatbots can also be routed through third-party platforms, such as WeChat, or Facebook Messenger.

Another form of social bot is a fraudulent account on social media. This type of bot came to prominence during the 2016 American presidential election cycle. Often, these accounts feature profile images and details that make them appear as if they are real people. However, they interact on social media at a rate that no human possibly could. In a 2018 article for *Wired* magazine, Paris Martineau gave the example of a Twitter bot account that had tweeted more than 2,000 times in three days, averaging 660 retweets and seven original tweets per day.

This type of social bot is often referred to as a troll due to its programmed behavior, usually political. A well-programmed bot of this variety can be very difficult to discern from an actual person, even for social media companies themselves. Two prominent platforms for bots of this variety, Facebook and Twitter, have both launched campaigns to rid themselves of bots following bad press in the aftermath of the 2016 presidential race.

These types of social bots are widely regarded as malicious; however, some function as news aggregators and might retweet articles that feature certain keywords. Others are used to archive threads on social media (e.g., Thread Reader App), or for parody (e.g., Think Piece Bot, HaikuBot), and can be helpful or even commercial. Helpful or commercial bots, however, usually disclose that they are bots. Malicious social bots attempting to impersonate genuine accounts typically will not disclose this.

Another variety of malicious bot is represented by "botnets," a portmanteau of "robot" and "internet." Botnets are comprised of a number of internet-connected devices, each of which is running a particular bot application. Devices can be part of a botnet without their users knowing. The botnets can then be used to perform a variety of tasks including Distributed Denial of Service (DDoS) attacks, cryptocurrency mining, and data mining.

Computers compromised by a botnet are often referred to as zombie computers. Their users may have no idea that they are being employed for malicious purposes. Often, computers are infected via spam email or fraudulent downloads. They can also be infected by visiting an infected website, or by exploited vulnerabilities in a web browser. The decentralized nature of botnets make them difficult to quarantine after a number of machines have been infected. Moreover, after zombie computers have reconnected to the botnet's "home," malicious software download packets often delete themselves, leaving little visible evidence of the botnet's presence on the zombie machine.

Legally, there is not much precedent for bots or botnets. Until 2016, many gaps existed in the Federal Rules of Criminal Procedure, creating substantial obstacles both for prosecuting the creators of botnets and also when attempting to de-infect zombie computers. With the new regulation, which went into effect on December 1, 2016, investigators are allowed to bring a single warrant to search infected computers to one federal court rather than being required to craft identical warrants in up to ninety-four jurisdictions. Previously, individual warrants had to be issued for each computer, regardless of whether or not they were in the same jurisdiction, making the process slow and ineffectual.

The State of California passed a law that went into effect in July 2019 requiring chatbots to identify themselves as not being human. While most commercial chatbots already do this, the law's author, State Senator Robert Herzberg, said that the measure was particularly targeted at "deceptive commercial and political bots." Some legal scholars have questioned whether or not this might constitute "compelled speech," either from the bot, its programmer, or the company that owns it. Moreover, as the law is at the state level, it is unclear whether or not it will have the intended effect. Companies that do not already have their bots disclose that they are not human will likely simply reprogram their bots to do so in order to do business within California. However, malicious bots are unlikely to comply regardless of the legislation.

More legislation is likely to focus on bots, particularly as home assistants like Amazon's Alexa, Google's Assistant, and Apple's Siri become more prevalent. Questions have already been raised about the potential for Alexa to monitor its users in order to gain marketing information on them. At present, however, most users seem to privilege the convenience of such bots over their potential negative side effects. Moreover, data protection laws in the United States have been tepid in keeping pace with technology.

—*J. N. Manuel*

References

"Ensuring BotNets Are Not 'Too Big to Investigate." *US Department of Justice*, 22 Nov. 2016, www.justice.gov/archives/opa/blog/ensuring-botnets-are-not-too-big-investigate.

Gershgorn, Dave. "A California Law Now Means Chatbots Have to Disclose They're Not Human." *BotLaw. Quartz*, 3 Oct. 2018, qz.com/1409350/a-new-law-means-californias-bots-have-to-disclose-theyre-not-human/.

Matineau, Paris. "What Is a Bot?" *Wired*, 16 Nov. 2018, www.wired.com/story/the-know-it-alls-what-is-a-bot/.

Sacharoff, Laurent. "Do Bots Have First Amendment Rights?" *Politico*, 27 Nov. 2018, www.politico.com/magazine/story/2018/11/27/bots-first-amendment-rights-222689

Shah, H., K. Warwick, J. Vallverdú, and D. Wu. "Can Machines Talk? Comparison of Eliza with Modern Dialogue Systems." *Computers in Human Behavior*, vol. 58, 2016, pp. 278–95.

Swaine, Jon. "Twitter Admits Far More Russian Bots Posted on Election Than It Had Disclosed." 19 Jan. 2018, www.theguardian.com/technology/2018/jan/19/twitter-admits-far-more-russian-bots-posted-on-election-than-it-had-disclosed.

Weizenbaum, J. *Computer Power and Human Reason: From Judgement to Calculation*. W. H. Freeman, 1976.

BOYD, DANAH MICHELE

Introduction

Danah Boyd was born November 24, 1977, in Altoona, Pennsylvania. In 1982, after her parents divorced, her mother relocated to New York with Danah and her brother. Her mother remarried while Danah was in third grade at school, and the family relocated again, this time to Lancaster, Pennsylvania. Danah's education continued at Manheim Township High School from 1992 through 1996. There she became familiar with the social media of the time, known as "internet relay chat" (IRC) and UseNet. These became important components of both her education and her social life, essentially melding together to become the focus of her postsecondary career.

Boyd began her postsecondary career at Brown University. To complete her Bachelor's degree (BA) in computer science, she presented her undergraduate thesis on the topic of three-dimensional (3D) computer graphics. The argument of her thesis was that 3D graphics systems used cues that were inherently sexist. This thesis was titled "Depth Cues in Virtual Reality: Understanding Individual Differences in Depth Perception by Studying Shape-from-shading and Motion Parallax."

From Brown, Boyd went on to complete a master's degree in sociable media studies at the

Danah Boyd. Photo courtesy of Boyd, via Wikimedia Commons.

Massachusetts Institute of Technology (MIT) Media Lab. She then went to the University of California at Berkeley (UC Berkeley) where she completed a doctoral degree in 2008, at the UC Berkeley School of Information. Her doctoral dissertation was titled *Taken Out of Context: American Teen Sociality in Networked Publics*. The focus of her doctoral research was an examination of how US teens used the large social networking sites Facebook and Myspace. She maintained a blog on the Boing Boing platform to document her research, and she has continued to blog her research notes to the present day.

In addition to her academic studies, Boyd held a position as a fellow at the Annenberg Center for Communication at University of Southern California (USC) in 2006–7 while undertaking her doctoral research. She later held a fellowship at Harvard University's Berkman Center for Internet and Society. There she was codirector of the Internet Safety Technical Task Force, as well as serving on the Youth and Media Policy Working Group.

In her research published in 2007, Boyd argued the principle of homophily was pervasive in large networking sites, particularly Facebook and Myspace. "Homophily" is essentially the birds-of-a-feather-flock-together paradigm, by which membership of those sites demonstrates cultural bias based on perceived ethnicity. The youth user base of both Myspace and Facebook appeared to represent two different, identifiable socioeconomic classes, and tended to maintain social divisions rather than promote social inclusion. Furthermore, Boyd's research considered the concept of so-called white flight, in which white privileged teens either abandoned or avoided the predominantly lower-class black youth population of Myspace by joining their peers on Facebook, with encouragement from their white privileged parents.

In 2009, following completion of her PhD degree, Boyd joined Microsoft Research, in Cambridge, Massachusetts, as a social media researcher. Four years later, she founded Data & Society Research Institute. Since then, she has become a partner researcher at Microsoft Research, a position she continues to hold as of 2022. She is also president of Data & Society Institute, and a visiting professor at Georgetown University and New York University. Outside of academia and professional work, she provides service on the Board of Directors of Crisis Text Line; as a trustee of the National Museum of the American Indian; on the board of the Social Science Research Council; and on the advisory board of the Electronic Privacy Information Center (EPIC).

Professional History

Boyd has published several academic works in peer-reviewed journals, and four books (including her PhD dissertation). She has also been the recipient of a number of awards and accolades, having been called one of the most influential women in technology (2009) and the smartest academic in the technology field (2010). Her awards include the Award for Public Sociology (American Sociological Association, Communication and Information Technologies section, 2010), and the Barlow/Pioneer Award (Electronic Frontier Foundation, 2019). She has also spoken on the use, value, and manipulation of data at several academic conferences.

Danah Boyd is married, has three children with her partner, and resides with her family in Altoona, Pennsylvania.

—*Richard M. Renneboog*

References

Boyd, Danah. *It's Complicated: The Social Lives of Networked Teens*. Yale UP, 2014.

Ito, Mizuko, et al. *Hanging Out, Messing Around, and Geeking Out: Kids Living and Learning with New Media*. MIT Press, 2010.

Lankshear, Colin, and Michele Knobel, editors. *Digital Literacies: Concepts, Policies and Practices*. Peter Lang, 2008.

Valkenberg, Patti M., and Jessica Taylor Piotrowski. *Plugged In: How Media Attract and Affect Youth*. Yale UP, 2017.

Varnelis, Kazys, editor. *Networked Publics*. MIT Press, 2008.

BRAIN-COMPUTER INTERFACING (BCI)

Introduction

Broadly speaking, any direct communication link between the brain and an external device is referred to as brain-computer interfacing (BCI). Brain-computer interfacing implies that a user's brain signals are directly involved in the communication process, thus allowing for a more immediate interface between a user and a device. This differs, of course, from traditional computer interfacing, where a user might, say, use a keyboard, a mouse, or even their voice to access a computer. The world of adaptive or assistive technology in particular utilizes BCI, where a lesser-abled user can directly manipulate their world using any of several computer devices.

BCI devices provide a direct access to the user's brain-wave patterns, and this allows the device to act upon those patterns. Based on its widespread growth and technological use in neurological advancements, BCI provides medical professionals and information technology (IT) development professionals with unrestricted and unregulated access to the brain. This cranium access may pose an

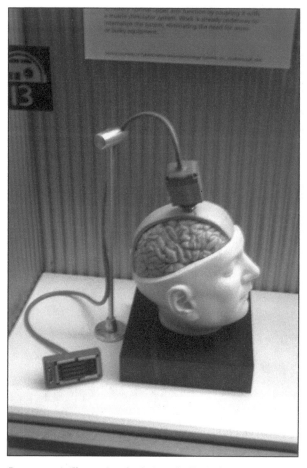

Dummy unit illustrating the design of a BrainGate interface. Photo by PaulWicks at English Wikipedia, via Wikimedia Commons.

increasing risk to individual privacy rights or private thoughts.

Background

Assistive technology includes screen-reading software, speech synthesizers, and eye-gaze and head-pointing software, among many others. Adaptive devices enable people to work on standard computers or other devices by altering existing equipment. Most famously, prominent physicist Dr. Stephen Hawking was disabled by amyotrophic lateral sclerosis. As his muscles gradually atrophied as a result of the disease, Hawking lost mobility and the ability to speak; yet assistive technology using BCI elements enabled him to continue his research, travel, and writing. Hawking operated his computer using switches controlled by one thumb or by blinking his eyes. These early technologies approached BCI, though they did still require elements of active participation on Hawking's part. Remembered most for his scientific contributions, Hawking also brought such technologies and devices into the mainstream and demonstrating that those with disabilities need not be confined by them.

More recent innovations—and the technology is truly in its infancy—bypass any need for conscious user input. A twenty-first-century BCI system directly monitors a user's brainwaves and converts those waves into any of several automated outputs on the part of the device so connected. The process is said to first measure brain activity, then "extract features from that activity, and convert those features into outputs that replace, restore, enhance, supplement, or improve human functions," according to Schalk and Allison. Schalk and Allison then go on to identify that lost functions such as speaking or moving can be replaced by a device that therefore speaks or moves for the user; or that muscles and nerves may be stimulated to allow the user to move their hand, for example; or that BCI's can help train "users to improve the remaining function of damaged pathways required to grasp." In other cases, they may simply enhance a user's life experiences, wherein, for example, a driver drifting into sleep can be stirred into waking up. Finally, supplements to the human experience may be provided by BCIs, such as the use of a third hand in complex textile operations. Most such interactions are, of course, complicated, for the measurement of brain activity needs to be converted into an "understanding" of the device's part as to what the user is attempting to accomplish. In any case, electrodes are necessary to detect the brain's electrical signals, and they are either placed inside the user's skull, or on the scalp's surface, although early work with magnetic resonance imaging (MRI) is proving to be effective in evaluating electrical impulses.

Dangerous Implications

If one considers possible nefarious motives, "brain spyware" is a risk when BCI is used via computer applications or software. For example, the software or computer application may track information such as the likes, dislikes, interests or disinterests of an individual who is participating in an educational study. This collection is done without the knowledge or awareness of the participant and may be sold for

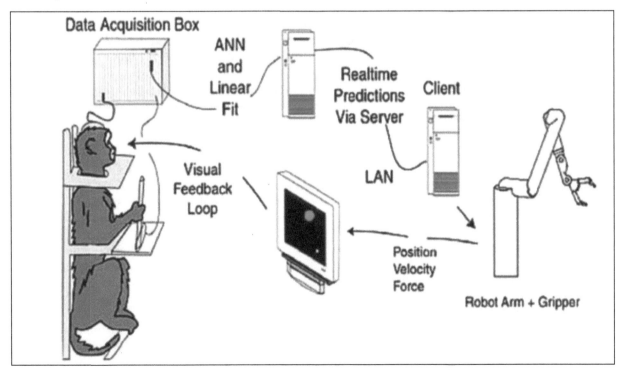

Diagram of the BCI developed by Miguel Nicolelis and colleagues for use on rhesus monkeys. (PLoS Biology, 1, 2003). Image via Wikimedia Commons.

something other than the researcher and participant originally intended. This example points to a potential risk of invasive or noninvasive BCI.

Another potential risk to individual privacy is the participant's financial institution information may become vulnerable to fraudulent and unauthorized financial transactions. When BCI is used, the interface opens exposure to manipulation or extraction of personal information such as home address, personal identification numbers (PINs), and banking information. Scientists at the Laboratory of Adaptive Intelligence commented that BCI leaves the mind open to hacking and allows researchers to "*secretly extract sensitive information from the brain.*"

As BCI expands, it becomes difficult for the government to regulate to protect privacy. Just like the educated use of the internet and information that individuals protect by controlling what is posted, searched, and used the same can be exercised as BCI is used for a variety of purposes. An educated participant makes for a participant that should be responsible for protecting what is explored in their minds to the extent possible. Harmless information may be extracted that does not necessarily give a tremendous amount of insight into the individual's private thoughts, however, just as a targeted group that does not make their private financial information at risk. In other words, limiting and policing use BCI may assist in how much harm or how much private information may be extracted and individual judgment of the line of private information can be drawn voluntarily.

—*Shaunté Chácon, Nancy W. Comstock, and James F. Nicosia*

References

Bonaci, T., and H. Chizack. "Privacy by Design in Brain-Computer Interfaces." *U of Washington*. Department of EE, www.ee.washington.edu/techsite/papers/documents/UWEETR-2013–0001.

Geekwire.com, www.geekwire.com/2014/geekwire-radiobraincomputer-interfaces-future-personal-privacy.

Luber, B., C. Fisher, P. S. Appelbaum, et al. "Noninvasive Brain Stimulation in the Detection of Deception: Scientific Challenges and Ethical Consequences." *Behavioral Sciences & the Law*, vol. 27, no. 2, 2009, pp. 191–208.

Martinovic, Ivan, Doug Davies, Mario Frank, et al. "On the Feasibility of Side-Channel Attacks with Brain-Computer Interfaces." *The Proceedings of the 21st USENIX Security Symposium*. USENIX, 2012.

Schalk, Gerwin, and Brendan Z. Allison. *Neuromodulation: Comprehensive Textbook of Principles, Technologies, and Therapies*. 2nd ed., Academic Press, 2018.

BROWSERS

Introduction

A web browser is a software application is utilized to access data and information on the World Wide Web. When someone initiates a search on the internet, the browser retrieves and culls information for the user to access. It is this stage of an internet search that helps users think critically about online information—its authenticity, validity, authoritativeness, and relevancy.

Browsers display documents, website URLs, articles, journals, and hyperlinks. It is up to the user to use critical thinking and reading skills to gauge the value of the results of the search. While browsers and internet searches are intended to be neutral in presenting information, many browsers accept advertisements (and sometimes/often) privilege promoted pages over others sources.

Multiple web pages can be opened at one time in tabs (which serve as file folders to organize discrete collections of data. This makes research easy and convenient for those who like to multitask and have access to information available concurrently.

There are numerous browser applications available. A quick search using Google or any other search engine will very quickly reveal at least fifty browser applications, and while they all function in the same way each one has its own unique appearance and built-in capabilities. Each one has its own strengths, weaknesses and configurability, and therefore its own usefulness.

Background

One of the most versatile browser applications for use with the Microsoft Windows operating system in the 1990s was Netscape Navigator, produced by Netscape Communications Corporation. As befit

Popular browsers have included Firefox, Chrome, Safari, and Opera. Image by EpiDor, via Wikimedia Commons.

the graphics capabilities of the time, the on-screen appearance of Navigator was simple in design. Navigator was essentially limited to an HTML-based display of text and still images. Within that limitation though, Navigator was a very capable and reliable browser with excellent operating speed. It also had one unique feature that no other browser application offered; its users could design and compose their own HTML-based web pages using native HTML code or with Navigator's built-in HTML coding functions and then view those pages before uploading them to a website.

Navigator also introduced a number of user-friendly features that made accessing the internet during the times of blazingly slow dial-up modem transfers almost tolerable for users. One such feature was the ability to view web pages as they were downloading rather than having to wait for the entire page to download before any of it could be viewed. Netscape also introduced the use of cookies, frames, proxy-auto configuration, and JavaScript, a kind of intermediate language that augmented mark-up languages by providing computational functionality that mark-up languages do not possess on their own.

Navigator, and its successor Netscape Communicator, were widely available at no cost through 2007, but can still be found today as legacy applications. They were written to run on a variety of operating platforms that included Windows, Linux, OS/2, Macintosh, and many of the UNIX variants. They looked and operated almost exactly the same on each operating system. Netscape's great success with Navigator and Communicator however, ultimately lead to its downfall as browsers developed to compete with them, chiefly Microsoft's Internet Explorer (IE), eventually displaced Netscape's browsers from

their position as the leading browser applications of the time.

Given the power of Microsoft's marketing strategies, it should come as no surprise that the IE browser that came with every single personal computer (PC) operating on Microsoft Windows would displace Netscape's browsers at some point. Explorer was introduced in 1995 to compete with Netscape Navigator, and in 2003 Netscape stopped supporting both Navigator and Communicator while IE held a 95 percent usage share of browser applications. In 2022, this had dropped to just 0.5 percent, as other competing browser applications had taken over. Explorer existed throughout its lifetime as a series of graphical web browsers developed by Microsoft since 1995 for inclusion with the concurrent Microsoft Windows operating systems. It was replaced in 2015 by Microsoft Edge.

Firefox

According to Mozilla.org, the producer of the browser application, Firefox is not just a browser, but a collection of products designed for users to promote safer and smarter browsing while online. The main feature of the Firefox family of products however, is the Firefox browser application itself. The browser is produced for desktop and laptop computers, mobile systems such as cell phones and tablets, and for enterprise computing systems and mainframes. In all iterations, the browser automatically blocks more than 2000 known data trackers, small third-party programs that monitor a user's online activity and returns a record of that activity to the data trackers' sources for different purposes.

Firefox was created in 2002, when Microsoft's IE 6 was the dominant browser in general use. The beta version of Firefox proved to be faster, more secure, and with better add-on features than IE 6. By 2009, Firefox had exceeded IE's share of browser usage, before both fell behind Google's Chrome browser in popularity. Originally part of a collection of utility programs called Mozille Suite, Firefox (originally called Phoenix) was developed to be a stand-alone application in order to reduce what was thought of as Mozille Suite's bloated code. The term refers to program code that requires so many coded instructions to run all of the program's features that it causes program functioning to bog down or become too slow to be useful. Firefox quickly proved itself to be a fast, efficient browser that is easy to use, with user-friendly usability and security features.

Google Chrome

By far the best-known browser in use as of April 2022 is the Chrome browser from Google. So well-known has searching through Google become that *google* has become an active verb around the world as millions of people everywhere "google" something every day. Google's Chrome browser was first released in 2008 to compete with Firefox and quickly displaced both Firefox and IE as the browser of choice. It is currently the default browser for all of Microsoft, Apple, Mac, iOS, and Android operating systems. Of course, users of those systems are able to load and use other browsers, but some of the embedded applications for those systems have been written to default to Chrome when accessing external information and data. Chrome currently holds a 65 percent browser usage share across all operating systems, down slightly from its peak of just over 72 percent.

Chrome is a fast, robust browser that is exceedingly simple to use due to its minimalist presentation, although that minimalism has been augmented recently by the presentation of a selection of topical links each time a new tab is opened. Until that happened, new tabs in Chrome displayed only a wallpaper screen image and the search bar/address bar called the "omnibox." Users type in a web address, search term or keyword, and Chrome uses the Google search engine to call up every instance of the word that it can locate.

Chrome is readily configured and maintained by its users, with numerous preference settings and "housekeeping" utilities. Chrome also has a large library of extensions available as add-ons, allowing users to add features such as other languages, translation, mathematics and others that are not part of the basic structure of Chrome's provided release. Many such extensions are written and produced by third-party developers and may not be entirely compatible with a particular version of Chrome.

Safari

Because Safari was developed to run on Mac computers rather than PCs, it is a graphics-based browser and unique to the MacOS, iOS, and iPadOS operating systems. A Windows version was offered in 2007, but was discontinued three years later in 2010.

Safari was initially offered in 2003 and as of 2022 is in its fifteenth iteration. Its performance in the 2020 version was 50 percent faster than Google Chrome and consumed significantly less power than its competitors. In 2021, Safari usage was second only to Google Chrome, with about 18.5 percent usage share worldwide and 39 percent in the United States. New versions of Safari were released every two years from 2003 to 2007, but, since 2012, updates have been released yearly.

Safari functions like all web browsers, the essential difference being that internet connections and data are displayed through graphics processing rather than the text-based processing of other computers. In graphics processing the hyperlinks to other web pages may be embedded within the digital code of graphics images, whereas in text-based processing the hyperlinks are merely associated with a string of text that typically identifies the URL of the target of the hyperlink, or is perhaps just an underlined word or an instruction such as "click here." The hyperlinks in both text-based and graphics processing can also be associated with an image.

Chromium

As the name would suggest, Chromium is also a product of Google. Though not a browser per se, it is a free and open-source browser project representing the very large codebase used by Chrome. As such, Google does not provide an official stable version of Chromium. While the program codes within the Chromium codebase are the property of Google, it is available freely for use by other developers and has been utilized to produce other web browsers, including Opera, Microsoft Edge and Samsung Internet. Users of Chromium code are able to develop and enhance the code they use, and add those new features to the Chromium codebase. In addition, they can use their features with the Chrome brand attached.

Brave

Brave is one of the several web browsers that have been constructed using the Chromium codebase. Brave recaptures the minimalistic appearance of new tabs, displaying only a beautifully composed high-resolution photographic wallpaper background, an omnibox search bar, and a small number of quick access icons linked to as many web locations as the user has accessed frequently. The icons are unobtrusive and can be removed either manually or when the browser cache is cleared. Brave tabs also often display a promotion for crypto currency as the wallpaper image, which users may or may not find annoying. The promotion is due to the fact that Brave users are also provided the opportunity to garner a type of crypto currency called BAT that they can choose to pass on to developers, charitable organizations, keep for themselves, or just simply ignore. This is an interesting feature not provided by other web browsers.

Brave's main attractions are its built-in automatic blocking of ads and data trackers, and its high user security capabilities. In normal use Brave runs the Chrome browser, but with enhanced user security features. Chrome itself gives the option of using a private window for browsing, as do other browsers, that does not log the browsing history of the user's current session. When the option to open a new private window is selected in Brave, however, the user is presented with a choice to use either Chrome's basic private window service or Brave's private window with Tor connectivity. With Tor connectivity, the user's IP address is completely masked as the browsing requests are passed through any number of other Tor server nodes.

Accordingly, this may slow down browser response, and Brave warns that some websites may not function through Tor and so will not be accessible. The Tor connectivity option also requires that the Tor browser be resident on the user's device.

Brave was first launched in 2016, and in 2021 claimed to have more than 50 million users per month. Not surprising, considering the browser's many features and its availability for use with different operating systems, including Android.

Duck Duck Go

The newest browser to break into the market in any significant way, Duck Duck Go was created in February 2008 by its creator, Gabriel Weinberg. Weinberg self-funded the deployment of Duck Duck Go, with the help of a handful of private investors. The site had the express intention of being the first browser/search engine to resist tracking users' visits to the internet. In 2010, the site was able to fulfill that goal by initiating privacy terms for users. As such, it has continued to break ground in an area of computing where users (and other browsers) have been resistant to trying something new.

The site now averages 100 million search queries each day and boasts a peak of a billion searches. In 2022, it is the second most popular search engine for mobile devices and employs over 120 workers.

Opera

Opera is one of the oldest web browsers, having been developed in 1995 by its namesake company. Until 2005, Opera was available only as commercial software based on Opera's Presto engine. Opera was switched from Presto to Chromium in 2013, and continues to develop from the Chromium codebase. In 2016, the Opera brand was sold to a consortium of Chinese investors.

The Opera browser has many of the features common to Chromium-based browsers, such as ad blocking, tabbed browsing, private browsing, and others. A particular feature of interest in Opera is that an unlimited number of recently viewed web pages are shown as thumbnail views when a new tab is opened. Opera also has embedded links to social media messaging applications, including Facebook Messenger, WhatsApp, Telegram, Twitter, Instagram, and V Kontakte (VK). Opera is contracted to use the Google search engine as its default. Opera runs on Windows, Mac, Linux, iOS, and Android operating systems.

—*Richard M. Renneboog and Jake D. Nicosia*

References

Dean, Brian. "DuckDuckGo: Usage Stats for 2022." *Backlinko*, Apr. 2022, backlinko.com/duckduckgo-stats#key-duckduckgo-stats.

Gralla, Preston. *How the Internet Works*. 4th ed., Que Publishing, 1998.

Hofmann, Chris, Marcia Knous, and John V. Hedke. *Firefox and Thunderbird Garage*. Prentice Hall Professional Technical Reference, 2005.

Huddleston, Rob. *HTML, XHTML, and CSS: Your visual Blueprint for Designing Effective Web Pages*. John Wiley & Sons, 2009.

La Counte, Scott. *The Ridiculously Simple Guide to Surfing the Internet with Google Chrome*. GOLGOTHAPressNC, 2020.

LeJeune, Urban A., and Jeff Duntemann. *Netscape and HTML Explorer*. Coriolis Group Books, 1995.

Markelo, Steve. *Microsoft Edge: A Beginner's Guide to the Widows 10 Browser.* Conceptual Kings, 2015.

McDaniel, Adam. *HTML 5: Your Visual Blueprint for Designing Rich Web Pages and Applications.* John Wiley & Sons, 2011.

Mehta, Prateek. *Creating Google Chrome Extensions.* Springer Science + Business Media, 2016.

Stockson, Eric. *Brave Browser: Blockchain Internet Browsing Made Easy.* First Rank, 2019.

Wilton, Paul, and Jeremy McPeak. *Beginning JavaScript.* 4th ed., John Wiley & Sons, 2011.

C

CATFISHING

Introduction

Catfishing refers to intentionally using a false online identity in order to trick someone into engaging in an emotional and/or romantic relationship. In documented cases of catfishing, the motivation for deception varies and can include boredom, loneliness, revenge, and simple curiosity. The term was first coined in the documentary *Catfish* (2010), in which the filmmaker learns that the woman with whom he believes he is having an online relationship is in reality someone completely different.

Background

The use of false or anonymous online identities has been commonplace since use of the internet became widespread in the early 1990s. People have used fake identities when writing book or film reviews, commenting on blogs, and when intending to aggravate or escalate online arguments. What distinguishes catfishing is its end goal of cultivating an online romantic relationship.

With the rise in popularity of social media networks in the 2000s, catfishing became more advanced and elaborate. Through websites such as Myspace and Facebook, users could create deceptive accounts using fabricated biographical information and photographs that were downloaded from the internet. Additional social media accounts were often created to give the illusion of a network of family members and friends.

The rise in popularity of online dating also led the way for an increase in catfishing. According to a study performed by the Pew Research Center in 2016, nearly six percent of internet users in a committed relationship first met their partner online. This figure was twice that of those polled in 2005. A 2013 Pew study also found that 54 percent of those polled believed that they had also been given false biographical information by others online at some point.

Motivation: Why Catfish?

The motivation for people to catfish others varies. Sometimes catfishers are lonely or feel ostracized by their peers or community, so they turn to online companionship. Other times there are malicious reasons, such as a drive for aggression or for revenge. Some catfishers create a false online profile in order to explore aspects of their sexuality they are afraid to reveal or confront in real life. Catfishing is also considered by experts as a form of cyberstalking

A 2012 study in the *Journal of Adolescence* found that young people are increasingly using social networking websites as a means for identity exploration. By creating fake profiles, users can explore different facets of their personality. The study states that while this exploration helps adolescents measure and understand themselves and form an identity, it can grow harmful if the user isolates from reality in order to nurture intimate relationships online, which then leads to negative psychological patterns. There have

Fictional identities and correspondence are used to create a sense of trust with a victim of catfishing. Photo via iStock/Tero Vesalainen. [Used under license.]

been various studies done on the psychology of both the catfisher and the victim as well as numerous articles on the warning signs of being catfished.

In the wake of the popularity of the *Catfish* documentary and television series, there have also been several publicized catfishing incidents involving sports and entertainment personalities. The term's position in the cultural lexicon was further cemented when its definition was amended in 2014 by Merriam-Webster to include a person who uses a deceptive social networking profile.

Catfish the Documentary and the Series

The term catfish was first coined in the documentary *Catfish* (2010), which followed photographer Yaniv "Nev" Schulman as he developed a romantic relationship online. He believed he was in a relationship with a single young woman named Megan, but when Schulman and the filmmakers tracked her down, they unveiled a series of untruths culminating in the realization that Megan was actually Angela Wesselman, an older married woman with two handicapped sons. In the film, an anecdote is told about how fisherman place catfish in shipping tanks with live cod when sending the fish overseas. The catfish harass the cod, thereby keeping them active and their meat firmer and better tasting. People who act as catfish, the documentary explains, keep others alert and never bored.

The success of the documentary led to the cable network MTV producing *Catfish: The Series* in 2012. In each episode, Schulman and *Catfish* filmmaker Max Joseph connect people who have an online relationship in order to determine whether someone in the relationship is catfishing the other.

Manti Te'o and Thomas Gibson

University of Notre Dame linebacker Manti Te'o led his team in an exciting upset against Michigan State University in September 2013. Fans were especially inspired by his performance because three days before, Te'o had learned that his grandmother and girlfriend, Lennay Kekua, had both died. Te'o and Kekua had met online and had developed a romantic relationship without ever having met in person, and Te'o's ability to overcome adversity garnered a tremendous amount of national attention. Following Kekua's reported death, journalists discovered that, unbeknownst to Te'o, Lennay Kekua did not exist, and that the religious musician

Ronaiah Tuiasosopo had been pretending to be Kekua because, as he later admitted, he was secretly in love with Te'o.

Also in 2013, it was revealed that actor Thomas Gibson, who stars on the popular television series *Criminal Minds*, was the victim of an elaborate catfish scam. The news broke when an entertainment news agency released an embarrassing video that Gibson took of himself in a hot tub. Reports indicated that Gibson and his catfisher had been exchanging photos and videos of themselves for at least two years, with Gibson's catfisher sending him images she downloaded from pornographic websites.

—*Patrick G. Cooper*

References

Caspi, Avner, and Paul Gorsky. "Online Deception: Prevalence, Motivation, and Emotion." *CyberPsychology & Behavior*, vol. 9, no 1, 2006, pp. 54–59.

D'Costa, Krystal. "Catfishing: The Truth about Deception Online." *Scientific American*. Nature America, 25 Apr. 2014.

Israelashvili, Moshe, et al. "Adolescents' Over-Use of the Cyber World: Internet Addiction or Identity Exploration?" *Journal of Adolescence*, vol. 35, no. 2, 2012, pp. 417–24.

McCarthy, Ellen. "What Is Catfishing? A Brief (and Sordid) History." *The Washington Post*, 9 Jan. 2016.

Moss, Caroline. "Strangers Have Been Using This Woman's Photos to Catfish People Online for Ten Years." *Business Insider*, 21 Jan. 2015.

Scott, A. O. "The World Where You Aren't What You Post." *The New York Times*, 16 Sept. 2010.

Smith, Aaron, and Maeve Duggan. "Online Dating & Relationships." *Pew Research*, 21 Oct. 2013.

CHILDREN'S ONLINE PRIVACY PROTECTION ACT

Introduction

The Children's Online Privacy Protection Act was signed into law on October 21, 1998, by President Bill Clinton. In October 1999, the Federal Trade Commission (FTC) issued the Children's Online Privacy Protection Act Rule (the "COPPA Rule") (15

C.F.R. § 312), which became effective on April 20, 2000. The FTC administers and enforces the Children's Online Privacy Protection Act (COPPA).

Background

The FTC's 1998 report, *Privacy Online: A Report to Congress,* contained findings related to its study of the practices of websites directed toward children. Among other pertinent findings, the report revealed that, while 89 percent of websites collected personal information directly from children, only 10 percent of these sites offered any mechanisms for parental control over the collection and use of such information. Based on these findings, the FTC recommended that Congress pass comprehensive legislation that would provide parents with greater control over the collection and dissemination of children's personal information.

According to the lead sponsor of COPPA, Senator Richard Bryan, Congress had four related aims in creating this legislation: (1) to enhance parental involvement in children's online activities as a way to protect children's privacy, (2) to protect children's safety when they engage in online activities, (3) to maintain the security of children's personal information collected online, and (4) to limit the collection of personal information from children without parental consent. Toward that end, COPPA initially imposed requirements on two groups of operators of commercial websites and online services: operators or websites and online services that are directed to children under the age of thirteen that collect, use, or disclose personal information from children, *and* operators of websites; and online services intended for a general audience but who have actual knowledge that they are collecting, using, or disclosing personal information from children under the age of thirteen.

"Personal information," as broadly defined under COPPA, incudes an individual's name, physical address, email address, telephone number, and Social Security number, as well as any other identifier (as determined by the FTC) that permits an individual to be contacted in person or online. Excluded from the definition of "operator" are nonprofit websites and personal homepages. In determining whether a website is "directed to children," the FTC considers factors including subject matter, visual or audio content (including use of animated characters), age of models, and language.

Key requirements imposed on covered operators include the provision of an effective notice as to its data use and collection policies with regard to children, the receipt of verifiable parental consent prior to collection of information, the disclosure to parents of information collected with respect to their children, procedures for parents to revoke consent and have information deleted, and limitations on the use of games and prizes directed toward children. Requirements of "effective notice" include the clear labeling and prominent placement of links to the privacy policy on the homepage. Also, the policy must provide the contact information of website operators collecting and maintaining information, indicate whether the information is disclosed to third parties, and specify how such information is used. "Verifiable parental consent" requires operators to use a consent method that is reasonably calculated, in light of available technology, to ensure that the person providing consent is the child's parent.

The COPPA rule has a safe harbor provision, whereby industry groups can seek FTC approval of self-compliance programs that implement protections of the COPPA rule. Under this provision, the FTC must act within 180 days of the request. Since 2000, the FTC has approved the safe harbor programs offered by the Entertainment Software Rating Board; Aristotle International, Inc.; the Children's Advertising Review Unit of the Council of Better Business Bureaus; PRIVO, Inc.; TRUSTe; kidSAFE; and iKeepSafe.

Enforcement

Congress delegated all enforcement duties to the FTC, granting it the power to bring forward adjudicatory actions against websites and the power to levy fines for violations. The FTC is authorized to treat a violation of the COPPA rule as a violation of a rule defining an unfair or deceptive act or practice prescribed under section 18(a)(1)(B) of the Federal Trade Commission Act. COPPA does not provide parents or children with a private right of action. It does, however, grant states and certain federal agencies the authority to enforce compliance with respect to entities over which they have jurisdiction. To date, only Texas and New Jersey have brought COPPA enforcement actions. Violators of COPPA are liable for civil penalties of up to $16,000 per violation. By 2010, the FTC had collected $3.2 million through fourteen COPPA enforcement actions.

Notable COPPA enforcement actions were filed against Xanga.com in 2006 (a $1 million civil penalty) and Sony BMG Music Entertainment ($1 million civil penalty) in 2008.

Recent Developments

Pursuant to COPPA and § 312.11 of the COPPA rule, the FTC was required to initiate a review no later than five years after the rule's effective date to evaluate the rule's implementation. After initiating this review in April 2005, the FTC considered extensive public comment on the COPPA rule, ultimately reaching a decision in March 2006 to retain the COPPA rule without change. In March 2010, however, the FTC sought public comment on whether it was necessary to re-examine the COPPA rule given ongoing changes in the online environment—notably, children's increasing use of mobile technology to access the internet.

The COPPA rule was amended effective July 2013. The amended rule takes into account technological developments, including mobile devices, interactive gaming, and social networking, that alter how children use and access the internet. Thus, under the revised rule, COPPA now applies to third-party service, including ad networks and plug-ins, that collect information from users of a website or online service directed to children under the age of thirteen. It now also applies to mobile apps that send or receive information online and internet-enabled gaming platforms. In addition, the amended COPPA rule adds four new categories of information to the definition of "personal information": geolocation information, photographs and video files containing a child's image as well as audio files containing a child's voice, a screen or username that reveals an individual's email address or a similar identifier that enables direct online contact with an individual, and persistent identifiers that may be used to recognize a user over time or across different websites or online services.

With the revelations of privacy lapses among the large social media companies like Facebook and Google during the late 2010s, the question of the sufficiency of COPPA's provisions have resurfaced. In an April 2018 congressional hearing on privacy for children and teens, Senator Ed Markey proposed a privacy bill of rights for teenagers that would cover the gap between COPPA, which covers children up to age thirteen, and adult privacy laws. Facebook chief executive officer (CEO) Mark Zuckerberg argued against such additional laws, calling them unnecessary. The timing of this assertion was difficult, as it came close upon the heels of the controversy Facebook faced due to the sharing of information on 87 million users with Cambridge Analytica, a social media consulting firm hired by Donald J. Trump's 2016 presidential campaign. During that same month, the video sharing site YouTube, which is owned by Google, faced charges by consumer advocacy groups that they did not comply with COPPA in the way they handled children's data.

—*Ursula Gorham*

References

Boyd D., E. Hargittai J. Schultz, and J. Palfrey J. "Why Parents Help Their Children Lie to Facebook about Age: Unintended Consequences of the 'Children's Online Privacy Protection Act.'" *First Monday*, vol. 16, no. 11, 2011.

Davis, J. J. "Marketing to Children Online: A Manager's Guide to the Children's Online Privacy Protection Act." *S.A.M. Advanced Management Journal*, vol. 67, no. 4, 2002, pp. 11–21.

Delaney, E. "The Children's Online Privacy Protection Act and Rule: An Overview." *Journal of Civil Rights and Economic Development*, vol. 16, no. 3, 2012, pp. 641–48.

Madden, M., S. Cortesi, U. Gasser, A. Lenhart, and M. Duggan. *Parents, Teens, and Online Privacy*. Pew Internet & American Life Project, 2012.

Maheshwari, S. "YouTube Is Improperly Collecting Children's Data, Consumer Groups Say." *The New York Times*, 9 Apr. 1028, www.nytimes.com/2018/04/09/business/media/youtube-kids-ftc-complaint.html.

Stanaland, A. J. S., M. O. Lwin, and S. Leong. "Providing Parents with Online Privacy Information: Approaches in the U.S. and the UK." *Journal of Consumer Affairs*, vol. 43, no. 3, 2009, pp. 474–94.

Whittaker, Z. "At Hearing, Facebook's Zuckerberg Rejects Law to Protect Privacy of Children." *ZDNet*, 10 Apr. 2018, www.zdnet.com/article/at-hearing-zuckerberg-rejects-law-to-protect-the-privacy-of-children/.

CLICKBAIT

Introduction

In online journalism, clickbait refers to headlines on online content that entice readers to click on a link to a story. Online news and commentary websites rely on clickbait to drive up the number of clicks to their articles, thereby increasing traffic to their sites and attracting advertisers.

Clickbait headlines are often provocative, written to arouse curiosity or stir outrage. The headlines attempt to lure readers through forward referencing, suspenseful wording, and the use of images. The term has taken on a negative connotation. Readers may feel manipulated after clicking to stories that overdramatize events, mischaracterize content, or advertise products.

Background

Websites use clickbait to promote content that readers can share across social media platforms, generating instant clicks. The content may include news articles, think pieces, quizzes, or viral videos. Clickbait exists in many different forms.

Mashable and *Buzzfeed* are early examples of websites that create and curate online content for the main purpose of distributing it on social media platforms such as Facebook and Twitter. Readers often share content from *Mashable* and *Buzzfeed* because it provides entertainment; this sort of clickbait is sometimes called "sharebait." *Buzzfeed's* quizzes are a popular draw. For example, its "What State Do You Actually Belong In?" quiz attracted 41.4 million views as of November 2014, according to *The Atlantic.*

Other kinds of clickbait appeal to people's inquisitive nature; they grab readers' attention by using forward referencing, which includes phrases such as, "You won't believe what happens next." *Upworthy,* another content-curating website, gained notice by using these types of headlines, which may mix in pronouns to add a mysterious slant. An example is the headline of the site's 2013 article, "Calling Them 'Girls' Was Their First Mistake. What Happened Next Is a Great Moment in Fierceness." The practice, sometimes known as "curiosity bait," spread to other sites.

Curiosity bait can let down readers if "what happens next" in the story fails to surprise them or sensationalizes the news. According to the *Washington Post,* news source CNN has come under fire for using the technique. In 2014, the network sent the following tweet on Twitter about one of its articles: "14-year-old girl stabbed her little sister 40 times, police say. The reason why will shock you." Many readers thought the network's promotional tactic was in poor taste.

Trickbait is used by websites that do not produce their own content to encourage people to click on their links. Trickbait often appears as a grid of stories, often called "sponsored content" or "promoted stories," at the bottom of legitimate news websites. The strategy is called "trickbait" because the

Leading Doctor Reveals the No. 1 Worst Carb You Are Eating
Mediconews

The $$$ Moneymaking Secret that Banks Don't Want You To Know
Bankfacts

These 12 Impossible Pet Rescue Stories Will Melt Your Heart!
Cutepups Inc

Fictional examples of clickbait style adverts. Image by Lord Belbury, via Wikimedia Commons.

sponsored stories can be mistaken for those of the news site. Visual trickbait refers to a story that appears in the "sponsored" grid accompanied by a photo that has no connection whatsoever to the article. The image misleads readers into clicking on the link.

Backlash is growing over the use of clickbait. Readers have expressed frustration when articles do not deliver the content they promised. In response, Facebook announced in 2014 that it would crack down on stories fronted by clickbait headlines. In 2015, Upworthy announced that it would stop using clickbait and instead produce original stories.

—*Rebecca Kivak*

References

Chowdhry, Amit. "Facebook Is Going to Suppress 'Click-Bait' Articles." *Forbes*, 26 Aug. 2014, www.forbes.com/sites/amitchowdhry/2014/08/26/facebook-is-going-to-suppress-click-bait-articles/#51f7bf8b47b0.

Closs, Wyatt. "Calling Them 'Girls' Was Their First Mistake: What Happened Next Is a Great Moment in Fierceness." *Upworthy*, 11 July 2013, www.upworthy.com/calling-them-girls-was-their-first-mistake-what-happens-next-is-a-great-moment-in-fierceness.

Council of Europe. *Journalism at Risk: Threats, Challenges and Perspectives*. Council of Europe, 2015.

Frampton, Ben. "Clickbait: The Changing Face of Online Journalism." *BBC News*, 14 Sept. 2015, www.bbc.com/news/uk-wales-34213693.

Hamblin, James. "It's Everywhere, the Clickbait." *The Atlantic*, 11 Nov. 2014, www.theatlantic.com/entertainment/archive/2014/11/clickbait-what-is/382545/.

Hollows, Joanne. *Media Studies: A Complete Introduction*. Hodder & Stoughton, 2016.

Klinger, Lauren, and Kelly McBride. "Stop Calling Every News Article Clickbait." *Poynter*, 22 Feb. 2016, www.poynter.org/2016/clickbait/397841/.

Levy, Nicole. "Once the Web's Fastest Growing Aggregator, Upworthy Pivots." *Politico*, 17 June 2015, www.politico.com/media/story/2015/06/once-the-webs-fastest-growing-aggregator-upworthy-pivots-003881.

McFarland, Matt. "Dear CNN: Please Be Careful about Copying Our Headlines. Sincerely, Upworthy." *The Washington Post*, 5 Feb. 2014, www.washingtonpost.com/news/innovations/wp/2014/02/05/dear-cnn-please-be-careful-about-copying-our-headlines-sincerely-upworthy/?utm_term=.7a2ebcd38cbe.

Rubin, Victoria L. "Deception Detection and Rumor Debunking for Social Media." *The SAGE Handbook of Social Media Research Methods*, edited by Luke Sloan and Anabel Quan-Haase, Sage Publications, 2017, pp. 342–64.

Tomar, David A. "11 Reasons We're Too Dumb to Resist Clickbait." *The Quad*, The Best Schools, 5 Aug. 2018, thebestschools.org/magazine/why-clickbait-works/.

CLOUD COMPUTING

Introduction

Cloud computing is a networking model in which computer storage, processing, and program access are handled through a virtual network. Cloud computing is among the most profitable information technology (IT) trends. A host of cloud-oriented consumer products are available through subscription, and allow users to save their work universally "in the cloud" for use anytime, anywhere, on any device. Several major internet service and content providers offer cloud-based storage for user data. Others provide virtual access to software programs or enhanced processing capabilities. Cloud computing is

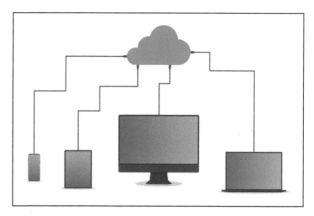

Cloud computing uses remote servers hosted on the internet to store and manage data instead of a local server or a personal computer. Image via iStock/Oleksandr Hurtovyi. [Used under license.]

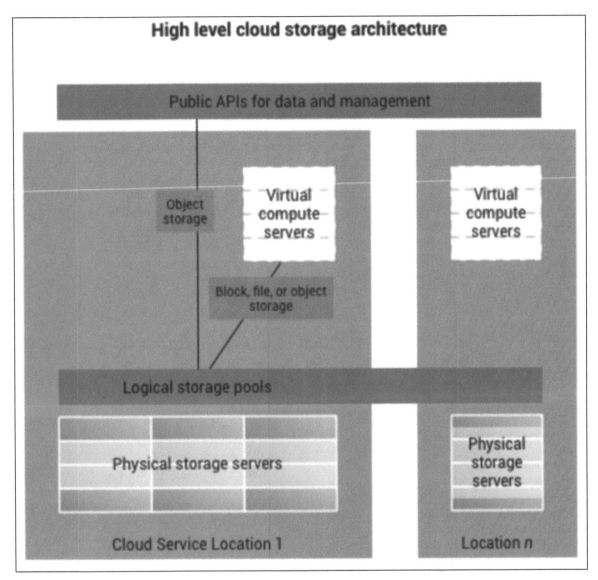

A high level architecture of cloud storage. Image by Leoinspace, via Wikimedia Commons.

among the fastest-growing areas of the internet services industry and has also been adopted by government and research organizations.

Background

Private clouds are virtual networks provided to a limited number of known users. These are often used in corporations and research organizations. Operating a private cloud requires infrastructure (software, servers, etc.), either on-site or through a third party. Public clouds are available to the public or to paying subscribers. The public-cloud service provider owns and manages the infrastructure.

Unlike private clouds, public clouds provide access to an unknown pool of users, making them less secure. Public clouds tend to be based on open-source code, which is free and can be modified by any user.

The hybrid cloud lies somewhere between the two. It offers access to private cloud storage or software services, such as database servers, while keeping some services or components in a public cloud. Set-up costs may be lower with hybrid cloud services. A group using a hybrid cloud outsources some aspects of infrastructure investment and maintenance but still enjoys greater security than with a public cloud.

Hybrid clouds have become widespread in the health care, law, and investment fields, where sensitive data must be protected on-site.

Cloud Computing as a Service

The infrastructure as a service (IaaS) model offers access to virtual storage and processing capability through a linked network of servers. Cloud-based storage has become popular, with services such as Apple's iCloud, Microsoft's OneDrive, and Dropbox offering storage alternatives beyond the storage available on users' physical computers. IaaS can also give users greater computing power by allowing certain processes to run on virtual networks, rather than on the hardware of a single system. Using IaaS enables companies to create a corporate data center through third-party data centers. These third-party centers provide expert IT assistance and server resources, generally for subscription fees.

The platform as a service (PaaS) model mainly offers access to a specific platform that multiple users can use to develop software applications, or apps. Many apps require access to specific development programs. The Google App Engine, for example, provides an environment that stores, supports, and runs web apps. PaaS allows software developers to create apps without investing in infrastructure and data center support. Providers may also offer virtual storage, access to virtual networks, and other services.

The software as a service (SaaS) model offers users subscription-based or shared access to software programs through a virtual network. Adobe's Creative Cloud provides access to programs such as Photoshop, Illustrator, and Lightroom for a monthly or yearly fee. Users pay a smaller amount over time rather than paying a higher cost up front to purchase the program. SaaS supports multitenancy, in which a single copy of a program is available to multiple clients. This allows software providers to earn revenue from multiple clients through a single instance of a software program.

Advantages and Disadvantages of the Cloud

Cloud networking allows small companies and individuals access to development tools, digital storage, and software that once were prohibitively expensive or required significant management and administration. By paying subscription fees, users can gain monthly, yearly, or as-used access to software or other computing tools with outsourced administration. For service providers, cloud computing is cost effective because it eliminates the cost of packaging and selling individual programs and other products.

Data security is the chief concern among those considering cloud computing. The private and hybrid cloud models provide a secure way for companies to reap the benefits of cloud computing. Firewalls and encryption are common means of securing data in these systems. Providers are working to increase the security of public clouds, thus reducing the need for private or hybrid systems.

—*Micah L. Issitt*

References

Huth, Alexa, and James Cebula. "The Basics of Cloud Computing." *US-CERT*, 2011, www.us-cert.gov/sites/default/files/publications/Cloud-ComputingHuthCebula.pdf.

Kale, Vivek. *Guide to Cloud Computing for Business and Technology Managers*. CRC Press, 2015.

Kruk, Robert. "Public, Private and Hybrid Clouds: What's the Difference?" *Techopedia*, vol. 22 Feb. 2017, www.techopedia.com/2/28575/trends/cloud-computing/public-private-and-hybrid-clouds-whats-the-difference.

Ramachandran, Muthu, and Zaigham Mahmood, editors. *Software Engineering in the Era of Cloud Computing*. Springer International, 2020.

Rountree, Derrick, and Ileana Castrillo. *The Basics of Cloud Computing*. Elsevier, 2014.

Sanders, James, and Conner Forrest. "Hybrid Cloud: What It Is, Why It Matters." *ZDNet*, 1 July 2014, www.zdnet.com/article/hybrid-cloud-what-it-is-why-it-matters/.

Surianarayanan, Chellammal, and Pethuru Raj. *Essentials of Cloud Computing: A Holistic Perspective*. Springer International, 2019.

Vacca, John R., editor. *Cloud Computing Security: Foundations and Challenges*. CRC Press, 2017.

CODING IN THE CURRICULUM

Introduction

In the twenty-first century, educators increasingly face the daunting task of instructing schoolchildren, beginning as early as five years old, in the systematic thinking essential to writing code. The goal is to teach schoolchildren how to become not merely passive consumers of computer technology but rather active designers of computer programs and applications. The knowledge base and problem-solving skills developed in learning computer programming are a way to prepare students for future job opportunities but, more important, to expand their intellect and their creativity.

Background

The rigorous field of computer science, which has emerged since 2000 as one of the most attractive postsecondary education programs, is simply not able to produce sufficient numbers of qualified computer programmers to meet the needs of the digital workplace. The related field of information technology, which emphasizes the discipline of setting up and then maintaining network computer systems, does not produce programmers qualified to create the programs necessary to keep pace with the needs of a digital workplace. Because the field of computer science is always evolving—a network's information systems can be rendered obsolete in a single fiscal year—the global business market demands workers competent in not only computer technology but also programming as a way to keep computer systems up to date and be able to address problems as they come up.

In classrooms, computers engaged students with learning; computers assisted with visual presentation of material; computers were essential to doing research, reports, and homework. The concept that computers could be instructed to solve problems and do original work, however, was not an element of technology in the classroom curricula. Computers in the classrooms were essentially assisting in a process of education that itself remained unchanged.

Beginning in the late 1990s, educators, particularly in Canada, the United States, Japan, South Korea, and the United Kingdom, began to explore the shortcomings of the education system in terms of producing graduates with competent and useful computer coding skills. Although classrooms routinely used software to engage students, the students themselves had little grasp of what the computer did or how to communicate directly to a computer's hardware using the discipline of binary logic and algorithms.

Coding advocates promoted a radical revisioning of the classroom itself that would make education equal to the demands of the contemporary digital workplace. The skills gap would have to be addressed by introducing children at a young age to the complexities of computer programming and taking the mystery out of communicating with a computer. This would be achieved by making computer science a fundamental element of the school curriculum. The earlier this skill set was introduced, advocates believed, the better. Encouraged initially by tech advocates in the business world (particularly in the field of video gaming) as well as by government agencies that monitored the expanding influence of technology into all career fields, the campaign to introduce coding into the curriculum gained widespread momentum through a variety of websites devoted to helping schools integrate coding into their curriculum.

Advocates of introducing coding into the curriculum (among them Facebook founder Mark Zuckerberg, President Barack Obama, and Bill Gates) faced an enormous public relations problem: The stereotype of computer programming as a field was largely negative. Computer programming was seen as boring, repetitive work that appealed largely to nerdy types. The challenges of the field, the feel of being a pioneer in a cutting-edge discipline, the exhilarating problem-solving dimension of the work were seldom extolled. Teaching the careful logic of computer coding would introduce young minds to the rigors of reasoning and how to think through a problem in careful step-by-step fashion.

Whether students pursued computer science, a curriculum element centered on computer coding would introduce students to a way of thinking about the process of thinking itself—after all, computer programs merely mimic human reasoning but at much greater speed. Far from simply introducing students to the potentially intimidating logic of computer communication and the ancient science of logic, learning the basics of coding—much like learning the basics of a musical instrument—would in fact encourage genuine creativity. Students would come to understand that every function of a computer, every expression of its considerable data reserves and its intellectual reach, began with a programmer designing the code to instruct the computer to execute that very function.

Applications

Although experimental pilot programs have been launched in the United States, success has been limited to a handful of private schools and to restricted access programs in a relatively small number of public school systems, most of them in the New York City area. School systems across the country have offered what is known as the "Hour of Code" program in which students are offered programming tutorials after school or in place of a study hall, roughly an hour of week. Several European and Asian nations have begun to work out a comprehensive national program for introducing coding into the public school curriculum, and the United Kingdom has already moved to introduce coding in a sweeping—and controversial—reformation of its public school system.

In the UK, the government's guide to the new program asserts that, "Pupils who can think computationally are better able to conceptualize… and use computer-based technology," a necessary requisite for students who will enter a globally connected, digitally dependent economy (Berry). In this landmark program, coding, not merely computer use, will become an intrinsic element of education, like English, science, math, and foreign languages.

School children everywhere can reap the benefits of learning coding at a young age. Doing so develops: logic and organization to solve problems; data gathering skills; accounting for variables; thinking through and sustaining a basic sequence of actions, such as tying a shoe. Further they are introduced to repetition and loop logic, which is the basis for creating and executing routine tasks.

Problems faced by the UK program indicate potential dilemmas for any such sweeping reformation of public education. The initiative was derided as a gimmick designed to create the illusion of a country leaping into the twenty-first century when the reality, critics charged, would be that few students, certainly under the age of ten, would be able to grasp the intricacies of algorithmic logic and the precise language skills necessary for writing effective code.

Advocates countered that error is an inevitable element of the curriculum and that students would quickly be taught the value of trial and error in developing code. Parents were reassured, however, and encouraged to take an interest in the class projects and homework assignments and to ask their kids questions about computers to bridge the technology gap between the generations.

Viewpoints

Programs have been developed that would introduce students at the middle school and high school levels to the rigors of coding through interactive projects in classes already established within the curriculum. A math class, for instance, could develop a program to instruct a computer to generate a particular graph or to determine a range of variables to solve a particular equation; a history class could instruct a computer to work through the variable outcomes of a particular battle and the options a general might face; an English class or a foreign-language class could instruct a computer to test the syntactical arrangements of words to test the difference between a run-on and a fragment; a music class could instruct a computer to work out the harmonics of a simple original melody.

Such exercises, though still directed by an instructor, would replace traditional instructional methodologies (i.e., the thin dynamic of lecture, note-taking, examinations, and controlled discussion).

Students and instructors would work together—indeed teachers would learn from students whose familiarity with technology routinely exceeds that of their teachers. Digital thinking and problem solving could supplement, even replace rote memorization or note-taking. Here students would produce something original while learning through hands-on interaction with the very technology that defines their immediate world of experience.

The applications of coding within an existing curriculum offering would help a student see that computer programming is not so much a field as it is a way of thinking, specifically a way of thinking about thinking. In addition, teachers from widely differing disciplines would find common ground—history teachers could discuss coding problems with biology teachers, music teachers could solicit advice from geometry teachers. Although such an introduction of coding into classes has been tested in limited pilot programs in the United States, it is likely that across-the-board implementation would require a complete revamping of the educational system. Every teacher would need to be competent in the basics of coding, school systems would have to provide cutting edge computer equipment and tutorial apps, and parents, administrators, and politicians would have to be convinced of the efficacy and value of the endeavor.

Computer literary cuts along age, gender, economic class, and ethnic lines, and because any reformation of a nation's education system would have to be cooperative, the reality of introducing coding across the curriculum is at best a working ideal. But coding in the curriculum is gathering momentum as a global education enterprise that recognizes not only the value but also the necessity of educating the next generation in the logic, organization, and thought processes of the computers upon which they routinely rely.

—Joseph Dewey

References

Bellanca, J. *21st Century Skills: Rethinking How Students Learn*. Leading Edge, 2010.

Berry, M. "Computing in the National Curriculum: A Guide for Primary Teachers." *Computingatschool.org*, www.computingatschool.org.

Cellan-Jones, R. "A Computing Revolution in Schools." *BBC Online*. www.Bbc.com.

Collins, A., and R. Halverson. *Rethinking Education in The Age of Technology: The Digital Revolution and Schooling in America*. McGraw, 2009.

Dredge, S. "Coding at School: A Parents' Guide to England's New Computing Curriculum." *The Guardian*, www.theguardian.com.

Farber, M. "Coding Across the Curriculum." *Edutopic.org*, www.edutopia.org.

Gardiner, B. "Adding Coding to the Curriculum." *The New York Times*. www.nytimes.com.

Green, M. *3-2-1 Code It*. Cengage, 2011.

Larson, E. "Coding the Curriculum: How High Schools Are Reprogramming Their Classes. Mashable Online." *Mashable, Inc.*, mashable.com.

Mak, J. "Coding in the Elementary School Classroom." *Learning & Leading with Technology*, vol. 41, no. 6, 2014, pp. 26–28.

Pinkston, G. "Forward 50, Teaching Coding to Ages 4-12: Programming in the Elementary School." *Annual International Conference on Education & E-Learning*, 2015, pp. 34–39.

COLLABORATIVE SOFTWARE (GROUPWARE)

Introduction

Collaborative software, or groupware, is a category of computer software applications that allow users to share information and communicate with one another as easily as possible. Used primarily in business settings, groupware makes it possible for both on-site and remote workers to collaborate over the internet and maximize their productivity. Most forms of groupware incorporate features such as email, instant messaging, task scheduling, and meeting management.

Some of the most commonly used examples of groupware include IBM Notes and Microsoft Exchange Server. These programs serve as a virtual office hub where important information is store and shared, and all employees can connect with one another. Although groupware has existed since the 1970s, it did not enjoy widespread use until computers began to be connected together through local area networks and the internet in the late 1980s and early 1990s. Since that time, groupware has become a popular tool for businesses across the country and around the world.

Background

The early development of groupware began with computer engineer Ray Tomlinson's creation of the first email system in 1971. Originally available through the Advanced Research Projects Agency Network (ARPANET), Tomlinson's email system and the concept of email in general eventually grew to enjoy widespread popularity as the internet took hold in the late 1980s and early 1990s. While most people used email to facilitate one-on-one communication, the gradual addition of mailing list tools and other group-oriented features helped turn it into a basic form of groupware.

Another feature that played a key role in the early development of groupware was real-time chat. First introduced with the launch of the ARPANET "talk" command in 1972, this feature allowed computer users to communicate directly with one another in real time. Most early real-time chat systems only allowed users to converse in a one-on-one format. The release of CompuServe's CM Simulator in 1984 introduced group chat capabilities for the first time and turned real-time chat into a form of groupware. CM Simulator's widespread popularity eventually led to the development of Internet Relay Chat (IRC), America Online Instant Messaging (AIM), and many similar real-time chat-based groupware systems.

One of the most important steps forward in groupware's continuing evolution was the debut of Lotus Notes in 1989. Now known as IBM Notes, Lotus Notes was a comprehensive groupware package that included a wide variety of features such as email, calendaring and scheduling, document sharing, and workflow management. A hypertext markup language (HTML)-based version of Lotus Notes that could be accessed through a web browser was introduced in 1996. Because of its immensely beneficial offerings, Lotus Notes quickly became popular in corporate settings and soon emerged as one of the most widely used groupware packages of its kind. Another early groupware package that rivaled Lotus Notes was the Microsoft Exchange Server. Much like Lotus Notes, the Microsoft Exchange Server, which was first released in 1996, offered email, document sharing, and calendaring. Unlike its biggest competitor, however, Microsoft Exchange Server runs on the Windows Server operating system. In any event, IBM Notes and Microsoft Exchange Server remain among the world's most popular groupware packages.

Overview

Groupware is a type of software that is specifically designed to provide an online environment in which group members can work together from any location. In most cases, groupware is used to allow a number of coworkers to collaborate on a given project or to complete ongoing tasks. It can, however, also be used to share information with clients, contractors, and others. The features included in different groupware packages can vary, but most include a number of standard components. These include email, calendaring and scheduling, reference libraries, and discussion databases.

Email is the most common and widely used of these components. It primarily serves as a quick and efficient means of communication that keeps users as connected with one another as possible. The inclusion of calendaring and scheduling tools helps users keep track of deadlines, appointments, and other important dates. These tools also often allow users to arrange and invite other users to meetings and keep track of who is planning to attend. Reference libraries serve as an easily accessible repository of essential reference materials such as employee handbooks and user manuals. Discussion databases provide a forum where users can discuss any ideas or questions that arise during the course of a project. These databases are often used to gather comments or solicit new ideas from the users. Many groupware packages also give users the ability to create their own database applications based on their specific needs.

There are two categories of groupware: server and client. In larger settings, groupware is typically installed on two or more network computers called "servers." These servers, which can be located in or out of the office, house the actual groupware applications and the data entered into them. They also communicate with one another to make sure that all information is as up-to-date as possible. Each individual person that accesses the groupware applications does so by installing its client software on his or her personal computer. This client software allows the users to interact with the groupware applications.

Functionally, groupware can be classified as either synchronous or asynchronous. Synchronous groupware allows users to interact with one another and collaborate in real time. This requires real-time coordination among the various clients that use a given groupware server. Synchronous groupware provides users with the most interactive and connected interface possible. Asynchronous groupware facilitates collaboration that is carried out in a non-real-time format. Although it offers many of the same features as other types of groupware, asynchronous groupware does not provide a real-time environment and instead supports communication and collaboration at different times. Because of the complications involved in a system to which different users connect and make changes at different times, asynchronous groupware packages typically work best when steps are taken to ensure that contributions can be made without any unnecessary restrictions. This often requires the use of replicated data management systems with full read and write data access.

Regardless of the type, groupware packages have many potential benefits. In addition to connecting group users and facilitating collaboration, groupware allows users to store important information in a central hub. It also provides a useful interface through which companies can connect and interact with off-site employees and other parties with whom they work.

—Jack Lasky

References

Duffy, Jill. "The Best Online Collaboration Software of 2017." *PCMag*, 3 Aug. 2017, www.pcmag.com/article2/0,2817,2489110,00.asp.

Green, Jason. "The Promise, Progress and Pain of Collaboration Software." *TechCrunch*, 24 May 2014, techcrunch.com/2014/05/24/the-promise-the-progress-and-the-pain-of-collaboration-software/.

"Groupware." *Inc.*, www.inc.com/encyclopedia/groupware.html.

"Groupware." *Techopedia*, www.techopedia.com/definition/7481/groupware.

Hausman, Kalani Kirk, and Susan L. Cook. *IT Architecture for Dummies.* John Wiley & Sons, 2010.

"Lotus Notes." *PCMag*, www.pcmag.com/encyclopedia/term/46341/lotus-notes.

Pinola, Melanie. "What Is Groupware?" *Lifewire*, 22 Aug. 2017, www.lifewire.com/what-is-groupware-2377429.

Rouse, Margaret. "Microsoft Exchange Server." *TechTarget*, searchwindowsserver.techtarget.com/definition/Microsoft-Exchange-Server.

COMMUNITY OF PRACTICE

Introduction

A community of practice is any group of people engaged in a similar activity who share knowledge about the activity in order to increase expertise and solve problems. Although first articulated in the late 1980s and early 1990s, the term describes a type of social learning that has always taken place, whether among professionals or hobbyists or members of a tribe. It recognizes learning as not just a cognitive process in which a learner passively absorbs information delivered by an instructor, but as a social, relational process in which knowledge spreads through group interaction and exchange.

In today's internet-enabled learning environments, there are numerous online communities that interact to form new collaborative knowledge, to advance and adapt traditional modes of discourse, and to agree on new standards of communication. Language (e.g., standardized English grammar) is constantly evolving and online communities of practice are advancing new grammars, new cultural literacies, and new standards of etiquette. Peter Kittle explains his experiment with students exploring the *I Can Has Cheezburger* website as the exploration of and formation of an expanding meme community: "[Students] developed literacy conventions that are counter to standardized English...saw that literacy evolves from communities of practice. It likewise provided a model for students to examine with a critical eye the communication practices of other online communities, and it gave them a lens for thinking about the complex and subtle ways that literacy is adapted by groups of people."

In short, communities of practice in digital realms are not entirely different than social groups in the "real" environment of brick-and-mortar buildings. We need to recognize that online social groups move, grow, and evolve perhaps more rapidly than nineteenth- and twentieth-century school environments, and the ripple effects of these digital communities of practice are felt across vast geographic environments.

Background

The first formal elaboration of the concept of communities of practice (CoP) is attributed to social anthropologist Jean Lave and educational theorist Etienne Wenger in their 1991 book *Situated Learning: Legitimate Peripheral Participation.* As part of their research, Lave and Wenger traveled to Africa and studied local apprenticeship practices among tailors; the researchers found that in learning their trade, apprentices gained more knowledge from other apprentices and journeymen than they did from the master tailors. They found this same pattern of informal group learning, which they described as "communities of practice," in widely divergent areas of endeavor, from naval quartermasters to participants in Alcoholics Anonymous.

Lave and Wenger described a process whereby novices enter a group and learn from more senior members, gradually increasing their level of participation until they themselves are experienced enough to impart knowledge to other newcomers. At the same time, discoveries and novel approaches by any member of the group are spread to other members, so that the practice in question advances and improves. Wenger went on to develop the CoP concept further, identifying three key elements: a domain, or common area of activity; a community, or group of people engaged in the activity and sharing information about it; and a practice, or body of tools, resources, and knowledge about the activity that advances it. CoPs typically arise spontaneously, and in the twenty-first century, they can take place in person or may develop online.

However, CoPs—initially of interest mainly to learning theorists—can also be actively fostered, and the idea has drawn the attention of organizational theorists interested in knowledge management in the twenty-first-century business context. CoPs have come to be seen as valuable organizational assets that can bypass cumbersome hierarchies and ensure that knowledge is shared as efficiently as possible, thus improving business performance. In this way, "community of practice" has to some extent moved from a descriptive term identifying a naturally occurring style of learning to a knowledge-management principle actively promoted by organizations. The latter development gained sufficient currency that by the 2010s, CoP initiatives were commonplace in large organizations from corporations to educational institutions to international agencies. With the increase of online learning, institutions are exploring virtual CoPs as a way to provide opportunities for peer-to-peer professional development.

These CoP initiatives are now taking place in both brick-and-mortar and digital environments and are facilitated by various information technologies, collaborative technologies, and social media platforms.

—*Adam Groff and Laura Nicosia*

References

Bond, M. Aaron, and Barbara B. Lockee. *Building Virtual Communities of Practice for Distance Educators*. Springer, 2014.

Hoadley, Christopher. "What Is a Community of Practice and How Can We Support It?" *Theoretical Foundations of Learning Environments*, edited by David H. Jonasson and Susan M. Land, 2nd ed., Routledge, 2012, pp. 287–300.

Kittle, Peter. "Online Literacy and Communities of Practice." 11 Sept. 2010, www.thecurrent. educatorinnovator.org/resource/ online-literacy-and-communities-of-practice.

Lave, Jean, and Etienne Wenger. *Situated Learning: Legitimate Peripheral Participation*. Cambridge UP, 1991.

Orsmond, Paul, Stephen Merry, and Arthur Callaghan. "Communities of Practice and Ways to Learning: Charting the Progress of Biology Undergraduates." *Studies in Higher Education*, vol. 38, no. 66, 2013, pp. 890–906.

Ranmuthugala, Geetha, et al. "How and Why Are Communities of Practice Established in the Healthcare Sector? A Systematic Review of the Literature." *BMC Health Services Research*, vol. 11 supp. 1, 2011, pp. 273–88.

Rathnappulige, Sasikala, and Lisa Daniel. "Creating Value through Social Processes: An Exploration of Knowledge Dynamics in Expert Communities of Practice." *International Journal of Technology Management*, vol. 63, no. 3-4, 2013, pp. 169–84.

Wenger, Etienne. *Communities of Practice: Learning, Meaning, and Identity*. Cambridge UP, 1998.

Wenger, Etienne, Richard A. McDermott, and William Snyder. *Cultivating Communities of Practice: A Guide to Managing Knowledge*. Harvard Business School, 2002.

COMPUTER ADDICTION

Introduction

Obsessive use of computer programs, especially video games, has been proposed as a behavioral addiction similar to compulsive gambling. Disregarding internet use, computer addiction is a concern of industries that lose productivity, and of parents and teachers who see a decrease in the academics and social skills of children and teenagers, especially boys, who are more likely to develop a computer addiction.

Background

With personal computers becoming commonplace in the 1990s came an increase in the numbers of children who appeared to be obsessive computer users, primarily focused on video games. Children and teenagers moved from nonelectronic fantasy games to video arcades to home computers and smartphones, dramatically increasing the numbers of children and teens playing video games.

These games are purchased or are resident programs in desktop computers, laptop computers, smartphones, and dedicated video gaming units, or consoles. Many games may also be available with livestreaming, allowing the users to interact with other players worldwide and in real time. While some video games are available over the internet, many are sold in packaged software for use with a general-purpose computer or a dedicated computer unit; other computers are designed and advertised as gaming computers.

Computer addiction and particularly video game addiction continues to expand as electronic media use increases and as more computers come in smaller and more portable sizes, such as tablets and smartphones. A 2016 report by Common Sense Media reported that teens spend almost nine hours per day on electronic devices viewing entertainment media (watching videos, gaming, or using social media). Preteens (aged eight to twelve) consume approximately six hours of content. That does not include the additional time that children spend using media for school or homework.

Students have been able to extend their electronic life by several hours by multitasking with electronic devices. Tasks that tend to take more of their time on the phone include texting (text messaging), watching other media, and video gaming. According to a 2016 survey from the Centers for Disease Control and Prevention, 84 percent of American households contain at least one smartphone. Eighty percent of households own a desktop or laptop computer, 68 percent contain a tablet, 39 percent contain a streaming media device such as Apple TV, Google Chromecast, or Amazon Fire TV.

Much like drug or alcohol addiction, individuals can compulsively use the internet or play games to alleviate depression or anxiety or to alleviate loneliness. Image via iStock/reklamlar. [Used under license.]

Also problematic is gaming in the workplace. Depending on the availability of computers, work time and productivity lost to video games and other nonwork-related computer use can exceed 10 percent.

Risk Factors

Researcher Douglas A. Gentile published a survey of eight- to eighteen-year-olds in the United States and found that 12 percent of boys were addicted to video games. Only 3 percent of girls were addicted to video games. Also, insofar as computers require a level of affluence, computer addiction is a problem mainly for developed and advanced-developing countries.

A Kaiser Family Foundation survey found that while daily use of all electronic media did not vary much by gender (11:12 for boys versus 10:17 for girls), girls lost interest in computer video games and played less as teenagers, averaging only three minutes per day. Some researchers suggest that computer addiction is a major cause of the worldwide "boy problem," in which boys are dropping out of academics and girls predominating in the higher levels of education. The decline in boys in academics parallels the rise of personal computer technology.

Symptoms

Researcher Margaret A. Shotton was the first to extensively document computer addiction and dependency, although primarily through anecdotal cases and with references to early video arcade games. Ricardo A. Tejeiro Salguero proposed a problem video-game-playing (PVP) scale in 2002. Because problematic video gaming is a behavioral addiction (in contrast with a chemical addiction), video gaming was more closely associated with compulsive gambling. Gentile developed a similar scale of eleven self-reported negative factors. Having a minimum of six symptoms of the eleven on the scale was set as the threshold for addiction.

The correlation between computer addiction as determined by Gentile's scale and poorer grades in school, for example, could have been an indication of comorbidity; that is, a child might spend more time on the computer and get poor grades because of a separate but common factor.

Proof that pathological video game addiction causes a decline in academics was established by Robert Weis and Brittany C. Cerankosky. After establishing a group of boys' academic baseline achievement, they gave one-half of the boys access to computer video games and saw their academics decline. The control group continued on with solid schoolwork.

An extensive Kaiser Family Foundation survey found an inverse relationship between electronic media use and good grades, with 51 percent of heavy users getting good grades versus 66 percent of light users getting good grades. Heavy users were less likely to get along with their parents, were less happy at school, were more often bored, got into trouble at twice the average rate, and were often sad or unhappy compared with light users.

Internet gaming disorder has been proposed as a "Condition for Further Study" in the fifth edition of the *Diagnostic and Statistical Manual of Mental Disorders* published by the American Psychiatric Association (*DSM-5*), and centers to treat individuals who display symptoms of excessive internet use are opening in the United States signaling a response to a perceived problem.

Screening and Diagnosis

Salguero and Gentile both proposed a multiple-factor scale to designate pathological computer video gaming. Extensive time spent playing computer games is not a sufficient indicator of addiction. However, when combined with risk factors of low social competence and higher impulsivity, there is a greater chance of pathological gaming that can result in anxiety, depression, social phobia, and poor school performance. There may be a correlation of computer addiction and attention deficit hyperactivity disorder that may be related to a child's difficulty relating normally in social settings, but these are a minority of cases.

Treatment and Therapy

At the public policy level, Western countries appear little concerned with computer addiction beyond lost workplace productivity. The main societal concerns are in Asia, where there is much more focus on the pool of intellectual talent and more concern with children's academic success. Several Asian nations have attempted to place limits on the amount of time that teenagers can spend on computers per day; most indications are that these limits are easily circumvented by tech-savvy students.

Modeled on summer camps for overweight children are China's experimental summer camps for weaning students from computer addiction. Programs beginning in the United States attempt to use counseling to treat, for example, the psychological problems and antisocial feelings that may coexist with computer addiction. Other programs use outdoor wilderness experiences. Limited evidence exists of the success of these types of programs.

Prevention

Because computers and the evolving tablets, e-readers, cell phones, and other media that are primarily small computers are presumed to be technical advances, little likelihood exists of establishing regulatory measures or controls on the availability of computers and video games. In 2011, the US Supreme Court rejected regulation of violent computer video games in the United States. There is a rating system developed by the Entertainment Software Rating Board (ESRB) similar to that used in the entertainment industry that suggests age appropriateness, content descriptors, and interactive elements present in apps and video games, and rated on a scale. But this leaves the control of children's access in the hands of teachers and parents. Surveys show many parents have a low level of concern about or have little desire to regulate their children's computer activities although that may continue to be revised as more studies are conducted.

—John Richard Schrock

References

Chiu, Shao-I, Jie-Zhi Lee, and Der-Hsiang Huang. "Video Game Addiction in Children and Teenagers in Taiwan." *Cyberpsychology and Behavior,* vol. 7, 2004, pp. 571–81.

Gentile, Douglas A. "Pathological Video-Game Use among Youths Ages 8 to 18: A National Study." *Psychological Science,* vol. 20, 2009, pp. 594–602.

Gentile, Douglas A., et al. "Pathological Video-Game Use among Youths: A Two-Year Longitudinal Study." *Pediatrics,* vol. 127, 2011, pp. 319–29.

Madden, Mary, et al. "Teens and Technology 2013." *Pew Research Center.* Pew Research Center, 13 Mar. 2013.

Nielsen. "An Era of Growth: The Cross-Platform Report Q4 2013." *Nielsen.* Nielsen, 5 Mar. 2014.

Rideout, Victoria J., Ulla G. Foehr, and Donald F. Roberts. "'Generation M2': Media in the Lives of 8- to 18-Year-Olds—A Kaiser Family Foundation Study." *Kaiser Family Foundation,* Jan. 2010.

Salguero, Ricardo A. Tejeiro, and Rosa M. Bersabe Moran. "Measuring Problem Video Game Playing in Adolescents." *Addiction,* vol. 97, 2002, pp. 1601–6.

Shotton, Margaret A. *Computer Addiction? A Study of Computer Dependency.* Taylor, 1989.

Shotton, Margaret A. "The Costs and Benefits of 'Computer Addiction.'" *Behaviour and Information Technology,* vol. 10, 1991, pp. 219–30.

Weis, Robert, and Brittany C. Cerankosky. "Effects of Video-Game Ownership on Young Boys' Academic and Behavioral Functioning: A Randomized, Controlled Study." *Psychological Science,* vol. 21, 2010, pp. 463–70.

COMPUTER-AIDED DESIGN

Introduction

Computer-aided design (CAD) allows engineers, scientists, architects, manufacturers, and others to use computer software and technology to carry out and document the design process. Using points, lines, planes, curves, and set shapes, a user can create a detailed description of an item, create schematics and blueprints, render three-dimensional (3D) models, or even create 3D-printed prototypes. By the third decade of the twenty-first century, the Autodesk-produced CAD software AutoCAD had become one of the most popular software packages for CAD. To appreciate everything AutoCAD offers fully, one must have an understanding of the history of CAD and the early technologies out of which AutoCAD arose.

Of the many CAD software packages available in the third decade of the twenty-first century, AutoCAD by Autodesk is one of the most popular and is often seen as an industry standard. It offers a wide range of tools suitable for an equally wide range of purposes, from manufacturing to animation.

Background

Engineering drawings have been around for a long time. They have helped build such diverse items and structures as churches, war machines, scientific instruments, and nearly all modern electronic devices, from radios to medical scanning machines. For a long time, schematics and plans were drawn out by hand on paper. By the 1940s, however, general-purpose computers were beginning to come into use. The potential for computers to handle complex equations and design was immediately noted.

First coined in the 1950s, the term "computer-aided design" and the abbreviation CAD are typically attributed to Douglas T. Ross, a pioneering computer scientist who led the Computer-Aided Design project at the Massachusetts Institute of Technology (MIT). Early innovations in the development of CAD systems included Sketchpad, described by MIT doctoral student Ivan Sutherland in his 1963 dissertation, and Design Augmented by Computer (DAC-1), a product of a collaboration between General Motors (GM) and International Business Machines (IBM). Sketchpad enabled users to draw and manipulate shapes on a screen. DAC-1, among other functions, facilitated the digitization and sharing of drawings that already existed on paper. Over the subsequent decades, advances in computing technology and software development led to the creation of increasingly complex CAD software packages that offered an array of advanced features, AutoCAD among them.

Types of CAD

Since emerging in the 1960s, CAD software has been subject to constant development and improvement.

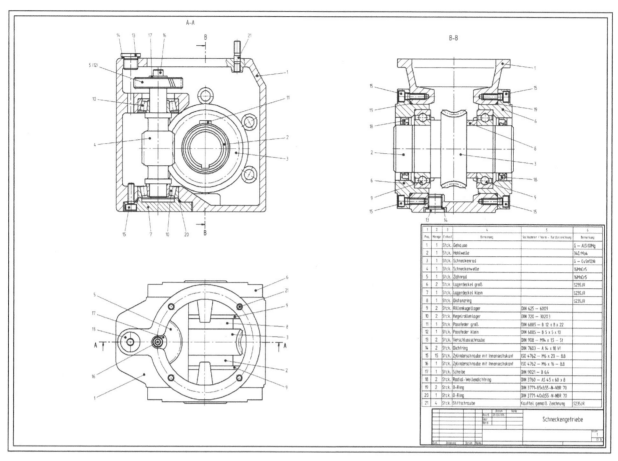

Example: 2D CAD drawing. Image by Thorsten Hartmann, via Wikimedia Commons.

Broadly, CAD encompasses several distinct forms of design.

Two-dimensional (2D) CAD images are essentially digital versions of hand-drawn technical drawings, blueprints, or sketches. Images are printed or plotted on a flat surface and depict only two dimensions.

Three-dimensional CAD models are drawn in three dimensions. All sides of the object exist in the model, even if they are not visible at a given time due to the model's orientation. 3D CAD models can typically be rotated or otherwise moved to allow the designer to view any side, angle, or component of the model.

Wireframe models represent 3D objects by outlining all edges of an object. However, the surfaces of the object are not modeled, and the model itself is not solid. As they do not rely on surface textures and shadowing, wireframe models can be displayed quickly and can be rotated, sized, and adjusted without waiting for surfaces or solid sections to be rendered. In surface modeling, the external surfaces of the object are modeled and can be viewed from any external angle. However, the model is not solid, and the interior of the model is typically hollow.

In contrast to wireframe and surface modeling, solid modeling entails the modeling of a solid object, not merely the object's outlines or surfaces. Designers can test the viability of their designs through the use of simulation tools that analyze how the modeled object fares when subjected to pressure, motion, or other forces.

Introducing AutoCAD

Due to the intense processing power required, early CAD packages required large time-sharing computers to operate. While that worked for a while in some industries and government settings, there was a great need for CAD technology for smaller engineering and mechanical design firms.

In 1982, the California-based computer software company Autodesk released a full-featured program called AutoCAD. Initially developed for CP/M (a precursor to DOS [disk operating system]) machines, it was later utilized on many microcomputer workstations, including those running Microsoft Windows, UNIX, and Macintosh operating systems. AutoCAD soon became a popular choice for CAD projects due to its numerous add-ons and enhanced functionality. Its DXF file format became importable and exportable to a wide range of graphics programs.

Uses and Advantages of AutoCAD

AutoCAD is primarily used to develop preliminary design concepts and layouts; work with different design options; make calculations; and create drawings, schematics, and 3D models. Like other CAD programs, AutoCAD can output to formats required for machine manufacturing and interact with analysis and marketing tools.

One of the many advantages of using AutoCAD is that editing and reviewing technical details becomes more efficient than attempting the same acts by hand. AutoCAD streamlines the manufacturing process by converting detailed information about items into a format that can be universally accessed. Using AutoCAD, users can view an object from any angle. CAD software such as AutoCAD can also reduce design time by allowing designers to run precise simulations before taking the time and expense involved in constructing physical prototypes or models.

With AutoCAD's advanced rendering and animation capabilities, engineers and designers can further visualize product designs with various textures and shading. These options are utilized heavily in computer-generated animated features. Artists can use select object descriptors to draw, render, and shade anything from a nail to a skyscraper and allow animators to move, scale, and rotate images with ease.

Impact of AutoCAD

In the twenty-first century, CAD software is used in a broader variety of industries than it was when first

Example: 3D CAD model. Image by Freeformer, via Wikimedia Commons.

introduced in the 1960s. In addition to the aerospace, electronics, and manufacturing industries, CAD is used in the film and game-design industries, in urban planning, and elsewhere. Overall, AutoCAD software encourages efficiency and design quality, increases productivity, and helps improve documentation and record keeping throughout the design and testing process.

Because AutoCAD software can increase productivity and nurture creativity, it has become a vital tool for visualizing products and mechanical interactions before introducing a manufacturing process. Autodesk provides extensive support for AutoCAD, including image and texture libraries, subscription licenses, and more. As technology improves, AutoCAD software will likely continue to have relevance and usefulness in even more fields and industries.

—*John Teehan*

References

Alton, Larry. "How CAD Software and 3D Printing Are Allowing Customized Products at Scale." *Inc.*, 1 Feb. 2020, www.inc.com/larry-alton/how-cad-software-3d-printing-are-allowing-customized-products-at-scale.html.

Bernstein, Larry. "What Is Computer-Aided Design (CAD) and Why It's Important." *Jobsite*, 11 Oct. 2021,www.procore.com/jobsite/what-is-computer-aided-design-cad-and-why-its-important.

"Computer-Aided Design (CAD) and Computer-Aided Manufacturing (CAM)." *Inc.*, 6 Feb. 2020, www.inc.com/encyclopedia/computer-aided-design-cad-and-computer-aided-cam.html.

Goldstein, Phil. "How Computer-Aided Design Is Used in Government." *FedTech*, 24 June 2020, fedtechmagazine.com/article/2020/06/how-computer-aided-design-used-government-perfcon.

"The History of Design, Model Making and CAD." *Creative Mechanisms*, 14 Dec. 2015, www.creativemechanisms.com/blog/the-history-of-design-model-making-and-cad.

Ziden, Azidah Abu, Fatariah Zakaria, and Ahmad Nizam Othman. "Effectiveness of AutoCAD 3D Software as a Learning Support Tool." *International Journal of Emerging Technologies in Learning (JET)*, vol. 7, no. 2, 2012, pp. 57–60.

COMPUTER-AIDED DESIGN IN EDUCATION

Introduction

Already a major tool used by engineers, designers, researchers, manufacturers, urban planners, architects, landscapers, and technologists, computer-aided design (CAD) software has become increasingly important in education during the twenty-first century. Students at nearly all levels of education, from primary school to college, have been introduced to a wide array of CAD programs as well as related technology such as three-dimensional (3D) printers. When selecting a CAD software for use in a school environment, educators must determine which software best meets both student needs and the educator's own goals.

Computer-aided design (CAD) appears at nearly all levels of education, from primary and middle school to high school and college. Its increased presence in schools provides considerable advantages to many students. Students planning a future in design or engineering will be better prepared for higher education and entry into the job market. In addition, students looking to enter fields such as art, medicine, landscaping, and manufacturing will have

the necessary head start when 3D tools become more present in their fields.

Background

Whatever the level or goal of a student's education, CAD software is finding ways to adapt and serve students' needs. If students begin with simple programs designed for beginners, their early work can serve as a valuable foundation for more complex projects and software. When presented with CAD software with easily understandable instructions and friendly interfaces, many children quickly pick up the concepts. From there, children can design and draft any number of projects, either for school or personal satisfaction. Such projects encourage creativity and acting on inspiration, which can then, in turn, be applied to other areas of schooling. In addition, early introduction to CAD software helps students stay ahead and learn a skill that is becoming increasingly practical.

Even if a student has no interest in pursuing a career in a CAD-heavy field such as automotive or aerospace design, CAD knowledge can be valuable. General computer knowledge was once considered a skill applicable to only a narrow range of fields; by the early twenty-first century, however, computers had become an integral part of daily life. Those who grew up with little or no basic computer education thus found themselves at a distinct disadvantage in the professional world and everyday life. While knowledge in CAD may not be quite as far-reaching, CAD knowledge is still a helpful tool for any student to have at the ready.

Numerous fields make use of 3D modeling and related functions. There are even practical applications for CAD knowledge in creative fields such as fashion design, sculpture, illustration, and film. With more CAD education available in schools, students are better equipped to develop creativity and take on the jobs of the future.

Selecting CAD Software for Schools

There are a number of factors that go into selecting the best CAD software for a particular school setting. These range from the age of the students to the academic and personal goals they have set.

CAD can be difficult to use at first for many people. Therefore, it is essential to choose software appropriate for students of a given age. Some tools have highly intuitive interfaces that allow students to learn and complete simple design tasks. As students get older, they can be introduced to more functional software with full suites of editing tools. It is also important to select software that meshes with the projects the students will take on as well as the goals the individual educator has set for the students.

Cost can also be a factor. Some CAD software packages can be expensive, particularly those widely used in industry. However, there is a wealth of less expensive and sometimes free options. Many of these are available online for either download or in-browser use. Hardware may also be something to consider. CAD software that focuses more on detailed rendering can take up significant processing power and may not run efficiently on older computers. It can be beneficial for an educator to consult with an information technology (IT) professional to ensure that the computers available meet the desired CAD software's technical requirements.

CAD Programs for Use in Schools

In the third decade of the twenty-first century, numerous software options are available to educators and schools seeking to incorporate CAD into their curricula.

For students on the elementary level, popular CAD programs available as of 2021 include the simple and versatile software 3D Slash and Solid-Works Apps for Kids, a software package that includes the applications Style It, Shape It, and Print It, among others. Other popular options include LeoCAD, which shows students how to build models using digital LEGO bricks.

CAD options for use in middle schools and high schools as of 2021 include SculptGL, an intuitive 3D browser-based introduction to sculpting software, and SketchUp for Schools, which offers a full selection of CAD tools specifically designed for classrooms. Tinkercad, a product of the software developer Autodesk, likewise provides a strong introduction to CAD design.

Options available to students on the college level, as well as advanced high school students, as of 2021 include BricsCAD, a complete CAD software that is free for students and schools, and Rhino3D, a software that is optimal for students looking to work in 3D design. Some students may also make use of AutoCAD, a professional and widely used CAD package, and SolidWorks for Students.

As CAD becomes increasingly important to a diverse range of fields, it is more important than ever to ensure that educators integrate CAD software into schools to prepare students for careers and encourage creativity and innovation. Affordable resources are more readily available than many think, and the benefits of CAD in education are immeasurable.

—John Teehan

References

Asperl, Andreas. "How to Teach CAD." *Computer-Aided Design & Applications*, vol. 2, no. 1-4, 2005, pp. 459–68.

Brown, William Christopher. "An Effective AutoCAD Curriculum for the High School Student." *CSUSB ScholarWorks*, 1999, scholarworks.lib.csusb.edu/etd-project/1791/.

Duelm, Brian Lee. "Computer Aided Design in the Classroom." *LearnTechLib*, Dec. 1986, files.eric.ed.gov/fulltext/ED276885.pdf.

Gaget, Lucie. "How to Learn CAD in Schools: Top 15 of the Best Educational Software." *Sculpteo*, 26 Dec. 2017, www.sculpteo.com/blog/2017/12/26/how-to-learn-cad-in-schools-top-15-of-the-best-educational-software/.

Poggenpohl, Sharon, and Keiichi Sato. *Design Integration: Research and Collaboration*. Intellect, 2009.

Segura, Diana. "13 Best CAD Programs for Kids." *3DPrinterChat.com*, 8 Feb. 2020, 3dprinterchat.com/13-best-cad-programs-for-kids/.

COMPUTER-ASSISTED INSTRUCTION

Introduction

Computer-assisted instruction (CAI) is the use of computer technology as a means of instruction or an aid to classroom teaching. The instructional content may or may not pertain to technology. CAI often bridges distances between instructor and student and allows for the instruction of large numbers of students by a few educators. With the onset of the

2020 COVID-19 (coronavirus) pandemic, CAI almost instantaneously became the worldwide norm for education, at least for the better part of two years.

Background

It was in 1963 when Stanford University initiated its research into the ways computers could assist teaching and learning. Over the decades since its inception, Stanford's investigations have been funded by various organizations, including the Carnegie Corporation, the US Department of Education, and even the National Science Foundation. Their programs began on a very small scale with one computer that was usable by no more than six researchers or students. Its initial successes have enabled the program to expand worldwide with impacts felt on equally large scales.

Computer-Assisted vs. Traditional Instruction

In a traditional classroom, a teacher presents information to students using basic tools such as pencils, paper, chalk, and a chalkboard. Most lessons consist of a lecture, group and individual work by students, and the occasional hands-on activity, such as a field trip or a lab experiment. For the most part, students must adapt their learning preferences to the teacher's own pedagogy, because it would be impractical for one teacher to try to teach to multiple learning styles at once.

CAI supplements this model with technology, namely a computing device that students work on for some or all of a lesson. Some CAI programs offer limited options for how the material is presented and what learning strategies are supported. Others, known as learner-controlled programs, are more flexible. A typical CAI lesson focuses on one specific concept, such as long division or the history of Asia. The program may present information through audio, video, text, images, or a combination of these. It then quizzes the student to make sure that they have paid attention and understood the material. Such instruction has several benefits. First, students often receive information through several mediums, so they do not have to adapt to the teacher's preferred style. Second, teachers can better support students as they move through the lessons without having to focus on presenting information to a group.

Educational computer programs are widely available and can enhance teacher instruction. Photo via iStock/Drazen Zigic. [Used under license.]

Advantages and Disadvantages

CAI has both benefits and drawbacks. Certain software features make it easier to navigate the learning environment, such as word prediction to make typing easier and spell-checking to help avoid spelling mistakes. Copy-and-paste features save users time that they would otherwise spend reentering the same information over and over. Speech recognition can assist students who are blind, have physical disabilities, or have a learning disability that affects writing. Other helpful features are present despite not having been intended to benefit students. For example, CAI video lessons include the option to pause playback, skip ahead or back, or restart. These functions can be vital to a student who is struggling to grasp an especially difficult lesson or is practicing notetaking. They can stop the video at any time and restart it after catching up with the content that has been presented. By contrast, in a regular classroom, the lecturer often continues at the same pace regardless how many students may be struggling to understand and keep up.

Learning is rarely a one-size-fits-all affair. Different topics pose greater or lesser challenges to different students, depending on their natural abilities and study habits. In regular classrooms, teachers can often sense when some students are not benefiting from a lesson and adapt it accordingly. With some CAI, this is not an option because the lesson is only presented in one way.

Adaptive Instruction

Some forms of CAI address different learning rates by using adaptive methods to present material. These programs test students' knowledge and then adapt to those parts of the lesson with which they have more difficulty. For instance, if a math program notices that a student often makes mistakes when multiplying fractions, it might give the student extra practice in that topic. Adaptive programs give teachers the means to better assess students' individual needs and track their progress. As the technology improves, more detailed and specific results may bolster teachers' efforts to tailor instruction further.

Adaptive instruction tends to focus on the instructional methods educators use in their pedagogical approaches to support their students' differing learning styles and abilities through repetition, engagement, and immediate feedback. Consequently, this type of teaching enables individuation and customization for students with less stress for the teachers.

Distance Education

CAI is especially important to the growing field of online education. Online instructors often use elements of CAI to supplement their curricula. For example, an online course might require students to watch a streaming video about doing library research so that they will know how to complete their own research paper for the course. Online education also enables just a few instructors to teach large numbers of students across vast distances. Tens of thousands of students may enroll in a single massive open online course (MOOC). CAI and online education proved particularly crucial amid the COVID-19 pandemic of 2020, during which schools throughout the United States and many other countries transitioned from classroom-based educational models to distance-learning programs that relied heavily on computer and internet technology.

Course Technology Being Added to the Classroom

- **Blogs:** A short form of "web log," and describes an online journal. Bloggers (people who contribute to a blog) do not need to have any technical knowledge to update a blog, and blogging (the act of posting to a blog) is generally done daily.
- **Tablets:** Handheld devices are computers that can be held in one hand, and they are gaining popularity because of the ease of accessing information from anyplace. Tablets represent, along with other mobile devices such as laptops and cell phones, the new frontier of computing as desktop computers become less desirable to everyday users.
- **Personal digital assistant (PDA):** A type of handheld computer that typically functions as a cellular phone, fax sender, and personal organizer (e.g., calendar, contact lists, etc.). Many PDAs incorporate handwriting and/or voice recognition features.
- **Podcasting:** a term derived from the Apple iPod, the world's first mobile music player. Podcasting is when a content provider allows users to download compatible files to their iPods or other brand of mobile player. Newer versions of the iPod also play videos.
- **Social networking sites:** Popular websites such as Facebook and Twitter that are changing the way people, especially teens, interact on the web. Facebook is the cyberspace equivalent of hanging out with friends, and Twitter is a microblogging service that allows users to send and receive limited-character texts. Publishers of these sites earn money by having banner ads or text ads, but there is no assurance that these sites will remain popular, and the long-term outlook is not certain.
- **Web 2.0:** Refers to the seeming second generation of Web-based services—version 2.0 of the Web. Web 2.0 sites tend to emphasize collaboration and sharing among users as well as personalized interactions. Delicious is a Web 2.0 service that allows you to store your bookmarks online so that you can retrieve them from any computer. Last.fm recommends music for users based on the user's listening habits. Pinterest is a photo-sharing website to create and manage theme-based collections. Tumblr, another popular social media site, allows users to post multimedia material and microblog.
- **Wiki:** A term from the Hawaiian language ("wiki-wiki") that means "fast." A wiki is

generally a collaborative website, created perhaps by one user but designed to allow anyone to edit content. The most notable example of a wiki is Wikipedia—a free online encyclopedia. However, accuracy is always a concern as anyone can edit or add material at any time.

—*Scott Zimmer, Kathryn Cook, and Laura Nicosia*

References

Abramovich, Sergei, editor. *Computers in Education.* 2 vols. Nova Science, 2012.

Brief History of Computer-Assisted Instruction at the Institute for Mathematical Studies in the Social Sciences. Stanford UP, 1963, eric. ed.gov/?id=ED034420.

Collins, Allan, and Richard Halverson. *Rethinking Education in the Age of Technology: The Digital Revolution and Schooling in America.* 2nd ed., Teachers College Press, 2018.

Dreamson, Neal. *Critical Understandings of Digital Technology in Education.* Routledge, 2020.

Huang, Ronghuai, J. Michael Spector, and Junfeng Yang. *Educational Technology: A Primer for the 21st Century.* Springer Singapore, 2019.

Krahmer, Shawn M., Ginette McManus, and Rajneesh Sharma. "Ensuring Instructional Continuity in a Potential Pandemic." *Inside Higher Ed*, 4 Mar. 2020, www.insidehighered. com/advice/2020/03/04/ preparing-instructional-continuity-advent-covid-19-pandemic-opinion.

Miller, Michelle D. *Minds Online: Teaching Effectively with Technology.* Harvard UP, 2014.

Roblyer, M. D., and Aaron H. Doering. *Integrating Educational Technology into Teaching.* 6th ed., Pearson, 2013.

Tatnall, Arthur, and Bill Davey, editors. *Reflections on the History of Computers in Education: Early Use of Computers and Teaching about Computing in Schools.* Springer-Verlag Berlin Heidelberg, 2014.

COMPUTER ETHICS

Introduction

Computer ethics is the study of moral and immoral uses of computer technology and the application of that knowledge. The study of computer ethics is decades old, however, it has grown exponentially in modern times because of the increased use of computers and related technology. Computer ethics includes a variety of issues, such as online piracy, hacking, online privacy, and electronic surveillance.

Background

Massachusetts Institute of Technology (MIT) professor Norbert Wiener is widely regarded as the founder of computer ethics. Wiener was a prominent engineer famous for his work in cybernetics, the science of making one part of a machine communicate with another part. Though he never called his work "computer ethics," his 1950 book *The Human Use of Human Beings* introduced a variety of concepts that would become essential to computer ethics. Wiener believed that the spread of computer technology would begin a second industrial revolution, altering every aspect of civilized life.

The study of computer ethics grew slowly during the 1950s and 1960s. As computer technology became widely available, the field began to attract more attention. Deborah Johnson published *Computer Ethics*, the first textbook in the field, in 1985. She also published and edited a variety of essays on the topic. Johnson asserted that as computer ethics grew, others would use it as a springboard for writings that would influence all types of ethics. She cited the writings of famous ethical philosophers Immanuel Kant and Jeremy Bentham, whose writings were originally a response to the invention of the printing press, as evidence.

Intellectual Property

Today, computers have become involved in most aspects of people's daily lives. Many people even carry portable computers with them in the form of laptops, smartphones, or tablets. Consequentially, the field of computer ethics has grown to cover a variety of legal and social issues. Several of these issues, such as piracy, involve intellectual property laws.

Intellectual property is the ownership of something that isn't a physical object. It is divided into two schools: industrial property and copyright. Industrial property deals with items such as trademarks, which identity a company or product, and patents, which protect inventions.

Copyright deals primarily with artistic works, such as music, films, writings, artwork, and computer code. Computers have made selling and distributing intellectual property easy. Additionally, theft of intellectual property has become extremely widespread because of computers.

Computer piracy is the act of downloading copyrighted materials without the permission of the copyright holder. With modern technology, pirating media takes minimal amounts of effort and costs next to nothing. Experts estimate that more than 46 percent of Americans have pirated copyrighted content, with more than 70 percent of these people being between the ages of eighteen and twenty-nine. Though downloading copyrighted content without the permission of or without compensating the copyright holder is morally wrong, experts assert that legally cracking down on the problem has done little to stop it. Despite increased prosecution, the number of people who pirate copyrighted media has continued to rise. Instead, experts advise corporations to provide less expensive and more convenient alternatives to piracy. Evidence has shown that people are significantly less likely to pirate content when presented with convenient, legal alternatives.

Privacy

Most people keep a large amount of personal information on their computers. They communicate through email and other messaging services, use credit cards to make online purchases, and leave records of websites routinely visited. When using their own hardware, most computer users expect that their data will remain private. However, this is not always the case.

Hackers—computer experts who specialize in accessing private data—have the potential to steal passwords or sensitive information. According to computer ethicists, viewing private information without permission is considered unethical. Experts

continue to debate whether it is ethical for internet service providers and government agencies to copy and store this data without the knowledge and consent of users. Some argue that this surveillance is needed because surveillance helps authorities find and apprehend criminals. Others assert that the government should only be able to acquire and search an individual's data with a warrant.

An ethical examination of a computer user's expectation of privacy becomes significantly more complicated when the individual is using a computer at a workplace. On one hand, a work computer is not considered an employee's property. Additionally, the employer is paying employees to spend their time working. For example, employees playing games on their computers or browsing the internet might be in violation of their work contracts. Checking what an employee does on an employer-owned computer should be acceptable, however, the information collected in these circumstances could have the potential to lead to greater abuses.

If employees use personal email accounts on work computers, monitoring software could allow the employer to intercept emails, read them, modify them, and even acquire usernames and passwords to employees' personal accounts. Many workplaces are not required to alert employees that their computers are monitored. Some computer ethicists argue that this practice violates the privacy of users. They argue that if an individual wrote a letter with a company-owned pen on company-owned paper—as long as it was done during a break or lunch—the company would not be entitled to open the letter, read it, make a copy of it, or decide if it should be sent. These ethicists assert that the same rules should apply to digital communications. Others argue that any data on an employer-owned machine should be considered the property of the employer, and the employer should have the right to access it. They also assert that employees should completely refrain from entering any personal data on work computers to avoid privacy concerns.

Many other cases involving online privacy have developed as computers have become more advanced and more ubiquitous. Often these issues are complicated by a lack of government regulation or legal guidelines, allowing the ethical debate to come to the forefront. One prominent example is the ongoing controversy regarding the collection of user information by search engines, such as Google.

Search engine companies can collect detailed information about what users search for, and then use or sell this information to create customized advertisements or for other means. Other ethical questions of privacy and censorship in the early twenty-first century include the potential for social media companies to exert power over public opinion by selective display of news and other content, which could in turn impact politics; the line between illegal hacking and whistleblowing activity, as in the cases of WikiLeaks; and the use of the deep web (or dark internet) as both a tool for criminal activity and social justice.

Still other issues of computer ethics continue to arise or encounter new complications. Many ethical debates center on the pervasiveness of the internet in everyday life and its potential to profoundly impact aspects of life even beyond actually using a computer. These include the implications of big data in areas such medical research and concerns over internet access as a socioeconomic problem and possibly a human right.

—*Tyler Biscontini*

References

Anderson, Nate. "It's Official: America a Land of Young, Casual Pirates." *Ars Technica.* Condé Nast, 16 Nov. 2011, arstechnica.com/tech-policy/2011/11/its-official-america-a-land-of-young-casual-pirates/.

___. "Report: Piracy a 'Global Pricing Problem' with Only One Solution." *Ars Technica.* Condé Nast, 14 Mar. 2011, arstechnica.com/tech-policy/2011/03/report-piracy-a-global-pricing-problem-with-only-one-solution/.

Arquilla, John. "In Defense of PRISM." *Foreign Policy.* Graham Holdings Company, 7 June 2013, foreignpolicy.com/2013/06/07/in-defense-of-prism/.

Bynum, Terrell Ward. "A Very Short History of Computer Ethics." *APA Newsletter on Philosophy and Computers.* Research Center on Computing & Society, 2008, web.archive.org/web/20080418122849/http://www.southernct.edu/organizations/rccs/resources/research/introduction/bynum_shrt_hist.html.

Kizza, Joseph Migga. *Ethics in Computing: A Concise Module.* Springer International, 2016.

Quinn, Michael J. *Ethics for the Information Age.* Pearson, 2016.

Roberts, Eric. "The Ethics (or Not) of Massive Government Surveillance." *Stanford Computer Science Department.* Stanford University, cs.stanford.edu/people/eroberts/cs181/projects/ethics-of-surveillance/ethics.html.

Schulman, Miriam. "Little Brother Is Watching You." *Markkula Center for Applied Ethics.* Santa Clara University, www.scu.edu/ethics/publications/iie/v9n2/brother.html.

Vanacker, Bastiaan, and Don Heider. *Ethics for a Digital Age.* Peter Lang, 2016.

"What Is Intellectual Property?" *Ohio University,* www.ohio.edu/people/tl303308/intellectual-property1.html.

COMPUTER FRAUD

Introduction

Computer fraud is a type of crime that involves using computers to defraud businesses, governments, or individuals. This could include stealing money, identity theft, illegally accessing private information, or intentionally preventing revenue. It is primarily carried out through viruses, phishing, distributed denial-of-service (DDoS) attacks, and social engineering.

Computer fraud refers to any attempt to use computers or computer software to defraud governments, corporations, or individuals. It may involve the theft of private or important information, such as internet histories, bank account numbers, and contacts. It may also involve the theft of money or other valuable resources. In the United States, computer fraud is illegal under the Comprehensive Crime Control Act. The act was passed on October 12, 1984 and was updated in 2008.

Background

Computer fraud comes in many forms. These include phishing, malware, DDoS attacks, and social engineering. Computer users should be wary against attacks and take a number of precautions to keep their digital information safe from criminals. Operating systems and antimalware software should be kept up to date, passwords should be crafted in a manner that makes both guessing and cracking them difficult, and anyone who asks for log-in information should be carefully scrutinized. Most legitimate businesses will never ask for a customer's username and password.

Phishing is a type of email scam perpetrated by a criminal intending to steal personal information, such as bank account numbers, usernames, passwords, or Social Security numbers. It involves creating a falsified email, usually claiming to belong to a reputable online store or banking institution. This email asks for the log-in or purchasing information of the user. Because users erroneously believe the email is from a reputable source, they are likely to enter their information into the email. In some cases, the email links to a false page designed to look like the impersonated website. Users then attempt to log into the fake website, and transmit their credentials to the criminal. This information can be used to steal money or perpetrate identity theft, or can be sold to other criminals.

Malware is malicious programming installed on individuals' computers without their knowledge or consent. It includes viruses, spyware, adware, and any other variety of malicious software.

Viruses are computer programs or scripts that modify the files on computers in disadvantageous or unethical ways. The malware may steal information, delete files, display messages, send false emails, or cause a computer to run slowly. Viruses spread by copying themselves to other computers through emails or other forms of file sharing.

Spyware is software designed to illegally spy on a computer user. It keeps a record of the user's activities, including keystrokes and browser history. This information is sent to a remote computer, where it can be used or sold. Adware is malware designed to show advertisements to a computer user. It is often coupled with spyware, allowing the malware to use an individual's search history to show targeted advertisements.

All varieties of malware can be extremely damaging to a computer. Users should run reputable antivirus or antimalware software to stop infections before they occur. If computer users suspect their devices may be infected by malware, they should take the equipment to a professional for proper removal of the virus. Failure to remove malicious software could result in identity theft, loss of personal files, or monetary theft.

DDoS attacks are used to disrupt a website or digital service. They utilize a botnet, or a network of computers remotely controlled through software. In many cases, botnets are created by viruses. They infect computers without the knowledge of the users, allowing criminals to control the users' computers without their knowledge or consent. To orchestrate a DDoS attack, botnet controllers order their botnets to attack a small number of servers or computers. The large botnet is able to overwhelm its target, disabling it. This is most commonly used to temporarily disable the web presence of certain news outlets, stores, businesses, and government agencies.

Social engineering involves tricking a person into providing important information used for cybercrime. For example, a criminal could trick an employee of a company into believing he is from the company's information technology division. The criminal could use this deception to convince the employee to allow the criminal to use his computer account, granting the criminal access to a company's computer network. Other common social engineering techniques include pretending to be a parent, spouse, or student to gain access to accounts or computer networks.

Computer fraud can be prevented in a number of ways. Proper cybersecurity measures will stop most attempts at computer fraud. These include keeping antimalware software updated, creating difficult to crack passwords, and utilizing two-factor authentication for important accounts. Two-factor authentication involves linking a cell phone with a specific computer account. If the computer fails to recognize a user's password, or suspects that someone may have hacked into the account, the computer can send a code to the cell phone linked with the account. Without this code, the account cannot be accessed. While it is possible for criminals to acquire a password, it is extremely unlikely that they also have access to the cell phone linked to it.

In addition to these steps, users should verify that important information being transmitted, such as passwords and credit card numbers, are only sent through encrypted channels. Encryption means that even if the information is intercepted by a third party, it will be extremely difficult for that party to unlock any important data.

—Tyler Biscontini

References

"Computer Fraud." *Computer Hope,* www.computer-hope.com/jargon/c/computer-fraud.htm.

"Computer Internet Fraud." *Cornell U,* July 2017, www.law.cornell.edu/wex/computer_and_internet_fraud.

"Distributed Denial of Service Attacks." *Imperva Capsula,* www.incapsula.com/ddos/denial-of-service.html.

"How to Protect Yourself While on the Internet." *Computer Hope,* 15 Sept. 2017, www.computer-hope.com/issues/ch000507.htm.

"How to Recognize Phishing Email Messages, Links, or Phone Calls." *Microsoft,* www.microsoft.com/en-us/safety/online-privacy/phishing-symptoms.aspx.

"Phishing." *Computer Hope,* 11 Oct. 2017, www.computerhope.com/jargon/p/phishing.htm.

"Social Engineering Fraud." *Interpol,* www.interpol.int/Crime-areas/Financial-crime/Social-engineering-fraud/Types-of-social-engineering-fraud.

"Tech Support Scams." *Federal Trade Commission,* July 2017, www.consumer.ftc.gov/articles/0346-tech-support-scams.

COMPUTER FRAUD AND ABUSE ACT

Introduction

As amended in 1994, the Computer Fraud and Abuse Act (CFAA) allows a private party who suffers damages or loss as a result of hacking, or unauthorized computer access, to bring a civil action and obtain compensatory damage, injunctive relief, or other equitable relief.

Background

The US Congress enacted the first version of the CFAA in 1984. It was originally entitled the Counterfeit Access Device and Computer Fraud and Abuse Act. This act imposed criminal sanctions on hackers and other criminals who accessed computers without authorization. Ratified during the dawn of the internet era, the statute prohibited hacking of certain types of information, such as matters concerning national security, foreign relations, and financial credit.

In 1986, the act was renamed the Computer Fraud and Abuse Act. In 1994, the CFAA underwent a notable expansion and established a private right of action for individuals harmed by certain violations of the CFAA. But for an individual to be exposed to civil liability, the individual's actions must meet one of at least six additional factors listed in the statute.

The six bases for civil liability include: loss aggregating to at least $5,000 in value; the modification or impairment, or potential modification or impairment, of the medical examination, diagnosis, treatment, or care of one or more individuals; physical injury to any person; a threat to public health or safety; damage affecting a computer used by or for the US government to further the administration of justice, national defense, or national security; or damage affecting ten or more protected computers during any one-year period.

CFAA claims are most often brought under 18 U.S.C. §1030(a)(2), §1030(a)(4), and §1030(a)(5). Each of these sections includes either the phrase "without authorization" or the phrase "exceeds authorized access." While the phrase "exceeds authorized access" is defined in the statute as "to access a computer with authorization and to use such access to obtain or alter information in the computer that the accessor is not entitled to so obtain or alter," the term "authorized" is never defined. Consequently, courts in different federal circuits have used varying definitions of *"authorized."*

The different interpretations of the term "authorization" are relevant because, under a broad interpretation, more conduct constitutes a federal crime. Under a narrow interpretation, only a small subset of conduct that meets that definition is prohibited. In federal circuits that adopt a broad definition of authorization, employers have been able to bring lawsuits under the CFAA for conduct such as unfair competition and trade secret misappropriation. However, in circuits that had adopted a narrow definition, less conduct has qualified as lacking or exceeding authorization, and fewer types of lawsuits have been successful.

The Fourth and Ninth Circuits have adopted a narrow definition of authorization. Under this definition, only a *technical* breach of access is deemed to lack or exceed authorization. The reason behind this narrow view is discussed at length in the seminal Ninth Circuit case *United States v. Nosal* (9th Cir. 2012). In that case, current employees of an executive search firm used their employer-granted access to the company database to obtain and pass along confidential information to a former employee who was setting up a competing business. The Ninth Circuit held that, because the current employees had logged into the firm database with their valid log-in credentials, they had proper authorization and did not violate the CFAA, despite the fact that their ultimate use of the information breached the company's policies. The court stated that any other meaning would turn a serious federal criminal hacking statute into "sweeping internet-policing mandate" and "make criminals of large groups of people who would have little reason to suspect they are committing a federal crime."

In contrast to this, other legal courts have adopted broad definitions of authorization. To do so, they have creatively adapted agency theories, contract theories, and use-based theories to find CFAA liability in situations in which computer users had been given technical access but were violating an employment contract or company policy. Thus, in the case *Shurgard Storage Centers, Inc. v. Safeguard Self Storage, Inc.* (W.D. Wash. 2000), the District Court held that the plaintiff lost authorization and breached the CFAA when he became an agent of a direct competitor and used his former employer's proprietary information in a way that damaged his former employer.

Several courts have both employed an "intended use" analysis. These courts looked at the underlying purpose of certain company policies to determine whether an employee breached or exceeded technically authorized access. This theory resembles contract theory but is broader because it considers how employees used the information they attained, even if there was no direct contradiction of a written policy or contract. Thus, in *United States v. John* (2010), the Fifth Circuit held that an employee violated the statute when she used data from Citigroup's internal computer system to attain customer account information, which she then shared with others in order to engage in fraudulent activities.

The court reasoned that such use was *unlikely* to be what the company intended when it granted her access.

Ultimately, as society's dependency on computers continues to grow, there is a growing need for the judiciary to offer clearer guidance for applying this statute.

—Myra Din

References

Bernescu, Laura. "When Is a Hack Not a Hack: Addressing the CFAA's Applicability to the Internet Service Context." *University of Chicago Legal Forum*, 2013, p. 633.

Kerr, Orin S. "Cybercrime's Scope: Interpreting 'Access' and 'Authorization' in Computer Misuse Statutes." *New York University Law Review*, vol. 78, 2003, p. 1596.

___. "Vagueness Challenges to the Computer Fraud and Abuse Act." *Minnesota Law Review*, vol. 94, 2010, p. 1561.

Murray, Ryan Patrick. "Myspace-ing Is Not a Crime: Why Breaching Terms of Service Agreements Should Not Implicate the Computer Fraud and Abuse Act Written February 2, 2009." *Loyola of Los Angeles Entertainment Law Review*, vol. 29, no. 3, June 2009, p. 475.

Olivenbaum, Joseph M. "Ctrl-Alt-Delete: Rethinking Federal Computer Crime Legislation." *Seton Hall Law Review*, vol. 27, 1997, p. 574.

Patterson, Kelsey T. "Narrowing It Down to One Narrow View: Clarifying and Limiting the Computer Fraud and Abuse Act." *Charleston Law Review*, vol. 7, no. 3, Mar. 2013, p. 489.

Rosen, David J. "Limiting Employee Liability under the CFAA: A Code-Based Approach to 'Exceeds Authorized Access.'" *Berkeley Technology Law Journal*, vol. 27, 2012, p. 737.

Schieck, Glenn R. "Undercutting Employee Mobility: The Computer Fraud and Abuse Act in the Trade Secret Context." *Brooklyn Law Review*, vol. 79, no. 2, 2014, p. 831.

COMPUTER VIRUSES AND WORMS

Introduction

Computer viruses and worms are malicious computer programs, sometimes more generally referred to as malware, that use embedded instructions to carry out destructive behavior on computers, computer networks, and digital devices.

Computer viruses and worms have the potential to disrupt computer networks and thus to cause great damage to a nation's economy. The US Department of Justice has devoted significant resources to investigating and prosecuting persons who release viruses or worms on the internet. In addition, government agencies investigate connections between malware and organized crime, identity theft, and terrorism.

Given the capacity of computer viruses and worms to spread to millions of computers within minutes and cause billions of dollars in damage, the distribution of malware is a criminal act. In the United States, causing damage to a computer connected to the internet is a federal crime that carries substantial penalties for those convicted. The principal US law enforcement weapon against malware is the Computer Fraud and Abuse Act of 1984.

Background

Many dangerous computer viruses have been spread through email attachments and files downloaded

Computer worms spread from computer to computer, and can replicate without any human interaction. Photo via iStock/solarseven. [Used under license.]

from websites, and a rise has been seen in the numbers of professional virus writers—that is, people who are paid to infect computers with malware. Tracking down and catching virus authors is extremely difficult. The investigative methods used in this work include analyzing virus code for clues about the authors; searching online bulletin boards, where virus authors may boast of their accomplishments; and reviewing network log files for originating internet protocol (IP) addresses of viruses. Even when law enforcement agencies make concerted efforts in applying these techniques, it is still extremely difficult to track down virus and worm authors.

Some malware authors have been apprehended, however. When the Melissa virus overwhelmed commercial, government, and military computer systems in 1999, the Federal Bureau of Investigation (FBI) launched the largest internet manhunt in history. Investigators succeeded in tracking down the virus creator by following several evidence trails. They identified David L. Smith of Aberdeen, New Jersey, as the suspect by analyzing the virus and the e-mail account used to send it, by searching America Online (AOL) log files that showed whose phone line had been used to send the virus, and by searching online bulletin boards intended for people interested in learning how to write viruses. Smith tried to hide the electronic evidence related to Melissa by deleting files from his computer and then disposing of it. The FBI found the computer, however, and used computer forensics techniques to recover incriminating evidence. Smith was caught within two weeks. He was the first person prosecuted for spreading a computer virus.

In August 2005, Turkish and Moroccan hackers released an internet worm named Zotob, intended to steal credit card numbers and other financial information from infected computers. Zotob crashed innumerable computer systems worldwide. Investigators gathered data, including IP addresses, email addresses, names linked to those addresses, hacker nicknames, and other clues uncovered in the computer code. Less than eight days after the malicious code hit the internet, two suspects, Farid Essebar and Attila Ekici, were arrested. Computer forensic experts on the FBI's Cyber Action Team (CAT) verified that the code found on seized computers matched what was released into cyberspace. Sixteen accomplices were later identified in the scheme.

Computer viruses, once executed, replicate by modifying other computer programs and inserting code that can damage a host computer. Photo via iStock/Credit:Rawf8. [Used under license.]

Government responses to hacking have become more intense following several high-profile computer security breaches targeting government servers in the 2010s. In 2014, the US government charged five Chinese military hackers working for the Chinese military's Unit 61398 for cyberespionage against American corporations, which was undertaken to gain a competitive advantage. The indictment marked the first time that criminal charges were filed against known state actors for hacking. In 2015, the Chinese military's Unit 61398 was again implicated in cyberattacks against the Australian Bureau of Meteorology, in which hundreds of terabytes of data were stolen. In 2016, the US Central Intelligence Agency (CIA) reported that the Russian government was behind a hack of the Democratic National Convention in which nearly 20,000 emails were stolen and leaked. The CIA told US legislators that the agency had concluded Russia carried out the hack with the aim of influencing the 2016 US presidential election.

As hacking becomes more common, the targets more prominent, and the stakes higher, computer forensics techniques will need to become ever more advanced to prevent and prosecute hackers.

—*Linda Volonino*

References

Dwight, Ken. *Bug-Free Computing: Stop Viruses, Squash Worms, and Smash Trojan Horses.* TeleProcessors, 2006.

Entous, Adam, Ellen Nakashima, and Greg Miller. "Secret CIA Assessment Says Russia Was Trying to Help Trump Win White House." *The Washington Post,* 9 Dec. 2016, www.washingtonpost.com/world/national-security/obama-orders-review-of-russian-hacking-during-presidential-campaign/2016/12/09/31d6b300-be2a-11e6-94ac-3d324840106c_story.html.

Erbschloe, Michael. *Trojans, Worms, and Spyware: A Computer Security Professional's Guide to Malicious Code.* Butterworth-Heinemann, 2005.

International Council of E-Commerce Consultants. *Computer Forensics: Investigating File and Operating Systems, Wireless Networks, and Storage.* 4 vols. 2nd ed., Cengage, 2016.

Maras, Marie-Helen. *Computer Forensics: Cybercriminals, Laws and Evidence.* Jones and Bartlett, 2015.

"U.S. Charges Five Chinese Military Hackers for Cyber Espionage Against U.S. Corporations and a Labor Organization for Commercial Advantage." *US Department of Justice,* 19 May 2014, www.justice.gov/opa/pr/us-charges-five-chinese-military-hackers-cyber-espionage-against-us-corporations-and-labor.

CONSTRUCTIVISM

Introduction

Constructivism has received a great deal of recent attention in the educational literature, and as a result, has been defined in multiple ways. So many different definitions currently exist some scholars believe constructivism has been emptied of meaning altogether. There are two identifiable strands of constructivism: cognitive constructivism, as outlined in the work of Jean Piaget, and social constructivism, as outlined in the work of Lev Vygotsky. Implications for teaching are introduced, as well as an example of a constructivist classroom activity. The summary also introduces the larger epistemological debate surrounding constructivism.

In recent years, constructivism has become one of the most often cited theories of learning in the educational literature. Its popularity has achieved such heights that it has been referred to by various scholars as fashionable, faddish, and even by some, as a religion. The frequent discussion of constructivism isn't a problem per se, but it has created some confusion regarding its exact meaning. As Harlow, Cummings, and Aberasturi acknowledge, "constructivism has taken on as many different definitions as the number of people attempting to define it." As a result, they argue, it has also been "emptied of meaning." Others concur, suggesting that there is such a wide range of interpretations of terminologies that too few people even agree on the term constructivism, even when they utilize it.

Background

Perhaps more solid ground can be established by first recognizing the philosophical foundations of constructivism. Although a relatively recent development in education, the issues addressed are ones that have been debated for thousands of years. At its core, constructivism is about epistemology, a branch of philosophy that studies the nature of knowledge: what it is that we know, and how we know what we know. Although oversimplified, philosophers have generally fallen into two camps; those who believe knowledge is an approximation of an independent reality—a reality separate from the knower and representative of the ultimate Truth—and those who believe that knowledge is created by human minds. Constructivists fall in the second camp, arguing that knowledge is constructed by individuals through their experience, and is not necessarily representative of 'the real world.'

The notion of knowledge as a construction helps bring some clarity to this elusive concept, as does the recognition of one of its main pioneers. Although constructivism has roots in ancient philosophy, and its ideas have been extended by many modern-day learning theorists, Piaget is most often credited with its development. As Prouix states, "Even if many other authors have contributed to numerous aspects of the theory in a tacit or indirect way (e.g., Dewey, Kant, Rousseau, Vico, etc.) the main pioneer of constructivism is without question Jean Piaget." The following summary, therefore, will focus largely on the work of Piaget. In addition, the theoretical work of Vygotsky will be introduced. Vygotsky's social constructivism is often contrasted with Piaget's cognitive constructivism, but the following will focus on the way in which these two strands are complementary.

Piaget and Cognitive Constructivism

In order to understand the significance of Piaget's contribution, we must first place it within the context of the epistemological debate referenced in the introduction. For the past several centuries, those who believe that knowledge is an approximation of an independent reality representative of the ultimate Truth have held sway in the philosophical courts. For equally as long, however, skeptics have argued that we cannot know the truth of our knowledge, because "we would need access to the world that does not involve our experiencing it" (von Glasersfeld, qtd. in Prouix).

What Piaget's theory does, however, is "make it possible to accept the skeptics' logical conclusion without diminishing the obvious value of knowledge" (von Glasersfeld). More specifically, Piaget introduced the concept of adaptation to epistemology. Having trained first as a biologist, Piaget studied the relationship between mollusks and their environment; the ability to adapt, he concluded, was simply the ability to survive in a given environment. Knowledge, then, is not important to the extent that it represents an external reality, but is important to the extent that it is *viable*. "Simply put, the notion of viability means that an action, operation, conceptual structure, or even a theory, is considered 'viable' as long as it is useful in accomplishing the task or in achieving a goal that one has set for oneself" (von Glasersfeld, qtd. in Prouix). In other words, "truth" is what works.

The question of what knowledge is, from a constructivist perspective, has now been answered to some extent—it is *not* a representation of external reality or objective truth, but rather *is* "truthful" to the extent it is viable and adaptive—but the exact mechanisms by which knowledge is constructed have not yet been explained. As Harlow et al. argue, those who overuse the term in the literature often ignore the "how" of constructivism. In other words, educators often pay lip service to the idea that people make meaning, but fail to understand the processes by which this occurs. Even teachers with the best intentions sometimes forget that cognitive conflict (also referred to as cognitive dissonance), for example, is essential for new knowledge construction.

According to Piaget, all learning is motivated by a desire to maintain a state of equilibrium. When an individual is confronted by information or an experience that contradicts his or her prior knowledge, the learner is motivated to modify or adapt prior knowledge in order to return to equilibrium. Therefore, those things that cause disequilibrium—sometimes referred to a perturbations or cognitive conflicts—play a critical role in the learning process.

In the digital realm and considering digital literacy, when learners, especially those using computers or educational technologies, encounter something new, if they choose to modify their prior knowledge to assimilate the new information, and hence reestablishing equilibrium—they have followed the Piaget model. Assimilation occurs when new experiences or information fit into our existing mental structures. Therefore, assimilation is largely an unconscious process, one in which we make new experiences fit into what we already know.

However, as C. T. Fosnot argues, in order to fully understand the concept of equilibration, one should understand its dynamic nature—"it is a dynamic 'dance'…of growth and change.'" The dance occurs between two polar tendencies: our tendency to assimilate information and our tendency to accommodate information.

Accommodation, on the other hand, takes place in the face of perturbations. When new knowledge or experiences contradict what was previously known, the learner must modify her existing cognitive structures, the new knowledge/experience, or both. According to Prouix, "the [digital] learner tries to deliberately adapt—or accommodate—what is already known (previous knowledge) to a new experience that interrupts or contradicts established interpretations." In general, the mind tends to assimilate; only when we have to accommodate does learning occur.

Digital Learning Is an Active and Selective Process

Although the basic structure of Piaget's theory of knowing has been put forth, it's worth noting a few other points of emphasis. First and foremost, for Piaget and other constructivists in general, learning is always an *active* process. Importantly, however "active" implies both physical and *mental* activity; that is, active in the sense of creating new mental structures and not just active in the sense of physically moving one's body. As Prouix explains, "The word 'active' should then not be read in the literal sense because it has a broader meaning in constructivism. The idea that the learners have to be active does not imply that they have to construct a model physically with their hands, but instead that they develop their structures of knowledge—by reflecting, analyzing, questioning themselves, working on problems, and so on."

Second, Piaget's theory highlights the significant role of prior knowledge in the learning process, and the implications this has for teaching as well. Students are not blank slates, and everything they experience in a classroom is interpreted in light of what they already know. As a result, teachers should recognize that learners possess knowledge already, and use that source of knowledge to build new understandings. Simply transmitting information to students, as some teachers do in a lecture-based classroom, does not acknowledge the learner as either active, or as an individual with preestablished cognitive structures. Teaching and learning in digital environments are activities that are useful, engaging, and challenging

As the previous points imply, constructivists conceive the classroom as learner-centered as opposed to teacher-centered. Learner-centered does not suggest, however, that students are free to create *any* meaning, to construct *any* knowledge. In other words, constructivists are often charged with promoting relativism, a charge they dismiss with reference to the concept of fit and viability. "Constructivism, with its concept of viability and 'fitting' does not imply that anything goes but merely that theories or explanations construed have to fit and be compatible with experiences lived" (Prouix). In other words, knowledge that is useful is "more truthful" than knowledge that is not.

Lev Vygotsky and Social Constructivism

Much of the current literature suggests that different strands of constructivism—mainly, cognitive constructivism as outlined by Piaget and social constructivism as outlined by Vygtosky—are at odds with one another. "Thus there is currently a dispute over whether. . . learning is primarily a process of active cognitive reorganization or a process of enculturation into a community of practice" (Cobb). Others argue, however, that Piaget recognized the importance of social interaction in learning, even if he focused on it less than Vygotsky. Thus the two theories are complementary more than they are competitive, and learning should be understood as a cognitive *and* a social process, not either-or.

Thus, although much of Vygotsky's work overlapped with Piaget's, he did in fact focus more heavily on the role of culture, language and social interaction in the construction of knowledge. Like Piaget, he believed learning to be developmental, but he made a distinction between what he viewed as the construction of spontaneous concepts (also known as "pseudoconcepts") and the construction of scientific concepts. Spontaneous concepts, he believed, were developed by children during their everyday activities, in the course of everyday life; these pseudoconcepts were similar to those studied by Piaget. On the other hand, scientific concepts, he suggested, originate in more formal settings—like the classroom—and represent culturally-agreed upon concepts. On their own, children would be unlikely to develop scientific concepts, but with the help of adults and older children, they can master ideas and thought processes that extend their knowledge. The space where children extend their current knowledge with adult assistance has become known as the zone of proximal development.

Vygotsky is undoubtedly best known for the zone of proximal development, but two other concepts are also worthy of mention. Like Piaget, Vygotsky studied the language of preschoolers, but what Piaget concluded was "egocentric" speech, Vygotsky concluded was social from the very beginning. He argued that inner speech was the mechanism by which "culturally prescribed forms of language and reasoning find their individualized realization" (qtd. in Fosnot). Vygotsky also concluded that inner speech plays an important role in the development of spontaneous concepts, and in particular, the attempts by children to *communicate* the concept to others.

Finally, Vygotsky was most interested in the role of other people in the development and learning processes of children. He emphasized the cooperative nature of the learning task to such an extent, for example, that "he viewed tests or school tasks that

only looked at the child's individual problem solving as inadequate, arguing instead that the progress in concept formation achieved by the child in cooperation with an adult was a much more viable way to look at the capabilities of learners" (Fosnot). He referred to cooperation as the dialogical nature of learning; others have since extended this idea through the notion of scaffolding. Scaffolding is best exemplified by an infant/mother interaction, during which the mother at times imitates the baby, and other times, varies her response to further develop the child's response.

Further Insights

One of the important distinctions theorists make about constructivism is that it is a theory of learning—and is even, at times, called a theory of knowing—and is *not* a theory of teaching. As a result, constructivism doesn't tell teachers what they should do, but rather provides a general framework within which they can work with students. As Prouix explains, "It is argued that constructivism brings a proscriptive discourse on teaching, one that sets boundaries in which to work, but does not prescribe teaching actions." von Glasersfeld elaborates, "It means that constructivism...cannot tell teachers very much about what they should do, but it can specify a number of things which they certainly should not do" (qtd. in Prouix). Within the realm of what they should do, he further argues, the possibilities are limitless.

Therefore, providing a specific example of constructivist teaching in the classroom might be the best way to introduce its application to the classroom. Before we proceed with the example, however, it might be worthwhile to outline what Prouix refers to as "implications" for teaching (as opposed to directives), as well as some pitfalls to be avoided. For example, constructivist teaching does not suggest that teachers should stop explaining information; while teachers are encouraged to create disequilibrium, or perturbations, for their students, this should not occur at the expense of explanation and elaboration.

As Prouix argues, "[C]onstructivism is not saying that teachers should not explain, it only renders problematic the assumption that by 'telling' or explaining the learners will automatically understand." He further suggests that constructivism does not imply students are always right or that students will always learn on their own without guidance from teachers. Finally, he encourages teachers to acknowledge the importance of prior knowledge in the learning process, as well as the role of mistakes. "Mistakes inform the learning process enormously and enable a better understanding of the domain…" Mistakes should not, he continues, be viewed as "humiliating blunders" never "to be repeated again" (Prouix).

When contemporary students engage with digital media, platforms, or technologies, they constructivism asserts they should be encouraged to explore, to question, and to test their own experiences in ways that are both assimilating and accommodating. If they do so, they are engaging in the cognitive dissonance that creates new knowledge.

—*Jennifer Kretchmar and Laura Nicosia*

References

Alexander, H. A. "A View from Somewhere: Explaining the Paradigms of Educational Research." *Journal of Philosophy of Education*, vol. 40, 2006, pp. 205–21.

Al-Huneidi, A. M., and J. Schreurs. "Constructivism Based Blended Learning in Higher Education." *International Journal of Emerging Technologies in Learning*, vol. 7, 2012, pp. 4–9.

Bächtold, M. "What Do Students 'Construct' According to Constructivism in Science Education?" *Research in Science Education*, vol. 43, 2013, pp. 2477–96.

Brown, T. H. "Beyond Constructivism: Exploring Future Learning Paradigms." *Education Today*, vol. 2, 2005, pp. 14–30.

Bruner, J. *Acts of Meaning*. Harvard UP, 1990.

Cardellini, L. "The Foundations of Radical Constructivism: An Interview with Ernst Von Glasersfeld." *Foundations of Chemistry*, vol. 8, 2006, pp. 177–87.

Cobb, P. "Where Is the Mind? A Coordination of Sociocultural and Cognitive Constructivist Perspectives." *Constructivism: Theory, Perspectives, and Practice*, edited by C. T. Fosnot, Teachers College Press, 1996, pp. 72–89.

Elkind, D. "Response to Objectivism and Education." *Educational Forum*, vol. 69, 2005, pp. 328–34.

Ertmer, P. A., and T. J. Newby. "Behaviorism, Cognitivism, Constructivism: Comparing Critical Features from an Instructional Design Perspective." *Performance Improvement Quarterly*, vol. 26, 2013, pp. 43–71.

Fostnot, C. T. *Constructivism: Theory, Perspectives, and Practice*. Teachers College Press, 1996.

Harlow, S., R. Cummings, and S. Aberasturi. "Karl Popper and Jean Piaget: A Rationale for Constructivism." *Educational Forum*, vol. 71, 2006, pp. 41–48.

Henson, K. T. *Curriculum Planning: Integrating Multiculturalism, Constructivism, and Education Reform*. Waveland Press, 2015.

Moford, J. "Perspectives Constructivism: Implications for Postsecondary Music Education and Beyond." *Journal of Music Teacher Education*, vol. 16, 2007, pp. 75–83.

Null, J. W. "Is Constructivism Traditional? Historical and Practical Perspectives on a Popular Advocacy." *Educational Forum*, vol. 68, 2004, pp. 180–88.

Prouix, J. "Constructivism: A Re-Equilibration and Clarification of Concepts, and Some Potential Implications for Teaching and Pedagogy." *Radical Pedagogy*, vol. 7, 2006, p. 5.

Schrader, D. E. "Constructivism and Learning in the Age of Social Media: Changing Minds and Learning Communities." *New Directions for Teaching and Learning*, vol. 144, 2015, pp. 23–35.

Von Glasersfeld, E. "Introduction: Aspects of Constructivism." *Constructivism: Theory, Perspectives, and Practice*, edited by C. T. Fosnot, Teachers College Press, 1996.

CREATIVE COMMONS

Introduction

Creative Commons (CC) is an international non-profit organization that provides easy access to creative works that others can legally build upon and share through its range of copyright licenses known as Creative Commons licenses. These licenses, which are completely free of charge, allow the makers of various creative works to easily communicate with others which rights to their works they reserve and which they voluntarily waive. In other words, CC licenses are a standardized way for creators of all types to grant permission for the public to legally use their work within the structure of established copyright law. Since it was originally founded in 2001, CC has worked to overcome the legal obstacles involved with copyright law to make it easier for people around the world to share information and creativity. CC licenses enjoy widespread use, notably serving as the default license of Wikipedia and covering millions of Flickr images (a for-pay platform) and YouTube videos.

Background

CC was primarily created to simplify the sometimes-complicated concepts of copyright and copyright law. Copyright is the legal right of owners of intellectual property to reproduce their creations as they see fit. Put another way, copyright means that the creators of intellectual property and those to whom they grant permission are the only people allowed to make copies of the work in question. Copyright law, which varies from country to country, is the legal framework that governs how copyright works.

The basic idea of copyright is relatively straightforward. When someone uses significant mental effort to create an original product, that product is automatically viewed as intellectual property. To ensure that the creator gets appropriate credit and compensation for their work, it is necessary for their

Creative Commons logo. Image via Wikimedia Commons. [Public domain.]

work to be protected from unauthorized duplication. Many things can be considered intellectual property, including books, films, music, and art. Copyright law is the mechanism through which intellectual property is protected.

Copyright law defines original works as those created entirely through independent thought and without any reliance on duplication. A work produced in this manner is referred to as an original work of authorship (OWA). When an OWA is created, it automatically becomes copyrighted. This means that no one else has the right to use or duplicate the work without the creator's consent. It is important to note, however, that the concept of copyright applies only to tangible works. Intangible creations like ideas, names, and logos may instead be protected through trademarks or patents.

The specifics of American copyright law clearly define the rights enjoyed by the holders of copyrights. According to the law, the creator of a copyrighted work has the exclusive right to reproduce the work, create new works derived from the original, publicly distribute copies of the work, display or perform the work publicly in various ways as applicable, and authorize others to exercise these same rights in relation to the work. Further, copyright law establishes that the legal copyright protection of an OWA lasts throughout the lifetime of its creator, plus an additional seventy years. This period is shorter when copyrighted material is owned by a corporation.

Overview

As an organization, Creative Commons provides an alternative to traditional copyright law that makes it easier for the creators of OWAs to allow others to use and share their works. It accomplishes this feat by offering a collection of CC licenses that afford creators the ability to decide for themselves how others are permitted to use their work. By releasing their work under the CC license of their choice, creators clearly define what the public can and cannot do with the work in question. From the other side of the equation, the use of CC licenses gives members of the public the ability to freely use a copyrighted work without having to seek permission from the creator unless they want to do so in a way that is not covered by the specific CC license in play. On top of all that, CC licenses are also advantageous because they all allow the open use of covered works for educational

Open access logo, originally designed by Public Library of Science. Image via Wikimedia Commons. [Public domain.]

purposes. This affords teachers and students the opportunity to duplicate, share, and in some cases even modify CC works without having to seek permission.

The six distinct types of CC licenses place different restrictions on how a work may be used, but all share some common characteristics. All CC licenses allow users to copy a work, distribute a work, display or perform a work, communicate a work, and format shift verbatim copies of a work. Beyond that, each type of CC license varies in its degree of permissiveness. The six types of CC licenses include: CC BY, CC BY-SA, CC BY-NC, CC BY-NC-SA, CC BY-ND, and CC BY-NC-ND.

Each license is denoted by special symbols that appear on or near a licensed work. CC BY, the most permissive CC license, allows users to copy, distribute, change, and build upon an existing work in virtually any way as long as the work is properly attributed to the original creator. It also allows for commercial use. CC BY-SA licenses allow users to do all of the same things that a CC BY license does, except that it requires users who change or build upon an existing work to license the modified materials under the same terms. CC BY-SA licenses allow for commercial uses as well. CC BY-NC licenses are the same as CC BY licenses, but the works they protect can only be used for noncommercial purposes. CC BY-NC-SA licenses are the same as CC BY-SA licenses, except that they prohibit commercial uses. CC BY-ND licenses allow users to copy and distribute a work in any medium or format, but only in unaltered form. Commercial use is permitted. CC BY-NC-ND licenses are the same as CC BY-ND, except commercial uses are not permitted.

CC's work goes well beyond issuing licenses. The organization also provides helpful public domain tools, works with other institutions and governments to create and implement open licensing protocols, develops technologies that make it easier to find and use open license materials, offers a course for those who wish to become open license experts, and more.

—*Jack Lasky*

References

"About CC Licenses." *Creative Commons*, 2021, creativecommons.org/about/cclicenses.

Bailey, Jonathan. "What Is Creative Commons Anyway?" *Plagiarism.org*, 24 July 2018, www.plagiarism.org/blog/2018/07/24/what-is-creative-commons-anyway.

Kenton, Will. "Copyright." *Investopedia*, 13 Sept. 2020, www.investopedia.com/terms/c/copyright.asp.

Park, Jane. "What Is Creative Commons and Why Does It Matter?" *Common Sense Education*, 4 May 2016, www.commonsense.org/education/articles/what-is-creative-commons-and-why-does-it-matter.

"What Is a Creative Commons License?" *Copyright Alliance*, 2021, copyrightalliance.org/faqs/what-is-creative-commons-license.

"What Is Copyright?" *Copyright.gov*, 2021, www.copyright.gov/what-is-copyright.

"What Is Creative Commons?" *Smartcopying*, 2021, smartcopying.edu.au/what-is-creative-commons.

"What We Do." *Creative Commons*, 2021, creativecommons.org/about.

CYBERBULLYING

Introduction

The advent of any new communication technology has historically brought with it new forms of bulling. Newspapers presented bullying on a widespread basis via the printed word; telephones created prank calls; the internet has presented an even quicker, broader form of harassment. Intimidation transpiring via the latest computer technologies is dubbed cyberbullying. Cyberbullying is especially prevalent on social networking websites, and is most commonly experienced by young people.

Background

The term "cyberbullying" was first used by educator Bill Belsey in 2004 in an essay detailing the emerging threat of harassment through the use of information and communication technologies. He described cyberbullying as a pervasive form of intentional harassment by a group or individual acting with hostility toward another person, aided by the internet's invasive capabilities. The act of cyberbullying, however, was present long before it was given a name. When the internet became a significant source of connectivity near the close of the twentieth century, a new kind of rapport developed between people. Individuals communicating through a computer screen were able to behave and interact differently than they could or normally would face to face. Technology allowed for an anonymity that made bullying easier. Paired with the distancing effect many experienced through the use of such devices, bullying had the potential to be even more vicious than it would be in face-to-face situations.

As awareness of cyberbullying increased, researchers began surveying students about their personal experiences to learn more about the incidence of such harassment among American youth. Teenagers seemed to be the main demographic affected by cyberharassment. In 2000, the Crimes Against Children Research Center interviewed 1,501 young people ages ten to seventeen. At that time, the survey found that one in seventeen children—about 6 percent—had experienced threats or harassment online. This number increased to 9 percent five years later and to 11 percent in 2011. Other studies supported these findings. In 2004, the internet safety

Cyberbullying has become increasingly common, especially among teens. Photo via iStock/SolStock. [Used under license.]

education website i-Safe surveyed the same number of students between grades four and eight and found that 42 percent of students had been bullied online; 35 percent of those surveyed had been threatened and many said it had happened more than once.

Many researchers showed rising rates of cyberbullying through the 2010s, as internet access and portable electronic devices became increasingly common with young people. As part of its biannual nationwide survey Youth Risk Behavior Surveillance, the Centers for Disease Control and Prevention reported that in 2017, 14.9 percent of high school students surveyed stated that they had been bullied electronically in the previous twelve months. Similarly, the National Center for Education Statistics reported in 2019 that during the 2016–17 school year, 15 percent of the 20 percent of students between the ages of twelve and eighteen who had reported being bullied had experienced this bullying online or by text; this marked an increase over the 2015–16 school year, during which time 11.5 percent of bullied students were bullied online or by text.

A Pew Research Center survey published in September 2018 found that 59 percent of US teens had experienced cyberbullying. The same survey revealed that the most common type of online harassment reported by American teens was name calling, with 42 percent of those surveyed saying they had experienced this type of bullying online or on their cell phone; another 32 percent reported that someone had spread false rumors about them online. Because of the anonymity provided by online platforms, there was a rise in hate speech used to cyberbully during the late 2010s.

In 2013, elevated concern over the possibly devastating effects of unchecked cyberbullying occurred following the suicides of at least seven teenagers in both the United States and the United Kingdom that were linked to incidents of bullying taking place on a largely unfamiliar social application, Ask.fm. The application, which did not have the privacy settings associated with popular social media sites such as Facebook, offered an open forum for questions and answers that allowed for anonymous bullying. However, even more prominent social media platforms such as Instagram, Facebook, and Snapchat struggled to limit cyberbullying.

Legislation against Cyberbullying

In late 2006, thirteen-year-old Megan Meier of Missouri committed suicide after a campaign of harassment over the internet. After an investigation, Meier's death was attributed to repeated cyberbullying via the then-popular social networking website Myspace. There were no laws against cyberbullying at the time, so the offenders—including an adult neighbor—were indicted on charges of "unauthorized access of a computer system with intent to harm another person." The case incited intense public outrage and prompted many states to take legislative action against cyberbullying; soon, many had passed laws criminalizing it.

Inspired by the case, Congresswoman Linda Sanchez proposed a bill referred to as the Megan Meier Cyberbullying Prevention Act in an attempt to decrease such tragic incidents at the federal level. However, the bill largely stalled as several congressional members argued that the legislation would conflict with the constitutional right to free speech. According to the Cyberbullying Research Center, by early 2021, forty-eight US states had legislation and/or policies that specifically addressed cyberbullying. All fifty states and the District of Columbia had more general antibullying legislation in place.

Schools, too, began taking steps to prevent cyberbullying, and many instituted programs of awareness and established punishments for those found guilty. However, although most schools in the United States block social networking sites from school computers, not all have programs teaching students responsible internet use. Additionally, states that do have laws addressing cyberbullying and even school codes often do not include any

insight into whether and how schools should intervene in such cases, or even clearly define cyberbullying. Principals are also often conflicted as to whether they have any power to discipline students if the cyberbullying is conducted outside of the school. Some states have statutes reflecting the fact that "federal case law allows schools to discipline students for off-campus behavior that results in a substantial disruption of the learning environment at school," as per the Cyberbullying Research Center. Yet the application of such legislation can be unclear and sometimes controversial.

Campaigns against Cyberbullying

To increase understanding of the issue, many international organizations have dedicated themselves to bringing awareness to the problem of cyberbullying as well as preventing it. Founded in 2005, the STOMP Out Bullying campaign helped over 100,000 students through their HelpChat Line and partnered with over 15,000 schools to raise awareness of cyberbullying by 2020. In 2007, the US-based National Crime Prevention Council created a public advertising campaign and initiated a contest that challenged entrants to create their own public service announcements. Stopbullying.gov, a US government website, provides information on cyberbullying and how to prevent and report it. The Cybersmile Foundation is an international nonprofit organization committed to reducing incidents of cyberbullying and helping victims of cyberbullying

Cyberbullying can include posting negative, harmful, or false information about an individual as well as issuing threats using electronic means. Photo via iStock/asiandelight. [Used under license.]

regain control of their lives. Several countries, such as Canada and Spain, have a national antibullying day in order to bring awareness to the problem.

People worldwide also use social networking websites to combat cyberbullying. For example, Sarah Ball, who was once cyberbullied, created a Facebook page called "Hernando Unbreakable" in order to help other victims. She earned attention by posting uplifting messages, updates on antibullying legislation, and examples of hate-based websites on the internet. The video-sharing website YouTube created an antibullying channel designed to encourage teens to speak out against internet harassment. As part of the "Be Best" campaign she officially launched in May 2018, First Lady Melania Trump held a summit on cyberbullying in August of that year; the importance of educating the American youth, particularly, about proper online etiquette was one of the foundations of her initiative. However, some commentators expressed concern regarding the effectiveness of her campaign, as her husband, then President Donald Trump, was often seen using his social media posts to bully and to disparage his opponents and others.

Impact

The rise of cyberbullying in America has led to increased awareness among the public and in the government and has inspired legislation intended to prevent such offenses.

Though cyberbullying is predominantly seen among teenagers, all age groups are affected by this type of harassment. Cyberbullying has had distressing effects on victims and is damaging to their mental and emotional health. Many experience anxiety, depression, and other related stress disorders. Victims have also been known to become isolated and undergo severe changes in behavior and mood. Some have committed suicide as a result of being relentlessly cyberbullied. Anticyberbullying campaigns have raised public awareness of different forms of harassment that occur both online and offline.

—*Cait Caffrey*

References

Alejandro Arzate, Hector. "Cyberbullying Is on the Rise among Teenagers, National Survey Finds." *Education Week*, 15 July 2019, /blogs.edweek.org/ edweek/District_Dossier/2019/07/ cyberbullying_is_on_the_rise_a.html.

Anderson, Monica. "A Majority of Teens Have Experienced Some Form of Cyberbullying." *Pew Research Center*, 27 Sept. 2018, www.pewinternet. org/2018/09/27/a-majority-of-teens-have-experienced-some-form-of-cyberbullying/.

Bagwell, Karen. "Teaching, Not Technology, Needed to Enforce Internet Rules." *Education Daily*, vol. 40, no. 212, 2007, p. 2.

Belsey, Bill. "Cyberbullying: An Emerging Threat to the 'Always On' Generation." *Bullying.org*, 2004, cyberbullying.ca/pdf/Cyberbullying_Article_by_ Bill_Belsey.pdf.

"Bullying Laws across America." *Cyberbullying Research Center*, cyberbullying.org/bullying-laws.

Cloud, John. "Bullied to Death?" *Time*, 18 Oct. 2010, pp. 60–63.

"Cyberbullying: Definition." *Pacer's National Bullying Prevention Center*. Pacer Center, 2020, www.pacer. org/bullying/resources/cyberbullying/.

Cyberbullying and Hate Speech." *Ditch the Label | Brandwatch*, 2016, www.ditchthelabel.org/ wp-content/uploads/2016/11/Cyberbullying-and-hate-speech.pdf. "Cyberbullying: What Is It and How to Stop It." UNICEF, www.unicef.org/ end-violence/how-to-stop-cyberbullying.

Donegan, Richard. "Bullying and Cyberbullying: History, Statistics, Law, Prevention and Analysis." *Elon Journal of Undergraduate Research in Communications*, vol. 3, no. 1, 2012, pp. 34–36.

Hern, Alex. "Ask.fm's New Owners Vow to Crack Down on Bullying or Shut the Site." *The Guardian*, 19 Aug. 2014, www.theguardian.com/tech-nology/2014/aug/19/askfm-askcom-bullying.

Hinduja, Sameer, and Justin W. Patchin. *Cyberbullying Prevention and Response: Expert Perspectives.* Routledge, 2012.

Hoffman, Jan. "Online Bullies Pull Schools into the Fray." *The New York Times*, 27 June 2010, www. nytimes.com/2010/06/28/style/28bully.html.

Mahdawi, Arwa. "Melania Trump Rails against Cyberbullying—But She Is Using Social Media to Gaslight the World." *The Guardian*, 21 Aug. 2018, www.theguardian.com/commentisfree/2018/ aug/21/melania-trump-rails-against-cyberbullying-social-media-gaslight-world.

"Parents: Cyber Bullying Led to Teen's Suicide." *ABC News*, 19 Nov. 2007, abcnews.go.com/GMA/ story?id=3882520.

Polanin, Joshua R., et al. "A Meta-analysis of School-Based Bullying Prevention Programs' Effects on

Bystander Intervention Behavior." *School Psychology Review*, vol. 41, no. 1, 2012, pp. 47–65.

Schneider, Shari Kessel, et al. "Cyberbullying, School Bullying, and Psychological Distress: A Regional Census of High School Students." *American Journal of Public Health*, vol. 102, no. 1, 2012, p. 171.

Siegel, Lee. "The Kids Aren't Alright." *Newsweek*, 15 Oct. 2012, pp. 18–20.

STOMP Out Bullying, 2020, www.stompoutbullying. org/.

"What Is Cyberbullying." *StopBullying.gov*, 21 July 2020. www.stopbullying.gov/cyberbullying/ what-is-it.

Ybarra, Michele L., and Kimberly J, Mitchell. "How Risky Are Social Networking Sites? A Comparison of Places Online Where Youth Sexual Solicitation and Harassment Occurs." *Pediatrics*, vol. 121, no. 2, 2008, pp. e350–e357.

Youth Risk Behavior Surveillance—United States, 2017. *Centers for Disease Control and Prevention.* US Department of Health and Human Services, 15 June 2018, www.cdc.gov/healthyyouth/data/ yrbs/pdf/2017/ss6708.pdf.

CYBERCRIME

Introduction

Cybercrime refers to any crime that uses a computer, often attached to the internet, as a target, weapon, or accessory for attacking individuals, groups, or their property.

There are many examples of cybercrime—including identity theft, denial-of-service (DoS) attacks, internet fraud, online predators, and theft of intellectual property—that have appeared in the media, but none is better known than identity theft. Identity theft is the use of personal identifying information to take actions regarding that person, usually by someone intent on performing an illegal act. While illegally impersonating someone is an old type of crime, the increasing use of the internet for business and pleasure in the 2000s resulted in the creation of a digital identity, made up of names, Social Security number, credit card numbers and the like, and identity thieves developed many ways of stealing these digital identities. According to the Bureau of Justice Statistics, in 2014 an estimated 17.6 million people in the United States were victims of at least one incident of identity theft.

Background

With the advent of computers in the 1950s, criminals immediately began exploiting the technology in creative ways. The introduction of the internet in the 1980s led to a marked increase in cybercrime, but the development of the ubiquitous World Wide Web in the 2000s—with access from home, work, and mobile devices—led to exponential growth of all types of cybercrime.

One of the most popular digital identity attacks of the 2000s was phishing with email. In a phishing attack, the thief sends an email to an unsuspecting victim, requesting their digital information under false pretenses, such as pretending to be the victim's bank and asking for their Social Security and back account numbers. Once the thief has the banking information, they then empty the victim's bank account. Thieves also steal identities by placing spyware in a victim's computer to secretly log their private information. Protection from an identity theft attack is tailored to the attack. For example, training has helped reduce phishing attacks, while internet security programs that specialize in antispyware are the best protection against a spyware attack.

Accessing and storing child pornography on a computer is another common type of cybercrime that increased as the web became more popular and accessible. Sites exhibiting a wide range of images and videos of child pornography are easily accessible from a web browser unless some type of blocking software has been installed. Many public libraries and home computers installed blocking software over the course of the 2000s. Social medial sites generally tried to control improper content by carefully monitoring their sites. Law enforcement personnel involved in computer forensics spent much of their time searching computers for child pornography and then testifying in court.

One of the most popular uses of the internet is to download and listen to music. The 2000s saw the creation of hundreds of sites where one can download all types of music in several formats like MP3, and many artists began marketing their music from their own websites. For example, the Apple iTunes site downloaded millions of recordings and albums to iPhones and personal computers. In spite of the large number of legal websites to download and play music, there were even more illegal sites created. These illegal sites have greatly reduced the profitability of the recording industry. The Recording Industry Association of America (RIAA), initially founded in 1952 to administer standards of frequency during recording, focused in the 2000s on helping to fight the illegal downloading of music. The RIAA became a leader in developing ways to secure the music downloading process, using special formats to protect music files and taking legal action at the discovery of illegal downloading sites.

Illegal downloading of motion pictures is another common form of cybercrime. Some popular films of the 2000s were recorded with cell phones and placed on illegal websites within days of their release. The Motion Picture Association of America (MPAA) is a trade group that has increasingly worked to combat this type of theft, using technology and lawsuits. The theft of music and motion pictures on the internet is just one example of the theft of intellectual property that became pandemic in the 2000s. Theft of software, images, and even company secrets also became a major problem for industry. To protect against such attacks, companies have implemented expensive network and computer software, conducted massive training programs, and employed many computer security specialists.

Attacks on Computers

The most common form of attack on a computer is an intrusion attack. These have many forms: viruses, codes that can replicate themselves and damage computers; worms, programs that can replicate themselves and damage computers; bots, programs that help attack other computers; and spyware, programs that collect and forward private information. Trojan horses are one of the most dangerous forms of intrusion attack, as they are often launched from a hacker website, masquerading as a useful site. For example, starting in 2007, the Trojan horse ZeuS was used to steal online banking information after infecting a user through a download from a website—whether a malicious site or an infected legitimate site—or by a link in an email to such a site. Almost all intrusion attacks constitute a crime, although some are simply attempts to irritate the attacked user.

Training about how to avoid attacks and protecting software—antivirus, antispyware, and intrusion protection systems—provided reasonable protection from intrusion attacks in the 2000s, but hackers still found vulnerabilities to attack.

Another well-known type of attack on computers is a DoS attack, during which a hacker sends a massive volume of messages to a server, usually on the internet, that interfere with the server's ability to function properly. A 2007 attack that interrupted electric service in Estonia is probably the best-known DoS attack of the 2000s, but there were many others. DoS attacks are generally cybercrimes, but they can be hard to prosecute. DoS attacks were also sometimes mounted by nations as a part of cyberwarfare, and in these cases were not technically a crime. A variety of defenses are used to combat DoS attacks. One of the most effective is to employ a honeypot, a computer that appears to be the server under attack, and let it draw the attacking traffic to it; intelligent firewalls and routers have also proven to be effective.

Attacks Using Computers

Fraud has always been a major problem for law enforcement, and in the 2000s it largely migrated to the internet. Digital identities can be hard to recognize and validate on the internet. For example, customers can log in to what they think is the rewards site for their credit card and give all their credit card information to a thief who proceeds to buy the maximum amount with their card.

In another famous example of internet fraud during the decade, a criminal or criminals posed as a Nigerian lawyer who solicited victims via email by promising to transfer an inheritance into their bank accounts upon receipt of their account numbers, and instead took all their money. Consumer education is one of the best defenses against internet fraud, but has needed to be combined with improved authentication techniques. One example is to give each internet user or site a digital certificate, thus creating a digital identity for all on the internet, so that cybercriminals intent on committing internet fraud can be detected and stopped.

Cyberbullying and Pharming

Cyberbullying is the use of communications devices or the internet to verbally abuse or threaten another individual, was recognized as a major problem after the shooting at Columbine High School in 1999. During the 2000s, many laws were passed to limit cyberbullying, but it has continued to be a difficult type of cybercrime to control, especially on social media sites.

The first two decades of the 2000s saw an increase in an additional form of cyberattack known as pharming, which, like phishing, is a type of digital scam that allows an individual to steal a user's personal information via the internet. Rather than using email to lure in victims, pharming targets a person's web browser by using a malicious code installed on the computer and browser to redirect the unsuspecting user away from a legitimate website (such as PayPal or eBay) to another, similar but fraudulent site. When the user visits the site and makes financial transactions or exchanges personal information under the impression that they are using a legitimate service, the hacker then actually receives the information instead of the intended company. This form of cyberattack has largely been considered even more dangerous, as users are not required to click on a link or respond to an email but instead are automatically redirected without their knowledge. While software has been created to help detect a fraudulent website, hackers have continued to come up with alternative methods of illegally acquiring digital information.

Impact

The twenty-first century has seen rapid growth in using the internet to communicate, transact business, access entertainment, and obtain information. Along with this growth came a proportionate increase in cybercrimes. Initially, most internet users paid little attention to these cybercrimes. However, publicity about the financial losses incurred by identity theft victims, the physical harm suffered by cyberbullying victims, and damage done to companies and nations by DoS attacks made people aware of the dangers of cybercrime. As a result, by the end of the 2000s, internet users had developed a healthy fear of cybercrime. Industry, educational institutions, and individuals purchased security software and hardware to protect their systems, greatly increasing the cost of using the internet.

—*George M. Whitson*

References

Bradbury, David. "When Borders Collide: Legislating Against Cybercrime." *Computer Fraud and Security*, vol. 2, 2012, pp. 11–15.

Cilli, Claudio. "Identity Theft: A New Frontier for Hackers and Cybercrime." *Information Systems Control Journal*, vol. 6, 2005, pp. 1–4.

Doyle, Charles. *Cybercrime: An Overview of the Federal Computer Fraud and Abuse Statute and Related Federal Criminal Laws*. Congressional Research Service, 2010.

Holt, Thomas J., et al. *Cybercrime and Digital Forensics: An Introduction*. Routledge, 2015.

McLaurin, Joshua. "Making Cyberspace Safe for Democracy: The Challenge Posed by Denial-of-Service Attacks." *Yale Law and Policy Review*, vol. 30, no. 1, 2011, p. 11.

Schell, Bernadette H., and Clemens Martin. *Cybercrime: A Reference Handbook*. ABC-CLIO, 2004.

"17.6 Million U.S. Residents Experienced Identity Theft in 2014." *Bureau of Justice Statistics*, 27 Sept. 2015, www.bjs.gov/content/pub/press/vit14pr.cfm.

Singer, P. W., and Allan Friedman. *Cybersecurity and Cyberwar: What Everyone Needs to Know*. Oxford UP, 2014.

Wall, David. *Cybercrimes: The Transformation of Crime in the Information Age*. Polity, 2007.

"What Is Pharming?" *Kaspersky Lab*, usa.kaspersky.com/internet-security-center/definitions/pharming#.WDXNKLIrJQI.

THE CYBER INTELLIGENCE SHARING AND PROTECTION ACT

Introduction

Proposed amendments to the National Security Act of 1947, 61 Stat. 495, which currently lacks provisions on cybercrime. Cyber Intelligence Sharing and Protection Act (CISPA), as introduced in the US Congress, would: (1) facilitate the sharing of information relating to internet information between the US government and technology and manufacturing companies and remove obstacles to such sharing; and (2) enhance the US government's ability to investigate cyberthreats and ensure the security of networks against cyberattacks. Privacy advocates opposed the bill all three times it was introduced citing privacy concerns.

CISPA defines "cyber threat intelligence" as "information in the possession of an element of the intelligence community directly pertaining to a vulnerability of, or threat to, a system or network of a government or private entity, including information pertaining to the protection of a system or network from either "efforts to degrade, disrupt, or destroy such system or network."

Much of CISPA focused on information sharing between agencies. CISPA authorizes the Director of National Intelligence to issue rules and regulations that would allow intelligence agencies to share cyberthreat intelligence with private-sector entities and encourage the sharing of such intelligence.

Background

Effective and efficient information sharing in the name of cybersecurity is crucial for protecting information systems from unauthorized access. Commentators have argued that undue barriers to information sharing on threats, attacks, and vulnerabilities is a significant weakness to effective cybersecurity, especially regarding critical infrastructure, such as the financial system and the electric grid.

Private-sector entities have stated that they are reluctant to share such information among themselves because of issues including legal liability, potential misuse of information, such as trade secrets and other proprietary information. Perceived barriers to sharing with the government include concerns about risks of disclosure and the ways governments might use the information it receives.

The provision on information sharing, however, gave rise to serious privacy and civil liberties. The issues, in this case, involve understanding the risks to privacy rights and civil liberties of individual citizens associated with sharing different types of cybersecurity information, and what are the best ways to protect these rights.

Privacy Concerns and Big Data

Privacy concerns, especially those related to the protection of personal and proprietary information and uses of shared information, endangered the bill

from the beginning. Although the legislation had provisions that sought to reduce risks of inappropriate sharing and misuse of such information, some observers argued that privacy-related information is seldom required in sharing cybersecurity information, suggesting that privacy concerns may be limited and relatively easy to address.

Various factors made the process more complicated, including potential impacts of advances in data analytic capabilities (which is commonly known as "big data"). A presidential advisory panel reported that "By data mining and other kinds of analytics, nonobvious and sometimes private information can be derived from data that, at the time of their collection, seemed to raise no, or only manageable, privacy issues." There are many potential sources, unrelated to the information-sharing activities addressed in the bills, from which an individual's personal information in cyberspace could be identified and acquired by various entities.

While CISPA opponents acknowledged that certain national security threats are genuine, also stressed the need to balance security concerns with those of individual privacy. Several security experts, engineers and other industry experts told Congress, expressed strong concern for national security, but added that, effective computer and network security does not mean that internet users should have to surrender their liberties. They argued, then, not whether internet security should be improved or better monitored, but rather, that the original CISPA bill lacked sufficient privacy protections for those it seeks to protect.

For example, the bill was prefaced with "Notwithstanding any other provision of law," which suggested to some privacy advocates that CISPA was intended to abolish or limit privacy protections or limitations on government access to private or personal information. Additionally, another section grants immunity to private entities for sharing information that would have previously required a warrant. This provision would protect parties liable for the sharing of network data (this was one of issues in the AT&T wiretapping incident in 2006). While CISPA does not explicitly legalize warrantless wiretapping such as that in the AT&T incident, it appears to allow private companies such as AT&T to share that same type of data with the government without liability. The legislation also explicitly limits oversight, stating that any information shared with a federal agency, is not required to comply with the Freedom of Information Act (FOIA), 80 Stat. 250 (1967).

CISPA was criticized by several internet privacy and civil liberties, such as the Electronic Frontier Foundation, the American Civil Liberties Union (ACLU), as well as various conservative and libertarian groups including the TechFreedom, FreedomWorks, and the American Conservative Union. These groups argue CISPA inadequately restricted the government regarding how and when the government would be allowed monitor a private individual's internet browsing information. Additionally, they expressed concerns that as such the government would use its powers under the act for general surveillance on Americans, rather than to pursue hackers.

Some critics argued that provisions included in CISPA were another attempt to protect intellectual property after Congress stopped action on the Stop Online Piracy Act in the face of opposition to that legislation. At first, provisions on the theft of intellectual property were included in the bill as possible justifications for sharing web traffic information with the government. These provisions, however, were struck from subsequent drafts.

Promoted to enhance network security, privacy advocates expressed concerns that CISPA was overly vague and would erode individual privacy rights. Some critics of the bill claimed that if CISPA passed, private sector companies could engage in surveillance on the electronic communications of millions of internet users and then share this information with the government with no oversight. They criticized the fact that no guidelines were developed for companies on the scope of data to be collected and transferred. Further, they were concerned that the bill offers companies broad immunities if they act in good faith, granting them exemption from liability for all decisions made based on cyberthreat information—a term the bill did not adequately define.

In addition to civil liberty groups, the Obama administration opposed the legislation, and criticized CISPA, asserting that any cybersecurity bill "must include robust safeguards to preserve the privacy and civil liberties of our citizens." The administration further said it would oppose any bill that would "sacrifice the privacy of our citizens in the name of security."

Due to strong opposition to CISPA, the cosponsors offered to amend the bill to address many privacy-related concerns, including limiting the bill's coverage to more restricted types of cyberthreats, and stating that the theft of intellectual property refers to the theft of research and development. Also, the bill was amended to impose fines if private companies or the government misappropriates data from CISPA for purposes not related to cyberthreats.

Privacy advocates, however, were not appeased. Many of them argued that the proposed amendments fell short in remedying the civil liberties threats posed by the bill. They continued to oppose CISPA. Rainey Reitman, of the Electronic Frontier Foundation (EFF), claimed that the bill's sponsors dismissed serious concerns on how the bill could adversely affect the privacy rights of internet users. While acknowledging that some positive changes were made to the legislation, Kendall Burman of the Center for Democracy and Technology (CDT) said that none of the changes reached addressed the core privacy concerns of privacy advocacy groups. The CDT and other privacy rights groups actively opposed CISPA and supported a competing House bill sponsored by Rep. Dan Lungren (R-CA).

In opposing CISPA, the ACLU said it "would create a cybersecurity exception to all privacy laws and allow companies to share the private and personal data they hold on their American customers with the government for cybersecurity purposes.... Beyond the potential for massive data collection authorization, the bill would provide no meaningful oversight of, or accountability for, the use of these new information-sharing authorities."

CISPA also faced opposition from conservative groups such as the American Conservative Union because they believed that the legislation would greatly increase federal power, interfere with free enterprise, and harm US competitiveness.

Media groups such as Reporters Without Borders opposed the legislation, arguing that in the name of fighting cybercrime, CISPA would authorize the government and private companies to use harsh measures to monitor and perhaps censor internet traffic. The group also suggested that the government would be granted the power to shut sites that publish classified files or information.

—Jane E. Kirtley

References

Chander, Anupam. *Securing Privacy in the Internet Age.* Stanford Law Books, 2008.

Kostopoulos, George K. *Cyberspace and Cybersecurity.* CRC Press, 2013.

Lee, Newton. *Counterterrorism and Cybersecurity: Total Information Awareness.* Springer, 2013.

CYBER MONDAY

Cyber Monday is the onine retail version of Black Friday; both take place after Thanksgiving. Photo via iStock/ MicroStockHub. [Used under license.]

Introduction

An integral part of the holiday shopping season, Cyber Monday occurs on the Monday immediately following Thanksgiving. Like Black Friday (the day after Thanksgiving), Cyber Monday is touted as a critical shopping day for consumers to take advantage of purportedly extraordinary sales and deep discounts on merchandise. However, whereas Black Friday's sales are offered to customers in-person at retail establishments, Cyber Monday's sales are exclusively available online through merchants' websites. Due to the proliferation of the internet, widespread access to home computers and smartphones, and the preference of some customers to avoid the frenetic and sometimes confrontational nature of shopping in person on Black Friday, sales on Cyber Monday have dramatically increased over the course of its relatively short history.

Background

Cyber Monday is relatively new compared to Black Friday. Although debate surrounds the exact origins of the term "Black Friday," the earliest attested use of the term was in the 1950s, and may have been originally used by police in Philadelphia to describe the traffic jams accompanying the start of the shopping season. An alternate explanation holds that it was the day on which retailers began to show a profit, from the accounting tradition of recording profits in black ink and losses in red, but though officially sanctioned, this version of the term's origin is considered less likely. On the other hand, Cyber Monday's origins are much clearer. Marketers at the National Retail Federation coined the term in 2005 in effort to brand the Monday following Black Friday, which had seen an increase in online purchases in previous years. Some experts credited this surge in online sales on this particular Monday as reflecting employees who were at work, but still found themselves in the mood to shop.

Efforts to establish Cyber Monday as a major retail event have succeeded tremendously. In 2005, the first officially designated Cyber Monday brought in sales revenue totaling nearly $500 million. In 2013, Cyber Monday purchases exceeded $2 billion. Financial experts estimate that more than 180 million customers now buy merchandise on Cyber Monday. In 2015, the total revenue of Cyber Monday sales passed the $3 billion mark, setting a new record and exceeding even the most optimistic predictions for the year. Numerous retailers, such as Target, Walmart, JCPenney, and Kohl's, among many others, now announce their Cyber Monday deals months in advance to entice customers. On November 28, 2017, Adobe Analytics, which tracks online transactions, reported that that year's Cyber Monday (which fell on November 27) had been the biggest online shopping day in US history, with online purchases totaling a record $6.59 billion—a 16.8 percent increase over the previous year.

Financial analysts debate whether, from a customer's standpoint, it is more advantageous to shop in person on Black Friday or online on Cyber Monday. Many experts seem to agree that there are pros and cons to each, with the answer often varying depending on what type of products the customer intends to purchase. Black Friday offers much larger discounts to customers on electronics such as televisions, video games and gaming systems, digital cameras, and computer goods; however, there is often a much more limited number of these highly valued items in a store's inventory. These items sell out quickly, sometimes resulting in short-tempered customers fighting with one another to procure this discounted merchandise.

For example, on Black Friday in 2011, a woman used pepper spray on customers who attempted to wrest an Xbox system from her two sons at a Los Angeles Walmart. Supporters of Black Friday also claim that the adrenaline rush that shoppers often feel when waiting for the doors to open at stores on Black Friday is a powerful emotional experience whose excitement cannot be replicated when shopping online. On the other hand, advocates for Cyber Monday point out that, generally speaking, ordering clothing and shoes on Cyber Monday offers greater savings than can be gained by purchasing these items on Black Friday. Moreover, proponents of Cyber Monday assert that shopping online offers many more options for customers than does in-person shopping on Black Friday; customers are able to peruse multiple retailers' stocks of merchandise and then make their selections, rather than feel rushed or compelled to make impulsive purchases on Black Friday due to the tremendous volume of other customers eager to get their hands on deals.

—*Justin D. García*

References

Bonebright, Marcy. "Thanksgiving vs. Black Friday vs. Cyber Monday: What to Buy Each Day." *The Christian Science Monitor*, 7 Nov. 2015, www.csmonitor.com/Business/Saving-Money/2015/1107/Thanksgiving-vs.-Black-Friday-vs.-Cyber-Monday-what-to-buy-each-day.

Geddes, James. "The Short History of Cyber Monday Is Still Being Written." *Tech Times*, 30 Nov. 2015, www.techtimes.com/articles/111779/20151130/the-short-history-of-cyber-monday-is-still-being-written.htm.

Gustafson, Krystina. "Cyber Monday Sales Top $3 Billion, Beat Forecast." *CNBC*, 1 Dec. 2015, www.cnbc.com/2015/12/01/cyber-monday-sales-top-3-billion-beat-forecast.html.

Masunaga, Samantha. "Cyber Monday Sales on Record Pace to Crack $3 Billion." *Los Angeles Times*, 30 Nov. 2015, www.latimes.com/business/la-fi-cyber-monday-numbers-20151130-htmlstory.html.

Pruitt, Sarah. "What's the Real History of Black Friday?" *History*. A+E Networks, 24 Nov. 2015, www.history.com/news/whats-the-real-history-of-black-friday.

Rao, Leena. "Cyber Monday Is the Biggest Online Sales Day Ever." *Fortune*, 1 Dec. 2015, fortune.com/2015/11/30/record-cyber-monday/.

Thomas, Lauren. "Cyber Monday Becomes Largest Online Shopping Day in US History." *CNBC*, 28 Nov. 2017, www.cnbc.com/2017/11/28/a-record-6-point-59-billion-spent-online-on-cyber-monday-making-us-history.html.

CYBERSECURITY

Introduction

By the late 1990s the internet dominated the global communication landscape. In 1993, only about 1 percent of telecommunications networks sent information over the internet, but by 2000 over 51 percent of these networks did. By 2007 the internet conveyed over 97 percent of telecommunications information. The internet continues to grow in the twenty-first century, propelled by massive amounts of online information, commerce, entertainment, and social networking.

Cyberspace is a key aspect of contemporary life, with broadband signals, wireless networks, local networks in schools and businesses, and heavy use of the power grid to support millions of computers, tablets, and cell phones. The military and intelligence networks protecting the United States depend on the internet for their operations, which is now a permanent, key feature of most countries' communications networks. Cybercriminals have grown as sophisticated as the computer systems worldwide, and the United States and the major countries of the world are joining forces to stop them.

Background

Cyberattacks are as old as the internet. Some accounts state that Steve Wozniak and Steve Jobs, the founders of Apple Computer, were originally "phone phreaks" in the 1970s who hacked computerized telephone systems so they could make free long-distance calls. The Federal Bureau of Investigation (FBI) named hacker Kevin Mitnick a top target in the late 1990s when he broke into academic and corporate computer systems and caused millions of dollars in damage. Virus creators have produced increasingly more sophisticated and harmful computer viruses, morphing from the relatively harmless "Melissa" and "I Love You" viruses of the late 1990s and early 2000s to the Stuxnet virus of 2009, which was designed to damage Iran's uranium enrichment facility. Viruses and other cyberthreats, such as identity theft, have fostered the multibillion-dollar security software industry.

A major form of hacking called denial of service (DoS) is designed to paralyze websites, financial networks, and computer systems by flooding them with data from outside computers. A fifteen-year-old Canadian boy orchestrated the first documented DoS attack in 2000 against several e-commerce sites, including eBay and Amazon, shutting some down and disrupting others at an estimated cost of $1.7 billion dollars.

Computer hackers and thieves have increasingly targeted government and private web networks in the United States. In 2006, the Pentagon reported six million attempts to break into its networks. This number has increased yearly, including a successful attempt supposedly originating in China to hack into the $300-billion-dollar Joint Strike Fighter project and copy data about its design and electronics systems. According to computer experts, computer criminals in China and Russia have infiltrated the US electrical grid by installing software capable of damaging it at any time.

Shortly after taking office in 2009, President Barack Obama named cybersecurity as a serious economic and national security challenge and ordered a review of government efforts to defend US information and communications systems. Obama accepted the recommendations of the Cyberspace Policy Review, which included appointing a high-level Cyber Security Coordinator. The Executive Branch of the government also vowed to work closely with US cybersecurity experts in state and local governments and the private sector. Their goal is to provide an organized and unified response to future cyberthreats, to strengthen public and private partnerships, find technological solutions to enhance US security and prosperity, and invest in the cutting-edge research and development. The Cyberspace Policy Review also called for a campaign to promote cybersecurity awareness and digital literacy from boardrooms to classrooms and to improve the twenty-first century digital workforce. Obama stated that cyberpolicy be created and implemented in a way consistent with enduring the privacy rights and civil liberties guaranteed to all Americans in the Constitution.

Following the Cyber Security Policy Review's mandate, the Department of Homeland Security (DHS) coordinated the interagency, state, and local government and private sector working groups to improve the cooperation between agencies and international partners during cyberattacks. In October 2009, the DHS launched the National Cyber Security and Communications Integration Center, a twenty-four-hour watch and warning center and the country's principal hub for organizing cyberresponse efforts and maintaining a comprehensive national picture.

In 2010, the DHS and the Department of Defense signed an agreement to cooperate to counter threats to critical military and civilian computer systems and networks. The agreement embedded Department of Defense cyberanalysts within the DHS and DHS personnel within the Department of Defense's National Security Agency.

Led by its US Computer Emergency Readiness Team (US-CERT), the DHS also forged vital partnerships with antivirus companies to develop and share threat potential, prevention, mitigation, and response information products. In 2011, US-CERT responded to more than 106,000 cybersecurity threats and released more than 5,000 viable cybersecurity alerts to public and private sector partners.

—Kathy Warnes

References

Amoroso, Edward. *Cyber Security.* Silicon Press, 2006.

Betz, David J., and Timothy C. Stevens. *Cyberspace and the State: Towards a Strategy for Cyberpower.* Routledge, 2012.

Brenner, Joel. *America the Vulnerable: Inside the New Threat Matrix of Digital Espionage, Crime, and Warfare.* Penguin, 2011.

Britz, Marjie T. *Computer Forensics and Cyber Crime: An Introduction.* 2nd ed., Prentice, 2008.

Burns, Nicholas, Jonathon Price, and Joseph S. Nye, Jr. *Securing Cyberspace: A New Domain for National Security.* Aspen Institute, 2012.

Casey, Eoghan. *Digital Evidence and Computer Crime: Forensic Science, Computers, and the Internet.* 3rd ed., Academic, 2011.

Dunn Cavelty, Myriam. "Breaking the Cyber-Security Dilemma: Aligning Security Needs and Removing Vulnerabilities." *Science & Engineering Ethics,* vol. 20, no. 3, 2014, pp. 701–15.

Hunter, Philip. "Cyber Security's New Hard Line." *Engineering & Technology,* vol. 8, no. 8, 2013, pp. 68–71.

Morozov, Evgeny. *The Net Delusion: The Dark Side of internet Freedom.* PublicAffairs, 2012.

Poulsen, Kevin. *Kingpin: How One Hacker Took Over the Billion-Dollar Cybercrime Underground.* Broadway, 2011.

Schmitt, Michael N. "The Law of Cyber Warfare: Quo Vadis?" *Stanford Law & Policy Review,* vol. 25, no. 2, 2014, pp. 269–99.

Stamp, Mark. *Information Security: Principles and Practice.* Wiley, 2011.

CYBERSTALKING

Introduction

Harassing or threatening behavior that one individual engages in repeatedly against another is referred to as either physical stalking or cyberstalking. Both physical stalking and cyberstalking may or may not be accompanied by a "credible threat of serious harm," depending on the facts of the case. Both types of stalking are intended to control or intimidate the victim through instilling fear, stress, and/or anxiety. Both the physical stalker and the cyberstalker intend to cause psychological harm and distress to the victim. Both types of stalking have the potential to escalate and lead to the stalker assaulting and/or killing the victim. Cyberstalking may even result in physical stalking.

Background

The National Institute of Justice describes physical stalking as a series of actions by the stalker against a particular person, which includes repeated instances of the stalker seeking visual or physical proximity to the victim; nonconsensual communication; or verbal, written, or implied threats or a combination

of such acts, which would instill fear in a reasonable person. Physical stalking involves repeated harassing or threatening behavior, such as following a person, appearing at one's house or work, sending written messages or objects, or vandalizing another person's property.

In 2012, the US Department of Justice (DOJ) reported that an estimated 1.5 percent of persons age eighteen or older were stalking victims. Individuals who were divorced or separated are at the greatest risk of being stalked compared to those who are married, never married, or widowed. While more females were stalked than males, females and males were equally likely to experience harassment. Men reported stalking incidents as often as women. Those less than thirty-five years old were more likely to be stalked than older people.

According to the Privacy Rights Clearinghouse, most victims know their stalker. Slightly more than 30 percent of stalking offenders are a known, intimate partner: a current or former spouse, a cohabiting partner, or a date. Approximately 45 percent of stalking offenders are acquaintances other than intimate partners. Just under 10 percent of all stalkers are strangers. In approximately 15 percent of stalking cases, the victim does not know the identity of the stalker and thus cannot report whether he or she might be an intimate partner, acquaintance, or stranger.

Stalking victims may be forced to resort to changing a phone number, moving, replacing damaged property, obtaining a restraining order, and/or testifying in court. In the 2012 DOJ report, almost 13 percent had to take time off from work to deal with their cases. Over 100,000 victims reported that they had been terminated from or had been asked to

Cyberstalking uses electronic communications to harass or threaten someone with physical harm. Photo via iStock/ MacXever. [Used under license.]

leave their jobs because they were being stalked. Stalkers may also commit identity theft against victims, including opening or closing accounts, removing money from accounts, or charging purchases to a victim's credit card.

Cyberstalking

The internet has proven to be a highly efficient way for stalkers to intimidate, terrorize, and harm their victims. Cyberstalking is the repeated use of an electronic or internet-capable device to pursue or harass an individual or group of people. Cyberstalking is viewed as the most dangerous type of internet harassment because of a credible threat of harm to the victim. Some of the key differences between physical and cyberstalking are that, with the latter, (1) a message communicated online can be sent to anyone with internet access, is present immediately, and cannot be taken back or deleted; (2) the stalker could be anywhere in the world; (3) the stalker may easily impersonate another individual to communicate with the victim; and (4) the stalker may use third parties to contact or communicate with the victim.

Cyberharassment differs from cyberstalking because the former does not usually involve a credible threat. Examples of cyberharassment include sending threatening or harassing email messages, instant messages, or blog entries or websites that are intended to harass a specific person.

Cyberstalkers post messages on various sites using the victim's personal information, including home address, phone number, and/or Social Security number. These posts are often lewd or intended to be embarrassing, and result in the victim receiving several emails, calls, or visits from individuals who read the online posts. The cyberstalkers also sign up for several online mailing lists and services using a victim's personal information.

Stalkers abuse the anonymity provided by the internet to harass their victims. Because the identity of the stalker is often unknown to the victim, the victim often becomes more fearful. Cyberstalking is difficult to curtail and prosecute because the stalker could be far removed or very close to the victim. Because of the internet's anonymity, it is difficult to verify a stalker's identity, gather the necessary evidence for an arrest and trace the cyberstalker to a physical location.

Stalkers almost always stalk someone they know or believe they know, as is the case with stalkers of celebrities or other public persons. While stalkers believe they know the celebrity, the celebrity most often does not know a stalker. One drawback of being a celebrity or public figure is having to deal with stalkers, who could be obsessed fans.

Corporate cyberstalking is when a company harasses a person online, or an individual or group of people harasses an organization. Corporate cyberstalking could be motivated by ideology, greed, or revenge.

Cyberstalkers are motivated by many factors: envy; pathological obsession (professional or sexual); unemployment or failures with their own job or life; the desire to intimidate and make others feel inferior; delusion, which makes the stalker believe that he or she knows the target; desire to instill fear in a person to justify the stalker's status; belief in remaining anonymous and thus getting away with it; intimidation for financial advantage or business competition; revenge over perceived or imagined rejection.

Cyberstalking evolves as technology changes. A technologically proficient cyberstalker can cause severe problems for the victim, especially because an increasing number of people use the internet to pay bills, make social connections, do their work, share ideas, and seek employment.

Cyberstalking victims should attempt to gather as much physical evidence as possible and document each contact from the perpetrator. While cyberstalking doesn't involve physical contact, it can be more dangerous than physical stalking. A proficient internet user can easily locate enough of the victim's personal information, such as phone number or place of business, to determine his or her physical location.

Social networking, through websites such as Facebook, Twitter, and LinkedIn, presents security issues for victims of stalking. A social network profile might include a victim's contact information, birthday, legal name, names of family members, and even updates on a victim's location. If a victim has a public online profile, a stalker could easily access any information posted to the social networking account, according to Privacy Clearinghouse. Even with strong privacy settings or a private profile, a stalker might be able to access a victim's account by:

- hacking the victim's bank accounts.
- creating a false profile and sending a friend request or follow request. The request may even appear to be from a known friend or family member.
- gaining access to the victim's social media accounts.

Stalking victims should consider suspending their social networking accounts until the stalking has been resolved. If the victim continues to use social networking sites, he or she should:

- use privacy settings; many social networking sites allow the user to make his or her profile completely private simply by checking a box.
- use any available security settings, including two-factor authentication; when a user enables this, the account requires another user to provide something the user knows (such as a password) that goes with something you have (such as a particular device). Therefore, if someone else obtains the password, he or she will be unable to log into the account without the specific code that the service sends to the computer.
- limit how much personal information is posted to the account, for example, the user should not include contact information, birth date, place of birth, or names of family members.
- refrain from accepting friend requests and follow requests from people he or she does not know; if the user recognizes the individual sending the request, contact him or her offline to verify that he or she sent the request.
- warn friends and acquaintances not to post personal information about the victim, especially contact information and location; the victim should also abstain from participating in activities, particularly those requesting personal information.
- refrain from posting photographs of his or her home that might indicate its location; for example, users should refrain from posting photographs showing a house number or an identifying landmark.
- be cautious when joining online organizations, groups, or fan pages.
- be cautious when connecting his or her cellphone to a social networking account.

- always use a strong, unique password for every social networking site.
- resist providing live updates on her or his location or activities.
- avoid posting information about current or future locations or providing information that a stalker may later use locate the user.

Victims most likely will be unaware that a stalker has accessed an online social networking account. Victims should post only information that would not expose them to harm if the stalker should read it. Cyberstalkers attempt to gather information about the victim. They may approach their victim's friends, family member, and work colleagues to obtain personal information. They may advertise for information on the internet or hire a private detective, and they often monitor their target's online activities and attempt to trace an internet protocol (IP) address to gather more information about their victims, and/or encourage others to harass the victim.

Cyberstalking of intimate partners includes the online harassment of a current or former romantic partner. It is a form of domestic violence, and experts say that its purpose is to control the victim by forcing social isolation and creating dependency. Harassers may send repeated insulting or threatening emails to their victims, or disrupt their victims' email use, and use the victim's account to send emails to others posing as the victim or to purchase goods or services the victim does not want. They may also use the internet to research and compile personal information about the victim and then use that information to harass him or her.

Federal Antistalking Laws

The most important federal statutes intended to deter and prosecute cyberstalking are the Interstate Stalking Act, the Interstate Communications Act, the Federal Telephone Harassment Statute, and the Protection of Children from Sexual Predators Act.

Interstate Stalking Act

President Bill Clinton signed the Interstate Stalking Act into law in 1996. That act made it a federal crime to travel across state lines with "the intent to kill, injure, harass, or place under surveillance with intent to kill, injure, harass, or intimidate another person" (18 U.S.C. 2261A). Several serious stalking cases have been prosecuted under Section 2261A, but the requirement that the stalker physically travel across state lines makes it largely inapplicable to cyberstalking cases. In addition, the travel must result in reasonable fear of death, serious bodily injury, or substantial emotional distress either to a victim or a victim's family member, spouse, or intimate partner. The act was amended in 2006 and 2013.

Section 2261A (2) makes it a federal crime to stalk another person across state, tribal, or international lines, using regular mail, email, or the internet. The stalker must have the intent to kill, injure, harass, intimidate, and/or cause substantial emotional distress, or to place a victim or a victim's family member, spouse, or intimate partner in fear of death or serious bodily injury.

Protection of Children from Sexual Predators Act

A federal statute (18 U.S.C. 2425) enacted in October 1998, it protects children against online stalking. The statute makes it a federal crime to use any means of interstate or foreign commerce (such as a telephone line or the internet) to communicate with any person with the intent to solicit or entice a child into unlawful sexual activity. While this statute provides important protections for children, it does not cover harassing phone calls to minors that do not include intent to entice or solicit the child for illicit sexual purposes.

While current federal statutes cover many instances of cyberstalking, there remain major inadequacies in federal cyberstalking law, including that the law generally applies only to direct communication between the cyberstalker and the victim. When the cyberstalker persuades other individuals to join the harassment, the current law is grossly inadequate. While a federal stalking law is in place, it applies only to interstate travel. The perpetrator must travel across state lines, which makes the law frequently inapplicable in prosecuting stalkers.

—*Jane E. Kirtley*

References

Bell, Mary Ann, and Bobby Ezell. *Cybersins and Digital Good Deeds: A Book about Technology and Ethics.* Haworth Press, 2007.

Bocij, Paul. *Cyberstalking: Harassment in the internet Age and How to Protect Your Family.* Praeger, 2004.

Curtis, George E. *The Law of Cybercrimes and Their Investigations.* CRC Press, 2012.

Cyberstalking, a New Challenge for Law Enforcement and Industry a Report from the Attorney General to the Vice President. Department of Justice, 1999.

Deibert, Ronald. "Black Code: Surveillance, Privacy, and the Dark Side of the Internet." *Internet Law & Policy,* edited by Janine Hiller and Ronnie Cohen, Prentice Hall, 2002.

Holtzman, David H. *Privacy Lost: How Technology Is Endangering Your Privacy.* Jossey-Bass, 2006.

"The Impact of Recent Cyberstalking and Cyberharassment Cases: Leading Lawyers on Navigating Privacy Guidelines and the Legal Ramifications of Online Behavior." *Cyberstalking and Cyberbullying,* edited by Samuel C. McQuade and Sarah Gentry, Chelsea House, 2012.

Reyns, Bradford W. *The Anti-social Network: Cyberstalking Victimization among College Students.* LFB Scholarly Publishing, 2012.

US Department of Justice. *1999 Report on Cyberstalking: A New Challenge for Law Enforcement & Industry.* DOJ, 1999.

Yar, Majid. *Cybercrime and Society.* SAGE, 2006.

CYBERTERRORISM

Introduction

The term "cyberterrorism" was coined in the late twentieth century to denote security threats arising from acts of sabotage perpetrated via networked computers. Determining whether or not a cyberterrorist attack has ever taken place is controversial, because scholars, politicians, and members of the media do not always agree on what constitutes cyberterrorism. However, fears about cyberterrorism reached new heights after al-Qaeda's terrorist attacks on the United States on September 11, 2001, and presidential administrations following President George W. Bush's continued to claim protecting national cybersecurity as a major priority.

Strategies concerning cybersecurity were consistently reassessed, especially after further high-profile cyberattacks such as those that occurred against the Democratic National Committee prior to the 2016 presidential election and against a crucial, large pipeline in 2021. Criminals choose to engage in cyberterrorism over traditional forms of terrorism due to its inherent anonymity, its ability to do major damage from any distance to large areas or groups simultaneously, and the fact that it is relatively easy and inexpensive to carry out.

Background

"Cyberterrorism" was coined in the 1980s by Barry Collin, a researcher at California's Institute for Security and Intelligence. Since then, two schools of thought on cyberterrorism have arisen. The first is represented by Dorothy Denning, a professor of computer science and an internationally renowned expert on information security. Denning has identified cyberterrorism as illegal and highly damaging attacks that target computers, networks, and digitally stored information for the purposes of causing harm to people or property or generating fear.

The second school of thought includes the military, government officials, and others who define cyberterrorism as virtually any cyberattack that threatens computers and networks. Myriam Dunn-Cavelty, a security information expert and the head of Switzerland's New Risks Research Unit at the Center for Security Studies, divides those who analyze cyberterrorism into "hypers"—those who believe that cyberattacks have occurred—and "de-hypers"—those who believe that no such attack has ever occurred.

The growth of personal computing in the 1990s made the World Wide Web available to individuals all over the world. Simultaneously, computer hackers began exploiting website and software security holes to gain access to information, chiefly targeting governments, banks, large corporations, academic institutions, and research centers. A 1991 report by the National Research Council and other agencies maintained in *Computers at Risk: Safe Computing in the Information Age* that cyberterrorists could wreak more havoc with a computer keyboard than with a bomb. In 2007 the Department of Homeland Security (DHS) announced that more than 840 attempts had been made to hack into DHS computers over the past two years. Most of the DHS attacks involved failed attempts to access classified information.

Those like Denning who define cyberterrorism narrowly believe that cyberterrorism should not be confused with hacktivism, the term associated with computer hackers who insist they are motivated by politics rather than maliciousness or desire for financial gain. Activities carried out by hacktivists include denial of service (DoS) attacks, email attacks, hacking into computer networks to steal information and make it public, and destroying data through viruses and worms. Many would consider the activities of WikiLeaks, the online organization founded by Australian Julian Assange that publishes secret information from anonymous sources, and Anonymous, a loose association of hackers who came to light after engaging in high-profile distributed DoS attacks, as hacktivism, not cyberterrorism.

Cyberterrorism Today

By the early twenty-first century, most nations acknowledged that the threat of cyberterrorism had become a major national security issue. Many were particularly alarmed about national power grids, which are especially vulnerable to cyberattacks and have the potential to cripple large areas if they go offline.

In a 2008 article for *Information Security Journal: A Global Perspective*, Jonathan Matusitz identifies seven types of cyberterrorist activity: destroying the machinery of an infrastructure; commandeering controls of nuclear power plants or hazardous waste facilities; using computers to control dams; hacking into power grids; using technology to commit sabotage; initiating protests that involve hacking into government computers; and compromising information illegally accessed through computers.

Incidences that are often cited as examples of cyberterrorist attacks include an incident in 1999 when the North Atlantic Treaty Organization (NATO) forces allegedly bombed the Chinese Embassy in Bombay by accident. In 2000, a Filipino man launched the so-called Love Bug virus that attacked the Pentagon, a number of government agencies, banks, and international corporations, causing millions of dollars in damages. Because the Philippines had no cyberlaws, the perpetrator walked free. That same year, a disgruntled employee hacked into a local government system in Queensland, Australia, causing 264,000 gallons of raw sewage to contaminate rivers and parks.

The cyberterrorist attack usually identified as the event that focused international attention on cyberterrorism is the Stuxnet computer worm incident of July 2010. In what came to be known as Iraq Net, Iranian computers were hacked in order to destroy plutonium enrichment plants, thus hampering the country's efforts to develop a nuclear bomb. It was rumored that the attacks were engineered through a joint effort between the United States and Israel. Allegedly, Iran responded by launching a cyberattack on US financial institutions. In 2007, the Eastern European nation of Estonia was hit with a massive DoS attack that affected government and corporate websites. Estonia blamed the Russian government, which denied responsibility.

Fears of cyberterrorism have been heightened through depictions in popular novels and movies. As early as 1983, the spotlight was turned on cyberterrorism with *WarGames*, a film in which a young hacker breaks into a US military supercomputer and sets in motion a chain of events that will start World War III. *Goldeneye*, the seventeenth James Bond film, also dealt with cyberterrorism. Novels that feature cyberterrorism include Tom Clancy's Net Force series and several works by Winn Schwartau, particularly *Pearl Harbor.com* (2002).

Efforts to pass federal legislation on cyberterrorism have typically led to partisan wrangling over increased government regulation, and Congress has repeatedly failed to pass them. On February 18, 2013, President Barack Obama responded to those failures by issuing an executive order titled "Improving Critical Infrastructure Cybersecurity," which encouraged voluntary implementation of improved computer security measures among those involved in critical infrastructures.

In November 2014 US-based Sony Pictures Entertainment suffered a cyberattack in which its computer networks were hacked. A group calling itself Guardians of Peace leaked data from Sony's computers, including embarrassing emails and personal information about its actors. The group also threatened movie theater chains that were planning to screen *The Interview*, a comedic satire about North Korea, with a September 11–style terror attack. In response, President Obama and the Federal Bureau of Investigation (FBI) blamed the attack on North Korea, which praised the cyberattack but refused to take responsibility for it. On January 2, 2015, Obama signed an executive order to impose largely symbolic sanctions on North Korean organizations and ten individuals.

National and international debate around cybersecurity next became more prominent in the lead-up to the 2016 presidential election, as it was discovered that an orchestrated cyberattack campaign had been employed by Russian hackers that had involved a breach of the Democratic National Committee's computer system as well as email accounts within Democratic candidate Hillary Clinton's campaign; other targeted attempts against some Republican politicians and organizations had also been made. The level of this cyberattack, in addition to questions regarding whether there had been any link between Republican candidate and eventual president-elect Donald Trump and the Russian interference in this democratic institution, resulted in lengthy federal investigations.

In 2018, Trump, as president, signed a bill that established a new agency, the Cybersecurity and Infrastructure Security Agency (which rebranded the former National Protection and Programs Directorate launched in 2007), to put more emphasis on and resources toward cybersecurity. Between 2020 and mid-2021, a series of major cyberattacks hit different sectors. These included the technology sector with Microsoft's announcement that its software for its Exchange Server email, used worldwide by a number of businesses, had been hacked, and the energy sector with the report that Coastal Pipeline had been compelled to shut down its pipeline responsible for transporting a significant percentage of jet fuel and gasoline across the country due to a ransomware attack on its central networks. In May 2021, President Joe Biden signed an executive order that outlined specific actions to be taken to make the country's defenses against such attacks stronger.

There is no widespread consensus on how to fight cyberterrorism, and information experts tend to agree that the United States lacks the capability of preventing all such attacks. However, most accept that basic security measures, such as implementing defense mechanisms, identifying potential cyberterrorists, eliminating known threats, and instituting international cooperation designed to mitigate damage and bring perpetrators to justice, are necessary steps in battling cyberterrorism.

—*Elizabeth Rholetter Purdy*

References

Abrams, Abigail. "Here's What We Know So Far about Russia's 2016 Meddling." *Time*, 18 Apr. 2019, time.com/5565991/russia-influence-2016-election/.

Assante, Mike. *CyberSkills Task Force Report Fall 2012*. Department of Homeland Security, 2012.

Colarik, Andrew Michael. *Cyber Terrorism: Political and Economic Implications.* IGI Global, 2006.

Collin, Barry. "The Future of Cyberterrorism." *Crime and Justice International,* vol. 13, no. 2, 1997, pp. 15–18.

Conway, Maura. "Against Cyberterrorism." *Communications of the ACM,* vol. 54, no. 2, 2011, pp. 26–28.

Denning, Dorothy. "A View of Cyberterrorism Five Years Later." *Internet Security: Hacking, Counterhacking, and Society,* edited by Kenneth Elinor Himma, Jones, 2007.

Dunn-Cavelty, Myriam. *Cyber-Security and Threat Politics: U.S. Efforts to Secure the Information Age.* Routledge, 2008.

Herbert, Lin. "A Virtual Necessity: Some Modest Steps toward Greater Cybersecurity." *Bulletin of the Atomic Scientists,* vol. 68, no. 5, 2012, pp. 75–87.

Matusitz, Jonathan. "Cyberterrorism: Postmodern State of Chaos." *Information Security Journal: A Global Perspective,* vol. 17, no. 4, 2008, pp. 179–87.

National Research Council, et al. *Computers at Risk: Safe Computing in the Information Age.* National Academy, 1991.

Ordoñez, Franco. "In Wake of Pipeline Hack, Biden Signs Executive Order on Cybersecurity." *NPR,* 12 May 2021, www.npr.org/2021/05/12/996355601/in-wake-of-pipeline-hack-biden-signs-executive-order-on-cybersecurity.

Sanger, David E., et al. "Cyberattack Forces a Shutdown of a Top U.S. Pipeline." *The New York Times,* 8 May 2021, www.nytimes.com/2021/05/08/us/politics/cyberattack-colonial-pipeline.html.

"Sony Cyber-Attack: North Korea Faces New US Sanctions." *BBC News.* BBC, 3 Jan. 2015.

Tafoya, William L. "Cyber Terror." *FBI Law Enforcement Bulletin.* FBI, n.d.

D

DARK WEB

Introduction

As the name suggests, the term dark web refers to a section of the internet that is not easily seen. People using the most common software tools and browsers to search or conduct business on the internet do not normally encounter the dark web. Although news accounts focus on the dark web's sinister aspects and controversial sites, of which there are many, some uses of and sites on this area of the internet do not fit that description.

Since communications undertaken on the dark web are not easily intercepted by any person, company, or government (hence, its use as a venue for illegal activities), any individual, government, or group not wanting others to have easy access to their communications can make use of the dark web. It does not differentiate between someone placing an order for illegal drugs or weapons and another person sending a grocery list for items to be purchased at a regular grocery store, although the former would be a much more likely use of the dark web. In addition to the dark web's common use for illegal commerce, it is also used for political ends by terrorist, revolutionary, and opposition groups desiring to evade governmental restrictions. Ironically, the initial development of many dark web tools was for all diplomatic, military, and other governmental security forces to have a secure form of electronic communication.

Background

In the mid-1960s the first long-distance, two-computer network allowed digital communications between the machines via normal telephone wires. As what eventually became known as the internet grew, advances in both the hardware and software used in the system began to allow a virtually unlimited number of computers to communicate via the web. Early in this process it was recognized that not all information should be available to every computer and user, resulting in systems of encryption being developed and put into use in the 1970s. Originally established to secure military and civilian governmental data and computer systems, private companies expanded their computer networks and needed to secure their data as well. The spread of encryption was the foundation for what is called the deep web: sites and information not available to the general user. (It is estimated that significantly less than ten percent of the World Wide Web is visible to internet users via popular browsers or search engines.) Encryption of the deep web is the foundation for internet commerce, as the encryption keeps data, such as credit card numbers, safe from those seeking to steal this type of information. However, given the type of encryption and security necessary for commerce and deep web communication, it was only a small step to strengthen the encryption and bury sites deeper, to create the dark web.

The dark web is generally seen as beginning in the 1990s with not only the explosion of internet availability and usage, but also the development of new, relatively easy-to-use, free programs for the

The dark web is only accessible with special software, allowing a greater degree of anonymity to users and transactions. Image via iStock/thomaguery. [Used under license.]

encryption and decryption of data. The two major systems/programs developed during the 1990s were Freenet and The Onion Router (TOR). Freenet was established as an alternative to the mainstream internet, as an attempt to allow uncensored, private communication among its users. The amount of security and anonymity one has depends on whether one uses the open or the darknet mode, with the latter being the most secure. For many ordinary purposes, the separation from other, larger sections of the internet makes this mode less useful, yet many users find that it meets certain needs. Nevertheless, bridges to the mainstream internet have been developed, and these tend to negate much of the security available using Freenet.

TOR was developed by the US Navy as a means for secure communication, with it becoming available to the general public in the early twenty-first century, although still partially funded by the American and Swedish governments. TOR can work within the general internet, but it strengthens its encryption by sending information through several routers/relays that encrypt/decrypt the information several times before it reaches the desired destination. Having multiple layers of encryption (hence the onion analogy in its name) makes breaking the security of any given transmission through the system, as well as finding the physical location of the sender, extremely difficult. In addition to the network aspects of TOR, it can be used to create generally inaccessible websites (which have a .onion suffix) that can only be reached using the TOR browser.

More recently, I2P has gained popularity among those attempting to avoid government surveillance, especially in light of some governmental success against selected TOR dark websites and malware released into the system. As with TOR, I2P uses multiple intermediary points where the information is encrypted and decrypted, making it difficult to intercept or locate the origin of the information. While the general internet can be reached using I2P, some functions such as email are secure only when sent between two computers that are both running I2P. As with TOR, I2P has its own section of the internet that uses the .i2p suffix.

Uses

Although most people do not think too much about it, general use of the internet results in records to which government agencies, as well as internet providers, browser owners, and operators of search engines have access. Thus, there is a small segment of people obsessed with privacy who go to the extreme of using the dark web for what most people would see as mundane purposes. They are not intentionally using the web for any illegitimate or illegal purposes; they only want complete privacy, if possible, when accessing the internet. Such users make up a relatively small portion of dark web users, yet they often complain loudly when any government or international action is contemplated regarding possible dark web restrictions.

While the deep web is an area in which many secretive yet legitimate/legal communication/data files are located, the dark web appeals to those seeking even greater security along with those seeking to conduct illicit activities. The main purpose for which the US Navy developed TOR, namely, secure communications between government entities, still exists; secure electronic communications between people in Washington, DC, and various agents of the government, whether military or civilian, is still needed and conducted on part of the dark web. Additionally, some private commercial interests have similar needs and make use of the dark web for these purposes.

Reliable statistics regarding dark web usage do not exist, and yet many experts agree that illegal, or at least illicit, activities seem to be its greatest use. This would principally be divided between politics and commerce, although there is an overlap on sites dealing with weapons or weapon technology. Terrorist groups and other extremist organizations make extensive use of the dark web for internal communications as well as recruitment. While obviously a recruitment ad on a general internet site would reach more people, it would quickly be shut down and the site owner located with relative ease. Thus, in addition to coded ads on the general internet, these organizations make more explicit information available to individuals drawn to their message on the dark web.

Dark web commerce incorporates all manner of illegal product and service offerings. Illegal drugs, almost any type of gun or tactical weapon, illegal forms of pornography, stolen goods (including numbers for credit cards, banks, or the totality of a person's ID), and other things that require the transaction being outside government surveillance are found on the dark web. Services that must be discreetly arranged, whether sexual, or a wide range of illegal or violent acts, are on dark web sites. The first iteration of Silk Road, one of the earliest large-scale dark web marketplaces, ran for about two years. It has been estimated that over $1 billion passed through the site during this period. Numerous other sites, large and small, also operated during this time with an unknown amount of money changing hands.

In addition to encryption techniques and basic legal protections such as the right to privacy, the development that has done the most to boost dark web commerce is the reliance on cryptocurrencies such as bitcoin. As with many other things associated with the dark web, cryptocurrencies are not illegal but they do make illegal transactions easier. Bitcoins, and other cryptocurrencies, can be transferred in such a manner as to conceal the identity of the sender, thus making it ideal for dark web transactions. Using markets like Silk Road has proved beneficial to both buyers and sellers, in that the market acts as a kind of intermediary entity that holds the cryptocurrency and guarantees to the seller that adequate funds are available, and then sends it to the seller once the buyer has acknowledged that the goods or service has been delivered. (The method is similar to PayPal, although the currency is different and there is no bank involved.)

Although efforts by a variety of law enforcement agencies around the world have diminished the illegal activities occurring on the dark web in recent years, human ingenuity has allowed many criminal entrepreneurs to transform their operations and continue exploiting the less well-known recesses of the internet.

—*Donald A. Watt and Nathan A. B. Watt*

References

Choudhury, Saheli Roy and Arjun Kharpal. "Beyond the Valley: A Look Inside the Mysteries of the dark web." *CNBC*, 6 Sept. 2018, www.cnbc.com/2018/09/06/beyond-the-valley-understanding-the-mysteries-of-the-dark-web.html.

Gehl, Robert W. *Weaving the Dark Web: Legitimacy on Freenet, Tor, and I2P.* (The Information Society Series). MIT Press, 2018.

Patterson, Dan. "Dark Web: A Cheat Sheet for Business Professionals." *TechRepublic*, 26 Oct. 2017, www.techrepublic.com/article/dark-web-the-smart-persons-guide/.

Porolli, Matias. "Cybercime Black Markets: Dark Web Services and Their Prices." *welivesecurity by eset*, 31 Jan. 2019, welivesecurity.com/2019/01/31/cybercrime-black-markets-dark-web-services-and-prices/.

Retzkin, Sion. *Hands-On Dark Web Analysis: Learn What Goes on in the Dark Web, and How to Work with It.* Packt Publishing, 2018.

DATA HARVESTING

Introduction

Data harvesting (also known as web harvesting, data scraping, data aggregation, or data mining) is the process of digitally compiling large amounts of information such as search results, purchasing preferences, commercial offerings, product prices, and demographic data from the internet. Data harvesting is usually done through the use of magnetic robots known as web harvesters or screen scrapers that collect data, filter inappropriate content, and present it to consumers in easy-to-use formats, such as graphs, tables, and indexes.

Businesses, banks, credit card bureaus, and even certain public-sector agencies often hire experts to design sophisticated web harvesters to collect data that is hard to retrieve manually. Indeed, most web harvesters can translate various computer languages, such as hypertext markup language (HTML), JavaScript, and PHP: Hypertext Preprocessor (PHP), among others.

Background

Experts at web harvesting are highly sought after by businesses because they can engage in data collection and data translation at warp speeds. Most web harvesters can retrieve several pages on a server simultaneously and can automatically access target websites repeatedly throughout the day. As such, web harvesting allows businesses to create reports, presentations, and profiles about individuals and groups of consumers quickly.

Because many web harvesters are quite inexpensive and can be accessed easily through a basic internet search, many individuals engage in web harvesting as well. The use of web harvesters has recently grown so much that internet users frequently interact with harvesters without even knowing that they are doing so. Common examples of web harvesters that consumers frequently come into contact with include: search engines, business advertisers, auction compilers, price aggregators, real estate listing services, financial data aggregators, financial money management applications, and social media websites. The websites that are targeted by web harvesting are usually referred to as data hosts.

Legal and Social Implications

Whether web harvesting is a socially beneficial or harmful activity often depends on the collateral damage that the web harvester causes to a data host. For example, certain web harvesters, such as price amalgamators and targeted advertisers, cause minimal or no damage to data hosts and allow businesses to match consumer needs with commercial offerings efficiently. In fact, web harvesters such as price amalgamators and targeted advertisers often benefit both consumers and data hosts because, in addition to causing the data hosts at most minimal harm, they increase the visibility of the data hosts' products and services.

Another example of a web harvester that internet users frequently interact with is a search engine. These web harvesters are almost universally lauded for the benefits they provide to end users through constant accessing of thousands of websites, pulling bits of information from these websites, and presenting the data in the form of easily readable search engine results. Search engines are also particularly useful web harvesters because they can collect archived data that is stored on a system but that can no longer be accessed due to the incompatibility of an old system or internet website with newer computer hardware or software.

On the other hand, web harvesting can also cause extensive damage to data hosts. If a web harvester is designed to overcome a technical barrier such as a password or other code barrier, the web harvester may end up undercutting a competing business's revenue, gaining access to confidential company information, or damaging the physical infrastructure of the data host. Indeed, some web harvesting has caused data hosts to suffer extensive damage, such as increased bandwidth usage, system crashes, the need to purchase anti-spam devices, the need to erect technical barriers, the need to clear up consumer confusion, and damage to reputation.

Because of some of the negative effects caused by web harvesting, it is not surprising that there have been many lawsuits involving web harvesting and data scraping in recent years. In addition to the prevalent use of web harvesters, a primary reason for these lawsuits is that many websites are poorly equipped to fend off web harvesting and want to deter web harvesters from gaining unfettered access to their data.

For example, in *eBay v. Bidder's Edge,* 100 F. Supp. 2d 1058 (N.D. Cal. 2000), a federal lawsuit that was litigated in Northern California in 2000, eBay complained that Bidder's Edge (BE) was unlawfully compiling eBay's auction listings and copying eBay's auction format on its own website without incurring any of the investment and operating costs that eBay incurs. eBay showed the court that it had unavailingly tried to block BE's data scrapers through telephonic and written communications and by trying to block BE's internet protocol (IP) addresses. The court sided with eBay and held that BE was liable for aggregating data from eBay's servers without attaining prior authorization and that BE was free-riding on the time, effort, and money that eBay had invested in its system.

A similar situation was litigated the following year in *EF Cultural Travel BV v. Explorica, Inc.,* 274 F.3d 577 (1st Cir. 2001). In this case, EF Cultural Travel BV (EF), a company that offered tour guides for groups of teenagers, complained that Explorica was unlawfully scraping information about EF's tour prices in order to undercut EF from the teenage tour market. The First Circuit sided with EF and approved an injunction against Explorica to prohibit further scraping that would be to EF's detriment.

During the 2016 US election, a major scandal involving data harvesting became headline news when a company named Cambridge Analytica harvested personal data from millions of people's Facebook profiles without their knowledge or consent. The campaigns of US Senator Ted Cruz (R-TX) and presidential candidate Donald Trump both used Cambridge Analytica's data to target their campaign efforts. Eventually, Facebook chief executive officer (CEO) Mark Zuckerberg was called to testify before Congress about the compromising of the privacy rights of over 80 million users.

Facebook was once again in the news for data harvesting in 2019, when a virtual private network (VPN) app they owned named Onavo, was revealed to actually be collecting user data rather than protecting it, which is the entire purpose of a VPN. VPNs are gateways through which users' internet traffic goes in order to protect the identity of the user. But rather than protecting the user, it was used by Facebook as a source of information concerning users' web and app use habits.

Because of the ubiquity of web harvesters, and in light of the numerous benefits that they provide, it is critical for users of web harvesters to become familiar with the laws governing web harvesting. Again, many uses of web harvesting are considered harmless to data hosts and beneficial to consumers. Such uses are unlikely to lead to legal disputes. But given that some data hosts are opposed to unknown web harvesting, it is critical for users of web harvesters to know what types of web harvesting may expose them to liability. Similarly, it is important for data hosts that are opposed to web harvesting to stay abreast of the capabilities of web harvesters so that they can erect technical barriers and other sophisticated blockades to protect their data.

—Myra Din

References

Chadwick, Paul. "How Many People Had Their Data Harvested by Cambridge Analytica?" *The Guardian*, 16 Apr. 2018. www.theguardian.com/commentisfree/2018/apr/16/how-many-people-data-cambridge-analytica-facebook.

Feldman, Brian. "Even If Facebook Stops Aggressively Collecting Data, Developers Will Still Supply It." *New York Magazine*, 22 Feb. 2019, nymag.com/intelligencer/2019/02/why-facebooks-data-collection-practice-is-so-messy.html.

Fibbe, George H. "Screen-Scraping and Harmful Cyber-trespass after Intel." *Mercer Law Review*, vol. 55, no. 1011, 2004.

Gladstone, Julia Alpert. "Data Mines and Battlefields: Looking at Financial Aggregators to Understand the Legal Boundaries and Ownership Rights in the Use of Personal Data." *Journal of Marshall Computer and Information Law*, vol. 19, no. 313, 2001.

Hirschey, Jeffrey Kenneth. "Symbiotic Relationships: Pragmatic Acceptance of Data Scraping." *Berkeley Technical Law Journal*, vol. 29, no. 897, 2014.

Rubin, Aaron. "How Website Operators Use CFAA to Combat Data-Scraping." *Law360*, www.law360.com/articles/569325?utm_source=rss&utm_medium=rss&utm_campaign=articles_search.

What Is a Screen Scraper? wiseGEEK, www.wisegeek.com/what-is-a-screen-scraper.htm.

Wierzel, Kimberly L. "If You Can't Beat Them, Join Them: Data Aggregators and Financial Institutions." *North Carolina Banking Institute*, vol. 5, no. 457, 2001.

DATA LITERACY

Introduction

Data literacy refers to the ability to access, read, understand, and effectively use data. Data, a raw form of information that may be difficult to interpret, includes numbers, letters, words, images, or any other material that contains knowledge. Individuals and organizations rely on data to conduct daily operations, make informed decisions, and perform important tasks. People who are data literate are skilled in viewing data and grasping its importance. They can then use the data themselves or translate it and communicate it into more accessible forms for use by others. Many businesses value data-literate employees and may offer training programs to help people become more proficient in data usage.

Background

Data consists of information that contains facts, figures, and other useful knowledge. People and organizations may rely on different forms of data. Individuals might use data when making purchases, while governments may use data to draft laws or set tax rates. Computers use data in the form of ones and zeroes to perform its programmed functions.

Data is essential for most modern businesses. For instance, a delivery company might maintain several sources of data to keep its operation running smoothly. It would likely need data such as inventories, pick-up points, customer addresses, available delivery vehicles, best delivery routes, and so on. This data might be transmitted verbally, digitally, on paper, in lists, on maps, or in any other fashion.

Although this large amount of data may seem overwhelming, it is necessary to gather, organize, understand, analyze, and use this data, or the company cannot run efficiently.

Defining Terms

Some people use the words "data" and "information" interchangeably. However, these concepts have an important difference. Data is a raw form of information that has not yet been processed, interpreted, or otherwise made easier for people to understand. For this reason, data can be difficult to read. It may be even harder to find the meaning of data, or use data to its maximum potential, making data literacy essential in many fields.

Data literacy refers to the ability to read, understand, and use data in a timely and efficient manner. Without proper use and interpretation, even the most important data will be meaningless. People who are data literate approach data almost like a new form of language. They understand data sources, how they work, and how they present their knowledge. These people can interpret data, decide how best to use it, and communicate it clearly to others. In this way, people who are data literate are able to translate raw data into information that could be understood by less specialized workers or laypeople.

Data can be analyzed in several ways. The first basic step in the process is the ability to ask the right questions about the data. Understanding the data that are relevant and finding ways to test that data are also fundamental in data literacy. The process requires someone to interpret the results and visually present them to others in a clear way. Data literacy also entails being able to help the decision-makers understand what the results mean so they can take the proper course of action.

—Mark Dziak

References

Bersin, Josh, and Marc Zao-Sanders. "Boost Your Team's Data Literacy." *Harvard Business Review*, 12 Feb. 2020, hbr.org/2020/02/boost-your-teams-data-literacy.

Data Literacy Project, 2021, thedataliteracyproject. org.

Herzog, David. *Data Literacy: A User's Guide.* Sage, 2015.

Knight, Michelle. "What Is Data Literacy?" *Dataversity*, 14 Oct. 2020, www.dataversity.net/what-is-data-literacy/.

Mandinach, Ellen B., and Edith S. Gummer. *Data Literacy for Educators: Making It Count in Teacher Preparation and Practice.* Teachers College P/West Ed, 2016.

Morrow, Jordan. *Be Data Literate: The Data Literacy Skills Everyone Needs to Succeed.* Kogan Page, 2021.

Panetta, Kasey. "Champion Data Literacy and Teach Data as a Second Language to Enable Data-Driven Business." *Gartner*, 6 Feb. 2019, www. gartner.com/smarterwithgartner/a-data-and-analytics-leaders-guide-to-data-literacy/.

Smalheiser, Neil R. *Data Literacy: How to Make Your Experiments Robust and Reproducible.* Academic Press, 2017.

DATA MANAGEMENT

Introduction

When thinking about managing electronic information, many people first think about an electronic analogy of conventional business processes. However, information technology also helps businesses transform their processes and perform tasks in new ways. To be effective, information systems need to manage both content and data. Content management systems manage entire documents or parts of documents.

Database management systems deal with a much finer level of granulation than content management systems. Database management systems are software programs that allow users to manage the data in a database. These systems allow users to share data, thereby cutting down on costs and improving consistency across the organization.

Background

The advent of computers and the ensuing Information Age has changed the way that many of people live their lives and do business in the twenty-first century. At home, technology cooks the TV dinner in the microwave and automatically turns on the porch lights at dusk. At the office, the ubiquitous computer workstation on the desktop allows employees to write and distribute documents and communicate not only with those across the street, but across the globe. Many tasks that were previously done by hand—writing letters, balancing the monthly books, inputting time card information—have been automated.

However, these are not just cosmetic changes that allow people to do the same things with different technology. In many cases, the very business processes that an organization uses have been transformed through the application of information technology. For example, producing a document no longer requires handwritten drafts and multiple submissions to a typing pool for changes. Today, the pencils often stay in the drawer and composition and correction of documents is done directly on the computer, bypassing the need for the secretary or typist. Further, documents no longer need to be printed out for distribution, but can be electronically transmitted to whomever needs them. Comments can be made and tracked electronically then returned electronically to the original author for coordination and finalization. Document storage and retrieval have also been made easier through technology. No longer does one have to search through piles of documents, file drawers, or dusty cardboard boxes, but one can easily retrieve documents off of a hard drive, the cloud, or other storage device.

Information technology allows organizations to do all this and more. Information technology includes the use of computers, communications networks, and knowledge in the creation, storage, and dispersal of data and information. Information technology comprises a wide range of items and abilities for use in the creation, storage, and distribution of information. Information technology can be linked together into an information system that facilitates the flow of information and data between people or departments. However, as anyone who has ever experienced a computer crash knows, these technologies are only useful to the extent that they allow one to actually retrieve the data that is stored within them.

Functions of Information Technology

Information technology has several basic functions that may occur sequentially or simultaneously. First, the information system captures data by compiling detailed records of activities for later analysis or processing. For example, data capture might include the collection of patron information and book information when a book is checked out of the library, the assignment of seats on an airplane or in a theatre, or the collection of customer information for orders taken over the internet. These data are then processed by converting, analyzing, or synthesizing them into information that can be used by the organization and its employees.

This function includes handling and transforming data into information. For example, word processing allows users to create documents and other text-based documents and image processing converts visual information such as graphics and photographs into a format that can be stored or manipulated in the information system and/or transmitted across the network. Information technology can also be used to generate data through processing by organizing data and information into a useful form such as in the generation of a document or multimedia presentation. In addition, data and information must also be stored on a computer so that they can be retrieved and processed at a later time. They can also be transmitted by information systems and distributed to other parties via a communications network.

When thinking about managing electronic information, many people first think about an electronic analogy of conventional business processes. For example, most businesses need to generate, store, and access various documents (e.g., word processing documents, spreadsheets, images, and graphics). In the past, this would be done through manual means: a document might be typed, a ledger might be handwritten and manually computed, and photographs might be available as negative or positive images. These documents would then be stored in various physical filing systems and retrieved by hand. However, information technology allows people to perform these tasks using computers and other mobile devices. Information also allows the electronic storage and retrieval of these items. These processes are handled by electronic document management systems that track and store electronic documents and/or images of paper documents or by content management systems that allows users to manage the content of a collection of data including computer files, audio files, graphics and images, electronic documents, and web content.

Data Management Systems vs. Content Management Systems

In addition to managing documents, most information systems also have data that need to be managed. Data management systems allow the management of the data housed in an information system at a more granular level. There are a number of parameters on which data management systems and content management systems differ. Content management systems manage items on a high level and are used both as electronic repositories for operational data and as archives for long-term data storage. Historically, these tasks were performed using a library (card catalogs, for example, are a nonelectronic type of content management system) or filing cabinet or system. The goal of content management systems is to respond to user queries by identifying documents that may contain information of interest and presenting a list of these documents to the user. This information is readable and accessible by humans and includes various documents such as files used for business that are primarily text or image-based. An example of an item managed by a content management system would be a document such as a memo or report that contains text, photos, or graphics that humans can understand without further processing. Major users of content management systems include industries that need to be able to access documents. For example, the insurance industry needs to keep various documents on file such as policies, claims, reports, and photos of damage. To perform their tasks, content management systems rely on metadata that enable them to track documents. Examples of metadata include key words, titles, and time stamp information that allow the system to track the documents.

Content management systems manage entire documents or parts of documents. Data management systems, on the other hand, deal with a much finer level of granulation than content management systems. In fact, data management systems deal with individual data values, not of value on their own to most humans, but which are heavily computational. These values are analogous not to something stored in the stacks of a library or in a file cabinet, but to those that are contained in a ledger. In fact, industries such as banking that previously did much of their record keeping in the form of ledgers rather than text documents are the primary users of data management systems. Examples of the kinds of data

managed in these systems are account codes, names, shipment dates, and balance in formation. The data tend to be short (e.g., numbers, dates, short character strings) and do not include much natural language or rich-media data. This type of data is used in applications such as automatic teller machines or point-of-sales devices in retail stores. As opposed to documents and other content, data are used by software applications programs or by information technology specialists. The level of granularity of a data management system is much finer than that of a content management system.

There are other differences between content management and data management as well. Content management is used to archive and retrieve information whereas data management is used to analyze or otherwise manipulate data. Content searches are parametric and text-based, and are used to find documents. Data searches, on the other hand, are primarily parametric and are used to find data values. Reflecting the differences in the users and use, there are also differences in how content and data managements systems' effectiveness is judged. Content management systems are rated by how quickly they respond to user requests. Because these systems need to deal with large volumes of unstructured data, transaction time can be relatively long compared to that of data management systems.

The performance of data management systems, on the other hand, is evaluated by its throughput (e.g., how many transactions or queries they can handle per second). The size of the two types of systems also differs. Content management systems can deal with data sets on the order of petabytes. This larger size is needed because the content management system needs more than the simple tabulated format and must maintain various relationships. Data management systems, on the other hand, do not have this requirement and typically deal with data sets that are on the order of terabytes.

Range and Purpose of Data

Organizations acquire and use a wide range of data for various purposes. For example, it may collect and store identifying information about its customers (e.g., name, address, phone number, account number) as well as other attributes (e.g., account balance, customer status). Frequently, these data are shared between users in the organization. For example, the billing department may need this information in order to send out a monthly statement. The accounting department may need the same data in order to track whether or not the bill was paid. The marketing department may use these data to distribute catalogs or other sales literature. Although each department could have its own database that housed only the information that it needed for its interactions with the customer, many of the data items are used by more than one department. As capturing, storing, and maintaining data in a database can be expensive, a company can save money by using a shared database rather than separate databases. In addition, sharing data means that everyone is working off the same data set. This practice will also ensure more consistency and everyone who needs access to the data will have the information that s/he needs.

However, not everyone in the organization will need the same data from the database. For example, although the accounting department may need to know the status of a customer's account, the marketing department may not. In addition, even when multiple people or departments need the same data, they frequently need it organized in different ways. Although both accounting and billing may need the same inputs, the latter will need the information generated in the form of a bill or invoice whereas the former will not.

Database Management Systems

Database management systems are software programs that allow users to manage the data in a database. Database management systems are designed to increase the accessibility of data and the productivity of the user. Database management systems work in tangent with other programs on the information system, maintaining the structure of the data and working with the other programs so that the data can be located and retrieved. Database management systems also accept new data from application programs and write these into the appropriate storage location on the system.

There are five functions to database management systems. First, database management systems integrate databases to provide the information required to solve problems or perform operations. Second, database management systems reduce data redundancy across the various databases so that a datum need only be stored in the system in one

location rather than in multiple locations. Third, database management systems enable the information system to give access to and share information between employees at various locations. Fourth, database management maintains the integrity of the various databases by controlling access to data, providing security, and ensuring that data are available when they are needed. Finally, database management systems help databases evolve so that they continue to meet the needs of their users.

—*Ruth A. Wienclaw*

References

Biesdorf, S., D. Court, and P. Willmott. "Big Data: What's Your Plan?" *Mckinsey Quarterly*, vol. 2, 2013, pp. 40–51.

Drnevich, P. L., and D. C. Croson. "Information Technology and Business-Level Strategy: Toward an Integrated Theoretical Perspective." *MIS Quarterly*, vol. 37, no. 2, 2013, pp. 483–509.

Francalanci, C., and V. Piuri. "Designing Information Technology Architectures: A Cost-Oriented Methodology." *Journal of Information Technology*, vol. 14, no. 2, 1999, pp. 181–92.

Helland, P. "If You Have Too Much Data, then 'Good Enough' Is Good Enough." *Communications of the ACM*, vol. 54, no. 6, 2011, pp. 40–47.

Mackie, M. "Proven Practices for Content Management." *KM World*, vol. 22, no. 7, 2013, pp. S3–S4.

Marchand, D. A., and J. Peppard. "Why IT Fumbles Analytics." *Harvard Business Review*, vol. 91, no. 1, 2013, pp. 104–12.

Senn, J. A. *Information Technology: Principles, Practices, Opportunities*. 3rd ed., Pearson, 2004.

Somani, A., D. Choy, and J. C. Kleewein. "Bringing Together Content and Data Management Systems: Challenges and Opportunities." *IBM Systems Journal*, vol. 41, no. 4, 2002, pp. 686–96.

Rahman, N. "Refreshing Data Warehouses with Near Real-Time Updates." *Journal of Computer Information Systems*, vol. 47, no. 3, 2007, pp. 71–80.

Winer, L. R., and M. A. Carrère. "Qualitative Information System for Data Management." *Qualitative Sociology*, vol. 14, no. 3, 1991, pp. 245–62.

DATA PROTECTION

Introduction

Globally, there are two broad approaches taken to protect personal information. One may be generally described as sectoral in nature: There are various legislative regimes that create standards and rules in discrete areas of the economy. Beyond those areas, privacy protection is left purely to the free market: If people desire privacy, then they can (in theory) pay for it. Different jurisdictions regulate different areas, and at different levels of protection.

The United States, for instance, has legislated privacy protections in various areas—including, but not limited to, telecommunications, health information, credit reporting, and websites aimed at children—but there is little consistency as to the kind of privacy protection offered in each area. Vietnam has also adopted a sectoral approach, choosing to regulate only e-commerce and consumer transactions. India goes further into this realm, having no data privacy regulation whatsoever. Proponents of a sectoral or free-market approach argue that excessive privacy laws impose costs on business and are therefore a threat to technological innovation and economic growth.

But the sectoral model is a global outlier. Critics argue that it leaves gaps in the law and creates confusing inconsistencies. Leaving privacy protections to the free market in those gaps is ineffective since there are great disparities in bargaining power between individuals and large organizations that seek to profit off their personal information. As a result, the approach adopted by much of the rest of the world is to legislate a single data protection regime applicable to all organizations that seek to collect, use, or disclose personal information. Broad state involvement through data protection regimes is justified because privacy is understood as a human right connected to individuality, dignity, and autonomy; while there may be economic costs to robust privacy rights, they are justified because of the values at play.

Background

The origin of comprehensive data protection regimes may be found in the 1980 Organisation for Economic Co-operation and Development (OECD) Privacy Guidelines, the core of which was the adoption of eight "fair information practice principles" (FIPPS) intended to give direction to the collection, use, and disclosure of personal information. Though having jointly developed the OECD Guidelines, the United States and Europe went in two different directions regarding their applicability in the years that followed.

The United States saw them as a framework of useful guidelines that could be freely adopted by industry if they so choose, while in Europe they were gradually strengthened and made directly enforceable. This strengthening culminated in the passage of the EU (European Union) Data Protection Directive. In one form or another, an enforceable version of the FIPPS can be found in all other modern data protection regimes, such as Canada's Personal Information & Protection of Electronic Documents Act, Hong Kong's Personal Data (Privacy) Ordinance, South Africa's Protection of Personal Information Act, and so on.

Because of this common ideological heritage, data protection regimes typically share some general features. These include a usually wide definition of "personal information" (such as any information that can lead to an identifiable individual) and of activities that count as "data processing" (both manual and automatic). Data protection regimes place a heavy emphasis on the knowledge of and/or consent to collection of personal information by the data subject and a strict limitation on the purposes to which collected information can be put. In other words, an individual must generally be informed at the time of collection of her or his information as to the purpose of the collection, and any new purpose must receive new consent.

Theory and Practice

Generally speaking, under a data protection regime, *all* organizations that collect, use, or disclose personal information will be subject to the same rules; this is in clear contrast to the sectoral approach. Some jurisdictions, however, may choose to have two separate regimes for public and private organizations. Likewise, while all data protection regimes grant exemptions for data processing or collection in specified areas such as journalism, statistical research, or public security, only some may grant exemptions to all noncommercial or personal use of information. Finally, while the definition of "personal information" tends to be broad, some regimes treat certain classes of information as particularly sensitive (e.g., medical information, financial records, and political opinions) and thus deserving of additional protections, while others do not.

Data protection regimes are also typically supervised by an independent commissioner, though the exact power of that commissioner may vary. Canada's Privacy Commissioner, for instance, lacks the power to issue fines directly to violators of the relevant law, while under the EU General Data Protection Regulation (adopted in 2016 and implemented in 2018) national data protection authorities are granted the power to issue sanctions to organizations found to be in noncompliance of up to 2 percent of their worldwide turnover. Beyond sanctioning, other powers that may vary across regimes include the possibility of an independent lawsuit absent public complaint, compelling reporting of data breaches, strength of independence from government, and so on.

Further, shared features most data protection regimes include a right of individual access to information held about them, and the right to seek erasure or correction of information where it is incorrect. However, differing interpretations of this basic principle (drawn from the FIPPS) can be found in the recent discussion over the right to be forgotten—whether individuals can request online sources to remove information about them. Interpretation of the Data Protection Directive by the European Court of Justice has found such a right to exist.

In *Google Spain v. Gonzalez* (2014), the Court found that existing provisions that granted the data subject the right to erasure of irrelevant data could support the right to be forgotten and required the well-known search engine to delete links to a news story regarding the complainant's financial difficulties from some fifteen years prior. The current General Data Protection Regulation explicitly recognizes and expands the application of this right. But no other jurisdiction with data protection regimes has yet announced any intention to introduce similar amendments or recognized such a right in its courts, arguing that as long as the information is true, forcing its deletion is incompatible with the right to free expression.

Indeed, the debate over the right to be forgotten is indicative of a new set of challenges that data protection regimes face. The FIPPS were developed in the 1970s in response to a particular set of privacy issues relevant at the time. In 2019, we live in age of "always-on" internet-connected devices that are carried voluntarily in our pockets, and an economy the lifeblood of which is information. There are thus disputes about whether data protection regimes can be adapted (or need to be adapted) to respond to these changes. In the coming years, we may a split within data protection regimes over some of these issues, just as the 1980s saw a split between interpreting the FIPPS as "useful guidelines" (the free market/sectoral approach) and as the basis for directly enforceable laws (the data protection regime approach).

—*Stuart A. Hargreaves*

References

Bygrave, Lee A. "The Place of Privacy in Data Protection Laws." *University of New South Wales Law Journal*, vol. 24, no. 1, 2001, pp. 277–83.

___. *Data Privacy Law, an International Perspective.* Oxford UP, 2014.

Cate, Fred. "The Changing Face of Privacy Protections in the European Union and the United States." *Indiana Law Review*, vol. 33, 1999, pp. 173–232.

Koops, Bert-Jaap. "The Trouble with European Data Protection Law." *International Data Privacy Law*, vol. 4, no. 4, 2014, pp. 250–61.

Levin, Avner, and Mary Jo Nicholson. "Privacy Law in the United States, the EU, and Canada: The Allure of the Middle Ground." *University of Ottawa Law & Technology Journal*, vol. 2, no. 2, 2005, pp. 357–95.

Mantlero, Alessandro. "The EU Proposal for a General Data Protection Regulation and the Roots of the 'Right to Be Forgotten.'" *Computer Law & Security Review*, vol. 29, no. 3, June 2013, pp. 229–35.

Shoenberger, Allen. "Privacy Wars." *Indiana International & Comparative Law Review*, vol. 17, 2007, pp. 355–93.

Whitman, James Q. "Two Western Cultures of Privacy: Dignity versus Liberty." *Yale Law Journal*, vol. 113, no. 6, Apr. 2004, pp. 1151–221.

DEEPFAKE

Introduction

The term deepfake refers to emerging technology that allows computer users to create fabricated but highly convincing sounds, static images, and moving pictures. Deepfake technologies are assisted by advanced artificial intelligence (AI), mostly from a class of AI known as "generative adversarial networks" (GANs). Using sophisticated algorithms, GANs manipulate user-supplied input to generate sounds, images, and videos, resulting in strikingly realistic simulated content. The word deepfake was derived from the advanced AI words "deep learning" and "fake."

As of this publication date, persuasive deepfakes are largely confined to sounds, static images, and a genre of content commonly known as "talking head videos," which depict immobile individuals speaking. However, as the underlying technologies continue to advance and improve, experts have voiced concerns that deepfake technology heralds the impending arrival of a dangerous virtual landscape. Its potential criminal and political applications are particularly worrisome to many observers. The consensus among experts is that deepfake technology is likely to introduce unprecedented complications to the problem of "fake news" through artificially manufactured but believable video clips featuring politicians and other high-profile public figures.

Background

The invention of deepfake technology is generally credited to Ian Goodfellow, a machine-learning expert who created his first GAN-powered deepfakes in 2014 while he was a PhD student at the University of Montreal. Goodfellow went on to work as a research scientist at Google before joining Apple in March 2019, where he accepted a role as the company's director of machine learning. He was named to the Massachusetts Institute of Technology's "35 Innovators Under [Age] 35" in 2017 and ranked among *Foreign Policy* magazine's "100 Global Thinkers" in 2019.

Deepfake technology relies on algorithms, which are systematized sequences of programming instructions that tell a computer how to handle a complex task. In particular, it uses advanced AI-powered GAN processes that push the limits of conventional algorithms. Most algorithms are focused on simply sorting or classifying data, while GANs use multiple algorithms that try to trick each other into categorizing a manufactured sound, image, or video as real. Specifically, they function by simultaneously adopting the roles of generator and discriminator, where the generator is responsible for drawing on user input to manufacture a fake sound clip, image, or video clip and the "discriminator" is responsible for comparing the simulated content against the authentic input. GANs are capable of testing simulated content against millions of evaluative parameters very quickly, ultimately allowing users to generate fake sounds, images, and videos realistic enough to convince viewers of their authenticity.

One definitive aspect of deepfake technology is that it does not require much initial input to create a believable result. A *Popular Mechanics* article from August 2019 noted that GANs only need a few images to generate output that appears genuine to the untrained eye.

The Ease of Deepfaking

Deepfake software is openly available for download on the internet, enabling any user with the requisite computer skills to use it to produce fake audio, image, and video content. According to a *BBC News* report published in October 2018, which drew on data supplied by the cybersecurity firm DeepTrace, approximately 15,000 deepfake videos are currently online, marking a sharp rise from the nearly 8,000 the firm counted in December 2018. Observers and analysts believe that amateur computing hobbyists are responsible for a large majority of existing deepfake content and emphasize that deepfake production is a worldwide phenomenon. The BBC report also noted that Deeptrace's analysis found 96 percent of deepfakes to be pornographic in nature, with most simulated videos superimposing the likenesses of famous actresses onto the bodies of adult performers.

Deeptrace's report also addressed claims that deepfake videos were used in recent political campaigns in Malaysia and Gabon. According to the firm, allegations that deepfake videos were used to influence voters in both countries did not withstand scrutiny and can be dismissed as false. Deeptrace did note that deepfake videos have the potential to be weaponized for political purposes. However, as of the report's October 2019 publication date, the firm's expert analysts believe the most current pressing threat comes from the technology's potential misuse as a cybercriminal and cyberbullying tactic.

E-commerce entrepreneurs moved quickly in their bid to monetize deepfake technology. According to the Deeptrace review, the four top-ranking adult websites featuring deepfake videos generated approximately 134 million views between February 2018 and the report's finalization in the autumn of 2019. Software developers have also created mobile apps that allow smartphone users to create deepfakes, with the website of one such app attracting a massive spike in traffic after media sources published unfavorable reports about it. The website's owners voluntarily took down the site and discontinued distribution of the app in the controversy's immediate aftermath.

A different analysis, conducted in February 2019 by a collaborative group known as Witness Media Lab, reported that current deepfake technologies require a significant level of specialized knowledge to use effectively. However, Witness Media Lab researchers also stated that the end-user landscape was changing quickly, with increasingly advanced deepfake technologies requiring less and less user skill. Witness Media Lab's conclusions matched the Deeptrace analysis, with both organizations agreeing that the production of simulated, personalized, and highly sophisticated fake content represents a pressing threat to individual users, and particularly to girls and women who face the risk of having their likenesses imposed on explicit adult videos for the purposes of phishing, extortion, harassment, and cyberbullying.

With authorities on the topic agreeing that the technology poses new dangers in the virtual environment, many experts believe that it is only a matter of time before deepfakes become a central part of political disinformation campaigns and cyberwarfare. Some experts believe that deepfakes will almost certainly be weaponized during the 2020 US presidential election campaign in a bid to influence voters. In the meantime, US government agencies and other cybersecurity stakeholders are actively working to develop technology capable of recognizing deepfakes in what some observers have described as a kind of virtual arms race meant to limit or prevent deepfakes from exerting a disruptive or damaging influence on society.

—*Jim Greene*

References

Cellan-Jones, Rory. "Deepfake Videos 'Double in Nine Months.'" *BBC News,* 7 Oct. 2019, www.bbc.com/news/technology-49961089.

Chen, Angela. "Three Threats Posed by Deepfakes that Technology Won't Solve." *MIT Technology Review,* 2 Oct. 2019, www.technologyreview.com/s/614446/deepfake-technology-detection-disinformation-harassment-revenge-porn-law/.

Gregory, Sam, and Eric French. "How Do We Work Together to Detect AI-Manipulated Media?" *Witness Media Lab,* 2019, lab.witness.org/projects/osint-digital-forensics/.

Libby, Kristina. "This Bill Hader Deepfake Video Is Amazing. It's Also Terrifying for Our Future." *Popular Mechanics,* 13 Aug. 2019, www.popularmechanics.com/technology/security/a28691128/deepfake-technology/.

Porup, J. M. "How and Why Deepfake Videos Work—And What Is at Risk." *CSO,* 10 Apr. 2019, www.csoonline.com/article/3293002/deepfake-videos-how-and-why-they-work.html.

Shao, Grace. "What 'Deepfakes' Are and How They May Be Dangerous." *CNBC,* 13 Oct. 2019, www.cnbc.com/2019/10/14/what-is-deepfake-and-how-it-might-be-dangerous.html.

Simonite, Tom. "Prepare for the Deepfake Era of Web Video." *Wired,* 6 Oct. 2019, www.wired.com/story/prepare-deepfake-era-web-video/.

"What Is a Deepfake?" *The Economist,* 7 Aug. 2019, www.economist.com/the-economist-explains/2019/08/07/what-is-a-deepfake.

DESKTOP AND E-PUBLISHING

Introduction

Desktop publishing is the process of producing a book, report, or other publication on a home or work computer. E-publishing, short for electronic publishing, often employs desktop publishing, especially by individuals or independent publishers, but it also refers to e-book releases by traditional publishers. E-publishing and Amazon's dominant role in distribution have put pressure on traditional publishers to adapt to a changing market in which authors can exercise control over when, how, and for what cost their works are released. These changes have also put pressure on writers, who must become experts in cover and page design; hiring editors, proofreaders, indexers, and other professional contractors; and marketing and distribution— elements of publishing that involve costs absorbed by a traditional publisher that fall squarely on an "indie," who publishes their own work. Additionally, desktop and e-publishing have forced readers to evaluate publications in a new way. Open-source journals, for example, give researchers access to a vast number of scientific and academic articles, but the reader must assess a publication for quality or peer-review in the absence of an editorial process that ensures a paper has been thoroughly reviewed.

Desktop and e-publishing are fascinating to many writers because they allow an author's voice to be expressed in a direct, more or less unfiltered way. Publications that are released from large presses often undergo considerable editing and revision, especially if the author is not highly skilled as a writer but possesses information the publisher is interested in publishing. Even skilled and experienced authors receive varying degrees of editorial guidance in the areas of craft and story development before a publisher will consent to publish a manuscript and may find their work ultimately rejected if the publisher remains unsatisfied with it. While such revisions are generally approved by the author, they do tend to smooth over characteristics of an author's style, word choice, and, at times, opinion.

Background

While desktop and e-publishing are often considered together, other non-traditional forms of publishing occurred long before e-publishing was possible. Access to photocopying machines made it possible for individuals and collectives to publish local newspapers, fliers, and magazines from home or by using photocopiers located in schools, libraries, grocery stores, and other community centers or local businesses. Small magazines, often called zines, were produced by individuals or small groups to express political opinions, engage in popular culture and music, and/or distribute art.

Many zines had low distribution numbers, often less than 1,000 copies, and were either sold in local bookstores or given away for free. There are examples of zines from as early as the 1920s that were printed in small runs by professional print shops. It was, however, the access to photocopy machines that made it possible for many more individuals to produce the entire publication themselves. This allowed individuals to express a wide array of opinions, commentary, and perspectives. Oftentimes a zine was associated with musical groups and zines were particular popular among fans and producers of punk music who appreciated that zines could be published without relying on mainstream media.

Zines were popular in the United States as well as developing countries such as Turkey where zines were a form of alternative media where they specialized in music, literature, and cultural topics. Zines continue to exist, but their production has been made easier by the introduction of desktop publishing—that is, a computer and some publishing software. Some zines are produced using photocopy machines or printers, and others are produced through online self-publishing houses, which provide access to a wide variety of papers, inks, and bindings.

Popularizing Media

The internet has made it easier to buy and sell zines in both their physical and electronic forms. To organize and encourage future research about this form of desktop publishing, many libraries have begun collecting zines. This is a significant step and acknowledgment of the significance of zines as publications. The collection of these publications requires a new form of filing and storage to accommodate the differences and creativity found in these publications. For example, zines do not always include information regarding the authors, publication dates, or publishing houses, which librarians typically use to record and organize materials (Cox, 2018). Therefore, librarians have had to catalog zines based on limited information—sometimes by the date on which the library was given the zine—or else by topic.

The emergence of computer-based desktop publishing and e-publishing have enabled writers to produce professional-looking publications. Access to personal computers and the development of software programs such as Microsoft Word and

PageMaker rapidly expanded the ability of writers to publish their own work. For many writers, access to personal computers and publishing software occurred before the internet was available, or was fast enough to allow consistent online publication. This means that there was a period in which publications produced on personal computers were printed and distributed, or sent to print shops. Then, as the internet developed, many of those publications moved to online forums, blogs, and journals. The emergence of technology that encouraged portability, such as laptops, tablets, and smartphones, further encouraged online publication.

Changes Going Forward

As a result of all of these changes and the number of publications emerging each year, the number of questions that scholars and researchers need to address before they analyze a publication has expanded. Some scholars are concerned with variables regarding the type of publication software that is used, the platforms which publication occurs on, the ways in which the publication is edited, how distribution occurs, and in what ways writers, editors, and graphic designers are paid for their work.

The emergence of desktop and e-publishing has caused a good deal of skepticism among scholars and professional journalists. The primary concern is that academic and journalistic works have not been properly vetted through a process known as peer review. Most professional news outlets and academic publications go through a process of peer review in which the work read and evaluated by experts in the subject of the publication (in the case of journalism, traditionally that person is an editor).

In the case of scholarly journals, experts evaluate the publication to ensure that the information is accurately presented, that research has been ethically conducted, and that the manuscript advances research and scholarship within the subject. Often, this process is done anonymously though blind-peer review in which the reviewers do not know the identity of the writer and therefore their judgments are not be clouded by their like or dislike of the writer. This process takes a long time, especially if the reviewers suggest revisions and then want to see the manuscript again before they agree to publish the text. The amount of time that this takes, and the selectivity of reviewers means that some scholars have difficulty publishing their work as quickly as they would like. They may be pressured because they have findings that they would like to be released immediately, or because their annual review requires that they have published a number of articles or books each year. These pressures have made desktop and e-publishing attractive to academics, although the quality of such publishing is often dubious.

Problems have emerged as the number of online journals rapidly expands. While older journals are attached to universities or publishing houses with long reputations, some new journals are organized by untraceable offices. These publications may charge academics to publish their work, whereas older journals typically publish research without a charge to the author. These "pay-to-publish" publications are sometimes labeled as predatory journals because they prey on academics that need to quickly publish to keep or secure their job. Clark and Smith's editorial regarding predatory journals outlines some of the ways in which this form of e-publishing harms academics and the advancement of science. Their reasons include the loss of important scientific findings because they are published in unproven or untrusted journals and the prohibitive costs which make it harder for academics from developing nations who cannot pay high rates for publication but need to publish to present their information to international audiences. In both ways, the publication structure has negatively affected academic institutions, researchers, and readers.

Other Issues

Communications scholars and researchers are interested in the ways that desktop and e-publishing are affecting reading and communication in multiple public spheres. For example, do desktop and e-publishing make it possible for readers to find a wider diversity of texts? Or are readers continuing to focus on texts published by traditional publishing houses but now available in electronic formats?

Many textbooks have been made available in electronic formats, which enable students to carry all of their textbooks on a tablet, computer, or phone. This certainly makes packing for a day of classes easier, but academics are still researching if these electronic texts are as effective as paper publications. They ask if using electronic texts change the ways that students take notes, study, and pay attention to their assignments. Because these texts are so new, researchers are still working to determine what questions should be asked and how to measure student learning via electronic texts. It is clear that electronic texts will continue to exist for a long time. Further, there are many advantages to desktop and e-publishing. Therefore, communication researchers are searching for ways to take advantage of these new tools and capabilities while ensuring that the public is still able to evaluate the information presented to them, and that academics are able to determine if the information they are reviewing has been properly reviewed.

—*Allison Hahn*

References

Al-Khatib, A., and J. A. T. da Silva. "Stings, Hoaxes and Irony Breach the Trust Inherent in Scientific Publishing." *Publishing Research Quarterly,* vol. 32, no. 3, 2016, pp. 208–19.

Ashuri, T. "When Online News Was New." *Journalism Studies,* vol. 17, no. 3, 2016, pp. 301–18.

Clark, J., and R. Smith. "Firm Action Needed on Predatory Journals." *BMJ* 350, 2015, p. h210.

Cox, D. "Developing and Raising Awareness of the Zine Collections at the British Library." *Art Libraries Journal,* vol. 43, no. 2, 2018, pp. 77–81.

Finn, J. C., R. Peet, S. Mollett, and J. Lauermann. "Reclaiming Value from Academic Labor: Commentary by the Editors of Human Geography." *Fennia-International Journal of Geography,* vol. 195, no. 2, 2017, pp. 182–84.

Henrie, C. R., L. R. Halverson, and C. R. Graham. "Measuring Student Engagement in Technology-Mediated Learning: A Review." *Computers & Education,* vol. 90, 2015, pp. 36–53.

Luther, J., F. Farmer, and S. Parks. "Special Issue Editors' Introduction: The Past, Present, and Future of Self-Publishing: Voices, Genres, Publics." *Community Literacy Journal,* vol. 12, 2017, pp. 1–4.

Oral, A. E., and E. B. Güzelo lu. "Zines as an Alternative Media: An Analysis on Female Zinsters in Turkey." *Communication & Media Researches,* vol. 219, 2017.

Tandoc, Jr., E. C., and J. Jenkins. "The Buzzfeedication of Journalism? How Traditional News Organizations Are Talking About a New Entrant to the Journalistic Field Will Surprise You!" *Journalism,* vol. 18, no. 4, 2017, pp. 482–500.

Wilson, B. "Innovators Ignite Revolution in Desktop Publishing and Scholastic Media." *Communication: Journalism Education Today,* vol. 47, no. 4, 2014, pp. 3–17.

DIGITAL CITIZENSHIP

Introduction
Digital citizenship can be defined as the norms and rules of behavior for persons using digital technology in commerce, political activism, and social communication. Digital citizenship is a unique phenomenon of the digital age, reflecting the growing importance of digital literacy, digital commerce, and information technology in global culture. A person's digital citizenship begins when they engage with the digital domain, for instance, by beginning to use a smartphone or email. However, digital citizenship exists on a spectrum based on an individual's level of digital literacy. This can be defined as their familiarity with the skills, jargon, and behaviors commonly used to communicate and conduct commerce with digital tools.

Background
Educational theorist Marc Prensky suggested that the modern human population can be divided into two groups: digital natives and digital immigrants. Digital natives were raised in the presence of digital technology. They learned how to use it in childhood. They absorbed the basics of digital citizenship during their early development. Digital immigrants were born before the digital age or have limited access to technology. They adapt to digital technology and communication later in life. Given the growing importance of digital technology, educators and social scientists believe that teaching children and adults to use digital technology safely and ethically is among the most important goals facing society.

An Evolving Paradigm
Digital communication enables people to have relationships online or on mobile devices. The degree to which these digital relationships affect IRL relationships, or those that occur "in real life," is an

important facet of digital citizenship. For instance, research suggests that people who spend more time communicating through smartphones or who feel they need constant access to digital media have more difficulty forming and maintaining IRL relationships. Good digital citizenship can help people use digital technology in positive ways that do not detract from their IRL relationships and well-being.

Digital technology has had a powerful, democratizing force on culture. Social media, for instance, has enabled small, local social movements to have national and even international impact. Even a simple tweet or viral video can quickly spread to millions of social media users. Small-scale behaviors can thus have larger, often unexpected consequences, both good and bad. This is sometimes called the butterfly effect. The potential impact of even a single user in the digital domain highlights the importance of learning and teaching effective digital behavior and ethics.

Ethics of Digital Citizenship

In *Digital Citizenship in Schools*, educational theorist Mike Ribble outlines nine core themes that characterize digital citizenship. These themes are: digital access, digital commerce, digital communication, digital literacy, digital etiquette, digital law, digital rights and responsibilities, digital health and wellness, and digital security. They address appropriate ways of interacting with the technology, information, government, companies, and other citizens in the digital world. Ribble writes that well-adjusted digital citizens help others become digitally literate. They strive to make the digital domain harmonious and culturally beneficial.

He also argues that digital citizens are responsible for learning about and following the laws and ethical implications of all digital activities. Piracy, for example, is the unauthorized digital reproduction of copyrighted media. It violates laws that protect creative property. It has become one of the most controversial issues of the twenty-first century. Other common digital crimes and forms of misconduct include:

- plagiarizing content from digital sources;
- hacking (gaining unauthorized access to computer networks or systems);
- sending unwanted communications and spam messages; and
- creating and spreading destructive viruses, worms, and malware.

Such behaviors violate others' rights and so are considered unethical, illegal, or both.

Digital Security and Responsibility

The rights and responsibilities of digital citizenship differ by political environment. In the United States, individuals have the right to free speech and expression. They also have a limited right to digital privacy. The ownership of digital data is an evolving subject in US law.

One responsibility of digital citizenship is to learn about potential dangers, both social and physical, and how to avoid them. These include identity theft, cyberstalking, and cyberbullying. Strong digital security can help protect one's identity, data, equipment, and creative property. Surge protectors, antivirus software, and data backup systems are some of the tools digital citizens use to enhance their digital security. Though the digital world is a complex, rapidly evolving realm, advocates argue that the rules of digital citizenship can be reduced to a basic concept: respect oneself and others when engaging in digital life.

—*Micah L. Issitt*

References

Hintz, Arne, Lina Dencik, and Karin Wahl-Jorgensen. *Digital Citizenship in a Datafied Society.* Polity Press, 2019.

Ribble, Mike. *Digital Citizenship in Schools: Nine Elements All Students Should Know.* International Society for Technology in Education, 2015.

Ribble, Mike, and Marty Park. *The Digital Citizenship Handbook for School Leaders: Fostering Positive Interactions Online.* International Society for Technology in Education, 2019.

Rogers-Whitehead, Carrie. *Digital Citizenship: Teaching Strategies and Practice from the Field.* Rowman & Littlefield, 2019.

Vromen, Ariadne. *Digital Citizenship and Political Engagement.* Palgrave Macmillan, 2017.

Wells, Chris. *The Civic Organization and the Digital Citizen: Communicating Engagement in a Networked Age.* Oxford UP, 2015.

DIGITAL DIVIDE

Introduction

The term "digital divide" refers to the division between individuals able to access computer and internet technology—typically in their homes—and those unable to do so. Such a lack of access can occur for several reasons. These may include the absence of reliable infrastructure, such as broadband internet, in a particular geographical area; the cost of internet service; or a lack of computer ownership. In some cases, an individual may have partial access to internet and computing technologies but nevertheless struggle to complete certain tasks. For example, an individual may be able to access the internet using a mobile device such as a smartphone but may experience spotty connectivity or be unable to use websites not optimized for mobile use.

As access to computer technology, internet service, and wireless telecommunications networks expanded throughout the United States over the late twentieth and early twenty-first centuries, awareness rose of the growing division between the portion of the population able to access that technology and the portion unable to do so. Known as the "digital divide," that division has in many ways corresponded with existing axes of inequity, as people of color, residents of rural communities, and low-income households were statistically less likely to have access to computers or to broadband internet service than their white, urban or suburban, and higher-income counterparts.

The issue of the digital divide became particularly pressing in 2020 with the spread of the global COVID-19 pandemic. The crisis prompted abrupt transitions to virtual learning for students and telecommuting for many workers and thus placed individuals with little to no access to computer technology or internet service at a severe disadvantage.

Policymakers, educators, and advocacy groups throughout the United States largely agree on the need to lessen the digital divide but were split in regard to the best means of doing so. Some individuals and organizations have called for reform on the national level. They argue that the federal government was the body best suited to bringing affordable broadband internet service, among other technologies, to the public. Others, however, have asserted that state and local governments should take the lead in closing the digital divide. They argued that state and local officials have the best understanding of the specific technological needs of their constituents.

Background

Information and communication technology (ICT) has pervaded almost every aspect of society, from dating and the labor market to governance and shopping. However, not every member of society has been successfully integrated into the information society. The increasing isolation of those suffering from this digital inequality continues to deepen the divide. While information technology (IT) persists in conquering ever more aspects of social life, the new form of inequality is affecting the social and economic prospects of those left without ICT knowledge or access. Without access to digital information or resources, these people face a digital divide that sociologists are working to overcome.

The term digital divide rose to fame in the mid-nineties, predominantly due to its use by Vice President Al Gore in a 1996 speech. Originally, it referred to the distribution of personal computers in American households. With the turn of the century, however, the question of internet access became a crucial aspect of the debate in the United States and around the world.

IT Access

In a global perspective, the difference between developed and developing nations in regard to IT access is immense. While in developed countries it is perfectly normal for more than half of households to own computers, in many developing nations it may be nearly impossible to find more than two people out of a hundred who own a computer. This disparity became the topic of two World Summit on the Information Society conferences hosted by the United Nations in Geneva and Tunis (2003, 2005) as well as a series of further related events. The continuing aim of these conferences, whose reports can be found online, is to find workable solutions for bridging the international digital divide. In the same spirit, a group of faculty members of the Massachusetts Institute of Technology (MIT) began an initiative called "One Laptop per Child," which builds inexpensive, rugged, energy-efficient laptop computers and distributes them to children in countries such as Uruguay, Rwanda, and Mongolia. These computers enable teachers worldwide to better educate children about technology and their world.

But the term "digital divide" does not just describe a global disparity. Within developed nations, too, access to IT can be unequal, and this inequality's effects are becoming increasingly grave. Within the United States itself, attempts have been made to bridge the gap in internet access, including trying to regulate the companies supplying this access. In 2011, one of the nation's largest internet providers, Comcast, released a product called "Internet Essentials" as part of a Federal Communications Commission (FCC) mandate issued upon the company's acquisition of NBC Universal. Internet Essentials, priced at ten dollars per month, was designed to allow low-income families the ability to purchase an affordable subscription. While many argued that the company did not make a genuine effort to reach out and market this product and initially included too many restrictions, leading to a minimum impact, Comcast did loosen one of the eligibility requirements and ran a special back-to-school promotion for the program in 2014. As IT continues to pervade everyday life and the job market, those without access are left further and further behind.

Causes of the Digital Divide

The causes behind the national digital divide are manifold. Poverty and social class are issues that come into play even within the most developed nations. These issues can be described in terms of access to cultural capital or symbolic capital, a theoretical conception originally formulated by French sociologist Pierre Bourdieu. According to Bordieu's model, members of a lower social class have little or no opportunity to acquire the traits, habits, or information necessary to accomplish a rise in status, income, class, or livelihood. In the worst cases, a lack of information, which is increasingly available only online, would bar these classes from informed participation in civic life and democracy.

In the case of the digital divide, a lack of cultural capital would make it much harder for children born into low socioeconomic classes to gain the knowledge necessary to command IT. Possessing this command, according to the Bourdieu theory, is a necessary form of capital if one is to be a part of modern society, which increasingly relies on the use of technology such as email and internet videophones. From arranging a date to securing job information to handling client agendas, the demands of everyday private and professional life require not only the capability to use IT but also the ability to do so with ease.

From the point of view of those already fluent in the use of this technology, it may seem very simple to be able to handle technology. But even something as simple as reading a website and finding its significant content requires a thorough initiation and consistent access.

Media Multitasking

The requirements have reached a level designated as media multitasking. Successfully performing a variety of simultaneous tasks, such as coordinating activities on a cell phone while simultaneously surfing the internet, requires a great deal of prior learning. Further, the learning process for such habitual routines is fairly time-consuming and gets harder with the increased age of the learner.

Therefore, we have to think of other factors besides mere class status when considering the digital divide, such as those of age and generation. Elderly people often have difficulty adjusting to swift changes in technology. The two major problems they are facing, even when they are presented with access, are (a) their own fear or resentment, and (b) a form of technological illiteracy. As Foehr and Roberts have argued, reading web content requires a multitude of learned skills (2008). For those who weren't educated into this cultural technique at an early age, the learning process can be long and difficult.

Symbolic-Capital Theory

The symbolic-capital theory applies in these cases, too. Consider the following analogy: buying into a fledgling market requires only a small amount of start-up capital, but once a market has gained momentum, it becomes much more difficult and requires an even higher margin of investment to buy into it. It is the same with IT. If a person has not grown up within the development of the technology, then more effort and more symbolic capital will be required of them in order to obtain even a moderate amount of technological knowledge.

In other words, those on the losing side of digital inequality will face a widening gap between themselves and the technologically literate as well as an increasingly steep learning curve as they try to catch up.

This effect is visible in the impact that internet use has on US workers, as Paul DiMaggio and Bart Bonikowski have shown. Just demonstrating the ability to use internet technology, whether at work or at home, has a significant positive impact on workers' earnings and chances on the job market. The ability to use the internet, symbolized, for example, by possessing one's own email address, can not only serve as an indicator to employers that a worker is computer literate and therefore more employable but also enable workers to find better job opportunities.

In sum, it is necessary to shrink the digital divide, for knowledge of ICT must now be considered a condition of participation not only in the labor market, but also within the political and social spheres in the forms of access to certain markets as well as government services. However, ICT must not be seen as only a mechanism of exclusion. ICT can also be a means to empower those who have been excluded. Many citizens, previously barred from certain forms of political and social participation, or, because of age or disability, dependent on others when it comes to fulfilling certain administrative requirements, now have a chance at participation and independence through technology in the form of e-government. Even if this goal is not equally realized across all US states, as Rubaii-Barret and Wise have shown, efforts are being made all over the United States to ensure that more people have easy access to government information and services (2008).

Applications

Because spreading information about consumer products becomes more difficult in a globalizing market, consumer empowerment has become increasingly important. Take the example of health care: a number of cheap generic medical products, for example, are only available through internet sources. Studies, like one undertaken by Rains, have shown that internet access and use can be positively correlated with personal health care. Specifically, access to broadband internet in correlation with age and area of residence (whether rural or urban) are factors that contribute to personal health. In this regard, the promotion of personal health is negatively affected by digital inequality. On the other hand, though, access and use can be linked to better health

as well as increased opportunities for social and economic participation. Enabling access to e-health is therefore a crucial factor to reduce the effects of digital inequality.

According to Matusitz and Breen, e-health now covers a wide range of fields. As an ever-greater number of aspects of healthcare are relocated to the internet (which increases digital inequality), the amount of actual discourse between patients and doctors is decreasing, making e-health an often-problematic social transformation. Notwithstanding, those on the downside of digital inequality, who have less access to internet technology or no accurate knowledge of how to use the internet, are unable to access new developments in treatments or the comparative resources and support offered by patient groups.

This question of e-health touches upon the basic question of citizens as consumers, not only of healthcare products, but of products in general. Social participation has transformed in large part into consumption. Therefore, it can be said that in a global, political economy that is increasingly dominated by so-called multinational corporations, the remaining counterpower, as Ulrich Beck suggests, lies not so much in the hands of national governments, but in those of the consumers themselves, who ultimately decide which products they will buy. The currency they use to exercise this power is information. The role of national governments, therefore, lies in ensuring that consumers can obtain and distribute information about products and services. Nation-states must then create IT access for everyone, or bridge the digital divide, if they wish to restore the democratic power of the people.

One group of actors in particular is struggling with the new digital age and represents a special dimension of the digital divide: the print media. Newspapers, magazines, and journals have in the past been perceived as the agents that upheld a system of critical control over political and commercial developments. But, faced with the free-floating information of the web, print media have a hard time adapting. With every major paper now maintaining its own website, readers are beginning to question whether buying a paper at the newsstand is truly an efficient way of accessing up-to-date information. Further, with dwindling sales and subscribers, the number of advertisers willing to financially support quality publishing is also decreasing.

The effect on journalism has been fairly grave, most importantly in the dimension of the quality. The quality of information (including contextualization, critical perspectives, reliability, validity, and thoroughness of research) is one of the least explicitly discussed, yet most important, factors in the functioning of modern economies and political systems. To some commentators, iconic publications such as the *New York Times* and *New Republic* have represented the shift from organized, in-depth editorial content to providing more space for images in conjunction with coverage of popular trends and even trending online games like Wordle. The quality of information itself also contributes to the digital divide, since those who have access to or can afford high quality information can more easily increase their activities and gains.

Bridging the Digital Divide

On the global scale, bridging the digital divide will be an effort that is wrought with conflict. One must factor in questions of gender, ethnicity, race, and religion, all of which are addressed differently from one nation to another. In some countries, internet access is regulated by the state, and content considered harmful, whether for political or ideological reasons, is banned. Governments often fear the internet's potential for aiding democratic and revolutionary movements in spreading their ideas and creating a coherent power base. This fear was proven to be warranted when dissenters used the internet to organize and report on massive protests during the Arab Spring uprisings that began in late 2010 and early 2011.

But at the same time, the progress of IT itself makes it much harder to bridge this divide. More and more intricate internet content demands not only better hardware, but also ever faster broadband connections. Delivering these to every region in the world is an enormous challenge.

The circuits of modern societies are in a state of transformation in regard to time, space, and meaning. The shipping and transportation of material goods is of less importance than the access and distribution of information. These circuits constitute the economies of social relations in regard to questions of ethnicity, gender, social justice, etc. In the transformation of the circuits, the social

relations are also being transformed, as Lash and Urry predicted in their analysis of the "economies of signs and space" in 1994.

We are witnessing a profound change in the way our societies and democracies are functioning. In 1962, the German sociologist and philosopher Juergen Habermas published his groundbreaking study *The Structural Transformation of the Public Sphere.* Habermas described the transformation of the bourgeois public sphere, which emerged in the eighteenth century, came to full bloom in the nineteenth century, and then fell into decline. Within this process of the rise and fall of a culture or form of public discourse, Habermas argued, were the two major social and political transformations that shaped modern western societies: the shift from a feudalistic society to a liberal public sphere on the one hand, and, on the other, yet another shift from the liberal bourgeois public discourse to the democratic social welfare state.

Following Habermas's account, it can be argued that we are witnessing another structural transformation of the public sphere. The looming question for this transformation, which is of course reflected in the emergence of the public sphere of the digital age or information society, is the problem of mechanisms of inclusion and exclusion in participation. Inclusion means herein the acquisition of cultural capital or the means to gain access to knowledge of the use of IT. Exclusion describes either a lack of access, either through indigence or through intentional separation. Nondemocratic regimes may find incentives for providing access only to a privileged few who are assumed to be loyal to the regime. Neo-Marxist critics, however, hold that even in democratic societies, forces exist that supposedly keep mechanisms of exclusion in place.

Several economic theorists subscribing to rather simple accounts of the digital divide often hold to theories of access, claiming that merely providing everyone with technology such as personal computers and broadband connections will eventually solve the problem of exclusion. But studies like Habermas's and Bourdieu's have shown that just providing technological access is not enough to guarantee inclusion. Even in the nineteenth century, simply being literate was not sufficient for active civic, social, or political participation. In the same regard, owning a computer with internet access is unlikely to solve the problems of poverty either globally or nationally.

Additionally, the problems caused by the digital divide on the one hand, and by IT itself on the other—for example, information overload, invalid information distribution, identity theft, etc.—lead to a transformation of the political structure of modern societies themselves.

The Digital Divide Today—and Tomorrow (Postpandemic)

By 2019 the United States faced significant disparities in broadband adoption, often along socioeconomic, racial, and ethnic lines. According to a 2019 survey by the Pew Research Center, 94 percent of US adults living in a household with an annual income of more than $100,000 had broadband internet at home, and 94 percent also owned a desktop or laptop computer. However, only 56 percent of adults living in households making $30,000 or less per year—defined by Pew as lower-income households—had home broadband access, and only 54 percent owned a desktop or laptop computer. About 26 percent of lower-income households relied on smartphones as their sole means of accessing the internet at home. Further, while 79 percent of white adults had broadband internet at home, only 66 percent of black adults and 61 percent of Hispanic adults did. Geographical disparities also persisted. The 2019 Pew survey found that only 63 percent of rural adults had broadband internet at home, as compared to 75 percent of urban adults and 79 percent of suburban adults.

The issue of the digital divide took on particular significance beginning in early 2020, when the COVID-19 pandemic prompted many businesses to shift to telecommuting and schools to transition to virtual-learning programs. Those shifts, carried out quickly and suddenly, highlighted the challenges facing those without reliable access to computer technology or the internet. A Pew Research Center survey found in April 2020 that 53 percent of US adults described the internet as "essential" during the pandemic, yet for many, that essential tool was effectively out of reach.

In addition, the shift to virtual learning for many schoolchildren underscored the ways in which the digital divide interfered with students' ability to attend online classes and complete assignments. Surveying parents whose children's schools had shifted to virtual learning by April 2020, Pew found that 36 percent of lower-income parents answered that it

was very or somewhat likely that their children would be unable to complete work because they had no access to a computer at home. In addition, 40 percent of lower-income parents stated that it was very or somewhat likely that the children would need to use public internet services, such as public wireless hotspots, because they had no reliable internet service at home.

Because of the inequities that the COVID-19 pandemic illuminated, government bodies throughout the United States introduced a number of new initiatives designed to close the digital divide, many of them focusing on increasing access to broadband internet. During late 2020 and early 2021, the federal government passed multiple COVID-relief bills that, along with other forms of financial aid, funded programs such as the Emergency Broadband Benefit, a new FCC subsidy program that took effect in May 2021. Under that temporary program, most eligible households would receive a broadband subsidy of up to $50 per month. Households located on tribal lands could receive up to $75 per month. This benefit expanded upon the existing Lifeline program, which, prior to the pandemic, had offered monthly broadband subsidies of $9.25 to most participants.

The FCC also announced the launch of the Emergency Connectivity Fund Program. That $7.17 billion initiative would provide schools and libraries with the funds to pay for computers and mobile devices, networking equipment, and internet services that could be used by students and others who needed such technology.

In addition to the initiatives carried out at the federal level, states such as Texas and Alabama introduced new programs designed to supply devices, internet access, or both to students in need. Cities likewise introduced new programs. Phoenix, Arizona, for example, began a pilot program that would bring internet service to apartment complexes where local students lived, while Philadelphia, Pennsylvania, and Chicago, Illinois, offered free internet service to public-school students. School districts throughout the country worked to address the lack of computers in some homes, in many cases lending devices such as laptops and tablets to students engaged in virtual learning.

—Alexander Stingl and Joy Crelin

References

Anderson, J. "Fighting to Bridge the Digital Divide." *Social Policy*, vol. 44, 2014, pp. 56–57, search. ebscohost.com/login.aspx?direct=true&db=sih&AN=95858812&site=ehost-live&scope=site.

Anderson, Monica, and Madhumitha Kumar. "Digital Divide Persists Even as Lower-Income Americans Make Gains in Tech Adoption." *Pew Research Center*, 7 May 2019, www.pewresearch. org/fact-tank/2019/05/07/ digital-divide-persists-even-as-lower-income-americans-make-gains-in-tech-adoption/.

Baudrillard, J. *Simulations*. Semiotext(e), 1983.

Beck, U. *Power in the Global Age: A New Global Political Economy*. Polity Press, 2006.

Bourdieu, P. "The Forms of Capital." *Handbook of Theory and Research in the Sociology of Education*, edited by J. C. Richardson, Greenwood Press, 1986, pp. 241–58.

Cantù, D. Antonio. "Initiatives to Close the Digital Divide Must Last beyond the COVID-19 Pandemic to Work." *The Conversation*, 27 Oct. 2020, theconversation.com/ initiatives-to-close-the-digital-divide-must-last-beyond-the-covid-19-pandemic-to-work-146663.

Castells, M. *The Internet Galaxy: Reflections on the Internet, Business and Society*. Oxford UP, 2001.

Chen, W. "The Implications of Social Capital for the Digital Divides in America." *Information Society*, vol. 29, 2013, pp. 13–25, search.ebscohost.com/ login.aspx?direct=true&db=sih&AN=84917786.

Crossley, N., and J. Roberts. *After Habermas: New Perspectives on the Public Sphere*. Blackwell, 2004.

Crouch, C. *Post-Democracy*. Polity Press, 2004.

Epstein, D., E. C. Nisbet, and T. Gillespie. "Who's Responsible for the Digital Divide? Public Perceptions and Policy Implications." *Information Society*, vol. 27, 2011, pp. 92–104, search.ebscohost.com/login.aspx?direct=true&db=sih&AN=59132055.

Fung, B. "Comcast Is Expanding Its $10-A-Month Internet Program for the Poor." *The Washington Post*, 4 Aug. 2014, www.washingtonpost. com/blogs/the-switch/wp/2014/08/04/ comcast-is-expanding-its-10-a-month-internet-program-for-the-poor/.

Goldstein, Phil. "How Cities Are Forging Partnerships to Close the Digital Divide." *StateTech*, 10 Dec. 2020, statetechmagazine.com/article/ 2020/12/how-cities-are-forging-partnerships-close-digital-divide.

Habermas, J. *The Structural Transformation of the Public Sphere*. MIT Press, 1991.

Hadley, G., and M. Mars. "Postgraduate Medical Education in Paediatric Surgery: Videoconferencing—A Possible Solution for Africa?" *Pediatric Surgery International*, vol. 24, 2008, pp. 223–26.

Hollander, P. "Popular Culture, the New York Times and the New Republic." *Society*, vol. 51, 2014, pp. 288–96, search.ebscohost.com/login.aspx?direct =true&db=sih&AN=96203565&site=e host-live&scope=site.

Horrigan, J. "Home Broadband Adoption 2008." *Pew Internet & American Life Project*, pewinternet. org/PPF/r/257/report%5fdisplay.asp.

Kong, S. C. "A Curriculum Framework for Implementing Information Technology in School Education to Foster Information Literacy." *Computers & Education*, vol. 51, 2008, pp. 129–41.

Lash, S., and J. Urry. *Economies of Signs and Space*. SAGE, 1994.

Logue, D., and M. Edwards. "Across the Digital Divide." *Stanford Social Innovation Review*, vol. 11, 2013, pp. 66–71, search.ebscohost.com/login.asp x?direct=true&db=sih&AN=91718527&site=e host-live&scope=site.

Masic, I., and E. Suljevic. "An Overview of E-Health Implementation in Countries, Members of the European Union." *Acta Informatica Medica*, vol. 15, 2007, pp. 242–45, search.ebscohost.com/ login.aspx?direct=true&db=a9h&AN=27747476 &site=ehost-live.

Matusitz, J., and G. M. Breen. "E-health: A New Kind of Telemedicine." *Social Work in Public Health*, vol. 23, 2007, pp. 95–113, search.ebsco-host.com/login.aspx?direct=true&db=sih&AN=3 0012503&site=ehost-live.

McLuhan, M. *The Gutenberg Galaxy: The Making of Typographic Man*. U of Toronto P, 1962.

Pick, J. B., and R. Azari. "Global Digital Divide: Influence of Socioeconomic, Governmental, and Accessibility Factors on Information Technology." *Information Technology for Development*, vol. 14, 2008, pp. 91–115, search.ebscohost.com/ login.aspx?direct=true&db=a9h&AN=31581293 &site=ehost-live.

Rains, S. A. "Health at High Speed: Broadband Internet Access, Health Communication, and the

Digital Divide." *Communication Research*, vol. 35, 2008, pp. 283–97, search.ebscohost.com/login.as px?direct=true&db=a9h&AN=31987928&site=e host-live.

Romm, Tony. "Millions of Low-Income Americans Will Receive Internet Access Rebates under New $7 Billion Broadband Stimulus Plan." *The Washington Post*, 22 Dec. 2020, www.washington-post.com/technology/2020/12/22/ internet-rebate-coronavirus-stimulus.

Sanz, E., and G. Turlea. "Downloading Inclusion: A Statistical Analysis of Young People's Digital Communication Inequalities." *Innovation: The European Journal of Social Sciences*, vol. 25, 2012, pp. 337–53, search.ebscohost.com/login.aspx?di rect=true&db=sih&AN=83467960&site=e host-live&scope=site.

Tate, Emily. "The Digital Divide Has Narrowed, but 12 Million Students Are Still Disconnected." *EdSurge*, 27 Jan. 2021, www.edsurge.com/ news/2021-01-27-the-digital-divide-has-narrowed-but-12-million-students-are-still-disconnected.

Vogels, Emily A., et al. "53% of Americans Say the Internet Has Been Essential during the COVID-19 Outbreak." *Pew Research Center*, 30 Apr. 2020, www.pewresearch.org/ internet/2020/04/30/53-of-americans-say-the-internet-has-been-essential-during-the-covid-19-outbreak/.

Wei, L., and D. Hindman. "Does the Digital Divide Matter More? Comparing the Effects of New Media and Old Media Use on the Education-Based Knowledge Gap." *Mass Communication & Society*, vol. 14, 2011, pp. 216–35, search.ebsco-host.com/login.aspx?direct=true&db=si h&AN=59131821.

"World Summit on the Information Society." *WSIS Stocktaking*, 2005, www.itu.int/wsis/docs2/tunis/ off/5.pdf.

DIGITAL ECONOMY

Introduction

The digital economy is the network of communications and economic transactions that takes place across the world via the internet. Although only decades old, the industry is already worth trillions of dollars. It has fueled the technological growth of personal computing devices, including home computers, smartphones, internet networks, and business computing software. It has brought new conveniences and tools to consumers across the world.

As the digital economy grows, some experts worry that it may be forming a bubble. Should the bubble burst, it will cause the digital economy to enter a sudden and severe downturn. This would have serious repercussions for industries affected by or reliant upon the digital economy. Others worry that the information harvested by participation in the digital economy will result in further violations of personal privacy.

Background

In the early 1970s, business computers slowly became commonplace. Early computers utilized punch-card technology to input information. However, this process was slow, complex, and difficult. For this reason, computers were not commonly utilized by businesses that did not do large amounts of calculations.

Punch-card technology was replaced with vacuum tubes and magnetic tape. These methods allowed individuals to interface with a computer in a more convenient manner. They made computers more useful for tasks such as analytics and data insight. As technology advanced, computer chips and hard drives took the place of vacuum tubes, magnetic tape, and punch cards. These forms of computer memory were much faster, more efficient, and smaller than their predecessors were.

As computers developed, they became easier for the average individual to use. This allowed businesses to use computers more, as employees needed less specialized training to interact with them. Additionally, more user-friendly technology helped the personal computer spread beyond the office to people's homes. As computers grew in popularity, several computer and software companies saw great success. These included Microsoft and Apple. Over the years, these companies produced successful software, operating systems, personal computers, and other digital devices. As computers continued to evolve, several other computer manufacturers and companies enjoyed economic success as well. As these companies grew, they formed some of the largest and most powerful sectors of the digital economy.

As personal computers became ubiquitous in First World economies, companies in the digital economy began to provide additional services targeted toward home-based users. One of the largest sectors of the digital economy, and one of the fastest growing, was online shopping. Consumers could digitally purchase goods without leaving their homes. The goods would then be delivered to the home. This revolutionary concept permanently altered the way in which business was conducted around the world.

Today's Digital Economy

The digital economy makes up a large portion of the world's economy. Collectively, the digital economy is worth more than $3 trillion. Unlike most industries, which grew slowly over time, much of the digital economy's value has been created in the last two decades. The world has adopted digital technology at an incredibly rapid pace, which has driven the growth of the digital economy.

The most important part of the digital economy is the connectivity enabled by the internet. Cell phones, personal computers, and business computers can all conveniently exchange information at any given time. These devices can be used for personal communication, business coordination, consuming media, viewing advertisements, finding new products, making purchases, or any number of other activities.

Many experts believe that the success of corporations and companies in a digital economy is dependent upon four factors. The first factor is customer expectations. Digital communication makes it easy for customers to interact with companies, raising the standards for interaction between customers and companies. Many customers expect proactive company policies that attempt to fix potential problems before they occur.

The second factor is product enhancement. Customers are now able to digitally compare products among multiple competitors at once, making markets more competitive. Successful companies must broaden their product line or provide services that stand out to the customers, such as on-demand services.

The third factor is collaborative innovations. Companies must continually innovate to maintain an edge over their competitors. To succeed in this regard, many companies work with other companies to combine their services. Potential collaborative partners include universities, start-ups, researchers, and customers.

The fourth and final factor is organizational leadership. Many companies may need to adjust their leadership structure to account for sudden innovations and new market environments. The traditional, hierarchical business structure may not succeed in a digital economy. It may be slower to analyze data and may place undue value on the opinions of executives instead of the opinions of experts.

While it has driven significant technological advancement, the spread of the digital economy is not without drawbacks. For example, despite large numbers of small digital firms existing within the digital economy, much of the economic power is concentrated in a few massive corporations. Just nine companies collectively control more than 90 percent of the profits in the digital economy.

Issues and Concerns

Many economic experts look at the rapid growth of the digital economy as a negative sign. They theorize that the growth indicates an economic bubble. In hindsight of the dot-com bubble, they believe that the digital economy will experience a sudden and severe downturn when the bubble bursts.

Some experts are also concerned with personal privacy in a digital economy. User information—such as browsing habits, page views, and purchase history—can be sold to advertising firms for a profit and utilized for digital marketing purposes. It can be used to craft targeted advertisements, tempting consumers with products related to their personal interests. Ultimately, consumers can do little to prevent their data from being harvested and sold. In many cases, consumers are unaware that this process even occurs.

—*Tyler Biscontini*

References

"About Us." *MIT Initiative on the Digital Economy*, ide. mit.edu/about-us.

Anderson, Lindsey, and Irving Wladawsky-Berger. "The 4 Things It Takes to Succeed in the Digital Economy." *Harvard Business Review*, 24 Mar. 2016, hbr.org/2016/03/the-4-things-it-takes-to-succeed-in-the-digital-economy.

Foroohar, Rana. "Money, Money, Money: Silicon Valley Speculation Recalls Dotcom Mania." *Financial Times*, 17 July 2017, www.ft.com/content/968f2022-6878-11e7-9a66-93fb352ba1fe.

Gada, Kosha. "The Digital Economy in 5 Minutes." *Forbes*, 16 June 2016, www.forbes.com/sites/koshagada/2016/06/16/what-is-the-digital-economy/#14397bc37628.

"History, Data, and Success in the Digital Economy." *SAPInsider*, 19 Oct. 2017, sapinsider.wispubs.com/Assets/Blogs/2017/October/SAP-Database-and-Data-Management.

"The New Digital Economy and Development." *United Nations Conference on Trade and Development*, Oct. 2017, unctad.org/en/PublicationsLibrary/tn_unctad_ict4d08_en.pdf.

Rouse, Margaret. "Digital Economy." *TechTarget*, Sept. 2017, searchcio.techtarget.com/definition/digital-economy.

"What Is Digital Economy?" *Deloitte*, www2.deloitte.com/mt/en/pages/technology/articles/mt-what-is-digital-economy.html.

Anyone who uses the internet creates a unique set of traceable activities and communications, known as a digital footprint. Photo via iStock/alengo. [Used under license.]

DIGITAL FOOTPRINT

Introduction

The term "digital footprint" refers to any information about a person that is available online. Digital footprints include many types of data, including social media information, credit card histories, and search engine histories. The more information that is available about a person, the larger the person's digital footprint is. Most people's digital footprints are larger than they realize, and many organizations are making an effort to inform people about this.

Background

There are two types of digital footprints: active and passive. An active digital footprint includes all the information a person has volunteered about him- or herself. A passive digital footprint includes information that was collected about a person by a third party. A digital footprint usually refers to both a person's active and passive footprints. Digital footprints can be very revealing and contain information collected and stored by other people.

A person's active digital footprint consists of his or her social media. This includes communication and networking websites, such as Facebook, LinkedIn, and in the past Myspace, in addition to blogs or websites the person actively contributes to. Any personal information posted online through these sources, such as relationships, interests, work histories, addresses, and contact information make up most of a person's active digital footprint. This information is usually stored by the website it was posted on and is sometimes sold to corporations for advertising. Facebook, in particular, has had multiple lawsuits brought against it for the sale of users' personal information.

Active and Passive Footprints

While a person's active digital footprint reveals personal information, it usually does not contain as much information as his or her passive digital footprint. Passive digital footprints include banking statements and bank account information, credit scores, purchase histories, criminal records, education records, internet browsing habits, and physical locations the person has visited. The act of collecting this information in bulk is called data mining. Data can be mined in several ways.

Corporations often store their customer's personal information, such as credit and debit card numbers and purchasing history, for long periods of time. Even though most companies take reasonable security measures, these servers can still be broken into. Hackers target them to steal large amounts of information at once, which they then sell. Victims often face serious consequences, such as identity theft.

Websites also use tools called cookies to track their users' browsing history, internet protocol (IP) addresses, and general location. They use this information to create individual profiles of each user for advertising. The more information websites collect for a profile, the more the advertisements will reflect the user's personal preferences.

Lastly, smartphones provide a great deal of information about their users to anyone who knows how to look for it. The global position system (GPS) and applications with location services often track, save, and broadcast the user's location even when they are not in use. Several companies monitor and use these signals to provide constant, up-to-date information of traffic in cities—but these signals can also be used to track a person's location. Other applications routinely request access to users' contact lists, message history, and various other personal details. Many applications will fail to function properly unless these requests are granted. Additionally, credit and debit card information is often stored in smartphones for music and application purchases. Histories of these purchases are stored by content providers and used for profile building similar to that of the advertisers mentioned previously. Even pictures taken on a camera phone can be stored online without the user's knowledge and stolen by others.

This data is all included in someone's digital footprint and is almost all of value to others. Internet browsing histories are valuable to online retailers and webmasters looking to increase the number of people who visit their pages. Employment histories, criminal records, and information displayed through social networking are valuable to employers for screening new job applicants. Credit card information, phone numbers, addresses, and other personal identifiers are valuable to criminals looking to steal identities. Institutions studying human psychology analyze this data and search for patterns within it. This is often called reality mining.

People should be aware that digital footprints are most likely permanent. It can be difficult, if not impossible, for people to find all the data that has been collected about them. And, even if they manage to find the data, having it removed is a long and difficult process. Even if they remove the data from active websites, it still probably exists in the form of cached pages, which are recorded copies of old versions of websites archived by a computer program and put in a database. Removing data from cached pages is sometimes impossible.

While it is likely impossible for people to eliminate their digital footprint, it is possible to minimize it and control it and maintain some online privacy. People should avoid putting personal data such as phone numbers, addresses, and major life events on social media. They should be careful about what permissions an application on a smartphone has and disable location services on a phone when they are not being used. Additionally, caution should be exercise when making online purchases with a credit or debit card, and make use of internet privacy tools such as browsers that do not track your online activities (such as DuckDuckGo).

—*Jane E. Kirtley*

References

Boyle, Justin. "11 Tips for Students to Manage their Digital Footprints." *TeachThought*, 8 Mar. 2014. www.teachthought.com/ technology/11-tips-for-students-tomanage-their-digital-footprints/.

Lambert, Jeffrey A. "How to Erase Your Digital Footprint." *MaximumPC*. Future US, Inc., 10 Nov. 2011, www.maximumpc.com/article/features/ how_erase_your_digital_footprint.

Singer, Natasha. "Ways to Make Your Online Tracks Harder to Follow." *The New York Times*. Arthur Ochs Sulzberger, Jr., 19 June 2013, bits.blogs. nytimes.com/2013/06/19/ ways-to-make-your-online-tracks-harder-to-follow-2/?_php=true&_type=blogs&_r=0.

Trotman, Andrew, and Katherine Rushton. "Facebook Mined Private Messages to Advertisers, Lawsuit Claims." *The Telegraph*. The Telegraph Media Group, 2 Jan. 2014, www.telegraph.co.uk/ technology/facebook/10548196/Facebook-mined-private-messages-to-advertisers-lawsuit-claims.html.

US Department of Homeland Security. "Digital Footprint: Assessing Risk & Impact." *US Department of Homeland Security*, 18 Feb. 2014, www. urmc.rochester.edu/MediaLibraries/URMC-Media/flrtc/documents/IT-20140218_Digital-Footprint.pdf.

DIGITAL FORENSICS

Introduction

Digital forensics is a branch of science that studies stored digital data. The field emerged in the 1990s but did not develop national standards until the 2000s. Digital forensics techniques are changing rapidly due to the advances in digital technology. The science of recovering and studying digital data was initially reserved for that engaged in the course of criminal investigations, primarily to investigate cybercrimes. These crimes target or involve the use of computer systems. Examples include identity theft, digital piracy, hacking, data theft, and cyberattacks. The Scientific Working Group on Digital Evidence (SWGDE), formed in 1998, develops industry guidelines, techniques, and standards.

Background

Digital forensics emerged in the mid-1980s in response to the growing importance of digital data in criminal investigations. The first cybercrimes occurred in the early 1970s. This era saw the emergence of hacking, or gaining unauthorized access to computer systems. Some of the first documented uses of digital forensics data were in hacking investigations.

Prior to the Electronic Communications Privacy Act (ECPA) of 1986, digital data or communications were not protected by law and could be collected or intercepted by law enforcement. The ECPA was amended several times in the 1990s and 2000s to address the growing importance of digital data for private communication. In 2014, the US Supreme Court ruled that police must obtain a warrant before searching the cell phone of a suspect arrested for a crime. In light of widespread concerns regarding digital privacy and government surveillance, legal policies regarding warrants and searches of digital files or communications remained in flux as of 2020.

Digital Forensics Techniques

Once forensic investigators have access to equipment that has been seized or otherwise legally obtained, they can begin forensic imaging. This process involves making an unaltered copy, or forensic image, of the device's hard drive. A forensic image records the drive's structures, all of its contents, and metadata about the original files.

A forensic image is also known as a physical copy. There are two main methods of copying computer data, physical copying and logical copying. A physical copy duplicates all of the data on a specific drive, including empty, deleted, or fragmented data, and stores it in its original configuration. A logical copy, by contrast, copies active data but ignores deleted files, fragments, and empty space. This makes the data easier to read and analyze. However, it may not provide a complete picture of the relevant data.

After imaging, forensics examiners analyze the imaged data. They may use specialized tools to recover deleted files using fragments or backup data, which is stored on many digital devices to prevent accidental data loss. Automated programs can be used to search and sort through imaged data to find useful information. Because searching and sorting are crucial to the forensic process, digital forensics organizations invest in research into better search and sort algorithms.

Information of interest to examiners may include emails, text messages, chat records, financial files, and various types of computer code. The tools and techniques used for analysis depend largely on the crime. These specialists may also be tasked with interpreting any data collected during an investigation. For instance, they may be called on to explain their findings to police or during a trial.

Challenges for the Future

Digital forensics is an emerging field that lags behind fast-changing digital technology. For instance, cloud computing is a developing technology in which data storage and processing is distributed across multiple computers or servers. In 2014, the National Institute of Standards and Technology (NIST) identified sixty-five challenges that must be addressed regarding cloud computing. These challenges include both technical problems and legal issues.

The SWGDE works to create tools and standards that will allow investigators to effectively retrieve and analyze data while keeping pace with changing technology. It must also work with legal rights organizations to ensure that investigations remain within boundaries set to protect personal rights and privacy. Each forensic investigation may involve accessing personal communications and data that might be protected under laws that guarantee free speech and expression or prohibit unlawful search and seizure. The SWGDE and law enforcement agencies are debating changes to existing privacy and surveillance laws to address these issues while enabling digital forensic science to continue developing.

—*Micah L. Issitt*

References

Gogolin, Greg. *Digital Forensics Explained.* CRC Press, 2013.

Holt, Thomas J., Adam M. Bossler, and Kathryn C. Seigfried-Spellar. *Cybercrime and Digital Forensics: An Introduction*, 2nd ed., Routledge, 2017.

Kävrestad, Joakim. *Fundamentals of Digital Forensics: Theory, Methods, and Real-Life Applications.* Springer International, 2018.

Le Khac, Nhien An, and Kim-Kwang Raymond Choo, editors. *Cyber and Digital Forensic Investigations: A Law Enforcement Practitioner's Perspective.* Springer International, 2020.

Pollitt, Mark. "A History of Digital Forensics." *Advances in Digital Forensics VI.* Edited by Kam-Pui Chow and Sujeet Shenoi. Springer Berlin Heidelberg New York, 2010, pp. 3–15.

Sachowski, Jason. *Digital Forensics and Investigations: People, Process, and Technologies to Defend the Enterprise.* CRC Press, 2018.

DIGITAL LIBRARIES AND ARTIFACTS

Introduction

In the early 1990s, when traditional library systems were first galvanized by the sweeping possibilities of digitalizing centuries of paper artifacts and documents into computer databases, library scientists believed a global network of digitalized materials was just around the corner. This grand digital library would be accessible to individual users anytime on any computer, thus rendering obsolete the notion of a library as a public building servicing a given community.

However, that bold vision proved to be a significant challenge to bring to fruition. Computer software experts and library scientists charged with devising the systems, system links, and databases and

A scan of a drawing with large areas of whitespace; the diamond Moiré pattern is a scanning artifact. Photo via Wikimedia Commons. [Public domain.]

amassing the archives to create digital libraries realized that reaching their goal would involve overcoming a myriad of complexities that still remained unresolved in the early twenty-first century.

Background

Not every available archive of information, documents, specialized publications, and data is a digital library; by that definition, any internet search engine would qualify. Instead, much like traditional libraries, digital libraries stress organization of the materials in addition to the traditional functions of long-term storage and preservation.

Digital libraries offer an important strategy for extending the reach of traditional libraries, and public and university libraries routinely subscribe to global databases for patron use in addition to participating in ongoing projects to convert centuries of print material into digital format. Although library science is well on its way to catching up to the possibilities of digital collections, distinctions have been established between materials that have to be digitalized—a process that is relatively quick, cheap, and applicable to basically to any publication from before 1990—and materials that are "born digital."

Those charged with developing the templates for digital libraries stress the virtual system's need to organize the ever-growing body of materials to permit efficient and transparent access to users worldwide, given that there will be no central digital library, simply links that connect databases and archives around the world. Such a system would require well-trained professionals to move users smoothly through an often-intimidating network of information.

The development of digital libraries poses a number of significant challenges, including designing the superstructure of an architecturally sound interrelated network of systems, rewriting existing international copyright laws for reproduction and distribution of materials, and generating metadata—that is, data that describes and can be used to catalog primary materials, much like traditional card catalogs or indexes.

In addition, libraries must keep up with the ever-expanding body of data that includes not only traditional print materials, such as books and periodicals, but also films, music, government records, and scientific and research data. Coordinating a theoretically unlimited number of digital libraries, each storing and organizing a specific area of available materials, and putting that network within reach of users ably assisted by digital librarians is the challenge that remains for library scientists and computer engineers.

—*Joseph Dewey and Laura Nicosia*

References

Calhoun, Karen. *Exploring Digital Libraries: Foundations, Practice, Prospects.* Facet. June 2018.

Cleveland, Gary. "Digital Libraries: Definitions, Issues and Challenges." *IFLA Core Programme*, Mar. 1998, archive.ifla.org/VI/5/op/udtop8/udt-op8.pdf.

Lanagan, James and Alan Smeaton. "Video Digital Libraries: Contributive and Decentralized." *International Journal on Digital Libraries*, vol. 12, no. 4, 2012, pp. 159–78.

Trivedi, Mayank. "Digital Libraries: Functionality, Usability, Accessibility." *Library Philosophy and Practice*, 2010, digitalcommons.unl.edu/libphilprac/381.

"What Is Digital Libraries?" *IGI Global*, igi-global.com/dictionary/fol-learning-knowledge-discovery-documents/7657.

DIGITAL NATIVES AND DIGITAL IMMIGRANTS

Introduction

A digital native is someone who was born during or after the Information Age, a period of emerging digital technology. The term "digital native" most commonly refers to those born at the end of the twentieth century and into the twenty-first century. Digital natives began interacting with digital technology at a young age and are unfamiliar with life without tools such as the internet, cell phones, and computers. Digital natives (often identified as millennials, generation Y, and generation Z) stand in contrast to digital immigrants, who were born before the prevalence of digital technology and had to adopt it later in life.

Background

The term "digital native" was coined by writer Marc Prensky in 2001 in an article for the journal *On the Horizon* about an emerging issue in education; he also created the term "digital immigrant" in the same article. In the article, he was writing about the changing nature of teaching—students have grown up around digital technology, while their teachers did not—and how it is affecting the educational system. He argued that the discontinuity has changed how students think critically and process information, which has widened the gap between them and their teachers, who must adapt to the new environment. Prensky further noted that digital immigrants often retain an "accent" that blends outdated language and behavior, highlighting their struggle to reconcile the new and the old.

One of the primary traits of digital natives is the ability to receive information rapidly, often through parallel processes and multitasking, taking on many things at once. Digital natives, who became used to these skills through their formative years, have entirely different frameworks for learning from those of the digital immigrants who are their teachers.

This can be as simple as a student being able to read and watch television at the same time or a much wider divide related to communication, networking, and connectivity in instruction. Another related issue is the disconnect between the attention of natives and the methodology of immigrants.

Beyond education, the concept of digital natives has become, in the broader sense, related to demographic and generational differences. The differences between the two groups—occasionally referred to as "analog versus digital"—are increasingly important as technology development continues to accelerate. Digital natives adapt to new technology almost instinctively, utilizing prior experience to intuit how to use something new; digital immigrants often struggle to keep up and often fail when they attempt to apply more traditional styles of thinking to new contexts.

That being said, generational gaps between natives and immigrants often reveal that digital immigrants—who have had to learn the technology rather than being born into its presence—often are more successful at manipulating the technology. Digital natives are more likely to rely on one source of information (hence, the verb "to google"), and are less likely to differentiate reliable from unreliable sources of information.

The gap between digital natives and digital immigrants has further implications when examined on a global scale. Poverty in developing nations is a potent example of this gap between the connected and disconnected, making it clear that it is not just a generational concern and instead runs the risk of being an ever-widening issue. The concept of digital natives is not without some controversy, however, with some critics noting that learning the use of digital technology is more simply a matter of access and cultural capital.

In their 2015 book, *The New Digital Natives: Cutting the Chord*, Dylan Seychell and Alexiei Dingli draw a distinction between first-generation digital natives and second-generation digital natives (2DNs). First-generation digital natives grew up before the advent of smartphones, tablets, social networking, and widespread Wi-Fi and laptop use. Their web access started only when they were able to use a mouse or read, unlike their children, the 2DNs, many of whom first accessed the web via touchscreens as toddlers.

—*Kehley Coviello*

References

Bennett, Sue, and K. Maton. "Beyond the 'Digital Natives' Debate: Towards a More Nuanced Understanding of Students' Technology Experiences." *Journal of Computer Assisted Learning*, vol. 26, no. 5, 2010, pp. 321–31.

Bittman, Michael, Leonie Rutherford, Jude Brown, and Lens Unsworth. "Digital Natives? New and Old Media and Children's Outcomes." *Australian Journal of Education*, vol. 55, no. 2, 2011, pp. 161–75.

Dingli, Alexiei, and Dylan Seychell. *The New Digital Natives: Cutting the Chord*. Springer, 2015.

Joiner, Richard, et al. "Comparing First and Second Generation Digital Natives' Internet Use, Internet Anxiety, and Internet Identification." *CyberPsychology, Behavior & Social Networking*, vol. 16, no. 7, 2013, pp. 549–52.

Jones, Chris. "A New Generation of Learners? The Net Generation and Digital Natives." *Learning, Media & Technology*, vol. 35, no. 4, 2010, pp. 365–68.

Pentland, Alex. "The Data-Driven Society." *Scientific American*, vol. 309, no. 4, 2013, pp. 78–83.

Ransdell, Sarah, Brianna Kent, Sandrine Gaillard-Kenney, and John Long. "Digital Immigrants Fare Better than Digital Natives Due to Social Reliance." *British Journal of Educational Technology*, vol. 42, no. 6, 2011, pp. 931–38.

Teo, Timothy. "An Initial Development and Validation of a Digital Natives Assessment Scale (DNAS)." *Computers & Education*, vol. 67, 2013, pp. 51–57.

Thompson, Penny. "The Digital Natives as Learners: Technology Use Patterns and Approaches to Learning." *Computers & Education*, vol. 65, 2013, pp. 12–33.

DIGITAL STORYTELLING

Introduction

Digital storytelling refers to the tendency of individuals to narrate aspects of their daily lives with the use of new media technology such as podcasts, videos, blogs, and social networks. It has also been described as multimedia creations that combine several digital aspects to construct a narrative. These tools through which people share their lives with others are growing in number, diversity, and sophistication. Although the expression may sound like an oxymoron, with "storytelling" recalling oral traditions and "digital" evoking modern technology, digital storytelling constitutes the postmodern adaptation of the ancient art of narrating stories. It is expanding both in terms of practitioners and audience and has also acquired a relevant status in all levels of education due to its engaging and interactive characteristics.

Background

Digital storytelling is made possible in large part by the accessibility and user-friendliness of new media hardware, such as digital cameras, digital voice recorders, and software such as Windows MovieMaker and Apple iMovie. Through these means, people who are not necessarily professional storytellers produce accounts of their lives or of things that have happened to them. These accounts are then shared with larger communities on the internet via video-sharing websites such as YouTube and Vimeo, as well as other means of electronic distribution such as various images, video, and audio, maps, and Tweets.

In digital storytelling, the ancient art of constructing a narrative is given a new angle through technology that allows storytellers to use multimedia techniques to intertwine words and digitized stills, moving images, music, and animation. Narrative techniques are therefore blended with technological resources to construct digital stories. This gives the storytelling a new form, as these narratives are often nonchronological, nonsequential, and much shorter than conventional narratives. In addition, new media technology allows for a greater interaction with the audience.

Because of these qualities, digital storytelling has attracted increasing numbers of authors and audiences. Evidence of this is the growing popularity of the Center for Digital Storytelling (CDS) in Berkeley, California. Founded in 1988, the center has worked to develop digital storytelling techniques and competencies that appeal to hundreds of organizations and thousands of people all over the world.

The interaction that digital storytelling affords makes it particularly well suited for the education sector as well as for the service sector, where stories have been used to carry out programs in the areas of prevention, inclusion, welfare, and health services.

Moreover, teachers and instructors can also use digital stories to generate interest and engagement for their digital-native students. Digital stories can appeal to diverse learning styles, allowing instructors to present abstract or conceptual information in a more understandable way.

Digital storytelling allows students to become creators in the classroom. They acquire technological skills, synthesize information, and write for an authentic audience with a meaningful or entertaining message. The benefits of digital storytelling are certainly verifiable by the passion with which students approach this kind of composition process.

—Luca Prono and Laura Nicosia

References

Alexander, Bryan. *The New Digital Storytelling: Creating Narratives with New Media.* ABC-CLIO, 2011.

Bouchrika, Imed. "Digital Storytelling: Benefits, Examples, Tools & Tips." *Research.com*, research.com/education/digital-storytelling.

Frazel, Midge. *Digital Storytelling Guide for Educators.* ISTE, 2010.

Hartley, John, and Kelly McWilliam, editors. *Story Circle: Digital Storytelling around the World.* Blackwell, 2009.

Lambert, Joe. *Digital Storytelling: Capturing Lives, Creating Community.* 4th ed., Routledge, 2013.

Miller, Carolyn Handler. *Digital Storytelling: A Creator's Guide to Interactive Entertainment.* 3rd ed., Focal, 2014.

Miller, Lisa C. *Make Me a Story: Teaching Writing through Digital Storytelling.* Stenhouse, 2010.

Ohler, Jason B. *Digital Storytelling in the Classroom: New Media Pathways to Literacy, Learning, and Creativity.* 2nd ed., Sage, 2013.

Sylvester, Ruth, and Wendy-lou Greenidge. "Digital Storytelling: Extending the Potential for Struggling Writers." *Reading Teacher*, vol. 63, no. 4, 2009, pp. 284–95.

DISCORD

Introduction

Discord is a software application (app) developed in the United States and used by tens of millions of people around the world. The app allows users to message each other using free voice, video, and text messaging on the platform.

Background

Two gaming engineers named Jason Citron and Stan Vishnevskiy worked together to create Discord. The friends first collaborated in 2013 to work on making video games together. However, they were unhappy with their games. The friends decided to create a platform for gamers to communicate with each other, and they launched Discord together in 2015. In part because of the demographics of gamers in America, Discord's early users were mostly young to middle-aged white men.

However, the demographics of the app changed as the app became more popular. Citron and Vishnevskiy developed desktop and mobile versions of the app, and they made it available to users for free. These advantages made it attractive, and by July 2017 it had 45 million registered users. Users can chat—through text, video, or audio—while they played their games. As of 2020, thousands of users communicate through group communication channels and through direct messages every day.

How It Works

Discord is a voice, video, and text chat app that is free to use for anyone thirteen years old and older. Users create unique user IDs and sign onto the application. Inside the application, users can communicate with each other by building and joining servers, or communities. Any user can create a server, and different servers deal with different ideas and topics. For example, some servers are intended for players of specific video games.

The user who creates the server chooses a name for it and makes decisions about what rules people have to follow and which users will be invited to join the server. Inside the server, the users create channels. Each server usually has multiple channels, and each channel will deal with a different topic and can have different rules. Users have created thousands

Discord logo. Image via Wikimedia Commons. [Public domain.]

of different Discord servers that deal with countless topics. The app is known for its simple design and high-tech features.

After a user makes a server, the user can invite other users to the server. The creator can also set up rules that apply to communication in the server. Some servers ban bullying, for example, but other servers require users to follow fewer rules. Server creators can also set up mods, or moderators, who can watch the content being shared to ensure it does not violate the server's rules. Servers are invite-only spaces, but the creator of the server can remove users from it if they break the rules.

Users can also communicate with each other through direct messages. Users can change the settings on their profiles to limit who can direct message them. They can also block specific users at any time to stop receiving messages from those users. Users can also send each other friend requests, and they have options to limit who can send them requests. Users who no longer want to use their Discord accounts can also delete their accounts. Users are supposed to be thirteen years old or older, but preventing a child younger than thirteen from joining the service often proves difficult, if not impossible.

People signing up for Discord accounts do not have to provide their real names. They also do not have to share personal information with other users. They can connect their Discord profiles to accounts on other apps and platforms, such as YouTube, Twitch, and Spotify. Although most people use the free version of Discord, the company also offers Discord Nitro, which is a paid service that, among other things, gives users increased video and audio quality.

Because all the content on Discord is created by users, the app is not immune to explicit language, sexual content, bullying, racism, and crude jokes. Some experts believe that teenagers who use the platform should be monitored by their parents or guardians because they could be influenced or harmed by some of the content. Users can limit which other users they communicate with, though, so users of any age can use settings to prevent unwanted communications from others.

Discord's Reputation

Although the app is very popular, it also has the reputation of being a site for attracting radical right-wing members who promote racist and xenophobic ideals. In 2017 members of the alt-right and of the political right planned a protest on the app and subsequently gathered in Charlottesville, Virginia, for a protest they called Unite the Right. After a counter protester was murdered, Discord was contacted about the role their application played in planning the event.

As of 2020, Discord user demographics had shifted, especially as people began using the Discord message function for countless topics in addition to gaming. During the 2020 COVID-19 pandemic, the app became even more popular as groups—such as school groups, scouting groups, and book clubs—used the app's free video and voice messaging to communicate. By June of that year, Discord had roughly 300 million registered users.

—Elizabeth Mohn

References

Brown, Abram. "Discord Was Once the Alt-Right's Favorite Chat App: Now It's Gone Mainstream and Scored a New $3.5 Billion Valuation." *Forbes*, 30 June 2020, www.forbes.com/sites/abram-brown/2020/06/30/discord-was-once-the-alt-rights-favorite-chat-app-now-its-gone-mainstream-and-scored-a-new-35-billion-valuation/#67cef99b6b2e.

Delfino, Devon. "What is Discord? Everything You Need to Know About the Popular Group-Chatting Platform." *Business Insider*, 26 Mar. 2020, www.businessinsider.com/what-is-discord#~:text=Discord%20is%20a%20group%2Dchatting,for%20all%20sorts%20of%20communities.&text=Discord%20also%20allows%20users%20to,other%20programs%20from%20their%20computers.

"Discord Safety Center." *Discord*, 2019, discord.com/safety.

Hornshaw, Phil. "What Is Discord?" *Digital Trends,* 1 Sept. 2020, www.digitaltrends.com/gaming/what-is-discord/.

Jargon, Julie. "The Dark Side of Discord, Your Teen's Favorite Chat App." *The Wall Street Journal*, 11 June 2019, www.wsj.com/articles/discord-where-teens-rule-and-parents-fear-to-tread-11560245402.

Lorenz, Taylor. "How an App for Gamers Went Mainstream." *The Atlantic*, 12 Mar. 2019, www.theatlantic.com/technology/archive/2019/03/how-discord-went-mainstream-influencers/584671/.

Minor, Jordan. "What Is Discord and How Do You Use It?" *PC Mag*, 11 May 2020, www.pcmag.com/how-to/what-is-discord-and-how-do-you-use-it.

Ucciferri, Frannie. "Parents' Ultimate Guide to Discord." *Common Sense Media*, 1 Mar. 2020, www.commonsensemedia.org/blog/parents-ultimate-guide-to-discord.

"What Is Discord?" *Discord*, discord.com/safety/360044149331-What-is-Discord.

DOXING

Introduction

Doxing (sometimes spelled doxxing) is the sharing of someone's personal information on the internet without their consent. Information shared in doxing is personal, such as cell phone numbers and work or home addresses. Sometimes it includes more sensitive material, such as social security numbers, personal messages, and photos.

Background

The word "dox" derives from having someone's documents, or information, which was shortened to "docs" and then to "dox." It is an abbreviation of "dropping dox," a revenge tactic used on hacker bulletin boards in the 1990s. As much of hacker culture depended on anonymity, disclosing someone's personal information (or PI) was a way to retaliate against them in an argument, show them to be vulnerable, and open them up to harassment or prosecution if they were breaking any laws. While initially doxing mostly revealed user profile information, the tactic expanded as the internet grew.

In 2006, a YouTube channel called Vigilantes was created. Its mission was to locate and publish the

Publicly revealing private personal informaiton about an individual or organization, usually with malicious intent, is known as doxing. Image via iStock/invincible_bulldog. [Used under license.]

personal information of other YouTube channels that posted what Vigilantes deemed to be hateful or racist content. In January 2007, the head of the Vigilantes group was doxed by members of *Encyclopedia Dramatica*. The information included her name, address, and personal posts she made to a newsgroup.

At this point in time, the hacker collective Anonymous and associated groups, such as Chan Enterprises LLC and Lulzsec, began to use doxing in targeted campaigns. One of the first documented doxing campaigns focused on white nationalist and radio host Hal Turner. Turner shared the telephone numbers of prank callers that phoned in to his radio show in December 2006. In response, Anonymous members calling themselves Chan Enterprises LLC began a doxing investigation that discovered Turner's criminal record, home address, and phone number, which they posted. Turner filed several lawsuits against the online forums and websites that posted his dox, such as 4chan, eBaums World, and 7chan, in January 2007. However, all the cases were dismissed by December of that year.

Forums like 4chan and 7chan are similar to Reddit, except that they have no user names and few rules. They are considered to be the antithesis of social media, where people anonymously say and post whatever they wish with few or no consequences. These forums are often hosts to doxing campaigns or other anonymous postings. For instance, 4chan was blamed for the leaks of many female celebrity nudes.

In January 2008, anonymous hackers started Project Chanology, a doxing campaign that targeted members of Scientology. The hackers published the personal information of high-ranking members and internal memos from the church. This doxing campaign received international coverage.

By 2008, the term "doxing" had become more widely known and was added to Urban Dictionary, which defined it as personal information leaked by a third party. Wiktionary added a doxing definition in 2011. Today, the term appears in mainstream dictionaries such as the Oxford British and World English Dictionary, which added the term in 2015.

The definition of doxing is generally perceived to be negative, as it violates privacy and was historically used for retaliation. However, there is some debate about whether doxing is, at times, warranted, when the goals achieved outweigh a person's privacy and anonymity. There are a wide variety of motives for doxing someone.

Internet vigilantism often uses doxing, where those who disagree with an individual's actions publish the person's personal information so that they are subject to harassment and criticism. Groups on both the left and the right of the political spectrum have employed this technique. It is not just political or hacker groups that use doxing. In July 2015, newspapers reported that Cecil the Lion was illegally killed by a hunter from Minnesota. *The Telegraph*, a British newspaper, identified the hunter as a dentist from Minnesota. His address, website, work, and vacation homes were vandalized and he received death threats and protests.

Doxing can serve as a tool for protest or exposing corruption. Government corruption in China was the target of the Human Flesh Search Engine, a group of internet citizens who search for and publish information about government wrongdoing. One of their doxes exposed government officials using public funds for recreational trips.

Sometimes doxing is used to expose perceived wrongdoing. In 2015, a group of hackers called the "Impact Team" breached the Ashley Madison database. The online dating site catered to married people wishing to have affairs. The hackers demanded that the site shut down permanently or they would dox the information they obtained. When the site remained up, the hackers released 30 million user email addresses and profiles. The doxing led to several suicides, extortion attempts, and general embarrassment.

Certain types of investigative journalism can have the effect of doxing, such as the disclosure of the identity of the presumed Bitcoin inventor, Satoshi Nakamoto. This has spurred debate about where the line between investigative journalism and doxing lies, and whether and when it might be acceptable to disclose the names of individuals that are making efforts to remain anonymous.

Doxing is most commonly understood to be a means of harassment or a form of cyberbullying. It is intended to threaten someone and make them feel vulnerable. In the worst cases, it is used in cyberstalking and makes someone fearful for their safety or life to the point where they need to go into hiding.

A Pew Research Center survey in 2014 stated that 40 percent of adult internet users have experienced some form of harassment and 7 percent have experienced "sustained" periods of harassment. Since information on the internet is difficult to erase, a dox may haunt the targeted person both personally and professionally for years. All one has to do is enter the person's name into a search engine for the material to come back up.

Due to the difficult task of fighting this sort of harassment, numerous groups have formed to offer support to victims of doxing. For instance, Crash Override Network is "a crisis helpline, advocacy group and resource center for people who are experiencing online abuse." The group was formed by two victims of doxing during Gamergate, a 2014–15 campaign of online harassment against women gamers, developers, and videogame critics.

Since the launch of the service, they have assisted over 400 clients. They offer the assistance of social workers, lawyers and computer security professionals. Doxing is the most frequent sort of harassment they encounter, as it is relatively easy to find information about someone on the internet and it has a strong impact. The harasser is also able to rationalize doxing actions as benign and deny responsibility for other's actions, even though the intention is to violate another's personal space and sense of security.

As the internet has evolved, opportunities to share personal data have increased in myriad ways, such as through social media, online shopping, and other means. Doxing, through its use and misuse, highlights the challenge of balancing online interconnection with anonymity and privacy, both personally and in relation to others.

—*Noëlle Sinclair*

References

Citron, Danielle Keats. *Hate Crimes in Cyberspace.* Harvard UP, 2014.

Crash Override Network. "So You've Been Doxed: A Guide to Best Practices." Crashoverridenetwork. com, crashoverridenetwork.com/soyouvebeen-doxed.html.

Douglas, David M. "Doxing: A Conceptual Analysis." *Ethics and Information Technology*, vol. 18, no. 3, 2016, pp. 199–210.

Harcourt, Bernard E. *Exposed: Desire and Disobedience in the Digital Age.* Harvard UP, 2015.

Li, Lisa Bei. "Data Privacy in the Cyber Age: Recommendations for Regulating Doxing and Swatting." *Federal Communications Law Journal*, vol. 70, no. 3, 2018, pp. 317–28.

Pew Research Center. "The Future of Free Speech, Trolls, Anonymity, and Fake News Online, 2017." Elon.elon.edu/docs/e-web/imagining/surveys/2016_survey/Pew%20and%20Elon%20University%20Trolls%20Fake%20News%20Report%20Future%20of%20internet%20 3.29.17.pdf.

DVDS

Introduction

Digital video discs (DVDs) are a form of optical disc storage format primarily used by consumers to watch films and television programs. They are quickly becoming obsolete in favor of Blu-ray discs, cloud storage, and other optical storage

Background

Digital video discs arrived in the mid-1990s and soon overtook the supremacy of videocassettes for home viewing. In the 1970s and 1980s, the Video Home System (VHS) videocassette recorder (VCR) revolutionized home entertainment by allowing viewers to videotape television programs and watch them at their leisure and to rent or buy films on videotape. This viewing flexibility was undercut for some because the picture and sound quality of videocassettes was generally inferior to what could be seen and heard on television and especially in movie theaters.

DVD logo. Image via Wikimedia Commons. [Public domain.]

Then, DVDs were developed to offer viewers considerably improved picture and sound.

Format Development

Two years after its introduction in 1976, VHS had a challenger in the laser disc, which offered much sharper images, offering 425 lines of horizontal resolution in contrast to VHS's 240. With Criterion's special edition release of *Citizen Kane* (1941) in 1985, which provided supplemental material about the film (generally referred to as bonus materials, or extras), another advantage was introduced. Laser discs never caught on with the public, however, because of their cumbersome size (comparable to long-playing records), their susceptibility to damage, their high cost, and their inability to record television programs.

Three million laser disc players had been sold in the United States by 1997. Consumers waited patiently while a cheaper, more adaptable technology was developed. By 1993, Philips and Sony had developed the smaller MultiMedia Compact Disc, while Toshiba had created its Super Density Disc. Philips and Sony, wanting to avoid a format war, eventually decided to proceed with the specifications of the Toshiba disc, and the DVD was born. Though the industry initially insisted that DVD stood for "digital versatile disc," most consumers believed it meant "digital video disc," and the nomenclature was changed.

Digital video discs and DVD players entered the US market in late 1997. At first, only recent popular films were offered, with older and more esoteric films becoming available late in the 1990s. Some consumers were hesitant at first because the first DVDs were not recordable, but those who had been reluctant to buy laser discs quickly embraced the cheaper, smaller (the same size as audio compact discs), and easier-to-store discs. These buyers found that the picture, with the same resolution as laser discs, was vastly superior to that of videocassettes, and when connected to the proper equipment (receiver, speakers), multichannel audio was possible. As a result, Pioneer, the main champion of laser discs, abandoned this format in June, 1999.

Quick Success

Though DVDs were initially slow to catch on with the general public, matters soon changed as more and more consumers heard about the improved audiovisual quality and saw it demonstrated in electronics stores. The entertainment industry had assumed that DVDs would slowly supplement or perhaps even replace VHS, but experts underestimated the public by assuming that consumers would continue to rent much more than they purchased. Though some had developed VHS collections of their favorite films, the bulky tapes took up considerable room. Digital video discs occupied much less space, were at first only slightly costlier than VHS cassettes, and were generally more durable (though prone to scratching), inviting multiple viewings. They also did not require rewinding as VHS tapes did.

Contributing to this early success was the inclusion of extras. Following the lead of laser discs, the makers of DVDs offered commentaries by filmmakers and film scholars. Viewers could watch films either with or without commentaries, which explained the production details of the films and, with older films, placed them in a historical context. Consumers wanted more and more extras, and soon many films included things like on-set interviews, documentaries about the making of the films, deleted scenes, and more.

Digital video discs also offered viewers the option, for many films made since the mid-1950s, of watching them in a full-screen format—which filled every inch of screen space but cut off the corners of the images—or in the film's original wide-screen format, meaning that the tops, bottoms, and sides of images were no longer excised. This pleased many cinephiles who had lamented the formatting changes to classic films upon VHS release. As television screens became larger, the wide-screen format option became more important.

In 1998, 2 million DVD players were sold in the United States, three thousand titles were available,

Example of a DVD disc. Photo by Marcin Sochacki (Wanted), via Wikimedia Commons.

and 9.3 million DVDs were sold. In 1999, 4 million players were sold, 6,300 titles were available, and 20 million DVDs were sold. Digital video discs and DVD players had an advantage that VHS and VCRs did not: the internet. By the late 1990s, consumers had discovered the ease of purchasing online, finding that players and DVDs could be found at lower prices than in stores. By the end of 1999, four titles had sold over a million copies each: *Austin Powers: The Spy Who Shagged Me* (1999), *The Matrix* (1999), *Saving Private Ryan* (1998), and *Titanic* (1997).

Internet commerce and DVDs have been linked since the introduction of the format. While videocassettes had been rented from stores such as the Blockbuster chain, DVDs could be rented online from Netflix starting in April, 1998. When the company introduced a flat monthly fee for unlimited rentals of DVDs delivered quickly by mail in September 1999, online renting of DVDs took off.

Impact

Because DVDs were introduced relatively late in the 1990s, their full impact did not become clear until the early twenty-first century. Once the initial consumer excitement over improved picture, sound, and storage subsided, more and more titles were demanded, especially classic and obscure films, along with increased extras. Many enthusiastic DVD collectors built libraries of hundreds and thousands of titles. Digital video disc producers were pleasantly shocked by the number of people wanting to own complete seasons of their favorite television shows. What began as an alternative to VHS eventually changed America's viewing habits as much as the earlier innovation. As a result, VHS itself slowly faded, with the last mass-market VHS title issued in 2006.

However, DVDs themselves soon faced challenges from newer technologies. Blu-ray Discs, which use blue lasers instead of the red lasers of DVDs, were officially introduced in 2006 and allow much higher resolution images and a greater amount of data. Cooperation from companies such as Sony and Philips again led to a standardization of formats, beating out Toshiba's HD DVD competitor. Ultra-high-definition Blu-ray technology later followed. These discs and players competed with DVDs, and retailers promoted special Blu-ray releases of films with new special features in order to attract consumers who may already have purchased the DVD version. Though Blu-ray technology was initially expensive compared to DVDs, and therefore less popular, it eventually ate into the market share of DVDs. Perhaps even more importantly, the 2010s also saw consumers increasingly turn to online streaming services for video content. Netflix pivoted from its DVD-mailing business to focus on streaming films and television shows, for example, and sales of DVDs declined.

—Michael Adams

References

Barlow, Aaron. *The DVD Revolution: Movies, Culture, and Technology.* Praeger, 2005.

Bennett, James, and Tom Brown, editors. *Film and Television After DVD.* Routledge, 2008.

Fitzpatrick, Eileen. "DVD POV: Perspective on a Deep-Pocketed Market." *Billboard,* 27 May 2000, p. 129.

Taylor, Jim. *Everything You Ever Wanted to Know About DVD: The Official DVD FAQ.* McGraw-Hill, 2004.

E-BOOKS AND EDUCATION

Introduction

An e-book is any text, originally written for print media or created specifically for reading on a device, that is available for consumption on a computer or mobile device. E-books use computer software to store and display the contents of a traditional book. Depending on the type of technology an e-book vendor uses, it may be possible to read an e-book on a computer screen or on a device specially designed to accommodate users of e-books; these devices have numerous brand names but in general are referred to as e-readers. E-readers usually consist of a screen on which the text of the book is displayed, and they often have navigation features that seek to replicate many of the features of a traditional, printed book, such as a table of contents and the option to turn virtual pages of the e-book just as one would turn a paper book's pages.

Background

Schools made major advances in providing access to information and technology beginning in the 1990s. With government assistance and donations from private foundations and other organizations, schools expose students to some of the latest technology and to the research goldmine that is the internet. Several innovations are of importance to literacy development, such as the introduction of software programs and mobile apps that help students learn to read, to think critically about what they have read, and to apply their insights about their reading to answer thought-provoking questions. Some of these programs even have special features designed for the benefit of students with learning disabilities such as dyslexia.

E-books have numerous features that interest librarians, educators, and teachers. For example, an

Ebook usage in schools has increased dramatically. Photo via iStock/urfinguss. [Used under license.]

institution can build up a library of hundreds of thousands of volumes without needing to dedicate physical space to house shelves for printed books. E-books also can be transmitted electronically over computer networks just like any other type of digital information, and can even be stored on a central server for access by users all over the world.

This is a huge advantage to schools whose students are widely dispersed over a large region; instead of each student having to make the journey to the school's library to locate books for research, students can simply log on to the school's online library and access books from anywhere there is an internet connection. E-books can also be enhanced versions of their printed counterparts, offering features that paper books do not have. For example, the bibliography of a print book offers useful references to other materials, but the reader will need to try to locate them elsewhere in the library, or even in another library; an e-book's bibliography can contain hyperlinks that will take the reader to the cited material by connecting to it through an internet browser.

Despite these advantages, the ways in which e-books can and should be used within the sphere of education are still unclear. Questions remain as to whether having access to e-books instead of or in addition to printed volumes has a significant, positive effect on the educational attainment of students. Critics argue that schools should not rush to adopt them without first evaluating both the benefits and the total cost of operation and making rational plans for how to best make use of them in the service of student learning.

The Efficacy of E-books

Ironically, while e-readers and e-books have exploded in popularity over the last few years, there has been relatively little reliable research conducted into how the use of these technologies improves reading ability. Of the studies that have been performed, many suffer from some form of selection bias. That is, they are conducted on groups that have essentially self-selected by opting to acquire or use e-books or e-readers in the first place, so the participants in the study are likely to be biased in favor of emphasizing the benefits of the technology and minimizing or ignoring its drawbacks.

For example, a school district that invests heavily in buying a certain brand of e-reader for its teachers and students will have done so in the believe that acquiring the technology was a wise decision and may exhibit resistance toward information that challenges that perspective. Several researchers have pointed out the need for more objective studies in which subjects are randomly assigned to control and study groups rather than recruited on a voluntary basis.

Comprehension

Other research has demonstrated that there is a common effect produced on students when they are exposed to e-readers and e-books, though it is not necessarily the effect that educators might have hoped for. In several studies, results have shown that students' motivation to read increases significantly with the introduction of e-books and/or e-readers, even when the content of the books being read is the same as that available to the students in print form. It appears that this is due to the novelty of the e-book experience and in some cases to the appeal of the e-reader that has been generated by its manufacturer's advertising and other forms of media exposure.

However, despite the laudable improvement in student motivation, these same studies show much lower levels of comprehension by the students using e-books, suggesting that the students were more interested in using the e-book and its interactive multimedia capabilities than they were in using a printed book, but that when it came to extracting meaning from what they were reading, they did not perform as well as students using paper books. These findings will have great relevance to manufacturers of e-books and e-readers, whom educators have urged to focus less on entertaining gimmicks designed to capture children's attention, and more on the cognitive psychology that describes how children learn and how that learning can be supported by technology.

Gender Bias

Another aspect of the way e-books may influence students' reading habits raises concerns not only of effectiveness but also of equity between genders. Research outside the field of e-books and literacy has tended to show that girls are more hesitant to experiment with new technologies such as those presented by e-readers and e-books, while boys tend to show greater enthusiasm for these pursuits. Without inquiring into whether this is due to environment and the effects of socialization or to some other factors, this insight suggests that when e-books are introduced into the curriculum, teachers and parents must do so with consideration.

Interestingly, the effects of gender on e-books and vice versa may in some ways compensate for what has otherwise been a decades-long trend in the opposite direction: Ordinarily girls express more interest in reading and report spending more of their time each day reading than do boys, so perhaps e-books can be a way of increasing male interest in reading.

E-books' Impact on Libraries

A common assumption is that as more and more educational institutions move to adopt e-readers and to convert their physical library collections to online repositories of e-books, there will be less need for physical libraries. The idea behind this notion is that because students will essentially be able to carry around the books they could possibly need on their tablet computers or e-readers, it would be pointless to keep librarians around to shelve books that no one reads. Research suggests, however, that this conclusion may be somewhat premature.

Studies have shown, to the surprise of many, that there is not much correlation between the academic performance of a school's students and the size of the school's library. Further research, however, has shown that what does make a difference in the ability of students to excel academically is the availability of library staff and other instructors who are able to assist students with navigating the world of online information. Further, special education teachers and students with various impairments or disorders find additional resources in digital collections. Online libraries, such as Bookshare, take advantage e-book features to provide increased accessibility for people with disabilities that prevent them from utilizing traditional, printed books.

Thus, what appears to produce the best outcome for students is not merely the conversion of print libraries to e-books, but the provision of instruction to the students in how to go about using e-books, print books, and other information sources to gather data, organize and evaluate it, and then synthesize it for their own understanding and to present it to others. In other words, the benefit of e-books seems to be the same benefit provided by print books. While e-books may be more effective at helping students interact with information and use it to their advantage, much of their attraction is derived from their novelty.

Viewpoints

E-books have been the subject of a great deal of hype in the media, and they do have some very real and important applications, particularly in serving disabled persons and in providing greater access to information to those of lower socioeconomic status. At the same time, it is important for schools to exercise caution in how e-books are used and in what expectations are created around that use. Projects that expect e-books to magically capture the attention of children and convert them into avid readers at a fraction of the cost of a well-stocked physical library are certain to result in disappointment.

On the other hand, initiatives that have a well-thought-out plan for how e-books will be used, what they are expected to accomplish, and why they are the best tool for the job, are much more likely to achieve their goals. Educators need to use their professional judgment and their knowledge of students' diverse learning modalities to select e-books that do not rely on distracting "eye candy" to enthrall children, but instead leverage the advantages of the e-book's multimedia platform to help children engage with a text without distracting them from that text. Once appropriate works have been selected, instructors' work is not over; they must also guide students through the process of learning to navigate the e-book.

Study after study has shown that e-books are not a "magic bullet" for defeating illiteracy. Students need their teachers' guidance and scaffolding with using e-books every bit as much as they need it in other types of activities. In the end, e-books are a type of tool—information delivery devices, just like books. They may be more versatile than books, because a single e-reader can hold several e-books while a traditional book only contains one literary work. E-books have great potential to help students learn, but only if teachers have the training and resources to help those students to do so.

—*Scott Zimmer*

References

Bartos, J. *What Is the Role of Technology in Education?* Greenhaven Press, 2013.

Felvégi, E., and K. I. Matthew. "Ebooks and Literacy in K-12 Schools." *Computers in the Schools*, vol. 29, no. 1/2, 2012, pp. 40–52.

Fisher, M. "Digital Learning Strategies: How Do I Assign and Assess 21st Century Work?" *ASCD*, 2013.

Harpur, P., and N. Suzor. "The Paradigm Shift in Realising the Right to Read: How Ebook Libraries Are Enabling in the University Sector." *Disability & Society*, vol. 29, no. 10, 2014, pp. 1658–71.

Johnson, D. *The Classroom Teacher's Technology Survival Guide.* Jossey-Bass, 2012.

Mcleod, S., and C. Lehmann. *What School Leaders Need to Know About Digital Technologies and Social Media.* Jossey-Bass, 2012.

Miller, C., and A. H. Doering, editors. *The New Landscape of Mobile Learning: Redesigning Education in an App-based World.* Routledge, 2014.

Murphy, D., R. Walker, and G. Webb. *Online Learning and Teaching with Technology: Case Studies, Experience and Practice.* Taylor and Francis, 2013.

Pacansky-Brock, M., and S. S. Ko. *Best Practices for Teaching with Emerging Technologies.* Routledge, 2013.

Passey, D. *Inclusive Technology Enhanced Learning: Overcoming Cognitive, Physical, Emotional, and Geographic Challenges.* Routledge, 2014.

Rowan, L., and C. Bigum, editors. *Transformative Approaches to New Technologies and Student Diversity in Futures Oriented Classrooms: Future Proofing Education.* Springer, 2012.

Sunghee, S. "Ebook Usability in Educational Technology Classes: Teachers and Teacher Candidates' Perception Toward Ebook for Teaching and Learning." *International Journal of Distance Education Technologies*, vol. 12, no. 3, 2014, pp. 62–74.

ENCRYPTION

Introduction

Encryption is a process in which data is translated into code that can only by read by a person with the correct encryption key. The original, unencrypted data is called the plaintext. Encryption uses an algorithm called a cipher to convert plaintext into ciphertext. The ciphertext can then be deciphered by using another algorithm known as the decryption key or cipher key. Encryption focuses on protecting data content rather than preventing unauthorized interception. Encryption is essential in intelligence and national security and is also common in commercial applications. Various software programs are available that allow users to encrypt personal data and digital messages. The study of different encryption techniques is called cryptography.

A key is a string of characters applied to the plaintext to convert it to ciphertext, or vice versa. Depending on the keys used, encryption may be either symmetric or asymmetric. Symmetric-key encryption uses the same key for both encoding and decoding. The key used to encode and decode the data must be kept secret, as anyone with access to the key can translate the ciphertext into plaintext. The oldest known cryptography systems used alphanumeric substitution algorithms, which are a type of symmetric encryption. Symmetric-key algorithms are simple to create but vulnerable to interception.

Background

In asymmetric-key encryption, the sender and receiver use different but related keys. First, the receiver uses an algorithm to generate two keys, one to encrypt the data and another to decrypt it. The encryption key, also called the public key, is made available to anyone who wishes to send the receiver a message. (For this reason, asymmetric-key encryption is also known as public-key encryption.) The decryption key, or private key, remains known only to the receiver. It is also possible to encrypt data using the private key and decrypt it using the public key.

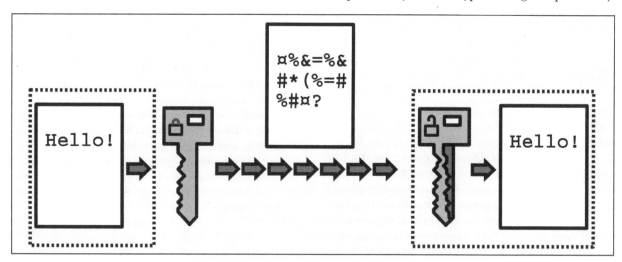

A simple illutration of public-key cryptography, one of the most widely used forms of encryption. Image by Johannes Landin, via Wikimedia Commons

However, the same key cannot be used to both encrypt and decrypt.

Asymmetric-key encryption works because the mathematical algorithms used to create the public and private keys are so complex that it is computationally impractical determine the private key based on the public key. This complexity also means that asymmetric encryption is slower and requires more processing power. First developed in the 1970s, asymmetric encryption is the standard form of encryption used to protect internet data transmission.

Authentication and Security

Authentication is the process of verifying the identity of a sender or the authenticity of the data sent. A common method of authentication is a hashing algorithm, which translates a string of data into a fixed-length number sequence known as a hash value. This value can be reverted to the original data using the same algorithm. The mathematical complexity of hashing algorithms makes it extremely difficult to decrypt hashed data without knowing the exact algorithm used. For example, a 128-bit hashing algorithm can generate 2^{128} different possible hash values.

For the purpose of authenticating sent data, such as a message, the sender may first convert the data into a hash value. This value, also called a message digest, may then be encrypted using a private key unique to the sender. This creates a digital signature that verifies the authenticity of the message and the identity of the sender. The original unhashed message is then encrypted using the public key that corresponds to the receiver's private key. Both the privately encrypted digest and the publicly encrypted message are sent to the receiver, who decrypts the original message using their private key and decrypts the message digest using the sender's public key. The receiver then hashes the original message using the same algorithm as the sender. If the message is authentic, the decrypted digest and the new digest should match.

Encryption Systems in Practice

One of the most commonly used encryption programs is Pretty Good Privacy (PGP). It was developed in 1991 and combines symmetric- and asymmetric-key encryption. The original message is encrypted using a unique one-time-only private key called a "session key." The session key is then encrypted using the receiver's public key, so that it can only be decrypted using the receiver's private key.

This encrypted key is sent to the receiver along with the encrypted message. The receiver uses their private key to decrypt the session key, which can then be used to decrypt the message. For added security and authentication, PGP also uses a digital signature system that compares the decrypted message against a message digest.

The PGP system is one of the standards in personal and corporate security and is highly resistant to attack. The data security company Symantec acquired PGP in 2010 and subsequently incorporated the software into many of its encryption programs.

Encryption can be based on either hardware or software. Most modern encryption systems are based on software programs that can be installed on a system to protect data contained in or produced by a variety of other programs. Encryption based on hardware is less vulnerable to outside attack. Some hardware devices, such as self-encrypting drives (SEDs), come with built-in hardware encryption and are useful for high-security data. However, hardware encryption is less flexible and can be prohibitively costly to implement on a wide scale. Essentially, software encryption tends to be more flexible and widely usable, while hardware encryption is more secure and may be more efficient for high-security systems.

—*Micah L. Issitt*

References

Ciesla, Robert. *Encryption for Organizations and Individuals: Basics of Contemporary and Quantum Cryptography*. Apress, 2020.

"A Deep Dive on End-to-End Encryption: How Do Public Key Encryption Systems Work?" *Surveillance Self-Defense*, 29 Nov. 2018, ssd.eff.org/en/module/deep-dive-end-end-encryption-how-do-public-key-encryption-systems-work.

Delfs, Hans, and Helmut Knebl. *Introduction to Cryptography: Principles and Applications*. 3rd ed., Springer-Verlag Berlin Heidelberg, 2015.

Dotson, Chris. *Practical Cloud Security: A Guide for Secure Design and Deployment*. O'Reilly Media, 2019.

Lackey, Ella Deon, et al. "Introduction to Public-Key Cryptography." *Mozilla Developer Network*, 21 Nov. 2019, developer.mozilla.org/en-US/docs/Archive/Security/Introduction_to_Public-Key_Cryptography.

Lewis, James A., Denise E. Zheng, and William A. Carter. *The Effect of Encryption on Lawful Access to Communications and Data.* Center for Strategic & International Studies/Rowman & Littlefield, 2017.

Nagelhout, Ryan. *Digital Era Encryption and Decryption.* Rosen, 2017.

ETHICS OF ALGORITHMS

Introduction

Algorithms—crucial to the field of computer science since the advent of computing—took on even greater importance during the first decades of the twenty-first century as technology companies explored new applications for algorithms within subfields such as artificial intelligence (AI) and machine learning. During the 2000s and 2010s, algorithms came to be used for a wide range of purposes, including serving social media users with relevant content, analyzing and identifying images of human faces, predicting criminal activity, and assessing job applicants.

At the same time, however, a debate arose regarding how best to manage the ethical implications of algorithmic technologies, which at times raised moral quandaries and made questionable decisions based on biased data. Some individuals and organizations concerned about those ethical ramifications have argued that technology companies and their programmers should take the lead in promoting and using ethical algorithm design and in combating bias through means such as human-led audits. Some, on the other hand, have asserted that the technology industry cannot regulate itself and that the US government must intervene and regulate algorithms to ensure that they are being designed and implemented in an ethical manner.

Background

The term "algorithm" originated in mathematics and was subsequently brought into widespread use within the field of computer science. It refers to a sequence of instructions a computer follows to perform a specific task. The concept of computer algorithms predates the physical creation of computers in the modern sense, arising as early as the mid-nineteenth century in the form of early programs written for proposed—though not yet built—computing devices. Perhaps the most famous of those early algorithms was a program written by the English mathematician Ada Lovelace, created for use with the Analytical Engine computing device proposed by inventor Charles Babbage. Lovelace's algorithm, published in 1843 as a note in her annotated translation of an Italian paper on the Analytical Engine, was designed to calculate the numbers known as Bernoulli numbers.

As computer technology developed from theoretical to physical, algorithms designed for computing devices became increasingly complex, rendering computers capable of performing a variety of complicated tasks. One of the first recorded uses of algorithms with computers was by Alan Turing, a mathematician best known for breaking the Enigma code during World War II, who published a computational theory to explain the patterns seen in nature. Turing's goal to capture general processes led to the creation of the Turing Machine, which in turn led the way for general purpose computers. Those machines were the first computers able to execute arbitrary sets of instructions.

Following those early successes, computer scientists made significant strides in the areas of computer technology and AI—algorithm-based computer technology that performs intelligence-based tasks, such as analyzing information and making decisions, that have historically been carried out within human minds. Some AI technologies function based on specific instructions coded by programmers, while others fall within the realm of machine learning, in which algorithms process large sets of data, learn from that data, and adapt accordingly without further human instruction.

During the early twenty-first century, algorithms came to play crucial roles in both programs and services used regularly by the public and in more experimental technologies under development. In the 2000s, social media services, such as Facebook and Twitter, began to use algorithms to determine which posts would appear in a user's newsfeed and in what order, as well as to identify trending content. Algorithms were also created to supply users of a content-providing service, such as a music- or video-streaming application, with relevant content. The music-streaming service Spotify, for instance, uses algorithms to recommend new music to a user based on that individual's past listening habits, while the video-streaming website YouTube uses algorithms to recommend videos related to one that the user has just watched.

Another common use of algorithms is the analysis and tagging of images. The service Google Photos, for example, could use algorithms to determine that a specific image was a photograph of a cat and could then tag the photograph accordingly. Image-analyzing algorithms were also key to the development of facial-recognition technology, which can locate a human face in an image, analyze its features, and compare that face against images of faces in a central database to find a match. Such technology came into regular use both as a personal security feature, enabling users to unlock their mobile devices with their faces rather than passcodes or fingerprints, and as a form of surveillance and policing technology, allowing authorities to identify individuals of interest based on sources such as security camera footage.

In addition to using facial-recognition technology, law enforcement and corrections officials in some areas experimented with a practice known as predictive policing, in which algorithms were used to predict the areas in which crimes were most likely to occur, which individuals were likely to commit crimes, and which imprisoned individuals seeking parole were likely to commit further crimes if released.

Some technological innovations based on AI and machine technologies earned praise and demonstrated the potential of algorithms to increase the efficiency, accuracy, and profitability of certain processes for companies and convenience or a better quality of life for users. However, their emergence into the mainstream likewise called attention to the ethical drawbacks of some such technologies. Content-serving algorithms, such as those used by Facebook and Twitter, drew criticism for exerting undue control over users' newsfeeds and thereby further polarizing the public politically, and Facebook's algorithm to highlight trending news stories struggled to discern factual articles from so-called fake news.

Facial recognition programs made more errors when trying to identify women and people of color than they did when identifying white men, a phenomenon that prompted researchers to investigate the diversity of the datasets used when training such programs and to speak out against the use of facial recognition technology in policing, as flawed programs could produce false matches. Predictive policing also drew criticism, with some scholars and advocacy groups asserting that the algorithmic approach to law enforcement was based on flawed data, disproportionately targeted black people and residents of poor neighborhoods, and ultimately perpetuated systemic racism. Additional technologies that presented ethical challenges included an experimental recruiting algorithm tested by the retailer Amazon, which penalized applications that included the word "women's." Ethical problems also arose around the use of algorithms in medicine and finance.

Ethics of Algorithms Today

In light of growing concerns regarding the ethical implications of AI, machine learning, and other algorithm-based technologies, the ethics and implicit biases of algorithms became the subject of extensive research throughout the United States, including at colleges and universities such as the Massachusetts Institute of Technology (MIT), Harvard University, and Stanford University. Researchers affiliated with such institutions not only looked into the causes and ramifications of algorithmic bias, but also explored means of mitigating such biases and tackling the numerous other ethical quandaries the continuously developing AI industry raised.

In response to the increased emphasis on ethics, a number of major technology companies developed boards or committees dedicated to ethics, particularly regarding their AI research. Microsoft founded its AI and Ethics in Engineering and Research (AETHER) Committee in 2017. Google launched an Advanced Technology External Advisory Council (ATEAC) to oversee its AI work in March 2019 but disbanded the council less than two weeks later. Social media companies also began ethics-oriented self-regulation initiatives, with Facebook selecting the first group of members of its Oversight Board, a group focused primarily on content-moderation disputes, in 2020.

Although scholars, organizations, and industry leaders with a diverse array of perspectives widely agreed that the use of algorithm-driven technology raised serious ethical concerns, opinions regarding the best means of addressing those concerns were split. Many individuals and trade organizations within the technology industry argued that technology companies should take the lead in addressing the issue and could regulate their own products and practices. In addition to recommending that companies perform regular audits to detect bias or other ethical issues in their technologies, some proponents of industry-led reform suggested that the technology industry could also benefit from greater diversity in staffing, which might help mitigate implicit racial or gender bias. By contrast, some experts argued that industry self-regulation was ineffective and that existing means of government oversight were incapable of keeping up with the ever-changing technological landscape. Such individuals argued that the US government should introduce new regulations to protect the public from the misuse of algorithms and to ensure that further developments in AI, machine learning, facial recognition technology, and related areas would be implemented ethically.

—*Joy Crelin*

References

Brogan, Jacob. "What's the Deal with Algorithms?" *Slate*, 2 Feb. 2016, slate.com/technology/2016/02/whats-the-deal-with-algorithms.html.

DeAngelis, Stephen F. "Artificial Intelligence: How Algorithms Make Systems Smart." *Wired*, Sept. 2014, www.wired.com/insights/2014/09/artificial-intelligence-algorithms-2.

Heaven, Will Douglas. "Predictive Policing Algorithms Are Racist: They Need to Be Dismantled." *MIT Technology Review*, 17 July 2020, www.technologyreview.com/2020/07/17/1005396/predictive-policing-algorithms-racist-dismantled-machine-learning-bias-criminal-justice.

Kearns, Michael. "How to Build an Ethical Algorithm." Interview by Dan Costa. *PCMag*, 27 Feb. 2020, www.pcmag.com/news/how-to-build-an-ethical-algorithm.

Kearns, Michael, and Aaron Roth. "Ethical Algorithm Design Should Guide Technology Regulation." *Brookings*, 13 Jan. 2020, www.brookings.edu/research/ethical-algorithm-design-should-guide-technology-regulation.

___. "Who Is Responsible for Biased and Intrusive Algorithms?" *Knowledge@Wharton*. University of Pennsylvania, 2 Dec. 2019, knowledge.wharton.upenn.edu/article/who-is-responsible-for-biased-and-intrusive-algorithms.

Kowalkiewicz, Marek. "How Did We Get Here? The Story of Algorithms." *Towards Data Science*, 10 Oct. 2019, towardsdatascience.com/how-did-we-get-here-the-story-of-algorithms-9ee186ba2a07.

Rainie, Lee, and Janna Anderson. "Code-Dependent: Pros and Cons of the Algorithm Age." *Pew Research Center*, 8 Feb. 2017, www.pewresearch.org/internet/2017/02/08/code-dependent-pros-and-cons-of-the-algorithm-age.

ETHICS OF SOCIAL MEDIA: FREE SPEECH

Introduction

In the United States the issue of how and whether free speech protections should apply in the online realm of social media has existed since the introduction of these communication platforms in the early 2000s. However, it became more relevant and significant as the accessibility, popularity, and influential reach of social media had grown by the beginning of the 2020s. A wider range of individuals spent large amounts of time on the sites and turned to them more regularly as a source for news and information. Some expressed concerns over the amount of disinformation and misinformation easily spread through social media and the potential societal consequences.

Background

The debate around free speech and social media became especially prominent after January 6, 2021, when thousands of people believed to be supporters of then-President Donald Trump stormed the US Capitol as lawmakers certified the Electoral College votes that confirmed Joe Biden as the winner of the contested 2020 presidential election. Trump had repeatedly claimed on social media that the election had been fraudulently stolen from him. When Trump was subsequently impeached based on allegations that he held responsibility for what was considered insurrection, the prosecution used his social media posts as key evidence.

Though Trump had eventually posted to encourage the rioters to leave the Capitol, he continued to praise their actions, calling them "great patriots" and reiterating unfounded claims of a stolen election. In the aftermath of the incident, as many social media sites instituted bans against Trump and others seen as engaging in harmful communication, some decried such bans as violations of free speech, renewing debate as others noted that the First Amendment offers powerful but narrow protection for such speech. Though the amendment prohibits government from "abridging the freedom of speech," the state action doctrine adopted by the Supreme Court maintains that private entities, be they people or companies, are not constitutionally limited, as the US Constitution has the power only to constrain government actions.

The Issue In-Depth

Supporters of extending free speech protections to social media platforms argue that these digital private entities have effectively replaced physical public spaces typically used as forums in the past by providing a platform for vast numbers of people to communicate, interact, and exchange ideas. Seen as having some of the greatest speech control in modern society, social media companies are viewed as particularly threatening by free speech proponents, who also note that some censorship efforts have gone very publicly awry. Others, however, argue that social media platforms, if largely unmoderated, can become hotbeds of hate speech and baseless conspiracies and, in some cases, can incite violence and extremist behavior; instead, content moderation improvements could be made. If users do not like the terms of the platform, they argue, they are free to go elsewhere.

History

First Amendment protections have been repeatedly tested judicially, and landmark cases have offered guidelines to what kind of speech or expression is included. In 1919, for example, the US Supreme Court upheld the espionage conviction of Socialist Party activist Charles Schenck, who had distributed antidraft material during World War I. His speech was not protected because the Supreme Court saw it as a "clear and present danger" to national security. In 1990, however, a Supreme Court decision upheld flag burning as a form of symbolic speech; state laws that prohibited burning the American flag were overturned. When it comes to government

regulation, the standard of "content neutrality" was developed. This means that the government must be neutral in its position on the content or subject of speech; in other words, material that is generally seen as offensive is still protected. Still, there are types of speech that the Supreme Court has ruled as largely outside of First Amendment protection, mainly those that cause direct harm. Defamation, obscenity, threats, and inciting criminal actions, for instance, are not protected.

To establish the boundaries of protection under the US Constitution, legal cases rely on the doctrine of "state action," as defined by the Supreme Court in Civil Rights Cases in 1883: state (government) actions are limited by the Constitution, while individual (private) actions are not. Several landmark cases have tested the boundaries between government (public) and private, however. Notably, in the 1946 case of *Marsh v. Alabama*, a town owned by a private company was held to First Amendment principles because it was functioning as a "state actor." At issue was the right of people to hand out religious materials on a street in the town.

According to Supreme Court justice Hugo Black, if a private entity performs a public function traditionally performed by the state, it may be considered a state actor. In the 1968 case of *Amalgamated Food Employees Union Local 590 v. Logan Valley Plaza*, the Supreme Court similarly concluded a trespassing injunction had violated the First Amendment rights of people picketing over a labor issue directly related to the operation of a business on the premises of a privately owned mall that was generally open to the public. Some states have confirmed the precedence of the broader rights of their citizens to protected speech in private settings, as in New Jersey's 2012 *Mazdabrook Commons Homeowners' Association v. Khan* decision.

Another relevant law governing free speech is Section 230 of the 1996 Communications Decency Act. Section 230 was developed in the 1990s as a response to cases that sought to determine the liability of internet companies for the content generated on their platforms. The intent of the law is to allow internet companies the ability to regulate themselves to some extent without making themselves liable for user content on their platform. Section 230 states that internet providers and platforms are not treated as publishers of the content produced by others on their platforms and may take actions in good faith to moderate or edit content. Though Section 230 has been targeted by some for encouraging censorship and suppressing free speech, others maintain that the liability protection offered by this law allows for a much freer exchange of speech on the internet. Additionally, some criticize Section 230 for fostering an environment where hate speech and extremism can thrive, since the platforms are largely not liable for their users' activities.

In the 2000s and 2010s, the rise of social media platforms as primary outlets of communication added another layer to the complicated free speech debate. Some argued that a transition from the exchange of ideas occurring in conventional public venues to privately owned online platforms like social media sites had occurred. As private entities, and with the protection of Section 230, social media companies employed content moderation efforts sometimes deemed inconsistent or questionably effective, without regulation. At times, that meant the removal of content or banning of users, causing some to express concern over peoples' loss of access to such crucial platforms for public speech and expression. In providing justifications for such actions over the years, including bans of figures like Nation of Islam leader Louis Farrakhan and conservative provocateur Alex Jones, social media companies often cited the promotion of hatred and violence and their possible negative offline impact.

Free Speech and Social Media Today

Though the issues around free speech and social media were contested before the 2016 presidential election, they became a focus of the Donald Trump administration, and of the American people, during his four years in office. Twitter was a crucial platform employed by Trump, in a much larger way than any of his predecessors, to communicate with the American people. His followers reportedly numbered around 90 million at their highest point, and billions more saw his posts shared in other media.

In 2017 Trump was at the center of a groundbreaking lawsuit, *Knight First Amendment Institute at Columbia University v. Trump*, that accused him of being a state actor on social media and unlawfully suppressing protected speech. Trump and a staffer were accused of blocking people critical of the president on his Twitter account. In 2018 the US District Court for the Southern District of New York ruled for the plaintiffs, finding Trump had violated First Amendment rights. The judge reasoned that despite the speech's occurrence on a private platform, Trump and his staff had operated the account in an official state capacity open to the public and therefore their control of the content of these Twitter posts was unlawful. Perhaps most importantly, the ruling, which was upheld in a 2019 appeal, found that Twitter was a public forum.

Trump posted on Twitter over twenty-five thousand times throughout his presidency. He was particularly active during and after the 2020 presidential election, repeating baseless charges of election fraud and sharing information that fact-checked as false. Twitter was criticized both for allowing the rampant spread of disinformation and, when it began flagging posts as unfounded or misleading, for suppressing free speech. In May 2020, as others, particularly conservative politicians who made claims of censorship bias by social media companies, denounced Section 230, Trump issued an executive order seeking to limit Section 230. In December 2020, after losing the election but before the Electoral College results had been certified, he vetoed the National Defense Authorization Act (NDAA) funding bill in part because he had demanded that it include language revoking Section 230. In the meantime, Republican senators Marsha Blackburn, Lindsey Graham, and Roger Wicker introduced bills attempting to narrow Section 230's protections.

After five people were killed and many injured in the storming of the US Capitol on January 6, 2021, Trump was "deplatformed" from his preferred social media accounts. As Twitter and other social media companies such as Facebook chose to suspend or ban Trump, Twitter also removed approximately seventy thousand accounts connected to the conspiracy theory QAnon, which had contributed to the Capitol insurrection. The debate over social media and free speech thus continued to rage.

—Bethany Groff Dorau

References

Brannon, Valerie C. *Free Speech and the Regulation of Social Media Content.* Congressional Research Service, 27 Mar. 2019, fas.org/sgp/crs/misc/R45650.pdf.

Denham, Hannah. "These Are the Platforms That Have Banned Trump and His Allies." *The Washington Post*, 14 Jan. 2021, www.washingtonpost.com/technology/2021/01/11/trump-banned-social-media.

Goodman, Ryan, et al. "Incitement Timeline: Year of Trump's Actions Leading to the Attack on the Capitol." *Just Security*, 11 Jan. 2021, www.justsecurity.org/74138/incitement-timeline-year-of-trumps-actions-leading-to-the-attack-on-the-capitol.

Hudson, David L., Jr. "Free Speech or Censorship? Social Media Litigation Is a Hot Legal Battleground." *ABA Journal*, 1 Apr. 2019, www.abajournal.com/magazine/article/social-clashes-digital-free-speech.

Lakier, Genevieve. "The Great Free-Speech Reversal." *The Atlantic*, 27 Jan. 2021, www.theatlantic.com/ideas/archive/2021/01/first-amendment-regulation/617827.

Romano, Aja. "Kicking People Off Social Media Isn't about Free Speech." *Vox*, 21 Jan. 2021, www.vox.com/culture/22230847/deplatforming-free-speech-controversy-trump.

Wakabayashi, Daisuke. "Legal Shield for Social Media Is Targeted by Lawmakers." *The New York Times*, 28 May 2020, www.nytimes.com/2020/05/28/business/section-230-internet-speech.html.

F

FACEBOOK

Introduction

The world's largest online social networking website where users can connect and share with other people, called on the site "friends." Reaching an average of approximately 1.93 billion daily active users around the world in September 2021, the social networking site Facebook has brought people together in unprecedented ways and provided innovative sharing and communication tools. Nevertheless, the site and its policies have also raised concerns about privacy and safety.

When Facebook was first released in 2004, several predecessors and early competitors already existed. Friendster, a social network for finding people with similar interests (with the possible intention of dating), was founded in 2002 by Jonathan Abrams and Rob Pazornik. The year 2003 saw the launch of Myspace, a media-heavy site that let users customize their profile pages. LinkedIn, a social networking site for business professionals, was also launched in 2003.

In addition to more general social networking sites, campus-specific social networks were founded at many colleges and universities in the early 2000s. The first was Club Nexus, launched at Stanford University in 2001, but Columbia University and several other schools also offered similar services, many created and managed by students. There were also several social networks aimed at college students in general, including the Daily Jolt and Collegester.com. Despite Facebook's late start compared to its competitors, the site ultimately gained the largest user base of all social networking sites, becoming one of the highest-trafficked sites of the decade.

Background

Harvard University student Mark Zuckerberg developed two websites in 2003 that would set the stage for the service that became Facebook. CourseMatch, which helped students determine their courses based on what others were taking, and Facemash, which allowed people to compare images of fellow students, were immediate hits and proved that college students were ready to take their socializing online.

Based on the popularity of these two sites and Zuckerberg's initial experiments with image-commenting capabilities, the first version of Facebook was launched on February 4, 2004, at TheFaceBook.com, allowing students to create profiles and connect with other students. Within a day of the launch, between twelve hundred and fifteen hundred people had signed up for the service.

Facebook icon. Image via Wikimedia Commons. [Public domain.]

Beyond Harvard

After approximately one month of exclusive access for Harvard students, Facebook opened up to Stanford, Columbia, and Yale universities. By June, the site had extended its access to users at forty different colleges and universities.

The early popularity of Facebook stemmed from a number of factors, including widespread internet access, which was initially greater on college campuses than in the general population, and a focused target demographic of college students who constantly socialized, had numerous social connections, and were willing to share personal information online with others. Additionally, the site was frequently updated by its users, prompting nearly 60 percent of Facebook's users to visit the site daily and some 20 percent of users to visit the site more than five times a day.

Facebook grew quickly. Zuckerberg and cofounder Moskovitz moved to California's Silicon Valley and received their first funding—$500,000 from PayPal cofounder Peter Thiel—in June 2004. The site reached 1 million users by November 2004, narrowly missing a goal set by Thiel of 1.5 million users for the year. In Palo Alto, Zuckerberg connected with Sean Parker, founder of the online music-sharing service Napster, who served as Facebook's president for a short, but influential, time.

Following Thiel's initial investment, Facebook continued to grow, attracting investment interest from venture capital companies. Zuckerberg turned down several acquisition offers, some from large and profitable companies such as Viacom, which wanted to combine the service with MTV.com. Interest in Facebook was sparked by its huge user base, rapid growth, high levels of repeat usage, and attractive demographic of users: young college students. Even the *Washington Post* displayed interest in investing in Facebook, but the venture capital firm Accel Partners outbid the news outlet by offering $12.7 million in funding in exchange for a 15 percent stake in the company. The investment would be crucial in acquiring the staff to develop the features and partnerships that would ultimately help Facebook become the dominant social network of the 2000s.

Basic Features

Facebook added many capabilities throughout its evolution, but early core Facebook features included the user's profile, wall, status update, and notifications.

Facebook logo. Image via Wikimedia Commons. [Public domain.]

Facebook user profiles include basic personal information, such as name, age, and gender; background information, such as hometown or schools attended; interests and hobbies; and other customizable information. Unlike many other social networking sites, Facebook does not make it easy to find people through shared interests; the emphasis is on maintaining existing connections, not creating new ones. A user's wall is a profile section where other users can post greetings, links, or photos. A status update is a message that a user can post to Facebook to be displayed to their friends on the site.

Users can receive notifications, get "tagged" in photos, send and receive private messages, and chat with friends/acquaintances. Other ways to communicate on Facebook include groups and events. Users can create groups for general communication around a particular topic or cause, or they can schedule events such as birthday parties or protests. The vast range of Facebook events and groups shows the flexibility and power of the platform, which has often been used for purposes of political organization and activism.

Facebook Platform and Facebook Connect

By May 2007, 1 percent of all internet time was spent on Facebook. In the same month, Facebook launched the Facebook Platform at its first annual F8 Developers Conference. The platform enabled software developers to create applications that integrated with the service, such as online games that could be played within Facebook. This move accelerated the company's rise, as its users began to download more and more applications that prompted them to log in to Facebook multiple times a day. By November 2007, more than 8,000 apps had been developed on the platform, a number that would rise to 33,000 by July 2008.

The success of the platform showed that Facebook's primary value proposition was not its features but was instead the connections between its users.

The platform also offers a social graph, which features the connections between users and their shared interests. It then offered access to the social graph to other software developers, a move that had nothing to do with risking its own success but rather with ensuring it: by selling its social data to other companies and developers, Facebook no longer needed to develop multiple types of functionality for the site. Instead, it could serve as the platform for myriad applications developed by others.

In late 2008, Facebook released Facebook Connect, a secure single sign-on system that allowed people to access any website using their Facebook login. This was not only convenient for its users; it also enabled the social graph to track users' activity on other websites.

Advertising, Business Model, and Corporate Culture

By the fall of 2007, Facebook had 50 million users. Microsoft invested $240 million in the company as part of an advertising deal, taking a 1.6 percent stake in Facebook. As the company continued to grow, Facebook hired Google executive Sheryl Sandberg in 2008 to serve as chief operating officer (COO). The company was first cash-flow positive in 2009, due mostly to advertising.

Facebook represented a revolution in advertising, because it provided not only a platform to broadcast product messages, but it also generated marketing and usage data to inform the successful targeting of those messages. For example, Facebook made it possible to target an advertisement about a running shoe sale in San Francisco only to users who live in the area and have indicated interest in running. This type of market targeting was unprecedented and prompted significant experimentation by other advertisers. However, many Facebook users eventually expressed discomfort with the degree to which the information they share on the service could be used to gear specific advertisements to them. This lack of user control and transparency factored heavily into widespread criticisms of Facebook in the late 2010s, especially in relation to the numerous scandals that emerged during that time.

Privacy, Criticism, and Blocking

In addition to providing user data for advertisement targeting, Facebook has been widely criticized for perceived privacy infringements. Although users are typically able to limit the content they post to be visible only to friends on the site, these settings often default to sharing information publicly. This not only aggravates some users, but it has allegedly resulted in serious situations of people losing their jobs, not being hired for a job, or not being accepted to a college because of content posted on Facebook.

In December 2009, Facebook changed all profiles to be public—meaning visible to anyone, even nonusers and nonfriends—by default, requiring users to change their individual settings if they wanted to keep their information private. Because many users preferred to keep their information visible to friends only, the switch angered many users and caused some to stop using the service. Several organizations joined a US Federal Trade Commission (FTC) complaint against Facebook for its lack of privacy protections.

Facebook's ability to open up connections between people who have fallen out of touch and to facilitate communication between such parties also proved to have negative aspects. For example, the platform has been blamed for playing a role in divorces, with spouses discovering information such as private messages between users. A December 2009 study found that 20 to 33 percent of all divorce filings in the United Kingdom cited Facebook as a reason for the separation, reflecting a potential downside of widespread sharing. Other researchers and advocates turned attention to the social media platform's role in bullying and other damaging behavior. Meanwhile, some individuals and organizations began to suggest that users can form an addiction to social media, with potentially harmful mental and even physical effects.

Other concerns about Facebook have come from various sources. The site has been blocked in many countries, including China and Iran in 2009, due to concerns about its role as a tool for political activism in opposition to parties in power.

Initial Public Offering

In July 2010, Facebook announced that it had 500 million users, making it the world's largest online social network. By the end of 2011, based on page views, Facebook was second only to Google as the most-used website in the United States. Then, on May 17, 2012, after years of rebuffing acquisition offers and urgings to go public, Facebook staged an

Mark Zuckerberg, co-creator of Facebook, in his Harvard dorm room, 2005. Photo by Elaine Chan and Priscilla Chan, via Wikimedia Commons.

initial public offering (IPO) on the NASDAQ stock exchange, raising some $16 billion by selling more than 400 million shares at $38 a share in what was the third largest IPO in US history.

Fake News, Misinformation, and Other Content Concerns

In August 2016, Facebook fired their team of editors responsible for their trending news section. This decision was made following accusations that the trending articles had a liberal political bias. The human editors were replaced with algorithms that determined what the biggest trending stories were. This turned out to not be an effective alternative, however. The algorithms allowed fake news stories to be at the top of Facebook's trending stories. These fake news stories would have previously been caught by editors.

Surveys in the mid- to late-2010s showed that increasing numbers of Facebook users got their news through posts on the social media site. In the aftermath of the 2016 US presidential election, Facebook was the subject of great criticism for allowing fake news stories, particularly ones that had to do with the election, to proliferate unchecked. In mid-November 2016, Zuckerberg announced that the company would not allow fake news sites to advertise and asked users for their help in catching fake news articles. However, media reports suggested the company's initiatives had little immediate success. Indeed,

criticisms grew as investigations exposed Russian interference in the 2016 election. Many commentators suggested that fake news stories, often created by or with support from Russian agents seeking to support Republican presidential candidate Donald Trump and undermine Democratic candidate Hillary Clinton, may have had a considerable effect on the controversial election.

In early 2017, Zuckerberg announced a shift in the company's focus from connecting friends and family to creating a social infrastructure that would connect a global community. In an over five-thousand-word letter posted to his own Facebook page on February 16, Zuckerberg announced revised company goals of globally promoting peace and understanding as well as prosperity and freedom. He stated that through the use and implementation of artificial intelligence (AI) technology, Facebook would be helping to make the world safer by removing fake news stories, blocking terrorist propaganda, and helping those suffering from mental illness or bullying.

Despite these efforts, high-profile criticism of Facebook's treatment of fake news, conspiracy theories, hate speech, and similar content continued. For example, many mainstream media outlets considered the temporary suspension of the personal account of Alex Jones, head of the notoriously inaccurate and inflammatory right-wing site InfoWars, in July 2018 to be an inadequate response to the damage caused by his discourse. Facebook did subsequently ban several prominent InfoWars related pages over violations of its hate speech policy. In May 2019, the company officially banned Nation of Islam leader Louis Farrakhan, Jones, and a handful of prominent right-wing extremists and white supremacists from the site.

The year 2020, which saw the worldwide spread of the coronavirus disease 2019 (COVID-19) pandemic as well as a highly contentious US presidential election, was also marked by criticism of the amount of harmful misinformation, disinformation, and hateful or even inflammatory speech communicated through social media platforms, particularly Twitter and Facebook. While Facebook, along with other platforms, began making efforts in late 2020 to make changes to aspects such as algorithms and protocols to help limit or prevent the spread of misinformation, disinformation, and inflammatory posts, many critics argued that the company had not done enough quickly enough, as President Trump himself as well as his supporters and general conspiracy theorists had long been posting content that included baseless or false claims regarding the election process as well as COVID-19.

After a large group of Trump supporters considered to have been persuaded by Trump's rhetoric as recently as a rally held by the outgoing president that same day stormed the US Capitol building on January 6, 2021, to disrupt Congress's certification of Joe Biden's election win, Facebook promptly announced that it had taken Trump's Instagram and Facebook accounts down. By June, in response to its independent Oversight Board, the company announced that it had issued a formal two-year suspension of Trump's accounts; as Facebook also indicated that it was working on protocols to be more transparently judicious, regardless of the account holder, of its content, Trump argued that it was unfair censorship.

Controversy over Facebook Live

After Facebook's livestreaming feature, Facebook Live, was made available for public use in January 2016 (having previously been restricted to verified VIP users), the company began drawing criticism for allowing users to stream videos of criminal activity, violence, and even deaths. Facebook's control over and reaction time with regard to such content was limited, as it relied primarily on AI algorithms and user reports to moderate user content. Mathew Ingram reported for *Fortune* magazine that "in some cases, the company has taken swift action to remove the videos, but in others it has chosen to leave them up with a warning about the disturbing content."

Videos that were allowed to remain with a warning included one in which Chicago resident Antonio Perkins was killed in a drive-by shooting and another in which Minneapolis resident Philando Castile was fatally shot by police while his girlfriend (who filmed and livestreamed the encounter) and her young daughter remained in their pulled-over car. Other violent and otherwise disturbing videos were removed with varying reaction times.

On April 16, 2017, Cleveland resident Robert Godwin Sr. was shot and killed in a video that the killer livestreamed on Facebook. The killer had also posted an earlier video announcing his intention to commit the murder, and he posted one afterward in which he confessed to the crime. Facebook was criticized for leaving the videos up for around two hours, during which time they went viral across multiple social media platforms. Later the same month, a man in Thailand posted videos that showed him killing his eleven-month-old daughter and then hanging himself. The videos remained on Facebook for around twenty-four hours until they were removed. Both cases renewed questions about Facebook's responsibility for the content of its users and how the company could do more to prevent such tragedies. Statements by Facebook personnel disavowed the killers' actions and acknowledged the need for the site to do better in preventing such content from being seen.

Cambridge Analytica, the "Ugly Truth" Memo, and Other Scandals

With considerable negative publicity already surrounding Facebook over livestreamed killings, the proliferation of fake news and its role in US and world politics, and other issues, additional scandals involving the social media giant emerged in late 2017 and early 2018. Content from the leaked documents known as the "Paradise Papers" revealed in November 2017 indicated parties linked to the Russian government had made considerable investments in Facebook (and Twitter). One of the individuals involved in the investments, Yuri Milner, was noted to have connections to Jared Kushner, son-in-law of President Donald Trump and an aide in his administration. The revelation further concerns over Facebook's political influence and manipulation by those seeking to sway public opinion.

A larger scandal, however, unfolded beginning in March 2018 when it was revealed that tens of millions of Facebook users' personal data had been sold to the British political analysis firm Cambridge Analytica, which had worked on the Trump campaign. Much of the private user data was harvested through apps, with users often unaware. Facebook initially did not acknowledge the data breach, and then suggested the data had been recovered when in fact Cambridge Analytica still had access to it. Facebook also reportedly attempted to stop news of the story from being published. When details of the episode broke, it garnered significant public backlash against Facebook as well as attention from lawmakers in both the United States and Great Britain, who wanted explanations for the data leak and its political ramifications.

In July 2019, it was announced that Facebook had agreed to pay a $5 billion settlement with the FTC reached in response to the company's mishandling of user privacy. As part of the settlement, the company also acquiesced to instituting new oversight policies, particularly setting up an independent privacy committee on Facebook's board to limit Zuckerberg's control over decisions related to the issue. Criticism followed over whether this regulation was strict enough. Later that year, on November 17, the banking data for about 29,000 Facebook employees—which was stored on unencrypted hard drives—was stolen. The hard drives were not reported to be missing until November 20, and Facebook did not inform employees about the data breach until December 13.

Corporate Name Change

While the Facebook site and app had continued to remain one of the most popular among social media platforms, in October 2021 its parent company announced that it was changing its longtime name of Facebook and rebranding as Meta (though, as of mid-2022, it was still transitioning as "Facebook from Meta"). Zuckerberg argued that the corporation had extended its reach and conceptual goals so far past just social networking platforms that it did not make sense to continue operating under the name, considered wholly unrepresentative, of just one of its apps. Facebook the app, which would keep its name, was one part, its company's chief executive officer (CEO) stressed, of a concentrated effort toward creating a "metaverse" in which the technologies of augmented reality and virtual worlds would be combined. This development was widely discussed in the media, with some commentators noting that the move likely had a role in the company's desire to distance itself from past scandals, particularly after highly publicized accusations of a conscious disregard for protecting users' safety had been made by former employees that same month.

Impact

In becoming one of the largest social networks in the world, Facebook revolutionized online communications, human connections, activism, and advertising. The site has helped people maintain connections with others in unprecedented ways and has even been used to mobilize grassroots political efforts. However, it has also exposed significant challenges that come with the great influence of social media, including issues of privacy, free speech, and even impacts on physical and mental health. As the social network continues to evolve, it will undoubtedly have further new applications (and implications) for corporations, advertisers, governments, law enforcement, and individuals.

—*Craig Belanger and Kerry Skemp*

References

Almasy, Steve. "Thailand Baby Killing: Facebook Removes Video." *CNN.com*, 26 Apr. 2017, www.cnn.com/2017/04/25/asia/thailand-baby-killed-facebook-live-trnd/.

Chokshi, Niraj. "Facebook Helped Drive a Voter Registration Surge, Election Officials Say." *The New York Times*, 12 Oct. 2016, www.nytimes.com/2016/10/13/us/politics/facebook-helped-drive-a-voter-registration-surge-election-officials-say.html.

Collins, Ben. "Facebook to Restrict Livestream Feature after Christchurch Attack." *NBC News*, 14 May 2019, www.nbcnews.com/tech/tech-news/facebook-restrict-livestream-feature-after-christchurch-attack-n1005741.

Dwoskin, Elizabeth, and Craig Timberg. "Facebook Wanted 'Visceral' Live Video. It's Getting Live-Streaming Killers and Suicides." *The Washington Post*, 17 Apr. 2017, www.washingtonpost.com/business/technology/facebook-wanted-visceral-live-video-its-getting-suicides-and-live-streaming-killers/2017/04/17/a6705662-239c-11e7-a1b3-faff0034e2de_story.html.

"Facebook Reports Third Quarter 2021 Results." *Facebook Investor Relations*, 25 Oct. 2021, investor.fb.com/investor-news/press-release-details/2021/Facebook-Reports-Third-Quarter-2021-Results/.

Feiner, Lauren, and Salvador Rodriguez. "FTC Slaps Facebook with Record $5 Billion Fine, Orders Privacy Oversight." *CNBC*, 24 July 2019, www.cnbc.com/2019/07/24/facebook-to-pay-5-billion-for-privacy-lapses-ftc-announces.html.

Griffin, Andrew. "Facebook Live: Site Adds Huge New Update to Feature That Lets People Stream in Their Timeline." *The Independent*, 6 Apr. 2016, www.independent.co.uk/life-style/gadgets-and-tech/news/facebook-live-site-adds-huge-new-update-to-feature-that-lets-people-stream-in-their-timeline-a6971566.html.

Hern, Alex. "Mark Zuckerberg's Letter Annotated: What He Said and What He Didn't." *The Guardian*, 17 Feb. 2017, www.theguardian.com/technology/ng-interactive/2017/feb/17/mark-zuckerberg-facebook-letter-annotated-what-he-said-what-he-didnt.

Herrman, John. "What Happens When Facebook Goes the Way of Myspace?" *The New York Times*, 12 Dec. 2018, www.nytimes.com/2018/12/12/magazine/what-happens-when-facebook-goes-the-way-of-myspace.html.

Hill, Kashmir. "Facebook's Mark Zuckerberg: 'We've Made a Bunch of Mistakes.'" *Forbes*, 29 Nov. 2011, www.forbes.com/sites/kashmirhill/2011/11/29/facebooks-mark-zuckerberg-weve-made-a-bunch-of-mistakes/.

Ingram, Mathew. "Facebook Killing Another Example of Live Video Feature's Dark Side." *Fortune*, 17 Apr. 2017, fortune.com/2017/04/17/facebook-killing/.

Isaac, Mike. "Facebook Renames Itself Meta." *The New York Times*, 28 Oct. 2021, www.nytimes.com/2021/10/28/technology/facebook-meta-name-change.html.

Kirkpatrick, David. *The Facebook Effect: The Inside Story of the Company That Is Connecting the World.* Simon & Schuster, 2010.

Klein, Ezra. "Mark Zuckerberg on Facebook's Hardest Year, and What Comes Next." *Vox*, 2 Apr. 2018, www.vox.com/2018/4/2/17185052/mark-zuckerberg-facebook-interview-fake-news-bots-cambridge.

Lacy, Sarah. *Once You're Lucky, Twice You're Good: The Rebirth of Silicon Valley and the Rise of Web 2.0.* Gotham Books, 2008.

Lincoln, Sian, and Brady Robards. "10 Years of Facebook." *New Media & Society*, vol. 16, no. 7, 2014, pp. 1047–50, doi:10.1177/1461444814543994.

Mezrich, Ben. *The Accidental Billionaires: The Founding of Facebook, a Tale of Sex, Money, Genius and Betrayal.* Doubleday, 2009.

Moscaritolo, Angela, and Chloe Albanesius. "Zuckerberg's Vision for Facebook: A Global Community Backed by AI." *PC Magazine*, 16 Feb. 2017, www.pcmag.com/news/351809/zuckerbergs-vision-for-facebook-a-global-community-backed.

Newitz, Annalee. "Facebook Fires Human Editors, Algorithm Immediately Posts Fake News." *Ars Technica*, 29 Aug. 2016, arstechnica.com/business/2016/08/facebook-fires-human-editors-algorithm-immediately-posts-fake-news/.

Olson, Parmy. "Facebook Wants Users to Help It Weed Out Fake News." *Forbes*, 6 Dec. 2016, www.forbes.com/sites/parmyolson/2016/12/06/facebook-users-fake-news/.

Osnos, Evan. "Can Mark Zuckerberg Fix Facebook Before It Breaks Democracy?" *The New Yorker*, 17 Sept. 2018, www.newyorker.com/magazine/2018/09/17/can-mark-zuckerberg-fix-facebook-before-it-breaks-democracy.

Rosenberg, Matthew, and Sheera Frenkel. "Facebook's Role in Data Misuse Sets of Storms on Two Continents." *The New York Times*, 18 Mar. 2018, www.nytimes.com/2018/03/18/us/cambridge-analytica-facebook-privacy-data.html.

Stinson, Liz. "Facebook Reactions, the Totally Redesigned Like Button, Is Here." *Wired*, 24 Feb. 2016, www.wired.com/2016/02/facebook-reactions-totally-redesigned-like-button/.

Sulleyman, Aatif. "Facebook Live Killings: Why the Criticism Has Been Harsh." *The Independent*, 27 Apr. 2017, www.independent.co.uk/life-style/gadgets-and-tech/features/facebook-live-killings-ai-artificial-intelligence-not-blame-fatalities-murders-us-steve-stephens-a7706056.html/.

Ziobro, Paul, and Jeff Horwitz. "Facebook Suspends Donald Trump for at Least Two Years." *The Wall Street Journal*, 4 June 2021, www.wsj.com/articles/facebook-suspends-donald-trump-for-two-years-11622825480.

Zuckerberg, Mark. "Building Global Community." *Facebook*, 16 Feb. 2017, www.facebook.com/notes/mark-zuckerberg/building-global-community/10103508221158471/.

FILE TRANSFER PROTOCOL

Introduction

File Transfer Protocol (FTP) is a program that allows the transfer of files from one computer to another over the internet. FTP is most often used to share files between an individual, or client computer, and a network server. A protocol is a set of common rules developed so that different computers can communicate with one another. FTP is one of the oldest network protocols, developed in the 1970s during the

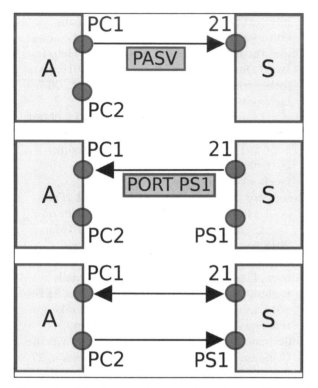

Illustration of starting a passive connection using port 21.
Image by Michael Lorer, via Wikimedia Commons.

earliest days of the internet. Some modern computers allow users to access FTP to download simple files directly through their web browsers. Uploading files or downloading more complex data often requires a user to log on to an FTP server to orchestrate the transfer.

Background

The precursor to the modern internet was developed as a joint effort between scientists and the United States military during the 1960s. It was considered a backup communications plan in case an attack by the Soviet Union destroyed the nation's infrastructure. The concept was originally proposed as a "galactic network" of computers that could communicate with one another without the use of the telephone system. The problem occurred in finding an information-transfer method that would be less vulnerable to enemy attack. In 1965, a scientist at the Massachusetts Institute of Technology (MIT) developed a system called "packet switching," which breaks down data into smaller blocks and transmits it to its destination over various routes. Once there, it is reassembled into its original form.

By 1969, the government's network was operational and soon grew to include computers in universities and research centers around the world. With many computers now part of the fledgling network, sharing information was often difficult because computers did not always speak the same technological language. The first set of standard rules, or protocols, for transferring files among systems was developed in 1971 to allow computers at MIT to communicate with one another. The protocols were developed by a standards group called the Internet Engineering Task Force and labeled RFC 141 (short for Request for Comments 141). The standards were improved several times until 1985 when RFC 959 was formalized. While these protocols have been amended, RFC 959 was still in place as the FTP standard as of 2016.

The Prevalence of FTP

Most computer users have used FTP at some point without even noticing. Many web browsers, such as the ones used by Microsoft Windows, come with a text-based version of the FTP program to allow for simple downloads. This version is called Trivial File Transfer Protocol (TFTP). In most cases, transferring larger files or uploads requires a connection between a client computer and an FTP server. A computer user installs an FTP client program on his or her individual device that allows the computer to communicate with an FTP server at another location. The server acts as a storage unit for files and data and allows the client computer to send or receive information from the server.

The initial contact between the client and server is typically made over an open port, or connection, called "TCP port 21." TCP stands for Transmission Control Protocol and is one of the fundamental sets of technological rules for running the internet. Servers contain a number of ports, each with its own specific function. The initial connection is referred to as the "command connection" or "command channel." Before any transfer of data can occur, the client computer must first identify itself to the server. In many cases, the user needs to enter a username and password to proceed. Some public FTP servers use an automatic default name and password to allow access.

Once the user's identity has been established, the client computer sets up a random port on itself to communicate with the server. The two computers then inform each other of the connection so that data transfer can begin. This connection is used only to transmit files and information from the client computer to the server. To receive data from the server, the client computer must open a new port and inform the server where to send the information. The server then opens a new connection, port 20, and transmits the data. Most software allows data transfers to be performed by dragging and dropping files from the server to the computer and vice versa. Once the process is finished, the client computer severs the connection to the server.

FTP can support two kinds of data exchanges. The first is plain text, or American Standard Code for Information Interchange (ASCII), an encoding standard used for the transfer of text files over the internet. The other is a binary file, a numeric data file that can be read only by a computer. Binary files are typically used to transfer larger amounts of data such as a program or music. Before files are transferred, the client computer must inform the server of the type of file being sent. Sending a text or binary file while in the opposite mode will make the file unusable.

In addition to the basic form of FTP, two variations are available that add extra security to the process to protect users' personal information. FTPS is similar to the basic FTP method but adds an extra layer of security called Secure Sockets Layer (SSL) encryption to the transfer. Before the user sends a username or password, the client computer requests the server open an SSL encrypted connection, and the information exchange and data transfer proceeds through this port. Information sent through this connection is "scrambled" at the source by a computer algorithm and deciphered at the other end. Another security protocol, SFTP, is a more modern method and is considered more reliable than FTPS. SFTP also establishes a protected connection between client and server but uses Secure Shell (SSH) protocols to secure the connection. This method breaks the files into packets of data and transmits them over the secured connection. It also removes the ability to bypass or turn off encryption filters manually.

—*Richard Sheposh*

References

Blank, Andrew G. *TCP/IP Foundations*. SYBEX, 2004.

"FTP Protocol (File Transfer Protocol)." *CCM Benchmark Group*, 16 Oct. 2008, ccm.net/contents/272-ftp-protocol-file-transfer-protocol.

Hacker, Scot. "Tutorial: FTP Made Simple." *UC Berkeley Graduate School of Journalism*, 2014, multimedia.journalism.berkeley.edu/tutorials/ftp/.

"The Invention of the Internet." *History.com*, www.history.com/topics/inventions/invention-of-the-internet.

Miller, Philip. "File Transfer Protocols." *TCP/IP: The Ultimate Protocol Guide*, Vol. 2. Brown Walker Press, 2009, pp. 607–38.

Mitchell, Bradley. "FTP—File Transfer Protocol." *Lifewire*, 19 Oct. 2016, www.lifewire.com/file-transfer-protocol-817943.

Pstatz. "FTP for Beginners." *Wired*, 15 Feb. 2010, www.wired.com/2010/02/ftp_for_beginners/.

"A Short History of FTP with Resources." *WhoIsHostingThis.com*, www.whoishostingthis.com/resources/ftp/.

FIREWALLS

Introduction

A firewall is a program designed to monitor the traffic entering and leaving a computer network or single device and prevent malicious programs or users from entering the protected system. Firewalls may protect a single device, such as a server or personal computer (PC), or even an entire computer network. They also differ in how they filter data. Firewalls are used alongside other computer security measures to protect sensitive data.

Background

In the early twenty-first century, increasing cybercrime and cyberterrorism made computer security a serious concern for governments, businesses and organizations, and the public. Nearly any computer system connected to the internet can be accessed by malicious users or infected by harmful programs

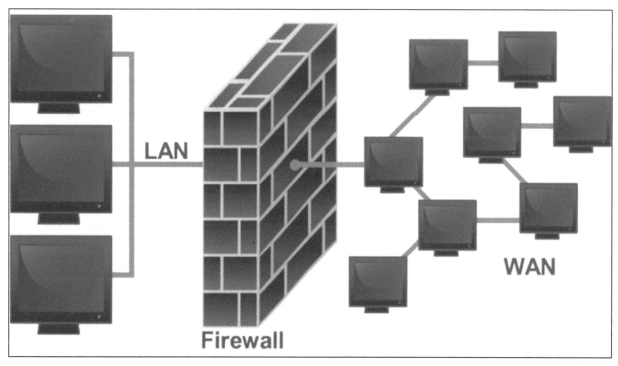

An illustration of a network-based firewall within a network. Image by Bruno Pedrozo, via Wikimedia Commons.

such as viruses. Both large networks and single PCs face this risk. To prevent such security breaches, organizations and individuals use various security technologies, particularly firewalls. Firewalls are programs or sometimes dedicated devices that monitor the data entering a system and prevent unwanted data from doing so. This protects the computer from both malicious programs and unauthorized access.

The term "firewall" is borrowed from the field of construction/building safety. In that field it refers to a wall specially built to stop the spread of fire within a structure. Computer firewalls fill a similar role, preventing harmful elements from entering the protected area. The idea of computer firewalls originated in the 1980s. At that time, network administrators used routers, devices that transfer data between networks, to separate one network from another. This stopped problems in one network from spreading into others.

By the early 1990s, the proliferation of computer viruses and increased risk of hacking made the widespread need for firewalls clear. Some of the advances in that era, such as increased access to the internet and developments in operating systems, also introduced new vulnerabilities. Early firewalls relied heavily on the use of proxy servers. Proxy servers are servers through which all traffic flows before entering a user's computer or network. In the twenty-first century, firewalls can filter data according to varied criteria and protect a network at multiple points.

Types of Firewalls

All firewalls work to prevent unwanted data from entering a computer or network. However, they do so in different ways. Commonly used firewalls can be in various positions relative to the rest of the system. An individual computer may have its own personal firewall, such as a firewall built into that computer's operating system. Other networked devices, such as servers, may also have personal firewalls. These are known as host-based firewalls because they protect a single host rather than the whole network. They protect computers and other devices not only from malicious programs or users on the internet but also from viruses and other threats that have already infiltrated the internal network, such as a corporate intranet, to which they belong. Network firewalls, on the other hand, are positioned at the entrance to the internal network. All traffic into or out of that network must filter through them. A network firewall may be a single device, such as a router or dedicated computer, which serves as the entrance point for all data. It then blocks any data that is malicious or otherwise unwanted. Application-level firewalls, which monitor and allow or disallow data transfers from and to applications, may be host based or network based.

Firewalls also vary based on how they filter data. Packet filters examine incoming data packets individually and determine whether to block or allow each one to proceed. They decide this based on factors such as the origin and destination of the packets. Stateful filters determine whether to admit or block incoming data based on the state of the connection. Firewalls that use stateful filtering can identify whether data packets trying to enter the computer system are part of an ongoing, active connection and determine whether to let them in based on that context. This allows them to examine and filter incoming data more quickly than their stateless counterparts.

Firewalls and Computer Security

By preventing malicious programs or users from accessing systems, firewalls protect sensitive data stored in or transmitted via computers. They are used to protect personally identifying information, such as social security numbers, as well as proprietary trade or government information. Both the technology industry and the public have put increased emphasis on such protections in the early twenty-first century, as identity theft, fraud, and other cybercrimes have become major issues. In light of such threats, firewalls play an essential role in the field of computer security. However, experts caution that a firewall should not be the sole security measure used. Rather, firewalls should be used along with other computer security practices. These practices include using secure passwords, regularly updating software to install patches and eliminate vulnerabilities, and avoiding accessing compromised websites or downloading files from suspicious sources.

—*Joy Crelin*

References

"About Firewalls." *Indiana University Knowledge Base*, 15 Feb. 2019, kb.iu.edu/d/aoru.

Easttom, Chuck. *Computer Security Fundamentals*. 4th ed., Pearson, 2019.

"How Firewalls Work." *Boston University Information Services and Technology*, www.bu.edu/tech/about/security-resources/host-based/intro/.

Kizza, Joseph Migga. *Guide to Computer Network Security*. 5th ed., Springer Nature Switzerland, 2020.

Musa, Sarhan M. *Network Security and Cryptography*. Mercury Learning and Information, 2018.

Stallings, William, and Lawrie Brown. *Computer Security: Principles and Practice*. 4th ed., Pearson, 2018.

Vacca, John, editor. *Network and System Security*. 2nd ed., Elsevier, 2014.

FIRMWARE

Introduction

Firmware occupies a position in between hardware, which is fixed and physically unchanging, and software, which has no physical form apart from the media it is stored on. Firmware is stored in nonvolatile memory in a computer or device so that it is always available when the device is powered on. An example can be seen in the firmware of a digital watch, which remains in place even when the battery is removed and later replaced.

Background

Many consumer devices have become so complex that they need a basic computer to operate them. However, they do not need a fully featured computer with an operating system (OS) and specially designed software. The answer to this need is to use embedded systems. These systems are installed on microchips inside devices as simple as children's toys and as complex as medical devices such as digital thermometers. The term "embedded" is used because the chips containing firmware are ordinarily not directly accessible to consumers. They are installed within the device or system and expected to work throughout its lifespan.

Computers also use firmware, which is called the "basic input/output system," or BIOS. Even though the computer has its own OS installed and numerous programs to accomplish more specific tasks, there is still a need for firmware. This is because, when the computer is powered on, some part of it must be immediately able to tell the system what to do in order to set itself up. The computer must be told to check the part of the hard drive that contains the start-up sequence, then to load the OS, and so on. The firmware serves this purpose because, as soon as electric current flows into the system, the information stored in the computer's nonvolatile memory is loaded and its instructions are executed. Firmware is usually unaffected even when a different OS is installed. However, the user can also configure the BIOS to some extent and can boot the computer into the BIOS to make changes when necessary. For example, a computer that is configured to boot from the compact disc-read only memory (CD-ROM) drive first could have this changed in the BIOS so that it would first attempt to read information from an attached universal serial bus (USB) drive.

Modifying and Replacing Firmware

Sophisticated users of technology sometimes find that the firmware installed by a manufacturer does not meet all of their needs. When this occurs, it is possible to update the BIOS through a process known as flashing. When the firmware is flashed, it is replaced by a new version, usually with new capabilities. In some cases, the firmware is flashed because the device manufacturer has updated it with a new version. This is rarely done, as firmware functionality is so basic to the operation of the device that it is thoroughly tested prior to release. From time to time, however, security vulnerabilities or other software bugs are found in firmware. Manufacturers helping customers with troubleshooting often recommend using the latest firmware to rule out such defects.

Some devices, especially gaming consoles, have user communities that can create their own versions of firmware. These user-developed firmware versions are referred to as homebrew software, as they are produced by users rather than manufacturers. Homebrew firmware is usually distributed on the internet as free software, or freeware, so that anyone can download it and flash their device. In the case of gaming consoles, this can open up new capabilities. Manufacturers tend to produce devices only for specialized functions. They exclude other functions because the functions would increase the cost or make

it too easy to use the device for illegal or undesirable purposes. Flashing such devices with homebrew software can make these functions available.

Automobile Software

One of the market segments that has become increasingly reliant on firmware is automobile manufacturing. More and more functions in cars are now controlled by firmware. Not only are the speedometer and fuel gauge computer displays driven by firmware, but also cars come with firmware applications for music players, real-time navigation and map display, and interfaces with passengers' cell phones.

Firmware as Vulnerability

Although firmware is not very visible to users, it has still been a topic of concern for computer security professionals. With homebrew firmware distributed over the internet, the concern is that the firmware may contain "backdoors." A backdoor is a secret means of conveying the user's personal information to unauthorized parties. Even with firmware from official sources, some worry that it would be possible for the government or the device manufacturer to include security vulnerabilities, whether deliberate or inadvertent.

—*Scott Zimmer*

References

Bembenik, Robert, et al., editors. *Intelligent Tools for Building a Scientific Information Platform: Advanced Architectures and Solutions.* Springer-Verlag Berlin Heidelberg, 2013.

Beningo, Jacob. *Reusable Firmware Development: A Practical Approach to APIs, HALs and Drivers.* Apress, 2017.

Dice, Pete. *Quick Boot: A Guide for Embedded Firmware Developers.* 2nd ed., Walter de Gruyter, 2018.

Khan, Gul N., and Krzysztof Iniewski, editors. *Embedded and Networking Systems: Design, Software, and Implementation.* CRC Press, 2014.

Sun, Jiming, et al. *Embedded Firmware Solutions: Development Best Practices for the Internet of Things.* Apress, 2015.

Yao, Jiewen, and Vincent Zimmer. *Building Secure Firmware: Armoring the Foundation of the Platform.* Apress, 2020.

FREEDOM OF INFORMATION ACT

Introduction

The Freedom of Information Act (FOIA), 5 U.S.C. § 552 (1966) is an openness-in-government or "government access" statute enacted by the US Congress in 1966. The Freedom of Information Act (FOIA) took effect on July 4, 1967, and became only the third such law in the world, after one that was enacted in Sweden (and later devolved to Finland) exactly 200 years earlier. The US FOIA allows the American public (or even "any person" in the world, with only limited exceptions for "intelligence community" files) to request access to any record or information maintained by any agency of the executive branch of the federal government (that is, not including Congress or the federal judiciary), except for (due to constitutional reasons) the records of the "inner White House" (that is, those of the president and his or her closest advisers).

If a FOIA "requester" is not satisfied with the agency's response to his or her request, he or she (or it) may file a lawsuit in federal court to enforce this right. There have been an estimated 10,000 such FOIA lawsuits filed thus far, with thirty-two of them ultimately adjudicated through decisions issued by the US Supreme Court. The most significant of these is the Supreme Court's landmark *Reporters Committee* decision (489 U.S. 749), issued in 1989, which established several key principles for the balancing of personal privacy interests against the public interest in disclosure under FOIA's two privacy exemptions, Exemptions 6 and 7(C), which by far are the exemptions most frequently invoked (that is, in more than 53 percent of cases between the two). Most recently, in 2011, the Supreme Court's decision in *Milner v. Department of the Navy* (562 U.S. 562 [2011]) flatly rejected the broad interpretation of Exemption 2 that had prevailed for nearly three decades, leaving that exemption effectively eviscerated and the government unable to protect some information of particular homeland security sensitivity.

Most fundamentally, FOIA has become a key foundation for the democratic form of government, fostering democracy by allowing Americans to be more aware of "what their government is up to" and thereby to become a more informed electorate. It also promotes government accountability to its citizenry, indirectly supports the freedom-of-the-press mandate of the First Amendment to the US Constitution, and in recent years has become an increasingly vital tool in combating government corruption. In fact, while other nations were slow to embrace the freedom-of-information principle (for instance, only two more countries had such laws by the time of FOIA's fifteenth anniversary), today more than 100 nations of the world have followed the United States' example in enacting and effectively implementing their own FOIA-type laws—thus creating a vibrant, worldwide openness-in-government community and establishing "transparency" (a term imported to the United States from Europe in the mid-2000s) as an important new societal norm. And in the United States, similar laws exist for the records of all states and many government localities as well.

Background

The operation of FOIA is relatively simple: A FOIA requester sends a letter (or an email message or a website submission, where permitted) to an agency of the federal government seeking access to identifiable records that exist within that agency's control in either paper or electronic (e.g., database or email) form. (In 1996, Congress enacted the Electronic Freedom of Information Act Amendments, which in effect brought FOIA into the twenty-first century by updating its provisions for the electronic age.) The requester's obligation is only to "reasonably describe" the records sought so that they can be located efficiently. Under the law, an agency is not required to create a record in order to satisfy a request (though agencies sometimes do so, as a matter of administrative discretion), nor is an agency required to comply with any request framed in the form of a question or without respect to existing records or information at that agency.

Apart from that—and the possible payment of applicable fees for the direct costs of record searches, duplication, and (for commercial requesters) document review—the burden is entirely on the agency to do what is necessary to satisfy the request, usually by mailing the disclosed records in paper form but sometimes in requested electronic form. In the United States, hundreds of thousands of FOIA requests are filed with the approximately 100 federal departments and agencies each year, at an annual cost that now exceeds $500 million. Almost since its inception, however, FOIA generally has been underfunded by Congress, resulting in large backlogs of pending FOIA requests at many agencies, particularly those with law enforcement, national security, or international responsibilities; this alone can be the cause of considerable, seemingly intractable conflict between requesters and agencies.

Beyond FOIA's procedural aspects—which include a basic response deadline of twenty working days, special provisions for media requesters, automatic "electronic reading room" disclosure, and the right to appeal administratively to a higher-level agency official any "adverse determination"—the heart of FOIA lies in its exemptions to required disclosure, which have been the greatest focus of dispute, policy interpretation, amendment, and litigation over the years. FOIA's exemptions, which total fourteen (nine enumerated ones, with one comprised of six subparts), encompass certain types of records (or portions thereof) that hold particular sensitivity under the US legal system.

The FOIA was amended by Congress in 1986 to include three special record "exclusions" for matters of exceptionally acute law enforcement or national security sensitivity. The language of FOIA's exemptions has been amended five times, most recently in 2016, and its exact contours have been shaped greatly over the years by authoritative judicial decisions as well. An example of the latter, and a case to watch, is *Food Marketing Institute v. Argus Leader Media*, a non-FOIA case that nevertheless offers the Supreme Court the opportunity, for the first time, to interpret the terse language of FOIA's fourth exemption.

While journalists make up only a surprisingly small percentage of FOIA requesters (the vast majority of FOIA requesters are commercial entities or individuals seeking records about themselves), the most striking use of FOIA is when it contemporaneously compels the disclosure of records pertaining to matters of government "scandal," including the files of internal investigations, where controversy over the very handling of a FOIA request itself can "add fuel to a fire." This was so during the Clinton administration, and the subsequent administrations of George W. Bush, Barack Obama, and Donald Trump have been plagued by disclosure controversies as well. More

than anything else, the steps taken by the United States in the wake of 9/11 have spawned intense FOIA activity at, and subsequent criticism of, many federal agencies.

In summary, FOIA is a vital and continuously developing government disclosure mechanism that over the past half century has served as a pillar of democracy. With refinements over time to accommodate both technological advancements and society's maturing interests in transparency, it has truly enhanced, and will continue to enhance, the American way of life.

—*Daniel J. Metcalfe*

References

"Alphabetical and Chronological Lists of Countries with FOIA Regimes." *Freedominfo.org*, 28 Sept. 2017.

American University. *Web Site of the Collaboration on Government Secrecy*, edited by Professor Daniel J. Metcalfe, Washington College of Law, 2014, www.wcl.american.edu/lawandgov/cgs/.

"Department of Justice Guide to the Freedom of Information Act." *US Department of Justice*, 2009, www.justice.gov/oip/doj-guide-freedom-information-act-0\.

Hammitt, Harry A., et al., editors. *Litigation under the Federal Open Government Laws*. Electronic Privacy Information Center, 2010, epic.org/bookstore/foia2010/.

Metcalfe, Daniel J. "Amending the FOIA: Is It Time for a Real Exemption 10?" *Administrative and Regulatory Law News*, vol. 37, no. 16, Summer 2012, www.wcl.american.edu/faculty/metcalfe/ABA.article.2012.pdf.

___. "Hillary's E-Mail Defense Is Laughable." *POLITICO Magazine*, 16 Mar. 2015, www.politico.com/magazine/story/2015/03/hillaryclinton-email-scandal-defense-laughable-foia-116116.html#.VXw6lvlViko.

Metcalfe, Daniel J. "The History of Transparency." *Research Handbook on Transparency*, edited by Padideh Ala'i and Robert G. Vaughn, Edward Elgar, 2014.

Metcalfe, Daniel J. *"The Nature of Government Secrecy."* *Government Information Quarterly*, vol. 26, no. 305, 2009, www.wcl.american.edu/faculty/metcalfe/nature.pdf.

"Supreme Court Grants Cert. in Case that May Redefine Scope of FOIA Exemption 4…" *Dashboard Insights,* 29 Jan. 2019.

ThinkProgress. "Post-shut Down, an Ocean of Outrage Greets Interior's Proposed Changes…" *thinkprogress.org,* 30 Jan. 2019.

US Department of Justice. "OIP Gives FOIA Implementation Advice to Other Nations." *FOIA Post,* 12 Dec. 2002, www.justice.gov/archive/ oip/ foiapost/2002foiapost30.htm.

G

GAME-BASED LEARNING

Introduction

While cognitive theories and intuition point to game-based learning as holding a great deal of promise, games are not fitting into the educational landscape with the ease anticipated by champions of game-based learning. Several technical, cultural, and ethical factors demand attention as the role of game-based learning in formal education evolves. Games of all stripes have long been of interest by educators as a way to engage and motivate students to learn new concepts and apply their knowledge in a meaningful context. Learning theories from the sociocultural cognition family of learning theories points to the potential games have to motivate, engage, and provide authentic learning experiences.

Despite this promise, however, games (particularly video games) have struggled to penetrate the formal education marketplace. Furthermore, some scholars have suggested that the application of game mechanics towards nongame environments is a manipulative and exploitive practice. Nonetheless, games are an increasingly important medium where school-aged children spend much of their time. As such, it is important for educators and educational researchers to understand games in the context of this greater media landscape, and what it means for the future of learning.

Background

Game-based learning is sometimes mistakenly referred to as game theory, but the term "game theory" refers to the use of mathematical models to study decision making, and is not related to game-based learning. The relationship between games and learning and the use of games as a vehicle for learning has long been of interest to educators.

Game-based learning uses gaming principles to engage users. Photo via iStock/Svetlana_Smirnova. [Used under license.]

Interest in game-based learning among scholars, funding agencies, educational technology start-ups, large educational publishing companies, and the White House has increased since the beginning of the twenty-first century. Leading theorists in the field are exploring the intersection of games and learning, and what games can teach us about learning.

Applications

Learning is a lifelong endeavor for humans and can occur via a designed experience (such as at a workshop, in a classroom, via a museum exhibit, or by watching a documentary) or via un-designed experiences such as free play or personal reflection. Game-based learning is typically discussed in the context of designed learning experiences both in terms of what learning designers can glean from game design and in terms of how to utilize games as part of a designed learning experience.

Sociocultural Learning Theories

There are numerous theories about learning, and in understanding game-based learning the family of theories that are of greatest use are the sociocultural learning theories. These theories of learning emphasize the roles that communities and tools play in how humans learn. Scholars from education, psychology, anthropology, and sociology have contributed and built upon this body of knowledge, which has its origin in the work done by Lev Vygotsky in the early part of the twentieth century.

Vygotsky's emphasis on the role adults and peers play in learning, along with how cultural context affects learning and the importance of play in cognitive development have been fruitful in generating learning theories that suggest game-based learning to be worthy of deeper investigation. One of Vygotsky's most enduring ideas was that of the zone of proximal development (ZPD). Cognitive tasks that a learner cannot perform on his own but can perform with outside assistance are said to lie within the ZDP. Understanding where a learner's ZPD is for learning objectives is critical for scaffolding learners through mastery in that learning objective. As research into learning moved toward more constructivist models, the role of mentors, peers, society, and culture could not be ignored. To be sure, the basic idea behind ZPD emerges frequently in sociocultural learning research, sometimes under other names such as cognitive apprenticeships or legitimate peripheral participation.

To accept that learning and cognition are social phenomenon is also to accept that cognition is distributed. An individual's knowledge is distributed among an individual's social network and the tools in the environment. People often use tools that make them work more efficiently or boost their knowledge base. Distributed cognition and sociocultural learning theories are critical for understanding the arguments behind game-based learning.

Games and Learning Experiences

T. Fullerton compares two very different experiences that are recognized as games (as opposed to toys, puzzles, or dramatic play): The card game Go Fish and the video game *Quake*. Through this comparison, Fullerton draws out what she identifies as the essential components of a game:

- **Players:** A game is designed for players. Unlike other forms of entertainment, games demand active participation;
- **Objectives:** Games lay out specific goals for players. Whether it is collecting the most cards or shooting the most enemies or getting a basket in a net, games provide players with goals;
- **Rules:** All games explain what players can or cannot do in pursuit of the goals;
- **Resources:** Games provide players with resources to draw upon to achieve the goals. For example, a puck, a scrabble tile, or a chance card;
- **Conflict:** In a game, the player should work against something or someone to obtain the goals. Other players might pose conflict. Hazards in a video game are another example of conflict;
- **Boundaries:** These can be physical boundaries such as the lines on the floor of a basketball court, or they can be conceptual boundaries via the social agreement of a game. For instance, players agree that only in the Go Fish game are they discussing and bargaining over the cards involved; and
- **Outcomes:** Games involve uncertain and unequal outcomes. Players will lose or win, but that is not certain from the outset of the game. That uncertainty is important as it drives the players through the game.

Students can interact with educational materials in a playful or more dynamic way. Photo via iStock/izusek. [Used under license.]

In examining these components, the overlaps between games and well-designed learning experiences become apparent. Learning experiences are designed with learners in mind. There is an objective that learners are working toward in the interest of specific outcomes. Well-designed learning experiences will likely provide learners with resources, such as videos, pencils, workbooks, Erlenmeyer flasks, or audiotapes to support the learner.

The degree to which learning and games overlap on those elements is arguable and there are certainly less apparent overlaps such as boundaries and conflict. One can find a detailed exploration of these arguments in Gee's *What Video Games Have to Teach Us About Learning and Literacy* (2007). Gee unpacks thirty-six learning principles that are manifest in both "good" games and effective learning experiences. By examining social learning and linguistic theories around situated cognition, distributed cognition, cultural models, multimodal principles, identity, self-knowledge, and others, Gee weaves all of Fullerton's elements into a schema for effective learning design.

Educational Video Games

Gee's work speaks to what makes any designed learning experience an effective one, it is not an explicit advocacy of the use of games in general or video games as learning tools. Rather, Gee's argument centers on the fact that modern video games are challenging and cognitively demanding. Players are often frustrated at many junctures in trying to reach the video games objectives. Yet, through the forces of a competitive market place, game designers need to figure out how to make their games just challenging enough to be compelling while providing rewards, help, hints, and reinforcement to keep players from quitting or giving up in frustration. These competing pressures yield the most popular video games on the shelves as the product would otherwise not thrive, people would not purchase those products. Gee poses a similar challenge to educators, schools, and curriculum designers: Design learning experiences that are challenging yet pleasurable.

Gee's contribution revived an interest in educational video games, but interest in games for learning began in the 1970s, with the earliest personal computers. In a white paper from the Joan Ganz Cooney Center, Richards, Stebbins, and Moellering (2013) note that older titles such as *Math Blaster, Oregon Trail, Where in the World Is Carmen Sandiego?,* and *Sim City* enjoyed tremendous success in both the K-12 institutional market as well as the commercial markets. A new generation of educational games has had a harder time achieving similar. Companies such as BrainPop and Discovery Education have begun to aggregate and deliver games to fill curricular niches across all the grade and subject areas. The challenge these companies have faced in finding profitable models for educational games underscores a fundamental disconnect.

The stigma of using games as tools for learning has all but fallen away, but schools are not yet buying learning games in a commercially viable way. With all the enthusiasm around game-based learning and the mutual vision educators seem to share for their potential, why has market success been such a challenge? Richards et al identify several potential issues, including uneven technological capabilities among schools, supplementary curricular budgets that are in flux, and the wide, confusing range of game products of varying quality.

Gamification

"Gamification," a term coined in the early 2000s, refers to the use of video-game logic and psychology in real-world environments, most prominently in marketing, education, and the corporate world. The theory of gamification holds that people—whether consumers, coworkers, or students—respond naturally and efficiently to competition, reward, and simulated risk of the type that have made video games such a cultural phenomenon since the 1980s.

The concept applies especially to the generation of Americans born after 1975, many of whom were raised playing video games, who began assuming positions of prominence in businesses and organizations in the early twenty-first century. These video-game aficionados brought with them many of the assumptions and strategies of gaming—incentivized decision making, rapid problem solving, the self-evident logic of specific tasks and short-term rewards, an adrenaline response to simulated risk, and the perception of achievement as a measure of self-expression—all guided by the assumption that operating in such a matrix is both fun and profitable.

Gamification assumes that productivity and efficiency can be enhanced by creating artificial narratives and a game feel around otherwise routine endeavors, thus increasing engagement, raising skill levels, and positively influencing those who are participating. Though the paradigm of gamification emerged in a very short time through weekend seminars, online training sessions, and social media, its application soon became widespread. Examples of gamification include fast-food restaurants that offer a free meal after ten visits, community organizations that attract volunteers by creating an artificial system of participation levels, and banks that create automated teller machine (ATM) games that award points for savvy deposit decisions.

Psychologists point out that the essential strategy of gamification is just a newer version of old-school operant conditioning that leverages desired behavior in manipulative ways. Some companies and educational institutions that must consider long-term developments fear that gamification narrows people's focus to short-term gains and to necessarily limited, even vague, objectives. A number of educators in particular have expressed concerns that the emphasis on external rewards may decrease students' intrinsic motivation for learning, although the extent to which this is a genuine concern remains in dispute; many argue that proper gamification of learning involves using extrinsic rewards to support, rather than supplant, intrinsic motivation.

Some more traditional individuals, particularly those born before the advent of video games, find the premise of gamification insulting and do not believe that the serious work of real life should mimic the simulated thrills of video games. Critics of gamification believe that simply motivating people to act in a certain way—whether customers, students, or coworkers—is a potentially catastrophic strategy because motion can be mistaken for progress, activity for achievement, and competition for teamwork.

Games and Behavior Modification

As formal learning scholars grappled with the ideas presented by Gee and others researching and developing games for use in the classroom, many in the private and commercial sector began to consider how game mechanics can be used for motivation and behavior modification. This application of game mechanics to areas where behavior modification is desirable such as in marketing, training, and education, have come to be known as gamification. Gamification leverages individuals' desire for such things

Image via iStock/Andrey Suslov.

as self-expression, mastery, competition, status, and achievement in pursuit of a desired objective.

Game designer J. McGonigal championed the role games can play in addressing global and society problems such as poverty and climate change. Games and gamified experiences hold potential for solving cognitively complex problems. For example, the game *Foldit* is an online game about protein folding. The game received special attention and acclaim when it was noted that human players could outperform the computationally demanding, algorithmically generated solutions to questions in protein folding.

Gamification has been utilized across a variety of efforts, including employee recruitment and retention, physical fitness, social network participation, ideation, and customer loyalty. Concerns emerged, however, that gamification techniques began to encourage unintended behaviors, as people would try to, for lack of a better term, "game the system." That is, maximize desired quantitative outputs for the outputs themselves, or, to revisit Fullerton's framework, to obtain the desired outcomes without pursuing the intended objective. Critics such as Ian Bogost have been adamant and vocal in their warnings that gamification is exploitive and manipulative, particularly when employed as a marketing strategy in for-profit commercial endeavors. Bogost described efforts as a type of "exploitationware."

Transmedia in the Learning Landscape

While the use of game mechanics to sculpt human behavior continues to garner critics and champions, other scholars are pointing out the ubiquitous role video games play in the American childhood media landscape. To be sure, where some critics of gamification criticized the movement's emphasis on mechanics over narrative, other scholars turned their attention to the value of narrative in games. Video games are a critical part of the transmedia experience common to children in many parts of the Western world. Transmedia defines the play, storytelling, and learning of most American children ages six to eleven. As is implied by the name, transmedia describes phenomena that cross media platforms: books, televisions, movies, live action, and games. Because of their interactive nature, video games play a key role in the transmedia landscape. As such, Jenkins has distilled what it is about transmedia that is of import to educators and in doing so has challenged educators to consider the role games (and particularly video games) can play in the transmedia learning landscape:

- **Spreadability vs. drillability:** Spreadability refers to the ability to scan a media landscape for bits of interesting information or data. This is the way traditional survey or introductory courses have typically approached information. Drillability refers to the ability and opportunity to dig deeper into content and asks educators to think carefully about motivation, what motivates students to try and learn more about a subject?

- **Continuity vs. multiplicity:** Continuity refers to the coherent story told by a media landscape. In education, this commonly manifests itself as a cannon. Multiplicity, on the other hand, asks learners to think about perspectives other than that of the established cannon. As an example, educational technology scholar Squire used the computer game *Civilization* to invite players to think about alternate histories: What if North America had colonized Europe, for example? How might the world be different today?

- **Immersion vs. extraction:** Immersion refers to the ability of media (theme parks, simulations, online worlds, video games) to immerse students in a different world. Extraction refers to the students' ability to take those lessons and experiences back with them to their own everyday world;

- **World building:** Since transmedia experiences are often outside of the core narrative, they can provide richer environments in which these peripheral narratives play out. In a school setting, for instance, this might mean that students read historical fiction to accompany a history lesson thus moving away from stories of presidents or generals to understanding or imagining the everyday life of citizens of those eras;

- **Seriality:** With the seriality principle, Jenkins asserts that educators can learn from good, serial storytellers. In a serial, chapters are satisfying as units but entice the reader to continue onto the next chapter with a cliffhanger. Classrooms should offer an equivalent of cliffhangers to motivate learners;

- **Subjectivity:** Transmedia experiences allow audiences to explore a central narrative through new eyes. A good example of this is the book *Wicked*, which tells a story from the perspective of the antagonist from *Wizard of Oz*. As such, they offer new perspectives. Using the example of a history class, this means students get to examine a battle from the perspective of the Greeks and the Persians, for example;

- **Performance:** Transmedia experiences lead audiences into wanting to participate and develop their own performance of the material. Jenkins uses much of his scholarship on fandom and fan experiences for this principle. Jenkins points to communities such as *Star Trek* fans (but more recent examples include multiple *Harry Potter* or *Buffy* fans) wherein the media becomes so meaningful to fans that the narrative of the media lives on with fans long after the media property has been retired. Performance is a point of interest as it points to issues of motivation and involvement that are of interest to the formal education community. To extend on the historical example used above, this could include asking students to dress up in period costumes and reenact important or even quotidian moments in history.

Viewpoints

Where Fullerton discusses the role of the game designer to establish rules, boundaries, and goals, Jenkins paints a media ecosystem in which learners become the rule makers and the rule breakers, where learners test boundaries and push past them. As such, Jenkins points the way to a postgames way of looking at games-based learning, one in which games are one piece of a media puzzle that must be mastered by children of the so-called information economy.

Games, particularly video games, will continue to be part of the rich media ecosystem inhabited by the distributed, situated minds of school-aged children. While anyone who has played an immersive game can intuit the power games have to shape knowledge, ideas, and values, the role of games in formal education settings remains to be seen.

—*Marjee Chmiel and Joseph Dewey*

References

Afari, E., J. Aldridge, B. Fraser, et al. "Students' Perceptions of the Learning Environment and Attitudes in Game-Based Mathematics Classrooms." *Learning Environments Research*, vol. 16, no. 1, 2013, pp. 131–50.

Bourgonjon, J., F. De Grove, C. De Smet, et al. "Acceptance of Game-Based Learning by Secondary School Teachers." *Computers & Education*, vol. 67, 2013, pp. 21–35.

Disessa, A. A. *Changing Minds: Computers, Learning, and Literacy*. MIT Press, 2011.

Flanagan, M., and H. Nissenbaum. *Values at Play in Digital Games*. MIT Press, 2014.

Fullerton, T. *Game Design Workshop: A Playcentric Approach to Creating Innovative Games*. CRC Press, 2014.

Gee, James Paul. *What Video Games Have to Teach Us About Learning and Literacy*. Rev. and Updated ed., Macmillan, 2007.

Hamari, J., and J. Koivisto. "Social Motivations to Use Gamification: An Empirical Study of Gamifying Exercise." *Proceedings of the 21st European Conference on Information Systems, Utrecht, Netherlands, June 5-8, 2013*.

Jenkins, Henry. "Transmedia Storytelling and Entertainment: An Annotated Syllabus." *Continuum: Journal of Media & Cultural Studies*, vol. 24, no. 6, 2010, pp. 943–58.

McGonigal, J. *Reality Is Broken*. Jonathan Cape, 2011.

Richards, J., L. Stebbins, and K. Moellering. "Games for a Digital Age: K-12 Market Map and Investment Analysis." 2013, joanganzcooneycenter.org.

Werbach, K., and D. Hunter. *For the Win: How Game Thinking Can Revolutionize Your Business*. Wharton Digital Press, 2012.

GEE, JAMES PAUL

Introduction

A principal aspect of James Paul Gee's work is based in the principles of Discourse. A particular distinction is drawn between ordinary discourse and the broader principles of Discourse as they relate to social communication and linguistics. In normal discourse, the concept applies only to the language in use, the spoken words used to communicate with others. By Discourse, however, the concept applies not only to the language and words being used, but also to the milieu in which discourse is taking place. This includes the community in which the language is being used and the many parts thereof, such as: individual and community values, the behaviors of community members and the community as a whole, the various ways of thinking, the kinds of clothes being worn, foods, customs, perspectives, and other aspects that comprise a particular community.

Any number of Discourse communities can exist, both virtually and in the real world. Groups on Facebook and other social media platforms are Discourse communities, as are those platforms themselves. A group of friends and acquaintances that meet up at the local bar is a Discourse community, as is the neighborhood bowling team or the local baseball team, the group of soccer moms that meets at the pitch to watch their kids play, the Sunday church group, etc. Each Discourse community develops with a set of characteristics that is unique to that community, although similar characteristics may exist in many other Discourse communities.

Background

James Paul Gee was born April 15, 1948, in San Jose, California. He began his postsecondary education at University of California at Santa Barbara (UC Santa Barbara), where he completed his bachelor's degree in philosophy. From UC Santa Barbara he undertook graduate studies at Stanford University, where he studied and conducted research in linguistics, completing both a master's degree and a doctorate in that field.

His postgraduate career work focused on theoretical linguistics, particularly related to the theoretical aspects of syntax and semantics. At Stanford, he taught linguistics for a time before moving on to the

School of Language and Communication at Hampshire College, in Amherst, Massachusetts. From there he moved to Northeastern University in Boston, and then to the Max Planck Institute for Psycholinguistics in Netherlands, conducting research in psycholinguistics at both institutions.

Professor Gee's research focus switched from psycholinguistics to sociolinguistics, discourse analysis, and the application of linguistics to literacy and education. At the School of Education in Boston University, he became chair of the Department of Developmental Studies and Counseling, where he worked to establish graduate programs that used an integrated approach to language and literacy. These combined programs focused on reading, writing, bilingual education, English as a Second Language (ESL), and applied linguistics. At Clark University, Gee held the post of Jacob Hiatt Chair in Education, at the Hiatt Center for Urban Education, from 1993 through 1997. In 1997, he was appointed as the Tashia Morgridge Professor of Reading, at University of Wisconsin–Madison, and held that position until 2007. In 2007, he became the Mary Lou Fulton Presidential Professor of Literacy Studies, in the Department of Curriculum and Instruction, a position he held until his retirement in 2019.

Discourse Communities

Discourse communities span the entire range of social structures, generally with advantages for the members of the particular Discourse community vis-a-vis the overall society. For example, being raised in a family of devout faith facilitates Discourses of religion, philosophy, and related social constructs. Inherently, all Discourses are of equal value, since all Discourses are neutral definitions of their respective Discourse communities with neither a positive nor negative value delimiter attached. Thus, no particular Discourse is inherently better or worse than any other Discourse.

Where Discourses differ is in their ability to distribute powers within the overall society. This, of course, depends on how power is defined. A Discourse community of charitable and nonprofit organizations, for example, has one kind of power within society, a street gang has another kind of power, and so on, such that each Discourse community that can be identified has its own peculiar power within society as a whole, and therefore its own particular contribution to the nature of the overall society.

Literacy

Coupled to the concept of Discourse is that of literacy, as each Discourse inherently contains its own type of literacy built upon the many different kinds of literacy that have been defined apart from the basic ability to read and write. The members of a Discourse community have to be able to speak the language and walk the walk of that community, as it were. Whereas the 3Rs basis of literacy was, and still is, fundamental to communication, one can add any number of other literacies. The use of sign language, for example, represents a different visual literacy.

Digital literacy, communication using digital media, is another type of new literacy. It is perhaps the most important of any new literacies given its global applicability and its ability to enable Discourse communities that may encompass members from far reaches of the world. According to Professor Gee, literacy of any sort should not be seen merely as a mental exercise, but as something that is fundamental to any society, enabling society to develop and evolve. Digital literacy, for example, not only facilitates communication between humans in their various Discourse communities, it is also facilitating communication between humans and machines, and even between humans and other animal species. This alone broadens the concept of Discourse to the eventual inclusion of robots and artificial intelligences in human-based Discourse communities. It is an entirely new concept in sociology and the evolution of human societies.

—*Richard M. Renneboog*

References

Gee, James Paul, and Elisabeth R. Hayes. *Language and Learning in the Digital Age*. Routledge, 2011.

___. *What Video Games Have to Teach Us About Learning and Literacy*. 2nd ed., Macmillan, 2014.

___. *Social Linguistics and Literacies: Ideology in Discourses*. Routledge, 2014.

___. *How to Do Discourse Analysis: A Toolkit*. 2nd ed., Routledge, 2014.

___. *An Introduction to Discourse Analysis: Theory and Method*. 4th ed., Routledge, 2014.

___. *Literacy and Education*. Routledge, 2015.

___. *Introducing Discourse Analysis: From Grammar to Society*. Routledge, 2017.

___. *What Is a Human?: Language, Mind, and Culture*. Springer Nature, 2020.

GMAIL

Introduction

Gmail is a free email service that is managed by Google, Inc. The service offers many features that make using email fast, easy, and efficient. These features include a large storage capacity, a search feature, and an inbox with customizable tabs. Over a billion people throughout the world use Gmail.

Background

Paul Buchheit, a Google employee, created Gmail. He began working on the email service in 2001, two years after joining Google. Over the next several years, he and other Google employees developed the service before it was launched in 2004.

A common misconception surrounding Gmail is that Buchheit developed it as part of Google's 20 percent time, a policy that allows Google engineers to spend up to 20 percent of their work hours working on personal projects. It was revealed, however, that the email service was an official project given to Buchheit and not a personal project. Buchheit had begun creating an email program on his own several years before he started working at Google, but he never completed that program. The early Gmail program was called Caribou after a top-secret project referenced in the comic strip *Dilbert*.

Gmail was officially launched on April 1, 2004. That day, Google issued a press release announcing the launch and stating that the company was testing a preview version of the service. Although rumors about the email service circulated the day before, many people thought the press release was a hoax since it was released on April Fools' Day—but the press release and new email service were real. Gmail marked the first significant service Google launched since 1998, when the company debuted its search engine.

Initially, Google gave Gmail accounts to about one thousand people and asked them to invite friends to make accounts. Desire for Gmail invitations grew quickly. In fact, people began selling their invites on eBay, and websites such as Gmail Swap were launched, allowing people to swap goods and services for Gmail invites. Finally, in 2007, Google made Gmail available to everyone. By 2012—just five years later—Gmail had about 425 million users around the world. Its usage continued to grow every

Gmail logo. Image via Wikimedia Commons. [Public domain.]

year since this time. As of 2020, there were 1.8 billion active Gmail users.

Features

When Gmail was first launched, it had several features that set it apart from other free email services such as Yahoo! and Hotmail, the latter of which became Outlook in 2013. Gmail introduced a much larger storage capacity than the other services; a feature that automatically organizes emails; and a feature that searches emails. At its inception, Gmail offered one gigabyte (1 GB), or one thousand megabytes (1000 MB), of storage—about one hundred times more storage than that of most other services.

As of 2018, the storage capacity of a user's entire Google Account, which includes Gmail, Google Drive, Google+, and Google Photos, among other applications, was 15 GB. This large storage capacity eliminates the need to delete emails, allowing users to keep every email. The feature that automatically organizes emails by grouping emails and their replies into "conversations." One benefit of this feature is that a user does not need to place emails into folders. Gmail's search feature is based on Google search technology. It allows a user to search each and every email that was both sent and received. The feature uses keywords, as well as advanced search features, to search the content of all the user's emails.

Some other features of Gmail are an inbox with customizable tabs, custom themes, and integration with Google Drive (a storage drive) and Google Hangouts (an application for messaging and video calls). The five customizable tabs—Primary, Social, Promotions, Updates, and Forums—group emails of the same type into one of the tabs, allowing a user to decide which emails he or she would like to read. The user also can move emails by dragging and dropping them into a chosen tab. Additionally, the user has the option of customizing specific tabs for specific senders, for example, so emails from friends always get placed in the Primary tab. The custom themes feature enables a user to select a personal image or a photo from a collection as his or her theme. Google Hangouts allows face-to-face conversations with up to ten people simultaneously. The feature that allows integration with Google Drive enables a user to easily email files as large as 10 GB.

While Gmail is free, it is supported by advertising. When people use the email service, they are shown ads that are relevant to their emails and searches. The company makes money by scanning messages for information about users and then uses this information to tailor ads to users. It does not provide any of its users' personal information to advertisers. The company has faced criticism and lawsuits for this practice, and in 2017, Google announced that Gmail would no longer scan user's emails for personalized ads.

Gmail is one of the most widely used free email service in the world and in the United States for both desktop computers and mobile devices. The number of Gmail users more than doubled from 2012 to 2015 and had a 92 percent share of US start-up businesses.

—*Michael Mazzei*

References

"Features." *Google*. Google, Inc., www.gmail.com/intl/en_us/mail/help/features.html.

"Gmail." *Google*. Google, Inc., www.gmail.com/intl/en_us/mail/help/about.html.

"Google Gets the Message, Launches Gmail." *Google*. Google, Inc., 1 Apr. 2004, googlepress.blogspot.com/2004/04/google-gets-message-launches-gmail.html. Accessed 28 Aug. 2015.

Kelly, Heather. "Why Gmail and Other E-mail Services Aren't Really Free." *Cable News Network*. Turner Broadcasting System, Inc., 1 Apr. 2014, www.cnn.com/2014/03/31/tech/web/gmail-privacy-problems/.

McCracken, Harry. "How Gmail Happened: The Inside Story of Its Launch 10 Years Ago." *Time*. Time, Inc., 1 Apr. 2014, time.com/43263/gmail-10th-anniversary/.

Nester, Gilbert. "Number of Active Gmail Users 2022/2023: Statistics, Demographics, & Usage." *Finances Online*, financesonline.com/number-of-active-gmail-users/.

Smith, Craig. "Eighteen Amazing Gmail Facts and Statistics (January 2018)/By the Numbers." *DMR*, 31 Mar. 2018, expandedramblings.com/index.php/gmail-statistics/.

GOOGLE

Introduction

Google is the most widely used search engine around the globe, and many of the company's communication and publishing tools and services continue to be among the market leaders, including its email service Gmail, video-sharing service YouTube, blogging platform Blogger, and file-sharing service Google Drive. As Google—which set out to "organize the world's information and make it universally accessible"—rose to become one of the world's most powerful technology companies, concerns about the company's protection of privacy also began to rise. While Google's web crawlers have been caching and indexing billions of web pages, the company has also been storing vast amounts of personal information on its servers. In 2007, the watchdog organization, Privacy International, rated Google as "hostile" to privacy in a report that ranked internet companies by how they handle the protection of personal data.

Background

In 2004, in response to the launch of Gmail, thirty-one privacy and civil liberties organizations wrote a letter to Google's cofounders urging them to suspend the Gmail service until the company clarified its privacy protection policies and made its practices more transparent. The signers were concerned about Google's plan to scan the text of all incoming messages so that companies could place targeted ads based on keywords. In addition, they warned about the risks of misuse posed by the unlimited period for data retention.

In 2004, the Online Privacy Protection Act, Cal. Bus. & Prof. Code §§ 22575–22579 (2004), became effective in California. The initial bill prohibited the provider of electronic mail to scan email without the consent of all parties. Google, however, had initiated a public relations and lobbying campaign against the proposed bill and was ultimately successful in convincing lawmakers to remove the major consent provisions. Gmail was implemented as planned.

Google Street View, introduced in 2007 as a feature of Google maps, has been particularly controversial. Street View allows users to view panoramic photographic images of locations and to zoom in and out on specific locations. Google has been collecting these images by dispatching a fleet of assorted vehicles equipped with specialized surveillance cameras to the areas that have been mapped. After being uploaded to the internet, the photos are merged to create seamless panoramic views. Street View, initially introduced in a few US cities, was quickly expanded and is now available for locations around the globe.

The controversies surrounding Street View also highlight the challenges of confronting Google's data-collecting practices while establishing and affirming international safeguards for the protection of privacy. Lauren H. Rakower, an expert in technology law, has argued that Street View violates the international right to privacy as stated by the Universal Declaration of Human Rights and the International Covenant on Civil and Political Rights. Several European countries, as well as Australia, temporarily banned the implementation of Street View, and citizens in several countries formed grassroots campaigns against dispatching Google's Street View fleet in their neighborhoods. Protests increased after a European data protection agency discovered that Google has been collecting vast amounts of Wi-Fi data in addition to collecting images for Street View. In response, privacy advocates called for a Federal Communications Commission (FCC) investigation into whether Google's practices violated the federal Wiretap Act.

Subsequently, more than twelve countries investigated Google's practices, and the company was ultimately charged with violating privacy laws in at least nine countries. In the class action suit *Joffe v. Google, Inc.*, 729 F.3d 1262 (9th Cir. 2013), Google was sued for intercepting private communications from millions of users on unencrypted networks. The US Ninth Circuit Court of Appeals affirmed the ruling that intercepting unencrypted Wi-Fi broadcasts violates the Wiretap Act. Google attempted to appeal to the US Supreme Court. The Court declined to hear the case, however, affirming the lower court's decision. The company reached a $7 million settlement with the attorneys general of thirty-eight states and the District of Columbia over the Street View collection from unprotected Wi-Fi networks.

Defending its practices, Google claimed that it collected the data by accident, yet it also admitted that it did not adequately protect the privacy of consumers. While Google stopped collecting Wi-Fi data through its Street View fleet, concerns about the company's data collection practices have not been alleviated. Indeed, the privacy issues are closely linked to the very nature of Google's operation and mission: The company "makes money because it harvests, copies, aggregates, and ranks billions of Web contributions by millions of authors," according to Siva Vaidhyanathan. Google collects information when users use its services; it copies and disseminates information about people that has been published on the internet; and it continues to collect images for Street View, potentially exposing private views to the public. While Google has made it easier to control one's privacy settings by introducing a central portal under the "My Account" settings, controlling the information that the company retains about individual users remains daunting.

Google's privacy policies frequently change as the company evolves and develops new features such as Google Glass, opening up new privacy concerns. Subsequently, Google has had to respond to tens of thousands of requests to remove personal information from its index.

Privacy advocates have been calling for establishment of the right to be unlinked in the United States as well. The movement to establish international regulations to safeguard the protection of privacy by Google and other companies that collect vast amounts of user data continues to gain ground.

—Katharina Hering

References

"31 Privacy and Civil Liberties Organizations Urge Google to Suspend Gmail." *Privacy Rights Clearinghouse*, www.privacyrights.org/ ar/GmailLetter. htm.

Bennett, Colin J. *The Privacy Advocates: Resisting the Spread of Surveillance*. MIT Press, 2008.

Electronic Privacy Information Center. *Ben Joffe v. Google, Inc.*, epic.org/amicus/ google-street-view/.

Rakower, Lauren. "Blurred Line: Zooming in on Google Street View and the Global Right to Privacy." *Brooklyn Journal of International Law*, vol. 37, no. 1, 2011, pp. 317–47.

Sarpu, Bridget A. "Google: The Endemic Threat to Privacy." *Journal of High Technology Law*, vol. 15, no. 1, 2014, pp. 97–134.

Vaidhyanathan, Siva. *The Googlization of Everything (And Why We Should Worry)*. U of California P, 2011.

GOOGLE SLIDES

Introduction

Google Slides is one of the leading online presentation applications available in 2022. Like other Google services, Google Slides is a free-to-use online service that can be used by anyone with internet access and a web browser. The application can be accessed by any browser, and comes in two versions: a free, basic version for personal use, and a more versatile and feature-rich business version.

Background

Essentially all of Microsoft's Office Suite software packages include a presentation application. Users are able to compose slide show presentations consisting of any number of slides, with many possible options for the appearance of each slide and for other functions. Each presentation exists as an individual file, allowing the presentation to be ported to other computers and devices for display. The problem with this, however, is that any other computer or device that would be used to display a particular presentation must have compatible presentation software installed in order for the file to be read and utilized.

For an application such as Microsoft Power-Point, for example, the presentation file will be in one of PowerPoint's proprietary file formats, and can only be displayed by other presentation applications that are capable of reading and interpreting those file formats. Other presentation applications have their own presentation file formats that are not recognized by Microsoft PowerPoint and its equivalent applications such as Apple's Keynote. This is why many creators and users often save their slide presentations as portable document formats (PDFs) to increase chances of readability across computers and operating systems.

Many software brands and developers now offer internet-based versions of their presentation software, generally on a fee-for-use or subscription basis. The programs and applications are accessed from cloud storage, and the presentations created with them can be downloaded, stored in the cloud, or shared and displayed to a defined audience group.

Usability

Google Slides is an integral part of the Google Docs suite, along with the Docs, Sheets, Drawings, Forms, Sites, and Keeps applications. Presentation files produce in Google Slides are fully compatible with Microsoft PowerPoint, and the application can be accessed for use with any of the Chrome, Firefox, Internet Explorer, Microsoft Edge and Apple Safari browsers. Initially released in 2006, the coding for Google Slides is written in JavaScript and is supported in machines running on Windows, Android, iOS, Blackberry, macOS and ChromeOS operating systems, on Chrome, Apple and Microsoft platforms. The Google Slides application currently supports eighty-three user languages, enabling worldwide usability.

Google Slides functions like all presentation applications in that users compose, create, and organize slides to construct a presentation. Editing is carried out online, but can also be cone offline using the Google Chrome browser with the Google Docs Offline extension added. This extension effectively turns Google Docs into a stand-alone software package residing on the user's computer, allowing the user to work with Google Docs without having to be connected to the internet.

Files produced in Google Slides are by default saved in the .gslide format unique to Google Slides. The application supports a number of other file types though, including PowerPoint template and slideshow formats (.pot, .potm, .potx, .pps, .ppsm, .ppsx, .ppt and .pptm), OpenDocument presentation format (.odp), Portable Document Format (.pdf), Plain Text (.txt) and several graphics file formats (.jpg, .jpeg, .png, .gif and .svg). Files to be saved in the .gslide format cannot exceed 100Mb in size. Inserted image files cannot exceed 50Mb in size.

Google Slides and Security

Google has had a history of security issues—as have all technology companies and institutions. Many users increasingly do not trust cloud-based sites with the protection of users' identities, but Google has been quick to deflect that criticism. According to Google, along with password protection to access presentations, Slides uses industry-leading security features such as advanced malware protection to prevent malicious code from being surreptitiously introduced into a user's presentation files.

Malicious codes can carry out many different undesirable actions from simply interfering with productivity by delivering pop-up ads to causing catastrophic physical damage, and could spread into the computer systems of any who would access the file in which the code resides. This includes both the creator and the end user(s). With Google Slides, the spread of malware is also facilitated because the application and the files it was used to produce are stored in the cloud, the massive depositories of servers and memory banks maintained by Google and other companies like Apple and Microsoft. This eliminates the need for individual users to store files in their own machines and maintain their security through firewalls and third-party security software. Instead, the trust is placed in the major technology players like Google—external to those who access or download the presentations.

Users' Google Slides files are fully encrypted, both while stored and when being transferred. In this way the file and the information it contains can only be reproduced properly by computers that have the correct encryption key to allow the scrambled coding to be unscrambled. As an enterprise system, Google Slides is subject to regular independent verification of its security, privacy, and compliance controls, as are all Google services.

—*Richard M. Renneboog and Jake D. Nicosia*

References

LaCounte, Scott. *The Ridiculously Simple Guide to Google Slides: A Practical Guide to Cloud-Based Presentations.* Ridiculously Simple Books, 2019.

Lentzner, Rémy. *Google Slides Online: Professional Training.* Editions Rémylent, 2021.

Obendorf, Hartmut. *Minimalism: Designing Simplicity.* Springer Science + Business Media, 2009.

Roberts, Barrie. *Step-by-Step Guide to Google Slides.* Independently published, 2020.

Rossington, Richard. "Is It Safe to Use Google Docs?" *CEO Today,* 9 Oct. 2019, ceotodaymagazine.com/2019/10/is-it-safe-to-use-google-docs/.

GRAPHICAL USER INTERFACE

Introduction

Graphical user interfaces (GUIs) are human-computer interaction systems. In these systems, users interact with the computer by manipulating visual representations of objects or commands. Graphical user interfaces are part of common operating systems such as Windows and macOS. They are also used in other applications.

A user interface is a system for human-computer interaction. The interface determines the way that a user can access and work with data stored on a computer or within a computer network. Interfaces can be either text based or graphics based. Text-based systems allow users to input commands. These commands may be text strings or specific words that activate functions. By contrast, GUIs are designed so that computer functions are tied to graphic icons (like folders, files, and drives). Manipulating an icon causes the computer to perform certain functions.

Background

The earliest computers used a text-based interface. Users entered text instructions into a command line. For instance, typing "run" in the command line would tell the computer to activate a program or process. One of the earliest text-based interfaces for consumer computer technology was known as a disk operating system (DOS). Using DOS-based systems required users to learn specific text commands, such as "del" for deleting or erasing files or "dir" for listing

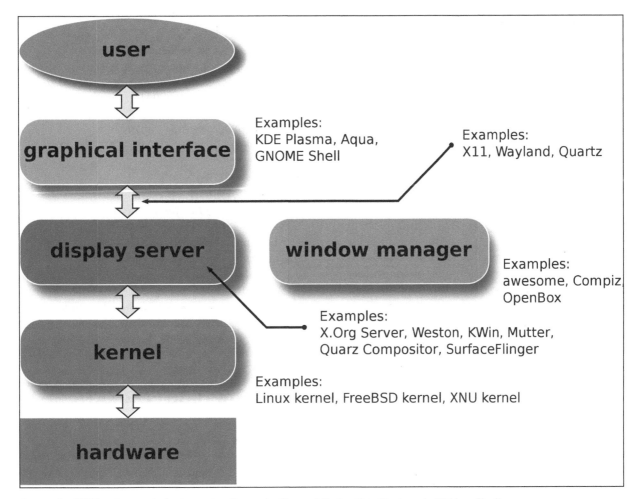

Layers of a GUI based on a windowing system. Image by Shmuel Csaba Otto Traian, via Wikimedia Commons.

the contents of a directory. The first GUIs were created in the 1970s as a visual "shell" built over DOS system.

Graphical user interfaces transform the computer screen into a physical map on which graphics represent functions, programs, files, and directories. In GUIs, users control an onscreen pointer, usually an arrow or hand symbol, to navigate the computer screen. Users activate computing functions by directing the pointer over an icon and clicking on it. For instance, GUI users can cause the computer to display the contents of a directory (the "dir" command in DOS) by clicking on a folder or directory icon on the screen. Modern GUIs combine text-based icons, such as those found in menu bars and movable windows, with linked text icons that can be used to access programs and directories.

Elements of GUIs and Other Object Interfaces

Computer programs are built using coded instructions that tell the computer how to behave when given inputs from a user. Many different programming languages can be used to create GUIs. These include C++, C#, JavaFX, XAML, XUL, among others. Each language offers different advantages and disadvantages when used to create and modify GUIs.

User-centered design focuses on understanding and addressing user preferences, needs, capabilities, and tendencies. According to these design principles, interface metaphors help make GUIs user friendly. Interface metaphors are models that represent real-world objects or concepts to enhance user understanding of computer functions. For example, the desktop structure of a GUI is designed using the metaphor of a desk. Computer desktops, like actual desktops, might have stacks of documents (windows) and objects or tools for performing various functions. Computer folders, trash cans, and recycle bins are icons whose functions mirror those of their real-world counterparts.

Object-oriented user interfaces (OOUIs) allow a user to manipulate objects onscreen in intuitive ways based on the function that the user hopes to achieve. Most modern GUIs have some object-oriented functionality. Icons that can be dragged, dropped, slid, toggled, pushed, and clicked are "objects." Objects include folders, program shortcuts, drive icons, and trash or recycle bins. Interfaces that use icons can also be direct manipulation interfaces (DMI). These interfaces allow the user to adjust onscreen objects as though they were physical objects to get certain results. Resizing a window by dragging its corner is one example of direct manipulation used in many GUIs.

Current and Future of Interface Design

GUIs have long been based on a model known as "WIMP." WIMP stands for "windows, icons, menus, and pointer objects," which describes the ways that users can interact with the interface. Modern GUIs are a blend of graphics-based and text-based functions, but this system is more difficult to implement on modern handheld computers, which have less space to hold icons and menus.

Touch-screen interfaces represent the post-WIMP age of interface design. With touch screens, users more often interact directly with objects on the screen, rather than using menus and text-based instructions. Touch-screen design is important in a many application-specific GUIs. These interfaces are designed to handle a single process or application, such as self-checkout kiosks in grocery stores and point-of-sale retail software.

Computer interfaces of the early twenty-first century typically require users to navigate through files, folders, and menus to locate functions, data, or programs. However, voice activation of programs or functions is also available on many computing devices. As this technology becomes more common and effective, verbal commands may replace many functions that have been accessed by point-and-click or menu navigation.

—Micah L. Issitt

References

"Graphical User Interface (GUI)." *Techopedia*, 13 Jan. 2017, www.techopedia.com/definition/5435/graphical-user-interface-gui.

Johnson, Jeff. *Designing with the Mind in Mind.* 2nd ed., Morgan Kaufmann, 2014.

Long, Simon. *An Introduction to C & GUI Programming.* Raspberry Pi Press, 2019.

Reimer, Jeremy. "A History of the GUI." *Ars Technica*, 5 May 2005, arstechnica.com/features/2005/05/gui/.

Tidwell, Jenifer, Charles Brewer, and Aynne Valencia. *Designing Interfaces: Patterns for Effective Interaction Design.* 3rd ed., O'Reilly Media, 2020.

"User Interface Design Basics." *Usability.gov*, www.usability.gov/what-and-why/user-interface-design.html.

Wood, David. *Interface Design: An Introduction to Visual Communication in UI Design.* Fairchild Books, 2014.

GRAPHICS FORMATS

Introduction

Graphics formats are standardized forms of computer files used to transfer, display, store, or print reproductions of digital images. Digital image files are divided into two major families, vector and raster files. They can be compressed or uncompressed for storage. Each type of digital file has advantages and disadvantages when used for various applications.

Background

A digital image is a mathematical representation of an image that can be displayed, manipulated, and modified with a computer or other digital device. It can also be compressed. Compression uses algorithms to reduce the size of the image file to facilitate sharing, displaying, or storing images. Digital images may be stored and manipulated as raster or vector images. A third type of graphic file family, called metafiles, uses both raster and vector elements. The quality and resolution (clarity) of an image depend on the digital file's size and complexity.

In raster graphics, images are stored as a set of squares, called pixels. Each pixel has a color value and a color depth. This is defined by the number of bits allocated to each pixel. Pixels can range from 1 bit per pixel, which has a monochrome (two-color) depth, to 32-bit, or "true color." 32-bit color allows for more than 4 billion colors through various combinations. Raster graphics have the highest level of color detail because each pixel in the image can have its own color depth. For this reason, raster formats are used for photographs and in image programs such as Adobe Photoshop. However, the resolution of a raster image depends on size because the image has the same number of pixels at any magnification. For this reason, raster images cannot be magnified past a certain point without losing resolution.

Vector graphics store images as sets of polygons that are not size-dependent and look the same at any magnification. For relatively simple graphics, like logos, vector files are smaller and more precise than raster images. However, vector files do not support complex colors or advanced effects, like blurring or drop shadows.

Two basic color models are used to digitally display various colors. The RGB color model, also called additive color, combines red, green, and blue to create colors. The CMYK model, also called subtractive color, combines the subtractive primary colors cyan, magenta, yellow, and black (key) to absorb certain wavelengths of light while reflecting others.

Image Compression

Image compression reduces the size of an image to enable easier storage and processing. Lossless compression uses a modeling algorithm that identifies repeated or redundant information contained within an image. It stores this information as a set of instructions can be used to reconstruct the image without any loss of data or resolution. One form of lossless compression commonly used is the Lempel-Ziv-Welch (LZW) compression algorithm developed in the 1980s.

The LZW algorithm uses a "code table" or "dictionary" for compression. It scans data for repeated sequences and then adds these sequences to a "dictionary" within the compressed file. By replacing repeated data with references to the dictionary file, space is saved but no data is lost. Lossless compression is of benefit when image quality is essential but is less efficient at reducing image size. Lossy compression algorithms reduce file size by removing less valuable information. However, images compressed with lossy algorithms continue to lose resolution each time the image is compressed and decompressed. Despite the loss of image quality, lossy compression creates smaller files and is useful when image quality is less important or when computing resources are in high demand.

Common Graphic Formats

Joint Photographic Experts Group (JPEG) is a type of lossy image compression format developed in the early 1990s. JPEGs support RGB and CMYK color and are most useful for small images, such as those used for display on websites. JPEGs are automatically compressed using a lossy algorithm. Thus, some image quality is lost each time the image is edited and saved as a new JPEG.

GIF (graphics interchange format) files have a limited color palette and use LZW compression so that they can be compressed without losing quality. Unlike JPEG, GIF supports "transparency" within an image by ignoring certain colors when displaying or printing. GIF files are open source and can be used in a wide variety of programs and applications. However, most GIF formats support only limited color because the embedded LZW compression is most effective when an image contains a limited color palette. PNGs (portable network graphics) are open-source alternatives to GIFs that support transparency and 24-bit color. This makes them better at complex colors than GIFs.

SVGs (Scalable Vector Graphics) are an open-source format used to store and transfer vector images. SVG files lack built-in compression but can be compressed using external programs. In addition, there are "metafile" formats that can be used to share images combining both vector and raster elements. These include PDF (portable document format) files, which are used to store and display documents, and the Encapsulated PostScript (EPS) format, which is typically used to transfer image files between programs.

—Micah L. Issitt

References

Brown, Adrian. "Graphics File Formats." *National Archives*, Aug. 2008, www.nationalarchives.gov. uk/documents/information-management/ graphic-file-formats.pdf.

Costello, Vic, Susan Youngblood, and Norman E. Youngblood. *Multimedia Foundations: Core Concepts for Digital Design.* 2nd ed., Routledge, 2017.

Dale, Nell, and John Lewis. *Computer Science Illuminated.* 6th ed., Jones & Bartlett Learning, 2016.

"Introduction to Image Files Tutorial." *Boston University Information Services and Technology,* www.bu.edu/tech/support/research/training-consulting/online-tutorials/imagefiles/.

Marschner, Steve, et al. *Fundamentals of Computer Graphics.* 4th ed., CRC Press, 2016.

Prust, Z. A., and Peggy B. Deal. *Graphic Communications: Digital Design and Print Essentials.* 6th ed., Goodheart-Willcox, 2019.

GRAPHICS TECHNOLOGIES

Introduction

Graphics technology, which includes computer-generated imagery (CGI), has become an essential technology of the motion picture and video-gaming industries, of television, and of virtual reality. The production of such images, and especially of animated images, is a complex process that demands a sound understanding of not only physics and mathematics but also anatomy and physiology.

While graphics technologies include all of the theoretical principles and physical methods used to produce images, the term more specifically refers to the principles and methods associated with digital or computer-generated images. Digital graphics are displayed as a limited array of colored picture elements, or pixels. The greater the number of pixels that are used for an image, the greater the resolution of the image and the finer the detail that can be portrayed. The data that specifies the attributes of each individual pixel are stored in an electronic file using one of several specific formats.

Each file format has its own characteristics with regard to how the image data can be manipulated and utilized. Because the content of images is intended to portray real-world objects, the data for each image must be mathematically manipulated to reflect real-world structures and physics. The rendering of images, especially for photorealistic animation, is thus a calculation-intensive process. For images that are not produced photographically, special techniques and applications are continually being developed to produce image content that looks and moves as though it were real.

Background

Imaging is as old as the human race. Static graphics have historically been the norm up to the invention of the devices that could make a series of still pictures appear to move. The invention of celluloid in the late nineteenth century provided the material for photographic film, with the invention of motion picture cameras and projectors to follow. Animated films, commonly known as cartoons, have been produced since the early twentieth century by repeatedly photographing a series of hand-drawn cells. With the development of the digital computer and color displays in the second half of the twentieth century, it became possible to generate images without the need for hand-drawn intermediaries.

Computer graphics in the twenty-first century can produce images that are indistinguishable from traditional photographs of real objects. The methodology continues to develop in step with the development of new computer technology and new programming methods that make use of the computing abilities of the technology.

How It Works

Images are produced initially as still or static images. Human perception requires about one-thirtieth of a second to process the visual information obtained through the seeing of a still image. If a sequential series of static images is displayed at a rate that exceeds the frequency of thirty images per second, the images are perceived as continuous motion. This is the basic principle of motion pictures, which are nothing more than displays of a sequential series of still pictures. Computer-generated still images (now indistinguishable from still photographs since the advent of digital cameras) have the same relationship to computer animation.

Images are presented on a computer screen as an array of colored dots, or pixels.

The clarity, or resolution, of the image depends on the number of pixels that it contains within a defined area. The more pixels within a defined area, the smaller each pixel must be and the finer the detail that can be displayed. In the 2010s, digital cameras typically captured image data in an array of between eight and fifty megapixels, though some specialty digital cameras manufactured later in the decade were capable of capturing that data in 100 megapixels or more. The electronic data file of the image contains the specific color, hue, saturation, and brightness designations for each pixel in the associated image, as well as other information about the image itself.

To obtain photorealistic representation in computer-generated images, effects must be applied that correspond to the mathematical laws of physics. In still images, computational techniques such as ray tracing and reflection must be used to imitate the effect of light sources and reflective surfaces. For the virtual reality of the image to be effective, all of the actual physical characteristics that the subject would have if it were real must be clearly defined as well so that when the particular graphics application being used renders the image to the screen, all of the various parts of the image are displayed in their proper positions.

To achieve photorealistic effects in animation, the corresponding motion of each pixel must be coordinated with the defined surfaces of the virtual object, and their positions must be calculated for each frame of the animation. Because the motions of the objects would be strictly governed by the mathematics of physics in the real world, so must the motions of the virtual objects. For example, an animated image of a round object bouncing down a street must appear to obey the laws of gravity and Newtonian mechanics. Thus, the same mathematical equations that apply to the motion and properties of the real object must also apply to the virtual object.

Other essential techniques are required to produce realistic animated images. When two virtual objects are designed to interact as though they are real, solid objects, clipping instructions identify where the virtual solid surfaces of the objects are located; the instructions then mandate the clipping of any corresponding portions of an image to prevent the objects from seeming to pass through each other. Surface textures are mapped and associated with underlying data in such a way that movement corresponds to real body movements and surface responses. Image animation to produce realistic skin and hair effects is based on a sound understanding of anatomy and physiology and represents a specialized field of graphics technology.

Software

The vast majority of products and applications related to graphics technology are software applications created specifically to manipulate electronic data so that it produces realistic images and animations. The software ranges from basic paint programs installed on most personal computers (PCs) to full-featured programs that produce wireframe structures, map surface textures, coordinate behaviors, movements of surfaces to underlying structures, and 360-degree, three-dimensional (3D) animated views of the resulting images.

Other types of software applications are used to design objects and processes that are to be produced as real objects. Computer-assisted design (CAD) is commonly used to generate construction-specification drawings and to design printed-circuit boards, electronic circuits and integrated circuits, complex machines, and many other real-world constructs. The features and capabilities of individual applications vary. The simplest applications produce only a static image of a schematic layout, while the most advanced are capable of modeling the behavior of the system being designed in real time. The latter are increasingly useful in designing and virtual-testing such dynamic systems as advanced jet engines and industrial processes. One significant benefit that has accrued from the use of such applications has been the ability to refine the efficiency of systems such as production lines in manufacturing facilities.

Hardware

The computational requirements of graphics can quickly exceed the capabilities of any particular computer system. This is especially true of PCs. Graphics technology in this area makes use of separate graphics processing units (GPUs) to handle the computational load of graphics display. This allows the PC's central processing unit (CPU) to carry out the other computational requirements of the application without having to switch back and forth between graphic and nongraphic tasks.

Many graphics boards also include dedicated memory for exclusive use in graphics processing. This eliminates the need for large sectors of a PC's random-access memory (RAM) to be used for storing graphics data, a requirement that can render a computer practically unusable.

Another requirement of hardware is an instruction system to operate the various components so that they function together. For graphics applications, with the long periods of time they require to carry out the calculations needed to render a detailed image, it is essential that the computer's operating system (OS) be functionally stable. The main operating systems of PCs are Microsoft Windows, the Apple macOS, the open-source OS Linux, and Google's Chrome OS. Some versions of other operating systems, such as Oracle Solaris, have been made available but do not account for a significant share of the PC market.

The huge amounts of graphics and rendering required for large-scale projects such as motion pictures demand the services of mainframe computers. The operating systems for these units have a longer history than do PC operating systems. Mainframe computers function primarily with the UNIX operating system, although many run under some variant of the Linux operating system. UNIX and Linux are similar operating systems, the main difference being that UNIX is a proprietary system whereas Linux is open source.

Motion Pictures and Television

Graphics technology is a hardware- and software-intensive field. The motion picture industry of the twenty-first century would not be possible without the digital technology that has been developed since 1980. While live-action images are often recorded on standard photographic film in the traditional way, motion picture special effects and animation have become the exclusive realm of digital graphics technologies. The use of CGI in motion pictures has driven the development of new technology and continually raised the standards of image quality. Amalgamating live action with CGI through digital processing and manipulation enables filmmakers to produce motion pictures in which live characters interact seamlessly with virtual characters, sometimes in entirely fantastic environments. Examples of such motion pictures are numerous in the science-fiction and fantasy film genres, but the technique is finding application in all areas, especially in educational programming. In addition, motion capture technology combines graphics with recorded human movement to create animated characters.

Video Gaming and Virtual Training

The most graphics-intensive application is video gaming. All video games, in all genres, exist only as the graphic representation of complex program code. The variety of video game types ranges from straightforward computer versions of simple card games to complex 3D virtual worlds.

Many graphics software applications are developed for the use of game designers, but they have also made their way into many other imaging uses. The same software that is used to create a fictional virtual world can also be used to create virtual copies of the real world. This technology has been adapted for use in pilot- and driver-training programs in all aspects of transportation. Military, police, and security personnel are given extensive practical and scenario training through the use of virtual simulators. A simulator uses video and graphic displays of actual terrain to give the person being trained hands-on experience without endangering either personnel or actual machinery.

Social Context and Future Prospects

Graphics technology is inextricably linked to the computer and digital electronics industries. Accordingly, graphics technology changes at a rate that at minimum equals the rate of change in those industries. Since 1980, graphics technology using computers has developed from the display of just sixteen colors on color television screens, yielding blocky image components and very slow animation effects, to photorealistic full-motion video, with the capacity to display more colors than the human eye can perceive and to display real-time animation in intricate detail. The rate of change in graphics technology exceeds that of computer technology because it also depends on the development of newer algorithms and coding strategies. Each of these changes produces a corresponding new set of applications and upgrades to graphic technology systems, in addition to the changes introduced to the technology itself.

Each successive generation of computer processors has introduced new architectures and capabilities that exceed those of the preceding generation, requiring that applications update both their capabilities and the manner in which those capabilities are performed. At the same time, advances in the technology of display devices require that graphics applications keep pace to display the best renderings possible. All of these factors combine to produce the unparalleled value of graphics technologies in modern society and into the future. With advances in 3D computer graphics and products such as smart glasses in the 2010s, graphics technologies became even more immersive, allowing for a continually growing range of functions from education to game play.

—*Richard M. Renneboog*

References

Brown, Eric. "True Physics." *Game Developer,* vol. 17, no. 5, 2010, pp. 13–18.

Jimenez, Jorge, et al. "Destroy All Jaggies." *Game Developer,* vol. 18, no. 6, 2011, pp. 13–20.

Marschner, Steve, et al. *Fundamentals of Computer Graphics.* 4th ed., CRC Press, 2016.

Prust, Z. A., and Peggy B. Deal. *Graphic Communications: Digital Design and Print Essentials.* 6th ed., Goodheart-Willcox, 2019.

Ryan, Dan. *History of Computer Graphics: DLR Associates Series.* AuthorHouse, 2011.

Wang, Yongtian, Qingmin Huang, and Yuxin Peng, editors. *Image and Graphics Technologies and Applications.* Springer Singapore, 2019.

Zhao, Pengfei, et al., editors. *Advanced Graphic Communications and Media Technologies.* Springer Singapore, 2017.

GREEN COMPUTING

Introduction

Green computing refers to efforts to manufacture, use, and dispose of computers and digital devices in ecologically friendly ways. Concerned with the effects of computer-related pollution and energy use on the environment, various government bodies and industry organizations have sought to promote more sustainable computing practices and the recycling of electronic waste.

Background

As pollution and climate change have become more pressing concerns, the need to consider the effects of industry and daily life on the environment has become apparent. As an especially fast-growing field, technology attracted particular notice from

Energy Star logo. Image via Wikimedia Commons. [Public domain.]

lawmakers, nonprofit organizations, and members of the public concerned with sustainability. "Green computing" describes the attempts to address the environmental impacts of widespread digital technology use.

Proponents have highlighted the excessive energy use by large computer systems such as data centers as a particular concern. Data centers in the United States and throughout the world consume large amounts of energy, due in part to inefficient operating practices. Such centers used about 200 terawatt hours of electricity per year by 2018, about 1 percent of all electricity used worldwide. On average, data centers use only a portion of that power for computing data. The bulk of it is used to maintain idle servers in case of a sudden spike in activity. In addition, such data centers often rely on diesel generators for backup power. They thereby emit greenhouse gases that contribute to climate change.

Another concern is the effects of the computer manufacturing process. Digital devices contain minerals such as rare earth elements that must be mined from the earth and processed, which can create toxic waste. Waste is also a matter of concern when an obsolete or otherwise unwanted device is discarded. The resulting electronic waste, or e-waste, often contains materials that may contaminate the surrounding area. Cathode-ray tube (CRT) monitors, for instance, contain lead, which can leach into soil and water from a landfill. Many computer parts are also not biodegradable. This means that they do not break down over time and will thus continue to be a cause of concern for decades.

Oversight and Certifications

A number of government and nonprofit organizations promote green computing and address issues such as environmentally responsible energy use and manufacturing. The US Environmental Protection Agency (EPA) launched the Energy Star program in 1992 to reduce air pollution. In the 2000s and 2010s, it focused on reducing greenhouse-gas emissions through energy efficiency. To earn the Energy Star certification for their products, computer manufacturers must demonstrate that their devices meet the EPA's energy efficiency standards.

TCO Development, a Swedish nonprofit, offers TCO certification. This credential was originally devised in 1992 and modernized on numerous occasions over the subsequent decades. It is granted to computers, mobile phones, and peripherals that meet certain sustainability requirements in all stages of their life cycle, from manufacture to disposal. The 2018 incarnation of the TCO credential particularly emphasized the importance of repairing or recycling electronic products rather than simply disposing of them and called for improved durability of devices and peripherals.

The nonprofit Green Electronics Council manages the Electronic Product Environmental Assessment Tool (EPEAT), created in 2005. Manufacturers provide the council with product information covering an item's life cycle. That information is then compared against other products and listed on the public EPEAT registry, which buyers can access.

Green Computing Initiatives

Perhaps the most common green computing initiatives have been efforts to educate corporations and the public about the environmental effects of computer use, particularly in regard to energy consumption. Computer users can save energy through techniques such as putting a computer in hibernation mode. When a computer enters this mode, it essentially shuts down and stops using power. It still retains the contents of its random-access memory (RAM), allowing the user to resume their previous activities after exiting hibernation mode.

Another technique, called "undervolting," lowers the voltage of the computer system's central processing unit (CPU). The CPU does need a minimum voltage to function, but decreasing the voltage by a small amount can improve the system's energy efficiency. In a mobile device, heat is reduced while battery life is prolonged. Other measures including turning off devices when not in use and enabling power-saving settings when available.

Present and Future Concerns

E-waste is one of the most significant computer-related environmental issues. Advances in computer and mobile technology continue apace, and new devices constantly replace obsolete or outmoded ones. Because of this, the disposal of discarded devices represents a serious and growing environmental problem, in large part because of parts that do not biodegrade and are environmentally hazardous. To prevent unwanted devices from entering landfills, major electronics companies such as Apple, Motorola, and Nintendo have offered take-back programs in which owners may return their devices to the manufacturers. Firms sometimes offer a payment or a discount on a new device in exchange. In some cases, the collected devices are refurbished and resold. In others, they are recycled in an eco-friendly manner.

Another major concern is that as the amount of data being created, stored, and accessed continues to grow, more numerous and powerful data centers will be needed. Unless the issue is addressed, the energy inefficiency of such centers will lead to ever-greater amounts of electricity being wasted in the future.

—*Joy Crelin*

References

Dastbaz, Mohammad, Colin Pattinson, and Bakbak Akhgar, editors. *Green Information Technology: A Sustainable Approach.* Elsevier, 2015.

Jones, Nicola. "How to Stop Data Centres from Gobbling Up the World's Electricity." *Nature,* 13 Sept. 2018, www.nature.com/articles/d41586-018-06610-y.

Kharchenko, Vyacheslav, Yuriy Kondratenko, and Janusz Kacprzyk, editors. *Green IT Engineering: Social, Business and Industrial Applications.* Springer Nature Switzerland, 2019.

Pritchard, Sara B., and Carl A. Zimring. *Technology and the Environment in History.* Johns Hopkins UP, 2020.

Smith, Bud E. *Green Computing: Tools and Techniques for Saving Energy, Money, and Resources.* CRC Press, 2014.

"The Story of TCO Certified." *TCO*, 2020, tcocertified.com/the-story-of-tco-certified/.

Wu, Jinsong, Sundeep Rangan, and Honggang Zhang, editors. *Green Communications: Theoretical Fundamentals, Algorithms and Applications.* CRC Press, 2013.

HACKING

Introduction

Hacking is using programming knowledge to illegally access a computer or network. The word "hack," by most accounts, originated at the Massachusetts Institute of Technology (MIT), where the Tech Model Railroad Club (TMRC) was founded in 1946. The members of the club created automated model trains that operated using telephone relays; they used the word *hack* to mean a creative way of solving a problem. A second meaning of *hack*, also in use at MIT, was "an ingenious, benign, and anonymous prank or practical joke, often requiring engineering or scientific expertise and often pulled off under cover of darkness."

This sense of hacking as a creative solution with an element of humorousness or mischievousness has remained steady through time. Like the multiple meanings within the etymology of the term, the various meanings of computer hacking have evolved as our technological world has evolved.

Background

In 1961, MIT purchased the first programmed data processor (PDP)-1. While it was a large computer that filled much of a room and cost (at the time) a whopping $120,000, it was compact and inexpensive compared to the hulking mainframe computers previously available. The members of the TMRC were fascinated with the new computer, and many of the club members formed MIT's computer science department. These students spent a great deal of time exploring and expanding the PDP-1's capabilities. They developed programming tools for it, composed and played music on it, and even played chess on it. In 1962, they created the very first videogame, called *Spacewar!*

The precursor to today's internet, Advanced Research Projects Agency Network (ARPANET), appeared in 1969. Built by the US Department of Defense (DoD) as an experiment in digital communications, ARPANET was the first transcontinental high-speed computer network. It linked universities, contractors, and labs, providing students and researchers a place to communicate with each other without regard to geographical boundaries. A hacker community formed through these networks, sharing hardware and software hacks and developing a shared vocabulary.

The earliest hackers were known as phreakers and explored the telephone system. The term *phreakers* comes from the combination of "phone" and "freak." In 1971, John Draper discovered that a prize whistle from Cap'n Crunch cereal (the origin of his nickname) could reproduce the 2,600-hertz tone needed to access AT&T's long-distance system in "operator mode." This allowed phreakers to explore proprietary aspects of the system, as well as make free calls. Draper was arrested many times over the following few years for phone tampering.

Hacking refers to compromising the security of digital devices like computers, smartphones, or even entire networks to steal data. Image via iStock/WhataWin. [Used under license.]

In 1975, two members of the Homebrew Computer Club in California started selling blue boxes, tone producers based on Draper's discovery, to allow people to make free long-distance phone calls. Their names were Steve Wozniak and Steve Jobs, who would go on to start Apple Computers in 1977.

While exploring the phone system was not illegal, stealing long-distance telephone service was. In spite of the involvement of the Federal Bureau of Investigation (FBI) at this point, hackers continued exploring new technologies without much legal or law enforcement interference.

When hackers were prosecuted, they were often given probation and a small fine. Hackers often sought to share what they discovered, either through publication or online bulletin boards, much to the chagrin of companies whose security flaws or functions were discovered. As technology advanced at a rapid pace, hacker knowledge and ability to locate weaknesses in systems outpaced the law. This somewhat antiauthoritarian spirit of exploration and sharing of knowledge would remain in the nuances of hacking's definition, although the technological universe was about to change.

Personal Computing Revolution

The early 1980s saw the first personal computers: The IBM PC, running MS-DOS, appeared in 1981, and Apple's Macintosh appeared in 1984. These computers sold for as low as $1,500, a fraction of the cost of the mainframe or PDP computers of the past. Computers were no longer confined to universities and laboratories—they were affordable enough for people have them in their homes. ARPANET was still in service, so these desktop computers (instead of whole-room computers) could be hooked up to the telephone network and talk with each other.

The potential universe for hackers to explore grew exponentially. The demand for new software applications and faster computers continued to grow as computer software companies sprung up. People could now explore the new technology easily on their desktop computers. Consequently, the hacker community grew, and online bulletin-board systems thrived where groups could meet to share tips. With the growth of the computer and software industry, many security flaws could be found, and hackers were interested to see what they might unlock.

In 1983, the movie *WarGames*, starring Matthew Broderick, was released. He played a teenage hacker who accesses a Pentagon supercomputer and narrowly avoids starting a nuclear war. The computer is named WOPR (War Operation Plan Response), supposedly a pun on an early NORAD computer that was called BRGR. While the idea of teenager starting a nuclear war was perhaps far-fetched, it illustrated a growing concern about what these new technologies and the information they controlled might do should they be compromised.

In a case of life imitating art, that same year the FBI arrested six teenagers in Milwaukee who referred to themselves as the 414s, after the city's area code. They were accused of breaking into over sixty computer networks, including the Los Alamos National Laboratory. One hacker received immunity for testifying against the others; the rest received probation.

Hackers already had a tradition of publishing and sharing their discoveries, and in 1984 a hacker magazine, *2600: The Hacker Quarterly*, began publication. The magazine's name comes from the 2,600-hertz tone that John Draper used to hack into AT&T's operator mode. The editor, Eric Corley, goes by the pen name Emmanuel Goldstein, a reference to the narrator in George Orwell's *1984*. The magazine publishes articles on a variety of topics, including privacy issues, computer security, and the digital underground.

By the mid-1980s, repeated break-ins into government and corporate databases and networks forced Congress to respond. The Counterfeit Access Device and Abuse Act (18 U.S.C. § 1030) was passed in 1984. It was the first federal law designed specifically to prosecute computer crimes. It focused on prosecuting computer activity that accessed government information protected for national defense or foreign relations, financial information from financial institutions, and government computers. In 1986, the Computer Fraud and Abuse Act (CFAA) amended the Counterfeit Access Device and Abuse Act and expanded the law's coverage from a "federal interest computer" to *any* "protected computer."

The first known computer virus, called Brain, appeared in 1987. It infected MS-DOS systems and was released through the internet. It was benign compared to the viruses we see today: The virus simply put a small file on the computer's hard drive with business card information for Brain Computer Services in Pakistan.

Hackers were not just limited to computers; changes in hardware and software on media players and game consoles could allow these devices to use media that was homemade, pirated, or free. In 1988, the Digital Millennium Copyright Act (DMCA) was passed; it criminalized the creation and distribution of hardware and software that disabled copyright protections on digital media.

In 1988, twenty-three-year-old Cornell University graduate student Robert Morris created the internet's first worm. The son of a National Security Agency (NSA) computer security expert, he wrote ninety-nine lines of code and released them to the internet as an experiment. The self-replicating software multiplied more quickly than anticipated and infected more than 6,000 systems. Almost one-tenth of the entire internet at the time was affected, and the network was out of service for days. The first person tried under the CFAA, Morris was arrested and sentenced to three years of probation, 400 hours of community service, and a $10,000 fine. He later formed an internet start-up, Viaweb, which he sold in 1998 for almost $49 million. A hacker going under the moniker "The Mentor" published what is now a classic treatise on hacking, *The Conscience of a Hacker*, in 1989. The last line reads: "You may stop this individual, but you can't stop us all."

The Rise of the Internet

In the late 1980s and early 1990s, commercial internet service providers (ISPs) began to emerge. They replaced ARPAnet, the first internet, which was decommissioned in 1990. Online retailers began to appear, such as Amazon.com in 1995. Personal information began flowing through the internet—hackers noticed. Enthusiasm for the growing internet led to more serious hacks, some just for exploration, and some for criminal gain.

Four hackers calling themselves the Legion of Doom were arrested in 1990 for stealing technical information on BellSouth's 911 emergency telephone network. While they did not do anything with it, the information could have disabled 911 service for the entire country. Three of the hackers were found guilty and received prison sentences ranging from fourteen to twenty-one months, along with almost $250,000 in damages.

In 1990, the Secret Service and Arizona's organized crime unit joined forces to create Operation Sundevil, a crackdown on illegal computer hacking activities. It resulted in three arrests and the confiscation of computers, the contents of electronic bulletin board systems (BBSs), and floppy disks. The arrests and following court cases resulted in the creation of the Electronic Frontier Foundation (EFF), which focuses on defending civil liberties issues affected by technology.

The 1990s also saw the first hacker breach of big banking. In 1994, Russian hacker Vladimir Levin had Citibank's computers transfer an estimated $10 million to his accounts; Citibank recovered all but $400,000 of what was stolen. In January 1998, Levin pled guilty in federal court to charges of conspiracy to commit bank, wire, and computer fraud. He admitted using passwords and codes stolen from Citibank customers to make the transfers. Levin was sentenced to three years in prison and was ordered to pay Citibank $240,000.

The first "Defcon" hacker conference was held in Las Vegas, Nevada, in 1993 and continues as an annual event. The term comes from the movie *WarGames* and references the US Armed Forces Defense Readiness Condition (DEFCON). In the movie, Las Vegas was selected as a nuclear target. It also references DEF, the letters on the number 3 on a standard phone, with "con" meaning conference.

Defcon and the other big hacker conferences (such as Black Hat or RSA) focus on so-called "ethical hacking." There are demonstrations of security flaws, such as an eleven-year-old child hacking into a replica of Florida's election website and changing votes in under 10 minutes in 2018, or the takeover of a Jeep's computer system while it was driving (which led to a recall of over 1 million cars). Bug bounties are offered by companies large and small (such as Facebook, Microsoft, and the Justice Department) for hackers that turn in security flaws.

Shame boards list those who attend and find themselves hacked, as well as an award for the most epic fail. In 2018, some of the contenders were Under Armour's MyFitnessPal for compromising personal information for over 150 million people, and the Facebook website hack, that exposed "access tokens" affecting the accounts of 29 million people.

Despite the CFAA, hackers continued to break into government computers. In 1996, the General

Accounting Office reported that hackers tried to break into DoD files more than 250,000 times in 1995; about 65 percent of the attempts succeeded. In August, hackers added swastikas and a picture of Adolph Hitler to the US Department of Justice (DOJ) website and renamed it the Department of Injustice. The next month, hackers broke into the Central Intelligence Agency's (CIA's) website and changed the department's name to Central Stupidity Agency.

By 1998, the Symantec AntiVirus Research Center estimated that 30,000 computer viruses were circulating on the internet. That same year, federal prosecutors charged a juvenile for the first time with computer hacking after a boy shut down an airport communications system in Massachusetts. No accidents occurred and his name was not released; however, he pled guilty and was sentenced to two years of probation, 250 hours of community service, and restitution to Bell Atlantic for $5,000.

A hacker think tank called "L0pht" (pronounced "loft") testified before Congress in 1998 that it could shut down the internet in half an hour. (The congressional hearings were about software and internet security flaws.) With the government, retailers, and financial institutions utilizing the internet, more personal and financial data than ever before had become accessible to hackers who had an interest in finding it.

Hacking Today

Verizon's *2018 Data Breach Investigations Report*, the best-known annual study of data breaches, indicated that the majority of the breaches, about three out of every four attacks, were due to criminals looking to steal money in some fashion.

Thieves use more than payment systems to steal money. In 2017, the use of ransomware increased, accounting for 40 percent of malware incidents. Ransomware locks a victim's data and then threatens to erase or publish it if money, or a "ransom" is not paid. Ransom demands in 2017 averaged about $500.

Information is also a valuable commodity to thieves. For instance, in August 2015, nine people were charged in the largest known computer hacking and securities fraud scheme to date. They stole over 150,000 press releases from three major

newswire companies about publicly traded companies and made insider stock trades, which generated over $30 million, based on the information. The defendants were in Ukraine and various locations in the United States In addition to stealing information and money, sometimes hacks cost money simply because of their disruption. As of 2000, a new computer virus was created every hour, according to the Symantec AntiVirus Research Center. In 2017, denial-of-service (DDoS) attacks continued to be the leading cause of security breaches. DDoS attacks overwhelm a server with requests so that it cannot accept more traffic and sometimes crashes.

While large attacks tend to make the news, such as the February 2000 DDoS attack on Yahoo!, eBay, CNN, Amazon.com, and E*Trade, even short-lived smaller attacks can cause security issues. The FBI estimated that such attacks cost about $1.7 billion in lost business and other damages. To counteract this trend, in 2003, Microsoft started a $5 million bounty on hackers attacking Windows. It continues a bug bounty program to this day. These bounties provide balance to the black market for unpatched bugs because members of organized crime and others are willing to pay well for these access points.

Viruses and malware have also shown that they can wreak havoc on systems ranging from phones to appliances, to nuclear power plants. These systems are managed and maintained by computers and internet connections. For example, between 2009 and 2010, Iran's nuclear program was infected by a virus named Stuxnet. This virus was unlike any other because it caused physical destruction of the equipment controlled by the computers. Stuxnet targeted the rotation speeds of centrifuges and caused one-fifth of them to destroy themselves, which delayed the progress of Iran's nuclear program.

The attackers also took over the facilities' workstations and blasted "Thunderstruck" by AC/DC at highest volume. It is suspected that the virus was developed by the US and Israeli governments, but in the digital realm, reliable attribution of any hack is very difficult.

Hacking has also taken on social and political purposes (this kind of hacking is called hacktivism). Hactivists sometimes work alone, like The Jester, who takes down Islamic jihadist websites. Some work in loose groups, such as Anonymous and Lulz

Security (abbreviated to LulzSec). Their targets have been varied, ranging from the Church of Scientology to PayPal.

There is no defined leadership for such groups, and sometimes their actions are condemned by others within the group. Quinn Norton of *Wired* wrote of Anonymous in 2011: "[Y]ou're never quite sure if Anonymous is the hero or antihero. The trickster is attracted to change and the need for change, and that's where Anonymous goes . . . And when they do something, it never goes quite as planned. The internet has no neat endings." It would appear that as technology evolves, hacking will do likewise. Both are works in progress and are inextricably interwoven as ongoing works in progress.

—*Noëlle Sinclair*

References

Carlin, John P. *Dawn of the Code War: America's Battle Against Russia, China, and the Rising Global Cyber Threat.* Hachette, 2018.

Coleman, E. Gabriella. *Coding Freedom: The Ethics and Aesthetics of Hacking.* Princeton UP, 2013.

Goldstein, Emmanuel. *Best of 2600: A Hacker Odyssey.* Wiley, 2008.

Greenberg, Andy. *Sandworm: A New Era of Cyberwar and the Hunt for the Kremlin's Most Dangerous Hackers.* Doubleday. 2019

Lapsley, Phil. *Exploding the Phone: The Untold Story of the Teenagers and Outlaws who Hacked Ma Bell.* Grove Press, 2013.

Levy, Steven. *Hackers: Heroes of the Computer Revolution—25th Anniversary Edition.* O'Reilly Media, 2010.

Mitnick, Kevin. *Ghost in the Wires: My Adventures as the World's Most Wanted Hacker.* Little, Brown and Company, 2011.

Olson, Parmy. *We Are Anonymous: Inside the Hacker World of LulzSec, Anonymous, and the Global Cyber Insurgency.* Little, Brown and Company, 2012.

Peterson, T. F., and Institute Historian. *Nightwork: A History of Hacks and Pranks at MIT.* Updated ed., MIT Press, 2011.

Smith, Jeremy N. *Breaking and Entering: The Extraordinary Story of a Hacker Called "Alien."* Eamon Dolan/Houghton Mifflin Harcourt, 2019.

Zetter, Kim. *Countdown to Zero Day: Stuxnet and the Launch of the World's First Digital Weapon.* Broadway, 2014.

HOLOGRAPHIC TECHNOLOGY

Introduction

Holographic technology employs beams of light to record information and then rebuilds that information so that the reconstruction appears three-dimensional (3D). Unlike photography, which traditionally produces fixed two-dimensional (2D) images, holography re-creates the lighting from the original scene and results in a hologram that can be viewed from different angles and perspectives as if the observer were seeing the original scene. The technology, which was greatly improved with the invention of the laser, is used in fields such as product packaging, consumer electronics, medical imaging, security, architecture, geology, and cosmology.

Holography is a technique that uses interference and diffraction of light to record a likeness and then rebuild and illuminate that likeness. Holograms use coherent light, which consists of waves that are aligned with one another. Beams of coherent light interfere with one another as the image is recorded and stored, thus producing interference patterns. When the image is re-illuminated, diffracted light allows the resulting hologram to appear 3D.

Several basic types of holograms can be produced. A transmission hologram requires an observer to see the image through light as it passes through the hologram. A rainbow hologram is a special kind of transmission hologram, in which colors change as the observer moves his or her head. This type of transmission hologram can also be viewed in white light, such as that produced by an incandescent lightbulb. A reflection hologram can also be viewed in white light. This type allows the observer to see the image with light reflected off the surface of the hologram. The holographic stereogram uses attributes of both holography and photography. Industry and art utilize the basic types of holograms as well as create new and advanced technologies and applications.

Background

Around 1947, Hungarian-born physicist Dennis Gabor developed the basics of holography while attempting to improve the electron microscope. Early efforts by scientists to develop the technique were restricted by the use of the mercury arc lamp as a monochromatic light source. This inferior light source contributed to the poor quality of holograms, and the field advanced little throughout the next decade. Laser light was introduced in the 1960s and was considered stable and coherent. Coherent light contains waves that are aligned with one another and is well suited for high-quality holograms. Subsequently, discoveries and innovations in the field began to increase and accelerate.

In 1960, American physicist Theodore Harold Maiman of Hughes Research Laboratories developed the pulsed ruby laser. This laser used rubies to operate and generated powerful bursts of light lasting only nanoseconds. The pulsed ruby laser, which acted much like a camera's flashbulb, became ideal for capturing images of moving objects or people. In 1962, while working at the University of Michigan, scientists Emmett Leith and Juris Upatnieks decided to improve on Gabor's technique. They produced images of 3D objects—a toy bird and train. These were the first transmission holograms and required an observer to see the image through light as it passed through the holograms.

Also in 1962, Russian scientist Yuri Nikolaevich Denisyuk combined his own work with the color photography work of French physicist Gabriel Lippmann. This resulted in a reflection hologram that could be viewed with white light reflecting off the surface of a hologram. Reflection holograms do not need laser light to be viewed. In 1968, electrical engineer Stephen Benton developed the rainbow hologram. When an observer moves his or her head, he or she sees the spectrum of color, as in a rainbow. This type of hologram can also be viewed in white light.

Holographic art appeared in exhibits beginning in the late 1960s and early 1970s, and holographic portraits made with pulsed ruby lasers found some favor beginning in the 1980s. Advances in the field have continued, and many and varied types of holograms are used in many different areas of science and technology, while artistic applications have lagged in comparison. Although a number of concerts and other live events during the second decade of the twenty-first century were advertised as featuring performing holograms of entertainers, the technology used in such events relied on alternative methods of visual projection and was not true holographic technology.

How It Works

A 3D subject captured by conventional photography becomes stored on a medium, such as photographic film, as a 2D scene. Information about the intensity of the light from a static scene is acquired, but information about the path of the light is not recorded. Holographic creation captures information about the light, including the path, and the whole field of light is recorded.

A beam of light first reaches the object from a light source. Wavelengths of coherent light, such as laser light, leave the light source "in phase" (in sync) and are known collectively as an "object beam." These waves reach the object, are scattered, and then are interfered with when a reference beam from the same light source is introduced. A pattern occurs from the reference beam interfering with the object waves. This interference pattern is recorded on the emulsion. Re-illumination of the hologram with the reference beam results in the reconstruction of the object light wave, and a 3D image appears.

Light Sources

An incandescent bulb generates light in a host of different wavelengths, whereas a laser produces monochromatic wavelengths of the same frequency. Laser light, also referred to as coherent light, is used most often to create holograms. The helium-neon laser is the most commonly recognized type. Types of lasers include all gas-phase iodine, argon, carbon dioxide, carbon monoxide, chemical oxygen-iodine, helium-neon, and many others.

To produce wavelengths in color, the most frequently used lasers are the helium-neon (for red) and the argon-ion (for blue and green). Lasers at one time were expensive and sometimes difficult to obtain, but twenty-first-century lasers can be relatively inexpensive and are easier to use for recording holograms.

Recording Materials

Light-sensitive materials such as photographic films and plates, the first resources used for recording holograms, still prove useful. Since the color of light is determined by its wavelength, varying emulsions on the film that are sensitive to different wavelengths can be used to record information about scene colors. However, many different types of materials have proven valuable in various applications.

Other recording materials include dichromated gelatin, elastomers, photoreactive polymers, photochromics, photorefractive crystals, photoresists, photothermoplastics, and silver-halide sensitized gelatin.

Applications and Products

Holographic art, prevalent in the 1960s through the 1980s, still exists. Although fewer artists practice holography exclusively, many artistic creations contain holographic components. A small number of schools and universities teach holographic art.

Digital holography is one of the fastest-growing realms and has applications in the artistic, scientific, and technological communities. Computer processing of digital holograms lends an advantage, as a separate light source is not needed for re-illumination.

Digital holography first began to appear in the late 1970s. The process initially involved two steps: first writing a string of digital images onto film, then converting the images into a hologram. Around 1988, holographer Ken Haines invented a process for creating digital holograms in one step.

Digital holographic microscopy (DHM) can be used noninvasively to study changes in the cells of living tissue subjected to simulated microgravity. Information is captured by a digital camera and processed by software.

Different types of holograms can be displayed in store windows; as visual aids to accompany lectures or presentations; in museums; at art, science, or technology exhibits; in schools and libraries; or at home as simple decorations hung on a wall and lit by spotlights.

Embossed holograms, which are special kinds of rainbow holograms, can be duplicated and mass produced. These holograms can be used as means of authentication on credit cards and driver's licenses as well as for decorative use on wrapping paper, book covers, magazine covers, bumper stickers, greeting cards, stickers, and product packaging.

The field of dentistry provided a setting for an early application in medical holography. Creating holograms of dental casts markedly reduced the space needed to store dental records for the United Kingdom's National Health Service (NHS). Holograms have also proved useful in regular dental practice and dentistry training.

The use of various types of holograms has proved beneficial for viewing sections of living and nonliving tissue, preparing joint replacement devices, noninvasive scrutiny of tumors or suspected tumors, and viewing the human eye. A volume-multiplexed hologram can be used in medical-scanning applications. While moving holograms can be made, limitations exist for the production of motion pictures. Somewhat more promising is the field of holographic video and possibly television.

Security

A recurring issue in world trade is that of counterfeit goods. Vendors increasingly rely on special holograms embedded in product packaging to combat the problem. The creation of complex brand images using holographic technology can offer a degree of brand protection for almost any product, including pharmaceuticals. Security holography garners a large segment of the market. However, makers of security holograms, whose designs are used for authentication of bank notes, credit cards, and driver's licenses, face the perplexing challenge of counterfeit security images. As time progresses, these images become increasingly easier to fake; therefore, this area of industry must continually create newer and more complex holographic techniques to stay ahead of deceptive practices.

Holographic stereograms, unique and divergent, use attributes of both holography and photography. Makers of stereograms have the potential of creating both very large and moving images. Stereograms can be produced in color and also processed by a computer.

Types of holography exist that use waves other than light. Some examples include acoustical holography, which operates with sound waves; atomic holography, which is used in applications with atomic beams; and electron holography, which utilizes electron waves.

Social Context and Future Prospects

Holography in one form or another is prevalent in society, whether as a security feature on a credit card, a component of a medical technique, or a colorful wrapping paper. Holograms have been interwoven into daily life and will likely continue to increase their impact in the future.

Next-generation holographic storage devices have been developed, setting the stage for companies to compete for future markets.

Data is stored on the surface of digital versatile discs (DVDs) and Blu-rays; however, devices have been invented to store holographic data within a disc. The significantly enlarged storage capacity is appealing for customers with large storage needs who can afford the expensive discs and drives, but some companies are also interested in targeting an even larger market by revising existing technology. Possible modification of existing technology, such as DVD players, could potentially result in less expensive methods of playing 3D data. In 2018, researchers affiliated with China's Northeast Normal University announced the creation of nanoparticle films capable of storing holographic data, further advancing the development of holographic storage technology.

—*Glenda Griffin*

References

Blanche, Pierre-Alexandre. *Optical Holography: Materials, Theory and Applications.* Elsevier, 2019.

Hariharan, P. *Basics of Holography.* Cambridge UP, 2010.

Hu, Jane C. "The Whitney Houston of the 3D Hologram Tour Will Be Neither 3D nor a Hologram." *Slate*, 22 May 2019. slate.com/technology/2019/05/whitney-houston-3d-hologram-tour-technology.html.

Johnston, Sean F. "Absorbing New Subjects: Holography as an Analog of Photography." *Physics in Perspective*, vol. 8, no. 2, 2006, pp. 164–88.

Poon, Ting-Chung, and Jung-Ping Liu. *Introduction to Modern Digital Holography: With MATLAB.* Cambridge UP, 2014.

"Researchers Develop Nanoparticle Films for High-Density Data Storage." *OSA: The Optical Society*, 3 Apr. 2018. www.osa.org/en-us/about_osa/newsroom/news_releases/2018/researchers_develop_nanoparticle_films_for_high-de/.

Richardson, Martin J., and John D. Wiltshire. *The Hologram: Principles and Techniques.* John Wiley & Sons, 2017.

Saxby, Graham, and Stanislovas Zacharovas. *Practical Holography.* 4th ed., CRC Press, 2016.

HTML

Introduction

HTML, which stands for hypertext markup language, is a code used by computer programmers to control the functionality of web pages. It was invented in the late twentieth century and has become an indispensable part of online technology. Hypertext consists of a set of instructions for the creation of display pages on browsers, which made the World Wide Web possible. By the mid-1990's, HTML embedded codes that defined fonts, layouts, graphics, and hypertext links provided a standard protocol that allowed web page designers to distribute content to any computer.

Background

Timothy Berners-Lee developed HTML over several years during the 1980s while working as a software engineering consultant at the Conseil Européen pour la Recherche Nucléaire (CERN; later known as the Organisation Européen pour la Recherche Nucléaire, or the European Organization for Nuclear Research) in Geneva, Switzerland. He attempted to organize laboratory research documents and statistics from incompatible computer systems submitted by physicists from around the world. In order to pool all of these files for sharing information, Berners-Lee developed a set of formatting codes to work with hypertext protocol by linking text within the files. Hypertext enables the computer user to cross-reference information and link formats together through multiple gateways on the World Wide Web.

His invention was called hypertext. Later in the decade, he invented systems that enabled computers within the same network to communicate with each other. And, in 1989, he proposed developing a network that would allow computers all over the world to connect. Rather than communicating by email, files could be located on a page on the web, where they could be accessed by anyone with the right technology and credentials—the code that would make this possible was HTML. Although the specific name for this language has changed significantly since its invention, its purpose has remained the same: to facilitate the smooth operation of web pages of all types.

Hypertext enables the computer user to cross-reference information and link formats together through multiple gateways on the World Wide Web. Each page is provided with a unique location address known as a universal document locator (URL). Robert Cailliau, who worked in the Office Computing Systems, Data Handling Division, at CERN, collaborated with Berners-Lee to get the web under way. Cailliau's contributions were essential to the development of the web. He rewrote the original proposal, lobbied administrators for funding, presented papers at conferences, and got programmers to work on the project.

Berners-Lee derived hypertext markup language (HTML) from standard generalized markup language. Standard generalized markup language (SGML), an international standard that emphasizes document structure and textual relationships. However, SGML proved too complex for the average web page creator, so HTML was developed as a nonproprietary format in order to embed code for text, images, and other files to make them easily accessible through the web. Berners-Lee's prototype for hypertext was the NeXT computer station, but he encouraged others to program, design, and improve software for displaying HTML documents. In 1993, Marc Andreessen, an undergraduate student at the National Center of Supercomputing Applications (NCSA) at the University of Illinois, designed a web browser to display HTML documents, called Mosaic, which was widely adopted and accelerated internet traffic over the following three years.

Function

Although the language of HTML is not necessarily second-nature to all users, it is extremely systematic, with a few basic, important components. The file in which HTML code is written is called a document, which usually has an .html extension. The term HTML is in brackets that look like this—<60><62>— at the beginning and end of a document. The words inside the brackets are called tags. Tags are a crucial component of an HTML document.

Tags are generally in pairs. The first tag, called the start tag, looks like this: <60>tag<62>, and the second tag, called the end tag, looks like this: <60>/tag<62>. Keywords, the text between tags, depend on the content of a page. Keywords may be of many different types, with many different degrees of significance. Many tags will simply designate the exact words and phrases that will appear on a page. For example, the words <60>title<62>My Favorite Job

Ever<60>/title<62> would probably appear at the top of the screen on the web version of an html document. This code might appear in the first paragraph under the title: <60>p<62> I have had many jobs. But one stood out as a favorite. <60>/p<62>

It is important to remember that HTML is a unique language. The text within tags is read and interpreted by a computer's software, so the rules of the language must be followed. For example, the tag <60>!DOCTYPE html<62> must be used at the beginning of an HTML document to indicate the document type. When an HTML document is opened within a web browser, the language of the document guides the appearance and function of the page. The tags <60>title<62>text<60>/title<62> indicate the title of a document, <60>body<62> and<60>/body<62> indicate the start and end of the main text of a document, and <60>p<62>text<60>/p<62> indicate the starting and ending points of a paragraph within a document. To place headers within a document, these tags must be used: <60>h1<62> and<60>/h1<62>. To create headers of different sizes, these tags are used: <60>h2<62> and <60>/h2<62>, <60>h3<62> and <60>/h3<62>. Images to be inserted in a document are preceded and followed with the tags <60>img<62> and <60>/img<62>.

The characteristics of an HTML document, such as the font, the color of the font, or the size of an image, are called attributes. They are usually placed between the brackets of a start tag and are followed by an equals (=) sign; the exact attribute itself is in quotes. For example, to display an image that is 600 pixels wide, this text would be used: width="600." Attributes such as color or font are referred to as *styles* and they must be designed in a specific way. A font is indicated with the phrase "font-family." For example, to create a title in Times font, these tags would be used: <60>title font-family="Times"<62>The Best Job I Ever Had<60>/title<62>. Every element of a web page and every characteristic of every element has its own designation in HTML. HTML has codes for tables, animations, different tabs within a page, and the size and shape of a page. Once an HTML document is complete, it is opened in a browser, which is when the person writing the HTML code can see whether or not the code has been properly written.

As time has passed, HTML has been modified and used in different ways, such as in mobile devices.

A notable development is XHTML. The X stands for Extensible, indicating that the language can be used in a wider variety of situations than web development. As programmers continue to write code and as the internet continues to become more pervasive in daily life, the true significance of Berner-Lee's invention becomes more and more evident.

Significance

The World Wide Web became a global, economic, and social phenomenon by the end of the 1990's. However, American businesses shied away from the internet in the early part of the decade, believing that it would be used only for research in the academic environment. In 1994, Berners-Lee, who was now working at the Massachusetts Institute of Technology (MIT), founded the World Wide Web Consortium (W3C) to promote guidelines regarding the growth of network infrastructure and strict language syntax with HTML, especially with the emerging browser battles between Netscape and Microsoft Explorer. HTML promoted interoperability, causing internet traffic to explode.

Search engines had difficulty trying to track all of the pages found on the web. Companies soon embraced the World Wide Web for commercial ventures, and in response, HTML continued to improve support. Browsers adopted cascading style sheets to improve document appearance. Dynamic HTML added capabilities to respond interactively with JavaScript. Extensible markup language (XML), a relative of HTML, created additional tags to identify structures and relationships within a document. XML had two important features. First, web page creators had more flexibility to create their own tags. Second, XML separated content from formatting through the use of sophisticated style sheets, ensuring that all data structures and relationships were identified within the XML tags in which they were enclosed. XML made search engines more powerful for cataloging contents, enabling computers to become even more interactive and responsive to user actions.

—Max Winter and Gayla Koerting

References

Bell, Mary Ann, Mary Ann Berry, and James L. Van Roekel. *Internet and Personal Computing Fads.* Haworth Press, 2004.

Berners-Lee, Tim. *Weaving the Web: The Original Design and Ultimate Destiny of the World Wide Web by Its Inventor.* Harper, 1999.

Boudreaux, Ryan. "HTML 5 Trends and What They Mean for Developers. *Web Designer,* 9 Feb. 2012, www.techrepublic.com/blog/web-designer/html-5-trends-and-what-they-mean-for-developers/.

Cailliau, Robert, and Helen Ashman. "Hypertext in the Web: A History." *ACM Computing Surveys,* vol. 31, Dec. 1999, pp. 1–6.

Henderson, Harry. *Encyclopedia of Computer Science and Technology.* Facts On File, 2003.

"The History of HTML." *Ironspider,* www.ironspider.ca/webdesign101/htmlhistory.htm.

"The History of HTML." *Landofcode.com,* landofcode.com/html-tutorials/html-history.php.

"HTML Basics." *MediaCollege.com,* www.mediacollege.com/internet/html/html-basics.html.

"HTML Introduction." *W3Schools.com.* W3 Schools, www.w3schools.com/html/html_intro.asp.

"HTML Tutorial." *Refsnes Data,* www.w3schools.com/html/default.asp.

Mobbs, Richard. "HTML Developments." *University of Leicester,* Oct. 2009, www.le.ac.uk/oerresources/bdra/html/page_04.htm.

Morris, Mary. *HTML for Fun and Profit.* SunSoft Press, 1995.

Mowery, David C., and Timothy Simcoe. "Is the Internet a U.S. Invention? An Economic and Technological History of Computer Networking." *Research Policy,* vol. 31, Dec. 2002, pp. 1369–87.

Musciano, Chuck, and Bill Kennedy. *HTML and XHTML: The Definitive Guide.* 4th ed., O'Reilly, 2000.

Nielsen, Jakob. *Multimedia and Hypertext: The Internet and Beyond.* SunSoft Press, 1995.

Ralston, Anthony, Edwin D. Reilly, and David Hemmendinger, editors. *Encyclopedia of Computer Science.* 4th ed., Nature Publishing Group, 2000.

"A Short History of HTML." *W3C-HTML.com,* W3C Foundation, w3c-html.com/html-history.html.

HUMAN-COMPUTER INTERACTION

Introduction

Human-computer interaction (HCI) is a field concerned with the study, design, implementation, evaluation, and improvement of the ways in which human beings use or interact with computer systems. The importance of HCI within the field of computer science has grown in tandem with technology's potential to help people accomplish an increasing number and variety of personal, professional, and social goals. For example, user-friendly interactive computer interfaces, websites, games, home appliances, office equipment, art installations, and information distribution systems such as advertising and public awareness campaigns are all applications that fall within the realm of HCI.

Background

Human-computer interaction, sometimes referred to as person-computer interaction, is an interdisciplinary science with the primary goal of harnessing the full potential of computer and communication systems for the benefit of individuals and groups. Human-computer interaction researchers design and implement innovative interactive technologies that are not only useful but also easy and pleasurable to use and anticipate and satisfy the specific needs of the user. The study of HCI has applications throughout every realm of modern life, including work, education, communications, health care, and recreation.

The fundamental philosophy that guides HCI is the principle of user-centered design. This philosophy proposes that the development of any product or interface should be driven by the needs of the person or people who will ultimately use it, rather than by any design considerations that center around the object itself. A key element of usability is affordance, the notion that the appearance of any interactive element should suggest the ways in which it can be manipulated.

For example, the use of shadowing around a button on a website might help make it look three-dimensional (3D), thus suggesting that it can be pushed or clicked. Visibility is closely related to affordance; it is the notion that the function of all the controls with which a user interacts should be clearly mapped to their effects. For example, a label such as "Volume Up" beneath a button might indicate exactly what it does. Various protocols facilitate the creation of highly usable applications. A cornerstone of HCI is iterative design, a method of development that uses repeated cycles of feedback and analysis to improve each prototype version of a product, instead of simply creating a single design and launching it immediately. To learn more about the people who will eventually use a product and how they will use it, designers also make use of ethnographic field studies and usability tests.

History

Before the advent of the personal computer, those who interacted with computers were largely technology specialists. In the 1980s, however, more and more individual users began making use of software such as word-processing programs, computer games, and spreadsheets. Human-computer interaction as a field emerged from the growing need to redesign such tools to make them practical and useful to ordinary people with no technical training. The first HCI researchers came from a variety of related fields: cognitive science, psychology, computer graphics, human factors (the study of how human capabilities affect the design of mechanical systems), and technology.

Among the thinkers and researchers whose ideas have shaped the formation of HCI as a science are John M. Carroll, best known for his theory of minimalism (an approach to instruction that emphasizes real-life applications and the chunking of new material into logical parts), and Adele Goldberg, whose work on early software interfaces at the Palo Alto Research Center (PARC) was instrumental in the development of the modern graphical user interface.

In the early days of HCI, the notion of usability was simply defined as the degree to which a computer system was easy and effective to use. However, usability has come to encompass a number of other qualities, including whether an interface is enjoyable, encourages creativity, relieves tension, anticipates points of confusion, and facilitates the combined efforts of multiple users. In addition, there has been a shift in HCI away from a reliance on theoretical findings from cognitive science and toward a more hands-on approach that prioritizes field studies and usability testing by real participants.

How It Works

The essential goal of HCI is to improve the ways in which information is transferred between a user and the machine he or she is using. Input and output devices are the basic tools HCI researchers and professionals use for this purpose. The more sophisticated the interaction between input and output devices—the more complex the feedback loop between the two directions of information flow—the more the human user will be able to accomplish with the machine.

An input device is any tool that delivers data of some kind from a human to a machine. The most familiar input devices are the ones associated with personal computers: keyboards and mice. Other commonly used devices include joysticks, trackballs, pen styluses, and tablets. Still more unconventional or elaborate input devices might take the shape of head gear designed to track the movements of a user's head and neck, video cameras that track the movements of a user's eyes, skin sensors that detect changes in body temperature or heart rate, wearable gloves that precisely track hand gestures, or automatic speech recognition devices that translate spoken commands into instructions that a machine can understand. Some input devices, such as the sensors that open automatic doors at the fronts of banks or supermarkets, are designed to record information passively, without the user having to take any action.

An output device is any tool that delivers information from a machine to a human. Again, the most familiar output devices are those associated with personal computers: monitors, flat-panel displays, and audio speakers. Other output devices include wearable head-mounted displays or goggles that provide visual feedback directly in front of the user's field of vision and full-body suits that provide tactile feedback to the user in the form of pressure.

Perceptual-Motor Interaction

When HCI theorists speak about perceptual-motor interaction, what they are referring to is the notion that users' perceptions—the information they gather from the machine—are inextricably linked to their physical actions, or how they relate to the machine. Computer systems can take advantage of this by using both input and output devices to provide feedback about the user's actions that will help him or her make the next move. For example, a word on a website may change in color when a user hovers the mouse over it, indicating that it is a functional link.

A joystick being used in a racing game may exert what feels like muscular tension or pressure against the user's hand in response to the device being steered to the left or right. Ideally, any feedback a system gives a user should be aligned to the physical direction in which he or she is moving an input device. For example, the direction in which a cursor moves on screen should be the same as the direction in which the user is moving the mouse. This is known as kinesthetic correspondence.

Another technique HCI researchers have devised to facilitate the feedback loop between a user's perceptions and actions is known as augmented reality. With this approach, rather than providing the user with data from a single source, the output device projects digital information, such as labels, descriptions, charts, and outlines, on the physical world. When an engineer is looking at a complex mechanical system, for example, the display might show what each part in the system is called and enable him or her to call up additional troubleshooting or repair information.

Applications

At one time, interacting with a personal computer required knowing how to use a command-line interface in which the user typed in instructions—often worded in abstract technical language—for a computer to execute. A graphical user interface, based on HCI principles, supplements or replaces text-based commands with visual elements such as icons, labels, windows, widgets, menus, and control buttons. These elements are controlled using a physical pointing device such as a mouse. For instance, a user may use a mouse to open, close, or resize a window or to pull down a list of options in a menu in order to select one.

The major advantage graphical user interfaces have over text-based interfaces is that they make completing tasks far simpler and more intuitive. Using graphic images rather than text reduces the amount of time it takes to interpret and use a control, even for a novice user. This enables users to focus on the task at hand rather than to spend time figuring out how to manipulate the technology itself. For instance, rather than having to recall and then correctly type in a complicated command, a user can print a particular file by selecting its name in a window, opening it, and clicking on an icon designed to look like a printer. Similarly, rather than choosing options from a menu in order to open a certain file within an application, a user might drag and drop the icon for the file onto the icon for the application.

Consumer Appliances

Besides computers, a host of consumer appliances use aspects of HCI design to improve usability. Graphic icons are ubiquitous parts of the interfaces commonly found on cameras, stereos, microwave ovens, refrigerators, and televisions. Smartphones such as Apple's iPhone rely on the same graphic displays and direct manipulation techniques as used in full-sized computers. Many also add extra tactile, or haptic, dimensions of usability such as touch-screen keyboards and the ability to rotate windows on the device by physically rotating the device itself in space.

Entertainment products such as video game consoles have moved away from keyboard and joystick interfaces, which may not have kinesthetic correspondence, toward far more sophisticated controls. The Joy-Con controller devices that accompany the Nintendo Switch, for instance, feature motion controls that allow players to control the movement of avatars within some games through the movements of their own bodies. Finally, HCI research influences the physical design of many household devices. For example, a plug for an appliance designed with the user in mind might be deliberately shaped so that it can be inserted into an outlet in any orientation, based on the understanding that a user may have to fit several plugs into a limited amount of space, and many appliances have bulky plugs that take up a lot of room.

Increasingly, HCI research is helping appliance designers move toward multimodal user interfaces. These are systems that engage the whole array of human senses and physical capabilities, match particular tasks to the modalities that are the easiest and most effective for people to use, and respond in tangible ways to the actions and behaviors of users. Multimodal interfaces combine input devices for collecting data from the human user (such as video cameras, sound recording devices, and pressure sensors) with software tools that use statistical analysis or artificial intelligence (AI) to interpret these data (such as natural language processing programs and computer vision applications).

For example, a multimodal interface for a global positioning system (GPS) system installed in an automobile might allow the user to simply speak the name of a destination aloud rather than having to type it in while driving. The system might use auditory processing of the user's voice as well as visual processing of his or her lip movements to more accurately interpret speech. It might also use a camera to closely follow the movements of the user's eyes, tracking his or her gaze from one part of the screen to another and using this information to helpfully zoom in on particular parts of the map or automatically select a particular item in a menu.

Similarly, in 2015, Amazon took the technology of the Bluetooth speaker one step further with its release of the Echo device. This speaker featured a built-in program that allowed the user to give voice commands to instruct the device to play certain music or to sync up with other applications and devices. A variety of competing "smart speaker" devices were released over the next several years, including the Apple HomePod and the devices in the Google Home and Google Nest product lines. In addition to their use of voice commands, some such products incorporated touch-screen displays that offered further usability options.

Workplace Information Systems

Human-computer interaction research plays an important role in many products that enable people to perform workplace tasks more effectively. For example, experimental computer systems are being designed for air traffic control that will increase safety and efficiency. Such systems work by collecting data about the operator's pupil size, facial expression, heart rate, and the forward momentum and intensity of his or her mouse movements and clicks. This information helps the computer interpret the operator's behavior and state of mind and respond accordingly. When an airplane drifts slightly off its course, the system analyzes the operator's physical modalities. If his or her gaze travels quickly over the relevant area of the screen, with no change in pupil size or mouse click intensity, the computer might conclude that the operator has missed the anomaly and attempt to draw attention to it by using a flashing light or an alarm.

Other common workplace applications of HCI include products that are designed to facilitate communication and collaboration between team members, such as instant messaging programs, wikis (collaboratively edited websites), and videoconferencing tools. In addition, HCI principles have contributed to many project-management tools that enable groups to schedule and track the progress they are making on a shared task or to make changes to common documents without overriding someone else's work.

Education and Training

Schools, museums, and businesses all make use of HCI principles when designing educational and training curricula for students, visitors, and staff. For example, many school districts are moving away from printed textbooks and toward interactive electronic programs that target a variety of information-processing modalities through multimedia. Unlike paper-and-pencil worksheets, such programs also provide instant feedback, making it easier for students to learn and understand new concepts.

Businesses use similar programs to train employees in such areas as the use of new software and the company's policies on issues of workplace ethics. Many art and science museums have installed electronic kiosks with touch screens that visitors can use to learn more about a particular exhibit. Human-computer interaction principles underlie the design of such kiosks. For example, rather than using a text-heavy interface, the screen on an interactive kiosk at a science museum might display video of a museum staff member talking to the visitor about each available option.

Social Context and Future Prospects

As HCI moves forward with research into multimodal interfaces and ubiquitous computing, notion of the computer as an object separate from the user may eventually be relegated to the archives of technological history, to be replaced by wearable machine interfaces that can be worn like clothing on the user's head, arm, or torso. Apple released its fifth version of a smartwatch in 2019, which is designed to have all of the features of smartphones in a wearable, theoretically more convenient format. Much like other wearable gadgets such as the Fitbit,

playing into society's increased concern with exercise and overall health, the watch has the ability to track human components such as heart rate and serve as a GPS that can map running, walking, and biking routes.

Virtual reality interfaces have been developed that are capable of immersing the user in a 360-degree space that looks, sounds, feels, and perhaps even smells like a real environment—and with which they can interact naturally and intuitively, using their whole bodies. As the capacity to measure the physical properties of human beings becomes ever more sophisticated, input devices may grow more and more sensitive; it is possible to envision a future, for instance, in which a machine might "listen in" to the synaptic firings of the neurons in a user's brain and respond accordingly. Indeed, it is not beyond the realm of possibility that a means could be found of stimulating a user's neurons to produce direct visual or auditory sensations. The future of HCI research may be wide open, but its essential place in the workplace, home, recreational spaces, and the broader human culture is assured.

—*M. Lee*

References

Horton, Sarah, and Whitney Quesenbery. *A Web for Everyone: Designing Accessible User Experiences.* Rosenfeld Media, 2014.

Jacko, Julie A., editor. *The Human-Computer Interaction Handbook: Fundamentals, Evolving Technologies, and Emerging Applications.* 3rd ed., CRC Press, 2012.

Jeon, Myounghoon, editor. *Emotions and Affect in Human Factors and Human-Computer Interaction.* Academic Press, 2017.

Jokinen, Jussi P. P. "Emotional User Experience: Traits, Events, and States." *International Journal of Human-Computer Studies,* vol. 76, 2015, pp. 67–77.

Moallem, Abbas. *Human-Computer Interaction and Cybersecurity Handbook.* CRC Press, 2019.

Purchase, Helen C. *Experimental Human-Computer Interaction: A Practical Guide with Visual Examples.* Cambridge UP, 2012.

Sharp, Helen, Jennifer Preece, and Yvonne Rogers. *Interaction Design: Beyond Human-Computer Interaction.* 5th ed., John Wiley & Sons, 2019.

Shneiderman, Ben, et al. *Designing the User Interface: Strategies for Effective Human-Computer Interaction.* 6th ed., Pearson Education, 2018.

Soegaard, Mads, and Rikke Friis Dam, editors. *The Encyclopedia of Human-Computer Interaction.* 2nd ed., Interaction Design Foundation, 2014.

Weyers, Benjamin, et al., editors. *The Handbook of Formal Methods in Human-Computer Interaction.* Springer International, 2017.

HYPERMEDIA IN EDUCATION

Introduction

In contrast to printed books, newspapers and magazines, hypermedia is a fusion of computer text, audio, video, graphics and hyperlinks that combines to present information in a nonlinear fashion while facilitating the active engagement between users and technology. The term hypermedia was coined in 1965, two decades before the invention of the World Wide Web. Beginning in the 1990s, schools were wired for high-speed broadband internet access, which enabled them to not only access the web, which has become the greatest embodiment of hypermedia ideas, but to take full advantage of a rich bounty of hypermedia in the form of linked online multimedia content requiring higher bandwidth. Today hypermedia drives variants of e-learning such as blended learning, computer-based learning, online learning, and distance education.

Background

In his seminal *Atlantic Monthly* article "As We May Think," V. Bush in 1945 writes "wholly new forms of encyclopedias will appear, ready-made with a mesh of associative trails running through them, ready to be dropped into the memex [an early conception of the internet] and there amplified." Two decades later in 1965, Ted Nelson coined the term hypermedia in his equally seminal 1965 article "Complex Information Processing: a File Structure for the Complex, the Changing and the Indeterminate."

Reflecting on his work decades later, Nelson wrote: "In 1960, I had a vision of a worldwide system of electronic publishing, anarchic and populist, where anyone could publish anything, and anyone could read it. (So far, sounds like the web.) But my approach is about literary depth—including side-by-side intercomparison, annotation, and a unique copyright proposal. I now call this 'deep electronic literature' instead of 'hypertext,' since people now think hypertext means the web." Nelson's conceptualization became realized through a community of contributors to the global, distributed, and multisensory knowledge base residing on the worldwide web. The worldwide web itself was not invented until 1989.

What Is Hypermedia?

Hypermedia took hypertext's simple, established concept of linking from one text page on the internet to related pages—which itself was patterned after the human experience of one thought leading to another—and extended it beyond the passive exercise of reading words on the (digital) page. As Hughes put it, "Hypermedia is hypertext with a difference—hypermedia documents contain links not only to other pieces of text, but also to other forms of media—sounds, images, and movies. Images themselves can be selected to link to sounds or documents. Hypermedia simply combines hypertext and multimedia."

Hypermedia encourages the consumer of electronic information to become an active participant in the quest for connections between related pieces of information—even as that information cuts across the boundaries of text, audio, and video. By appealing to more of our senses simultaneously, hypermedia promises a richer intellectual experience through a deeper engagement with technology and the experience it can deliver.

Any discussion of hypermedia must get beyond the realm of abstractions and theory. Hughes provides some examples of hypermedia:

- You are reading a text on the Hawaiian language. You select a Hawaiian phrase, then hear the phrase as spoken in the native tongue.
- You are a law student studying the California Revised Statutes. By selecting a passage, you find precedents from a 1920 Supreme Court ruling stored at Cornell. Cross-referenced hyperlinks allow you to view any one of 520 related cases with audio annotations.
- Looking at a company's floor plan, you select an office by touching a room. The employee's name and picture appear with a list of their current projects.

- You are a scientist doing work on the cooling of steel springs. By selecting text in a research paper, you view a computer-generated movie of a cooling spring. By selecting a button, you can receive a program that will perform thermodynamic calculations.
- A student reading a digital version of an art magazine can select a work to print or display in full. Rotating movies of sculptures can be viewed. By interactively controlling the movie, the student can zoom in to see more detail.

This hypermedia engagement is simpler in the sense that this multisensory approach is more akin to how we interact with our environment—our brains creating a rich, three-dimensional (3D) and coherent virtual reality from innumerable bits of sensory inputs—yet it is dependent upon a whole series of advances in computer technology that needed to be made before the dream of hypermedia could become a reality.

One of those advances was the prevalence of increasingly inexpensive broadband internet connections that enable bits of data to be exchanged at rates that were once experienced only within government or university computer networks. Because images, audio and video take up more physical computer bits than text, hypermedia has blossomed as more and more users, particularly in the West and in Asia, have begun to use broadband.

Hypermedia in Education

Hypertext and hypermedia have been used in education in the United States since advances in computer technology and internet connectivity made it possible. First came the personal computer. By the 1980s, computer technology had advanced to the point where more and more Americans were buying personal computers. Popular models such as the Apple IIe, the Apple Macintosh Plus/SE, and various IBM personal computer (PC) clones began to transform how students and their parents lived and worked. Educational software began to proliferate as increasingly powerful computers found their way into K-12 classrooms.

While examples of hypermedia date back to the *Aspen Movie Map* (a virtual driving tour of Aspen, Colorado made at the Massachusetts Institute of Technology [MIT] in 1978), the first popular use of hypermedia in education came in 1987, with the introduction of Apple's HyperCard application for the Macintosh, a widely used computer in schools. HyperCard consisted of a series of electronic index cards that contained related pieces of text and images. Most notably, it also featured a collaborative tool that later would become known as a "wiki," but naturally this pre-World Wide Web version lacked the online collaborative functionality.

Therefore, despite the advances made by computer technology in the 1980s, there were limitations to be overcome. Hypertext and hypermedia still had not yet arrived in force, though HyperCard and educational software titles such as *Reader Rabbit, Where in the World is Carmen San Diego?* and *Oregon Trail* incorporated a limited version of the hypermedia in terms of their multisensory approach to conveying information to a student audience.

In the early 1990s, a new phenomenon known as the "internet" began to transform hypermedia and e-learning, making it web-based rather than simply computer-based. Using the internet, students could tap into a global community—a worldwide web—of teachers and learners to expand their educational horizons. In addition, textbooks that once had been limited to the contents contained between the covers were augmented with online resources for use by students and teachers. Some cultural critics however, noted that many textbooks were becoming more visual, and they argued that the growing number of photos and other illustrations per page was dumbing down textbooks by crowding out some important text-based content.

These trends paint a clear picture of wired teachers and wired students, and they form a backdrop for the advent of hypertext and hypermedia in the later 1990s. As fast, reasonably priced, and accessible internet access became available to more and more K-12 students, both in and out of school, many in the education community began to conceive of ways to use it to improve education in America. Educators noted that new technologies were changing the face of the entertainment industry—from movies to television to video games—and they sought ways to incorporate those technologies in their lesson planning. Blogs have been created to keep educators up to date on the latest online resources.

Web-based Instruction: Hypermedia 2.0

One growing use of hypermedia in education is web-based instruction, which was one of the ideas discussed during the national conversation about education reform and outcome-based education culminating in the passage of the historic No Child Left Behind Act of 2001. Allen and Seaman's 2006 research reveals that web-based learning can take three main forms: online, blended/hybrid, and web-facilitated:

- **Online:** Course where most or all the content is delivered online. Defined as at least 80 percent of seat time being replaced by online activity;
- **Blended/Hybrid:** Course that blends online and face-to-face delivery. Substantial proportion (30 to 79 percent) of the content is delivered online (Allen and Seaman, 2006);
- **Web-facilitated:** Course that uses web-based technology (1 to 29 percent of the content is delivered online) to facilitate what is essentially a face-to-face course.

According to statistics compiled by Watson and Ryan, web-based instruction is a trend that shows no signs of abating.

Online learning continues to grow rapidly across the country as an increasing number of educators and policymakers recognize the benefits of learning unconstrained by time and place. The growth of online education in the United States can be attributed to the increasing patronage among students. It is estimated that more than 30 percent of American students are enrolled in at least one online course. This is especially true for the period during the COVID-19 pandemic when up to 70 percent of all students in the world attended classes online or in hybrid fashion. It has been estimated that even during non-COVID times, that 67 percent of American university students used mobile devices (cell phones, tablets) to navigate part or all of their coursework and school-related activities.

As for K-12 students, the statistics gathered by Bouchrika are telling:

- 57 percent of all K-12 students in the United States are using digital learning tools for their daily education in 2019;
- 65 percent of K-12 teachers are already using digital learning tools to teach their students every day; and

- Online educational videos (67 percent) are the most commonly used learning materials in K-12 classrooms, followed by educational software or apps (65 percent). Only 17 percent of K-12 classes use e-books and 2 percent use e-magazines.

A footnote in a recent US Department of Education statistical report notes an important trend in web-based instruction across the United States: students can take delivery of content in different, but mutually reinforcing ways. The type of web-based instruction that is used is often determined by factors such as the classroom instructor's familiarity with web-based tools and the student's level of comfort with self-paced learning. Another factor is the level of concern school administrators have regarding quality control.

Blogs and Wikis in Education

Blogs (short for "weblogs") are another example of hypermedia in action, particularly when they contain text, audio, photos and video. Schools can use blogs to reach out to the local and global community by posting classroom projects and encouraging feedback.

Wikis are collaborative websites that can be edited by any web user with something to contribute to the ongoing conversation. The leading example of the wiki concept, of course, is Wikipedia, the user-developed encyclopedia. Several elementary, middle, and high schools are using wikis as tools to collaborate on school assignments, report on school news and so on.

The hope and expectation are that use of such hypermedia tools will increase students' interest in—followed swiftly by their competence in—basic skills like math, reading and writing. This is precisely the point argued by both Diane Penrod, professor of writing arts at Rowan University in Glassboro, New Jersey, (author of U*sing Blogs to Enhance Literacy: The Next Powerful Step in 21st-Century Learning*) and Laura Nicosia, professor of English at Montclair State University, New Jersey (author of *Educators Online: Preparing Today's Teachers for Tomorrow's Digital Literacies*).

In short, blogging might turn out to be the tipping point in education for lifelong learning. Its adaptive nature, malleability, and ease of use make blogs a killer application. Like its predecessor, email, blogs might soon develop into a ubiquitous communication tool in schools. For literacy, this will be an important event: having an inexpensive, ever-present, easy-to-use method for transmitting information, knowledge, and meaning across student populations, suggesting that it is indeed possible to teach and upgrade the literacies students need right now and will continue to need in the future.

Audio Hypermedia and the MP3 Revolution

While some public schools have distributed laptops to middle or high school students for use in their classes, there's no report of high schools or middle schools using MP3 players in education. Duke University in North Carolina broke new ground in 2004 by distributing iPods to incoming freshman for use in their studies. Carvin (2007) reports that in the 3 years the program has been running, more than 1,300 students and professors are using the devices in 71 courses, mostly within the language and humanities realms. The professors use the iPods to send copies of lectures and other course related materials such as video or books on tape.

Video Games as Educational Hypermedia

There is some research indicating that video games, when handled properly, are effective learning tools for young people. According to the BBC News (2002) researchers from the group Teachers Evaluating Educational Multimedia (TEEM) study went further:

- Computer games could become part of the school curriculum after researchers found they had significant educational value;
- [A] UK study concluded that simulation and adventure games—such as *Sim City* and *Roller-Coaster Tycoon*, where players create societies or build theme parks, developed children's strategic thinking and planning skills;
- Parents and teachers also thought their children's mathematics, reading and spelling improved (BBC News).

James Paul Gee, a reading professor at the University of Wisconsin-Madison, wrote in *Wired* magazine that schools must begin to accept that video games are a valid learning tool. He believes that since kids basically devour information, concepts and skills via media and television every day after school, they are experiencing a much more powerful form of learning than that offered in the classroom. However, since most video games are considered violent, they are often discouraged as learning tools. Gee believes that the skills used in many video games teach kids to problem solve, carry out missions, and shape worlds, micromanaging a huge array of elements.

—*Matt Donnelly*

References

Allen, I. E., and J. Seaman. *Making the Grade: Online Learning in the United States, 2006.* The Sloan Consortium. 2006.

BBC News. "Video Games 'Valid Learning Tools.'" *News.bbc.co.uk*, 29 Apr. 2000.

___. "Video Games 'Stimulate Learning.'" *News.bbc.co.uk*, 18 Mar. 2002.

Bouchrika, Imed. "50 Online Education Statistics: 2021/2022 Data on Higher Learning & Corporate Training." *Research.com*, 30 June 2020, research.com/education/online-education-statistics.

___. "66 Elearning Statistics: 2021/2022 Data, Analysis & Predictions." *Research.com*, 23 June 2020, research.com/education/elearning-statistics#k-12.

Bush, V. "As We May Think." *The Atlantic Monthly*, July 1945, theatlantic.com.

Frazier, M., and D. Hearrington. *The Technology Coordinator's Handbook.* International Society for Technology in Education, 2017.

Kahraman, H., S. Sagiroglu, and I. Colak. "A Novel Model for Web-Based Adaptive Educational Hypermedia Systems: SAHM (Supervised Adaptive Hypermedia Model)." *Computer Applications in Engineering Education*, vol. 21, 2013, pp. 60–74.

Moos, D. "Examining Hypermedia Learning: The Role of Cognitive Load and Self-Regulated Learning." *Journal of Educational Multimedia & Hypermedia*, 22, 2013, pp. 39–61.

National Center for Education Statistics. "In Brief: Computer and Internet Access in Private Schools and Classrooms: 1995 and 1998." *US Department of Education*, Feb. 2000, nces.ed.gov.

___. *US Department of Education*, nces.ed.gov.

Nicosia, Laura. *Educators Online: Preparing Today's Teachers for Tomorrow's Digital Literacies.* Peter Lang, 2013.

Penrod, Diane. *Using Blogs to Enhance Literacy: The Next Powerful Step in 21st-Century Learning.* Rowman & Littlefield, 2007.

Picciano, A. G., and J. Seaman. "K-12 Online Learning: A Survey of U.S. School District Administrators." *The Sloan Consortium,* 2007, sloan-c.org.

Rowsell, J. *Working with Multimodality: Rethinking Literacy in the Digital Age.* Routledge, 2013.

Sandars, J., M. Homer, K. Walsh, and A. Rutherford. "Don't Forget the Learner: An Essential Aspect for Developing Effective Hypermedia Online Learning in Continuing Medical Education." *Education for Primary Care,* vol. 23, 2012, pp. 90–94.

US Census Bureau. "The 2007 Statistical Abstract: 1143—Households with Computers and Internet Access: 1998 and 2003." *US Census Bureau,* 2007, census.gov.

Wells, J., and M. Lewis. *Internet Access in U.S. Public Schools and Classrooms: 1994–2005.* US Department of Education, 2006.

IDENTITY THEFT

Introduction

Identity theft is the most frequent consumer complaint reported to the Federal Trade Commission (FTC), a relatively new crime that is often perpetrated through various familiar crimes, such as forgery; counterfeiting; and check, credit, and computer fraud. In 2016, 15.4 million people were victims of identity theft, up from 2015's figure of 13 million, according to Javelin's *2018 Identity Fraud Study*. The losses from identity theft totalled $16.8 billion. Part of this increase is due to some significant changes in data breaches. According to the FTC's *Consumer Sentinel Data Book*, in 2017 almost a third of US consumers were notified of a breach, an increase of 12 percent from 2016.

According to the recent studies (2021), the number of data compromises (1,862) has risen to more than 68 percent as the numbers from 2020. The new number of data breaches is 23 percent more than the previous record (1,506 in 2017). The number of data breaches for Social Security numbers, for example, increased also in 2020 (83 percent vs. 80 percent). For the first time, Social Security numbers (35 percent) were compromised more than credit card numbers (30 percent). The National Crime Victimization Survey (NCVS) defines identity theft as (1) unauthorized use or attempted use of an *existing* account; (2) unauthorized use or attempted use of personal information to open a *new* account; and (3) misuse of personal information for a *fraudulent purpose*.

Background

The term "identity theft" did not appear in federal laws until 1998. Prior to 1998, crimes related to identity theft were charged under late nineteenth-century false personation statutes. False personation

As banking and other financial transactions increasingly take place online, keeping personal identifying information safe is becoming more challenging. Photo via iStock/Vertigo3d. [Used under license.]

refers to impersonating another individual, such as a police officer or other official, and does not have the financial connotations that the term "identity theft" now carries. The late 1990s saw a staggering increase in reporting on identity theft. TransUnion, one of the three major national credit bureaus, reported that the total number of identity theft inquiries to its fraud department rose from about 35,000 in 1992 to almost 523,000 in 1997. While these numbers did not indicate what percentage of the inquiries were actual identity thefts, they did indicate a growing concern on the part of consumers. In 1998, Congress responded to these growing numbers and passed the Identity Theft and Assumption Deterrence Act, 112 Stat. 3007, making identity theft a federal crime. It expanded 18 U.S.C. § 1028, "Fraud and related activity in connection with identification documents," to make it a federal crime to "knowingly transfer or use, without lawful authority, a means of identification of another person with the intent to commit, or to aid or abet, any unlawful activity that constitutes a violation of Federal law, or that constitutes a felony under any applicable State or local law."

According to the Office for Victims of Crime, the Identity Theft and Assumption Deterrence Act accomplished four things:

> Identity theft became a separate crime against the person whose identity was stolen. Previously, victims were defined as those who had financial losses, so the emphasis was on banks and other financial institutions rather than on individuals.

> It made the FTC the federal government's point of contact for reporting instances of identity theft by creating the Identity Theft Data Clearinghouse.

> Criminal penalties for identity theft and fraud were increased, providing for up to fifteen years' incarceration as well as substantial fines.

The Act closed loopholes so it became a crime to steal another person's identifying information. Previously, it was a crime only to produce or possess false identity documents. The act has been updated several times. The Identity Theft Penalty Enhancement Act of 2004, Pub. L. 108–275 § 1028A, established penalties for aggravated identity theft, which is when a stolen identity is used to commit felony crimes, including immigration violations, theft of another's Social Security benefits, and acts of domestic terrorism.

The Identity Theft Enforcement and Restitution Act of 2008 amended 18 U.S.C. § 3663(b) to clarify that restitution for identity theft cases may include the value of the victim's time spent repairing harm from the identity theft. It also allows federal courts to prosecute even if the criminal and the victim live in the same state. Under the previous law, federal courts had jurisdiction only if the thief used interstate communication to access the victim's information. In addition to the federal laws, state laws help victims of identity theft. Because most crimes are prosecuted at the state level, the Identity Theft Resource Center has a list of state-specific laws that deal with identity theft.

Evolving Targets

Identity thieves continue to target individuals, but in recent years they have also used security flaws to break into retailer and other databases to steal personal and financial information. For instance, in 2017 Equifax, one of the three credit reporting agencies, was breached. As of March 2018, over 148 million people had credit card, driver's license, Social Security numbers and other personal information compromised.

The data breach was so massive, the FTC devoted a web page to it: www.ftc.gov/equifax-data-breach. The breach went undetected for 76 days and Equifax waited another six weeks to disclose it.

In May 2018, President Donald Trump signed a bill that made freezing your credit easier and requires the three credit agencies to share fraud reports among themselves. However, a September 2018 report issued by the US General Accounting Office (GAO) which investigated the Equifax breach indicated that there were still many unresolved issues and sensitive data remains at risk.

Selling large collections of account information on the black market to thieves who then use the information has become lucrative. It is extremely difficult to identify the perpetrators in these data breaches; when they then sell the stolen data to third parties, the waters become even more muddied.

For instance, in December 2013, in the final shopping days before Christmas, the department store Target had the credit and debit card information of 40 million customers stolen. While Target's security software set off alarms when the offending malware was uploaded, it was not fully investigated. Because the breach was not identified quickly, additional personal information, including email and mailing addresses, for about 70 million people was compromised. The same Eastern European group that attacked Target is also suspected in breaches at Neiman Marcus and Michaels. Millions of people had to cancel and replace their credit and debit cards; many also became victims of identity theft due to the breach.

In August 2014, the *New York Times* reported that a Russian crime ring had assembled the largest known collection of stolen internet information, including 1.2 billion username and password combinations and more than 500 million email addresses. So far, the information has been used only to send spam, for which the group collects a fee.

Another method identity used by thieves to steal money is tax fraud. The Internal Revenue Service (IRS) publishes an annual list of its so-called dirty dozen tax scams. In 2011, only one involved identity theft. By 2015, about one-quarter of all IRS criminal investigations focused on identity theft.

In 2015, the IRS itself became a victim of an online attack that stole personal information, including Social Security numbers, and diverted tax refunds from over 610,000 taxpayers. The breach occurred through a new online service that provided access to past tax returns. The stolen data was subsequently used to file fraudulent tax returns totalling about $39 million. The IRS believes the identity thieves are part of a criminal group from Russia.

The IRS's attempts to modernize and increase taxpayer convenience with online resources highlight the challenge any business faces—how to outpace criminals, provide online convenience, and still keep data secure. The IRS is an interesting combination of old and new in this respect, and some of its seemingly outdated practices actually serve a protective function. For instance, the IRS communicates with taxpayers only by snail mail; it never initiates any contacts by phone or email. Commissioner John Koskinen acknowledged, at a Tax Policy Center conference, that the agency's database software is so old that hackers do not have the programming knowledge to break in.

Methods of Stealing Data

Both low- and high-tech methods are used to steal personal information, although recent years have seen growth in scams resulting from our increasing use of computers, including email and the internet. Low-tech methods include purse snatching or digging through trash, known as "dumpster diving." High-tech methods use technology to acquire information, such as phishing emails, spyware, and malware. According to Verizon's annual *Data Breach Investigations Report*, the majority of computer hacks occur because people click on links in emails, companies do not apply patches to software flaws in a timely fashion, and computer systems are improperly configured (which includes failure to install updated security software).

Scams that occur through email are called "phishing." Phishing scams target people by sending an email that seems to be from a trustworthy source, such as a well-known store or a bank. It asks the recipient to enter personal information, often indicating that there is a problem with an account, or enticing the recipient with coupons or other gains. Once the phishing target has entered his or her personal information, the scammer can use it to open new accounts or access existing accounts. Emails and pop-up messages that request personal and financial information should be viewed with suspicion; calling a business or contacting it through its official website to verify the request can help keep personal information safe. Many institutions, such as the IRS, have policies where they do not ask for personal information through email. Malware is short for "malicious software."

There are many types of malware, including viruses and spyware, that can steal personal information; use a computer for unauthorized activities, such as sending spam; or cause damage to a computer. Computers without security software are especially vulnerable to malware attacks. Spyware is another type of malware that records your computer use. It is often used to display targeted advertisements, redirect internet surfing to certain websites, monitor internet surfing, or record keystrokes to obtain passwords and other personal information. Malware can infect your computer in a variety of ways, and antivirus software is constantly struggling to identify and protect against the most recent malware.

Buying and Selling Data

An entire industry exists to acquire and sell stolen personal data. The *Christian Science Monitor* reported that black market forums and stores that trade in stolen personal information were increasing. With names like Rescator, Republic of Lampeduza, Mc-Dumpals, and Blackstuff, they sell stolen Social Security numbers, bank account information, credit card data, and other personal and financial information. They also offer hardware and malware meant to steal this type of information.

In July 2015, a hacking forum called "Darkode," which allowed users to buy and sell cybercrime tools and services such as malware, spam services and other items, was infiltrated by the Federal Bureau of Investigation (FBI) and dismantled. Twenty-eight people were arrested, and twelve were charged as a result of international law enforcement efforts involving twenty countries. Indictments included charges such as authoring and selling malware to steal bank account credentials, selling access to botnets (a group of compromised computers used to send spam and other malware), and money laundering.

The only way to become a member of Darkode was to convince existing members of the value of the abilities or products that an individual could bring to the forum. Membership had to be approved by the other members. Just weeks after the indictments, however, Darkode was ready to reopen with a different domain suffix (Darkode.cc instead of the original Darkode.me). Most of the staff members appeared to be untouched by the arrests, and the forum implemented even more stringent membership requirements to keep out informants.

A report entitled *Markets for Cybercrime Tools and Stolen Data* by the RAND Corporation predicts that the future will see an expansion of darknets, in terms of both numbers and activity. It also anticipates that, while greater attention will be paid to encrypting and protecting communications and transactions, the ability to generate successful cyberattacks will likely outpace the ability to defend against them. "Crime will increasingly have a networked or cyber component, creating a wider range of opportunities for black markets; and that there will be more hacking for hire, as-a-service offerings, and brokers."

The report says that there is disagreement on who will be the target of the black market (e.g., small or large businesses, or individuals), what products will be on the rise in the black markets (e.g., fungible goods, such as data records and credit card information; nonfungible goods, such as intellectual property), and which types of attacks will be most prevalent (e.g., persistent, targeted attacks; opportunistic, mass smash-and-grab attacks).

Identity Protection Services

As the black market that facilitates identity theft grows, so does another market—companies that offer protection against identity theft. The increasing number and size of data breaches causes concern and is fueling a growth in identity protection services from companies such as LifeLock, ezShield, and IdentityForce. In 2015, consumers spent $3.8 billion on identity protection services, an 18 percent increase from the previous year, according to Javelin Strategy & Research. These services may check to see if customer data is being

bought and sold on darknets or other places that are difficult for an average person to access. Another possible benefit of such a service may be the remediation services some offer in case of theft. It is a great deal of work to repair the damage once an identity has been stolen. While an individual can do it, having assistance may make a difficult situation easier. Some insurance companies, banks, and employers offer these services for little or no cost.

It appears that the companies that are looking to help prevent identity theft, however, are not without their own problems. In a suit against LifeLock, the FTC asserted that, from 2012 to 2014, the company failed to alert customers as soon as their identities were used by thieves and also failed to protect data with the same high-level safeguards used by financial institutions, both claims the company has made to its customers. The company has since settled the lawsuit with the FTC.

Another concern about identity theft and the need for protection services is that it may not be as dire a problem as it appears in recent news. The *New York Times* reported that it is the type of data stolen that actually determines the seriousness of a data breach. The theft of Social Security numbers can allow thieves the opportunity to open new accounts in the victim's name, a particularly damaging type of identity theft. These types of theft are also difficult to discover and fix before significant damage occurs.

Many times, however, large breaches expose data that is available through other, legal means, such as email and home addresses, or information that is shared willingly, such as through social media. The size and surreptitious nature of the breach are alarming and leads to concern, even though breaches of this type of data do not often lead to crimes of identity theft. The *Times* reported that, according to the American Bankers Association, the largest expense that occurred from the 2013 Target breach was the cost of reissuing compromised debit and credit cards and assisting affected customers. Also, merchants and banks, rather than individual consumers, generally bear the financial cost of stolen credit card numbers. Because of their interest in keeping these losses to a minimum, banks and merchants are investing in better ways to find and prevent fraudulent purchases.

The government is taking the increased reporting of identity theft seriously. An entire FTC website, www.identitytheft.gov, has been created to assist those dealing with identity theft. It offers step-by-step advice on detecting identity theft, as well as how to repair the various types of damage that may be the result. The FTC also provides resources on their website for law enforcement, attorneys assisting victims of identity theft, and businesses trying to prevent future data breaches.

—*Noëlle Sinclair*

References

"2018 Data Breach Investigations Report." *Verizon*, verizonenterprise.com.

Abagnale, Frank W. *Stealing Your Life: The Ultimate Identity Theft Prevention Plan.* Broadway Books, 2008.

Ablon, Lillian, Martin C. Libicki, and Andrea A. Golay. *Markets for Cybercrime Tools and Stolen Data.* RAND Corporation, 2014. www.rand.org/pubs/research_reports/RR610.html.

Copes, Heith, and Lynne M. Vieraitis. *Identity Thieves: Motives and Methods.* Northeastern UP, 2012.

Hastings, Glen, and Richard Marcus. *Identity Theft, Inc.: A Wild Ride with the World's #1 Identity Thief.* The Disinformation Company, 2006.

Hoofnagle, Chris Jay. "Identity Theft: Making the Known Unknowns Known." *Harvard Journal of Law and Technology*, vol. 21, no. 1, 2007, pp. 97–122.

McNally, Megan. *Identity Theft in Today's World.* Praeger, 2012.

Poulsen, Kevin. *Kingpin: How One Hacker Took Over the Billion-Dollar Cybercrime Underground.* Broadway Paperbacks, 2011.

"Victims of Identity Theft, 2016." *Bureau of Justice Statistics.* bjs.gov, 2019, www.bjs.gov/index.cfm?ty=pbdetail&iid=6467.

IMAGE EDITING

Introduction

Image-editing software uses computing technology to change digital images. Image editing can involve altering the appearance of an image, such as showing a hot air balloon underwater, or improving the quality of a low-resolution image. Images may also be compressed so that they require less computer storage space.

Background

There are as many ways of digitally altering images as there are uses for digital art. The first step in image editing is to obtain an image in digital format. The easiest method is to use a digital camera to take a photograph and then transfer the photograph to a computer for editing. Another approach that is occasionally necessary is to scan a print photograph or film negative. This converts the photo to a digital image ready for editing. It is even possible to create an image by hand in native digital format, by using a tablet and stylus to draw and paint. Finally, rendering makes it possible for a computer to produce a digital image from a two-dimensional (2D) or three-dimensional (3D) model.

Once the digital image is available, the next step is to determine what will be done to it. Most often, the image will be enhanced (improving the image quality through interpolation or other techniques), compressed (decreasing the file size by sacrificing some image quality or clarity), or altered (made to depict something that was not originally there). These changes may be through destructive or nondestructive editing. In destructive editing, the changes are applied to the original file. By contrast, in nondestructive editing, they are saved in a separate version file.

In the early days of the internet, image compression was an especially important type of image editing. Bandwidth was limited then, and it could take several minutes to transmit even a medium-sized image file. Image compression algorithms were invented to help reduce the size of these files, with some loss of quality. Lossless compression can avoid degradation of the image, but in most cases, it does not reduce file size as much as lossy compression does.

How Compression Works

Computers store image data as sets of numeric values. Each pixel onscreen is lit in a particular way when an image is displayed, and the colors of each pixel are stored as numbers. For example, if the color black were represented by the number eight, then anywhere in a picture that has three black pixels in a row would be stored as 8, 8, 8. Because an image is composed of thousands of pixels, all of the

An example of selective color changes made in an image editing program. Photo via Wikimedia Commons. [Public domain.]

numbers needed to describe the colors of those pixels, when combined, take up a lot of storage space.

One way to store the same information in less space is to create substitutions for recurring groups of numbers. The symbol *q1* could be used to represent three black pixels in a row, for instance. Thus, instead of having to store three copies of the value "8" to represent each of the three black pixels, the computer could simply store the two-letter symbol *q1*, thus saving one-third of the storage space that otherwise would be required. This is the basis for how digital images are compressed.

Most images are compressed using lossy compression algorithms, such as Joint Photographic Experts Group (JPEG). Compression thus usually requires that the sacrifice of some image quality. For most purposes, the reduction in quality is not noticeable and is made up for by the convenience of more easily storing and transmitting the smaller file. It is not uncommon for compression algorithms to reduce the file size of an image by 75 to 90 percent, without noticeably affecting the image's quality.

A Numbers Game

Image enhancement typically relies on the mathematical adjustment of the numeric values that represent pixel hues. For instance, if an image editor were to desaturate a photograph, the software would first recognize all of the pixel values and compare them to a grayscale value. It would then interpolate new values for the pixels using a linear operation. Similarly, a filtering algorithm would find and apply a weighted average of the pixel values around a given pixel value in order to identify the new color codes for each pixel being adjusted. The median or the mode (most common) value could also be used. The type of filter being applied determines which mathematical operation is performed. Filters are often used to correct for noise, or unwanted signal or interference.

Image Editing Goes Mobile

Image editing is even possible on mobile platforms. Certain programs work only on personal computers (PCs), others strictly on mobile devices, and still others on both. Besides the well-known Adobe Photoshop, other programs, including Apple's Photos and the open-source software Gimp, also provide image editing for desktop computers. Fotor and Pixlr Editor work across platforms, giving users flexibility between their desktop, mobile device, and the web. Similarly, photo collaging software abounds. Among these programs are Photoshop CC and CollageIt on desktops, Ribbet and FotoJet online, and Pic Stitch and BeFunky on mobile devices.

Companies such as Nokia and Apple have developed the capability to create "live photos" with their smartphones. These are a hybrid of video and still images in which a few seconds of video are recorded prior to the still photo being taken. This feature represents yet another direction for image capture, alteration, and presentation.

—*Scott Zimmer*

References

Adobe Photoshop: Quick Guide and Quick Reference. CreativeCloud Publications, 2020.

Freeman, Michael. *Digital Image Editing & Special Effects: Quickly Master the Key Techniques of Photoshop & Lightroom.* Focal Press, 2013.

Galer, Mark, and Philip Andrews. *Photoshop CC Essential Skills: A Guide to Creative Image Editing.* Focal Press, 2014.

Goelker, Klaus. *Gimp 2.8 for Photographers: Image Editing with* Open Source *Software.* Rocky Nook, 2013.

Nichols, Robin. *Mastering Adobe Photoshop Elements.* Packt, 2019.

Whitt, Phillip. *Beginning Pixlr Editor: Learn How to Edit Digital Photos Using This Free Web-Based App.* Apress, 2017.

IMGUR

Introduction

Online media sites that enable posting of pictures and videos, as well as messaging, have become very popular. Such sites as Facebook, TikTok, and Instagram are very well-known venues for pictures, videos, and other features of digital communication. In 2009, Alan Schaaf developed such an application for a project while studying computer science at The Ohio University. His goal was to produce an online image sharing and hosting service that could avoid the usability problems users were encountering with other such services. Initially, his service held only pictures and images that had gained a lot of traction on other sites such as Reddit. Traction is acquired by garnering high numbers of views and popularity votes, or even going viral on those sites.

According to Schaaf, his IMGUR (which may be pronounced as imager) site became very popular very quickly, garnering a million total page views within five months of its release. The service was financed initially by donations toward the cost of hosting the service's website. Revenue from display ads, introduced in 2009, added to the level of support funding, and this was further augmented by the introduction of sponsored images and self-service ads in 2013. As of January 2022, IMGUR had 300 million users, with 85 percent of those users identifying as male, and 35 percent of all users being younger than thirty-five years old.

Background

The first years of IMGUR's existence were full of change. Three different web-hosting services were used in the first year alone, until Schaaf settled the site with Voxel as the hosting service. That lasted until late 2011, when the hosting service was switched again from Voxel to Amazon Web Services. In 2012, IMGUR introduced direct image sharing so that users could share images directly to IMGUR without the need to first become popular on Reddit and other sites. This followed the move of the company from Ohio to San Francisco in 2011.

The success of the service earned it the 2012 Crunchies Award as the Best Bootstrapped Startup, and in June, 2013, IMGUR had a total of 40 employees. In 2014, IMGUR raised a $40 million-funding boost from Andriessen Horowitz, which was subsequently represented on IMGUR's board of directors by Lars Dalgaard. IMGUR's popularity and success was, at the time, generating good profits from advertising revenue and the sale of 'Pro' subscriptions. The nature of business competition, however, guarantees that profitability is fleeting. When Reddit introduced native image hosting in 2016, the number of submissions to IMGUR decreased by a substantial amount and IMGUR's popularity, as listed in Alexa's Top Sites in the United States, dropped from 16th place in 2016 to 51st over the next five years. In 2021, IMGUR was acquired by MediaLab AI Incorporated, its current owner.

Features

A logical way of organizing images is to arrange them in galleries, a feature that became part of the IMGUR structure as IMGUR Accounts in 2010. This was improved by the addition of Albums later the same year. The user account provides complete image management that includes image editing, deletion, creation and embedding of Albums, and allows users to comment on viral images and submit them to the public gallery. Users could then view their past public activity as well, much like Facebook's personal timelines.

With paid Pro IMGUR accounts, added in 2010, users were not subject to image upload restrictions and could store an unlimited number of images. Initially, images posted to IMGUR were hosted indefinitely unless they went for a period of three months without being viewed, at which time they would become subject to removal from the site. In 2015, IMGUR chose instead to host all images permanently unless the poster specifically requested removal, even if they had not been posted from a Pro account.

Memes are popular images that are often posted to media sites. A meme is typically a regular image or screen grab that has a pithy quote or a humorous comment applied to it. Since June, 2013, IMGUR has maintained a built-in meme generator that allows users to create and share their own memes for posting.

The public gallery in IMGUR collects the most viral of images from around the web. It uses an algorithm that calculates the number of times an image has been viewed, the number of times it has been shared, and the number of votes it has received from IMGUR users relative to time. Users have been allowed to browse the entire public gallery at random since 2012. Since 2014, IMGUR has automatically converted animated .gif files to WebM and MP4 video files, and since 2015 users have been able to link video URLs to create .gif files directly via IMGUR. Also, since 2015, by using IMGUR's Topics utility, users are able to search and view specific images according to the tags that have been applied to them. Mobile apps for iOS and Android were also introduced in 2015.

In use, the IMGUR website opens directly to a simple landing screen displaying public content that users can scroll through indefinitely. This is reminiscent of an individual's Timeline in Facebook, but is much broader in scope, and presumably in extent as well. The image stream is interspersed with unobtrusive ads that scroll along with the image stream. Visitors have the choice of opening the website with specific purposes or ordering of the image stream. A visitor can also open the website at the sign-in page to either log into their existing account or to open a new account.

—*Richard M. Renneboog and Jake D. Nicosia*

References

"The Magic of the Internet." *IMGUR*, imgurinc.com.

Pollard, Barry *HTTP/2 in Action*. Simon & Schuster, 2019.

Sadun, Erica. *The Advanced iOS 6 Developer's Cookbook*. Addison-Wesley, 2013.

Smith, Craig. "IMGR Statistics, User Count and Facts: 2022." *DMR Publisher*, expandedramblings.com/index.php/imgur-statistics/.

Summers, Danny. *Imgur: 42 Success Secrets–42 Most Asked Questions–Imgur: What You Need to Know.* Emereo Pty Ltd., 2014.

Swarts, Jason. *Wicked, Incomplete and Uncertain: User Support in the Wild and the Role of Technical Communication*. UP of Colorado, 2018.

INFORMATION ETHICS

Introduction

As its name suggests, information ethics is the branch of ethics dealing with information. It is a vast field and includes questions of applied and normative ethics. The field is also broad because it examines ethical questions in many categories, including the use of artificial intelligence (AI), the philosophy of information, ethics in mass media, privacy and anonymity, and access to information. Because many parts of information ethics deal with technology, the field is constantly changing and evolving. Information ethics is also broad because it concerns people all over the world, and the influence of various cultures and perspectives is essential for a better understanding of the subject.

Background

The broadness of information ethics has also led to questions about its history and origin. Some contend that the field emerged in the 1940s, while others believe it did not originate until the 1980s. The earliest ideas to be part of the broader information ethics field were related to librarianship and library science. In the 1940s, scholars published books about various topics dealing with library science and ethics. For example, some publications dealt with the ideas of censorship, privacy, and access to information. These topics were related to information and its use and access. Also in the 1940s, scholars began publishing articles about computer ethics, which is another important part of information ethics.

One of the most important early scholars in computer ethics was Norbert Wiener, an engineer at MIT (Massachusetts Institute of Technology). Wiener helped develop some of the first electronic computers. While he and his colleagues worked with this technology, Wiener realized that it had huge ethical implications because of the major changes it could bring to society. He believed that computers and similar technologies would revolutionize human work and life. He published a number of books on the subject, which became important texts in the early field of computer ethics. Two of which are: *Cybernetics* (1948), which described the ethical of using electronic computers and T*he Human Use of Human Beings* (1950), which discussed the ethical issues that technology could create.

The ideas that were published in the 1940s and 1950s developed over time, and eventually the field of information ethics emerged from both librarianship and computer ethics. By the late 1980s and early 1990s, the field of information ethics was fully established. It was a large field that was concerned with many topics and disciplines. In 1988, scholar Rafael Capurro published an article on the topic, "Informationethos und Informationsethik" ("Information Ethos and Information Ethics"). In 1992, the *Journal of Information Ethics* was created. As technology advanced, the field of information ethics expanded with it, causing the number of professionals concerned with information ethics to significantly increase.

Overview

Information is sometimes compared to traditional Western ethical theories such as virtue ethics and utilitarianism. However, the field is not limited by Western philosophy and its definitions. Information ethics is influenced by ethical and philosophical traditions from around the world.

Information ethics is an extremely broad category incorporating many disciplines, such as librarianship. Librarians focus on data that can be sorted and classified. For example, books have authors, titles, publishers, and publication dates. This information can be used to organize groups of books. The individual pieces of information can themselves be organized into citations. Librarianship also deals with metadata, which is data about data. Many types of metadata exist, with some being as long as a piece of writing and including genre and keywords that help describe it.

Taxonomy, which is the classification of information based on groups or sets, is also an important part of information ethics because it helps people organize and make use of information. Information ethics can be used to discuss the use of certain classification and taxonomic systems. For example, a common classification system used in Western libraries is the Dewey classification system. This system has certain biases that affect users' experiences. Discussing these biases and their effects on those using a library is a question of information ethics.

Computer ethics and cyberethics make up another important discipline in information ethics. The field first dealt with electronic computers and focused on issues such as automation, or replacing human work with the work of computers and machines. This topic remains an important issue in computer ethics. The discipline expanded rapidly throughout the twentieth century as technology also rapidly changed. Two important topics in the discipline of computer ethics are privacy and anonymity.

These topics are related to computer ethics because computers and the internet have fundamentally changed people's privacy. Anonymity—which can help ensure safety but can also allow people to avoid accountability—is another important topic in the field. Computer ethics also deals with AI. The ethics of using the technology, replacing human workers with robots, and the treatment of AI devices are all considered in information ethics. Computer crime is yet another relevant topic. It includes hacking, spying, using computer viruses, and implementing security.

Media ethics is another important discipline in computer ethics. This field deals with the collection, preparation, and dissemination of information using the mass media. Mass media include print sources, such as books and magazines, and electronic sources, such as television and the internet. The media have a huge influence on human beliefs and, therefore, actions, so this topic is also an important part of information ethics. People who study media ethics consider many topics, including the appropriate ways to collect information, the use of violent images or descriptions, and objectivity and fairness.

The field of information ethics includes countless other disciplines. Intellectual property, which involves intangible items that people create, is part of the field. Intellectual property is easier to take and use without permission, making it much harder to protect than tangible objects. Access to information, including the difference in access between rich nations and poor nations, is also a topic in the field of information ethics.

—*Elizabeth Mohn*

References

Adams, Andrew A., Kiyoshi Murata, and Yohko Orito. "The Japanese Sense of Information Privacy." *AI & Society,* vol. 24, no. 4, 2009, pp. 327–41.

Bynum, Terrell. "Computer and Information Ethics." *Stanford Encyclopedia of Philosophy,* 2008, meinong.stanford.edu/entries/ethics-computer/index.html.

Froehlich, Thomas. "A Brief History of Information Ethics." *Biblioteconomia i Documentació Universitat de Barcelona,* 2004, bid.ub.edu/13froael2.htm.

Foundations of Information Ethics, edited by John T. F. Burgess and Emily J. M. Knox, ALA Neal-Schuman, 2019.

"Media Ethics." *Purdue Online Writing Lab,* owl.purdue.edu/owl/subject_specific_writing/journalism_and_journalistic_writing/media_ethics.html.

Muller, Vincent C. "Ethics of Artificial Intelligence and Robotics." *Stanford Encyclopedia of Philosophy,* 30 Apr. 2020, plato.stanford.edu/entries/ethics-ai/.

"News Values and Principles." *Associated Press,* 2021, www.ap.org/about/news-values-and-principles/.

Raval, Vasant. "Information Ethics: Information Ethics in the Mid-21st Century." *ISACA Journal,* vol. 6, 2016.

INFORMATION TECHNOLOGY

Introduction

Information technology is a discipline that stresses systems management, use of computer applications, and end-user services. Although information technology professionals need a good understanding of networking, program development, computer hardware, systems development, software engineering, website design, and database management, they do not need as complete an understanding of the theory of computer science as computer scientists do. Information technology professionals need a solid understanding of systems development and project management but do not need as extensive a background in this as information systems professionals. In contrast, information technology professionals need better interpersonal skills than computer science and information systems workers, as they often do extensive work with end users.

Information technology is a major discipline with ties to computer science, information systems, and software engineering. In general, information technology includes any expertise that helps create, modify, store, manage, or communicate information. It encompasses networking, systems management, program development, computer hardware, interface design, information assurance, systems integration, database management, and web technologies. Information technology places a special emphasis on solving user issues, including helping everyone learn to use computers in a secure and socially responsible way.

Background

During the second half of the twentieth century, the world moved from the industrial age to the computer age, culminating in the development of the World Wide Web in 1990. The huge success of the web as a means of communications marked a transition from the computer age, with an emphasis on technology, to the information age, with an emphasis on how technology enhances the use of information. In the early twenty-first century, the web is used in many ways to enhance the use and transfer of information, including telephone service, social networking, email, teleconferencing, and even radio and television programs. Information technology contains a set of tools that make it easier to create, organize, manage, exchange, and use information.

The first computers were developed during World War II as an extension of programmable calculating machines. John von Neumann added the stored program concept in 1944, and this set off the explosive growth in computer hardware and software during the remainder of the twentieth century. As computing power increased, those using the computers began to think less about the underlying technology and more about what the computers allowed them to do with data. In this way, information, the organization of data in a way that facilitates decision making, became what was important, not the technology that was used to obtain the data. By 1984, organizations such as the Data Processing Management Association introduced a model curriculum defining the training required to produce professionals in information systems management, and information systems professionals began to manage the information of government and business.

In 1990, computer scientist Tim Berners-Lee developed a web browser, and the web soon became the pervasive method of sharing information. In addition to businesses and governmental agencies, individuals became extensive users and organizers of information, using applications such as Google and Facebook. In the early 2000s, it became clear that a new computer professional, specializing in information management, was needed to complement the existing information systems professionals. By 2008, the Association of Computing Machinery and the IEEE Computer Society released their recommendations for educating information technology professionals, authenticating the existence of this new computing field.

The field of information technology has become one of the most active areas in computer science. The principal activity of information technology is the creation, storage, manipulation, and communication of information. To accomplish these activities, information technology professionals must have a background from a number of fields and be able to use a wide variety of techniques.

Networking and Web Systems

Information is stored and processed on computers. In addition, information is shared by computers over networks. Information technology professionals need to have a good working knowledge of computer and network systems to assist them in acquiring, maintaining, and managing these systems. Of the many tasks performed by information technology professionals, none is more important than installing, updating, and training others to use applications software. The web manages information by storing it on a server and distributing it to individuals using a browser, such as Google Chrome, Microsoft Edge, Firefox, or Safari. Building websites and applications is a major part of information technology and promises to increase in importance as more mobile devices access information provided by web services.

Component Integration and Programming

Writing programs in a traditional language such as Java continues to be an important task for information technology professionals, as it had been for other computer professionals in the past. However, building new applications from components using several web services appears to be poised to replace traditional programming. For all types of custom applications, the creation of a user-friendly interface is important. This includes the careful design of the screen elements so that applications are easy to use and have well thought-out input techniques, such as allowing digital camera and scanner input at the appropriate place in a program, as well as making sure the application is accessible to people with visual or hearing impairments.

Databases

Data storage is an important component of information technology. In the early days of computers, most information was stored in files. The difficulty of updating information derived from a file led to the first database systems, such as the information management system created by International Business Machines (IBM) in the 1960s. In the 1970s, relational databases became the dominant method of storing data, although a number of competing technologies are also in use. For example, many corporate data are stored in large spreadsheets, many personal data are kept in word-processing documents, and many web data are stored directly in web pages.

Information Security, Privacy, and Assurance

Regardless of how information is collected, stored, processed, or transferred, it needs to be secure. Information security techniques include developing security plans and policies, encrypting sensitive data during storage and transit, having good incident response and recovery teams, installing adequate security controls, and providing security training for all levels of an organization. In addition to making sure that an organization's data are secure, it is also important to operate the data management functions of an organization in such a way that each individual's personal data are released only to authorized parties. Increasingly, organizations want information handled in such a way that the organization can be assured that the data are accurate and have not been compromised.

End-User Support

One of the most important aspects of information technology is its emphasis on providing support for

247

a wide variety of computer users. In industrial, business, and educational environments, user support often starts immediately after someone is given access to a computer. An information technology professional assists the user with the login procedure and shows him or her how to use email and various applications. After this initial introduction, technology professionals at a help desk answer the user's questions. Some companies also provide training courses. When hardware and software problems develop, users contact the information technology professionals in the computer support department for assistance in correcting their problems.

The Electronic Medical Record (EMR)

A major use of information technology is in improving the operation of hospitals in providing medical services, maintaining flexible schedules, ensuring more accurate billing, and reducing the overall cost of operation. In much the same way, information technology helps doctors in clinics and individual practices improve the quality of their care, scheduling, billing, and operations. One of the early successes in using computers in medicine was the implementation of e-prescribing. Doctors can easily use the internet to determine the availability of a drug needed by a patient, electronically send the prescription to the correct pharmacy, and bill the patient, or their insurance company, for the prescription. Another success story for medical information technology is in the area of digital imaging. Most medical images are created digitally, and virtually all images are stored in a digital format.

Geographic Information Management (GIS)

Maps have been used by governments since the beginning of recorded history to help with the process of governing. Geographic information systems are computerized systems for the storage, retrieval, manipulation, analysis, and display of geographic data and maps. In the 1950s, the first GIS were used by government agencies to assist in activities such as planning, zoning, real estate sales, and highway construction. They were developed on mainframes and accessed by government employees on behalf of those desiring the information contained in the systems. The early GIS required substantial computing resources because they used large numbers of binary maps but were relatively simple as information retrieval systems.

Geographic information systems still serve the government, but they are also used by industry and educational institutions and have gained many applications, including the study of disease, flood control, census estimates, and oil discovery. Geographic information systems information is easily accessed over the internet. For example, zoning information about a particular city is often readily available from that city's website. Many general portals also provide GIS information to the public. For example, Google Maps allows travelers to map their routes on their portable devices and provides a curbside view of the destination. Twenty-first-century GISs are complex, layered software systems that require expertise to create and maintain.

Database Management

One of the major functions of information technology is the storage of information. Information consists of data organized for meaningful usage. Both data and information regarding how the data are related can be stored in many ways. For example, many corporate data are stored in word-processing documents, spreadsheets, and emails. Even more corporate data are stored in relational databases such as Oracle Database. Many businesses, educational institutions, and government agencies have database management specialists who spend most of their time determining the best logical and physical models for the storage of data.

Mobile Computing and the Cloud

Mobile phones and tablets have become so powerful that they rival computers, and web services and applications for computers or mobile devices are developed at a breathtaking rate. These two technological developments work together to provide many web applications for smartphones. Smartphones are capable of sharing all manner of data.

Cloud computing and storage has changed how people use computers in their homes. Rather than purchasing computers and software, some home users pay for computing as a service and store their data in an online repository. Numerous companies offer cloud storage, including Google, Apple, and Amazon.

Computer Integrated Manufacturing

Computer integrated manufacturing (CIM) provides complete support for the business analysis, engineering, manufacturing, and marketing of a manufactured item, such as a car. CIM has a number of key areas including computer-aided design (CAD), supply chain management, inventory control, and robotics.

Computer Security Management

One of the most active areas of information technology is that of computer security management. As theoretical computer scientists develop new techniques to protect computers, such as new encryption algorithms, information technology specialists work on better ways to implement these techniques to protect computers and computer networks. Learning how to acquire the proper hardware and software, to do a complete risk analysis, to write a good security policy, to test a computer network for vulnerabilities, and to accredit a business's securing of its computers requires all the talents of an information technologist. For information technology professionals specializing in end-user support, ensuring user compliance with security policies such as password requirements is particularly key.

Website Development

The World Wide Web was first introduced in 1990, and since that time, it has become the most important information distribution technology available. Information technology professionals are the backbone of most website development teams, providing support for the setup and maintenance of web servers, developing the hypertext markup language (HTML) pages and graphics that provide the web content, and assisting others in a company in getting their content on the web.

Social Context and Future Prospects

The growth in the use of the internet and mobile devices requires the support of robust networks, and this, in turn, will require a large number of information technology professionals to install, repair, update, and manage networks. The ever-increasing use of the internet and mobile devices also means that there will be a large number of new, less technically aware people trying to use the web and needing help provided by information technology end-user specialists.

The Future of Information Technology

A large number of new applications for information technology are being developed. One of the areas of development is in medical informatics. This includes the fine-tuning of existing hospital software systems, development of better clinical systems, and the integration of all of these systems. The United States and many other nations are committed to the development of a portable electronic health record for each person. The creation of these electronic health records is a massive information technology project and will require a large workforce of highly specialized information technology professionals.

The use of mobile devices to access computing from web services is another important area of information technology development. Web-based software and storage, or cloud computing, is increasingly becoming the dominant form of computing, which means more jobs for information technology professionals. Another important area of information technology is managing information in an ethical, legal, and secure way, while ensuring the privacy of the owners of the information. Security management specialists must work with network and database managers to ensure that the information being processed, transferred, and stored by organizations is properly handled. As technology use becomes increasingly ubiquitous, the ethical and other logistics of maintaining systems becomes increasingly important.

—George M. Whitson

References

Evans, Alan, Kendall Martin, and Mary Anne Poatsy. *Technology in Action.* 16th ed., Pearson, 2020.

O'Leary, Timothy, Linda O'Leary, and Daniel O'Leary. *Computing Essentials 2021.* McGraw-Hill, 2020.

Miller, Michael. *Cloud Computing: Web-Based Applications That Change the Way You Work and Collaborate.* Que Publishing, 2009.

Rainer, R. Kelly, Brad Prince, and Hugh J. Watson. *Management Information Systems: Moving Business Forward.* 4th ed., John Wiley & Sons, 2016.

Rains, Tim. *Cybersecurity Threats, Malware Trends, and Strategies.* Packt Publishing, 2020.

Senn, James. *Information Technology: Principles, Practices, and Opportunities.* 3rd ed., Prentice Hall, 2004.

Wager, Karen A., Frances W. Lee, and John P. Glaser. *Health Care Information Systems: A Practical Approach for Health Care Management.* 4th ed., Jossey-Bass, 2017.

INSTAGRAM

Introduction

Instagram (sometimes abbreviated as IG) is a photograph-sharing and social media mobile application (app) for smartphones and tablets that launched in October 2010. The app takes photos in a square shape, rather than the 4:3 aspect ratio typically found on smartphone cameras. Users can then apply filters to their photographs to achieve a desired look. Instagram also supports videos, which can last up to fifteen seconds. Users can then share their photographs or videos on other social media services such as Facebook and Twitter.

Instagram rapidly grew in popularity, seeing 1 million users within two months of its launch. Within four years, that number reached approximately 200 million active monthly users and 20 billion photos shared. As of January 2021, the app had 1 billion monthly active users (MAUs), making it even more popular than Twitter, and had been used to share more than 40 billion photos. To put the MAUs into perspective, that number is greater than the populations of North America and Europe combined.

Background

Software engineer Kevin Systrom developed the basis of Instagram while attending Stanford University in Stanford, California. After working a day job, Systrom learned how to code and built a hypertext markup language (HTML) prototype app called Burbn. This app allowed users to check in at locations, make plans, and earn points for hanging out with other users and posting pictures.

Systrom met backers from venture capital investment firms Baseline Ventures and Andreessen Horowitz. Two weeks after meeting with these investors, Systrom had raised $500,000. Engineer Mike Krieger was brought on as a partner, and a team of other engineers was assembled. Systrom and Krieger decided that if they wished to establish themselves as a legitimate company among the many other app developers, they would have to focus on their app performing one task very well. They chose to focus on the mobile photograph aspect of Burbn and spent eight weeks developing a new photography app, which they called Instagram, a combination of the words, "instant" and "telegram."

After beta testing and fixing some malfunctions of the app, Instagram was launched on October 6, 2010. Within hours, over ten thousand users had downloaded the app and by the end of the first week, it had over 100,000 downloads. By the end of 2010, over a million users were using the app. In February 2011, Instagram was valued at $20 million and was receiving a great amount of media coverage.

Investors continued to finance Instagram, and in April 2012 Facebook acquired the company for $1 billion in cash and stock. In 2021, Instagram had more than 2 billion active monthly users (MAUs), following Facebook's 2.91 MAUs. It is predicted that Instagram's revenue is projected to exceed 30 percent over the next year to attain over $17 billion.

Growing the App

For several years, Instagram went through only slight changes in its features. Users can take a photograph, add a filter to it to give it a desired effect, share it, and "like" and comment on other users' photographs. In June 2014, the app added ten new features so that users could modify their photographs even further.

These additional features allow users to adjust the contrast, brightness, and saturation of their photographs. In addition, they can also use a slide bar to adjust the intensity of the preset filters. For these additional features, Instagram engineers examined film cameras to study how light is affected by different lenses. In August 2014, Instagram introduced the Hyperlapse app, which allows users to post time-lapse videos.

In August 2015, through the company blog, Instagram announced its biggest change up until that point: support for the posting of images in a format other than those in a square shape. Despite the app's beginnings as a program dedicated to preserving the nostalgia of the historical square photograph format, the company acknowledged that a large number of photos are rectangular, causing frustrated users to turn to outside apps to format for posting. With this change, users can share both photos and videos in portrait and landscape orientation. Just as Facebook had changed its "feed" method in 2009, Instagram also followed suit in March 2016 and began testing an algorithm that arranges items in a user's feed according to photos users would most want to see based upon who they follow rather than in reverse chronological order.

In further recognition of such transformations, the app instituted another large and controversial alteration only weeks later when it presented a new logo. The company replaced its iconic retro camera logo with a more modern pink, purple, and orange logo, which a spokesperson explained is meant to capture the "diverse storytelling" for which the app has come to serve as a platform. These changes were met with mixed reviews from users and commentators.

After its launch, Instagram users quickly adapted the use of hashtags to enhance their photograph commenting. The hashtag is a word or words grouped together without spaces and prefixed with the hash (#) symbol. Users can then search for the hashtag on various social media networks and find posts concerning the topic.

One of the most popular hashtags used on Instagram is #selfie, a term for when people use their smartphone's camera to photograph themselves. By December 2014 more than 200 million photos on Instagram were tagged "#selfie." *The Oxford English Dictionary* even named "selfie" its 2013 word of the year. Numerous studies have been undertaken concerning their effect on ego and self-image. For example, some believe that since Instagram is image-driven, it can have a negative effect on self-esteem when users do not "like" a person's selfie.

Another prevalent hashtag is #TBT, an abbreviation for "Throwback Thursday." Using this hashtag, users post old photographs of themselves. Posting baby photographs is a popular practice with this hashtag. Other frequently used hashtags on Instagram include #WCW ("Woman Crush Wednesday," in which users post photographs of women they admire), #MCM ("Man Crush Monday," in which users post photographs of men they admire), and #blessed, in which users post photographs of people or things for which they feel grateful.

In 2016, Instagram introduced the ability to create Stories, collections of photos and videos that expire after a day. This functionality is similar to that of the app Snapchat, one of Instagram's competitors. The feature quickly became popular; Instagram stated in 2017 that over 250 million people used Stories every day.

Instagram announced in June 2018 that the company would soon be launching a long-form video hub similar to YouTube, which is advantageous for those people seeking to grow their social media influence and outreach. Consequently, numerous celebrities use Instagram, and many of them take frequent selfies, which some attribute to the rise in the hashtag's popularity. As of January 2022, the most popular celebrity accounts on Instagram were soccer player Cristiano Ronaldo, actor The Rock, singers Ariana Grande, Selena Gomez and Taylor Swift, and television personalities Kylie and Kim Kardashian. Celebrities commonly use their accounts to offer a glimpse into their private lives, communicate with fans, and promote causes they support.

Many major brands also use Instagram for marketing purposes. Retailers, restaurant chains, and sports teams are examples of some of the types of brands that widely use Instagram to market themselves. Ways of marketing that have been embraced on Instagram include posting behind-the-scenes photographs, holding contests in which users are asked to repost photographs and hashtags, promoting new products, and displaying customers using their products. In 2016, Instagram began adding "shoppable tags," small icons of a shopping bag appearing on advertising posts that users can click to find out how to buy products depicted in that post, to posts made by a small number of corporate partners. Use of shoppable tags expanded over the next several years, and in 2018 they were introduced into Stories.

Instagram has also made an impact on the world of photography. It widely popularized the art of photography and exposed people who did not regularly take photographs to it. While some see this as a positive movement, some professional photographers believe Instagram has undermined the true art of photography and created a homogenized brand of photograph.

In May 2017, a survey of nearly fifteen hundred people between the ages of fourteen and twenty-four, conducted by the UK Royal Society of Public Health, found that of all social networking apps, Instagram was the most detrimental for young people's mental health. The survey, called "#StatusofMind," reported that Instagram negatively affected body image (especially among young women) and sleep patterns and contributed to "fear of missing out," or FOMO, a term coined by Patrick McGinnis in 2004. The author of the survey report, Matt Keracher, noted that young women who use Instagram are more driven to "compare themselves against unrealistic, largely curated, filtered, and photoshopped versions of reality." In response, the report called for social media platforms to identify images that have been digitally altered. Despite these negative effects, however, the survey also found that Instagram had a positive effect on self-expression and self-identity for many of those surveyed.

In 2021, Instagram introduced Reels (to compete with TikTok). Users post fifteen-second videos for all sorts of information, entertainment, communication. This allows content creators to reach more users and to get out their messages and influence to larger and more engaged audiences.

—*Patrick G. Cooper and Laura Nicosia*

References

Aslam, Salman. "Instagram by the Numbers: Stats, Demographics & Fun Facts." *Omnicore*, 21 June 2017, www.omnicoreagency.com/instagram-statistics/.

Bevan, Kate. "Instagram Is Debasing Real Photography." *The Guardian*, 19 July 2012, www.theguardian.com/technology/2012/jul/19/instagram-debasing-real-photography

Bradford, Alina. "Everything You Need to Master Instagram Stories." *CNet*, 24 Apr. 2018, www.cnet.com/how-to/how-to-use-instagram-stories/.

Constine, Josh. "Instagram Plans June 20th Launch Event for Long-Form Video Hub." *TechCrunch*, 11 June 2018, techcrunch.com/2018/06/11/instagram-long-form-video/.

Constine, Josh, and Kim-Mai Cutler. "Facebook Buys Instagram for $1 Billion, Turns Budding Rival into Its Standalone Photo App." *TechCrunch*. AOL, 9 Apr. 2012, techcrunch.com/2012/04/09/facebook-to-acquire-instagram-for-1-billion/.

Coulthard, Charissa. "Self-Portraits and Social Media: The Rise of the 'Selfie.'" *BBC News*. BBC, 7 June 2013, www.bbc.com/news/magazine-22511650.

Dean, Brian. "Instagram Demographic Statistics: How Many Users Use Instagram in 2022?" *Backlinko*, 5 January 2022, backlinko.com/instagram-users.

Fox, Kara. "Instagram World Social Media App for Young People's Mental Health." *CNN.com*, 19 May 2017, www.cnn.com/2017/05/19/health/instagram-worst-social-network-app-young-people-mental-health/index.html.

Gillett, Rachel. "How the Most Successful Brands Dominate Instagram, and You Can Too." *Fast Company*. Mansueto Ventures, 22 Apr. 2014, www.fastcompany.com/3029395/how-the-most-successful-brands-dominate-instagram-and-you-can-too.

Hamburger, Ellis. "Instagram's New Editing Features Could Make It Your Only Photo App." *The Verge*. Vox Media, 3 June 2014, www.theverge.com/2014/6/3/5771860/instagram-new-editing-features-could-make-it-your-only-photo-app-vsco-cam-afterlight.

Hatmaker, Taylor. "Instagram Adds Shopping Tags Directly into Stories." *TechCrunch*, 12 June 2018, techcrunch.com/2018/06/12/instagram-adds-shopping-tags-directly-into-stories/.

"Instagram 2022—What You Need to Know!" *Lounge Lizard*, 8 Feb. 2022, loungelizard.com/blog/instagram-2022-what-you-need-to-know/.

Isaac, Mike. "Instagram May Change Your Feed, Personalizing It with an Algorithm." *The New York Times*, 15 Mar. 2016, www.nytimes.com/2016/03/16/technology/instagram-feed.html.

Leonard, Tom. "Instacash: The Nerds Who Made a Billion in 551 Days from Camera App." *Daily Mail Online*, 11 Apr. 2012, www.dailymail.co.uk/sciencetech/article-2128518/Instagram-The-nerds-billion-551-days-camera-app.html.

Markowitz, Eric. "How Instagram Grew from Foursquare Knock-Off to $1 Billion Photo Empire." *Inc.* Mansueto Ventures, 10 Apr. 2012, www.inc.com/eric-markowitz/life-and-times-of-instagram-the-complete-original-story.html.

Monckton, Paul. "Instagram Makes Biggest Ever Photo Changes." *Forbes*, 27 Aug. 2015, www.

forbes.com/sites/paulmonckton/2015/08/27/
instagram-makes-biggest-ever-photo-changes/.

Titcomb, James. "Instagram Is Changing Its Iconic
Logo—Here's Why." *The Telegraph*, 11 May 2016,
www.telegraph.co.uk/technology/2016/05/11/
instagram-is-changing-its-iconic-logo–heres-why/.

INSTRUCTIONAL DESIGN

Introduction

Instructional design (ID) can be defined as the systematic development of instructional specifications using learning theory to ensure the quality of instruction. It includes the analysis of learning needs and objectives and the development of a delivery system including instructional materials and activities to meet those objectives. In this digital age with online courses, Zoom meetings, web-based research, it is imperative that sound ID is implemented. Evaluation of all instruction and learner activities is central to the theory. Its main foundation is that of an objective-oriented model for managing the instructional process, which is rooted in theories that specify how high-quality instruction should be performed. A successful learning situation is one in which behavior goals are reached through mastery of a series of small steps or tasks which represent a larger objective. Each step or task is clearly defined and outcomes and activities are continually assessed to evaluate efficiency.

Instructional design theory has evolved over many decades and consists of several different models which can be applied to many types of learning situations. The concept of ID was adopted as a means of organizing learning and providing objective-based methodologies for conveying knowledge. Instructional Design theories and models are still changing over time, as educational philosophies and current trends in modern education evolve. This article presents an overview of the concept of ID in American education, and provides further insights into specific aspects of ID such as the behaviorist, programmed instruction, constructivist and direct instruction approaches which are still used in some form today. Instructional systems design is used in technological, computer and industrial learning for training in the rapidly changing environments of the modern information age.

Background

As a discipline, ID developed slowly from the time of Plato and Socrates to the philosophers of the seventeenth and eighteenth centuries. By the turn of the twentieth century, the concepts of learning theory and educational psychology were beginning to take form in modern thought. The turmoil of the first half of the twentieth century brought political and social changes which in turn encouraged new ways to look at the purpose and functions of our education system. By the 1950s, educational theories abounded, and ID was quickly adapted to many theories and models.

Theories that were used to approach ID were originally conceived in the military. During World War II, personnel had to be trained quickly and efficiently to perform their duties. Military researchers developed training films and corresponding programs to get the troops ready. The development of this task-oriented method of instructional technology spurred further research into the formulation of theoretical models of learning.

Influence of Behaviorism

The developers of early ID models were associated with the Behaviorist school of learning theory. Behaviorism looked at learning as a stimulus, response, and reinforcement process (S-R-R), first outlined by Ivan Pavlov's Classical Conditioning theory, and continued by B. F. Skinner. Such reactive behavior was documented in animals and adapted to human learning situations, positing that all behavior is explained by external events. The influence of behaviorism on learning led to a form of ID that incorporated immediate feedback and reinforcement with drill and practice procedures and programmed instruction that allowed the learner to repeat tasks that were not performed correctly until they were mastered. Behavioral outcomes were directly connected to instruction systems.

The 1950s in America were characterized by a huge economic boom that followed World War II. The launch of the Soviet satellite Sputnik triggered an education panic in the United States, prompting politicians and educators to send large amounts of federal money to research on education, especially concentrating on studies in cognition and instruction. In universities around the country, theoretical models of learning were being developed by educational theorists and psychologists such as B. F. Skinner and Benjamin Bloom.

Skinner's work in Operant Conditioning and Stimulus-Response-Reinforcement theory ultimately led to what is considered a first incarnation of ID, called programmed instruction (PI). Programmed instruction emphasized formulating behavioral objectives, breaking down instructional content into smaller units and rewarding correct responses early and often. Benjamin Bloom's 1956 taxonomy of educational objectives (Bloom's Taxonomy) and theory of mastery learning formed the basis of a standardized design process introduced by Robert Glaser in 1962. Glaser's model linked learner analysis to the design and development of instruction. His 'instructional systems' assessed students' entry-level behavior to determine the extent to which they would learn needed objectives. This not only tested the learners, but tested the learning system as well.

Also in 1962, Robert Mager developed the idea of Learning or Behavioral Objectives. His central concept was that training needs should be analyzed and the learning goals (objectives) of the program be defined. Each objective should then be broken down into smaller tasks. Each behavioral objective should have three criteria: behavior, condition and standard. In 1965 Robert Gagné introduced the Nine Events of Instruction, a series of distinct steps necessary for learning to occur. Gagné also introduced the concept of task analysis, previously used in military training, which broke each task to be mastered down to its most basic components, or subtasks. The theories of both of these scholars are still used today in modern ID systems.

Instructional Design in the Schools and Beyond

During the 1960s and 1970s, ID in one form or another was widely adopted in the public schools as the most effective teaching process available. Robert Morgan and Leslie Briggs conducted several studies which demonstrated that an instructionally designed course could yield up to a 2:1 increase over conventionally designed courses in terms of achievement, reduction in variance, and reduction of time-to-completion. This was four times greater than that of a control group which received no training. New

teachers were extensively trained in ID, primarily with the Behaviorist approach.

Instructional design models flourished in the 1970s and into the 1980s, with many researchers contributing to the field, such as Robert Branson and W. Dick and L. Carey. With the onset of the Information Age, many organizations established formal education and training departments to educate employees in the rapidly developing uses of computers and technology. Instructional design programs proved effective and efficient in introducing employees to new technological methods and concepts and training them to perform the new skills needed.

Instructional systems design (ISD), as the field is now sometimes called, has become a significant tool in the computer and technology training fields, as well as in computer-aided education in the schools. It has also been adopted in one form or another in corporate training programs for technical and other employees. Today, the ADDIE Model of ISD is widely used in all forms of instruction, particularly web-based and online computer instruction. Second to ADDIE is the Dick and Carey Model of ID, although it has recently been criticized as rigid.

Since the 1990s, the models have moved away from the behaviorist approach and adopted a constructivist approach to creating learning environments with less formal structure and facilitated by teachers. These are based on the theory of constructivism, which differs vastly from behaviorism in that it holds that knowledge is internal and tested by the individual in reality. Instructional design models in today's school classroom are vastly different from their behavioral roots, but still valuable tools for effective teaching.

Computer-Assisted Learning

With the increase in new media, especially the explosion of the internet, computer-assisted learning has become widely adopted in schools. Instructional design for computer-aided education has also evolved quickly. Originally, computer enhanced programs employed a basic Behaviorism-based approach with heavy emphasis on PI. Today, like in most classrooms, a constructivist approach has become the norm. One of the leading educational theorists in the computer-aided learning field is Seymour Papert. Known as the father of artificial intelligence

(AI), Papert has developed a learning approach called constructionism, an offshoot of constructivism. He was one of the first to bring information technology to the classroom. His Logo computer language and Massachusetts Institute of Technology (MIT) Media Lab are at the forefront of developing instruction for computer learning.

—*Karen A. Kallio*

References

Cates, W. M. "Instructional Technology: The Design Debate." *Clearing House,* vol. 66, 1993.

Chevalier, R. D. "When Did ADDIE Become Addie?" *Performance Improvement,* vol. 50, 2011, pp. 10–14.

Christie, N. V. "An Interpersonal Skills Learning Taxonomy for Program Evaluation Instructors." *Journal of Public Affairs Education,* vol. 18, 2012, pp. 739–56.

Gagné, Robert M., Leslie Briggs, and Walter W. Wager. *Principles of Instructional Design.* 4th ed., Harcourt Brace Jovanovich College Publishers, 1992.

Luebke, S., and J. Lorié. "Use of Bloom's Taxonomy in Developing Reading Comprehension Specifications." *Journal of Applied Testing Technology,* vol. 14, 2013, pp. 1–27.

Ryder, M. "Instructional Design Models: Instructional Technology Connections." www.carbon.cudenver.edu.

Shibley, I., K. E. Amaral, J. D. Shank, et al. "Designing a Blended Course: Using ADDIE to Guide Instructional Design." *Journal of College Science Teaching,* vol. 40, 2011, pp. 80–85.

Spector, J. M. "Philosophical Implications for the Design of Instruction." *Instructional Science,* vol. 29, no. 4/5, 2011, pp. 381–402.

Wiburg, K. M. "An Historical Perspective on Instructional Design: Is It Time to Exchange Skinner's Teaching Machine for Dewey's Toolbox?" *Internettime.com.*

INTELLECTUAL PROPERTY

Introduction

Intellectual property is the set of rules that governs creations of the mind, including, but not limited to, copyrights, patents, music, books, art, designs and more. Intellectual property may trigger privacy concerns in connection with aggregation and dissemination of personal information, database protection, freedom of speech under the First Amendment to the US Constitution, and liability of internet service providers (ISPs).

Background

Intellectual property rules grant monopolies over intellectual creations. Original works are protected by copyright law, whereas patent law protects inventions. In both cases, the creator or inventor is entitled to a bundle of exclusive rights, enabling him or her solely to control the use and distribution of the work or invention. This monopoly is limited in time, lasting for several decades after the life of the creator, or around twenty years since the invention was patented. This time limitation on copyright is why certain classic novels often revert to the public domain and become accessible without fees or prices.

Many of the international agreements that define the global design of current intellectual property regimes have been negotiated in connection with trade agreements. For this reason, many of the intellectual property norms and regulations that affect privacy rights are negotiated in trade arenas and reflect normative and policy choices designed to promote trade goals.

Privacy rights are at stake in situations in which intellectual property directly or indirectly affects access to proprietary information. This is the case of databases, or similar compilations of facts, which contain personal information. Aggregation of personal data can be conducted by private agents, with or without commercial purposes, or by the government. In the case of aggregation of data conducted by private agents, there has been a sharp rise in the economic exploitation of databases over the last two decades. Certain countries, especially in Europe, grant extensive intellectual property rights over databases or other compilations of facts. In the United States, the threshold for the ability to copyright compilations of facts is tied to requirements of minimal originality, which means that acquisition of monopolistic rights over compilations of personal information is subject to slightly more stringent standards.

Control over personal information is therefore affected by laws governing ownership of and access to databases or other compilations. When personal information enclosed in databases or compilations is transmitted, a potential clash might occur between intellectual property–created rights and privacy rights if the person to whom said information pertains is unaware of the transmission or is unable to prevent it. On the other end of the spectrum, intellectual property rights may help strengthen privacy in the sense that they grant ownership over information, making it harder for other parties to access proprietary content. From this viewpoint, the creation of layers of intellectual property protection over data may function as a deterrent against misappropriation of personal information by erecting legal barriers to access and/or use of personal information and nonpersonal information, such as copyrighted content.

The rise of digital technologies has significantly affected the relationship between content or data protection and privacy, especially where exchanges of copyrighted works in the online environment are concerned. Legal mechanisms entitling copyright holders to prevent unauthorized use or distribution of their works tend to require access to and sharing of personal data of individuals. In addition to copyright holders, ISPs play a relevant role in this process.

Liability of ISPs was regulated following several copyright infringement lawsuits when peer-to-peer technologies enabled the uploading and downloading of copyrighted works at almost no cost. Through peer-to-peer networks, users can easily share digital files containing film, music, or literary works protected by copyright law. When that sharing has not been authorized, copyright holders may request the internet protocol (IP) address of the infringing user from the ISP. The IP address, together with user information stored by the ISP, can be used to track and identify the user. In many cases, either the copyright holder or the ISP and the copyright holder jointly send cease and desist letters to reputedly infringing users, asking them to take down the material and informing them of their intention to enforce their rights.

Another area in which intellectual property interacts with privacy rights is regulation of freedom of speech, governed in the United States by the First Amendment to the US Constitution. The First Amendment shields one's ability to convey information without extraneous interference. Intellectual property, in the form of copyright law, protects creative speech through the grant of exclusive rights. For an extended period of time, the author of a copyrighted work possesses a wide array of control mechanisms over that work, including the ability to allow others to copy and distribute the work, with or without compensation, and the ability to prevent them from doing so.

Copyright law includes exceptions and limitations, however, that apply to situations in which part of the creative work may be copied regardless of the will of its author. Some of the most common situations include criticism, commentary, or parody. Many countries recognize situations of public interest in access to specific kinds of information as well. Political speech, in particular, or works conveying the personal (and, in some cases, even private) opinions of political figures may override copyright-based monopolies, meaning that parts of the work might be copied, reprinted, or circulated by others. In these and similar situations, privacy expectations and privacy rights may recede to favor freedom of speech or other copyright-sanctioned goals.

Because of the historical connection between intellectual property and trade, many of the negotiations of privacy-related aspects of intellectual property are connected to sweeping trade agreements. These agreements—which seek, for instance, to impose more stringent sanctions for intellectual property violations, including seizure and destruction of suspected counterfeit or pirated goods—also regulate subjects that may directly affect privacy rights, especially in the case of unlawful uses of copyrighted works in the digital environment.

One of the most salient examples of this was the negotiation process surrounding the Anti-Counterfeiting Trade Agreement (ACTA), a multilateral agreement on enforcement of intellectual property rights that set forth international standards to address the problems raised by piracy and counterfeiting, and regulated ex novo the enforcement of intellectual property rights in the digital environment. ACTA was also one of the first instances of international regulation of intellectual property in which privacy and data protection were explicitly mentioned.

This is a major departure from classical normative approaches to international intellectual property because neither the Paris Convention on patents nor the Berne Convention on copyrights covered those issues. While one of ACTA's main goals was to promote expeditious identification and disclosure of the identity of internet users suspected of copyright infringement, it also urged countries to preserve privacy rights. This requirement was generically anchored, however, on observance of fundamental principles, such as the principle of proportionality in implementing ACTA provisions, which does not detract significantly from the core obligations surrounding user identification in the online environment. The emphasis on expeditious identification of the personal information of internet users is one of the constants around which contemporary regulation of digital intellectual property revolves.

The association between copyright ownership and the ability to seek and obtain information about the identity of users, an ability that emerged with the democratization of internet access, may also bring about other kinds of chilling effects that touch on privacy. As laws permit identification of supposedly infringing users of copyrighted content, there might be cases in which the wrong user is identified. Another possibility is that a user might be identified following a request by a copyright holder, but because no determination has been made as to the actual unlawfulness of the use of the copyrighted work, it is possible that the use in question might have been permissible under applicable copyright laws. In addition to peer-to-peer networks, the growth and popularization of social media, among other types of platforms that enable online dissemination of content, has greatly expanded the number of internet users that may be subject to identification by copyright holders and/or ISPs.

Social media are digital platforms, such as Facebook or YouTube, which enable users to share information electronically. Copyright protects a significant amount of content currently shared on social media. When that sharing has not been authorized, the rights holder may request the disclosure of the identity of a specific internet user through a process similar to the one applicable to peer-to-peer exchanges. Unlike peer-to-peer platforms, whose relevance has faded, the exponential expansion of social media over the last decade has given popular social media an extra incentive to monitor user activity to avoid costly copyright litigation, which in turn raises further concerns about privacy rights in cyberspace.

—*Ana Santos Rutschman*

References

Marlin-Bennett, Renée. *Knowledge Power: Intellectual Property, Information, and Privacy*. Lynne Rienner, 2004.

Moore, Adam, editor. *Information Ethics: Privacy, Property, and Power*. U of Washington P, 2005.

Samuelson, Pamela. "Privacy as Intellectual Property?" *First Amendment Handbook*, edited by James L. Swanson, C. Boardman, 2002.

Silva, Alberto J. Cerda. "Enforcing Intellectual Property Rights by Diminishing Privacy: How the Anti-Counterfeiting Trade Agreement Jeopardizes the Right to Privacy." *American University International Law Review*, vol. 26, no. 3, 2011, pp. 601–43.

Zittrain, Jonathan. "What the Publisher Can Teach the Patient: Intellectual Property and Privacy in an Era of Trusted Privication." (Symposium: Cyberspace and Privacy: A New Legal Paradigm?) *Stanford Law Review*, vol. 52, no. 5, May 2000, pp. 1201–50.

INTELLIGENT TUTORING SYSTEMS

Introduction

Intelligent tutoring systems (ITS) are computer-based training programs that use artificial intelligence (AI) to tailor multimedia learning by providing individualized instruction. Intelligent tutoring systems tries to imitate the help that a live tutor would provide to an individual student. Intelligent tutoring systems offer a way to identify, remediate, and track all students separately. The goal of

ITS is to provide the benefits of individualized instruction without the cost and time it takes to provide personalized instruction with teachers.

Background

The concept of ITS has been studied for more than thirty years by researchers in education, psychology, and AI. Schools and universities have been looking for ways to increase learning for students and improve test scores. Since computer technologies have made their ways into both homes and schools, computer tutoring systems are viewed as a potential solution to this problem.

In the early 1990s, Jay Liebowitz imagined a world in which students of all grade levels and abilities used video-conferencing in schools, employed voice-activated programs, and enrolled in distance learning courses. It turns out he was right. By the early years of the twenty-first century, Intelligent Tutoring Systems were providing interactive instruction to support K-12 education, college education, corporate training and military preparation.

What Are Intelligent Tutoring Systems?

Intelligent tutoring systems are computer-based training programs that use AI to tailor multimedia learning by providing individualized instruction. They are also referred to as intelligent computer-aided instruction (ICAI) and have been a breakthrough in the field of instructional technology. Before, ITS, computer-based training (CBT) and computer aided instruction (CAI) were the only computer teaching systems. In systems like these, the directions were not specified to meet the individual needs of each learner, and transitioning a student through the material was formulaic and inflexible. Prior knowledge and learning style were not considered. As a result, their impact on learning was mediocre.

Intelligent tutor systems are more advanced, allowing learners to hone their abilities by completing assignments within interactive academic settings. Intelligent tutor systems can answer questions and provide personalized assistance to the learner. Intelligent tutor systems, unlike other educational technologies, evaluate every student's response to assess his/her knowledge and skills. Intelligent tutor systems can then modify instructional strategies, give explanations, examples, demonstrations, and practice exercises where necessary. Intelligent tutor

systems offer more options in the presentation of material and have the capability to specialize information to cater to a student's needs.

The typical ITS model does the following:

- Identifies learning objectives and their context
- Acknowledges gaps in individual student's knowledge
- Trains each student according to the areas in which they lack knowledge
- Guides the student through the relevant parts of the book, or provided material
- Assesses students on the learning objectives
- Gives the student feedback on his/her responses and provides explanation as to why an answer is correct or incorrect
- Provides each student with more questions in the specific areas where they lack knowledge.

The inception of the No Child Left Behind Act put pressure on schools to deliver high-quality instruction to all their students. As a result, schools were trying to utilize technological advancements such as ITS to teach their subjects, practice tests, and track progress. Intelligent tutoring systems provide motivation, modeling, interactivity, feedback, and consistency like no other tool before.

Why Use Intelligent Tutoring Systems?

Many academic courses are attended by a heterogeneous group of students who have come from different backgrounds and have attended different courses in the past; some even speak in different languages. Some students may simply be at varying skill levels. Effectively teaching a heterogeneous student population is a challenge in education because most traditional methods target the average student. This is a definite disadvantage for advanced students, students with disabilities, and students who lack certain prior knowledge.

Unfortunately, class sizes and instructor loads often make it impossible for teachers to tutor every student individually. Intelligent tutoring systems try to imitate the help that a live tutor would provide to an individual student. Intelligent tutoring systems offer a way to identify, remediate, and track all students separately.

The primary initiative of ITS is giving personalized instruction without the cost and time it takes to provide personalized instruction with teachers. Intelligent tutoring systems can be thought of as a virtual training assistant that collects the wisdom and experience of trained teaching professionals and distributes the content to students electronically. Adaptive ITS may help to support learning for a heterogeneous group of students.

Research on prototype ITS indicated that students who used ITS generally learned faster and demonstrated improved performance compared to classroom-trained participants. In the 1980s, Benjamin Bloom determined "that students who receive one-on-one instruction perform two standard deviations better than students who receive traditional classroom instruction. An improvement of two standard deviations means that the student performed in the top 2 percent of those receiving instruction."

In a more recent study conducted at Carnegie Mellon University, college students used an ITS called the LISP Tutor to learn computer programming skills. "Students who used the ITS scored 43 percent higher on the final exam than the control group." In addition, the control group needed 30 percent more time to solve complex programming problems. In another example, students using Smithtown, an ITS for economics, did not perform better than students in a traditional learning environment, but they required less time to cover the material Performance was equal but more efficient.

In 2011, Vanlehn compared computer tutors and human tutors for their impact on learning gains, particularly focusing on experiments that compared one type of tutoring to another while attempting to control all other variables, such as the content and duration of the instruction. He concluded that students should use ITS instead of seatwork or homework since ITS seems to be as effective as human tutors. However, Vanlehn also concluded that the traditional, face-to-face classroom experience is still the superior environment for the best learning.

How Intelligent Tutoring Systems Work

Many traditional teaching methods introduce learners to facts and concepts and follow up with test questions to assess understanding. "These methods are effective in exposing people to large amounts of information and testing their recall but learners often" are not taught how to correctly apply their new knowledge. By contrast, ITS uses highly interactive learning environments, including simulations, that require students to use the skills they have just acquired. This type of learning is effective in helping students retain and apply knowledge more effectively in the future.

To provide such specialized guidance to students, ITS typically uses three kinds of knowledge, arranged into the following software components:

- The expert model (also known as the "domain model")
- The student model
- The instructor model (also known as the "adaptive or pedagogical model").

"The expert model represents subject matter expertise and provides the ITS with knowledge of what it's teaching." The student model shows the student what he or she knows as well as what he or she has yet to learn, letting the system know what type of learner it is teaching. The instructor model uses information from the other two models and assembles appropriate content and provides the necessary instructional strategies through the ITS user interface.

The Expert Model

The expert model is the backbone of the ITS structure. It possesses the content that the instructor is teaching. The knowledge in the expert model provides the system with information with which to compare the learner's selections so that the ITS can evaluate the learner's previous knowledge as well as the knowledge gained using the system. For that purpose, the expert model is more than just a representation of data; it is a prototype of how someone skilled in a subject area applies knowledge This allows the ITS to more accurately pinpoint a learner's problem areas.

The Student Model

By maintaining a record of each user's skills and drawbacks, the ITS can provide effective, individualized instruction. The student model keeps its individualized content in its electronic storage, allowing for easy access to each user The information gathered shows what the system sees as the learner's current skill level. For the learner to achieve training, the student model should improve for each learning objective with which the user is presented and after a user completes a module, the student model should be on a satisfactory level for each learning objective.

A student model should contain a record of the student's understanding of the material, as well as more general information about the student such as learning preferences, acquisition and retention. Acquisition calculates the time it takes for students to learn new material. Retention evaluates the recall of the learning content over time. A more intuitive ITS, such as the one used in Naval Officer training, can monitor student's electronic actions to determine where his or her level of comprehension lies. That system uses "pattern matching to detect sequences of actions that track whether the student does or doesn't understand."

The Instructor Model

The instructor model provides the instructional strategies that are determined to be most effective for teaching the assigned material to "the learner based on its knowledge of the user's strengths and weaknesses and preferred learning styles." One concern for the instructor model of "an ITS is the selection of a meta strategy for teaching the domain. For example, the system could decide to use the Socratic method or it could select a series of problem-solving examples."

This component uses data from the student model to provide an appropriate model for teaching the specific user types of information that are regulated by the instructor model are when to review, "when to present a new topic, and which topic to present" If a student was determined to be a novice in a certain area of instruction, then this model might include a review or show a step-by-step demonstration before asking the student to apply his or her own knowledge.

The instructor model may also give constructive feedback and detailed coaching while the learner complete relevant exercises. As a learner develops his/her skills, the instructor model may scale back on hints and examples and present increase the complexity of the exercises.

Types of ITS Instruction

Recent work in organizing information has been derived from the idea that instructional goals should vary according to the type of information learned. In addition to this, goals should be set with regards to what the student will be able to do when they complete the lesson.

Most ITS interactions tend to focus on teaching procedural skills. The instructional aim is for learners to complete a certain task Systems designed with this objective are often called cognitive tutors. They are usually structured around a set of guidelines that are part of the expert model. This set of expert rules also can serve as the knowledge domain for the instructor model. If a student approaches difficult or trying questions, the expert model can determine the most effective way to assist Many systems try to teach procedures by taking on the appearance and manner of a real educational environment A simulated learning environment can help improve the benefits of educational training and diminish the costs

Contrary to the simulation-based tutors are the teachers of information that lies outside of the real-world context. These ITS focus on teaching concepts. These systems are referred to as knowledge-based tutors and require more substantial domain knowledge. They promote complex problems that the student can solve without requiring a connection to real life issues. Intelligent tutoring systems of this type use general teaching strategies and emphasize the explication and presentation system to accomplish educational objectives. They are arranged to provide students with abstract knowledge that can correlate with other, future situations.

Challenges Associated with Intelligent Tutoring Systems

Intelligent tutors are available but not used as much as Jay Liebowitz had predicted in *The Explosion of Intelligent Systems by the Year 2000* due to the labor-intensive programming required to effectively and intuitively deliver course material. Development of ITS are not only time-consuming but require specific knowledge and advanced computer skills. This can take months or years and often a design team is necessary to create a successful system.

Ansari and Sykes proposed the use of "enthymemes," a manner of presenting a deductive argument, in programming tutors and suggest that the framework of an ITS could benefit greatly by incorporating enthymemes in the transfer of knowledge to the interactive users of such systems. The study authors assert that "by including enthymemes and transformation rules, Intelligent Tutoring Systems may in the near future offer what they have always intended to do—provide personalized instruction comparable to a domain expert tutor."

Another challenge with ITS is that is limited in terms of communication with the user Therefore, it is difficult to get an accurate representation of learner's abilities and progress. As a result, the student model of the ITS may not be accurate. An ITS that has misread a learner's abilities may offer too much assistance to a learner who is performing satisfactorily and vice versa. Yet, even an imperfect student model can be valuable in tailoring education methods to a student's individual abilities. This is what happened with earlier CBT and CAI systems, which could not individualize instruction.

One of the biggest challenges with using ITS is responding to the user's request for assistance. "When faced with a problem, the student must wait for help from technical support or an online instructor who may take a long time to respond."

While the potential for using ITS in schools and other learning environments continues to grow, there are limits to what can be achieved. There can be inconsistencies in operating systems, technology support, and computer literacy among students. In addition, sociological, political, and economic variables influence the effect of ITS on the learning environment. All these factors can affect the success or failure rates of ITS in schools.

Potential Solutions

A common alternative to the expensive process of customizing ITS is to allow instructors or schools to supply much of the knowledge needed to achieve learning goals. This method avoids having to cover all possible problems in an ITS. Rather, it needs only a way to indicate that what the learner needs to know is corresponding with how to apply the knowledge in real setting.

Authoring tools are a great technology to help make customizing ITS easier and more efficient. The goal of authoring tools is to allows educators to use a basic development shell to author their own course material within an ITS and to allow programmers to input more to the expert, student and instructor models. Effective authoring tools could empower teachers to have more control over the material presented and would allow them to quickly modify and update material as needed. It would also allow fewer developers to design software.

Although the planning and implementation phase of ITS development can be time-consuming, research has shown that, once designed, ITS can help minimize an instructor's workload compared to face-to-face instruction.

Technologies for learning environments are a vital tool for the ever-changing field of education. Computer-based tutoring programs have been designed to model direct instruction while using the technical ability to provide effective feedback, remediation, and guided practice to all learners. Intelligent tutoring systems have proven their extreme efficiency and aid in increasing student education. In addition to developing and enhancing systems, an important consideration in the advancement of ITS is reducing development time and expense Solving this problem would allow more systems to be created and could redirect research foci on how to make ITS more effective. The current emphasis on standardized testing and accountability has created opportunities for ITS to enhance traditional instruction and maximize both the learner and the educator's time.

—*Jennifer Bouchard*

References

Ansari, S., and E. R. Sykes. "Towards Smarter Intelligent Tutoring Systems: A Proposal for the Inclusion of Enthymemes in Their Design." *Technology, Instruction, Cognition & Learning*, vol. 9, no. 1/2, 2012, pp. 9–29.

Gong, Y., J. E. Beck, and N. T. Heffernan. "How to Construct More Accurate Student Models: Comparing and Optimizing Knowledge Tracing and Performance Factor Analysis." *International Journal of Artificial Intelligence in Education*, vol. 21, no. 1/2, 2011, pp. 27–46.

Karlin, S. "Futurist Liebowitz Looks at Tomorrow's Schools Today." *American School Board Journal*, vol. 194, 2007, p. 36.

Magliaro, S., B. Lockez, and J. Burton. "Direct Instruction Revisited: A Key Model for Instructional Technology." *Educational Technology Research & Development*, vol. 53, 2005, pp. 41–55.

Montalvo, G. "Online Design Elements: Improving Student Success and Minimizing Instructor Load." *Mid-Western Educational Researcher*, vol. 19, 2006, pp. 35–39.

Scandura, J. M. "Comments on Ansari & Sykes and Gogus, and Suggestions for Future Research."

Technology, Instruction, Cognition & Learning, vol. 9, no. 1/2, 2012, pp. 51–56.

Sessink, O., H. Beeftink, J. Tramper, et al. "Proteus: A Lecturer-Friendly Adaptive Tutoring System." *Journal of Interactive Learning Research,* vol. 18, 2007, pp. 533–54.

Troussas, C. C., and M. M. Virvou. "Information Theoretic Clustering for an Intelligent Multilingual Tutoring System." *International Journal of Emerging Technologies in Learning,* vol. 8, 2013, pp. 55–61.

Vanlehn, K. "The Relative Effectiveness of Human Tutoring, Intelligent Tutoring Systems, and Other Tutoring Systems." *Educational Psychologist,* vol. 46, 2011, pp. 197–221.

Wijekumar, K. "Implementing Web-Based Intelligent Tutoring Systems in K-12 Settings: A Case Study on Approach and Challenges." *Journal of Educational Technology Systems,* vol. 35, 2006, pp. 193–208.

INTERNET PRIVACY

Introduction

Among the considerations of privacy include privacy as a social value, privacy as a democratic value, privacy as a human right, and privacy as data protection. Although the latter seems like the only one explicitly concerned with the online world, all are important. In general, internet or online privacy is less about hiding and concealment and more about personal autonomy and the power to determine the intimacy levels of one's relationships (as mediated by the internet).

Background

In April 2013 in Nova Scotia, Canada, a young woman named Rehtaeh Parsons committed suicide after four young men allegedly sexually assaulted her and distributed explicit pictures of the act online. This brought the issue of cyberbullying to the forefront in Canada, although it also carries clear implications for the state of online privacy. In the last several years, coverage of people fired for their social media activities has almost become a genre of journalism unto itself. These terminated employees include teachers who used social media to post photos their employers deemed inappropriate, and fast-food workers who posted photos of mishandled food that was then served to customers. While the latter is not a new phenomenon, the documentation and broadcast of such acts is. With the profusion and rapid diffusion of social networks such as Facebook, Twitter, Instagram, Snapchat, and YouTube, the "making public" of one's self has reached new heights and created problems with privacy as well as implications affecting mental health, law, business, politics, and security.

Online social networks enable the sharing of text, images, sound files, and video files instantly. Because most cell phones are equipped to create some, if not all, of these types of files, no "live" moment is spared the potential for broadcast online. While the motivations for sharing these files are often well-intentioned, the potentially negative and harmful consequences are often given little thought.

The mobility of internetworked multimedia means that phenomena previously called "private," such as family photography, now have a public dimension once shared on social media. Facial recognition technology, global positioning systems (GPS), and personal information disclosure (i.e., demographics) enables "re-identification," whereby sets of data without personal information (legal name, address, birth date) can be connected to data with clear identifiers through common attributes. Information revealed via social media leaves users vulnerable to risks such as stalking, state surveillance and targeting, identity theft and related forms of fraud, employer surveillance, and harassment by unwanted solicitors.

The predominant business model for social media cashes in on personal information that is collected and then often sold to marketers. In the early days of social media, very few users took advantage of privacy options, although awareness campaigns and lobbying efforts of organizations such as the American Civil Liberties Union (ACLU) have improved the situation somewhat. Also, public pressure on services such as Facebook has made them revamp the privacy section of users' profiles. Often social media sites discourage the use of heightened privacy settings by putting the word "recommended" beside lower privacy settings.

Overview

Governments and technologists have begun to address privacy concerns in the online world. Some browsers include a do-not-track feature that reduce a user's data trails, although these are by no means foolproof. In the United States, the Federal Trade Commission (FTC) filed a report in December 2010 recommending a new regulatory framework for consumer privacy, which would include a do-not-track mechanism to allow internet users to opt out of behavioral advertising entirely. Subsequently, a number of bills were introduced in Congress to restrict user tracking by websites and advertisers, by Democrats and Republicans alike, some of which incorporated the FTC's recommendations. Many consider privacy an essential feature of democracy to maintain individual autonomy and lament its erosion in a networked environment.

Another online privacy issue that has emerged recently is the livestreaming of closed-circuit television (CCTV) surveillance cameras. The British-based website Internet Eyes, for example, functions as a node where policing, business, and the public at large intersect. Users watch CCTV and are paid for alerting police and businesses to crimes such as shoplifting and burglaries. What services such as this lack is consideration for the privacy of the majority of people not committing crimes, although their proponents contend such services reduce crime and associated risks. In addition, some technologists have hacked into CCTV networks and streamed their cameras online for entertainment purposes. New technologies, such as forward-looking infrared cameras, also allow state agencies to circumvent traditional barriers, such as search warrants, to access private spaces.

The awareness of social media practices can have an inhibitory effect on personal conduct for some, and self-censorship is one of the results. Indeed, psychologists have identified a new neurosis that could never have existed without technological media, the "Truman Show syndrome," which is named after the 1998 movie about a television show that secretly broadcast all the details of one man's life without his consent or awareness.

Social media is also a source for marketers and advertisers to glean information on consumers' personal tastes and interests. In 2015, the *Wall Street Journal* reported that the United States and six European nations strongly objected to Facebook's use of user monitoring for the sole purpose of tracking user browser habits. This monitoring in turn would influence advertising displayed to consumers. Consumer tracking and data sharing has been commonplace among internet marketers and advertisers for many years, but the tactics used by Facebook and other online sources are often viewed by consumers as overly aggressive, and antitracking technologies are becoming more and more popular.

In February 2015, news broke that Samsung was warning consumers to be careful what they said aloud in front of their Smart TVs because any and all spoken information had the potential to be recorded and then supplied to a third party, admitting that the television would eavesdrop on private conversations. (A "smart" TV is any television with internet capabilities.) The US Senate got involved and questioned both Samsung and LG regarding their privacy and data sharing policies. Samsung responded that speech-to-text information would only be gathered when the consumer pressed an activation button on the remote control. The company also provided the public with directions on disabling the voice-recognition feature in the televisions, thereby disengaging the television's ability to recognize and record voice commands in any form.

Data Security

Another element of online privacy is data security, and in many places the security of people's health information is increasingly put in jeopardy. Multiple Canadians have been refused entry to the United States by US border guards because information related to their mental health, such as attempted suicides and certain forms of psychiatric care, had been uploaded to the Canadian Police Information Centre (CPIC), to which US federal law enforcement officials have access. To one such woman, who was denied entry in 2013 because she had previously been hospitalized for clinical depression, the guard "cited the US Immigration and Nationality Act, which denies entry to people who have had a physical or mental disorder that may pose a 'threat to the property, safety or welfare' of themselves or others," according to a report on the CBC News website.

The Future of Privacy

The future promises many more challenges to privacy in the online world. The emergence of internet-enabled objects (such as keys that contact their owners automatically if they turn up in an unusual or unexpected location) will most likely present a new onslaught of privacy concerns. The US National Security Agency (NSA) has developed and launched a program called QUANTUM that can turn any online communication into an attack vector in information warfare. The agency devised the means to intercept any message sent online through internet traffic routers in the United States and send falsified responses, making the target act on such responses as if they came from a real person.

In October 2016, near the end of US president Barack Obama's final term, the US Federal Communications Commission (FCC) issued new rules that would require internet service providers (ISPs) to obtain customer approval before selling their browsing data to advertisers and other third parties. The rules, titled "Protecting the Privacy of Customers of Broadband and Other Telecommunication Services" in their final form, were intended to take effect near the end of 2017. However, a bill to repeal the new rules was passed by the Republican-dominated Congress in March 2017 and was signed into law by new president Donald Trump at the beginning of April. Because oversight of ISPs had been transferred from the FTC to the FCC, the latter having declared ISPs to be common telecommunications carriers in 2015 in an effort to preserve net neutrality, the repeal of the FCC rules left the ability of ISPs to collect and disseminate consumer data largely unregulated.

In early 2018, a scandal broke involving the security of user information on Facebook that caused further discussion regarding internet privacy. After nearly three hundred thousand users of the social media site took part in what was believed to be a personality survey in 2014 and it was discovered that data obtained from that survey (which was estimated to have involved more than fifty million users and their friends) was then sold to the data research firm Cambridge Analytica and was possibly used to target political advertising during the 2016 presidential election, questions were raised about Facebook's commitment to protecting its users' data.

Cybercrime

Cybercrime is on the rise and the potential consequences can be disastrous for individuals and businesses. Attacks on e-commerce sites are on the rise exponentially; according to Justin Lee for the Whir,

between 2010 and 2011, e-commerce sites saw a 153 percent increase in attacks during the winter holiday season. In 2012, over 90 percent of organizations had reported some loss of sensitive or confidential data and information over the preceding twelve-month period. One strategy that businesses use to protect user and company information and safeguard internet privacy is defense in depth, which utilizes the capabilities of current available technology to guard against and monitor intrusions. Security measures are multilayered and intended to thwart an attack, slow down an attack that is not thwarted, and in turn accelerate the detection of and response to the attack.

Firewalls are another method to protect privacy. Firewalls are special-purpose software programs or pieces of computer hardware that are designed to prevent unauthorized access to a private network from the internet, or to the internet from a private network.

—Trevor Cunnington

References

Bennett, Colin J., and Rebecca Grant, editors. *Visions of Privacy: Policy Choices for the Digital Age.* U of Toronto P, 1999.

Bernal, Paul. *Internet Privacy Rights: Rights to Protect Autonomy.* Cambridge UP, 2014.

"Canadians' Mental-Health Info Routinely Shared with FBI, US Customs." *CBC News.* CBC/Radio-Canada, 14 Apr. 2014, www.cbc.ca/news/canada/windsor/canadians-mental-health-info-routinely-shared-with-fbi-u-s-customs-1.2609159.

Derene, Glenn. "Samsung, LG, and Vizio Smart TVs Are Recording—and Sharing Data about—Everything You Watch." *Consumer Reports,* 27 Feb. 2015, www.consumerreports.org/cro/news/2015/02/samsung-lg-vizio-smart-tvs-watch-everything-you-watch/index.htm.

Erramilli, Vijay. "The Tussle around Online Privacy." *IEEE Internet Computing,* vol. 16, no. 4, 2012, pp. 69–71.

Friedewald, Michael, and Ronald J. Pohoryles, editors. *Privacy and Security in the Digital Age.* Routledge, 2014.

Granville, Kevin. "Facebook and Cambridge Analytica: What You Need to Know as Fallout Widens." *The New York Times,* 19 Mar. 2018, www.

nytimes.com/2018/03/19/technology/facebook-cambridge-analytica-explained.html.

Gross, Ralph, and Alessandro Acquisti. "Information Revelation and Privacy in Online Social Networks." *WPES '05: Proceedings of the 2005 ACM Workshop on Privacy in the Electronic Society; November 7, 2005, Alexandria, Virginia, USA (Co-located with CCS 2005)*, edited by Sabrina De Capitani di Vimercati and Roger Dingledine, ACM Press, 2005, pp. 71–80.

Humphries, Matthew. "Internet Eyes Will Pay You to Watch Security Camera Feeds." *Geek.com*, Ziff Davis, 6 Oct. 2010, www.geek.com/news/internet-eyes-will-pay-you-to-watch-security-camera-feeds-1288416/.

Lee, Justin. "Prolexic Study Offers E-Commerce Website Strategies to Combat Holiday DDoS Attacks." *The Whir*. Penton, 29 Oct. 2012, www.thewhir.com/web-hosting-news/prolexic-study-offers-e-commerce-website-strategies-to-combat-holiday-ddos-attacks.

Pressman, Aaron. "What Really Happens When the FCC's Online Privacy Rules Are Cancelled." *Fortune*, 3 Apr. 2017, fortune.com/2017/04/03/fcc-online-privacy-faq/.

Schechner, Sam. "Facebook Privacy Controls Face Scrutiny in Europe." *The Wall Street Journal*, 2 Apr. 2015, www.wsj.com/articles/facebook-confronts-european-probes-1427975994.

Sweeney, Latanya. "k-Anonymity: A Model for Protecting Privacy." *International Journal of Uncertainty, Fuzziness and Knowledge-Based Systems*, vol. 10, no. 5, 2002, pp. 557–70.

Trepte, Sabine, and Leonard Reinecke, editors. *Privacy Online: Perspectives on Privacy and Self-Disclosure in the Social Web*. Springer, 2011.

INTERNET SAFETY

Introduction

Internet usage has exploded among children and adolescents in recent years as the medium provides them with both educational and social opportunities. According to the Child Trends Data Bank, in 2003, approximately 76 percent of children had access to a computer at home; by 2021, that figure had increased to 95 percent according to the National Center for Education Statistics. Additionally, children with access to the internet in the home rose from 42 percent in 2003 to 62 percent in 2012. Of these users, just 10 percent report using the computers for reading magazines or newspapers online, while the remainder play games or watch videos. Child Trends further reports that according to their 2009 survey, 36 percent of children report having a computer with internet access in their bedroom and spend almost ninety minutes (in addition to schoolwork) per day with a computer. This figure is up from just over sixty minutes in 2004.

Besides keeping an eye on the content that kids access, parents and educators should also be aware of what kids do and say online so that they do not compromise their privacy or safety. Over the past few years, social networking sites like Twitter, Facebook, and Pinterest have become enormously popular among teenagers. Facebook, in particular, has grown at an enormous rate and reported 1.39 billion monthly active users in 2014. These sites can offer many benefits to their users, but some teens may not take sufficient care in protecting their privacy or may find themselves exposed to inappropriate content. Parents and educators can use internet control software to block youths from accessing inappropriate content, but they should also be sure to educate themselves and their children or students about internet safety.

Background

The internet can be an extremely useful tool at home and in the classroom, but parents and schools must be careful to monitor children's and adolescents' online activities. The internet does not house more predators than the real world, but online there are fewer visual or auditory warning signs to alert a teen that a person may be dangerous. People may not be who they say they are, and many experts advise parents to limit their children's online friends to their real-life friends. Children and teens can easily be exposed to online victimization, or situations in which they encounter intimidating and inappropriate sexual content, solicitation, or harassment.

Though millions of people who use social networking sites are harmless, some are sexual predators. The nonprofit internet safety organization, Enough is Enough, offers some sobering insights into online predators:

- Eighteen percent of young people use chat rooms to interact with other youth, but the majority of internet-initiated sex crimes against children are begun in chat rooms;
- In 82 percent of online sex crimes against minors, the offender used the victim's social networking site to gather information on the victim's likes and dislikes; 65 percent use the victim's social networking site to gather home and school information; 26 percent gain information on the victim's whereabouts at a specific time; and
- Fewer than half (44 percent) of online sexual solicitors were under the age of eighteen.

One study estimates that one in seven youth nationwide have received online sexual solicitations and sexual solicitation of youth occurs most frequently in chat rooms, via instant or Facebook messaging, or through online gaming devices. Wolak reports that the majority of victims of internet-initiated sex crimes in 2007 were between the ages of thirteen and fifteen.

Although anyone can be targeted by a predator, adolescents, particularly girls, are more likely to be victimized than younger children. Youths who share personal information, meet online acquaintances in person, or communicate in a sexual manner, as well as youths who are depressed, questioning their sexuality, or have poor family relationships are also at a greater risk. Additionally, the more time a youth spends on the internet, the more likely it is that he or she will become an online victim or engage in high-risk behaviors.

Online harassment, or cyberbullying, defined as "willful and repeated harm inflicted through the medium of electronic text," can also harm children and teens. Thirty-four percent of youth, ages ten through fifteen, reported being harassed online, and the majority report these incidences to friends or a parent/guardian. Cyberbullies harass their victims by posting insults, taunts, threats, or slanderous statements on the internet or by directly sending them to their victims through digital communications like email, text messaging, and instant messaging. Because of the media's nature, these bullies can easily remain anonymous, and the psychological impact of online harassment can lead to increased levels of fear, stress, and depression among victims. Hate groups also use the internet to promote harassment. These groups may use websites and online communications to target adolescents and spread their message to a mass amount of people.

Besides these very large dangers, teens also need to be careful about how they present themselves online. Social networking sites, instant messaging, and email are where kids today hang out, gossip, and assert their independence. The difference between real-world hang outs and cyber hang outs, however, is that cyberspace is open twenty-four hours a day and is vaster and, in some cases, much more public. In a few widely publicized cases, teenagers have been arrested after chatting about or posting pictures of illegal activities online; colleges and employers checking an applicant's profile may also find evidence of drug use, underage drinking, or inappropriate behavior.

What Is Being Done to Promote Internet Safety?

The federal government has been studying the problem of child internet safety for many years. One result of these studies has been the passage of the Children's Internet Protection Act of 2000 (CIPA), which requires any school or library that receives federal discounts for internet access to "have an internet safety policy and technology protection measures in place" (Federal Communications Commission). As of 2007, approximately one-third of public libraries in the United States opted not to apply for federal internet discounts in order to avoid CIPA restrictions.

The Children's Online Privacy Protection Act (COPPA) was passed in 1998, banning websites from gathering personal information from children under the age of thirteen without parental consent. COPPA has been revised twice (in 2011 and 2012) since it was put into effect in 2000. The revisions expand on and further define what it means to collect data, present data retention and deletion rules, and create additional parental notice and consent requirements. Agencies like the Federal Bureau of Investigation (FBI), the Department of Justice, and the National Center for Missing and Exploited Children have also created internet safety guides and websites.

Although Facebook has been criticized for being too lax in its privacy settings, a Carnegie Mellon study revealed that of the 540 Facebook users profiled, the majority had not altered their privacy settings, which allowed unknown users access to their personal profile information.

While current approaches tend to favor legislation and restriction, some groups are advocating for education. A school safety survey conducted by researchers at Quality Education Data discovered that although most school districts across the nation block inappropriate websites from school computers, only 8 percent teach students responsible internet usage.

General Recommendations to Promote Safe Use of the Internet

Unfortunately, many parents and schools rely solely on online blockers to prevent children and adolescents from accessing inappropriate or dangerous content, and they seldom observe children's online activity directly. According to one survey of metropolitan Los Angles parents, over 60 percent had never talked with their teens about their social networking use. Just over a third had never viewed their child's profile. While online blockers or filtering devices can be helpful, they should not be the only line of defense, as parents need to be aware of what their children are posting and who they are talking to, as well as what they are accessing. Teachers and parents should have open and honest discussions with children to educate them about internet victimization. Parents need to be on the lookout for strangers who contact their children online, as well as observe their child's behavior for actions that might make them easy targets for predators.

Youth may pose as wild or promiscuous and post suggestive content or use provocative screen names like "sexygirl." Adults need to step in and help kids understand the dangerous image they may be projecting. Teaching youth prevention strategies can help them self-monitor their time online and reduce victimization.

Parents should also set limits on the amount of time children can spend online and emphasize the importance of balancing internet use with other interests and activities. To promote safe internet use, children and adolescents should be supervised when online. They should also be advised to stay away from chat rooms and sites where they can easily interact with strangers, and they should be made aware of the consequences of making acquaintances online and sharing personal information (pictures, birth dates, addresses, etc.) with strangers. Youths need to know how to exit a situation if victimization occurs or seems likely to occur, and reporting incidents of victimization to the police may help prevent future incidents. Schools should also develop and follow acceptable-use policies and procedures for student and faculty use of the internet.

Websites and Internet Control Software

Parents and schools may wish to investigate the following websites that provide information on internet safety education and internet control software packages. However, it should be remembered that no software provides total security.

- SafeSurf is an internet content rating system that helps parents and schools to filter content they find inappropriate for children and adolescents. The software takes great care to distinguish between types of content (i.e., a violent news photograph meant to inform and a gratuitously violent video meant to entertain or shock) and allows users to customize their settings.
- Net Nanny, produced by ContentWatch, Inc., is an internet-control software that blocks children's access to inappropriate websites, put time limits on computer use, and block specific desktop personal computer (PC) games. Net Nanny also flags potentially dangerous instant messaging conversations.
- Cyber, part of the Center for Safe and Responsible Internet Use, offers news and information on cyber and cyberthreats to parents and educators.
- i-SAFE is a nonprofit foundation that aims to educate youth about safe and responsible internet use. It works with students, parents, teachers, communities, and law enforcement to spread awareness about internet safety and security, and offers a variety of free educational resources.
- CyberSmart! offers online workshops geared toward online safety and security, avoiding cyber, online manners and ethics, using the internet for effective researching, and understanding the digital challenges of the twenty-first century.
- "A Parent's Guide to Internet Safety" is an FBI handbook parents can use to minimize their

children's risk for victimization, detect signs that child may be in contact with an online predator, and take action against a predator.

- GetNetWise, sponsored by the Internet Education Foundation, grew out of a collaboration between public interest groups and industry leaders from companies like Google and Microsoft. Along with information on privacy and security for adults, the site also offers kids and parents child safety information and tools.
- Children's Privacy, created by the Federal Trade Commission, provides parents, teachers, and kids with information on the 1998 Children's Online Privacy Protection Act. Parents and teachers can how to read a website's privacy policy and decide if they will consent to a website collecting personal information about a child. Children can learn about how to protect their personal information, and when they should ask an adult for help.
- WiredSafety.org posts internet safety information for parents, educators, and kids. Parents can learn how to monitor and understand their children's internet use; educators can learn how to teach students internet safety; and kids can learn how to safely use email and instant messaging, as well as how to respond to cyberbullies.

—Jennifer Bouchard

References

Andrews, M. "Decoding MySpace." *U.S. News & World Report*, 18 Sept. 2006, pp. 46–60.

Bagwell, K. "Teaching, Not Technology, Is Key to Enforcing Internet Safety." *Education Daily*, vol. 40, 2007, p. 2.

Contentwatch. *Netnanny.com*.

Cybersmart Education Company. "About Us."

Dorman, S. "Internet Safety for Schools, Teachers, And Parents." *Journal of School Health*, vol. 67, 1997, p. 355.

Durflinger, D. "Balancing Student Empowerment with Online Safety." *School Administrator*, vol. 72, no. 10, 2015, p. 11.

"Enough Is Enough: Internet Safety 101: Educate, Equip, Empower." *Internetsafety101.org*.

Family Online Safety Institute. "About ICRA." *Fosi. org*.

Federal Bureau of Investigation. "A Parent's Guide to Internet Safety." *Fbi.gov*.

Federal Communications Commission. "Children's Internet Protection Act." *Fcc.gov*.

Federal Trade Commission. "Children's Privacy." *Business.ftc.gov*.

Gashi, L., and K. Knautz, K. "Somebody That I Used to Know—Unfriending and Becoming Unfriended on Facebook." *Proceedings of the European Conference on E-Learning*, 2015, pp. 583–90.

Greifner, L. "Students from U.S., Europe Collaborate on Internet Safety." *Education Week*, vol. 26, 2017, p. 9.

Gross, Ralph, and Allessandro Acquisti. "Information Revelation and Privacy in Online Social Networks: The Facebook Case." *Heinz.cmu.edu*, 2005.

Hockenson, Lauren, and Rani Molla. "Facebook Grows Daily Active Users by 25 Percent, Mobile Users by 45 Percent." *Gigaom.com*, 13 Oct. 2013.

Joseph, L. "Keeping Safe in Cyberspace." *Multimedia & Internet@Schools*, vol. 14, 2007, pp. 17–20.

Kardell, Nicole. "FTC Will Propose Broader Children's Online Privacy Safeguards." *Natlawreview. com*, 2 Dec. 2011.

Ktoridou, D., N. Eteokleous, and A. Zahariadou. "Exploring Parents' and Children's Awareness on Internet Threats in Relation to Internet Safety." *Campus-Wide Information Systems*, vol. 29, 2012, pp. 133–43.

McClure, Charles R., and Paul T. Jaeger. *Public Libraries and Internet Service Roles: Measuring and Maximizing Internet Services*. American Library Association, 2009.

Melgosa, A., and Scott, R. "School Internet Safety: More Than 'Block It to Stop It.'" *Education Digest*, vol. 79, 2013, pp. 46–49.

National Center for Education Statistics. "Fast Facts: Access to the Internet." *US Department of Education*, 2021, nces.ed.gov/fastfacts/display. asp?id=46.

Percival, Lynn C., and Poyner Spruill. "New Children's Online Privacy Protection Act (COPPA) Rule Now in Effect." *Natlawreview.com*, 1 July 2013.

Safesurf. "The Safesurf Internet Rating Standard." *Safesurf.com*.

"Senate Considers Internet Safety." *American Libraries*, vol. 38, 2007, pp. 23–24.

Tucker, C. "Creating A Safe Digital Space." *Educational Leadership*, vol. 73, no. 2, 2015, pp. 82–83.

Tynes, B. "Internet Safety Gone Wild? Sacrificing The Educational and Psychosocial Benefits of Online Social Environments." *Journal of Adolescent Research*, vol. 22, 2007, pp. 575–84.

Waterman, C. "Online Safety Still Not Good Enough but Who Cares Enough to Act?" *Education Journal*, 2014, pp. 17–18.

Weiss, Daniel. "Cyber And Online Harassment." *Myrocktoday.org*, 11 Apr. 2007.

Wolak, J., D. Finkelhor, K. J. Mitchell, et al. "Online 'Predators' and Their Victims: Myths, Realities, and Implications for Prevention and Treatment." *American Psychologist*, vol. 63, 2008, pp. 111–28.

Young, A., A. Young, and H. Fullwood. "Adolescent Online Victimization." *Prevention Researcher*, vol. 14, 2007, pp. 8–9.

INTRANET

Introduction

An intranet, also known as a private business network, is a generic term for a private computer network within an organization. An intranet network utilizes internet protocol (IP) technologies to safely facilitate communication between individuals or work groups. They are used to share project management tools, corporate directories, and teleconferencing. This helps improve an organization's data sharing capabilities by making them more efficient, safe, and quick.

An intranet generally includes internet access with strict firewalls so that outside computers cannot directly reach users of the network. Smaller companies sometimes protect their intranet using private IP address ranges. Typical services of an intranet include internal email systems, a message board service, and databases that store the organization's forms and personnel information. An intranet can also host several private websites and have an extension called an extranet, where approved outside parties can access the intranet.

Background

The first intranet networks developed out of static websites that were used by employees to access information at an organization's central location. Frontier Technologies released the first intranet software in 1996. Called Intranet Genie, this early program was a client server application that contained server software and a series of software components that allowed users to securely share documents and other communications. Similar products followed from other software companies, and the term intranet eventually became the official term for content shared on a private computer network.

As the internet began to expand, intranet software changed as well. The dominant design became web portals, which are specially designed web pages that collect information from various sources in an unvarying manner. This helped simplify installation and management of intranets and only required an organization to have a uniform web browser on their computers.

Web-based intranet products helped to reduce the cost of development and application. In the mid-2000s, the functionality of intranets improved so that they could be further customized. Users could now build custom websites, tests and surveys, and more dynamic forms.

As social media outlets such as Facebook became increasingly popular in the 2000s, online communication became quicker and easier. With these developments, more social features began to be integrated into intranet software. These features included instant chat functions, communication walls, and the ability for employees to see when another employee they follow has made a post or updated information. Features like these have improved communication speeds and interactivity, as employees could now correspond with one another much like they would on their personal social media at home.

Intranet products continued to increase in their functionality and complexity into the 2010s. For many large organizations, in-house web pages grew to such a degree that separate departments exist to edit, manage, and maintain them. Internet metrics can be used on these large intranets to measure overall user activity.

Intranet vs. Internet

An organization's intranet and public website on the internet are two different spaces for information. The main difference is that an intranet can only be accessed by in-house employees and approved outside users, while the public website can be accessed by anyone with an internet connection. They contain different user interface designs and many different applications.

The public internet website is essentially used by customers and other outside parties who are interested in purchasing a product from the organization or gathering information that the organization is sharing with the public. Employees use the intranet for their everyday work within the organization, which can range from instant messaging and teleconferencing to managing reports and documents.

An intranet's main function is for employees to perform tasks and manage projects. The public website is more for promotional purposes. Because of this, an intranet network should look different than the public site. This way employees know which network they are using and do not inappropriately share information.

A company's intranet is generally more complex than its public website and often contains anywhere from ten to several hundred or thousands of pages. This is due to the large amount of in-house work that is contained within the intranet. Since intranets contain more information than single websites, they typically run at greater bandwidth speed than the public internet.

Advantages

An intranet offers an organization several advantages over the public internet. When an intranet is managed well, an organization's highly sensitive information is secured from any nonemployees. Information stays within the intranet network through encrypted computer security systems. This security also applies to communication between employees and the documents that may share. Any teleconferencing done within an intranet is also secure.

Intranets ensure that employees can easily view the tasks and information relevant to their responsibilities. The databases contained within an intranet allow for employees to store and retrieve documents easily and from any of the company's workstations. When information is updated on an intranet, the relevant employees can instantly see it, leading to more efficient turnarounds and real-time updates. All of these advantages may subsequently lead to higher productivity, a more efficient business operation, and the promotion of a common corporate culture.

Disadvantages

Employees who are not comfortable with technology might get frustrated when trying to use an intranet network. For this reason, training is crucial, but it can come at a large cost. Sometimes the cost of setting up an intranet can be considerable. This cost depends on the size of the organization and the complexity of the network they wish to establish. After an intranet network is set up, there are typically frequent upgrades and maintenance that can cost a significant amount annually.

Intranets that are too complex may not be used to their greatest potential, which can lead to decreased productivity. This complexity can also increase the need for a full-time information technology (IT) department, which adds further costs. The more complex a system is, the greater the chance for network failures as well.

Intranets may also limit access to computers in certain physical locations, such as the company's office. Although virtual private networks (VPNs) and other systems may circumvent this, it can still provide a challenge for remote employees. Internet-based technologies, such as cloud computing, offer greater flexibility, though they are potentially less secure.

—*Patrick G. Cooper*

References

Blackmore, Paul. *Intranets: A Guide to Their Design, Implementation and Management.* Aslib-IMI, 2001.

Chadha, Peter. "The Return of the Intranet: Old-School Tech Complements the Cloud." *Tech Radar.* Future US, 27 Feb. 2015.

Comer, Douglas. *Computer Networks and internets.* 6th ed., Pearson, 2015.

Conroy, Kevin. "Collaboration in the New Age of Intranets." *CMS Wire.* Simpler Media Group, 2 Apr. 2015.

___. "The New Age of Intranets: Planning & Corporate Communications." *CMS Wire.* Simpler Media Group, 30 Jan. 2015.

Hall, Ryan. "The History and Evolution of Intranet Software." *Intranet Connections*. Intranet Connections, 12 Sept. 2013.

Knudson, Julie. "What Can an Intranet Do for Your Small Business?" *Small Business Computing.com*. QuinStreet, 31 July 2014.

Oppliger, Rolf. *Internet and Intranet Security*. 2nd ed., Artech House, 2002.

Robertson, James. *Essential Intranets: Inspiring Sites That Deliver Business Value*. Step Two Designs, 2013.

IOS

Introduction

Apple's iPhone operating system (iOS) is an operating system designed for mobile computing. It is used on the company's iPhone and iPod Touch products and was previously used on the iPad. The system, which debuted in 2007, is based on the company's OS X. iOS was the first mobile OS to incorporate advanced touch-screen controls.

Background

Apple's iOS is an OS designed for use on Apple's mobile devices, including the iPhone and iPod Touch. In 2020, iOS was the world's second most popular mobile OS after the Android OS. Between 2010 and 2019, Apple's iPad tablet devices also used iOS. However, Apple renamed the variant of iOS used for the iPad the iPadOS in mid-2019.

Introduced in 2007, iOS (then known as iPhone OS) was one of the first mobile OSs to incorporate a capacitive touch-screen system. The touch screen allows users to activate functions by touching the screen with their fingers. The Apple iOS was also among the first mobile OSs to give users the ability to download applications (apps) to their mobile devices. The iOS is therefore a platform for numerous apps, including the more than 1.8 million apps available in the App Store by early 2020.

The first iOS system and iPhone were unveiled at the 2007 Macworld Conference. The original iOS had a number of limitations. For example, it was unable to run third-party apps, had no copy and paste functions, and could not send email attachments. It was also not designed for multitasking, forcing users to wait for each process to finish before beginning another. However, iOS introduced a sophisticated capacitive touch screen. The iOS touch features allowed users to activate most functions with their fingers rather than needing a stylus or buttons on the device. The original iPhone had only five physical buttons. All other functions, including the keyboard, were integrated into the device's touch screen. In addition, the iOS system supports multitouch gestures. This allows a user to use two or more fingers (pressure points) to activate additional functions. Examples include "pinching" and "stretching" to shrink or expand an image.

Jailbreaking

Computer hobbyists soon learned to modify the underlying software restrictions built into iOS, a process called "jailbreaking." Modified devices allow users greater freedom to download and install apps. It also allows users to install iOS on devices other than Apple devices. Apple has not typically pursued legal action against those who jailbreak iPhones or other devices. In 2010, the US Copyright Office authorized an exception permitting users to jailbreak their legally owned copies of iOS for select legal purposes. However, jailbreaking iOS voids Apple warranties.

Version Updates

The second version of iOS was launched in July 2008. With iOS 2, Apple introduced the App Store, where users could download third-party apps and games. In 2009, iOS 3 provided support for copy and paste functions and multimedia messaging. A major advancement came with the release of iOS 4 in 2010. This update introduced the ability to multitask, allowing iOS to begin multiple tasks concurrently without waiting for one task to finish before initiating the next task in the queue. The iOS 4 release was also the first to feature a folder system in which similar apps could be grouped together on the device's home screen (called the "springboard"). FaceTime video calls also became available with iOS 4.

The release of iOS 5 in 2011 integrated the voice-activated virtual assistant Siri as a default app. Other iOS 5 updates include the introduction of iMessage, Reminders, and Newsstand. In 2012, iOS 6 replaced Google Maps with Apple Maps and redesigned the App Store, among other updates.

Released in 2013, iOS 7 featured a new aesthetic and introduced the Control Center, AirDrop, and iTunes Radio.

Innovations

With the release of iOS 8, Apple included third-party widget support for the first time in the company's history. Widgets are small programs that do not need to be opened and continuously run on a device. Examples including stock tickers and weather widgets that display current conditions based on data from the web. Widgets had been a feature of Android and Windows mobile OSs for years. However, iOS 8 was the first iOS version to support widgets for Apple. Since their release, Apple has expanded the availability of widgets for users.

The release of iOS 9 in 2015 marked a visual departure for Apple. This update debuted a new typeface for iOS called San Francisco. This specially tailored font replaced the former Helvetica Neue. The release of iOS 9 also improved the battery life of Apple devices. This update introduced a low-power mode that deactivates high-energy programs until the phone is fully charged. Low-power mode can extend battery life by as much as an hour on average.

Coinciding with the release of iOS 9, Apple also debuted the iPhone 6S and iPhone 6S Plus, which introduced 3D Touch. This new feature is built into the hardware of newer Apple devices and can sense how deeply a user is pressing on the touch screen. 3D Touch is incorporated into iOS 9 and enables previews of various functions within apps without needing to fully activate or switch to a new app. For instance, within the camera app, lightly holding a finger over a photo icon will bring up an enlarged preview without needing to open the iPhoto app.

Apple added additional features to iOS over the subsequent years, including implementing the use of apps within iMessage in iOS 10. The OS continued to evolve through the releases of iOS 11 and iOS 12, the latter of which introduced a function known as Screen Time, used to track and limit an individual's time using a device or a specific app. Released in September of 2019, iOS 13 introduced Dark Mode as well as a variety of tweaks to existing apps and features. In June of 2020, Apple announced that iOS 14 would introduce features such as home-screen widgets, pinned conversations in Messages, and an App Library. As of this writing, the most recent iOS is version 15. In 2021, Apple announced its iOS 15 at its

World Wide Developers Conference with many additions and bug fixes.

—*Micah L. Issitt*

References

Clement, J. "Number of Apps Available in Leading App Stores 2020." *Statista*, 4 May 2020, www.statista.com/statistics/276623/number-of-apps-available-in-leading-app-stores/.

Costello, Sam. "The History of iOS, from Version 1.0 to 13.0." *Lifewire*, 11 Mar. 2020, www.lifewire.com/ios-versions-4147730.

Heisler, Yoni. "The History and Evolution of iOS, from the Original iPhone to iOS 9." *BGR*, 12 Feb. 2016, bgr.com/2016/02/12/ios-history-iphone-features-evolution/.

"iOS." *AppleInsider*, 27 June 2020, appleinsider.com/inside/ios.

"iOS 14." *AppleInsider*, 25 June 2020, appleinsider.com/inside/ios-14.

"iOS: A Visual History." *Verge*, 16 Sept. 2013, www.theverge.com/2011/12/13/2612736/ios-history-iphone-ipad.

Williams, Rhiannon. "Apple iOS: A Brief History." *Telegraph*, 17 Sept. 2015, www.telegraph.co.uk/technology/apple/11068420/Apple-iOS-a-brief-history.html.

Wuerthele, Mike. "Apple Unveils iPadOS, Adding Features Specifically to iPad." *AppleInsider*, 2 June 2019, appleinsider.com/articles/19/06/03/apple-supplements-ios-13-with-new-tablet-specific-ipad-os-branch.

IPADS IN THE CLASSROOM

Introduction

Since Apple introduced the iPad in 2010, it has come to dominate the world of mobile computing. Applications for the iPad are designed to help preschool users learn basic skills such as counting and colors. The iPad is also used in K-12 and college classrooms for everything from note taking to embarking on virtual tours to learning about outer space. Teachers across disciplines have used iPads to teach literacy, literature, writing, language, social science, history, mathematics, science, geography, computing, medicine, pharmacology, business, art, drama, and music. The iPad has also been used successfully with special needs students.

Background

Personal computers first appeared on the scene in the 1970s, but it took another two decades before the home computer became part of the American mainstream. During the 1990s, colleges and university students wholeheartedly adapted to using technologies that included everything from email and instant messaging to podcasts and personal digital assistants (PDAs). K–12 classrooms were more likely to provide desktop computers in a computer laboratory setting, requiring teachers to sign up for computer time for their classes.

On January 27, 2010, Apple introduced the iPad, which had been designed by Apple's founder Steve Jobs. The marketing campaign for the iPad revolved around the theme "Reinventing Textbooks." Jobs saw the iPad as the answer to expensive and bulky textbooks because the iPad could essentially put an entire library at the fingertips of any user. Apple also announced that it was partnering with McGraw-Hill, Pearson PLD, and Houghton Mifflin Harcourt to publish textbooks for use in grades K-12. Jobs believed that ultimately every schoolchild in the United States should have his/her own iPad.

From the outset, the iPad was intended to be both educational and fun. For a generation that had exposed to computers, cell phones, and video gaming for all or much of their lives, the iPad was viewed as a means of "playing" during school hours. The iPad had the added benefit of preparing students for eventual entry to an increasingly technology dependent workplace.

Released in April 2010, the cost of the first-generation iPad was $499. Marketing the iPad as "a world of content," Apple offered 80,000 educational applications by 2014. Key features included Pages, an application designed to help students write term papers; Numbers, which provided tools for creating tables, charts, and graphs; and Keynote, a presentation application. All three applications were compatible with Microsoft Office, which meant that students could move files back and forth between their iPads and desktop/laptop computers. Other iPad features that made the device popular in classrooms included iPhoto, for keeping video journals; Garage-Band, for recording and mixing music; and iBooks

iPads offer many advantages to a learning environment, but some argue that students can get distracted by games and social media. Photo via iStock/lisegagne. [Used under license.]

Author, for creating original interactive classroom material. Through iTunes University, users of the iPad, the iPhone, and the iPod Touch had access to a wealth of educational material on everything from computing to chemistry. Connecting an iPad to an Apple TV allowed teachers to stream content to an entire class using Air Play.

The use of mobile technology by college students rose from 1.2 percent in 2005 to 62.7 percent in 2010 when the first-generation iPad was introduced. By 2012, 80 percent of internet users were accessing web portals through mobile devices such as iPads and smartphones. Experts predicted that tablet computers would become more common than desktop computers by 2015. However, a 2015 Pew Research Center study found that 73 percent of American adults owned a desktop or laptop computer while only 45 percent owned a tablet. The success of the iPad, however, contributed to what came to be known as the digital divide, the educational gap that separated those who could afford mobile devices and internet access from those who could not.

In 2011, it was estimated that only 2 percent of low-income students had access to mobile tablets as compared to 17 percent of middle- and higher-income students. Because of the wide range in access to iPads or other such devices, knowledge of technology in classrooms varied greatly along socioeconomic lines. Another digital divide has been identified separating the richer nations of the world from countries that lack access to modern technology. A generational divide also exists, separating older people who may distrust technology or lack technological skills from younger people for whom technology has been an important part of their daily lives.

Applications

School systems immediately saw the advantage to using iPads in the classroom. New York was the first city to come on board, and the school system spent $1.3 million to purchase two thousand iPads for classroom use. Chicago used federal grant money to place iPads in two hundred schools. At Indiana University-Purdue University (IUPU), iPads were placed in classrooms for use across disciplines, encouraging teachers to seek out ways to improve learning experiences. At the University of Minnesota, first-year instructors and first-year students were given iPads in 2011. They were used for everything from writing in English classes to analyzing data in math classes. The experience was highly successful. Business schools around the country saw the advantage to iPads immediately, and business majors were among the first to endorse the use of iPads in the classroom.

Within a year of the iPad's initial release, more than three-fourths of respondents in a survey conducted by the International Society for Technology identified iPads as the leading technology in education. While iPads in the classroom are chiefly intended to promote academic performance, they also allow students to access games, music, videos, and the internet. While some educators view nonacademic use of school-issued iPads as wasteful, others see such activities as essential tools in promoting student confidence, decreasing differences in students with and without home access, and familiarizing students with the technologies of the twenty-first century.

School districts have found that it is cheaper to provide iPads for the classroom than to buy either desktop or laptop computers. Costs can be reduced even further by purchasing refurbished iPads that have been discarded as newer models have entered the market. While the chief focus in education has been on iPads, cheaper tablet computers of high quality are also available for classroom use. With iPads in the classroom, teachers no longer wait their turns for scarce computer laboratory time since iPads can be assigned to each classroom.

Several other advantages have also been attributed to using iPads in the classroom.

Teachers have complete flexibility of location since iPads can be moved around the room or from one room to another. Flexibility of use is provided by the wide range of applications available. The iPad is pre-equipped with applications designed to handle photographs, music, and videos, and teachers may choose to use the iPad's note, clock, calculator, maps, and weather applications to enhance learning experiences (Banister, 2010). Educators have also hailed the iPad's e-reader capabilities, contending that it encourages students to read. Because it is more difficult to use copy/paste functions on the iPad or other tablet computers than on desktops or laptops, some advocates suggest that students may be likely to commit plagiarism.

Educators have also found that the video conferencing capability of the iPad can become an essential tool in helping homebound students participate in classroom discussions and activities. Thousands of applications for the iPad are free, and others are relatively inexpensive. Other advantages include reduced teacher training time since software applications tend to be more user friendly than traditional software used on desktops and laptops. The opportunity for teacher experimentation is considered one of the chief advantages of the iPad.

Educators have found that the iPad is ideal for helping preschoolers and special needs students learn basic skills since the device promotes both visual and tactile learning. Applications such as Monkey Math and Bridge Basher are designed to begin teaching students basic concepts involved in the science, technology, engineering, and mathematics (STEM) curriculum that are viewed as essential to career success. Because even preschoolers are already involved with interactive and touch screens through daily activities such as smartphones, video gaming, and supermarket displays, they are generally viewed as accessible technologies. The ideal scenario is workstations where teachers or aides work with students using iPads in small groups.

Critics of iPads in the classroom insist that the biggest obstacle to success is not Apple's technology but the lack of technological training for teachers. This is particularly true of older teachers who may have not grown up using devices such Apple's iPod or cell phones. While one of the advantages of the iPad is that it does away with the need for permanent technical support staff, it is recommended that schools have someone on hand to provide information or advice when untrained teachers run into problems. Some researchers insist that schools need to do more to improve functionality of the iPad by providing back-up and battery charging capabilities. They also suggest that students need to be prevented from installing or uninstalling applications.

Discourse

Virtually all developed countries and many developing countries are using iPads to enhance learning experiences for students and prepare them for participation in the technological revolution. One of the issues with the iPad as a universally implemented educational device is its price. iPads are more expensive than many other mobile devices. Several schools have instituted a Bring Your Own Device policy that allows students to use a wide range of personal mobile devices such as smartphones and tablet computers at school. The availability of retired models, pre-owned devices, and lower-priced tablet computers and mobile phones has enabled most students to have access to these devices even where districts do not adequately provide them. That does, however, introduce complexity into the process of ensuring every student is on the same (virtual) page, and it also introduces the need for technological support in the classroom, something that is almost never provided.

Research of the 2010s reveals that learning to use iPads in the classroom is making it easier for students to understand difficult concepts. A 2014 study conducted by Matthew Schneps and a team of researchers at Harvard University's Smithsonian Center for Astrophysics found that using the iPad or another tablet computer for only twenty minutes raised neurocognitive abilities. Students receiving guided instruction revealed the highest increases in neurocognitive scores. The research team studied 152 students at a Massachusetts high school using second generation iPads and Solar Walk, a three-dimensional (3D) simulation of outer space, and tested their knowledge of the solar system in comparison with 1,184 students who had studied the same material taught in traditional ways. Since iPads and other tablets have the "pinch" function, students could zoom the screen in for a close look and zoom out to see the solar system to scale. By contrast, students viewing traditional tools for viewing outer space were exposed to a solar system in which the

size of the earth and other planets were greatly exaggerated.

—*Elizabeth Rholetter Purdy*

References

Aronin, S., and K. Floyd. "Using an iPad in Inclusive Preschool Classrooms to Introduce STEM Concepts." *Teaching Exceptional Children*, vol. 45, no. 4, 2013, pp. 34–39.

Banister, S. "Integrating the iPod Touch in K-12 Education: Visions and Vices." *Computers in the Schools*, vol. 27, no. 2, 2010, pp. 121–31.

Bers, M. *Designing Digital Experiences for Positive Youth Development: From Playpen to Playground.* Oxford UP, 2012.

Falloon, G. "What's the Difference? Learning Collaboratively Using iPads in Conventional Classrooms." *Computers & Education*, vol. 84, 2015.

Ferguson, J., and J. Oigara. "iPads in the Classroom: What Do Teachers Think?" *International Journal of Information & Communication Technology Education*, vol. 13, no. 4, 2017.

Gillispie, M. *From Notepad to iPad: Using Applications and Web Tools to Engage a New Generation of Students.* Taylor and Francis, 2013.

Harrington, K. "From Tablet to Tablet, from Mesopotamia to Galway." *Adult Learner*, 2014, pp. 94–102.

Howard, J., P. Vu, and L. Vu. "How Do Undergraduate Students Use Their iPad?" *Journal of Technology Integration in the Classroom*, vol. 4, no. 3, 2012, pp. 5–12.

Khalid, S., O. Jurisic, H. S. Kristensen, et al. "Exploring the Use of iPads in Danish Schools." *Proceedings of the European Conference on E-Learning*, 2014, pp. 264–72.

Laidlaw, L., and J. O'Mara. "Rethinking Difference in the Iworld: Possibilities, Challenges and 'Unexpected Consequences' of Digital Tools in Literacy Education." *Language & Literacy: A Canadian Educational E-Journal*, vol. 17, no. 2, 2015, pp. 59–74.

Levin, B., and L. Schrum. *Leading Technology-Rich Schools: Award-Winning Models for Success.* Teachers College Press, 2012.

Rossing, J., W. Miller, A. Cecil, et al. "Ilearning: The Future of Higher Education? Student Perspectives on Learning with Mobile Tablets." *Journal of the Scholarship of Teaching and Learning*, vol. 12, no. 2, 2012, pp. 1–26.

Schneps, M., J. Ruel, G. Sonnert, et al. "Conceptualizing Astronomical Scale: Virtual Simulations on Handheld Tablet Computers Reverse Misconceptions." *Computers and Education*, vol. 70, 2014, pp. 269–80.

Wardley, L. L., and C. Mang. "Student Observations: Introducing iPads into University Classrooms." *Education & Information Technologies*, vol. 21, no. 6, 2016, pp. 1715–32.

ITUNES

Introduction

iTunes is a type of digital media software developed by Apple Inc. It allows users to add, organize, and play digital, or online, media files such as songs, videos, television shows, movies, audiobooks, or podcasts. These can be accessed on a computer or portable device such as the iPod portable media player or iPhone. Apple launched iTunes in 2001 with just a few hundred thousand songs, and since then, it has added millions of media files as well as the streaming service Apple Music and the storage service iCloud.

Background

To commercialize on the digital music industry, computer technology company Apple Inc. debuted iTunes in January of 2001. iTunes was software that allowed Macintosh users to add, organize, and play digital media files on their computers. Less than a year later, the company introduced the iPod, a portable digital media player that worked exclusively with iTunes to permit customers to download and play media files. Apple also released the second version of iTunes to coincide with the introduction of the iPod.

The third upgrade came soon after and included audiobooks. In 2003, Apple debuted its iTunes Store, allowing customers to access to two hundred thousand different types of digital files. In just one week, the iTunes Store sold more than 1 million songs. A few months later, more than 1 million people were seen sporting the iconic white iPod earbuds, a testament to how popular the iPod had become in such a short period. At this time, however, only Mac users could utilize iTunes. To widen its market, Apple released a Windows version of iTunes.

The iTunes 4 update came in 2004 and included a shuffle feature as well as support for digital photos and videos. The following year, Apple released an upgrade that permitted consumers to access podcasts. iTunes 6, which debuted in 2006, added minor enhancements, fixed bugs, and introduced users to video streaming. iTunes 7 launched in September of 2006 and featured iPod games and gapless (or uninterrupted) playback of music files.

In 2007, the company released its first iPhone smartphone, which linked to iTunes and the iTunes Store—and later to the App Store. Upgrades iTunes 8 and iTunes 9 followed, both of which helped to streamline all of Apple's services. People were able to rent and purchase television shows and movies, download courses from iTunes U, and buy digital books.

iTunes 10 came in 2010 and included a new social media network called Ping; however, Ping failed to attract followers and was quickly discarded. In 2011, Apple debuted iTunes Match, which worked with iCloud and iTunes in the Cloud to help match songs with subscribers. The iTunes 11 upgrade launched in 2012 with the addition of iTunes Radio and minor enhancements and fixes to the software. In 2014, Apple debuted iTunes 12, which changed the interface to make the software easier to navigate.

The following year, Apple released an updated version of iTunes 12 to embrace digital music streaming with the debut of Apple Music. Throughout 2016, the company continued to release other versions of iTunes 12 in an effort to fix several weaknesses in the system. It also worked on streamlining its iTunes and other services to make them more user friendly.

iTunes as titled, was, for all intents and purposes, phased out in 2019, in favor the more generally named iMusic. Because iMusic also referred to Apple's music subscription service, however, iTunes continued to be used popularly as a title for the app, to differentiate it from the service.

—Angela Harmon

References

"iTunes." *Apple Inc.*, www.apple.com/itunes.

Jarnow, Jesse. "Apple's iTunes Is Alienating Its Most Music-Obsessed Users." *Wired*, 17 Nov. 2015, www.wired.com/2015/11/itunes-alternatives.

Layton, Julia, and Jonathan Strickland. "How iTunes Works." *HowStuffWorks.com*, 20 Mar. 2006, electronics.howstuffworks.com/itunes.htm.

McElhearn, Kirk. "15 Years of iTunes: A Look at Apple's Media App and Its Influence on an Industry." *Macworld*, 9 Jan. 2016, www.macworld.com/article/3019878/software/15-years-of-itunes-a-look-at-apples-media-app-and-its-influence-on-an-industry.html.

McGarry, Caitlin. "How Apple Plans to Make iCloud, Siri, and iTunes Better." *Macworld*, 6 Oct. 2016, www.macworld.com/article/3128754/software/how-apple-plans-to-make-icloud-siri-and-itunes-better.html.

Pepitone, Julianne, and David Goldman. "The Evolution of iTunes." *CNN Money*, 26 Apr. 2013, money.cnn.com/gallery/technology/2013/04/25/itunes-history.

Perez, Sarah. "Redesigned Version of iTunes Launches with iCloud Music Glitches." *Tech Crunch*, 13 Sept. 2016, techcrunch.com/2016/09/13/redesigned-version-of-itunes-launches-with-icloud-music-glitches.

Thompson, Derck. "The Death of Music Sales." *The Atlantic*, 25 Jan. 2015, www.theatlantic.com/business/archive/2015/01/buying-music-is-so-over/384790.

J

JENKINS, HENRY

Introduction

Henry Jenkins III was born on June 4, 1958, in Atlanta, Georgia. Following completion of high school, he attended Georgia State University, where he completed a bachelor's degree in political science and journalism. He then went to the University of Iowa, where he completed a master's degree in communication studies, and then to University of Wisconsin–Madison to complete a PhD in communication arts. A sense of the nature of his studies and his approach to them may be discerned from the title of his 1989 PhD dissertation *What Made Pistachio Nuts?: Anarchistic Comedy and the Vaudeville Aesthetic.*

Background

Jenkins' research interests in media communications are both extensive and eclectic, delving into such areas as vaudeville theater, television, comic book culture, video game studies, cinema, and transmedia communication. All of these represent forms of popular culture, each with its own characteristic mode of media communication. Transmedia refers to a framework for the design and communication of content across different types of media, as for example when vaudeville acts that appeared in live vaudeville theater productions are communicated through television broadcasts or in motion pictures. This, in actuality, was the principal focus of Jenkins' doctoral studies in which he examined the influence of live vaudevillean comedy on the development of 1930s-era cinematic comedy.

Comic books, another area of interest to Jenkins, can be thought of as an abstract of motion pictures. Motion pictures depend on the visual element to show the actions of characters in real time, and on the aural element of spoken dialogue typically combined with background music and sound effects. In a similar way, comics present a story visually by using only still pictures rather than motion pictures. The aural element is instead represented by written words and symbols. Comic book readers experience what is a two-dimensional (2D) representation of the story being communicated, while the same story is experienced by cinemagoers in what is effectively three dimensions.

The communication of the story taking place within a video game has far more in common with cinema than with comic books, though the story content itself may, in fact, be identical. This has

Henry Jenkins. Photo courtesy of the Peabody Awards, via Wikimedia Commons.

always been true, ever since the development of the original *Pong* video game, but has become increasingly true as computing technology has advanced and become capable of producing ever more realistic video game presentations. The most recent video games have become so well animated and immersive that the game play feels more like the user is actually taking part in a cinematic production as the star of the show. In Jenkins's view, video games were, and still are, a crucial component for the development of digital interactive culture and digital communication.

Video game culture involves much more than just how a story is communicated from within the context of a video game. As an interactive medium, video game culture studies include such things as gender depiction within the games, audience gender bias in the player audience, marketing—what demographic is the game marketing directed towards—and how player gender determines how the game is played, to name just a few aspects. As a case in point, a global debate revolves around whether or not the depiction of violence in video games contributes to the incidence of real-world violence.

Transmedia

Jenkins coined the term transmedia storytelling in 2003, describing it as the process of distributing integral components of a story through multiple kinds of media in order to produce a single unified story. This could be likened to reading a book in which part of the story is presented in comic book format, while another part requires the reader to watch a specific video clip located at a particular web address as one of the paragraphs or chapters of the book, and to listen to the lyrics of a particular vocal or instrumental performance as another of the chapters in the book. Transmedia studies seek to identify and understand how this use of different media to tell a single, unified story—or, in some cases, multiple, competing canonical and noncanonical stories— can be carried out most effectively.

The study of transmedia storytelling has had important applications, particularly in the field of advertising. One may consider just how showing different advertisements for the same product, such as a new movie, on different media outlets builds a unified story of the product. Consider, for example, the product advertisements that are released on the giant video screens at the Super Bowl football games

each year, are then followed by their presentation in whole or in part on television, on YouTube, on the radio, in movie theaters and other venues; different media and different presentations. Using different media outlets builds a unified story in which the dénouement is that the audience understands how important it is to them that they see the movie or buy the product. It is also of interest to note that each part of an effective transmedia storytelling approach adds layers to a story that theoretically has no end.

Active Participants

Underlying all of the aspects of digital media studied by Jenkins, and other researchers, is the concept that users of digital media are not merely passive consumers, but are in fact active participants in the development of digital media culture. Their use of digital media both drives and is driven by the ongoing development of the various components of media culture. This is the essence of the theory of what Jenkins calls "convergence culture."

Jenkins analyzes *The Matrix* franchise as a seminal example of transmedia storytelling. The franchise consists of three movies by the American film directors, screenwriters, and producers the Wachowskis: *The Matrix* (1999), *The Matrix Reloaded* (May 2003), and *The Matrix Revolutions* (November 2003). It also includes *The Animatrix* (June 2003), a series of nine animated short films set in the world of the Matrix. The Wachowskis were involved in the creation of a series of comic books set in the world of the Matrix, written and illustrated by different artists, including Geof Darrow, concept artist on all three Matrix movies. Video games include *Enter the Matrix*, *The Matrix: Path of Nemo*, and a massively multiplayer online role-playing game. Each piece of the world contributes something new and connects to other elements. Only viewers who had played the video game could interpret some clues in the films, and backstory was accessible only to those who had watched animated shorts via web downloads or on digital video disc (DVD). The multiple texts work together to create what Jenkins describes as "a narrative so large it cannot be contained within a single medium."

Other such examples include the multiple incarnations of Marvel and D.C. Comics, Star Wars, and Harry Potter franchises, the latter of which includes feature films, music, toys, clothing, food items, video games, videos, podcasts, mobile apps, a theme park, museum exhibits, conferences, ancillary books, an online archive of Harry Potter fanfiction that boasts more than eighty thousand stories, and websites like *Pottermore*, an interactive joint venture that offers exclusive content, including alternate endings and original short stories about the characters by Rowling.

The Star Trek universe is another strong example of the evolving world of transmedia storytelling. Originally a television series in the 1960s, the original story line of the television series became augmented by a series of feature films involving the same characters. But with a very large break in the timeline between the end of the original series and the period of time in which the movies are set, fans and documented writers of the series began to produce more adventures of the Starship Enterprise crew to fill in those gaps. The tales they produced fill well over a hundred individual novels, a small number of "photonovels" made up of still pictures taken from the television series. Subsequent to these novels, a new television series, *Star Trek: The Next Generation*, was produced, and ran for seven years. That story line then expanded into feature films, one of which fused both the original and Next Generation characters/timelines, and overlapping these, three follow-up series were created, all of which intertwined characters and story lines from previous series. In some cases, characters—and their concomitant actors—transferred from one series to another.

In the twenty-first century, the story line continued with an original series "reboot," which reconsidered the original characters and revised the events that had previously been established as those characters' backstories. As such, this is an example of the ability of transmedia storytelling to create conflicting story lines that cannot coexist with one another.

Jenkins is a professor at University of Southern California, a position he has held since 1992.

—Richard M. Renneboog, Wylene Rholetter, and Jake D. Nicosia

References

Jenkins, Henry. *Comics and Stuff.* NYU P, 2020.

___. *Confronting the Challenges of Participatory Culture: Media Education in the 21st Century.* MIT Press, 2009.

___. *Convergence Culture: Where Old and New Media Collide.* NYU P, 2008.

___. *Sam Ford and Joshua Green. Spreadable Media: Creating Value and Meaning in Networked Culture.* NYU P, 2018.

___. *Textual Poachers. Television Fans and Participatory Culture.* Updated 20th Anniversary ed., Routledge, 2013.

___, Mizuko Ito, and Danah Boyd. *Participatory Culture in a Networked Era: A Conversation on Youth.* John Wiley & Sons, 2015.

K

KEYNOTE

Introduction

Keynote is a presentation software application produced by Apple. It runs only on MacOS and iOS operating systems, and is provided as part of the iWorks suite of applications. Before it was created, Apple cofounder Steve Jobs had used the Concurrence presentation software and applications produced by Lighthouse Design that ran on the NeXTSTEP and OPENSTEP platforms. But for the chief executive officer (CEO) of a company who believed in designing the best possible, and most efficient, products for the Mac OS, he felt that using a non-Mac application for presentations to shareholders and the general public were counter to the goals of Apple. He therefore had the Keynote application made for MacOS systems. The name Keynote was made for its relation to the term "keynote speaker," who is ostensibly the most relevant or important speaker at any convention or meeting. While generally believed to be more powerful, efficient, and user-friendly than the industry standard Microsoft PowerPoint application, Keynote remains a distant second in terms of popularity, even on the Mac platform.

Background

Keynote was initially released in 2003 to compete with presentation software applications from other companies, and those from various open-source developers, that had been made compatible with the Mac platform. With the success and popularity of "suites" of productivity applications, particularly Microsoft Works and the open-source packages such as StarOffice, Apple's proprietary suite iWorks was developed over the following years with the addition of the Pages word processing application in 2005, and the Sheets spreadsheet application in 2007. In 2013, ten years after its initial release, Keynote was redesigned for its sixth version, and has since been provided as a free application to anyone purchasing a new Apple computer or iOS-based device (e.g., iPhone, iPad). In 2021, Keynote was released in its eleventh version.

The Apple Way

In accord with the Apple approach to doing technology differently, Keynote was designed to be unlike other existing presentation software applications. From the start, Apple founder Steve Jobs and Steve Wozniak designed personal computers (PCs) from the ground up, rather than adapting previous architectures. The long line of PCs had its start in Microsoft's use of the Intel microprocessors designated 8088 and 8086. Essentially all PCs since then have been based on the x86 microprocessor line of integrated circuits (IC) chips, and have had a native disk operating system (DOS) as its principal operating system or as the underlying support system for Windows.

For Apple computer systems, however, Jobs and Wozniak eschewed the text-based DOS processors in favor of an entirely graphics-based approach that DOS-based processors were not capable of carrying out. They instead chose Motorola's 6804 IC and subsequently the 68004 IC as the basis for Apple computers. This distinctly made Mac and PC computers, and hence their software, incompatible. Over time, and the realization that neither Microsoft nor Apple could eliminate each other from the computer market, and amid growing complaints from customers about the inability to port files between Apple and Windows computers, concessions were made that would allow files produced on either system to "play nice" with the other system. The concessions also allowed the development of competitors' products to run on their nonnative operating system software.

Keynote continued in the Apple way of doing things differently. As it is at its base a presentation software application, Keynote and all other presentation applications have the same overall functionality with which users compose, generate, and organize "slide shows" for presentation. Keynote, of course, does this on the native graphics basis of macOS and iOS systems. It has also been developed recently to run on PC systems using Windows 10 and later versions. Prior to this, users of Keynote had to save files in PowerPoint file formats if they were to be shared. Keynote runs on Windows systems through a modern web browser with internet access, but the majority of its users run the program on Apple's own computer systems.

Versatility

Keynote supports no fewer than thirty-three world languages, as befits a global enterprise application. Consistent colors and fonts throughout a presentation are provided through the use of the Themes function, and these apply as well to any charts, graphs, and tables in the presentation. Animated transitions between slides can be shown as fades, as a flipping page, or even as the face of a rolling cube. Keynote presentations can be displayed on two screens simultaneously, one of which displays the actual slideshow while the presenter's screen displays both the slides and their accompanying notes.

Keynote can export files in several file formats, including PowerPoint, Portable Document Format (.pdf), QuickTime (.qt), hypertext markup language (HTML), and the .jpg, .tif, and .png graphics formats. QuickTime video formats are supported in Keynote slideshows, and presentations can be exported to Apple's iDVD application. Keynote is also compatible with the Apple Remote system. Keynote remote allows control of a presentation using an iPhone, iPad or iPad Touch, via a Wi-Fi or Bluetooth connection. Users of Keynote for Mac find that the usability and flexibility of the program are superior to that of PowerPoint. This is especially true for those with memory constraints, for Windows programs are notorious for being "bloated," that is, having excessive codes to account for their ability to be used in a variety of machines. As a Mac-native application, Keynote runs more smoothly as a matter of course. Though users also claim to prefer the look of Keynote's themes to those of PowerPoint, that remains a matter of personal preference.

—*Richard M. Renneboog*

References

Clark, Josh. *Sharing Keynote Slideshows: The Mini Missing Manual.* O'Reilly Media Inc., 2010.

___. *Creating Keynote Slideshows: The Mini Missing Manual.* O'Reilly Media Inc., 2010.

Dummett, Paul, Helen Stephenson, and Lewis Lansford. *Keynote 4.* Cengage Learning, 2020.

K, Toly. *Keynote Survival Guide: Step-by-Step User Guide for Apple Keynote: Getting Started, Managing Presentations, Formatting Slides and Playing a Slideshow.* MobileReference, 2012.

Lentzner, Rémy. *Getting Started with Keynote: Professional Training.* Editions Rémylent, 2022.

Wise, Donny. *Using Apple Keynote for the Classroom.* Lulu.com, 2015.

L

LIGHT-EMITTING DIODES

Introduction

Light-emitting diodes (LEDs) are diodes, semiconductor devices that pass current easily in only one direction, that emit light when current is passing through them in the proper direction. Light-emitting diodes are small and are easier to install in limited spaces or where small light sources are preferred, such as indicator lights in devices. Light-emitting diodes are also generally much more efficient at producing visible light than other light sources. As solid-state devices, when used properly, LEDs also have very few failure modes and have longer operational lives than many other light sources. For these reasons, LEDs are gaining popularity as light sources in many applications, despite their higher cost compared with other more traditional light sources.

Background

Diodes act as one-way valves for electrical current. Current flows through a diode easily in one direction, and the ideal diode blocks current flow in the other direction. The very name *diode* comes from the Greek meaning "two pathways." The diode-like behavior comes from joining two types of semiconductors, one that conducts electricity using electrons (n-type semiconductor) and one that conducts electrons using holes, or the lack of electrons (p-type semiconductor). The electrons will try to fill the holes, but applying voltage in the proper direction ensures a constant supply of holes and electrons to conduct electricity through the diode.

The electrons and holes have different energies, so when the electrons combine with holes, they release energy. For most diodes this energy heats the diode. However, by adjusting the types and properties of the semiconductors making up the diodes, the energy difference between holes and electrons can be made larger or smaller. If the energy difference corresponds to the energy of a photon of light, then the energy is given off in the form of light. This is the basis of how LEDs work.

Light-emitting diodes are not 100 percent efficient, and some energy is lost in current passing through the device, but the majority of energy consumed by LEDs goes into the production of light. The color of light is determined by the semiconductors making up the device, so LEDs can be fabricated to make light only in the range of wavelengths

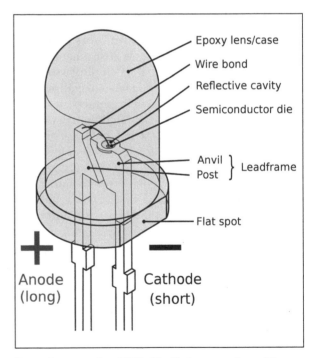

Parts of a conventional LED. The flat bottom surfaces of the anvil and post embedded inside the epoxy act as anchors, to prevent the conductors from being forcefully pulled out via mechanical strain or vibration. Image via Wikimedia Commons. [Public domain.]

desired. This makes LEDs among the most energy-efficient sources of light.

Background and History

In 1907, H. J. Round reported that light could be emitted by passing current through a crystal rectifier junction under the right circumstances. This was the ancestor of the modern LED, though the term diode had not yet been invented. Though research continued on these crystal lamps, as they were called, they were seen as impractical alternatives to incandescent and other far less expensive means of producing light. By 1955, Rubin Braunstein, working at RCA, had shown that certain semiconductor junctions produced infrared light when current passed through them. Scientists Robert Biard and Gary Pittman, however, managed to produce a usable infrared LED, receiving a patent for their device.

Nick Holonyak, Jr., a scientist at General Electric, then created a red LED—the viable and useful visual spectrum LED—in 1961. Though these early LEDs were usable, they were far too expensive for widespread adoption. By the 1970s, Fairchild Semiconductor had developed inexpensive red LEDs. These LEDs were soon incorporated into seven segment numeric indicators for calculators produced by Hewlett Packard and Texas Instruments. Red LEDs were also used in digital watch displays and as red indicator lights on various pieces of equipment.

Early LEDs were limited in brightness, and only the red ones could be fabricated inexpensively. Eventually, other color LEDs and LEDs capable of higher light output were developed. Developing a blue LED proved to be particularly difficult, and for decades this prevented scientists from creating the white LED lights necessary for purposes such as normal indoor lighting. In the late 1980s and early 1990s, scientists at last succeeded in creating and refining a blue LED; three of these researchers, Isamu Akasaki, Hiroshi Amano, and Shuji Nakamura, were awarded the 2014 Nobel Prize in Physics for their efforts. As the capabilities of LEDs expanded, they began to see more uses. By the early twenty-first century, LEDs began to compete with other forms of artificial lighting.

Efficiency

Most light sources emit light over a wide range of wavelengths, often including both visual and nonvisual light as well as heat. Therefore, only a portion of the energy used goes into the form of light desired. For an idealized LED, all of the light goes into one color of light, and that color is determined by the composition of the semiconductors making the p-n junction. For real LEDs, not all of the light makes it out of the material. Some of it is internally reflected and absorbed.

Furthermore, there is some electrical resistance to the device, so there is some energy lost in heat in the LED—but nowhere near as much as with many other light sources. This makes LEDs very efficient as light sources. However, LED efficiency is temperature dependent, and they are most efficient at lower temperatures. High temperatures tend to reduce LED efficiency and shorten the lifetime of the devices.

Indicator Lights

Among the first widespread commercial use of LEDs for public consumption was as indicator lights. The early red LEDs were used as small lights on instruments in place of small incandescent lights. The LEDs were smaller and less likely to burn out. Light-emitting diodes are still used in a similar way, though not with only the red LEDs. They are used as the indicator lights in automobile dashboards and in aircraft instrument panels. They are also used in many other applications where a light is needed and there is little room for an incandescent bulb.

Another early widespread commercial use of LEDs was the seven-segment numeric displays used to show digits in calculators and timepieces. However, LEDs require electrical current to operate, and calculators and watches would rather quickly discharge the batteries of these devices. Often the display on the watches was visible only when a button was pressed to light up the display. However, the advent of liquid crystal displays (LCDs) has rendered these uses mostly obsolete since they require far less energy to operate, and LEDs are needed to light the display at night only.

Replacements for Colored Incandescent Lights

Red LEDs have become bright enough to be used as brake lights in automobiles. Red, green, and yellow LEDs are sometimes used for traffic lights and for runway lights at airports. Light-emitting diodes are even used in Christmas-decoration lighting. They are also used in message boards and signs.

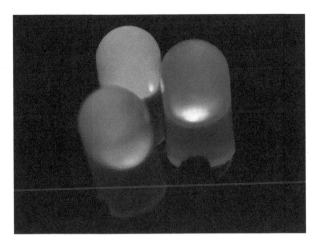

Blue, green, and red LEDs in 5 mm diffused cases. Photo by PiccoloNamek, via Wikimedia Commons.

Light-emitting diodes are sometimes used for backlighting LCD screens on televisions and laptops. Colored LEDs are also frequently used in decorative or accent lighting, such as lighting in aquariums to accentuate the colors of coral or fish. Some aircraft use LED lighting in their cabins because of energy efficiency. Red LEDs are also used in pulse oximeters used in a medical setting to measure the oxygen saturation in a patient's blood.

The biggest obstacle to replacing incandescent lights with LEDs for room lighting or building lighting is that they produce light of only one color. Several strategies are in development for producing white light using LEDs. One strategy is to use multicolored LEDs to simulate the broad spectrum of light produced by incandescent lights or fluorescent lights. However, arrays of LEDs produce a set of discrete colors of light rather than all colors of the rainbow, thus distorting colors of objects illuminated by the LED arrays. This is aesthetically unpleasing to most people. Another strategy for producing white light from LEDs is to include a phosphorescent coating in the casing around the LED. This coating would provide the different colors of light that would mimic the light of fluorescent bulbs; however, such a strategy removes much of the efficiency of LEDs. Research continues to produce a pleasing white light from LEDs.

Despite the color problems and the higher initial cost of LEDs, LEDs have many properties that make them attractive replacements for incandescent or fluorescent lights. LEDs typically have no breakable parts and, being solid-state devices, are very durable and have low susceptibility to vibrational damage. Light-emitting diodes are very energy efficient, but they tend to be less efficient at high power and high light output. Light-emitting diodes are slightly more efficient, and more expensive, than high-efficiency fluorescent lights, but research continues.

Nonvisual Uses for LEDs

Infrared LEDs are often used as door sensors or for communication by remote controls for electronic devices. They can also be used in fiber optics. The rapid switching capabilities of LEDs makes them well suited for high-speed communication purposes. Ultraviolet LEDs are being investigated as replacements for black lights for purposes of sterilization, since many bacteria are killed by ultraviolet light.

The Future of LEDs

Light-emitting diodes are used in many industries, not just in electronics, which means that there are many different degree and coursework pathways to working with LEDs. The development of new types of LEDs requires detailed understanding of semiconductor physics, chemistry, and materials science. Typically, such research requires an advanced degree in physics, materials science, or electrical engineering. Such degrees require courses in physics, mathematics, chemistry, and electronics. The different degrees will have different proportions of those courses.

Utilization of LEDs in circuits, however, requires a quite different background. Technicians and assembly workers need only basic electronics and circuits courses to incorporate the LEDs into circuits or devices. Lighting technicians and lighting engineers also work with LEDs in new applications. Such careers could require bachelor's degrees in their field. New LED lamps are being developed and LEDs are seen as a possible energy-efficient alternative to other types of lighting. They also have long operational lives, so there is continual development to include LEDs in any type of application where light sources of any sort are used.

At first, LEDs were a niche field, with limited uses. However, as LEDs with greater capabilities and different colors of emitted light were produced, uses began to grow. Light-emitting diodes have evolved past the point of simply being indicator lights or alphanumeric displays.

Developments in semiconductor manufacturing have driven down the cost of many semiconductor devices, including LEDs. The reducing cost combined with the energy efficiency of LEDs has led these devices to become more prominent, particularly where colored lights are desired. Research continues to produce newer LEDs with different colors, different power requirements, and different intensities. Newer techniques are being developed to produce white light using LEDs. These technological developments will make LEDs even more practical replacements for existing light sources, despite their higher initial up-front costs.

Research continues on LEDs to make them more commercially and aesthetically viable as alternatives to more traditional light sources. In the United States, the Department of Energy promoted the use of energy-efficient LED lighting and projected that the adoption and use of LEDs could save consumers more than 340 terawatt-hours of energy and US$30 billion by the year 2027. However, research is also continuing on other alternative light sources. The highest-efficiency fluorescent lights have similar efficiencies to standard LEDs, but they cost less and are able to produce pleasing white light that LEDs do not yet produce. Light-emitting diodes will continue to play an increasing role in their current uses, but it is unclear if they will eventually become wide-scale replacements for incandescent or fluorescent lights.

—*Raymond D. Benge*

References

Chi, Nan. *LED-Based Visible Light Communications.* Springer-Verlag Berlin Heidelberg, 2018.

Held, Gilbert. *Introduction to Light Emitting Diode Technology and Applications.* Auerbach, 2019.

Kitai, Adrian, editor. *Materials for Solid State Lighting and Displays.* John Wiley & Sons, 2017.

"LED Lighting." *Energy.gov*, www.energy.gov/energysaver/save-electricity-and-fuel/lighting-choices-save-you-money/led-lighting.

Lee, Cheng-Chung, editor. *The Current Trends of Optics and Photonics.* Springer Netherlands, 2015.

Mottier, Patrick, editor. *LEDs for Lighting Applications.* John Wiley & Sons, 2009.

Paynter, Robert T. *Introductory Electronic Devices and Circuits: Conventional Flow Version.* 7th ed., Prentice Hall, 2006.

Razeghi, Manijeh. *Fundamentals of Solid State Engineering.* 4th ed., Springer International, 2019.

LINKEDIN

Introduction

LinkedIn is an online social networking website that is used for professional business networking. Unlike other social media sites such as Facebook and Twitter that cater to general social interests, LinkedIn is designed specifically for professional networking based upon the reality that business connections remain significant factors for starting and progressing careers. On LinkedIn profiles, which serve as a kind of digital résumé, users can list their job experience, skills, education, and business connections. The service allows people to search for a job, connect with professional partners in a wide range of fields, and a variety of other business-related tasks. Employers can use the site to list jobs and search for potential new hires.

Alongside the professional networking aspects of LinkedIn, the service allows users to post images, share articles and videos, and take advantage of other functions common to social-networking websites. Companies can also make their own business pages for users to follow that include their information and job listings. Other features supported on LinkedIn include interest groups where users discuss specific business-related topics, and the LinkedIn Influencers program where professionals share their insights with members.

Background

Entrepreneur and investor Reid Hoffman founded LinkedIn in late 2002. Previously, Hoffman was executive vice president in charge of development at the e-commerce service PayPal. After PayPal was sold to the online shopping platform eBay, Hoffman decided to start LinkedIn with his share of the money. When he founded the company, the United States was experiencing an economic downturn, which Hoffman believes added to LinkedIn's competitive advantage.

He recruited a team of colleagues from PayPal and SocialNet to help him create the service and build the company. These colleagues included Allen Blue, Lee Hower, and David Eves. After six months of development, LinkedIn officially launched on May 5, 2003. Growth was slow during the first few weeks, with thirteen of the company's employees inviting 112 people to join the service. However, the growth was enough to draw the attention of venture capital firm Sequoia Capital, which became the company's first investor.

LinkedIn continued to grow and in 2008 the company opened its first international office in London, United Kingdom, and launched French and Spanish language versions. By late 2010, the company was valued at $1.575 billion and employed almost one thousand people in ten offices around the world. The following year, LinkedIn filed for an initial public offering (IPO), so its stock could be traded on the open market. The first shares were sold on May 19, 2011, and the price of shares increased as much as 171 percent during the first day of trading on the New York Stock Exchange.

Recent statistics indicate that LinkedIn has generated $8 billion revenue in 2020 and boasts over 756 million members. However, it is not accurately known how many users are active daily or even every month.

How It Works

LinkedIn is a professional-networking service that allows users to build business connections, look for jobs, and find potential job candidates. As of January, 2015, it is the world's largest professional network on the internet. The users of the service range from people searching for a job to executives of Fortune 500 companies. The site contains several features that enable users to connect and engage with their professional network. While many features are provided free of charge, premium subscriptions are available so that professionals can better manage their networks and business identity.

A LinkedIn professional profile contains a user's basic information and work experience. It acts as a résumé, with a focus on employment and education. There is also a section where users can provide information on certifications, specific skills, affiliated groups, and other honors. After creating a profile, users can then search for contacts by uploading their e-mail address book and by performing a general search. LinkedIn also finds colleagues based on the

employment information and education history users provide.

Unlike other social media services where a person is added as a casual "friend," network "connections" on LinkedIn typically mean that the two people know each other well as trusted business associates and can vouch for their work experience and skills. Contacts who accept a user's invitation to connect are known as "direct connections." Everyone a direct connection is affiliated with becomes a part of his or her network. How directly a user is connected to another user dictates how they can communicate with each other.

LinkedIn Groups allows users to hold a discussion about a specific business-related topic. While other social media services such as Facebook allow users to create their own groups without hindrance, a panel of professionals must first review new groups that wish to be added to LinkedIn. Once a group is allowed, that group's manager can accept or reject applications from users to join.

Many users rely on LinkedIn to stay in touch with colleagues or classmates. Others use it to actively search for jobs and post job listings. Companies that post job listings on the website must pay a fee to do so. LinkedIn's audience goes beyond employees and employers as well. Salesmen also use LinkedIn to engage with contacts in their target industry, and entrepreneurs can use the site to look for potential business partners and investors.

Popularity

Since its launch, LinkedIn has become immensely popular around the world. Initially, LinkedIn's user adoption was slow. In its first week the service had 2,500 users and after the first month this grew to 6,000. By November 2003, there were 37,000 users. After two years, the service had more than 1.7 million registered users. The company's chief executive officer, Jeff Weiner, reported that one new user was joining the site every second as of November 2010, bringing the total to 85 million.

From there LinkedIn's popularity increased dramatically as its reputation as a legitimate professional network continued to grow. In 2015, the service boasted over 400 million users in over two hundred countries and territories. As of 2020, LinkedIn reports over 690 million individual users.

—Patrick G. Cooper

References

Anders, George. "How LinkedIn Has Turned Your Resume into a Cash Machine." *Forbes*. Forbes.com, 27 June 2012.

___. "LinkedIn Reprices Premium Services, Hoping Users Won't Turn Furious." *Forbes*. Forbes.com, 6 Jan. 2015.

Blodget, Henry. "LinkedIn's CEO Jeff Weiner Reveals the Importance of Body Language, Mistakes Made Out of Fear, and One Time He Really Doubted Himself." *Business Insider*, 22 Sept. 2014.

Chang, Alexandra. "The Most Important LinkedIn Page You've Never Seen." *Wired*. Condé Nast, 15 Apr. 2013.

Duffy, Jill. "LinkedIn." *PC*. Ziff Davis, 27 Nov. 2013.

Gershbein, J. D. "LinkedIn Publishing: A New Era of Social Influence." *The Huffington Post*. HuffingtonPost.com, 28 Apr. 2014.

Goel, Vindu. "LinkedIn Wants to Be Your Soapbox, Not Just Your Résumé." *The New York Times*, 19 Feb. 2014.

Iqbal, Monsoor. "LinkedIn Usage and Revenue Statistics: 2022." *BusinessofApps*, www.businessofapps.com.

Pozin, Ilya. "200 Million Users? LinkedIn Is Just Getting Started." *Forbes*. Forbes.com, 18 Apr. 2013.

Yeung, Ken. "LinkedIn Now Has 400M Users, but Only 25% of Them Use It Monthly." *VentureBeat*, 29 Oct. 2015.

LIQUID CRYSTAL TECHNOLOGY

Introduction

Liquid crystal devices are the energy efficient, low-cost displays used in a variety of applications in which information or images are presented. The operation of the devices is based on the unique electrical and optical properties of liquid crystal materials. Liquid crystal technology is the use of a unique property of matter to create visual displays that have become the standard for modern technology.

Background

Originally discovered as a state existing between a solid and a liquid, liquid crystals were later found to have applications for visual display. While liquid crystals are less rigid than something in a solid state of matter, they also are ordered in a manner not found in liquids. As anisotropic molecules, liquid crystals can be polarized to a specific orientation to achieve the desired lighting effects in display technologies.

Liquid crystals themselves can exist in several states. These range from a well-ordered crystal state to a disordered liquid state. In-between states are known as the smectic phase, which have layering, and the nematic phase, in which the separate layers no longer exist but the molecules can still be ordered. Liquid crystal displays (LCDs) at this point typically use crystals in the nematic state. They also use calamitic liquid crystals, whose rodlike shape and orientation along one axis allow the display to lighten and darken.

Over time, researchers have made advances in the materials used for LCDs and the route of power for manipulating the crystals, allowing for the low-cost, high-resolution, energy-efficient displays that have become the dominant technology for displays such as computers and television sets. Future research should allow for improvements in the response time of the displays and for better viewing from different angles.

History

Liquid crystals were discovered by Austrian botanist and chemist Friedrich Reinitzer in 1888. While working with cholesterol, he discovered what appeared to be a phase of matter between the solid (crystal) state and the liquid state. While attempting to find the melting point, Reinitzer observed that within a certain temperature range he had a cloudy mixture, and only at a higher temperature did that mixture become a liquid. Reinitzer wrote of his discovery to his friend, German physicist Otto Lehmann, who not only confirmed Reinitzer's discovery—that the liquid crystal state was unique and not simply a mixture of solid and liquid states—but also noted some distinct visual properties, namely that light can travel in one of two different ways through the crystals, a property known as birefringence.

After the discovery of liquid crystals, the field saw a lengthy period of dormancy. Modern display applications have their roots in the early 1960s, in part because of the work of French physicist and Nobel laureate Pierre-Gilles de Gennes, who connected research in liquid crystals with that in superconductors. He found that applying voltages to liquid crystals allowed for control of their orientation, thus allowing for control of the passage of light through them.

In the early 1970s, researchers, including Swiss physicist and inventor Martin Schadt at the Swiss company Hoffman-LaRoche, discovered the twisted-nematic effect—a central idea in LCD technology. (The year of invention is typically said to be 1971, although patents were awarded later.) The idea was patented in the United States at the same time by the International Liquid Xtal Company (now LXD), which was founded by American physicist and inventor James Fergason in Kent, Ohio. (Fergason was part of the Liquid Crystal Institute at Kent State University. The institute was founded by American chemist Glenn H. Brown in 1965.) Licensing the patents to outside manufacturers allowed for the production of simple LCDs in products such as calculators and wristwatches.

In the 1980s, LCD technology expanded into computers. LCDs became critical components of laptop computers and smaller television sets. With research continuing on liquid crystals into the twenty-first century, LCD televisions overtook cathode ray tubes (CRTs) as the dominant technology for television sets.

How It Works

Liquid crystal displays have a similar structure, whether in a digital watch or in a 40-inch (102-centimeter) television. The liquid crystals are held between two layers of glass. A layer of transparent conductors on the liquid crystal side of the glass allows the liquid crystal layer to be manipulated. Polarized film layers are placed on the outside ends of the glass, one of which will face the viewer and the other will remain at the back of the display.

Polarizers alter the course of light. Typically, light travels outward in random directions. Polarizers present a barrier, blocking light from traveling in certain directions and preventing glare. The polarizers in an LCD are oriented at 90-degree angles from each other. With the polarizers in place alone, all light would be blocked from traveling through an LCD, but the workings of liquid crystals allow that light to come through.

The simplest LCD displays, such as calculators and watches, typically do not have their own light sources. Instead, they have what is known as passive display. In back of the LCD display is a reflective surface. Light enters the display and then bounces off the reflective surface to allow for the screen display. Simple LCDs are monochromatic and have specific areas (typically bars or dots) that become light or dark. While these devices are lower-powered, some do still use a light source of their own. Alarm clocks, for example, have light-emitting diodes (LEDs) as part of their display so that they can be seen in the dark.

For larger monitors that display complex images in color, the setup for an LCD becomes more complicated. Multicolor LCDs need a significant light source at the back of the display. The glass used for more sophisticated LCD displays will have microscopic etchings on the glass plates at the front and back of the display. As with the polarizing filters and the conductors, the etchings are at 90-degree angles from each other, vertical on one plate and horizontal on the other. This alignment forms a matrix of points in each location where the horizontal and vertical etchings cross, resulting in what are known as pixels. Each pixel has a unique address for the electronic workings of the display. Many television sets are marketed as having 1080p, referring to 1,080 horizontal lines of pixels.

An active matrix (AM) display will have individual thin film transistors (TFTs) added at each pixel to allow for control of those sites. Three transistors are actually present at each pixel, each accompanied by an additional filter of red, green, or blue. Each of those transistors has 256 power levels. The blending of the different levels of those three colors (16,777,216 possible combinations) and the number of pixels allows for the full-color LCD displays.

While light is displayed as a combination of red, green, and blue on screens, printing is typically done on a scale that uses cyan, magenta, yellow, and black as base colors. This accounts for some discrepancy between colors that appear on screen and those that show up on paper.

Applications and Products

Liquid crystals are used in displays for a number of products. Early uses included digital thermometers, digital wristwatches, electronic games, and calculators. As the power needed for an LCD display and resolution improved, LCDs came to be used in computer monitors, television sets, car dashboards, and cellphones.

Watches and calculators use what is known as a seven-segment display, wherein each of the seven segments that make up a number are "lit" or "unlit" to represent the ten digits. Looking closely at an LCD will reveal that most numbers come from seven segments, which can be lit to display the ten different digits. Without the polarizing layer, the display would not work. Placing the polarized layers in parallel on the surface would, for example, cause the outlines of all the numbers and other areas on the display to illuminate (appearing as 8s) and leave as blanks the rest of the display.

Early electronic games also used a segment display. Fixed places on the display would be either lit or unlit, allowing game characters to appear to move across the screen.

Because of their sensitivity to heat, liquid crystals have been studied for their use as temperature monitors. Molecules in the smectic liquid crystal state rotate around their axes, and the angle at which they rotate (the pitch) can be temperature sensitive. At different temperatures, the wavelength of light given off will change. Some liquid crystal mixtures are fairly temperature sensitive, and so the mixture of the colors will change with relatively small changes in the temperature. Because of this, they can be used for displays such as infrared or surface temperatures.

Liquid crystal displays have been, and will likely remain, the standard for laptop computers. They have been used for monitors since the notebook computer was introduced. Because of the low power consumption and thinness of the monitor, their use is likely to continue.

There are several developments that could affect LCD technology in the near future. One example is the development of LEDs for use as backlighting for LCDs. By using LEDs rather than a fluorescent bulb, as LCD technology now uses, LCDs can manifest greater contrast in different areas of the screen. Other areas of LCD development include photoalignment and supertwisted nematic (STN) LCDs.

Grooves are made in glass used for LCDs, but this has raised some concern about possible electric charges, reducing the picture quality. Additionally, photoalignment—a focus on the materials used to align the liquid crystals in the display—should ultimately allow for liquid display screens that are flexible or curved, rather than rigid (as are glass panels).

STN LCDs are modified versions of TN LCDs. Rather than twisting the crystals between the layers a total of 90 degrees, STN LCDs rotate the crystals by 270 degrees within the display. This greater level of twisting allows for a much greater degree of change in the levels of brightness in a display. At the same time, it presents a challenge because the response time for the screen is significantly slower.

Social Context and Future Prospects

Some of the concerns and problems with LCDs are being confronted by society as a whole. One concern is the high energy consumption of fluorescent lamps used by LCDs. In contrast, LED lights, which use less energy, are being used more and more in LCDs. There is concern, however, about the environmental hazards LEDs may create when they are disposed of in landfills. Another possibility is the use of carbon nanotubes, which would provide LCD backlighting but would use even less energy than LEDs.

Durability concerns may also come to play a role. The grooves in the glass necessary for high-definition LCDs also lead to physical wear and tear on the product. Refining the technology further may produce more durable sets while also alleviating some of the concerns about electronics disposal. Future work on LCDs also will involve altering components to overcome picture quality and durability concerns. Given the prominence of the products that utilize liquid crystals, the technology is likely to be important for development for the foreseeable future.

—*Joseph I. Brownstein*

References

Chigrinov, Vladimir G., Vladimir M. Kozenkov, and Hoi-Sing Kwok. *Photoalignment of Liquid Crystalline Materials.* John Wiley & Sons, 2008.

Collings, Peter J., and Michael Hird. *Introduction to Liquid Crystals.* CRC Press, 2017.

Delepierre, Gabriel, et al. "Green Backlighting for TV Liquid Crystal Display Using Carbon Nanotubes." *Journal of Applied Physics*, vol. 108, no. 4, 2010.

Gross, Benjamin. *The TVs of Tomorrow: How RCA's Flat-Screen Dreams Led to the First LCDs.* U of Chicago P, 2018.

Sluckin, Timothy J., David A. Dunmur, and Horst Stegemeyer. *Crystals That Flow: Classic Papers from the History of Liquid Crystals.* CRC Press, 2004.

Souk, Jun, et al., editors. *Flat Panel Display Manufacturing.* John Wiley & Sons, 2018.

M

MAC OS

Introduction

Mac OS is a family of operating systems—programs used to run computers—pioneered by the Apple computer company and utilized on a wide variety of Apple systems. Noted for being the first successful graphical interface operating system and for making its debut on the original 1984 Macintosh, Mac OS played a key role in the emergence of the personal computer as a popular consumer product. Though later overshadowed by Microsoft Windows, Mac OS continued to be one of the most recognized and widely used operating systems on the market. Over the years, it evolved through a variety of iterations, each of which has offered new features and an improved user experience.

Background

Although Mac OS often receives credit for being the first graphical interface operating system, it actually had two predecessors. The first of these was the operating system featured on the Xerox Alto. The Alto was a computer manufactured in the 1970s with a graphical operating system that was the first of its kind. This software replaced the traditional command-line operating system that required users to issue text commands. However, its staggering cost of $32,000 ensured that it would never be a commercial success. Regardless, after visiting Xerox's facilities in the early 1980s, Apple engineers recognized the potential of the graphical interface to the future of computing. Eventually, the Apple team members incorporated lessons from Xerox when they produced the Lisa, the first Apple computer to feature a graphical interface operating system. Like the Xerox Alto, however, the Lisa was a commercial failure.

Still determined to make an affordable personal computer that would appeal to the average consumer,

Apple introduced the Macintosh in 1984. Powering the Macintosh was a graphical interface operating system that, although unnamed at the time, would eventually become known as System 1, the first version of Mac OS. With a virtual desktop, windows, icons, menus, scrollbars, a file manager called Finder, and mouse control, System 1 represented a revolutionary shift in the user experience that would soon become the industry standard.

Evolution

When the Macintosh proved to be a success, Apple engineers began working to improve its operating system. The result of their efforts was System 2,

Apple logo. Image via Wikimedia Commons. [Public domain.]

released in 1985. Though very similar to System 1, System 2 featured several key upgrades, such as the inclusion of key-commands for creating new folders and shutting down the computer, as well as an enhanced version of Finder. Thanks to these and other tweaks, System 2 ran 20 percent faster than System 1.

After Microsoft released the inaugural version of Windows in late 1985, Apple once again revisited the design of its own operating system. When System 3 debuted the following year, it included a new version of Finder that came equipped with file-nesting capabilities that allowed users to create folders within folders for the first time. It also included Disk Cache, a program that improved performance by storing commonly used commands in memory. While these improvements were helpful for users, System 3 was plagued by bugs and, as a result, did not work as well as hoped.

Apple released System 4 in 1987. Among other updates, System 4 offered support for disk drives and multiple monitors. It also included MultiFinder, a new version of Finder that allowed systems with enough memory to run more than one program at a time. The following year, Apple skipped System 5 and jumped ahead to System 6. The most notable improvement in System 6 was the inclusion of color support. Although the desktop and Finder were still rendered in black and white as they had been since System 1, System 6 made it possible for third-party applications to run in full color.

With the release of System 7 in 1991, Mac OS took its first major step forward. In addition to including a new version of Finder that combined the previously separate Finder and MultiFinder into a single file manager, System 7 introduced virtual memory, which turned unused disc drive space into random-access memory (RAM), a type of memory designed to improve system performance. Until the release of Mac OS X in 2001, System 7 was Apple's longest running operating system.

In 1997, Apple made the decision to officially rename its operating system series Mac OS. Thus, Mac OS 8 was the first title in the series not to bear the "System" name. Along with a number of other upgrades, Mac OS 8 featured the debut of Sherlock, an integrated web search function that worked in tandem with Finder.

Although not substantially different from Mac OS 8, 1999's Mac OS 9 offered several key improvements. Most notably, it allowed multiple users to create individual accounts on a single machine. Mac OS 9 also gave users the ability to download system updates from the internet.

The launch of Mac OS X in 2001 marked the debut of the modern Mac OS. Touting a completely redesigned user interface and a brand-new code base, Mac OS X radically changed the Apple experience. Along with several new features, Mac OS X also introduced the concept of protected memory, which prevented applications from corrupting one another's data. The debut of Mac OS X also enabled the creation of an array of new programs, including the Safari web browser. OS X, the tenth version of the Macintosh OS, was released on March 24, and it combined a stable Unix-based platform with a visually appealing user interface called Aqua. For software developers, OS X introduced the Carbon application programming interface (API) and the X-code integrated development environment (IDE) for writing code. OS X was a key step in making Macs a central focus of consumer computing culture. Cat-themed names for OS X releases were popular with enthusiasts and eventually became marketing devices. OS X versions progressed from Cheetah (version 10.0) and Puma (10.1) in 2001 to Jaguar (10.2) in 2002, Panther (10.3) in 2003, Tiger (10.4) in 2005, Leopard (10.5) in 2007, Snow Leopard (10.6) in 2009, Lion (10.7) in 2011, and Mountain Lion (10.8) in 2012.

Beginning with Mavericks (10.9) in 2013, the company moved away from the cat-themed names to names associated with California, subsequently introducing Yosemite (10.10) in 2014 and El Capitan (10.11) in 2015. In 2016, macOS Sierra was released, representing Apple's attempt to bring some consistency to the naming of operating systems for all of its products, such as iOS and watch OS. MacOS High Sierra followed in 2017 and macOS Mojave followed in 2018. Each update has brought new features, including chat programs, customizable widgets (such as a calculator or dictionary), a file and application search, or a simple backup system.

In 2018, Mac moved to OS 10 (Mojave) which allowed for Dark Mode uses. In 2019, iTunes was dismantled, and OS 10.15 (Catalina) allowed users to connect an iPad screen to their Mac. In 2020, Big Sur rolled out OS11.0 which allowed users to run iOS apps natively on their Mac computers. These are called universal apps. Shortly afterward, in fall 2021

Monterey OS 12 enabled Shortcuts and a wide range of FaceTime augmentations.

—Jack Lasky

References

Edwards, Benj. "The Little-Known Apple Lisa: Five Quirks and Oddities." *Macworld*, 30 Jan. 2013, www.macworld.com/article/2026544/the-little-known-apple-lisa-five-quirks-and-oddities.html.

"An Illustrated History of Mac OS X." *Tower*, 12 Jan. 2016, www.git-tower.com/blog/history-of-osx/.

Moretti, Marcus. "Before Mac OS X, There Was OS 1 Through 9: A History of Apple's Operating System." *Business Insider*, 10 July 2012, www.businessinsider.com/mac-os-i-through-x-2012-7?op=1.

Warren, Christina. "The Evolution of Mac OS, From 1984 to Mountain Lion." *Mashable*, 17 Feb. 2012, mashable.com/2012/02/17/mac-os-timeline/#KKsyA8f26qqR.

MALWARE

Introduction

Malware, or malicious software, is a form of software designed to disrupt a computer or to take advantage of computer users. Creating and distributing malware is a form of cybercrime. Criminals have frequently used malware to conduct digital extortion.

Malware is a name given to any software program or computer code that is used for malicious, criminal, or unauthorized purposes. While there are many different types of malware, all malware acts against the interests of the computer user, either by damaging the user's computer or extorting payment from the user. Most malware is made and spread for the purposes of extortion. Other malware programs destroy or compromise a user's data. In some cases, government defense agencies have developed and used malware. One example is the 2010 Stuxnet virus, which attacked digital systems and damaged physical equipment operated by enemy states or organizations.

Hex dump of the Blaster worm, showing a message left for Microsoft co-founder Bill Gates by the worm's programmer. Photo via Wikimedia Commons. [Public domain.]

Background

The earliest forms of malware were viruses and worms. A virus is a self-replicating computer program that attaches itself to another program or file. It is transferred between computers when the infected file is sent to another computer. A worm is similar to a virus, but it can replicate itself and send itself to another networked computer without being attached to another file.

The first viruses and worms were experimental programs created by computer hobbyists in the 1980s. As soon as they were created, computer engineers began working on the first antivirus programs to remove viruses and worms from infected computers.

Public knowledge about malware expanded rapidly in the late 1990s and early 2000s due to several well-publicized computer viruses. These included the Happy99 worm in 1999 and the ILOVEYOU worm in May 2000, the latter of which infected nearly 50 million computers within ten days.

According to research from the cybersecurity company PurpleSec, more than 812 million malware infections took place during 2018, and the majority of malware was delivered via email. PurpleSec further reported that malware specifically targeting mobile devices had become increasingly prevalent during the second decade of the twenty-first century and that the majority of mobile malware was hosted by third-party app stores.

Types of Malware

One of the most familiar types of malware is adware. This refers to programs that create and display unwanted advertisements to users, often in pop-ups or uncloseable windows. Adware may be legal or illegal, depending on how the programs are used. Some internet browsers use adware programs that analyze a user's shopping or web browsing history to present targeted advertisements. A 2014 survey by Google and the University of California, Berkeley, showed that more than 5 million computers in the United States were infected by adware at that time.

Another type of malware is known as spyware. This is a program that is installed on a user's computer to track the user's activity or provide a third party with access to the computer system. Spyware programs can also be legal. Many can be unwittingly downloaded by users who visit certain sites or attempt to download other files.

One of the more common types of malware is scareware. Scareware tries to convince users that their computer has been infected by a virus or has experienced another technical issue. Users are then prompted to purchase antivirus or computer-cleaning software to fix the problem.

Although ransomware dates back as far as 1989, it gained new popularity in the 2010s. Ransomware is a type of malware that encrypts or blocks access to certain features of a computer or programs. Users with infected computers are then asked to pay a ransom to have the encryption removed.

Addressing the Threat

Combating malware is difficult for various reasons. Launching malware attacks internationally makes it difficult for police or national security agencies to target those responsible. Cybercriminals may also use zombie computers to distribute malware. Zombie computers are computers that have been infected with a virus without the owner's knowledge. Cybercriminals may use hundreds of zombie computers simultaneously. Investigators may therefore trace malware to a computer only to find that it is a zombie distributor and that there are no links to the program's originator. While malware is most common on personal computers, there are several malware programs that can be distributed through tablets and smartphones.

Often creators of malware try to trick users into downloading their programs. Adware may appear in the form of a message from a user's computer saying that a driver or other downloadable update is needed. In other cases, malware can be hidden in social media functions, such as the Facebook "Like" buttons found on many websites. The ransomware program Locky, which appeared in February 2016, used Microsoft Word to attack users' computers.

Users would receive an email containing a document that prompted them to enable macros to read the document. If the user followed the instructions, the Locky program would be installed on their computer. Essentially, users infected by Locky made two mistakes. First, they downloaded a Word document attachment from an unknown user. Then they followed a prompt to enable macros within the document—a feature that is automatically turned off in all versions of Microsoft Word. Many malware programs depend on users downloading or installing programs.

Therefore, computer security experts warn that the best way to avoid contamination is to avoid opening emails, messages, and attachments from unknown or untrusted sources.

—*Micah L. Issitt*

References

Bettany, Andrew, and Mike Halsey. *Windows Virus and Malware Troubleshooting.* Apress, 2017.

Brandom, Russell. "Google Survey Finds More than Five Million Users Infected with Adware." *Verge*, 6 May 2015, www.theverge.com/2015/5/6/8557843/google-adware-survey-ad-injectors-security-malware.

Franceschi-Bicchierai, Lorenzo. "Love Bug: The Virus That Hit 50 Million People Turns 15." *Motherboard*, 4 May 2015, www.vice.com/en_us/article/d73jnk/love-bug-the-virus-that-hit-50-million-people-turns-15.

Gallagher, Sean. "'Locky' Crypto-Ransomware Rides in on Malicious Word Document Macro." *Ars Technica*, 17 Feb. 2016, arstechnica.com/information-technology/2016/02/locky-crypto-ransomware-rides-in-on-malicious-word-document-macro/.

Hudak, Heather C. *Cybercrime.* Abdo, 2020.

Kleymenov, Alexey, and Amr Thabet. *Mastering Malware Analysis.* Packt, 2019.

Rains, Tim. *Cybersecurity Threats, Malware Trends, and Strategies.* Packt, 2020.

"The Ultimate List of Cyber Security Statistics for 2019." *PurpleSec*, 2019, purplesec.us/resources/cyber-security-statistics/.

MEDIA LITERACY

Introduction

Media literacy is defined as the ability to access, communicate, interpret, and evaluate messages or texts across a range of digitally mediated forms. Individuals who are media literate can identify how, why, and for what purposes messages or texts are constructed. Young people around the world are spending more time consuming and producing multimedia texts, such as blogs, chat forums, wikis, videos, and video games.

An infographic on how to spot fake news. Image by the International Federation of Library Associations and Institutions (IFLA), via Wikimedia Commons.

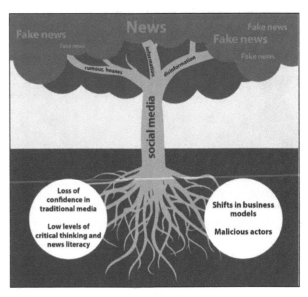

The roots of "fake news," UNESCO's World Trends Report. Image by UNESCO, via Wikimedia Commons.

Scholars and educators are calling for the development of new media literacy: a form of critical literacy that attends to the ongoing development of media and information and communication technologies (ICTs), multimodality, and the convergence of media toward the privatization and commercialization of knowledge.

Background

The relationship between media, ICTs, and young people has evolved over time and across disciplines. The first wave of research in the 1960s and 1970s was primarily concerned with investigating the ideological messages embedded in print and digital texts. The second wave of research, in the 1980s, shifted the focus to the reader or the audience of texts. In 1982, the UNESCO Grünwald Declaration established media literacy as a global concern. It called for educational and political systems to promote the development of a critical understanding of communication and information technologies for all citizens, specifically in relation to images, words, and sounds. The third wave, in the 1990s, highlighted the ways in which audiences negotiate the meaning of various texts in relation to their social locations—for example, their social class, gender, ethnicity, and sexuality—and social and cultural contexts.

Deliberately false stories can appear to come from credible, journalistic sources. Photo via iStock/Tero Vesalainen. [Used under license.]

The rise of the internet in the 1990s catalyzed debates regarding how to use digital technology for learning and education. Since 2000, governmental, educational, and institutional support for media literacy has continued to grow, as has the everyday use of ICTs for communication, corporate and domestic labor, education, and entertainment. New media literacy highlights, among other things, the convergence of media ownership and the privatization and commercialization of media over time.

Media literacy builds on a foundation of active inquiry and critical thinking and includes the ability to access, communicate, interpret, evaluate, create, reflect on, and interact with digitally mediated texts. Interdisciplinary research has contributed literature that examines the relationships between media literacy and cultural practices, public health and well-being, societal norms and values, and education and work opportunities.

The following themes were identified across research: (1) mass media influences both individuals and society; (2) this influence is perceived to be subtle and individuals who are passive consumers are more susceptible to media influence; (3) a goal of media literacy is to enable individuals to become aware of the role and influence that media has on their lives and to empower them to use media as a tool through which they can achieve their own goals; (4) media literacy is learned and develops over time, and; (5) to increase media literacy individuals must be engaged in active knowledge construction and skill development.

Media shapes individually lived experiences, cultures, and societies. Cultural and corporate norms, values, ideologies, and practices are mediated by modern day modes of storytelling from movies, videogames, television, music, and the internet. Drawing on educational reformer John Dewey's argument in the early twentieth century that a strong democracy relies on an educated and literate citizenry, scholars of new media position media literacy as a vital ability for a democratic citizenry and socially just world.

—*Kristen P. Goessling and Jennifer A. Vadeboncoeur*

References

Alvermann, Donna E., and Margaret C. Hagood. "Critical Media Literacy: Research, Theory, and Practice in 'New Times.'" *Journal of Educational Research*, vol. 93, no. 3, 2000, pp. 193–205.

Buckingham, David. *The Media Literacy of Children and Young People: A Review of the Research Literature on Behalf of Ofcom.* Ofcom, 2005.

Luke, Carmen. "As Seen on TV or Was That My Phone? *New Media* Literacy." *Policy Futures in Education,* vol. 5, no. 1, 2007, pp. 50–58.

___. "Cyberpedagogy." *The International Handbook of Virtual Learning Environments,* edited by Joel Weiss, Jason Nolan, Jeremy Hunsinger, and Peter Pericles, Springer, 2006, pp. 269–77.

"Media Literacy: A Definition and More." *Medialit. org.* Center for Media Literacy, n.d.

National Association for Media Literacy Education. "Core Principles of Media Literacy Education in the United States." *NAMLE.net.* NAMLE, n.d.

Potter, James W. "Review of Literature on Media Literacy." *Sociology Compass,* vol. 7, no. 6, 2013, pp. 417–35.

Rideout, Victoria J., et al. "Generation M2: Media in the Lives of 8- to 18- Year Olds." *Kaiser Family Foundation.* Kaiser Family Foundation, 2010.

Share, Jeff. *Media Literacy Is Elementary: Teaching Youth to Critically Read and Create Media.* Lang, 2009.

MICROSCALE 3D PRINTING

Introduction

Microscale three-dimensional (3D) printing is a type of 3D printing that makes it possible to construct objects at an extremely small scale. Some processes can create objects as small as 100 micrometers. 3D printing at this scale has a number of applications for computing and medicine. It makes it possible to produce microscopic structures out of organic materials for biomedical applications.

Three-dimensional printing is a relatively new technology. However, it has already revolutionized manufacturing. It takes its name from traditional computer printers that produce pages of printed images. Regular printers operate by depositing small amounts of ink at precise locations on a piece of paper. Instead of ink, a 3D printer uses a material, such as a polymer, metallic powder, or even organic material. Following a digital design, it builds an object by depositing small amounts of that material in successive layers; this process is also known as additive manufacturing (AM). In some cases, 3D printing fastens materials to a substrate using heat, adhesives, or other methods. 3D printing can produce incredibly intricate objects that would be difficult or impossible to create through traditional manufacturing methods.

Background

Microscale 3D printing advances the innovation of standard 3D printing to create microscopic structures. The potential applications for microscale 3D printing are still being explored. However, microscale 3D printing presents the possibility of creating tissue for transplant. For example, full-scale 3D printing has already produced some types of tissue, such as muscle, cartilage, and bones. One problem is the printed tissue sometimes did not survive because it had no circulatory system to bring blood and nutrients to the new tissue. Microscale 3D printing makes it possible to create the tiny blood vessels needed in living tissue, among other potential applications.

3D Printing Methods

The basic approach used by 3D printing is to build an object by attaching tiny amounts of material to each other at precise locations. Some materials are melted before they are deposited. Material extrusion heats polymer filament. The melted plastic material is then extruded through nozzles and deposited in a layer. The materials then harden into place, and another layer is added. With vat photopolymerization, a light-sensitive liquid polymer is printed onto a platform within a vat of liquid resin. An ultraviolet (UV) laser then hardens a layer of resin. More liquid polymer is then added, and the process is repeated. With material jetting, a printer head deposits liquefied plastic or other light-sensitive material onto a platform. The material is then hardened with UV light.

Other methods melt or fuse materials after they have been deposited. In powder bed fusion, the printer heats a bed of powdered glass, metal, ceramic, or plastic until the materials fuse together in the desired locations. Another layer of powder is then added and fused onto the first. Binder jetting uses a printer head to deposit drops of glue-like liquid into a powdered medium. The liquid soaks into and solidifies the medium. Sheet lamination fuses together thin sheets of paper, metal, or plastic with an adhesive. The layers are then cut with a laser into the desired shape. In directed energy deposition, a metal wire or powder is deposited in thin layers before being melted with a laser.

The method used depends on the physical properties of the material being printed. Metal alloys, for example, cannot easily be liquefied for vat polymerization, material jetting, or material extrusion. Instead, they are printed using binder jetting, powder bed fusion, or sheet lamination.

Microscale Methods

Microscale 3D printing requires more exact methods to create objects that are just a few micrometers wide. Microscopic objects require tiny droplets of materials and precise locations of deposition. One microscale 3D printing technique is optical lithography. This technique uses light to create patterns in a photosensitive resist, where material is then deposited. Optical transient liquid molding (TLM) uses UV light patterns and a custom flow of liquid polymer to create objects that are smaller than the width of a human hair. Optical TLM combines a liquid polymer, which will form the structure of the printed object, with a liquid mold in a series of tiny pillars. The pillars are arranged based on software that determines the shape of the liquids' flow.

Patterned UV light then cuts into the liquids to further shape the stream. The combination of the liquid mold and the UV light pattern allow the creation of highly complex structures that are just 100 micrometers in size.

Microscale 3D printing makes it possible to create extremely small circuits. This will enable the creation of new devices, such as "smart clothing" that can sense the wearer's body temperature and adjust its properties based on this information. Microscale 3D printing may also revolutionize the creation of new medicines. Because drug uptake by cells is shape-dependent, the precision of microscale 3D printing may allow researchers to design custom drugs for specific brain receptors.

A New Type of "Ink"

Some refer to the build materials used in 3D printing as inks because they take the place of ink as it is used in regular document printers. This can stretch the definition of "ink." Most people think of ink as either the liquid in a pen or the toner of a computer printer. In microscale 3D printing, however, the ink might be human cells used to create an organ or metallic powder that will be fused into tiny circuits.

—*Scott Zimmer*

References

"About Additive Manufacturing." *Additive Manufacturing Research Group*, 2021, www.lboro.ac.uk/research/amrg/about/.

Bernier, Samuel N., Bertier Luyt, Tatiana Reinhard, and Carl Bass. *Design for 3D Printing: Scanning, Creating, Editing, Remixing, and Making in Three Dimensions.* Maker Media, 2014.

Bitonti, Francis. *3D Printing Design: Additive Manufacturing and the Materials Revolution.* Bloomsbury, 2019.

Brockotter, Robin. "Key Design Considerations for 3D Printing." *HUBS*, www.hubs.com/knowledgebase/key-design-considerations-3d-printing/.

Horvath, Joan. *Mastering 3D Printing: Modeling, Printing, and Prototyping with Reprap-Style 3D Printers.* Apress, 2014.

Hoskins, Stephen. *3D Printing for Artists, Designers and Makers.* Bloomsbury, 2013.

Lipson, Hod, and Melba Kurman. *Fabricated: The New World of 3D Printing.* Wiley, 2013.

V., Carlotta. "What Is the Current State of Microscale 3D Printing?" *3DNatives*, 16 Apr. 2020, www.3dnatives.com/en/what-is-the-current-state-of-microscale-3d-printing/.

MICROSOFT EXCEL

Introduction

Microsoft Excel is a computer software program that allows users to create spreadsheets, or displays of rows and columns in which data is recorded. After early innovations in computerized spreadsheets in the 1960s and 1970s, technology company Microsoft first released Excel in 1985. Unlike prior spreadsheet programs, Excel offered a convenient interface and easy data entry. By the early 1990s, Excel had established itself as the foremost spreadsheet application, and a long series of updated versions continually modified and improved its offerings for users.

Background

Traditionally, a spreadsheet is a large, wide paper divided into rows and columns. People use these rows and columns to record information, generally numbers pertaining to transactions. Placing all the data on one sheet makes the information easier to view, sort, and analyze. For centuries, mathematicians, record keepers, accountants, and businesspeople have used spreadsheets to document important numbers and other facts.

In the middle of the twentieth century, computers started to become increasingly important to society. Many designers began finding ways to translate tasks formerly done with paper and ink into the digital realm. One of these pioneers was Richard Mattessich, who in 1961 developed a computerized spreadsheet. This program was useful in its ability to organize and store information, but later designers would add calculating functions that would pave the way for Microsoft Excel.

In 1978, a student named Dan Bricklin was preparing a report that involved a large amount of numeric data. To help speed the process, Bricklin

Excel logo. Image via Wikimedia Commons. [Public domain.]

designed a computer program that allowed users to type in and manipulate information in twenty rows and five columns. Another student, Bob Frankston, perfected the program, which was soon marketed as VisiCalc (a shortened form of "Visible Calculator") at VisiCorp. Although an early success, VisiCalc soon began to struggle in the marketplace. It was over-taken by a competing program called Lotus 1-2-3, which offered many new features, including the ability to turn spreadsheet data into charts.

Creation of Microsoft Excel

Around 1982, engineers at Microsoft developed their own spreadsheet program, Multiplan. This program was successful among some users but was, like VisiCalc, ultimately overwhelmed by the popu-larity of Lotus 1-2-3. In the coming years, Microsoft examined the strong points of Lotus and began de-signing a new competing product that would perfect the idea of an effective and easy-to-use computerized spreadsheet. The result was Microsoft Excel, a spreadsheet program that featured capabilities sim-ilar to Lotus but with the addition of a much more user-friendly platform.

Previous spreadsheet programs required users to input information through command-line text prompts, not directly into the cells of the spread-sheet rows and columns. This process was unwieldy and sometimes confusing. Excel, on the other hand,

was based on a new interface, or a system by which users interact with computers, that used graphics and direct user interaction. An Excel user could use a mouse to point and click on particular fields, rows, columns, or cells and input information directly into them. Further, mouse clicking could access drop-down menus that displayed Excel's various tools and features.

Excel's ease of use and many capabilities made it a favorite among computer users in the early 1980s. The first version, released in 1985, was for the Apple Macintosh. Excel proved so popular that many people purchased the Macintosh primarily to access the program. In 1987, when Microsoft revealed its own operating system, Windows, engineers provided a compatible version of Excel. By the time Windows became the standard operating system in the early 1990s, Excel had outdone Lotus 1-2-3 and cemented its place as the world's premiere spreadsheet program.

Excel's Evolution

Microsoft and Windows became some of the most successful and recognizable brands of the modern era. Excel, too, prospered greatly, particularly after Microsoft began bundling it with a program suite called Microsoft Office. The Office programs were all related by their usefulness to businesses, large and small, as well as to students and other individ-uals looking to perform documentation and com-munication tasks. Some other integral Office pro-grams included Microsoft Word (a word-processing program) and Microsoft PowerPoint (a presenta-tion-making program).

Every few years, Microsoft releases updated ver-sions of Excel, both for Windows and Macintosh op-erating systems. Each new version boasted some im-provements over the last. Excel 2.0 (1987) was the first version to operate on Windows. Excel 3.0 (1990) included improved menus and toolbars and in-creased drawing and chart-making capabilities. Excel 4.0 (1992) streamlined previous versions, and Excel 5.0 (1993) instituted two important improve-ments. One was a multisheet design, which allowed users to flip between multiple spreadsheets within a single file. The other improvement was the ability to create macros, or user-defined shortcuts that could reduce repetitive tasks. For example, a user might create a macro to automatically format all new entries as dollar figures, rather than doing so manually.

Subsequent updates to Excel, such as Excel 95 (1995) and Excel 2000 (1999) added new features, such as an animated "office assistant" character that could provide help to users as well as the means by which users could restore or repair lost information. Excel 2007 (2007) updated menu systems and added new available file types. Excel 2010 (2010) added increased graphical capabilities and formatting options. Excel 2013 (2013), offers an array of new functions. These include Power View, a display of multiple charts based on the same data, and Flash Fill, a feature that detects and replicates patterns in data. In 2016, Excel began using the same name for both the Mac and Windows versions with updates being automatic for users of Office 365. The latest version (as of this publication) is the 2019 version which added more robust charts (both map charts and funnel charts) and the ability to include 3D visuals.

—Mark Dziak

References

"History of Microsoft Excel." *Haresoftware*, www. haresoftware.com/ExcelHistory.htm.

Kaul, Ankit. "History of Microsoft Excel 1978–2013 (Infographic)." *Excel Trick*, www.exceltrick.com/ others/history-of-excel/.

Leung, K. Ming. "History of Microsoft Excel?" *K. Ming Leung.* New York University Polytechnic School of Engineering, cis.poly.edu/~mleung/ CS394/f06/week01/Excel_history.html.

Power, D. J. "A Brief History of Spreadsheets." *Museum of User Interfaces.* Department of Computer Science, University of Maryland, www. cs.umd.edu/class/spring2002/cmsc434-0101/ MUIseum/applications/spreadsheethistory1. html.

Weber, Thomas E. "How Microsoft Excel Changed the World." *Business Insider.* Business Insider, Inc., 28 Dec. 2010, www.businessinsider.com/ how-microsoft-excel-changed-the-world-2010-12.

"What's New in Excel 2013." *Office.* Microsoft, support.office.com/en-us/article/What-s-new-in-Excel-2013-1cbc42cd-bfaf-43d7-9031-5688ef1392f d?CorrelationId=e75af659-e5a8-4d3c-a810-9a8017781cf5&ui=en-US&rs=en-US&ad=US.

MICROSOFT POWERPOINT

Introduction

Microsoft PowerPoint is a computer software program that allows users to create presentations using words, images, sounds, and animations. Developed between 1984 and 1987 by programmers at Forethought, Inc., the program was later purchased and promoted by the technology company Microsoft. Throughout the years and after many updates, PowerPoint became the world's top presentation software and one of the best-known programs in modern computing. It has also, however, garnered some criticism for its arguably harmful effects on its users' public speaking abilities.

Background

Prior to the early 1980s, people had few technological aids for making presentations. Businesspeople and educators generally relied on notes and copied handouts to convey their data. Some used basic overhead projectors with transparent plastic sheets, or slide projectors with slide shows, to display information for audiences. While generally effective, these methods were still limited in their capacity and sometimes difficult to design and execute. Although computers were becoming increasingly common in companies as well as in schools and homes, digital technology had little impact on the traditional forms of presentations.

Starting in 1984, a small team of programmers including Dennis Austin, Robert Gaskins, and Thomas Rudkin began developing plans to digitize presentations for overhead projection. These programmers were employed at the technology company Forethought, Inc., based in Sunnyvale, California. Their proposals set out plans for a program called Presentation that would be compatible with the popular Apple Macintosh computer.

One of the earliest proposals, made by Gaskins in August of 1984, laid out the goals and approaches for the new product. It would be designed to appeal to anyone who had to make presentations, including business managers, teachers, and salespeople. Gaskins noted that people spent $3.5 billion on business presentations in 1982, largely to create millions of slides and transparencies. Computer-based presentations, he posited, could create and present more information faster and less expensively than traditional means.

The Presentation program, even in its earliest manifestations, was designed around the concept of creating projectable slides with customizable borders, graphics, tables, fonts, and other features for display on computer screens. The program would also help presenters create personal notes as well as handouts for audiences and provide some guidance to help in the design of effective presentations. All of this would be contained within a single master file, easy to store and operate.

The programmers believed their creation would make complex presentations clearer and more effective, allow users greater control and ability to make changes, and greatly reduce the time and costs involved in the entire process. Forethought, Inc. approved the project, and the programmers got to work in late 1985. The first version of the program was completed by spring of 1987.

Immediate Success

In 1987, due to a conflict over trademarks, Presentation was renamed PowerPoint. Later that year, burgeoning technology company Microsoft purchased Forethought for $14 million and absorbed PowerPoint into its own offerings. In its first year, PowerPoint proved a modest success, with about a million dollars in sales. When it was moved from the Apple Macintosh onto the PC (personal computer) platform, however, its sales increased tenfold.

Now under the Microsoft banner, PowerPoint grew from a success into a phenomenon. The program was bundled in with many Microsoft products, including the program suite known as Microsoft Office, which also came with word-processing (Microsoft Word) and spreadsheet (Microsoft Excel) applications. Over time, PowerPoint became nearly ubiquitous among computer users. By 1993, PowerPoint was the premier presentation software for PCs. By the twenty-first century, PowerPoint controlled about 95 percent of the presentation-software market.

Every few years, Microsoft introduced updated versions of PowerPoint, each of which expanded the program's offerings. For instance, the original version only allowed slides to be printed in black and white, whereas the second version allowed color

printouts. By 1992, the program had evolved into a virtual slide show, and later versions incorporated animations, transitions, sound and video clips, and other increasingly advanced features.

According to Microsoft, as of 2009 more than 500 million people used PowerPoint, with about 30 million PowerPoint presentations taking place each day around the world. Although originally designed mainly for business uses, PowerPoint quickly began appearing in schools and various community organizations. It became a new standard for presentation giving, although its dominance in this field has been met with deeply mixed reactions by experts and the public alike.

As of 2019, there are over 500,000,000 users of PowerPoint worldwide, with over 350 presentations being started every second and over 300 million presentations being made daily.

Praise and Criticism

PowerPoint has won great popularity among people who might otherwise be anxious about public speaking, or who might have trouble organizing thoughts in an effective manner. Generally, when used properly, PowerPoint has proven to be a very valuable tool for supporting and enhancing a speaker's points during a presentation. Many analysts suggest that the best use of PowerPoint is in providing supporting graphics and key words, and that presentations done that way can be of great benefit to companies and individuals.

The popularity of the program has also brought about a large amount of criticism. Many critics feel the program is overused and that poor presenters use it as a crutch rather than a springboard to more dynamic and meaningful presentations. Ineffective PowerPoint presentations may be confusing, boring, or distracting to audiences. Some are too laden with information or are simply too long—Microsoft estimates that the average PowerPoint session lasts 250 minutes. Critics also note that poorly made PowerPoint presentations may simply employ a tedious series of bulleted lists instead of promoting truly insightful and comprehensive discussions of the issues being presented.

—Mark Dziak

References

Austin, Dennis. "Beginnings of PowerPoint: A Personal Technical Story." *Computer History Museum*, archive.computerhistory.org/resources/access/text/2012/06/102745695-01-acc.pdf.

Austin, Dennis, Tom Rudkin, and Robert Gaskins. "Presenter Specification—May 22, 1986." *Robert Gaskins Home Page*, www.robertgaskins.com/powerpoint-history/documents/austin-rudkin-gaskins-powerpoint-spec-1986-may-22.pdf.

Gaskins, Robert. "Sample Product Proposal: Presentation Graphics for Overhead Projection." *Robert Gaskins Home Page*, www.robertgaskins.com/powerpoint-history/documents/gaskins-powerpoint-original-proposal-1984-aug-14.pdf.

___. "Viewpoint: How PowerPoint Changed Microsoft and My Life." *BBC*, 31 July 2012, www.bbc.com/news/technology-19042236.

Parks, Bob. "Death to PowerPoint!" *Bloomberg Business.* Bloomberg L.P., 30 Aug. 2012, www.bloomberg.com/bw/articles/2012-08-30/death-to-powerpoint.

"PowerPoint." *Office.* Microsoft, products.office.com/en-US/powerpoint?legRedir=true&CorrelationId=1e6f9d59-6693-4d10-aff3-e1ce0ae02d22.

"The Problem with PowerPoint." *BBC News Magazine.* BBC, 19 Aug. 2009, news.bbc.co.uk/2/hi/uk_news/magazine/8207849.stm.

MICROSOFT WORD

Introduction

Microsoft Word is a computer software program intended for word processing. With this program, users can create, format, edit, and store documents on their computers and print them out as hard copies. The development of Microsoft Word began in the early 1980s when programmers with the technology company Microsoft began trying to enter the word-processing market. Although early versions of Microsoft Word received mixed reviews, it eventually became a top seller due largely to its revolutionary user-friendly design. By 1994, Microsoft Word had become the world's foremost word-processing program, and its market dominance has continued through the latest version, Word 2013.

Background

Prior to the 1980s, most people did their writing manually with pen and paper or with simple machines such as typewriters. As computers began to become common fixtures in businesses, schools, and homes, however, programmers sought to create word processors, computer software programs for writing. With a word processor, a person could type, edit, and store large amounts of information much more quickly and efficiently than by hand or typewriter.

By 1986, a strong competition had developed between software companies making word processors. The market leaders that year were WordPerfect and WordStar, although other contenders included Samna Word, MultiMate, DisplayWrite, and a little-known program called Microsoft Word. The creation of Microsoft Word began in 1981, when technology company Microsoft hired word-processing pioneer Charles Simonyi. Previously, Simonyi had created a prototype computer writing system called BRAVO for the Xerox Corporation. After working on a spreadsheet program for Microsoft, Simonyi took on the difficult task of designing a new word processor. With help from programmer Richard Brodie, Simonyi completed the new program in October of 1983.

Immediately, the first version of Microsoft Word proved to be unlike its competitors. It was designed for use with a mouse or other pointing devices. It processed information so quickly it could format words even as a user was typing them. It also allowed users to flip between multiple screens, undo mistakes, change font sizes, and add footnotes to text. Despite these benefits, many reviewers found it frustratingly unlike the norm and difficult to learn how to use. It also cost $495.

This early version of Microsoft Word was designed for the DOS operating system, which limited the program's capabilities. Despite this fact, by the end of the 1980s, Microsoft Word for DOS had reached the number two spot in the marketplace. However, it was still far behind the industry leader, WordPerfect.

Move to Microsoft Windows

In 1989, Microsoft released its own operating system, Windows, to replace the text-based DOS system. Windows was revolutionary in that it used a graphical interface, which meant users could interact directly with menus, icons, and other symbols on the screen using a mouse or other pointing device. The new interface setup made the system much easier to use and much more popular with the growing demographic of personal computer owners. By 1990, Windows had already become a major player in the computer market.

Microsoft released new versions of its programs that were compatible with Windows. Microsoft Word was one of the foremost of these programs, and it quickly skyrocketed in popularity. Subsequent versions of the program, each with updates and new capabilities, added to its acclaim. In the early 1990s, it outpaced other Windows-compatible word processors such as WordPerfect and Ami Professional, and by 1994 it completely ruled the word-processing market. By 1997, Microsoft Word accounted for about 95 percent of market share for all word processors, due largely to the near-monopoly Windows had on the operating systems of the time, and the weight of Microsoft's marketing

Continual upgrades to the product added new features and revised old shortcomings. In the late 2000s, updated versions improved menus and other forms of navigation within the program, added new file types and compatibility features, and offered additional layouts and images. The latest version, Word 2013, is configured to operate on the latest mobile devices and to safeguard files using cloud technology, which is a means of sharing files between interconnected devices. In 2016, Word was subscription based with annual renewals. Word 2019 was released late in 2018 and included text-t0-speech and Focus Mode (which blocks out distractions for improved productivity).

Successes and Analysis

The overwhelming success of Microsoft Word for Windows was due to several factors. One was Microsoft's ability to market its offerings effectively. Advertisements touted the unique features of the program and promoted each subsequent upgrade. The inclusion of Word into the popular Microsoft Office program suite provided another major push for the program. Microsoft Office, introduced in 1990, was a box set of programs intended to assist in office-style tasks for businesses, organizations, and individuals. Microsoft Office also included Microsoft Excel (a spreadsheet program) and Microsoft PowerPoint (a presentation program), and was regularly updated and reissued.

Another factor in Word's success was that it was relatively user-friendly. It used clickable menus and graphics where previous word processors had used complex codes and laborious text prompts. It also used a WYSIWYG (What You See Is What You Get) approach, meaning that whatever a user created on the screen would be exactly duplicated on the final printed version.

These features made Word the clear choice for most users, including nonprofessionals. As computers became widely available in schools and homes, Word emerged as the clearest option for the general public. Continual updating of the program with new features to meet current technology trends provided consumers with a steady stream of revised products to purchase and Microsoft with millions of dollars in revenue.

—*Mark Dziak*

References

"A History of Windows." *Windows*. Microsoft, windows.microsoft.com/en-us/windows/history#T1=era0.

Kumar, Arun. "History & Evolution of Microsoft Office Software." *The Windows Club*, 28 Jan. 2013, www.thewindowsclub.com/history-evolution-microsoft-office-software.

Liebowitz, Stan. "Word Processors." *University of Texas at Dallas*, www.utdallas.edu/~liebowit/book/wordprocessor/word.html.

Shustek, Len. "Microsoft Word for Windows Version 1.1a Source Code." *Computer History Museum*, www.computerhistory.org/atchm/microsoft-word-for-windows-1-1a-source-code/.

"Word: Write On." *Office*. Microsoft, 15 July 2015, products.office.com/en-US/word?legRedir=true&CorrelationId=2a80dbed-2adc-4646-bcf2-439ad39b8911.

MOBILE OPERATING SYSTEMS

Introduction

Mobile operating systems (OSs) are installed on mobile devices such as smartphones, tablets, and portable media players. Mobile OSs differ from ordinary computer OSs in that they must manage cellular connections and are configured to support touch screens and simplified input methods. Mobile OSs tend to have sophisticated power management features as well, since they are usually not connected to a power source during use.

Background

The mobile computing market is one of the fastest-growing sectors of the technology field. Its growing popularity began in the late 1990s with the release of the Palm Pilot 1000, a personal digital assistant (PDA). The Pilot 1000 introduced Palm OS, an early mobile operating system (OS). The Palm OS was later extended to smartphones. Smartphones combined the features of PDAs, personal computers (PCs), and cell phones. Prior to smartphones, many people had cell phones, but their functionality was extremely limited, and many people owned both a PDA and cell phone. The Ericsson R380, released in 2000, was the first cell phone marketed as a smartphone. The Ericsson R380 ran on Symbian. Symbian was the dominant mobile OS in the early smartphone market.

The arrival of the iPhone in 2007 changed this. The sleek, simple design of Apple's mobile OS, called iOS, gave the device an intuitive user interface. Despite the success of the iPhone, some felt that Apple devices and its App Store were too locked down. Apple does not allow users to make certain changes to the iOS or to install apps from unofficial sources. In response, a community of iPhone hackers began releasing software that could be used to jailbreak Apple devices. Jailbreaking removes some of the restrictions that are built into the iOS in order to give users root access to the iOS. Jailbreaking gives users greater control over their mobile devices.

Google released a mobile OS called Android in 2008. Unlike Apple's iOS, Android's source code is open source. Open-source software is created using publicly available source code. The Android Open Source Project (AOSP) develops modified versions of the Android OS using the open-source code.

Android's status as an open system means there is no need to jailbreak. Android quickly became the dominant OS worldwide. However, Apple's iOS remained particularly popular in the United States, with about 47 percent of the US subscriber share as of mid-2019.

Mobile Features

Mobile OSs share many similarities with desktop and laptop OSs. However, mobile OSs are more closely integrated with touch-screen technology. Mobile OSs also typically feature Bluetooth and Wi-Fi connectivity, global positioning system (GPS) navigation, and speech recognition. Furthermore, many smartphones are equipped with hardware that supports near-field communication (NFC). NFC allows two devices to exchange information when they are placed close to one another. NFC uses radio frequency identification (RFID) technology to enable wireless data transfers.

A major benefit of NFC is its low power usage, which is particularly critical to mobile devices. Mobile technology such as NFC facilitates numerous business transactions, including mobile payment systems at the point of sale.

Although there remain some significant differences between desktop OSs and mobile OSs, they are rapidly converging. Cloud computing enables users to share and sync data across devices, further narrowing the differences between smartphones and PCs.

Security Concerns

Features such as NFC and Bluetooth come with privacy and security concerns. Many of the mobile OS features that make smartphones so convenient also make them vulnerable to access by unauthorized users. For example, hackers have been able to collect users' private information by scanning large crowds for mobile devices with unsecured Bluetooth connections. The ability to capture private data so easily creates major vulnerabilities for identity theft. To combat this threat, mobile OSs have incorporated various forms of security to help make sure that the private data they contain can only be accessed by an authorized user. For example, Apple has integrated fingerprint recognition into its mobile OS, as have manufacturers of Android smartphones.

Both Android and iOS also include features that help a user to locate and recover a mobile device that has been lost or stolen. Mobile owners can go online to geographically locate the device using its GPS data. The owner can also remotely lock the device to prevent its use by anyone else. In some cases, users can even cause the device to emit a loud alarm to alert those nearby to its presence.

Impact

Mobile OSs and the apps that run on them have revolutionized the way in which people conduct their daily lives. Thanks to mobile OSs, users can track personal health data, transfer funds, connect with social media, receive GPS and weather data, and even produce and edit photo and audiovisual files, among other activities. As the popularity of mobile devices (and, by extension, mobile OSs) has increased, many have questioned the future of the PC. However, PCs and desktop OSs continued to dominant the business sector throughout the second decade of the twenty-first century.

—*Scott Zimmer*

References

Collins, Lauren, and Scott Ellis, editors. *Mobile Devices: Tools and Technologies.* CRC Press, 2015.

Dutson, Phil. *Responsive Mobile Design: Designing for Every Device.* Addison-Wesley, 2015.

Elenkov, Nikolay. *Android Security Internals: An In-Depth Guide to Android's Security Architecture.* No Starch Press, 2015.

Neuburg, Matt. *Programming iOS 13: Dive Deep into Views, View Controllers, and Frameworks.* O'Reilly Media, 2019.

O'Dea, S. "U.S. Smartphone Subscriber Share by Operating Platform 2012-2019, by Month." *Statista*, 28 Feb. 2020, www.statista.com/statistics/266572/market-share-held-by-smartphone-platforms-in-the-united-states/.

Phillips, Bill, et al. *Android Programming: The Big Nerd Ranch Guide.* 4th ed., Big Nerd Ranch Guides, 2019.

Silberschatz, Abraham, Peter Baer Galvin, and Greg Gagne. *Operating System Concepts.* 10th ed., John Wiley & Sons, 2018.

MUSIC EDITING

Introduction

Music editing involves the use of computer technology to alter files of recorded sound. Music files can be compressed, enhanced, combined, or separated through editing software. Both the recording and film industries rely on music editing software to create their products. Compression has enabled the music industry to move away from physical media and has driven the growth of online music transfer. The sharing of audio files has also led to a more collaborative music scene.

Background

Music editing software is used by sound engineers working with musicians to record and produce music for commercial purposes. Performers record their music in studios, often in separate sessions. Once all the recording has been completed, sound engineers begin mixing the tracks together. Mixing combines different sounds into a single audio recording. One track might include the vocals, another the backup singers, and a third the instruments. Recording these separately can help preserve the full depth of sound produced by each source (or input). Sound engineers mix these recordings together such that they support and enhance one another instead of competing. Mixers allow them to adjust the volume of each input (channel), equalize frequencies, reduce noise, add effects, and control channel subgroups (buses). Music editing software usually includes a virtual mixer and a timeline with a scroll bar, allowing the editor to move back and forth along an audio track in a process called scrubbing. Scrubbing is particularly helpful for aligning vocal tracks with other audio tracks or with film visuals.

When the mixing stage has been completed for an album, the next step is mastering. This is the creation of a master recording that can be used to produce copies for sale thereafter. Mastering was much more complex when music was mainly sold on physical media, such as record albums or cassette tapes. The recording master had to be protected from theft, damage, and the ravages of time. In the twenty-first century, most music editing is done entirely digitally. In digital mastering, the mixed audio recording is checked for errors, reformatted for distribution, and then subtly adjusted for the best sound quality possible.

Compression and Transmission

Music editing can be destructive, meaning that changing a recording destroys the original version of the recording. It can also be nondestructive, in which editing preserves the original recording. The technology that made it possible for music to move away from physical media was compression, specifically the MPEG Audio Layer3 (MP3) compression algorithm and file type. MP3 was developed in the early 1990s as a type of lossy compression for audio files. It can greatly reduce the size of an ordinary audio file while losing only a negligible amount of sound quality. MP3 is an audio codec that makes music portable by compressing it into files small enough for transfer over the internet and for digital storage. A codec can reduce the size of audio files by using shorthand to describe repeated data within the file more concisely.

When a compressed recording is played back, it is decoded by the device playing it, provided that the device is equipped with the proper codec (an apparatus or program capable of performing manipulations on a data stream or signal). The recording's fidelity (similarity to the original) depends on how much information is kept and how much of the original frequency and dynamic range are captured. For instance, 16 bits of data are encoded for a high-fidelity compact disc (CD) as compared to 24 bits in a studio recording.

Motion Picture Music Editing

Motion pictures rely on the skills of sound engineers to mix the film's dialogue, musical score and soundtrack, and sound effects into a single audio accompaniment to the visuals. The process is like that used in a recording studio. However, there is the added complication that the audio tracks must not only all be in harmony but also follow the timing of the movie's scenes. Usually the dialogue takes priority, with the music and sound effects being mixed in later.

Culture of Remixing

The development and adoption of the MP3 audio codec made it easier and more common than ever for music to be shared illegally. People found it preferable to make illegal copies of music than to buy it, since those copies essentially retain the same quality as the original. Despite this, some praise the sharing of music online as giving rise to a new culture of remixing. Artists release their creative output into the world for audiences to enjoy it and other artists to build off it and even transform it. In remixing, other artists add their own perspectives to produce a collaborative work that is greater than the sum of its parts. Consumer audio editing software, such as Audacity, Adobe Audition, GarageBand, and Pro Tools, enables such artists to record and mix music using just their personal computer (PC) instead of a studio.

—Scott Zimmer

References

Collins, Mike. *Pro Tools 11: Music Production, Recording, Editing, and Mixing.* Focal Press, 2014.

Cross, Mark. *Audio Post Production for Film and Television.* Berklee Press, 2013.

Jackson, Wallace. *Digital Audio Editing Fundamentals.* Apress, 2015.

Kuehnl, Eric, Andrew Haak, and Frank D. Cook. *Ableton Live 101: An Introduction to Ableton Live 10.* Rowman & Littlefield, 2019.

Pinch, T. J., and Karin Bijsterveld, editors. *The Oxford Handbook of Sound Studies.* Oxford UP, 2013.

Saltzman, Steven. *Music Editing for Film and Television: The Art and the Process.* Focal Press, 2015.

Zala, Paul. *How to Make Great Music Mashups.* Routledge, 2018.

MYSPACE

Introduction

Myspace was the premier online social-networking site from 2005 to 2009, known especially for music. Myspace was one of the most innovative and lucrative websites of the first decade of the twenty-first century, and the first social-networking site to gain widespread popularity. By the end of the decade, however, its reputation was in decline, its popularity had been surpassed by Facebook, and it became known mostly as a music and entertainment site.

Myspace was one of the most innovative and lucrative websites of the decade and the first social-networking site to gain widespread popularity. Its popularity has been surpassed by Facebook, and it became known mostly as a music and entertainment site.

Background

Myspace (originally styled "MySpace") was launched by American internet entrepreneurs Chris DeWolfe and Tom Anderson in August 2003. Designed to compete with Friendster and other social-networking sites, it offered profile pages that could be individually customized, the ability to upload photos and videos, and, most importantly, an opportunity for members to socialize with friends and other like-minded people, all paid for with advertising revenues. What set it apart from the other social networks was its openness. Members could "friend" any other member, and, if desired, could even fake their own identification.

By June 2004, Myspace was claiming 1 million unique visitors each month, and by July 2005, the site had more than 22 million members. That same month, media conglomerate News Corporation bought out Myspace's parent company, Intermix Media (formerly eUniverse Inc.), for $580 million.

Much of the site's success came from a business decision to turn Myspace into a music site where established musicians could promote their recordings and fans could "friend" the musicians. At the time, Myspace had become known as the world's largest online hangout for teenagers, where they could share music, meet potential dates, and chat. It also became known as a hangout for sexual predators. (In 2009, Myspace admitted they had blocked ninety thousand sex offenders during 2007 and 2008.) Lawsuits brought by the families of victimized minors, as well as a 2006 lawsuit brought by Universal Music Group over copyright infringement, and various other lawsuits began to taint the site's reputation.

While Myspace fought back, a formidable competitor, Facebook, was beginning to edge ahead. (Facebook surpassed Myspace in number of users in June 2008.) In 2009, DeWolfe stepped down as the website's chief executive officer (CEO), and Myspace went on to lay off the majority of its employees by 2011. As the decade came to a close, the future of Myspace was uncertain, particularly with the increased popularity of additional media-sharing sites

such as YouTube ; however, it appeared to be focused on music and entertainment. In 2011, News Corporation sold Myspace at a significant loss; the advertising firm Specific Media Group bought out the social-networking site for $35 million. In the sale and in their plans to relaunch the site, Specific Media partnered with pop star Justin Timberlake, who was involved in creating and promoting the site's redesign.

The revamped Myspace debuted in 2013, no longer focused on social networking between users, but instead emphasizing music, recording artists, and other forms of entertainment, including articles and videos, and new ways for artists and fans to connect with one another. The new site featured an embedded music player at the bottom of the page with access to 53 million tracks—billed by the company as the web's largest music streaming library. Specific Media's parent company Interactive Media Holdings became known as Viant Technologies in 2015. In February 2016, the publishing and media company Time Inc., which owns *Time*, *Sport Illustrated*, and *Fortune* magazines, purchased Viant Technology for a reported $87 million. Three years later, the site's credibility suffered a blow when it was revealed that, during a server migration process, photo, video, and audio files from the first twelve years of the site's existence had been lost.

Impact

As the first social-networking site to host millions of people with billions of hits worldwide each day, Myspace set the bar for future business collaborations and innovation. It built an unprecedented community of established and amateur musicians, many of whom were given a boost through Myspace Records or special concerts. After several high-profile incidents involving sexual predators, Myspace supported the passage of the Keeping the Internet Devoid of Sexual Predators Act of 2007, which requires sex offenders to register their email addresses and instant-messaging aliases with the sex offender registries.

The revamped, music-oriented Myspace then forged numerous brand partnerships and promised to remain an enduring web presence, if in a slightly different space than the one in which it started out. It remains, in the third decade of the twenty-first century, an attractive, if fringe site, primarily because of its reputation as an "old" platform for previous generations of users. Adolescent and young adult users, who predominate in the social media market, have exhibited an ongoing tendency to seek out ever-new platforms, if only to stay ahead of older generations of users. Myspace is anything but an ever-new platform.

—*Sally Driscoll*

References

Angwin, Julia. *Stealing MySpace: The Battle to Control the Most Popular Website in America.* Random, 2009.

Barr, Jeremy. "SEC Filing Gives Clues to Price Time Inc. Paid for MySpace Parent Viant." *Advertising Age,* 9 May 2016, adage.com/article/media/time-s-purchase-price-myspace-parent-87-million/303898.

Glazer, Eliot. "Assessing Second-Tier Social-Media Sites." *New York Times Magazine,* 16 Feb. 2014, p. 9.

Nusca, Andrew. "Myspace Acquired by Time Inc, Fortune's Publisher." *Fortune,* 11 Feb. 2016, fortune.com/2016/02/11/myspace-acquired-time-inc/.

Robinson, Matthew. "Myspace Apologizes after Losing 12 Years' Worth of Music." *CNN,* 18 Mar. 2019, www.cnn.com/2019/03/18/us/myspace-lost-12-years-music-uploads-apology-intl-scli/index.html.

O

ONLINE ANONYMITY

Introduction

Online anonymity is a phenomenon encouraged by the technological orientation of the internet, although people take an active role in attempting online anonymity with little tech savvy as well. Anonymity, at its core, means the separation of one's activities from identifying features such as legal name, location, birth date, and family information. Internet users may employ a range of strategies to achieve anonymity, from using a dummy email address or a fictional social media profile to using proxy servers. There are also various levels of anonymity, ranging from full identification to pseudonym usage, in which a person adopts a name that cannot be linked to their legal identity, to full anonymity.

Background

In 1996, John Perry Barlow typed out the Declaration of the Independence of Cyberspace in a frenzy of utopian sentiment. In it, he described how the anonymity of the internet permitted a new egalitarianism to emerge beyond the boundaries of race, creed, ethnicity, nationality, gender, and sexual orientation. He thought that people's contributions would be valued solely on merit. He also predicted the erosion of government power.

However, the anonymity possible in the online world has in reality caused considerable controversy and led to challenges both for individual users and for larger social and political concerns. The masking of identities behind digital avatars or pseudonymous usernames means that users must be aware that others may not be who or what they appear to be. Anonymity leaves many channels open to fraud and other online crimes, the rates of which increased substantially throughout the early twenty-first century.

Additionally, the rise of social media in particular was accompanied by instances of bullying and racism enabled by anonymity and the lack of repercussions, as seen in the phenomenon of trolling, in which users post intentionally offensive, instigating, or irrational messages within an online community to generate arguments.

Specific examples of the impact of online anonymity—including instances where assumed anonymity is revealed to be compromised—have often attracted considerable media interest and public controversy. In 2007, a popular World of Warcraft fan video outed characters in the game as "gold farmers," professional players who make real money from selling virtual goods. Not only did this video out the previously anonymous players, it targeted them with a vitriolic racist discourse because many of them were Chinese.

In an even more obviously sociopolitical example, it was revealed that the US National Security Agency (NSA) had access to the online communications of millions of US citizens, as well as to domestic and foreign telephone metadata, sparking concerns that most online activity could in fact be traced back to its source, potentially violating individuals' privacy.

Some contend that the norm on the internet is anonymity. Others, however, note that most online business and social media require some sort of identity verification. Anonymity is an orientation of the technological features of the internet; one has to have a fairly high level of expertise to link an IP address with other identifiers such as name and location. However, the values encoded in one layer of the internet are not necessarily found in others.

Thus, though relative anonymity is a feature of the infrastructural layer with regards to transmission protocols, this does not mean it necessarily figures largely in the control software and applications layer. Facebook, for example, strongly discourages anonymity. Arguments against anonymity include the tendency for people to vent socially unacceptable feelings and actions to escape responsibility. A quick visit to the comment sections of news articles is often unpleasant enough to give weight to this argument.

Overview

A study of a news website that transitioned from a comment platform that allowed anonymity to one that did not, showed that identified users tended to have their comments liked by others more than anonymous users. Anonymous users tended to use profanity and angry language more often than identified users. The researchers noted that computer-mediated communication in general tends to encourage deindividuation, which means that people are less aware of how their actions are socially situated, which results in less concern about what others think and do.

To be fair, the internet has resulted in greater political transparency with the emergence and continued activities of groups such as WikiLeaks, which publicizes leaked documents online that expose various wrongdoings of governments and government agencies. WikiLeaks depends upon protecting its suppliers' anonymity, and it does this technologically with an online, electronic drop-box that has so far proved difficult to trace. The flow of information between those who hold political power and the governed has traditionally been tilted in the former's favor; therefore, WikiLeaks needs to protect their informants from prosecution. They also need reliable data storage, which they have found in an underground nuclear bunker.

WikiLeaks' organizational headquarters is in Sweden, where the act of revealing journalists' sources is a criminal offense. With regards to transmission security, WikiLeaks has had to bolster their encryption and has adopted "onion routing," which scrambles the encoded locations of the sources, destinations, and dates in their internet traffic. To do this they use the Tor network. However, information weapons of the QUANTUM program have been used by the NSA to reveal the identities and locations of members of this network.

Aside from WikiLeaks and other "hacktivist" groups such as Anonymous, ordinary people also feel the need to secure some degree of anonymity in their online activities. The reasons for this include fear of judgment from family and friends; fear of discovery by an abusive ex-partner, family member, or any other person an individual has reason to believe would cause them harm if their true identity were revealed; self-protection from prosecution in the case of activities such as illegal downloading; solicitation of honest, uncoerced input and critique of creative works; entertainment and/or practical jokes; and fear of political, social, or workplace persecution. In one study, researchers found that while some people used anonymity to conceal some wrongdoings, they used it just as often to help or support another with no enduring commitments. Contrary to the saying that "honest people should have nothing to hide," many people seek anonymity because of prior negative experiences.

It should be noted, however, that anonymity is rarely absolute. Even on sites such as 4chan.org, which is credited with originating such popular online memes as LOLcats and where anonymity is assumed as the norm, it is possible to recognize patterns of form and content in the writing, images, and links shared on the site. This is true despite the site culture that sometimes even scorns contributors who use "tripcodes" or pseudonyms. Furthermore, a person would have to be a top-notch hacker in order to evade the identification techniques of a powerful organization such as the NSA.

The American Civil Liberties Union (ACLU) describes "the right to remain anonymous" as "a fundamental component of our right to free speech," which it extends to online anonymity as well. The organization has taken on a number of cases against government and corporate efforts to identify anonymous critics and political dissidents online.

In one case, the US Department of Homeland Security (DHS) sent a summons to the social media platform Twitter demanding it reveal records regarding the account @ALT_USCIS, which had been critical of the Donald Trump administration, with a focus on US Citizenship and Immigration Services (USCIS), a department under the DHS. In response, Twitter sued the federal government to block the unmasking, citing the First Amendment right to free speech, and the ACLU assigned lawyers to represent the anonymous user and announced their intent to file on the user's behalf. The DHS immediately withdrew the summons, and in response Twitter voluntarily dismissed its lawsuit. In addition to defending anonymous users against "overbroad or unjustified efforts to unmask" them, the ACLU also "monitor[s] occasional efforts to establish verified online identities" to ensure that any such efforts do not infringe on the right to anonymous speech online.

—*Trevor Cunnington*

References

"Anonymity." *Electronic Frontier Foundation*, www.eff.org/issues/anonymity.

Bernstein, Michael S., et al. "4chan and /b/: An Analysis of Anonymity and Ephemerality in a Large Online Community." *Proceedings of the Fifth International Conference on Weblogs and Social Media, AAAI Press, 2011*. Association for the Advancement of Artificial Intelligence, www.aaai.org/ocs/index.php/ICWSM/ICWSM11/paper/view/2873.

Krotoski, Aleks. "WikiLeaks and the New, Transparent World Order." *Political Quarterly*, vol. 82, no. 4, 2011, pp. 526–30, search.ebscohost.com/login.aspx?direct=true&db=a9h&AN=66793319&site=ehost-live.

Marx, Gary T. "What's in a Name? Some Reflections on the Sociology of Anonymity." *Information Society*, vol. 15, no. 2, 1999, pp. 99–112, search.ebscohost.com/login.aspx?direct=true&db=a9h&AN=2030997&site=ehost-live.

McKenna, Katelyn Y. A., and John A. Bargh. "Plan 9 from Cyberspace: The Implications of the Internet for Personality and Social Psychology." *Personality and Social Psychology Review*, vol. 4, no. 1, 2000, pp. 57–75, search.ebscohost.com/login.aspx?direct=true&db=a9h&AN=3176644&site=ehost-live.

Morozov, Evgeny. "WikiLeaks' Relationship with the Media." *The New York Times*. Room for Debate, 11 Dec. 2010, www.nytimes.com/roomfordebate/2010/12/09/what-has-wikileaks-started/wikileaks-relationship-with-the-media.

North, Anna. "The Double-Edged Sword of Online Anonymity." *The New York Times*. Taking Note, 15 May 2015, takingnote.blogs.nytimes.com/2015/05/15/the-double-edged-sword-of-online-anonymity/.

Omernick, Eli, and Sara Owsley Sood. "The Impact of Anonymity in Online Communities." *2013 International Conference on Social Computing (SocialCom 2013)*. IEEE, pp. 526–35.

"Online Anonymity and Identity." *American Civil Liberties Union*, 10 Apr. 2017, www.aclu.org/issues/free-speech/internet-speech/online-anonymity-and-identity.

Suler, John. "The Online Disinhibition Effect." *CyberPsychology & Behavior*, vol. 7, no. 3, 2004, pp. 321–26, Academic Search Complete, search.ebscohost.com/login.aspx?direct=true&db=a9h&AN=13621589&site=ehost-live.

Tufekci, Zeynep. "Can You See Me Now? Audience and Disclosure Regulation in Online Social Network Sites." *Bulletin of Science, Technology & Society*, vol. 28, no. 1, 2008, pp. 20–36, doi:10.1177/0270467607311484.

Zajácz, Rita. "WikiLeaks and the Problem of Anonymity: A Network Control Perspective." *Media, Culture & Society*, vol. 35, no. 4, 2013, pp. 487–503, doi:10.1177/016344371348379.

ONLINE COMMUNICATION

Introduction

The project that ultimately become the internet was launched in 1969 by the US Department of Defense, but it was not until the late 1980s that the general public became aware of its existence. By the late twentieth century, online interactions had become a major means of communication in everyday lives. Online communication includes such avenues as email, chat, instant messaging, short-message service (SMS), web pages, forums, bulletin boards, mailing lists, newsletters, video conferencing, blogs (online journals), vlogs (video journals), virtual worlds, online gaming communities, and virtual classrooms. In addition, 37 percent of workers telecommute at least part of the time (even more so due to the COVID-19 pandemic), which means that much of their work time is spent in online communication. Online communication may be either written, oral, or a combination of the two. It may be interactive, as with Facebook posts in which a "thread" continues to lengthen as various users react to other users' comments or with tweets and retweets among Twitter users.

Within the field of communications, the growth of online communication has sometimes caused scholars to reexamine their approaches to scholarship. Instead of focusing on mass communication by studying television, radio, and newspapers or on personal communication that dealt with dialogue, origins, and nonverbal language, communications scholars have been forced to study a field in which divisions have been blurred by rapidly changing technologies. The internet has been labeled an "existential bubble" by scholars who insist that online communication allows individuals to become the center of their own online worlds in response to the assumption that everyone else is interested in what they have to say. Some scholars have labeled millennials the "app generation" because of their dependence on smartphones and computers and their expectation that, when needed, there is sure to be an application that offers assistance for every possible activity.

For millions of users throughout the world, Facebook, Twitter, YouTube, Instagram, Snapchat, and other online services have become their chief form of communication with the rest of world. By 2001, 72 percent of American adults were regular participants in social media. In 2013, 85 percent of American adults regularly used email and the internet. By 2020, Facebook was claiming more than one 1.9 billion daily users globally, and Twitter boasted 396.5 million users.

It is true that online communication has eroded walls between celebrities and their fans with Donald Trump shattering presidential convention by regularly addressing the public from his private Twitter account. In the first year of his administration, Trump had 32 million followers, though 11. 6 percent of those were considered dormant or were run by bots,—automated accounts without a human profile. Eventually, Trump was banned from the site for misinformation and fomenting violence. As of 2021, the top Twitter accounts (in the millions) were: Barack Obama (129.9 followers), Justin Bieber (113.9 followers), Katy Perry (108.7 followers).

Written forms of online communication eliminate verbal cues such as voice tones and nonverbal cues such as the widening of the eyes or the raising of the eyebrows that increase understanding of person-to-person communication. In online communication, symbols such as emoticons, or emojis, which convey emotions pictographically, and acronyms such as LOL (laughing out loud to denote amusement or joking) attempt to serve the same

purpose. Online communication has also introduced new words to language. English-speaking Facebook users have become familiar with the concepts of "friending," which refers to the acceptance of a friendship offer from another user, as well as their corollaries, "defriending" or "unfriending," which refer to removing another user from one's list of friends and ensuring that they no longer have access to postings and photographs. Many individuals differentiate between their offline (real-life) and online friends.

Background

Before the World Wide Web became ubiquitous, online bulletin board systems (BBS) were the chief form of online communication. BBS had been invented by Ward Christensen and Randy Seuss in 1978. By 1994, there were 60,000 BBS online. Online communication occurred when a user composed a message, and other users responded by "pinning" or "posting" a response. Chat rooms, where semiprivate conversations occurred, first appeared at the University of Illinois in 1973 and became more common as computer access increased. Allowing for multiple simultaneous users, internet relay chat (IRC), the invention of Finnish graduate student Jarkko Oikarinen, was introduced in 1988.

General online access was initially limited because personal computers were not common, and a home computer was most likely to be used for word processing, spreadsheets, or simple games. Computer use was also cumbersome; early Microsoft software required a disc operating system, or DOS, which was stored on a floppy drive and had to be inserted before the computer could boot up. Home computing changed drastically in the mid-1980s, with the advent of Apple's Macintosh computer, and in 1995 with the release of Microsoft's Windows 95.

For the first time, users could turn on a computer and have immediate access to the information superhighway. Windows 95's user-friendly interface, modeled after Apple's pioneering OS, was designed to make using computers more intuitive, and companies such as America Online and CompuServe were available to assist users in learning how to explore the vast opportunities offered via online communication. Most early internet access, however, was through dial-up modems that used telephone land lines and often required long wait periods, and tied up the home or office phone when in use. Except for the more stable Macintosh computers (which held no more than 10 percent of the market at any time in the 1990s), computers frequently lost contact with the web and were increasingly subject to viruses,

The virtual classroom has become increasingly common in the twenty-first century, with students taking courses or earning certifications and degrees through distance learning. In 2014, the National Center for Educational Statistics reported that 28.5 percent of students had taken at least part of their required coursework online. The number was greater for graduate students (32.7 percent) than for undergraduate students (27.7 percent). Fourteen percent of students had obtained degrees exclusively through distance learning. Of those, 24.9 percent were graduate students, and 12.2 percent were undergraduate students. While making learning more accessible, some critics claim that students do not always get the full benefit of traditional education from distance learning. There is also significant concern about opportunities for cheating, particularly during examinations, when students illegally use smartphones or tablet computers, plagiarize material from online sources, and seek outside help without authorization. Some colleges and universities have dealt with these problems by turning to online proctoring companies that monitor students through video technologies.

Applications

Online communication has proved advantageous for protest groups, allowing them to rally support for causes even in countries that restrict speech and press. In early 2011, an online protest movement surfaced in Egypt in response to the tyrannical activities of President Hosni Mubarak. The protest also spread offline, gathering members and ultimately leading to Mubarak's ousting. Z. Papacharissi notes that the protest was vastly different from traditional protests because no single leader or political faction appeared to rally followers for the cause. Instead, it involved a wave of popular support that allowed Egyptians to work together to achieve their goals. Similarly, the Occupy movement began in the United States in the spring of that same year. Protesters were involved in a grassroots effort to call public attention to the increasing divide between the most affluent top one percent and the rest of the people. Because of instant online communication,

the movement quickly spread throughout the United States and Europe.

In late 2017, the #MeToo movement surfaced in the United States on Twitter and quickly gained steamed, leading to women speaking out and resulting in the ousting of powerful men such as film producer Harvey Weinstein, news anchor Matt Lauer, and Congressman Al Franken and renewed accusations of sexual misconduct by Donald Trump. The #MeToo movement became global. In China, a group of Chinese women began speaking out about the problem of sexual harassment. As the movement gained support among both online and traditional media sources, governments essentially continued to ignore the problem. Women in Congress established #MeToo Congress, and four of ten female members of Congress insisted that sexual harassment/sexual assault was a major problem in Congress itself. There was also an upsurge in the number of women running for political office.

Online communities sometimes allow members to be what they would like to be rather than who they are offline. With online communication, social boundaries may be removed, and people from all races, age groups, and social classes may interact with one another. In online communities, members may be judged by what they contribute to the online venue rather than by how they look, how much money they make, or what kind of car they drive or clothes they wear.

Virtual Communities

Virtual communities that have surfaced online have provided a fertile field of study for scholars. Anthropologist Tony Boellstorff has conducted an in-depth study of *Second Life*, a virtual world that allows users to create alternate versions of themselves. His study introduced him to "Fran," an eight-five-year-old woman debilitated by Parkinson's disease, who is able to dance, ride horses, and walk on the beach as her online persona, an avatar that lives on Namaste Island, which was created by Fran's daughter Barbie to reflect their former home, Nettles Island on the Florida coast. Fran also runs an online support group for Parkinson's patients.

Boellstorff argues that virtual worlds may seem realistic to their participants, and insists that identities, relationships, and cultures may evolve as participants interact with one another. When *Second Life* was launched in 2003 by Linden Lab, there were 2,500 active members, and around 200 of those might have been online at a given time. At its peak, *Second Life* grew to more than a million users. In 2015, half a million people were registered, and 30,000 to 60,000 users might be online at one time. Real names are not used to protect privacy. In 2018, possible destinations in *Second Life* included Arcade Gacha, Bailey's Norge, The Secret Garden, I Still Love the 80s, ASMR Library, and the Butterfly Conservatory.

Large online gaming communities have developed with thousands of members from around the world whose only form of communication with one another may be online. In 2008, it was estimated that 47 million players regularly participated in massively multiplayer online games (MMOGs). To test the level of trust found among online gaming communities, Rabindra A. Ratan, Jae Eun Chung, Cuihua Shen, Dmitri Williams, and Marshall Scott Poole (2010) looked at 3,500 players who regularly play the MMOG *Everquest III*.

They found that the highest levels of trust were found among members of particular teams. Other *Everquest III* players were trusted more than the online community at large because of the need to cooperate within the game when performing such activities as forming guilds and providing in-game assistance. Trust among teammates was strong enough that players generally felt comfortable sharing details of their private lives with one another. Some scholars who study online communication have found that as trust in online communities has increased, it has declined in traditional associations with unions, clans, and neighborhoods.

Viewpoints

A large body of literature has been generated about the negative impacts of online communication, and most critics bemoan the loss of one-on-one contact, suggesting, for example, that email lacks the personal touch of a handwritten letter. Some critics argue that online communication has opened new behaviors for teenagers such as cyberbullying, which refers to taunting, derogatory comments, and untruths posted on social media about individuals. In some cases, this behavior has been so psychologically damaging that victims have committed suicide.

Several studies have found links between the rise in online communication and the increase in social alienation, particularly among teenagers. Others insist that online communication promotes shyness. Kathleen Long, Ben Judd, Joan O'Mora, and Jerry Allen (2006) examined 270 students at a medium-sized university in the northeastern United States and 152 adults employed at the middle-management level or above, discovering no evidence of a link between communication apprehension and computer anxiety. Their studies did, however, indicate that individuals with high levels of communication anxiety were more likely than others to perceive other online users as more emotional, less verbally immediate, more inclined to be domineering, or were less capable of intimacy.

Advocates of online communication laud the ease with which it allows instant communication across the globe. Online communication has allowed individuals instant access to daily news, healthcare information, banking accounts, research resources such as e-books and online databases, and online ordering that requires no shopping trips. One of the biggest advantages of online communication is its ability to allow separated families and friends to remain in touch with one another. Facebook, the top social media site, reported in 2018 that 25.5 million of its users were between 55 and 64 and another 21.1 million were over the age of 65. That participation is due in large part to the desire of older users to brag about their grandchildren and to remain in contact with high school or college friends or with former colleagues. Grandparents who live in separate states or countries are able to see photographs of their grandchildren growing up and follow the daily lives of their children and grandchildren. Online communication has also become an integral part of the communication process for separated military families. Therapists working with these families find that online communication is useful in dealing with psychological situations involving marital conflict, depression, posttraumatic stress disorder (PTSD), alcohol abuse, and vulnerability to suicide.

More than any other forum for online communication, Facebook has been alternately praised and vilified. Critics complain of the inanities involved in reading about what someone is having for dinner every night. Three-fourths of Facebook users are female. Its population is made up of users from all ages, races, ethnicities, religious and political alliances, and sexual orientations. In 2017, 1.40 billion people logged on daily to the social media giant to discover what their "friends" were doing. Facebook users "friend" someone for a number of reasons and not necessarily because of friendship. Deborah Chambers found that some of the most cited reasons for responding to a friend request were because the person is a friend in the real world; because the person is a family member, friend, or colleague; because having a lot of friends makes one appear popular to others; to support a brand or follow a celebrity, writer, or cause; to look cool; and to gain access to posts written by online friends.

Online communication faced a major challenge that threatened the status quo of Facebook and conceivably social media in general in March 2018 when news broke that the social media giant had enabled the Britain-based data analysis firm Cambridge Analytica, hired to help Donald Trump win the 2016 election, to access personal information about more than 50 million users. Responding to public outcry, founder Mark Zuckerberg agreed to appear before Congress to answer questions, and Facebook announced new privacy policies. Government agencies in both the United States and Europe launched investigations into the firm, and the #DeleteFacebook movement gained momentum.

—*Elizabeth Rholetter Purdy*

References

Boellstorff, T. *Coming of Age in Second Life: An Anthropologist Explores the Virtually Human.* Princeton UP, 2015.

Chambers, D. *Social Media and Personal Relationships: Online Intimacies and Networked Friendships.* Palgrave Macmillan, 2013.

Franklin, M. *Digital Dilemmas: Power, Resistance, and the Internet.* Oxford UP, 2013.

Goggin, G., and Mark McLelland, editors. *The Routledge Companion to Global Internet Histories.* Routledge, 2017.

Long, K., B. Judd, J. O'Mara, et al. "Orientations Toward Communication, Computer Anxiety, and the Development of Personal and Professional Relationships Face-to-Face and Online: Conference Papers–International Communication Association." *International Communication Association, 2006 Annual Meeting,* pp. 1–4.

Papacharissi, Z. *Affective Publics: Sentiment, Technology, and Politics.* Oxford UP, 2015.

Paz, V., M. Moore, and T. Creel. "Academic Integrity in an Online Business Communication Environment." *Journal of Multidisciplinary Research,* vol. 9, no. 2, 2017, pp. 57–72.

Perloff, R. M. "Mass Communication Research at the Crossroads: Definitional Issues and Theoretical Directions for Mass and Political Communication Scholarship in an Age of Online Media." *Mass Communication and Society,* vol. 18, no. 5, 2015, pp. 531–56.

Ratan, R. A., J. E. Chung, C. Shen, at al. "Schmoozing and Smiting: Trust, Social Institutions, and Communication Patterns in an MMOG." *Journal of Computer-Mediated Communication,* vol. 16, no. 1, 2010, pp. 93–114.

Rea, J., A. Behnke, N. Huff, et al. "The Role of Online Communication in the Lives of Military Spouses." *International Journal,* vol. 37, no. 3, 2015, pp. 329–39.

ONLINE ENTERTAINMENT AND MUSIC DATABASES

Introduction

Online entertainment and music databases are storehouses of information found in one location that purport to house a complete record of all available records for their respective industries. One such database is the Internet Movie Database, IMDb. Allmusic.com historically has been the music depository leader for over twenty years. In each case, users can access a plethora of information about productions from the most popular to the most obscure.

Databases are structured using the tags of XML and other mark-up languages to provide specific field identification markers. Tags are user-defined for specific field entries so that by selecting or specifying the desired master file, such as a movie title, the database program will return all of the data fields associated with that master file. The user can then select a specific tag, such as one of the actors, to see the information about that actor. This is the basic operating principle of all databases.

The IMDb website is an online database that is the repository of a massive amount of information about a large number of movies, as well as of TV movies and episodic TV series, and video games, including the actors, musicians, and others involved in those productions. In February, 2022, the IMDb site covered more than 8.7 million titles in those categories, and 11.5 million actor and personnel records, serving some 88 million registered users worldwide.

Background

IMDb was started in 1990 as the rec.arts.movies database on Usenet by Col Needham. Needham initiated the movie database with its first post being his piece, titled "Those Eyes," in a category he defined as "actresses with beautiful eyes." He also became the database's lead programmer, while allowing for other movie fans to participate in the open-source project (similar to more recognizable encyclopedic databases like Wikipedia). As the database grew, it became more difficult for users to search the more than 10,000 entries, which required knowing how to use a number of UNIX shell scripts to accomplish.

In 1993, the database was moved from Usenet to become part of the World Wide Web, and in 1996 the IMDb website was incorporated as a business entity in the United Kingdom as Internet Movie Database Limited, with Col Needham as its principal owner. Advertising, licensing, and partnerships provided the income needed to maintain the company and the operation of the website. Two years later, in 1998, the IMDb company was purchased by Jeff Bezos and Amazon. It continues to operate as an independent subsidiary of Amazon and functions as an advertising resource for sales of movies and other entertainment products on Amazon. It also serves to track new projects still in development for a number of fans' favorite actors, writers, directors, and so forth.

IMDb and the World

The IMDb website was originally programmed using the Perl programming language, but for reasons of security IMDb no longer reveals what programming language is currently used for its programming. All IMDb websites are presented primarily in English, though there are translated sites in ten other languages. IMDb uses a mathematical algorithm to assign weighted ratings to movies in its database, and registered visitors to the IMDb website offer a rating for entries on a 1-to-10 scale.

The average of these ratings, multiplied by the number of votes the entry has received, is added to the required vote minimum, multiplied by the overall average score for the entry, and the resulting number is divided by the number of votes the movie received plus the minimum number of votes required. The value obtained by this calculation is the "weighted average rating" for the movie. There is also a Bottom 100 rating for movies, and a Top 25 rating for television shows. Only votes provided by regular voters—registered IMDb users who have voted a certain number of times on IMDb—are used for the ratings calculations. IMDb does not disclose the minimum number of times a registered user must have voted in order to be considered a regular voter.

Particular pages in the IMDb website, as well as corporate IMDb, are readily accessible through any web browser. If, for example, one searched the title of a movie or the name of an actor or director, the corresponding IMDb page becomes available for viewing. The IMDb page provides a wealth of information about the particular entry, including complete cast biographies, movie trailers, story and plot synopses, episode descriptions, all supporting production personnel, suggestions for similar entries, user reviews, and more. Given the extent of the database and the depth of the information it provides, IMDb is the go-to source for anyone researching cinema, television, music, and video games.

Other Databases

There are several other online databases that are primarily related to movies and television, each with its own area of focus. Of the online databases, IMDb holds the top spot. OMDb, the Open Movie Database, provides a service similar to that of IMDb, but all OMDb content is provided by its users rather than through a corporate entity like Amazon. The Television Database, TVDb, focuses exclusively on television shows. The Rotten Tomatoes database provides brief overviews and cast lists of movies, but is primarily concerned with the critique of movies. The Complete Index to World Film, CITWF, is as the name suggests, the world's largest film database. It references every movie made since 1895, and also provides print versions of its content. Almost all movies in certain genres and even some in other genres involve firearms of some kind. BCD, the Big Cartoon Database, contains information about more than 100,000 cartoon productions and animated features. The Box Office Mojo website focuses on tracking the financial aspects of movies rather than their actors and production values. The site Metacritic collects reviews of its entries, much like Rotten Tomatoes does. However, Metacritic covers television, music, and video games in addition to its movie coverage.

There are, as of March 2022, at least sixty-three known databases dedicated to the many aspects of cinema, television, animation, music, and video games that can be found online.

—*Richard M. Renneboog*

References

Hutchison, Tom, Paul Allen, and Amy Macy. *Record Label Marketing.* Taylor & Francis, 2012.

Sickels, Robert C. *The Business of Entertainment.* 3 vols. ABC-CLIO, 2009.

Wacholtz, Larry. *Monetizing Entertainment: An Insider's Handbook for Careers in the Entertainment and Music Industry.* CRC Press, 2016.

Williams, Joe. *Entertainment on the Net.* Que, 1995.

ONLINE GAMES: ROLES, RULES, AND ETIQUETTE

Introduction

Online gaming occupies an ever-growing place in the daily lives of all kinds of people, and has grown from a small-population's leisure activity to a global, multibillion-dollar industry. There are academic journals and college majors devoted to the topic of game studies, and universities have even begun offering eSports athletic scholarships for players to represent their schools in national and international eSports competitions. It is no surprise, therefore, that online gaming has become an object of study among academics across disciplines as diverse as business management, communications, anthropology, sociology (including digital sociology), linguistics, psychology, game studies, neurology, and many more.

Each discipline has its own terminology and is grounded in its own foundational theories, but there can also be a great deal of overlap. For example, since the goal of sociology is to learn about society, a sociologist might explore the role that gaming plays within a given society or culture (perhaps viewing language as manifestation of that role). The goal of linguistics, on the other hand, is to learn about language. A linguist might therefore study how the language of gaming reflects or reinforces social structures. Both involve language and both involve gaming, but they approach them in different ways and with different purposes. While this paper highlights the linguistic research on gaming (using linguistic citations and terminology), it is important to remember that the underlying themes are cross-disciplinary and therefore overlap with other fields.

While many believe that online games are an entertaining leisure activity, others express concern that games provide an environment that allows (and perhaps even encourages) negative behaviors such as rudeness, aggression, bullying, and face-to-face (f-t-f) violence away from the keyboard (AFK). Impoliteness and other toxic behaviors in online gaming are therefore an area that is heavily discussed by parent groups, the gaming industry, and players, each of which has a different perspective.

Background

In 1994 in the United States, in part because of parent lobbyists, the Entertainment Software Rating Board (ESRB), established a rating system that ranks video games according to their levels of violence, nudity, and explicit language. Despite these types of regulations, however, the gaming industry is still perceived by many as a destructive environment that encourages negative/immoral behavior, and calls for censorship of violent or otherwise controversial games continue.

Linguistic Research on Digitally Mediated Discourse

Before discussing online conflict, it is necessary to provide an overview of the features of digital communication more broadly. Since the 1990s, linguists have been researching interaction in digital contexts. Initially labeled computer-mediated communication (CMC), a key focus in this early research was an attempt to discover the ways that CMC differed from f-t-f interaction—for example, how people adapted oral communication to a written transmission format. Later research questioned how (or if) CMC was different from spoken interaction, and largely concluded that the differences were not as great as was initially assumed. More recent research has argued that making such a distinction is impossible in any event, since our current communicative practices blur the boundaries between digital practice and life that takes place AFK.

Nevertheless, some features of CMC do distinguish it from oral communication. Susan Herring, a pioneer in CMC research, proposed a faceted classification scheme to categorize the interwoven characteristics of digital communication with regard to (1) technical parameters, and (2) social attributes of interaction (Herring, 2007). Some of the technical categories she proposed were:

- **a/synchronicity:** how much delay—if any—there might be between the time a message was sent and the time it was received;
- **message format:** how the platform requires messages be composed and transmitted (e.g., email has unlimited length and known recipients, while Twitter has limited length and unknown recipients);
- **anonymity:** how/whether the platform allows pseudonyms or nontraceable usernames;
- Some of the social and situational factors were:
  - **participant characteristics:** characteristics that participants share—which to some extent determines the tone of the group (e.g., knowledgeable, engaged, informal, business-like, topic-focused);
  - **topic:** the reason that brought the participants together (e.g., discussion of horses, books, or politics);
  - **norms:** features of behavior that are expected and seen as normal—which differ from group to group (e.g., teasing, joking, markers of respect, formal titles).

By using these categories to classify digital environments we can assess the ways that digital interactions unfold and gain a more thorough understanding of how the digital medium(s) affect conflict and perceptions of impoliteness.

A second development in digital discourse research relates to multimodality. Whereas the label CMC was adequate for initial explorations, it is now the norm to use devices and platforms far beyond those used in early CMC research. Rather than being restricted to a computer, communication now may also include interaction via mobile phones, tablets, televisions, and smart devices (such as Apple's artificial intelligence [AI] assistant Siri).

Researchers have therefore modified the CMC label to reflect this evolving complexity, proposing labels such as digitally mediated communication (DMC) and digitally mediated discourse (DMD). While to some degree we might argue that these labels are unimportant, the underlying idea—that digital-communicative practices go far beyond the limited facets and capabilities of an "old-style" computer—it is an important concern when examining digital conflict and impoliteness.

What Is Impolite?

As with research on the nature of DMD overall, conflict and impoliteness have also been the subject of academic inquiry for decades. One prominent area of exploration has focused on the phenomena of "flaming" and "trolling"—two of the terms most commonly used to describe digital conflict. Much of the early research on flaming and trolling saw them as being destructive and often intentionally harmful behaviors that took advantage of the characteristics of the digitally mediated environment (e.g., anonymity) to avoid consequences for problematic behavior.

A critical component of this process is identifying conflict/impoliteness in the first place. Since the 1990s, researchers in pragmatics have debated the nature of (im)politeness—whether it could be identified by predictive rules, or whether it must be identified according to the contextual influences of the given interaction. Although online sites do not necessarily use the label "impolite," many have frequently asked questions (FAQs), codes of conduct, or other guidelines outlining what constitutes unacceptable behavior. It is common for these guidelines to include an explicit prohibition of racist, sexist, or other discriminatory language, as well as spamming, flaming, trolling and other negative actions specific to the community.

The difficulty is that these terms, while common in DMD, do not always come with definitions, and may vary widely in interpretation from community-to-community.

Flaming, for example, is often defined as communication in which an individual or group is targeted with negative or harmful messages, but it is unclear what, in a given digital community, might be classified as negative or harmful. Similarly, spamming can be defined very differently among different groups. And while it may be a marker of a hoax (and therefore highly problematic) in some instances, it may be expected and even positive in others.

There are also behaviors that go far beyond spamming, flaming, and trolling that can have dire consequences. Some examples include doxing (releasing someone's physical contact information or address), DDoSing (overloading their electronic resources to make them unusable), and swatting (falsely reporting illegal behavior to authorities resulting in arrival of a SWAT team to their physical address). While it seems obvious that acts such as doxing, DDoSing, and swatting go far beyond what might normally be classified as impolite, a recurrent question in impoliteness research is where lines should be drawn between behavior that is impolite, insulting, aggressive, threatening, or downright violent. It is clear, then, that vague and inconsistent definitions of conflict and/or impoliteness can be problematic and may require knowledge of the norms of a given digital community of practice to evaluate whether impoliteness has occurred.

Online Gaming as a Communicative Environment

As a venue that continues to grow exponentially each year, online gaming is a fertile environment for research on communicative practice. At the forefront of linguistic research in this area is the work of James P. Gee who has explored online gaming's relationship to teaching literacy since the mid-1990s. As online gaming has become more varied and complex, his investigations have broadened to focus on both the use of games in the classroom and games as an avenue through which social structures more generally are developed, enacted, and (re)negotiated. Gee's research presents gaming as a lens through which we can evaluate not only teaching practices, but also argues that gaming (and research on it) is a vital activity because it is there that we conceptualize our societies and our roles within them. As Ensslin and Balteiro put it, video games "carry enormous ideological weight that can inform people's views and behaviors inside and outside the fictional gameworlds they inhabit."

The focus on gaming as an avenue through which to establish and negotiate social relationships has led to a great deal of research that takes a constructivist approach to topics such as identity and community in gaming. Such studies often examine the ways that the preset characteristics of a given game influence the ways we form relationships and craft our in-game identities (which we then communicate to others). These studies examine questions such as how the genre of a game (First-Person Shooter, Massively Multiplayer Online Role-Playing Game, and Multiplayer Online Battle Arena, etc.) affects communicative practices and how the game features (e.g., choice of avatars, ability to communicate with teammates) affect our practices both in-game and away from the keyboard.

Increasingly, there is also growing research on game broadcasts either on mainstream television (e.g., ESPN) or via personal channels on platforms such as YouTube or Twitch.tv. Research on communication in traditional competitive sports is well established, but research on live-broadcast game streams and eSports is also growing. These investigations attempt to enhance our understanding of the way streamers balance multiple (multimodal) demands amidst the rituals that are inherent in competitive sports. Game streamers who broadcast their matches, for example, must balance communicating via chat with viewers while simultaneously sending written messages to teammates and playing the game by directing images on the screen. It is reasonable to expect that, as online gaming continues to grow in popularity and complexity, research on multimodal communication and language use in this highly dynamic setting will continue to grow.

How Impoliteness & Conflict "Play Out" in Online Gaming

Finally, within the larger context of online gaming research, there are many studies that focus more specifically on conflict, impoliteness, and "toxic" communication. One area that has received attention is role of gender in online gaming. The gaming industry has been recognized by many researchers as being the domain of the straight white male, with other groups being either un(der)represented, or relegated to stereotyped roles and tropes. Gender is frequently acknowledged as fuel for conflict, where women are often ostracized or attacked with misogynistic insults when other players discover that they are female.

Gamergate

In August of 2014, Anita Sarkesian published a series of YouTube videos where she noted that females in games were represented as stereotypical tropes: the powerless damsel-in-distress who must be saved by male characters (e.g., Princess Peach), and the slutty warrior who fights battles with flowing hair and impractical "armor" that leaves her arms and midriff exposed and vulnerable (e.g., Xena, Warrior Princess). After publishing her exposé, Sarkesian's private address was doxed (i.e., leaked to the public) and she received harassment and death threats severe enough that she moved to a hotel for a period of time.

This case, which was labeled Gamergate in the media, led to a flurry of research across many disciplines where scholars set out to assess impolite and conflictual behavior as they intersected with gender in online gaming. Some studies assessed how women adopted invisibility in response to impolite/aggressive behavior. Amanda Cote, for example, in her 2017 study of gender and online harassment of female gamers, found that females were active participants in gaming subculture. She also determined, however, that they carefully navigated their participation within the gaming community so as to not expose themselves as "outsiders" and risk further harassment. Other research has determined that females take advantage of the stereotypes and expectations of the male-centric gaming environment. Graham, for example, found that some female gamers fight harassment by adopting hypersexualized identities. This strategy allows them to control the narrative and thereby co-opt the power of the stereotype that placed them in a disadvantaged position.

Looking to the Future

Expansion of research on online gaming is inevitable as gaming takes on increasing prominence in society. Constructivist explorations of gaming as a force for identity building and social action will no doubt continue to expand, including an evolving examination of conflict, aggression, and impoliteness. Given rising awareness of demographic disparities in the online gaming community, we can hope for increased research examining demographic groups that have historically been invisible in this context. A rising awareness of multimodal strategies is also likely to direct future research, including greater attention to the role of AI/bot-generated communication as a component of online gaming.

—*Sage L. Graham*

References

Benwell, B., and E. Stokoe. *Discourse & identity*. Edinburgh UP, 2006.

Eckert, P., and J. McConnell-Ginet. "Communities of Practice: Where Language, Gender, and Power All Live." *Readings in Language and Gender*, edited by Jennifer Coates, Blackwell, 1992, pp. 573–82.

Ensslin, A. *The Language of Gaming*. Palgrave, 2012.

Ensslin, A. I., and I. Balteiro. "Locating Videogames in Medium-Specific, Multilingual Discourse Analysis." *Approaches to Videogame Discourse*. Bloomsbury Academic, 2019, pp. 1–10.

Garcés-Conejos Blitvich, P. "The Status Quo and Quo-Vadis of Impoliteness Research." *Intercultural Pragmatics*, vol. 7, no. 4, 2010, pp. 535–59.

Garcés-Conejos Blitvich, P., and M. Sifianou. "Im/politeness in Discursive Pragmatics." *Quo Vadis Pragmatics? Recent Developments in the Field of Pragmatics*, edited by Michael Haugh and Marina Terkourafi, Special Issue of *Journal of Pragmatics*, vol. 145, 2019, pp. 91–101.

Gee, James Paul. *Unified Discourse Analysis: Language, Reality, Virtual Worlds, and Video Games*. Routledge, 2015.

Graham, S. "Interaction and Conflict in Digital Communication." *Routledge Handbook of Language in Conflict*, edited by M. Evans, L. Jeffries, and J. O'Driscoll, Routledge, 2019, pp. 310–28.

___. "Impoliteness and the Moral Order in Online Gaming." *Internet Pragmatics*, vol. 1, no. 2, 2018, pp. 303–28.

Graham, S., and C. Hardaker. "(Im)Politeness in Digital Communication." *The Palgrave Handbook of Linguistic (Im)Politeness*, edited by J. Culpeper, M. Haugh, and D. Z. Kádár, Palgrave Macmillan, 2017, pp. 785–814.

Grey, K. L. "Intersecting Oppressions and Online Communities: Examining the Experiences of Women of Color in Xbox Live." *Information, Communication and Society*, vol. 15, no. 3, 2012, pp. 411–28.

Herring, S. "A Faceted Classification Scheme for Computer-Mediated Discourse." *Language@ Internet*, vol. 4, 2007, Urn:Nbn:De:0009-7-7611.

Heyd, T. "Email Hoaxes." *Pragmatics of Computer-Mediated Communication*, edited by S. Herring, Mouton Degruyter, 2013, pp. 387–410.

Lavé, J., and Wenger, E. *Situated Learning: Legitimate Peripheral Participation*. Cambridge UP, 1991.

Locher, M., B. Bolander, and N. Höhn. "Introducing Relational Work in Facebook and Discussion Boards." *Pragmatics*, vol. 25, no. 1, 2015, pp. 1–21.

Locke, John L. *The De-Voicing of Society: Why We Don't Talk to Each Other Anymore.* Simon & Schuster, 1998.

Maccallum-Stewart, E. *Online Games, Social Narratives.* Routledge, 2014.

Newon, L. "Online Multiplayer Games." *Routledge Handbook of Language and Digital Communication*, edited by A. Georgakopoulou and T. Spillioti, Routledge, 2015.

Salter, A., and B. Blodgett. *Toxic Geek Masculinity in Media: Sexism, Trolling, and Identity Policing.* Palgrave Macmillan, 2017.

Salter, M. "From Geek Masculinity to Gamergate: The Technical Rationality of Online Abuse." *Crime Media Culture*, vol. 14, no. 20, 2018, pp. 247–64.

Shaw, A. "Do You Identify as a Gamer? Gender, Race, Sexuality and Gamer Identity." *New Media and Society*, vol. 14, no. 1, 2011, pp. 28–44.

Yates, S. "Oral and Literate Aspects of Computer Conferencing." *Computer-Mediated Communication: Linguistic, Social, and Cross-Cultural Perspectives*, edited by S. Herring, John Benjamins Press, 1996, pp. 29–46.

ONLINE PIRACY

Introduction

As the internet has continued to grow more technologically sophisticated, online piracy has kept pace. A study funded by the UK.gov and released by the Intellectual Property Office, found that during January 2021, the overall level of infringement for all content categories (excluding digital visual images) was at 23 percent, which is 2 percent lower than where it had been for the previous four years. Hundreds of millions of internet users around the world infringed on copyrighted content. Targeted content includes films, television, music, games, and books, and piracy of this content has become so commonplace that some people consider it a right instead of a crime. The significant financial impact of online piracy on copyright holders has become the concern of individuals, businesses, and the US Congress, while advocates for internet freedom of speech are just as concerned about remedies that might unduly restrict online expression and legitimate use of content.

Background

While the use of the term "piracy" in reference to intellectual property has a long history, it only entered widespread use with the advent of the internet, especially when compact disc (CD) burners made copying and distributing music, software, and other material from the internet as easy as a few clicks. The most commonly pirated content includes music, films, television shows, e-books, and software. Digital music files, typically in MP3 format, were one of the first types of files to be extensively copied, due to the development of several file-sharing programs in the 1990s that made it easy to transfer such files both legally and illegally.

Internet pirates have turned illegal copying and sharing of intellectual property into thriving businesses, with several websites specializing in hosting pirated files for download. One popular site was megaupload.com, hosted by the Hong Kong–based company Megaupload Limited. In 2012, the US Department of Justice shut down the company's sites and indicted its owners for allegedly operating an organization based on copyright infringement, and Hong Kong's Customs and Excise Department froze the company's $42 million worth of assets.

As quickly as authorities shut down pirating services, others just as quickly spring up to take their place. According to a report by Digimarc, a company that provides antipiracy technology for publishers

Napster logo. Image courtesy of Napster, via Wikimedia Commons.

Naptser runing on an iBook, circa 2001. Image by Njahnke, via Wikimedia Commons.

and authors, in the first month after Megaupload shut down, two other sites, Putlocker and Rapidshare, raised the total of pirated books to 13 percent. Digimarc also identified the twenty best websites for downloading free e-books. In another piracy report, brand-protection firm NetNames reported that in Europe and North America, the peer-to-peer file-sharing protocol BitTorrent is the most popular method of downloading pirated material, while in the Asia-Pacific region, pirates prefer direct-download websites.

Software piracy has also continued to advance as technology has improved.

The main types of software piracy include "softlifting," in which users share their software with other, unauthorized users; uploading and downloading; software counterfeiting; OEM unbundling, in which OEM (original equipment manufacturer) software is separated from the hardware it was originally sold with and distributed independently; and hard disk loading, in which unauthorized software is preinstalled on hardware before it is sold.

The New Pirates of the Twenty-First Century

According to a 2011 study by Envisional, a subsidiary of NetNames, digital piracy of music, movies, and other copyrighted material accounted for 23.76 percent of internet bandwidth worldwide and 17.53 percent of bandwidth in the United States. Commenting on the study, Republican senator Orrin Hatch of Utah, cochair of the International Anti-Piracy Caucus, argued that online piracy hijacks the earnings of artists and creators of movies, television, and music, which discourages reinvestment in new job-creating projects and thus weakens the American economy.

Internet book piracy affects millions of writers and publishers whose books have been scanned or their digital files copied and uploaded to websites that feature pirated works, sometimes alongside legitimate uploads. A study published in January 2010 by Attributor, which has since been acquired by Digimarc, found that writers and publishers had lost an estimated $2.8 billion to date because of internet piracy, assuming that each illegal download represented a lost sale.

Internet theft of music is a constant challenge. The volume of pirated music and the drop in music industry revenues is significant, with rising digital sales not closing the gap. The Recording Industry Association of America (RIAA) reports that a decade after Napster introduced its file-sharing site in 1999, music sales in the United States dropped from $14.6 billion to $7.7 billion. In 2003, with the launch of the Apple iTunes Store, steady options for legal digital music downloads became available. It is illegal to download copied music files in the United States but legal to do so in Canada and Europe. In most Western countries, it is illegal to copy movies through internet piracy.

The Motion Picture Association of America (MPAA) reports that in 2005, the major US motion-picture studios lost $6.1 billion worldwide to internet piracy, and the worldwide motion-picture industry, including foreign and domestic producers, distributors, theaters, video stores, and pay-per-view operations, lost $18.2 billion. With these statistics in mind, the entertainment industry has countered internet piracy of music, television, and movies with more legal options. As broadband speeds have increased, so too have the opportunities to legally watch television shows and movies online, whether via download or streaming video files.

Netflix, which offers video-streaming services in addition to digital video disc (DVD) rentals, announced in 2015 that it had over 57 million subscribers around the world, while also in 2015, the music-streaming service Spotify totaled over 75 million active users.

In 2013, major internet service providers and the entertainment industry announced a partnership to attempt to curb piracy of copyrighted material online. Under the Copyright Alert System (CAS) or "six strikes" system, internet subscribers accused of online piracy will receive a series of alerts each time they are found pirating material. The sixth copyright violation may result in the user being punished by the internet provider. Subscribers who illegally share movies or songs can be punished by losing their internet access or having the speed of their broadband downloads reduced to a crawl.

Responding to an outcry from internet users and technology companies including Google, Congress defeated the Stop Online Piracy Act (SOPA) and the PROTECT IP Act (PIPA) in 2012. SOPA and PIPA would have imposed strict penalties on websites carrying copyright-violating material, which Google and other critics claimed would curtail free speech.

Reputable companies who advertise on the internet have also been pulled into the online piracy problem. Because most internet ad placement is generated automatically through algorithms, companies cannot always control where their ads are placed. Often these ads appear on sites that offer illegal downloads of music and films. A 2015 report issued by Digital Citizens alliance and MediaLink, a consulting firm, found that "theft" websites earned more than $200 million from advertising placed on their pages in 2014. This phenomenon has been termed "ad fraud" and is an effect of online piracy, illustrating the ubiquity of the problem.

—Kathy Warnes

References

Fisk, Nathan W. *Understanding Online Piracy: The Truth about Illegal File Sharing.* ABC-CLIO, 2009.

Gordon, Sherri Mabry. *Downloading Copyrighted Stuff from the Internet: Stealing or Fair Use?* Enslow, 2005.

Hamedy, Saba. "Report: Online Piracy Remains Multi-Hundred-Million-Dollar Business." *Los Angeles Times,* 19 May 2015.

Hinduja, Sameer. *Music Piracy and Crime Theory.* LFB, 2005.

Husak, Douglas. *Overcriminalization: The Limits of the Criminal Law.* Oxford UP, 2008.

Johns, Adrian. *Piracy: The Intellectual Property Wars from Gutenberg to Gates.* U of Chicago P, 2009.

Murray, Brian H. *Defending the Brand: Aggressive Strategies for Protecting Your Brand in the Online Arena.* AMACOM, 2004.

Nhan, Johnny. *Policing Cyberspace: A Structural and Cultural Analysis.* LFB, 2010.

"Research and Analysis: Online Copyright Infringement Tracker Survey (10th Wave) Executive Summary." *Intellectual Property Office,* gov.uk/government/publications/online-copyright-infringement-tracker-survey-10th-wave/online-copyright-infringement-tracker-survey-10th-wave-executive-summary.

Riley, Gail Blasser. *Internet Piracy.* Cavendish, 2010.

Torr, James D. *Internet Piracy.* Greenhaven, 2004.

ONLINE SAFETY

Introduction

Online safety, also known as internet safety, refers to considerations of any possible risks, including emotional and financial, involved with browsing and using the web, especially concerning any exchange of private or sensitive information. This concept became prevalent in the beginning of the 2000s as internet crimes advanced alongside computer and online technology. The amount of information users entrusted to the internet also grew exponentially during this time, as people began turning online to handle more transactions such as banking, bill paying, and shopping. An increasing variety of cybercrimes, including identity theft, credit card scams, spam, and phishing, in which users are tricked into disclosing sensitive information, became a serious issue.

The rise of the internet as well as social media websites also brought about an influx of cyberbullying, where a person, typically a child or teenager, is harassed by peers or even strangers online. Due to the anonymity afforded by some internet sites, this bullying is often severe and, in some cases, has led to the victim committing suicide.

Background

The concept of online safety has been established to some extent since the internet became available to the public in the 1990s. Around the same time, the crime of phishing began to develop, though it did not become well known until the mid-2000s. Hackers and others who traded pirated software formed communities online where they developed these phishing scams. The first form of this crime used algorithms to create randomized credit card numbers that were then used to open accounts with America Online (AOL), one of the first providers of internet access. Those accounts were used to further scam people until 1995 when AOL created security measures to prevent the use of generated credit card numbers.

In 2001 phishers began targeting online payment systems to steal users' information. The first attack in June 2001 was on E-Gold, a website that allowed users to open accounts denominated in grams of gold and make transfers to other accounts. Two years later phishers began setting up websites that resembled legitimate ones like the online payment service PayPal in order to trick people into providing their sensitive information. Since 2003 phishers have been using other sophisticated methods to target banking websites and their users. According to Javelin Strategy and Research, fraud, phishing, and other forms of online identity theft led to a loss of over $56 billion in 2021 and $43 billion in 2020.

Cyberbullying and cyberstalking have also become major topics regarding online safety. In 2018, Comparitech conducted a survey of over 1,000 parents of children over the age of five. It found:

- 47.7 percent of parents with children ages six to ten reported their children were bullied;
- 56.4 percent of parents with children ages eleven to thirteen reported their children were bullied;
- 59.9 percent of parents with children ages fourteen to eighteen reported their children were bullied; and
- 54.3 percent of parents with children ages nineteen and older reported their children were bullied.

It is clear that cyberbullying was a major form of harassment facing youth. Over 82 percent of bullying occurs during and at the school, nearly 20 percent of students in grades six to twelve experienced bullying on social media sites, and 11 percent through text messages. Most cyberbullying prevention and safety programs stress the monitoring of a child's online activity by a parent, but schools are also involved in teaching our children safe and caring practices while online.

Overview

Several issues regarding security have continued to plague both young and adult users of the internet alike, especially as the convenience of and reliance upon this service has increased. The accessibility of pornographic materials was especially debated, and with the Communications Decency Act of 1996, Congress attempted to regulate it. The anti-indecency provisions of this act were struck down the following year. In 1998 Congress passed the Child Online Protection Act, which restricted online access by minors to material that could be considered harmful. The law failed to take effect and was shut down in 2009.

Aside from the harmful effects of pornographic materials on children, the spread of cyberbullying became an important issue starting in the early 2000s. This form of bullying takes place online, typically on social media websites but also via chat rooms and other websites. The bullying usually involves cruel messages, rumors, pictures, or even fake social media profiles meant to harm an individual. Surveys have shown that youths who are cyberbullied are more likely to skip school, use alcohol or drugs, and develop low self-esteem. In some tragic cases, it has led to suicide. One high-profile case involved the suicide of thirteen-year-old Megan Meier, a student in Missouri who hanged herself after being cyberbullied by classmates on the social media website Myspace.

To combat cyberbullying and reinforce online safety, the US government established the website Stop Bullying, which provides an overview of what cyberbullying is and how to prevent it. Numerous other websites and organizations, including the American Humane Association, have developed programs and educational websites to help prevent and report cyberbullying. Many schools have added cyberbullying to their anti-bullying policies to help prevent and regulate it as well. Online safety discussions concerning children also typically include warnings against sexual predators who target youth and attempt to arrange meetings in person.

Other online threats come in the form of hacking. Many internet users employ some form of antivirus software and firewalls to protect their sensitive information from theft through computer viruses and malicious programs known as malware. However, with consistently changing and evolving technology, hackers often manage to find ways around these safeguards, and antivirus software and firewalls require frequent updates. Many forms of viruses record users' keystrokes, which could eventually record their personal information. Spyware is a common form of software used to gather users' information without their knowledge. To monitor users' movements online, hackers typically install these programs covertly, so users are unaware that their system has been invaded.

A form of computer malware program that grew increasingly popular amongst hackers during the 1990s was known as a Trojan horse. These programs usually acted as undetected gateways into users' computers. Hackers could execute a Trojan horse to perform a number of malicious tasks, including taking control of the computer, corrupting and stealing data, or simply crashing the computer. Another form of malware program similar to a Trojan horse is a computer worm, which replicates itself and spreads to other users via a computer network.

Due to the variables and technology involved, it has remained difficult to find a way to guarantee total safety when browsing the web. However, as the internet is a necessary tool, efforts will continue to be made to curb cybercrime and protect users.

—*Patrick G. Cooper*

References

Anderson, Nate. *The Internet Police: How Crime Went Online—and the Cops Followed.* Norton, 2013.

Brandon, John. "Making the Internet Safe for Kids." *Fox News.* Fox News Network, 14 May 2011.

Cloherty, Jack, and Pierre Thomas. "'Trojan Horse' Bug Lurking in Vital US Computers since 2011." *ABC News.* ABC News Internet Ventures, 6 Nov. 2014.

Cook, Sam. "Cyberbullying Facts and Statistics for 2018-2022." *Comparitech,* 29 Jan. 2022, comparitech.com/internet-providers/cyberbullying-statistics/.

Jacobs, Bruce. "Cyberbullying a Growing Concern." *HTRNews.com.* HTR Media, 5 Dec. 2014.

Kay, Russell. "How-To: Phishing." *Computerworld,* 19 Jan. 2004.

Legon, Jeordan. "'Phishing Scams Reel in Your Identity." *CNN*. Cable News Network, 26 Jan. 2004.

Menn, Joseph. "US and Russian Experts Turn Up Volume on Cybersecurity Alarms." *Chicago Tribune*. Tribune Media, 27 Sept. 2012.

Scheff, Sue. "Online Safety: What Does It Mean to You?" *The Huffington Post*. TheHuffingtonPost.com, 21 Nov. 2014.

OPEN SOURCE

Introduction

Software with source code that anyone is able to modify or enhance because its design is publicly accessible. Source code is the code used to manipulate or change how a program or application functions. Individuals who have access to a computer program's source code can improve that program by adding features to it or adjusting parts with performance issues.

Background

While the term "open source" was not invented until 1989, some of the concepts surrounding it have existed since the early 1980s. The Open Source Initiative (OSI) maintains the Open Source Definition (OSD) and is recognized worldwide as the authority on determining whether a particular software is a truly open source.

Open-source software differs from proprietary or closed source software because, with the latter, the person, team, or organization who created it and maintain exclusive control over the software are the individuals that are able to modify the source code. Because the source code of proprietary software is considered the property of its original authors, they are the only individuals legally authorized able to copy or modify it. Microsoft Word and Adobe Photoshop are examples of proprietary software. To use proprietary software, users must agree (usually by signing a license that comes with the software) that they will not modify the software in ways that the software company has not explicitly allowed.

Open-source software has been commercially available since the mid-1990s. Currently, open source is being used by many organizations that operate large-scale or critical infrastructure. Open-source software differs from proprietary software because its authors make the source code freely available to others. Open-source software includes: LibreOffice and the GNU Image Manipulation Program (GIMP). Like proprietary software, users must accept the terms of a license when they begin using the open-source software. The terms of open-source licenses, however, differ significantly from those of proprietary licenses. Open-source software licenses promote collaboration and sharing by allowing others to modify the source code and incorporate those changes into their own work. Some open-source licenses require that any individual who modifies and then shares a particular program must also share the program's source code without imposing a licensing fee on it. Computer users may freely access, view, and modify open-source software as long as they allow others the same right when they share their work. Users could violate provisions of some open-source licenses if they fail to comply with this stipulation.

Open-source software is licensed under terms allowing the users to practice the four so-called freedoms: (1) Use the software without access restrictions and within the terms of the license applied; (2) view the source code; (3) improve and add to the object and source code; and (4) distribute the source code. Because much of the internet itself is constructed on many open-source technologies, including the Linux operating system and the Apache Web server application, anyone using the internet benefits from open-source software.

Open-source software has the following current and potential benefits: (1) encourages reuse, (2) enables easy innovation and flexibility; (3) drives the price of software down to nothing; (4) because there is no vendor or service monopoly, there is no reason to hide defects and security vulnerabilities; (5) there is no single vendor, meaning there is no reason to avoid free and open standards; (6) key software is improved through a process analogized to Darwinian evolution; and (7) with lower barriers to entry, there is wider participation.

Remote computing is frequently referred to as cloud computing, so-called because it entails functions (including storing files, sharing photos, or watching videos) that incorporate not only local devices but also the global network of remote computers that form an "atmosphere" around them. Cloud computing has grown increasingly popular. Some cloud-computing applications, such as Google Docs, are closed source programs. Others, such as Etherpad, are open-source programs.

Cloud-computing applications run over additional software, which helps them operate smoothly and effectively. The software that runs "underneath" cloud-computing applications is a platform for those applications. Cloud-computing platforms may be open source or closed source. OpenStack is one form of an open-source cloud-computing platform.

Many users prefer open-source software because it gives them more control. They can examine the code to ensure that it is functioning properly and make modifications as needed. Users who are not programmers also benefit from open-source software because they can use this software for any purpose they would like. Some software users prefer open-source software because it improves their programming skills. Open-source code is publicly accessible, so users can learn to make better software by studying what others have written.

Some users prefer open-source software because they view it as more secure and stable than proprietary software. Anyone can view and modify open-source software, and anyone might spot and correct errors or omissions overlooked by the program's original authors. Because so many programmers can work on some open-source software without seeking approval from the original authors, open-source software is generally fixed, updated, and upgraded quickly.

Many users prefer open-source software to proprietary software for significant, long-term projects because the source code for open-source software is publicly distributed. Users that rely on software for critical tasks can ensure that their software will remain functional even if the original creators cease their participation in the project.

The term "open source" does not mean that the program is distributed without charge. Programmers may charge for the open-source software they create or when they cooperate with others in its creation. However, most open-source licenses require users to release their source code when they sell software to others, so many open-source software programmers find that charging users money for software services and support (as opposed to the software itself) is more profitable. With this method,

their software remains free of charge; instead, they earn money by assisting others install, use, and troubleshoot it.

There is a misconception that open-source software is not as secure as proprietary software. Many individuals are concerned that open-source software is inherently less secure and riskier than closed source software because the source code is easily available to all. There is, in fact, no particular type of software that is inherently more or less secure than others. Each must be considered on its own merits.

—*Gretchen Nobahar*

References

DiBona, Chris. *Open Sources Voices from the Open Source Revolution.* O'Reilly, 1999.

Dixon, Rod. *Open Source Software Law.* Artech House, 2004.

Feller, Joseph. *Perspectives on Free and Open Source Software.* MIT Press, 2005.

Kavanagh, Paul. *Open Source Software Implementation and Management.* Elsevier Digital Press, 2004.

Lerner, Joshua, and Mark Schankerman. *The Comingled Code: Open Source and Economic Development.* MIT Press, 2010.

OPTICAL STORAGE

Introduction

Optical storage refers to a variety of technologies that are used to read and write data. It employs special materials that are selected for the way they interact with light (an optical, or visible, medium). Most optical storage devices being manufactured are digital, though some analogue systems remain in use. Both the computer and entertainment industries offer numerous practical applications of optical storage devices. Common optical storage applications are compact discs (CDs), digital video discs (DVDs), and Blu-ray discs (BDs). A variety of data can be stored optically, including audio, video, text, and computer programs. Data are stored in binary form.

Optical storage differs from other data storage technologies such as magnetic tape, which stores data as an electrical charge. Most optical storage is in the form of optical discs, which are flat and circular. They contain binary data in the form of microscopic pits, which are nonreflective and have a binary value of 0, and smooth areas, which are reflective and have a binary value of 1. Optical discs are both created and read with a laser beam. The discs are encoded in a continuous spiral running from the center of the disc to the perimeter. Some discs are multilayer: with these discs, after reaching the perimeter, another spiral track is etched back to the center.

The amount of data storage is dependent upon the wavelength of the laser beam. The shorter the wavelength, the greater the storage capacity (shorter-wavelength lasers can read a smaller pit on the disc surface). For example, the high-capacity BD uses short-wavelength blue light. Lasers can be used to create a master disc from which duplicates can be made by a stamping process. Another, less common form of optical storage is optical tape, which consists of a long, narrow strip of plastic upon which patterns can be written and from which the patterns can be read back.

Optical media is more durable than electromagnetic tape and is less vulnerable to environmental conditions. However, with early formats such as CDs and DVDs, the speed of data retrieval is considerably slower than that of a computer hard drive. The storage capacity of most optical discs is also significantly less than that of hard drives, though experimental formats continue to expand capacity.

Background

Optical storage originated in the nineteenth century. In 1839, English inventor John Benjamin Dancer produced microphotographs with a reduction ratio of 160:1. Microphotography progressed slowly for almost a century until microfilm began to be used commercially in the 1920s. Between 1927 and 1935, more than 3 million pages of books and manuscripts in the British Library were microfilmed by the Library of Congress. Newspaper preservation on film had its onset in 1935 when Kodak's Recordak division filmed and published the *New York Times* on 35-millimeter (mm) microfilm reels.

Analogue optical discs were developed in 1958 by American inventor David Paul Gregg, who patented the videodisc in 1961. In 1969, physicists at the Netherlands-based Royal Philips Electronics began experimenting with optical discs. Subsequently, Philips and the Music Corporation of America (MCA) joined forces to create the laser disc (Laser-Disc), which was first introduced in the United States in 1978. Although the laser disc achieved greater popularity in Asia and Europe than it did in the United States, it never successfully competed with video home system (VHS) tape.

In 1980, Philips partnered with Sony to develop the CD for the storage of music. A few years later, the CD had evolved into a compact disc read-only memory (CD-ROM) format, which in addition to audio, could store computer programs, text, and video. In 1996, the DVD format was first introduced by Toshiba in Japan; it first appeared in the United States in 1997; in Europe in 1998; and in Australia in 1999. Several different versions of the DVD would follow.

A format war between two higher-capacity data storage technologies emerged in 2006 when Sony's Blu-ray and Toshiba's high-definition (HD) DVD players became commercially available for the recording and playback of high-definition video. Two years later, Toshiba conceded to Sony; Blu-ray was based on newer technology and had a greater storage capacity. Other variants of optical storage were also introduced over the years, often for specialized use or in pursuit of greater capacity, but none proved as popular as CDs, DVDs, or Blu-ray.

How It Works

CDs, DVDs, and BDs are produced with a diameter of 120 mm. The storage capacity is dependent upon the wavelength of the laser: the shorter the wavelength, the greater the storage capacity. CDs have a wavelength of 780 nanometers (nm), DVDs have a wavelength of 650 nm, and BDs have a wavelength of 405 nm. Some disc drives can read data from a disc while others can both read and write data.

In a disc reader, the optical system consists of pickup head (which houses a laser), a lens for guiding the laser beam, and photodiodes that detect the light reflection from disc's surface. The photodiodes convert the light into an electrical signal. An optical disc drive contains two main servomechanisms: one maintains the correct distance between the lens and the disc while it ensures that the laser beam is focused on a small area of the disc; the other servomechanism moves the head along the disc's radius, keeping the beam on a continuous spiral data path.

The same servomechanism can be used to position the head for both reading and writing. A disc writer employs a laser with a significantly higher-power output. It burns data onto the disc by heating an organic dye layer, which changes the dye's reflectivity. Higher-writing speeds require a more powerful laser because of the decreased time the laser is focused on a specific point. Some discs are rewritable—they contain a crystalline metal alloy in their recording layer. Depending on the amount of power applied, the substance may be melted into a crystalline form or left in an amorphous form. This enables the creation of marks of varying reflectivity. The number of times the recording layer of a disc can be reliably switched between its crystalline and amorphous states is limited. Estimates range from 1,000 to 100,000 times, depending on the type of media. Some formats may employ defect-management schemes to verify data as it is written and skip over or relocate problems to a spare area of the disc.

Double-layer (DL) media has up to twice the storage capacity of single-layer media. DL media have a polycarbonate first layer with a shallow groove; a first data layer, a semi-reflective layer; a second polycarbonate spacer layer with a deep groove; and a second data layer. The first groove spiral begins on the inner diameter and extends outward; the second groove starts on the outer diameter and extends inward. If data exists in the transition zone, a momentary hiccup of sound and/or video will occur as the playback head changes direction. Formats with more than two layers have also been produced.

Many commercial optical discs are copy protected; in some cases, a limited number of copies can be made. Discs produced on home or business computers can be readily copied with inexpensive (or included) software. If two optical drives are available, a disc-to-disc copy can be made. If only one drive is available, the data is first stored on the computer's hard drive and then transferred to a blank disc placed in the same read-write drive. For copying larger numbers of discs, dedicated disc-duplication devices are available. The more expensive ones incorporate a robotic disc-handling system, which automates the process. Some products incorporate a label printer. Industrial processes are used for mass replication of more than 1,000 discs, such as DVDs, CDs, or computer programs. These discs are manufactured from a mold and are created via a series of industrial processes including pre-mastering, mastering, electroplating, injection molding, metallization, bonding, spin coating, printing, and advanced quality control.

Applications and Products

Numerous applications and products are focused on optical storage. Most applications are geared toward the computer and entertainment industries, though archival needs are another important field.

Most optical discs are read-only; however, some are rewritable. They are used for the storage of data, computer programs, music, graphic images, and video games. Since the first CD was introduced in 1982, this technology has evolved markedly. Optical data storage has in large part supplanted storage on magnetic tape. Although optical storage media can degrade over time from environmental factors, they are much more durable than magnetic tape, which loses its magnetic charge over time. Magnetic tape is also subject to wear as it passes through the rollers and recording head. This is not the case for optical media, in which the only contact with the recording surface is the laser beam.

CDs are commonly used for the storage of music: A CD can hold an entire recorded album and supplanted cassette tapes and vinyl records, which are more easily subject to wear and degradation. (However, those formats, especially vinyl, have seen a resurgence due to a perceived superiority of their sound quality.) A limitation of the CD is its storage capacity, which is typically 700 megabytes (MB) of data (eighty minutes of music).

The DVD, which appeared in 1996, rapidly gained popularity and soon outpaced VHS tape for the storage of feature-length movies. The standard DVD can store 4.7 gigabytes (GB) of data in single-layer format and 8.5 GB in dual-layer format. The development of high-definition television fueled the development of higher-capacity storage media. The BD can store about six times the amount of data as a standard DVD: 25 GB of data in single-layer format and 50 GB of data in dual-layer format. An evolution of the BD disc is the 3D format; the increased storage capacity of this medium allows for the playback of video in three dimensions.

Computer Applications

Many computers contain one or more optical drives, although tablets and some laptops do not due to size considerations and some computer makers have moved away from optical drives altogether. A computer's optical drive may be used to load computer programs stored on an optical disc onto a hard drive, for data storage and retrieval, and for playback of CDs and DVDs. If a computer's optical drive is write-capable, data from the computer can be written (burned) onto blank or rewritable optical discs. As the price of Blu-ray technology fell, some computers also began to include Blu-ray readers. Most internal drives for computers are designed to fit in a 5.25-inch drive bay and connect to their host via an interface. External drives can be added to a computer through various connectivity standards, such as universal serial bus (USB).

Entertainment Applications

Stand-alone optical disc players are a common component of home entertainment systems. Most play DVDs as well as CDs, though some are specific to one format. As with computer applications, the presence of Blu-ray devices increased as prices fell. Some devices load a single optical disc at a time; others load a magazine holding multiple optical discs, from which users can select using an interface on the device or a remote control. CD, DVD, and Blu-ray players contain audio and video outputs to interface with home entertainment systems. If attached to an audio-video receiver (AVR), surround-sound audio playback can be enjoyed. Many later generations of players also have internet connectivity, moving beyond their optical data reading capability to allow for online streaming of content and other forms of interconnectivity with the entire entertainment system.

Many automobiles contain a CD player for playback of audio, and in the early twenty-first century in-vehicle DVD drives became more common. DVD video is typically displayed to backseat passengers for safety reasons, though the rise of dashboard touch screens made front-seat viewing capability more common. Some vehicle navigation systems have incorporated optical drives as well to load route information. Portable stand-alone CD, DVD, and Blu-ray players are also available. These range from small devices that can be strapped on an arm to systems similar in size to a laptop computer.

Games

Although a wealth of games can be played on a computer, many devices in the marketplace are designed strictly for game playing. Most of these devices attach to a television set or monitor and are interactive; thus, the player can immerse oneself in the action. Some accommodate more than one player. Although earlier devices had proprietary cartridges for data storage, these were generally superseded by DVDs and BDs.

Data Backup and Archival Storage

While entertainment and other consumer applications are the most familiar applications of optical storage, the technology has also been explored for other means. Prominent among these is the archival storage of data. Microfilm is still held by some libraries to archive newspapers and other publications, though digital formats now dominate. CDs and DVDs have commonly been used as a method of backing up data from computers, though solid-state technology such as USB flash drives have become more popular as their capacity has grown and prices have fallen. Researchers continue to experiment with different formats of optical storage that provide greater capacity. However, the ultimate longevity of optical media is uncertain due to the relative youth of the technology.

Social Context and Future Prospects

Within decades after optical-storage devices appeared on the market, they and their playback systems became innumerable and ubiquitous. Stand-alone DVD and CD players remain common household items, though they saw some decline in popularity as computers became cheaper and therefore more widespread. In the United States and other highly developed countries, most households contain one or more computers with optical drives, often including a CD and DVD burner. Video game systems using optical discs are also extremely popular, though the games themselves have often stirred cultural debate over issues such as violence and addiction.

However, while optical storage technology rose to popularity extremely quickly, it faced serious challenges by the 2010s. In particular, the rise of digital downloads and then streaming media quickly eroded the consumer market for CDs, DVDs, BDs, and their respective players. In 2014 global revenue from downloaded and streaming music overtook CD sales for the first time, and streaming services such as Spotify especially continued to grow in popularity at the expense of physical discs. In 2016 DVDs in turn were surpassed in sales by streaming video content on services such as Netflix and Hulu, according to the Entertainment Retailers Association. Those trends continued over the subsequent years, with sales of physical media declining further amid the rising popularity of streaming services.

Meanwhile, the falling costs of solid-state hard-disc storage systems such as flash drives, which have desirable features such as fast retrieval speeds and no moving parts, changed the face of the computer industry. Online stores for downloading software and other applications largely replaced the model of buying software on CD or DVD and uploading it onto a computer's hard drive. Personal computer makers such as Apple began to phase out optical drives from laptops and other products altogether, while tablet computers without optical drives gained in popularity. Even some automobiles stopped including built-in CD players in favor of connectivity with smartphones and other internet-based multimedia systems.

Still, CDs, DVDs, and BDs all remain in use. High-capacity optical media are used not only for entertainment, such as high-definition movies, but also for data storage. Technology companies have developed various optical formats that exceed the capacity of Blu-ray, but as of 2020 these have not been widely adopted. The technologies are often not economically viable, and they are often quickly superseded by other formats with even more potential. Among the optical formats being researched are Ultra HD Blu-ray, Sony's Archival Disc (AD), stacked volumetric optical disc (SVOD), and holographic data storage.

—*Robin L. Wulffson*

References

McDonald, Paul. *Video and DVD Industries.* British Film Institute, 2008.

Meinders, Erwin R., et al. *Optical Data Storage: Phase-Change Media and Recording.* Springer Netherlands, 2011.

"Optical Storage." *Computer History Museum,* 2020, www.computerhistory.org/revolution/memory-storage/8/262.

Taylor, Jim, Mark R. Johnson, and Charles G. Crawford. *DVD Demystified.* 3rd ed., McGraw-Hill, 2006.

Taylor, Jim, et al. *Blu-ray Disc Demystified.* McGraw-Hill, 2009.

Wroot, Jonathan, and Andy Willis. *DVD, Blu-ray & Beyond: Navigating Formats and Platforms within Media Consumption.* Palgrave MacMillan, 2017.

Xu, Duanyi. *Multi-Dimensional Optical Storage.* Springer Singapore, 2016.

P

PEER-TO-PEER PAYMENT APPS

Introduction
Peer-to-Peer Payment (P2P) is a monetary transaction that is accomplished through the use of applications tied to one's bank account, credit card, or PayPal account. These apps (notably Cash App, Venmo, Zelle, PayPal, Google Pay, Apple Pay, WeChat Wallet, and Facebook Pay) allow the registered user to send or receive an instant payment to/from a friend or acquaintance. Many businesses began using P2P options during the COVID-19 pandemic to reduce the physical exchange of paper money and to speed up what is usually a longer process for checking out customers.

P2P payments have become commonplace when acquaintances are out to dinner (for example) and rather than splitting the bill or asking for individual checks, the users can pay their fair share by directly sending payment to one person who will pay the bill to cover the group's tab.

Background
As populations grow ever-more impatient and desire more rapid forms of commerce and banking, banking institutions have continued to adopt more nimble financial technologies that are cost-effective and decentralized. Consumers have grown accustomed to digital technologies and have become dissatisfied with writing checks (which incurs costs for the consumer and impacts the environment) and with making trips to brick-and-mortar banks to make deposits, payments, or withdrawals. Consequently, internet banking and mobile payments have become the wave of the future without the need of third-party institutions.

Some may identify the progenitor of P2P payments as Napster (the 1999 file-sharing program that allowed users to directly download files from one computer to another). Though Napster was shut down in 2001 after legal issues regarding royalties, intellectual property, and copyright infringement, the technology continued to develop and mature through various protocols and applications. Such applications continue to redefine methods of sharing and exchanging currencies and of consuming entertainment. The most recent form of P2P sharing and payment apps is the birth of Bitcoin in 2009. This has become what many consider to be a new category of financial and investment transactions.

Given the growing importance of P2P technologies, learning how and when to use these apps technology safely and ethically is among the most important goals facing society. Each P2P app has its niche and best practices. It is up to consumers to identify with app is best suited for their needs. Bessette identifies in her article for *Nerdwallet:*

- Best for instant transfers: Zelle
- Best for social groups: Venmo
- Best for investors: Cash App
- Best for online shoppers: PayPal
- Best for digital wallet users: Google Pay
- Best for Apple users: Apple Pay Cash
- Best for social media users: Social media money transfers

Potential Issues Associated with P2P apps
While the ease and speed of P2P payment apps make them appealing and favorable for everyday transactions, the rates and terms of each P2P app varies in use and transaction fees. So, it is imperative to become familiar with each app's terms of use before committing to monetary exchanges through the app.

Some of the more important limitations of P2P apps are: very few P2P apps allow users to send payments to overseas users; one must use a smartphone and download a proprietary app in order to initiate the P2P transaction; some apps require both parties to have monetary or financial accounts with the creators of the app to access their funds; some apps have fees for each payment, while other apps have fees once users reach a certain number of transactions; the danger of making payments to the wrong party (someone who may share the same name as the intended recipient). Consequently, it is the responsibility of the users to ensure they are making payment to the correct party by validating the name, title, and address of the receiver. Once funds are paid out, it is exceptionally difficult (if not impossible) to retrieve those payments. Care must be used proactively—not retroactively.

Additionally, while most P2P apps are technically safe to use, fraud and scammers are always lurking for an opportunity to steal one's identity or funds. Users must be certain to secure their account information, log-ins, passwords, and payment recipients for every use. Consequently, users (on both ends) must keep the apps up-to-date since old or outdated apps are both vulnerable to digital theft and to obsolescence. Some apps also make payments between parties public to anyone using their app, and this practice needs to be examined before users partake in any transaction made with that application.

—*Laura Nicosia*

References

Bessette, Chanelle. "Top Peer-to-Peer Payment Apps: Pros, Cons and How to Use them." *Nerdwallet,* 1 Apr. 2021, nerdwallet.com/article/banking/peer-to-peer-p2p-money-transfers.

Blanco, Octavio. "The Truth About Those Peer-To-Peer Payment Apps." *Consumer Reports,* May 2022, p. 48.

Kern, Kirsten, and Naticia Chetty. "Peer-to-Peer Payments in the Fintech Revolution." *Fintech Weekly,* 5 Jan. 2022, fintechweekly.com/magazine/articles/peer-to-peer-payments-in-the-fintech-revolution.

Klein, André. "A Brief History of Peer-to-Peer Networks." *Learnoutlive,* 20 Oct. 2020, learnoutlive.com/a-brief-history-of-peer-to-peer-networks/.

Paratii. "A Brief History of P2P Content Distribution, in 10 Major Steps." *Paratii,* 25 Oct. 2017, medium.com/paratii/a-brief-history-of-p2p-content-distribution-in-10-major-steps-6d6733d25122.

Peratello, Gabriela. "What Are Peer-to-Peer (P2P) Payments?" *Wise,* 10 Apr. 2022, wise.com/us/blog/p2p-payments.

PHISHING

Introduction

Phishing is the act of using various communication devices such as email and telephones in an attempt to trick individuals into either revealing their personal information, including passwords and Social Security numbers, or installing malicious software (malware). Phishing is used by identity thieves to acquire the confidential personal and financial information of victims. The term is a variation of "fishing" and refers to identity thieves fishing for victims. Identity thieves, also referred to as "phishers," pose as representatives from banks, credit card companies, or other financial institutions and email or call victims requesting their personal information. Phishers offer several fraudulent reasons for why the victim must enter their personal information. Phishing raised many concerns over online security in the 2000s.

Background

Phishing first became popular during the early days of America Online (AOL), one of the first widely used internet service providers (ISPs). Phishers would pretend to be AOL employees and send users instant messages requesting their passwords for confirmation purposes. Once they procured users' passwords, phishers could use them to access their accounts for spamming or other nefarious purposes. AOL eventually put policies into place to delete the accounts of anyone involved with phishing and to quickly detect any instant messages that contained phishing-related words.

After AOL's security increased, phishers started to pretend to be financial institutions such as banks and credit card companies. The first known phishing attempt in which the perpetrator pretended to be a financial institution was in June 2001. A phisher posed as e-gold, a website that allowed users to instantly transfer gold currency. Although this attempt was unsuccessful, it was used by phishers as a test to develop more successful methods.

Following the terrorist attacks of September 11, 2001, phishers began sending out fraudulent identification check emails. Recipients were asked to enter their personal information to confirm their identities for reasons of national security. These attempts were also seen as failures but were used to test new methods of phishing.

Online Phishing

After unsuccessful attempts in the early part of the 2000s, phishers started implementing more sophisticated methods to acquire victims' personal information. By 2004, phishing was seen as a serious and lucrative criminal activity. It led to heightened online security, increased awareness, and several lawsuits and government actions.

Many phishers pose as social media websites such as Facebook. They send users e-mails claiming that they noticed a security issue on the account and that, as a result, users must fill out legal forms, such as terms of use or copyright law forms. These phishers typically state that if users do not comply and fill out the form, their account will be suspended or terminated. A link is usually included in the e-mail that is disguised with a legitimate address, such as Facebook's web address; in reality, the link will download an executable file if clicked. This kind of trickery is how phishers get victims to download malicious software that exposes personal information and passwords.

Oftentimes phishers include company logos in their emails to make them look legitimate. There are several ways to tell whether an e-mail is a phishing scam or not. Common indicators of scam emails include misspelled words and threats of account deletion. In 2006, phishers began using emails to pose as the US Internal Revenue Service (IRS). In response, the IRS issued several consumer warnings about the use of the IRS logo for phishing and identity-theft purposes. Several of these IRS-related email phishing scams claimed that the individual was owed a tax refund. The individual was then asked to enter personal information in order to receive the money owed them. The IRS established several ways for consumers to report suspicious emails that might be phishing scams.

Some phishers set up fraudulent or replica websites to pose as financial institutions. Once one of these fake websites is visited, users can unknowingly receive malicious software. Even on legitimate websites, phishers can alter the sites' scripts and security aspects to fool users. This is a particularly successful phishing method, because the fraudulent websites are nearly undetectable to average online users.

In 2006, this type of phishing was done on the website PayPal, which allows users to easily transfer money to merchants or other individuals online. Phishers used the PayPal website to trick users into going to a uniform resource locator (URL) hosted on the legitimate PayPal website. Phishers created a warning message that appeared when users visited the website that said the user's account was disabled because it may have been accessed unlawfully by a third party. Users were then redirected to a fraudulent PayPal log-in page that looked extremely similar to the actual log-in page.

This technique has also frequently been used on the websites of banks. When users visit the sites, a pop-up window appears, requesting their personal log-in information for security purposes. Financial institutions responded by increasing online security measures through the use of security questions and images. For example, in 2008, Bank of America implemented a SiteKey system on its website, in which users choose an image that appears every time they log in. If the image does not appear during the log-in process, the user has been led to a fraudulent site. Other companies hit with phishing attacks during the 2000s included Best Buy, the United Parcel Service (UPS), and First Union Bank.

File-sharing websites and services such as RapidShare have also been used by phishers to harvest information or leave computers vulnerable to later attack. Phishers would use fake websites or alter legitimate ones to sell users RapidShare upgrades that did not exist. Sometimes phishers would send out e-mail newsletters posing as file-sharing websites or would post in forums, encouraging users to pay for fake upgrades. Both of these phishing methods were used to steal victims' credit card information.

A majority of online phishing in the 2000s was traced to the Russian Business Network (RBN). RBN is a cybercrime organization based in Russia that performs identity theft on a large scale. It undertook some of the largest and most successful phishing scams of the decade, oftentimes selling personal information to criminals for use in identity theft. RBN developed malicious software such as the MPack, which is a kit that was sold to hackers to infect hundreds of thousands of personal computers.

Among the most notable phishing attacks in the 2010s were a 2013 attack on the big-box retailer Target, in which over 100 million customer credit card numbers were stolen, and a similar-sized 2014 attack on the home-improvement chain Home Depot.

Phone Phishing

Phishers also use phones to acquire personal financial information. This method became known as "vishing" (voice phishing). Sometimes they email messages posing as financial institutions or internet providers. At other times, phishers may steal a list of phone numbers from financial institutions and call the victims themselves. Once victims are on the phone, they may be asked to enter their debit card pin number, Social Security number, or other personal information. The phone numbers victims call are owned by the phishers, who typically use voice over internet protocol (VoIP) to disguise the location of their numbers, making the phishers difficult to locate. A VoIP number allows phishers to make and receive phone calls using their computer and internet connection.

Phishers can even use VoIPs to disguise the caller identification on the victims' end. They can call a victim and have the caller identification information correspond to that of a trusted bank or other entity. This makes vishing hard to monitor. Other phishers use phones to pose as technical support departments from internet providers or software companies such as Microsoft. Phishers use this method to install malware to gain access to sensitive information. Frequently, once the malicious software has been installed, phishers charge victims to remove it from their computer.

Phishers also use this method to adjust the settings on victims' computers to leave them vulnerable to further unlawful access. In response, financial institutions, internet providers, and software companies have released several warnings stating that they will never call and request information or make charges via the phone. They have stated that if anyone calls claiming to be from their institution,

that individuals should hang up and report the number.

Combating Phishing

The rise of phishing and the massive financial losses it has caused has led to several antiphishing responses on public and private levels. The most basic method of combating phishing has been to educate the public on how to recognize these scams. The IRS has released several consumer warnings throughout the decade, and software companies, including Microsoft, have published materials online to inform the public about phishing. Along with online consumer warnings, the IRS has released informational videos and podcasts and provided consumers with emails and telephone numbers they can contact if they suspected they have been the target of phishing attempts.

Because of phishing, several websites, financial institutions, and other entities have changed the way they handle emails and information online. For example, PayPal began to include users' log-in names in emails to let them know they were not being phished. Typically, PayPal phishing emails would address users with generic greetings, such as "Dear PayPal user." In a similar fashion, banks have started to include partial account numbers in emails.

Many popular internet browsers have implemented measures for what is known as secure browsing. Several internet browsers now also include antiphishing technology as part of their browsers and services. If a user attempts to visit a website that is not recognized as secure by Firefox, for example, a warning box will appear or Firefox will simply block the website.

Email servers such as Gmail have increased their email spam filters to help combat phishing. Many of these filters utilize language processing to recognize and block emails that include common phishing words and sentences.

The US Federal Trade Commission (FTC) has set up services to help reduce telephone phishing scams. Their services encourage users to report suspicious phone calls and phone numbers. The FTC then passes this information on to appropriate law enforcement officials. Individuals can also register their phone number on the National Do Not Call Registry, which limits the number of telemarketers and potential phishers that can call the number.

Federal Responses

In 2004, the FTC filed a lawsuit against a seventeen-year-old in California who was suspected of perpetrating phishing scams to acquire credit card information. This was the first law-enforcement action brought against a phisher. In 2006, the Federal Bureau of Investigation (FBI) enacted an operation code-named Cardkeeper that led to the arrest of seventeen people involved with international phishing scams in the United States, Poland, and Romania. This group allegedly stole identities, credit card information, and bank information. Four suspects from the group were arrested in the United States and were in possession of machines used to encode cards with victims' bank information.

On December 16, 2003, President George W. Bush signed the Controlling the Assault of Non-Solicited Pornography and Marketing Act (CAN-SPAM Act). This act established national standards for the distribution of commercial email. The FTC was given authority to enforce the provisions put forth by the act. It was created to reduce the amount of unwarranted and unwanted emails, including phishing-related messages. Although many critics saw it as a failure, the first individual convicted under its provisions was sentenced in 2007. This individual, Jeffrey Brett Goodin, sent thousands of emails posing as the AOL billing department and requesting users' personal information. He was sentenced to serve seventy months in prison.

Impact

Phishing has raised many concerns about the security of valuable personal information that is frequently used online by banks and other entities. During the 2000s and 2010s, various phishing methods managed to successfully rob victims of millions of dollars. Businesses affected by phishing also lost millions of dollars. Phishing was the most successful cybercrime method of the early twenty-first century and changed the way information is distributed online. Its rise has also led to an increase in awareness and heightened security on several fronts.

—*Patrick G. Cooper*

References

Hong, Jason. "The State of Phishing Attacks." *Communications of the ACM*, vol. 55, no. 1, 2012, pp. 74–81, search.ebscohost.com/login.aspx?direct=true&db=a9h&AN=71678156.

Jakobsson, Markus, and Steven Myers, editors. *Phishing and Countermeasures: Understanding the Increasing Problem of Electronic Identity Theft.* John Wiley & Sons, 2007.

James, Lance. *Phishing Exposed.* Syngress Publishing, 2005.

Krebs, Brian. "Shadowy Russian Firm Seen as Conduit for Cybercrime." *The Washington Post*, 13 Oct. 2007, www.washingtonpost.com/wp-dyn/content/article/2007/10/12/AR2007101202461.html.

Lininger, Rachael, and Russell Dean Vines. *Phishing: Cutting the Identity Theft Line.* Wiley, 2005.

"Phishing." *OnGuardOnline.* US Federal Trade Commission, Sept. 2011, www.consumer.ftc.gov/articles/0003-phishing.

PRIVACY SETTINGS

Introduction

Privacy settings are the means by which users of a website or application manipulate and control the amount and type of personal information about them that is collected and disseminated. Forms of privacy settings range from the ability to control what other users see to what information might be passed on to third parties for targeted advertising or other purposes by the company providing the service.

Privacy settings have become essential in the digital world. An option to enable standard privacy settings or the ability to manipulate and personalize privacy settings is available on almost every form of digital platform—from operating systems to applications and websites. Google, Facebook, and even web browsers include options to determine what data users reveal to third parties—to an extent—during their time online.

Privacy settings became important as a way to implement the fair information practice principles (FIPPs) drafted by the Federal Trade Commission (FTC) in May 2000. No company is legally required to have privacy settings that consumers can manipulate or to have privacy settings at all, but companies are required to comply with the principles. Nearly ten years after FIPPs were created, websites began to experiment with more substantial and customizable privacy settings.

Currently, in the digital world, most websites and software provide privacy policies that detail whether a user has the ability to manipulate his or her privacy settings. The most significant and often cited example of privacy policies online is Facebook's policy. Many Facebook users know that the website allows users to manipulate privacy settings to a certain degree. Users may decide with whom to share their posts and information—from a small group of friends to the general public. Because it is so simple to disseminate information online, privacy settings are essential to the preservation of an individual's personal information and online image, which may affect his or her personal and professional life, especially on a site as widely used as Facebook. Privacy settings have been controversial, however, since their inception because the existence of privacy settings does not mean that the settings are actually followed or enforced.

Background

The issue of privacy settings is a largely unregulated area. No government agency is authorized to govern all the areas of cyberspace. In online services such as Google and Facebook, the FTC has the ability only to enforce the privacy settings, which companies disclose to consumers, to alleviate consumer fraud. In some controversial cases, the FTC may enter into legal agreements with companies to preserve consumer privacy and security. Google currently has an agreement with the FTC stating that the company will honor user privacy settings and will not circumvent them.

Specifically, the FTC ordered Google "not [to] misrepresent in any manner, expressly or by implication . . . the extent to which consumers may exercise control over the collection, use or disclosure of covered information." Although the FTC seems to exert control over one of the world's most significant online companies through this 2011 order, this contract demonstrates the current limit of the FTC's power. The FTC can only ensure that Google and other corporations do not engage in consumer fraud. Beyond this, the FTC is powerless to control how these massive online corporations handle private consumer data.

Privacy settings are also controversial because consumers face many challenges even when privacy settings are in place. First, consumers often ignore privacy settings or do not have the technical skills that may be necessary to take advantage of the available protections. Under current law, privacy settings tend to be opt-in rather than opt-out provisions, which means that, unless requested, users' privacy settings will be off or set to the least restrictive settings. To protect privacy rights, consumers must be proactive and search for additional protection. Each update to a company's privacy policy may result in an individual's personal privacy settings are no longer as active or as restrictive as the user requested prior to the policy change.

Despite the controversy over privacy settings, only one bill is currently pending in Congress that will affect privacy settings. The bill, known as the Do Not Track Kids Act of 2015 (H.R. 2734, 2015), is not the first bill to attempt to regulate privacy settings. In fact, a broader bill, Do Not Track Me Online Act of 2011 (H.R. 654, 2011), was originally introduced in 2011. This previous bill would have required the FTC to "establish standards for the required use of an online opt-out mechanism," which would have been placed within an application or website's privacy settings. This bill did not gain sufficient support in 2011 but was reintroduced in 2015 with a focus on children. The pending bill requires companies to gain verifiable consent from parents before the companies are able to track any of the information within the application regarding children. The parents, via privacy settings, would be able to control exactly what information about their children is collected and how companies may then use the information. However, the Do Not Track Kids Act of 2015 was not enacted, so privacy settings continue to be a largely unregulated area with the potential danger to privacy rights that this entails. The most recent (re)introduction of the Do Not Track Act (2019) applies to more than merely web browsers and extends to all online activities, including mobile and phone applications. The bill would allow individuals to prevent organizations and companies from collecting any data beyond that which is necessary to supporting its goods and services. Likewise, the bill enforces rigorous consequences for any violations.

Many of the most ubiquitous web presences in modern society including Facebook, Apple, and Google, continue to have a contentious relationship with users who want their data, browsing habits, and purchasing habits kept private. Turning off location services may prevent some parts of the companies' services from working but can keep people's private information more secure. Apps that use augmented reality or virtual reality rely on location services as well. Many apps, such as Facebook, track users' movements whether or not the app itself is open unless users change their privacy settings to prevent it.

Currently, privacy settings remain a legally murky area. The FTC has little power to regulate the way in which privacy settings are presented or enforced. Consumers must trust that online companies provide users with options to safeguard their privacy while still being able to apprise themselves of the benefits of the various services. As the digital landscape has evolved, privacy settings began and continue to be a point of contention among consumers, government administrations, and online corporations.

—Ashley Baker

References

Datta, Anwitaman, et al. *Social Informatics: Third International Conference, SocInfo, 2011, Singapore, October 2011*. Springer-Verlag, 2011.

Trepte, Sabine, and Leonard Reinecke. *Privacy Online: Perspectives on Privacy and Self-Disclosure in the Social Web*. Springer-Verlag, 2011.

"Windows 10 Privacy Settings: How to Stop Microsoft from Spying on You." *The Star*, 16 Feb. 2019.

Zetlin, Minda. "Want to Make Facebook Stop Tracking Your Location When Not in Use? Here's How." *Inc.*, 22 Feb. 2019.

Q

QR CODES

Introduction

QR, short for "quick response," codes are a two-dimensional (2D) barcode invented in Japan in 1994 that serve as identifiers, but most popularly are scanned by users' internet-capable devices. Once scanned, QR codes automatically link users to a particular website without the need of surfing the web to find it, or even typing the URL into the browser. Traditional one-dimensional (1D) barcodes consist of a series of vertical lines, or "bars," differing in widths and spacing. A laser device is used to scan the barcode of an object such as a grocery item and pass the barcode structure to a computer application that interprets that data and correlates it with the object's identity and purchase price or another piece of information about the object that has been stored in memory. A standard barcode is read only in one direction by the scanner, which is horizontally across the lines of the barcode, although the scanning device may be held in any orientation that allows the reading to take place. QR codes, on the other hand, are read in two directions, both horizontally and vertically, which allows them to contain much more information than standard barcodes.

A typical QR code is a square or rectangular design that vaguely resembles a chess board. The square, black dots look to be positioned in an entirely random manner. They are not, however. Each tiny square dot is precisely located according to a QR code-generating algorithm. A greatly oversimplified way of understanding QR codes is to think of them as two standard barcodes overlaid at right angles to each other. Where the barcode lines and spaces cross, a value is assigned to that location according to Boolean logic, which will determine whether the location will appear as a black square or a white square in the corresponding QR code which will be read as a bit of binary code (a 0 or a 1) when it is scanned.

This cross-hatched placement effectively creates a square with an equal number of horizontal and vertical lines, each of which can be thought of as a separate barcode in its own right. In this way, a pair of 10-line barcodes would generate a QR code with 10 readable lines instead of just one line. While this is certainly not the way a QR code is actually generated, it does give an idea of how a QR code works relative to a standard barcode. This is what allows a QR code to contain many times more information than a standard barcode is able to contain.

Background

The QR code was invented by Masahiro Hara, for the Japanese automaker Denso Wave, in 1994. The Japanese manufacturing industry is the birthplace

Sample QR Code. Image via iStock/alexsl. [Used under license.]

of the "lean" manufacturing process of quality control, in which parts are rigorously tracked as they are moved through manufacturing facilities. Time is saved and productivity is enhanced in this process by eliminating the need to create and read paper certificates that must be filled out by hand at every stage of the process. The use of barcodes could be read and processed so much more quickly than paper certificates. Unfortunately, a barcode cannot contain the amount of information complete tracking required. However, the QR code, once it was put into use, carried far more information making the process efficient. Since that time, the use of QR codes has become ubiquitous for tracking goods and encapsulating information that requires more capacity than a simple barcode can provide.

QR codes are commonly scanned with a camera device, such as a smart phone's built-in camera, and interpreted by a QR code reader application. The app then connects to a network or a website location specified within the QR code, where the user is able to find detailed information about the particular product or service. For example, as part of its efforts to mitigate the spread of the COVID-19 virus government of the Province of Ontario, Canada, required residents of the province to install a QR code image on their cell phones to show as proof of vaccination.

They were to show the QR code to screeners at establishments requiring proof of vaccination for entry to the premises. The screeners scanned the QR codes with their own scanning device, which then received a confirmation message from the government's Ministry of Health website. Prior to this, the people were only required to carry the paper verification documents they had been provided with when they had received their vaccinations. However, a significant number of false documents began to appear, allowing people who had not been vaccinated to get past screeners and into places where they would otherwise not have been admitted.

While it is debatable that screening had any real mitigating effect on the spread of the COVID-19 virus, the institution of the QR code effectively eliminated the false documentation problem. Unfortunately, people who didn't have cell phones or who had cell phones that were not capable of obtaining the QR code were still reliant on their paper documentation.

QR Code Structure and Appearance

QR codes can be generated in several ways and in different sizes. The vast majority are produced in black and white to take advantage of the high optical contrast of the two colors. But QR codes can also be produced using any two highly contrasting colors. Part of the reason the colors must have high contrast to each other is due to the nature of pixel coloration for displaying and scanning purposes. A common feature in computer graphics is the occurrence of a feathering effect at the edges of adjacent colored areas in an image. In effect, the color of one area bleeds slightly into the other area where they are in contact. In this way there is a narrow outline in which the color is indistinct, neither one color nor the other. In graphics, colors have an assigned value. If even on bit of the value is not correct, a scanner would identify it only as not the color it expects and therefore will not recognize it. Thus, if a scanner encounters feathered edges in a QR code made with poorly contrasting colors, the program that interprets the color value cannot assign the correct value, resulting in misinterpretation of the QR code's information content. When highly contrasting colors are used, especially black and white, feathering of the edges does not occur and the transitions between colors cannot be misinterpreted.

QR codes contain square structures of different sizes in specific locations. The largest squares, found in three of the corners of a QR code, define the correct positioning of the QR code for the scanning program. Three corners of a square can only be correctly positioned one way, while one, two or four corners allow for multiple incorrect positions. A number of smaller squares set in a regular array within the QR code define the correct alignment of the code for the scanning program. This array also uses the "missing corner" method for proper alignment. The smallest squares, which make up the remainder of the QR code, are timing markers that the scanning program interprets as data content. A small number of these squares in a specific location within the QR code define error checking and correction data for the scanning program.

How much data can be contained within a QR code depends on the type of data character being used, such as common text, Japanese kanji, Arabic script, or another data character type. The maximum storage capacity of 7,089 characters requiring

3½ bits per character is obtained in the Version 40 QR code with the lowest level of error correction. The array size for QR codes ranges from 21 X 21 in Version 1 QR codes to 177 X 177 in Version 40 QR codes.

QR code structure and use is very complex, with many different functional components. It is easy for anyone to generate a QR code, as the process has been automated with QR code-generating applications, some of which are free to use. Alternatively, one can install a QR code generator application on a suitable device.

—*Richard M. Renneboog*

References

Aktaş, Calalettin. *The Evolution and Emergence of QR Codes.* Cambridge Scholars, 2017.

Burns, Monica. *Deeper Learning with QR Codes and Augmented Reality: A Scannable Solution for Your Classroom.* Corwin Press, 2016.

Dutson, Phil. *Creating QR and Tag Codes.* Sams Publishing, 2013.

Kato, Hiroki, Keng T. Tan, and Douglas Chai. *Barcodes for Mobile Devices.* Cambridge UP, 2010.

Pless, Vera. *Introduction to the Theory of Error-Correcting Codes.* John Wiley & Sons, 2011.

Winter, Mick. *Scan Me—Everybody's Guide to the Magical World of QR Codes.* Westsong, 2011.

R

RANDOM-ACCESS MEMORY

Introduction

Random-access memory (RAM) is a form of memory that allows the computer to retain and quickly access program and operating system data. RAM hardware consists of an integrated circuit chip containing numerous transistors. Most RAM is dynamic, meaning it needs to be refreshed regularly, and volatile, meaning that data is not retained if the RAM loses power. However, some RAM is static or nonvolatile.

Background

The speed and efficiency of computer processes are among the most areas of greatest concern for computer users. Computers that run slowly (lag) or stop working altogether (hang or freeze) when one or more programs are initiated are frustrating to use. Lagging and freezing are often due to insufficient computer memory, typically RAM. Random-access memory is an essential computer component that takes the form of small chips. It enables computers to work faster by providing a temporary space in which to store and process data. Without RAM, this data would need to be retrieved from direct-access storage or read-only memory (ROM), which would take much longer.

Computer memory has taken different forms over the decades. Early memory technology was based on vacuum tubes and magnetic drums. Between the 1950s and the mid-1970s, a form of memory called "magnetic-core memory" was most common. Although RAM chips were first developed during the same period, they were initially unable to replace core memory because they did not yet have enough memory capacity.

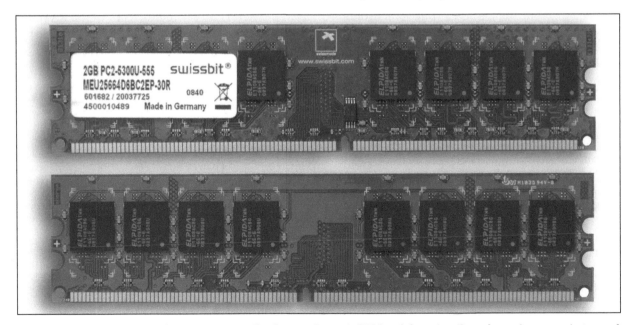

Example of writable volatile random-access memory: Synchronous Dynamic RAM modules, primarily used as main memory in personal computers, workstations, and servers. Photo by An-d, via Wikimedia Commons.

A major step forward in RAM technology came in 1968, when International Business Machines (IBM) engineer Robert Dennard patented the first dynamic random-access memory (DRAM) chip. Dennard's original chip featured a memory cell consisting of a paired transistor and capacitor. The capacitor stored a single bit of binary data as an electrical charge, and the transistor read and refreshed the charge thousands of times per second. Over the following years, semiconductor companies such as Fairchild and Intel produced DRAM chips of varying capacities, with increasing numbers of memory cells per chip. Intel also introduced DRAM with three transistors per cell, but over time the need for smaller and smaller computer components made this design less practical. By the 2010s, commonly used RAM chips incorporated billions of memory cells.

Types of RAM

Although all RAM serves the same basic purpose, there are a number of different varieties. Each type has its own unique characteristics. The RAM most often used in personal computers is a direct descendant of the DRAM invented by Dennard and popularized by companies such as Intel. DRAM is dynamic, meaning that the electrical charge in the memory cells, and thus the stored data, will fade if it is not refreshed often. A common variant of DRAM is speed-focused double data rate synchronous DRAM (DDR SDRAM), the fourth generation of which entered the market in 2014.

Random Access Memory that is not dynamic is known as static random-access memory (SRAM). SRAM chips contain many more transistors than their DRAM counterparts. They typically use six transistors per cell: two to control access to the cell and four to store a single bit of data. As such, they are much more costly to produce. A small amount of SRAM is often used in a computer's central processing unit (CPU), while DRAM performs the typical RAM functions.

Just as the majority of RAM is dynamic, most RAM is also volatile. Thus, the data stored in the RAM will disappear if it is no longer being supplied with electricity—for instance, if the computer in which it is installed has been turned off. Some RAM, however, can retain data even after losing power.

Such RAM is known as nonvolatile random-access memory (NVRAM).

Using RAM

RAM works with a computer's other memory and storage components to enable the computer to run more quickly and efficiently, without lagging or freezing. Computer memory should not be confused with storage. Memory is where application data is processed and stored. Storage houses files and programs. It takes a computer longer to access program data stored in ROM or in long-term storage than to access data stored in RAM. Thus, using RAM enables a computer to retrieve data and perform requested functions faster. To improve a computer's performance, particularly when running resource-intensive programs, a user may replace its RAM with a higher-capacity chip so the computer can store more data in its temporary memory.

Shadow RAM

While RAM typically is used to manage data related to the applications in use, at times it can be used to assist in performing functions that do not usually involve RAM. Certain code, such as a computer's basic input/output system (BIOS), is typically stored within the computer's ROM. However, accessing data saved in ROM can be time consuming. Some computers can address this issue by copying data from the ROM and storing the copy in the RAM for ease of access. RAM that contains code copied from the ROM is known as "shadow RAM."

—Joy Crelin

References

Dieny, Bernard, Ronald B. Goldfarb, and Kyung-Jin Lee. *Introduction to Magnetic Random-Access Memory.* IEEE Press/John Wiley & Sons, 2017.

Hey, Tony, and Gyuri Pápay. *The Computing Universe: A Journey Through a Revolution.* Cambridge UP, 2015.

McLoughlin, Ian. *Computer Systems: An Embedded Approach.* McGraw-Hill, 2018.

O'Leary, Timothy, Linda O'Leary, and Daniel O'Leary. *Computing Essentials 2021.* McGraw-Hill, 2020.

Siddiqi, Muzaffer A. *Dynamic RAM: Technology Advancements.* CRC Press, 2013.

RANSOMWARE

Introduction

Ransomware is a form of malicious software used by cybercriminals to hijack a user's computer or mobile device and keep it under their control until the user pays for its release. Cybercriminals use various strategies to try to extort money from unsuspecting users with ransomware, such as encrypting files saved on the user's device; threatening to erase important files; denying access to key programs and applications; and entrapping the user by linking him or her to extreme or illegal pornographic material. The user will then be instructed to submit some form of untraceable payment to the cybercriminals behind the ransomware attack, though antifraud authorities stress that making such a payment does not guarantee the release of the user's device.

When it first appeared as a widespread internet phenomenon, ransomware tended to indiscriminately target individuals. However, according to a 2021 report released by the US Department of Health and Human Services, the criminal networks using ransomware are becoming more sophisticated and are increasingly targeting businesses. They are said to be "liars, thieves, extortionists and members of a global criminal enterprise, and they take extreme technological measures to conceal any trace of their identity and location."

Background

The first known example of ransomware was launched by Dr. Joseph Popp, a Harvard-educated evolutionary biologist who distributed an estimated 20,000 virus-infected floppy disks to attendees of the World Health Organization's (WHO's) international acquired immunodeficiency syndrome (AIDS) conference in December, 1989. Popp's program, known as the AIDS Trojan, used a technique known as "symmetric cryptography" to encrypt files after users loaded the infected disks into their computers. No reason was ever given for Popp's actions, though media reports stated that Popp had been rejected for a job with the WHO just prior to the attack.

A ransomware platform known as Archievus was one of the earliest such programs to be widely distributed over the internet. Archievus first appeared in 2006 and targeted Microsoft's Windows operating system by encrypting all the files saved in the infected computer's "My Documents" directory. To secure the release of their files, victims were instructed to purchase specific products in exchange for the decryption password.

Ransomware became more prevalent with the advent of anonymous internet-based payment-processing platforms, which made it easier for cybercriminals to extract ransoms directly from their victims. Since 2011, there has been a sharp rise in the frequency and scale of ransomware attacks, as well as in the number of malicious programs used to infect victims' computers. One particularly noteworthy campaign began in 2014 with the launch of the CryptoDefense and CryptoWall ransomware platforms. These programs infected computers and encrypted victims' saved files, using anonymity network internet browsing and the untraceable Bitcoin cryptocurrency to secure payments. According to a 2015 report published by the Cyber Threat Alliance, the CryptoDefense and CryptoWall campaigns generated $325 million in revenues for the criminal network behind the software.

Ransomware has since extended beyond personal computing to affect smartphones and other mobile devices. Smartphone-specific forms of ransomware initially locked users out of their phones but have evolved to encrypt files and folders saved on affected devices. Advancements in cloud computing technology have also led to the rise of a malware distribution strategy known as Ransomware as a Service, or RaaS. RaaS first appeared in 2015, enabling individuals to purchase ransomware platforms on digital black markets. Buyers could then distribute the malicious programs on their own, sharing a percentage of their revenues with the malware's anonymous vendors.

Ransomware Today

According to statistics in 2021, since 2016, over 4000 ransomware attacks have been detected in the United States. In its 2016 report, Microsoft also stated that the five most common ransomware families were Tescrypt (accounting for 42 percent of detected attacks), Crowti (17 percent), Fakebsod (15 percent), Brolo (9 percent), and Locky (7 percent). These malware families use a range of techniques to extort payments from users, but most fall into two broad categories known as "lockscreen ransomware" and "encryption ransomware."

Lockscreen ransomware hijacks a user's device, displaying a full-screen message that cannot be closed, minimized, or otherwise removed. The full-screen message prevents a user from accessing files and programs on his or her device and may also use scare tactics, such as allegations that the device has been associated with illegal or extreme pornographic material, with an accompanying threat to report the activity to authorities. In other cases, ransomware appropriates the names and logos of local law enforcement agencies, claiming to represent the agency and demanding that the user submit payment to avoid fines or criminal prosecution for illegal online activity. A variant strategy sees the ransomware use sexually explicit images in the lockscreen message, claiming that the images cannot be removed unless the user complies with the criminal's demands.

Encryption ransomware targets specific files saved on the device, which the ransomware distributors often identify beforehand by employing phishing techniques to research the end user. Once the files are encrypted, the user will be instructed to submit payment in exchange for the decryption key. This technique typically targets confidential, sensitive, or important information saved on the user's device and is a favored form of ransomware for attacking businesses.

According to Symantec Corporation's comprehensive 2016 report, criminal networks using ransomware are becoming increasingly sophisticated and are displaying very high levels of expertise. The report stated that the average ransomware demand in 2016 was $679, representing a sharp year-over-year increase from 2015 demands, which averaged $294. Symantec also reported that more than one hundred new ransomware families were identified in 2015.

Users usually unwittingly install ransomware on their own devices. Cybercriminals use various strategies to spread ransomware; it may be embedded in unsafe websites or installed on a user's computer after the user is redirected to a fake website designed to mirror a legitimate one. Email, social media, and personal communication platforms are also used to distribute links that will install ransomware on a user's device if they are clicked.

While individual users are still falling afoul of ransomware distributors, there is also a growing trend toward the victimization of businesses. Attacks on businesses are usually targeted, and Symantec reports that 38 percent of ransomware infections in 2016 affected enterprises in the services sector. Manufacturing, finance, real estate, and public administration organizations were also leading targets of enterprise-oriented attacks in 2016. Between 2015 and 2016, the number of detected ransomware attacks peaked in October, 2015, when 150,000 such incidents were reported.

A major worldwide ransomware attack occurred in May 2017, using software known as WannaCry. This encryption program locked users out of many documents on their computers and demanded US$300 in Bitcoin to restore access. Within days over 300,000 computers in over 150 countries were infected, with Europe and Asia seeing higher rates than the United States. Individuals and businesses were both targeted, and the impact on major companies led to travel delays and other serious consequences. Perhaps most notable was the targeting of the National Health Service (NHS) in Great Britain, with tens of thousands of NHS computers affected and many services disrupted.

The WannaCry software used a vulnerability in the Microsoft Windows operating system to infect computers. Not long after the spread of WannaCry died down, another ransomware program, NotPetya (derived from an older program known as Petya), spread by exploiting the same vulnerability. It was later revealed that the US National Security Agency (NSA) had previously discovered the vulnerability, but exploited it for its own work rather than alerting Microsoft, creating a "backdoor" known as Double-Pulsar to allow them to access computers running Windows. This backdoor was stolen by hackers in 2016, and is thought to have been used in the WannaCry attack. Microsoft eventually released security updates to address this vulnerability. In addition, a computer security researcher discovered a section of the ransomware's code that was able to be used as a kill switch, effectively slowing down the rate at which WannaCry could spread.

In June 2018, McAfee, a company that produces antivirus software, reported that ransomware attacks were down 32 percent from the previous quarter, while cryptojacking—infecting computers with malware that makes the target machine mine cryptocurrency (such as Bitcoin) that is then deposited into the attacker's cryptocurrency wallet—has increased by 300 percent. Some technology commentators have theorized that this shift is the result of low-level criminals turning from ransomware to cryptojacking as a safer way of obtaining money; ransomware by definition involves the victim knowing they have been attacked, while cryptojacking often goes undetected. However, high-profile ransomware attacks continue to occur; for example, in 2018, the computer systems of the City of Atlanta were infected with the ransomware program SamSam.

—*Jim Greene*

References

Boatman, Kim. "Beware the Rise of Ransomware." *Symantec Corporation*, ca.norton.com/yoursecurityresource/detail.jsp?aid=rise_in_ransomware.

Cabaj, Krzysztof, and Wojciech Mazurczyk. "Using Software-Defined Networking for Ransomware Mitigation: The Case of CryptoWall." *IEEE Network*, vol. 30, no. 6, Nov.-Dec. 2016, pp. 14–20.

Francis, Ryan. "The History of Ransomware." *CSO Online*, 20 July 2016, www.csoonline.com/article/3095956/data-breach/the-history-of-ransomware.html#slide10.

HHS Cybersecurity Program. "Ransomware Trends 2021." *US Department of Health and Human Services*, hhs.gov/sites/default/files/ransomware-trends-2021.pdf.

Kharaz, Amin, et. al. "UNVEIL: A Large-Scale, Automated Approach to Detecting Ransomware." *USENIX: The Advanced Computing Systems Association*, 2016, www.usenix.org/system/files/conference/usenixsecurity16/sec16_paper_kharraz.pdf.

Liska, Allan, and Timothy Gallo. *Ransomware: Defending Against Digital Extortion*. O'Reilly Media, 2016.

"Ransomware and Businesses 2016." *Symantec Corporation*, 2016, www.symantec.com/content/en/us/enterprise/media/security_response/whitepapers/ISTR2016_Ransomware_and_Businesses.pdf.

"Ransomware Facts." *Microsoft Corporation*, 2016, www.microsoft.com/en-us/security/portal/mmpc/shared/ransomware.aspx.

Samani, Raj. "'McAfee Labs Threats Report' Spotlights Innovative Attack Techniques, Cryptocurrency Mining, Multisector Attacks." *McAfee*, 26 June 2018, securingtomorrow.mcafee.com/other-blogs/mcafee-labs/mcafee-labs-threats-report-spotlights-innovative-attack-techniques-cryptocurrency-mining-multisector-attacks/.

Sobers, Rob. "81 Ransomware Statistics, Data, Trends and Facts for 2021." *Inside Out Security*. Varonis Blog, varonis.com/blog/ransomware-statistics-2021.

Stobing, Chris. "Ransomware Is the New Hot Threat Everyone Is Talking About; What Do You Need to Know?" *Digital Trends*, 6 June 2015, www.digitaltrends.com/computing/what-is-ransomware-and-should-you-be-worried-about-it/.

Whittaker, Zack. "Atlanta, Hit by Ransomware Attack, Also Fell Victim to Leaked NSA Exploits." *ZDNet*, 27 Mar. 2018, www.zdnet.com/article/atlanta-hit-by-ransomware-attack-also-fell-victim-to-leaked-nsa-exploits/.

Woollaston, Victoria. "WannaCry Ransomware: What Is It and How to Protect Yourself." *Wired*, 22 May 2017, www.wired.co.uk/article/wannacry-ransomware-virus-patch.

REDDIT

Introduction

Reddit is a social networking and news website that allows registered users, or redditors, to post and discuss content such as news reports, entertainment, images, and personal stories. Reddit was founded in 2005 by Steve Huffman and Alexis Ohanian. The pair later sold the site to Condé Nast, and it became an independent subsidiary of Condé Nast in 2011. The site's name is a play on the words "read it." At the end of 2020, Reddit reported that it had over 52 million daily active users.

The Reddit home page is organized in a bulletin board system with posts shown as a bulleted list. The most popular posts are at the top of the page. The Reddit community views and comments on user posts, and other users can vote on whether the content is good or bad by issuing the poster what is known as an upvote or a downvote. Posts that receive the most upvotes populate the very top of Reddit's front page, making it the first post the user reads when accessing Reddit. The pages constantly update with newer posts every day. Users can also vote on the comments section of each post, with the most popular comment showing up directly beneath the post. Reddit's software also allows users to interact through public message boards and private messaging.

Apart from its home page, Reddit also organizes posts by the areas of interest in which they are related. These separate pages are known as subreddits. Users can post their content to varying subreddits containing similar content. Since they were first introduced in 2008, thousands of subreddits have been created related to a broad range of topics. Any registered user can create a subreddit. By 2013, there were more than five thousand subreddits on Reddit. As of 2021, there are 2.9 million subreddits in existence—though not all may be active.

Currently, Reddit has more than 52 million daily active users (worldwide), and tallies over 46.7 million searches each day. Users are generally highly educated (15 percent with a college degree), range from eighteen to twenty-nine years old (36 percent), with nearly 50 percent of users living in the United States. Approximately 70 percent of all videos uploaded come from mobile devices.

One of Reddit's most popular subreddits is known as "IAmA." The titles of these posts usually begin with "IAmA" followed by whatever the poster claims to be. Users with a unique skill or story often post AMAs (Ask Me Anything) to this subreddit, where other users ask questions about their life and skills. Many professionals and celebrities have answered users' questions in this subreddit.

Background

Steve Huffman and Alexis Ohanian first met while studying at the University of Virginia. The twenty-two-year-olds wanted to create a website that made it easier for internet users to sift through the vast amount of news and information available online. Reddit was developed to allow users to post content they found to the site, and other users could then gauge the post's popularity by giving it their upvote or downvote. Users who continually posted popular content built up karma points, giving them higher credibility among Reddit users, while the opposite effect befell unpopular posters.

When the site first launched, Huffman and Ohanian posted content under fabricated accounts to attract internet traffic. The site eventually gained enough momentum to interest outside investments.

Reddit merged with a company called Infogami in January 2006. Infogami was headed by Aaron Swartz, who received a portion of Reddit's ownership. By October 2006, Reddit had five hundred thousand daily viewers. This attracted the attention of Condé Nast, which purchased Reddit for a reported $20 million in 2006. Swartz was fired shortly after Condé Nast acquired Reddit.

Reddit added many new team members in the years following. It also introduced new site features as traffic continued to grow. In July 2010, the Reddit team launched Reddit Gold, a subscription membership that gave paying users access to more site features. By 2011, Reddit had accumulated more than 1 billion monthly page views and boasted more than 80 million users. Numbers continued to grow dramatically, rising from 5 billion total views in 2013 to 82 billion total views in 2015. The site's popularity garnered it multiple high-profile investors, including venture capitalists Peter Thiel and Marc Andreessen as well as celebrities Snoop Dogg and Jared Leto. The site continued to launch new features and content, including a podcast, newsletter, and its own web-based editorial publication known as "Upvoted," which allows users to write and upload original stories, videos, art, and podcasts. Reddit also engaged in a number of philanthropic efforts and played an active part in raising money for several charities throughout the years.

Controversies

The site has had to initiate several policy changes since its inception to ensure controversial content stays off its pages. Despite heavy moderation by the Reddit team, the website has sparked controversy several times due to user-related incidents. The Reddit community became known for its failed attempts at internet vigilantism, which led to real-life harassment and consequences for several people. A famous example of Reddit's sometimes-dangerous influence involved the 2013 Boston Marathon bombings. Redditors misidentified several people as possible suspects, leading to massive witch hunts against innocent people. Such incidents have forced Reddit to censor or ban user-posted content at times, causing backlash from redditors.

In January 2021, Reddit drew nationwide attention when one of its subreddits had a very real impact in the financial world. As part of an effort to compete with professional investors, several individual amateur stock traders who follow the sub-reddit r/WallStreetBets had begun using the platform to create hype around shares for the company GameStop, which many investors, including large hedge funds, had bet on falling. This led to GameStop's stock increasing dramatically as a large number of these individual traders purchased GameStop shares. As some hedge funds reported experiencing losses due to this rise, a debate immediately erupted in which some raised concerns about such types of coordinated efforts, considering them to be a potentially inappropriate manipulation of the market; the inconsistent and largely unregulated oversight of social media sites such as Reddit also remained an issue.

—*Cait Caffrey and Jake D. Nicosia*

References

"About." *Reddit*, www.redditinc.com/.

Adams, Richard. "Reddit.com." *The Guardian*. The Guardian News and Media, 7 Dec. 2005, www.theguardian.com/technology/2005/dec/08/innovations.guardianweeklytechnologysection1.

Alden, William. "With Reddit Deal, Snoop Dogg Moonlights as a Tech Investor." *The New York Times*, 1 Oct. 2014, dealbook.nytimes.com/2014/10/01/with-reddit-deal-snoop-dogg-moonlights-as-a-tech-investor/.

Buncombe, Andrew. "Family of Sunil Tripathi—Missing Student Wrongly Linked to Boston Marathon Bombing—Thank Well-Wishers for Messages of Support." *Independent*. Independent Digital News and Media, 26 Apr. 2013, www.independent.co.uk/news/world/americas/family-of-sunil-tripathi-missing-student-wrongly-linked-to-boston-marathon-bombing-thank-well-8586850.html.

"Frequently Asked Questions." *Reddit*, n.d., 23 Jan. 2016, www.reddit.com/wiki/faq#Whatdoes-thenamredditmean.

"On Reddit, Unlike Other Social Sites, It's About the Topic, Not the Brand." *PR News*. Access Intelligence, 28 Oct. 2013, www.prnewsonline.com/topics/social-media/2013/10/28/on-reddit-unlike-other-social-sites-its-about-the-topic-not-the-brand/.

Pengue, Maria. "Reddit Statistics: Traffic, Subreddits, Demographics, and More." *Writers Block Live*, 16 June 2021, writersblocklive.com/blog/reddit-statistics/.

Phillips, Matt, and Taylor Lorenz. "'Dumb Money' Is on GameStop, and It's Beating Wall Street at Its Own Game." *The New York Times*, 25 Feb. 2021, www.nytimes.com/2021/01/27/business/gamestop-wall-street-bets.html.

"Reddit.com." *SimilarWeb*, n.d., www.similarweb.com/website/reddit.com#referrals.

Singel, Ryan. "Feds Charge Activist as Hacker for Downloading Millions of Academic Articles." *Wired*. Condé Nast, 19 July 2011, www.wired.com/2011/07/swartz-arrest/.

S

SCIENTIFIC LITERACY

Introduction

Scientific literacy refers to a having a core understanding of scientific concepts. Though literacy does not require someone to become an expert in a given topic, individuals must maintain a conversational level of competency. They must also demonstrate a capacity to research new topics and effectively evaluate source materials. Scientifically literate individuals can demonstrate a working knowledge of the scientific method, the method by which reliable research is conducted.

Scientific literacy in adults is important for many reasons. Such individuals are better informed on important issues and more likely to identify misleading or fraudulent sources of information.

Background

Scientific literacy refers to a specific standard of scientific understanding. In an academic context, science is both a process and a body of knowledge. It is a systematic approach to discovering new knowledge about the world and the universe. Science differs from other ways of learning about the universe because of its methods. Whereas philosophers and theologians may try to learn about the universe through thought, scientists seek to learn about the world through repeated, measurable testing and analysis.

To attain reputable results, scientists use the scientific method, which has six steps. First, they make an observation about the world around them. This observation can be complex, such as observing that a star is moving through space in an unusual way, but it can also be simple, such as observing that a particular object is a certain color. Second, scientists ask questions about the observation and begin to gather information about the topic. For example, scientists might ask why an object is a certain color and then begin researching how colors function.

After asking questions, scientists carefully form a hypothesis, which is a theory about a given subject. Scientists often suspect that a hypothesis might be correct but cannot be certain. To test their hypothesis, scientists perform experiments and study the data provided by their tests. If the scientists believe that the data provided by the experiments supports their hypothesis, they will note that the hypothesis is most likely correct. However, if the data does not support the hypothesis, they may modify their original theory. Scientists will continue to experiment, refining their hypothesis and ensuring that they did not make any mistakes.

Scientific theories are very rarely proven. Instead, it simply becomes more likely that a theory is correct. However, in rare cases, scientific theories become laws that are accepted as true by the scientific community. For example, the law of conservation of matter states that matter can never be destroyed, only changed.

Overview

Scientific literacy refers to a working knowledge and understanding of scientific concepts. A minimum amount of scientific literacy is required for individuals to effectively participate in modern society. People who have attained this level of scientific literacy should have a conversational familiarity with important scientific concepts. They should be able to take science into account when discussing current issues such as climate change and vaccines.

In addition to a basic working knowledge of major scientific issues, scientific literacy refers to the ability to actively pursue new topics. Scientifically literate individuals should be able to research new information, including the ability to find and comprehend articles about most subjects. This does not require that individuals gain mastery of complex topics, but they must be able to competently discuss basic ideas.

Another important hallmark of scientific literacy is the ability to evaluate data. People who have attained a degree of scientific literacy should be reasonably skilled at identifying properly conducted research. This allows literate individuals to separate false or misleading information from legitimate, reliable sources.

Lastly, scientifically literate individuals should be able to pose effective arguments about life-science concepts. These arguments should be logically sound and reliably sourced. Similarly, literate individuals should be able to reliably identify unscientific arguments and practices.

Traditionally, scientific literacy begins in schools. From a young age, children are taught the scientific method, as well as many of the core concepts of life sciences. As they grow and enter more advanced schooling, children will be required to learn to research new topics, cite sources, and present their thoughts eloquently. However, it is important to note that scientific literacy does not end with school. Literate individuals should continue learning throughout their lives, remaining up to date on advancements in important fields.

Rapid advances in modern technology and expanded access to the internet make developing and maintaining scientific literacy easier than ever before. In the past, students and scholars had to travel to libraries or academic institutions to educate themselves on scientific topics. Additionally, staying current on scientific advancements was particularly difficult. The internet allows modern students to access a wide range of academic materials from their personal computers or smart phones. However, because so much information can be found online, students should ensure that any information they research is based on reliable sources.

A scientifically literate populace is less likely to be swayed by false information, even if that information is delivered by a charismatic leader. Additionally, scientific literacy allows voters to competently research important topics before deciding upon their opinions, leading to a more effective, well-informed electorate.

—*Tyler Biscontini*

References

Bradford, Alina. "What Is Science?" *LiveScience*, 2017, www.livescience.com/20896-science-scientific-method.html.

Drummond, Caitlin, and Fischoff, Baruch. "Individuals with Greater Science Literacy and Education Have More Polarized Beliefs on Controversial Science Topics." *PNAS*, 2017, www.pnas.org/content/114/36/9587.

Grant, Maria, and Lapp, Diane. "Teaching Science Literacy." *Educational Leadership*, 2011, www.ascd.org/publications/educational-leadership/mar11/vol68/num06/Teaching-Science-Literacy.aspx.

Kirshenbaum, Sheril. "What Is Scientific Literacy?" *Discover Magazine*, www.discovermagazine.com/the-sciences/what-is-scientific-literacy-02.

Lombrozo, Tania. "Scientific Literacy: It's Not (Just) About the Facts." *NPR*, 2015, www.npr.org/sections/13.7/2015/09/14/440213603/scientific-literacy-it-s-not-just-about-the-facts.

"Scientific Literacy." *Literacynet*, www.literacynet.org/science/scientificliteracy.html.

"Scientific Literacy: Definition and Examples." *Study.com*, 2020, study.com/academy/lesson/scientific-literacy-definition-examples.html.

Zen, E-an. "Science Literacy and Why It Is Important." *Journal of Geological Education*, 2018, www.tandfonline.com/doi/abs/10.5408/0022-1368-38.5.463?journalCode=ujge19.

SEARCH ENGINES

Introduction

Search engines are software programs or networks of programs that search the internet for terms entered by a user and that compile a list of internet locations at which the term is found. A search engine appears to users as a search box at the top of the computer page. Many search engines are available, including Google, DuckDuckGo, Bing, Yahoo! Search, Ask, AOL Search, Wow, WebCrawler, and many more. All these search engines serve as users' convenient path to the content on the internet;

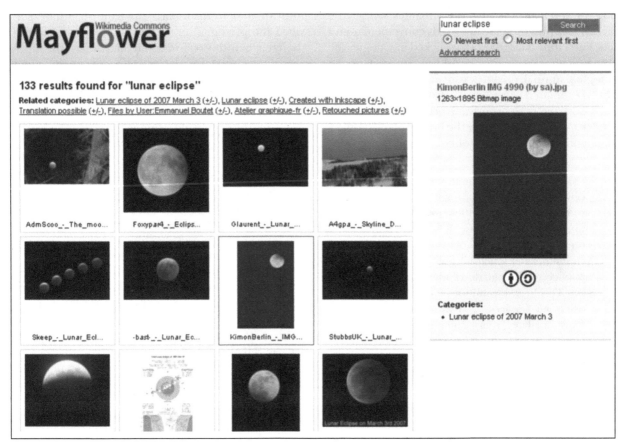

The results of a search for the term "lunar eclipse" in a web-based image search engine. Image by Tangotango, via Wikimedia Commons

however, many search engines also serve as a convenient path for marketers and even less scrupulous persons and groups to learn a great deal about users' formerly private lives.

Google, the world's leading search engine at present, with an estimated 1.1 billion users per month, routinely forwards users' search histories, identities, and shopping patterns—for a fee—to marketers around the world. From one perspective, there is an advantage to that for the users, who receive targeted advertisements and whose search results are returned in a personally relevant order based on the user's browsing history. Even Edward Snowden, who tipped off the world to the National Security Agency's (NSA's) cell phone telephone metadata collection program that captures and retains the phone call history of millions of Americans, has warned us all that users must stop using Google to protect users' privacy in this digital age. And Tim Cook, CEO of Apple Computers, derided Google

and other search engines by claiming that at least Apple doesn't "read your email or your messages to get information to market to you."

If the upside of search engines is convenience, the downside is the user privacy that is lost in the process. Search engines operate by applying rather complex search algorithms to interpret users' search queries, then seek information on the internet that is relevant to those queries. How can search engine companies make any money doing that? Well, they sell priority placements so that entities willing to pay for the service will end up prominently displayed on the first page of the search results on all relevant queries. A business school in Ohio can purchase priority placement from Google to highlight their school whenever a Google user query in Ohio and contiguous states includes the words *business school*. Once a user has searched for, say, a laptop computer, a barrage of ads for laptop computers will appear on that user's screen. Those pop-up targeted ads are bought and paid for by the companies selling the laptop computers. That all sounds convenient—and it is. Each time a targeted ad is clicked in Google, the company that sponsored the ad pays a fee to Google. Google's annual income from its advertising business is estimated to be approximately $50 billion.

Users pay a steep privacy price for that convenience. As disclosed among the fine print of Google's all-encompassing privacy policy:

> When you upload, submit, store, send or receive content to or through our Services, you give Google (and those we work with) a worldwide license to use, host, store, reproduce, modify, create derivative works ..., communicate, publish, publicly perform, publicly display and distribute such content. . . . This license continues even if you stop using our Services. . . . Our automated systems analyze your content (including emails) to provide you personally relevant product features, such as customized search results, tailored advertising, and spam and malware detection. This analysis occurs as the content is sent, received, and when it is stored.

In other words, in exchange for the convenience and robust search features of Google, the user must give up a great deal of privacy. To make matters worse, data captured and stored by Google can be retained by Google indefinitely, just as information on the internet can almost never be removed. That huge store of personal data is a tremendous draw for law enforcement agencies, who can use the third-party doctrine to access that data quite easily and without notice to the user whose data were accessed.

The third-party doctrine provides that (1) only the individual whose constitutional rights were violated has standing to contest violation; (2) a search of data on an individual that is stored by a third-party did not violate the individual's constitutional right to be free from unreasonable searches and seizures (the individual's physical property was not invaded or searched); and therefore, (3) upon a lawful demand from law enforcement, a third-party must turn over to law enforcement the data they seek on the

individual. The third-party doctrine may have survived the predigital era relatively intact, but in the digital age, with users so freely sharing so much private data with third parties—as a convenience and almost as a necessity—the third-party doctrine can no longer prevail. Until it is abandoned by the courts or rendered impermissible through legislation, however, the third-party doctrine will remain the law of the land, and digital age privacy will be the victim left in its wake.

Some search engines have begun to offer more private services, and that is a sound development. DuckDuckGo, with monthly users at just two-hundredths of one percent of Google's monthly user rate, offers private web searching that does not use cookies or log internet protocol (IP) addresses. Ixquick, touting itself as the most private search engine, does not record users' IP addresses or track cookies, and guarantees that it will not share users' information with any third party. StartPage, too, holds itself out as having "state-of-the-art privacy protection." If these more private search engines can begin to take at least some of the search engine business away from Google and other low-privacy search engines, perhaps Google and the rest will have to add more privacy protections to their search services or at least create different tiers of privacy so that users can select their preferred privacy tier.

Some of these so-called private search engines (PSE) started as direct competitors to Google and Bing but have begun to specialize in providing additional privacy features. StartPage actually uses Google search results, but without the tracking that Google includes. Similarly, DuckDuckGo uses Yahoo! search results without the tracking. One PSE, Search Encrypt, uses AES-256 and Secure Sockets Layer (SSL) encryption to secure data being transmitted. Gibiru bills itself as being what Google was in the beginning, avoiding the cookies that track your movements across the internet. Another PSE called Swisscows offers similar protections but also uses artificial intelligence to learn the context of users' searches. Almost all PSEs do not track users searches or store any information about them. Along with providing security, by offering searches done in isolation from company algorithms, these PSEs return a wider variety of less demographically targeted results. This can be an advantage in an age where companies like Google and Facebook curate information to present users exactly what they expect and what aligns with their values.

Information once on the internet seems always to be on the internet, not susceptible to masking or erasure. Data relevant to a foreclosure process that occurred and was resolved many years before is still on the internet years later, with the potential to harm the reputation of the one foreclosed against. That was the actual situation in Spain, and the injured party sued Google Spain and Google Inc. to have that irrelevant entry removed from Google's information stores. The lawsuit was transferred to the Court of Justice of the European Union, which ultimately held that (1) the European Union's (EU's) rules apply wherever Google has a branch or subsidiary that markets its services there; (2) the EU's data protection rules, which had been issued as an EU Directive in 1995, did apply to search engines; and (3) under certain circumstances, internet users and persons about whom information is placed on the internet, have a "right to be forgotten" and to have the search engine remove the private information and render it inaccessible. That "right to be forgotten" movement was violently opposed by Google in the EU, and Google is fighting even harder to keep that movement from reaching the United States.

It appears, in the digital age, that the United States has largely abdicated its responsibility to create and administer nationwide privacy determinations and protections, or have delegated those decisions to software engineers or to the entities that hire them and control—and sell—access to so much private data on individuals. That may seem like inertia, or it may seem inevitable, but the European Union and its Court of Justice proved otherwise in the case out in Spain. Congress, the courts, and individuals in the United States can take a similar stand and reset the privacy bar. We need not all be victims of the next technology that will decimate our privacy while making the technology designers and search engines a fortune.

Of course, the "right to be forgotten" movement, especially in the United States, has been attacked as a variant of censorship and antithetical to free speech, but the EU has attacked those challenges as myths set up by the movement's opponents

but devoid of substance. On opponents' claims that the "right to be forgotten" is a form of censorship, the EU maintains, "The right to be forgotten does not allow governments to decide what can and cannot be online and what should or should not be read. It is a right that citizens will invoke to defend their interests as they see fit. Independent authorities will oversee the assessment carried out by the search engine operators." On opponents' claims that the "right to be forgotten" violates free speech, the EU responds, "the right to be forgotten applies where the information is inaccurate, inadequate, irrelevant, or excessive for the purposes of data processing . . . This assessment must balance the interest of the person making the request and the public interest to have access to the data by retaining it in the list of results. [It] does not give the all-clear for people or organizations to have search results removed from the web simply because they find them inconvenient."

It is time for this dialogue in the United States. We need not be victims of technology in the digital age. We can resume control over technology, allowing it to be used in socially responsible and constitutional ways but, in the process, limiting its ability to damage the privacy rights of us all.

—*Charles E. MacLean*

References

Efrati, Amir. "Google's Data-Trove Dance." *The Wall Street Journal,* 30 July 2013, www.wsj.com/articles/SB10001424127887324170004578635812623154242.

Goodale, Gloria. "Privacy Concerns? What Google Now Says It Can Do with Your Data." *The Christian Science Monitor,* 16 Apr. 2014, www.csmonitor.com/ USA/2014/0416/ Privacy-concerns-What-Google-nowsays-it-can-do-with-your-data-video.

"Myth-Busting: The Court of Justice of the EU and the 'Right to be Forgotten.'" *European Commission,* ec.europa.eu/justice/data-protection/files/factsheets/factsheet_rtbf_mythbusting_en.pdf.

Stewart, Christian. "The Best Private Search Engines—Alternatives to Google." *Medium,* 8 Feb. 2018, hackernoon.com/ untraceable-search-engines-alternatives-to-google-811b09d5a873.

SEXTING

Introduction

Any digital transmission of a sexually explicit image created by a sender and sent to a recipient falls under the category of sexting. Sexting usually involves only two parties, and the images depict either the recipient or the sender.

Although sexting is technically a criminal offense, it appears to be common practice among a wide spectrum of individuals, including well-known individuals. Sexting is becoming increasingly common among teenagers. In a landmark study in 2021, Katz found that 17 percent of fifteen-year-olds used their cell phones to share explicit images, videos, or livestreams. It has been evidenced that many of those teens who are sexting are some of the most vulnerable youths (physically, emotionally, economically). The National Campaign to Prevent Teen and Unplanned Pregnancy reported that 19 percent of survey participants aged thirteen to nineteen had sent a sexually suggestive picture or video of themselves through email, cell phone or other medium and 31 percent had received a nude or seminude picture. Sexting becomes a legal issue because approximately 20 percent of all teenagers are involved in conduct that could result in imprisonment and sex offender registration. Also, a large percentage of sexters have been pressured or even blackmailed (emotionally or socially) to do so—leading to more vulnerabilities offline as well as online.

Sending sexually explicit digital images or messages can lead to sexual exploitation, and it can also affect future career choices. Photo via iStock/grinvalds. [Used under license.]

The most controversial aspects of sexting are when it involves a minor. Most of the discussion in this entry involves sexting as related to teenagers. The narrow scope of sexting occurs between two teenagers, either as part of courtship or a relationship, and when they act in a flirtatious or romantic manner. The pictures are consensually sent and received within the agreed upon boundaries of the relationship. The wide scope of sexting involves those cases when a minor sends an image they made of themselves to multiple recipients or sends an unsolicited sext that is not part of a romantic relationship.

Background

Under current law, sexting poses a difficult legal issue because minors technically violate state and federal law when they sext. Child pornography law prohibits any visual depiction that involves a minor engaging in sexually explicit conduct. No exceptions have been recognized on the context. Child pornography statutes currently prohibit sexting-related images, despite the fact that the statutes are intended to prosecute "sexual exploitation and other abuse of children" by predatory adults. Under current circumstances, prosecutors are punishing minors for intimate sexual decisions, not for conduct that abuses children.

Despite the potential of harsh punishment, the National Campaign's 2008 survey appears to indicate that sexting has become a "normal" part of life for many teenagers. Usually, the recipient of sexts is a significant other of the sender. Teens most frequently engage in sexting for fun or to be flirtatious. A majority of teen recipients of sexts reported that they were amused or aroused. Less than 10 percent of the respondents reported they were scared, angry, or disappointed, and only 15 percent said they were disgusted. Sexting appears to have also become part of courtship among contemporary American teenagers. After receiving a sext, 22 percent of recipients said were more interested in dating compared to 13 percent that were less interested.

Current criminal statutes, however, associate sexted images with child predators. This could result in the prosecution of minors for creating what is technically child pornography, when they view sexting as merely expressing their sexuality through a new medium.

Some teenage sexting has led to serious consequences and tragic results. In 2008, Jessica Logan, a high school senior, took some provocative pictures of herself using her cell phone and transmitted the images to her boyfriend. After the relationship had ended, he sent the photographs to Jessica's classmates, who disseminated both the photos, along with vile comments about her. As a result of this torment, Jessica committed suicide shortly after her graduation.

Critics of sexting argue that because there are negative consequences when minors are forced into child pornography, there are also dangers when the teenagers produce the pornography themselves. In most cases, however, adult exploitation is absent from teen sexting. It may be a difficult argument to make that teenagers are abused when they created sexual images through their own free will.

There are three commonly made arguments stressing that sexting is harmful. First, the government believes that teen sexual activity is always inherently "abusive" because minors are incapable of consent. This argument would assert that individuals under the age of consent do not accurately perceive all the ramifications of engaging in sexual activities. Children who engage in sexual intercourse, therefore, are victimized regardless if they perceive themselves as a victim. Privacy rights advocates have criticized this argument because sexting does not result in issues such as pregnancy or sexually transmitted diseases. These privacy advocates also argue that any harms such as bullying and the harmful dissemination are committed by third parties, not by the creators of the sexts.

Another argument is that there is the possibility that embarrassing images may be widely disseminated, beyond what the sender had intended. While this is a potential danger, privacy advocates argue, criminalizing sexting does not answer the actual risk. Cases of bullying or harassment may be dealt with statutes directed at the wrongdoers. Opponents of sexting also argue that sexting is potentially harmful to minors because other individuals might use these images inappropriately. Opponents of sexting offer a rebuttal that it is more effective and efficient for the government to eliminate sexting entirely rather than seeking to identify and punish difficult to find third party disseminators of the images. When an item appears on the internet, it is almost impossible to stop its spread.

Last, many sexting opponents argue that any production of child pornography is potentially dangerous because it may later be used to encourage predators or entice children into unwanted sexual activity. Privacy advocates, however, argue that just because an activity may have harmful side effects, however, does not necessarily justify a blanket prohibition of an activity that involves fundamental rights. Privacy advocates invoke Justice Kennedy, who wrote a majority opinion that invalidated the Child Pornography Prevention Act of 1996. He wrote that "[t]here are many things innocent in themselves, however, such as cartoons, video games, and candy, that might be used for immoral purposes, yet we would not expect those to be prohibited because they can be misused," *Ashcroft v. Free Speech Coalition*, 535 U.S. 234 (2002). Privacy advocates, thus, argue that the sexual abuse of children should be fought by prosecuting predatory adults as opposed to suppressing of teenage sexting.

Although no court has held that sexting is constitutionally protected speech, some privacy rights advocates argue that courts could consider the rights of privacy raised by prosecuting minors who engage in sexting. Privacy advocates argue that courts should balance governmental regulations against sexting against their costs to individual liberty. These advocates offer *Lawrence v. Texas*, 539 U.S. 558 (2003) as a workable framework to determine whether state interests justify state involvement in the personal decisions involved with teenage sexuality, as exemplified in sexting.

—*Jane E. Kirtley and Laura Nicosia*

References

Katz, Adrienne, and Aiman El Asam. "Look at Me: Teens, Sexting, and Risks." *Internet Matters.org*, 2020. internetmatters.org/about-us/sexting-report-look-at-me/.

Kreimer, Seth F. "Sex, Laws, and Videophones: The Problem of Juvenile Sexting Prosecutions." *Children, Sexuality, and the Law*, edited by Sacha M. Coupet and Ellen Marrus, New York UP, 2015, pp. 133–62.

Sweeny, Jo Anne. "Sexting and Freedom of Expression: A Comparative Approach." *Kentucky Law Journal*, vol. 102, 2013–2014, pp. 103–46.

SNAPCHAT

Introduction

Snapchat is a social networking service that allows users to share photographs and videos through their mobile devices. Snapchat users, often referred to as Snapchatters, are able to send and receive picture and video messages, which are called snaps. What makes the application unique is that the snaps can be viewed only for a few seconds before they disappear. In addition to sending snaps, Snapchat offers a My Story feature, which allows users to post snaps for up to twenty-four hours on their story. A story can be viewed by other users an unlimited number of times during that twenty-four-hour period. Snapchat also offers text and video chat functions, a multiuser-input Our Story, and an electronic payment system called Snapcash. Snapchat is one of the most popular social media applications available, with estimates of over 290 million active daily users, as of 2022.

Snapchat is notable for its prominent use of augmented reality "filters" and "lenses." Snapchat allows users to modify the subject in the camera by altering their face or providing overlays onto the world "in camera." Popular examples include the addition of animal ears and noses, enlarging the eyes, and smoothing facial features. Although these changes are primarily cosmetic, some offer more practical functionality, such as overlaying the local temperature or the speed at which the user is traveling. The latter, the so-called speed filter, has implicated Snapchat in lawsuits where Snapchat users used the filter while operating a vehicle at dangerous speeds, resulting in traffic accidents.

Snapchat's central feature is that all snaps are ephemeral. Snapchat therefore allows users to communicate and express themselves through an online medium with the knowledge that they will not create a permanent record that can be subjected to future scrutiny. Snapchat cocreator Evan Spiegel has claimed that Snapchat differs from other social media by removing the requirement to cultivate an idealized online identity, instead allowing for a less inhibited form of expression. This ephemerality of snaps is also perceived to provide more robust privacy and security than more traditional forms of online communication, although Snapchat cannot ultimately guarantee that the content of snaps will be deleted.

Background

Snapchat was founded by Evan Spiegel and Robert Murphy in 2011. Spiegel and Murphy, the chief executive officer (CEO) and chief technology officer (CTO) of Snapchat, respectively, were students at Stanford University when they met. Spiegel studied product design, and Murphy studied mathematical and computer science. While at Stanford, the college friends began developing a disappearing image application. Snapchat, which was originally called Picaboo, was soon born. The application attracted many users from the outset.

Snapchat's usage grew so quickly that in just two years, it caught the attention of Facebook, the popular social networking service. Just two years after the launch of Snapchat, Mark Zuckerberg, cofounder and CEO of Facebook, approached Spiegel and Murphy about buying the company in November 2013. Zuckerberg offered the cofounders $3 billion for the company. Given their ownership in the company at the time, this meant that Spiegel and Murphy would each earn $750 million in the deal. However, not wanting to settle for a short-term gain, the cofounders turned down Zuckerberg's offer. Rejecting the offer seemed to be the right move, as Snapchat raised $485 million from twenty-three investors in late 2014. At the time, the company was valued at $10 billion to $20 billion.

How It Works

A Snapchat user who wishes to send a snap to a friend must first take a photograph or video with their mobile phone. The sender can then set the timer for the snap, which means they can choose the amount of time it can be viewed before it disappears. The timer may be set for no more than ten seconds. The sender also has the option of adding a caption to or drawing on the snap. Once the sender is satisfied with the snap, he sends it to the other user. The recipient can then view the snap on their mobile phone, but only for the time period the sender has allotted, and only if that recipient has been approved as a "friend" of the sender. After this time is up, the snap will disappear from the recipient's phone. Although snaps also can be sent to a particular geolocation for public viewing, it requires further setup.

Primarily, Snapchat remains a privately shared communication app.

Snapchat also offers a chat feature. This feature, which is accessed through the Chat screen, allows two users to send messages back and forth. The chat feature also allows users to share live video with each other. As with snaps, the messages and videos disappear after they are viewed.

Yet another aspect of Snapchat is the stories feature. A story is a string of snaps that acts as a narrative. The user creating the story chooses who can view it. For example, the user can decide that all Snapchatters can view the story or that only the user's friends can view it. A story can be viewed for twenty-four hours.

Issues with Security

Indeed, Snapchat's ephemeral quality can be undermined through several methods, all allowing users to produce lasting copies of snaps. These include taking a screenshot of the phone while an image is being shown (although Snapchat will notify the sender if a recipient screenshots), taking a picture of the phone with another camera, or using one of several third-party apps designed specifically to store the transient snaps. One of these third-party "Snapchat scraper" apps was the subject of a massive data breach in 2014, dubbed the "Snappening," which led to an estimated 100,000 snaps being publicly leaked on the internet.

Snapchat's claim that it deletes all snaps stored on its servers is also subject to certain limitations, such as law enforcement warrants requesting file retention and the temporary retention of files on redundant backup servers. These shortcomings led the Federal Trade Commission (FTC) to bring an enforcement action against Snapchat in 2013, claiming that it had misled its users about the privacy and security the app provided. In addition, Snapchat has been frequently criticized for poor privacy and security practices, being voted "most unreliable" by the Electronic Frontier Foundation in its 2014 report on privacy policies.

Notwithstanding these security concerns, Snapchat has proved to be a popular means for sending pictures or videos that are considered privacy-sensitive, such as those called "sexting." Sexting (a portmanteau of "sex" and "texting"), refers to sexually explicit personal messages and can include anything from merely suggestive text to actual nude photographs. Considering the sexually explicit nature of sexts, sending or receiving sexts often carries serious legal ramifications, particularly if the subject is under the age of consent. And because Snapchat's primary demographic is younger users, sexting among these users may violate child pornography laws. Thus, Snapchat has frequently been criticized for facilitating child pornography. Snapchat refutes these claims, however, pointing out that almost all photomessaging applications create the potential for underage sexting.

Despite these concerns with teen sexting, research conducted by the University of Washington found that the majority of users claim to use Snapchat primarily for "funny content," such as taking selfies with funny faces or drawn-on mustaches, not for sexting. This usage suggests less a desire for privacy than it does a desire to prevent snaps from being subjected to lasting scrutiny. And indeed, many respondents cited not privacy but different social standards as their primary reason for using Snapchat. Online media entails a permanence that can stifle expression, and Snapchat offers a means of recapturing this freedom of expression that other forms of social media inhibit.

Snapchat may be viewed more broadly as an attempt to use technology to solve privacy and security problems created by the digital age. One of the many concerns among social media users is that their actions leave a permanent digital record, and that record is often owned and controlled by a third party. Even social media platforms that provide much control over content still retain records of that user's activity, and this threat of a permanent record for all online activity can seriously stifle free speech and uninhibited expression. Snapchat represents an attempt to circumvent this problem by creating a medium that utilizes the benefits of technology while also limiting some of these perceived negatives. Although Snapchat's technical solution is imperfect, it represents a novel approach to information sharing. Its success suggests that a market for similar privacy-protecting apps has strong consumer support.

Thus, Snapchat is part of the broader trend in privacy that attempts to regulate data retention. Snapchat's primary appeal is that it inherently limits how long personal data is stored, both by itself and among its users. While Snapchat's data retention limits are integral to its design, some suggest these limitations should be imposed on all companies that manage personal data. Considering the amount of personal data that is shared with and controlled by third parties and the ease of storage, data retention limits are a proposed mechanism to reduce the extent this data can be subjected to lasting scrutiny. While there is currently no federal law limiting data retention by private companies generally, there are some limits for government agencies, and broader regulations are increasingly common abroad, most notably the European Union's "Right to Be Forgotten" and the corresponding provisions in the General Data Protection Regulation (GDPR).

Popularity

Snapchat has become a hugely popular application. By 2021, over 20 percent of all iPhone owners in the United States were using Snapchat and it was the most downloaded photo application among those users. One survey found that 60 percent of US smartphone owners between the ages of thirteen and 34 used Snapchat. It is particularly popular with teenagers and young adults; 60 percent of Snapchat users were between the ages of thirteen and twenty-four in 2016. Women used the application more than men, as about 70 percent of all Snapchatters were women. As of August of 2014, Snapchat had about 100 million users. By the end of that year, four months later, the number of users had nearly doubled and was closer to 200 million. Many Snapchatters used the application on a daily basis, as hundreds of millions of snaps were sent every day. Snapchat's usage was almost as high as the usage of Facebook and Twitter. However, the number of daily active users of the application had reportedly grown at a slower rate as of May 2018, only increasing 2 percent from the 187 million reported in its previous quarter; experts speculated that the decrease may have been a result of dissatisfaction with a major redesign of the application that had been carried out in February 2018. By 2022, Snapchat estimated that over two-thirds of its users were based outside of North America, and over 5 billion snaps were created daily.

Controversies

Since becoming a popular social networking application, Snapchat has experienced some controversies. In 2013, the company was sued by Frank Brown, a college friend of both Spiegel and Murphy. Brown claimed that he had conceived the idea for Snapchat, designed its logo, and came up with the

original Picaboo name. The case was settled in September 2014. Another controversy occurred in late 2013, when Snapchat was hacked. About 4.6 million users were affected, and their usernames and part of their phone numbers were hacked.

Yet another controversy associated with Snapchat is the idea that the application is used as a sexting tool. Spiegel denies these claims, as he believes the media overplays the use of Snapchat as a sexting tool.

—*Scott Russell, Michael Mazzei, and Jake D. Nicosia*

References

Ahmad, Irfan. "The Timeline of #Snapchat—#infographic." *Digital Information World*, 26 Sept. 2014, www.digitalinformationworld.com/2014/09/the-history-of-snapchat-infographic.html.

Cardoza, Nate, Cindy Cohn, Parker Higgins, et al. *Who Has Your Back?: Protecting Your Data from Government Requests*. Electronic Frontier Foundation, 15 May 2014.

Chafkin, Max, and Sarah Frier. "How Snapchat Built a Business by Confusing the Olds." *Bloomberg*, 3 Mar. 2016, www.bloomberg.com/features/2016-how-snapchat-built-a-business/.

Colao, J. J. "Snapchat: The Biggest No-Revenue Mobile App since Instagram." *Forbes*, 27 Nov. 2012.

Crump, Catherine. "Data Retention: Privacy, Anonymity, and Accountability Online." *Stanford Law Review*, vol. 56, no. 1, 2003, p. 191.

Dean, Brian. "Snapchat Demographic Stats: How Many People Use Snapchat in 2022." *Backlinko*, backlinko.com/snapchat-users.

D'Onfro, Jillian. "Snapchat Now Has Nearly 100 Million Daily Users." *Business Insider*, 26 May 2015, www.businessinsider.com/snapchat-daily-active-users-2015-5.

"How Snaps Are Stored and Deleted." *Snapchat Blog*, 9 May 2013.

McBride, Sarah, and Alexei Oreskovic. "Snapchat Breach Exposes Flawed Premise, Security Challenge." *Reuters*, 14 Oct. 2014.

Meyer, Robinson. "The New Terminology of Snapchat." *The Atlantic*, 2 May 2014.

Morrison, Kimberlee. "Snapchat Is the Fastest Growing Social Network." *Adweek*, 28 July 2015, www.adweek.com/digital/snapchat-is-the-fastest-growing-social-network-infographic/.

Roesner, Franziska, Brian T. Gill, and Tadayoshi Kohno. "Sex, Lies, or Kittens? Investigating the Use of Snapchat's Self-Destructing Messages." *Financial Cryptography and Data Security, Lecture Notes in Computer Science*, vol. 8437, 9 Nov. 2014, pp. 64–76.

Shontell, Alyson. "Snap Is a Lot Bigger Than People Realize and It Could be Nearing 200 Million Active Users." *Business Insider*, 3 Jan. 2015.

Strassberg, Donald, Ryan K. McKinnon, Michael A. Sustaíta, and Jordan Rullo. "Sexting by High School Students: An Exploratory and Descriptive Study." *Archives of Sexual Behavior*, vol. 42, no. 1, 2012, pp. 15–21.

Wolverton, Troy. "Snapchat Users Hate the Redesign So Much, It Could Have Turned Away Millions of Users." *Business Insider*, 1 May 2018, www.businessinsider.com/snaps-daily-active-users-flatlined-then-fell-in-the-first-quarter-2018-5.

SOCIAL IMPACTS OF CYBERCRIME

Introduction

Cybercriminals take full advantage of the anonymity, secrecy, and interconnectedness provided by the internet, therefore attacking the very foundations of the modern information society. Cybercrime can involve botnets, computer viruses, cyberbullying, cyberstalking, cyberterrorism, cyberpornography, denial of service (DoS) attacks, hacktivism, identity theft, malware, and spam. Law enforcement officials have struggled to keep pace with cybercriminals, who cost the global economy billions annually. Police are attempting to use the same tools cybercriminals use to perpetrate crimes in an effort to prevent those crimes and bring the guilty parties to justice. This essay begins by defining cybercrime and then moves to a discussion of its economic and social impacts. It continues with detailed excursions into cyberbullying and cyberpornography, two especially representative examples of cybercrime, and concludes with a discussion of ways to curtail the spread of cybercrime.

Background

Computer-related crime dates to the origins of computing, though the greater connectivity between computers through the internet has brought the concept of cybercrime into the public consciousness of the information society.

Cybercrime, as distinguished from computer crime, is an umbrella term for the various crimes committed using the World Wide Web, such as:

- The theft of one's personal identity (identity theft) or financial resources;
- The spread of malicious software code such as computer viruses;
- The use of others' computers to send spam email messages (botnets);
- Denial of Service attacks on computer networks or websites by the hacker;
- Hacktivism, or attacking the computer servers of those organizations felt by the hacker to be unsavory or ethically dubious;
- Cyberstalking, by which sexual predators use internet chat rooms, social networking sites, and other online venues to find and harass their victims;
- Cyberbullying, where individuals are harassed by others, causing severe mental anguish;
- Cyberpornography, the use of the internet to spread child and adult pornography;
- Internet gambling and software piracy; and
- Cyberterrorism, the use of the internet to stage intentional, widespread attacks that disrupt computer networks; using the internet to spread violent messages, recruit terrorists, and plan attacks.
- Cybertrespass (hacktivism, viruses, denial of service attacks)
- Cyberdeceptions (identity theft, fraud, piracy)
- Cyberpornography
- Cyberviolence (cyberbullying, cyberstalking)

Several of these activities have a long history that predates the internet, and they also have technological antecedents.

Media reports since the 1990s have documented the many methods by which criminals have used the internet to commit crimes. Cyberthieves have become skilled at using the anonymity and secrecy of the internet to defraud their victims of their money, their peace of mind, and indeed even their lives. When victims let their guard down by muting a healthy skepticism and caution, cybercrime takes place.

The Scope of Cybercrime

Law enforcement officials have struggled to identify, arrest, and prosecute these tech-savvy offenders, even as sociologists have sought to get to the root of cybercrime. The Federal Bureau of Investigation (FBI) created a special cyber division in 2002 to address cybercrime in a coordinated and cohesive manner with cybersquads in each of its fifty-six field offices, "cyberaction teams" that travel worldwide to address cyberattacks, and nationwide computer task forces. The field of cybercrime has spawned the field of cybercriminology.

The scope of cybercrime remains staggering, and it continues to grow. In 2012, for instance, the US economy lost $525.5 million to cybercrime, an increase of over 40 million from 2011, with the most common complaints in 2012 being impersonation email scams, intimidation crimes, and scams that attempted to extort money from computer users. In 2012, cybercrime cost British businesses 21 billion pounds, and over 1 million computer users in the European Union (EU) were affected every day by cybercrime. According to the Federal Bureau of Investigation's Internet Crime Complaint Center's 2016 report, victims of cybercrime lost a total of $1.33 billion that year; by that point, the organization was receiving an average of 280,000 complaints of cybercrime victimization per year.

As more and more people have used the internet to do their shopping, communicating, banking, and bill paying, they have become targets for cybercriminals. There are common-sense steps that can prevent or reduce having one's financial information stolen online, as well as to avoid other scams and threats, but cybercrime in these areas persists largely due to a lack of consumer education.

Some varieties of cybercrime, such as hacktivism, are ostensibly motivated by noble intentions, such as protest against perceived abuses by governments and corporations. Often these attacks involve posting comments on official government websites and are not motivated by a desire for monetary gain. However, other forms of cybercrime have a much more violent intent. These include cyberstalking, cyberbullying, and cyberterrorism.

Cybercrime and Society

While the economic impact of cybercrime is beyond dispute, rather less attention has been given to the social implications of cybercrime. Psychologists and psychiatrists can help victims cope with the fallout from identity theft, sexual abuse, or financial ruin, whereas sociologists are well-positioned to look at the broader social impacts and explanations of cybercrime.

Cybercrime attacks the very foundations of modern, technological societies, bound up as they are with the rapid flow of computer data facilitated by the internet. At the most basic level, cybercriminals often take advantage of technologically unsophisticated individuals who nonetheless find themselves in a world where the internet plays an increasingly central role in both community and private life. Cybercrime depends, at this level, on the ability of those who are more technologically sophisticated to use that knowledge to trick others into surrendering vital information, such as their bank account information or Social Security number. While it is possible in some situations for the victim of cybercrime to restore stolen money or even their personal online identity, the event often leaves the victim traumatized and deeply suspicious of the internet and other trappings of modern life. In this way the cybercriminal deprives his or her victim of many of the conveniences of today's information economy.

Experts in cybercrime have noted that its impact occurs on multiple levels. First, on a purely economic level, cybercrime involves the theft of millions, and in some instances billions, of dollars every year. In addition, cybercrime requires individuals and institutions to take on the added cost of security software and other means by which to frustrate the cybercriminals.

Second, on a broader cultural level, cybercrime helps to sour general perceptions about the internet in particular and new technology in general. Paradoxically, it can also make those who have been victims of one type of cybercrime more vulnerable to other types of cybercrime because of their lack of awareness of new and evolving cybercrime methods.

Third, and perhaps most alarming of all, cybercrime creates traumatized individuals who are less able to cope with the demands of life. Whether one is the victim of identity theft, a credit card scam, or cyberbullying, and regardless of whether restitution is made, the effects of cybercrime can impact the psyche as much as any crime.

Stopping Cybercrime

In his 1995 essay, Gene Stephens offered what one might call a traditionally libertarian way to combat cybercrime that fits well with the open ethos of cyberspace. Given the massive proliferation of cybercrime since 1995, Stephens began in 2008 to see things differently and argued that stopping cybercrime will depend largely on two factors: a more secure internet infrastructure, redesigned with security foremost in mind; and coordinated, global policing of cyberspace to back up other security methods such as biometrics. Stephens also argued that fighting cybercrime involves tackling a larger and more fundamental issue: How can one police an area, such as cyberspace, that very obviously no one person owns and has jurisdiction over? The answer, he argues, is voluntary, multinational policing, with the price of failure being too great to ignore.

The exponentially improving capabilities of emerging web technologies spotlights the long-ignored issues of who owns the World Wide Web, who manages it, and who has jurisdiction over it. The answer now is: Nobody! Can the world's most powerful socio-politico-economic network continue to operate almost at random, open to all, and thus be excessively vulnerable to cybercriminals and terrorists alike? Yet any attempt to restrict or police the web can be expected to be met by extreme resistance from a plethora of users for a variety of reasons, many of which seem contradictory. Biometrics and more-advanced systems of ID will need to be perfected to protect users and the network. In addition, multinational cybercrime units will be required to catch those preying on users worldwide, as web surfers in Arlington, Virginia, and Victoria, British Columbia, may be victims of cyberscams perpetrated in Cairo or Budapest.

Although the task is daunting, governments worldwide are taking steps. In 2012, the EU announced the establishment of a cybercrime center aimed at stopping identity thieves and other online criminals. The policymaking arm of the EU, the European Commission, proposed mandatory jail time for online crimes and the cybercrime center was expected to staff fifty-five personnel with an annual budget of 3.6 billion.

Can one be optimistic about the containment of cybercrime? If history is any judge, the same internet technology that empowers criminals to evade the law can enable law enforcement to defend the law.

—Matt Donnelly

References

"2007 Internet Crime Report." *The National White Collar Crime Center.* Bureau of Justice Assistance, Federal Bureau of Investigation, www.ic3.gov/media/annualreports.aspx.

"2012 Internet Crime Report Released: More Than 280,000 Complaints of Online Criminal Activity Reported in 2012." *Federal Bureau of Investigation*, 14 May 2013, www.fbi.gov/sandiego/press-releases/2013/2012-internet-crime-report-released.

"Battling the Online Bullies." *BBCNews.* 27 June 2008, news.bbc.co.uk/2/hi/programmes/click&#x005F;online/7477008.stm.

Duggan, M. "Online Harassment 2017." *Pew Research Center*, 11 July 2017, www.pewinternet.org/2017/07/11/online-harassment-2017/.

Dupont, B. "Bots, Cops, and Corporations: On the Limits of Enforcement and the Promise of Polycentric Regulation as a Way to Control Large-Scale Cybercrime." *Crime, Law and Social Change*, vol. 67, no. 1, 2017, pp. 97–116, search.ebscohost.com/login.aspx?direct=true&db=sxi&an=120927470&site=ehost-live&scope=site.

"EU Prepares to Launch First Cybercrime Centre." *Euractive*, 29 Mar. 2012, www.euractiv.com/infosociety/eu-prepares-launch-cybercrime-ce-news-511823.

Federal Bureau of Investigation. "Cybercrime: Computer Intrusions." *Federal Bureau of Investigation*, 2012, www.fbi.gov/about-us/investigate/cyber/computer-intrusions.

Heath, N. "FBI Cybercrime Chief on Botnets, Web Terror and the Social Network Threat." *Management.silicon.com*, 16 Apr. 2008, www.fbi.gov/about-us/investigate/cyber/computer-intrusions.

Internet Crime Complaint Center. "2016 Internet Crime Report." *Federal Bureau of Investigation*, pdf. ic3.gov/2016_ic3report.pdf.

"Internet Porn 'Increasing Child Abuse.'" *The Guardian*, 12 Jan. 2004, www.guardian.co.uk/technology/2004/jan/12/childprotection.childrensservices.

Jaishankar, K. "Cyber Criminology: Evolving a Novel Discipline with a New Journal." *International Journal of Cyber Criminology*, vol. 1, 2007, www.geocities.com/cybercrimejournal/editorialijcc.pdf.

Johnston, C. "Brave New World or Virtual Pedophile Paradise? Second Life Falls Foul of Law." *The Age*, 10 May 2007, acrime/2007/05/09/1178390390098.html.

Lenhart, A. "Cyberbullying And Online Teens." *Pew Internet and American Life Project*, 27 June 2007, www.cyberlaw.pro/docs/pewcyberbullying.pdf.

Levi, M. "Assessing the Trends, Scale and Nature of Economic Cybercrimes: Overview and Issues." *Crime, Law and Social Change*, vol. 67, no. 1, 2017, pp. 3–20, search.ebscohost.com/login.aspx?direct=true&db=sxi&AN=120927472&site=ehost-live&scope=site.

Liebowitz, M. "Online Bullying Rampant Among Teens, Survey Finds." *Security News Daily*, 9 Nov. 2011, www.technewsdaily.com/3396-online-bullying-teens-facebook.html.

Marcum, C., G. Higgins, T. Freiburger, et al. "Exploration of the Cyberbullying Victim/Offender Overlap by Sex." *American Journal of Criminal Justice*, vol. 39, 2014, pp. 538–48, search.ebscohost.com/login.aspx?direct=true&db=sih&an=97320502.

Morris, H. "Europe Cracks Down on Cybercrime." *International New York Times*, 12 Mar. 2012, rendezvous.blogs.nytimes.com/2012/03/29/europe-cracks-down-on-cybercrime,

"National Economies Threatened by Cybercrime, according to EU Information Security Agency." *AVG Anti-Virus and Internet Security*, 9 June 2008, www.grisoft.com.

Pokin, S. "'My Space' Hoax Ends with Suicide of Dardenne Prairie Teen." *Suburban Journals*, 11 Nov. 2007, suburbanjournals.stltoday.com/articles/2007/11/13/news/sj2tn20071110-1111stc&#X005f.

Simmons, C. "Losses Rise in Internet-Related Scams." *CIO Today*, 7 Apr. 2008, www.newsfactor.com"xlink:type="simple">http://www.newsfactor.com.

Simons, M. "Dutch Say a Sex Ring Used Infants on Internet." *The New York Times*, 19 July 1998, query.nytimes.com/gst/fullpage.html?res=990de3da1330f93aa25754c0a96e958260&scp=1&sq=dutch+sex+ring&st=nyt.

Stanglin, D., and W. M. Welch. "Sheriff Says He Made Arrests After One Suspect Posted on Facebook That She Didn't Care the Victim Had Died." *USA Today*, 16 Oct. 2013, www.usatoday.com/story/news/nation/2013/10/15/florida-bullying-arrest-lakeland-suicide/2986079.

Stephens, G. "Crime in Cyberspace." *Futurist*, vol. 29, 1995, pp. 24–31.

___. "Cybercrime in the Year 2025." *Futurist*, vol. 42, 2008, pp. 32–36, retrisearch.ebscohost.com/login.aspx?direct=true&db=aph&an=32526239&site=ehost-live.

Swartz, J. "Online Crime's Impact Spreads." *USA Today*, 11 Apr. 2008.

Wall, D. *Cybercrime: The Transformation of Crime in the Information Age*. Polity, 2007.

Wall, D. S., and M. L. Williams. "Policing Cybercrime: Networked and Social Media Technologies and the Challenges for Policing." *Policing and Society*, vol. 23, 2013, pp. 409–12, search.ebscohost.com/login.aspx?direct=true&db=sih&an=91557437.

Wayne L., A., and L. A. Johnson. "Current United States Presidential Views on Cyber Security and Computer Crime with Corresponding Department of Justice Enforcement Guidelines." *Journal of International Diversity*, 2011, pp. 116–19, search.ebscohost.com/login.aspx?direct=true&db=sih&an=72324633.

Yar, M. *Cybercrime and Society*. SAGE, 2006.

SOCIAL MEDIA

Introduction

Internet-based applications and websites that promote the sharing of user-generated content, communication, and participation on a large scale, are grouped into the general term of "social media." Since the early 2000s social media has taken the internet by storm, and by February 2019, according to the Pew Research Center, approximately 72 percent of adults in the United States used some type of social media. A large variety of user-generated applications make up what is considered social media. These applications include blogs, social networks such as Facebook, and audio podcasts. Over time, social media has become used for marketing and as an alternative news source. Although the aim of social media is to make it easier for individuals to communicate and engage in conversations, many argue that it has led to a reduction in human interaction.

Background

The idea of social media began in the mid-to-late 1990s, when internet users were first given the ability to make their own websites through servers such as Geocities. Blogging and social networks also began around that time. Sixdegrees.com, launched in 1997, was one of the first websites that allowed users to create a profile and add lists of friends. It was not until 2002 and the launch of Friendster that the concept of a social network become highly popular. Within three months of its launch, Friendster had gained 3 million users. Other popular social media applications launched around this time include the social networking platforms MySpace (currently stylized as Myspace) and LinkedIn, the music service iTunes, and the image-hosting website Flickr.

Social media is classified in several ways. Any application that allows users to create a profile and build a friend list is considered a social network. The most popular example of this is Facebook, which was launched in 2004 and had grown to more than 1 billion daily active users by mid-2020. Blogs allow users to generate a variety of content for publication on the internet. Several websites are devoted to hosting users' blogs; one of the most popular of these servers is WordPress. Forums are another classification that allows users to voice their opinion on a range of topics. Video and audio podcasts allow users to record themselves discussing different topics. Internet users can then download or stream these recordings. Collaborative websites known as wikis, which allow users to generate informational content on a variety of topics, also became very popular; the most famous of these is Wikipedia, a crowdsourced encyclopedia.

Multiplayer online games are also a prevalent type of social media. These games, such as the popular *World of Warcraft*, allow users to communicate with other players while participating in a virtual world. Other popular examples of these games are *The Sims* and *Second Life*, which allowed users to create avatars and interact with other users. Other more general categories that can be considered social media include emails, instant messaging, and video sharing. Many of these varieties have been aggregated with social networks.

The rise in smartphone and tablet computer technology allowed individuals to access an array of social media applications while mobile. Geographic tagging applications allowed users to "tag" themselves at specific locations such as restaurants and stores and post these tags on social media websites such as Facebook and Foursquare.

By the late 2010s, many social media platforms had banned hate speech. Several platforms like Telegram, Parler, and Gab, however, did not, and so became popular with right-wing extremist groups who used the sites to communicate and organize events. In January 2021, such sites were used to coordinate the storming of the US Capitol building in Washington, DC.

Following the storming of the Capitol, many mainstream social media platforms, including Facebook and Twitter, banned President Donald Trump for allegedly inciting the violent event. The sites also banned many more users who violated their rules against hate speech and inciting violence.

Myspace and Facebook

The most popular social media and networking tool in the world is Facebook. The website was launched on February 4, 2004, by computer programmer and Harvard sophomore Mark Zuckerberg. When the website was first created, it was exclusively for students of Harvard University and others with college-based email addresses. It was opened to everyone on September 26, 2006, and quickly gained hundreds of millions of users. Although the website requires users to be at least thirteen years old, it has been reported that several million users are under age thirteen.

Facebook allows users to build a personal profile that includes pictures and cultural interests, to exchange messages, and to share thoughts, pictures, and videos. The website initially drew comparisons with Myspace, an earlier social networking website. However, Facebook allows for more customization and requires users to give their true identity, which Myspace did not.

Myspace was launched even before Facebook, in August 2003, and quickly became one of the most visited websites in the United States. It was surpassed by Facebook in 2008 but, as of 2015, it still had 50 million users. The website shifted its focus to cater heavily to musicians and was revamped to make it easy for users to upload and share music from established and upcoming artists. However, by 2020, competition and a 2019 report that a server migration initiative had resulted in the loss of a significant amount of early user data meant that the site had continued to fail to attract new users.

Twitter

The social networking and microblogging website Twitter has risen to immense popularity since it was launched in 2006. It allows users to create a small profile, follow other users, and post brief messages, originally restricted to 140 characters long. (As of November 2017, Twitter users can post messages of up to 280 characters.) These messages are known as tweets. Twitter further encourages interaction and online conversations through the use of hashtags. A hashtag, represented by the pound symbol before a word or group of words, allows users to search for and view every tweet with that specific hashtag attached. The most popular current hashtags are known as "trending topics." The application was launched by web developer Jack Dorsey, and by mid-2020 had around 186 million active monthly users, with hundreds of millions of tweets being sent every day from computers and various mobile devices.

The application is significant for the way it allows people to organize quickly. For example, Twitter was used to rally individuals for political protests around the world, as in the Egyptian Revolution in 2011. Politicians utilized it as a way to garner support and interact with voters. US president Barack Obama used it heavily during his 2008 campaign. He encouraged voters to ask him questions via Twitter and Facebook throughout the campaign. This innovative use was expanded to an unprecedented level by television celebrity Donald Trump, who used his personal Twitter account as a main form of communication during his successful presidential campaign in 2016. During his presidency, he continued to use the platform heavily to express his views to the public, and it became particularly prominent again throughout the 2020 presidential campaign.

Twitter has also been used to report breaking news, although many critics argue that Twitter users rarely perform fact checking before sending out news tweets. For example, during the 2016 US presidential election Twitter served as a highly influential news source for millions of Americans, but it and other social media sites were plagued by accounts spreading misleading or outright false news and analysis. Twitter has also been frequently used in police investigations, education, and public relations. As of 2020, the microblogging service remained one of the world's most-visited websites.

Social Media Marketing

Since social media is accessible through a broad range of applications, it has become a heavily used tool in marketing. Companies can manufacture advertisements that social media users can easily share at no cost to the company, making it an inexpensive alternative to traditional marketing. Additionally, by 2020 many businesses and brands had begun taking advantage of influencer marketing, which typically entailed the involvement of individuals with a large number of social media followers.

Social networking sites such as Facebook allow companies to join them and create a profile for marketing purposes. On Facebook, users can "like" the page of companies to get updates and offers from them, as well as communicate with them. This approach was especially successful for small businesses that used Facebook to promote their brand through special events and offers.

Brands utilize Twitter to market and interact on a more individual level. When users "follow" brands online, short messages posted by the brand appear on the users' main Twitter feed page. Many times, these messages include links that a user could click on to learn more about offers and specific products. This too is a very inexpensive method of online marketing.

Foursquare was another influential social media application frequently used by businesses in online marketing. This application originally allowed users to "check-in" at the location of a store, restaurant, or other business. Their check-in was then posted on the Foursquare website as well as on other applications such as Facebook. Businesses encouraged return customers by offering incentives for checking in many times. While Foursquare itself eventually abandoned this model in favor of focusing on personalized, localized search services, the "check-in" concept was taken up by other social media applications.

The video-sharing website YouTube has become another popular place for advertisers. Marketing on YouTube is personalized through various language-detection programs that analyze users' individual interests and market to them accordingly. Advertisers are able to attach specific advertisements to relevant videos being searched, making it easy for them to reach a target audience. Another popular method of no- or low-cost advertising on YouTube is through "viral videos." These videos, which are oftentimes humorous and culturally relevant, are created with the goal of having users spread them across the web, to gain monetary compensation or temporary fame.

Other popular social media applications that are heavily used in marketing are blogs where advertisements can be posted, business-profile websites such as Yelp, and the business-networking website LinkedIn.

Privacy Concerns

One of the biggest debates concerning social media remains over online privacy and protection of user information. Those concerned with these issues argue that social networking sites such as Facebook and Twitter do not take the proper steps to protect the information users share with each other. Debates have looked at ownership of the content on social networking websites. Users generate it onto these websites, but corporations own the websites.

In November 2007, Facebook came under heavy negative criticism for implementing Beacon, a system that allowed partner websites to send information concerning the actions of Facebook users on their own websites. This information included items purchased at online retailers and games users played online. Beacon aroused concerns over privacy of information and users' lack of control over how their information was used. Facebook spokespersons argued that it allowed users to further share their interests with friends and help refer them to online retailers. Beacon was discontinued in September 2009, but the company came under similar scrutiny in 2014 for major privacy policy changes as well as for an emotion study that drew the attention and ire of privacy watchdog organizations and individuals.

There also have been concerns over federal and local authorities using Facebook to acquire personal information in the investigation of crimes. Facebook's privacy policy states that they may turn over any information they believe may be related to an illegal or criminal activity, but many argued that personal information has been harvested even when authorities lacked reasonable suspicion. This has raised further questions about what online information falls under the US Electronic Communications Privacy Act (ECPA) of 1986, which regulates what electronic messages and information can be legally seized or intercepted by authorities. Critics argue that the bill is very loose in its language and outdated with respect to contemporary information sharing.

The concept of data mining to extract user information has been another serious concern for social network users. Many worry that companies and individuals have been allowed to freely harvest information and use it for various purposes without necessarily obtaining the consent of users. In 2005, as part of a project on Facebook privacy, two students from the Massachusetts Institute of Technology (MIT) demonstrated the possibility of simple data mining on Facebook. They used an automated script to download the Facebook profiles of over seventy thousand users.

Facebook has since developed higher security methods for their users, including customizable security, but privacy continued to be a concern. Challenges of Facebook's operations and policies were heightened once more in 2018 when it was revealed that the political data firm Cambridge Analytica had been able to harvest a large amount of user data from the site without their knowledge. In early 2020, the platform made concerted efforts to emphasize the importance of information privacy.

Impact

Since its inception, social media has changed everything from politics to public relations, from telecommunications to theater. It has fundamentally shifted the way many people experience everyday life, including friendship, shopping, and job searching. While it helps connect people and share their ideas, it continues to come under heavy negative criticism and skepticism. Critics argue that it only creates the illusion of connection and in reality, decreases the need for actual human interaction. Others state that it leads to an increase in cyberbullying, in which people are harassed on social networks.

Many employers have banned social media at work due to concerns that it decreases productivity. The ultimate concern is now one of privacy and the misuse of personal information. Yet supporters of social media claim that these downsides are far outweighed by the social and economic benefits of increased interaction over the internet, a field with ever-growing potential as technology and access improves around the world. For better or worse, social media continues to increase in popularity, particularly with the rise and influx of mobile applications. In 2020, during the global COVID-19 pandemic, many people turned increasingly to social media platforms to stay connected while in-person contact was limited in an effort to slow the spread of the virus.

—*Patrick G. Cooper*

References

Bryfonski, Dedria. *The Global Impact of Social Media.* Greenhaven, 2012.

Denham, Hannah. "These Are the Platforms that Have Banned Trump and His Allies." *The Washington Post*, 14 Jan. 2021, www.washingtonpost.com/technology/2021/01/11/trump-banned-social-media/.

"Facebook Reports Second Quarter 2020 Results." *Facebook*, 30 July 2020, s21.q4cdn.com/399680738/files/doc_financials/2020/q2/Q2'20-FB-Financial-Results-Press-Release.pdf.

Highfield, Tim. *Social Media and Everyday Politics.* Polity, 2016.

Humphreys, Ashlee. *Social Media: Enduring Principles.* Oxford UP, 2016.

Kirkpatrick, David. *The Facebook Effect: The Inside Story of the Company That Is Connecting the World.* Simon, 2011.

Lovink, Geert. *Networks without a Cause: A Critique of Social Media.* Polity, 2011.

Moe, Wendy, and David A. Schweidel. *Social Media Intelligence.* Cambridge UP, 2014.

Morozov, Evgeny. *The Net Delusion: The Dark Side of Internet Freedom.* Public Affairs, 2011.

Nicosia, Laura. *Educators Online: Preparing Today's Teachers for Tomorrow's Digital Literacies.* Peter Lang, 2013.

Qualman, Erik. *Socialnomics: How Social Media Transforms the Way We Live and Do Business.* Wiley, 2010.

"Q2 2020 Letter to Shareholders." *Twitter*, 2020, s22.q4cdn.com/826641620/files/doc_financials/2020/q2/Q2-2020-Shareholder-Letter.pdf.

Shirky, Clay. *Here Comes Everybody: The Power of Organizing without Organizations.* Penguin, 2009.

"Social Media Fact Sheet." *Pew Research Center*, 12 June 2019, www.pewresearch.org/internet/fact-sheet/social-media/.

Tuten, Tracy L., and Michael R, Solomon. *Social Media Marketing.* Pearson, 2013.

SOCIAL MEDIA ADDICTION

Introduction

Social media addiction represents a constellation of uncontrollable, impulsive, and damaging behaviors caused by persistent social media usage that continues despite repeated negative consequences.

The rise in popularity of social media websites, such as Facebook, Snapchat, Instagram, and Twitter, has spawned an age of social media consumption that is difficult to quantify. In April 2021, Hootsuite, a major platform for social media management, reported that around 4.3 billion people, or around 55 percent of the global population, were actively using social media. Rather than point to specific numbers or trends in everyday use, perhaps a better way of considering the effect of social media on society is to consider that professional journals began chronicling the ongoing relationship with social media and are relevant to studies of the effects of social media on human behavior.

Facebook, for example, has changed the way that people communicate and maintain social relationships, both in productive and nonproductive ways. Twitter has become a global vehicle through which people collect, report, and share the news of the moment. Communicating with other people has become easier and more immediate, while the boundaries, rules, and language that govern this communication have become more convoluted. As a result, research aimed at how and why people find

The most widely recognized causes of social media addiction include low self-esteem, dissatisfaction with one's personal life, and depression and hyperactivity. Photo via iStock/ ViewApart. [Used under license.]

themselves using social media, and technology in general, has been on the rise. For instance, psychologist Julia Hormes hypothesizes that the unpredictable updates on social media platforms and self-disclosures inherent in the process both activate the brain's reward circuitry, reinforcing the behaviors. Other research has suggested that people use social media for a sense of belonging, much as they would join social groups in the real world.

Furthermore, features of one's personality that predict heavy, or limited, social media use have been under investigation. For instance, poor emotion regulation, impulsivity, alcohol abuse, and internet addiction were associated with social media dependence among young adults in one 2014 study. The merits of what widely interconnected, online relationships mean for face-to-face communication, intimacy, and privacy have become the objects of study as well.

Background

Social media researcher Sherry Turkle has been exploring the interaction of human relationships and technology for decades. Her work has developed a collective understanding of how human beings interface with a technological society. Her seminal works applying self and interpersonal theories to social media relationships were predictive and formative. Turkle has shown that technological advances have made it virtually impossible to isolate oneself from complex interpersonal relationships.

Additionally, technology has done as much to challenge self-representation as it has challenged

interpersonal relationships; for instance, many Facebook users report feeling anxiety in trying to manage their self-representation to varying audiences of friends, family, and professional connections on the site. Social media sites also encourage attention-seeking behaviors. In so doing, the ways in which one's real life aligns with one's virtual life are telling and have become useful fodder for ongoing research.

Psychological Addiction? Loneliness, Anxiety, Shyness

Because of the long-held assumption that social media helps to foster meaningful, online relationships, and because of the ease through which one can build a relationship with someone previously unknown to them, three psychological concerns in particular have been studied: loneliness, anxiety, and shyness. No consensus exists on how these factors intersect with one's proclivity for social media use (or for social media addiction), though there are a few interesting points to highlight.

First, research has revealed mixed findings regarding people who self-identify as "lonely" and people who self-identify as "anxious." Some research has indicated that lonely people prefer face-to-face interaction (they find that social media lacks intimacy), whereas anxious people prefer electronic modes of communication. As such, loneliness could be better understood as something self-representational (with concerns hovering around issues of the self rather than of a specific fear of others or of socializing with others).

According to a University of Wisconsin–Milwaukee meta-analysis of loneliness and Facebook use, lonelier people spend more time on the site despite not feeling their loneliness lessen while using it. Anxious people prefer social media because of the anonymity involved, making it easier to rationalize possible disapproval while having more control over how the other person experiences them. Studies have also suggested that those with low self-esteem are particularly vulnerable to dysfunctional social media usage, as they repeatedly seek the rewards of self-disclosure, but often discourage their social media contacts with negative sharing.

Second, shyness is not something that inhibits social media usage despite the likelihood that shy people will experience the same minimal amount of social contact online as they would otherwise.

Despite reported difficulty maintaining online relationships, shy people report heightened satisfaction in their virtual worlds. This is likely because they are spending a greater amount of time seeking, surveying, and considering positive social encounters while online. Additionally, social media provides a rather safe and secure outlet for heightened social interaction.

Third, the issue of locus of control has come under scrutiny as it relates to potential social media addiction. Specifically, research has examined closely the types of reinforcements experienced by heavy social media users. People are less likely to become addicted to social media if they feel that they have control over their own lives both online and off, whereas people are more likely to be addicted to social media if they feel as though others have greater control over them both online and off.

Turkle's analysis of the internet and social media as seductive is especially relevant here, particularly when one considers the fluid nature of a person's experience of social media. That is, a person can update, alter, change, or redefine their online identity in the click of a button. Additionally, ephemeral media, or content that has only a fleeting existence and then self-deletes such as videos or photos posted on Snapchat, heightens the illusion of anonymity. At the same time, because there is a limited window of viewing opportunity, ephemeral media could be seen as even more addictive as it is necessary for the user to interact even more frequently. Research suggests that the high engagement of social networking users could be due to users' apprehension about missing out on an experience. A study at the University of Chicago found that social media can be more addictive than cigarettes and alcohol.

During the coronavirus disease 2019 (COVID-19) pandemic, addiction to social media use took on yet another meaning due to the changed context of that use. The quarantines and lockdowns implemented to attempt to stop the spread of the virus meant that many people relied on social media even more than before to connect with even those people closest to them on a regular basis as well as to get real-time insight into discussions around the pandemic and its effects. At the same time, research tended to show an even more drastic increase in new users of social media as well as the amount of average time spent on the platforms, furthering the hypothesis that social media had become, for many, a crucial, perhaps addictive, digital replacement for the loss of in-person interactions and an escape from feelings of isolation caused by the pandemic.

—Joseph C. Viola

References

Beard, Keith W. "Internet Addiction: A Review of Current Assessment Techniques and Potential Assessment Questions." *Cyberpsychology and Behavior*, vol. 8, no. 1, 2007, pp. 7–14.

Chak, Katherine M., and Louis Leung. "Shyness and Locus of Control as Predictors of Internet Addiction and Internet Use." *Cyberpsychology and Behavior*, vol. 7, no. 5, 2004, pp. 559–70.

Chia-Yi, Mba, and Feng-Yang Kuo. "A Study of Internet Addiction through the Lens of the Interpersonal Theory." *Cyberpsychology and Behavior*, vol. 10, no. 6, 2007, pp. 799–804.

Feiler, Bruce. "For the Love of Being 'Liked': For Some Social-Media Users, an Anxiety from Approval Seeking." *The New York Times*, 9 May 2014.

Forest, Amanda L., and Joanne V. Wood. "When Social Networking Is Not Working: Individuals with Low Self-Esteem Recognize but Do Not Reap the Benefits of Self-Disclosure on Facebook." *Psychological Science*, vol. 23, no. 3, 2012, pp. 295–302.

Hawi, Nazir S., and Maya Samaha. "The Relations Among Social Media Addiction, Self-Esteem, and Life Satisfaction in University Students." *Social Science Computer Review*, vol. 35, no. 5, 2017, pp. 576–86.

Hormes, Julia M., Brianna Kearns, and C. Alix Timko. "Craving Facebook? Behavioral Addiction to Online Social Networking and Its Association with Emotion Regulation Deficits." *Addiction*, vol. 109, no. 12, 2014, pp. 2079–88.

Kemp, Simon. "WhatsApp Is the World's Favorite Social Platform (and Other Facts)." *Hootsuite*, 22 Apr. 2021, blog.hootsuite.com/simon-kemp-social-media/.

Lam, Lawrence T., et al. "Factors Associated with Internet Addiction among Adolescents." *Cyberpsychology and Behavior*, vol. 12, no. 5, 2009, pp. 551–55.

Molla, Rani. "Posting Less, Posting More, and Tired of It All: How the Pandemic Has Changed Social Media." *Recode*, Vox Media, 1 Mar. 2021, www.vox.com/recode/22295131/social-media-use-pandemic-covid-19-instagram-tiktok.

Muise, Amy M., Emily Christofides, and Serge Desmarais. "More Information Than You Ever Wanted: Does Facebook Bring Out the Green-Eyed Monster of Jealousy?" *Cyberpsychology and Behavior*, vol. 12, no. 4, 2009, pp. 441–44.

Orr, Emily S., et al. "The Influence of Shyness on the Use of Facebook in an Undergraduate Sample." *Cyberpsychology and Behavior*, vol. 12, no. 3, 2009, pp. 337–40.

Rosen, Larry D. *iDisorder: Understanding Our Dependency on Technology and Overcoming Our Addiction.* Palgrave, 2012.

Stevens, Sarah, and Tracy Morris. "College Dating and Social Anxiety: Using the Internet as a Means of Connecting to Others." *Cyberpsychology and Behavior*, vol. 10, no. 5, 2007, pp. 680–88.

Turkle, Sherry. "Whither Psychoanalysis in Computer Culture." *Psychoanalytic Psychology*, vol. 21, no. 1, 2004, pp. 16–30.

University of Wisconsin-Milwaukee. "Does Facebook Make You Lonely?" *ScienceDaily*, 9 Oct. 2014.

SOCIAL MEDIA AND DEPRESSION

Introduction

The Pew Research Center, which has been tracking social media use in the United States since 2005, reported that in 2015, 65 percent of adults used social networking sites, an increase of almost 60 percent over a decade. As recently as 2021, a study showed that Americans spend between five and six hours on their cell phones with 145 minutes of that time spent on social media. Young adults between ages eighteen and twenty-nine and teens were the heaviest users, with 90 percent of young adults and 92 percent of teens self-identifying as social media users. At the other end of the age spectrum, more than one third of adults sixty-five and older reported using social media. The purpose of social media is to connect people, and while this sounds benevolent,

Social media can have a direct impact on emotional and mental health. Photo via iStock/martin-dm. [Used under license.]

researchers have questioned whether social media can have harmful effects. The number of stories concerning cyberbullying and harassment has increased interest in the finding an answer. The effects of social media on those suffering from depression have been of particular concern.

With the advent of the virus COVID-19 in 2020, social distancing with some mandated stay-at-home orders caused an increasing sense of isolation. Without physical contact with others that can trigger stress-relief hormones, work relationships, and other social outlets, humans, who are social creatures, face a serious mental health threat. Multiple social media platforms have replaced real-world contacts until such time as quarantine requirements ease. Unfortunately, too much time on social media can make the individual feel lonely and isolated and enhance feelings of anxiety and depression. While excessive use may impact feelings and mental health, it can still be a positive way to stay engaged with others and enhance well-being. Going forward, the habit of too much time on social media may need to be broken.

The use of social media may not have the same psychological benefits of in-person contact, but there are multiple positives such as staying connected with others, even virtually. For some, staying up-to-date with friends and family around the world when visits and travel are limited is a significant positive. Finding new groups online, promoting worthwhile causes and seeking or providing emotional support is also important in the use of social media especially if the individual lives in a rural or isolated area. Finding an outlet for creativity such as writing, sharing craft ideas, decorating tablescapes and posting pictures, and even selling artwork or crafts online may be a benefit. Hobbies can even be monetized and social media platforms such as eBay and Etsy may be great selling sites.

There are negative consequences of social media that must be considered. Safety is always an issue. With minimal regulation, posts may be untrue, misleading or even dangerous. Sufficient research exists that demonstrate a strong relationship between heavy social media use and an increased risk for depression and other mental health issues, including suicidal thoughts. When reading others' posts, it may cause the individuals feelings of inadequacy about their lives or appearance. A fear of missing out (FOMO) may occur, with Facebook and Instagram heavy contributors to FOMO.

The University of Pennsylvania conducted a study that demonstrated that excessive use of Facebook, Snapchat, and Instagram may increase feelings of loneliness. They also showed that decreasing or controlling the use of social media could improve overall well-being. Oversharing, such as too many selfies and too much sharing of inner thoughts and feelings, may create a distancing from real-life connections and cause the individual to become too self-centered. Social media may also mask problems such as stress, depression, and boredom or it may become a security blanket in a social situation.

If an individual spends more time on social media than in-person contacts, it may adversely affect mental health. The year 2020 has been an exception since in-person contacts have been limited. Using Zoom, a video chat, or meeting platform, has helped to allow both work and personal contacts a way to stay connected. There are actions to limit social media exposure. Turning off social media notifications, putting the phone away for periods during the day and doing other activities, using an app to track time on social media, leaving devices in another room when going to bed, and even removing some apps from the phone are all strategies to control how smartphones and other devices are used.

The warning is if the individual is using social media as a substitute for real life or if social media causes feelings of inadequacy or sadness, actions must be taken to gain control of use time. Spend time with people in person where possible, reach out to offline friends as not everyone uses social media, join a club, practice mindfulness and take time for reflection, or even consider working as a volunteer. Monitor children's use of social media and don't be afraid to speak to a significant other or friend if they are spending too much time online to the detriment of personal relationships. And most importantly, realize that social media may present an unrealistic view of life.

Background

The beginnings of social media date back to 1979 and Usenet, but Myspace (2003) and Facebook (2004) are more familiar starting points. In 2016, Facebook alone had a population larger than that of many countries. The young with their smartphones were the heaviest users. Depression is a global problem, and the number of people affected by it is increasing. Since around 2005, researchers have studied social media use to determine if there is a connection between depression and heavy social media use. Excessive social media use can make feelings of depression, anxiety, and isolation worse.

Researchers looking at the connection between depression and social media have found mixed results. Some studies suggest that social media users experience increased depression. Others have found that social media use offers certain benefits to depressed individuals. Evidence is strongest for a connection between depression and cyberbullying and other negative experiences.

Facebook, with several billion users and accounting for more than 40 percent of all social media visits as of 2021, has been the focus of most studies. In 2011, the American Academy of Pediatrics (AAP) released a report in which the authors coined the term "Facebook depression." They cautioned against the risks of social media, noting depression as a specific risk. The report stated that heavy social media use among preteens and teens could trigger depressive symptoms, citing six studies as evidence for the claim. The American Academy of Pediatrics advised that those suffering from Facebook depression could become socially isolated and were in danger of turning for help to internet sources that might encourage self-destructive behaviors.

Popular media broadcast the news, warning parents that Facebook depression could bring about the realization of their worst fears: teens involved in substance abuse, unsafe sex, or self-destructive behaviors. The report stirred considerable controversy among experts. Some researchers charged that the authors of the report had misinterpreted the cited research, insisting that although social media could exacerbate existing depression, it did not cause depression. Others supported the report, acknowledging that negative experiences on Facebook could contribute to depression and that children and teens who needed social media to affirm their self-worth were especially vulnerable.

Facebook Envy

"Facebook envy," is a term coined to identify the feeling that Facebook friends are enjoying greater happiness and more success than oneself. Depressed individuals are more likely to experience envy, and they are more likely to compare themselves with their friends frequently, view themselves more negatively, and suffer more negative feelings as a consequence of comparisons than are people with no depressive symptoms. Because social media provide extensive opportunities for social comparisons, depressed individuals should be made aware of the risk of low self-esteem and exacerbated depression. Although less controversial than Facebook depression, the identification of Facebook envy also created a firestorm online and offline with pundits, some seriously and some tongue-in-cheek, cautioning the public about the dangers of social comparison. *Slate* even argued that image-driven Instagram was a greater cauldron of envy than Facebook.

Substantial research indicates that greater perceived social support (assistance and comfort one believes to be available) correlates with a decrease in depression and a higher quality of life. Facebook users report social support as a purpose for logging on to the site, and research suggests that Facebook is unique among social media in providing this support. Anecdotal evidence and some research indicate that perceived social support provided by a user's Facebook community has a similar effect to that offered by real-life communities.

Because of the paucity of empirical evidence for the similarity, one group of researchers developed the Facebook Measure of Social Support (FMSS), a measure specifically designed to test Facebook's features more reliably than the previously used general instruments modified for the purpose. These researchers found that the correlation between negative support and increased depressive symptoms and lower quality of life was strong, but other results were inconclusive. The researchers were left with the question of whether Facebook use contributed to depression in some cases or whether depressed individuals were more likely to seek community on Facebook.

Lin and colleagues were left with the same uncertainty. This study moved beyond Facebook users to look at a diverse sample of young adults from nineteen to thirty-two and their use of eleven widely used social media platforms: Facebook, Twitter, YouTube, LinkedIn, Instagram, Pinterest, Tumblr, Vine, Snapchat, and Reddit. Median total time on social media was sixty-one visits per day; median social media site visits per week across all platforms was thirty. Slightly more than 3 percent of the sample reported no social media use. Although this study found a strong and significant association between social media use and depression, the nature of the association was open to speculation.

The association between depression and social media use that Lin and colleagues found, like the association other researchers found, may be a result of depressed individuals turning to social media communities to confirm their self-worth. Those with depressive symptoms may find social interactions provided via social media preferable to face-to-face interactions. On the other hand, social media use may foster the development of depression. Passive users may be more likely than those who actively engage the community to become depressed, or the social comparison that is part of social media use may stir feelings of inferiority, envy, and depression. Internet addiction and cyberbullying may be associated with depression.

Further Insights

Researchers at Brown University offered an answer to the question that shadowed the conclusions of other studies linking depression and social media use. Looking at a group of young adults who for several years had been participants in the New England Family Study (NEFS), a long-running research project, found that people with negative Facebook experiences were 3.2 times more likely to develop depression that those who had no negative experience. A substantial majority (82 percent) of participants had at least one negative Facebook experience, and well over half reported four or more experiences. The latter group had a considerably higher risk of depression.

Cyberbullying

Mean or bullying posts were most strongly related to depression; recipients were 3.5 times more likely to develop depression. Participants targeted by cyberstalking and others initiating unwanted contacts were more than twice as likely to have depression. Because the researchers in the Brown University study worked with young adults they knew through NEFS and controlled for such factors as depression as adolescents and parental mental health, they could conclude without reservations that negative experiences on Facebook led to increased levels of depression.

The negative experience that has attracted the most attention is cyberbullying. Estimates of students who have been cyberbullied range from 15 to 35 percent of the population, and 10 to 20 percent have bullied someone else. A National Institutes of Health (NIH) study released in 2010 found that the risk for depression was greater for those involved in cyberbullying than for those who were not, and the greater risk held true regardless of the nature of the attack. Threats of physical violence, verbal taunts, social exclusion, and cyberaggression all increased the likelihood of depression. Whether the bully uses Facebook pages, online chat groups, or text messages, victims feel depressed. Unlike face-to-face bullying where the victim can identify his or her attacker, the cyberbully, as likely to be female as male, may remain anonymous, increasing the victim's feelings of isolation and helplessness. The NIH study found that more frequent attacks increased levels of depression. Although victims scored highest for depressive symptoms, bullied victims and bullies were more likely to be depressed than students not involved in bullying in any capacity.

Media coverage of the suicides who were victims of cyberbullies has increased awareness of the association between cyberbullying, depression, and suicide. These tragic deaths have been labeled "cyberbullicide." Cyberbullying cannot be identified as the single cause of suicide in adolescents and young adults, but research suggests that it does heighten the risk of suicide by magnifying feelings of isolation and hopelessness for those already depressed or stressed from complicating conditions. The NIH researchers expect that with the ubiquity of smartphones and the increased use of multiple social media, cyberbullying will increase, and so will depression.

Adults and Excessive Use

Not all studies of social media and social media focus on adolescents and young adults. It has been found that adults who spent excessive amounts of time online and those who devoted more than average time to tasks (such as updating profiles) that contributed to their Facebook impression were more likely to report depressive symptoms than those who did not. Feinstein and colleagues cite several studies that suggest an association between depression in both adolescents and adults and internet use so excessive that individuals become socially isolated and neglectful of real-life responsibilities.

However, some studies with adults indicate a connection between social media use and a decrease in depression. Rosen and colleagues found that adults with more friends on Facebook exhibited lower rates of depression. Studies have found that adults who increased use of the internet to communicate with family and friends from several days each week to daily contact showed lower rates of depression and Cotton, Ford, Ford, and Hale found that retired adults who spent time online for email and related activities had a twenty to twenty-eight percent reduction in the likelihood of receiving a depression diagnosis.

Self-Harm Sites

Another common concern surrounding social media use by children and adolescents is that those already suffering from depression may find information or encouragement in online communities that would lead them to harm themselves. For example, studies have consistently shown that media coverage of a suicide is likely to provoke others to commit suicide. Adolescents have proved particularly vulnerable. Perhaps the best-known example of the negative potential of social media is the number of groups and websites devoted to helping anorexics maintain their disorder. Some go so far as to offer advice on how to defeat the programs designed to help them overcome the disorder.

A group of Oxford University researchers examined fourteen studies (eleven from Western countries and three from Asia) that focused on the internet's influence on adolescents at risk of self-harm or suicide. They concluded that higher exposure to suicide and self-harm material seemed to be linked to increased depression, suicidal ideation and self-harm. Experts estimate that between 8 and 25 percent of teens harm themselves through cutting, burning, or other life-threatening acts. Such practices have been viewed as predictive of suicide risk. Some question if the increase in such behaviors can be partially attributed to portrayals on social media sites.

Popular social media sites such as Facebook, Instagram, Twitter, YouTube, Tumblr and Pinterest since 2012 have had policies in place that ban images and posts about self-harm, including cutting, suicide, and eating disorders such as anorexia and bulimia. Some sites go further, having such posts link to a public service announcement or to prevention resources. For example, Tumblr redirects searches that indicate a problematic interest in depression or suicide to a message that asks "Everything okay?" and provides links to helpful resources. Nevertheless, often the sites can take down the material only after it has been posted, and policing efforts are never completely effective.

Providing a Sense of Community

Research also reveals the benefits social media can offer. Perhaps the primary benefit is a sense of community for youth who feel isolated and alienated. Social media may also provide valuable support for those who refuse conventional treatment and support. Daine and colleagues found that internet forums were especially helpful as a coping mechanism for troubled teens. Adolescents are engaged in the exploration of identity, and social media provides a platform for such exploration. At its best, social media allows teens to relate to others whose experiences or interests mirror theirs. Chandra argues that given this role as well as legitimate concerns about the time teens spend on social media, discussions about social networking should become as significant an area in clinical settings as discussions about an adolescent patient's life at home and in school.

The future may hold even more innovative uses of social media in the treatment of depression. Robert Morris, who studied psychology at Princeton under Nobel laureate Daniel Kahneman, used crowdsourcing to develop Panoply in the Massachusetts Institute of Technology (MIT) Media Lab. The research was mixed concerning the efficacy of online peer support groups, with some studies suggesting they could be detrimental. For example, one criticism of Whisper, the popular social platform that allows users to anonymously share secrets, is that even though the opportunity to speak candidly and anonymously can be beneficial, many whispers from depressed individuals and others seeking help do not elicit productive community response.

Panoply adapted existing technology into a platform that combined elements of peer-to-peer interaction with therapeutic content based on cognitive-behavioral theories. Participants were asked to identify a negative idea and view it less subjectively, a process therapists term "reappraisal." Panoply invited users, whose anonymity was protected, to write first a description of an incident they found disturbing and then to write their interpretation of the incident. The post prompted crowdsourced responses.

The first messages offered sympathy and acceptance. The second responders pointed out specific points in the original post where the thought became illogical or failed to reflect reality accurately. The third group rewrote the original message from a more positive perspective. Morris, Schueller, and Picard found that the system reduced depression symptoms and that the control platform involving expressive writing did not. The study also suggested that users of Panoply were engaged with the platform at double the rate of those using the control platform.

—*Wylene Rholetter and Patricia S. Edens*

References

Appel, H., J. Crusius, and A. L. Gerlach. "Social Comparison, Envy, and Depression on Facebook: A Study Looking at the Effects of High Comparison Standards on Depressed Individuals." *Journal of Social and Clinical Psychology*, vol. 34, no. 4, 2015, pp. 277–89.

Cavazos-Rehg, P. A., M. J. Krauss, S. Sowles, et al. "A Content Analysis of Depression-Related Tweets." *Computers in Human Behavior*, vol. 54, 2016, pp. 351–57.

Chandra, A. "Social Networking Sites and Digital Identity: The Utility of Provider-Adolescent Communication." *Brown University Child and Adolescent Behavior Letter*, vol. 32, no. 3, 2016, pp. 1–7.

Daine, K., K. Hawton, V. Singaravelu, et al. "The Power of the Web: A Systematic Review of Studies of the Influence of the Internet on Self-Harm and Suicide in Young People. *PLOS One*, vol. 8, no. 10, 2013, pp. 1–6.

Dyson, M. P., L. Hartling, J. Shulhan, et al. "A Systematic Review of Social Media Use to Discuss and View Deliberate Self-Harm Acts." *PLOS One*, vol. 11, no. 5, 2016, pp. 1–15.

English, Cameron. "Social Media Use Causes Depression and Suicide? It's a Surprisingly Difficult Question to Answer. "*American Council on Science and Health,* 24 June 2021, acsh.org/news/2021/06/24/social-media-use-causes-depression-and-suicide-its-surprisingly-difficult-question-answer-15628.

Feinstein, B., V. Bhatia, J. Latack, et al. "Social Networking and Depression." *The Wiley Handbook of Psychology, Technology, and Society*, edited by L. D. Rosen, N. A. Cheevery, and L. M. Carrier, Wiley Blackwell, 2015, pp. 273–86.

Jelenchick, L., J. Eickhoff, and M. Moreno. "Facebook Depression?: Social Networking Site Use and Depression in Older Adolescents." *Journal of Adolescent Health*, vol. 52, 2013, pp. 128–30.

Kross, E., P. Verduyn, E. Demiralp, et al. "Facebook Use Predicts Declines in Subjective Well-Being in Young Adults." *PLOS One*, vol. 8, no. 8, 2013, pp. 1–6.

Lin, L., J. E. Sidani, A. Shensa, et al. "Association between Social Media Use and Depression among U.S. Young Adults." *Depression and Anxiety*, vol. 33, no. 4, 2016, pp. 323–31.

McCloskey, W., S. Iwanicki, D. Lauterbach, et al. "Are Facebook 'Friends' Helpful? Development of a Facebook-Based Measure of Social Support and Examination of Relationships among Depression, Quality of Life, and Social Support." *Cyberpsychology, Behavior and Social Networking*, vol. 18, no. 9, 2015, pp. 499–505.

Moreno, M., D. Christakis, K. Egan, et al. "A Pilot Evaluation of Associations between Displayed Depression References on Facebook and Self-Reported Depression Using a Clinical Scale." *Journal of Behavioral Health Services and Research*, vol. 39, no. 3, 2012, pp. 295–304.

Morris, R. R., S. M. Schueller, and R. W. Picard. "Efficacy of a Web-Based, Crowdsourced Peer-to-Peer Cognitive Reappraisal Platform for Depression: Randomized Controlled Trial." *Journal of Medical Internet Research*, vol. 17, no. 3, 2015, p. e72.

O'Keeffe, G. S., and K. Clarke-Pearson. "Clinical Report—The Impact of Social Media on Children, Adolescents, and Families." *Pediatrics*, vol. 127, no. 4, 2011, pp. 800–804.

Rosen, L. D., K. Whaling, S. Rab, et al. "Is Facebook Creating Idisorders"? The Link between Clinical Symptoms of Psychiatric Disorders and Technology Use, Attitudes and Anxiety." *Computers in Human Behavior*, vol. 29, no. 3, 2013, pp. 1243–54.

Rosenthal, S. R., S. Buka, B. D. L. Marshall, et al. "Negative Experiences on Facebook and Depressive Symptoms among Young Adults." *Journal of Adolescent Health*, vol. 59, no. 5, 2016, pp. 570–76.

"Social Media and Mental Health." *HelpGuide*, www.healthguide.org/articles/mental-health/social-media-and-mental-health.htm.

"Social Media Use Increases Depression and Loneliness." *University of Pennsylvania.* PennToday, penntoday.upenn.edu/news.social-media-use-increases-depression-and-loneliness.

SOCIAL MEDIA AND ISOLATION

Introduction

Social media use continues to expand as existing sites grow and new sites are created. In a Pew Research Center study in 2018, the most popular sites for all adults were YouTube (73 percent) and Facebook (68 percent). Among young adults eighteen to twenty-four, Snapchat (78 percent), and Instagram (71 percent) dominated. Scholars have identified significant connections between social media use and social isolation. Some have praised social media as a method of ameliorating isolation, but others insist that it is frequently used to avoid human contact. Some scholars have identified a negative link between mental and physical health and extensive social media use.

Background

Social media is generally identified as social interactive platforms like Facebook, Twitter, YouTube, Instagram, Snapchat, Pinterest, LinkedIn, and Reddit. Scholars tend to broaden the definition to encompass email, blogs, and instant messaging. Each medium provides channels of communication between individuals and/or groups. Since the early days of social media, scholars have studied the link between social media platforms and social isolation, the sense of being an outsider surrounded by insiders. As early as the 1920s, theorists at the Chicago School of Professional Psychology, including noted philosopher, psychologist, and educational reformer John Dewey (1859–1952), identified the role of communication in social interaction and social integration.

As the century advanced, media took on the role of facilitating the formation of a sense of community through newspapers, radio, and television, connecting individuals and households to the outside world. With the rise of the internet, that sense of community was transformed as the meaning of time and space became more fluid. Scholars have used data from the United States General Social Survey to report that the average number of close friends with whom Americans feel free to discuss their lives and feelings dropped from three to two between 1985 and 2004. The number of Americans who reported having no close friends at all rose from 8 percent to 23 percent during that same period, and the rate of social isolation climbed from 10 percent to 23 percent. Not all scholars agree with this assessment. Anthony Paik and Kennethy Sanchagrin, for instance, maintain that interview bias may have inadvertently affected the results. In the United Kingdom, scholars have identified a "crisis of friendship" as larger numbers of individuals live on their own, as the sense of community life continues to erode, and as populations become increasingly mobile.

Sherry Turkle, a psychologist trained in psychoanalysis, suggests that access to the internet had changed the nature of American life by 1985 with the rise of chat rooms, forums, bulletin boards, user groups, and other interactive online platforms. She suggests that some people, particularly those who were socially inadept or who had few real-life friends who shared their interests found online interaction more satisfying than real-life interaction. She argues that over the next decade that social isolation increased with the infinite landscape provided by the World Wide Web, the easy accessibility of mobile connections, and the global robotic revolution.

Communication studies indicate that 89 percent of Americans have had personal conversations interrupted by the use of cell phones, and 82 percent of those who have been interrupted describe those interruptions as having a negative impact on personal interaction. While interruptions may consist of family or work calls considered important, others are simply social media or email notifications that have no immediate relevance. In other studies, even the presence of a cell phone on a lunch table has been shown to interfere in personal interactions, leading to less meaningful conversations and less investment in personal contact with others.

Graham Crow has examined the role of social networks in social exclusion, which may be closely linked to social isolation, by building on sociological studies of theories of group solidarity within the context of insiders versus outsiders. Crow maintains that in order to understand the true impact of social media, scholars must pursue appropriate methodologies, understand the diverse influences exerted by social networks, and consider both the prosocial and antisocial natures of social networks. Crow contends that social networks may be stronger or weaker in response to the number of people who belong to the network, the level of connections among members, and the broader impact of social network settings.

Crow acknowledges that social networks are chiefly successful because they provide users with what is needed, offering a sense of shared culture, common language, and adherence to both written and unwritten rules. As in real life, the most enduring relationships on social media tend to be between individuals who already have a common bond, such as family, friends, former classmates, or those who share a common interest, such as hobbies or sports. However, the antisocial nature of social media is also evident in the presence of "closed groups" that allow or deny membership according to stated criteria and in the desire of some users and groups to keep knowledge away from outsiders.

Peer Pressure from the Internet

Teenagers are more likely to use social media than any other age group, and 92 percent of them access at least one social media site daily. Facebook was established by Mark Zuckerberg, Chris Hughes, and a group of friends at Harvard University in 2004. Even though it was not the first social media site, Facebook is credited with transforming social media. Six Degrees had been established in 1997, and Myspace in 2003. In 2006, American teenagers reported an average of 137 social network contacts each. Within three years, that number had skyrocketed to 440. The average teenager had three hundred Facebook friends and 79 Twitter followers. Information, images, and comments, both positive and negative, are posted and reposted, tweeted and retweeted multiple times, sometimes increasing their impact by the hundreds or thousands.

Because peer pressure is strong among adolescents, social media is being used to strengthen the differences being insider and outsider groups, thereby contributing to incidences of social isolation among teens who perceive of themselves as socially isolated. Insider/outsider status is closely linked to incidences of cyberbullying and harassment of outsiders. A number of factors have been linked to social isolation in teens, but cyberbullying presents a unique set of problems because teens do not always know who is behind the cyberbullying. Thus, they do not always know how to confront it, and they may learn to distrust classmates and even friends because of this. When teens share information among their friends, the cyberbullying may increase, exacerbating the problem still further. In some cases, teens have turned to suicide when there seemed to be no other way of dealing with the problem.

In a 2017 study of perceived social isolation (PSI) among 1,898 Americans aged nineteen to thirty-two years, Brian A. Primack and his colleagues found that PSI was linked to greater morbidity and mortality. They defined social isolation as a sense of not belonging, the feeling of being an outsider, or not being involved in meaningful relationships. Social media was identified as Facebook, Twitter, Google+, YouTube, LinkedIn, Instagram, Pinterest, Tumblr, Vine, Snapchat, and Reddit. Perceived social isolation was measured by using the Patient-Reported Outcomes Measurement Information System. Primack and colleagues found that social media use may sometimes mitigate the effects of PSI, but the study also revealed that young adults with the highest levels of social media use often feel more socially isolated than less frequent users.

High levels of social media use were also correlated with higher incidences of obesity, increased cortisol levels, disrupted sleep, impaired immune functions, impaired cognition, threats to vascular mental health and gene expression, and higher rates of depression. Those individuals most likely to be helped by extensive social media use are generally identified as those suffering from rare diseases and conditions, stigmas, the elderly, the temporarily isolated, and those with special interests. Primack et al. found that 90 percent of American adults in this age group use social media daily. Slightly more than half of all users are female. Some 57.5 percent are white, 13 percent are African American, 20.6 percent are Hispanic, and 8.9 percent are biracial or multiracial. More than 55 percent are in a committed relationship, and 35.6 percent live with a significant other. Some 38 percent come from families with annual incomes of $75,000 or more. Around 26 percent have college degrees or higher.

A number of scholars in various countries have found that the use of social media may exacerbate loneliness because some users interact on social media in order to avoid actual human contact. Some scholars have also reported that narcissists are attracted to social media because it gives them opportunities to increase their own sense of importance. US president Donald Trump is frequently quoted as an example of this phenomenon as evidenced by his "Twitter storms" in response to widespread negative reactions to his many controversial actions and statements.

Ameliorating Isolation?

When signing up to use social media sites, users create profiles or social avatars of themselves to display to others. On Facebook, for instance, information requested includes name, birthdate, place of residence, marital or relationship status, religious and political affiliation, education and employment data. Users ignore any information they do not wish to make public, and they choose whether they want to make information available to the public, to friends and friends of friends, or only to friends. Scholars have found that what is posted and what exists may vary widely because people may not be who they say they are. They may belong to a different sex, age group, race or ethnicity, be of a different sexual persuasion, and so on. Media scholars suggest that, at best, social media users tend to present their ideal selves. For other users, comparing themselves to unrealistic ideals may lead to envy of others and dissatisfaction with their own lives. In worst cases, it may strengthen the belief that one is an outsider being purposefully excluded from the larger group.

Some scholars believe that social media might be more helpful in alleviating a temporary sense of isolation than in ameliorating entrenched loneliness. For example, a study conducted in the Netherlands revealed that social media may be successful in helping individuals to deal with nighttime loneliness because it is always available, even when other individuals, perhaps within the user's own household, may be sleeping. Others have found that social media is also helpful in strengthening existing ties and in maintaining contact among family and friends who are geographically separated.

Communication scholars find that social media has been successfully used to ameliorate a sense of isolation in distinct groups. New mothers, particularly those who have been used to working or who have been socially active, may feel a strong sense of isolation when spending weeks or months caring for an infant. In a 2012 study, McDaniel, Coyne, and Holmes examined the impact of social media in dealing with this sense of isolation among 157 new mothers. The average age of the mothers was twenty-seven, and the average age of their infants was 7.9 months. These mothers spent an average of three hours each day on the internet, often writing or perusing "mommy blogs" that allowed them maintain contact with family, friends, and other new mothers. They found that blogging had a positive impact on marital satisfaction, couple conflict, parenting stress, and depression. A German study of 7,837 individuals over the age of forty who did not live in institutions, examined the use of Facebook to mitigate social isolation. It found that daily users felt less socially isolated than occasional users or those who never used Facebook.

Social media has proved to be useful in relieving loneliness among those who are isolated from society by ill health, geography, or circumstances. For many, social media sites such as Facebook have provided a connection to the rest of the world. The anthropomorphization of products is also being used in much the same way. Amazon's Alexa, Apple's Siri, and Microsoft's Cortana are all examples of twenty-first-century interactive technologies that provide individuals with a human voice that responds to requests and demands. Like social media, the anthropomorphizing of electronic devices may give some users the sense of belonging that is necessary to human well-being.

Communication scholars have long understood the need to belong as a basic need, and they suggest that in the absence of contact with others, humans may lead individuals to search for ways to connect with others though a sense of belonging to insider groups. This may be done through such behaviors as contributing to charities, choosing to buy high-status rather than low-status consumer products, purchasing larger sizes when selecting food items, or buying nostalgic items that remind them of childhood and family memories.

On Facebook, such individuals may overestimate their number of friends or accept friend requests from people they do not know. To test the use of social media among lonely individuals, Mourey, Olson, and Yoon studied 118 undergraduates at the University of Michigan, discovering that while the use of anthropomorphic products served specific purposes for socially isolated individuals, they were less useful than interactions with other humans over the long term.

—*Elizabeth Rholetter Purdy*

References

Bond, M. "Friends in High-Tech Places." *New Scientist*, vol. 222, no. 2970, 2014, pp. 40–43.

Brunskill, D. "The Dangers of Social Media for the Psyche." *Journal of Current Issues in Media and Telecommunications*, vol. 6, no. 4, 2014, pp. 391–415, search.Ebscohost.Com/Login.Aspx?Direct=True&Db=Ufh&AN=108921776&Site=Ehost-Live.

Crow, G. "Social Networks and Social Exclusion: An Overview of the Debate." *Social Networks and Social Exclusion: Sociological and Policy Perspectives*, edited by C. Phillipson, G. Allan, and D. Morgan, Routledge, 2017, pp. 7–19.

Freitas, D. *The Happiness Effect: How Social Media Is Driving a Generation to Appear Perfect at Any Cost.* Oxford UP, 2017.

Hajek, A., and H. H. König. "The Association Between Use of Online Social Network Sites and Perceived Social Isolation Among Individuals in the Second Half of Life: Results Based on a Nationally Representative Sample in Germany." *BMC Public Health*, vol. 19, no. 1, 2019, pp. 1–7.

Kisselburgh, L., and S. Matei. "The Role of Media Use, Social Interaction, and Spatial Behavior in Community Belonging." *Conference Papers—International Communication Association 2007 Annual Meeting*, 2007, pp. 1–50, search.Ebscohost.Com/Login.Aspx?Direct=True&Db=Ufh&AN=26951131&Site=Ehost-Live.

McDaniel, B., S. Coyne, and E. Holmes. "New Mothers and Media Use: Associations between Blogging, Social Networking, and Maternal Well-Being." *Maternal and Child Health Journal*, vol. 16, no. 7, 2012, pp. 1509–17.

Mourey, J. A., J. G. Olson, and C. Yoon. "Products as Pals: Engaging with Anthropomorphic Products Mitigates the Effects of Social Exclusion." *Journal of Consumer Research*, vol. 44, no. 2, 2017, pp. 414–31, Search.Ebscohost.Com/Login.Aspx?Direct=True&Db=Ufh&AN=124308268&Site=Ehost-Live.

Primack, A., A. Shensa, J. E. Sidani, et al. "Social Media Use and Perceived Social Isolation in the U.S." *American Journal of Preventive Medicine*, vol. 53, no. 1, 2017, pp. 1–8.

Turkle, Sherry. *Alone Together: Why We Expect More from Technology and Less from Each Other*. Basic Books, 2017.

SOCIAL MEDIA AND JOB HUNTING

Introduction

According to the Reuters for December 2021, there were 11 million job vacancies in the United States, which was the highest level of job openings since January 2001. These openings are largely due to the COVID-19 pandemic. Despite the increase in openings, with 1.5 jobs for every American seeking work, American workers are quitting their current positions in large numbers. As is often the case, when there are more people in search of jobs than there are jobs to fill, it is important for applicants to utilize as many tools as possible. In the case of current, COVID-related unemployment, workers are seeking to change careers and are looking for a different kind of job satisfaction. For both cases, a growing number of job seekers are turning to social media to share résumés, apply for work, and enhance their marketability to prospective employers. Websites such as LinkedIn, Twitter, and Facebook enable individuals to widen their professional network, research and apply for career opportunities, and build relationships with potential employers.

In the prepandemic competitive job market, recruiters and employers turned to social media to verify facts on an applicant's résumé, and assess an applicant's communication skills, background, and personality. Workers were often required, in fact, to apply to jobs online, and those who hadn't aligned their résumés to enormously narrow considerations for jobs, were unable to even gain access to interviews. Such was the case for many big-name corporations, who didn't need to sift through the hundreds of applicants but could have programs weed out candidates based on a narrow algorithm term set and still find many people who could do the work required.

Postpandemic, an immediate shift in social media professional networking occurred, where employers found themselves short-staffed and now sought out workers to fill many needs. In short, social media and employment application software was quickly transformed from an employer-prejudiced environment to an employee-centered asset.

Background

The birth of social media is rooted in the desire to facilitate communication. During the 1980s and 1990s, the Bulletin Board System (BBS) was the first version of today's social media. It was accessed over telephone lines via a modem, and although very slow, it gave users a platform to share information and files, post announcements, and download games.

The 1980s was also a time of accelerated internet evolution as home computers became more prevalent in American households. Prodigy Communications Corporation was the first provider to offer home computer users online access (via telephone lines) to weather reports, stock market numbers, and breaking news. At the end of the 1980s, Tim Berners-Lee, a British scientist at the European Organization for Nuclear Research (CERN), created the very first website, which explained how to access information online and how to create a website. This then led to what was called the "World Wide Web" in the 1990s with millions of people having access to over 1 million sites.

Among the myriad websites available on the internet in the mid-1990s was Classmates.com, which allowed users to take part in virtual class reunions using instant messaging and blogging. Other websites, many of which were short-lived, allowed users to create profiles in order to better connect with others. Widely believed to be the first social networking site, Six Degrees was launched in 1997 and allowed users to send messages to and post bulletin board items to family, friends, and acquaintances

At the turn of the twenty-first century, handheld devices with web capabilities (such as Palm Pilots and, later, smartphones) increased the availability of internet access. Meanwhile, the evolution of social networking sites like Friendster and Myspace made social networking commonplace. In the early 2000s, two of the most dominant social networking sites, LinkedIn and Facebook, went online. LinkedIn has since become the most popular site for business and professional networking.

Social Media as a Professional Resource

Social media is used by employers and by individuals seeking employment. As of 2021, LinkedIn remained the most popular site for employers and recruiters to post job openings and to screen and contact candidates. As of June 2021, the site boasted a total of over 756 million users, with 310 million monthly users. There were over 15 million job openings posted on the site, accruing over 8 billion dollars in annual revenue for LinkedIn. It is also one of the most necessary sites for viewing and responding to job postings (using the site's cover-letter feature and uploading a résumé). Other popular social media sites used for employment searches are Facebook, and Twitter. In 2017, SmartRecruiters.com reported that more than 60 percent of job postings are submitted to specialty job boards.

Job postings are viewed and acted on by hundreds and perhaps thousands of candidates. In order to attract the most qualified candidates for a position, employers and recruiters have to ensure that any job postings, company profiles, blog entries, or other social media communications are informative and clearly written. Similarly, candidates must ensure that their personal profiles are also well-written and relevant since individual profiles, as an extension of the résumé, should highlight professional development and demonstrate the pertinent qualifications prospective employers would seek. Many career counselors recommend that LinkedIn profiles be geared toward the job the candidate wants rather than the job the candidate has. Profiles should also be geographically relevant. LinkedIn postings, for example, can be organized by country, state, and municipal region.

Social media sites can also be venues for candidates to learn about the culture and management of prospective employers that interest them. Similarly, such platforms may allow candidates to learn about and discuss business trends and topics of interest within their industry or an industry they wish to join. Finally, sites like LinkedIn enable users to connect and communicate with friends, colleagues, or other professional networking contacts who may introduce them to prospective employers or recruiters.

An important distinction of job searching via social media sites is that information is shared among an individual's network. Postings can be potentially deleterious to one's job pursuits, but an informative, well-constructed, and relevant post can be valuable and set a candidate apart in the eyes of a potential employer.

Trends in Social Media and Job Hunting

According to a July 2016 survey by the social recruiting software company Jobvite, 87 percent of recruiters polled assessed prospective candidates through LinkedIn and 43 percent of respondents did so using Facebook while nearly 60 percent of job seekers research prospective employers through social media platforms. LinkedIn is also a popular social networking site for professional development. Facebook, blogs, and Instagram are used less often by recruiters and employers. Traditional job-search websites like Indeed, Glassdoor, and Monster also provide social media venues where recruiters, employers, and candidates can network, share information, and post and respond to job openings. Despite its 140-character limit, Twitter is also used by job hunters and employers. It is especially important that posts or tweets are well-written, clear, and use proper spellings.

Appearances matter greatly to recruiters and employers, both online and in person. According to the Jobvite survey, 41 percent of respondents felt that candidate photographs influenced their first impressions and were sensitive to casual dress in particular. Other assessment factors include photographs of a candidate's alcohol or marijuana use, oversharing of personal information, typographical errors, self-portraits ("selfies"), and even political affiliation shared on social media sites.

The volume and diversity of employment-related social media outlets can sometimes cause confusion for job seekers and employers alike since the medium seems to continually evolve with websites using increasingly cutting-edge techniques to effectively connect businesses and candidates. Before the pandemic, many qualified employees who did not amend their resumés and cover letters to contain app buzzwords specific to jobs were immediately rejected from consideration—a severe limitation of such simplistic algorithms that the corporate world seemed unconcerned about. Postpandemic, however, the job market shifted. Jobs suddenly became plentiful for employees who now had choices. Employers became dependent instead upon the restrictive algorithm-based applications (apps), and suddenly were faced with the reality that good people were available but could no longer be accessed.

—*Michael Auerbach*

References

Adams, Susan. "LinkedIn Still Rules as the Top Job Search Technology Tool, Survey Says." *Forbes*, 12 Aug. 2013.

Aslam, Salam. "81 LinkedIn Statistics You Need to Know in 2022." *Omnicore*, 4 Jan. 2022, omnicore-agency.com/LinkedIn-statistics/.

Ceniza-Levine, Caroline. "10 Ways to Use Social Media to Supercharge Your Job Search." Time, 4 Apr. 2016, time.com/money/4278588/10-ways-to-use-social-media-to-supercharge-your-job-search.

"Economic News Release: Job Openings and Labor Turnover Summary." *BLS*. US Bureau of Labor Statistics, 8 May 2018, www.bls.gov/news.release/jolts.nr0.htm.

"The Employment Situation—April 2018." *BLS*. US Bureau of Labor Statistics, 4 May 2018, www.bls.gov/news.release/pdf/empsit.pdf.

"Jobvite Recruiter Nation Report 2016: The Annual Social Recruiting Survey." *Jobvite*, July 2016, www.jobvite.com/wp-content/uploads/2016/09/RecruiterNation2016.pdf.

Liu, Aaron. "The History of Social Networking." *Digital Trends*. Designtechnica, 5 Aug. 2014.

Langmia, Kehbuma, et al. *Social Media: Pedagogy and Practice.* University Press of America, 2014.

McAlister, Matthew. "How Social Media Helps Your Job Search." *Career Glider*, 7 Jan. 2015.

Mutikani, Lucia. "U.S. Job Openings Jump to 11 Million; Fewer Workers Voluntarily Quitting." *Reuters*, 8 Dec. 2021, reuters.com/business/us-job-openings-jump-11-million-october-2021-12-08/.

Sinacole, Patricia Hunt. "Use Social Media Wisely When Job Hunting." *Boston Globe*. Boston Globe Media Partners, 26 Oct. 2014.

SOCIAL MEDIA AND LAW ENFORCEMENT

Introduction

Law enforcement engages with social media by using it as a means of public outreach as well as an investigative tool. Agencies face new challenges in policing crimes conducted on or with the assistance of social media and formulating social media policies to govern department employees' behavior. Because phones capable of recording and broadcasting citizens' encounters with law enforcement are ubiquitous, social media has become a means of challenging police accounts that differ from eyewitness testimony.

Background

Since the advent of the World Wide Web in the early 1990s and the rise of social networking services in the twenty-first century, social media has become an important aspect of the world of law enforcement. On the one hand, it offers new tools for crime fighting, crime prevention, and engagement with the public; on the other hand, it has made law enforcement officers and others vulnerable in new ways to harassment and online abuse and has changed the demands of off-duty behavior. By 2013, one survey showed that 96 percent of police departments were using social media in some capacity.

In the 1970s through the 1980s, local police departments across the country increased their spending precipitously in order to follow the directives of the Richard Nixon and Ronald Reagan administrations (primarily) in prioritizing the War on Drugs. The rising crime rates, which peaked in the 1990s and have subsequently substantially declined, were used to justify these expenditures, leading to police departments modernizing their equipment and expanding arsenals. In the twenty-first century, one of the new areas of expenditure for police departments has been computer software and hardware, including extensive software packages that are designed for or can be used to monitor social media for crime prevention and criminal investigation purposes.

The relationship between social media and law enforcement can be considered in three broad areas: the ways social media enables crime, commonly including harassment and fraud; the ways social media is used by law enforcement to investigate or prevent crime; and the interactions between police and the public on social media. Law enforcement may use social media to investigate crimes that have occurred on social media, and public engagement on social media is frequently part of a missing persons investigation.

Social networking sites can make members of the public vulnerable to a number of crimes, ranging from burglars who target their homes knowing that they are not home, to phishing and other forms of fraud that depend on getting specific personal information (passwords, financial information, or just the biographical information necessary to answer security questions) from victims. Making the public aware of better social media security and privacy practices is a form of opportunity blocking, which prevents crimes of opportunity and has become an important enough part of law enforcement's public engagement that some graduate programs in criminal justice now offer courses on opportunity blocking (not limited to social media applications).

Social media can be valuable for certain kinds of investigations, especially when information needs to be circulated or gathered quickly. It is common for police in the twenty-first century to circulate photos on social media bearing on missing persons and suspected child abduction cases, for example, as well as photos of suspects or persons of interest in criminal investigations. This is particularly true with the rise of ubiquitous digital photography, as more and more private residences are equipped with low-cost digital security cameras. An investigation into neighborhood theft and vandalism may be assisted by half a dozen photos of suspects provided by residents. Time-sensitive notifications can also be issued on social media about road closures, accidents impacting traffic, weather-related emergencies, and police situations in progress (such as a vehicle pursuit, or an armed suspect on the loose).

The internet has also impacted the sale of illegal goods. Pawn shops and other used-goods shops, which used to be the default means for burglars to sell their stolen goods, are considerably less common than they were in the twentieth century, because of the rise of eBay, Craigslist, and other venues for e-commerce. The internet—in part because of its anonymity—has enabled new vectors of selling illegal goods and services. While robust commercial auction sites like eBay are vigorous in enforcing their terms of service in order to prevent the sale of illegal goods, many smaller services, and services not specifically intended for e-commerce, are more lax about it or rely on user reporting to discover rule breaking. While the "dark web"—networks of web content not appearing in normal search engine results—has become infamous for anonymous market sites selling firearms and drugs, often using bitcoin and other cryptocurrency as the medium of exchange in order to safeguard transactors' identities, there are also illegal transactions found throughout social media.

In essence, law enforcement faces a problem similar to what they faced with the War on Drugs: the policing of activities that primarily take place in private spaces, such as homes and cars. To secure arrests, police disproportionately targeted public spaces in predominantly low-income minority neighborhoods and housing projects. Craigslist has similarly suffered disproportionate levels of attention, simply because it is identifiable and accessible, compared with the difficulty of finding someone offering prescription drugs for sale for recreational use in a friends-locked Facebook post. Social media platforms, however, are believed to offer safe spaces for considerable criminal activity. There have been a number of prominent cases involving Facebook groups distributing child pornography or illegally obtained nude photographs of nonconsenting adults, for example.

A wide variety of crimes occur or begin online, grouped under the rubric "cybercrime," or in the language of some laws, "computer crime." Originally referring principally to hacking, cybercrime also refers to the dissemination of child pornography, numerous forms of fraud, extortion and blackmail conducted online, and predation on minors. Whether or not cyberbullying is a crime, and what constitutes cyberbullying for legal purposes, varies by jurisdiction, though harassment laws often apply.

Social media is often involved in hacking attempts—many people whose personal accounts are hacked were not hacked in the sense that their passwords were figured out by computer software, but because they were fooled into revealing their password or other information to a hacker talking to them on social media, generally posing as someone else, such as a Facebook employee or a family member. Social media can also be used to organize offline crime, whether this means the flash crime of 2011, whereby "flash robs" were organized by teenagers in Chicago, Philadelphia, and Cleveland to shoplift local businesses en masse, or a sexual predator grooming a minor online before persuading them to meet somewhere.

Sometimes the role of social media in law enforcement is simple: A criminal is caught because he posts about his crimes, thinking no one will know. Police with information about where and when a crime was committed can use geotagging to compare a suspect's social media check-ins—but sometimes people are caught simply because their confession is reported by a social media connection to police.

Strengths and Dangers

Social media contributes to the growth of subcultures, the spread of ideas, and the making of social connections that might not otherwise be possible. This is both its strength and the danger it represents. Social media has been a boon for everyone from hobbyists who are able to find more people to talk to about, for instance, vintage record collecting or non-western fantasy novels, to lesbian, gay, bisexual, transgender, and queer (LGBTQ) youth in rural or otherwise remote communities who are able to find an online community that accepts and validates them. It has also engendered the spread of rumors, personal attacks, death threats, and calls to violence.

Social media has a demonstrable impact on suicides both because cyberbullying has precipitated a number of teen and youth suicides and because of behavioral contagion, whereby vulnerable young people are spurred to suicide by the suicide of others. In the case of suicide trends and other cases of behavioral contagion leading to harmful or criminal behavior, public engagement is critically important, both on social media and through other vectors (local or national media, for instance, and in-person interactions such as "Coffee with a Cop" or other public outreach events hosted by local police departments).

In the twenty-first century, local, state, and federal law enforcement agencies have relied on social media monitoring as a controversial form of crime prevention. This likely began at the federal level; the PATRIOT Act passed after 9/11 grants broad powers of surveillance to the federal government in the name of national security, including surveillance of American citizens (in specific circumstances). While the National Security Agency and other bodies concerned with fighting terrorism may monitor e-mail, online messaging, and web browsing, smaller agencies like state and local police departments are limited to the monitoring of social media. Originally, this meant infiltration of online groups by undercover agents, such as to uncover information about local criminal activity, smuggling rings, or attempted terrorist activity. Expensive software packages have allowed for different forms of monitoring, by gathering up large amounts of data and analyzing them for specific patterns. As of 2016, the International Association of Police Chiefs reported that at least 550 state and local police agencies in forty-four states were using such packages, with agencies like the Texas Department of Public Safety and the County of Sacramento spending about $70,000 on software alone over three years.

Many civil rights groups have raised concerns about the infringement of citizens' rights by such monitoring projects, but the most alarming development in this trend, accelerated since 2016, is the use of social media monitoring to keep tabs on protest and political activist groups, especially those concerned with police violence or affiliated with the Black Lives Matter movement. The Oregon Department of Justice, for instance, used the Digital Stakeout software package to monitor people who used any of about thirty hashtags on social media, one of which was #BlackLivesMatter.

Police were also alleged to have monitored Facebook and other geo-tagged social media check-ins in their handling of the Standing Rock Sioux Reservation oil pipeline protests of 2016–17. Hashtag and geo-tagged monitoring is relatively simple. Much more involved is sentiment analysis, which sifts through social media data (or any other text) in order to determine the emotional state or affective attitudes of the author. Data which has been subject to sentiment analysis can then be searched: for Twitter users in Oklahoma who have expressed hostility to the police, for example, or for Facebook users in Rhode Island who have discussed planned protests using language suggesting anger or violence.

In the aftermath of many mass shootings, an examination of the shooters' social media profiles has revealed numerous red flags that, hindsight suggests, should have been noticed and acted on by someone. In some cases, this has literally meant announcing the intent to commit murder, while in others it has meant posting or reposting hateful content, violent sentiments, and showing an allegiance to white supremacist or even to incel groups (which often leads to violence against women and/or to suicide).

Many have called for social media companies to do more to control the use of their platforms as a vector for hate—for instance, bomber Cesar Sayoc had been reported for harassment and violent threats, which Twitter had ruled not to be a violation of their policies. Some representatives of law enforcement have pushed for broader access to social media in order to have a richer stream of data to analyze in search of potential crime.

Social Media and Social Welfare

More and more police departments and law enforcement agencies have adopted social media policies to guide the conduct of their employees online, whether during work hours or while off-duty. Policies are usually divided into sections bearing on investigative use, official community engagement (such as the conduct of the official department Twitter or Facebook account), and off-duty employee use. Such policies are usually fairly straightforward and common-sensical: Employees should not post offensive or abusive content, should not engage with members of the public in abusive ways, should watch their use of language, and should not discuss job matters in an unprofessional or unbecoming manner, for instance.

Though called "social media policies," most guidelines are not actually limited in scope to social networking services; the Department of Defense's policy explicitly includes image- and video-hosting web services, Wikis, blogs, and data mash-ups, in addition to social networks, as well as clarifying that policy about official communications applies both to department websites and to official presences on external sites, such as the chairman of the joint chiefs of staff's Twitter account. Policies also address the use of agency internet resources for personal use (such as checking Facebook or Twitter on the office computer while at work).

The larger the agency, the more likely that policy governing the official social media presence of the agency is both strict and detailed. A small local police department may use broad language like "appropriate," both because the department's exposure is limited and because the staff is small. Federal agencies, on the other hand, represent an important part of the American government and have strict and often granular policies governing their public-facing activities. Even local agencies may be specific in some of their policy points, though. For instance, the police department of Northampton, Massachusetts, a small college town, has a brief social media policy but uses specific language in noting that any photos of on-duty personnel or police property must be approved for display by the chief before being posted anywhere online; that no employee may gossip about internal matters with nonemployees; and that any information released about any crime, accident, or violation must be approved by the Public Information Function. Further, employees are reminded that any of their interactions online may have consequences during cross-examination or future employment.

Unlike in-person conversations, online activity leaves a record and is visible to people who were not part of the original intended audience. Even posts made "friends-only" may be screenshotted and shared by people within that circle to people outside it. There have been a number of high-profile cases in which police officers or other police department employees have been criticized for social media posts expressing opinions inappropriate for their profession. In 2017, Officer Tom Newberry of West Linn, Oregon, was fired for a number of social media posts expressing hostility toward African Americans and the Black Lives Matter movement, including references to running protestors over and using protestors for target practice. He subsequently sued the city and was awarded over $100,000 in lost wages. In 2018, rookie police officer Sean Bostwick was fired for posting a Snapchat photo of himself, in uniform, with a racist caption about the nature of his work. Unlike Newberry, Bostwick had little recourse; as a rookie officer, he was still in the probation period, which expedited his being fired.

Police officers, in encountering the public, are aware of the likelihood that someone is recording their activity on a camera phone and may be posting the video on social media. The 2016 shooting death of Philando Castile during a traffic stop was partially broadcast on Facebook Live, a feature of the platform that allows the streaming of events in real time. Some researchers believe the potential for this level of scrutiny may act as a curb on police violence. Officers' testimony is often met with skepticism where a witness video shows use of force in an arrest or police shooting. Police departments after the shooting death of Michael Brown in 2014, began adopting the use of body cameras to provide more context, this from the perspective of the officers involved, to visual presentations of disputed accounts.

—Bill Kte'pi

References

Bejan, V., M. Hickman, W. S. Parkin, and V. F. Pozo. "Primed for Death: Law Enforcement-Citizen Homicides, Social Media, and Retaliatory Violence." *PLOS One*, vol. 13, no. 1, 2018, pp. 1–23.

Beshears, M. "Effectiveness of Police Social Media Use." *American Journal of Criminal Justice*, vol. 42, no. 3, 2017, pp. 489–501. search.ebscohost.com/login.aspx?direct=true&db=sxi&an=124485166&site=ehost-live.

Brown, G. R. "The Blue Line on Thin Ice: Police Use of Force Modifications in the Era of Cameraphones and YouTube." *British Journal of Criminology*, vol. 56, no. 2, 2016, pp. 293–312, search.ebscohost.com/login.aspx?direct=true&db=sxi&an=113170632&site=ehost-live.

Goldsmith, A. "Disgracebook Policing: Social Media and the Rise of Police Indiscretion." *Policing & Society*, vol. 25, no. 3, 2015, pp. 249–67, rsearch.

ebscohost.com/login.aspx?direct=true&db=sxi&an=101347947&site=ehost-live.

Jones, M. J. "Shady Trick or Legitimate Tactic—Can Law Enforcement Officials Use Fictitious Social Media Accounts to Interact with Suspects?" *American Journal of Trial Advocacy*, vol. 40, no. 1, 2016, pp. 69–81.

Owen, S. "Monitoring Social Media and Protest Movements: Ensuring Political Order Through Surveillance and Surveillance Discourse." *Social Identities*, vol. 23, no. 6, 2017, pp. 688–700, search.ebscohost.com/login.aspx?direct=true&db=sxi&AN=125909013&site=ehost-live.

Prichard, J., P. Watters, T. Krone, et al. "Social Media Sentiment Analysis: A New Empirical Tool for Assessing Public Opinion on Crime?" *Current Issues in Criminal Justice*, vol. 27, no. 2, 2015, pp. 217–36, search.ebscohost.com/login.aspx?direct=true&db=sxi&an=111395844&site=ehost-live.

Schneider, C. J., and D. Trottier. "The 2011 Vancouver Riot and the Role of Facebook in Crowd-Sourced Policing." *BC Studies*, vol. 175, 2012, pp. 57–72.

Spizman, R. J., and M. K. Miller. "Plugged-In Policing: Student Perceptions of Law Enforcement's Use of Social Media." *Applied Psychology in Criminal Justice*, vol. 9, no. 2, 2013, pp. 100–123, search.ebscohost.com/login.Aspx?Direct=True&Db=Sxi&AN=95588738&Site=Ehost-live.

Stott, T. C., A. Maceachron, and N. Gustavsson. "Social Media and Child Welfare: Policy, Training, and the Risks and Benefits from the Administrator's Perspective." *Advances In Social Work*, vol. 17, no. 2, 2016, pp. 221–34, search.ebscohost.com/login.aspx?direct=true&db=sxi&an=121190728&site=ehost-live.

Trottier, D. "Coming to Terms with Social Media Monitoring: Uptake and Early Assessment." *Crime, Media, Culture*, vol. 11, no. 3, 2015, pp. 317–33, search.ebscohost.com/login.aspx?direct=true&db=sxi&an=111190330&site=ehost-live.

Williams, M. L., A. Edwards, A. Housley, et al. "Policing Cyber-Neighbourhoods: Tension Monitoring and Social Media Networks." *Policing & Society*, vol. 23, no. 4, 2013, pp. 461–81, search.ebscohost.com/login.aspx?direct=true&db=sxi&AN=91557440&site=ehost-live.

SOCIAL MEDIA AND RELIGION

Introduction

While the United States is generally considered one of the more religious countries in the West, this is not reflected in participation in organized religious services. The majority of members in most denominations (the exceptions being evangelical Protestants, historically black Protestants, Jehovah's Witnesses, and Mormons) attend services less than once a month, with about a quarter attending "seldom or never." It has become clear to religious studies scholars and other social scientists that in the age of social media, a lack of physical attendance does not always indicate a lack of religious engagement. Even before social media, television—especially for Protestants—had similarly offered an alternative means of engagement in the 1980s rise of televangelism.

Online outreach groups can help connect people to faith communities who have either felt alienated from communities in the past or have difficulty attending in person—such as housebound or elderly members, or soldiers stationed abroad. Many religious leaders have Facebook pages or Twitter accounts; the author and rabbi David Wolpe uses Facebook to respond to questions about faith and make motivational or thought-provoking posts. OurJewishCommunity.org is a global outreach launched in 2008 by Beth Adam, an independent Jewish congregation in Cincinnati, and reaches a community much larger than that of the local congregation. Twitter and Facebook have also been fertile grounds for interfaith dialogue; it has become common in the era of social media for the Muslim celebration of Ramadan to be greeted with Christians making shows of solidarity with the Muslim community, and similarly Muslims, especially in the United States, sometimes do the same during Lent, under hashtags like #Muslims4Lent.

Since the start of the COVID-19 pandemic, 30 percent of US adults reported attending services online via streaming services (YouTube or Facebook Live) with 57 percent of self-identifying religious adults who regularly attend services admitting to watching services online or on television during the COVID-19 period.

Background

Social media has also provided forums for religionists to reconnect with faith communities, particularly those who have no connection to a local community. Over the second half of the twentieth century, evangelical and Pentecostal forms of Christianity overtook the relatively moderate denominations of mainline Protestantism in the United States, with the net effect of making American Protestantism more conservative. This was exacerbated by the attrition of moderates and liberals raised in Christian traditions, as the social pressures to attend church were lessened over time, and for many it was easier to either consciously leave the church or drift away than to seek out a new and more compatible community.

In the twenty-first century, some of these lapsed or unaffiliated Christians found a new sense of community online. Facebook includes several Progressive Christian groups that receive thousands of posts a day, as well as a number Christian pages with thousands of likes that identify as Progressive, Christian Left, or lesbian, gay, bisexual, transgender, and queer (LGBTQ). Needless to say, there are also conservative Christian groups, though fewer of these seem to be made up of people returning to a faith community, and instead may represent an additional religion-adjacent activity for churchgoing Christians.

There is more to the intersection between social media and religion than outreach. Social media offer a rich body of data for looking at religious trends. Every year since 2008, Bible Gateway's Stephen Smith has compiled a top 100 list and word cloud about the things Twitter users publicly announce they are giving up for Lent. In 2011, for example, the most common choice was Twitter itself, followed by Facebook. While many of the top choices were unsurprising—various unhealthy foods like soft drinks or chocolate, vices like alcohol or swearing—other trends were much more interesting. Over a quarter of the top 100 results were jokes (e.g., giving up school for Lent, giving up "giving things up" for Lent), while many of those were either directly or indirectly antireligion: Lent itself ranked 8th, religion 14th, Catholicism 26th, and virginity 37th.

Social media have also been important in the study of the "nones." "Nones" is an increasingly common shorthand for those who respond to surveys about religious affiliation with any variation of "no religion" or "none of the above." It is not the same as atheism or agnosticism, but rather includes both nontheists and those who evince some kind of religious or spiritual beliefs ("spiritual but not religious" is a common self-descriptor) but reject affiliation with any specific organized religion. Historically a footnote in American religious demographics, in the 2010s nones grew to about a quarter of the population and over a third of millennials. In the twentieth century, nones were largely ignored both by the media and by many scholars; in a sense, they were taken at face value as having no religious belief. Their growing numbers attracted enough attention that studies have shown this could not be further from the truth; nones seem to have as many specific, concrete beliefs as religionists do, including supernatural beliefs. It is not the beliefs they reject as much as affiliation with, or the leadership of, religious institutions.

The study of nones on social media is often undertaken by people seeking to explain why Americans are supposedly "losing" their religion. While that is an erroneous characterization of the nones, those efforts have nonetheless produced a large body of data. The number of young people who say they have never attended religious services, for example, has steadily increased (though many of those who have never attended services nevertheless identify with a specific organized religion, usually that of their parents). Religious leaders sometimes blame social media for what they perceive as a lack of religious engagement; social media are condemned as narcissistic, superficial, or distractions. Analyses of the social media feeds of nones, however, shows this is off base—that many nones actively engage in discussions of religion or religion-adjacent ideas like morality.

A phenomenon closely related to the rise of the nones, also evinced mainly through studies of social media, is not yet well-defined but often described as "picking and choosing" religious beliefs. Whether it is meaningfully true or not, there is a received construction of religious belief as something that one picks up from one's family and local faith community. Implicit is the notion that religious belief is more or less standardized within a denomination or other religious grouping: There may be unanswered or unanswerable questions, but there is a specific viewpoint and framework from which religious issues are seen, held in common by all congregations and members of that grouping.

There are important exceptions that disprove this generalization: Even apart from the phenomenon of syncretism, there is the interest shown by many American Christians and Jews in Buddhism since the middle of the twentieth century, and the secularization-cum-commercialization of yoga and meditation as a means for Americans to adopt religious practices from outside their religious community.

Pick-and-choosers, rather than embrace the whole of religious teachings offered by a given denomination, adopt a customized set of beliefs from those to which they have been exposed. It should be pointed out that "picking and choosing" is a charge conservative and literalist members of most religions levy against liberal members, amounting to the accusation that a nonliteral interpretation of traditional beliefs is a piecemeal version of the faith.

That is a separate phenomenon from people who, for example, identify as Christian but believe in karma, reincarnation, or other concepts from Dharmic faiths, or who identify as Protestant but observe Lent and revere the Virgin Mary. (Studies of Lent on Twitter like the above have found that this Protestant observation of the liturgical season is surprisingly common.) There is some evidence that use of social media may be correlated with this kind of loose approach to religious practice, but without more rigorous research it can be difficult to separate out social media use from other demographic factors such as age, education level, and economic class.

Social Media Promoting Radicalization

Social media have provided a fertile ground for the radicalization of young people online, usually young men. Radicalization is a process whereby the individual's political, religious, and social ideas become increasingly extreme, especially when associated with an existing set of extreme ideas and practices. The media primarily associates radicalization with violent Muslim extremists, which has some justification in the fact that terrorist and other extreme groups have developed sophisticated recruitment approaches that very consciously use social media and online video to shift the opinion of potential recruits and isolate them from others.

However, some argue that there is a disproportionate focus on Islam, not simply because it exaggerates the presence of radicals within one of the world's largest religions by shining a light on those elements, but because when discussions of radicalization and terrorism focus so much on Islam, the terminology and norms involved in such discussions develop in such a way as to exclude non-Muslim manifestations. The most obvious example is the failure of the American government to categorize the Ku Klux Klan as a terrorist group, when experts agree it is the oldest such group in the country. This contributes to a tendency in the media to discuss terrorism and white supremacy as separate phenomena, rather than white supremacy as one type of terrorism.

Radicalization depends on group identity. People who feel alienated in their community or unhappy with their lives benefit from the support they receive from these groups, and from having other people affirm the beliefs that previously may have been the subject of criticism. As preradicalized people find a community of people who do not reject them for their extreme views, and even reward them for such and introduce them to new extensions of those views, they experience gratification that, on one hand, is as simple as the gratification of finding someone to discuss your favorite obscure band or movie with; and that on the other, has far more serious consequences. Social media is powerful here because it can connect people independent of distance.

White supremacists and the alt-right have flourished online, and developed elaborate sets of injokes, memes, and codes to identify and communicate with one another. The cartoon Pepe the Frog, taken from a web comic unaffiliated with the Far Right, became the unofficial mascot of the alt-right via message boards 4chan and Reddit. Crusader iconography was adopted to convey Islamophobic messages. The McDonald's commercial character Mac Tonight was used for memes about antiblack violence. And most notably, as conceived of by the neo-Nazi podcast *The Daily Shoah*, the "echo" was used as a tactic to mark Jewish journalists by surrounding their name in triple parentheses ((())). One of the main functions of all this coding is to escape content filters. Racial slurs and other language can be banned from message boards and social media, but images would need to be reported by a third party to result in action, and if the meaning of an image, term, or meme is known only to those familiar with the coding, action is unlikely to be taken. The echo serves the same purpose—it is essentially a way to refer to someone by an anti-Jewish slur through inventing a new one that filters cannot act against. Many Twitter users have fought back against the alt-right by echoing their own screen names.

—Bill Kte'pi

References

Cheong, P. H., P. Fischer-Nielsen, S. Gelfgren, et al., editors. *Digital Religion, Social Media, and Culture: Perspectives, Practices, and Futures.* Peter Lang, 2012.

Coman, I. A., and M. Coman. "Religion, Popular Culture and Social Media: The Construction of a Religious Leader Image on Facebook." *Essachess*, vol. 10, no. 2, 2017, pp. 129–43, search.ebscohost.com/login.aspx?direct=true&db=sxi&an=126979138&site=Ehost-live.

Douglas, C. "Religion and Fake News: Faith-Based Alternative Information Ecosystems in the US and Europe." *Review of Faith & International Affairs*, vol. 16, no. 1, 2018, pp. 61–73, doi:10.1080/15570274.2018.1433522.

Henry, G. B. "Are Social Media Changing Religion?" *USA Today*, 21 June 2010, search.ebscohost.com/login.aspx?direct=true&db=asn&an=j0e230620908010&site=ehost-live.

Ketelaar, P. E., R. Konig, E. G. Smit, et al. "In Ads We Trust: Religiousness as a Predictor of Advertising Trustworthiness and Avoidance." *Journal of Consumer Marketing*, vol. 32, no. 3, 2015, pp. 190–98, search.ebscohost.com/login.aspx?direct=true&db=bsu&an=102992949&site=ehost-live.

Mitchem, S. Y. "Editorial: Technologies of Religions." *Cross Currents*, vol. 65, no. 4, 2015, pp. 408–9, search.ebscohost.com/login.aspx?direct=true&db=asn&an=112708103&site=ehost-live.

Nortey, Justin. "More Houses of Worship Are Returning to Normal Operations, But In-Person Attendance Is Unchanged Since Fall." *PEW Research Center*, 22 Mar. 2022, pewresearch.org/fact-tank/2022/03/22/more-houses-of-worship-are-returning-to-normal-operations-but-in-person-attendance-is-unchanged-since-fall/.

Ott, K. "Hacking the System." *Journal of Feminist Studies in Religion*, vol. 31, no. 2, 2015, pp. 140–44, search.ebscohost.com/login.aspx?direct=true&Db=asn&an=110195289&site=ehost-live.

Ratcliff, A. J., J. Mccarty, and M. Ritter. "Religion and New Media: A Uses and Gratifications Approach." *Journal of Media & Religion*, vol. 16, no. 1, 2017, pp. 15–26, search.ebscohost.com/Login.Aspx?Direct=True&Db=Asn&AN=121290536&Site=Ehost-live.

Slama, M. "Practising Islam Through Social Media in Indonesia." *Indonesia & The Malay World*, vol. 46, no. 134, 2018, pp. 1–4, doi:10.1080/13639811.2018.1416798.

Wood, M., H. Center, and S. C. Parenteau. "Social Media Addiction and Psychological Adjustment: Religiosity and Spirituality in the Age of Social Media." *Mental Health, Religion & Culture*, vol. 19, no. 9, 2016, pp. 972–83, doi:10.1080/13674676.2017.1300791.

SOCIAL MEDIA AND THE SELF-ESTEEM OF ITS USERS

Introduction

Around the world, 3.03 billion people classify themselves as active social media users. For many, social media provides a channel of communication with family, friends, and colleagues. For others, it offers a sense of community that they lack in their daily lives. Because social media provides ample opportunity for users to express approval of one another's posts, tweets, comments, and images, scholars have found that social media use may be closely related to self-esteem. Studying the link between social media and self-esteem among teenagers is particularly important because 97 percent of teens have daily online access, and teenagers are particularly vulnerable to social media threats to self-esteem.

Background

Scholars who study social identity theory have long identified the innate need of human beings to belong to groups, allowing them to identify themselves as insiders rather than outsiders while developing a strong sense of self. Scholars have reported contradictory findings when examining the correlation between self-esteem and social media use. Excessive time on social media has been shown to increase incidences of low self-esteem, anxiety, depression, loneliness, eating disorders, somatic complaints, and cybervictimization.

Studies have also shown that heavy Facebook users, those who spend more than two hours a day on Facebook, are more likely than other users to have low self-esteem. Other studies have found that social media may improve physical and mental health by providing a sense of community and reducing individual stress. Some researchers have identified a link between low self-esteem and the attractiveness of images posted on social media. Other scholars have linked self-esteem to the frequency of status updates, comments, images uploaded, and participation in discussion groups, suggesting that users with high self-esteem are more likely to post frequently, receive positive comments, and engage in discussions with others.

While there may be significant fluidity in group membership, with individuals belonging to a number of different groups, self-esteem is higher when individuals belong to groups with which they are able to identify because such groups influence the way that individuals define their own worth. Within the field of computer mediated communication, scholars have used social identity theory to examine both self- and group esteem.

Between 2005 and 2015, the use of social media expanded dramatically. Studies indicate that social media use rose in all categories: from 55 percent to 76 percent among adolescents, 12 percent to 90 percent among adults eighteen to twenty-nine, from 8 percent to 77 percent among adults thirty to forty-nine, from 5 percent to 51 percent among adults fifty to sixty-four, and from 2 percent to 35 percent among adults sixty-five and over. According to the PEW Research Center's 2018 report, 73 percent of all American adults actively use YouTube, and 68 percent actively use Facebook. In smaller numbers, they also use Instagram (36 percent), Pinterest (27 percent), LinkedIn (25 percent), Twitter (24 percent), and WhatsApp (22 percent).

Social media sites use various methods to allow users to express affirmation, which is also called "paralinguistic digital affordances." On Facebook, for instance, a "like" may mean approval, or it may simply indicate acknowledgement that a post has been read or an image seen. Thus, a like is used to respond to a cancer diagnosis or a death in the family as well as to a photograph of a new baby or a wedding or prom picture. Studies conducted on social media suggest that online persona are frequently idealized versions of a user's actual self.

This may be unintentional as users strive to appear admirable to their friends or self-select what to share and what to hold back, such as only posting flattering photos. Some users may use imaging software to improve or touch up photos. Misleading profiles may also be the result of individuals consciously choosing to appear as someone extremely different from themselves. Facebook is frequently chosen as the focus of academic study because it has more than 2.27 billion users worldwide and is used by all age groups. Twitter, which has 300 million daily users, is also widely studied.

In a study conducted in Thailand, Yokfa Isaranon found that many Facebook users use the site to present their best selves to other members of their world, thereby boosting self-esteem through both wall posting and photo sharing. Self-esteem was measured in part by the role of affirmation, and Isaranon found that affirmation tends to be higher among moderate users than among occasional users. Self-esteem was highest when Facebook users constantly received positive feedback from other users. Affirmation rates may be boosted by such actions as controlling privacy settings, filtering out unwanted information, and careful selection of friends. Wohn, Carr, and Hayes found that Facebook users ascribe significant meaning to digital affordances, considering that a high number of likes indicates strong social support from friends. Users who rarely experience likes or other forms of affirmation are more likely than others to suffer from low self-esteem. However, Wohn et al., found only a weak link between perceived social media support and loneliness.

Applications

Technology and social media scholar Danah Boyd has spent considerable time among teenagers, and one of the things she has studied is their use of social media. She suggests that contemporary teens use social media to hang out with their friends in the same way that teens from earlier periods socialized at shopping malls or on city streets. Boyd finds that American teens find their sense of community on social media, causing them to consider access to Myspace, Facebook, Instagram, Snapchat, and Twitter an essential part of their lives. When they are together, adolescents continually post images of what they see and what they are doing; when they are not together, they use social media to discuss what they have seen, heard, and experienced. Teenagers also use social media to track favorite celebrities, feeling that it makes those celebrities a part of their own lives. However, celebrity friending, following, and sharing enhances the commonality of negative comparisons between young people and the idealized images presented by celebrities.

In 2015, Dove beauty brand decided to do something about the fact that four out of five Twitter tweets dealing with beauty express negative perceptions of body image, even though 82 percent of females acknowledge that popular body images are unrealistic. Three-fourths of teenagers also admitted to feeling injured by negative comments about them on social media. With its #SpeakBeautiful campaign, Dove promoted the use of positive affirmations to boost self-esteem and self-confidence. The night of the 2015 Academy Awards, Dove invited Boyd and child and adolescent psychologist Jen Hartstein to respond to negative comments made about on-camera celebrities.

Group identity among teenagers may be based on such characteristics as speech, dress, musical preferences, and appearances, and social media gives teenagers opportunities for sharing information and opinions on all of these. YouTube is the most accessed site among American teenagers (85 percent), followed by Instagram (72 percent), Snapchat (69 percent), Facebook (51 percent), and Twitter (32 percent). Social media provides individuals with a myriad of opportunities that allow them to boost self-esteem, such as having a large number of "friends" on Facebook or having a huge following on Twitter. Self-esteem is also boosted when other users approve of a post, tweet, comment, or image.

On the other hand, negative impacts of social media include decreased self-esteem levels. Some users may feel disconnected from others, some may feel increasingly dissatisfied with themselves when comparing their looks or their lives to those of other users, and some users may become unhappy or depressed. Some studies have revealed that the more friends a Facebook user has, the more likely that user is to engage in upward comparisons, increasing opportunities for decreased self-esteem. Julia Brailovskaia and Jürgen Margraf found both positive and negative impacts on a study of 790 Facebooks users and 155 non-Facebook users. Nonusers were somewhat more likely than users to experience depression.

A 2008 study undertaken by Valerie Barker looked at the impact of social media on group self-esteem in older adolescents. The vast majority (85 percent) of participants were eighteen years old, and 78 percent were female. More than half were Anglo Saxon, but the group also included African and Latin Americans, Asians, and Pacific Islanders. Barker found that among those with strong peer identification, the most common reasons given for using social media was passing time and entertainment. Individuals who had weak or negative peer identification were more likely to state that they used social media for the purpose of social identity gratification or for virtual companionship.

Issues

Tammy K. Vigil and H. Denis Wu examined college students who used Facebook from five to ten times a day for at least five to ten minutes on each visit. They found that females spent more time than males on Facebook. Ninety percent of students in the study reported having more than five hundred friends, and 20 percent stated that they have more than one thousand friends. The average number of friends for all Facebook users is 338. Anyone friended by a user and given access to posts, comments, and images is considered a friend. Some users friend anyone who sends them a friend request, even though some requests come from spammers and hackers. Despite the large number of friends reported by study participants, three-fourths of them acknowledged that they only had regular contact with about twenty friends. Vigil and Wu found that excessive Facebook use led to lower self-esteem and greater life dissatisfaction.

The term cyberbullying refers to threatening, humiliating, mocking, or hurtful behavior online. One of the most notorious incidents involved the suicide of a thirteen-year-old Myspace user who was tricked by the mother of a "friend," into believing that she was communicating online with a sixteen-year-old boy named Josh who had fallen for her. After weeks of online wooing, "Josh" told the victim in a 2006 post that the world would be better off

without her. The mother was indicted in 2008, but the indictment was later overturned. In a 2010 case of cyberbullying, a first-year college student from New Jersey committed suicide after his roommate posted online a surreptitiously captured video of the young man having sex with another male.

While such cases are extreme, cyberbullying occurs daily on social media, and it may lead to low self-esteem and to high depression and loneliness among victims. It may also be responsible for a host of other physical and mental problems. From 9 to 30 percent of undergraduates on college campus acknowledge that they have been victimized by cyberbullying at some time, and 8.6 percent report that they have cyberbullied others. Cyberbullying has the most impact on students who may already be suffering from mental health issues and/or low self-esteem. Strong relations with parents have been shown to modify the impact of cyberbullying, but some teens do not share their experiences with their parents.

In a 2014 study that compared 502 American and Korean students, Lee et al. found that the use of social media is negatively related to body satisfaction. However, social media use was positively related to self-status for Korean students but not for American students. Scholars use the concept of body image as a measurement of an individual's overall personal satisfaction, and body image is particularly important to teenagers because of the strong desire to fit in and to be approved by peers. Individuals with poor body image may contract eating disorders or may become obsessive about their appearance. Living in a collective society, Korean teenagers are pressured to live up to accepted standards of beauty, to comply with appropriate behaviors, and to compare themselves to one another. While Americans have more leeway than Koreans in expressing individuality, self-esteem is more important in America than in Korea.

Communication scholars have found that communication is a key factor in forming and maintaining body image perceptions. Mass media is widely accepted as a major factor in body image perceptions because the emphasis on thinness, particularly for females, is a key element in defining beauty. The need for young females to obtain unrealistic body images has been labeled the "Barbie doll syndrome." The lines between interpersonal communication and mass media have become increasingly blurred on social media, with users sharing images from mass media on a regular basis, so that teenaged social media users may be constantly comparing themselves with thin attractive models and celebrities. A careless comment on social media about someone might spread to large numbers of people through such methods as shares and retweets. Studies have shown that half of all Americans hold negative body images, and girls as young as eight have already begun to diet for weight loss.

Since Swiss psychiatrist Carl Jung introduced the concept of extroverts and introverts in the late twentieth century, the subject has been widely studied. The concepts entered mainstream culture with the introduction of the Myers-Briggs Type Indicator that used Jungian theory to explain personality types and help individuals understand themselves and their friends of opposite types. When comparing extroverts and introverts, they found that extroverts tended to spend more time on social media than introverts. Extroverts, who are commonly described as being people-oriented, also reported higher numbers of friends and shared more photographs. They also found that extroversion and self-esteem are negatively linked to depression and stress. Overall, Brailovskaia and Margraf reported that, when compared to nonusers, Facebook users have higher self-esteem as well as higher rates of narcissism, extroversion, life satisfaction, social support, and subjective happiness than non-Facebook users.

—Elizabeth R. Purdy

References

Barker, V. "Older Adolescents' Motivations for Use of Social Networking Sites: The Influence of Group Identity and Collective Self-Esteem." *Conference Papers—International Communication Association 2008 Annual Meeting*, pp. 1–39, search. ebscohost.com/login.aspx?direct=true&db=ufh &an=36956224&site=ehost-live.

Boyd, D. *It's Complicated: The Social Lives of Networked Teens.* Yale UP, 2014.

Brailovskaia, J., and J. Margraf. "Comparing Facebook Users and Facebook Non-Users: Relationship Between Personality Traits and Mental Health Variables—An Exploratory Study." *PLOS One*, vol. 11, no. 12, 2016, pp. 1–17, doi:10.1371/journal.pone.0166999.

Isaranon, Y. "The Role of Facebook Affirmation Towards Ideal Self-Image and Self-Esteem."

International Journal of Behavioral Science, vol. 14, no. 1, 2019, pp. 46–62.

Lee, H.-R., H. E. Lee, J. Choi, et al. "Social Media Use, Body Image, and Psychological Well-Being: A Cross-Cultural Comparison of Korea and the United States." *Journal of Health Communication*, vol. 19, no. 12, 2014, pp. 1343–58, search. ebscohost.com/login.aspx?direct=true&db=ufh &an=99907281&site=ehost-live.

Nick, E. A., D. A. Cole, S. J. Cho, et al. "The Online Social Support Scale: Measure Development and Validation." *Psychological Assessment*, vol. 30, no. 9, 2018, pp. 1127–43, doi:10.1037/pas0000558.

Varghese, M. E., and M. C. Pistole. "College Student Cyberbullying: Self-Esteem, Depression, Loneliness, And Attachment." *Journal of College Counseling*, vol. 20, no. 1, 2017, pp. 7–21, doi:10.1002/jocc.12055.

Vigil, T. T., and H. D. Wu. "Facebook Users' Engagement and Perceived Life Satisfaction." *Media and Communication*, vol. 3, no. 1, 2015, pp. 5–16, search.ebscohost.com/login.aspx?direct=true&d b=cms&an=111212352&site=ehost-live.

Wohn, D. Y., C. T. Carr, and R. A. Hayes. "How Affective Is A 'Like'? The Effect of Paralinguistic Digital Affordances on Perceived Social Support." *CyberPsychology Behavior and Social Networking*, vol. 19, no. 9, 2016, pp. 562–66, doi:10.1089/cyber.2016.0162.

SOCIAL MEDIA AS A TEACHING AND LEARNING TOOL

Introduction

In part because of greater social media participation rates among young people, social media's effects upon the education system have been especially noteworthy. In recent years, educators have begun to embrace various social media platforms not only for their personal use, but also as a tool to connect with their students and to help their students collaborate with one another. Social media is also helping educators find new ways for students to conduct research, because the information that people share in online communities represents a largely untapped source of data.

Social media has presented something of a mixed blessing for schools and teachers. It has several disadvantages that at first caused educators to be cautious about its use. One problem is that social media presents an additional distraction for many young people, who may prefer to spend their time interacting with their peers online instead of focusing on their studies. Social media also raises concerns among school administrators because it represents another medium in which some students will inevitably choose to behave irresponsibly. Incidents in which students are bullied by their peers on social media sites, as well as cases where students post threats of school violence on social media, have become items that regularly appear in the news media. There have also been incidents in which inappropriate relationships between educators and students are fostered through social media's tendency to flatten hierarchies and make people more accessible to one another.

Still, these problems are the exception rather than the norm. Most users of social media behave appropriately, and as society has adjusted to the availability of social media as a form of interaction, educators have begun to find innovative methods of putting online networks to work. One of the first ways in which social media was found to support education is in its ability to assist educators in communicating with one another, to share ideas, offer advice, and learn from one another about how to better serve their students.

Background

From the earliest days of personal computers, teachers have been pioneers in this regard, building websites for their colleagues, sharing lesson plans online, and emailing one another to organize professional conferences. The arrival of social media has made this process much easier than it was in the past. Teachers can, in a matter of minutes, research who the best-known experts on a subject are, organize an online group to include them, and begin sharing ideas. In the past, this might have taken weeks or months.

Apart from communication among professional educators, social media also represents another topic for instructors to teach students about. Because part of educating students includes helping them to develop the critical thinking skills necessary to evaluate media rather than blindly consume it, many educators are making social media the focus of at least part of their coursework. Just as students must be able to listen to news reports and read newspapers and magazines to be able to extract, evaluate, and synthesize information, they must be shown how to use that same lens of critical inquiry when they use Twitter, Facebook, and other social networking sites.

To help this process along, teachers will occasionally assign students to, for example, devote one day to counting the number of advertisements they see while using social media. This helps raise students' awareness that much of what they see on social media is there because companies want it to be seen, and that ads are purchased in online forums with that goal in mind.

Another common task is for students to spend a day counting the number of hours they spend on social media, the number of times they reach for their cell phones, and the number of times they post something to a social media site. This assignment also seeks to raise awareness of the extent of a student's own social media use, because if a person is not aware of their usage and in control of it, they are in a very real sense controlled by it.

Teachers who have the most comfort with social media have gone beyond using it as a professional tool and helping their students to evaluate its role in their lives, by incorporating social media into their own instructional practices. This often takes the form of an assignment that requires students to use social media in a certain way. Examples include opening a Twitter account and locating followers who are experts on a specific subject; creating a Facebook group to collaborate on an assignment with other classmates; and interacting with other classes of students across the country or across the world. Often this last type of assignment is used with language instruction, as it gives students in different countries the chance to interact with native speakers of the language they are learning.

Using social media for instruction requires that the teacher be adept with the selected social media platform, understanding how it works and what its limitations and strengths are. The teacher must also manage the students as they navigate the online environment and ensure that they behave appropriately with one another. In a sense, using social media to support content learning in this way is not significantly different from an instructor taking her class on a field trip—the teacher must guide the group, make sure everyone is safe, behaving properly, and paying attention to what they are supposed to be learning.

The Implications of Inclusion

Some in the education community have resisted the inclusion of social media in the educational experience. Social media involves a different form of communication than many people are used to. In the past, information was disseminated in controlled ways, typically using a "one to many" distribution method. Under such a method, an information outlet (typically a television or radio station, or a newspaper publisher) would gather information, use it to produce a coherent report of events, and then broadcast its reports to the public by means of radio and television signals and newspapers. Each person received the same information at the same time, and there was no convenient means of discussing the information on a large scale.

In contrast, social media is thought of as a "many to many" information dissemination medium. Every person on social media can broadcast information to people in his or her network, and each of these recipients is free to respond or to pass the message along to their own network, in effect creating a large, continuously spreading conversation. Instead of simply receiving information, members of social media sites are constantly participating in its generation and distribution. Many educators find this type of online environment too chaotic and stress-inducing, and they may have a difficult time simply navigating social media on their own, much less using it to teach others.

Others embrace what they call social media's "egalitarian atmosphere," because the ability for teachers and students to interact with one another online and to share information has had the effect of reducing some of the barriers that often separate these groups, flattening the educational hierarchy and making learning itself a many-to-many conversation even within a single classroom, with students communicating together to help one another construct their understanding of the world.

Once students become accustomed to having this sort of freedom to participate in their own learning, it can help to increase their motivation to participate in a class and to expand their own horizons. Part of this has to do with the fact that because

social media sites are built upon technology, using smartphones and computers in constantly changing ways, students are often more adept at its use than their teachers. For some students, this advantage in technological skill over their instructors can give them a sense of accomplishment and build their faith in their own ability to learn and discover new things. A student that has a habit of tuning out traditional lectures is may be surprisingly engaged when given the chance to help the class and the teacher figure out how to use Twitter to learn more about a subject. A watchful teacher can use this to his or her advantage by drawing the reluctant learner into the lesson with the lure of technology and social media. The student is fully engaged and excited about what the class is learning together.

Many teachers are also using social media with their students because of the unique ways it can help to prepare them to participate in the workforce as adults. Lessons of this sort may require students to construct online profiles that are intended to accomplish specific results, such as obtaining a job. This can be an important way to convey to students how important it is to think about how one comes across in online communication. People are familiar with the idea that "you never get a second chance to make a first impression," but online interactions are new enough in social relations that many people have yet to realize that the content they post online—photographs, status updates, or comments on political issues—will almost certainly stay online in some form permanently, despite their best efforts to remove it later. Since part of teachers' role, in addition to content instruction in core subjects, is to prepare students for the world of adulthood, it is crucial to include in students' lessons some time devoted to online reputation management. This may involve building a resumé using a site such as LinkedIn, reviewing one's online history to spot issues that could potentially be a source of concern in the future, and learning the niceties of online communication (where one must keep in mind that sarcasm and other means of communication are often not perceptible in the absence of nonverbal cues).

Some educators and parents have voiced atypical concerns about social media use in education. While most such concerns deal with cyberbullying and the distracting effects of social media, there are occasionally concerns raised about the extent to which the use of social media in education may further discourage young people from interacting with one another directly, in person. Those who express this view tend to see technology in general as having a widespread effect of isolating people from one another.

It is one of the ironies of the internet that even while it allows people on different continents to communicate with one another easily, it also takes away time that one might otherwise spend directly interacting with friends, family, and neighbors. Teachers who use social media must keep in mind the need to remind students that, as with most activities, moderation is the key to success.

—*Scott Zimmer*

References

Bartow, S. M. "Teaching with Social Media: Disrupting Present Day Public Education." *Educational Studies: Journal of the American Educational Studies Association*, vol. 50, no. 1, 2014, pp. 36–64.

Bryant, P., A. Coombs, and M. Pazio. "Are We Having Fun Yet? Institutional Resistance and the Introduction of Play and Experimentation into Learning Innovation Through Social Media." *Journal of Interactive Media in Education*, vol. 2, 2014, pp. 32–39.

Budra, P. V., and C. Burnham. *From Text to Txting: New Media in the Classroom*. Indiana UP, 2012.

Ciampa, M., E. H. Thrasher, and M. A. Revel. "Social Media Use in Academics: Undergraduate Perceptions and Practices." *Journal of Educational Technology*, vol. 12, no. 4, 2016, pp. 10–19.

Dotterer, G., A. Hedges, and H. Parker. "Fostering Digital Citizenship in the Classroom." *Education Digest*, vol. 82, no. 3, 2016, pp. 58–63.

Horowitz, M., D. M. Bollinger, and American Association of School Administrators. *Cyberbullying in Social Media within Educational Institutions: Featuring Student, Employee, and Parent Information*. Rowman & Littlefield, 2014.

Joosten, T. *Social Media for Educators: Strategies and Best Practices*. Jossey-Bass, 2012.

Junco, R. *Engaging Students Through Social Media: Evidence Based Practices for Use in Student Affairs*. Jossey-Bass, 2014.

Langmia, K., T. C. M. Tyree, P. O'Brien, et al. *Social Media: Pedagogy and Practice*. University Press of America, 2014.

Mcleod, S., and C. Lehmann. *What School Leaders Need to Know About Digital Technologies and Social Media*. Jossey-Bass, 2012.

Militello, M., and J. I. Friend. *Principal 2.0: Technology and Educational Leadership*. Information Age, 2013.

Neal, D. R. *Social Media for Academics: A Practical Guide*. Chandos, 2012.

Nicosia, Laura. *Educators Online: Preparing Today's Teachers for Tomorrow's Digital Literacies*. Peter Lang, 2013.

Noor, A. D. H. S., and J. A. Hendricks. *Social Media: Usage and Impact*. Lexington Books, 2012.

Seo, K. K. J. *Using Social Media Effectively in the Classroom: Blogs, Wikis, Twitter, and More*. Routledge, 2012.

SOCIAL MEDIA MINING

Introduction

Social media is made up of the numerous websites and online platforms where people share information while building virtual communities. Social media mining is the process of gathering and studying the immense amount of data collected from social media networks such as Facebook, Twitter, Instagram, Tumblr, and LinkedIn. Social media networks generate a massive amount of data through the interactions of individuals with each other and their surroundings. In the context of social media mining, individuals are known as social atoms, and the communities they form are known as social molecules. The data collected from the interaction of social atoms and social molecules can be extracted and analyzed—a process known as mining—in order to realize meaningful patterns that can be examined and used.

Through mining social media networks, social scientists are able to study how individuals interact with each other and their environments. They are also able to see how virtual communities are formed and maintained. Data mining of social media is also used for marketing and other commercial purposes.

Background

Since social media's advent in the early 2000s, people have been using it to upload videos, images, news stories, personal information, and other content in vast amounts to webpages for the purpose of sharing this content and thus interacting with others around the world. This information can be accessed immediately via computers or mobile devices. Viewers of the content can usually interact with the original poster by giving feedback through comments or by using onscreen features, such as Facebook's "like" button, to signal their approval or share the content with others. Despite the turnover in many of the second-tier social media sites, as a whole social media does keep growing.

According to the website eBizMBA, which provides information on e-business, the most popular social networking sites as of May 2016 were Facebook, YouTube, Twitter, LinkedIn, Pinterest, Google Plus, Tumblr, Instagram, Reddit, VK, Flickr, and Vine. The sites' popularity rankings are based on the estimated number of unique visitors each site receives on a monthly basis. Of these, Facebook is the most-used social media network, and the most recognized worldwide. By 2020, BroadbandSearch.net identified the top ten list, worldwide, as: Facebook, YouTube, WhatsApp, Facebook Messenger (as distinct from the primary service), WeChat, Instagram, LinkedIn, TikTok. In 2022, Kristen McCormick of WordStream noted Facebook, YouTube, WhatsApp, Instagram, and Facebook Messenger still at the top internationally. Pinterest and LinkedIn, continue, meanwhile, to attract a national audience in the middle of the top ten.

Because social media has a global audience, the information distributed on these networks is extensive, with billions of pieces of data. This data is disorganized and sporadic. Special techniques and a multidisciplinary approach are needed in order to gather, analyze, and present the information in a useful way. The data that is mined can then be used for marketing strategies, productivity, increased revenue, and understanding human social behavior.

Impact of Social Media Mining

The data that is mined from social media is so vast and from so many sources that it is considered "big data," which refers to data that exceeds petabytes (1 million gigabytes) in size. Big data may be structured, meaning that it is identifiable and retrievable, or unstructured, meaning it cannot be easily retrieved or analyzed.

According to IBM, roughly 2.5 quintillion bytes of data were created on an average day in 2012. Such a large amount of data cannot be analyzed by traditional data mining means. Database software on regular computers would take months to be able to make sense of any of it. That is why computer scientists must use supercomputers and new techniques of data mining to analyze and interpret much of the social media data that is generated.

Social media data differs from other data in several ways. For example, it relies on social relations and actions like friending and following, where users post content where others may comment on it, "like" it by clicking on a positive icon to highlight their approval, or repost it through sharing on their own social media pages. Therefore, making sense of the data requires a multidisciplinary approach to retrieving and interpreting it, one that combines the established technical algorithms and methods of data mining from computer science and mathematics with social network analysis, statistics, ethnography, behavioral theories, and machine learning.

Financial firms have a large stake in using social media networks. They want to deliver information to users quickly and efficiently. Firms want to be the trendsetters of their niche, and to be the center of the scattered information posted on the numerous social media platforms.

Although companies want to have an extensive social media presence, it does not always translate to more profits. Revenue from social media is not easily earned nor easily tracked. Increased traffic and interest on a company's Facebook or Twitter account, for instance, does not automatically translate to increased revenue, but mining social media data can provide valuable information. Companies mine social media tracking data to better understand users' spending habits and product desires. Companies can then use what they learn to better target their online marketing to customers who are more likely prospects.

Social media mining can also show politicians the political leanings and attitudes of users, based on demographic information. It can give city officials a better insight into their citizens' priorities and demands. By mining social networks, social scientists can examine either collective behavior (the behavior of groups of people) or individual behavior in order to better understand—and also predict—the behavioral patterns of people.

Social media mining is an emerging discipline, as is big data analysis. While analyzing and interpreting the data from social media mining has numerous implications, it can also be overwhelming because of the immensity of the data to be gathered. Nonetheless, these disciplines continue to grow and change.

—*Rich Stein*

References

Corley, Courtney D., et al. "Text and Structural Data Mining of Influenza Mentions in Web and Social Media." *International Journal of Environmental Research and Public Health*, vol. 7, no. 2, 2010, pp. 596–615.

Ganis, Matt, and Avinash Kohirkar. *Social Media Analytics: Techniques and Insights for Extracting Business Value Out of Social Media.* IBM, 2016.

Gundecha, Pritam, and Huan Liu. "Mining Social Media: A Brief Introduction." *INFORMS Tutorials in Operations Research.* INFORMS, 14 Oct. 2014.

Kennedy, Helen. *Post, Mine, Repeat: Social Media Data Mining Becomes Ordinary.* Palgrave Macmillan, 2016.

McCormick, Kristen. "The Six Biggest, Baddest, Most Popular Social Media Platforms of 2022." *WordStream*, www.wordstream.com/blog/ws/2022/01/11/most-popular-social-media-platforms.

"The Most Popular Social Networking Sites in 2022." *BroadbandSearch.net*, www.broadbandsearch.net/blog/most-popular-social-networking-sites.

Naone, Erica. "When Social Media Mining Gets It Wrong." *MIT Technology Review*, 9 Aug. 2011.

Rogow, Geoffrey. "In Social Media Mining, Some Go Slow." *The Wall Street Journal: Money Beat.* Dow Jones, 1 Dec. 2014.

Tang, Jiliang, Yi Chang, and Huan Liu. "Mining Social Media with Social Theories: A Survey." *ACM SIGKDD Explorations Newsletter*, vol. 15, no. 2, 2013, pp. 20–29.

"Top 15 Most Popular Social Networking Sites." *EBizMBA Guide.* EBizMBA, May 2016.

Zafarani, Reza, and Mohammad Ali Abbasi. *Social Media Mining: An Introduction.* Cambridge UP, 2014.

SOCIAL NETWORKING SERVICES

Introduction

Social networking services (SNS) are web-based and mobile services that connect users through user-defined social connections. Content of such services is generally created by users, including links to off-site content such as news stories or videos, and they are nearly always free to use. The popularity of such services has impacted the demographics, social dimension, and business model of the internet, as well as having long-lasting effects on the media and world politics.

Social networking services are online platforms in which much of the activity is centered around users' social connections to other users. These platforms range from services like Facebook or Twitter, in which these networked connections are the explicit focus of the service, to services like Goodreads or Letterboxed, which are primarily focused on user-created reviews of books and movies while offering social connections and interactions among users. In the case of the former, the conventional assumption is that most of a Facebook user's "friends" (the service's term for members who have formalized a connection between their accounts) are known to that user in "real life," whether they are social acquaintances, current or former classmates, coworkers, family members, etc. With sites like Goodreads, however, there is no such assumption; in fact, heavy users primarily connect and interact with other users because of their on-site contributions, not because of off-site relationships. Because of such differences, generalizations about and definitions of SNS pose many challenges. Other key differences include the expectations attached to user identity; Facebook users are presumed to identify themselves by their real names, whereas Tumblr users rarely do.

Norms vary widely, sometimes even among user groups within the same service. For some, Twitter is primarily used for microblogging anonymously; for others, it is primarily for engaging in site-wide conversations; for still others, it is primarily for reading others' posts with little or no interaction. SNS overlap with other types of sites, like blogging platforms, dating sites, and e-commerce sites. Amazon, for instance, allows users to add friends in order to see their wish lists. Many communications and media theorists describe the rise in both popularity and cultural importance of SNS as part of a postindustrial shift in society, away from the hierarchical organization of the nineteenth and twentieth centuries and towards a decentralized and more fluid organization.

Nearly all social networking services are free to use. Even sites that charge a subscription fee usually reserve it for a premium tier, as in LinkedIn's case. Even commercial accounts, such as the Facebook page for a business, are free on most services. The revenue from these services comes from two main sources: advertising (each free commercial account constitutes a new potential advertising customer) and data (marketable information about users, usage, engagement, etc.). There is a direct relationship here between the free service and the revenue model: advertising and demographic data are more valuable when the user base is larger and more active.

The business model of social networking services is sometimes summed up as "the user is the product." Modern SNS, after an early phase that included services like SixDegrees and Friendster, are products of Web 2.0 design, sometimes called the "social web," or "participatory web." While the early World Wide Web was primarily static, with interactive elements limited to specific corners of online culture (especially message boards and blog comments), Web 2.0 refers to the expectation that most web pages would involve user activity of some kind. This activity could range from a button letting the user share a page; the capacity to add comments, reviews, or ratings; or the richer, user-generated content of SNS. User-generated content is one of the defining characteristics of modern social media. Facebook and Twitter provide a structure for content, defining specific kinds of posts (images, links, text), as well as the nature of user profiles and the mechanisms governing social connections, but most of what users see when reading either service has been added or created by the other users they follow.

Background

The golden age of SNS can probably be considered to have started around 2008, when the growing popularity of Facebook resulted in online engagement by demographic groups that had not previously been very involved with the internet. Originally limited to college students, Facebook was soon considered "your grandmother's internet," a success that it enjoyed in part because of its emphasis on real names, family relationships, and photo sharing. Digital immigrants, those who had graduated high school before internet use had become as common as it is for Millennials and Generation Z, used Facebook in part to reconnect with the former classmates and childhood friends.

One of the key elements distinguishing this generation of social networks from the earlier decades of the internet is the degree to which so many people were now using the internet not as passive audience members but as active participants who not only engaged with content but actively create their own public identities through the use of social network profiles and other means.

This early rise of social networks was generally seen as positive, at least outside of complaints about increased smartphone usage and screen time. As smartphones became more common, the internet became more accessible or appealing to large swaths of people who had not participated heavily in online culture before, not only the aforementioned grandmothers but also people in rural areas where cable internet remained either unavailable or prohibitively expensive (different costs and incentives have resulted in cellular coverage expanding to many areas where other telecommunications infrastructure has not), and people in developing countries. The possibilities were promising.

Lesbian, gay, bisexual, transgender, and queer (or questioning) LGBTQ+ teenagers in remote communities could find an accepting, supportive community online. Grassroots movements could organize and recruit with less need for door-to-door campaigning; the 2008 presidential election campaigns, for instance, saw heavy use of Twitter and email. Throughout the world, mobile apps and social networks offered organizing capabilities to protesters and political movements, especially in authoritarian regimes.

Much of the early 2010s scholarly work on Twitter, for instance, focused on its role in the Arab Spring and similar antigovernment protests. At times, the rhetoric around social networks was almost utopian, resting on the contention that online communities made it harder for governments to censor the speech and assembly of their citizens, and that this greater amplification and connectivity would lead to more democratic results.

However, that optimism changed dramatically in the years surrounding the 2016 US presidential election. Concurrent with the Brexit vote in the United Kingdom and the rise of nationalist movements in Europe, the election saw a rise in the use of fake social media accounts by state and nonstate agencies for the purposes of manipulating voter sentiment. In the United States, the internet's relative anonymity offered all users the same benefits and networking abilities that had been used by antigovernment protesters during the Arab Spring.

Furthermore, for a variety of reasons, many of them contested, the presence of extremist groups on social networks had a significant impact on political discourse, as propaganda originating with fringe groups were disseminated through retweets and reached audiences that would not consciously identify with such groups or their views. The role of social media in the rise of extremist groups seems to require a separate explanation beyond the simple fact that SNS enable networking and organization. Scholar Derek Hrynyshyn has examined the ways in which authoritarian populism has thrived on social networks.

One factor in that rise is the response of social networks' management and moderation teams to the use of their services. Early in the 2020 election season, a video of US Speaker of the House Nancy Pelosi was circulated on social media, in which the sound and playback speed had been manipulated in order to give the impression that Pelosi was intoxicated and slurring her speech. It was not presented as a parody and was used to argue both explicitly and implicitly the ridiculousness of her position on President Donald Trump's refusal to cooperate with federal investigations. Despite the fact that Facebook had recently implemented new policies on fact checking and fake news, and had deplatformed a number of high-profile users because of their use of similar tactics, the social network decided not to delete the video. Facebook's statement on the decision not to delete the video read, in part, "We don't have a policy that stipulates that the information you post on Facebook must be true" (Harwell).

However, right after the insurrection on January 6, 2021, Twitter announced that (outgoing) President Trump was deplatformed (banned) from using the social media platform indefinitely. Within the next several days, other social media sites (Facebook, Instagram, Reddit, Shopify, and TikTok), banned Trump, also.

Issues

There are several reasons why Facebook's response to fake news is concerning, but among them is the impact that SNS in the late 2000s and 2010s had on journalism. Newspapers had been downsizing for years, both in response to declining subscriptions and ad sales and as the result of media conglomerations buying local papers and either merging them with others or sharing content across multiple papers in order to reduce the need for labor. The internet posed a frustrating challenge to print media. On one hand, there was a demand for putting news content online. On the other hand, from small locally owned papers to major papers like the *New York Times*, no one seemed to have much success with paywalls, which make some or all of the paper's online content available only to subscribers. In short, everyone wanted and expected to be able to read the news, but few were willing to pay to do so.

Sharing news articles on Facebook was helpful to newspapers and other outlets by creating more clicks for online ad revenue (and in theory attracting potential subscribers). As Facebook became more and more popular, having a Facebook presence and encouraging the sharing of articles on Facebook became not just desirable for newspapers, but necessary. Facebook began to wield a disproportionate influence on news media; its reports to news outlets about which articles attracted the most engagement impacted management decisions and, in turn, drove news content.

The rise of fake news is one subplot in this story. The other major one is the "pivot to video," a media term for the shift in the 2010s to creating more and more video content for the purpose of sharing online. Pivoting to video had a more dramatic effect on journalism than other trends, like the waxing and waning of lifestyle sections or the mix of local to national news, because video production requires specialized skills, equipment, and trained personnel. A video is substantially more expensive to produce than a story of text and photos, or even a dozen such stories. The pivot to video eliminated jobs across the country in order to make up for the increased cost.

In 2018, it was revealed that this shift in journalism, which had peaked around 2015 in the lead-up to the election, had been predicated on misinformation. Facebook had misrepresented—deliberately, according to documents filed as part of a potential class action lawsuit—the popularity of video because of its own interest in favoring video and multimedia links over text content. In its reports to news outlets and other business customers, it had overstated the popularity of videos by as much as 900 percent.

Furthermore, when calculating the average length of time that a user spent watching a video, an important engagement metric, it had ignored durations under three seconds, which both inflated the average and implied a much larger and more interested audience than actually existed, because no one who scrolled down a page and skipped the video was counted. (Facebook agreed with the claims about erroneous figures, but insisted it had been a simple mistake.) The new money sunk into video thus showed little return, and in the meantime an estimated five hundred jobs in American journalism had been lost just in the pivot.

The possibility of a class action lawsuit by journalists who had lost their jobs due to misreported data was seriously raised, though in the end not pursued. As with the Pelosi video decision, the pivot highlighted the most important fact about the intersection of social media and the news: the decisions that are smartest for business and best for revenue are not necessarily the ones that most accord to traditional journalistic ethics and values.

—Bill Kte'pi

References

Baker, L. R., and D. L. Oswald. "Shyness and Online Social Networking Services." *Journal of Social and Personal Relationships*, vol. 27, no. 7, 2010, pp. 873–89, search.ebscohost.com/login.aspx?direct=true&db=ufh&an=55209473&site=ehost-live.

Baym, N., and D. Boyd. "Socially Mediated Publicness: An Introduction." *Journal of Broadcasting & Electronic Media*, vol. 56, no. 3, 2012, pp. 320–29, search.ebscohost.com/login.aspx?direct=true&db=ufh&an=79830560&site=ehost-live.

Boyd, D. M., and N. B. Ellison. "Social Network Sites: Definition, History, and Scholarship." *Journal of Computer-Mediated Communication*, vol. 13, no. 1, 2007, pp. 210–30, search.ebscohost.com/login.aspx?direct=true&db=ufh&an=27940595&site=ehost-live.

Harwell, D. "Facebook Acknowledges Pelosi Video Is Faked but Declines to Delete It." *The Washington Post*, 24 May 2019, www.washingtonpost.com/technology/2019/05/24/facebook-acknowledges-pelosi-video-is-faked-declines-delete-it/.

Hrynyshyn, Derek. "The Outrage of Networks: Social Media and Contemporary Authoritarian Populism." *Democratic Communiqué*, vol. 28, no. 1, 2019, pp. 27–45, search.ebscohost.com/login.aspx?direct=true&db=ufh&an=135902018&site=ehost-live.

Macaulay, M. "Status Update: Celebrity, Publicity, and Branding in the Social Media Age." *Canadian Journal of Communication*, vol. 40, no. 1, 2015, pp. 143–46, search.ebscohost.com/login.aspx?direct=true&db=ufh&an=101106489&site=ehost-live.

Marwick, A. E., and D. Boyd. "Networked Privacy: How Teenagers Negotiate Context in Social Media." *New Media and Society*, vol. 16, no. 7, 2014, pp. 1051–67, search.ebscohost.com/login.aspx?direct=true&db=ufh&an=98993397&site=ehost-live.

Pitcan, M., A. E. Marwick, and D. Boyd. "Performing a Vanilla Self: Respectability Politics, Social Class, and the Digital World." *Journal of Computer-Mediated Communication*, vol. 23, no. 3, 2018, pp, 163–79, search.ebscohost.com/login.aspx?direct=true&db=ufh&an=129489443&site=ehost-live.

Yam, Caleb. "'Deplatformed': Trump's Social Media Suspension." *The Science Survey*, 21 Mar. 2021, thesciencesurvey.com/editorial/2021/03/21/deplatformed-trumps-social-media-suspension/.

SOFTWARE ARCHITECTURE

Introduction

Software architecture refers to the specific set of decisions that software engineers make to organize the complex structure of a computer system under development. Sound software architecture helps minimize the risk of the system faltering as well as optimizing its performance, durability, and reliability.

Building architects deal with static structures that maintain their structural integrity over the long term. In contrast, the architecture of a computer program must be able to change, grow, and be modified. The term "software architecture" refers to the internal operations of a system under development and how its elements will ultimately function together. It is a blueprint that helps software engineers avoid and troubleshoot potential problems. These problems are far easier to address while the system is in development rather than after it is operational.

Software architects examine how a system's functional requirements and nonfunctional requirements relate to each other. Functional requirements control what processes a system is able to perform. Nonfunctional requirements control the overall operation of a program rather than specific behaviors. They include performance metrics such as manageability, security, reliability, maintainability, usability, adaptability, and resilience. Nonfunctional requirements place constraints on the system's functional requirements.

The main challenge for the software architect is to determine which requirements should be optimized. If a client looking for a new software program is asked what requirements are most critical—usability, performance, or security, for instance—they are most likely going to say, all of them. Because this cannot be done economically, the software architect prioritizes the list of requirements, knowing that there must be trade-offs in the design of any application. If, for instance, the project is a long-term home-loan application program or a website for purchasing airplane tickets, the architect will most likely focus on security and modification. If the project is short term, such as a seasonal marketing campaign or a website for a political campaign, the architect will focus instead on usability and performance.

Background

Software architecture design is an early-stage abstract process that allows for the testing of an assortment of scenarios in order to maximize the functionality of a system's most critical elements. Well-planned software architecture helps developers ascertain how the system will operate and how best to minimize potential risks or system failures. In most cases, software architecture factors in modifiability, allowing the system to grow over time to prevent obsolescence and anticipate future user needs.

Software architecture projects can involve weeks, months, or even years of development. Software architects often develop a basic skeletal system early in the development process. While this early system lacks the depth and reach of the desired program, it provides critical insights into the system's developing functionality. Incremental modifications are then made and tested to ensure that the emerging system is performing properly. Multiple iterations of the system are made until full functionality is achieved. This approach is known as agile software development.

Software architects work to understand how the system will ultimately operate to meet its performance requirements. Programs should be designed to be flexible enough to grow into more sophisticated and more specialized operations. Plug-ins can be used to add features to existing systems. By designing software functions as discrete elements, software architects can make the system easier to adapt. This design principle is known as a separation of concerns. It allows one element of the program to be upgraded without dismantling the entire superstructure, for example. This has the potential to save considerable time and money. Component-based development is a related idea that borrows from the industrial assembly-line model. It involves using and reusing standardized software components across different programs.

Implications

Software architecture aims to balance the end user's needs with the system's behavioral infrastructure and the expectations of the company that will support the software. Software architects start the development process by looking at the broadest possible implications of a proposed system's elements and their relationships to one another. This distinguishes them from code developers, whose vision is often relatively narrow and specified. Software architects evaluate the critical needs of the software, consider the needs of both the client and the end user, and draft system blueprints that maximize those requirements while managing the practical concerns of time and cost.

—Joseph Dewey

References

Bass, Len, Paul Clements, and Rick Kazman. *Software Architecture in Practice.* 3rd ed., Addison-Wesley Professional, 2012.

Cervantes, Humberto, and Rick Kazman. *Designing Software Architectures: A Practical Approach.* Addison-Wesley Professional, 2016.

Hohpe, Gregor. *The Software Architect Elevator.* O'Reilly Media, 2020.

Mitra, Tilak. *Practical Software Architecture: Moving from System Context to Deployment.* IBM Press, 2015.

Mistrik, Ivan, et al., editors. *Software Architecture for Big Data and the Cloud.* Morgan Kaufmann, 2017.

Richards, Mark, and Neal Ford. *Fundamentals of Software Architecture: An Engineering Approach.* O'Reilly, 2020.

Sonmez, John Z. *Soft Skills: The Software Developer's Life Manual.* Manning, 2015.

SPAM

Introduction

Spam (formerly SPAM) is a general term for an abuse of email technology to transmit a large amount of unsolicited junk email in bulk, often for commercial reasons. Spam is often sent by "botnets"—networks of virus-infected computers—and this hinders the prosecution of spammers. Some estimates state that nearly 80 percent of all email sent worldwide is spam. For computer users, spam can be annoying. Spam is often used to send fraudulent offers or to disseminate malicious software such as viruses. Spammers harvest and compile bulk listings of email address through automated scanning of popularly used websites or by intercepting the transmission of electronic mailing lists.

Spam often has some form of false or misleading information and consistently offends recipients by promoting investment scams, pornography, or medications. The Federal Trade Commission (FTC) found that 66 percent of all spam has false, fraudulent, or misleading information somewhere in the email's routing information, subject line, or message content.

Most users agree that spam clutters email inboxes with unwanted communication and thus violates the privacy of email users and their "right to be let alone." Current Supreme Court jurisprudence on the right to privacy in one's home also grants email recipients a right to privacy in what they receive in their email inboxes.

Background

What is now known as spam has existed since the mid-1970s. It originated as postings to newsgroups, evolved into advertisements and solicitations, and soon got out of hand, with individual members receiving numerous unwanted emails. With the rapid expansion of the internet during the 1990s, the problem of unsolicited email began to grow exponentially. By 2005, most internet email users were receiving dozens—sometimes even hundreds—of pieces of spam every day. Its origin is said to come from a 1970 Monty Python's Flying Circus comedy troupe skit about an American diner that included SPAM, the canned meat, in each of its breakfast offerings, often in multiple helpings, each mentioned separately. Then the group broke into song with the repetitive lyrics: "SPAM, SPAM, SPAM, SPAM, SPAM, SPAM, SPAM, SPAM, lovely SPAM! Wonderful SPAM!"

Spam messages include legal and illegal solicitations of all kinds, running from advertisements—including a large proportion of pornographic advertisements—to chain letters and jokes. Volume is not the only problem that spam presents to computer users. Many spam messages contain computer viruses and worms that can inflict serious damage on the computers receiving the unwanted messages. The annoyance that spam causes computer users is difficult to exaggerate. In addition to offending users with unwanted—and often repugnant—solicitations, spam forces users to spend time and resources filtering and removing spam, while increasing their anxieties about the safety and security of their computers.

During the 1990s, increasing numbers of lawsuits were being filed against the purveyors of spam, known as spammers, in state and federal courts—primarily under fraud statutes. The Coalition Against Unsolicited Commercial E-mail (CAUCE) is one of a number of groups that have lobbied for criminalizing spam in the United States and Europe. During the 2003–4 session of the US Congress, at least six pieces of legislation designed to regulate spam were introduced. By the year 2005, no blanket national law made spam illegal, but by then as many as twenty-one states had passed, or were then considering, laws to criminalize spam.

One problem with criminalizing spam is the fact that much of it falls under laws protecting legitimate commerce and trade. The state of California found a way around this problem by enacting a law requiring that spam messages be labeled as advertising and that they offer ways for recipients to have their names removed from mailing lists. The California law was upheld by an appeals court as constitutional.

Existing federal and state laws protect citizens from fraud and illegal pornography. The FTC, the Federal Bureau of Investigation (FBI), the Internet Fraud Complaint Center, and the National White Collar Crime Commission all investigate complaints concerning spam. However, spam messages are difficult to trace back to their senders. Moreover, even when the senders are identified, they are rarely prosecuted or sued unless criminal activity and criminal intent can clearly be demonstrated.

On January 1, 2004, the federal Controlling the Assault of Non-Solicited Pornography and Marketing Act (CAN-SPAM) of 2003 took effect. A so-called opt out law, this legislation gave email users a way to remove themselves from mailing lists. In addition, the CAN-SPAM Act forbade fraudulent email subject lines, made it illegal to send email to addresses that are improperly "harvested," forbade sending email with pornographic content without clear identifying labels, and provided both criminal and civil penalties for violators.

Some critics warned that the CAN-SPAM Act would actually increase the volume of spam in the United States. The fear is that by signaling to the world that spam is legal in the United States, foreign spammers might send more messages than ever. Also, requiring recipients to read unwanted emails to opt out is considered unfair.

Most spam being sent in 2005 remained illegal. Nothing in the law will stop illegal spammers from sending spam. The general consensus toward fighting spam seems to be on the side of private sector response. Individual computer users should use devices such as firewalls and antivirus programs to protect their computers from invasive email threats; users can also set up filters within their email to detect and divert spam to a specific folder so that it does not clutter their inbox. Internet service providers are developing "black hole" technologies to help prevent spam from reaching subscribers. These are seen as more effective than additional layers of legislation.

According to the National Conference of State Legislatures, as of 2015, thirty-seven states had instituted laws designed to regulate spam. However, according to research, as of 2016, there were still billions of spam emails sent daily. Additionally, while traditional methods of bulk spamming are typically detected by antispam software and filters, some spammers have come up with more creative ways of fooling these common levels of protection. Referred to in the technology world as "snowshoe spamming," this technique, which has been used increasingly in the 2010s and is harder to detect, involves distributing the unsolicited advertising over several different IP addresses in lower volumes over a longer period of time.

In 1979, the US Supreme Court recognized an individual's "right to be let alone" and held that a mailer's right to communicate ends at the mailbox of an uninterested addressee. The law was challenged but was held to be constitutional similar to the laws that prohibited sexually explicit mailings on free speech grounds. The Court pointed to the necessity that the "right to be let alone" must balance with the right of others to communicate: "Individual autonomy must survive to permit every householder to exercise control over unwanted mail." Accordingly, the statute served to protect individuals' privacy and passed constitutional muster. The Court stated: "In effect, Congress allows each citizen to erect a wall that no advertiser may penetrate without his acquiescence....Nor should the householder have to risk that offensive material come into the hands of children before it can be stopped."

Similarly, the right of spammers to solicit others must end at the outer edge of each individual's private home. The sanctuary of the home in this case includes the mailbox *and* an email inbox, both are meant to send and receive communications. Individuals maintain a higher expectation of privacy in email addresses. Email addresses maintain anonymity and are not a matter of public record. Each recipient must have a password to access an inbox, just as one must have a key to enter a residence. Thus, an inbox must be considered part of the home and enjoy at least the same protected status as the mailbox. It follows that no one has the right to impose ideas on unwilling recipients in the sanctuary of his or her email inbox. Spammers do not have a fundamental right to send unsolicited commercial emails to individuals' inboxes. Consequently, spam encroaches upon the personal space of individuals and violates their "right to be let alone," their right to be free from objectionable intrusion, and their right to privacy.

Spam invades the privacy of email recipients by sending objectionable content to them, whether or not they want this type of material. Spam imposes significant costs on email users. By the first decade of the twenty-first century, spam cost both individuals and businesses a considerable amount of time and money. Both the privacy and cost issues contributed to demands that spam be curtailed, including by federal legislation.

Congress recognized the importance of email and the harms caused by spammers. To shift the costs of advertising to the spammer and to enhance the privacy of email users, Congress enacted the Controlling the Assault of Non-Solicited Pornography and Marketing Act of 2003. The statute became effective January 1, 2004. Finding that many spammers purposely mislead recipients and often conceal their identity, Congress justified the statute, asserting that there is a substantial government interest in regulating commercial email on a national level, spammers should not mislead recipients about the source or content of electronic messages, and recipients of commercial email have the right to decline additional spam messages. To enforce this statute, the FTC promulgated and enforced protocols for the commercial use of bulk email.

The statute prohibits predatory and abusive commercial email. The law penalizes those who knowingly engage in one or more of the following behaviors: (1) accessing a protected computer without authorization and intentionally initiating the transmission of multiple commercial email messages through that computer; (2) sending several multiple commercial email messages with the intent to deceive or mislead recipients, or any internet access service, as to the origin of such messages; (3) materially falsifying header information in several commercial emails and intentionally initiating the transmission of such messages; (4) registering for five or more email accounts or online user accounts or two or more domain names using false identification and intentionally sending spam from such

accounts or domain names; and (5) falsely representing oneself to be the registrant of five or more internet protocol addresses and intentionally initiating the transmission of spam. Individuals participating in these activities could be imprisoned for up to five years and be liable for a maximum of $6 million in fines.

The statute's opt-out provision requires commercial email messages to include a functioning return email address that a recipient may use to opt out of future spam from the sender. The email address provided must remain active for at least thirty days after the original message was transmitted. Once a consumer effectively chooses to opt out of future email messages, the sender must respect the decision. After this point, it would be unlawful for the initial sender or anyone acting on such person's behalf to transmit, or to assist in the transmission of, a commercial email message upon the expiration of ten business days after the receipt of the opt-out notice. The initial sender and any person with knowledge of the opt-out request must refrain from selling, leasing, exchanging, or transferring the recipient's email address. Also, commercial email messages must provide clear and conspicuous identification that the message is an advertisement or solicitation, notice of the opportunity to decline to receive further messages, and a valid physical postal address for the sender.

The CAN-SPAM statute also prohibits harvesting and dictionary attacks, and requires individuals to place warning labels on commercial emails with sexually oriented material. Email messages containing sexually explicit content must include in the subject line the marks or notices prescribed by the FTC. Such messages must further ensure that the message, when initially opened, contains only the content required by the opt-out provision and instructions on how to access the sexually explicit material, unless the sender receives the prior affirmative consent of the recipient. An individual in violation of this provision can face up to five years in jail and/or fines.

This legislative action enjoyed rare overwhelming bipartisan support. This support indicated a substantial legislative commitment to the spam issue and understanding of the severity of this problem. The act was a significant step forward in supporting the individual's "right to be let alone" in balancing privacy with free speech rights. The

CAN-SPAM Act will serve to deter spammers from sending fraudulent or misleading email messages, from concealing their identity, and from using intrusive methods to collect email addresses. Email users will be able to identify spam messages as advertisements generally and as pornographic messages specifically due to the provisions of the act. The CAN-SPAM Act has had a valuable role in initiating legislative action, which would restrict spam, increase the privacy of the email inboxes of Americans, and relieve Americans from the financial burdens of unwanted advertising.

Despite the promise of the law, some observers argue that the statute is not effective enough in fighting spam. These critics believe that spam needs to be subject to further restriction through a combination of market-based initiatives and additional restrictive statutes and regulations.

Opting in/Opting Out

The spam law debate shifted into a controversy over two conflicting approaches: the opt-in and the opt-out mechanisms. The opt-in approach requires that all spammers obtain express permission before transmitting any email addresses. The more lenient opt-out approach allows spammers to send messages as long as each message offers a legitimate link from which one can request that the spammer refrain from sending future emails. Congress favored the opt-out approach because it allowed marketers and businesses with the most leeway to conduct their work.

The opt-out method of regulation has failed, however, to protect individual privacy fully. It continues to allow uninvited and unwelcome messages to individual inboxes in homes and businesses. Under current law, to halt unwanted email, individual users must take an affirmative step against each piece of unwanted mail; such a move wastes more time and money than the underlying problem. By implementing the opt-out approach, Congress developed a method that imposed additional costs on individuals because it is a competitive, repetitive, and labor-intensive method to oppose spam.

In terms of privacy, the opt-in approach protects consumers to a significantly greater degree and in a more effective manner. The opt-in approach prohibits unsolicited intrusions and requires that spammers send invited messages only. Like a vaccine prevents a disease, the opt-in approach stops the widespread dissemination of spam. Rather than imposing the costs of the remedy on all email users for each uninvited message like the opt-out approach, the opt-in approach imposes costs on spammers and those interested in receiving spam. In other words, it shifts the burden of sending spam onto spammers. Spammers must ask permission to enter an inbox instead of entering and then being asked to leave. The opt-in approach would ultimately serve to reduce the enormous volume of spam clogging networks and flooding the email system, and would halt the widespread waste of time and money directed at eliminating spam. Congress should adopt the opt-in approach to protect the privacy of email users.

—Donald R. Dixon and Gretchen Nobahar

References

Beales, J. Howard. *Legislative Efforts to Combat Spam: Joint Hearing before . . . 108th Congress, 1st Session, July 9, 2003*. US Government Printing Office, 2003.

Clifford, Ralph D., editor. *Cybercrime: The Investigation, Prosecution, and Defense of a Computer-Related Crime*. Carolina Academic Press, 2001.

The Criminal Spam Act of 2003: Report (to Accompany S. 1293). US Government Printing Office, 2003.

Feinstein, Ken. *Fight Spam, Viruses, Pop-Ups and Spyware (How to Do Everything)*. McGraw-Hill, 2004.

Garfinkel, Simson, and Gene Spafford. *Web Security, Privacy & Commerce*. 2nd ed., O'Reilly Media, 2011.

Gelman, Robert B., and Stanton McCandlish. *Protecting Yourself Online: The Definitive Resource on Safety, Freedom, and Privacy in Cyberspace*. Harper-Edge, 1998.

Himma, Kenneth Einar. *The Handbook of Information and Computer Ethics*. Wiley, 2008.

Jasper, Margaret C. *The Law of Obscenity and Pornography*. 2nd ed., Oceana, 2009.

Jenkins, Simms. *The Truth about Email Marketing*. FT Press, 2009.

Manishin, Glenn B. *Complying with the CAN-SPAM Act and Other Critical Business Issues: Staying Out of Trouble*. Practicing Law Institute, 2004.

Reduction in Distribution of Spam Act of 2003: Hearing before the Subcommittee on Crime, Terrorism, and Homeland Security of the Committee on the Judiciary,

House of Representatives, One Hundred Eighth Congress, First Session, on H.R. 2214, July 8, 2003. US Government Printing Office, 2003.

Schwabach, Aaron. *Internet and the Law: Technology, Society, and Compromises.* ABC-CLIO, 2006.

Smith, Marcia S. *"Junk E-mail": An Overview of Issues and Legislation concerning Unsolicited Commercial Electronic Mail ("Spam").* Congressional Research Service, Library of Congress, 2001.

SPAM FILTERS

Introduction

Spam is an electronic version of junk mail, and has been around since the introduction of the internet. The senders of spam (called "spammers") are usually attempting to sell products or services. Sometimes, their intent is more sinister—they may be trying to defraud their message recipients. Since the cost of sending spam is negligible to spammers, it has been bombarding email servers at a tremendous rate. Some estimate that as much as 40 to 50 percent of all emails are spam. The cost to the message recipients and businesses can be considerable in terms of decreased productivity and unwelcome exposure to inappropriate content and scams. As frustrating and potentially damaging as spam email is, fortunately, much of it does not reach recipients thanks to spam filters.

Spam filters are computer programs that screen email messages as they are received. Any email suspected to be spam will be redirected to a junk mail folder so that it does not clutter up a user's inbox. How does the filter decide which messages are suspect? Spam filters are implementations of statistical models that predict the probability that a message is spam given its characteristics. The filter classifies messages with large predicted probabilities of being spam, as spam.

Background

Primitive filters designed to catch up to spammers who had perfected an early version of their craft simply classified a message as spam if it contained a word or phrase that frequently appeared in spam messages. However, spammers only need to adjust their messages slightly to outsmart the filter, and all legitimate messages containing these words would automatically be classified as spam. Modern spam filters are designed using a branch of statistics known as classification. Bayesian filtering is a particularly effective probability modeling approach in the war on spam. Bayesian methods are named for eighteenth-century mathematician and minister Thomas Bayes. He formulated Bayes' theorem, which relates the conditional probability of two events, A and B, such that one can find both the probability of A given that one already knows B (e.g., the probability that a specific word occurs in the text of an email given that the email is known to be spam); the reverse, the probability of B given that one knows A (e.g., the probability that an email is spam given that a specific word is known to appear in the text of the email).

The underlying logic for this type of filter is that if a combination of message features occurs more or less often in spam than in legitimate messages, then it would be reasonable to suspect a message with these features as being or not being spam. An extensive collection of email messages is used to build a prediction model via data analysis. The data consist of a comprehensive collection of message characteristics, some of which may include the number of capital letters in the subject line, the number of special characters (for example, "$", "*", "!") in the message, the number of occurrences of the word "free," the length of the message, the presence of html in the body of the message, and the specific words in the subject line and body of the message. Each of these messages will also have the true spam classification recorded. These email messages are split into a large training set and a test set. The filter will first be developed using the training set, and then its performance will be assessed using the test set. A list of characteristics is refined based on the messages in the training set so that each of the characteristics provides information about the chance the message is spam.

However, no spam filter is perfect. Even the best filter will likely misclassify spam from time to time. False positives are legitimate emails that are mistakenly classified as spam, and false negatives are spam that appear to be legitimate emails so they slip through the filter unnoticed. An effective spam filter will correctly classify spam and legitimate email messages most of the time. In other words, the misclassification rates will be small. The spam filter developer will set tolerance levels on these rates based on the relative seriousness of missing legitimate messages and allowing spam in user inboxes.

Spam filters need to be customized for different organizations because some spam features may vary from organization to organization. For instance, the word "mortgage" in an email subject line would be quite typical for emails circulating within a banking institution, but may be somewhat unusual for other businesses or personal emails. Filters should also be updated frequently. Spammers are becoming more sophisticated and are figuring out creative ways to design messages that will filter though unnoticed. Spam filters must constantly adapt to meet this challenge.

—*Bethany White*

References

Madigan, D. "Statistics and the War on Spam." *Statistics: A Guide to the Unknown.* 4th ed., Thompson Higher Education, 2006.

Zdziarski, J. *Ending Spam: Bayesian Content Filtering and the Art of Statistical Language Classification.* No Starch Press, 2005.

SPEECH-RECOGNITION SOFTWARE

Introduction

Speech-recognition software records, analyzes, and responds to human speech. The earliest such systems were used for speech-to-text programs. Speech recognition became commonplace in the 2010s through automated assistants. Speech recognition depends on complex algorithms that analyze speech patterns and predict the most likely word from various possibilities.

Speech-recognition software consists of computer programs that can recognize and respond to human speech. Applications include speech-to-text software that translates speech into digital text for text messaging and document dictation. This software is also used by automated personal assistants such as Apple's Siri, Microsoft's Cortana, Google Assistant, and Amazon's Alexa, which can respond to spoken commands. Speech-recognition software development draws on the fields of linguistics, machine learning, and software engineering. Researchers first began investigating the possibility of speech-recognition software in the 1950s. However, the first such programs only became available to the public in the 1990s.

Speech-recognition software works by recognizing the phonemes that make up words. Algorithms are used to identify the most likely word implied by the sequence of phonemes detected. The English language has forty-four phonemes, which can be combined to create tens of thousands of different words. A particularly difficult aspect of speech recognition is distinguishing between homonyms (or homophones). These are words that consist of the same phonemes but are typically spelled differently. Examples include "addition" versus "edition" and "taught" versus "taut." Distinguishing between homonyms requires an understanding of context. Speech-recognition software must be able to evaluate surrounding words to discern the most likely homonym intended by the speaker.

Some speech-recognition software uses training, in which the speaker first reads text or a list of vocabulary words to help the program learn particularities of their voice. Training increases accuracy and decreases the error rate. Software that requires training is described as speaker dependent. Speaker-independent software does not require training, but it may be less accurate. Speaker-adaptive systems can alter some operations in response to new users.

Background

Research into speech-recognition software began in the 1950s. The first functional speech-recognition programs were developed in the 1960s and 1970s. The first innovation in speech-recognition technology was the development of dynamic time warping (DTW). Dynamic time warping is an algorithm that can analyze and compare two auditory sequences that occur at different rates.

Speech recognition advanced rapidly with the invention of the hidden Markov model (HMM). The HMM is an algorithm that evaluates a series of potential outcomes to a problem and estimates the probability of each one. It is used to determine the "most-likely explanation" of a sequence of phonemes, and thus the most likely word, given options taken from a speaker's phonemes. Together, HMMs and DTW are used to predict the most likely word or words intended by an utterance.

Speech recognition is based on predictive analysis. An important part of developing a predictive algorithm is feature engineering. This is the process of teaching a computer to recognize features, or relevant characteristics needed to solve a problem. Raw speech features are shown as waveforms. Speech waveforms are the two-dimensional (2D) representations of sonic signals produced when various phonemes are said.

An emerging feature in speech recognition is the use of neural networks. These computing systems are designed to mimic the way that brains handle computations. Though only beginning to affect speech recognition, neural networks are being combined with deep learning algorithms, which make use of raw features, to analyze data.

Applications and Future Directions

Deep neural network algorithms and other advancements have made speech-recognition software more accurate and efficient. The most familiar applications for speech-recognition technology include the voice-to-text and voice-to-type features on many computers and smartphones. Such features automatically translate the user's voice into text for sending text messages or composing documents or emails. Most speech-recognition programs rely on cloud computing, which is the collective data storage and processing capability of remote computer networks. The user's speech is uploaded to the cloud, where computers equipped with complex algorithms analyze the speech before returning the data to the user.

Automated assistant programs such as Siri and Cortana can use an array of data collected from a user's device to aid comprehension. For instance, if a user tells a speech-recognition program "bank," the program uses the internet and global positioning systems (GPSs) to return data on nearby banks or banks that the user has visited in the past.

Experts predict that speech-recognition apps and devices will likely become ubiquitous. Fast, accented, or impeded speech and slang words pose much less of a challenge than they once did. Speech-recognition software has become a basic feature in many new versions of the Mac and Windows operating systems. These programs also help make digital technology more accessible for people with disabilities. In future, as voice recognition improves and becomes commonplace, a wider range of users will be able to use advanced computing features.

—*Micah L. Issitt*

References

"How Speech-Recognition Software Got So Good." *Economist*, 22 Apr. 2014, www.economist.com/the-economist-explains/2014/04/22/how-speech-recognition-software-got-so-good.

Hoy, Matthew B. "Alexa, Siri, Cortana, and More: An Introduction to Voice Assistants." *Medical Reference Services Quarterly*, vol. 37, no. 1, 2018, pp. 81–88.

Information Resources Management Association, editor. *Assistive Technologies: Concepts, Methodologies, Tools, and Applications*. Vol. 1. Information Science Reference, 2014.

Li, Jinyu, et al. *Robust Automatic Speech Recognition*. Academic Press, 2016.

Martindale, Jon. "Cortana vs. Siri vs. Google Assistant vs. Alexa." *Digital Trends*, 17 June 2020, www.digitaltrends.com/computing/cortana-vs-siri-vs-google-now/.

Pearl, Cathy. *Designing Voice User Interfaces*. O'Reilly Media, 2017.

Pinola, Melanie. "Speech Recognition through the Decades: How We Ended Up with Siri." *PCWorld*, 3 Nov. 2011, www.computerworld.com/article/2499980/speech-recognition-through-the-decades–how-we-ended-up-with-siri.html.

Sen, Soumya, Anjan Dutta, and Nilanjan Dey. *Audio Processing and Speech Recognition*. Springer Singapore, 2019.

SPOTIFY

Introduction

Spotify is a free and subscription streaming service that makes a vast library of digital music and other audio content available to play on smartphones, computers, tablets, video gaming consoles, and other electronic devices. The name *Spotify* is a portmanteau of the words "spot" and "identify." In the first decade of its existence, the streaming service transformed the way people listened to music and reshaped the way the music industry makes its money. By 2012, Spotify's success had increased founder Daniel Ek's worth to an estimated $290 million, and he was tenth on the *London Sunday Times* list of richest men; by April 2019, according to *Forbes*, his net worth had reached $2.3 billion. By 2022, Spotify had set up operations in over 180 countries around the world. Spotify went public in April 2018.

Background

Spotify was established in Stockholm, Sweden, in 2006 by Daniel Ek and Martin Lorentzon. Ek, who is considered the driving force behind Spotify, was already a millionaire when he came up with the idea of Spotify. At twenty-two, he had just sold his online marketing firm Advertigo for $1.2 million. Lorentzon was the cofounder of Tradedoubler, the digital marketing company that had acquired Advertigo. Daniel Ek envisioned Spotify as a legal version of Napster, the popular online service from the late 1990s that had offered music selections for free from users' personal databases. The service introduced online music piracy and helped drive a marked decline in music industry revenue. Ek convinced Napster's founder Sean Parker to serve on Spotify's board. Ek obtained an engineer for his new project by acquiring uTorrent, a torrent client service, and he gave cash advances to Swedish artists to convince them to sign deals with the new service.

Spotify operates on what has been termed the "freemium" model, offering both free and paid subscriptions. The free subscriptions offer somewhat limited services and are paid for by advertisements. While the free version of Spotify has a number of restrictions, premium users gain access to shuffle play; they are not required to listen to advertising; they can skip an unlimited number of songs; they may listen offline; and they may play any track from an artist's available songs.

All of these features are available for around $10 a month. A family plan is also available. Spotify struck deals with record companies and music publishers for the ability to stream their music. The record companies and artists are paid a certain percentage of the revenue from each song streamed. Spotify insisted that 70 percent of its budget was allotted to paying labels, publishers, and distributors for music rights. However, the amount Spotify paid and the ways the company and similar streaming services affected artists' income became a source of controversy.

For its first five years, Spotify built up its user base in Europe. After its creation in 2006, the service officially launched in 2008, after the process of development and establishing rights deals with record labels. Spotify soon offered millions of songs to fit every musical taste, and thousands of new selections were added each day. More than two billion playlists were created, including celebrity playlists.

By 2011, the service had grown to over a million subscribers in Europe and was prepping for release in the United States. In May of that year, the company partnered with Facebook. The partnership allowed existing Facebook users to establish a Spotify account through their existing Facebook account and share music with friends.

Spreading to the United States

After years of building the company up, Spotify launched in the United States in 2011. Building on the explosion of social media and its partnership with Facebook, Spotify allowed users to share musical preferences with a selected group of other users. Spotify also incorporated the popular social media concept of followers, allowing users to follow any artist, as well as other users.

As Spotify gained in popularity, it began to acquire other companies. In 2012, Spotify acquired Soundwave, a Dublin-based social network application for music lovers. Two years later, Spotify acquired the Cord Project, a New York-based operation that offers mobile messaging services. In January 2015, Spotify announced an exclusive partnership with Sony PlayStation, called Playstation Music, which offers users streaming access for Playstation 4, Playstation 3, and Xperia devices. Additionally, Spotify signed partnership deals with Starbucks and Nike.

In 2017, the company struck a deal with video streaming service Hulu to offer a bundled subscription service for US college students. By early 2019, Spotify was offering a general market bundle for a limited time in which premium subscribers would receive Hulu for free. Subscribers also have access to playlists created by professional deejays for use at parties. Whether searching by musical artist or song title, the service offers users the opportunity to create their own "radio stations" of songs by selected artists.

Initially, Spotify stood out because it is interactive, unlike other online music streaming services like Pandora. Other companies soon followed Spotify's example. Spotify was challenged by rivals including Apple Music, which had decades of trust already built up with both artists and users through its iTunes service. Other competition came from such services as Pandora, Amazon Prime Music, Google Play, Deezer, Rhapsody, and Jay Z's Tidal. Another potential threat to Spotify's success surfaced when Amazon launched its own full-catalog music streaming service, Amazon Music Unlimited, in October 2016 in the United States. Still, many observers suggested that there was room for many such services as the demand for digital music continued to increase throughout the world. According to *Billboard*, by 2018, Spotify accounted for 43 percent of all streaming music subscriptions worldwide and was valued at $8 billion.

On April 3, 2018, Spotify (SPOT) listed its shares on the New York Stock Exchange in an initial public offering (IPO), reaching a market capitalization of $26.5 billion. The IPO was considered nontraditional because Spotify offered shares directly to the public instead of indirectly via underwriters, and because the company did not impose a lockup period to prevent employees and investors from selling their shares immediately, causing some analysts to fear that the share price would become volatile with high-volume trading. Yet, despite the fact that 90 percent of Spotify's shares were immediately available for trade, trading did not become volatile and prices remained relatively stable. According to the company's website, by 2022 it had 180 million paying subscribers and 406 million active users in 184 markets.

In a further effort to compete with the likes of Apple Music, Spotify continued to diversify by making more investments in expanding its podcast offerings. By February 2019, it had been reported that the company had acquired the podcast production companies Gimlet Media and Anchor. In 2020 the service signed a major deal with popular comedian and podcaster Joe Rogan, with a reported value of over $100 million. *The Joe Rogan Experience* established itself as the most popular podcast on Spotify with over 11 million listeners to each episode.

Despite its steady growth, Spotify (and Joe Rogan) did attract considerable controversy. Along with ongoing complaints from some artists over royalties, the service drew scrutiny for some of its content, especially controversial podcasts. This issue was highlighted during the coronavirus disease 2019 (COVID-19) pandemic that began in 2020, as a variety of podcasts on Spotify were criticized for spreading misinformation about the disease. Other examples of controversial material included misinformation about the 2020 presidential election and various conspiracy theories. While Spotify stated that it made efforts to remove harmful material that violated its terms of agreement, many critics argued that it failed to do enough to prevent the circulation of false and damaging information.

In January 2022, over two hundred health officials and professors sent an open letter asking Spotify to better regulate COVID-19 misinformation, including by making its rules and policies more transparent. Soon after, musician Neil Young publicly criticized Spotify for allowing Rogan to spread falsehoods about COVID-19, and asked the company to remove his music in protest.

Several other prominent artists joined Young's boycott, notably including Joni Mitchell. In response, Spotify reiterated its commitment to removing any dangerous content and published its rules of conduct, but it also defended Rogan and its overall opposition to censorship. Rogan himself suggested he would attempt to feature more balanced viewpoints on his show but would also continue to spotlight controversial opinions. The incident ignited widespread debate over misinformation and the limits of free speech, feeding into the broader culture wars of the time.

Impact

Spotify was established in the post-Napster environment in which artists and labels demanded that copyrights be acknowledged and that they receive compensation for sales of their products. Despite the fact that Napster was forced to shut down, its presence ushered in changes in the music industry. Music users had become insistent that the price of compact discs (CDs) was unreasonable, and they demanded new ways of purchasing music. Spotify offered an alternative to the purchase of CDs by negotiating deals with all major music studios, following a model that Ek called access-based, versus transaction-based. The model proved immensely successful, effectively changing the way music is consumed for many people by ushering in the era of streaming.

Yet Spotify also proved controversial, with some artists insisting that they saw very little return for their songs being offered on the platform. A few prominent artists, perhaps most notably pop musician Taylor Swift, publicly denounced the service, and pulled all of their music from Spotify. (Swift pulled her music in 2014, but returned to Spotify in 2017.) Though the debate as to whether Spotify is helpful or harmful to artists continues, it is evident that the company had a huge effect on the music industry and making online streaming profitable.

—*Elizabeth Rholetter Purdy and Jake Nicosia*

References

"About Spotify." *Spotify*, newsroom.spotify.com/companyinfo/.

Andrew, Levshon. *Reformatted: Code, Networks, and the Transformation of the Music Industry.* Oxford UP, 2014.

Beer, Jeff. "What It Really Means That Spotify Has Lost Its Second Top Marketing Executive in a Week." *Fast Company*, 18 Sept. 2018, www.fastcompany.com/90238502/what-it-really-means-that-spotify-has-lost-its-second-top-marketing-executive-in-a-week.

"Company Overview of Spotify Technology S.A." *Bloomberg*, 7 Nov. 2018, www.bloomberg.com/research/stocks/private/snapshot.asp?privcapId=225595077.

Goodman, Shalom. "Neil Young, Joe Rogan Podcast and Spotify: What to Know." *The Wall Street Journal*, 2 Feb. 2022, www.wsj.com/articles/joe-rogan-podcast-neil-young-spotify-what-to-know-11643663216.

Heater, Brian. "Why Spotify Is Betting Big on Podcasting." *TechCrunch*, Verizon Media, 6 Feb. 2019, techcrunch.com/2019/02/06/why-spotify-is-betting-big-on-podcasting/.

Levine, Robert. "Billboard Cover: Spotify CEO Daniel Ek on Taylor Swift, His 'Freemium' Business Model and Why He's Saving the Music Industry." *Billboard*, 5 June 2015, www.billboard.com/articles/business/6590101/daniel-ek-spotify-ceo-streaming-feature-tidal-apple-record-labels-taylor-swift.

___. "Billboard Power 100's New No. 1: Spotify Streaming Pioneer Daniel Ek." *Billboard*, 9 Feb. 2017, www.billboard.com/articles/business/7685308/no-1-power-100-daniel-ek-spotify.

Linksy, Dorian. "Is Daniel Ek, Spotify Founder, Going to Save the Music Industry...or Destroy It?" *The Guardian*, 10 Nov. 2013, www.theguardian.com/technology/2013/nov/10/daniel-ek-spotify-streaming-music.

McGarry, Caitlin. "Hands On with the New Spotify: Still the Streaming Service to Beat." *Macworld*, vol. 32, no. 7, 2015, pp. 112–14.

Miller, James. "Spotify Controversy: What You Need to Know." *The Siskiyou*, 23 Feb. 2022, siskiyou.sou.edu/2022/02/23/spotify-controversy-what-you-need-to-know/.

Morris, Jeremy Wade. *Selling Digital Music, Formatting Culture.* U of California P, 2015.

Pisani, Bob. "Spotify's IPO Disrupted Wall Street. What Lies Ahead Now for Unicorns Looking to Go Public." *CNBC Disruptor/50*, 22 May 2018, www.cnbc.com/2018/05/22/spotifys-ipo-disrupted-wall-street-what-lies-ahead-now-for-unicorns-looking-to-go-public.html.

Seabrook, John. "Revenue Streams." *The New Yorker*, 24 Nov. 2014. www.newyorker.com/magazine/2014/11/24/revenue-streams.

Suhr, H. Cecilia. *Evaluation and Credentialing in Digital Music Communities: Benefits and Challenges for Learning and Assessment.* MIT Press, 2014.

SPYWARE

Introduction

Software that performs certain behaviors (like being downloaded to a user's computer without being given permission), is generally considered spyware, although the definition may be expanding to include any software, or website, that acts in any way without the user's content. These programs are aimed to obtain the owner's private information, such as lists of websites visited, passwords, and credit card numbers.

Some spyware gets installed onto a user's computer through electronic games, legitimate programs that have been tampered with, infected attachments, infected email links, even advertisements that seem innocent but are created to get users to click on buttons or links. Spyware can spread quickly if left unchecked.

With many types of malicious software on the internet, users must be aware of what spyware is and what spyware does. Spyware generally performs certain behaviors, including (1) advertising, (2) collecting personal information, and (3) changing the configuration of the user's computer. Spyware is often associated with software that displays advertisements (known as adware) or software that tracks personal or sensitive information.

Not all software that has advertisements or tracks user online activities is harmful. For example, a user may sign up for a free service and in return for the service, she or he must agree to receive targeted ads. If the user understands these terms and agrees to them, the user may decide that this trade-off is worthwhile. The user may also agree to let the company track his or her online activities to determine which ads to show the individual. For any software program, the user must understand what the software will do and have agreed to install the software on his or her computer.

Background

Detecting spyware can often be difficult process because most spyware is intended to be difficult to remove. Spyware that changes the computer's configuration can be annoying and can cause the computer to slow down or crash.

Spyware can alter the web browser's home page or search page, or add additional components to the browser that users may not want. Spyware also makes it difficult for the user to change the settings. One common tactic is that spyware is covertly installed along with the software a user may want, such as a music or video file-sharing program.

Whenever a user installs software on a computer, he or she must carefully read all disclosures, including the license agreement and privacy statement. Sometimes the inclusion of unwanted software in a given software installation is documented, but it might appear at the end of a license agreement or privacy statement.

—*Gretchen Nobahar*

References

Aycock, John Daniel. *Spyware and Adware.* Springer, 2011.

Bennett, Colin J. *The Privacy Advocates: Resisting the Spread of Surveillance.* MIT Press, 2008.

Erbschloe, Michael. *Trojans, Worms, and Spyware: A Computer Security Professional's Guide to Malicious Code.* Elsevier Butterworth Heinemann, 2005.

Marzolf, Julie Schwab. *Online Privacy.* Gareth Stevens, 2013.

T

TECHNICAL DRAWING

Introduction

A technical drawing is a precise representation of a physical object or space drawn to a specific scale of proportions and specifying all dimensions of its subject. There are many different types of technical drawings relating to different fields of endeavor and ranging in complexity.

Scientists may be required to include a drawing of the apparatus used for a particular operation such as distillation. Physicists and electricians may be required to produce a drawing showing the layout of a certain electrical circuit. Artists may be required to produce a drawing of a particular building or the design of the stage for a certain play, and so on. All are types of technical drawings, and the most basic types of a fairly complex process begin with orthographic representation and isometric projection.

An orthographic representation of an object consists of three views: the front, top, and side. Each view depicts essentially how the object appears as though the viewer is looking directly at it along one of its three major axes (length, width, or depth) using just one eye. As a very simple example, the front, top, and side orthographic views of a cube are simple, two-dimensional (2D) squares. No other parts of the cube can be seen in an orthographic view. But as objects represented in orthographic views become more complex, so too do the orthographic views. The key feature of all such views in an orthographic representation is that only the features of the object that are visible are drawn. Technical drawings using orthographic views are completed by indicating the dimensions of the actual object.

The other fundamental representation used in basic technical drawing is isometric projection. An isometric projection can be thought of as an orthographic view of an object that has been rotated toward the viewer by 15 degrees and then dextrorotated (turned clockwise) by 15 degrees as well. The isometry in an isometric projection is due to the fact that the scale of the drawing along all three-dimensional (3D) axes (length, width, and depth) is the same. An isometric projection is produced by transferring the dimensions of an orthographic drawing point by point to an isometric grid. The isometric grid, typically ruled on isometric graphing paper, is scaled with lines at mutual angles of 120 degrees corresponding to the three axes of the object. Transferring the main dimensions of the object in the orthographic drawing to the isometric grid generates the isometric view of the object in three dimensions, much as it would appear in reality. As with an orthographic view, the more complex the object, the more complex is the isometric drawing.

Orthographic drawings and isometric projections are the foundation of all forms of technical drawing. A completed technical drawing, such as an engineering blueprint or a drawing of a newly designed proprietary device, becomes the legal documentation of its subject, as well as being the key to its reproduction as an actual physical entity.

Background

Traditional, or manual, technical drawing is carried out using a set of precision-made instruments. The first of these is the drafting table. The tops of such tables are made to different dimensions to facilitate their use in different working spaces. Each tabletop is made perfectly even and is often covered with a sheet of dense vinyl that can be replaced when necessary. The tabletops can be tilted to provide a comfortable working position for the draftsperson. Each tabletop is bordered by a precisely engineered and machined hardwood frame. The purpose of this border is to provide a precise match for the second essential drafting tool, the T-square.

A T-square is made to fit squarely to the edge of the drafting table, allowing the draftsperson to draw perfectly parallel horizontal lines. Other lines are generated using standard precision-made 30-60 and 45-90 triangle templates in conjunction with the T-square. Setting the base of the template against the crossbeam of the T-square guarantees that the lines drawn are at precise angles. All other dimension lines in the drawing are made using an appropriate template as a straightedge. Circles are generally drawn using a drafting compass or precision-made circle and ellipse templates. Constructing an ellipse using a drafting compass is a technique that demands definite skill.

The remaining essential tools of basic technical drawing are also the simplest: very sharp pencils and a gum eraser. Through all progressive developments of manual drafting, these are the only tools that have remained constant. All of the other tools of manual drafting have been replaced by the mechanical drafting table. A mechanical drafting table has a precision-engineered articulated arm that ends with two orthogonal straightedges attached to a hub that can be rotated to any desired angle, enabling the draftsperson to make any desired line in the drawing.

The technical drawing itself begins when the draftsperson positions the drawing paper on the drafting table and inscribes a fixed border around it, typically one centimeter from all four sides of the paper. This border defines the area of the drawing that will contain the legal content of the drawing. The legal content of the drawing, as an intellectual property, exists only within the area bounded by the border, regardless of the nature of the drawing. The drawing may be a map, an architectural blueprint, a design for an engineered device, a flow chart, a patent sketch, or something else.

Sketching

A sketch is a type of technical drawing that is carried out freehand, without the use of any of the standard drafting tools. It is not meant to be an accurate representation of the subject matter and can be thought of as analogous to the first draft of an essay. Sketching is primarily used to capture the essence of the thing being drawn so that it can be rendered accurately in a formal technical drawing. A sketch may also be used simply as a guide to record the locations and dimensions of certain features of an actual object for comparison to those features in an existing technical drawing.

Since sketching does not employ precise drafting tools, perhaps not even the pencils, sketches appear in a range of quality, depending on the conditions under which they were produced. One can, for example, imagine a technician attempting to sketch the appearance of a part located underneath a large machine while lying supine and trying to make the sketch on a piece of paper held in the palm of one hand. Accordingly, the technique of sketching is intended to minimize the negative effects of environmental conditions. In a formal drawing, straight lines are drawn in a single fluid motion while holding the tip of the pencil against a straight edge and turning the pencil as it moves to keep the line of uniform thickness. But in sketching, straight lines are drawn using short, straight-line segments that one hopes will produce a line that is more-or-less straight overall. Sketching is very much an acquired skill that calls for a great deal of practice.

Computer-Aided Technical Drawing

Manual technical drawing continued to be the only accepted standard of technical drawing until well after computer graphic resolution became equal to that of manual drawing methods. It is still the preferred standard in many areas and applications that do not justify the cost or use of computer-aided drawing. That being said, however, nearly all graphics applications—whether incorporated into office software suites or existing as standalone applications—can be used to generate technical drawings. The benefits of such applications are their low cost and ease of use. Also beneficial is the ability to print out the drawing from any suitable printer on paper of the appropriate size. The applications typically have standard drafting line types and symbols that further enhance their capability as basic drafting implements.

High-end, and therefore high-cost, computer-aided drafting applications have far greater capabilities. Such applications are often referred to as either computer-aided design (CAD) or computer-aided design and drafting (CADD) tools. Software of that type is able to produce precise technical drawings on screen that can then be printed out as hard copies or be maintained as electronic files.

Computer-aided design and computer-aided design and drafting programs allow real-time manipulation of a drawing as an animation through the use of rotation matrix functions. These computational methods demand significant computing power and allow the user to rotate the object being drawn through any angle in three dimensions. This enables designers to observe the function and performance of the object in a simulated environment before the investment is made to produce the object, a process that may itself be very costly due to the materials and production methods required to produce the actual object.

With the object finally designed, CAD/CADD programs have a singularly valuable feature in their ability to interface with other programs such as product lifecycle management (PLM), computer-aided manufacturing (CAM), or computer-aided engineering (CAE) programs. CAM programs, for example, control the operations of production machines such as milling machines, lathes, and 3D printers. By such digital transfer of data, the CAM programs can perform a dimensional analysis of the object from its drawing parameters, determine the order of operations its machinery should carry out to produce the shape of the object, and then direct that machinery in carrying out those operations. This ensures that each unit of the object in question is produced in precisely the same way and to the same dimensions given in the technical drawing. PLM programs are used throughout the lifecycle of a product, from its inception and design to the end of its useful life. CAD programs are of primary importance at the beginning of that lifetime, but less so thereafter.

A large number of CAD/CADD software options are available, spanning a range of costs from free to several thousand dollars annually. Proprietary CAD software applications typically have the highest costs but also the greatest capability with regard to interconnection and usability. Many of the free-for-use CAD programs are scaled-down versions of the high-end proprietary programs, designed for organizations and users that do not require the full functionality of the high-end program. Often, these programs can be upgraded to the high-end version after the user has had the opportunity to assess their needs against the capability of the particular CAD program. Some CAD programs are provided as open-source software, for which the end user is allowed to alter the source code of the program to suit particular needs that may not be adequately covered. Proprietary software, on the other hand, can only be legally altered by the proprietor of the software. Open-source applications generally also have the advantage of a large number of users and developers globally who will seek to find ways to improve the software and enhance its usability, as opposed to the proprietor organization having to maintain a large stable of in-house developers for the same purpose.

—*Richard M. Renneboog*

References

McHenry, David. *Drawing the Line: Technical Hand Drafting for Film and Television*. Routledge, 2018.

Ostrowsky, O. *Engineering Drawing with CAD Applications*. Routledge, 2019.

Plantenberg, Kirstie. *Engineering Graphics Essentials with AutoCAD 2022 Instruction*. SDC Publications, 2021.

Simmons, Colin H., Dennis E. Maguire, and Neil Phelps. *Manual of Engineering Drawing: British and International Standards*. Butterworth-Heinemann, 2020.

Singh, Lakhwinder Pal, and Harwinder Singh. *Engineering Drawing: Principles and Applications*. Cambridge UP, 2021.

Szkutnicka, Basia. *Flats: Technical Drawing for Fashion: A Complete Guide*. Lawrence King, 2017.

TECHNOETHICS AND SOCIETY

Introduction

Technoethics is a portmanteau of the words "technology" and "ethics." New technologies in any age exploit what is possible to accomplish; the repercussions of powerful new tools are of interest to ethicists. Advances in the sciences, as with any rapidly evolving fields, such as genetic engineering, are not without ethical challenges. Twenty-first century medical and technical advances have led to both ethical and moral dilemmas—questions about patient and human rights, for instance—ethical considerations have accelerated along with the possibilities and certainties of humankind's increasingly online and digital abilities.

Technology concerns the development and use of tools to solve problems or to make life easier, while ethics concerns the study of what is right or wrong and what is fair or unfair. In the past, technology could refer to relatively simple things such as the wheelbarrow or a particular method of planting grain. More recently, technology tends to concern the use of computers, the internet, and advanced processes such as genetic engineering. Technology in the age of the internet grows at an ever-increasing pace as the availability of more information makes it possible for research to advance further and faster than ever before. This acceleration, however, is not without its ethical challenges. All too often, new technologies emphasize what it *is* possible to accomplish without considering whether or not it is desirable that this end *be* accomplished.

Background

Ethical debates concerning technology have been around for most of human history, but it is since the Industrial Revolution that they have become more frequent and more serious. This is not to suggest that older ethical debates were lacking in seriousness, but to emphasize that in the modern era the ethical implications of new technology and new uses of existing technology can have severe and immediate consequences in ways that were not always possible at earlier points in history. Because this is so, it is important to distinguish between consequences due to the use of technology that are undesirable and those that are unethical.

All too often, debates concerning technology and ethics confuse these two points, but it is important to remain aware of the distinction. For example, the case of making genetic modifications to human deoxyribonucleic acid (DNA) in order to produce offspring with or without specific characteristics has potential consequences that are both undesirable and of questionable ethics. Within the category of undesirable consequences is found the possibility that genetic modification of human DNA could produce unintended consequences that are difficult or impossible to contain, such as new diseases or new vulnerabilities to diseases. Although it may sound like science fiction, there remains the possibility that a seemingly innocuous alteration to human DNA, such as changing eye color, could potentially cause unpredicted results like increasing the frequency of certain birth defects or the chances of developing cancer or similar ailments.

Researchers in the field of technoethics have begun to distinguish between two broad areas of interest. The first of these concerns the technoethical implications of emerging technologies, while the second area concerns the ways in which technologies alter preexisting ethical questions by changing the scope of the individual's influence. The manipulation of human genetic material is an example of a new and still-developing technology that technoethicists are interested in, while an example of a preexisting ethical question being affected by technological developments can be found in the field of artificial intelligence.

Artificial intelligence (AI) refers to a computer that mimics features of a human mind—information seeking and decision-making, for example. Machine learning enables a computer to use information it already possesses to draw conclusions about a problem and carry out a task without explicit instructions from a human controller. As these systems become more complex, computer functions come closer to resembling human thought. This technology allows human beings to delegate high-risk, dangerous, or repetitive tasks, such as surgery, reconnaissance, and manufacturing, to artificial intelligence systems, or "robots." While fully humanlike artificial intelligence—capable of abstract thinking and self-awareness—has not yet arrived, the prospect of creating a disposable labor force recasts the previously settled ethical question, as to whether people can be enslaved. In other words, if human beings are able to create artificially intelligent machines that are functionally equivalent to living people, these machines may not wish to perform the tasks they were designed to do. (In this scenario, technological developments in computer science will have extended the ability of human beings to exert control over other completely new intelligences).

Advancements, Checks, and Balances

Large corporations specializing in the fields of biochemistry and agriculture produce grains that are genetically modified. The goal of these companies in developing modified grains is to increase the grains' agricultural outputs by, for example, making the grain more resistant to pests and disease. On its face this would appear to be a highly beneficial outcome, because growing more food would mean that more food is available for people around the world, vast numbers of whom do not have enough to eat. Ethical questions have nevertheless arisen.

For example, genetic modifications to crop seed frequently including one to ensure that purchased seed will produce only one generation of crops. This means that a farmer cannot use seed from a crop to replant the following year but must buy a quantity of seed every year. This feature disrupts the traditional model, in which farmers were able to perpetuate crops, developing and improving their own seed. Replanting is a low-cost option for farmers but a problem for commercial seed producers. This genetic modification ensures the corporation that developed the more productive grain will reap annual profits from sale of its seed.

A further complication arises due to the natural behavior of crops. Wind carries some of the genetically modified seeds from the land of a farmer who purchased them to the land of a farmer who did not. This is not something that the non-purchasing farmer had any control over; but in some instances, corporations have sought to obtain compensation from the farmers in order to protect their intellectual property. The entire issue speaks to the larger question of whether or not it is fair or right for an individual or corporation to have ownership rights over the genetic code of a plant or another organism.

Wind is also a factor in the destruction of nongenetically modified crops, as herbicides used on modified crops is carried to fields of non-modified crops. Use of modified seed at a single farm, therefore, applies pressure to neighboring farms to also use modified seed. The mere availability of genetically modified seeds has resulted in the necessity of using it, placing a financial burden on farmers because they must cope with the added expense of having to buy brand new seeds every year, which they had not needed to do in the past. Finally, the expanded use of pesticides on genetically modified crops, which is necessary to reap the benefits of the genetic modifications, comes with its own set of ethical questions.

In the field of medicine, ethical questions have arisen where researchers in a number of cases have encountered tissues from individuals that are uniquely able to produce certain biochemical substances that hold great promise for the treatment of diseases. Upon making this discovery, some researchers have sought to obtain patents over the creation of these substances, even though the creation was only made possible by the bodily tissue of a person who is not included in the patent protection and therefore will not derive any benefit from it. Ethical concerns surrounding this type of situation include whether or not it should be permissible to file a patent over a chemical substance produced by a living organism, particularly when that substance may be vitally important to the treatment of disease, as well as whether it is fair for the researchers to benefit financially from possessing a patent on the substance and not sharing those benefits with the person whose tissue made them possible.

Technological Conflicts

Technoethics frequently is the cause of conflict between various parties interested in a given topic. In many of these cases the essential nature of the conflict is that one party is in favor of the use of the technology or the development of technology, while the other party, composed of the technoethicists, is concerned about the consequences of the use of or development of the technology. The proponents of the technology tend to frame the issue as technoethicists putting up obstacles to progress. The technoethicists, on the other hand, feel that they are posing the underlying question of whether or not the technology could actually be accurately described as progress.

From the perspective of technoethicists, their role is not to stand in the way of progress but to help other segments of society more accurately identify what is and is not progress. Their view is that if a new technology or a new use of technology comes along with consequences that are undesirable, and undesirable in such a degree that they outweigh the benefits of the technology, then the technology does not represent progress and may actually be a step backward. The debate between technological progress and ethics is not a new one. In fact, it dates back to one of the ethical philosophies that has been around for hundreds of years. This is called utilitarianism.

Utilitarianism is an outlook based on the idea that whatever has the greatest benefit for the greatest number of people is the right thing to do, without regard to any other considerations. In debates between technoethicists and researchers, the researchers often have a utilitarian perspective because they are focused on what the specific technology can do and how it would benefit people, and because they consider this benefit to be significant, they tend to discount other considerations.

The example of genetically modified seeds is also an excellent example of utilitarianism and technoethics in conflict. The developers of the genetically modified seeds primarily are concerned with their utility. Because they have a greater output of food, this is seen as the overriding concern by this group. There is, however, another concern that they may not be aware of or sensitive to, and this is the issue of biodiversity. In nature there are often many different kinds of seeds for a particular plant or variety of crop. This would change if researchers develop a genetically modified version of the seed that is not only designed to produce more food but also designed to be genetically successful, essentially driving out competing versions of itself and leaving only a single type of seed to be used by human beings.

From the researchers' perspective this is most likely not a problem, but from the perspective of environmentalists and others it is dangerous to cause other variations of seeds to die out, because they may have unique properties that could be vitally important in the future. It is this unpredictability that always occurs in conjunction with technological development that concerns technoethicists above all else. Time and again throughout history, a scientific breakthrough has occurred that transforms the lives of people all over the world, providing them with incredible benefits, only for it to later be discovered that these benefits come at a high cost. For example, the invention of the internal combustion engine and other advances in energy technologies drove the fossil fuel industry, resulting is more comfortable and convenient living globally but at a cost of lasting environmental devastation of many areas and changes to the planet's climate.

In the hope of preventing humanity from repeating this scenario too many times, technoethicists consider new technologies in the light of not only what the benefits are known or expected to be but also what humanity may be expected to give up or suffer in order to receive those benefits. If the answer is that the cost is unknown or unpredictable or potentially too great, then the proper course of action is to apply restraints on development and commercial distribution or to reconsider the value of the technology.

If this type of discernment process had been followed when the combustion engine was first invented, technoethicists argue, it might very well be that the modern world would not be grappling with the effects of climate change caused by the emission of greenhouse gases through the burning of fossil fuels. While there may be tension between scientific and technological innovators and technoethicists, history makes a strong case for rigorous examination of technological consequences for the future of humankind.

—*Scott Zimmer*

References

Berman, F., V. G. Cerf, N. Horton, L., et al. "Technologies Do Have Ethics." *Communications of the ACM*, vol. 60, no. 6, 2017, pp. 8–9.

Brusoni, S., and A. Vaccaro. "Ethics, Technology and Organizational Innovation." *Journal of Business Ethics*, vol. 143, no. 2, 2017, pp. 223–26.

Bułat, R., and A. Zep. "Posthumanism, Androids and Artificial Intelligence: An Aspect Cultural, Biological and Ethical." *International Academic Conference on Social Sciences*, 2017, pp. 36–41.

Grebenshchikova, E. "NBIC-Convergence and Technoethics: Common Ethical Perspective." *International Journal of Technoethics*, vol. 7, no. 1, 2016, pp. 77–84.

Heller, P. B. "Technoethics: The Dilemma of Doing the Right Moral Thing in Technology Applications." *International Journal of Technoethics*, vol. 3 no. 1, 2012, pp. 14–27.

Klaus, C. L., and T. S. Hartshorne. "Ethical Implications of Trends in Technology." *The Journal of Individual Psychology*, vol. 71, no. 2 2015, pp. 195–204.

Lau, L. "A Postcolonial Framing of Indian Commercial Surrogacy: Issues, Representations, and Orientalisms." *Gender, Place and Culture: A Journal of Feminist Geography*, vol. 25, no. 5, 2018, pp. 666–85.

Parahakaran, S. "An Analysis of Theories Related to Experiential Learning for Practical Ethics in Science and Technology." *Universal Journal of Educational Research*, vol. 5, no. 6, 2017, pp. 1014–20.

Patrignani, N., and D. Whitehouse. "Slow Tech: Bridging Computer Ethics and Business Ethics. " *Information Technology and People*, vol. 28, no. 4, 2015, pp. 775–89.

Pavone, V., and L. Martinelli. "Cisgenics as Emerging Bio-Objects: Bio-Objectification and Bio-Identification in Agrobiotech Innovation." *New Genetics and Society*, vol. 34 no. 1, 2015, pp. 52–71.

Stahl, B. C., J. Timmermans, and C. Flick. "Ethics of Emerging Information and Communication Technologies: On the Implementation of Responsible Research and Innovation." *Science and Public Policy*, vol. 44, no. 3, 2017, pp. 369–81.

Sugarman, J., S., M. Shivakumar, J. F. Rook, C. Loring, et al. "Ethical Considerations in the Manufacture, Sale, and Distribution of Genome Editing Technologies." *American Journal of Bioethics*, vol. 18, no. 8, 2018, pp. 3–6.

Tran, B. "Machine (Technology) Ethics: The Theoretical and Philosophical Paradigms." *International Journal of Technoethics*, vol. 7, no. 2, 2016, pp. 77–99.

Upadhyay, P. "Climate Change as Ecological Colonialism: Dilemma of Innocent Victims. " *Himalayan Journal of Sociology and Anthropology*, vol. 7, 2016, pp. 111–40.

Young-Joo Lee, and Ji-Young Park. "Identification of Future Signal Based on the Quantitative and Qualitative Text Mining: A Case Study on Ethical Issues in Artificial Intelligence." *Quality and Quantity*, vol. 52, no. 2, 2018, pp. 653–67.

TELECOMMUNICATIONS

Introduction

The etymology of the term *telecommunications* is rooted in long-distance communication by means of technological devices. In the twenty-first-century, this means primarily electrical and electronic communications, including the technologies that make telecommunications possible, the applications that derive from this technology, and the organizations developing and using it.

In the Information Age, data, sound, and video are gathered, .stored, disseminated, and manipulated. Senders, receivers, and manipulators are often separated by miles, even continents.

Telecommunication is usually envisioned as taking place between two people, but it is just as likely that information will be transmitted from people to machines, machines to people, or even machines to machines. The first telecommunications were electrical (such as the telegraph) and not electronic. Later, almost all telecommunications came to involve electronics (such as cellular radio, the internet, and satellite communications systems). Because telecommunication involves distance, it is important to consider the transmission medium. Early transmissions were carried over copper wire. Then came radio, and still later came coaxial cable and fiber optics. Although telecommunications technology has continued to develop, none of these had become obsolete by the year 2020.

Background

Certainly, the progress in communication technology from smoke signals and semaphores was not without effort; it took the work of hundreds of men and women. In 1835, American Samuel F. B. Morse developed a rudimentary telegraph system, which he improved and demonstrated in 1837. In 1864, Scottish physicist and mathematician James Clerk Maxwell predicted that waves of oscillating electric and magnetic fields could travel through empty space at the speed of light. In 1887, German physicist Heinrich Hertz tested Maxwell's theory and successfully demonstrated the existence of electromagnetic waves. His work demonstrated that radio waves could be generated at one location and transmitted to a nearby spot.

American scientist Alexander Graham Bell received a patent for the first telephone system in 1876. Inventor Thomas Alva Edison developed an electrical telegraph known as the quadruplex telegraph, which allowed four signals to be sent and received on a single wire at the same time. In 1877 and 1878, he developed the carbon transmitter, a telephone microphone used in telephones until the 1980s. Almon Brown Strowger, an undertaker, invented the first automatic switching system, the

Strowger switch, which would allow telephone users to direct their own calls. He received a patent in 1891. In 1901, Guglielmo Marconi transmitted the first trans-Atlantic radio signal, from Poldhu, Cornwall, to St. John's, Newfoundland.

In 1904, English electrical engineer and physicist Sir John Ambrose Fleming developed the first diode vacuum tube, and American inventor Lee De Forest inserted a grid in the diode vacuum tube and created the first triode vacuum tube in 1906. In 1948, Bell Telephone Laboratories employees Walter Brattain and John Bardeen applied for a patent for the point-contact transistor, and William Bradford Shockley, who had earlier worked with Brattain, applied for a patent for the junction transistor. The three are credited with the invention of the transistor, an electronic device that essentially made the vacuum tube obsolete. In 1958, Jack Kilby, an engineer at Texas Instruments, invented the integrated circuit; six months later, Robert Noyce independently developed the integrated circuit; both are credited with its invention. Without these scientific discoveries and technological adaptations, modern telecommunications would not be possible.

How It Works

Communication involves the conveying of information; telecommunication is communication through a transmission media. For decades, the prevalent means of transmitting information was copper wire. Two wires formed a circuit, and millions of miles of copper wire were strung across the United States. Unfortunately, this copper wire had limitations; the desired signal could leak out, and undesirable noise could leak in.

One method of correcting these problems was to use coaxial cable. This type of cable has a single strand of copper at its center, surrounded by insulation and a sheath of conductor such as aluminum or copper. The capacity of coaxial cable is extremely high, and its most well-known application is cable television.

An additional land-based means of transmitting information is fiber optics. A hair-thin strand of glass (very pure and very flexible) does not carry electricity—it carries light. That light, however, is a huge extension of the electromagnetic spectrum and can be triggered on and off at gigabit rates.

Wireless communications (such as radio) have become a significant means of transmitting information. The primary tool of wireless communications, the transistor, was small, used little power, lasted a long time, and was inexpensive. Of equal importance was the speed at which it could operate—it, too, could turn on and off at gigabit rates.

The Transmission Scheme

Equally important is the structure of the signal being sent. Broadly speaking, a signal can be either analogue or digital. An analogue signal is a continuously varying electrical signal that replicates the amplitude or frequency of the originating signal. Thus, the signal being transmitted over a telephone channel is a sine wave that varies in both frequency and amplitude. Unfortunately, such a transmission scheme has inherent problems. A burst of noise (for instance electromagnetic static caused by a nearby motor starting) will be picked up by the channel. In addition, high-frequency signals (as might be used for data) leak out.

The alternative is a digital transmission scheme. An analogue signal is sampled, a process that changes a continuous signal into a discrete one. The magnitude of each sample is converted into a binary code—a series of ones and zeros—and transmitted down the line. It is possible to apply error-checking techniques to a group of ones and zeros and make corrections for any noise bursts that have entered the system. At the distant end, the digital signal is converted back to an analogue signal. Usually, the communications channel is capable of extremely high-speed operation. If so, many individual voice or data channels can be multiplexed at the transmitting end and separated at the receiving end.

The Network

Digitization and the use of fiber optics had a tremendous impact on telecommunications and enabled the internet and packet switching. The internet is a vast worldwide network of computers, and packet switching is the method used for transmitting data.

The transmission of a message from point A to point B can be done by establishing a path, or circuit, through this network. Establishing a circuit and transmitting a message is known as circuit switching. This method, however, is quite inefficient, so scientists developed a faster and more versatile method, packet switching.

In packet switching, a complete data message is broken up into thousands of packets. Each packet, in addition to carrying the requisite intelligence, carries information regarding its importance and its destination. A selected packet is sent toward its destination and is received by the node at the end of this particular link and analyzed. It is then sent over a new link to the next node along the way, and the previously used link is released.

Thus, each packet, in its trek across the network, can take a different path. It is left to the intelligence of the computers at each node, and especially to the computer at the receiving end of the overall circuit, to reassemble the packets and deliver them to the recipient. Because of the high speed of this transmission, the time the packet spends at each node (called "latency") is less than 1 millisecond.

Applications and Products

The telecommunications industry embraces a number of transmission media (twisted-pair copper, coaxial cable, fiber optics, wireless), a highly efficient transmission scheme (digitization), and a huge, evolving network (the internet). Uses for these technologies have expanded rapidly, and that trend is likely to continue.

The telephone network that serves much of the world is hierarchical in nature. A circuit from a calling party to a receiving party is extended through a series of telephone central offices—both up and down—until a complete circuit has been established. Transmission media most likely will consist of both copper wires and fiber optics. The information communicated starts out as analogue and is transmitted over the majority of its path as a digital signal.

Data in the public network use the internet—that vast array of nodes consisting of computer-like devices, interconnected by wire and fiber optics, and employing packet switching. There is no set path for an entire message to traverse, and transmission speed is so high that the cost of transmitting a single message (no matter where) approaches zero.

To receive email, a computer must be connected to the internet. Connection can be made by coaxial cable or a satellite, as would be the case from a cruise ship. In some cases, the computer is connected to a telephone line, and digital subscriber line (DSL)

technology is used. So that the telephone can be used at the same time as the computer, a DSL circuit using high frequencies is used for the computer and low frequencies for the telephone conversation. A filter is inserted in telephone lines to keep the two separated. A modulation scheme is used to combine the voice and data signals at the user's premises and to separate them at the central office.

Another means of connection is the fiber-to-the-home (FTTH) form of broadband connection, which uses fiber optics to transmit data to the home. Its advantages are faster speeds and greater capacity for data.

The telecommunications tool used the world over is the cell phone. A cell phone system employs a series of cells, about 10 square miles (26 square kilometers) in size. Each cell site, or base station, is equipped with a tower and an antenna and serves subscribers only within its bounds. A cell phone moving from one cell to another will change operating frequencies automatically to conform with the frequencies assigned to the adjacent cell. This scheme makes it possible to reuse frequencies over and over again as the user moves across the country.

The wireless network consists of the wireless (radio) channels connecting the cell phone to the base station. Once a cell phone signal reaches the base station, it travels through copper or fiber to the central office, where it enters the public switched telephone network, or the internet. The frequencies used for this transmission are extremely valuable, and electronic auctions conducted by the Federal Communications Commission bring in millions of dollars to the US Treasury. Technologies have been created to improve wireless networks. Wi-Fi (802.11 standard networking) allows connectivity between computers and printers. WiMax (based on the 802.16 standard) is a wireless network that tries to capture the benefits of wireless and broadband technologies. Long-term Evolution (LTE), a fourth generation (4G) wireless broadband technology for wireless networks, was introduced in 2010. The fifth generation of wireless technology, known as 5G, was introduced in select regions beginning in 2019.

For the most part, cable television employs coaxial cable to connect the head end to the subscribers' premises. Television is also received through satellites, DSL, and fiber optics. In addition to cable television, cable access providers started selling high-speed broadband internet access in the 1990s. Cable access internet service is transmitted over the cable television infrastructure.

Global positioning systems (GPSs) are built into many cell phones and smartphones, come with many new cars, and are available as handheld devices. They simply identify the user's longitude and latitude. Associated components—all computer based—translate the longitude and latitude to a location on an electronic map of the city or the area and generate a route to get from one place to another.

Perhaps the most sophisticated part of this is how the GPS determines the user's location. The GPS unit does not transmit a signal to one of the satellites that form a part of this program, nor does a satellite transmit a unique signal to any GPS unit. Instead, each of the very accurate clocks on board the satellites produce a pulse that will not miss a beat in thousands of years. A somewhat less accurate clock in each GPS unit will produce an equivalent pulse. The Earth-bound unit measures the time between the beep received from the satellite and the beep generated by the unit. This time difference is used to determine the distance separating the satellite and the Earth-bound unit. Thus, the Earth-bound unit, with its internal maps, can determine its distance from the satellite (although its location could be anywhere on the surface of a sphere with the satellite at its center). A second satellite repeats the process, narrowing the location to the circle that represents the intersection of the spheres around the two satellites, and a third satellite narrows the location of the GPS unit to two points, the intersection of a sphere around the third satellite and the circle formed by the intersection of the first two spheres. A fourth satellite would pinpoint the user's location, but usually one of the two possibilities given by the intersection of the spheres of the three satellites makes sense and the other is nonsensical.

Identification of automobiles, pets, and other items can be made by equipping them with a device called a tag, and using radio frequency identification (RFID). The tags are tiny (hardly larger than a piece of glitter) and cost as little as ten cents. A common use is to enable people to enter toll roads without stopping to pay each time. As an automobile passes through the tollgate, a transmitter mounted on the gate sends out a radio frequency signal that is received by a device in the automobile. The device captures a bit of the electrical power being transmitted and triggers a small transmitter. This transmitter reflects the signal it has received, adding identification.

This technology is also used for asset tracking, retailing, and security and access. The US Department of Defense requires all equipment being shipped overseas to carry a tag. The equipment can be tracked as if it had a bar code, although visual contact is not required. The technology permits up to fifty readings per second.

Walmart, Target, and Best Buy are among the retailers tagging their stock in an effort to better track inventory, and some retailers are requiring their vendors to provide the tags. US passports incorporate tags that contain a photograph and all other passport information. They can also track travel information. Identification chips are often implanted under the skin of dogs, cats, and horses, and ear tags are used to identify cattle and other farm animals.

Careers and Specialists

The telecommunications field encompasses many disciplines, including electrical and computer engineering. A knowledge of programming and software is extremely important, as it is software that drives the hardware. Certainly physics, and increasingly chemistry, play a role in telecommunications. For example, GPSs provided inaccurate results until Einstein's special and general theories of relativity were incorporated. Some segments of the telecommunications industry—such as statistical signal processing and antenna design—are so specialized that only a few will understand them.

Social Context and Future Prospects

Predicting the future—especially when the present is moving so quickly—is an impossible task.

In 1965, Gordon E. Moore, then director of engineering at Fairchild Semiconductor and later co-founder of Intel, observed that the power of the computer chip was doubling every eighteen months. Industry experts welcomed the rapid advances but thought the pace was unsustainable; however, that doubling of capability continues and has been dubbed Moore's law.

Telecommunications has been, and will continue to be, a driving force in the growth of nations. The treatment and transmission of intelligence is faster, cheaper, more comprehensive, and more convenient than ever before. People are aware of what is happening as it happens, and as a result, people are better able to deal with it. People are able to stay connected to work, home, and the world twenty-four hours a day. There are negative aspects to this trend, and one of the most insidious is privacy. The information being gathered and manipulated is often personal and private, and its availability to virtually any enterprising person is of great concern. In spite of this, data of every sort are flooding the world.

—*Robert E. Stoffels*

References

Crandall, Robert W. *Competition and Chaos: U.S. Telecommunications Since the 1996 Telecom Act.* Brookings Institution Press, 2005.

Curwen, Peter, and Jason Whalley. *Mobile Telecommunications Networks: Restructuring as a Response to a Challenging Environment.* Edward Elgar, 2014.

Dodd, Annabel Z. *The Essential Guide to Telecommunications.* 6th ed., Pearson, 2019.

Ezmailzadeh, Riaz. *Broadband Telecommunications Technologies and Management.* John Wiley & Sons, 2016.

Frenzel, Louis E., Jr. *Principles of Electronic Communication Systems.* 4th ed., McGraw-Hill, 2016.

Fulle, Ronald G. *Telecommunications History and Policy into the Twenty-first Century.* RIT Press, 2010.

Giambene, Giovanni. *Queuing Theory and Telecommunications: Networks and Applications.* 2nd ed., Springer, 2014.

Lathi, B. P., and Zhi Ding. *Modern Digital and Analog Communication.* 5th ed., Oxford UP, 2018.

Penttinen, Jyrki T. J. *The Telecommunications Handbook: Engineering Guidelines for Fixed, Mobile, and Satellite Systems.* John Wiley & Sons, 2015.

Tripathi, Nishith D., and Jeffrey H. Reed. *Cellular Communications: A Comprehensive and Practical Guide.* Wiley-IEEE Press, 2014.

TIKTOK

Introduction

TikTok is a social media app that allows users to share short-form video content. Owned by Chinese technology company ByteDance, the application was first launched in China under the name Douyin before being released to international markets as TikTok in 2017. The app started out as a music-based app on which users lip synced to clips of popular songs. It later evolved to include talent- and comedy-based videos. Uploaded videos are short in form and can only be between three and fifteen seconds in length.

The app is most popular in Asia but has grown in popularity among Western nations since 2018, when it became the most downloaded app in the United States. It was the third fastest-growing brand in 2020. Despite its popularity, some tech experts worry that the app is a cybersecurity risk for users due to the app's built-in biometrics and location-tracking features. News outlets have also called out TikTok for its use of censorship in certain parts of the world.

Background

Prior to the official launch of TikTok in the United States, the app was known by a different name in China, where it was created. The app was first launched as Douyin by the Chinese internet technology company ByteDance in 2016. Content initially involved users uploading videos of themselves lip syncing to various songs. As the app developed, users also uploaded videos featuring comedic scenes and talent exhibitions. Douyin was extremely popular from the get-go, garnering millions of users within months. Within a year, the app had 100 million users.

After one year of operation, ByteDance decided to take their product to international markets. The app was relaunched as TikTok in September 2017 for countries outside of China, retaining its Douyin moniker within China. It was free to download and quickly became one of the most downloaded apps across the globe. ByteDance acquired a similar short-form social video networking app named Musical.ly in late 2017 and shut down the app's operation the following year while migrating all of the app's users over to TikTok.

The app was similar to Musical.ly, allowing users to upload very short videos featuring background music tracks. By the end of 2018, TikTok had been downloaded more than 80 million times in the United States alone. On a global level, the app had been downloaded more than 800 million times, and this number did not include Chinese Android phone users. These numbers surpassed download totals for popular social networking sites Facebook, Instagram, and Snapchat. A number of celebrities also began using the app, including Jimmy Fallon and Tony Hawk.

By the following year, the app had grown so popular that it had become a common household name. The app was available in more than 150 global markets and in more than forty languages. It boasted hundreds of millions of monthly active users around the world, with more than 40 million monthly active users in the United States alone. In September 2019, the NFL announced it had agreed to a partnership with TikTok that included the launch of an official NFL TikTok account that users could access around the world for a variety of NFL content.

Overview

The TikTok app is a mobile app that users download onto their phones. Users create accounts with unique usernames on which they can upload short videos of themselves or other content. This content usually features background music that can be edited within the app. An example of a song edit is adjusting the play speed to either increase or decrease the pace of the song. Users have the option of choosing from a wide selection of inbuilt musical tracks, many of which are popular songs. A common form of TikTok content is a short video of a user lip-syncing to a popular song, often while in the midst of an unrelated activity. Users then add a filter to the video if desired and post the content to their account. Users can also post short comedic videos or videos recording a talent or activity.

User accounts can be set to public or private. Public accounts can be viewed by anyone on TikTok. Users also have the option of setting their accounts to private so only those accounts the user has authorized are able to access his or her content. Privacy settings can also be applied to individual posts, with users having the option to make their video public, private, or viewable by friends only. Users can also interact with each other on TikTok. The app has a "react" feature that allows users to film their own reactions to another user's videos. Users can also perform duets together by using the "duet" feature, which allows users to film one video next to another. TikTok has commenting and messaging features for interacting with users. TikTok also features a user feed called the "for you" page, which recommends videos to users based on videos they have previously watched. The "for you" page has age restrictions, however, and any user under the age of sixteen is not permitted to be featured on the page.

Since its launch, TikTok has become a hugely popular social media app that has shown itself capable of producing viral content. In 2019, a rapper named Lil Nas posted a video of an original song he wrote called "Old Town Road" that went on to become one of the biggest singles of the year. Media outlets credited TikTok for raising awareness of the song, which went on to receive six Grammy Award nominations in 2020. It also led to the viral popularity of new social media influencers, including Baby Ariel, Michael Le, Addison Rae, Charli and Dixie D'Amelio, and Spencer X.

Despite its success, some tech experts worried that the app could be considered a security risk given its usage of biometrics and location tracking, data that was directly conveyed to the app's Chinese parent company. The company later became a target of censorship by the Chinese government when users began posting anti-Communist content in the wake of the 2018 Hong Kong protests. Amid growing censorship concerns, the app began reviewing its content-moderation policies.

Such concerns led the app to be temporarily banned in Indonesia in July 2018; blocked from internet access in Bangladeshi in November 2018; and preliminarily banned in India in April 2019, followed by a complete ban in June 2020. In August

2020, President Donald Trump issued an executive order that would ban TikTok from the United States if ByteDance did not sell the app to a US distributor by September 15. Several critics, however, questioned the legality of the executive order.

On September 13, ByteDance announced that it would not sell TikTok's US operations to Microsoft, which had made an offer to buy the operation the previous month. The same day, it was reported that TikTok had entered a partnership with the US software company Oracle in an attempt to address concerns over data security. However, the company reaffirmed that it would not sell or give the source code of the app to any US buyers.

—*Cait Caffrey and Jake D. Nicosia*

References

"8 Lessons from the Rise of Douyin (Tik Tok)." *Technode,* 15 June 2018, technode.com/2018/06/15/8-lessons-douyin/.

Graziani, Thomas. "How Douyin Became China's Top Short-Video App in 500 Days." *Walk the Chat,* walkthechat.com/douyin-became-chinas-top-short-video-app-500-days/.

Hallanan, Lauren. "Is Douyin the Right Social Video Platform for Luxury Brands?" *Jing Daily,* 11 Mar. 2018, jingdaily.com/douyin-luxury-brands/.

Koble, Nicole. "TikTok is Changing Music as You Know It." *GQ,* 28 Oct. 2019, www.gq-magazine.co.uk/culture/article/what-is-tiktok.

Leskin, Paige. "Trump's Push to Ban TikTok in the US, Explained in 30 Seconds." *Business Insider,* 8 Aug. 2020, www.businessinsider.com/donald-trump-tiktok-ban-us-china-explained-in-30-seconds-2020-8.

Perez, Sarah. "The NFL Joins TikTok in Multi-Year Partnership." *TechCrunch,* 3 Sept. 2019, techcrunch.com/2019/09/03/the-nfl-joins-tiktok-in-multi-year-partnership/.

___. "TikTok Surpassed Facebook, Instagram, Snapchat & Youtube in Downloads Last Month." *TechCrunch,* 2 Nov. 2018, techcrunch.com/2018/11/02/tiktok-surpassed-facebook-instagram-snapchat-youtube-in-downloads-last-month/.

Rayome, Alison DeNisco. "10 Most-Downloaded Apps of the 2010s: Facebook Dominates the Decade." *CNET,* 16 Dec. 2019, www.cnet.com/news/10-most-downloaded-apps-of-the-decade-facebook-dominated-2010-2019/.

Spangler, Todd. "Musical.ly Is Going Away: Users to Be Shifted to Bytedance's TikTok Video App." *Variety,* 2 Aug. 2018, variety.com/2018/digital/news/musically-shutdown-tiktok-bytedance-1202893205/.

Yurieff, Kaya. "TikTok Is the Latest Social Network Sensation." *CNN,* 21 Nov. 2018, edition.cnn.com/2018/11/21/tech/tiktok-app/index.html.

TOUCH SCREENS

Introduction

Anyone who has used a tablet or smartphone of any kind is familiar with touch screens. Touch the screen and move the finger about to select items displayed on the screen or to make things happen. Using a touch screen for digital natives seems simple, indeed. Behind the scenes, however, there is a lot going on users are unaware of, and digital immigrants often find that the logic behind touch-screen gestures is not as intuitive as those who are familiar with the technology believe.

A touch screen is both an input device and an output device for the computer within the particular device being used. Whether it is a laptop, a desktop, a tablet, a cell phone, an automobile or a machine control panel, touch screens may be used. In this use, the fingertip effectively becomes the cursor used to select the action or content desired. In ordinary computer use, the user requires a mouse to control the cursor and navigate about the screen. Once a user finds the area of the screen desired, the user clicks a button on the mouse (or trackpad) to select the action the cursor indicates.

With a touch screen, touching the screen at the desired location often replaces the movement of the mouse—its navigation or button-click actions. Afterwards, the touch screen becomes an output device for displaying the selected action, just as any other screen. This is where the screen becomes the viewing medium to see what the user has accessed.

Background

How a touch screen identifies where it is being touched can be determined in a variety of ways: electrical resistance, electrical capacitance, pressure, infrared light, and ultrasonic waves, for example. In all cases, the method used locates the position of the input touch signal by calculating it using an X-Y grid built into the overall construction of the screen. The screen itself is not simply a sheet of thin, tempered glass, but a multilayer construct of which the outermost layer is made of very tough glass as a protective layer. In a touch screen that uses electrical resistance to determine position, the thin glass deflects sufficiently under pressure to bring two underlying conductive layers into contact with each other. This closes an electrical circuit between them and changes the electrical resistance accordingly. By alternating between the X and Y components of the grid repeatedly, the location of the touch is instantly isolated and identified.

A "capacitance screen" works in much the same way as a touch screen, but using electrical capacitance rather than electrical resistance. When two conducting materials are in close proximity, but separated by a nonconducting material such as a thin layer of air, there is a build-up of electrical charge. In a touch screen, two thin conductive sheets are separated by a nonconductive sheet, creating the condition for capacitance. When the screen is touched, the capacitance charge is shorted at that location, changing the overall capacitance within the structure. The location is calculated in the same way from the X-Y grid, and in either type of screen the user can touch with either a fingertip or a stylus. A stylus resembles an ordinary pen but has a soft rubber bulb at the end rather than an ink delivery ballpoint. The rubber tip acts as a nonconducting layer between the metal casing of the stylus and the conductive glass surface of the touch screen, creating a capacitance trigger point where it touches the screen or providing enough pressure to trigger the resistance change in a resistance-based touch screen.

While capacitance- and resistance-based touch screens are the most common, there are many other means of identifying position in the X-Y grid of a touch screen. Some use an X-Y array of infrared (IR) emitters. Another type of touch screen uses piezoelectricity to identify location. Some materials produce an electrical output when they are subjected to pressure. This allows piezoelectric glass to be used in the construction of a touch screen. At the point of contact a piezoelectric output is produced and is subsequently detected by the change it induces in the state of the X-Y grid. Still another means of touch detection uses triangulation of the small sonic pulses. The triangulation is carried out by at least three small transducers situated about the perimeter of the screen. Other detection systems that do not use this microacoustic method identify the touch position continuously, whether the indicator is moving or not.

—*Richard M. Renneboog*

References

Gray, Leon. *How Does a Touchscreen Work?* Rosen, 2013.

Gray, Tony. *Projected Capacitive Touch: A Practical Guide for Engineers.* Springer International, 2019.

Lonbere, Philip. *A History of Communication Technology.* Routledge, 2021.

Rogers, Scott. *Swipe This!: The Guide to Great Touchscreen Game Design.* Wiley, 2012.

White, Michele. *Touch Screen Theory: Digital Devices and Feelings.* MIT Press, 2022.

TRANSMEDIA STORYTELLING

Introduction

Transmedia storytelling is rooted in the distant past when storytellers first began to use media in addition to words to craft their tales, transmedia storytelling has expanded through the cross-platform development of franchised stories and through the participatory culture made possible by the internet. Educators have found the form particularly suited to fostering skills widely considered essential for students' success in college and the job market and have adopted it for classroom use.

The history of storytelling stretches back into ancient time, earlier than the eighteenth century BCE when the earliest version of the Epic of Gilgamesh was recorded, to a time when tales existed only in the oral tradition. For millennia, storytelling, whether oral or written, was text-based, but the late twentieth century saw tellers of tales incorporate technology into a new form known as transmedia storytelling, a weaving together of the elements of story across multiple media.

Transmedia storytelling is difficult to define in exact terms because it is an evolving concept that few agree on its tenets. The only reliable quality all transmedia storytelling has is that, simply put, it incorporates multiple media. As such, it can be as traditional as oral stories told around a fire, or as contemporary as internet gaming.

Background

The term transmedia storytelling was coined in stages. Henry Jenkins, a media scholar and a leading voice in transmedia studies, credits Marsha Kinder, another media scholar, with first using "transmedia" in 1991 to describe the cross-media systems that had developed around popular children's characters such as the Muppet Babies and the Teenage Mutant Ninja Turtles. Jenkins coined the term transmedia storytelling in 2003 when he was director of the Comparative Media Studies graduate degree program at the Massachusetts Institute of Technology (MIT). He argued that the generation who had grown up making connections in core narratives that moved across games, television programs, movies, and books, with no one medium viewed as superior to others, was likely to demand this feature in the entertainment these consumers enjoyed as adults. He later defined transmedia storytelling as a narrative that "unfolds across multiple media platforms, with each new text making a distinctive and valuable contribution to the whole."

The most immediate association with transmedia storytelling may be the entertainment products that have used multiple platforms to tell a story, but the twenty-first century has also seen educators employ transmedia storytelling in the classroom as a teaching and learning tool. They have discovered that transmedia narratives develop multiple literacies—textual, visual, and media. Building these literacies through transmedia play, a larger term than transmedia storytelling, fosters imagination, experimentation, and critical thinking.

Students engaged in transmedia play with stories and with non-narrative puzzles and video games become not merely consumers of information but also participants in creating new information through connections, explorations, collaborations, and other forms of imaginative—and productive—play. Such play is not limited to the regular classroom; it can also occur in after-school programs, on field trips, and at home. Hence it is often considered an important mode of articulating and experiencing one's world.

Transmedia and Pop Culture

Jenkins offers a detailed analysis of *The Matrix* franchise as a definitive example of transmedia story telling. The franchise consists of three movies by the American film directors, screenwriters, and producers the Wachowskis: *The Matrix* (1999), *The Matrix Reloaded* (May 2003), and *The Matrix Revolutions* (November 2003). It also includes *The Animatrix* (June 2003), a series of nine animated short films set in the world of the Matrix.

The Wachowskis were also heavily involved in the creation of a series of comic books set in the world of the Matrix, written and illustrated by different artists, including Geof Darrow, concept artist on all three Matrix movies. Video games include *Enter the Matrix*, produced in conjunction with the second and third films, *The Matrix: Path of Nemo*, and a massively multiplayer online role-playing game. From prerelease ads that sent consumers to the web seeking more information through the internet discussion groups, each piece of the world contributes something new and connects to other elements. Only viewers who had played the video game could interpret some clues in the films, and backstory was accessible only to those who had watched animated shorts via web downloads or on digital video disc (DVD). The multiple texts work together to create what Jenkins describes as "a narrative so large it cannot be contained within a single medium."

Once Jenkins explained his concept of transmedia storytelling, other scholars pointed out that although it may have been an unintentional move by their creators, other narratives had engaged in transmedia storytelling prior to *The Matrix. Star Trek*'s move from television series to feature films, toys, animation, games, novels, conferences, and a themed attraction in Las Vegas spanned three decades. Another wildly successful, albeit unintentional, example of transmedia storytelling is the *Harry Potter* franchise. What began as a seven-book children's fantasy series by British author J. K. Rowling expanded into a multibillion-dollar franchise to include feature films, music, toys, clothing, food items, video games, videos, podcasts, mobile apps, a theme park, museum exhibits, conferences, ancillary books, an online archive of Harry Potter fan fiction that boasts more than eighty thousand stories, and websites. Foremost among the last is *Pottermore*, an interactive joint venture of Rowling and Sony that offers exclusive content, including alternate endings and original short stories about the characters by Rowling.

The entertainment company Marvel provided another example in the early twenty-first century, with various film adaptations of its comic-book superheroes becoming some of the most popular and highest-grossing films of all time. While the central superhero characters had existed in comics, animated works, toys, and other forms for decades, the films, including *Iron Man* (2008) and *The Avengers* (2012), provided updated versions.

Meanwhile, some characters original to the films were later featured in comics, television, and other media, showing that the flow of adaptation went both ways. In addition, both network television shows and series on the streaming service Netflix were developed, set in the same "universe" as the films and occasionally overlapping with actors, characters, and plot points. The so-called Marvel Cinematic Universe (MCU) had enormous influence on the concept of franchises, impacting both Marvel's own comics line and the transmedia efforts of rival film studios.

Some transmedia storytelling is rooted in transformations of much older texts. The novels of Jane Austen have fueled a small industry of story transformations with Austen and her best-known characters reimagined in guises ranging from sleuths to vampire slayers in print novels, graphic novels, digital books, feature films, television episodes, and anime. In 2012, Austen's most popular novel, *Pride and Prejudice*, entered the world of twenty-first-century technology and transmedia storytelling with Bernie Su and Hank Green's *The Lizzie Bennet Diaries*. That story cuts the five Bennet sisters to three and transforms them into modern young women: Jane, a fashion merchandiser; Lizzie, a grad student in mass communications; and Lydia, a party girl at a community college. It also changes Charlotte Lucas to Charlotte Lu, who finds a fulfilling career at Collins & Collins, makes Bingley into Bing Lee, a wealthy

medical student, and transforms Pemberley from Darcy's estate to his digital company.

The series consists of more than nine hours of content on over 160 videos that ran on five YouTube channels plus 35 social media profiles. The story was further extended through characters' contributions to Facebook, Twitter, and other social media that allowed for interaction with fans.

Roots of Transmedia Play

Children, real and fictional, have routinely engaged in transmedia play. Some of the most famous children's books of the nineteenth century show young characters acting out their own versions of older stories. Louisa May Alcott's March sisters in *Little Women* (1868–69) are encouraged to see themselves as John Bunyan's Pilgrim in their lives in a manner like their acting out scenes from *The Pilgrim's Progress* (1678) when they were younger. The imaginative title character of Mark Twain's *Tom Sawyer* (1876) pretends to be Robin Hood (Tom's source is probably the 1841 *Robin Hood and His Merry Foresters* by Stephen Percy and Joseph Cundall). In the early twentieth century, the title character of Lucy Maud Montgomery's *Anne of Green Gables* (1908) dramatically and riskily reenacts a scene from Sir Walter Scott's 1833 poem "The Lady of Shalott." Davy Crockett's coonskin cap and his rifle "Old Betsy" treasured by millions of children in the mid-1950s may have been more marketing ploys by Walt Disney, who created the television series, than transmedia, but certainly the let's-pretend versions of Crockett's adventures acted out in backyards across America, often to the accompaniment of "The Ballad of Davy Crockett," the show's theme song, expanded the original and thus became transmedia storytelling.

Digital Books

The digital book is a prime example of an educational tool that encourages students to develop critical thinking, creativity, communication, and collaboration. These skills, known as the 4Cs, are emphasized by the framework developed by the Partnership for 21st Century Skills, an advocacy group of businesses (Time Warner, Ford, Microsoft, Cisco Systems, Dell, Verizon, and others); education-related organizations (American Association of School Librarians, American Federation of Teachers, Educational Testing Service, Pearson Education, and others); foundations (Intel Foundation and Oracle Education Foundation); and media groups (Corporation for Public Broadcasting, Cable in the Classroom, and more) that fosters the inclusion of technology in education. They are also key skills in the Common Core state standards.

Inanimate Alice, a digital book, has been effective worldwide in engaging students in a transmedia experience that involves an array of literacies—verbal, digital, media, visual, information, and critical. The online episodic story, created by author Kate Pullinger, digital artist Chris Joseph, and series producer Ian Harper, features a girl named Alice growing up as she travels around the world. Created as entertainment, Inanimate Alice was quickly adopted by teachers who saw the transmedia learning potential of the book that required students to determine meaning based on text, images, sounds, and actions and provided tools to create their own content, making it possible to incorporate text, images, and sound into interactive web presentations that could then be shared through applications for iPad, iPhone, Kindle Fire, and Android. *Inanimate Alice*, with its game-playing elements has been effective also in motivating reluctant readers, those with poor comprehension skills and those who have little interest in reading.

Not all transmedia storytelling has to be high-tech. One K-6 media specialist encouraged students to create a "storyworld" after reading *Weslandia*, a Newberry Medal-winning novel by Paul Fleischmann. Their storyworld included a Facebook page where students wrote and posted updates as the protagonist Wesley. It also included original music composed in a music class to accompany the fictional character's flute playing, and kids created games based on the novel created in physical education class.

Transmedia storytelling has proved to be a particularly effective format for young adult literature. An early and innovative example is *Cathy's Book: If Found Call 266-8233* by Sean Stewart and Jordan Weisman, published by Running Press, an imprint of Perseus Books Group, in 2006. The young adult (YA) mystery, which uses alternative reality game elements, includes Cathy's doodles and notes written in the margins of the book and incorporates an evidence package of letters, phone numbers, pictures, and birth certificates. The book was almost derailed by criticism from such heavy hitters as consumer advocate Ralph Nader and novelist Jane Smiley over its use of Cover Girl products in exchange for promotional ads, but it found its audience. Readers thronged to the interactive website to discuss what happened after the book's end. The paperback version, released in 2008, removed all references to Cover Girl products. Two sequels followed: *Cathy's Key* (2008) and *Cathy's Ring* (2009). A revamped version of the original book was released in 2010 as an app for the iPod Touch and iPhone.

Chopsticks (2012), a collaboration between author Jessica Anthony and designer Rodrigo Corral, is a transmedia text that in the enhanced e-book version immerses the reader in the lives of the characters by providing access to photo albums, postcards, paintings, highlighted pages of favorite books, video clips, favorite music, and instant messages. Readers are even allowed to shuffle the pages of the book, thereby changing the order of the story and creating a personalized version of the book. Amanda Havard's paranormal YA *The Survivors* (2011), the pilot for Chafie Press's trademark book app, enhances the story by including historical and mythological background information with images of documents dating back to the seventeenth century, a music soundtrack (including three original songs by Havard) music videos, and photographs and Google satellite maps of more than fifty locations that are part of the book.

Copyright Confusion and Fan Fiction

Given the many directions in which stories move as they cross platforms, it is hardly surprising that confusion and conflicts over copyrights sometimes develop. A classic example of the potential for confusion is *Splinter of the Mind's Eye* (1978) by Alan Dean Foster, the first *Star Wars* expansion novel published. The story's sexual tension between Luke Skywalker and Princess Leia was not a problem at the time, but five years later, in the film *Return of the Jedi*, Leia and Luke were revealed as being twins. To prevent a recurrence of contradictions, Howard Roffman, the executive in charge of what became known as Lucasfilm's *Star Wars Expanded Universe*, established a rule that anything new added to the world could not violate what came before. This policy served as a model for the intricate, complex storytelling that became the standard for transmedia stories.

The popularity of fan fiction has complicated copyright issues. Fan fiction has existed at least since the first decades of the twentieth century when admirers of Jane Austen added new storylines to her fictional worlds, but it proliferated with easy access to the internet. Fan fiction sites such as fanfiction.net have millions of users who post stories based on the characters and settings from popular novels and other media in dozens of languages with quality ranging from excellent to barely literate. Some authors have battled to prevent their characters from being used in this manner, but others have followed Harry Potter's creator in accepting fan fiction within limits. Rowling specifies that Potter fan fiction be noncommercial and nonpornographic.

Lawrence Lessig, the Roy L. Furman Professor of Law at Harvard Law School and director of the Edmond J. Safra Center for Ethics at Harvard University, argued that the technology that makes possible fan fiction, fan art, and remix videos that go viral is the result of the democratization of technology. He views the twentieth century as a period in which commercial interests stifled creativity and promoted a read-only culture. Digital technology in his view has reinstated a read-write culture that fosters creativity, especially among the young. He advocates a more liberal application of copyright laws in which creators concede noncommercial use of their content to avoid rigid dichotomy between any use of protected content and a wholesale ignoring of copyright protections.

—*Wylene Rholetter*

References

Evans, E. *Transmedia Television: Audiences, New Media, and Daily Life*. Routledge, 2011.

Hovious, A. S. *Transmedia Storytelling: The Librarian's Guide*. Libraries Unlimited, 2016.

Gutierrez, Peter. "Every Platform Tells a Story." *School Library Journal*, vol. 58, no. 6, 2012, pp. 32–34.

Herr-Stephenson, B., Alper, M., Reilly, E., & Jenkins, H. "T Is for Transmedia: Learning Through Transmedia Play." *USC Annenberg Innovation Lab and the Joan Ganz Cooney Center at Sesame Workshop*, annenberglab.com.

Hovious, A. "Inanimate Alice." *Teacher Librarian*, vol. 42, no. 2, 2014, pp. 42–46.

Jenkins, Henry. "Searching for the Origami Unicorn: The Matrix and Transmedia Storytelling." *Convergence Culture: Where Old and New Media Collide*, NYU P, 2006, pp. 93–130.

McDonald, R., and J. Parker. "When a Story Is More Than a Paper." *Young Adult Library Services*, vol. 11, no. 4, 2013, pp. 27–32.

Ramasubramanian, S. "Racial/Ethnic Identity, Community-Oriented Media Initiatives, and Transmedia Storytelling." *Information Society*, vol. 32, no. 5, 2016, pp. 333–42.

Rodrigues, P., and J. Bidarra. "Transmedia Storytelling and the Creation of a Converging Space of Educational Practices." *International Journal of Emerging Technologies in Learning*, vol. 9, no. 6, 2014, pp. 42–44.

TUMBLR

Introduction

Tumblr is a blogging outlet and social networking website owned by the -internet company Yahoo! Inc. The form of blogging done on Tumblr is known as "microblogging" or "tumblelogging"—terms referring to the sparse elements used in the blog, such as brief captions and video links. With Tumblr, users can upload images, text, video, or links to their blog. The interface is centered on a dashboard, where users can view a feed of posts from other Tumblr blogs they follow, which they can then comment on and share.

Since the website is highly visual with an emphasis on photos, companies use Tumblr as a marketing tool to showcase and share their products. It allows marketers to engage with their target audience in a quick manner. Due to the stripped-down presentation of Tumblr, companies typically use the website to link to their main page or other social media outlets such as Facebook or Twitter.

While Tumblr growth has slowed over the last few years, the site currently claims over 450 million active users and was worth an estimated $1.1 billion. It was purchased by Automattic (owner of WordPress) in 2019 for approximately $3 million.

Background

Web developer David Karp began developing Tumblr in 2006 while working at his own web development and consulting firm, Davidville. He had previously done some web development for Fred Seibert, the founder of Frederator Studios. Karp built Frederator's first multiuser blogging platform, but he found the blogging process a tedious one. This led Karp to create a web application that made creating and sharing digital content simple. He acquired the domain name Tumblr.com and then recruited web developer Marco Arment to help him build the platform.

Seibert introduced Karp to investors Bijan Sabet of Spark Capital and Fred Wilson of Union Square Ventures. After the site's official launch in February 2007, Tumblr raised $750,000 in initial funding, primarily through those two companies. Within two weeks of its launch, the site had 75,000 registered users, and by 2010 750,000 new users were signing up every month. Tumblr raised $4.5 million in a second round of funding in December 2008, followed by an additional $5 million in a third round in April 2010.

For the first year in operation, the only employees of Tumblr were Karp and Arment. In 2008 Marc LaFountain, a public relations employee living in Richmond, Virginia, emailed Karp, offering his services as technical support for Tumblr. He was hired as their third employee. Within three years, Tumblr established a support office in Richmond, and LaFountain had a team of eighteen people working with him there. In September 2010, Arment, who had been serving as Tumblr's acting chief technology officer and lead developer since the launch, left the company to concentrate on his web service Instapaper, which he had founded in 2008.

At first, the only monetization on Tumblr came from users who paid for premium blog layouts to enhance their visual display and features. To bring in new revenue, Karp announced in April 2012 that they would be opening up Tumblr to paid advertisements and sponsors. To help this process, Karp hired Lee Brown, a former employee of Yahoo!, as Tumblr's head of global sales in September 2012. The first company Tumblr opened up paid advertising for was Adidas in June 2012.

On June 20, 2013, Yahoo! officially acquired Tumblr for $1.1 billion. Karp remained chief executive officer of Tumblr, and Yahoo! stated that it did not intend to change the interface; however, many Tumblr users protested the deal. Yahoo! had fallen behind in revenue and popularity and hoped the purchase would connect them with a younger demographic.

Tumblr's Fading Popularity

According to online traffic analyst company Alexa Internet, Tumblr was the forty-sixth most trafficked website in the world and the twenty-second most trafficked website in the United States in May 2016. While it is considered a blogging platform, many use it more as a social networking website; users can follow friends, share content, and "like" posts, which creates a strong networking effect. Since then, it has tumbled in popularity, and does not appear on any top-ten social networking sites, though it is still somewhat popular for blogging.

Besides networking, Tumblr has other applications. The straightforward visual display lends itself to presenting an artist's portfolio. For this same reason, photography and travel blogging are other popular uses for Tumblr, as well as a way for musicians to present their content.

Tumblr grew quickly during its first year in service. Many experts agree that the website's sharp rise in popularity was due to its ease of use. A lot of people who start their own blog do not have the time to maintain it, but Tumblr's simple interface and stripped-down format make it easier for bloggers to maintain a steady stream of updates and posts.

Another reason cited for the website's popularity is the user's option to remain anonymous. Whereas social media networks such as Facebook require a real name, Tumblr users are allowed to use pseudonyms. The prevalence of pornography on Tumblr is also cited as a reason for its popularity. Settings can be changed to prohibit pornographic search results.

When users sign up for Tumblr, they create a username and pick from a variety of page layouts. Those wanting more customization can pay for a premium layout. From their dashboard, users can post photos, videos, links, and text. After they publish their content, other users can like, share, or comment on the post.

On the Tumblr main page, users can see real-time updates from blogs that they follow. There are also posts suggested by Tumblr based on the user's interests and followers. Also, companies and users can pay to have their posts featured on the main page or the suggested posts. A mobile version of Tumblr has been available since 2009.

Tumblr allows companies to easily create a brand presence while interacting and engaging with consumers. While the website does not enable users to purchase products directly, it does help draw in potential customers who may repost a product they are interested in or who may be redirected to the company's main website, thereby helping the company promote itself.

In November 2015, two significant updates were made to Tumblr. To address the problem in which a site whose users consistently post graphics interchange formats (GIFs) did not have a tool designed to create such GIFs, the company introduced a tool for making GIFs from video clips and image bursts on mobile devices—beginning with the iPhone. Additionally, spokespeople for the app explained that one of the biggest requests from users was to have an instant messaging capability on the site. Therefore, the company also implemented a messaging feature in an effort to allow users to talk with other users and followers—including people they do not know personally—about shared interests in real time.

—Patrick G. Cooper

References

Benkoil, Dorian. "Tumblr CEO David Karp's Wild Ride from 14-Year-Old Intern to Multimillionaire." *MediaShift*. PBS, 22 May 2013, mediashift.org/2013/05/tumblr-ceo-david-karps-wild-ride-from-14-year-old-intern-to-multimillionaire/.

Bercovici, Jeff. "Tumblr: David Karp's $800 Million Art Project." *Forbes*. Forbes.com, 2 Jan. 2013, forbes.com/sites/jeffbercovici/2013/01/02/tumblr-david-karps-800-million-art-project/?sh=556afdaa43f6.

Delo, Cotton. "Tumblr Announces First Foray into Paid Advertising." *Ad Age*. Crain Communications, 18 Apr. 2012, adage.com/article/special-report-digital-conference/social-media-tumblr-announces-foray-paid-ads/234214.

Lapowsky, Issie. "David Karp: Why I Sold Tumblr." *Inc.* Mansueto Ventures, 31 May 2013, inc.com/issie-lapowsky/david-karp-why-i-sold-tumblr-yahoo.html.

Lunden, Ingrid. "Tumblr Overtakes Instagram as Fastest-Growing Social Platform, Snapchat Is the Fastest-Growing App." *Tech Crunch*. AOL, 25 Nov. 2014, techcrunch.com/2014/11/25/tumblr-overtakes-instagram-as-fastest-growing-social-platform-snapchat-is-the-fastest-growing-app/.

Madrigal, Alexis. "How Tumblr Hired Its 3rd Employee, or, the Luckiest Cold 'Call' Ever." *The Atlantic*. Atlantic Monthly Group, 23 Oct. 2011, theatlantic.com/technology/archive/2011/10/how-tumblr-hired-its-3rd-employee-or-the-luckiest-cold-call-ever/247226/.

Mendoza, Menchie. "Facebook Popularity Drops among Teens as Tumblr, Pinterest, Snapchat Gain Steam." *Tech Times*, 1 Dec. 2014, techtimes.com/articles/45159/20150409/teens-still-prefer-facebook-instagram-snapchat-among-social-media-platforms.htm.

Moynihan, Tim. "Tumblr Finally Adds a GIF-Maker to Its iPhone App." *Wired*. Condé Nast, 17 Nov. 2015, wired.com/2015/11/tumblr-adds-gif-making-tools-to-its-iphone-app/.

___. "Tumblr's New Messanger Is Chat for the Cool Kids." *Wired*. Condé Nast, 10 Nov. 2015, wired.com/2015/11/tumblr-gets-its-very-own-messaging-app/.

Oreskovic, Alexei, and Jennifer Saba. "Yahoo Buying Tumblr for $1.1 Billion, Vows Not to Screw It Up." *Reuters*. Thomson, 20 May 2013, reuters.com/article/us-tumblr-yahoo-idUSBRE94I0C120130520.

Rifkin, Adam. "Tumblr Is Not What You Think." *Tech Crunch*. AOL, 18 Feb. 2013, techcrunch.com/2013/02/18/tumblr-is-not-what-you-think/.

"Tumblr Statistics, User, Demographics and Facts for 2021." *Saas Scout.org*, saasscout.com/statistics/tumblr-statistics/#Tumblr_Statistics_User_Demographics_And_Facts_For_2021.

TURKLE, SHERRY

Introduction

For the past three decades, Sherry Turkle, a sociologist of science at the Massachusetts Institute of Technology (MIT), in Cambridge, Massachusetts, and a licensed clinical psychologist, has been carefully observing how humans interact with computers. According to her, our interaction with computers can change our very identities. No longer is a person limited to a single, consistent, cohesive identity, Turkle has argued. Instead, with the help of computers, we can embrace another conception of the self—multiple, fluid, and without boundaries.

Sherry Turkle. Photo by jeanbaptisteparis, via Wikimedia Commons.

Background

Consider Doug. He is a college student and is one of the many people who enthusiastically participate in multiple user domains (MUDs) on the internet. In MUDs, he can assume any identity and act out any fantasy. He can meet other people in virtual bars, order virtual margaritas, flirt, visit players at their virtual homes, and even have virtual sex. He is not limited to a single character, either.

Doug has four personas: a seductive woman; a macho, cowboy type; and two furry animals. At any given moment when he is in front of his computer, he might be impersonating any of his characters or all of them simultaneously, while also doing his homework. "I just turn on one part of my mind and then another when I go from window to window. I'm in some kind of argument in one window and trying to come on to a girl in a MUD in another, and another window might be running a spreadsheet program or some other technical thing for school. . . . And then I'll get a real-time message [which flashes on the screen as soon as it is sent by another system user], and I guess that's RL [real life]. It's just one more window."

Doug's story is recounted in Sherry Turkle's book, *Life on the Screen: Identity in the Age of the Internet* (1995). While many might think of Doug as an isolated case, Turkle offers evidence that he is far from alone. Computers and a rapidly emerging "culture of simulation" increasingly affect almost all aspects of life. Everything from the movement of atomic particles to voter behavior can be modeled on computers; with the popular computer games *SimCity, SimAnt,* and *SimEarth,* children can entertain themselves by pretending to manage cities, insect colonies, and entire worlds. People can even date and, as the late talk-show host Rush Limbaugh did, meet their future spouses over the internet.

The intrusion of computers into more and more aspects of life, Turkle has noted, provokes many questions about the boundaries between computers and humans. A computer beats a human in chess; does the computer think? A computer program successfully administers psychotherapy; can the program experience empathy? A man's wife has an electronic "affair" with another man hundreds of miles away; is the affair just a diversion or is it a breach of her marriage vows? Using examples like these, Turkle questions whether one's biological self is really separate from one's electronic self. "Are we living life on the screen or life in the screen?" she wrote in her most recent book. "Our new technologically enmeshed relationships oblige us to ask to what extent we ourselves have become cyborgs, transgressive mixtures of biology, technology, and code."

Turkle has long been fascinated by questions of identity. Prominently displayed above the fireplace in her home in Boston is a portrait of the author Ann Beattie, in which Beattie is surrounded by panels that represent some of her stories. "That's how I feel about myself, sitting in the middle of all my stories," Turkle told Pamela McCorduck. "That's how we all are, in the center of our many stories." A brief laundry list of Turkle's own identities would include an English-speaking Sherry, a French-speaking Sherry, mother, teacher, pioneer ethnographer of the computer culture, and writer.

Biography

Sherry Turkle was born on June 18, 1948, in the New York City borough of Brooklyn. She never knew her biological father, whose surname was Zimmerman, and after her mother, Harriet Bonowitz, married Milton Turkle, Sherry's last name was changed to Turkle. The name change led to Sherry's first experience with dual identities: In school, she was Sherry Zimmerman, but within her extended family, she was Sherry Turkle.

In 1965, Turkle graduated from Abraham Lincoln High School, in Brooklyn, where she was the valedictorian of her class, and entered Radcliffe College (which later merged with Harvard University), in Cambridge, Massachusetts. In her junior year, her mother died, an event that led her to become briefly estranged from her stepfather.

Unable to concentrate on her studies, she dropped out of college and went to live in France, where she worked as a live-in cleaning woman for a year and a half. It was an auspicious time for her to be in France; French philosophers were leading the way in an intellectual movement that would later become known as poststructuralism. With a letter of introduction from Laurence Wylie, a Harvard expert on French culture, helping to open doors for her, Turkle attended seminars taught by such French luminaries as Roland Barthes and Michel Foucault.

Her experiences in Paris eventually left their mark on her personality: The shy Sherry was replaced by a self-confident Sherry who spoke fluent French. "In France during the late 1960s, I didn't have any way to talk about that sense of having other strengths to draw on," she told Pamela McCorduck. "I just knew that when I was in France—hey! I felt in touch with another aspect of my self. And I saw my job as bringing that through into English-speaking Sherry." Later, terms such as "fluidity," "multiplicity," and "social construction of identity," used by postmodern philosophers, would give her a vocabulary to describe those changes.

While in France, Turkle witnessed the massive student uprising of May 1968, which was at least partly inspired by civil unrest in the United States and Soviet satellite countries. The movement in France for societal reform eventually collapsed, leaving the French political system relatively unchanged. Turkle did notice subtle changes, however. French people started to become more introspective and more accepting of the ideas of the German psychoanalyst Sigmund Freud. Whereas before, the French had viewed Freud's ideas with suspicion, suddenly the jargon-loaded vocabulary of psychoanalysis was regularly used in talk shows, advice columns, and everyday conversation.

The changed intellectual landscape of France would become the subject of Turkle's research after she returned to the United States. After earning an AB in social studies, summa cum laude, from Radcliffe, in 1970, she spent one year with the University of Chicago's Committee in Social Thought; she then enrolled at Harvard, where she received an MA in sociology, in 1973, and a PhD in sociology and personality psychology, in 1976. For her dissertation, entitled "Psychoanalysis and Society: The Emergence of French Freud," she reflected on the French reception of Freud's theories after 1968.

If there was any one person in France who symbolized the newfound appreciation of Freud, it was Jacques Lacan, a psychoanalyst who is known for his structuralist and linguistic interpretation of Freud's ideas. Turkle had been initially reluctant to study the work of Lacan and his French followers. In fact, she didn't really understand his writings, which are peppered with cryptic but oft-quoted comments like "The unconscious is structured like a language." Laurence Wylie suggested that she "use this opportunity to talk about superficial knowledge, about why all these people have Lacan's book on their coffee tables, and what it means to them," as she recalled to Pamela McCorduck. Turkle followed her professor's advice, and in her first book, *Psychoanalytic Politics: Freud's French Revolution* (1978), which grew out of her doctoral dissertation, she noted how the psychoanalytic jargon of Freud and Lacan was appropriated by ordinary people as a tool for thinking about their own identities. Her study laid the groundwork for her future investigations on how the similarly technical discourse of computer users entered into society at large.

Turkle first encountered the strange discourse of computer users when, after completing her doctorate, she accepted a position as an assistant professor of sociology at MIT. Like an anthropologist who has come to a foreign country, she discovered that the culture at MIT was radically different from that which she had experienced either at Harvard or in France. "When I went to MIT and came upon students who talked about their minds as machines, I became intrigued by the way in which they were using this computer language to talk about their minds, including their emotions, whereas I used a psychoanalytic one," she told Pamela McCorduck.

MIT students talked of "debugging their relationships" during difficult times and "clearing their buffer" when they needed to get something off their minds; verbal gaffes were "information processing errors." Like a good anthropologist, Turkle started to take field notes. Soon, she had conceived a new book, one in which she would analyze this group more thoroughly. She spent the next six years interviewing more than 400 people involved with computers.

The title of her second book, *The Second Self: Computers and the Human Spirit* (1984), reveals its basic insight: that the computer is not just a tool—a calculating machine—but an "evocative object," as Turkle labeled it, with which we can have intense, almost intimate relations, as if it were a person. Drawing on her observations of personal computer (PC) owners, hackers, people working in the field of artificial intelligence (AI), and schoolkids, Turkle examined the variety of ways in which people interact with these "evocative objects." "The computer is like Don Corleone in *The Godfather*—it makes so many offers that many different kinds of people can't refuse," she told David Hellerstein for *Esquire* (December 1985). Video-game players, for instance, she explained, are not just mindless drones but are people who gain satisfaction out of mastery of a rule-bound system—a mastery that often isn't possible to achieve in real life. Similarly, hackers derive their sense of identity from the sense of power they gain from mastering complex computer systems.

The diversity of ways in which people crafted identities through computers led Turkle to rethink the popular conception that using computers requires a rigorous, logical, "hard" approach. As Turkle discovered, some people use a "soft" approach, which is "messy" but creative and interactive. With the "soft" approach, the psychological benefit derives not from mastery of programming rules, but from the risk and excitement of seeing something new emerge. The "soft" approach, Turkle argued, is associated with female ways of knowing.

As a child, Turkle had been discouraged from playing with electric or electronic toys, because of the prevailing "hard" view. "Being a girl came with a message about technology—'Don't touch it, you'll get a shock,'" she told David Hellerstein. Encouraging "soft" approaches, Turkle contended, would attract more females to computing. "I want educators to accept and exploit the fact that children can master the computer in many different ways," she told *U.S. News & World Report*. "This will allow the widest range of children to enter the computer culture."

In the course of her investigation, Turkle also discovered that using a computer often stimulates people to ask metaphysical questions about what it means to be human. Children who play with such electronic educational games as *Speak & Spell, Merlin,* and *Simon* sometimes have schoolyard debates on whether the machines have emotions and are capable of thought. Adults, too, can become motivated to redefine humanness after encountering computer programs that can beat them at chess or perform psychoanalysis.

Turkle closely followed debates in academic circles about whether computers can be considered human minds. Had the notions of free will and the self become outdated, like the notion that the world is flat? Are human minds sophisticated computational programs, and is consciousness simply a product of those programs? "Under pressure from the computer, the question of mind in relation to machine is becoming a central cultural preoccupation," Turkle wrote in *The Second Self*. "It is becoming for us what sex was to the Victorians—threat and obsession, taboo and fascination."

Turkle clarified the nature of this obsession and taboo in her third book, *Life on the Screen* (1995), for which she interviewed more than 1,000 people, 300 of them children. During the period between the publication of that book and her second book, the use of computers had dramatically increased, and with the emergence of new technologies, the issue of human identity in relation to the computer had grown more complex and controversial.

AI researchers, for example, had changed the way they conceived of intelligence. No longer did they liken the mind to a single program that can perform dizzying computations top-down. Rather, AI researchers compared intelligence to the interaction of several programs running simultaneously, with the outcome of their interactions impossible to predict. Turkle noted the effect this new AI paradigm had on thinking about the human mind. If the mind is not a single program but multiple programs that interact with one another to produce unpredictable results, can we still say that we have a single identity, or is our very identity decentered and multiple?

The issue of multiple identities comes out most forcefully in Turkle's chapters on MUD users. In MUDs, one can assume electronic personae and, like Doug, described at the beginning of this article, explore what it might be like to be different people, have a different gender, or even belong to other species. According to Turkle, MUDs dramatically highlight the shaky nature of unitary conceptions of the self, which she believes have been reinforced by print technology. "Print has been a transparent medium for expressing a unitary self," she told Pamela McCorduck. "Our cultural memory really doesn't go back to the time we felt we were inhabited by divinities, so we treat the sense of unitary self we've adapted from print as natural."

The internet, by contrast, encourages people to add facets to their personalities and create additional identities for themselves. Often, virtual dates allow people who usually feel ill at ease in social situations to be charming, funny, and seductive. Signing on as men may enable women to speak up more and thus become more assertive. (Interestingly, one study showed that women whose contributions to electronic dialogues amounted to 20 percent of the conversations were seen as "interrupting" the conversations.) For men, assuming a female identity can allow them to be more collaborative, or, in some instances, to act more assertively, as in the case of one man whom Turkle described who plays strong "Katharine Hepburn" types.

Critics of the rapidly expanding "culture of simulation" often accuse the technology of aiding escapist fantasies. In her study, Turkle addressed this criticism and pointed out the many ways in which virtual experiences may be an unhealthy substitute for real life. A man who couldn't transfer the social skills he learned in the virtual domain to real life, for example, felt even more depressed about his real life than he had before his social success on the internet. Others, though, can successfully apply lessons learned from the internet to real life, as happened in the case of a young man who became able to deal with both his father's and his own alcoholism after he took a position of responsibility in a virtual community. Turkle believes that "permeability" —in which online and offline experiences influence each other—is a mechanism of healthy psychological development. "We don't have to reject life on the screen, but we don't have to treat it as an alternative life either," she wrote in the *American Prospect* (1996). "Virtual personae can be a resource for self-reflection and self-transformation."

Turkle has pointed out that it isn't only computer users who are dealing with changes in identity. "We live in an increasingly multi-roled existence," she told Herb Brody for *Technology Review.* "A woman may wake up as a lover, have breakfast as a mother, and drive to work as a lawyer. . . . So even without computer networks, people are cycling through different roles and are challenged to think about their identities in terms of multiplicity." She cited as an example her own French-speaking and English-speaking identities, and her efforts to let the strengths of one complement the weaknesses of the other. She has pointed out as well the possible political consequences of taking our multiple identities seriously. "As we sense our inner diversity, we come to know our limitations," she wrote in *Life on the Screen.* "We understand that we do not and cannot know things completely, not the outside world and not ourselves. Today's heightened consciousness of incompleteness may predispose us to join with others."

—*Jack Lasky and Laura Nicosia*

References

Adams, Tim. "Sherry Turkle: 'I Am Not Anti-Technology. I Am Pro-Conversation." *The Guardian,* theguardian.com/science/2015/oct/18/sherry-turkle-not-anti-technology-pro-conversation.

Else, Liz. "Sherry Turkle. Living Online: I'll Have to Ask My Friends." *New Scientist,* no. 2569, 20 Sept. 2006, newscientist.com/article/mg19125691.600.

Fischetti, M. "The Networked Primate." *Scientific American,* vol. 311, no, 3, pp. 82–85.

Howard, Alex. "A Conversation with MIT's Sherry Turkle About Conscious Consumption of Tech." *Tech Republic,* 11 Apr. 2016, techrepublic.com/article/a-conversation-with-mits-sherry-turkle-about-conscious-consumption-of-tech/.McCorduck, Pamela. "Sex, Lies and Avatars: Sherry Turkle knows what role-playing in Cyberspace Really Means. A Profile." 1 Apr. 1996. *Wired.* www.wired.com/1996/04/turkle/.

Purtill, Corinne. "Sherry Turkle's Plugged-in Year." *The New Yorker,* 23 Mar. 2021, newyorker.com/culture/persons-of-interest/sherry-turkles-plugged-in-year.

TED Talk. *Sherry Turkle: Cultural Analyst.* Apr. 2012, ted.com/talks/sherry_turkle_connected_but_alone.

"Turkle, Sherry." *MIT,* sherryturkle.mit.edu.

TWITCH

Introduction

Twitch is a video livestreaming service operated by Amazon subsidiary Twitch Interactive. It is primarily known for hosting video game livestreaming. Twitch was first created in 2011 as a spin-off of Justin.tv, a popular general-interest streaming platform. In addition to featuring numerous channels that specialize in livestreaming video games like *League of Legends, Minecraft,* and *Fortnite,* Twitch also hosts eSports competition broadcasts, music broadcasts, and a vast array of other content.

Twitch has become enormously popular over time, eventually growing to boast more than 2 million unique broadcasters and millions upon millions of regular viewers, not to mention tens of thousands of partner channels. Using the trailblazing Twitch platform, many Twitch broadcasters have cultivated large followings and built wildly successful businesses that have earned them a great deal of money. Moreover, Twitch itself has grown to become one of the internet's most popular and most-visited websites since its inception.

Background

Twitch is built on the concept of streaming. Streaming is a method of distributing specially encoded content onto computers, tablets, smartphones, and other electronic devices through broadband or wireless internet connections. Content can be streamed in either video or audio format, though video streaming allows for a more robust experience and is generally the preferred format on most streaming websites.

Streaming first emerged as a unique concept just after podcasting took hold as a popular form of consumable media. While podcasting was an effective format for audio broadcasts, it proved to have serious drawbacks when it came to video broadcasts. At the time, technological limitations meant that it was difficult to send a strong, smooth video of reasonable quality over the internet. As broadband technology improved and devices capable of processing constant streams of data became widely available, however, streaming became a more viable alternative to podcasting where video was concerned.

Streaming is an approach to broadcasting that is similar to, but also decidedly unique from, podcasting and other broadcast formats. In terms of how it works, streaming can be said to fall somewhere between podcasting and more traditional broadcast formats such as television and radio. Television and radio programming is organized and broadcast according to a strict schedule. This means that the viewer or listener must tune in to a particular station at an established time to consume the content of their choice.

Podcasting, on the other hand, affords the consumer the freedom to watch or listen to whatever they want at any time or place they so desire. Streaming falls neatly into the middle of these two approaches. While livestreaming does follow a set schedule that requires the viewer to tune in at an appointed time, the fact that it is broadcast over the internet means that the stream can be accessed from anywhere as long as the viewer has an internet-connected device capable of connecting to said stream.

Twitch made its debut just as ongoing technological improvements allowed streaming to become a viable broadcast format. Thanks to this timing and its early embrace of video game content, Twitch quickly became one of the internet's premiere streaming destinations.

The Evolution of Twitch

The genesis of Twitch was tied directly to an experimental online reality show called "Justin.tv." Launched in 2007, Justin.tv was a unique show that essentially followed internet personality Justin Kan as he went about his daily life. Kan worked on Justin.tv alongside cofounder Emmet Shear. In building the Justin.tv show and website, Kan and Shear unintentionally created a new online video platform that allowed users to livestream content to an interactive audience.

When Justin.tv began to meet with success, Shear decided to broaden the site's focus to include video games. A long-time gamer himself, Shear believed that adapting the Justin.tv platform to serve as a place where other gamers could connect with high-level players could be of great interest to the broader gaming community. The subsequent introduction of gaming content caused the popularity of Justin.tv to soar. It was such a hit, in fact, that Shear and Kan decided to spin the gaming portion of Justin.tv off into its own website. That decision ultimately led to the creation of Twitch in 2011.

Twitch is a video livestreaming service that primarily focuses on gaming content. In essence, it is an online platform that allows users to broadcast live feeds for others to watch. Twitch can be accessed through the official Twitch website, as well as any of the Twitch apps that are available for smartphones, video game consoles, tablets, and other devices. Users do not have to pay to watch standard broadcasts and are not required to create an account. Users who do create an account gain access to a variety of additional features, such as the ability to subscribe to their favorite channels or participate in chatrooms.

Beyond that, finding something to watch on Twitch requires little more than a few clicks. In addition to a typical search feature, users can find new Twitch channels by checking out the channel suggestions listed on the website's main page or browsing through channel categories. Since many Twitch streamers also maintain an active presence on social media platforms like Twitter and Facebook, it is also possible to discover new Twitch channels without even visiting Twitch itself.

Using Twitch can be particularly advantageous for those who stream their own content. While most Twitch streamers simply choose to stream for fun, others do so to make money. In fact, some streamers make a full-time living just by streaming on the platform. The majority of those who stream for profit earn money through paid subscriptions, donations, sponsorships, and affiliate sales. A smaller number of streamers earn money by becoming Twitch Partners and Affiliates. Partners and Affiliates are special Twitch accounts that have monetized broadcasts. To qualify to become a Partner or Affiliate, streamers must be able to meet certain requirements related to popularity and follower count.

While video game content continues to be Twitch's biggest draw, other types of content have also become popular on the platform. Twitch hosts a variety of talk shows, cooking shows, and much more. The popular Creative category provides a place for users to showcase their talents in everything from music and art to programming and cosplay. Another popular category is IRL (in real life), which features streamers documenting various aspects of their daily lives and chatting with users in real time.

—*Jack Lasky*

References

Asarch, Steven. "What Is Twitch? Understanding the Explosive Live-Streaming Service." *Newsweek*, 3 May 2018, www.newsweek.com/2018/05/11/twitch-909594.html.

"Explained: What Is Twitch?" *WebWise*, 2020, www.webwise.ie/parents/explained-what-is-twitch.

Freeman, Will. "A Parents' Guide to Twitch." *Ask About Games*, 17 Aug. 2018, www.askaboutgames.com/a-parents-guide-to-twitch.

Good, James. "What Is Twitch? A Beginner's Guide to Live Streaming." *GameQuitters*, 9 Nov. 2019, gamequitters.com/what-is-twitch.

Morris, Tee. *Twitch for Dummies*. Wiley, 2019.

Stephenson, Brad. "Twitch: Everything You Need to Know." *Lifewire*, 9 Sept. 2019, www.lifewire.com/what-is-twitch-4143337.

Ward, Tom. "The Biggest Gamer in the World Breaks Down Twitch for Us." *Forbes*, 1 May 2018, www.forbes.com/sites/tomward/2018/05/01/the-biggest-gamer-in-the-world-breaks-down-twitch-for-us/#36132d0d5bb5.

"What Should Parents Know About Twitch?" *Common Sense Media*, 2020, www.commonsense-media.org/social-media/what-should-parents-know-about-twitch.

TWITTER

Introduction

Twitter is an online social networking tool that enables registered users send and read messages of up to 280 (originally 140, until 2017) characters. Unregistered users may read the messages called tweets, but they may not compose tweets themselves. Users may access Twitter through a website, Short Message Service (SMS), or mobile device application. As of June 2015, Twitter had more than 300 million active monthly users and had become influential in contemporary society. By March 2022, the number had dropped to a purported 217 million users, though the number has stabilized.

Background

Jack Dorsey, an undergraduate student at New York University, developed the concept of an individual using an SMS service to communicate with a small group. He originally referred to the project as twttr. Work on this idea began in March 2006. Initially, Dorsey and contractor Florian Weber developed the first Twitter prototype as an internal service for the podcasting company Odeo and its employees. The full public version was released on July 15, 2006.

Twitter has various features, with the most obvious being able to create and read tweets. The default setting is that they are visible to anyone online, but users can restrict their messages so that only followers can see them. Twitter users can tweet from the actual Twitter website or through external devices such as applications (apps) for a smartphone. Also, users can retweet messages and subscribe to view other users' feed, which is known as "following."

Also, Twitterers may place hashtags in their tweet. A hashtag uses the number symbol (#), and groups words together to indicate the topic of the tweet. This also allows other users to search for tweets by topic, and allows Twitter to list trending topics, which are popular topics shown on the sidebar of Twitter. Users may make a topic trend either by a concerted effort or because of recent events.

Users can also use web-based interfaces that allow them to post from multiple accounts, maintain various column views, track activities (like who is following the user), and schedule tweets to be posted in the future. Users may use Twitter to direct message (DM) one another, as long as both parties are following one another. Only the recipient, and not the general public, may see a DM. However, the message still restricts the recipient to 280 characters.

Over the years, individuals have begun to use Twitter in various different ways. For example, people have used Twitter to organize protests and social movements, connect with celebrities, receive emergency notifications, and read news. Also, the emergence of live tweeting has changed the way people sometimes watch television. Live tweeting usually consists of a television show's actor, producer or director tweeting about the show as fans are watching it.

Similarly, Twitter has changed the way fans interact with celebrities. Many celebrities have started

Twitter logo. Image by Twitter, Apache License 2.0, via Wikimedia Commons.

to use Twitter to promote themselves and reach out to fans, posting updates on various topics such as where they are vacationing and promoting a new television show. Most celebrities use a verified account, which shows up as a blue check, signifying that Twitter verifies that they are who they say they are. This is important for various public figures. Holding a verified account also gives the user additional features not available to unverified users, such as the ability to receive DMs from people they do not follow. You can tweet at a celebrity, or other user, by using the at sign (@) in front of a username. This also means that celebrities can tweet back at a fan, which often allows more fan access. Obviously, this can also create security and privacy risks for public figures because the general public has access to greater information about the public figure.

Twitter has also changed how people engage in politics and elections. The 2016 election was the first election that saw the rise of Twitter being used for campaigning, as well as "Twitter bots" attempting to influence the election. Twitter admitted that more than 50,000 Russian linked accounts used Twitter to post automated materials about the 2016 US election. In January 2018, congressional Democrats called on Twitter and Facebook to investigate the Russian influence, and the use of Twitter bots.

As is true of most online services, however, privacy and the use of data are a concern. Twitter's own website and privacy policy states: "When using any of our Services you consent to the collection, transfer, storage, disclosure, and use of your information as described in this Privacy Policy." Also, most are aware that what one tweets is for public view. There is an option to make one's account private and to choose who sees those tweets, but one's account name is still visible to the public.

Other serious privacy issues exist. For example, Twitter collects data from users when they tweet, but it also collects data when those users visit other sites. For example, many websites have embedded tweet buttons, which, even without tweeting the website, alerts Twitter to the fact that you have visited the website. Twitter has admitted that it uses this information to recommend people to follow in Twitter.

In 2013, Twitter acquired MoPub, a company that places ads within various mobile apps. This creates an advantage for Twitter because it allows advertisers not only to track internet usage but also to track it across all devices. Data security experts have also raised security concerns about this type of tracking because hackers could obtain a multitude of information through MoPub. Twitter's track record on privacy, however, has been largely unchallenged. It allows users to opt out of tracking functions and respects the do-not-track settings in browsers. Also, when government officials have attempted to subpoena Twitter users' data, Twitter has resisted exposing the data. The Electronic Frontier Foundation has even named Twitter the best large technology company for protecting data.

—*Melissa A. Gill and Ian Gill*

References

Curtis, Craig R., Michael C. Gizzi, and Michael J. Kittleson. "Using Technology the Founders Never Dreamed Of: Cell Phones as Tracking Devices and the Fourth Amendment." *University of Denver Criminal Law Review*, vol. 4, no. 61, 2014, pp. 61–101.

Harkinson, Josh. "Here's How Twitter Can Track You on All of Your Devices." *Mother Jones*, 24 Sept. 2013.

Swaine, Jon. "Twitter Admits Far More Russian Bots Posted on Election Than It Had Disclosed." *The Guardian*, 19 Jan. 2018, theguardian.com/technology/2018/jan/19/twitter-admits-far-more-russian-bots-posted-on-election-than-it-had-disclosed.

U

UNIVERSAL DESIGN FOR LEARNING

Introduction

Universal design for learning (UDL) is based on knowledge gained from the field of architecture as well as from recent advances in cognitive neuroscience. It capitalizes on the inherent flexibility of technology to meet the needs of diverse learners. The term universal does not mean a single solution; instead, it implies recognition of each learner's unique differences and creating learning experiences that support learners, maximizing their ability to progress. Recent national legislation calls for an emphasis on universal design (UD) in special education.

Background

Universal design for learning (UDL) has its roots in the field of architecture and cognitive neuroscience. It recognizes the promise of technology to meet the needs of individual learners because of the inherent and nearly limitless flexibility of technology itself. National legislation requires attention to UD in curriculum and assessment development.

Universal design for learning principles guide educators in finding innovative ways to make curricula accessible and appropriate for individuals with different backgrounds, learning styles, abilities, and disabilities in various learning situations and contexts. This paradigm for teaching, learning, assessment, and curriculum development focuses on adapting the curriculum to suit the learner rather than the other way around. University design for learning guides teachers and curriculum developers toward creating flexible materials and methods before they are put in students' hands, rather than waiting until students arrive and trying to retrofit inflexible materials to each learner.

Architecture and UDL

The UDL movement in education has roots in the field of architecture. Over forty years ago, architect Ronald Mace introduced the novel idea that physical environments could be designed from the start to meet the diverse needs of all the individuals who access such spaces. At the time, disability was not considered in design practice and aesthetics.

Universally designed products and environments provide a more functional environment or product for everyone, not just the disabled. Universally designed products and settings are increasingly common in all our lives. For example, TV closed captioning, which is necessary for individuals with hearing impairments, is also helpful to people in noisy settings such as airports or restaurants, and curb cuts which are required for wheelchair users are handy for kids on bicycles, parents with strollers and travelers pulling wheeled luggage.

In UD, the new paradigm in education for addressing the instructional needs of students with disabilities and those at risk for learning difficulties, "disability" is accepted as a normal phenomenon of human diversity rather than as an aberration.

In 1997, The Center of Universal Design at North Carolina State University defines UD as a way to design, create and manufacture products and environments that are usable by all people, to the greatest extent possible, without the need for adaptation or specialized design. The Center outlines seven basic principles:

- **Equitable use:** the design is useful and marketable to people with diverse abilities;
- **Flexibility in use:** the design accommodates a wide range of individual preferences and abilities;
- **Simple and intuitive use:** use of the design is easy to understand, regardless of the user's experience, knowledge, language skills or current concentration level;

- **Perceptible information:** the design communicates necessary information effectively to the user, regardless of ambient conditions or the user's sensory abilities;
- **Tolerance for error:** the design minimizes hazards and the adverse consequences of accidental or unintended actions;
- **Low physical effort:** the design can be used efficiently and comfortably and with a minimum of fatigue; and
- **Size and space for approach and use:** appropriate size and space is provided for approach, reach, manipulation and use regardless of user's body size, posture or mobility.

University design for learning has risen to the top of the alphabet soup in educational settings because it is based on recent developments in cognitive neuroscience that are becoming widely accepted views of how the human brain learns.

The Recognition Network of Learning

According to Meyer and Rose, the recognition network is the "what" of learning. The question, "What is it?" is associated with recognition. Located in the back of the brain, recognition networks "enable us to identify and interpret patterns of sound, light, taste, smell and touch. These networks allow us to recognize voices, faces, letters, and words, as well as more complex patterns, such as an author's style and nuance and abstract concepts like justice." Even though human brains all have the same basic recognition architecture and recognize things basically the same way, our recognition networks can be very different. Each of us has a brain that is slightly different from everyone else's.

A UDL curriculum activates diverse learners' recognition networks by offering multiple means of representation (e.g., supplement an oral lecture with visuals) to give learners various ways of acquiring information and knowledge.

The Strategic Network of Learning

The strategic network is the "how" of learning. A classic strategic question is, "How do I do it?" These neural networks are located primarily in the front part of the brain called the "frontal lobe." We use strategic networks to "plan, execute, and monitor our internally generated mental and motor patterns—actions and skills as diverse as sweeping the

floor, deciding a chess move, or choosing a college" (Meyer & Rose). During some activities, we may be aware that we are applying a strategy. However, conscious or not, we use strategy in essentially everything we do. Strategic brain networks vary widely between individuals. To meet diverse learner's strategic networks, a UDL curriculum allows for multiple means of expression to provide students with alternatives for demonstrating what they know.

The Affective Network of Learning

The affective network is the "why" of learning. A commonly heard affective question posed by learners is, "Why should I do it?" Affective networks are comprised of "many specialized modules, located predominantly at the core of the brain and associated with the limbic system" (Meyer & Rose). The affective network determines whether a student is engaged and motivated depending on the level of challenge, excitement and interest. Universal design for learning principles call for the provision of multiple means of engagement (e.g., small group projects instead of individual or whole class activities) to tap into diverse learners' interests, challenge them appropriately, and motivate them to learn.

These three brain networks show up clearly on magnetic resonance imaging (MRI) brain scans when people are given learning tasks that are new as well as practiced. When a learning task is novel, the brain "lights up" brightly in all three areas, demonstrating a high level of cognitive activity; conversely, when a learning task is practiced and familiar, the brain shows much less activity in these areas, because it has developed routines to reduce cognitive load. Interestingly, the brain also appears less engaged when a task is either too hard or too easy, thus supporting Lev Vygotsky's concept of the" zone of proximal development." University design for learning principles help educators differentiate their teaching for individual learners according to each of the three brain networks.

Technology and UDL

Universal design for learning has a prime focus on using computers in the curriculum because, unlike traditional learning materials such as books, computers are uniquely flexible. Through technology, learning materials can instantly be transformed into formats that are better matched with individual learners; for example, text fonts can be enlarged for individuals with visual impairments or even printed out in Braille. Likewise, learners with auditory challenges can have video clips captioned. Students with mild reading disabilities can have words, sentences, or texts read aloud via text-to-speech software, and learners who struggle to comprehend can have metacognitive prompts embedded within the text.

There is a misconception that UDL may eventually eliminate the need for traditional assistive technologies (AT) for students with disabilities. This is not accurate, since children with physical or language disabilities will still need properly designed wheelchairs, adaptive switches to control devices and speech synthesizers. Similarly, students with severe disabilities will still need some individualized special education services outside the general education classroom (dressing themselves, eating with utensils, using public transportation, etc.). However, there is an important philosophical difference between an exclusively AT approach and an inclusive UDL approach. A singular emphasis on AT places the burden of adaptation on the individual learner rather than on the curriculum itself. Assistive technology accepts an inflexible curriculum—say, a printed textbook—as a given, and then finds ways to make it accessible to learners. In contrast, a UDL approach posits that all aspects of the curriculum should be designed from the outset to be accessible to a wide range of learners rather than retrofitted after the fact.

Concurrent with the increasing focus on developing UDL curricula is a growing awareness that simply providing access to the general curriculum is insufficient to ensure optimal learning. There is an important distinction between access to information and access to learning. Therefore, researchers and designers are now emphasizing the need to provide access to learning itself. Just because a student can access a piece of content doesn't automatically mean s/he can understand or make sense of it. Mere access to the content is inadequate unless that access is mediated with instructional design supports appropriate for the specific disability of the user. Since instructional design elements that are suitable for one disability population might not be appropriate for someone with a different disability—the key is to build in maximum flexibility from the start. For example, it is generally believed that students with learning disabilities should not be exposed to overwhelming or distracting graphics in a computer program; conversely, some students with emotional disabilities prefer strong auditory and visual effects. However, since there is significant variation even within disability populations, assumptions about desirable design features cannot be made with complete confidence.

The design of universally accessible computer interfaces can have a positive social effect on individuals with disabilities. For instance, people with sensory disabilities can use computers to achieve face-to-face remote communication. Computers can assist those with "severe motor impairments to manipulate their environment and to enhance their mobility" through technologies such as smart wheelchairs, helping them to become more socially active and productive.

Legislation and UDL

Both the Individuals with Disabilities Education Act (IDEA 1997/2004) and the No Child Left Behind Act of 2001 (NCLB) legislate that all learners have a right to a high-quality standards-based education. These laws hold teachers, schools, districts, and states responsible for ensuring that challenged students demonstrate progress according to the same standards as their peers.

The 2004 reauthorization of IDEA refers to UD with a definition from the Assistive Technology Act (Section 602) and requirements to support the use of technology based on UD principles to "maximize accessibility to the general education curriculum (Section 611 (e)(C)(v); and the use of UD principles in developing and administering districtwide and alternative assessments (Section 612 (a)(E))" (McGuire et al.).

IDEA 2004 also calls for a National Instructional Materials Accessibility Standard (NIMAS) that requires textbook publishers to use a consistent file format when developing alternate versions of texts (e.g., CD-ROM [computer disc/read-only memory] or web-based) for students with print disabilities. This is an improvement over the earlier Chafee Amendment that gave permission for special educators to convert copyrighted print materials (e.g., to create Braille, audio, or digital versions), but which placed the burden of responsibility on educators rather than on publishers.

The Future of UDL

Ideally, a UDL curriculum will meet the needs of the full range of students who actively attend our schools; students with a wide range of abilities and disabilities and not just those students in the narrow middle of the bell curve. However, educators should be cautioned not to overstate the promise of UDL in educational settings. While the concept of UDL is intuitively appealing, it has not yet been fully researched across multiple instructional environments and with multiple populations. Further, there are limits on what modern technologies can accomplish to date. Most notably, speech recognition software has not yet reached its potential in educational environments because many children have difficulty "training" the software and there is often ambient classroom noise that interferes with the process. Regrettably, although many software publishers know that they should consult educational experts during the design process and are required *by law* to take into consideration how their software will interface with AT devices, many do not. There are also limits on what teachers and special educators can provide for students in terms of time, training, and funding.

Therefore, a more realistic perspective is to recognize that no single solution will provide all the accessibility and learning supports necessary for every learner. A combination of UDL and AT along with curriculum accommodations, curriculum modifications, and differentiated instruction will continue to play a role in the education of learners with disabilities.

—Maya Eagleton

References

Abascal, J., and C. Nicolle. "Moving Towards Inclusive Design Guidelines for Socially and Ethically Aware HCI." *Interacting with Computers,* vol. 17, 2005, pp. 484–505.

Basham, J. D., and M. T. Marino. "Understanding STEM Education and Supporting Students Through Universal Design for Learning." *Teaching Exceptional Children,* vol. 45, 2013, pp. 8–15.

Boone, R., and K. Higgins. "New Directions in Research: The Role of Instructional Design in Assistive Technology Research and Development." *Reading Research Quarterly,* vol. 42, 2007, pp. 135–40.

Center for Applied Special Technology (CAST), 2007, cast.org.

Center for Universal Design. *The Principles of Universal Design, Version 2.0.* NC State UP, 1997, design.ncsu.edu.

Davies, P. L., C. L. Schelly, C. L. Spooner, et al. "Measuring the Effectiveness of Universal Design for Learning Intervention in Postsecondary Education." *Journal of Postsecondary Education & Disability,* vol. 26, 2013, pp. 195–220.

Edyburn, D., K. Higgins, and R. Boone, editors. *Handbook of Special Education Technology Research and Practice.* Knowledge by Design, 2006.

Fisher, D., and N. Frey. "Access to the Core Curriculum." *Remedial & Special Education,* vol. 22, 2001, pp. 148–57.

Hitchcock, C., and S. Stahl. "Assistive Technology, Universal Design, Universal Design for Learning: Improved Learning Opportunities." *Journal of Special Education Technology,* vol. 18, 2003, pp. 45–52.

Individuals with Disabilities Education Act Amendments of 1997, 20 U.S.C. §1415 *Et Seq.*

Individuals with Disabilities Education Improvement Act of 2004, P.L. 108-446, 20 U.S.C. §1400 *Et Seq.*

Katz, J. "The Three Block Model of Universal Design for Learning (UDL): Engaging Students in Inclusive Education." *Canadian Journal of Education,* vol. 36, 2013, pp. 153–94.

Mcguire, J. M., S. S. Scott, and S. F. Shaw. "Universal Design and Its Applications in Educational Environments." *Remedial & Special Education,* vol. 27, 2006, pp. 166–75.

Mckenna, M. C., and S. Walpole. "Assistive Technology in the Reading Clinic: Its Emerging Potential." *Reading Research Quarterly,* vol. 42, 2007, pp. 140–45.

Meyer, A., and D. H. Rose. *Learning to Read in the Computer Age.* Brookline, 1998.

National Instructional Materials Accessibility Standard (2003). *NIMAS Report Executive Summary: National Instructional Materials Accessibility Standard Report–Version 1.0. NIMAS,* nimas.cast.org.

No Child Left Behind Act of 2001, P.L. 107-110, 107th Congress, 1st Session. Ed.gov.

Rappolt-Schlichtmann, G., S. G. Daley, L. Seoin, et al. "Universal Design for Learning and Elementary School Science: Exploring the Efficacy, Use, and Perceptions of a Web-Based Science Note-book." *Journal of Educational Psychology*, vol. 105, 2013, pp. 1210–25.

Rose, D. H., and A. Meyer, editors. *A Practical Reader in Universal Design for Learning*. Harvard Education P, 2006.

___. *Teaching Every Student in the Digital Age: Universal Design for Learning*, 2002.

US Department of Education, Office of Special Education and Rehabilitation Services. *A New Era: Revitalizing Special Education for Children and Their Families*. US Department of Education, 2002.

Wehmeyer, M. L. "Universal Design for Learning, Access to the General Education Curriculum, and Students with Mild Mental Retardation." *Exceptionality*, vol. 14, 2006, pp. 225–35.

UNIX

Introduction

UNIX is a computer operating system (OS) originally developed by researchers at Bell Laboratories in 1969. The term is also used to refer to later OSs based in part on its source code. Several of the original UNIX OS's features, such as its hierarchical file system and multiuser support, became standard in later systems.

Background

As computer technology rapidly developed in the mid-twentieth century, programmers sought to create means of interfacing with computers and making use of their functions in a more straightforward, intuitive way. Chief among the goals of many programmers was the creation of an OS. OSs are specialized programs that manage all of computers' processes and functions. Although many different OSs were created over the decades, UNIX proved to be one of the most influential. UNIX inspired numerous later OSs and continues to be used in various forms into the twenty-first century.

Development of the original UNIX OS began in 1969 at Bell Laboratories, a research facility then owned by American Telephone and Telegraph (AT&T). Researchers at Bell had been working on the Multiplexed Information and Computing Service (Multics) project in collaboration with the Massachusetts Institute of Technology (MIT) and General Electric (GE). The group had focused on creating systems that allowed multiple users to access a computer at once. After AT&T left the project, Bell programmers Ken Thompson and Dennis Ritchie began work on an OS. Thompson coded the bulk of the system, which consisted of 4,200 lines of code, in the summer of 1969, running it on an outdated PDP-7 computer.

The OS was initially named the Unmultiplexed Information and Computing Service, a play on the name of the Multics project. That name was later shortened to UNIX. Thompson, Ritchie, and their colleagues continued to work on UNIX over the next several years. In 1973 they rewrote the OS in the new programming language C, created by Ritchie. UNIX gained popularity outside of Bell Laboratories in the mid-1970s. It subsequently inspired the creation of many UNIX variants and UNIX-like OSs.

Understanding UNIX

While different editions of UNIX vary, the majority of UNIX OSs have some common essential characteristics. UNIX's kernel is the core of the OS. The kernel is responsible for executing programs, allocating memory, and otherwise running the system. The user interacts with what is known as the shell. The shell is an interface that transmits the user's commands to the kernel. The original UNIX shell was a command-line interpreter, a text-based interface into which the user types commands. Over time programmers developed a variety of different shells for UNIX OSs. Some of these shells were graphical user interfaces that enabled the user to operate the computer by interacting with icons and windows. Files saved to a computer running UNIX are stored in a hierarchical file system. This file system used a treelike structure that allowed folders to be saved within folders.

Using UNIX

In keeping with its origins as a project carried out by former Multics researchers, UNIX was designed to have multiuser capabilities. This enabled multiple people to use a single computer running UNIX at the same time. This was an especially important feature in the late 1960s and early 1970s. At that time, computers were not personal computers (PCs) but large, expensive mainframes that took up a significant amount of space and power. Multiuser capabilities made it possible for the organization using the UNIX OS to maximize the functions of their computers.

UNIX is also a multitasking system, meaning it can carry out multiple operations at once. One of the first programs designed for UNIX was a text-editing program needed by the employees of Bell Laboratories. Over time, programmers wrote numerous programs compatible with the OS and its later variants, including games, web browsers, and design software.

UNIX Variants and UNIX-Like OSs

At the time that UNIX was first developed, AT&T was prohibited from selling products in fields other than telecommunications. The company was therefore unable to sell its researchers' creation. Instead, the company licensed UNIX's source code to various institutions. Programmers at those many institutions rewrote portions of the OS's code, creating UNIX variants that suited their needs. Perhaps the most influential new form of UNIX was the Berkeley Software Distribution variant, developed at the University of California, Berkeley, in the late 1970s.

In the twenty-first century, the multitude of UNIX variants and UNIX-derived OSs are divided into two main categories. Those that conform to standards established by an organization known as the Open Group, which holds the trademark to the UNIX name, may be referred to as "certified UNIX OSs." Systems that are similar to UNIX but do not adhere to the Open Group's standards are typically known as "UNIX-like OSs." The latter category includes Apple's OS X and the free, open-source system Linux. The mobile OSs Android and Apple iOS also fall under this category and account for hundreds of millions of users, arguably making UNIX-derived OSs the most widely used systems ever.

—*Joy Crelin*

References

Gancarz, Mike. *The UNIX Philosophy*. Butterworth-Heinemann, 1995.

"History and Timeline." *Open Group*, www.unix.org/what_is_unix/history_timeline.html.

Kernighan, Brian W. *UNIX: A History and a Memoir*. Kernighan, 2019.

Ray, Deborah, and Eric Ray. *Unix and Linux*. 5th ed., Peachpit Press, 2015.

Raymond, Eric S. *The Art of UNIX Programming*. Addison-Wesley, 2008.

Stevens, W. Richard, and Stephen A. Rago. *Advanced Programming in the UNIX Environment*. 3rd ed., Addison-Wesley, 2013.

Taylor, Dave. *Learning Unix for OS X*. 2nd ed., O'Reilly Media, 2016.

Toomey, Warren. "The Strange Birth and Long Life of Unix." *IEEE Spectrum*, 28 Nov. 2011, spectrum.ieee.org/tech-history/cyberspace/the-strange-birth-and-long-life-of-unix.

"What Is Unix?" *Indiana University Knowledge Base*, 28 Nov. 2018, test.kb.iu.edu/kmssc-snd/d/agat.

V

VIRTUAL REALITY

Introduction

The applied science of virtual reality (VR) engages in the design and engineering of and research related to special immersive interactive computer systems. These VR systems synthesize environments, or worlds, which are simulations of reality that are usually rendered using three-dimensional (3D) computer images, sounds, and force feedbacks. Virtual reality applications are used for pilot and astronaut training, entertainment, communication, teleoperation, manufacturing, medical and surgery training, experimental psychology, psychotherapy, education, science, architecture, and the arts. This technology, which submerges humans into altered environments and processes, intensifies experience and imagination, thereby augmenting research and education. Virtual reality training systems can simplify and improve manufacturing and maintenance, while simultaneously reducing risk exposure.

Background

A VR system is an interactive technology setup (software, hardware, peripheral devices, and other items) that acts as a human-to-computer interface and immerses its user in a computer-generated 3D environment. Virtual reality is the environment or world that the user experiences while using such a system. Although the term "virtual" implies that this simulated world does not actually exist, the term "reality" refers to the user's experience of the simulated environment as being real. The more that the senses are involved in a compelling fashion, the more genuine the perceived experience will be, and the more intense the imagination. Most VR systems stimulate the senses of sight, hearing, touch, and other tactile-kinesthetic sense perceptions, such as equilibrioception, torque, and even temperature. Less often they include smell, and with existing technology, they exclude taste. Virtual reality must be almost indistinguishable from reality in some applications such as pilot training, but it can often differ significantly from the real world in, for example, games.

Virtual reality in a narrow sense (a computer-generated simulation that exists virtually but not materially) is not the same as augmented reality (enhanced reality) or telepresence (in the sense of teleconferencing). Augmented reality technology improves the perception of and supplements the knowledge about existing entities or processes (highlighting data of interest while abstracting the less important information). Telepresence (as teleconferencing) refers to a remote virtual re-creation of a real situation (e.g., to enable audio and visual interactions between people at diverse places). However, a wider notion of VR includes notions of both augmented reality and telepresence.

Ancient History

The idea of simulated reality is often traced back to the ancient Greek philosopher Plato's allegory of

Individuals can interact with three-dimensional computer-generated simulations in a seemingly real or physical way with the use of specialized equipment. Photo via iStock/ismagilov. [Used under license.]

the cave in *Politeia* (fourth century BCE; *Republic*, 1701). In the allegory, spectators observe images (shadows) of objects on a cave wall that they take for real objects. The term "virtual" is derived from the Latin word "virtue" (which means "goodness" or "manliness"). "Virtual," in the digital context, then means existing in effect or in essence but not in actuality. The notion of VR can be traced back to the French theater director, actor, playwright, and illustrator Antonin Artaud who described theater as *la réalite virtuelle* in his influential *Théâtre et son double* (1938; *The Theatre and Its Double*, 1958).

Computer scientist and artist Myron W. Krueger coined the technical term "artificial reality" in his book of the same title, published in 1983. Computer scientist and artist Jaron Lanier popularized the notion of VR as a technical term in the 1980s. Many artists, science-fiction authors, and directors incorporated concepts of computer-generated, simulated, or augmented reality in their creations. One of the most prominent examples is the holodeck, an advanced form of VR featured on the television program *Star Trek: The Next Generation* (1987–94).

Sight, Sound, and Space

In the late 1960s, computer scientist Ivan Sutherland created the first head-mounted device, which was capable of tracking the user's viewing direction. In the 1970s, Sutherland and David Evans developed a computer graphic scene generator. In the 1970s and 1980s, force feedback was incorporated into tactile input devices such as gloves and interactive wands. Lanier and Thomas Zimmerman developed sensing gloves, which recognized finger and hand movements.

This kind of VR technology was intended to improve flight simulators and applications for astronaut training. In 1981, the National Aeronautics and Space Administration (NASA) combined commercially available Sony liquid crystal display (LCD) portable television displays with special optics for a prototype stereo-vision head-mounted device called the Virtual Visual Environment Display (VIVED). NASA then created the first VR system, which combined a host computer, a graphics computer, a noncontact user position-tracking system, and VIVED.

Scott Fisher and Elizabeth Wenzel developed hardware for 3D virtual sound sources in 1988. Also, in the late 1980s, Lanier built a VR system for two simultaneous users that he named RB2 (Reality Built for Two). Fisher incorporated sound systems, head-mounted device technology, and sensor gloves into one system called the Virtual Interactive Environment Workstation (VIEW), also used by NASA. The first conference on VR, "Interface for Real and Virtual Worlds," was held in Montpellier, France, in March of 1992. That same year, scientists, engineers, and medical practitioners assembled in San Diego, California, for the "Medicine Meets Virtual Reality Conference." In September of 1993, the Institute for Electrical and Electronics Engineers (IEEE) organized its first VR conference in Seattle.

How It Works

To create a realistic computer-generated world, several high-end technologies must be integrated into a single VR system. This kind of high-end system is used at university, military, governmental, and private research laboratories. Adequate computing speed and power, fast image and data processors, broad bandwidth, and sophisticated software are essential. Other requirements include high-tech input-output devices or effectors (such as head-mounted devices), 3D screens, surround-sound systems, and tactile devices (such as wired gloves and suits, tracking systems, and force feedback devices, including motion chairs and multidirectional treadmills).

Input

The input devices used for VR systems—sensing gloves, trackballs, joysticks, wands, treadmills, motion sensors, position trackers, voice recognizers, and biosensors—are typically more complex than those used for personal computers. Biosensors recognize eye movement, muscle activity, body temperature, pulse, and blood pressure, all of which are vital to surgical applications. Position trackers and motion sensors identify and monitor the user's position and movements. The tracking systems used in VR systems are mechanical, optical, ultrasonic, or magnetic devices. Steering wheels, joysticks, or wands are used for pilot training and games. Sophisticated devices for research and experiments (such as those for molecular modeling) offer six-degrees-of-freedom input. Such input devices allow the computer to adjust the virtual environment according to the data received from the user.

When motion sensors and position trackers detect the user's movement, the data are processed by the computer in real time, and the display, also in real time, has to accurately render the image (such as the interior of a building). If slow data processing creates a time lag, the user may experience simulator sickness or motion sickness (nausea or dizziness), especially if the user's senses register conflicting data. In a VR parachute training session, for example, equilibrioception might be in conflict with visual perception if movement is represented faster by the display than by the force feedback system.

Output

Output devices are intended to stimulate as many senses as possible for a high degree of immersion. The important visual output devices are head-mounted devices, LCDs, and projectors and screens. Developers compete to make these displays the most immersive. All displays must be able to render 3D images. Other output devices are for sound and touch. Sound systems can assist in conveying the impression of 3D space. Force feedback systems give the user the sense of physical resistance (essential in surgical [VR] systems), torque, tilt, and vibration (appreciated for games and essential for pilot training).

The CAVE (Cave Automatic Virtual Environment) is a surround-sound, surround-screen, projection-based room-sized VR system developed by the Electronic Visualization Laboratory at the University of Illinois at Chicago (the name is trademarked by the University of Illinois Board of Regents). Users put on lightweight stereo glasses and walk around inside the room, interacting with virtual objects. One user is an active viewer, controlling the projection, and the others are passive viewers, but all users can communicate while in the CAVE. The system was designed to help with visualization of scientific concepts.

Hardware and Software

Standard personal computers have both limited memory capacity and limited performance capability for running professional VR applications. Therefore, high-end hardware and software have been developed for specific purposes such as games, research programs, and pilot, combat infantry, and medical training.

Computer languages such as C++, C#, Java, and Quest3D are used for programming VR software. Virtual reality computers handle tasks such as data

input and output and the interaction, integration, and recomposition of all the data required in virtual environment management. Because a VR system needs high computing, processing, and display speeds, the VR computer architecture can at times use several computers or multiple processors.

Aerospace and Military

One of the early applications of VR was in pilot training. Twenty-first-century flight simulators are convincingly close to real flight experiences, although the simulation of acceleration and zero gravity are still challenges. In the military, VR applications are used not only by pilots, paratroopers, and tank drivers but also by battle strategists and combat tacticians to enhance safety training and analyze battle maneuvers and positions.

These military applications make targeting more precise, thereby reducing human casualties and collateral damage. Virtual reality systems are also used to evaluate new weapons systems. In space exploration, VR systems help astronauts prepare for zero-gravity activities such as the repair of solar panels on the outside of a spaceship. Virtual reality training systems give the user the opportunity to review and evaluate specific sequences in a training session or the entire session.

Entertainment and Games

The military took commercial games and adapted them to create flight simulators and other professional VR applications, which, in turn, were adapted to use as games. Virtual reality game applications and the virtual games industry are not common in gaming arcades, but they are making significant headway into the home and in the mobile entertainment market, with estimated consumer spending of about US$7 billion in virtual and augmented reality software, hardware, and accessories worldwide during 2020, according to the market-research firm IDC. Virtual reality hardware released specifically for the consumer market during that period included the Sony PlayStation VR headset, Nintendo's Labo VR Kit, and several headsets manufactured by the brand Oculus.

Some companies lease VR game equipment (such as training applications for golf, racing, and shooting) to customers for entertainment or to corporations for internal team-bonding experiences. Some VR applications enable users to journey through fantastic and futuristic worlds. The common equipment for VR games—depending on the quality and level of sophistication of the games—includes head-mounted devices, several LCD screens, tracking systems, omnidirectional treadmills for walking, force feedback or rumbling seats (or platforms) for flight and race simulations, batons for tennis, and guns, wands, or sticks for shooting. The more sensory feedback provided, the more immersive the VR game application.

Education

The more senses that are involved in the process of learning and training, the more a student is able to become engaged in the subject matter and the better the educational impact, especially when it comes to learning skills or practical content. The employment of a VR system enables data and images to become interactive, colorful, 3D, and accompanied by sound. For example, a visitor to a virtual museum is able to virtually touch the artifacts, taking them from their shelves, turning them around, and viewing them from different perspectives. In an immersive experience, a user can witness, seemingly first-hand, historical events such as famous battles as they take place. Virtual reality applications exist in almost every area of education, including sports (such as golfing), sciences (such as astronomy, physics, biology, and chemistry), the humanities (such as history), and vocational training (such as medical procedures and mechanical engineering techniques).

Universities have used virtual world environments such as Second Life to create 3D learning sites populated by student-created avatars (called "residents"). Launched in 2003, Second Life grew to a peak of 1 million daily users in 2013. Avatars interact with each other, places and objects as individuals and in groups—just as students would behave in a class or school. While many people classify Second Life as a game, it does not fit the definition of such for there is no set conflict, no set goal or objective (unless designed by a leader, instructor, or individual avatar). The laws of physics are not bound by the grid within which Second Life is housed—objects and avatars can move freely, fly, or hover. This makes coding and building the in-world environment unique and instructive.

Art

Although classic artworks can be immersive, few of them are interactive. People are not allowed to touch exhibits in most art galleries and museums. In 1993, the Solomon R. Guggenheim Museum became the first major museum to dedicate an entire exhibition to VR art. The exhibition featured VR installations from Jenny Holzer, Thomas Dolby, and Maxus Systems International. Virtual reality technology enables artists to blur or combine genres (such as music, graphic arts, and video) and involves the viewer in the creation of art. Every viewer or user of the artwork perceives the work in a different way depending on his or her input into the VR work of art. A VR art exhibit can be programmed to produce sound or visual feedback according to, for example, a visitor's footsteps or voice input from an audience. Artworks thus become interactive, and viewers become cocreators of the art. VR technology has also been utilized by multimedia artists and animators for content creation and making 3D storyboards

Science, Engineering, and Design

Virtual reality systems can advance the creative processes involved in science, engineering, and design. Results can be tested, evaluated, shared, and discussed with other VR users. Chemists at the University of North Carolina, Chapel Hill, used VR systems for modeling molecules, and similar systems have been used to observe atoms. Buildings, automobiles, and mechanical parts can be designed on computers and evaluated using 3D modeling tools and visualization techniques in a VR environment. An architect can take a client on a virtual walk through a building before it is constructed, or the aerodynamics of a new automobile design can be evaluated before manufacturing a model or prototype. Virtual reality applications also can simulate crash tests. The use of VR applications reduces cost, waste, and risk.

Business

Business applications include stores on the internet featuring virtual showrooms and 360-degree, 3D views of products. Another important application is teleconferencing. In contrast to the traditional conference call, VR applications may permit multisensory evaluations of new products. Virtual reality systems also help network, combine, and display data from diverse sources to analyze financial markets and stock exchanges. In these situations, VR applications serve as decision support systems.

Medicine, Therapy, and Rehabilitation

Experienced surgeons as well as physicians in training use VR systems to practice surgery. The images for such training programs are taken from X-rays, computed tomography (CT) scans, and magnetic resonance imaging (MRI). Virtual operations can be recorded and repeated as many times as desired, in contrast to practice operations on animals or human corpses, which cannot be repeated. Force feedback gloves give practitioners the realistic feel and touch needed, for example, to determine how much force is needed for certain incisions.

Virtual reality environments are being developed for use in training patients as well as doctors. Virtual human limbs are being prototyped and studied for use in training patients to use and become comfortable with prosthetic limbs, as well as for patient rehabilitation. Some of the virtual prosthetics in development appear as avatars in a VR environment and are able to accept both kinematic and neural control inputs from the patient.

In psychotherapy, VR applications are often used an alternative therapy to help treat clients with disorders such as phobias, anxiety, and PTSD (post-traumatic stress disorder). Clients often undergo desensitization treatment, which is especially useful in treating phobias and PTSD. Virtual reality allows clients who fear enclosed spaces (claustrophobia), dirt and germs (mysophobia), or snakes (ophidiophobia) to gradually confront their fears without being exposed to the actual condition or object. Virtual reality applications can also help clinicians understand certain psychological problems better by enabling them to experience what the client or the patient experiences. For example, a psychiatrist, psychologist, or counselor may take a virtual bus ride in the role of a schizophrenic client, during which they experience some simulated symptoms of this disorder, such as distorted images viewed through the windows of the bus or strange voices that seem to appear from nowhere.

Careers and Coursework

Because the development of VR systems and applications involves many areas of applied science, students pursuing careers related to VR systems should be versatile. A bachelor of science in a field such as information technology, mechanical engineering, or electrical engineering is an appropriate foundation for a career in VR, but most positions in the field require multidisciplinary skills and experience with designing and developing 3D software. Therefore, the best approach is to take additional courses in other fields.

For high-level positions or to work as a researcher in industry or academia, a master of science degree or a doctorate is recommended. Work can also be found with governmental entities (such as NASA) and the military as well as manufacturers of VR systems and products (such as head-mounted devices, screens, force feedback systems, and tracking systems). The producers of VR software and hardware need skilled professionals such as electrical and mechanical engineers, roboticists, software developers, and information technologists. As of 2020, job opportunities related to VR technology and research are still somewhat limited because of the field's highly technical and specialized nature and also because VR applications are not yet in widespread use. It is generally believed, however, that as the VR industry grows, product managers and business development/sales representatives will be needed in addition to programmers and engineers.

Social Context and Future Prospects

Some experts believe that VR, like the computer and the internet, soon will become a commonplace and indispensable part of everyday life, but others do not see the potential for such a wide implementation. Most agree, however, that once computing speed and power, broad bandwidth, and peripheral systems become more affordable for average consumers, VR will be more widely used. Beyond science, education, and other professional applications, the entertainment industry is thought most likely to want affordable VR innovations. Critics of VR applications point to personal and societal risks such as isolation, desocialization, and alienation, but advocates emphasize the technology's proven potential for augmenting people's lives. Both critics and advocates agree that experiences in VR can alter people's perceptions of and responses to the real world. These changes are intentional and welcome in most cases but sometimes they take place in an unintended and potentially dangerous manner. Airplane pilots have reportedly made mistakes that could be linked to the limitations of training with a flight simulator, which, for example, is incapable of realistically simulating acceleration. However, VR applications are valuable in highly technical and precise areas of medicine, industry, business, and research and are likely to gain more users, despite the potential risks and the expense.

—*Roman Meinhold*

References

Al-Jumaily, A., and R. A. Olivares. "Bio-Driven System-Based Virtual Reality for Prosthetic and Rehabilitation Systems." *Signal, Image and Video Processing*, vol. 6, no. 1, 2012, pp. 71–84.

Craig, Alan B., William R. Sherman, and Jeffrey D. Will. *Developing Virtual Reality Applications. Foundations of Effective Design.* Morgan Kaufmann, 2009.

Jung, Timothy, and M. Claudia tom Dieck, editors. *Augmented Reality and Virtual Reality: Empowering Human, Place and Business.* Springer International, 2018.

Nicosia, Laura. *Educators Online: Preparing Today's Teachers for Tomorrow's Digital Literacies.* Peter Lang, 2013.

Parisi, Tony. *Learning Virtual Reality.* O'Reilly Media, 2015.

Rizzo, Albert "Skipp," and Stéphane Bouchard, editors. *Virtual Reality for Psychological and Neurocognitive Interventions.* Springer-Verlag New York, 2019.

Sherman, William R., and Alan B. Craig. *Understanding Virtual Reality: Interface, Application and Design.* 2nd ed., Morgan Kaufmann, 2018.

Vince, John. *Introduction to Virtual Reality.* Springer-Verlag London, 2004.

"VR Futures: Where Will Virtual Reality Take You?" *EandT*, 15 Mar. 2016, eandt.theiet.org/content/articles/2016/03/vr-futures-where-will-virtual-reality-take-you/.

Weiss, Patrice L. (Tamar), Emily A. Keshner, and Mindy F. Levin, editors. *Virtual Reality for Physical and Motor Rehabilitation.* Springer-Verlag New York, 2014.

"Worldwide Spending on Augmented and Virtual Reality Expected to Reach $18.8 Billion in 2020, According to IDC." *IDC*, 27 Nov. 2019, www.idc.com/getdoc.jsp?containerId=prUS45679219.

WEARABLE TECHNOLOGY

Introduction

Also known as wearable tech, wearable devices, or simply wearables, the term applies to electronics incorporated into clothing, wristwatches, eyeglasses, and other familiar and not-so-familiar methodologies of attachment to the human body. They are generally not permanently affixed to the body and may be removed. They may be viewed as the end designs for sensor and communications technology or as segues into more permanent invasive devices, such as cochlear implants that allow the deaf to hear. Wearables now include the potential use of surface tattoo and implanted microchip technology, but these categories may diverge as internal devices proliferate and become a separate category from externally worn devices.

Background

Wearable technology gathers data about the individual wearing it and uploads it to an application (app) or the internet, or it may gather data from the environment or the internet and display it for the user. Some wearables may store and process data locally in the device itself, or they may transmit it for analysis. Generally, wearables use wireless/Wi-Fi and/or cellular service for communication capabilities. Because wearables communicate with a network or the internet, they are considered members of the Internet of Things (IoT). Like many IoT devices, wearables often lack screens or other interfaces to facilitate notice and consent for privacy communications with the user.

Wearables in the Health Care Industry

Initial applications of this technology have been successful in the health care field. In this context, health care is construed broadly, incorporating general wellness concerns such as fitness, weight loss, and safety/location monitoring. Devices such as Fitbit monitor the user's physical activity in multiple dimensions and supersede the one-dimensional (1D) mechanical step counter. However, most information generated by fitness trackers is not regulated under the primary US regulatory scheme for health care information, the Health Insurance Portability and Accountability Act of 1996 (HIPAA), unless the data relates to the person's health condition, the provision of health care, or the payment of health care and the data collected is personal health information (PHI). This would be a legal disincentive to integrate unregulated fitness tracker data with regulated health records, even if it makes financial or medical sense.

Fitness wearables may still have some regulatory obligations. Wearable technology companies might incur obligations under the HITECH Act, which amended HIPAA to include business associates of regulated entities, if, for example, they contract with health insurance companies to share their customers' fitness data. The US Food and Drug

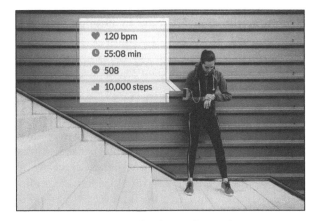

Smart jewelry—rings, wristbands, watches, or pins—are common examples of wearable tech. Photo via iStock/Todor Tsvetkov. [Used under license.]

Administration (FDA) has regulated traditional medical devices and may, as consumer fitness wearables become more mainstream, venture into this field as well. Faulty wearables are subject to review and recall by the Consumer Product Safety Commission (CPSC).

In one example, a Fitbit band was associated with skin irritations and approximately 1 million devices were recalled. The Federal Trade Commission (FTC) has launched several initiatives related to IoT, including wearable devices, focusing on concerns about appropriate notices to users under its mandate to seek out unfair and deceptive communications with consumers. The FTC has looked into the security of IoT devices and wearables to determine if companies offering such devices have established protocols guarding against unauthorized sale of consumer data and against breach of databases holding such data.

More traditional medical applications that would fit under FDA and/or HIPAA regulations are wearable insulin-, blood pressure–, heartbeat-, epileptic seizure–, and glucose-monitoring devices provided by medical providers to assist in monitoring patients. While not yet a substitute for medical attention, these devices have been lauded for allowing users to receive early alerts for life-threatening medical conditions and then to obtain the necessary medical treatment. There are concerns that some wearables are still primitive in their ability to measure body data as accurately as clinical devices do, and so research continues into increasing the accuracy and availability of such data. In addition, companies are continually looking at new ways to gather data from the human body. In development for medical and possibly for commercial markets, Google has researched the possibility of smart contact lenses and nanoscale cancer hunters for use in the human body.

A variety of companies have entered the wearables market, such as Google's experiment with Glass, a wearable eyepiece computer that may have failed to gain widespread acceptance because it was both visible and distracting to others. Criticisms of the device included its use to record video and audio of other parties without their knowledge and consent, copyright concerns, and the possibility of distracted driving or biking while wearing the device.

The Apple iWatch was launched with much fanfare, and quickly ushered in a new generation of watch-wearing that far exceeded mere timekeeping. Indeed, Apple competitors like Google and Samsung, though slow to catch up, did indeed issue forth their own versions of smart watches that could access users' phones and provide Inspector Gadget-like accessibility to text and email messages, as well as personal music, not to mention rudimentary health data. Companies already in the global positioning system (GPS) market, like Garmin, continually improved the functionality of GPS to be included on their watches, so athletes like runners, bicyclists and triathletes could access their routes and track their mileage. By 2020, start-up companies like Fitbit, Coros, and Polar had joined the fray, and as a result, quickly accelerated the implementation of features like wrist-detected heart rate monitors and weeklong battery life.

Wearable devices have begun to figure in insurance, employment, and legal cases as the temptation to use gathered data about individual's mounts. Cases may arise in which fitness devices are used to demonstrate that someone was not injured as claimed; an employment disability was not accurate; or, using the devices' GPS, a user was not where he or she claimed to be. In each scenario, the user's data would be subpoenaed or otherwise revealed in discovery in a way that the user of the wearable device did not intend on initial purchase or use of the device.

The impact of big data, including information on individuals collected by wearables, may affect insurance rates, potentially allowing fluctuations on a daily or minute-by-minute basis rather than adjustments made solely on renewal of an annual contract. Data aggregators and analysis companies can now look to wearables as one potential source of data that can be collected to create a health profile of an individual or a numerical score for that user. This information can be used to set insurance rates, determine employment, or inform marketing companies looking for individuals for whom certain pharmaceuticals or other medical products might be appropriate. Big data aggregated from wearables can also be used to create data maps of risky neighborhoods or types of individuals, and such data may affect individuals who do not use wearables at all.

Also, employers have begun offering free or low-cost wearable fitness or location trackers as a benefit or condition of employment to employees. These offerings are frequently included as part of an overall corporate wellness program. As a benefit, employee users may receive a discount on insurance or other financial benefit for using the device. As a condition of employment, some employees may be required to wear location trackers to determine if, for example, they are following a prescribed delivery route or taking only authorized breaks. On the rise is the use of body cameras by police officers, a measure that has the potential to increase safety for the police and for the public but may reduce privacy for the police officers and those who may cross their paths, whether suspect or bystander.

This fledgling use of wearables presents many layers of privacy concerns, most of which have been subsumed under the traditional legal methods of notice and consent in a written contract. If the wearable device in question does not fit into one of the usual regulatory frameworks, industry standards prevail, and customer concerns are embedded into privacy policies, terms of use, acceptable use policies, and other physical and digital contractual methods for obtaining consent from users. Employment law may reach this issue and establish some standards beyond voluntary contracts for what employers may do, and union negotiations may include wearable device parameters as part of the next cycle of labor contracts.

The aggregation of wearable data into databases presents a security risk to that data, especially if the data is not encrypted and made anonymous prior to database entry. The sheer volume of such data makes it a target for hackers who seek to discredit particular companies or countries, create valuable portraits of individuals for identity theft purposes, or resell the data to marketers. As with many IoT devices, the wearables market remains dispersed, and there is an opening for products that provide a platform to manage multiple wearables. That product would need to have even stricter security protocols because the stakes increase with the amount, specificity, and individually identifiable data collected. Risks include profiling by government and private companies, stalking, tracking, identification (ID) theft and other digital and physical theft like home burglaries, and miscellaneous and yet to be imagined losses of individual privacy. Additional regulatory plans for data security protocols and other minimum standards on the US federal level may include wearables explicitly or implicitly via the inclusion of provisions for IoT devices, big data, or network security.

—*Jill Bronfman and Jake D. Nicosia*

References

Barfield, Woodrow. *Fundamentals of Wearable Computers and Augmented Reality.* 2nd ed., Rowman and Littlefield, 2015.

"Consumer Generated and Controlled Health Data." *Federal Trade Commission*, 7 May 2014, www.ftc.gov/system/files/documents/public_events/195411/consumer-health-data-webcast-slides.pdf.

Ng, Cindy. "5 Things Privacy Experts Want You to Know About Wearables." *Varonis Blog*, 17 July 2014, blog.varonis.com/5-things-privacy-experts-want-youto-know-about-wearables/.

Tehrani, Kiana, and Andrew Michael. "Wearable Technology and Wearable Devices: Everything You Need to Know." *Wearable Devices Magazine*, 26 Mar. 26 2014. www.wearabledevices.com/what-is-a-wearable-device/.

WEB 2.0 IN THE SCHOOLS

Introduction

Web 2.0, or interactive programs/software that permit people to personalize their internet experiences, have had a great impact on how people communicate in the public domain. This technology, which includes blogs, wikis, and social networking sites, is also present in the classroom. As educators integrate Web 2.0 into their classrooms, two primary questions have emerged. First, what is the most effective way to use the technology with students? Second, how is the technology impacting knowledge construction? Although no definitive answers are yet available, this article provides a brief overview of the tentative conclusions educators are making as they experiment with new online tools and texts.

Background

Visit a first-grade classroom today and one might very well hear five-year-olds bragging about how many hits they have on their latest blog post or maybe watch as they send instant messages to their fourth-grade study buddies. In fact, hang out with elementary-school children long enough and one is likely to witness many innovations in writing technology being put to an array of educational uses.

Web 2.0, the term used to describe interactive programs/software that allow people to personalize their internet experiences, has already had a great impact in the public sphere. By allowing and inviting millions of new voices into publicly connected conversations, Web 2.0, which include blogs, wikis, and social networking sites, have reshaped and democratized public discourse. No longer do a few talking heads and a cadre of gatekeeping journalists solely determine what the public sees, hears, and talks about. Now the public, including anyone around the world with access to a computer and an internet connection, is free to thrust its voice into the fray of debate and expect to be heard.

The technology that inspired the revolution of public discourse has also entered the classroom, and the result, as one might expect, is producing a sea change in the way educators think about writing, collaboration, interaction, creativity, and knowledge construction. Two main categories of impact are emerging. The first is related to the application of the technology. How can educators best incorporate new online tools so that their students get the most benefit? The second is regarding the impact of the online writing environment on knowledge construction. In other words, how does the use of new technologies impact the way we understand writers, readers, and the texts and/or knowledge they create.

The answers to these questions are far from resolved. Technology is changing at dizzying speeds; new tools and ideas for using them can appear and disappear before teachers have a chance to implement them. Furthermore, the rapid pace at which new forms of text are being produced means few researchers have had adequate time to study the associated impacts on readers and writers or their writing processes. Thus, discussions of Web 2.0 technology use in education can leave one with an unsettled feeling. Obviously, the nexus of change is here. The technology is already available, and it will be used. But what writing will be in the future and the forms it will take is still somewhat murky. Therefore, educators are faced with the task—as they often are—of

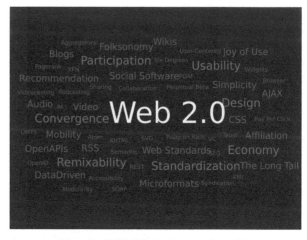

A tag cloud (a typical Web 2.0 phenomenon in itself) presenting Web 2.0 themes. Image by Markus Angermeier and Luca Cremonini, via Wikimedia Commons.

blending old concepts and skills with new technologies and ideas. In this process, they become part of the change that is reshaping the future.

Blogs, Wikis, Networks, and Podcasts

The core technologies having an impact in the classroom are those that allow students to produce texts—either oral or written—and share them online. The most popular of these include blogs, wikis, social networking sites, podcasts, and video sharing services such as YouTube. While teachers and instructors are experimenting with these tools, attempting to determine which are appropriate and effective for their students, blogs and wikis seem to be two of the most popular.

Blogs (a portmanteau of "web" and "log") are akin to online journals shared with the general public. Technically, they are spaces where individuals can post multiple written comments that are then presented in reverse chronological order. Individuals can enable their blog readers to comment on their posts, and additional tools, such as trackbacks and blog rolls, allow bloggers to connect their blogs to one another, creating a community of readers and respondents. While blogs began in the 1990s as a way for those with knowledge of the internet to post information about useful sites by listing links, improvements in technology quickly gave them a new purpose. Blogs became more personal in nature as individuals began writing about their daily activities or commenting on public events. Today, blogs remain individually produced texts with readers allowed to make comments on the text but not to change it.

Wikis, on the other hand, are collaboratively produced websites that permit anyone with access to the site to modify the content. Wikipedia is probably the most well-known wiki. This is an internet encyclopedia that allows anyone to update content on the site. Most wikis require the use of a simple text editing system although sites like have created wiki technology that provides simple point and click editing. A popular feature of wikis is that changes in the wiki can be easily tracked and earlier versions of a wiki can be reverted to in the event of unintentional loss.

Wikis and blogs are being used in the classroom to help students develop writing skills and demonstrate knowledge. Students use wikis to create group reports and for online writing workshops where drafts can be posted for review and feedback (Morgan & Smith, 2008). One common arrangement with blogs is for each student to have a blog that links to a classroom blog. Teachers post topics of discussion and links to relevant information on the class blog and then invite (or require) students to respond through their own blog and comments on those of their classmates.

The theoretical benefit of this activity is that students will develop their critical reading and thinking skills because of giving and receiving feedback in an authentic writing situation. Black provides an example of this kind of use. He suggests that law school professors use the main blog to post new legislation and court decisions as well as related news articles, blogs, and websites. As students comment on the unit material and reflect on the opinions of their classmates, they will revisit and revise their understanding of learned concepts and sharpen their critical thinking, analytical, reflective, and collaborative skills.

Some teachers ask students to explore the blogosphere (a collection of blogs) to gain insight into other cultures or to read a variety of opinions on a chosen controversial topic. In one project, university German and French students read blogs written by native speakers of the target language for a semester, recording new vocabulary and giving class reports on their chosen blogger. In the second semester, students became the bloggers, writing in the target language on topics related to classroom instruction and responding to each other's work through blog comments.

In a first-year composition class, students were required to read and critique the rhetorical style that several political figures used in their blogs. The goal was for the students, in their role of audience, to interpret and critique the writers. However, in the blogosphere, readers and writers quickly change roles. In this instance, both the instructor and the students were surprised when the subjects of the critique learned of the assignment through trackbacks and chose to respond to the assignments themselves. The instructor used the incident to discuss the importance of audience awareness, a key concept in rhetoric and composition.

Audience

For lessons using blogs, the presence of the audience presents benefits and challenges. The positive perspective is that having an interested audience is a strong motivator for many writers. This makes sense from a social constructivist position. From this perspective, writing is a social act, and words are meant to be read. In blogging, students know their work can be read by the world at large and this should motivate them to choose their words carefully and to write more. In many classrooms, especially those of the youngest writers, this appears to be true. In one elementary classroom, for example, emerging writers are excited to write in their blogs because they are paired with a preservice teacher who sends them regular feedback. Children also look forward to receiving comments from friends and family.

The challenge posed by audience, however, is that some audiences are more authentic than others. While students in the composition classroom became engaged in their discussions with the professional writers who responded to their critiques, students in the foreign language classroom indicated that the blog comments of their classmates were boring. While they enjoyed reading the works of the bloggers they followed in the blogosphere, they found they were less inspired by their classmates' work. Other instructors have noted a similar student reaction to classroom blogs that required students to write on specific topics. Dawson writes that she was disappointed by her students' responses to blogging assignments. "With few exceptions, the blogs would sit inactive until about 24 hours before our face-to-face class meetings (or 24 hours before the assignments were due in my online class), when a flurry of posts and comments would erupt. Then I would spend an excessive amount of time reading and commenting in the hours before class. Some students did the same, while others didn't bother to comment at all." She adds that few students continued posting in their blogs after the course ended, indicating little authentic engagement with the form. In this respect, the novelty of online writing did not seem to prompt writing in students any more than innovations of the past have.

Classroom Blogs vs. Personal Blogs

One possible reason for the lackadaisical response by older students to classroom blogs is that older students (adolescents through college) have been the primary users of blogs in the "real world." A study in 2003 by the Perseus Development Group found that 92.4 percent of all blogs were created by those thirty years old and younger. An Educause Report found that 28 percent of college students are bloggers compared to 7 percent of adults in the general population. By 2010, those in the twenty-one to thirty-five age group accounted for 53.3 percent of all bloggers. Bloggers twenty-years-old and younger were 20.2 percent of the blogging population.

Adolescent bloggers tend to prefer social blogging—using the blog to stay in touch with friends and family, arrange social gatherings, and maintain a social community. Unlike professors, who may envision blogs as forums for presenting polished pieces of writing, adolescents tend to see blogs as personal and experimental spaces where a free range of thought is the norm. Thus, they may find required response to a prompt to be uninteresting compared to their personal blogs.

The challenge for educators is to determine what kinds of blogs and associated activities will inspire students to interact in a meaningful way with their classmates. Fernheimer and Nelson contend that educators should use students' motivation to write expressively to challenge them to explore the more social, interactive, and collaborative potential of blogs. This can be accomplished, they believe, by creating a classroom virtual space that is governed by clearly articulated and enforced rules. In their college literature and composition classes, they deliberately plan and model for students the kind of

academic exchange they expect students to engage in when blogging. These expectations include students will read and acknowledge other writers' opinions in their own blog. Without teaching and modeling these expectations, students may not understand how classroom blogging should be different from personal blogging. This misunderstanding can lead students to produce noninteractive, noncollaborative writing, which is more typical of the personal, expressivist uses of blogs with which students are already familiar.

Discourse

While there is no doubt that more students are using Web 2.0 either as a component of an otherwise traditional class or as part of a class that is taught online, there are questions about what students are learning from using this technology. Research and anecdotal experiences indicate that Web 2.0 changes the way individuals construct knowledge. This seems to occur in part because the technology distributes the control of the learning process and responsibility for learning differently than a traditional classroom. Additionally, the texts that are produced in these environments are very different. Like conversations, they allow multiple voices to enter and leave an ongoing, fluid discussion, shifting topics and direction over time.

Like print media, they maintain a permanent record of ideas, allowing for reflection on statements that might have been otherwise lost in a face-to-face conversation. Where one begins to interact with the text—at the beginning of a conversation or half way to the end—impacts how one understands the knowledge produced by the exchanges. To add to all of this, online texts look different. They frequently use more visuals than traditional print media, and their inclusion of hyperlinks increases their intertextuality. To effectively create or interpret these texts requires new literacy skills including the ability to read nonlinearly, to synthesize sources, and to understand how visuals can augment the written word. Students without these skills may not be developing knowledge the way instructors intend.

Online Discussions

To understand the process of knowledge construction within the online environment, researchers have begun to examine the collaborative texts that are produced as participants engage in online discussion. Online discussions offer a good way to evaluate this process because it is generally accepted that knowledge is constructed when individuals explore issues, take and defend positions, and then reflect upon and reevaluate those positions based on contradicting evidence. In a face-to-face classroom, this process occurs through classroom discussions facilitated by an instructor. An online discussion, especially one undertaken for educational purposes, such as an online course, is supposed to substitute for these spoken interchanges. Thus, it offers a promising ground for examining the kind of knowledge generated by Web 2.0 experiences.

Asynchronous and Synchronous Discussions

Online discussions come in two basic forms: asynchronous and synchronous. Asynchronous discussions are those that do not occur in real time. Discussion boards that allow threaded discussions are an example of this form of discussion. In a discussion board, several topics are available and individuals can post comments to each topic separately at any time. Synchronous discussions are like face-to-face conversations. They occur in real time, such as videoconferencing or online chat (where participants post text that is immediately read by a user on another computer).

Both forms of discussion have been used as part of online learning courses, and each has positive and negative attributes for contributing to knowledge construction. Synchronous discussions, because they occur in real time, are most like face-to-face classroom discussion. Participants interacting within the same time space can immediately receive response to their comments and questions. Furthermore, just as in face-to-face conversation, the ideas presented may be fragmented or incomplete, allowing respondents more freedom to interpret what participants mean, thereby facilitating the processes important to individual meaning making.

On the other hand, some synchronous discussions, especially online chat, do not appear to create the feeling of community that is necessary for fostering deep knowledge construction. The obstacles to community building include that the contributions to an online chat discussion often occur out of sync, creating a disjointed feeling that prevents

negotiation of meaning; that people who are not good typists may be left out of the conversation; and that too many participants in the discussion can make the speed at which comments are made overwhelming.

Asynchronous conversations, some have argued, are more conducive to knowledge construction because they allow users time to think before responding. In an asynchronous discussion, participants read and respond at their convenience, meaning hours, days, weeks or even months can pass between responses. Lea argues that this lag time allows for more reflexive learning. She cites students who indicated that writing in an online conference made them solidify their thinking before responding because they had time to think and understanding that the response would last forever made them more careful. An additional benefit of these discussions is that they provide a way for shy students to respond, increasing the feeling of community building necessary for advanced negotiation of and coconstruction of meaning.

However, asynchronous discussions have been faulted for some of these same traits. Several studies have indicated that developing mutual understanding in an asynchronous environment is more difficult because individuals can ignore some messages in the conversation and because the responses occur over a range of time, making following a single train of thought difficult. Moreover, some students entering these discussions at their midpoint found them overwhelming due to the large number of messages they had to read to catch up with the conversation. These characteristics can make the discussion unsatisfying for some participants, and can prohibit knowledge construction because existing paradigms are more likely to remain unchanged.

While it might be tempting to fault the format of the discussion or the medium in which it occurs, research seems to indicate that the controlling factor in whether knowledge is constructed in the online environment is the instructor. When instructors are able to engage students in developing a sense of shared purpose and to intervene at crucial points during the online discussion (e.g., to provide corrective feedback or information), students are more likely to find the discussion satisfying and to reach higher levels of knowledge construction. Thus, it seems that while new technologies are impacting education, they are not replacing the need for inspired educators.

Web 2.0 has brought many changes to the world and is now affecting the classroom. While advances in this technology are still being developed and tested, the new technologies are changing the way students and teachers approach learning. At this point in time, the most pressing questions for teachers and researchers are how to most effectively integrate the technology and how integration will impact students' knowledge construction. As answers to these questions are still being explored, teachers continue to experiment with various options. In so doing, they bring new skills to their students in the hope that they will be prepared for the future.

—*Noelle Vance*

References

Asselin, M., and M. Moayeri. "The Participatory Classroom: Web 2.0 In the Classroom." *Australian Journal of Language & Literacy*, vol. 34, 2011, p. 45.

Barone, D. "Exploring Home and School Involvement of Young Children with Web 2.0 and Social Media." *Research in the Schools*, vol. 19, 2012, pp. 1–11.

Barone, D., and T. E. Wright. "Literacy Instruction with Digital and Media Technologies." *The Reading Teacher*, vol. 62, 2008, pp. 292–302.

Black, P. "Use of Blogs in Legal Education." *James Cook University Law Review*, vol. 13, 2006, pp. 8–29.

Bober, M. J., and V. P. Dennen. "Intersubjectivity: Facilitating Knowledge Construction in Online Environments." *Education Media International*, vol. 38, 2001, pp. 241–50.

Cassidy, K. "To Blog or not to Blog: That Is Not the Question." *Connect Magazine*, vol. 21, 2008, pp. 1–3.

Caverly, D. C., and A. Ward. "Techtalk: Wikis and Collaborative Knowledge Construction." *Journal of Developmental Education*, vol. 32, 2008, pp. 36–37.

Ducate, L. C., and L. L. Lomicka. "Adventures in the Blogosphere: From Blog Readers to Blog Writers." *Computer Assisted Language Learning*, vol. 21, 2008, pp. 9–28.

Fernheimer, J. W., and J. T. Nelson. "Bridging the Composition Divide: Blog Pedagogy and the Potential for Agonistic Classrooms." *Currents in Electronic Literacy*, vol. 9, 2005, www.currents.cwrl.utexas.edu.

Hou, H., K. Chang, and Y. Sung. "An Analysis of Peer Assessment Online Discussions within a Course That Uses Project-Based Learning." *Interactive Learning Environments*, vol. 15, 2007, pp. 237–51.

Jimoyiannis, A., P. Tsiotakis, D. Roussinos, et al. "Preparing Teachers to Integrate Web 2.0 in School Practice: Toward a Framework for Pedagogy 2.0." *Australasian Journal of Educational Technology*, vol. 29, 2013, pp. 248–67.

Lea, M. "Computer Conferencing and Assessment: New Ways of Writing in Higher Education." *Studies in Higher Education*, vol. 26, 2001, pp. 163–81.

Kilgore, D. "The Medium Is the Message: Online Technology and Knowledge Construction in Adult Graduate Education." *Adult Learning*, vol. 15, no. 3/4, 2004, pp. 12–15.

Luce-Kapler, R. "Radical Change and Wikis: Teaching New Literacies." *Journal of Adolescent and Adult Literacy*, vol. 51, 2007, pp. 214–23.

McEwan, B. "Managing Boundaries in the Web 2.0 Classroom." *New Directions for Teaching & Learning*, 2012, pp. 15–28.

Morgan, B., and R. D. Smith. "A Wiki for Classroom Writing." *The Reading Teacher*, vol. 62, 2008, pp. 80–82.

Nackerud, S., and K. Scaletta. "Blogging In the Academy." *New Directions for Student Services*, Winter 2008, pp. 71–87.

Nicosia, Laura. *Educators Online: Preparing Today's Teachers for Tomorrow's Digital Literacies*. Peter Lang, 2013.

Park, S. "The Potential of Web 2.0 Tools to Promote Reading Engagement in a General Education Course." *Techtrends: Linking Research & Practice to Improve Learning*, vol. 57, 2013, pp. 46–53.

Phirangee, K. "Beyond the Elementary Classroom Walls: Exploring the Ways Participation within Web 2.0 Spaces Are Reshaping Pedagogy." *Journal of Educational Multimedia & Hypermedia*, vol. 22, 2013, pp. 299–316.

Skinner, E. "Building Knowledge and Community Through Online Discussion." *Journal of Geography in Higher Education*, vol. 31, 2007, pp. 381–91.

Sysomos, Inc. "Inside Blog Demographics." June 2010, sysomos.com.

Tryon, C. "Writing and Citizenship: Using Blogs to Teach First-Year Composition." *Pedagogy*, vol. 6, 2006, pp. 128–32.

WIKIPEDIA

Introduction

Wikipedia is a multilingual, web-based, free-content encyclopedia project supported by the Wikimedia Foundation. This foundation administers and funds Wikipedia but does not exercise editorial control over the encyclopedia. Wikipedia is based on a model of openly editable content. Its entries are written collaboratively by largely anonymous volunteers, who write without compensation. Anyone with internet access can write and make changes to the entries, except in limited cases in which editing is deemed necessary, such as to prevent vandalism. Users may contribute anonymously, under a pseudonym, or, if they choose to, with their real identity.

Background

Since it was created in 2001, Wikipedia has become one of the world's largest reference sites, with over 21 billion page views per month as of April 2022. Wikipedia has more than 300,000 active contributors who have written more than 100 million entries in over 300 languages. Each day, millions of users worldwide make hundreds of thousands of edits and create thousands of new entries at Wikipedia; individuals of all ages, cultures, and backgrounds are allowed to add or edit article prose, references, images, and other media.

At Wikipedia, the contribution is considered more important than the background of the contributor. What Wikipedia retains as an entry depends on considerations such as copyright issues and whether the entry complies with Wikipedia's policies, such as being verifiable against a published reliable source, thereby notionally excluding the bias of editors and unsupported and unreviewed research. Wikipedia also has software that allows for correction of mistakes, and many experienced editors monitor the entries to ensure the quality of the editing work.

Wikipedia invites a large contributor base and attracts many editors from diverse backgrounds. This allows Wikipedia to reduce greatly regional and cultural bias and largely prevents any group from censoring or imposing bias. A large, diverse number of editors also provides access and breadth on subject matter that often is otherwise inaccessible or little documented. Several editors contributing at any given moment also means that Wikipedia can add entries on significant events shortly after they occur. Like any publication, however, Wikipedia may reflect the cultural, age, socioeconomic, and other biases of its contributors, and without any specific authorities overseeing topics, or scholarly peer review, the validity of any information can be questionable.

Currently, Wikipedia is one of the most popular sites for finding information on events or people. In 2009, two German men who killed the actor Walter Sedlmayr in 1990 sued the Wikimedia Foundation, claiming that their right to privacy was infringed by Wikipedia's inclusion of details about their crimes. The two men each received a life sentence in 1993, but one was released in 2007 and the other in 2008. The attorney representing the two ex-convicts filed lawsuits in German courts to demand that the Wikimedia Foundation remove their names from the English-language article. German Wikipedia editors had removed the killers' names from the German-language version. The lawyer for the convicts cited the suppression of publication of their names in Germany since 2006. He claimed that the German courts, including several courts of appeals, had held

Wikipedia is a free internet-based encyclopedia started in 2001. Photo via iStock/zmeel. [Used under license.]

that his clients' names and likenesses could no longer be published in connection with Sedlmayr's death.

The debate centered on whether the individuals' German court–determined right to privacy should take preeminence over the First Amendment to the US Constitution. Essentially it involved a conflict between the First Amendment, which guarantees freedom of speech, and German privacy and criminal laws, which stipulate that, after a given period, a crime is "spent" and may not be referred to by the media.

Striking a different balance than US courts between the right to privacy and the public's right to know, German courts allow a convict's name to be withheld in media reports after he or she has served his or her sentence and a set period has expired. The practice has been justified on the grounds that ex-convicts could return to society and not be publicly stigmatized for their crime. In other words, there is the belief that ex-criminals have a right to privacy, too, and a right to be left alone. The German law is based on a 1973 decision of Germany's highest court, the Federal Court of Justice, which led to German publications referring to people whose convictions are spent as, for example, "the perpetrator," or "Mr. G."

The American legal community generally finds the German law highly objectionable because American law holds that people must be allowed to publish truthful information about historical events and because foreign governments should not be able to censor publications in the United States. Under the American justice system, the Wikipedia article would undoubtedly receive First Amendment protection. First Amendment advocates make the slippery slope argument that once speech is suppressed, there is pressure to suppress still more speech.

The Wikimedia Foundation responded that it supported its German editors in removing the names of the convicts while also supporting its English-language editors in rejecting the German request. Wikipedia also noted that the ex-convicts were named in several other online sources in Germany. Because of the publicity accorded this case, the efforts of the two German plaintiffs had the opposite of the intended result of maintaining confidentiality. Instead, the controversy fed the publicity.

Despite its commitment to First Amendment freedoms, Wikipedia has restricted editing of the biographies of living individuals after instances of personal details being fabricated to create libelous misinformation. In another set of circumstances, such as when the Taliban seized a *New York Times* journalist in Afghanistan, Wikipedia founder Jimmy Wales personally asked the site's editors not to disseminate information on the incident.

Wikipedia also faced pressure to suppress reporting of stories that might cause embarrassment to prominent individuals. In 2011, Wales announced that he would resist pressure to censor Wikipedia entries in response to the success of an English family footballer who had received an injunction from England's High Court to enjoin the media from publicizing an alleged affair with the *Big Brother* contestant Imogen Thomas. Wales said that, as an encyclopedia, Wikipedia seeks to document facts obtained from reputable sources and should not be prevented from recording facts. Wales criticized the injunctions, claiming them to be an infringement of the right to free speech. He added that the public should object to the rich and powerful being able to censor media publications whenever they wanted.

Not all of Wikipedia's privacy clashes occurred overseas. The most prominent of these cases took place in the United States. Among the documents revealed by the whistleblower Edward J. Snowden were those indicating that the National Security Agency (NSA) was surveilling Wikipedia, along with other sites, such as Gmail and Facebook. A leaked slide from a classified PowerPoint presentation stated that monitoring these sites could allow NSA analysts to learn "nearly everything a typical user does on the internet." On March 10, 2015, the Wikimedia Foundation, along with several human rights and media organizations, responded by filing the lawsuit *Wikimedia Foundation et al. v. National Security Agency* in the US District Court of Maryland, C 1.15-CVv-00662-RDB. Wikimedia said that it was suing the NSA to protect the rights of the 500 million people who use Wikipedia monthly, asserting that that this was necessary in order to protect the free exchange of knowledge and ideas.

Specifically, the Wikimedia lawsuit claimed the NSA mass surveillance of internet traffic in the United States (frequently referred to as "upstream surveillance") violated both the Fourth Amendment, against unreasonable searches, as well as the First Amendment, which protects the freedom of expression. Wikimedia also argued that the NSA surveillance exceeds the authority granted by the Foreign Intelligence Surveillance Act (FISA), 92 Stat. 1783 (1978), as amended by Congress in 2008. Section 702 of the FISA Amendments Act of 2008 (FAA), 122 Stat. 2436, specifically states that the "Attorney General and the Director of National Intelligence may authorize . . . the targeting of persons reasonably believed to be located outside the United States to acquire foreign intelligence information."

Most people search and read Wikipedia anonymously because an account is not needed to use the service. Many of these users prefer anonymity, especially those who work on controversial issues or who live in countries with repressive governments. User anonymity was frustrated by NSA upstream surveillance that was intercepting and searching almost all of the international text-based traffic flowing across the internet backbone within the United States (that is, the network that connects Wikipedia with its global community of readers and editors). The NSA was tracking the content of what was read or typed, as well as other information that could be linked to the person's physical location and possible identity. Wikipedia maintained that these activities are sensitive and private. They can reveal everything from a person's political and religious beliefs to sexual orientation and medical conditions.

Wikimedia asserted that it and its users were harmed because pervasive surveillance has a chilling effect. It stifles freedom of expression and the free exchange of knowledge that Wikipedia was designed to enable. Specifically, Wikimedia and the plaintiffs say that known NSA surveillance of website users in other countries is discouraging online participation and "undermines their ability to carry out activities crucial to their missions."

Wikimedia, in its lawsuit, asked the court to order the NSA to end its unconstitutional dragnet surveillance of internet traffic, basing its argument on privacy as an essential right. Wales stressed that privacy makes freedom of expression possible and sustains freedom of inquiry and association. It empowers everyone to read, write, and communicate in confidence, without fear of persecution.

—Gretchen Nobahar

References

Barber, N. W. "A Right to Privacy?" *Human Rights and Private Law: Privacy as Autonomy*, edited by Katja S. Ziegler, Hart, 2007.

Fuchs, Christian. *Social Media: A Critical Introduction.* Sage, 2014.

Greenstein, Shane M., and Feng Zhu. *Collective Intelligence and Neutral Point of View: The Case of Wikipedia.* National Bureau of Economic Research, 2012.

Lee, Newton. *Facebook Nation: Total Information Awareness.* 2nd ed., Springer Science + Business Media, 2014.

Lih, Andrew. *The Wikipedia Revolution: How a Bunch of Nobodies Created the World's Greatest Encyclopedia.* Hyperion, 2009.

Palma, Paul. *Computers in Society 09/10.* 15th ed., McGraw-Hill Irwin, 2010.

Reagle, Joseph Michael. *Good Faith Collaboration: The Culture of Wikipedia.* MIT Press, 2010.

Rocha, Álvaro, Ana Maria Correa, Tom Wilson, and Karl A. Stroetmann. *Advances in Information Systems and Technologies.* Springer, 2013.

Schwartz, John. "Two German Killers Demanding Anonymity Sue Wikipedia's Parent." *The New York Times*, 12 Nov. 2009.

WINDOWS OPERATING SYSTEM

Introduction

Microsoft Windows is the most dominant group of operating systems available for personal computers. Operating systems are software programs that support and manage the basic functioning of the computer. Operating systems provide a graphical interface through which users can easily execute tasks by clicking on icons or typing into a command prompt.

Windows is designed to streamline and simplify the computing experience and endlessly expand the breadth of what computers can do. Since its initial release in 1985, Windows has evolved with consistently improved functionality that has kept the brand at the forefront of the market for decades. Despite occasionally being the target of vocal criticism, Windows continues to be the most popular operating system for personal computers and is installed on hundreds of millions of machines around the world.

Background

Prior to the mid-1980s, most early computers ran on simplistic operating systems that required users to input complex text-based commands into command prompts. Starting in 1981, the most common of these rudimentary operating systems was the Microsoft Disk Operating System (MS-DOS). Although MS-DOS was reasonably functional and reliable for its time, it was quickly overshadowed when Apple Computer's Macintosh debuted in 1984. Rather than using a text-based operating system like MS-DOS, the Macintosh featured one the earliest examples of a graphical interface-based operating system that allowed users to interact with the machine by clicking on icons.

The arrival of the graphical interface represented a major step forward in personal computing and presented a significant challenge for Microsoft. Undaunted, the company responded by developing its own graphical interface-based operating system. Referred to internally as Interface Manager, the new operating system featured a sort of virtual desktop on which programs ran in boxes called windows. These windows eventually became the inspiration for the operating system's official name when it was released in 1985. Even though the early Windows system offered mouse support; included features like drop-down menus and scroll bars; and came loaded with a range of basic programs such as Paint, Notepad, and Calculator, Windows 1.0 was generally considered inferior to the Macintosh operating system and was a commercial failure.

Evolution of Windows

Undeterred by the initial negative response to Windows 1.0, Microsoft worked to create a better product. In an effort to emulate its competitor's success, Microsoft entered a licensing agreement that allowed it to incorporate some of Apple's graphical interface features in Windows 2.0. With these added features, improved graphics, and the inclusion of additional software, Windows 2.0 clearly improved upon its predecessor and enjoyed a more positive reception upon its release in 1987.

While Windows 2.0 proved to be a step in the right direction, Microsoft's first real operating system breakthrough came with the 1990 debut of Windows 3.0 and the enhanced Windows 3.1 two years later. Touting an entirely new file management system, visual customization, alternative operating modes, and more bundled software, the new Windows was an immediate hit, selling 10 million copies in just two years. Crucially, Microsoft also released a software development kit with Windows 3.0 that made it easier for third-party software developers to write programs to run on the operating system. This effort helped to solidify the place of Windows in the personal computing market.

With the internet emerging as the driving force in the computer industry, Microsoft unveiled Windows 95 in 1995. This product featured a totally redesigned operating system with a unique look and feel. Unlike earlier releases that ran on top of MS-DOS and required a manual launch from the user, Windows 95 loaded automatically when the computer was started. Most notably, Windows 95 included the first taskbar and Start menus, which offered users easy access to programs, documents, and settings. Windows 95 also provided a gateway to the internet through the inclusion of the internet browser, Internet Explorer. With these new features, Windows 95 was a success, selling 7 million copies in only five weeks. Three years later, Microsoft returned with Windows 98, a release that was essentially an improved version of Windows 95.

Through the early 2000s, Microsoft released several new versions of Windows, including Windows 2000, which was an updated iteration of the professional Windows NT line, and Windows Millennium Edition. The latter was notoriously unstable, largely because it was rushed to the marketplace in anticipation of the debut of Windows XP in 2001. Windows XP was designed to address many of the issues that plagued Microsoft's previous releases and, as a result, offered significantly improved speed, stability, and file management. Thanks to these key tweaks, Windows XP became one of Microsoft's most widely used products.

Windows Vista (2007) was the next version of the product.

Though this product boasted the strongest security system and most impressive graphics that had yet been seen in a Windows operating system, it was critically panned. Much of the criticism was focused on Vista's extensive compatibility issues, which convinced many XP users to delay upgrading. Microsoft released Windows 7 in 2009. With better compatibility and even more new features, Windows 7 resolved the Vista issues and satisfied critics and customers alike.

Microsoft released Windows 8 in 2012, Windows 10 in 2015, and Windows 11 in 2021.

Move Toward Touchscreens

Acknowledging the growing consumer interest in tablets and smartphones, Microsoft radically changed its approach when it released Windows 8 in 2012. Specifically tailored for compatibility with touchscreen devices, Windows 8 rejected the traditional Start menu in favor of a tile-based layout. While tablet and smartphone users welcomed this design, traditional desktop and laptop users did not. Hoping to reconcile its new aesthetic design with the user desire for traditional functionality, Microsoft introduced Windows 10 in 2015. The was the first version of their OS to be offered as a free upgrade. Windows 10 also introduced a new service model in which the OS would continually receive updates to various features and functions. This model is similar to that employed by Microsoft's competitor Apple. Windows 10 was also the first version of Windows that had a universal application architecture. This means apps on Windows 10 can be used on smartphones, tablets, and the Xbox One gaming system as well. This package included options for both the Start menu and the new tile scheme. Windows 10 also featured the debut of Cortana, Microsoft's first digital personal assistant.

Dominance and Reinvention

More than 77 percent of desktop PCs worldwide ran some version of Windows by the end of 2019. The majority (about 72 percent) ran Windows 10, while some PCs continued to run older Windows OSs, including Windows 7 and Windows 8.1. Windows is sold around the world and comes formatted for a variety of languages. In addition, language interface packs are available for free download and offer support for languages not found in full versions. Each pack requires a base language that can be activated within the OS after installation.

Given the rising popularity of handheld computing devices, such as tablets and smartphones, the global computer market is no longer based solely on the PC market.

While Microsoft continued to dominate the PC market through 2019, the company controlled only about 0.03 percent of the global mobile OS market and 0.1 percent of the tablet OS market by the end of that year, falling far behind Android and Apple iOS (iPhone operating system). As a result, with the release of Windows 10, Microsoft has made changes to its basic strategy. The company has reduced its focus on proprietary software. Instead, it is increasingly embracing the potential of open-source software. Future versions of Windows will likely show an increased focus on cloud-based computing, intuitive touch-screen technology, and alternative interface controls such as voice activation and multitouch gestures.

—*Jack Lasky and Micah L. Issitt*

References

Brown, Michael. "Microsoft Windows Is 30: A Short History of One of the Most Iconic Tech Products Ever." *International Business Times*, 20 Nov. 2015, www.ibtimes.com/microsoft-windows-30-short-history-one-most-iconic-tech-products-ever-2194091.

Calore, Michael. "A History of Microsoft Windows." *Wired*, 10 Dec. 2008, www.wired.com/2008/12/wiredphotos31/.

Gibbs, Samuel. "From Windows 1 to Windows 10: 29 Years of Windows Evolution." *The Guardian*, 2 Oct. 2014, www.theguardian.com/technology/2014/oct/02/from-windows-1-to-windows-10-29-years-of-windows-evolution.

"A History of Microsoft Windows." *Microsoft*, Oct. 2015, windows.microsoft.com/en-US/windows/history#T1=era0.

Holcombe, Jane, and Charles Holcombe. *Survey of Operating Systems*. 6th ed., McGraw-Hill Education, 2020.

McLellan, Charles. "The History of Windows: A Timeline." *ZDNet*, 14 Apr. 2014, www.zdnet.com/article/the-history-of-windows-a-timeline/.

"Operating System Market Share Worldwide." *Statcounter*, May 2020, gs.statcounter.com/os-market-share/all/worldwide/2019.

Warren, Tom. "Windows Turns 30: A Visual History." *Verge*, 19 Nov. 2015, www.theverge.com/2015/11/19/9759874/microsoft-windows-visual-history-30-years.

"What Is the History of Microsoft Windows?" *Indiana University Knowledge Base*, 18 Jan. 2018, kb.iu.edu/d/abwa.

XML (EXTENSIBLE MARKUP LANGUAGE)

Introduction

Extensible markup language (XML) is a programming language used to categorize and describe data. As a type of markup language, XML uses tags or rules for tags to add information about data. Tags used in XML coding help describe the data inside the tags. XML does not rely on any particular software or hardware. It also is written in plain text, so it can be shared easily among different programs and devices.

Even though XML is a markup language, it is different from some other markup languages because it was created to label and categorize data rather than display data. One of the most popular markup languages is hypertext markup language (HTML). HTML adds information about the format and the appearance of text. XML, however, adds information about the data included inside the tags. The goal of HTML is to display text in a certain way while the goal of XML is to describe data.

XML and HTML have another important difference: XML tags are not predefined, but HTML tags are. A person using HTML has to memorize or look up specific tags to use to have data display in a particular way. XML users, however, can develop unique tags to describe data. One other difference between XML and HTML is that XML is more rigid. HMTL is a fairly flexible language and can tolerate some coding errors. XML, however, has to be formatted very specifically because errors can be introduced easily.

Background

The World Wide Web Consortium (W3C)—a group of volunteers and paid employees who create standards for the web—wanted to create a new type of markup language that was that useful on the internet. The group decided to base the new language on another type of markup language called "standard generalized markup language" (SGML). Standard generalized markup language is made up of elements, and these elements usually consist of a start tag, content, and an end tag (e.g., <60>firstname <62>Jose <60>/firstname <62>). The group from W3C structured XML in much the same way.

Members of W3C developed the first draft of XML in 1996. They distributed coding instructions in a twenty-five-page manual and released it to the public. The W3C recommended the use of XML in 1998. Soon, XML became an important markup language that many people used for different purposes. Some people used XML on the web, and others used it in electronic publishing, in databases, and in other types of documents. The W3C working group intended to create a markup language for the internet, but they created a markup language capable of being used in many different situations.

Throughout the history of XML, groups at W3C and other individuals and groups around the world have worked to further develop the language. Today a working group at W3C continues to refine the specifications for XML, though people and programmers outside W3C also influence it. The W3C publishes its work so others can use XML and make changes and enhancements to the language. Numerous conferences about XML, its standards, and its uses are held around the world each year, proving the language's continued popularity.

Uses of XML

One of the main uses of XML is to categorize data. XML can be used on the web to classify information. The idea of data categorization is especially important on the "semantic web," which is the web of data. XML also can be used to separate data from other elements on a web page. For example, a programmer can use XML to keep the data of a web page separate from the HTML coding on that page. This separation allows the programmer to update the data without updating the HTML.

Another important use of XML is data transport. At times, data has to be shared between two different programs that are incompatible with one another. Because XML does not rely on a specific type of software, it is compatible with many different programs. Sometimes XML can help two incompatible programs share data with each other. In a similar way, data sometimes has to be shared when a platform (either software or hardware) is being upgraded. These upgrades can be time consuming because of the large amount of data that needs to be shared. However, XML is useful because it can make transferring the data much simpler.

Adding XML to Documents

One way people use XML is to add markup to documents. Often in documents using XML, the first line of code is called the declaration line. The declaration line states that XML is being used and identifies the version of XML being used (e.g., <60>?xml version="1.0" encoding="UTF-8"? <62>). The line after the declaration is a line that describes the root element. This information tells what type of document is being coded (e.g., <60>note <62>). The lines after the root element contain the content of the document and can be coded to show the function of each piece of data (e.g., <60>heading <62>, <60>body <62>, <60>conclusion <62>). The document then ends with a tag that shows the text is complete (e.g., <60>/note <62>).

People using XML have to remember some important rules about the language. If any opening tag is used, a corresponding closing tag must also be used (e.g., <60>firstname <62> and <60>/firstname <62> or <60>note <62> and <60>/note <62>). Other markup languages, such as HTML, do not always require closing tags, but XML does. Along the same lines, XML tags have to be nested properly. That means the elements opened first must be closed last. For example, <60>i <62> <60>b <62>word <60>/i <62> <60>/b <62> is nested incorrectly, but <60>i <62> <60>b <62>word <60>/b <62> <60>/i <62> is nested correctly. Another factor people using XML have to remember is that the language is case sensitive, so the tag <60>Note <62> and the tag <60>note <62> are not the same.

—Elizabeth Mohn

References

"A Brief SGML Tutorial." *W3C*, 11 Aug. 2015, www.w3.org/TR/WD-html40-970708/intro/sgmltut.html.

"Definition of: XML." *PC Mag*. Ziff Davis, LLC, PCMag Digital Group, 13 Aug. 2015, www.pcmag.com/encyclopedia/term/55048/xml.

"Development History." *W3C*, 13 Aug. 2015, www.w3.org/XML/hist2002.

"Extensible Markup Language (XML)." *W3C*, 13 Aug. 2015, www.w3.org/XML/.

Hollander, Dave, and C. M. Sperberg-McQueen. "Happy Birthday, XML!" *W3C*, 13 Aug. 2015, www.w3.org/2003/02/xml-at-5.html.

Rouse, Margaret. "XML (Extensible Markup Language) Definition." *TechTarget*, 13 Aug. 2015, searchsoa.techtarget.com/definition/XML.

"XML Tutorial." *W3Schools*, 13 Aug. 2015, www.w3schools.com/xml/.

Y

YOUTUBE

Introduction

YouTube is a popular video streaming website that displays uploaded video files created or disseminated by its users. The types of videos uploaded to YouTube include user-created content, such as homemade videos and videoblogs, and short video clips from films, television, and copyrighted and noncopyrighted materials. YouTube has become very popular since its introduction in 2005 and is the video streaming website against which most others are measured. Since its launch, YouTube has become a touchstone in cultural debates about the internet. There has been controversy over the uploading of copyrighted materials. However, the popularity of YouTube has also brought favorable attention to some media outlets when users upload portions of copyrighted content. YouTube now offers television streaming services and exclusive content like sporting events. These are available, like YouTube's commercial-free version, as a for-pay subscription, and they are beginning to challenge traditional television services offered by cable and satellite companies.

YouTube's interface is relatively easy to use, but is designed to allow a complex array of activity. Users do not need to download software to use YouTube, but access to a high-speed internet connection does optimize the video streaming capabilities of the website. Users may respond to videos by posting a comment about the video (in writing or by video response), giving a video a thumbs-up or thumbs-down rating, or by voting a video a "favorite."

Users may also share videos by emailing them or linking them to another web page, such as a personal weblog (blogs) or social networking and bookmarking websites. Users may flag a video as inappropriate if the content is copyrighted or if the content

YouTube is the most popular video-hosting website. Photo via iStock/hocus-focus. [Used under license.]

is sexually or verbally explicit. Users can see the number of hits or visits a video has garnered, view the username of any individual who posted a video, and be notified whenever that person posts a new video. Users can also join user communities with similar interests or subscribe to channels with specific content.

YouTube has become associated with several controversies related to the internet, including copyright infringement and the display of violent or otherwise explicit content. However, YouTube has also resulted in celebrity status for several of its users who posted original, self-generated videos.

Background

YouTube was founded in February 2005 by three former PayPal employees: Chad Hurley, Steve Chen, and Jawed Karim. Venture capital firm Sequoia Capital funded the launch of YouTube in December 2005. The first video featured on YouTube was uploaded by "jawed" (presumably cofounder Jawed Karim) on April 23, 2005. The video is eighteen seconds in length and features an uneventful moment at a zoo. By July 2006, YouTube was receiving 20 million visitors per month. Of the 9 billion video clips watched in the United States that same month, more than a quarter of them (2.5 billion videos at an average length of 2.7 minutes each) were watched on YouTube.

By August 2008, the site boasted 74 million visitors per month. YouTube was immediately successful: the ease of use and open policy of the website, which allowed almost all forms of content (excluding copyrighted, pornographic, violent, or otherwise inappropriate content), combined with the fact that it was a free service, attracted millions of users. As of December 2014, more than 1 billion unique users were visiting the site each month. By 2017, the site had 1.5 billion logged-in users visiting YouTube each month, and logged-in users spent an average of more than one hour per day watching YouTube videos on mobile devices. YouTube was the second-most trafficked web page on the internet in 2017, following Google.

Videos featured at YouTube, most of which are ten minutes or less in length, span the spectrum of content, including instructional and how-to videos, clips from popular television shows, amateur and professionally produced motion pictures and music videos, home movies, film trailers, videos created especially for YouTube, and much more.

YouTube's rapid ascent to the top tier of internet websites in terms of popularity and number of visits was achieved partially as a result of several incidents that brought it to the attention of the wider public. Soon after launch, clips from popular television shows, such as a sketch from the comedy show *Saturday Night Live* and the 2006 Winter Olympics (both of which were owned by television broadcasting company NBC), made their way onto YouTube, allowing users to watch and share specific parts of those programs that they felt warranted attention on their own. This brought about charges of copyright infringement and subsequent litigation by NBC and others, something YouTube immediately began addressing in various ways, including a policy stating that it will remove any copyrighted materials when and if the copyright holder asks, and also by asking users to police the site for inappropriate content.

However, copyrighted material abounds on YouTube. Many media critics acknowledge that it is in the best interests of some copyright holders to allow such infringement because of the potential viral marketing benefits of being hosted on YouTube, which makes this content available to many viewers who might not otherwise be exposed to these products. One television show that appeared to take advantage (unofficially) of this type of publicity was *The Daily Show with Jon Stewart*, one of several shows airing on cable television network Comedy Central that were featured regularly on YouTube. However, with the launch of The MotherLoad, a competing video sharing website, Comedy Central and owner company Viacom have determined that they prefer providing the content at a dedicated website.

In 2007 YouTube launched its Partners Program. The program allows content creators who join to earn part of the revenue paid to YouTube by advertisers. The more popular the video, the more the partner is paid. YouTube also promotes the videos on its platform.

Several frequent YouTube posters have become famous as a result of the popularity of their videos. These have included Jessica Rose, an actress whose videos under the name of lonelygirl15 were long thought to be the real video diary entries of a teenage girl until it was disclosed that they were Rose's fictional creations; "Chad Vader," a *Star Wars* fan film series featuring a grocery store employee and his cohorts; Smosh, a pair of internet short film creators who produce comedy sketches and parodies of music videos; Lilly Singh, who operates a one-woman channel featuring comedy sketches and music videos; Roman Atwood, who posts humorous and occasionally distasteful videos of pranks; "Ask a Ninja," the comedic creation of Kent Nichols and Doug Sarine; and Felix Kjellberg, a Swedish video gamer known as PewDiePie and star of the YouTube channel *Let's Play* who ranked as the highest-paid YouTube star in 2016, with earnings of more than $15 million. Many of the YouTube celebrities were featured in mainstream media and have subsequently translated their popularity into lucrative multimedia deals outside YouTube. Pop band OK Go won a 2006 Grammy Award for a video that had originally achieved notoriety on YouTube rather than more traditional music video channels. In December 2014, Tad Friend reported in the *New Yorker* that in 2013 DreamWorks bought AwesomenessTV for 33 million dollars. AwesomenessTV is a talent management firm for YouTube celebrities. PewDiePie signed with the Disney-owned Maker

Studios in December 2012; however, this partnership was terminated in 2017 after the YouTube star posted anti-Semitic comments to his channel.

Among the most notorious incidents related to current events involving YouTube is the so-called Macaca video featuring former Virginia Senator George Allen and videos posted by a Finnish mass murderer. In 2006, Senator Allen was videotaped at a campaign funding rally in Virginia with Allen referred to a videographer from a rival campaign as "Macaca," which was taken by some to be a racial slur; footage of this incident was posted to YouTube and is widely regarded as a major factor in Allen's failure to be reelected to the Senate. In November 2007, YouTube removed dozens of videos posted by Pekka-Eric Auvinen, who days before had shot to death eight people at a Finnish high school before killing himself. Auvinen had posted many videos to YouTube under his various usernames, including clips of himself showing off his gun; one clip was entitled "Jokela High School Massacre–11/7/2007," the date of the incident.

Google Gets Larger

YouTube was purchased by leading internet search engine Google, Inc., in November 2006, for $1.65 billion. At the time of the purchase, YouTube held 46 percent of the online video market. As an independently operated subsidiary of Google, YouTube is a direct competitor with Google's video service, as well as other leading video sharing websites, such as Yahoo Video, Myspace, VideoEgg, Blip.tv, DailyMotion, and Break. These sites are all part of a burgeoning trend toward more and more user-generated websites, which are a part of a larger movement known as Web 2.0. "Web 2.0" is a term that describes the movement away from fixed, unchanging content toward websites that encourage and grow in functionality as a result of user participation. Social networking websites are an example of Web 2.0.

To encourage more interaction by users, YouTube introduced TestTube, a series of web tools that are still under development. TestTube features include a way to add licensed music to videos, a remixer for adding titles or otherwise altering videos, active sharing to communicate to other users which videos you have watched, and chatting with other users while watching videos.

Two years in terms of modern technology can be a very long time, and many internet websites have gone through the stages of launch, popularity, and then obscurity in that same time frame. Despite this, YouTube has withstood many types of criticism and fierce competition from other websites and promises to remain an important internet website for the foreseeable future. As of 2017, Susan Wojcicki is chief executive officer (CEO) of the company. Shortly after cofounding the company, Karim left the company to pursue a graduate degree at Stanford University. Hurley stepped down as CEO and was replaced by Salar Kamangar. Early Google employee and executive Wojcicki took over as YouTube CEO in February 2014. Chen joined Google Ventures in 2014.

In 2017, the number of hours viewed per day on YouTube increased to approximately 3 billion. In March 2013, the site reached 1 billion unique monthly visitors; by December 2014, it had more than 1 billion visitors who watched more than 6 billion hours of videos monthly. YouTube is by far the most popular video sharing website on the web, but others, such as Yahoo Video, Flickr, and Metacafe, offer alternatives.

YouTube experienced an increase in professionally produced channels in 2012.

There were channels designed for a number of topics, celebrities, and news outlets, including Justin Bieber, Nike Football, and ABC News. These channels were beginning to take precedence over more obscure videos, some of which have received millions of views—a video of a sneezing baby panda, for instance, has over 150 million views. Google announced plans to establish fifty original channels in 2012. To promote these channels and videos, a $200 million marketing campaign was planned with the intent of moving YouTube down the path to replacing television. As of December 2014, the site quoted a Nielsen report stating that US adults between the ages of eighteen and thirty-four watch YouTube more than they watch any cable network. YouTube also reported that it has more than a million YouTube Partners, creators who earn income from the videos they post on YouTube, and, of these, thousands earn six figures annually.

In August 2015, Google announced plans to launch YouTube Gaming to provide a site devoted solely to video-gaming content. The service allows users to view livestream videos for more than 25,000 different games as well as receive personalized recommendations for YouTube gaming channels to follow. Google developed the site to directly compete with the popular livestream gaming site Twitch, which is owned and operated by Amazon.

In October 2015, Google announced another YouTube expansion in its launch of YouTube Red, which is a paid, monthly service that allows subscribers to view any video, with the exception of paid content on YouTube, without being interrupted by advertisements. The service also includes the added incentive of free monthly subscriptions to Google Play Music. Similarly, anyone who purchases a subscription to Google Play Music will receive a free subscription to YouTube Red. YouTube Red is an optional service, and those who choose not to purchase a subscription will not see any change in their usual viewing or viewing options.

—*Craig Belanger and Marlanda English*

References

Artero, Juan P. "Online Video Business Models: YouTube vs. Hulu." *Palabra Clave*, vol. 13, no. 1, 201, pp. 111–23, search.ebscohost.com/login.Aspx?direct=true&db=a9h&AN=52258649&site=ehost-live.

Berg, Madeline. "The Highest-Paid YouTube Stars 2016: PewDiePie Remains No. 1 with $15 Million." *Forbes*, 5 Dec. 2016, www.forbes.com/sites/maddieberg/2016/12/05/the-highest-paid-youtube-stars-2016-pewdiepie-remains-no-1-with-15-million/#31d1dbfc7713.

Bloom, Kristen, and Kelly Marie Johnston. "Digging into YouTube Videos: Using Media Literacy and Participatory Culture to Promote Cross-Cultural Understanding." *Journal of Media Literacy Education*, vol. 2, no. 2, 2013, p. 3.

Chen, Chih-Ping. "Exploring Personal Branding on YouTube." *Journal of Internet Commerce*, vol. 12, no. 4, 2013, pp. 332–47.

Etherington, Darrell. "People Now Watch 1 Billion Hours of YouTube Per Day." *Tech Crunch*, 28 Feb. 2017, techcrunch.com/2017/02/28/people-now-watch-1-billion-hours-of-youtube-per-day.

Friend, Tad. "Letter from California: Hollywood and Vine." *The New Yorker*. Condé Nast, 15 Dec. 2014, www.newyorker.com/magazine/2014/12/15/hollywood-vine.

Gallardo-Camacho, Jorge. "The Low Interaction of Viewers of Video Clips on the Internet: The Case

Study of YouTube Spain." *Revista Latina de Comunicación de Social*, vol. 13, no. 65, 2010, pp. 1-14, search.ebscohost.com/login.Aspx?direct=true&db=a9h&AN=60167086&site=ehost-live.

Konijn, Elly A., et al. "YouTube as Research Tool—Three Approaches." *CyberPsychology, Behavior & Social Networking*, vol. 16, no. 5, 2013, pp. 1–7.

Kopacz, Maria A. "Rating the YouTube Indian: Viewer Ratings of Native American Portrayals on a Viral Video Site." *American Indian Quarterly*, vol. 35, no. 2, 2011, pp. 241–57, search.ebscohost.com/login.Aspx?direct=true&db=a9h&AN=59422220&site=ehost-live.

Lavaveshkul, Liz. "How to Achieve 15 Minutes (or More) of Fame through YouTube." *Journal of International Commercial Law & Technology*, vol. 7, no. 4, 2012, pp. 370–85.

Matney, Lucas. "YouTube Has 1.5 Billion Logged-In Monthly Users Watching a Ton of Mobile Video." *Tech Crunch*, 22 June 2017, techcrunch.com/2017/06/22/youtube-has-1-5-billion-logged-in-monthly-users-watching-a-ton-of-mobile-video.

Miller, Claire C. "YouTube to Serve Niche Tastes by Adding Channels." *The New York Times*, 7 Oct. 2012, www.nytimes.com/2012/10/08/business/media/YouTube-to-serve-niche-tastes-by-adding-channels.html.

Mitroff, Sarah. "Everything You Need to Know About YouTube Red." *CNET*. CBS Interactive, 28 Oct. 2015, www.cnet.com/how-to/youtube-red-details/.

Morreale, Joanne. "From Homemade to Store Bought: Annoying Orange and the Professionalization of YouTube." *Journal of Consumer Culture*, vol. 14, no. 1, 2014, pp. 113–128, search.ebscohost.com/login.aspx?direct=true&db=a9h&AN=94776861.

O'Neill, Megan." Video Infographic Reveals the Most Impressive YouTube Statistics of 2012." *SocialTimes*, 10 Sept. 2012, socialtimes.com/video-YouTube-statistics-2012%5Fb104480.

Rosenbaum, Steven. "YouTube Reveals a Curated Future."*Forbes*, 10 Oct. 2012, www.forbes.com/sites/stevenrosenbaum/2012/10/10/YouTube-reveals-a-curated-future-2/.

Sarker, Samit. "YouTube Gaming Launches Aug. 26 with Website and Mobile Apps." *Yahoo*. YAHOO/

ABC News Network, 25 Aug. 2015, www.polygon.
com/2015/8/25/9208245/youtube-gaming-
launch-date-web-android-ios#:~:text=Google%20
will%20launch%20YouTube%20Gaming,
looking%20for%20gaming%20video%20
content..

Saul, Roger. "KevJumba and the Adolescence of
YouTube." *Educational Studies*, vol. 46, no. 5,
2010, pp. 457–77, search.ebscohost.com/login.
Aspx?direct=true&db=a9h&AN=54166670&site=
ehost-live.

Shreekumar, Advik. "Rise of the YouTube Star."
Harvard Political Review, vol. 41, no. 1, 2014, p. 16,
search.ebscohost.com/login.aspx?direct=true&d
b=pwh&AN=95604237&site=pov-live.

Appendixes

DIGITAL LITERACY APPENDIX

The following pages highlight some current resources related to digital literacy produced by various organizations. Excerpts include:

Federal Trade Commission
February 2022

Introduction

The FTC takes in reports from consumers about problems they experience in the marketplace. The reports are stored in the Consumer Sentinel Network (Sentinel), a secure online database available only to law enforcement. While the FTC does not intervene in individual consumer disputes, its law enforcement partners – whether they are down the street, across the nation, or around the world – can use information in the database to spot trends, identify questionable business practices and targets, and enforce the law.

Since 1997, Sentinel has collected tens of millions of consumer reports about fraud, identity theft, and other consumer protection topics. During 2021, Sentinel received over 5.7 million consumer reports, which the FTC has sorted into 29 top categories. The 2021 Consumer Sentinel Network Data Book (Sentinel Data Book) has aggregated information about what consumers told us last year on the full range of fraud, identity theft and other consumer protection topics. The Consumer Sentinel data is also available online in an interactive format at ftc.gov/exploredata, with updates provided quarterly. The Sentinel Data Book is based on unverified reports filed by consumers. The data is not based on a consumer survey. Sentinel has a five-year data retention policy, with reports older than five years purged biannually.

In addition to taking consumer reports directly from people who call the FTC's call center or report online, Sentinel also includes reports filed with other federal, state, local, and international law enforcement agencies, as well as other organizations, like the Better Business Bureau and Publishers Clearing House.

In 2021, the FTC was pleased to welcome the data contributions of the Social Security Administration Office of the Inspector General and the Australian Competition & Consumer Commission. A full listing of data contributors is available in Appendices A3 and A4. Non-government organizations that contribute reports do not have access to Sentinel reports, as access is limited to law enforcement agencies.

For more information about the Consumer Sentinel Network, visit www.FTC.gov/Sentinel. Law enforcement personnel may join Sentinel at Register.ConsumerSentinel.gov.

Executive Summary

Overview
In 2021, the Consumer Sentinel Network took in over 5.7 million reports, an increase from 2020.
- Fraud: 2.8 million (49% of all reports)
- Identity theft: 1.4 million (25%)
- Other: 1.5 million (27%)

In 2021, people filed more reports about Identity Theft (25.0% of all reports), in all its various forms, than any other type of complaint. Imposter Scams, a subset of Fraud reports, followed with 984,756 reports from consumers in 2021 (17.2% of all reports). Credit Bureaus, Information Furnishers and Report Users (10.3% of all reports) rounded out the top three reports to Sentinel.

Fraud
There were over 984,000 imposter scam reports to Sentinel. Seventeen percent of those reported a dollar loss, totaling over $2.3 billion lost to imposter scams in 2021. These scams include, for example, romance scams, people falsely claiming to be the government, a relative in distress, a well-known business, or a technical support expert, to get a consumer's money.

Of the nearly 2.8 million fraud reports, 25% indicated money was lost. In 2021, people reported losing more than $5.8 billion to fraud – an increase of $2.4 billion over 2020.

The median loss for all fraud reports in 2021 is $500. Among the top 10 frauds reported, the median individual losses were highest in these categories:
- Investment Related ($3,000)
- Foreign Money Offers and Counterfeit Check Scams ($2,000)
- Business and Job Opportunities ($1,991)

Telephone was the method of contact for 36% of fraud reports with a contact method identified. Nine percent of those reports indicated a money loss – but that 9% reported an aggregate loss of nearly $692 million, and a $1,200 median loss.

Bank transfers and payments accounted for the highest aggregate losses reported in 2021 ($756 million), followed closely by Cryptocurrency ($750 million), while credit cards were most frequently identified as the payment method in fraud reports.

Of people who reported their age, those aged 20-29 reported losing money to fraud in 41% of reports filed with the FTC, while people aged 70 – 79 reported losing money in 18% of their reports and people 80 and over reported it in 17% of their reports. But when they did experience a loss, people aged 70 and older reported much higher median losses than any other age group.

Identity Theft
Government Documents or Benefits Fraud tops the list of identity theft types reported in 2021. The FTC received 395,948 reports from people who said their information was misused to apply for a government document or benefit, such as unemployment insurance.

Military
Military consumers reported over 110,000 fraud complaints, including 44,039 imposter scams that reportedly cost them over $103 million in 2021.

Top States
The states with the highest per capita rates of reported fraud in 2021 were Georgia, Maryland, Delaware, Nevada, and Florida. For reported identity theft, the top states in 2021 were Rhode Island, Kansas, Illinois, Louisiana, and Georgia.

CONSUMER SENTINEL NETWORK
DATA BOOK 2021

SNAPSHOT

5.7 MILLION REPORTS

TOP THREE CATEGORIES

1 Identity Theft

2 Imposter Scams

3 Credit Bureaus, Info Furnishers and Report Users

2.8 million fraud reports

25% reported a loss

$5.9 billion
total fraud losses

$500
median loss

Younger people reported losing money to fraud **more often than older people.**

41%
Age 20-29

18%
Age 70-79

But when people aged 70+ had a loss, **the median loss was much higher.**

$1,500

$800

$500

Age 20 - 29   70 - 79   80+

Imposter Scams

ABOUT
1 in 5
PEOPLE
LOST MONEY

$2,331 million
reported lost

$1,000 median loss

Identity Theft Reports

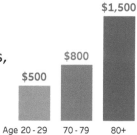

64% ⬆

Checking\Savings
Account - New

22% ⬇

Mobile
Telephone –
New Accounts

FEDERAL TRADE COMMISSION • ftc.gov/data

Number of Fraud, Identity Theft and Other Reports by Year

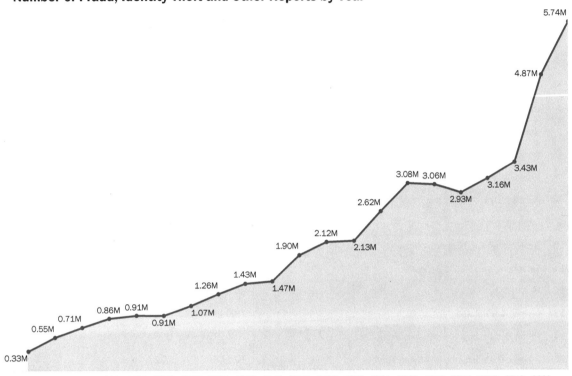

Year	# of Reports
2001	325,519
2002	551,622
2003	713,657
2004	860,383
2005	909,314
2006	906,129
2007	1,070,447
2008	1,261,124
2009	1,428,977
2010	1,470,306
2011	1,898,543
2012	2,115,079
2013	2,134,565
2014	2,620,931
2015	3,080,378
2016	3,060,824
2017	2,926,167
2018	3,160,199
2019	3,428,818
2020	4,865,023
2021	5,737,265

The reported figures exclude National Do Not Call Registry complaints.

Report Categories

Rank	Category	# of Reports	%
1	Identity Theft	1,434,676	25.01%
2	Imposter Scams	984,756	17.16%
3	Credit Bureaus, Information Furnishers and Report Users	592,928	10.33%
4	Online Shopping and Negative Reviews	398,283	6.94%
5	Banks and Lenders	195,370	3.41%
6	Debt Collection	151,335	2.64%
7	Prizes, Sweepstakes and Lotteries	148,243	2.58%
8	Auto Related	137,468	2.40%
9	Internet Services	121,445	2.12%
10	Business and Job Opportunities	104,019	1.81%
11	Telephone and Mobile Services	92,802	1.62%
12	Health Care	89,801	1.57%
13	Investment Related	78,988	1.38%
14	Home Repair, Improvement and Products	70,612	1.23%
15	Privacy, Data Security, and Cyber Threats	70,177	1.22%
16	Credit Cards	65,173	1.14%
17	Travel, Vacations and Timeshare Plans	53,891	0.94%
18	Television and Electronic Media	41,905	0.73%
19	Foreign Money Offers and Fake Check Scams	39,139	0.68%
20	Advance Payments for Credit Services	24,152	0.42%
21	Education	22,810	0.40%
22	Mortgage Foreclosure Relief and Debt Management	21,258	0.37%
23	Computer Equipment and Software	15,701	0.27%
24	Charitable Solicitations	9,270	0.16%
25	Magazines and Books	5,541	0.10%
26	Tax Preparers	5,424	0.09%
27	Grants	4,254	0.07%
28	Office Supplies and Services	3,609	0.06%
29	Funeral Services	1,310	0.02%

Percentages are based on the total number of 2021 Sentinel reports (5,737,265). 9% of the total were coded "Other Misc." See Appendix B3.

Report Type

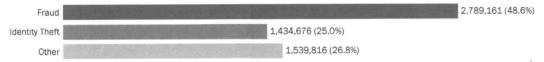

Fraud	2,789,161 (48.6%)
Identity Theft	1,434,676 (25.0%)
Other	1,539,816 (26.8%)

Top 10 Fraud Categories

Rank	Category	# of Reports	% Reporting $ Loss	Total $ Loss	Median $ Loss
1	Imposter Scams	984,756	17%	$2,331M	$1,000
2	Online Shopping and Negative Reviews	397,826	52%	$392M	$150
3	Prizes, Sweepstakes and Lotteries	148,243	12%	$255M	$968
4	Internet Services	103,501	23%	$216M	$500
5	Business and Job Opportunities	103,003	25%	$206M	$1,991
6	Telephone and Mobile Services	92,716	12%	$21M	$250
7	Investment Related	78,988	73%	$1,679M	$3,000
8	Health Care	63,333	13%	$17M	$197
9	Travel, Vacations and Timeshare Plans	53,891	24%	$95M	$1,112
10	Foreign Money Offers and Fake Check Scams	39,139	26%	$78M	$2,000

Identity Theft Types

Rank	Theft Type	# of Reports
1	Government Documents or Benefits Fraud	395,948
2	Credit Card Fraud	389,737
3	Other Identity Theft	377,102
4	Loan or Lease Fraud	197,914
5	Bank Fraud	124,388
6	Employment or Tax-Related Fraud	111,723
7	Phone or Utilities Fraud	88,813

Top 10 Other Categories

Rank	Category	# of Reports
1	Credit Bureaus, Information Furnishers and Report Users	592,928
2	Banks and Lenders	195,370
3	Debt Collection	151,335
4	Auto Related	137,468
5	Home Repair, Improvement and Products	70,612
6	Credit Cards	65,173
7	Television and Electronic Media	41,905
8	Education	22,810
9	Privacy, Data Security, and Cyber Threats	18,724
10	Computer Equipment and Software	15,701

Certain categories are comprised of subcategories that fall in both Fraud and Other report types. See Appendix B3. The Fraud rankings exclude subcategories that are not fraud, and the Other rankings exclude subcategories that are classified as fraud.

Number of Reports by Type

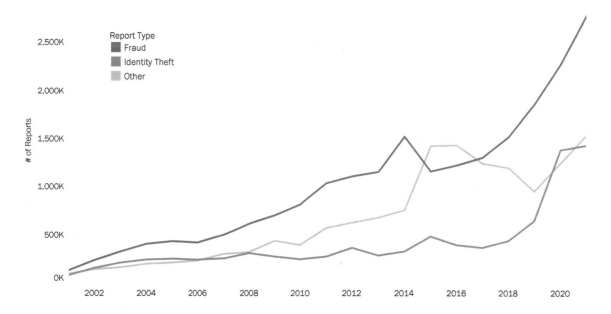

Number of Reports by Type

Year	Fraud	Identity Theft	Other
2001	137,306	86,250	101,963
2002	242,783	161,977	146,862
2003	331,366	215,240	167,051
2004	410,298	246,909	203,176
2005	437,585	255,687	216,042
2006	423,672	246,214	236,243
2007	505,563	259,314	305,570
2008	620,832	314,587	325,705
2009	708,781	278,360	441,836
2010	820,072	251,074	399,160
2011	1,041,517	279,191	577,835
2012	1,112,693	369,958	632,428
2013	1,159,115	290,098	685,352
2014	1,526,365	332,545	762,021
2015	1,165,393	490,085	1,429,676
2016	1,228,865	398,356	1,435,874
2017	1,310,003	370,915	1,247,309
2018	1,522,834	444,339	1,202,864
2019	1,862,871	650,523	956,682
2020	2,277,130	1,388,540	1,251,666
2021	2,789,161	1,434,676	1,539,816

The reported figures exclude National Do Not Call Registry complaints.

Fraud Reports by Amount Lost

2,789,161	692,376 (25%)
Number of Fraud Reports	# of Reports with $ Loss

$5,893,260,382	$500
Total $ Loss	Median $ Loss

Reported Fraud Losses in $1 - $10,000+ Range

Amount Lost	# of Reports
$1 - $1,000	447,732
$1,001 - $2,000	74,179
$2,001 - $3,000	35,101
$3,001 - $4,000	19,743
$4,001 - $5,000	16,112
$5,001 - $6,000	9,425
$6,001 - $7,000	6,804
$7,001 - $8,000	6,034
$8,001 - $9,000	4,215
$9,001 - $10,000	7,496
More than $10,000	65,535

Reported Fraud Losses in $1 - $1,000 Range

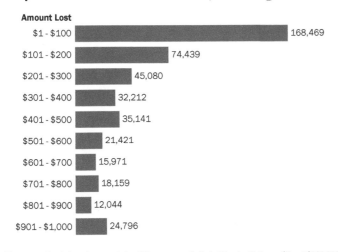

Amount Lost

$1 - $100	168,469
$101 - $200	74,439
$201 - $300	45,080
$301 - $400	32,212
$401 - $500	35,141
$501 - $600	21,421
$601 - $700	15,971
$701 - $800	18,159
$801 - $900	12,044
$901 - $1,000	24,796

The amount lost is based on reports in which consumers indicated they lost between $1 and $999,999.

Fraud Reports by Payment Method

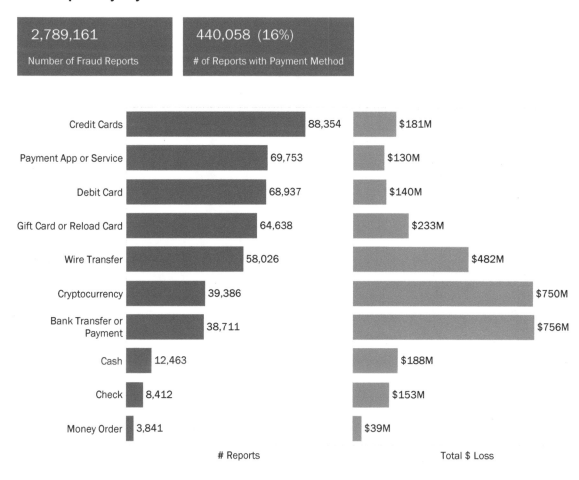

2,789,161	**440,058 (16%)**
Number of Fraud Reports	# of Reports with Payment Method

Payment Method	# Reports	Total $ Loss
Credit Cards	88,354	$181M
Payment App or Service	69,753	$130M
Debit Card	68,937	$140M
Gift Card or Reload Card	64,638	$233M
Wire Transfer	58,026	$482M
Cryptocurrency	39,386	$750M
Bank Transfer or Payment	38,711	$756M
Cash	12,463	$188M
Check	8,412	$153M
Money Order	3,841	$39M

Fraud Reports by Contact Method

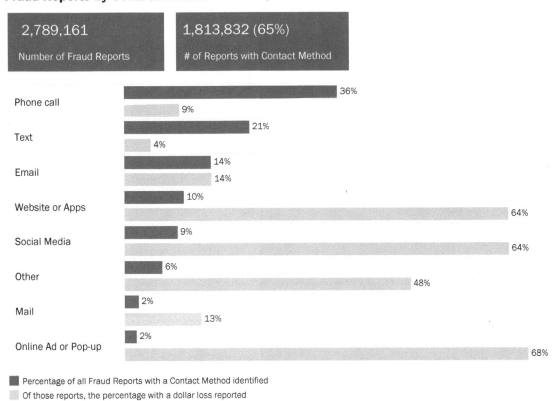

2,789,161	**1,813,832 (65%)**
Number of Fraud Reports	# of Reports with Contact Method

Phone call — 36% / 9%
Text — 21% / 4%
Email — 14% / 14%
Website or Apps — 10% / 64%
Social Media — 9% / 64%
Other — 6% / 48%
Mail — 2% / 13%
Online Ad or Pop-up — 2% / 68%

■ Percentage of all Fraud Reports with a Contact Method identified
▦ Of those reports, the percentage with a dollar loss reported

Number of Reports and Amount Lost by Contact Method

Contact Method	# of Reports	Total $ Lost	Median $ Lost
Phone call	644,048	$692M	$1,200
Text	377,840	$131M	$900
Email	260,818	$323M	$800
Website or Apps	177,777	$649M	$300
Social Media	159,423	$796M	$400
Other	114,354	$677M	$622
Mail	42,842	$65M	$823
Online Ad or Pop-up	36,730	$96M	$181

Other contact methods includes TV or radio, print, fax, in person, consumer initiated contact, and other methods consumers write in or that cannot be otherwise categorized.

Reported Frauds and Losses by Age

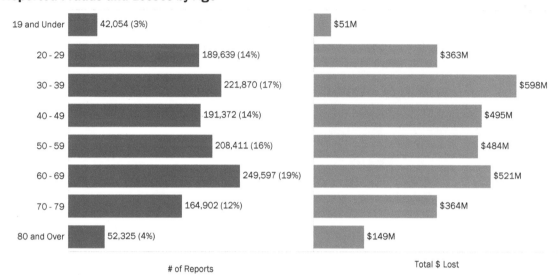

Percentages are based on the total number of 2021 fraud reports in which consumers provided their age: 1,320,170.

Percentage Reporting a Fraud Loss and Median Loss by Age

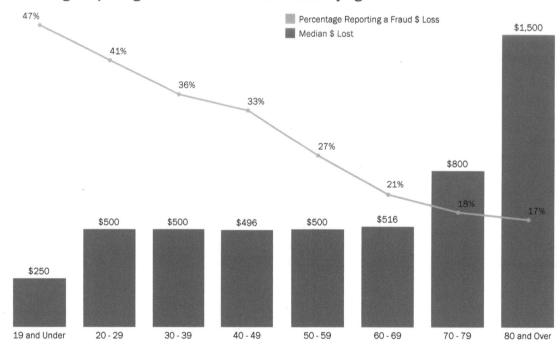

Of the 2,789,161 total fraud reports in 2021, 47% included useable consumer age information.

Identity Theft Reports by Type

Theft Type	Theft Subtype	# of Reports	% Difference from Previous Year
Credit Card Fraud	New Accounts	363,092	-1%
	Existing Accounts	32,204	-5%
Loan or Lease Fraud	Apartment or House Rented	13,166	-3%
	Auto Loan\Lease	70,710	-3%
	Business\Personal Loan	105,711	+6%
	Federal Student Loan	18,202	-34%
	Non-Federal Student Loan	13,897	-19%
	Real Estate Loan	9,087	-23%
Phone or Utilities Fraud	Landline Telephone – Existing Accounts	2,140	+2%
	Landline Telephone – New Accounts	11,503	-6%
	Mobile Telephone – Existing Accounts	5,433	-10%
	Mobile Telephone – New Accounts	37,795	-22%
	Utilities – Existing Accounts	1,642	-27%
	Utilities – New Accounts	41,004	-1%
Bank Fraud	Debit Cards, Electronic Funds Transfer, or ACH	33,248	+8%
	Existing Accounts	14,358	+5%
	New Accounts	83,721	+64%
Employment or Tax-Related Fraud	Employment or Wage-Related Fraud	24,004	-10%
	Tax Fraud	89,649	+0%
Government Documents or Benefits Fraud	Driver's License Issued\Forged	5,506	-11%
	Government Benefits Applied For\Received	385,264	-3%
	Other Government Documents Issued\Forged	8,366	-12%
	Passport Issued\Forged	1,117	-20%
Other Identity Theft	Email or Social Media	15,374	+9%
	Evading the Law	4,740	+1%
	Insurance	10,397	+21%
	Medical Services	42,773	-6%
	Online Shopping or Payment Account	15,207	+3%
	Other	300,244	+7%
	Securities Accounts	8,455	+122%

Consumers can report multiple types of identity theft. In 2021, 14% of identity theft reports included more than one type of identity theft.

Top Three Identity Theft Report Types by Year

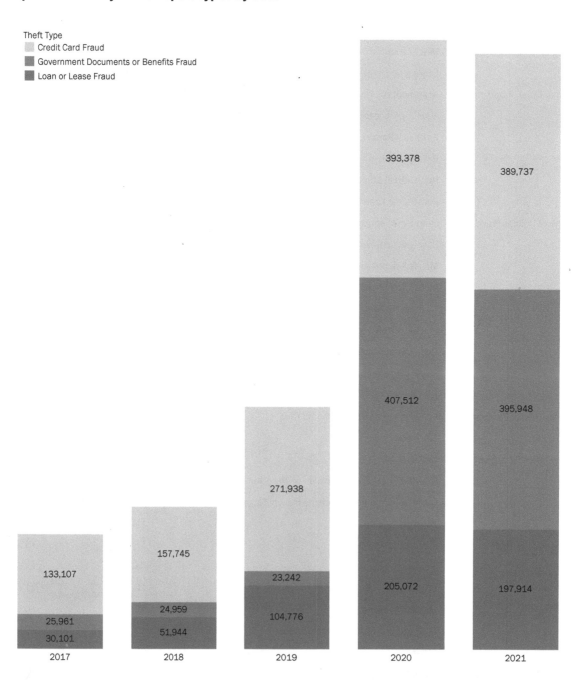

The top identity theft types can vary by year. This graph depicts the top three types of identity theft reported in 2021 and how those types changed over five years.

Identity Theft Reports by Age

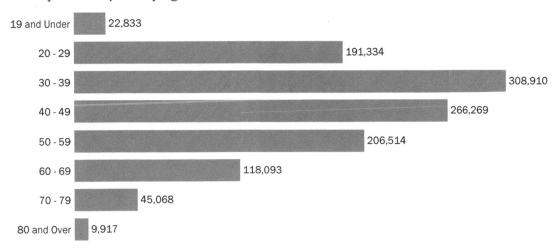

Age	Reports
19 and Under	22,833
20 - 29	191,334
30 - 39	308,910
40 - 49	266,269
50 - 59	206,514
60 - 69	118,093
70 - 79	45,068
80 and Over	9,917

Identity Theft Types by Age

Theft Type	19 and Under	20 - 29	30 - 39	40 - 49	50 - 59	60 - 69	70 - 79	80 and Over
Bank Fraud	1,664	15,333	25,802	25,461	23,795	17,647	7,580	1,961
Credit Card Fraud	1,707	65,269	108,592	76,693	45,741	21,992	7,507	1,954
Employment or Tax-Related Fraud	14,578	21,697	25,027	17,967	13,845	8,824	3,882	1,502
Government Documents or Benefits Fraud	2,467	15,873	32,390	65,693	77,270	49,094	19,153	3,038
Loan or Lease Fraud	1,003	41,239	65,163	41,855	21,936	9,105	2,465	505
Other Identity Theft	2,722	61,910	103,283	74,288	43,581	20,072	6,981	1,710
Phone or Utilities Fraud	696	20,134	27,161	17,330	10,069	5,026	1,839	457

Of the 1,434,676 total identity theft reports in 2021, 81% included consumer age information.

Fraud, Identity Theft, and Other Reports by Military Consumers

Reports by Status

Status	# of Reports	# of Fraud Reports	% Reporting Fraud Loss	Total Fraud Loss	Median Fraud Loss
Active Duty Service Member	18,544	8,670	38%	$34M	$881
Military Retiree/Veteran	162,067	87,343	24%	$177M	$570
Reserve/National Guard	10,914	6,015	34%	$25M	$758
Spouse/Dependent of Active Duty Service Member	14,771	8,799	34%	$30M	$536

Reports by Branch

Branch	# of Reports	# of Fraud Reports	% Reporting Fraud Loss	Total Fraud Loss	Median Fraud Loss
U.S. Air Force	38,343	21,353	22%	$42M	$550
U.S. Army	89,269	42,966	25%	$93M	$583
U.S. Coast Guard	3,128	1,689	28%	$7M	$600
U.S. Marines	18,518	9,306	27%	$21M	$545
U.S. Navy	40,104	22,127	24%	$45M	$550

Of the 207,816 total reports from military consumers in 2021, 91% provided military branch information.

Reports by Rank

Rank	# of Reports	# of Fraud Reports	% Reporting Fraud Loss	Total Fraud Loss	Median Fraud Loss
Enlisted	134,015	74,354	26%	$151M	$550
Officer	32,175	18,916	23%	$54M	$676

Of the 207,816 total reports from military consumers in 2021, 80% provided information about rank.

Reports by Military Consumers

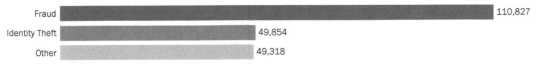

Fraud — 110,827
Identity Theft — 49,854
Other — 49,318

Top 10 Fraud Categories

Rank	Category	# of Reports	% Reporting $ Loss	Total $ Loss	Median $ Loss
1	Imposter Scams	44,039	20%	$103.9M	$1,031
2	Online Shopping and Negative Reviews	18,314	63%	$29.6M	$178
3	Prizes, Sweepstakes and Lotteries	5,201	19%	$23.7M	$2,000
4	Business and Job Opportunities	4,563	22%	$12.9M	$2,395
5	Investment Related	3,089	76%	$49.5M	$3,000
6	Foreign Money Offers and Fake Check Scams	2,447	28%	$7.8M	$2,498
7	Telephone and Mobile Services	2,304	28%	$2.3M	$225
8	Internet Services	1,778	16%	$2.0M	$500
9	Health Care	1,768	11%	$1.9M	$267
10	Mortgage Foreclosure Relief and Debt Management	1,257	24%	$4.6M	$1,120

Identity Theft Types

Rank	Theft Type	# of Reports
1	Government Documents or Benefits Fraud	17,407
2	Credit Card Fraud	9,379
3	Other Identity Theft	7,809
4	Bank Fraud	7,782
5	Loan or Lease Fraud	7,488
6	Employment or Tax-Related Fraud	4,295
7	Phone or Utilities Fraud	3,571

110,827
# of Fraud Reports

29,081 (26%)
# of Reports with $ Loss

Top 10 Other Categories

Rank	Category	# of Reports
1	Credit Bureaus, Information Furnishers and Report Users	12,315
2	Banks and Lenders	7,502
3	Debt Collection	5,897
4	Auto Related	3,609
5	Credit Cards	2,714
6	Privacy, Data Security, and Cyber Threats	1,306
7	Television and Electronic Media	1,114
8	Home Repair, Improvement and Products	987
9	Education	722
10	Computer Equipment and Software	107

$267M
Total $ Loss

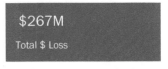

$600
Median $ Loss

Certain categories are comprised of subcategories that fall in both Fraud and Other report types. See Appendix B3. The Fraud rankings exclude subcategories that are not fraud, and the Other rankings exclude subcategories that are classified as fraud.

Military Consumer Identity Theft Reports by Type

Theft Type	Theft Subtype	# of Reports	% Difference from Previous Year
Credit Card Fraud	New Accounts	7,510	-20%
	Existing Accounts	2,230	-11%
Bank Fraud	New Accounts	5,121	+29%
	Debit Cards, Electronic Funds Transfer, or ACH	2,391	-5%
	Existing Accounts	758	-36%
Phone or Utilities Fraud	Mobile Telephone – New Accounts	1,595	-34%
	Utilities – New Accounts	1,300	-18%
	Landline Telephone – New Accounts	572	-9%
	Mobile Telephone – Existing Accounts	396	-19%
	Landline Telephone – Existing Accounts	168	-7%
	Utilities – Existing Accounts	87	-11%
Loan or Lease Fraud	Business\Personal Loan	5,607	+80%
	Auto Loan\Lease	1,184	-11%
	Non-Federal Student Loan	370	-5%
	Apartment or House Rented	334	-17%
	Real Estate Loan	310	-9%
	Federal Student Loan	225	-34%
Employment or Tax-Related Fraud	Tax Fraud	3,698	-16%
	Employment or Wage-Related Fraud	664	-43%
Government Documents or Benefits Fraud	Government Benefits Applied For\Received	16,885	-27%
	Other Government Documents Issued\Forged	481	-32%
	Driver's License Issued\Forged	321	-27%
	Passport Issued\Forged	77	+13%
Other Identity Theft	Other	4,787	-14%
	Online Shopping or Payment Account	1,060	-5%
	Email or Social Media	1,025	-6%
	Securities Accounts	667	+114%
	Medical Services	651	-19%
	Evading the Law	294	-19%
	Insurance	279	-4%

Consumers can report multiple types of identity theft. In 2021, 12% of Military identity theft reports included more than one type of identity theft.

State Rankings: Fraud and Other Reports

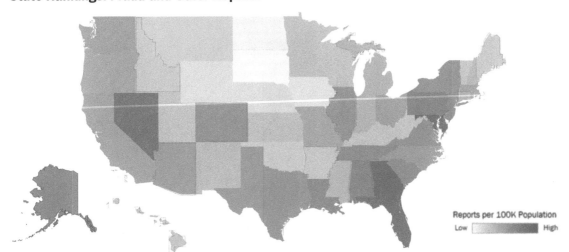

Reports per 100K Population
Low   High

Rank	State	Reports per 100K Population	# of Reports	Rank	State	Reports per 100K Population	# of Reports
1	Georgia	1,421	150,898	27	Connecticut	917	32,686
2	Maryland	1,415	85,568	28	New Hampshire	914	12,429
3	Delaware	1,410	13,726	29	Mississippi	906	26,958
4	Nevada	1,407	43,339	30	New Mexico	888	18,613
5	Florida	1,370	294,328	31	Michigan	881	87,996
6	Alabama	1,217	59,669	32	Indiana	861	57,988
7	Pennsylvania	1,205	154,313	33	Hawaii	851	12,051
8	Louisiana	1,193	55,456	34	Vermont	848	5,292
9	Tennessee	1,157	79,012	35	Kansas	845	24,615
10	Alaska	1,156	8,458	36	Utah	823	26,373
11	South Carolina	1,149	59,177	37	Maine	821	11,035
12	Colorado	1,119	64,464	38	Idaho	809	14,464
13	New Jersey	1,107	98,316	39	Minnesota	809	45,599
14	Virginia	1,099	93,763	40	Montana	806	8,612
15	New York	1,083	210,749	41	Wisconsin	803	46,755
16	Texas	1,080	313,044	42	Arkansas	801	24,176
17	Illinois	1,078	136,640	43	West Virginia	797	14,287
18	Rhode Island	1,066	11,289	44	Kentucky	796	35,544
19	Arizona	1,065	77,534	45	Oklahoma	783	30,996
20	North Carolina	1,036	108,698	46	Wyoming	731	4,230
21	Washington	1,013	77,128	47	Nebraska	697	13,475
22	California	991	391,517	48	Iowa	636	20,071
23	Massachusetts	980	67,515	49	North Dakota	608	4,637
24	Ohio	976	114,140	50	South Dakota	549	4,854
25	Oregon	970	40,908		District of Columbia	1,701	12,004
26	Missouri	953	58,485		Puerto Rico	260	8,315

The District of Columbia and Puerto Rico are included in the table but are not ranked. States are ranked based on the number of reports per 100,000 population. Population estimates are based on 2019 U.S. Census population estimates. Ranking excludes state-specific data contributor reports.

State Rankings: Identity Theft Reports

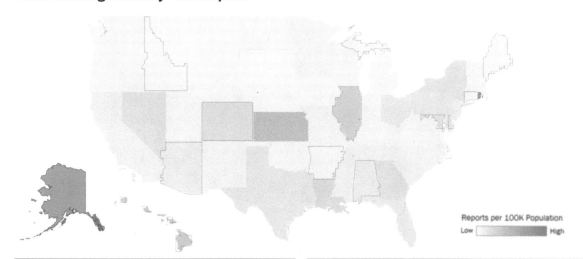

Reports per 100K Population
Low [   ] High

Rank	State	Reports per 100K Population	# of Reports	Rank	State	Reports per 100K Population	# of Reports
1	Rhode Island	2,857	30,270	27	Missouri	218	13,372
2	Kansas	1,355	39,461	28	Hawaii	211	2,993
3	Illinois	924	117,056	29	Arkansas	211	6,358
4	Louisiana	732	34,043	30	Michigan	206	20,556
5	Georgia	618	65,666	31	Wisconsin	193	11,253
6	Nevada	584	17,985	32	Oregon	190	8,016
7	Colorado	583	33,572	33	Utah	189	6,060
8	New York	563	109,466	34	Connecticut	187	6,666
9	Delaware	560	5,449	35	Indiana	176	11,866
10	Florida	515	110,675	36	Oklahoma	173	6,850
11	Texas	504	146,095	37	Washington	170	12,917
12	Maryland	493	29,778	38	Minnesota	168	9,457
13	Ohio	431	50,421	39	Maine	167	2,239
14	Pennsylvania	425	54,460	40	New Hampshire	162	2,205
15	Alabama	402	19,691	41	West Virginia	159	2,845
16	Arizona	386	28,108	42	Idaho	152	2,719
17	New Jersey	359	31,857	43	Vermont	132	825
18	South Carolina	343	17,642	44	North Dakota	131	999
19	California	337	133,119	45	Nebraska	125	2,409
20	Mississippi	333	9,906	46	Alaska	122	896
21	Tennessee	297	20,254	47	Iowa	119	3,758
22	North Carolina	289	30,318	48	Wyoming	107	620
23	Massachusetts	240	16,566	49	Montana	106	1,130
24	Kentucky	233	10,416	50	South Dakota	76	673
25	Virginia	225	19,214		District of Columbia	577	4,072
26	New Mexico	220	4,611		Puerto Rico	44	1,404

The District of Columbia and Puerto Rico are included in the table but are not ranked. States are ranked based on the number of reports per 100,000 population. Population estimates are based on 2019 U.S. Census population estimates.

Top 50 Metropolitan Areas: Fraud and Other Reports

Rank	Metropolitan Area	Reports per 100K Population	# of Reports
1	Tuscaloosa, AL Metropolitan Statistical Area	3,691	9,303
2	Memphis, TN-MS-AR Metropolitan Statistical Area	2,170	29,208
3	Lafayette, LA Metropolitan Statistical Area	1,908	9,333
4	Sebastian-Vero Beach, FL Metropolitan Statistical Area	1,812	2,898
5	Atlanta-Sandy Springs-Alpharetta, GA Metropolitan Statistical Area	1,769	106,521
6	Philadelphia-Camden-Wilmington, PA-NJ-DE-MD Metropolitan Statistical Area	1,690	103,131
7	Savannah, GA Metropolitan Statistical Area	1,657	6,516
8	Montgomery, AL Metropolitan Statistical Area	1,623	6,058
9	Las Vegas-Henderson-Paradise, NV Metropolitan Statistical Area	1,508	34,173
10	Miami-Fort Lauderdale-Pompano Beach, FL Metropolitan Statistical Area	1,497	92,338
11	Florence, SC Metropolitan Statistical Area	1,477	3,027
12	Jacksonville, FL Metropolitan Statistical Area	1,470	22,928
13	North Port-Sarasota-Bradenton, FL Metropolitan Statistical Area	1,467	12,280
14	Baltimore-Columbia-Towson, MD Metropolitan Statistical Area	1,454	40,722
15	Charleston-North Charleston, SC Metropolitan Statistical Area	1,448	11,612
16	Palm Bay-Melbourne-Titusville, FL Metropolitan Statistical Area	1,437	8,647
17	East Stroudsburg, PA Metropolitan Statistical Area	1,429	2,434
18	Orlando-Kissimmee-Sanford, FL Metropolitan Statistical Area	1,421	37,055
19	Homosassa Springs, FL Metropolitan Statistical Area	1,376	2,060
20	Tampa-St. Petersburg-Clearwater, FL Metropolitan Statistical Area	1,369	43,726
21	Washington-Arlington-Alexandria, DC-VA-MD-WV Metropolitan Statistical Area	1,328	83,429
22	Virginia Beach-Norfolk-Newport News, VA-NC Metropolitan Statistical Area	1,292	22,850
23	Dover, DE Metropolitan Statistical Area	1,289	2,330
24	Charlotte-Concord-Gastonia, NC-SC Metropolitan Statistical Area	1,284	33,852
25	Dallas-Fort Worth-Arlington, TX Metropolitan Statistical Area	1,283	97,143
26	Houston-The Woodlands-Sugar Land, TX Metropolitan Statistical Area	1,283	90,625
27	Gadsden, AL Metropolitan Statistical Area	1,282	1,311
28	Deltona-Daytona Beach-Ormond Beach, FL Metropolitan Statistical Area	1,280	8,555
29	Santa Fe, NM Metropolitan Statistical Area	1,262	1,897
30	Anchorage, AK Metropolitan Statistical Area	1,251	4,958
31	New Orleans-Metairie, LA Metropolitan Statistical Area	1,236	15,706
32	Huntsville, AL Metropolitan Statistical Area	1,233	5,816
33	Columbia, SC Metropolitan Statistical Area	1,228	10,299
34	Lakeland-Winter Haven, FL Metropolitan Statistical Area	1,225	8,877
35	Alexandria, LA Metropolitan Statistical Area	1,223	1,860
36	Columbus, OH Metropolitan Statistical Area	1,219	25,877
37	Colorado Springs, CO Metropolitan Statistical Area	1,219	9,090
38	Trenton-Princeton, NJ Metropolitan Statistical Area	1,218	4,477
39	Fayetteville, NC Metropolitan Statistical Area	1,214	6,397
40	Tallahassee, FL Metropolitan Statistical Area	1,213	4,697
41	Killeen-Temple, TX Metropolitan Statistical Area	1,205	5,545
42	Port St. Lucie, FL Metropolitan Statistical Area	1,203	5,888
43	Baton Rouge, LA Metropolitan Statistical Area	1,201	10,265
44	Birmingham-Hoover, AL Metropolitan Statistical Area	1,200	13,086
45	Austin-Round Rock-Georgetown, TX Metropolitan Statistical Area	1,194	26,593
46	Ocala, FL Metropolitan Statistical Area	1,188	4,343
47	Prescott Valley-Prescott, AZ Metropolitan Statistical Area	1,186	2,789
48	Cleveland-Elyria, OH Metropolitan Statistical Area	1,186	24,285
49	Myrtle Beach-Conway-North Myrtle Beach, SC-NC Metropolitan Statistical Area	1,183	5,879
50	Vallejo, CA Metropolitan Statistical Area	1,179	5,276

Metropolitan Areas are defined by the Office of Management and Budget, and population estimates are based on 2019 U.S. Census figures. Metropolitan Areas are ranked based on the number of reports per 100,000 population. Reports exclude state-specific data contributor reports.

Top 50 Metropolitan Areas: Identity Theft Reports

Rank	Metropolitan Area	Reports per 100K Population	# of Reports
1	Providence-Warwick, RI-MA Metropolitan Statistical Area	1,981	32,176
2	Lawrence, KS Metropolitan Statistical Area	1,779	2,175
3	Topeka, KS Metropolitan Statistical Area	1,548	3,591
4	Wichita, KS Metropolitan Statistical Area	1,378	8,825
5	Lafayette, LA Metropolitan Statistical Area	1,212	5,931
6	Baton Rouge, LA Metropolitan Statistical Area	1,184	10,126
7	Tuscaloosa, AL Metropolitan Statistical Area	1,153	2,907
8	Manhattan, KS Metropolitan Statistical Area	1,062	1,384
9	Chicago-Naperville-Elgin, IL-IN-WI Metropolitan Statistical Area	975	92,239
10	Memphis, TN-MS-AR Metropolitan Statistical Area	924	12,434
11	Atlanta-Sandy Springs-Alpharetta, GA Metropolitan Statistical Area	850	51,172
12	Miami-Fort Lauderdale-Pompano Beach, FL Metropolitan Statistical Area	839	51,751
13	Springfield, IL Metropolitan Statistical Area	833	1,723
14	Houston-The Woodlands-Sugar Land, TX Metropolitan Statistical Area	817	57,733
15	Kansas City, MO-KS Metropolitan Statistical Area	801	17,291
16	Kankakee, IL Metropolitan Statistical Area	786	863
17	Bloomington, IL Metropolitan Statistical Area	740	1,269
18	Rockford, IL Metropolitan Statistical Area	712	2,393
19	Syracuse, NY Metropolitan Statistical Area	682	4,423
20	Cleveland-Elyria, OH Metropolitan Statistical Area	675	13,833
21	Decatur, IL Metropolitan Statistical Area	670	697
22	Las Vegas-Henderson-Paradise, NV Metropolitan Statistical Area	664	15,055
23	New Orleans-Metairie, LA Metropolitan Statistical Area	654	8,311
24	Rochester, NY Metropolitan Statistical Area	648	6,929
25	Champaign-Urbana, IL Metropolitan Statistical Area	647	1,462
26	Fort Collins, CO Metropolitan Statistical Area	637	2,272
27	Philadelphia-Camden-Wilmington, PA-NJ-DE-MD Metropolitan Statistical Area	636	38,789
28	Denver-Aurora-Lakewood, CO Metropolitan Statistical Area	633	18,786
29	Peoria, IL Metropolitan Statistical Area	633	2,534
30	Dallas-Fort Worth-Arlington, TX Metropolitan Statistical Area	632	47,825
31	Tallahassee, FL Metropolitan Statistical Area	631	2,444
32	Boulder, CO Metropolitan Statistical Area	627	2,046
33	Albany-Schenectady-Troy, NY Metropolitan Statistical Area	599	5,272
34	Shreveport-Bossier City, LA Metropolitan Statistical Area	597	2,357
35	Poughkeepsie-Newburgh-Middletown, NY Metropolitan Statistical Area	592	4,022
36	Colorado Springs, CO Metropolitan Statistical Area	588	4,385
37	Columbia, SC Metropolitan Statistical Area	567	4,757
38	Orlando-Kissimmee-Sanford, FL Metropolitan Statistical Area	559	14,591
39	Lakeland-Winter Haven, FL Metropolitan Statistical Area	545	3,949
40	Buffalo-Cheektowaga, NY Metropolitan Statistical Area	541	6,105
41	Columbus, OH Metropolitan Statistical Area	540	11,452
42	Baltimore-Columbia-Towson, MD Metropolitan Statistical Area	536	15,013
43	Sumter, SC Metropolitan Statistical Area	531	746
44	Savannah, GA Metropolitan Statistical Area	526	2,071
45	Greeley, CO Metropolitan Statistical Area	521	1,690
46	Columbus, GA-AL Metropolitan Statistical Area	520	1,669
47	Montgomery, AL Metropolitan Statistical Area	512	1,913
48	Akron, OH Metropolitan Statistical Area	511	3,598
49	Los Angeles-Long Beach-Anaheim, CA Metropolitan Statistical Area	509	67,258
50	Albany, GA Metropolitan Statistical Area	508	746

Metropolitan Areas are defined by the Office of Management and Budget, and population estimates are based on 2019 U.S. Census figures. Metropolitan Areas are ranked based on the number of reports per 100,000 population.

FASTEST INTERNET CONNECTION, 2019

Select population of interest

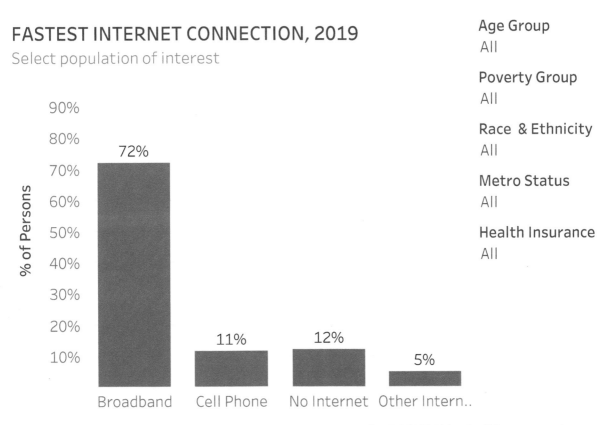

Age Group
All

Poverty Group
All

Race & Ethnicity
All

Metro Status
All

Health Insurance
All

Source: HHS-ASPE tabulations from the 2013-2019 American Community Survey, accessed via IPUMS USA, University of Minnesota, www.ipums.o..

ACCESS TO BROADBAND HAS INCREASED OVER TIME BUT MANY LIVE WITHOUT A FAST INTERNET CONNECTION..

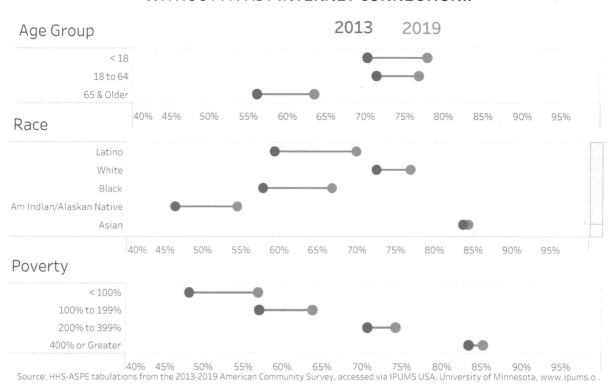

Source: HHS-ASPE tabulations from the 2013-2019 American Community Survey, accessed via IPUMS USA, University of Minnesota, www.ipums.o..

Office of the Assistant Secretary for Planning & Evaluation ● U.S. Department of Health & Human Services

People in Low-Income Households Have Less Access to Internet Services – 2019 Update

By Kendall Swenson and Robin Ghertner   March 2021

Many human services agencies and health providers rely on virtual communication with clients to provide services. In particular, in response to the current COVID-19 pandemic, agencies and service providers in many states have closed their offices to prevent transmission of the virus. To continue serving clients, many have transitioned to remote casework and to providing medical care through telehealth services. While much of this can be done over the telephone, some may require access to the internet. In these situations, access to the internet may be a factor in accessing critical benefits to support families dealing with the economic consequences of the response to the pandemic. In addition, populations with worse internet access also tend to have higher rates of chronic conditions and worse health outcomes, suggesting that they may be particularly vulnerable to the consequences from lapses in care.

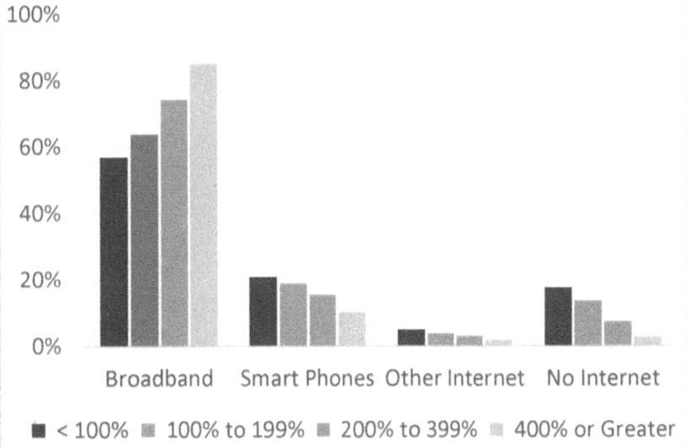

This factsheet updates previous estimates of access to internet services for low-income families, as well as differences by demographic characteristics and geography. The data in this brief come from the Census Bureau's 2019 American Community Survey (ACS), the most recent national data available.[1]

More than one in six people in poverty had no Internet access in 2019. People with higher incomes were more likely to have internet access in their households. As shown in Figure 1, 17 percent of people below 100 percent poverty lacked access to the internet.[2] For people at or above 400 percent poverty, only three percent lacked internet access. Likewise, people below 100 poverty were 28 percentage points less likely to have access to broadband than people at or above 400 percent poverty (57 percent compared to 85 percent).

Access to the internet varied by race and ethnicity. Asians and Whites were more likely to have internet access, and have access to broadband, than other race and ethnic groups, as shown in Figure 2. Compared to other groups, American Indians and Alaska Natives were the least likely to have access to the internet (80 percent) and to broadband services (54 percent).

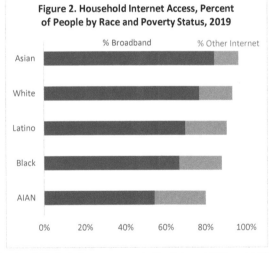

Figure 1. Fastest Household Internet Connection, Percent of People by Poverty Status, 2019

■ < 100% ■ 100% to 199% ■ 200% to 399% ■ 400% or Greater

Figure 2. Household Internet Access, Percent of People by Race and Poverty Status, 2019

% Broadband   % Other Internet

---

[1] Data were accessed via IPUMS USA, University of Minnesota, www.ipums.org.
[2] For this figure, broadband services are assumed to be the fastest internet connection, followed by smart phones, and then other internet services such as satellite and dial-up connections. People without internet access in their households may or may not have access outside of their households from libraries, businesses, homes of relatives, or other places.

Office of the Assistant Secretary for Planning & Evaluation ● U.S. Department of Health & Human Services

People living in nonmetropolitan areas had less access to the internet than those in metropolitan areas. People in low-income families living in nonmetropolitan areas were less likely to have access to the internet than those in metropolitan areas. As displayed in Figure 3, people below 100 percent of poverty were seven percentage points less likely to have access to the internet than people in poverty living in metropolitan areas.

Internet access was less common among older people in poverty. The access gap between lower and higher income people was much starker for adults age 65 and older than for other age groups, as shown in Figure 4. Among adults age 65 and older (light orange bars), 60 percent of those in poverty had access to the internet, 22 percentage points lower than those between 200 and 399 percent poverty. This gap was larger than the gap across poverty status for younger age groups. When focusing just on people in poverty, older adults were 15 percentage points less likely to have access than adults age 18 to 64. This gap was more than double the gap between different age groups in the 200 to 399 percent poverty group.

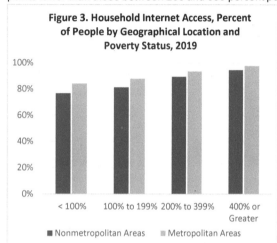

Figure 3. Household Internet Access, Percent of People by Geographical Location and Poverty Status, 2019

Access to the internet among people in poverty varied across states. In all states, access to the internet among people in poverty was lower than people not in poverty. However, there were important differences across states (Figure 5). For example, the percentage of people in poverty without access to the internet was 28 percent in New Mexico compared with 10 percent in Utah, a difference of 18 percentage points.

Internet access generally improved for poor Americans between 2016 and 2019. In 2019, the percent of people in poverty without internet access dropped from 24 percent to 17 percent, and the percent with broadband access increased from 51 percent to 57 percent.

For detailed estimates from these tables, and more information on internet access in specific states see https://aspe.hhs.gov/pdf-report/low-income-internet-access.

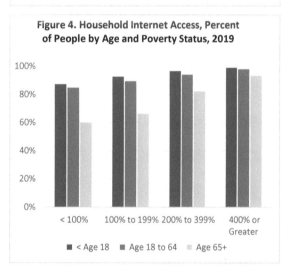

Figure 4. Household Internet Access, Percent of People by Age and Poverty Status, 2019

Office of the Assistant Secretary for Planning & Evaluation ● U.S. Department of Health & Human Services

Figure 5. Percentage of People in Poverty Who Have No Internet Access in their Households by State, 2019

NTIA Data Reveal Shifts in Technology Use, Persistent Digital Divide

June 10, 2020 by Evelyn Remaley, Associate Administrator, Office of Policy Analysis and Development

Today, NTIA is releasing results of its latest NTIA Internet Use Survey, which show that nearly 4 out of 5 Americans were using the Internet by November 2019, and are increasingly using a larger and more varied range of devices. Even as seniors and other demographic groups reported encouraging increases in Internet use, the data show that a persistent digital divide still exists based on income levels, age groups, and race, among other factors.

This is the fifteenth edition of the survey—the product of a partnership between NTIA and the U.S. Census Bureau that **spans a quarter century**—and it includes **over 50 detailed questions** about computer and Internet use administered to approximately 50,000 households across all 50 states and the District of Columbia. The NTIA Internet Use Survey is a vital data source for policymakers, researchers, and advocates seeking to understand critical questions related to Internet use and help bridge the digital divide.

Over the coming months, NTIA policy analysts will be digging into the new data to understand computer and Internet use in the United States. Because the survey was conducted this past November, it effectively serves as a snapshot of the country shortly before the COVID-19 pandemic began. NTIA is working to gain insights into how the pandemic has impacted the digital divide since November and what potential policy responses might address it.

We have also updated our **Data Explorer visualization tool** to include the latest estimates for dozens of tracked metrics, enabling users to easily see the latest results either on a state-by-state map or charted over time. And for those researchers who want to use NTIA Internet Use Survey data in their own studies, this summer we will continue **our long-standing practice** of publicly releasing a complete dataset, along with extensive technical documentation and sample code.

Internet Use in 2019

Overall, the proportion of Americans ages 3 and older using the Internet from any location increased modestly from 78 percent in 2017 to 79 percent in 2019. The pace of growth in Internet use has been relatively stable over the past decade, increasing by 11 percentage points since 2009. However, some demographic groups remained less likely to go online than their peers; for example, African Americans and Hispanics were 7 percentage points less likely to use the Internet, and Asian Americans were 4 percentage points less likely to do so, compared with White non-Hispanics (see Figure 1).

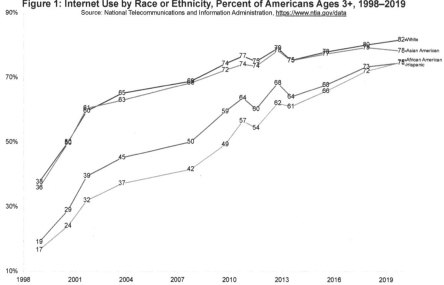

Figure 1: Internet Use by Race or Ethnicity, Percent of Americans Ages 3+, 1998–2019
Source: National Telecommunications and Information Administration, https://www.ntia.gov/data

The gaps between Whites and other groups in 2019 were statistically significant and require further study. Among Asian Americans in particular, there was also a small decline in estimated Internet use overall, though the difference from 2017 is within the margin of error. The trend across over two decades of NTIA Internet Use Surveys is encouraging, as disparities in Internet use based on race and ethnicity have narrowed significantly.

Breaking out Internet use along other demographic lines revealed largely similar trends. Internet use among Americans with family incomes below $25,000 per year increased from 62 percent in 2017 to 65 percent in 2019, though this was still far short of the 87 percent of those with annual family incomes of $100,000 or more. Seniors ages 65 and older experienced one of the largest gains in Internet use of any demographic group, increasing their use by 5 percentage points to 68 percent.

Evolution of Computing Devices

The popularity of different device types has changed dramatically since NTIA began tracking them separately in 2011. Back then, desktop PCs were the most commonly used type of computing device, utilized by 45 percent of Americans, while only 27 percent used a smartphone. By 2019, smartphones had soared in popularity and were used by 68 percent of Americans, while desktop use fell dramatically to 28 percent (see Figure 2).

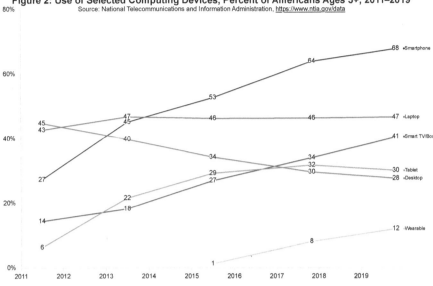

Figure 2: Use of Selected Computing Devices, Percent of Americans Ages 3+, 2011–2019
Source: National Telecommunications and Information Administration, https://www.ntia.gov/data

The use of smart TVs and TV-connected devices also increased rapidly over this period, and continued to grow quickly in the latest survey to 41 percent of Americans, from 34 percent in 2017 and just 14 percent back in 2011. Americans are also using more devices: 64% reported using at least two different types of devices in 2019, and 45% used at least three different types of devices. Both figures are somewhat higher than those **we reported two years ago**, and continue a long-term trend toward use of multiple devices.

Similar to Internet adoption rates, however, multiple device use was not consistent across demographic groups. For example, people with annual family incomes under $25,000 reported using an average of 1.4 different types of devices in 2019, compared with an average of 2.8 device types among those with family incomes of $100,000 or more.

NTIA will continue publishing findings as we explore the latest NTIA Internet Use Survey data in depth. There is a significant need for high-quality data and expert analysis of the challenges related to the digital divide. We will therefore strive to identify evidence-based policy solutions that ensure all Americans can enjoy the numerous economic, social, and educational opportunities these technologies enable.

More than Half of American Households Used the Internet for Health-Related Activities in 2019, NTIA Data Show

December 07, 2020 by Michelle Cao, Intern, and Rafi Goldberg, Policy Analyst, Office of Policy Analysis and Development

Telemedicine and telehealth-related activities are on the rise, according to NTIA's November 2019 Internet Use Survey, which found that more households are using the Internet to communicate with health professionals, access health records, and research health information.

Because the survey was conducted prior to the outbreak of COVID-19, it provides an important baseline for understanding the prevalence of telehealth usage among American households and the importance of Internet access for essential services.

The proportion of households that accessed health or health insurance records online grew from 30 percent in 2017 to 34 percent in 2019 (see Figure 1). Households communicating with a doctor or other health professional online grew by two percentage points, and households that researched health information online grew by one percentage point between 2017 and 2019.

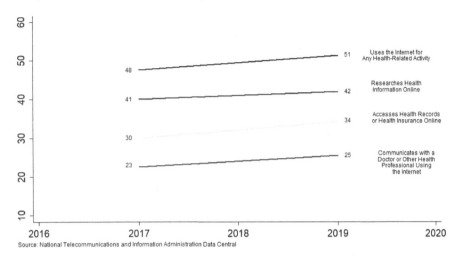

Figure 1: Percent of Households Using the Internet for Health-Related Activities, 2017-2019

Source: National Telecommunications and Information Administration Data Central

Our data reveal that telehealth and telemedicine users tend to have higher incomes, more education, and live in metropolitan areas. An Internet-using household in which the reference person lacked a high school diploma was half as likely as one with some college experience to research health information, such as with WebMD or similar services. The reference person is the first individual in each household who is identified as owning or renting the housing unit.

On average, Internet-using households with reference persons that were 65 years of age or older tended to use the Internet less to access health records and research health information compared to those between the ages of 25 to 64. However, compared to all other age brackets, those 65 or older had the highest adoption rate of electronic health monitoring services, which collect and send data to health care providers through the Internet, including connected devices that monitor vital statistics.

Higher Income is Generally Associated with Higher Rates of Telehealth Usage

Households with annual family incomes of $100,000 or more were substantially more likely to use the Internet to communicate with health professionals, access health records, research health information, and use electronic health monitoring services compared to those with annual family incomes less than $25,000 (see Figures 2 and 3).

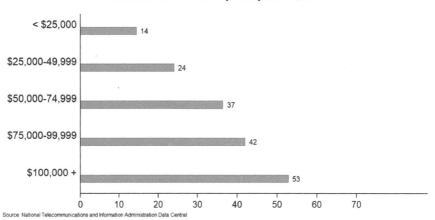

Figure 2: Percent of Households Accessing Health Records
or Health Insurance Online by Family Income, 2019

Source: National Telecommunications and Information Administration Data Central

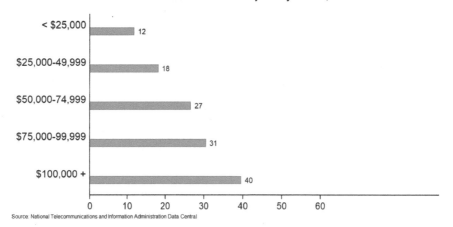

Figure 3: Percent of Households Communicating with a Doctor
or other Health Professional Online by Family Income, 2019

Source: National Telecommunications and Information Administration Data Central

Further, at every income bracket, women were slightly more likely to use the Internet to access health or health insurance records online compared to men. According to the data, this was also true for the other telehealth measures asked about in the NTIA Internet Use Survey.

Households in Metropolitan Areas Are More Inclined to Access Health Records Online

The proportion of households in urban areas that accessed health or health insurance records using the Internet grew by four percentage points from 2017 to 2019, while for those in rural areas, it grew by six percentage points in the same period. The 10-point gap between urban and rural households (see Figure 4) can mostly be explained by lower rates of Internet use in non-metropolitan areas, as discussed in a **previous NTIA analysis on the urban/rural digital divide**.

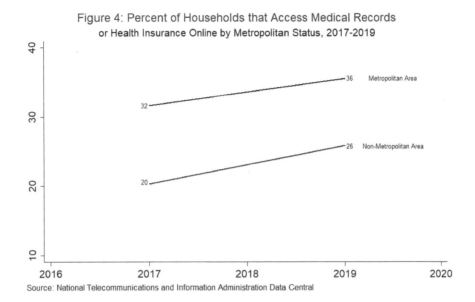

Figure 4: Percent of Households that Access Medical Records
or Health Insurance Online by Metropolitan Status, 2017-2019

Source: National Telecommunications and Information Administration Data Central

In general, we see higher overall rates of adoption in metropolitan areas compared to non-metropolitan areas but greater growth among groups in non-metropolitan areas.

Hispanic and American Indian/Alaska Native Households Experienced Greatest Growth in Online Health-related Activities

Comparing the rates of telehealth usage among different racial or ethnic groups showed substantial growth for Hispanic and American Indian/Alaska Native households from 2017 to 2019 (see Figure 5). While overall usage increased for all racial groups, there are still large disparities between groups that are consistent with results from the most recent **NTIA analysis of shifts in technology use**.

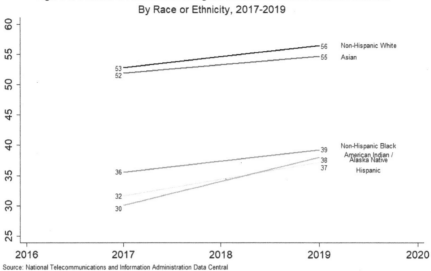

Figure 5: Percent of Households Using the Internet for Health-Related Activities By Race or Ethnicity, 2017-2019

Source: National Telecommunications and Information Administration Data Central

Comparing data from the next survey to what we see here, especially with increased measures for working from home and growth of e-health services, should lead to useful data for identifying adaptations in usage during the pandemic. NTIA will continue to analyze these trends and research how different populations are impacted by the rise in telehealth.

Nearly a Third of American Employees Worked Remotely in 2019, NTIA Data Show

September 03, 2020 by Rafi Goldberg, Policy Analyst, Office of Policy Analysis and Development

This summer, NTIA reported **initial results from our latest NTIA Internet Use Survey**, which showed that Americans were increasingly using a larger and more varied range of devices. But with **dozens of topics covered in the survey**, there is a lot more we can learn from this data collection, including questions about online activities such as checking email, watching videos and participating in the sharing economy.

Two online activities of particular importance right now are remote work and taking online classes. Our data show that approximately 51 million Americans reported using the Internet to work remotely in 2019, nearly a third of the estimated 160 million Americans who were employed in November. A smaller number, about 43 million Americans, said they used the Internet to take classes or complete job training last year. That represents about 20 percent of Internet users ages 15 or older.

Although our survey was conducted in November 2019, a few months before the outbreak of the coronavirus, the results can be helpful to understanding the extent to which Americans were prepared to work and learn online.

Working Remotely

As with many other online activities, there are significant disparities in the prevalence of teleworking via the Internet among particular demographic groups. For example, while 34 percent of White non-Hispanic employees and 38 percent of Asian American employees teleworked in 2019, only 26 percent of African American and 22 percent of Hispanic employees reported doing so. Part of this gap is due to lower rates of Internet use among African American and Hispanic employees, but Internet users in these groups were also less likely to telework (see Figure 1). Even when looking at those Americans who were both employed and using the Internet in some fashion, we still see significant racial disparities in rates of telework, consistent with **previous NTIA analysis of online activities**.

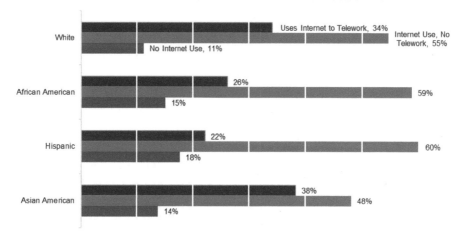

**Figure 1: Telework Status by Race or Ethnicity
Percent of Employed Americans Ages 15+, 2019**
Source: National Telecommunications and Information Administration, https://www.ntia.gov/data

Gaps in telework were also evident when looking at population density. Thirty-two percent of employed Americans living in urban areas teleworked in 2019, but only 22 percent of their counterparts in rural locales did so. While a small part of this gap is attributable to disparities in Internet use, most of the difference consisted of rural employees who used the Internet but did not work remotely.

Breaking out the employed population by occupation revealed some of the largest variations in telework. Some of these differences are unsurprising. Workers in scientific, legal, and finance fields were the most likely to telework. Over half of all employees in those categories reported that they worked remotely in 2019. At the other end of the spectrum were those who worked in transportation, agriculture, food preparation, manufacturing, and other fields where employees were both less likely to report teleworking and more likely than most to say they did not use the Internet at all (see Figure 2).

Figure 2: Telework Status by Occupation
Percent of Employed Americans Ages 15+, 2019
Source: National Telecommunications and Information Administration, https://www.ntia.gov/data

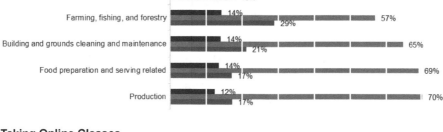

Taking Online Classes

NTIA first asked about Internet users taking online classes in 2001. At that time, only 4 percent of Internet users ages 15 and older said they took classes or training online. Although that number stands at 20 percent as of 2019, there are some significant demographic differences in the rate at which Internet users take courses online.

We previously detailed the **substantial demographic gaps in Internet use**, but among those Americans who already had an Internet connection, there was little difference across racial or ethnic groups in the likelihood of taking online classes. However, there was a substantial gap based on educational attainment. While 27 percent of Internet-using college graduates and 22 percent of those with some college credit took online classes in 2019, only 10 percent of those with only a high school diploma and 14 percent of those lacking a high school diploma reported doing so.

Moreover, participation in online classes or job training varied substantially with age. Relatively young Internet users were significantly more likely to take online classes than their older counterparts. For example, 30 percent of Internet users between the ages of 15 and 24 reported taking online classes or job training in 2019, compared with just 6 percent of those 65 and older (see Figure 3).

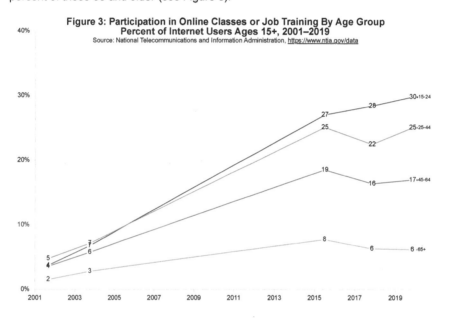

Figure 3: Participation in Online Classes or Job Training By Age Group
Percent of Internet Users Ages 15+, 2001–2019
Source: National Telecommunications and Information Administration, https://www.ntia.gov/data

Fifty-three percent of Internet-using college students said they participated in online classes or job training in 2019. This was especially common among part-time students who used the Internet, 60 percent of whom took online classes, compared with 50 percent of their full-time counterparts. In addition, 88 percent of all college students were Internet users, which is a significantly **higher adoption rate than the country overall**.

NTIA will continue to analyze results from out November 2019 survey to better understand today's connectivity challenges and how digital inclusion can help improve our nation's resiliency. We also plan to continue to track metrics on remote work and learning in our next survey to gauge the impact of COVID-19 on these activities.

Nearly Three-Fourths of Online Households Continue to Have Digital Privacy and Security Concerns

December 13, 2021 by Michelle Cao, Policy Analyst, Office of Policy Analysis and Development

The security and privacy landscape has continued to evolve since NTIA first asked about it in our 2015 Internet Use Survey. High-profile data breaches and debates about the role of technology in people's lives have kept concerns about privacy and security in the forefront. The spread of emerging technologies such as smart home devices and always-on voice assistants, as well as business models predicated on the collection, use, and sale of personal information, means these concerns have taken on increased urgency.

As NTIA will be exploring in **our listening sessions this week**, these concerns are especially acute for those in marginalized or underserved communities. These communities can sometimes face higher risks of harm from the loss of privacy or misuse of data.

In 2019, most Internet-using households in America expressed concerns regarding digital privacy, according to data from the NTIA Internet Use Survey. While fewer households had concerns about digital privacy and security and deterred online activities in 2015 vs. 2017, rates have held steady from 2017 to 2019. In 2019, 73 percent of Internet-using households in 2019 had significant concerns about online privacy and security risks, and 35 percent said such worries led them to hold back from some online activities (see Figure 1).

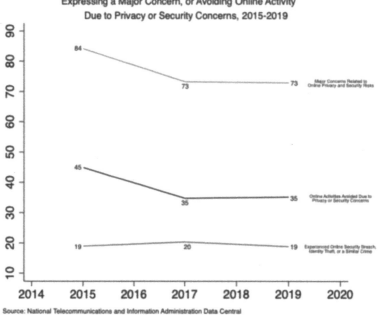

Figure 1: Percent of Internet-Using Households Experiencing Online Security Breach,
Expressing a Major Concern, or Avoiding Online Activity
Due to Privacy or Security Concerns, 2015-2019

Source: National Telecommunications and Information Administration Data Central

Overall, about 19 percent of Internet-using households experienced an online security breach, identity theft, or similar crime in 2019, a rate that has remained relatively steady since 2015. Reports of security breaches became more common as the range of computing devices used in a household increased, the data showed. Households reporting security breaches were also generally more common among those higher annual family incomes.

Concerns Regarding Identity Theft Have Declined

Although most categories of privacy and security concerns have either increased modestly or remained stable, the percentage of online households worried about identity theft and credit card or banking fraud declined over the four-year period (see Figure 4). There was a 9 percentage point decrease in the proportion of those households that named identity theft as a major concern from 2015 to 2019. This downward trend may be surprising given that the number of identity theft reports climbed from about 490,000 in 2015 to over 1.3 million reports in 2020, according to the **Federal Trade Commission (FTC) Consumer Sentinel Network**. Despite this surge, fewer Internet-using households considered identity theft a major concern in 2019.

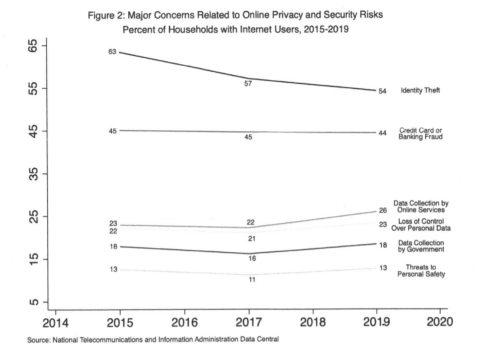

Figure 2: Major Concerns Related to Online Privacy and Security Risks
Percent of Households with Internet Users, 2015-2019

Source: National Telecommunications and Information Administration Data Central

In contrast, concerns about data collection by online services grew from 23 percent of online households in 2015 to 26 percent in 2019.

These digital privacy and security concerns also deterred millions of Americans from engaging in online activities at some point during the past year (see Figure 5). Although fewer households refrained from conducting financial transactions online – decreasing 6 percentage points over the course of four years – we found small increases in Internet-using households avoiding buying goods or services online, posting on social networks, and expressing a controversial opinion online between 2017 and 2019 following significant declines from 2015.

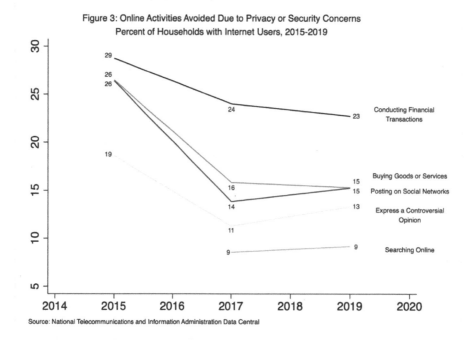

Figure 3: Online Activities Avoided Due to Privacy or Security Concerns
Percent of Households with Internet Users, 2015-2019

Source: National Telecommunications and Information Administration Data Central

The most recent survey data show that Americans are concerned about their privacy and security, especially when it comes to their personal data. The explosion of the marketplace for Internet-based services and applications, as well as Americans' growing engagement online, means it is more important than ever for policymakers to understand the digital landscape, to encourage the widespread deployment of encryption and other technologies to protect users, and to address structural disparities that persist in the digital economy.

This past month, the 2021 NTIA Internet Use Survey went into the field. We look forward to analyzing these results when they become available next year, as we continue our efforts to inform policies that build trust, confidence, and resilience among Internet users.

NTIA has now sponsored its Internet Use Survey 16 times since 1994, using the results for data-driven policy analysis and development. With its large sample size and more than 50 questions about Internet usage, it is the most comprehensive national survey of how Americans connect to the Internet and what they do when they're online. The Census Bureau administers the NTIA Internet Use Survey as a supplement to its Current Population Survey (CPS) and includes over 114,000 people living in nearly 50,000 households across all 50 states and the District of Columbia.

Would you like more of NTIA's analysis delivered to your inbox? **Sign up for the Data Central mailing list** *to receive the latest updates about the NTIA Internet Use Survey.*

Digital Equity Leaders Network
March 2022

What is the Digital Equity Leaders Network (DELN)?

The National Telecommunications and Information Administration's BroadbandUSA program convenes and facilitates the Digital Equity Leaders Network (DELN), a community of practitioners who work on increasing digital equity and digital inclusion and access at the local, county, state, government as well as the community level.

DELN participants meet virtually monthly. Participants share priorities and best practices and discuss emerging telecommunications policy issues at the federal and local level. The DELN provides a forum to strengthen policy and program connections among local, state jurisdictions and federal agencies, providing opportunities to improve funding coordination, align policies and address barriers to collaboration across states and agencies. BroadbandUSA works with DELN participants to support technical assistance offerings for communities, businesses and organizations at the local, regional and state level.

Who participates?

The DELN has experienced tremendous growth over the past several years, with staff from 48 cities, 11 counties, and 25 states and territories actively participating in the group. Since each locality and community approaches digital equity, digital inclusion, broadband access differently, a variety of local and state level offices participate in the DELN. Participants are usually part of a dedicated digital equity office or programs in their local or county government or have identified digital equity and broadband as a specific responsibility within their agency or department. The positions generally reside in the mayor's of county executive's offices, the offices of technology and innovation, economic development, the public library or local education offices, the public utility/public service commission,or newly formed digital equity offices. Many participants have also formed multi-partnered coalitions and partnerships that include other local government agencies, internet service providers, nonprofit and community based organizations, and members of the local community.

What digital equity and broadband activities happen at the local level?
The BroadbandUSA website lists digital inclusion programs across state, local, and county governments. While most programs focus on digital equity, digital inclusion, and workforce development, some address broadband access and infrastructure. Other topic areas include telehealth/telemedicine, education, digital literacy skill development and training, K-12 and adult STEM/STEAM programs, IT career advancement training and employment, economic development, digital equity and broadband mapping, digital equity investments, technical assistance, policy improvements and interventions, and innovation. Click on the local map to learn more.

For more information, contact BroadbandUSA@ntia.doc.gov.

FBI
Scams and Safety

CHARITY AND DISASTER FRAUD

Charity fraud schemes seek donations for organizations that do little or no work—instead, the money goes to the fake charity's creator.

While these scams can happen at any time, they are especially prevalent after high-profile disasters. Criminals often use tragedies to exploit you and others who want to help.

Charity fraud scams can come to you in many forms: emails, social media posts, crowdfunding platforms, cold calls, etc. Always use caution and do your research when you're looking to donate to charitable causes.

After a natural disaster or other emergency, unethical contractors and other scammers may commit insurance fraud, re-victimizing people whose homes or businesses have been damaged. Sometimes these fraudsters even pretend to be affiliated with the government, when they are not. If you need any post-disaster repairs, do your research before hiring any contractor.

Protect Yourself

The following tips can help you avoid these schemes:

- Give to established charities or groups whose work you know and trust.
- Be aware of organizations with copycat names or names similar to reputable organizations.
- Be wary of new organizations that claim to aid victims of recent high-profile disasters.
- Do your research. Use the Federal Trade Commission's resources to examine the track record of a charity.
- Give using a check or credit card. If a charity or organization asks you to donate through cash, gift card, virtual currency, or wire transfer, it's probably a scam. Learn more about this trick from the FTC.
- Practice good cyber hygiene:
- Don't click links or open email attachments from someone you don't know.
  - **Manually type out links instead of clicking on them.**
  - **Don't provide any personal information in response to an email, robocall, or robotext.**
  - **Check the website's address—most legitimate charity organization websites use .org, not .com.**
- After a natural disaster or other emergency, carefully vet any contractors before hiring them to work on your home or business.

Report Fraud

If you're a victim of charity or disaster fraud or have information about these types of schemes, you can:
- Contact your state consumer protection office
- Report fraud to the FBI at tips.fbi.gov
- Report online fraud to the FBI's Internet Crime Complaint Center (IC3)
- File a complaint with the Federal Trade Commission (FTC)
- Report suspected disaster-related fraud to the National Center for Disaster Fraud Resources

https://www.fbi.gov/scams-and-safety/common-scams-and-crimes/charity-and-disaster-fraud

ELDER FRAUD

Each year, millions of elderly Americans fall victim to some type of financial fraud or confidence scheme, including romance, lottery, and sweepstakes scams, to name a few. Criminals will gain their targets' trust and may communicate with them directly via computer, phone, and the mail; or indirectly through the TV and radio. Once successful, scammers are likely to keep a scheme going because of the prospect of significant financial gain.

Seniors are often targeted because they tend to be trusting and polite. They also usually have financial savings, own a home, and have good credit—all of which make them attractive to scammers.

Additionally, seniors may be less inclined to report fraud because they don't know how, or they may be too ashamed at having been scammed. They might also be concerned that their relatives will lose confidence in their abilities to manage their own financial affairs. And when an elderly victim does report a crime, they may be unable to supply detailed information to investigators.

With the elderly population growing and seniors racking up more than $3 billion in losses annually, elder fraud is likely to be a growing problem.

Former FBI Director William Webster and his wife were the targets of a Jamaican lottery scam in 2014. They assisted in the FBI's investigation, which led to the arrest and conviction of Keniel Thomas, who was sentenced in February 2019 to nearly six years in prison.

If you believe you or someone you know may have been a victim of elder fraud, contact your local FBI field office or submit a tip online. You can also file a complaint with the FBI's Internet Crime Complaint Center.

Common Elder Fraud Schemes

- **Romance scam:** Criminals pose as interested romantic partners on social media or dating websites to capitalize on their elderly victims' desire to find companions.
- **Tech support scam:** Criminals pose as technology support representatives and offer to fix non-existent computer issues. The scammers gain remote access to victims' devices and sensitive information.
- **Grandparent scam:** Criminals pose as a relative—usually a child or grandchild—claiming to be in immediate financial need.
- **Government impersonation scam:** Criminals pose as government employees and threaten to arrest or prosecute victims unless they agree to provide funds or other payments.
- **Sweepstakes/charity/lottery scam:** Criminals claim to work for legitimate charitable organizations to gain victims' trust. Or they claim their targets have won a foreign lottery or sweepstake, which they can collect for a "fee."
- **Home repair scam:** Criminals appear in person and charge homeowners in advance for home improvement services that they never provide.
- **TV/radio scam:** Criminals target potential victims using illegitimate advertisements about legitimate services, such as reverse mortgages or credit repair.
- **Family/caregiver scam:** Relatives or acquaintances of the elderly victims take advantage of them or otherwise get their money.

Protect Yourself

- Recognize scam attempts and end all communication with the perpetrator.
- Search online for the contact information (name, email, phone number, addresses) and the proposed offer. Other people have likely posted information online about individuals and businesses trying to run scams.
- Resist the pressure to act quickly. Scammers create a sense of urgency to produce fear and lure victims into immediate action. Call the police immediately if you feel there is a danger to yourself or a loved one.
- Be cautious of unsolicited phone calls, mailings, and door-to-door services offers.

- Never give or send any personally identifiable information, money, jewelry, gift cards, checks, or wire information to unverified people or businesses.
- Make sure all computer anti-virus and security software and malware protections are up to date. Use reputable anti-virus software and firewalls.
- Disconnect from the internet and shut down your device if you see a pop-up message or locked screen. Pop-ups are regularly used by perpetrators to spread malicious software. Enable pop-up blockers to avoid accidentally clicking on a pop-up.
- Be careful what you download. Never open an email attachment from someone you don't know, and be wary of email attachments forwarded to you.
- Take precautions to protect your identity if a criminal gains access to your device or account. Immediately contact your financial institutions to place protections on your accounts, and monitor your accounts and personal information for suspicious activity.

How to Report

If you believe you or someone you know may have been a victim of elder fraud, contact your local FBI field office or submit a tip online. You can also file a complaint with the FBI's Internet Crime Complaint Center.

When reporting a scam—regardless of dollar amount—include as many of the following details as possible:

- Names of the scammer and/or company
- Dates of contact
- Methods of communication
- Phone numbers, email addresses, mailing addresses, and websites used by the perpetrator
- Methods of payment
- Where you sent funds, including wire transfers and prepaid cards (provide financial institution names, account names, and account numbers)
- Descriptions of your interactions with the scammer and the instructions you were given

You are also encouraged to keep original documentation, emails, faxes, and logs of all communications.

https://www.fbi.gov/scams-and-safety/common-scams-and-crimes/elder-fraud

ELECTION CRIMES AND SECURITY

Fair elections are the foundation of our democracy, and the FBI is committed to protecting the rights of all Americans to vote.

The U.S. government only works when legal votes are counted and when campaigns follow the law. When the legitimacy of elections is corrupted, our democracy is threatened.

While individual states run elections, the FBI plays an important role in protecting federal interests and preventing violations of your constitutional rights.

An election crime is generally a federal crime if:

- The ballot includes one or more federal candidates
- An election or polling place official abuses their office
- The conduct involves false voter registration
- The crime intentionally targets minority protected classes
- The activity violates federal campaign finance laws

Protect Your Vote

- Know when, where, and how you will vote.
- Seek out election information from trustworthy sources, verify who produced the content, and consider their intent.
- Report potential election crimes—such as disinformation about the manner, time, or place of voting—to the FBI.
- If appropriate, make use of in-platform tools offered by social media companies for reporting suspicious posts that appear to be spreading false or inconsistent information about voting and elections.
- Research individuals and entities to whom you are making political donations.

Voter Suppression

Intentionally deceiving qualified voters to prevent them from voting is voter suppression—and it is a federal crime.

There are many reputable places you can find your polling location and registration information, including eac.gov and usa.gov/how-to-vote. However, not all publicly available voting information is accurate, and some is deliberately designed to deceive you to keep you from voting.

Bad actors use various methods to spread disinformation about voting, such as social media platforms, texting, or peer-to-peer messaging applications on smartphones. They may provide misleading information about the time, manner, or place of voting. This can include inaccurate election dates or false claims about voting qualifications or methods, such as false information suggesting that one may vote by text, which is not allowed in any jurisdiction.

- For general elections, Election Day is always the first Tuesday after November 1.
- While there are some exceptions for military overseas using absentee ballots by email or fax, you cannot vote online or by text on Election Day.

Always consider the source of voting information. Ask yourself, "Can I trust this information?" Look for official notices from election offices and verify the information you found is accurate.

Help defend the right to vote by reporting any suspected instances of voter suppression—especially those received through a private communication channel like texting—to your local FBI field office or at tips.fbi.gov.

Report Election Crime

If you suspect a federal election offense, contact the election crimes coordinator at your local FBI office, or submit a tip online at tips.fbi.gov.

Threats Against Election Workers

A threat to an election worker or volunteer is a threat to democracy. All election workers should be permitted to do their jobs free from threats and intimidation. The FBI is part of a law enforcement task force that investigates and prosecutes these threats. The FBI and the Cybersecurity Infrastructure Security Agency (CISA) offer security resources for election workers.

Visit tips.fbi.gov to report threats to election workers. If someone is in imminent danger or risk of harm, contact 911 or your local police immediately.

Federal Election Offenses

Fraud by the Voter

- Giving false information when registering to vote (such as false citizenship claims)
- Voting when ineligible to vote
- Voting more than once or using someone else's name to vote

Fraud by an Elections/Campaign Official or Other Individual:

- Changing a ballot tally or engaging in other corrupt behavior as an elections official
- Providing a voter with money or something of value in exchange for voting for a specific candidate or party in a federal election
- Threatening a voter with physical or financial harm if they don't vote or don't vote a certain way
- Trying to prevent qualified voters from voting by lying about the time, date, or place of an election (voter suppression)

Campaign Finance Crimes

- Excessive campaign contributions above the legal limit
- Conduit contributions or straw donor schemes (reimbursing someone for contributing to a campaign)
- Contributions from prohibited sources
- Coordination between Super PACs and independent expenditure organizations and a candidate's campaign
- Use of campaign funds for personal or unauthorized use

What is Not a Federal Election Crime?

While the examples below are not federal election crimes, states have their own election laws. If you are concerned about a possible violation of a state or local election law, contact your local law enforcement.

- Giving voters a ride to the polls or time off to vote
- Offering voters a stamp to mail an absentee ballot
- Making false claims about oneself or another candidate
- Forging or faking nominating petitions
- Campaigning too close to the polls

Scam PACs

Scam PACs are fraudulent political action committees designed to reroute political contributions for personal financial gain. This is a federal crime—and can be costly to victims who thought they were making legitimate campaign contributions.

Signs that a PAC is a scam include the PAC and its website disappearing and the phone number going out of service.

If you or someone you know has been targeted by a scam PAC, contact your local FBI field office and ask to speak to an election crimes coordinator.

https://www.fbi.gov/scams-and-safety/common-scams-and-crimes/election-crimes-and-security

HEALTH CARE FRAUD

Health care fraud is not a victimless crime. It affects everyone—individuals and businesses alike—and causes tens of billions of dollars in losses each year. It can raise health insurance premiums, expose you to unnecessary medical procedures, and increase taxes.

Health care fraud can be committed by medical providers, patients, and others who intentionally deceive the health care system to receive unlawful benefits or payments.

The FBI is the primary agency for investigating health care fraud, for both federal and private insurance programs.

The FBI investigates these crimes in partnership with:

- Federal, state, and local agencies
- Healthcare Fraud Prevention Partnership
- Insurance groups such as the National Health Care Anti-Fraud Association, the National Insurance Crime Bureau, and insurance investigative units

Tips for Avoiding Health Care Fraud

- Protect your health insurance information. Treat it like a credit card. Don't give it to others to use, and be mindful when using it at the doctor's office or pharmacy.
- Beware of "free" services. If you're asked to provide your health insurance information for a "free" service, the service is probably not free and could be fraudulently charged to your insurance company.
- Check your explanation of benefits (EOB) regularly. Make sure the dates, locations, and services billed match what you actually received. If there's a concern, contact your health insurance provider.

Common Types of Health Care Fraud

Fraud Committed by Medical Providers

- **Double billing:** Submitting multiple claims for the same service
- **Phantom billing:** Billing for a service visit or supplies the patient never received
- **Unbundling:** Submitting multiple bills for the same service
- **Upcoding:** Billing for a more expensive service than the patient actually received

Fraud Committed by Patients and Other Individuals

- **Bogus marketing:** Convincing people to provide their health insurance identification number and other personal information to bill for non-rendered services, steal their identity, or enroll them in a fake benefit plan
- **Identity theft/identity swapping:** Using another person's health insurance or allowing another person to use your insurance
- **Impersonating a health care professional:** Providing or billing for health services or equipment without a license

Fraud Involving Prescriptions

- **Forgery:** Creating or using forged prescriptions
- **Diversion:** Diverting legal prescriptions for illegal uses, such as selling your prescription medication
- **Doctor shopping:** Visiting multiple providers to get prescriptions for controlled substances or getting prescriptions from medical offices that engage in unethical practices

Prescription Medication Abuse

Creating or using forged prescriptions is a crime, and prescription fraud comes at an enormous cost to physicians, hospitals, insurers, and taxpayers. But the greatest cost is a human one—tens of thousands of lives are lost to addiction each year. Protect yourself and your loved ones by following this guidance:

- If you are taking opioids, take them exactly as prescribed by your doctor, ideally, for the shortest amount of time possible.
- Never share your medication with others.
- Explore non-opioid options with your doctor.
- Learn more about the risks of opioid use from the CDC.
- If you have unused or expired pain medications, take them to a DEA-approved take back site for disposal.

https://www.fbi.gov/scams-and-safety/common-scams-and-crimes/health-care-fraud

HOLIDAY SCAMS

When shopping online during the holiday season—or any time of year —always be wary of deals that seem too good to be true. Do your part to avoid becoming a scammer's next victim.

Every year, thousands of people become victims of holiday scams. Scammers can rob you of hard-earned money, personal information, and, at the very least, a festive mood.

The two most prevalent of these holiday scams are non-delivery and non-payment crimes. In a non-delivery scam, a buyer pays for goods or services they find online, but those items are never received. Conversely, a nonpayment scam involves goods or services being shipped, but the seller is never paid.

According to the Internet Crime Complaint Center's (IC3) 2020 report, non-payment or non-delivery scams cost people more than $265 million. Credit card fraud accounted for another $129 million in losses.

Similar scams to beware of this time of year are auction fraud, where a product is misrepresented on an auction site, and gift card fraud, when a seller asks you to pay with a pre-paid card.

The IC3 receives a large volume of complaints in the early months of each year, suggesting a correlation with the previous holiday season's shopping scams.

If You've Been Scammed

- Call your credit card company or your bank. Dispute any suspicious charges.
- Contact local law enforcement.
- Report the scam to the FBI's Internet Crime Complaint Center (IC3) at ic3.gov.

Tips to Avoid Holiday Scams

Whether you're the buyer or the seller, there are a number of ways you can protect yourself—and your wallet.

Practice good cybersecurity hygiene.

- Don't click any suspicious links or attachments in emails, on websites, or on social media. Phishing scams and similar crimes get you to click on links and give up personal information like your name, password, and bank account number. In some cases, you may unknowingly download malware to your device.
- Be especially wary if a company asks you to update your password or account information. Look up the company's phone number on your own and call the company.

Know who you're buying from or selling to.

- Check each website's URL to make sure it's legitimate and secure. A site you're buying from should have https in the web address. If it doesn't, don't enter your information on that site.
- If you're purchasing from a company for the first time, do your research and check reviews.
- Verify the legitimacy of a buyer or seller before moving forward with a purchase. If you're using an online marketplace or auction website, check their feedback rating. Be wary of buyers and sellers with mostly unfavorable feedback ratings or no ratings at all.
- Avoid sellers who act as authorized dealers or factory representatives of popular items in countries where there would be no such deals.
- Be wary of sellers who post an auction or advertisement as if they reside in the U.S., then respond to questions by stating they are out of the country on business, family emergency, or similar reasons.
- Avoid buyers who request their purchase be shipped using a certain method to avoid customs or taxes inside another country.

Be careful how you pay.

- Never wire money directly to a seller.
- Avoid paying for items with pre-paid gift cards. In these scams, a seller will ask you to send them a gift card number and PIN. Instead of using that gift card for your payment, the scammer will steal the funds, and you'll never receive your item.

- Use a credit card when shopping online and check your statement regularly. If you see a suspicious transaction, contact your credit card company to dispute the charge.

Monitor the shipping process.
- Always get tracking numbers for items you buy online, so you can make sure they have been shipped and can follow the delivery process.
- Be suspect of any credit card purchases where the address of the cardholder does not match the shipping address when you are selling. Always receive the cardholder's authorization before shipping any products.

And remember: If it seems too good to be true, it probably is.

https://www.fbi.gov/scams-and-safety/common-scams-and-crimes/holiday-scams

MONEY MULES
Don't Be a Mule: Awareness Can Prevent Crime

What Is a Money Mule?
A money mule is someone who transfers or moves illegally acquired money on behalf of someone else.

Criminals recruit money mules to help launder proceeds derived from online scams and frauds or crimes like human trafficking and drug trafficking. Money mules add layers of distance between crime victims and criminals, which makes it harder for law enforcement to accurately trace money trails.

Money mules can move funds in various ways, including through bank accounts, cashier's checks, virtual currency, prepaid debit cards, or money service businesses.

Some money mules know they are supporting criminal enterprises; others are unaware that they are helping criminals profit.

Money mules often receive a commission for their service, or they might provide assistance because they believe they have a trusting or romantic relationship with the individual who is asking for help.

If you are moving money at the direction of another person, you may be serving as a money mule.

What Are the Consequences?
Acting as a money mule is illegal and punishable, even if you aren't aware you're committing a crime.

If you are a money mule, you could be prosecuted and incarcerated as part of a criminal money laundering conspiracy. Some of the federal charges you could face include mail fraud, wire fraud, bank fraud, money laundering, and aggravated identity theft.

Serving as a money mule can also damage your credit and financial standing. Additionally, you risk having your own personally identifiable information stolen and used by the criminals you are working for, and you may be held personally liable for repaying money lost by victims.

Who Is at Risk?
Criminals often target students, those looking for work, or those on dating websites, but anyone can be approached to be a money mule.

What Are the Signs?

Work-from-Home Job Opportunities
- You received an unsolicited email or social media message that promises easy money for little or no effort.
- The "employer" you communicate with uses web-based email services (such as Gmail, Yahoo, Hotmail, Outlook, etc.).
- You are asked to open a bank account in your own name or in the name of a company you form to receive and transfer money.
- As an employee, you are asked to receive funds in your bank account and then "process" or "transfer" funds via: wire transfer, ACH, mail, or money service business (such as Western Union or MoneyGram).
- You are allowed to keep a portion of the money you transfer.
- Your duties have no specific job description.

Dating and Social Media Sites
- An online contact or companion, whom you have never met in person, asks you to receive money and then forward these funds to one or more individuals you do not know.

Protect Yourself
- Perform online searches to check the legitimacy of any company that offers you a job.

- Do not accept any job offers that ask you to use your own bank account to transfer money. A legitimate company will not ask you to do this.
- Be wary if an employer asks you to form a company to open up a new bank account.
- Be suspicious if an individual you met on a dating website wants to use your bank account for receiving and forwarding money.
- Never give your financial details to someone you don't know and trust, especially if you met them online.

Respond and Report
If you have received solicitations of this type, do not respond to them and do not click on any links they contain. Inform your local police or the FBI.

If you believe that you are participating in a money mule scheme:
- Stop communication with the suspected criminal(s).
- Stop transferring money or any other items of value immediately.
- Maintain any receipts, contact information, and relevant communications (emails, chats, text messages, etc.).
- Notify your bank and the service you used to conduct the transaction.
- Notify law enforcement. Report suspicious activity to the FBI's Internet Crime Complaint Center (IC3) at ic3.gov, and contact your local FBI field office.

Types of Money Mules

Unwitting or Unknowing
Individuals are unaware they are part of a larger scheme
- Often solicited via an online romance scheme or job offer
- Asked to use their established personal bank account or open a new account in their true name to receive money from someone they have never met in person
- May be told to keep a portion of the money they transferred
- Motivated by trust in the actual existence of their romance or job position

Witting
Individuals ignore obvious red flags or act willfully blind to their money movement activity
- May have been warned by bank employees they were involved with fraudulent activity
- Open accounts with multiple banks in their true name
- May have been unwitting at first but continue communication and participation
- Motivated by financial gain or an unwillingness to acknowledge their role

Complicit
Individuals are aware of their role and actively participate
- Serially open bank accounts to receive money from a variety of individuals/businesses for criminal reasons
- Advertise their services as a money mule, to include what actions they offer and at what prices. This may also include a review and/or rating by other criminal actors on the money mule's speed and reliability.
- Travel, as directed, to different countries to open financial accounts or register companies
- Operate funnel accounts to receive fraud proceeds from multiple lower level money mules
- Recruit other money mules
- Motivated by financial gain or loyalty to a known criminal group

https://www.fbi.gov/scams-and-safety/common-scams-and-crimes/money-mules

ROMANCE SCAMS

Romance scams occur when a criminal adopts a fake online identity to gain a victim's affection and trust. The scammer then uses the illusion of a romantic or close relationship to manipulate and/or steal from the victim.

The criminals who carry out romance scams are experts at what they do and will seem genuine, caring, and believable. Con artists are present on most dating and social media sites.

The scammer's intention is to establish a relationship as quickly as possible, endear himself to the victim, and gain trust. Scammers may propose marriage and make plans to meet in person, but that will never happen. Eventually, they will ask for money.

Scam artists often say they are in the building and construction industry and are engaged in projects outside the U.S. That makes it easier to avoid meeting in person—and more plausible when they ask for money for a medical emergency or unexpected legal fee.

If someone you meet online needs your bank account information to deposit money, they are most likely using your account to carry out other theft and fraud schemes.

Report Internet Crime to the FBI ic3.gov

If you suspect an online relationship is a scam, stop all contact immediately. If you are the victim of a romance scam, file a complaint with the FBI's Internet Crime Complaint Center (IC3).

Tips for Avoiding Romance Scams:

- Be careful what you post and make public online. Scammers can use details shared on social media and dating sites to better understand and target you.
- Research the person's photo and profile using online searches to see if the image, name, or details have been used elsewhere.
- Go slowly and ask lots of questions.
- Beware if the individual seems too perfect or quickly asks you to leave a dating service or social media site to communicate directly.
- Beware if the individual attempts to isolate you from friends and family or requests inappropriate photos or financial information that could later be used to extort you.
- Beware if the individual promises to meet in person but then always comes up with an excuse why he or she can't. If you haven't met the person after a few months, for whatever reason, you have good reason to be suspicious.
- Never send money to anyone you have only communicated with online or by phone.

https://www.fbi.gov/scams-and-safety/common-scams-and-crimes/romance-scams

SEXTORTION

An Online Threat to Kids and Teens

The FBI has seen a huge increase in the number of cases involving children and teens being threatened and coerced by adults into sending explicit images online—a crime called sextortion.

Sextortion can start on any site, app, or game where people meet and communicate. In some cases, the first contact from the criminal will be a threat. The person may claim to already have a revealing picture or video of a child that will be shared if the victim does not send more pictures. More often, however, this crime starts when young people believe they are communicating with someone their own age who is interested in a relationship or with someone who is offering something of value. The adult will use threats, gifts, money, flattery, lies, or other methods to get a young person to produce an image.

After the criminals have one or more videos or pictures, they threaten to share publish that content, or they threaten violence, to get the victim to produce more images. The shame, fear, and confusion children feel when they are caught in this cycle often prevents them from asking for help or reporting the abuse. Caregivers and young people should understand how the crime occurs and openly discuss online safety.

If young people are being exploited, they are the victim of a crime and should report it. Contact your local FBI field office, call 1-800-CALL-FBI, or report it online at tips.fbi.gov.

What Kids and Teens Need to Know

Why do young people agree to do this?

The people who commit this crime have studied how to reach and target children and teens.

One person the FBI put in prison for this crime was a man in his 40s who worked as a youth minister so he could learn how teens talked to each other. Then, he created social media profiles where he pretended to be a teenage girl. This "girl" would start talking to boys online and encourage them to make videos.

Another person offered money and new smartphones to his victims.

In one case, the criminal threatened a girl, saying he would hurt her and bomb her school, if she didn't send pictures.

Other cases start with the offer of currency or credits in a video game in exchange for a quick picture.

How do you know who can be trusted online?

That's what is so hard about online connections. The FBI has found that those who commit this crime may have dozens of different online accounts and profiles and are communicating with many young people at the same time—trying to find victims.

Be extremely cautious when you are communicating with anyone online. It's easy to think: I'm on my phone, in my own house, what could possibly happen? But you can very quickly give a criminal the information and material he or she needs to do you harm.

But how can this harm me?

It's true that these criminals don't usually meet up with kids in real life, but the victims of this crime still experience negative effects. The criminals can become vicious and non-stop with their demands, harassment, and threats. Victims report feeling scared, alone, embarrassed, anxious, and desperate. Many feel like there's no way out of the situation.

What do I do if this is happening to me?

If you are ready, reach out to the FBI at 1-800-CALL-FBI or report the crime online at tips.fbi.gov. Our agents see these cases a lot and have helped thousands of young people. Our goals are to stop the harassment, arrest the person behind the crime, and help you get the support you need.

If you're not feeling ready to speak to the FBI, go to another trusted adult. Say you are being victimized online and need help. Talking about this can feel impossible, but there are people who can help. You are not the one in trouble.

How can you say I won't be in trouble?

You are not the one who is breaking the law. This situation can feel really confusing, and the criminals count on you feeling too unsure, scared, or embarrassed to tell someone. Even if this started on an app or site that you are too young to be on. Even if you felt okay about making some of the content. Even if you accepted money or a game credit or something else, you are not the one who is in trouble. Sextortion is a crime because it is illegal and wrong for an adult to ask for, pay for, or demand graphic images from a minor.

How can I help someone else who is in this situation?

If you learn friends, classmates, or family members are being victimized, listen to them with kindness and understanding. Tell them you are sorry this is happening to them and that you want to help. Let them know that they are the victim of a crime and have not done anything wrong. Encourage them to ask for help and see if you can help them identify a trusted adult to tell.

How do I protect myself and my friends?

Your generation can be the generation that shuts down these criminals. Awareness and sensible safety practices online, along with a willingness to ask for help, can put an end to this exploitation.

The FBI agents who work on these cases want you to know these six things:

1. Be selective about what you share online. If your social media accounts are open to everyone, a predator may be able to figure out a lot of information about you.
2. Be wary of anyone you encounter for the first time online. Block or ignore messages from strangers.
3. Be aware that people can pretend to be anything or anyone online. Videos and photos are not proof that people are who they claim to be. Images can be altered or stolen. In some cases, predators have even taken over the social media accounts of their victims.
4. Be suspicious if you meet someone on one game or app and this person asks you to start talking on a different platform.
5. Be in the know. Any content you create online—whether it is a text message, photo, or video—can be made public. And nothing actually "disappears" online. Once you send something, you don't have any control over where it goes next.
6. Be willing to ask for help. If you are getting messages or requests online that don't seem right, block the sender, report the behavior to the site administrator, or go to an adult. If you have been victimized online, tell someone.

What Caregivers Need to Know

Why would any child or teen agree to do such a thing?

The individuals carrying out this crime are skilled and ruthless and have honed their techniques and approaches to maximize their chances at success. The entry point to a young person can be any number of mobile or online sites, applications, or games. The approach may come as compliments or flattery or the pretense of beginning a romantic relationship.

Another entry point is to offer the child something they value in exchange for a taking a quick picture. This could be the possibility of a modeling contract; online game credits or codes; or money, cryptocurrency, and gift cards.

The third common point of entry is to go right to threats by either claiming they already have an image of the young person that they will distribute or threatening to harm the child or other people or things the child cares about. Once the perpetrator has the first image, they use the threat of exposure or other harm to keep the child producing more and more explicit material.

But my child would never do that.

The FBI has interviewed victims as young as 8, and the crime affects children of both genders and crosses all ethnic and socioeconomic groups. The victims are honor-roll students, the children of teachers, student athletes, etc. The only common trait among victims is internet access.

Why don't the victims tell someone or ask for help?

The cycle of victimization continues because the child is afraid—afraid of the repercussions threatened by the criminal and afraid they will be in trouble with their parents, guardians, or law enforcement. By the time a child is a victim, they have done something that may be generating feelings of shame and embarrassment. The criminal may also be telling them they have produced child pornography and will be prosecuted for it. In addition, they may fear their access to their phone or computer will be taken away from them as a result of their actions.

How do I protect the young people I know?

Information-sharing and open lines of communication are the best defense. Young people need to know this crime is happening and understand where the risks are hiding. Explain to the children in your life that people can pretend to be anyone or anything online, a stranger reaching out to them online may be doing so with bad intent, and no matter what the platform or application claims, nothing "disappears" online. If they take a photo or video, it always has the potential to become public.

You may choose to place certain limits on your children's Internet use or spot check their phones and other devices to see what applications they are using and with whom they are communicating. This can be part of an open and ongoing conversation about what it and is not appropriate online. It also may be worth considering a rule against devices in bedrooms overnight or shutting off Wi-Fi access in the overnight hours. Caregivers may also want to review the settings on a young person's social media accounts with them. Keeping accounts private can prevent predators from gathering their personal information.

The other crucial element is to keep the door open to your children so that they know they can come to you and ask for help. Let them know that your first move will be to help—always. These predators are powerful because of fear, and the victims suffer ever more negative consequences as the crime carries on over days, weeks, and months. If you are the adult a child trusts with this information, comfort them, help them understand they have been the victim of a crime, and help them report it to law enforcement.

How can I talk to my kids about sextortion?

Here are three 30-second conversations you can have with your kids or kids you know.

The New Version of Don't Talk to Strangers

—When you're online, has anyone you don't know ever tried to contact or talk to you?

—What did you do or what would you do if that happened?

—Why do you think someone would want to reach a kid online?

—You know, it's easy to pretend to be someone you're not online and not every person is a good person. Make sure you block or ignore anything that comes in from someone you don't know in real life.

The Power of a Picture

—Has anyone you know ever sent a picture of themselves that got passed around school or a team or club?

—What's possible anytime you send someone a picture?

—What if that picture were embarrassing?

—Can you think about how someone could use that kind of picture against a person?

I'm Here to Help

　　—I read an article today about kids being pressured to send images and video of their bodies to a person they met online. Have you ever heard about anything like that?

　　—Sometimes they were being threatened and harassed—scary stuff.

　　—You know, if you are ever feeling like something is going on—online or off—that feels scary or wrong or over your head, my first concern is going to be helping you. You can always come to me.

https://www.fbi.gov/scams-and-safety/common-scams-and-crimes/sextortion

SKIMMING

Skimming occurs when devices illegally installed on ATMs, point-of-sale (POS) terminals, or fuel pumps capture data or record cardholders' PINs. Criminals use the data to create fake debit or credit cards and then steal from victims' accounts. It is estimated that skimming costs financial institutions and consumers more than $1 billion each year.

Fuel Pump Skimming

- Fuel pump skimmers are usually attached in the internal wiring of the machine and aren't visible to the customer.
- The skimming devices store data to be downloaded or wirelessly transferred later.

Tips When Using a Fuel Pump

- Choose a fuel pump that is closer to the store and in direct view of the attendant. These pumps are less likely to be targets for skimmers.
- Run your debit card as a credit card. If that's not an option, cover the keypad when you enter your PIN.
- Consider paying inside with the attendant, not outside at the pump.

Report

If you think you've been a victim of skimming, contact your financial institution immediately.

ATM and POS Terminal Skimming

- ATM skimmer devices usually fit over the original card reader.
- Some ATM skimmers are inserted in the card reader, placed in the terminal, or situated along exposed cables.
- Pinhole cameras installed on ATMs record a customer entering their PIN. Pinhole camera placement varies widely.
- In some cases, keypad overlays are used instead of pinhole cameras to records PINs. Keypad overlays record a customer's keystrokes.
- Skimming devices store data to be downloaded or wirelessly transferred later.

Tips When Using an ATM or POS Terminal

- Inspect ATMs, POS terminals, and other card readers before using. Look for anything loose, crooked, damaged, or scratched. Don't use any card reader if you notice anything unusual.
- Pull at the edges of the keypad before entering your PIN. Then, cover the keypad when you enter your PIN to prevent cameras from recording your entry.
- Use ATMs in a well-lit, indoor location, which are less vulnerable targets.
- Be alert for skimming devices in tourist areas, which are popular targets.
- Use debit and credit cards with chip technology. In the U.S., there are fewer devices that steal chip data versus magnetic strip data.
- Avoid using your debit card when you have linked accounts. Use a credit card instead.
- Contact your financial institution if the ATM doesn't return your card after you end or cancel a transaction.

https://www.fbi.gov/scams-and-safety/common-scams-and-crimes/skimming

ATM Skimming

Skimming is an illegal activity that involves the installation of a device, usually undetectable by ATM users, that secretly records bank account data when the user inserts an ATM card into the machine. Criminals can then encode the stolen data onto a blank card and use it to loot the customer's bank account.

1 Hidden camera

A concealed camera is typically used in conjunction with the skimming device in order to record customers typing their PIN into the ATM keypad. Cameras are usually concealed somewhere on the front of the ATM—in this example, just above the screen in a phony ATM part—or somewhere nearby (like a light fixture).

2 Skimmer

The skimmer, which looks very similar to the original card reader in color and texture, fits right over the card reader—the original card reader is usually concave in shape (curving inward), while the skimmer is more convex (curving outward). As customers insert their ATM card, bank account information on the card is "skimmed," or stolen, and usually stored on some type of electronic device.

3 Keypad overlay

The use of a keypad overlay—placed directly on top of the factory-installed keypad—is a fairly new technique that takes the place of a concealed camera. Instead of visually recording users punching in their PINs, circuitry inside the phony keypad stores the actual keystrokes.

SPOOFING AND PHISHING

Spoofing

Spoofing is when someone disguises an email address, sender name, phone number, or website URL—often just by changing one letter, symbol, or number—to convince you that you are interacting with a trusted source.

For example, you might receive an email that looks like it's from your boss, a company you've done business with, or even from someone in your family—but it actually isn't.

Criminals count on being able to manipulate you into believing that these spoofed communications are real, which can lead you to download malicious software, send money, or disclose personal, financial, or other sensitive information.

Phishing

Phishing schemes often use spoofing techniques to lure you in and get you to take the bait. These scams are designed to trick you into giving information to criminals that they shouldn't have access to.

In a phishing scam, you might receive an email that appears to be from a legitimate business and is asking you to update or verify your personal information by replying to the email or visiting a website. The web address might look similar to one you've used before. The email may be convincing enough to get you to take the action requested.

But once you click on that link, you're sent to a spoofed website that might look nearly identical to the real thing—like your bank or credit card site—and asked to enter sensitive information like passwords, credit card numbers, banking PINs, etc. These fake websites are used solely to steal your information.

Phishing has evolved and now has several variations that use similar techniques:

- **Vishing** scams happen over the phone, voice email, or VoIP (voice over Internet Protocol) calls.
- **Smishing** scams happen through SMS (text) messages.
- **Pharming** scams happen when malicious code is installed on your computer to redirect you to fake websites.

Spoofing and phishing are key parts of business email compromise scams.

How to Report

To report spoofing or phishing attempts—or to report that you've been a victim—file a complaint with the FBI's Internet Crime Complaint Center (IC3).

How to Protect Yourself

- Remember that companies generally don't contact you to ask for your username or password.
- Don't click on anything in an unsolicited email or text message. Look up the company's phone number on your own (don't use the one a potential scammer is providing), and call the company to ask if the request is legitimate.
- Carefully examine the email address, URL, and spelling used in any correspondence. Scammers use slight differences to trick your eye and gain your trust.
- Be careful what you download. Never open an email attachment from someone you don't know and be wary of email attachments forwarded to you.
- Set up two-factor (or multi-factor) authentication on any account that allows it, and never disable it.
- Be careful with what information you share online or on social media. By openly sharing things like pet names, schools you attended, family members, and your birthday, you can give a scammer all the information they need to guess your password or answer your security questions.

https://www.fbi.gov/scams-and-safety/common-scams-and-crimes/spoofing-and-phishing

ON THE INTERNET: BE CAUTIOUS WHEN CONNECTED

Everyday tasks—opening an email attachment, following a link in a text message, making an online purchase—can open you up to online criminals who want to harm your systems or steal from you. Preventing internet-enabled crimes and cyber intrusions requires each of us to be aware and on guard.

Protect Your Systems and Data

- Keep systems and software up to date and install a strong, reputable anti-virus program.
- Create a strong and unique passphrase for each online account you hold and change them regularly. Using the same passphrase across several accounts makes you more vulnerable if one account is breached.
- Do not open any attachments unless you are expecting the file, document, or invoice and have verified the sender's email address.

Protect Your Connections

- Be careful when connecting to a public Wi-Fi network and do not conduct any sensitive transactions, including purchases, when on a public network.
- Avoid using free charging stations in airports, hotels, or shopping centers. Bad actors have figured out ways to use public USB ports to introduce malware and monitoring software onto devices that access these ports. Carry your own charger and USB cord and use an electrical outlet instead.

Protect Your Money and Information

- Examine the email address in all correspondence and scrutinize website URLs. Scammers often mimic a legitimate site or email address by using a slight variation in spelling. Or an email may look like it came from a legitimate company, but the actual email address is suspicious.
- Do not click the link in an unsolicited text message or email that asks you to update, check, or verify your account information. If you are concerned about the status of your account, go to the company's website to log into your account or call the phone number listed on the official website to see if something does in fact need your attention.
- Carefully scrutinize all electronic requests for a payment or transfer of funds.
- Be extra suspicious of any message that urges immediate action.
- Make online purchases with a credit card for an extra layer of protection against fraud.
- Do not send money to any person you meet online or allow a person you don't know well to access your bank account to transfer money in or out.

If You are a Victim, File a Report with IC3

If you are the victim of an online or internet-enabled crime, file a report with the Internet Crime Complaint Center (IC3) as soon as possible.

Crime reports are used for investigative and intelligence purposes. Rapid reporting can also help support the recovery of lost funds.

Visit ic3.gov for more information, including tips and information about current crime trends.

Learn about other common scams and crimes. And discover more about the work of the FBI's Cyber Division.

If You Spot a Scam Message, Report It to the FTC

Receive a suspicious message? Report it to the Federal Trade Commission so they can help protect others.

Note: The FBI does not send mass emails to private citizens about cyber scams. If you received an email that claims to be from the FBI Director or other top official, it is most likely a scam.

https://www.fbi.gov/scams-and-safety/on-the-internet

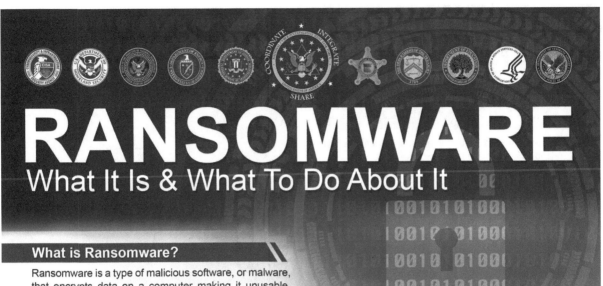

RANSOMWARE
What It Is & What To Do About It

What is Ransomware?

Ransomware is a type of malicious software, or malware, that encrypts data on a computer making it unusable. A malicious cyber criminal holds the data hostage until the ransom is paid. If the ransom is not paid, the victim's data remains unavailable. Cyber criminals may also pressure victims to pay the ransom by threatening to destroy the victim's data or to release it to the public.

Government Efforts to Combat Ransomware

While ransomware attacks impact all sectors, the federal government is particularly concerned about the impact of ransomware on the networks of state, local, tribal, and territorial governments, municipalities, police and fire departments, hospitals, and other critical infrastructure. These types of attacks can delay a police or fire department's response to an emergency or prevent a hospital from accessing lifesaving equipment. To combat this threat, the NCIJTF has convened an interagency group of subject matter experts to educate the public on ways to prevent ransomware attacks, to improve law enforcement coordination and response, and to enable and sequence whole-of-government actions that impose consequences against the criminals engaged in this malicious activity. The Cybersecurity and Infrastructure Security Agency (CISA) leads a number of efforts including —CISA Cyber Essentials—and—CISA Insights— to assist entities in protecting themselves from cyber incidents like ransomware. More about these efforts and the tools CISA offers can be found at https://www.cisa.gov/ransomware. The FBI's IC3.gov website has additional ransomware focused resources that can be found at https://ic3.gov/Home/Ransomware.

Common Infection Vectors

Although cyber criminals use a variety of techniques to infect victims with ransomware, the most common means of infection are:

■ Email phishing campaigns: The cyber criminal sends an email containing a malicious file or link, which deploys malware when clicked by a recipient. Cyber criminals historically have used generic, broad-based spamming strategies to deploy their malware, though recent ransomware campaigns have been more targeted and sophisticated. Criminals may also compromise a victim's email account by using precursor malware, which enables the cyber criminal to use a victim's email account to further spread the infection.

■ Remote Desktop Protocol (RDP) vulnerabilities: RDP is a proprietary network protocol that allows individuals to control the resources and data of a computer over the internet. Cyber criminals have used both brute-force methods, a technique using trial-and-error to obtain user credentials, and credentials purchased on dark web market - places to gain unauthorized RDP access to victim systems. Once they have RDP access, criminals can deploy a range of malware—including ransomware—to victim systems.

■ Software vulnerabilities: Cyber criminals can take advantage of security weaknesses in widely used software programs to gain control of victim systems and deploy ransomware.

RANSOMWARE
What It Is & What To Do About It

Best Practices To Minimize Ransomware Risks

1. Backup your data, system images, and configurations, test your backups, and keep the backups offline
2. Utilize multi-factor authentication
3. Update and patch systems
4. Make sure your security solutions are up to date
5. Review and exercise your incident response plan

How Ransomware Has Impacted The Public Sector

The examples below may show the impacts in terms of ransom paid or service restoration cost, but it is difficult to calculate the total impact/costs of a ransomware infection. In addition, paying a ransom does not guarantee that stolen sensitive data will not be sold on the dark web.

▮ A U.S. county was infected by Ryuk, taking almost all of the county's systems offline. The county had backup servers, but they were not isolated from the network, allowing them to be infected as well. The county paid a $132,000 ransom.

▮ A U.S. city's systems were infected by Robbinhood with a ransom demand of 13 Bitcoins ($76,000). The attackers entered the network through old, out-of-date hardware and software. The ransom was not paid, but service restoration was estimated to cost over $9 million.

▮ A U.S. county's computer systems were infected by Ryuk. The attackers demanded over $1.2 million in Bitcoin for a decryption key. Officials decided to rebuild their systems rather than pay the ransom and spent $1 million in new equipment and technical assistance. A user allegedly opened a malicious link or attachment which caused the infection.

Reporting Information

▮ The FBI does not encourage paying a ransom to criminal actors. Paying a ransom may embolden adversaries to target additional organizations, encourage other criminal actors to engage in the distribution of ransomware, and/or fund illicit activities. Paying the ransom also does not guarantee that a victim's files will be recovered. Regardless of whether you or your organization have decided to pay the ransom, the FBI urges you to report ransomware incidents to your local field office or the FBI's Internet Crime Complaint Center (IC3). Doing so provides investigators with the critical information they need to track ransomware attackers, hold them accountable under U.S. law, and prevent future attacks.

Victims of ransomware can file a complaint with law enforcement or report incidents by:

▮ **Contacting your local federal law enforcement field office**

▮ **Filing a complaint with the Internet Crime Complaint Center (IC3)** https://ic3.gov/Home/Ransomware

▮ **Contacting NCIJTF CyWatch 24/7 support at 1-855-292-3937**

▮ **Reporting incidents, phishing, malware or vulnerabilities with CISA** https://us-cert.cisa.gov/report

FEDERAL BUREAU OF INVESTIGATION

BY THE NUMBERS

IC3 Over 60 Victims by the Numbers [1]

2021

92,371
Victims

$1.7 Billion
Losses

74 Percent
Increase in losses from 2020

$18,246
Average dollar loss per victim

3,133
Victims losing more than $100K

[1] Accessibility description: Image depicts key statistics regarding Over 60 complaints. The total number of complaints received in 2021 was 92,371. Total losses of $1.7 billion were reported. Over 60 victims experienced 24 percent of the total loss of all IC3 complaints received in 2021. 3,133 victims lost more than $100,000. The average loss per victim was $18,246.

2021 VICTIMS BY AGE GROUP

VICTIMS		
Age Range[2]	Total Count	Total Loss
Under 20	14,919	$101,435,178
20 - 29	69,390	$431,191,702
30 - 39	88,448	$937,386,500
40 - 49	89,184	$1,192,890,255
50 - 59	74,460	$1,261,591,978
Over 60	92,371	$1,685,017,829

OVER 60 VICTIM REPORTING FOR PAST FIVE YEARS[3]

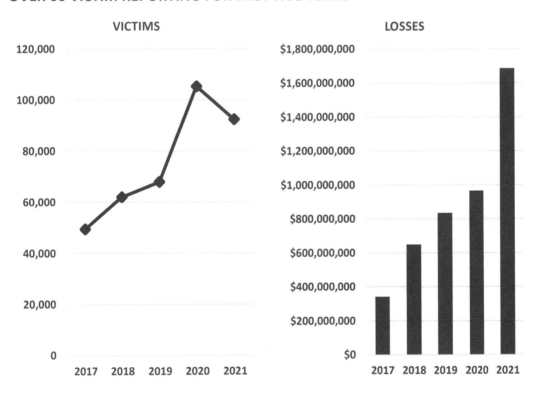

_____

[2] Not all complaints include an associated age range—those without this information are excluded from this table. Please see Appendix B for more information regarding IC3 data.

[3] Charts describe Over 60 Victim Counts and Losses from 2017 – 2021.

2021 – STATES BY NUMBER OF OVER 60 VICTIMS[4]

10,001+
5,001 – 10,000
2,501 – 5,000
1,000 – 2,500
501 – 1,000
0 – 500

2021 – STATES BY LOSSES OF OVER 60 VICTIMS

> $100M
>$50M - $100M
>$20M - $50M
>$10M - $20M
>$5M - $10M
$0 - $5M

[4] Accessibility description: Image depicts a map of the United States color-coded by victim counts and losses. Please see Appendix B for more information regarding IC3 data.

2021 CRIME TYPES

OVER 60 VICTIM COUNT

Crime Type	Victims	Crime Type	Victims
Tech Support	13,900	Investment	2,104
Non-payment/Non-Delivery	13,220	Real Estate/Rental	1,764
Identity Theft	8,902	Overpayment	1,448
Confidence Fraud/Romance	7,658	Employment	1,408
Personal Data Breach	6,189	Terrorism/Threats of Violence	719
Extortion	5,987	IPR/Copyright and Counterfeit	686
Phishing	5,831	Ransomware	365
Spoofing	3,936	Civil Matter	184
BEC/EAC *	3,755	Computer Intrusion	176
(Reporting a potential business victimization)	*2,143*	Corporate Data Breach	158
(Reporting a personal victimization)	*1,612*	Malware/Scareware/Virus	134
Government Impersonation	3,319	Re-shipping	76
Credit Card Fraud	3,164	Health Care Related	74
Advanced Fee	3,029	Denial of Service/TDos	61
Other	2,933	Crimes Against Children	42
Lottery/Sweepstakes/Inheritance	2,607	Gambling	19

Descriptors*

Social Media	3,951
Virtual Currency	5,109

These descriptors relate to the medium or tool used to facilitate the crime and are used by the IC3 for tracking purposes only. They are available as descriptors only after another crime type has been selected. Please see Appendix B for more information regarding IC3 data.

* Regarding BEC/EAC victim counts: A whole number is given to depict the overall victim count and is then broken out into separate counts to identify when an Over 60 victim may be reporting victimization on behalf of a business or personally.

2021 CRIME TYPES *Continued*

OVER 60 VICTIM LOSS

Crime Type	Loss	Crime Type	Loss
Confidence Fraud/Romance	$432,081,901	Spoofing	$19,473,060
BEC/EAC *	$355,805,098	Employment	$9,610,615
(Reporting a potential business loss)	*$277,547,598*	Overpayment	$9,214,129
(Reporting a personal loss)	*$78,257,500*	Phishing	$9,166,217
Investment	$239,474,635	Corporate Data Breach	$7,095,746
Tech Support	$237,931,278	Civil Matter	$6,530,661
Personal Data Breach	$103,688,489	IPR/Copyright and Counterfeit	$4,954,221
Real Estate/Rental	$102,071,631	Computer Intrusion	$4,575,956
Government Impersonation	$69,186,858	Health Care Related	$1,233,632
Identity Theft	$59,022,153	Malware/Scareware/Virus	$1,177,864
Lottery/Sweepstakes/Inheritance	$53,557,330	Ransomware **	$424,852
Non-Payment/Non-Delivery	$52,023,580	Terrorism/Threats of Violence	$361,549
Credit Card Fraud	$39,019,072	Re-shipping	$360,455
Advanced Fee	$36,464,491	Denial of Service/TDos	$119,840
Other	$22,196,542	Gambling	$20,116
Extortion	$19,533,187	Crimes Against Children	$550

Descriptors*

Social Media	$58,940,655	These descriptors relate to the medium or tool used to facilitate the crime and are used by the IC3 for tracking purposes only. They are available only after another crime type has been selected. Please see Appendix B for more information regarding IC3 data.
Virtual Currency	$241,143,166	

* Regarding BEC/EAC victim losses: A whole number is given to depict the overall victim loss and is then broken out into separate counts to identify when an Over 60 victim may be reporting victimization on behalf of a business or personally.

** Regarding ransomware adjusted losses, this number does not include estimates of lost business, time, wages, files, equipment, or any third-party remediation services acquired by a victim. In some cases, victims do not report any loss amount to the FBI, thereby creating an artificially low overall ransomware loss rate. Lastly, the number only represents what victims report to the FBI via the IC3 and does not account for victims directly reporting to FBI field offices/agents.

LAST 3 YEARS COMPARISON

OVER 60 VICTIM COUNT			
Crime Type	2021	2020	2019
Advanced Fee	3,029	3,008	4,038
BEC/EAC	3,755	3,530	3,792
(Reporting a potential business loss)	*2,143*		
(Reporting a personal loss)	*1,612*		
Civil Matter	184	170	150
Computer Intrusion	176	--	--
Confidence Fraud/Romance	7,658	6,817	5,871
Corporate Data Breach	158	285	133
Credit Card Fraud	3,164	3,195	2,716
Crimes Against Children	42	58	31
Denial of Service/TDos	61	52	40
Employment	1,408	1,867	1,670
Extortion	5,987	23,100	12,242
Gambling	19	16	28
Government Impersonation	3,319	4,159	4,038
Health Care Related	74	243	72
IPR/Copyright and Counterfeit	686	552	287
Identity Theft	8,902	7,581	2,744
Investment	2104	1,062	612
Lottery/Sweepstakes/Inheritance	2,607	3,774	2,764
Malware/Scareware/Virus	134	287	622
Non-payment/Non-Delivery	13,220	14,534	7,731
Other	2,933	3,259	3,340
Overpayment	1,448	2,196	2,913
Personal Data Breach	6,189	6,121	6,725
Phishing/Vishing/Smishing/Pharming	5,831	7,353	5,383
Ransomware	365	365	337
Re-shipping	76	114	141
Real Estate/Rental	1,764	1,882	1,754
Spoofing	3,936	7,279	6,260
Tech Support	13,900	9,429	6,781
Terrorism/Threats of Violence	719	1,699	1,941

LAST 3 YEARS COMPARISON, *Continued*

OVER 60 VICTIM LOSS			
Crime Type	2021	2020	2019
Advanced Fee	$36,464,491	$33,184,114	$49,079,064
BEC/EAC	$355,805,098	$168,793,903	$209,597,559
(Reporting a potential business loss)	*$277,547,598*		
(Reporting a personal loss)	*$78,257,500*		
Civil Matter	$6,530,661	$1,866,788	$3,198,653
Computer Intrusion	$4,575,956	--	--
Confidence Fraud/Romance	$432,081,901	$281,134,006	$233,839,738
Corporate Data Breach	$7,095,746	$10,148,817	$3,616,996
Credit Card Fraud	$39,019,072	$20,780,800	$19,449,560
Crimes Against Children	$550	$411,349	$22,149
Denial of Service/TDos	$119,840	$180,447	$205
Employment	$9,610,615	$16,092,611	$8,920,628
Extortion	$19,533,187	$18,503,168	$30,564,053
Gambling	$20,116	$17,450	$85,457
Government Impersonation	$69,186,858	$45,909,970	$47,982,075
Health Care Related	$1,233,632	$2,652,390	$38,900
IPR/Copyright and Counterfeit	$4,954,221	$479,375	$1,146,051
Identity Theft	$59,022,153	$39,006,465	$25,739,680
Investment	$239,474,635	$98,040,940	$79,100,961
Lottery/Sweepstakes/Inheritance	$53,557,330	$38,804,343	$35,744,579
Malware/Scareware/Virus	$1,177,864	$671,667	$277,806
Non-Payment/Non-Delivery	$52,023,580	$40,377,167	$50,538,448
Other	$22,196,542	$49,689,594	$39,149,129
Overpayment	$9,214,129	$11,212,323	$13,397,602
Personal Data Breach	$103,688,489	$24,641,539	$28,470,827
Phishing/Vishing/Smishing/Pharming	$9,166,217	$18,829,999	$12,919,831
Ransomware	$424,852	$5,332,312	$723,642
Re-shipping	$360,455	$588,553	$595,352
Real Estate/Rental	$102,071,631	$50,098,565	$47,579,324
Spoofing	$19,473,060	$40,886,040	$42,218,197
Tech Support	$237,931,278	$116,415,126	$38,410,435
Terrorism/Threats of Violence	$361,549	$1,112,825	$2,363,624

2021 OVERALL STATE STATISTICS

OVER 60 VICTIMS BY STATE*

Rank	State	Victims	Rank	State	Victims
1	California	12,951	30	Utah	917
2	Florida	9,645	31	Louisiana	860
3	Texas	6,798	32	New Mexico	785
4	New York	6,223	33	Arkansas	721
5	Ohio	4,166	34	Kansas	666
6	Nevada	3,712	35	Iowa	548
7	Pennsylvania	3,627	36	Alaska	546
8	Colorado	3,569	37	Idaho	508
9	Illinois	3,499	38	Maine	475
10	Arizona	3,175	39	New Hampshire	471
11	Massachusetts	3,129	40	Hawaii	470
12	Virginia	2,956	41	Mississippi	469
13	Washington	2,853	42	Montana	406
14	New Jersey	2,665	43	Delaware	394
15	North Carolina	2,594	44	West Virginia	380
16	Michigan	2,410	45	Nebraska	353
17	Georgia	2,189	46	District of Columbia	349
18	Maryland	2,096	47	Rhode Island	260
19	Oregon	1,773	48	Vermont	244
20	Tennessee	1,686	49	Puerto Rico	229
21	Missouri	1,566	50	South Dakota	217
22	Indiana	1,536	51	Wyoming	208
23	Minnesota	1,458	52	North Dakota	151
24	South Carolina	1,447	53	Virgin Islands, U.S.	29
25	Wisconsin	1,315	54	United States Minor Outlying Islands	18
26	Alabama	1,184	55	Guam	16
27	Connecticut	1,061	56	American Samoa	7
28	Kentucky	953	57	Northern Mariana Islands	4
29	Oklahoma	923			

*Note: This information is based on the total number of complaints from each state, American Territory, and the District of Columbia when the complainant provided state information. Please see Appendix B for more information regarding IC3 data.

2021 OVERALL STATE STATISTICS, *Continued*

OVER 60 VICTIM LOSSES BY STATE*

Rank	State	Loss	Rank	State	Loss
1	California	$427,263,948	30	Kentucky	$12,767,463
2	Florida	$224,205,716	31	Hawaii	$11,693,691
3	New York	$188,052,904	32	Iowa	$10,312,324
4	Texas	$159,614,547	33	Oklahoma	$10,003,612
5	New Jersey	$87,546,156	34	Kansas	$8,488,260
6	Pennsylvania	$77,027,656	35	Mississippi	$7,907,893
7	Virginia	$60,833,227	36	District of Columbia	$7,704,848
8	Arizona	$54,441,279	37	Delaware	$7,079,040
9	Nevada	$53,320,488	38	Arkansas	$6,597,200
10	Massachusetts	$51,358,532	39	New Mexico	$6,316,971
11	Illinois	$49,956,292	40	Rhode Island	$5,671,235
12	Washington	$49,354,985	41	Vermont	$5,664,535
13	Ohio	$45,244,016	42	Montana	$5,405,855
14	North Carolina	$40,553,429	43	South Dakota	$5,372,535
15	Maryland	$37,817,082	44	Alaska	$5,166,344
16	Colorado	$33,942,278	45	Wyoming	$5,004,298
17	Georgia	$33,548,909	46	Idaho	$4,165,655
18	Tennessee	$32,520,912	47	Puerto Rico	$3,786,418
19	Michigan	$31,852,632	48	North Dakota	$3,099,693
20	Wisconsin	$22,634,486	49	West Virginia	$3,050,335
21	Oregon	$20,862,388	50	New Hampshire	$2,960,234
22	Minnesota	$20,513,323	51	Maine	$2,561,129
23	Louisiana	$19,887,674	52	Nebraska	$2,499,945
24	Utah	$19,868,020	53	Guam	$1,583,587
25	Indiana	$18,637,905	54	Virgin Islands, U.S.	$314,574
26	South Carolina	$18,331,406	55	American Samoa	$148,600
27	Alabama	$17,627,526	56	United States Minor Outlying Islands	$38,063
28	Missouri	$16,290,136	57	Northern Mariana Islands	$3,000
29	Connecticut	$15,630,551			

*Note: This information is based on the total number of complaints from each state, American Territory, and the District of Columbia when the complainant provided state information. Please see Appendix B for more information regarding IC3 data.

COMMON FRAUDS AFFECTING OVER 60 VICTIMS

Tech Support Fraud

Tech Support Fraud is the most reported Fraud among Over 60 Victims. In 2021, the IC3 received 13,900 complaints related to Tech Support Fraud from elderly victims who experienced almost $238 million in losses. Elderly victims account for 58 percent of the total reports of tech support fraud to the IC3 and 68 percent of the total losses.

Tech support scammers continue to impersonate well-known tech companies, offering to fix non-existent technology issues or renewing fraudulent software or security subscriptions. However, in 2021, the IC3 observed an increase in complaints reporting the impersonation of customer support, which has taken on a variety of forms, such as financial and banking institutions, utility companies, or virtual currency exchanges.

Many victims report being directed to make wire transfers to overseas accounts, purchase large amounts of prepaid cards, or mail large amounts of cash via overnight or express services.

For additional information on tech support scams, refer to IC3 Tech Support Fraud PSA, I-032818-PSA[5]

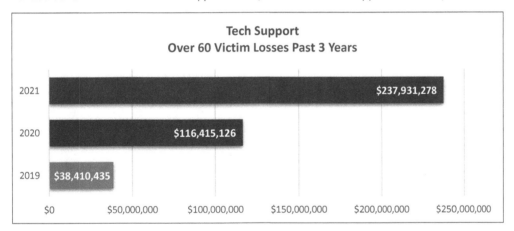

Confidence Fraud/Romance Scams

Confidence Fraud/Romance scams encompass those designed to pull on a victim's "heartstrings". In 2021, the IC3 received reports from 7,658 victims who experienced over $432 million in losses to Confidence Fraud/Romance scams. This type of fraud accounts for the highest losses reported by Over 60 victims.

---

[5] IC3 Tech Support Fraud PSA, I-032818-PSA, https://www.ic3.gov/Media/Y2018/PSA180328

Romance scams occur when a criminal adopts a fake online identity to gain a victim's affection and confidence. The scammer uses the illusion of a romantic or close relationship to manipulate and/or steal from the victim. The criminals who carry out Romance scams are experts at what they do and will seem genuine, caring, and believable. The scammer's intention is to quickly establish a relationship, endear himself to the victim, gain trust, and eventually ask for money. Scam artists often say they are in the military, or a trades-based industry engaged in projects outside the U.S. That makes it easier to avoid meeting in person—and more plausible when they request money be sent overseas for a medical emergency or unexpected legal fee.

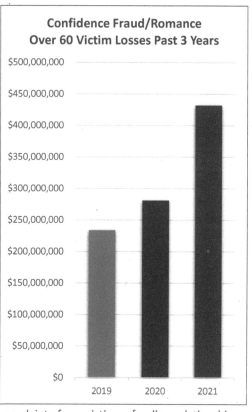

Grandparent Scams also fall into this category, where criminals impersonate a panicked loved one, usually a grandchild, nephew, or niece of an elderly person. The loved one claims to be in trouble and needs money immediately. In 2021, over 450 Over 60 victims reported Grandparent scams, with approximate losses of $6.5 million.

Con artists are present on most dating and social media sites. In 2021, the IC3 received thousands of complaints from victims of online relationships resulting in sextortion or investment scams.

- Sextortion occurs when someone threatens to distribute your private and sensitive material if their demands are not met. In 2021, the IC3 received over 2,100 sextortion-related complaints from victims over 60, with losses over $3 million. Please see the September 2021 IC3 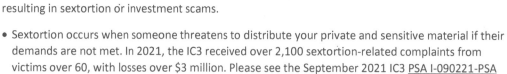 PSA I-090221-PSA on Sextortion for more information.[6]
- Many victims of Confidence Fraud/Romance scams also report being pressured into investment opportunities, especially utilizing cryptocurrency, called "pig butchering". This scam is most often reported among younger populations. However, in 2021, 791 over 60 victims lost almost $123 million from this scam. Additional information on "pig butchering" can be found in the September 2021 IC3 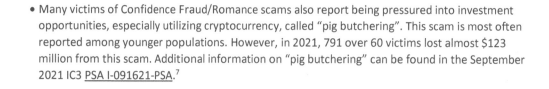 PSA I-091621-PSA.[7]

---

[6] FBI Warns about an Increase in Sextortion Complaints. https://www.ic3.gov/Media/Y2021/PSA210902

[7] Scammers Defraud Victims of Millions of Dollars in New Trend in Romance Scams. https://www.ic3.gov/Media/Y2021/PSA210916

Lottery/Sweepstakes/Inheritance

In 2021, the IC3 received over 2,600 reports of elderly victims in Lottery/Sweepstakes/Inheritance scams. Victims lost over $53 million to these types of fraud.

The initial contact in a lottery/sweepstakes scam is often a call, an email, a social media notification, or a piece of mail offering congratulations for winning a big contest, lottery, or sweepstakes the victim did not enter. To claim their prize, the victim is required to pay upfront fees and taxes. The subjects will continue to call victims for months or even years, promising the big prize is only one more payment away.

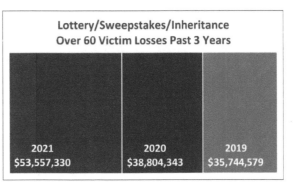

Inheritance scams function very similarly as the victim is informed an unknown, distant relative has left a large inheritance to the victim. The victim is required to pay taxes and fees to receive the inheritance money.

Government Impersonation

While government impersonation is not reported as often, millions of dollars are still lost by the elderly to criminals impersonating government officials. The criminals often extort victims with threats of physical or financial harm to obtain personally identifiable information.

In 2021, victims over the age of 60 reported this type of fraud over 3,300 times, with losses of $69 million. The subjects generally demand prepaid cards, wire transfers, or cash to be mailed or sent overnight.

Investment

Investment fraud involves the illegal sale or purported sale of financial instruments. The typical investment fraud schemes are characterized by offers of low or no-risk investments, guaranteed returns, overly consistent returns, complex strategies, or unregistered securities. Examples of investment fraud include advance fee fraud, Ponzi schemes, pyramid schemes, and market manipulation fraud.

These schemes often seek to victimize targeted individuals, such as groups with common interests, age, religion, or ethnicity, to build trust to effectively operate the investment fraud against them. The scammers' ability to foster trust makes these schemes so successful. Investors should use scrutiny and gather as much information as possible before considering any new investment opportunities.

More than 2,100 Over 60 victims reported Investment scams in 2021, with losses over $239 million.

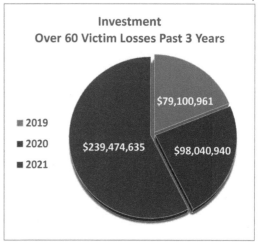

Investment
Over 60 Victim Losses Past 3 Years

- 2019
- 2020
- 2021

$79,100,961
$239,474,635
$98,040,940

Cryptocurrency

In 2021, the IC3 received more than 5,100 complaints from over 60 victims involving the use of some type of   cryptocurrency, such as Bitcoin, Ethereum, Litecoin, or Ripple. Losses of these victims totaled over $241 million.

Cryptocurrency is becoming the preferred payment method for all types of scams – SIM Swaps, tech support fraud, employment schemes, romance scams, even some auction fraud. It is extremely pervasive in investment scams, where losses can reach into the hundreds of thousands of dollars per victim.

Cryptocurrency ATMs: Automated Teller Machines (ATMs) used to purchase cryptocurrency are popping up everywhere. Regulations on the machines are lax and purchases are almost instantaneous and irreversible, making this payment method lucrative to criminals. The most common scams reported were Confidence Fraud/Romance, Investment, Employment, and Government Impersonation. Read more about crypto ATM scams in IC3 PSA I-110421-PSA.[8]

---

[8] The FBI Warns of Fraudulent Schemes Leveraging Cryptocurrency ATMs and QR Codes to Facilitate Payment
https://www.ic3.gov/Media/Y2021/PSA211104

APPENDIX A: DEFINITIONS

Advanced Fee: An individual pays money to someone in anticipation of receiving something of greater value in return, but instead, receives significantly less than expected or nothing.

Business Email Compromise/Email Account Compromise: BEC is a scam targeting businesses (not individuals) working with foreign suppliers and/or businesses regularly performing wire transfer payments. EAC is a similar scam which targets individuals. These sophisticated scams are carried out by fraudsters compromising email accounts through social engineering or computer intrusion techniques to conduct unauthorized transfer of funds.

Civil Matter: Civil litigation generally includes all disputes formally submitted to a court, about any subject in which one party is claimed to have committed a wrong but not a crime. In general, this is the legal process most people think of when the word "lawsuit" is used.

Computer Intrusion: Unauthorized access or exceeding authorized access into a protected computer system. A protected computer system is one owned or used by the US Government, a financial institution, or any business. This typically excludes personally owned systems and devices.

Confidence/Romance Fraud: An individual believes they are in a relationship (family, friendly, or romantic) and are tricked into sending money, personal and financial information, or items of value to the perpetrator or to launder money or items to assist the perpetrator. This includes the Grandparent's Scheme and any scheme in which the perpetrator preys on the complainant's "heartstrings".

Corporate Data Breach: A data breach within a corporation or business where sensitive, protected, or confidential data is copied, transmitted, viewed, stolen, or used by an individual unauthorized to do so.

Credit Card Fraud: Credit card fraud is a wide-ranging term for theft and fraud committed using a credit card or any similar payment mechanism (ACH. EFT, recurring charge, etc.) as a fraudulent source of funds in a transaction.

Crimes Against Children: Anything related to the exploitation of children, including child abuse.

Denial of Service/TDoS: A Denial of Service (DoS) attack floods a network/system, or a Telephony Denial of Service (TDoS) floods a voice service with multiple requests, slowing down or interrupting service.

Employment: An individual believes they are legitimately employed and loses money, or launders money/items during the course of their employment.

Extortion: Unlawful extraction of money or property through intimidation or undue exercise of authority. It may include threats of physical harm, criminal prosecution, or public exposure.

Gambling: Online gambling, also known as Internet gambling and iGambling, is a general term for gambling using the Internet.

Government Impersonation: A government official is impersonated in an attempt to collect money.

Health Care Related: A scheme attempting to defraud private or government health care programs which usually involving health care providers, companies, or individuals. Schemes may include offers for fake insurance cards, health insurance marketplace assistance, stolen health information, or various other scams and/or any scheme involving medications, supplements, weight loss products, or diversion/pill mill practices. These scams are often initiated through spam email, Internet advertisements, links in forums/social media, and fraudulent websites.

IPR/Copyright and Counterfeit: The illegal theft and use of others' ideas, inventions, and creative expressions – what's called intellectual property – everything from trade secrets and proprietary products and parts to movies, music, and software.

Identity Theft: Someone steals and uses personal identifying information, like a name or Social Security number, without permission to commit fraud or other crimes and/or (Account Takeover) a fraudster obtains account information to perpetrate fraud on existing accounts.

Investment: Deceptive practice that induces investors to make purchases based on false information. These scams usually offer the victims large returns with minimal risk. (Retirement, 401K, Ponzi, Pyramid, etc.).

Lottery/Sweepstakes/Inheritance: An Individual is contacted about winning a lottery or sweepstakes they never entered, or to collect on an inheritance from an unknown relative.

Malware/Scareware/Virus: Software or code intended to damage, disable, or capable of copying itself onto a computer and/or computer systems to have a detrimental effect or destroy data.

Non-Payment/Non-Delivery: Goods or services are shipped, and payment is never rendered (non-payment). Payment is sent, and goods or services are never received, or are of lesser quality (non-delivery).

Overpayment: An individual is sent a payment/commission and is instructed to keep a portion of the payment and send the remainder to another individual or business.

Personal Data Breach: A leak/spill of personal data which is released from a secure location to an untrusted environment. Also, a security incident in which an individual's sensitive, protected, or confidential data is copied, transmitted, viewed, stolen, or used by an unauthorized individual.

Phishing/Vishing/Smishing/Pharming: The use of unsolicited email, text messages, and telephone calls purportedly from a legitimate company requesting personal, financial, and/or login credentials.

Ransomware: A type of malicious software designed to block access to a computer system until money is paid.

Re-shipping: Individuals receive packages at their residence and subsequently repackage the merchandise for shipment, usually abroad.

Real Estate/Rental: Loss of funds from a real estate investment or fraud involving rental or timeshare property.

Spoofing: Contact information (phone number, email, and website) is deliberately falsified to mislead and appear to be from a legitimate source. For example, spoofed phone numbers making mass robo-calls; spoofed emails sending mass spam; forged websites used to mislead and gather personal information. Often used in connection with other crime types.

Social Media: A complaint alleging the use of social networking or social media (Facebook, Twitter, Instagram, chat rooms, etc.) as a vector for fraud. Social Media does not include dating sites.

Tech Support: Subject posing as technical or customer support/service.

Terrorism/Threats of Violence: Terrorism is violent acts intended to create fear that are perpetrated for a religious, political, or ideological goal and deliberately target or disregard the safety of non-combatants. Threats of Violence refers to an expression of an intention to inflict pain, injury, or punishment, which does not refer to the requirement of payment.

Virtual Currency: A complaint mentioning a form of virtual cryptocurrency, such as Bitcoin, Litecoin, or Potcoin.

APPENDIX B: ADDITIONAL INFORMATION ABOUT IC3 DATA

- Each complaint is reviewed by an IC3 analyst. The analyst categorizes the complaint according to the crime type(s) that are appropriate. Additionally, the analyst will adjust the loss amount if the complaint data does not support the loss amount reported.

- One complaint may have multiple crime types.

- Some complainants may have filed more than once, creating a possible duplicate complaint.

- All location-based reports are generated from information entered when known/provided by the complainant.

- Losses reported in foreign currencies are converted to U.S. dollars when possible.

- Complaint counts represent the number of individual complaints received from each state and do not represent the number of individuals filing a complaint.

- Victim is identified as the individual filing a complaint.

- Subject is identified as the individual perpetrating the scam as reported by the victim.

- "Count by Subject per state" is the number of subjects per state, as reported by victims.

- "Subject earnings per Destination State" is the amount swindled by the subject, as reported by the victim, per state.

- Victims are not required to provide an age range. This field is completely voluntary. Therefore, information in this report only reflects complaints where a victim provided an age range of "Over 60"

APPENDIX C: 2021 – STATE VICTIMS PER CAPITA

OVER 60 VICTIMS BY STATE *(per 100,000 People)*

Rank	State	Victims	Rank	State	Victims
1	Nevada	118.1	27	Illinois	27.6
2	Alaska	74.5	28	Utah	27.5
3	Colorado	61.4	29	Idaho	26.7
4	District of Columbia	52.1	30	Minnesota	25.5
5	Massachusetts	44.8	31	Missouri	25.4
6	Florida	44.3	32	North Carolina	24.6
7	Arizona	43.6	33	South Dakota	24.2
8	Oregon	41.8	34	Tennessee	24.2
9	Delaware	39.3	35	Michigan	24.0
10	Vermont	37.8	36	Arkansas	23.8
11	New Mexico	37.1	37	Rhode Island	23.7
12	Washington	36.9	38	Alabama	23.5
13	Montana	36.8	39	Oklahoma	23.2
14	Wyoming	35.9	40	Texas	23.0
15	Ohio	35.4	41	Kansas	22.7
16	Maine	34.6	42	Indiana	22.6
17	Virginia	34.2	43	Wisconsin	22.3
18	Maryland	34.0	44	West Virginia	21.3
19	New Hampshire	33.9	45	Kentucky	21.1
20	California	33.0	46	Georgia	20.3
21	Hawaii	32.6	47	North Dakota	19.5
22	New York	31.4	48	Louisiana	18.6
23	Connecticut	29.4	49	Nebraska	18.0
24	New Jersey	28.8	50	Iowa	17.2
25	Pennsylvania	28.0	51	Mississippi	15.9
26	South Carolina	27.9	52	Puerto Rico	7.0

*Note: This information is based on the total number of complaints from each state, Puerto Rico, and the District of Columbia when the complainant provided state information. Please see Appendix B for more information regarding IC3 data. Populations based on data available from the U.S. Census Bureau.

Per 100,000 people, based upon U.S. Census Bureau population estimates when available. https://www.census.gov

OVER 60 VICTIM LOSSES BY STATE *(per 100,000 People)*

Rank	State	Loss	Rank	State	Loss
1	Nevada	$1,695,949	27	Louisiana	$430,092
2	District of Columbia	$1,149,892	28	North Dakota	$399,987
3	California	$1,088,908	29	Illinois	$394,242
4	Florida	$1,029,358	30	North Carolina	$384,350
5	New York	$948,043	31	Ohio	$384,074
6	New Jersey	$944,695	32	Wisconsin	$383,902
7	Vermont	$877,447	33	Minnesota	$359,417
8	Wyoming	$864,594	34	South Carolina	$353,158
9	Hawaii	$811,187	35	Alabama	$349,761
10	Arizona	$748,198	36	Iowa	$322,959
11	Massachusetts	$735,298	37	Michigan	$316,916
12	Delaware	$705,517	38	Georgia	$310,651
13	Alaska	$705,136	39	New Mexico	$298,551
14	Virginia	$703,903	40	Kansas	$289,249
15	Washington	$637,769	41	Kentucky	$283,130
16	Maryland	$613,403	42	Indiana	$273,846
17	South Dakota	$600,031	43	Mississippi	$268,067
18	Utah	$595,212	44	Missouri	$264,099
19	Pennsylvania	$594,163	45	Oklahoma	$250,928
20	Colorado	$583,996	46	Idaho	$219,139
21	Texas	$540,554	47	Arkansas	$218,025
22	Rhode Island	$517,633	48	New Hampshire	$213,121
23	Oregon	$491,324	49	Maine	$186,638
24	Montana	$489,541	50	West Virginia	$171,083
25	Tennessee	$466,235	51	Nebraska	$127,308
26	Connecticut	$433,508	52	Puerto Rico	$116,020

*Note: This information is based on the total number of complaints from each state, Puerto Rico, and the District of Columbia when the complainant provided state information. Please see Appendix B for more information regarding IC3 data. Populations based on data available from the U.S. Census Bureau.

Per 100,000 people, based upon U.S. Census Bureau population estimates when available. https://www.census.gov

2021 – STATES BY NUMBER OF OVER 60 VICTIMS PER CAPITA[9]

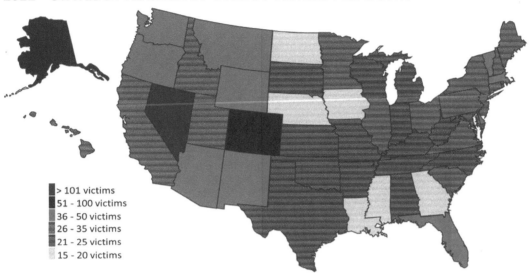

> 101 victims
51 - 100 victims
36 - 50 victims
26 - 35 victims
21 - 25 victims
15 - 20 victims

2021 – STATES BY LOSSES OF OVER 60 VICTIMS PER CAPITA

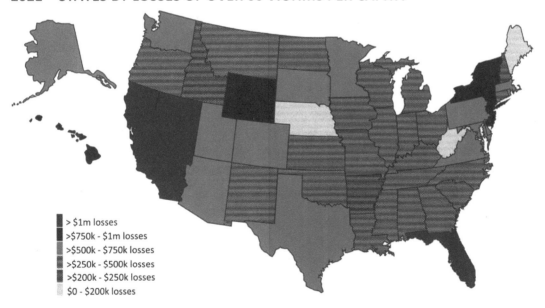

> $1m losses
>$750k - $1m losses
>$500k - $750k losses
>$250k - $500k losses
>$200k - $250k losses
$0 - $200k losses

[9]Per 100,000 people, based upon July 2021 U.S. Census Bureau population estimates. https://www.census.gov

FEDERAL BUREAU of INVESTIGATION

Internet Crime Report

2O21

INTERNET CRIME COMPLAINT CENTER

FEDERAL BUREAU OF INVESTIGATION

THE IC3

Today's FBI is an intelligence-driven and threat focused national security organization with both intelligence and law enforcement responsibilities. We are focused on protecting the American people from terrorism, espionage, cyber attacks and major criminal threats, and on supporting our many partners with information, services, support, training, and leadership. The IC3 serves those needs as a mechanism to gather intelligence on cyber and internet crime so we can stay ahead of the threat.

The IC3 was established in May 2000 to receive complaints of internet related crime and has received more than 6.5 million complaints since its inception. Its mission is to provide the public with a reliable and convenient reporting mechanism to submit information to the FBI concerning suspected cyber enabled criminal activity, and to develop effective alliances with law enforcement and industry partners to help those who report. Information is analyzed and disseminated for investigative and intelligence purposes for law enforcement and for public awareness.

To promote public awareness, the IC3 aggregates the submitted data and produces an annual report to educate on the trends impacting the public. The quality of the data is directly attributable to the information ingested via the public interface, www.ic3.gov, and the data categorized based on the information provided in the individual complaints. The IC3 staff analyzes the data to identify trends in cyber crimes and how those trends may impact the public in the coming year.

THE IC3 ROLE IN COMBATING CYBER CRIME[1]

What we do

 Partner with Private Sector and with Local, State, Federal, and International Agencies

 Host a Portal where Victims Report Internet Crime at www.ic3.gov

 Provide a Central Hub to Alert the Public

 Perform Analysis, Complaint Referrals, and Aid the Freezing of Assets

 Host a Remote Access Database for all Law Enforcement via the FBI's LEEP website

---

[1] Accessibility description: Image lists IC3's primary functions including partnering with private sector and with local, state, federal, and international agencies: hosting a victim reporting portal at www.ic3.gov; providing a central hub to alert the public to threats; Perform Analysis, Complaint Referrals, and Asset Recovery; and hosting a remote access database for all law enforcement via the FBI's LEEP website.

IC3 CORE FUNCTIONS²

COLLECTION	ANALYSIS	PUBLIC AWARENESS	REFERRALS
The IC3 is the central point for Internet crime victims to report and alert the appropriate agencies to suspected criminal Internet activity. Victims are encouraged and often directed by law enforcement to file a complaint online at www.ic3.gov. Complainants are asked to document accurate and complete information related to Internet crime, as well as any other relevant information necessary to support the complaint.	The IC3 reviews and analyzes data submitted through its website to identify emerging threats and new trends. In addition, the IC3 quickly alerts financial Institutions to fraudulent transactions which enables the freezing of victim funds.	Public service announcements, industry alerts, and other publications outlining specific scams are posted to the www.ic3.gov website. As more people become aware of Internet crimes and the methods used to carry them out, potential victims are equipped with a broader understanding of the dangers associated with Internet activity and are in a better position to avoid falling prey to schemes online.	The IC3 aggregates related complaints to build referrals, which are forwarded to local, state, federal, and international law enforcement agencies for potential investigation. If law enforcement investigates and determines a crime has been committed, legal action may be brought against the perpetrator.

---

² Accessibility description: Image contains icons with the core functions. Core functions - Collection, Analysis, Public Awareness, and Referrals - are listed in individual blocks as components of an ongoing process.

IC3 COMPLAINT STATISTICS

LAST 5 YEARS

Over the last five years, the IC3 has received an average of 552,000 complaints per year. These complaints address a wide array of Internet scams affecting victims across the globe.[3]

Complaints and Losses over the Last Five Years

2017 — 301,580 — $1.4 Billion
2018 — 351,937 — $2.7 Billion
2019 — 467,361 — $3.5 Billion
2020 — 791,790 — $4.2 Billion
2021 — 847,376 — $6.9 Billion

2.76 Million Total Complaints

$18.7 Billion Total Losses

■ Complaints ■ Losses

---

[3] Accessibility description: Chart includes yearly and aggregate data for complaints and losses over the years 2017 to 2021. Over that time, IC3 received a total of 2,760,044 complaints, reporting a loss of $18.7 billion.

TOP 5 CRIME TYPE COMPARSON[4]

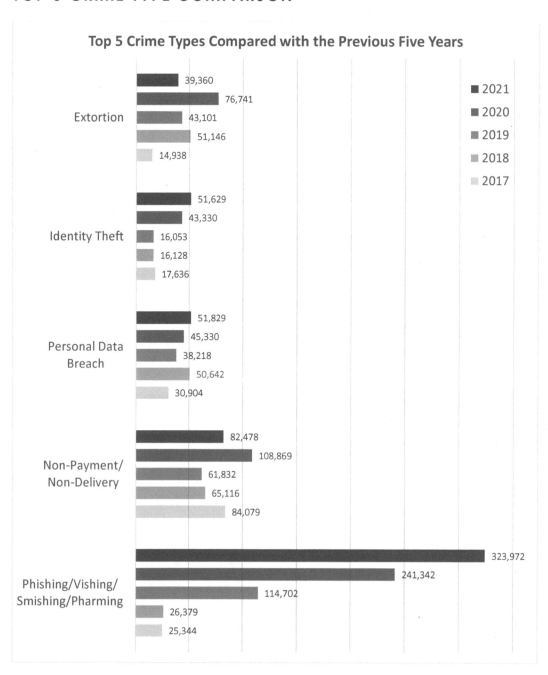

Top 5 Crime Types Compared with the Previous Five Years

- Extortion
  - 39,360
  - 76,741
  - 43,101
  - 51,146
  - 14,938
- Identity Theft
  - 51,629
  - 43,330
  - 16,053
  - 16,128
  - 17,636
- Personal Data Breach
  - 51,829
  - 45,330
  - 38,218
  - 50,642
  - 30,904
- Non-Payment/Non-Delivery
  - 82,478
  - 108,869
  - 61,832
  - 65,116
  - 84,079
- Phishing/Vishing/Smishing/Pharming
  - 323,972
  - 241,342
  - 114,702
  - 26,379
  - 25,344

Legend:
- 2021
- 2020
- 2019
- 2018
- 2017

---

[4] Accessibility description: Chart includes a victim loss comparison for the top five reported crime types for the years of 2017 to 2021.

THREAT OVERVIEWS FOR 2021

BUSINESS EMAIL COMPROMISE (BEC)

In 2021, the IC3 received 19,954 Business Email Compromise (BEC)/ Email Account Compromise (EAC) complaints with adjusted losses at nearly $2.4 billion. BEC/EAC is a sophisticated scam targeting both businesses and individuals performing transfers of funds. The scam is frequently carried out when a subject compromises legitimate business email accounts through social engineering or computer intrusion techniques to conduct unauthorized transfers of funds.

As fraudsters have become more sophisticated and preventative measures have been put in place, the BEC/EAC scheme has continually evolved in kind. The scheme has evolved from simple hacking or spoofing of business and personal email accounts and a request to send wire payments to fraudulent bank accounts. These schemes historically involved compromised vendor emails, requests for W-2 information, targeting of the real estate sector, and fraudulent requests for large amounts of gift cards. Now, fraudsters are using virtual meeting platforms to hack emails and spoof business leaders' credentials to initiate the fraudulent wire transfers. These fraudulent wire transfers are often immediately transferred to cryptocurrency wallets and quickly dispersed, making recovery efforts more difficult.

The COVID-19 pandemic and the restrictions on in-person meetings led to increases in telework or virtual communication practices. These work and communication practices continued into 2021, and the IC3 has observed an emergence of newer BEC/EAC schemes that exploit this reliance on virtual meetings to instruct victims to send fraudulent wire transfers. They do so by compromising an employer or financial director's email, such as a CEO or CFO, which would then be used to request employees to participate in virtual meeting platforms. In those meetings, the fraudster would insert a still picture of the CEO with no audio, or a "deep fake" audio through which fraudsters, acting as business executives, would then claim their audio/video was not working properly. The fraudsters would then use the virtual meeting platforms to directly instruct employees to initiate wire transfers or use the executives' compromised email to provide wiring instructions.

IC3 RECOVERY ASSET TEAM

The Internet Crime Complaint Center's Recovery Asset Team (RAT) was established in February 2018 to streamline communication with financial institutions and assist FBI field offices with the freezing of funds for victims who made transfers to domestic accounts under fraudulent pretenses.

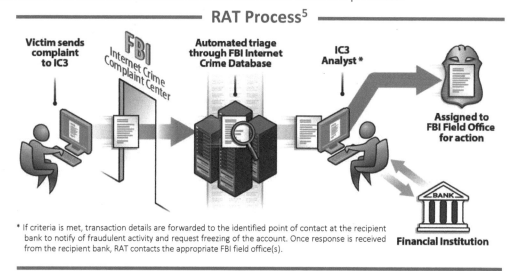

RAT Process[5]

* If criteria is met, transaction details are forwarded to the identified point of contact at the recipient bank to notify of fraudulent activity and request freezing of the account. Once response is received from the recipient bank, RAT contacts the appropriate FBI field office(s).

The RAT functions as a liaison between law enforcement and financial institutions supporting statistical and investigative analysis.

Goals of RAT-Financial Institution Partnership

- Assist in the identification of potentially fraudulent accounts across the sector.

- Remain at the forefront of emerging trends among financial fraud schemes.

- Foster a symbiotic relationship in which information is appropriately shared.

Guidance for BEC Victims

- Contact the originating financial institution as soon as fraud is recognized to request a recall or reversal and a Hold Harmless Letter or Letter of Indemnity.

- File a detailed complaint with www.ic3.gov. It is vital the complaint contain all required data in provided fields, including banking information.

- Visit www.ic3.gov for updated PSAs regarding BEC trends as well as other fraud schemes targeting specific populations, like trends targeting real estate, pre-paid cards, and W-2s, for example.

- Never make any payment changes without verifying the change with the intended recipient; verify email addresses are accurate when checking email on a cell phone or other mobile device

---

[5] Accessibility description: Image shows the different stages of a complaint in the RAT process.

RAT SUCCESSES[6]

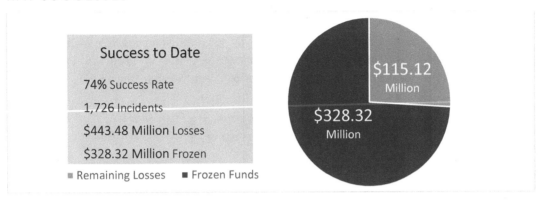

Success to Date

74% Success Rate

1,726 Incidents

$443.48 Million Losses

$328.32 Million Frozen

■ Remaining Losses ■ Frozen Funds

$115.12 Million

$328.32 Million

The IC3 RAT has proven to be a valuable resource for field offices and victims. The following are three examples of the RAT's successful contributions to investigative and recovery efforts:

Philadelphia

In December 2021, the IC3 received a complaint filed by a victim roadway commission regarding a wire transfer of more than $1.5 million to a fraudulent U.S. domestic bank account. The IC3 RAT quickly notified the recipient financial institution of the fraudulent account by initiating the financial fraud kill chain. Collaboration between the IC3 RAT, the recipient financial institution, and the Philadelphia Field office resulted in learning the subject quickly depleted the wired funds from the original account into two separate accounts held at the same institution. The financial institution was able to quickly identify the second-hop accounts and freeze the funds, making a full recovery possible.

Memphis

In June 2021, the IC3 received a complaint filed by a victim law office regarding a wire transfer of more than $198k to a fraudulent U.S. domestic account. IC3 RAT collaboration with the Memphis Field Office and the recipient financial institution resulted in learning the domestic account was a correspondent account for a fraudulent account in Nigeria. IC3 RAT immediately initiated the international FFKC to FinCEN and LEGAT Abuja, which resulted in freezing the full wired amount. The victim forwarded a note of gratitude for all the work put into their case.

Albany

In October 2021, the IC3 received a complaint filed by a victim of a tech support scam where an unauthorized wire transfer of $53k was sent from their account to a U.S. domestic custodial account held by a cryptocurrency exchange (CE). The IC3 RAT immediately notified the recipient financial institution and collaborated with the CE that held the account. With the knowledge that funds sent to cryptocurrency accounts will be depleted to crypto faster than the usual wire transfer gets depleted, the immediate efforts of initiating the financial fraud kill chain with the CE resulted in the freezing of the funds in the custodial account before they could be depleted to purchase or withdraw cryptocurrency. Further collaboration with the domestic financial institution and the Albany Field Office confirmed the funds were frozen in the account, making a full recovery possible.

---

[6] Accessibility description: Image shows Success to Date to include 74% Success Rate; 1,726 Incidents; $433.48 Million in Losses; and $328.32. Million Frozen.

CONFIDENCE FRAUD / ROMANCE SCAMS[7]

Confidence Fraud/Romance scams encompass those designed to pull on a victim's "heartstrings." In 2021, the IC3 received reports from 24,299 victims who experienced more than $956 million in losses to Confidence Fraud/Romance scams. This type of fraud accounts for the third highest losses reported by victims.

Romance scams occur when a criminal adopts a fake online identity to gain a victim's affection and confidence. The scammer uses the illusion of a romantic or close relationship to manipulate and/or steal from the victim. The criminals who carry out Romance scams are experts at what they do and will seem genuine, caring, and believable. The scammer's intention is to quickly establish a relationship, endear himself/herself to the victim, gain trust, and eventually ask for

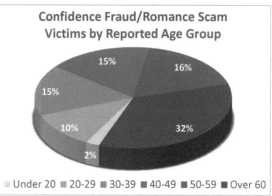

Confidence Fraud/Romance Scam Victims by Reported Age Group

■ Under 20 ■ 20-29 ■ 30-39 ■ 40-49 ■ 50-59 ■ Over 60

money. Scammers may propose marriage and make plans to meet in person, but that will never happen. Scam artists often say they are in the military, or a trades-based industry engaged in projects outside the U.S. That makes it easier to avoid meeting in person—and more plausible when they request money be sent overseas for a medical emergency or unexpected legal fee. Grandparent Scams also fall into this category, where criminals impersonate a panicked loved one, usually a grandchild, nephew, or niece of an elderly person. The loved one claims to be in trouble and needs money immediately.

Con artists are present on most dating and social media sites. In 2021, the IC3 received thousands of complaints from victims of online relationships resulting in sextortion or investment scams.

- Sextortion occurs when someone threatens to distribute your private and sensitive material if their demands are not met. In 2021, the IC3 received more than 18,000 sextortion-related complaints, with losses over $13.6 million. Please see the September 2021 IC3 PSA on Sextortion for more information.[8]
- Many victims of Romance scams also report being pressured into investment opportunities, especially using cryptocurrency. In 2021, the IC3 received more than 4,325 complaints, with losses over $429 million, from Confidence Fraud/Romance scam victims who also reported the use of investments and cryptocurrencies, or "pig butchering" –so named because victims' investment accounts are fattened up before draining, much a like a pig before slaughter. Additional information on "pig butchering" can be found in the September 2021 IC3 PSA I-091621-PSA.[9]

---

[7] Accessibility description: Chart shows Confidence Fraud/Romance Scam Victim by Reported Age Group. Under 20 2%; 20-29 10%; 30-39 15%; 40-49 15%; 50-59 16%; Over 60 32%

[8] FBI Warns about an Increase in Sextortion Complaints. https://www.ic3.gov/Media/Y2021/PSA210902

[9] Scammers Defraud Victims of Millions of Dollars in New Trend in Romance Scams.

CRYPTOCURRENCY (VIRTUAL CURRENCY)

In 2021, the IC3 received 34,202 complaints involving the use of some type of cryptocurrency, such as Bitcoin, Ethereum, Litecoin, or Ripple. While that number showed a decrease from 2020's victim count (35,229), the loss amount reported in IC3 complaints increased nearly seven-fold, from 2020's reported amount of $246,212,432, to total reported losses in 2021 of more than $1.6 billion.

Initially worth only fractions of pennies on the dollar, several cryptocurrencies have seen their values increase substantially, sometimes exponentially. Once limited to hackers, ransomware groups, and other denizens of the "dark web," cryptocurrency is becoming the preferred payment method for all types of scams – SIM swaps, tech support fraud, employment schemes, romance scams, even some auction fraud. It is extremely pervasive in investment scams, where losses can reach into the hundreds of thousands of dollars per victim. The IC3 has noted the following scams particularly using cryptocurrencies.

- Cryptocurrency ATMs: Automated Teller Machines (ATMs) used to purchase cryptocurrency are popping up everywhere. Regulations on the machines are lax and purchases are almost instantaneous and irreversible, making this payment method lucrative to criminals. In 2021, the IC3 received more than 1,500 reports of scams using crypto ATMs, with losses of approximately $28 million. The most common scams reported were Confidence Fraud/Romance, Investment, Employment, and Government Impersonation. Read more about crypto ATM scams in IC3 PSA I-110421-PSA.10

- Cryptocurrency support impersonators: Increasingly, crypto owners are falling victim to scammers impersonating support or security from cryptocurrency exchanges. Owners are alerted of an issue with their crypto wallet and are convinced to either give access to their crypto wallet or transfer the contents of their wallet to another wallet to "safeguard" the contents. Crypto owners are also searching online for support with their cryptocurrencies. Owners contact fake support numbers located online and are convinced to give up login information or control of their crypto accounts.

- Many victims of Romance scams also report being pressured into investment opportunities, especially using cryptocurrency. In 2021, the IC3 received more than 4,325 complaints, with losses over $429 million, from Confidence Fraud/Romance scam victims who also reported the use of investments and cryptocurrencies, or "pig butchering." The scammer's initial contact is typically made via dating apps and other social media sites. The scammer gains the confidence and trust of the victim, and then claims to have knowledge of cryptocurrency investment or trading opportunities that will result in substantial profits.

---

https://www.ic3.gov/Media/Y2021/PSA210916
[10] The FBI Warns of Fraudulent Schemes Leveraging Cryptocurrency ATMs and QR Codes to Facilitate Payment https://www.ic3.gov/Media/Y2021/PSA211104

RANSOMWARE[11]

In 2021, the IC3 received 3,729 complaints identified as ransomware with adjusted losses of more than $49.2 million. Ransomware is a type of malicious software, or malware, that encrypts data on a computer, making it unusable. A malicious cyber criminal holds the data hostage until the ransom is paid. If the ransom is not paid, the victim's data remains unavailable. Cyber criminals may also pressure victims to pay the ransom by threatening to destroy the victim's data or to release it to the public.

Ransomware tactics and techniques continued to evolve in 2021, which demonstrates ransomware threat actors' growing technological sophistication and an increased ransomware threat to organizations globally. Although cyber criminals use a variety of techniques to infect victims with ransomware, phishing emails, Remote Desktop Protocol (RDP) exploitation, and exploitation of software vulnerabilities remained the top three initial infection vectors for ransomware incidents reported to the IC3. Once a ransomware threat actor has gained code execution on a device or network access, they can deploy ransomware. Note: these infection vectors likely remain popular because of the increased use of remote work and schooling starting in 2020 and continuing through 2021. This increase expanded the remote attack surface and left network defenders struggling to keep pace with routine software patching.[12]

Immediate Actions You Can Take Now to Protect Against Ransomware:

- Update your operating system and software.
- Implement user training and phishing exercises to raise awareness about the risks of suspicious links and attachments.
- If you use Remote Desktop Protocol (RDP), secure and monitor it.
- Make an offline backup of your data.

Ransomware and Critical Infrastructure Sectors

In June 2021, the IC3 began tracking reported ransomware incidents in which the victim was a member of a critical infrastructure sector. There are 16 critical infrastructure sectors whose assets, systems, and networks, whether physical or virtual, are considered so vital to the United States that their incapacitation or destruction would have a debilitating effect on our security, national economy, public health or safety, or any combination thereof.

---

[11] Accessibility description: Image shows actions you can Take to Protect Against Ransomware: Update your operating system. Implement user training and phishing exercises to raise awareness, secure and monitor Remote Desktop Protocol (DDP) if used, and make an offline backup of our data.

[12] 2021 Trends Show Increased Globalized Threat of Ransomware. https://www.ic3.gov/Media/News/2022/220209.pdf

In October 2021, the IC3 posted a Joint Cybersecurity Advisory (CSA) to ic3.gov regarding ongoing cyber threats to U.S. Water and Wastewater Systems. In September 2021, the IC3 posted a Private Industry Notification (PIN) which warned that ransomware attacks targeting the Food and Agriculture sector disrupt operations, cause financial loss, and negatively impact the food supply chain. In May 2021, the IC3 posted an FBI Liaison Alert System (FLASH) report that advised the FBI identified at least 16 CONTI ransomware attacks targeting US Healthcare and First Responder networks, including law enforcement agencies, emergency medical services, 9-1-1 dispatch centers, and municipalities within the last year. And in March 2021, the IC3 posted a FLASH warning that FBI reporting indicated an increase in PYSA ransomware targeting education institutions in 12 US states and the United Kingdom.

The IC3 received 649 complaints that indicated organizations belonging to a critical infrastructure sector were victims of a ransomware attack. Of the 16 critical infrastructure sectors, IC3 reporting indicated 14 sectors had at least 1 member that fell victim to a ransomware attack in 2021.
[13]

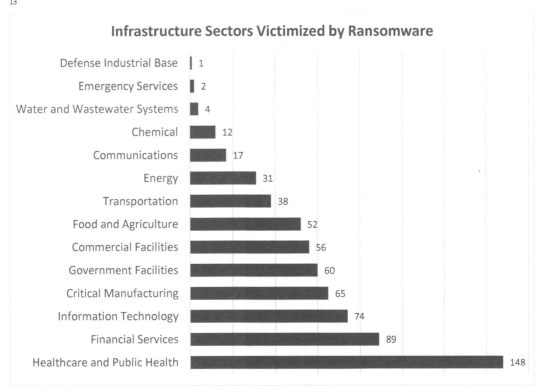

Infrastructure Sectors Victimized by Ransomware

Sector	Value
Defense Industrial Base	1
Emergency Services	2
Water and Wastewater Systems	4
Chemical	12
Communications	17
Energy	31
Transportation	38
Food and Agriculture	52
Commercial Facilities	56
Government Facilities	60
Critical Manufacturing	65
Information Technology	74
Financial Services	89
Healthcare and Public Health	148

---

[13] Accessibility description: Chart shows Infrastructure Sectors Victimized by Ransomware. Healthcare and Public Health was highest with 148 followed by Financial Services 89; Information Technology 74; Critical Manufacturing 65; Government Facilities 60; Commercial Facilities 56; Food and Agriculture 52; Transportation 38; Energy 31; Communications 17; Chemical 12; Water and Wastewater Systems 4; Emergency Services 2; Defense Industrial Base 1.

Of the known ransomware variants reported to IC3, the three top variants that victimized a member of a critical infrastructure sector were CONTI, LockBit, and REvil/Sodinokibi.

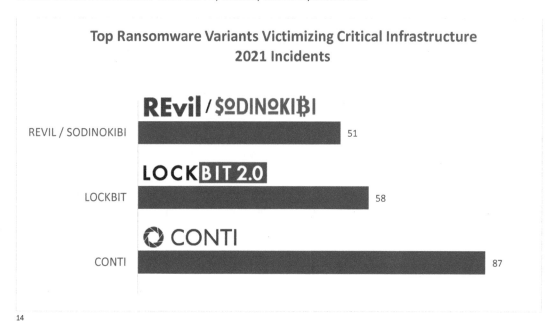

According to information submitted to the IC3, CONTI most frequently victimized the Critical Manufacturing, Commercial Facilities, and Food and Agriculture sectors. LockBit most frequently victimized the Government Facilities, Healthcare and Public Health, and Financial Services sectors. REvil/Sodinokibi most frequently victimized the Financial Services, Information Technology, and Healthcare and Public Health sectors.

Of all critical infrastructure sectors reportedly victimized by ransomware in 2021, the Healthcare and Public Health, Financial Services, and Information Technology sectors were the most frequent victims. The IC3 anticipates an increase in critical infrastructure victimization in 2022.

The FBI does not encourage paying a ransom to criminal actors. Paying a ransom may embolden adversaries to target additional organizations, encourage other criminal actors to engage in the distribution of ransomware, and /or fund illicit activities. Paying the ransom also does not guarantee that a victim's files will be recovered. Regardless of whether you or your organization have decided to pay the ransom, the FBI urges you to report ransomware incidents to your local FBI field office or the IC3. Doing so provides investigators with the critical information they need to track ransomware attackers, hold them accountable under U.S. law, and prevent future attacks.

---

[14] Accessibility description: Chart shows top variants Victimizing Critical Infrastructure 2021 Incidents. REvil/Sodinokibi, Locbit, and CONTI.

TECH SUPPORT FRAUD[15]

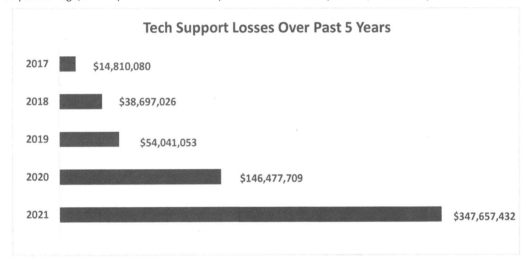

Tech Support Fraud involves a criminal claiming to provide customer, security, or technical support or service to defraud unwitting individuals. Criminals may pose as support or service representatives offering to resolve such issues as a compromised email or bank account, a virus on a computer, or a software license renewal.

Many victims report being directed to make wire transfers to overseas accounts or purchase large amounts of prepaid cards. In 2021, the IC3 received 23,903 complaints related to Tech Support Fraud from victims in 70 countries. The losses amounted to more than $347 million, which represents a 137 percent increase in losses from 2020. Most victims, almost 60 percent, report to be over 60 years of age, and experience at least 68 percent of the losses (almost $238 million).

Tech Support Losses Over Past 5 Years

2017	$14,810,080
2018	$38,697,026
2019	$54,041,053
2020	$146,477,709
2021	$347,657,432

Tech support scammers continue to impersonate well-known tech companies, offering to fix non-existent technology issues or renew fraudulent software or security subscriptions. However, in 2021, the IC3 observed an increase in complaints reporting the impersonation of customer support, which has taken on a variety of forms, such as financial and banking institutions, utility companies, or virtual currency exchanges.

---

[15] Accessibility description: Chart shows Tech Support Losses Over Past 5 Years.
2021 $347,657,432; 2020 $146,477,709; 2019 $54,041,053; 2018 $38,697,026; 2017 $14,810,080.

IC3 by the Numbers[16]

$6.9 Billion
Victim losses in 2021

2,300+
Average complaints received daily

552,000+
Average complaints received per year (last 5 years)

Over 6.5 Million
Complaints reported since inception

---

[16] Accessibility description: Image depicts key statistics regarding complaints and victim loss. Total losses of $6.9 billion were reported in 2021. The total number of complaints received since the year 2000 is over 6.5 million. IC3 has received approximately 552,000 complaints per year on average over the last five years, or more than 2,300 complaints per day.

2021 Victims by Age Group[17]

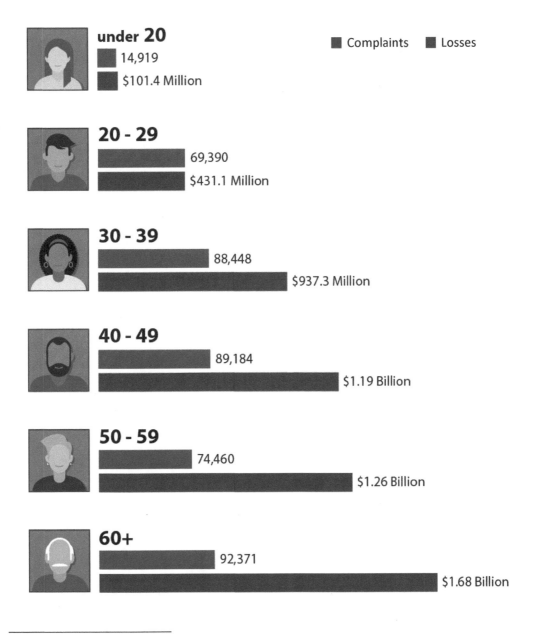

under 20
- ■ 14,919
- ■ $101.4 Million

■ Complaints ■ Losses

20 - 29
- 69,390
- $431.1 Million

30 - 39
- 88,448
- $937.3 Million

40 - 49
- 89,184
- $1.19 Billion

50 - 59
- 74,460
- $1.26 Billion

60+
- 92,371
- $1.68 Billion

[17] Not all complaints include an associated age range—those without this information are excluded from this table. Please see Appendix B for more information regarding IC3 data.

Accessibility description: Chart shows number of complaints and Loss for Victims by Age Group. Under 20 14,919 victims $101.4 Million losses; 20-29 69,390 Victims $431.1. Million losses; 30-39 88,448 Victims $937.3 Million losses; 40-49 89,184 victims $1.19 Billion losses; 50-59 74,460 Victims $1.26 Billion losses; 60+ 92,371 Victims $1.68 Billion losses.

2021 - Top 20 International Victim Countries[18]

Compared to the United States

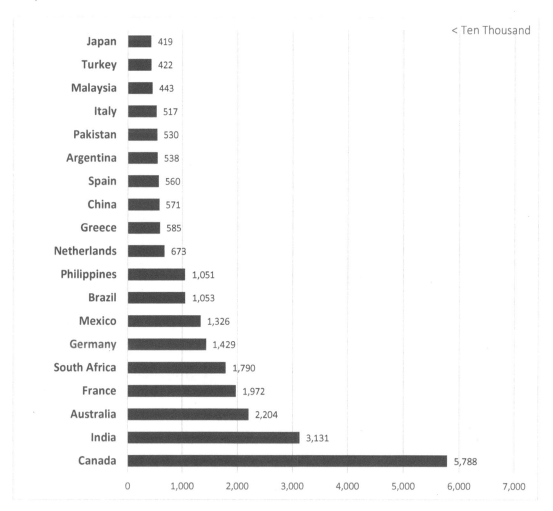

< Ten Thousand

Country	Value
Japan	419
Turkey	422
Malaysia	443
Italy	517
Pakistan	530
Argentina	538
Spain	560
China	571
Greece	585
Netherlands	673
Philippines	1,051
Brazil	1,053
Mexico	1,326
Germany	1,429
South Africa	1,790
France	1,972
Australia	2,204
India	3,131
Canada	5,788

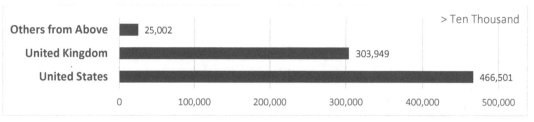

> Ten Thousand

Country	Value
Others from Above	25,002
United Kingdom	303,949
United States	466,501

[18] Accessibility description: The charts list the top 20 countries by number of total victims as compared to the United States. The specific number of victims for each country are listed in ascending order to the right of the graph. Please see Appendix B for more information regarding IC3 data.

2021 - Top 10 States by Number of Victims[19]

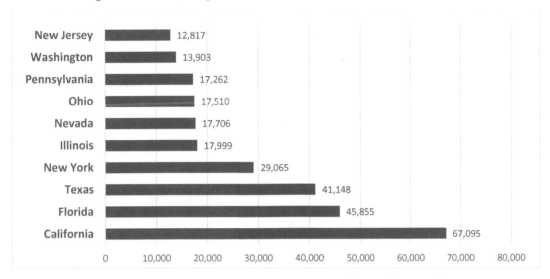

2021 - Top 10 States by Victim Loss in $ Millions[20]

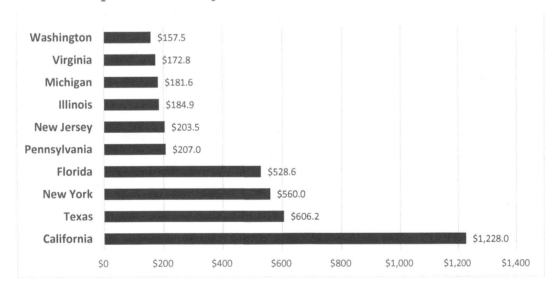

---

[19] Accessibility description: Chart depicts the top 10 states based on number of reporting victims are labeled. These include California, Florida, Texas, New York, Illinois, Nevada, Ohio, Pennsylvania, Washington, and New Jersey. Please see Appendix B for more information regarding IC3 data.

[20] Accessibility description: Chart depicts the top 10 states based on reported victim loss are labeled. These include California, Texas, New York, Florida, Pennsylvania, New Jersey, Illinois, Michigan, Virginia, and Washington. Please see Appendix B for more information regarding IC3 data.

2021 CRIME TYPES

By Victim Count

Crime Type	Victims	Crime Type	Victims
Phishing/Vishing/Smishing/Pharming	323,972	Government Impersonation	11,335
Non-Payment/Non-Delivery	82,478	Advanced Fee	11,034
Personal Data Breach	51,829	Overpayment	6,108
Identity Theft	51,629	Lottery/Sweepstakes/Inheritance	5,991
Extortion	39,360	IPR/Copyright and Counterfeit	4,270
Confidence Fraud/Romance	24,299	Ransomware	3,729
Tech Support	23,903	Crimes Against Children	2,167
Investment	20,561	Corporate Data Breach	1,287
BEC/EAC	19,954	Civil Matter	1,118
Spoofing	18,522	Denial of Service/TDoS	1,104
Credit Card Fraud	16,750	Computer Intrusion	979
Employment	15,253	Malware/Scareware/Virus	810
Other	12,346	Health Care Related	578
Terrorism/Threats of Violence	12,346	Re-shipping	516
Real Estate/Rental	11,578	Gambling	395

Descriptors*

Social Media	36,034	Virtual Currency	34,202

*These descriptors relate to the medium or tool used to facilitate the crime and are used by the IC3 for tracking purposes only. They are available as descriptors only after another crime type has been selected. Please see Appendix B for more information regarding IC3 data.

2021 Crime Types continued

By Victim Loss

Crime Type	Loss	Crime Type	Loss
BEC/EAC	$2,395,953,296	Lottery/Sweepstakes/Inheritance	$71,289,089
Investment	$1,455,943,193	Extortion	$60,577,741
Confidence Fraud/Romance	$956,039,740	Ransomware	*$49,207,908
Personal Data Breach	$517,021,289	Employment	$47,231,023
Real Estate/Rental	$350,328,166	Phishing/Vishing/Smishing/Pharming	$44,213,707
Tech Support	$347,657,432	Overpayment	$33,407,671
Non-Payment/Non-Delivery	$337,493,071	Computer Intrusion	$19,603,037
Identity Theft	$278,267,918	IPR/Copyright/Counterfeit	$16,365,011
Credit Card Fraud	$172,998,385	Health Care Related	$7,042,942
Corporate Data Breach	$151,568,225	Malware/Scareware/Virus	$5,596,889
Government Impersonation	$142,643,253	Terrorism/Threats of Violence	$4,390,720
Advanced Fee	$98,694,137	Gambling	$1,940,237
Civil Matter	$85,049,939	Re-shipping	$631,466
Spoofing	$82,169,806	Denial of Service/TDos	$217,981
Other	$75,837,524	Crimes Against Children	$198,950

Descriptors**

Social Media	$235,279,057	Virtual Currency	$1,602,647,341

* Regarding ransomware adjusted losses, this number does not include estimates of lost business, time, wages, files, or equipment, or any third-party remediation services acquired by a victim. In some cases, victims do not report any loss amount to the FBI, thereby creating an artificially low overall ransomware loss rate. Lastly, the number only represents what victims report to the FBI via the IC3 and does not account for victim direct reporting to FBI field offices/agents.

**These descriptors relate to the medium or tool used to facilitate the crime and are used by the IC3 for tracking purposes only. They are available only after another crime type has been selected. Please see Appendix B for more information regarding IC3 data.

Last 3 Year Complaint Count Comparison

By Victim Count		▼ ▲ = Trend from previous Year				
Crime Type	*2021*		*2020*		*2019*	
Advanced Fee	11,034	▼	13,020	▼	14,607	▼
BEC/EAC	19,954	▲	19,369	▼	23,775	▲
Civil Matter	1,118	▲	968	▲	908	▲
Confidence Fraud/Romance	24,299	▲	23,751	▲	19,473	▲
Corporate Data Breach	1,287	▼	2,794	▲	1,795	▼
Credit Card Fraud	16,750	▼	17,614	▲	14,378	▼
Crimes Against Children	2,167	▼	3,202	▲	1,312	▼
Denial of Service/TDoS	1,104	▼	2,018	▲	1,353	▼
Employment	15,253	▼	16,879	▲	14,493	▼
Extortion	39,360	▼	76,741	▲	43,101	▼
Gambling	395	▲	391	▲	262	▲
Government Impersonation	11,335	▼	12,827	▼	13,873	▲
Health Care Related	578	▼	1,383	▲	657	▲
Identity Theft	51,629	▲	43,330	▲	16,053	▼
Investment	20,561	▲	8,788	▲	3,999	▲
IPR/Copyright and Counterfeit	4,270	▲	4,213	▲	3,892	▲
Lottery/Sweepstakes/Inheritance	5,991	▼	8,501	▲	7,767	▲
Malware/Scareware/Virus	810	▼	1,423	▼	2,373	▼
Non-Payment/Non-Delivery	82,478	▼	108,869	▲	61,832	▼
Other	12,346	▲	10,372	▼	10,842	▲
Overpayment	6,108	▼	10,988	▼	15,395	▼
Personal Data Breach	51,829	▲	45,330	▲	38,218	▼
Phishing/Vishing/Smishing/Pharming	323,972	▲	241,342	▲	114,702	▲
Ransomware	3,729	▲	2,474	▲	2,047	▲
Real Estate/Rental	11,578	▼	13,638	▲	11,677	▲
Re-Shipping	516	▼	883	▼	929	▲
Spoofing	18,522	▼	28,218	▲	25,789	▲
Tech Support	23,903	▲	15,421	▲	13,633	▼
Terrorism/Threats of Violence	12,346	▼	20,669	▲	15,563	▼

Last 3 Year Complaint Loss Comparison

By Victim Loss		▼ ▲ = Trend from previous Year			
Crime Type	2021		2020		2019
Advanced Fee	$98,694,137 ▲		$83,215,405 ▼		$100,602,297 ▲
BEC/EAC	$2,395,953,296 ▲		$1,866,642,107 ▲		$1,776,549,688 ▲
Civil Matter	$85,049,939 ▲		$24,915,958 ▲		$20,242,867 ▲
Confidence Fraud/Romance	$956,039,739 ▲		$600,249,821 ▲		$475,014,032 ▲
Corporate Data Breach	$151,568,225 ▲		$128,916,648 ▲		$53,398,278 ▼
Credit Card Fraud	$172,998,385 ▲		$129,820,792 ▲		$111,491,163 ▲
Crimes Against Children	$198,950 ▼		$660,044 ▼		$975,311 ▲
Denial of Service/TDoS	$217,981 ▼		$512,127 ▼		$7,598,198 ▲
Employment	$47,231,023 ▼		$62,314,015 ▲		$42,618,705 ▼
Extortion	$60,577,741 ▼		$70,935,939 ▼		$107,498,956 ▲
Gambling	$1,940,237 ▼		$3,961,508 ▲		$1,458,118 ▲
Government Impersonation	$142,643.253 ▲		$109,938,030 ▼		$124,292,606 ▲
Health Care Related	$7,042,942 ▼		$29,042,515 ▲		$1,128,838 ▼
Identity Theft	$278,267,918 ▲		$219,484,699 ▲		$160,305,789 ▲
Investment	$1,455,943,193 ▲		$336,469,000 ▲		$222,186,195 ▼
IPR/Copyright and Counterfeit	$16,365,011 ▲		$5,910,617 ▼		$10,293,307 ▼
Lottery/Sweepstakes/Inheritance	$71,289,089 ▲		$61,111,319 ▲		$48,642,332 ▼
Malware/Scareware/Virus	$5,596,889 ▼		$6,904,054 ▲		$2,009,119 ▼
Non-Payment/Non-Delivery	$337,493,071 ▲		$265,011,249 ▲		$196,563,497 ▲
Other	$75,837,524 ▼		$101,523,082 ▲		$66,223,160 ▲
Overpayment	$33,407,671 ▼		$51,039,922 ▼		$55,820,212 ▲
Personal Data Breach	$517,021,289 ▲		$194,473,055 ▲		$120,102,501 ▼
Phishing/Vishing/Smishing/Pharming	$44,213,707 ▼		$54,241,075 ▼		$57,836,379 ▲
Ransomware	$49,207,908 ▲		$29,157,405 ▲		$8,965,847 ▲
Real Estate/Rental	$350,328,166 ▲		$213,196,082 ▼		$221,365,911 ▲
Re-Shipping	$631,466 ▼		$3,095,265 ▲		$1,772,692 ▲
Spoofing	$82,169,806 ▼		$216,513,728 ▼		$300,478,433 ▲
Tech Support	$347,657,432 ▲		$146,477,709 ▲		$54,041,053 ▲
Terrorism/Threats of Violence	$4,390,720 ▼		$6,547,449 ▼		$19,916,243 ▲

Overall State Statistics

Rank	State	Victims	Rank	State	Victims
1	California	67,095	30	Louisiana	4,248
2	Florida	45,855	31	Utah	4,242
3	Texas	41,148	32	Oklahoma	4,156
4	New York	29,065	33	Arkansas	2,745
5	Illinois	17,999	34	Kansas	2,693
6	Nevada	17,706	35	New Mexico	2,644
7	Ohio	17,510	36	Nebraska	2,407
8	Pennsylvania	17,262	37	Mississippi	2,170
9	Washington	13,903	38	West Virginia	2,135
10	New Jersey	12,817	39	Delaware	2,132
11	Arizona	12,375	40	District of Columbia	2,103
12	Virginia	11,785	41	Puerto Rico	1,923
13	Georgia	11,776	42	Idaho	1,882
14	Maryland	11,693	43	Alaska	1,787
15	Indiana	11,399	44	Hawaii	1,615
16	Michigan	10,930	45	New Hampshire	1,487
17	Colorado	10,537	46	Maine	1,402
18	North Carolina	10,363	47	Rhode Island	1,205
19	Missouri	9,692	48	Montana	1,188
20	Massachusetts	9,174	49	South Dakota	951
21	Iowa	8,853	50	Wyoming	735
22	Wisconsin	8,646	51	Vermont	715
23	Kentucky	7,148	52	North Dakota	670
24	Tennessee	7,129	53	Virgin Islands, U.S.	100
25	Oregon	5,954	54	U.S. Minor Outlying Islands	93
26	Minnesota	5,844	55	Guam	64
27	South Carolina	5,426	56	Northern Mariana Islands	29
28	Alabama	5,347	57	American Samoa	25
29	Connecticut	4,524			

*Note: This information is based on the total number of complaints from each state, American Territory, and the District of Columbia when the complainant provided state information. Please see Appendix B for more information regarding IC3 data.

Overall State Statistics continued

Rank	State	Loss	Rank	State	Loss
1	California	$1,227,989,139	30	Louisiana	$38,783,908
2	Texas	$606,179,646	31	Kentucky	$37,953,949
3	New York	$559,965,598	32	Iowa	$33,821,569
4	Florida	$528,573,929	33	Kansas	$26,031,546
5	Pennsylvania	$206,982,032	34	North Dakota	$21,246,355
6	New Jersey	$203,510,341	35	Mississippi	$20,578,948
7	Illinois	$184,860,704	36	District of Columbia	$20,096,921
8	Michigan	$181,622,993	37	Nebraska	$19,743,241
9	Virginia	$172,767,012	38	Hawaii	$18,964,018
10	Washington	$157,454,331	39	South Dakota	$18,131,095
11	Massachusetts	$150,384,982	40	Idaho	$17,682,386
12	Georgia	$143,998,767	41	Arkansas	$15,302,829
13	Ohio	$133,666,156	42	New Hampshire	$15,302,618
14	Colorado	$130,631,286	43	Delaware	$15,041,717
15	Arizona	$124,158,717	44	Puerto Rico	$14,650,062
16	Tennessee	$103,960,100	45	Alaska	$13,070,648
17	Maryland	$99,110,757	46	New Mexico	$12,761,850
18	North Carolina	$91,416,226	47	Rhode Island	$11,191,079
19	Nevada	$83,712,410	48	Wyoming	$10,249,609
20	Minnesota	$82,535,103	49	Montana	$10,107,283
21	Oregon	$75,739,646	50	Vermont	$9,826,787
22	Connecticut	$72,476,672	51	West Virginia	$9,453,607
23	Utah	$65,131,003	52	Maine	$7,261,234
24	Indiana	$60,524,818	53	Guam	$2,168,956
25	Missouri	$53,797,188	54	Virgin Islands, U.S.	$895,946
26	Wisconsin	$51,816,862	55	Northern Mariana Islands	$705,244
27	Oklahoma	$50,196,339	56	U.S. Minor Outlying Islands	$403,844
28	Alabama	$49,522,904	57	American Samoa	$177,533
29	South Carolina	$42,768,322			

*Note: This information is based on the total number of complaints from each state, American Territory, and the District of Columbia when the complainant provided state information. Please see Appendix B for more information regarding IC3 data.

Overall State Statistics continued

Rank	State	Subjects		Rank	State	Subjects
1	California	27,706		30	Nebraska	1,243
2	Texas	13,518		31	Kentucky	1,238
3	Florida	11,527		32	District of Columbia	1,107
4	New York	10,696		33	Utah	1,063
5	Maryland	5,244		34	Delaware	924
6	Ohio	5,182		35	New Mexico	893
7	Pennsylvania	5,168		36	Kansas	876
8	Illinois	4,587		37	West Virginia	863
9	Georgia	4,521		38	Arkansas	831
10	New Jersey	3,913		39	Iowa	723
11	Washington	3,586		40	Mississippi	714
12	Virginia	3,542		41	Montana	681
13	Arizona	3,485		42	Maine	507
14	North Carolina	3,316		43	Idaho	486
15	Nevada	3,308		44	New Hampshire	467
16	Colorado	2,885		45	Hawaii	435
17	Michigan	2,605		46	Alaska	429
18	Tennessee	2,384		47	Puerto Rico	346
19	Massachusetts	2,018		48	Rhode Island	318
20	Indiana	1,976		49	North Dakota	297
21	Oklahoma	1,929		50	Wyoming	251
22	Missouri	1,646		51	South Dakota	216
23	Oregon	1,598		52	Vermont	189
24	Minnesota	1,553		53	U.S. Minor Outlying Islands	34
25	Alabama	1,520		54	Virgin Islands, U.S.	14
26	Connecticut	1,499		55	Guam	11
27	Louisiana	1,398		56	Northern Mariana Islands	7
28	South Carolina	1,358		57	American Samoa	3
29	Wisconsin	1,316				

*Note: This information is based on the total number of complaints from each state, American Territory, and the District of Columbia when the complainant provided state information. Please see Appendix B for more information regarding IC3 data.

Overall State Statistics continued

Subject Earnings per Destination State*					
Rank	State	Loss	Rank	State	Loss
1	California	$404,965,496	30	South Carolina	$10,406,812
2	New York	$320,011,292	31	Iowa	$7,960,272
3	Florida	$174,884,203	32	Wyoming	$7,007,308
4	Texas	$168,153,129	33	Idaho	$6,879,088
5	Colorado	$96,949,691	34	Connecticut	$6,586,016
6	Illinois	$82,985,601	35	Kansas	$6,527,306
7	Ohio	$65,567,505	36	New Mexico	$6,441,444
8	Georgia	$62,682,196	37	Kentucky	$6,260,280
9	Washington	$49,643,646	38	Arkansas	$5,511,079
10	New Jersey	$46,773,594	39	Delaware	$5,404,683
11	Nevada	$46,441,562	40	Hawaii	$5,312,553
12	Pennsylvania	$44,661,540	41	Nebraska	$5,156,069
13	Arizona	$44,490,075	42	New Hampshire	$5,082,033
14	Louisiana	$43,427,842	43	Mississippi	$4,245,861
15	North Carolina	$43,281,815	44	Puerto Rico	$4,067,734
16	Virginia	$42,989,608	45	Maine	$3,445,411
17	Maryland	$33,912,104	46	Vermont	$3,357,692
18	Massachusetts	$29,327,619	47	Rhode Island	$3,307,726
19	Michigan	$28,857,054	48	North Dakota	$3,174,006
20	Oklahoma	$19,278,395	49	Montana	$2,946,504
21	Minnesota	$19,039,734	50	Alaska	$2,773,302
22	Tennessee	$18,580,987	51	South Dakota	$2,413,398
23	Utah	$17,137,321	52	West Virginia	$2,269,994
24	Missouri	$16,619,864	53	Northern Mariana Islands	$107,000
25	District of Columbia	$15,656,649	54	U.S. Minor Outlying Islands	$77,350
26	Wisconsin	$14,886,212	55	Virgin Islands, U.S.	$44,453
27	Alabama	$14,639,799	56	Guam	$3,932
28	Indiana	$14,634,699	57	American Samoa	$420
29	Oregon	$10,561,887			

*Note: This information is based on the total number of complaints from each state, American Territory, and the District of Columbia when the complainant provided state information. Please see Appendix B for more information regarding IC3 data.

Appendix A: Definitions

Advanced Fee: An individual pays money to someone in anticipation of receiving something of greater value in return, but instead, receives significantly less than expected or nothing.

Business Email Compromise/Email Account Compromise: BEC is a scam targeting businesses (not individuals) working with foreign suppliers and/or businesses regularly performing wire transfer payments. EAC is a similar scam which targets individuals. These sophisticated scams are carried out by fraudsters compromising email accounts through social engineering or computer intrusion techniques to conduct unauthorized transfer of funds.

Civil Matter: Civil litigation generally includes all disputes formally submitted to a court, about any subject in which one party is claimed to have committed a wrong but not a crime. In general, this is the legal process most people think of when the word "lawsuit" is used.

Computer Intrusion: Unauthorized access or exceeding authorized access into a protected computer system. A protected computer system is one owned or used by the US Government, a financial institution, or any business. This typically excludes personally owned systems and devices.

Confidence/Romance Fraud: An individual believes they are in a relationship (family, friendly, or romantic) and are tricked into sending money, personal and financial information, or items of value to the perpetrator or to launder money or items to assist the perpetrator. This includes the Grandparent's Scheme and any scheme in which the perpetrator preys on the complainant's "heartstrings".

Corporate Data Breach: A data breach within a corporation or business where sensitive, protected, or confidential data is copied, transmitted, viewed, stolen, or used by an individual unauthorized to do so.

Credit Card Fraud: Credit card fraud is a wide-ranging term for theft and fraud committed using a credit card or any similar payment mechanism (ACH. EFT, recurring charge, etc.) as a fraudulent source of funds in a transaction.

Crimes Against Children: Anything related to the exploitation of children, including child abuse.

Denial of Service/TDoS: A Denial of Service (DoS) attack floods a network/system, or a Telephony Denial of Service (TDoS) floods a voice service with multiple requests, slowing down or interrupting service.

Employment: An individual believes they are legitimately employed and loses money, or launders money/items during the course of their employment.

Extortion: Unlawful extraction of money or property through intimidation or undue exercise of authority. It may include threats of physical harm, criminal prosecution, or public exposure.

Gambling: Online gambling, also known as Internet gambling and iGambling, is a general term for gambling using the Internet.

Government Impersonation: A government official is impersonated in an attempt to collect money.

Health Care Related: A scheme attempting to defraud private or government health care programs which usually involving health care providers, companies, or individuals. Schemes may include offers for fake insurance cards, health insurance marketplace assistance, stolen health information, or various other scams and/or any scheme involving medications, supplements, weight loss products, or diversion/pill mill practices. These scams are often initiated through spam email, Internet advertisements, links in forums/social media, and fraudulent websites.

IPR/Copyright and Counterfeit: The illegal theft and use of others' ideas, inventions, and creative expressions – what's called intellectual property – everything from trade secrets and proprietary products and parts to movies, music, and software.

Identity Theft: Someone steals and uses personal identifying information, like a name or Social Security number, without permission to commit fraud or other crimes and/or (Account Takeover) a fraudster obtains account information to perpetrate fraud on existing accounts.

Investment: Deceptive practice that induces investors to make purchases based on false information. These scams usually offer the victims large returns with minimal risk. (Retirement, 401K, Ponzi, Pyramid, etc.).

Lottery/Sweepstakes/Inheritance: An Individual is contacted about winning a lottery or sweepstakes they never entered, or to collect on an inheritance from an unknown relative.

Malware/Scareware/Virus: Software or code intended to damage, disable, or capable of copying itself onto a computer and/or computer systems to have a detrimental effect or destroy data.

Non-Payment/Non-Delivery: Goods or services are shipped, and payment is never rendered (non-payment). Payment is sent, and goods or services are never received, or are of lesser quality (non-delivery).

Overpayment: An individual is sent a payment/commission and is instructed to keep a portion of the payment and send the remainder to another individual or business.

Personal Data Breach: A leak/spill of personal data which is released from a secure location to an untrusted environment. Also, a security incident in which an individual's sensitive, protected, or confidential data is copied, transmitted, viewed, stolen, or used by an unauthorized individual.

Phishing/Vishing/Smishing/Pharming: The use of unsolicited email, text messages, and telephone calls purportedly from a legitimate company requesting personal, financial, and/or login credentials.

Ransomware: A type of malicious software designed to block access to a computer system until money is paid.

Re-shipping: Individuals receive packages at their residence and subsequently repackage the merchandise for shipment, usually abroad.

Real Estate/Rental: Loss of funds from a real estate investment or fraud involving rental or timeshare property.

Spoofing: Contact information (phone number, email, and website) is deliberately falsified to mislead and appear to be from a legitimate source. For example, spoofed phone numbers making mass robo-calls; spoofed emails sending mass spam; forged websites used to mislead and gather personal information. Often used in connection with other crime types.

Social Media: A complaint alleging the use of social networking or social media (Facebook, Twitter, Instagram, chat rooms, etc.) as a vector for fraud. Social Media does not include dating sites.

Tech Support: Subject posing as technical or customer support/service.

Terrorism/Threats of Violence: Terrorism is violent acts intended to create fear that are perpetrated for a religious, political, or ideological goal and deliberately target or disregard the safety of non-combatants. Threats of Violence refers to an expression of an intention to inflict pain, injury, or punishment, which does not refer to the requirement of payment.

Virtual Currency: A complaint mentioning a form of virtual cryptocurrency, such as Bitcoin, Litecoin, or Potcoin.

Appendix B: Additional Information about IC3 Data

- Each complaint is reviewed by an IC3 analyst. The analyst categorizes the complaint according to the crime type(s) that are appropriate. Additionally, the analyst will adjust the loss amount if the complaint data does not support the loss amount reported.

- One complaint may have multiple crime types.

- Some complainants may have filed more than once, creating a possible duplicate complaint.

- All location-based reports are generated from information entered when known/provided by the complainant.

- Losses reported in foreign currencies are converted to U.S. dollars when possible.

- Complaint counts represent the number of individual complaints received from each state and do not represent the number of individuals filing a complaint.

- Victim is identified as the individual filing a complaint.

- Subject is identified as the individual perpetrating the scam as reported by the victim.

- "Count by Subject per state" is the number of subjects per state, as reported by victims.

- "Subject earnings per Destination State" is the amount swindled by the subject, as reported by the victim, per state.

What's New in Civic Tech: A Federal Digital Literacy Bill

By Zack Quaintance and Julia Edinger

Government Technology

January 13, 2022

The U.S. Congress has introduced a new bill that seeks to create a digital literacy and equity commission.

Rep. Brenda Lawrence, D-Mich., introduced the Digital Literacy and Equity Commission Act this week, announcing it via a press release. In that release, Lawrence notes that currently there is no commonly used metric to measure digital literacy. Part of the proposed commission's job would be to not only assess digital literacy in the U.S., but to suggest a way to measure it moving forward. Also on the agenda would be promoting interagency cooperation as it applies to digital literacy.

"As a result of the Bipartisan Infrastructure Law, we're investing billions to expand access to broadband. Laying down the fiber is a strong first step to connect Americans around the country, but this effort won't be as effective if people can't use the online tools they've been given," Lawrence said in a statement.

This new commission would be chaired by the secretary of education and the chair of the Federal Communications Commission (FCC). If passed, the bill would also require a report to Congress that would offer recommendations for how to improve digital literacy throughout the U.S. Finally, the new bill also notes that chief among the commission's concerns would be addressing digital equity by focusing on literacy within low-income and disadvantage areas, which have long found themselves on the wrong end of the digital divide.

Digital literacy has become an increasing focus of those who work on digital equity and digital inclusion. Along with fostering access to the Internet and to devices needed to access it, digital literacy represents a pillar of digital inclusion work. After the disruptions caused by the COVID-19 pandemic, support has flowed into government from the private sector, philanthropies and nonprofit groups for this work. In fact, in cities across the country efforts have been made to help families with school children in particular get Internet access at home.

Digital literacy—which is also being increasingly branded as digital skills training by advocates—involves helping folks who are now connected to the Internet learn how to use it in meaningful ways. It varies by individual on an almost granular level, but this sort of training ranges from helping folks setup email addresses to teaching them how to use Zoom in order to access telehealth.

The introduction of this new bill represents continued momentum at the federal level to support digital inclusion work across the U.S. To date, the most prominent instance of this is the $2.75 billion of digital inclusion funding already included in the infrastructure bill. Experts have described this investment as historic, noting that it will fall to states, cities and community groups to convey exactly where that money needs to go next.

A digital literacy commission would be a natural extension of this investment, doing the work of benchmarking the progress that's being made in the wake of this funding while helping to pinpoint continued areas of need for any potential future digital inclusion support at the federal level. (Zack Quaintance)

NTIA Requests Public Comment on Federal Broadband Programs

The U.S. Department of Commerce's National Telecommunications and Information Administration (NTIA) will be open for public comment on information and policy related to the broadband grant programs that will be funded by the Infrastructure Investment and Jobs Act (IIJA).

The specific programs being discussed are the Broadband Equity, Access and Deployment Program; the Enabling Middle Mile Broadband Infrastructure Program; and the State Digital Equity Planning Grant Program. NTIA plans to release an additional request for comment addressing the State Digital Equity Capacity Grant Program and Digital Equity Competitive Grant Program.

Comments can be submitted online using regulations.gov by the Feb. 4 deadline, and all submitted comments will be posted publicly. NTIA is also hosting a series of public virtual listening sessions regarding the programs funded by the IIJA. (Julia Edinger)

Maine Confirms First President of State's Connectivity Authority

Maine has sworn in Andrew Butcher as the first president of the Maine Connectivity Authority.

State officials announced Butcher's nomination to the role in October 2021, following the July 2021 confirmation of the nominees for the authority's seven-member board.

Butcher, unanimously confirmed by the Maine state Senate, had previously served as the leader of the Maine Broadband Coalition, which represents organizations, communities and other Internet users in efforts to expand broadband access. In addition, as director of innovation and resilience for the Greater Portland Council of Governments, Butcher took part in passing a 2020 bond proposal that raised $14 million for broadband expansion in the state.

Maine's previous work to expand broadband access includes funding from the Maine Jobs and Recovery Plan and the CARES Act Coronavirus Relief Fund, as well as an effort to put mobile hot spots and Internet-enabled devices in schools. Additionally, a broadband mapping initiative in the state aims to facilitate broadband expansion efforts to unserved and underserved areas. (Julia Edinger)

City Hall Teams with Jersey City Housing Authority to Bridge Digital Divide

The Jersey City, N.J., mayor's office and the Jersey City Housing Authority (JCHA) have teamed up to announce a new broadband expansion initiative. In partnership with the Internet service provider Andrena, the initiative aims to expand access through public housing developments with discounted Internet infrastructure and services—starting at $20 per month. This initiative will pair with the subsidies available through the FCC's Affordable Connectivity Program.

"The digital surge during the COVID-19 pandemic has changed the way we live, work and educate, and it has put an urgency on the need to close the digital divide," said Mayor Steven Fulop in the announcement.

Another key component of combating the digital divide is providing residents with the information they need, which JCHA and Andrena have delivered on by offering weekly community events to help Berry Gardens residents sign up for service, connect devices and obtain available Internet subsidies. The city also launched a public outreach campaign to educate residents on the resources available to them.

The program has gone live at the Berry Gardens senior housing development, and in the coming months, it will launch in Booker T. Washington, Curries Woods and Marion Gardens communities. (Julia Edinger)

https://www.govtech.com/civic/whats-new-in-civic-tech-a-federal-digital-literacy-bill

GLOSSARY

1-bit watermarking: a type of digital watermark that embeds one bit of binary data in the signal to be transmitted; also called "0-bit watermarking."

3D rendering: the process of creating a 2-D animation using 3-D models.

3D Touch: a feature that senses the pressure with which users exert upon Apple touch screens.

abstract learning: learning that involves the comprehension and manipulation of ideas without tangible reference points to aid understanding, such as higher mathematics, literature, philosophy, and so forth.

abstraction: a technique used to reduce the structural complexity of programs, making them easier to create, understand, maintain, and use.

accelerometer IC: an integrated circuit that measures acceleration.

acceptable-use policy (AUP): a document that communicates the expectation that school technology will be used responsibly and exclusively for educational purposes.

access level: in a computer security system, a designation assigned to a user or group of users that allows access a predetermined set of files or functions.

accommodation: According to Piaget's theory of knowing, humans attempt to maintain a state of equilibrium by either assimilating new information and experiences or accommodating them. Accommodation takes place when new information contradicts what was previously known, so that the learner must modify cognitive structures, modify the new information, or both.

actuator: a motor designed to control the movement of a device or machine by transforming potential energy into kinetic energy.

adaptation: Piaget transferred the concept of adaptation from his studies in biology to the studying of human learning. He defined adaptation as the ability to survive in one's environment; with regard to knowledge, he believed knowledge is 'true' to the extent that it's useful and adaptive, rather than the extent to which it mirrors an objective, independent reality.

address space: the amount of memory allocated for a file or process on a computer.

adware: software that generates advertisements to present to a computer user.

affective learning: learning that deals largely with the emotions and psychological outlook of students, drawing upon personal emotional responses rather than, traditionally, intellectual schemata.

agile software development: an approach to software development that addresses changing requirements as they arise throughout the process, with programming, implementation, and testing occurring simultaneously.

algorithm: a set of precise, computable instructions that, when executed in the correct order, will provide a solution to a certain problem.

alias: Two names or identifiers are aliases if they name or identify the same thing.

American National Standards Institute (ANSI): a nonprofit organization that oversees the creation and use of standards and certifications such as those offered by CompTIA.

amplifier: a device that strengthens the power, voltage, or current of a signal.

analog signal: a continuous signal whose values or quantities vary over time.

analytic combinatorics: a method for creating precise quantitative predictions about large sets of objects.

anchor activity: a management strategy used in differentiated classrooms to "anchor" a group of students, engaging them in a meaningful task directly related to the unit of study, while the teacher meets with a small group of students to introduce, re-teach, or assess a skill or understanding.

Android Open Source Project: a project undertaken by a coalition of mobile phone manufacturers and other interested parties, under the leadership of Google. The purpose of the project is to develop the Android platform for mobile devices.

animation variables (avars): defined variables used in computer animation to control the movement of an animated figure or object.

app: an application that executes on a small, handheld device.

applications: software installed on computers (or web-accessed) that allow users to perform a wide range of activities. The full term is usually used for desktop computing devices, while the shorter one (app) is always used for tablets and smart devices like phones and watches.

application-level firewalls: firewalls that serve as proxy servers through which all traffic to and from applications must flow.

application program interface (API): the code that defines how two pieces of software interact, particularly a software application and the operating system on which it runs.

application suite: a set of programs designed to work closely together, such as an office suite that includes a word processor, spreadsheet, presentation creator, and database application.

application-specific GUI: a graphical interface designed to be used for a specific application.

applied learning: any form of learning immediately put into the context of a real world, practical problem-solving context. It is often applied when analyzing vocational education programs.

artificial intelligence (AI): the intelligence exhibited by machines or computers, in contrast to human, organic, or animal intelligence.

ASCII: The original common character code for computers using 8 bits.

assimilation: According to Piaget's theory of knowing, humans attempt to maintain a state of equilibrium by either assimilating new information and experiences or accommodating them. Assimilation takes place when new information is consistent with what was previously known, so that it can be "taken in" without modifying existing cognitive structures.

assistive technologies (AT): any item, piece of equipment, or product system, whether acquired commercially off the shelf, modified, or customized, that is used to increase, maintain, or improve the functional capabilities of a person with a disability.

asymmetric-key encryption: a process in which data is encrypted using a public encryption key but can only be decrypted using a different, private key.

asynchronous discussion: any text-based conversation between parties that does not occur in real time. Discussion boards, where people's responses can be made hours, days or months apart, offer an example of an asynchronous discussion.

asynchronous learning: Asynchronous learning occurs when students and instructors can interact with one another at different times and from different places, rather than interacting at the same time. Asynchronous learning is a typical methodology for online classes, where students log on and participate according to their own schedules rather than at a set time.

attenuation: the loss of intensity from a signal being transmitted through a medium.

attributes: the specific features that define an object's properties or characteristics.

audio codec: a program that acts as a "coder-decoder" to allow an audio stream to be encoded for storage or transmission and later decoded for playback.

authentication: the process by which the receiver of encrypted data can verify the identity of the sender or the authenticity of the data.

automatic sequential control system: a mechanism that performs a multistep task by triggering a series of actuators in a particular sequence.

automaton: a machine that mimics a human but is generally considered to be unthinking.

autonomic components: self-contained software or hardware modules with an embedded capacity for self-management, connected via input/outputs (I/Os) to other components in the system.

autonomous: able to operate independently, without external or conscious control.

autonomous agent: a system that acts on behalf of another entity without being directly controlled by that entity.

backdoor: a hidden method of accessing a computer system that is placed there without the knowledge of the system's regular user in order to make it easier to access the system secretly.

base-16: a number system using sixteen symbols, 0 through 9 and A through F.

base-2 system: a number system using the digits 0 and 1.

BASIC: Beginners All-purpose Symbolic Instruction Code, a family of languages developed for teaching programming and given away with early IBM PCs.

battery: In electricity, any device for storing an electrical charge so that it can be used later to power a machine, heater, or light source.

behavioral marketing: advertising to users based on their habits and previous purchases.

behaviorism: a school of thought in psychology which holds that all behavior can be studied and explained scientifically through observable actions and responses. Internal thoughts and feelings are not considered, as they cannot be seen.

binary: Pertaining to 2. Binary operators have two operands. Binary numbers have base 2 and use 2 symbols.

binary number system: A mathematical system having only two numerals, 0 and 1, most commonly used in computer hardware and software, because at its most basic, a computer can turn a series of switches on (value = 1) or off (value = 0). *See also* computer.

bioethics: the study of issues surrounding advances in medicine and biology.

bioinformatics: the scientific field focused on developing computer systems and software to analyze and examine biological data.

bioinstrumentation: devices that combine biology and electronics in order to interface with a patient's body and record or monitor various health parameters.

biomarker: short for "biological marker"; a measurable quality or quantity (e.g., internal temperature, amount of iron dissolved in blood) that serves as an indicator of an organism's health, or some other biological phenomenon or state.

biomaterials: natural or synthetic materials that can be used to replace, repair, or modify organic tissues or systems.

biomathematics: The professional field concerned with applying mathematical techniques to analyze and model biological phenomena.

biomechanics: the various mechanical processes such as the structure, function, or activity of organisms.

bioMEMS: short for "biomedical micro-electromechanical system"; a microscale or nanoscale self-contained device used for various applications in health care.

biometrics: measurements that can be used to distinguish individual humans, such as a person's height, weight, fingerprints, retinal pattern, or genetic makeup.

bionics: the use of biologically based concepts and techniques to solve mechanical and technological problems.

biosignal processing: the process of capturing the information the body produces, such as heart rate, blood pressure, or levels of electrolytes, and analyzing it to assess a patient's status and to guide treatment decisions.

birthday problem: The birthday problem is a classic probability problem first presented by mathematician and scientist Richard von Mises in 1939. The problem asks: Given that there is some number of people (n) in a room, what is the probability that at least two of them share the same birthday? The answer is much different than what most people intuitively expect.

bit: a single binary digit that can have a value of either 0 or 1.

bit rate: the amount of data encoded for each second of video; often measured in kilobits per second (kbps) or kilobytes per second (Kbps).

bit width: the number of bits used by a computer or other device to store integer values or other data.

blended learning: Blended learning refers to an educational experience which is not entirely conducted through in person class meetings, nor through purely online interactions, but which uses a combination of both strategies.

blog: an online writing tool that allows an individual to post multiple written comments that are then published in reverse chronological order on the internet.

bookshare: an online library of ebooks formatted for use by people with print disabilities that prevent them from utilizing traditional, printed books. Bookshare operates under an exemption to U.S. copyright law that allows nonprofits to make books available to those with disabilities, without the need to acquire permission from the books' publishers or copyright holders.

Boolean search: A search in which different terms are combined using the operations "and," "or," and "not'; for instance, a search on "algebra AND software" would find documents containing both terms, while a search on "algebra OR software" would find documents containing either term, and "algebra NOT software" would find articles containing the term algebra but not the term software.

bootstrapping: a self-starting process in a computer system, configured to automatically initiate other processes after the booting process has been initiated.

botnet: a collection of computers that have been infected with software by computer hackers to force those computers to commit crimes, such as sending out computer viruses or unsolicited email (spam).

bridge: a connection between two or more networks, or segments of a single network, that allows the computers in each network or segment to communicate with one another.

broadcast: an audio or video transmission sent via a communications medium to anyone with the appropriate receiver.

butterfly effect: an effect in which small changes in a system's initial conditions lead to major, unexpected changes as the system develops.

byte: a group of eight bits.

caching: the storage of data, such as a previously accessed web page, in order to load it faster upon future access.

carrier signal: an electromagnetic frequency that has been modulated to carry analog or digital information.

cathode ray tube (CRT): a vacuum tube used to create images in devices such as older television and computer monitors.

central processing unit (CPU): electronic circuitry that provides instructions for how a computer handles processes and manages data from applications and programs.

channel capacity: the upper limit for the rate at which information transfer can occur without error.

character: a unit of information that represents a single letter, number, punctuation mark, blank space, or other symbol used in written language.

chat: a form of online discussion that takes places in real-time.

chatterbot: a computer program that mimics human conversation responses in order to interact with people through text; also called "talkbot," "chatbot," or simply "bot."

Children's Internet Protection Act (CIPA): a federal law enacted by Congress in 2000 to address concerns about access to offensive content over the internet in schools and libraries.

circular wait: a situation in which two or more processes are running and each one is waiting for a resource that is being used by another; one of the necessary conditions for deadlock.

clock speed: the speed at which a microprocessor can execute instructions; also called "clock rate."

cloud computing: a form of technology service where the user's data and applications are stored in and run on a server to which the user connects over the internet. This contrasts with the traditional model in which both data and application are housed on the local machine that the user has physical access to.

code: a piece of text that cannot be understood without a key, hence the source code for a program.

coding theory: the study of codes and their use in certain situations for various applications.

command line: a text-based computer interface that allows the user to input simple commands via a keyboard.

communication architecture: the design of computer components and circuitry that facilitates the rapid and efficient transmission of signals between different parts of the computer.

communication devices: devices that allow drones to communicate with users or engineers in remote locations.

competency-based learning: an approach to education that relies on the demonstrated acquisition of relevant skills by students as a means of evaluating progress, rather than the accumulation of hours of instruction time. This approach is lauded for its flexible approach to education, which allows students to learn in their own way and demonstrate that learning in their own way as well.

compliance: adherence to standards or specifications established by an official body to govern a particular industry, product, or activity.

component: A unit of composition with contractually specified interfaces and only explicit context dependencies; components can be deployed and composed by third parties, often a collection of objects with a given set of methods for handling them and abstract classes that can be defined by other people.

component-based development: an approach to software design that uses standardized software components to create new applications and new software.

compressed data: data that has been encoded such that storing or transferring the data requires fewer bits of information.

computational linguistics: a branch of linguistics that uses computer science to analyze and model language and speech.

computational mathematics: Also known as mathematics *in silico*, computational mathematics is the process of modeling systems quantitatively on computers.

computer: Any device that can be programmed to perform mechanical or electrical computation, processing numbers. Since the middle of the twentieth century, the term is commonly used for equipment that can be programmed using a binary number system to perform a variety of work. For a computer to process letters, words, graphic images, or maps, human programmers have to encode nonnumerical data in a numeric form. *See also* binary number system.

computer-aided instruction (CAI): less sophisticated than Intelligent Tutoring Systems, CAI refers to computer technology that assists the teaching and learning process.

computer algebra systems: A type of software that allows computers to solve problems that go beyond mere calculation, such as simplifying rational functions, factoring polynomials, and finding solutions to a system of equations.

computer-based training (CBT): any instruction and learning that takes place using computer technology.

Computer Fraud and Abuse Act (CFAA): a 1986 legislative amendment that made accessing a protected computer without authorization, or exceeding one's authorized level of access, a federal offense.

computer technician: a professional tasked with the installation, repair, and maintenance of computers and related technology.

constraints: limitations on values in computer programming that collectively identify the solutions to be produced by a programming problem.

constructivism: a school of thought in psychology which holds that knowledge is constructed internally within the individual, and that learners continually construct new knowledge through experience.

content management system: a software system that allows users to manage the content of a collection of data including computer files, audio files, graphics and images, electronic documents, and web content.

control character: a unit of information used to control the manner in which computers and other devices process text and other characters.

control statement: a statement that permits a processor to select the next of several possible computations according to various conditions.

cookie: a small data file that allows websites to track users.

cooperative multitasking: an implementation of multitasking in which the operating system will not initiate a context switch while a process is running in order to allow the process to complete.

core voltage: the amount of power delivered to the processing unit of a computer from the power supply.

counter: a digital sequential logic gate that records how many times a certain event occurs in a given amount of time.

coupling: the degree to which different parts of a program are dependent upon one another.

cracker: a criminal hacker; one who finds and exploits weak points in a computer's security system to gain unauthorized access for malicious purposes.

crippleware: software programs in which key features have been disabled and can only be activated after registration or with the use of a product key.

crosstalk: interference of the signals on one circuit with the signals on another, caused by the two circuits being too close together.

cryptology: The science of encrypting or decrypting information, including creating codes for privacy or security and finding means to break a code by working from a message in an unknown code to learn the pattern. Any code in which a symbol is substituted for each letter of the alphabet is particularly vulnerable to decryption, because in a large sample, there is a probability for how often each letter will appear, with "e" being used more often than any other. *See also* encoding.

cultural capital: a form of symbolic capital made popular by French sociologist Pierre Bourdieu. In his work, Bourdieu showed that besides money, other forms of capital regulate access to social classes. Cultural capital comprises knowledge, network connections, and experiences.

curriculum compacting: a methodology employed for students who demonstrate they have already mastered a skill or understanding. Rather than repeat mastered material, students are provided with the opportunity to work on alternative, more challenging assignments.

cyberbullying: the use of the internet and other Web-enabled mobile technologies to systematically harass someone, often in the presence of other members of an online community.

cybercrime: crime that involves targeting a computer or using a computer or computer network to commit a crime, such as computer hacking, digital piracy, and the use of malware or spyware.

cybersafety: a term used to describe information and actions taken to help keep users safe online.

cyberstalking: the use of the internet and other Web-enabled mobile technologies to track the movements of another individual, often with the intent of doing that person harm.

cyberterrorism: the use of the internet and other Web-enabled mobile technologies to plan terrorist activities.

database: a collection of data items used for multiple purposes that is stored on a computer.

database management system: a software program that allows users to manage the data in a database. Database management systems are designed to increase the accessibility of data and the productivity of the user.

data granularity: the level of detail with which data is collected and recorded.

data integrity: the degree to which collected data is and will remain accurate and consistent.

data mining: the process using algorithms to search for meaningful patterns in large collections of data, often without stating any kind of a hypothesis in advance. Data mining draws on the knowledge base of several fields of study, including statistics, artificial intelligence, and machine learning.

data source: the origin of the information used in a computer model or simulation, such as a

data width: a measure of the amount of data that can be transmitted at one time through the computer bus, the specific circuits and wires that carry data from one part of a computer to another.

datapath design: describes how data flows through the CPU and at what points instructions will be decoded and executed.

deep learning: an emerging field of artificial intelligence research that uses neural network algorithms to improve machine learning.

default: An item provided in place of an omitted item.

delta debugging: an automated method of debugging intended to identify a bug's root cause while eliminating irrelevant information.

demography: variations in human population that can be studied statistically, in defined groups, rather than individual behavior. Almost any characteristic can form the basis for demographic research: ethnicity, diet, religion, wealth, language, education, urbanization, occupation, marriage customs, class or caste distinctions.

denial of service attack: a method by which computer hackers send a swarm of data to a certain website to overwhelm its servers and prevent the company for transacting normal business online.

device: equipment designed to perform a specific function when attached to a computer, such as a scanner, printer, or projector.

device fingerprinting: information that uniquely identifies a particular computer, component, or piece of software installed on the computer. This can be used to find out precisely which device accessed a particular online resource.

device manager: an application that allows users of a computer to manipulate the device drivers installed on the computer, as well as adding and removing drivers.

differentiated instruction: a theory of instruction based on the premise that learning approaches should vary and be adapted relative to the abilities and learning styles of each individual student in the classroom.

digital citizenship: the use of technology and information to promote legal and ethical behavior regarding the application of information and technology to social and political issues.

digital commerce: the purchase and sale of goods and services via online vendors or information technology systems.

digital divide: a concept that describes the unequal access to technology that exists because of the stratification of society into different economic classes. Many families are unable to afford their own computers, tablets, smartphones, and similar gadgetry, and even when some of these devices are available (most libraries have computers for public use, for example), not everyone has the opportunity or educational background to make use of them.

digital legacy (digital remains): the online accounts and information left behind by a deceased person.

digital literacy: familiarity with the skills, behaviors, and language specific to using digital devices to access, create, and share content through the Internet.

digital immigrant: an individual born before the digital age who had to learn the intricacies of digital technology as it evolved.

digital native: an individual born during the digital age or raised using digital technology and communication.

digital society: a form of society in which electronically stored and processed information is a main constituent for the functions of society, replacing material constituents (e.g., products of craftsmanship) in most sectors. Is contrasted with the analog society, a form of society in which material objects constitute the main functions of society.

direct manipulation interfaces: computer interaction format that allows users to directly manipulate graphical objects or physical shapes that are automatically translated into coding.

direct-access storage: a type of data storage in which the data has a dedicated address and location on the storage device, allowing it to be accessed directly rather than sequentially.

discussion board: an online conversation/communication tool where writers post questions and comments under individual categories or threads. Respondents can respond at any time to the thread, and users can review responses at any time. Generally, answers remain available indefinitely.

disequilibrium: According to Piaget, learning is motivated by an individual's desire to maintain a state of equilibrium. Disequilibrium occurs when new information or experience conflicts with what was previously known, requiring the individual to modify or adapt in some way.

distance learning: an umbrella term for any instruction that occurs remotely, rather than in person. Teachers and students may communicate via mail, telephone, email or online programs.

distributed algorithm: an algorithm designed to run across multiple processing centers and so is capable of directing a concentrated action between several computer systems.

dynamic: Something that is done as the program runs rather than by the compiler before the program runs.

dynamic random-access memory (DRAM): a form of RAM in which the device's memory must be refreshed on a regular basis, or else the data it contains will disappear.

dynamic testing: a testing technique in which software input is tested and output is analyzed by executing the code.

ebook: an electronic book consisting of text, images, or both, to be read on computers, e-readers, and other digital devices, sometimes enhanced with sound, video, animation, and so on. Usually, to be considered an ebook, a text needs to be published/available in print form and/or be of such a length that it would qualify as a book (as opposed to an article or essay).

e-health: healthcare that is supported by information technology. This can take a variety of forms, from electronic medical records, to health-related websites for patients, to smartphones being used to accumulate a patient's heart activity over a set time period, to surgeons using robot arms to operate from remote locations.

e-learning: also known as online learning or virtual education, e-learning may use of a variety of electronic media, including, but not limited to: text, streaming video, instant messaging, document sharing software, online learning environments, webcams, blogging, and streaming video. Among other things, e-learning encompasses the integration of computer technology into the traditional classroom, online courses and online colleges, free online education resources, and online corporate learning tools.

Electronic Communications Privacy Act: a 1986 law that extended restrictions on wiretapping to cover the retrieval or interception of information transmitted electronically between computers or through computer networks.

electronic interference: the disturbance generated by a source of electrical signal that affects an electrical circuit, causing the circuit to degrade or malfunction. Examples include noise, electrostatic discharge, and near-field and far-field interference.

embedded system: a computer system that is incorporated into larger devices or systems to monitor performance or to regulate system functions.

emulator: a program that mimics the functionality of a mobile device and is used to test apps under development.

e-reader: a handheld computer designed for use in storing and displaying ebooks in one or more file formats.

e-waste: short for "electronic waste"; computers and other digital devices that have been discarded by their owners.

Electronic Communications Privacy Act: a 1986 law that extended restrictions on wiretapping to cover the retrieval or interception of information transmitted electronically between computers or through computer networks.

electronic interference: the disturbance generated by a source of electrical signal that affects an electrical circuit, causing the circuit to degrade or malfunction. Examples include noise, electrostatic discharge, and near-field and far-field interference.

encoding: Representing information by a system of symbols or characters. Encoding processes exist in human memory, heredity, computer programming, and in written or verbal communication, including military or business communications intended to be secret. The most common use is to take a message in a plain language and convert it into a sequence of characters that can be read only by a person instructed in the code—or by a cryptologist who can break the code by mathematically analyzing the pattern. Natural encoding processes include the genetic code, which stores in long molecules of DNA the structure, physiology, and metabolism of a complete living organism. *See also* binary number system, computer, cryptology, DNA.

engagement: a marketing term for the active involvement of a consumer with a brand or online content. Most people are familiar with "clicks," a measure of how often a specific web page (or file) is opened. Clicks are a measure of passive receiving of content. Engagement is more valuable to marketers; it is a measure of, in essence, the attention that is paid to content. Comment sections in online newspapers are encouraged because of the assumption that if a reader is engaging socially on the page, he/she is paying more attention and thus more likely to respond positively to advertisements on that page.

Environmental Protection Agency (EPA): US government agency tasked with combating environmental pollution.

firewall: a virtual barrier that filters traffic as it enters and leaves the internal network, protecting internal resources from attack by external sources.

fixed point: a type of digital signal processing in which numerical data is stored and represented with a fixed number of digits after (and sometimes before) the decimal point, using a minimum of sixteen bits.

flash memory: nonvolatile computer memory that can be erased or overwritten solely through electronic signals, i.e., without physical manipulation of the device.

floating point: a type of digital signal processing in which numerical data is stored and represented in the form of a number (called the mantissa, or significand) multiplied by a base number (such as base-2) raised to an exponent, using a minimum of thirty-two bits.

floating-point arithmetic: a calculation involving numbers that have a decimal point that can be placed anywhere through the use of exponents, as is done in scientific notation.

force-sensing touch technology: touch display that can sense the location of the touch as well as the amount of pressure the user applies, allowing for a wider variety of system responses to the input.

frames per second (FPS): a measurement of the rate at which individual video frames are displayed.

friend/follower/mutual: one of the central concepts of social networking services (SNS), a "friend" is not coequal with friend in the conventional sense of a member of one's social circle to whom one is especially close. A Facebook "friend" can include a celebrity or author the user has added, for instance, or an online acquaintance the user knows little about beyond enjoying his or her posts. Some services use follower/followed terminology: while a "friend" connection is mutual (on Facebook, a friend request is made by one user and must be accepted by the other). On Twitter and many other SNSs, users have two separate but overlapping lists: a list of the accounts they follow and a list of the accounts that follow them. In such cases, an account that is both a follower and is followed is a "mutual."

function: instructions read by a computer's processor to execute specific events or operations.

functional programming: a theoretical approach to programming in which the emphasis is on applying mathematics to evaluate functional relationships that are, for the most part, static.

game loop: the main part of a game program that allows the game's physics, artificial intelligence, and graphics to continue to run with or without user input.

game theory: a branch of mathematics dedicated to analyzing strategic behavior in which several people or entities must make choices even when the outcomes of their decisions rely on the choices made by others.

gateway: a device capable of joining one network to another that has different protocols.

gesture: a combination of finger movements used to interact with multitouch displays in order to accomplish various tasks. Examples include tapping the finger on the screen, double-tapping, and swiping the finger along the screen.

global positioning system (GPS): A system owned by the United States government and operated by the Air Force for determining the exact position on the surface of the Earth of any user or defined landmark. By receiving signals from any of 24 orbiting satellites that are in direct line of site to a user's position, GPS devices can calculate latitude, longitude, altitude, and time.

graphical user interface (GUI): an interface that allows users to control a computer or other device by interacting with graphical elements such as icons and windows.

Green Electronics Council: a US nonprofit organization dedicated to promoting green electronics.

GroupMe: a mobile group messaging service launched in 2010, which became popular in 2013, and continues to slowly attract more users. GroupMe members can join free and send free messages among groups of people, and as such the app has become popular for high school and college students to share notes and discussions for individual classes.

hacking: the use of technical skill to gain unauthorized access to a computer system; also, any kind of advanced tinkering with computers to increase their utility.

hacktivism: electronic attacks by computer attackers on certain business or electronic websites, with the aim of spreading their message about the organization through online graffiti.

hardware: the physical parts that make up a computer. These include the motherboard and processor, as well as input and output devices such as monitors, keyboards, and mice.

hardware interruption: a device attached to a computer sending a message to the operating system to inform it that the device needs attention, thereby "interrupting" the other tasks that the operating system was performing.

Harvard architecture: a computer design that has physically distinct storage locations and signal routes for data and for instructions.

Health Insurance Portability and Accountability Act (HIPAA): a 1996 law that established national standards for protecting individuals' medical records and other personal health information.

hibernation: a power-saving state in which a computer shuts down but retains the contents of its random-access memory.

hierarchical file system: a directory with a treelike structure in which files are organized.

homebrew: software that is developed for a device or platform by individuals not affiliated with the device manufacturer; it is an unofficial or "homemade" version of the software that is developed to provide additional functionality not included or not permitted by the manufacturer.

host-based firewall: a firewall that protects a specific device, such as a server or personal computer, rather than the network as a whole.

HTML: hypertext markup language; used to define pages on the WWW.

HTML editor: a computer program for editing web pages encoded in hypertext markup language (HTML).

humanoid: resembling a human.

hybrid cloud: a cloud computing model that combines public cloud services with a private cloud platform linked through an encrypted connection.

identifiers: measurable characteristics used to identify individuals.

imitation game: Alan Turing's name for his proposed test, in which a machine would attempt to respond to questions in such a way as to fool a human judge into thinking it was human.

immersive mode: a full-screen mode in which the status and navigation bars are hidden from view when not in use.

imperative language: language that instructs a computer to perform a particular sequence of operations.

imperative programming: programming that produces code that consists largely of commands issued to the computer, instructing it to perform specific actions.

individualized Instruction: a teaching practice that considers the needs of each individual student and customizes instruction accordingly.

information hiding: the doctrine that design choices should be hidden by the modules in which they are implemented.

information hierarchy: the relative importance of the information presented on a web page.

information society: a form of society in which the production, distribution, use, and conservation of knowledge and information is a main factor in all social aspects from the political and economic sectors to the cultural sector. The term is used to describe the economies in the United States and other First World nations, based as they are on the flow of information via the internet.

information technology: A broad professional field drawing on many disciplines, including computer science, information systems, and software engineering. information technology includes any expertise that helps create, modify, store, manage, or communicate information, including networking, systems management, program development, computer hardware, interface design, information assurance, systems integration, database management, and web technologies.

infrastructure as a service: a cloud computing platform that provides additional computing resources by linking hardware systems through the Internet; also called "hardware as a service."

Initiative for Software Choice (ISC): a consortium of technology companies founded by CompTIA, with the goal of encouraging governments to allow competition among software manufacturers.

input: data supplied to some program, subprogram, OS, machine, system, or abstraction.

input/output (I/O) instructions: instructions used by the central processing unit (CPU) of a computer when information is transferred between the CPU and a device such as a hard disc.

interface: the function performed by the device driver, which mediates between the hardware of the peripheral and the hardware of the computer.

interference: anything that disrupts a signal as it moves from source to receiver.

internal-use software: software developed by a company for its own use to support general and administrative functions, such as payroll, accounting, or personnel management and maintenance.

internet of things: a wireless network connecting devices, buildings, vehicles, and other items with network connectivity.

interpolation: a process of estimating intermediate values when nearby values are known; used in image editing to "fill in" gaps by referring to numerical data associated with nearby points.

interpreter: A program which executes another program written in a programming language other than machine code.

iOS: Apple's proprietary mobile operating system, installed on Apple devices such as the iPhone, iPad, and iPod touch.

iPads: small mobile computers manufactured by Apple that broke ground in the tablet computer market and pioneered mobile devices designed to enhance classroom learning.

IRL relationships: relationships that occur "in real life," meaning that the relationships are developed or sustained outside of digital communication.

jailbreak: the removal of restrictions placed on a mobile operating system to give the user greater control over the mobile device.

JavaScript: a flexible programming language that is commonly used in website design.

jQuery: a free, open-source JavaScript library.

kernel: the central component of an operating system.

keyframing: a part of the computer animation process that shows, usually in the form of a drawing, the position and appearance of an object at the beginning of a sequence and at the end.

language interface packs: programs that translate interface elements such as menus and dialog boxes into different languages.

laser: A light source that emanates from a well-defined wavelength; originally an acronym for light amplified by stimulated emission of radiation.

learner-controlled program: software that allows a student to set the pace of instruction, choose which content areas to focus on, decide which areas to explore when, or determine the medium or difficulty level of instruction; also known as a "student-controlled program."

learning strategy: a specific method for acquiring and retaining a particular type of knowledge, such as memorizing a list of concepts by setting the list to music.

learning style: an individual's preferred approach to acquiring knowledge, such as by viewing visual stimuli, reading, listening, or using one's hands to practice what is being taught.

lexicon: the total vocabulary of a person, language, or field of study.

light-emitting diode (LED): A diode constructed to provide illumination from the movement of electrons through a semiconductor, which is housed in a bulb that concentrates the light in a desired direction. Because there is no filament to warm up, as in a conventional electric light bulb, LEDs use ten percent or less electrical current to provide the same brightness of light and last up to twenty times longer. LEDs can be constructed to provide almost any desired color or hue of light.

linear predictive coding: a popular tool for digital speech processing that uses both past speech samples and a mathematical approximation of a human vocal tract to predict and then eliminate certain vocal frequencies that do not contribute to meaning. This allows speech to be processed at a faster bit rate without significant loss in comprehensibility.

livelock: a situation in which two or more processes constantly change their state in response to one another in such a way that neither can complete.

local area network (LAN): a network that connects electronic devices within a limited physical area.

local: Related to the current instruction rather than a larger context.

logic programming: A style or paradigm of computer programming exemplified by the language Prolog.

logical copy: a copy of a hard drive or disk that captures active data and files in a different configuration from the original, usually excluding free space and artifacts such as file remnants; contrasts with a physical copy, which is an exact copy with the same size and configuration as the original.

logotype: a company or brand name rendered in a unique, distinct style and font; also called a "wordmark."

lossless compression: data compression that allows the original data to be compressed and reconstructed without any loss of accuracy.

lossy compression: a method of decreasing image file size by discarding some data, resulting in some image quality being irreversibly sacrificed.

low-energy connectivity IC: an integrated circuit that enables wireless Bluetooth connectivity while using little power.

machine code: system of instructions and data directly understandable by a computer's central processing unit.

magnetic storage: a device that stores information by magnetizing certain types of material.

main loop: the overarching process being carried out by a computer program, which may then invoke subprocesses.

main memory: the primary memory system of a computer, often called "random access memory" (RAM), accessed by the computer's central processing unit (CPU).

malware: malicious software, a form of software designed to disrupt a computer or to take advantage of computer users.

mastering: the creation of a master recording that can be used to make other copies for distribution.

Medical Device Innovation Consortium: a nonprofit organization established to work with the US Food and Drug Administration on behalf of medical device manufacturers to ensure that these devices are both safe and effective.

medical imaging: the use of devices to scan a patient's body and create images of the body's internal structures to aid in diagnosis and treatment planning.

metadata: data that contains information about other data, such as author information, organizational information, or how and when the data was created.

microcontroller: a tiny computer in which all of the essential parts of a computer are united on a single microchip—input and output channels, memory, and a processor.

micron: a unit of measurement equaling one millionth of a meter; typically used to measure the width of a core in an optical figure or the line width on a microchip.

middle computing: computing that occurs at the application tier and involves intensive processing of data that will subsequently be presented to the user or another, intervening application.

million instructions per second (MIPS): a unit of measurement used to evaluate computer performance or the cost of computing resources.

mixing: the process of combining different sounds into a single audio recording.

mobile website: a website that has been optimized for use on mobile devices, typically featuring a simplified interface designed for touch screens.

modeling: the process of creating a 2-D or 3-D representation of the structure being designed.

module: A program that is linked with others to form a functioning application; one method of implementing a subroutine.

morphology: a branch of linguistics that studies the forms of words.

multi-agent system: a system consisting of multiple separate agents, either software or hardware systems, that can cooperate and organize to solve problems.

multiple intelligences: eight major intelligences including verbal / linguistic, logical / mathematical, visual / spatial, bodily / kinesthetic, musical / rhythmical, naturalist / environmental, interpersonal and intrapersonal. These intelligences serve as indicators to help assess learning preferences and styles.

multi-terminal configuration: a computer configuration in which several terminals are connected to a single computer, allowing more than one person to use the computer.

multibit watermarking: a watermarking process that embeds multiple bits of data in the signal to be transmitted.

multicast: a network communications protocol in which a transmission is broadcast to multiple recipients rather than to a single receiver.

multiplexing: combining multiple data signals into one in order to transmit all signals simultaneously through the same medium.

multiplier-accumulator: a piece of computer hardware that performs the mathematical operation of multiplying two numbers and then adding the result to an accumulator.

multiprocessing: the use of more than one central processing unit to handle system tasks; this requires an operating system capable of dividing tasks between multiple processors.

multitasking: in computing, the process of executing multiple tasks concurrently on an operating system (OS); in the mobile phone environment, allowing different apps to run concurrently, much like the ability to work in multiple open windows on a PC.

multitouch gestures: combinations of finger movements used to interact with touch-screen or other touch-sensitive displays in order to accomplish various tasks. Examples include double-tapping and swiping the finger along the screen.

multiuser: capable of being accessed or used by more than one user at once.

network: two or more computers being linked in a way that allows them to transmit information back and forth.

network firewalls: firewalls that protect an entire network rather than a specific device.

networking: the use of physical or wireless connections to link together different computers and computer networks so that they can communicate with one another and collaborate on computationally intensive tasks.

neural network: in computing, a model of information processing based on the structure and function of biological neural networks such as the human brain.

neuroplasticity: the capacity of the brain to change as it acquires new information and forms new neural connections.

neutron: A neutral particle within the nucleus of an atom, having neither a positive or negative electrical charge and a weight slightly more than that of a proton. *See also* atom, electron, proton.

nibble: a group of four bits.

node: any point on a computer network where communication pathways intersect, are redistributed, or end (i.e., at a computer, terminal, or other device).

noise: interferences or irregular fluctuations affecting electrical signals during transmission.

noise-tolerant signal: a signal that can be easily distinguished from unwanted signal interruptions or fluctuations (i.e., noise).

nondestructive editing: a mode of image editing in which the original content of the image is not destroyed because the edits are made only in the editing software.

nongraphical: not featuring graphical elements.

nonlinear editing: a method of editing video in which each frame of video can be accessed, altered, moved, copied, or deleted regardless of the order in which the frames were originally recorded.

nonvolatile memory: computer storage that retains its contents after power to the system is cut off, rather than memory that is erased at system shutdown.

nonvolatile random-access memory (NVRAM): a form of RAM in which data is retained even when the device loses access to power.

normalization: a process that ensures that different code points representing equivalent characters will be recognized as equal when processing text.

numerical analysis: The study of how to design, implement, and optimize algorithms that provide approximate values to variables in mathematical expressions.

object-oriented programming: a type of programming in which the source code is organized into objects, which are elements with a unique identity that have a defined set of attributes and behaviors.

object-oriented user interface: an interface that allows users to interact with onscreen objects as they would in real-world situations, rather than selecting objects that are changed through a separate control panel interface.

online community: a group that interacts primarily or exclusively online, especially one that has a specific site for doing so. While those online communities are explicitly defined—users usually need to either create accounts for the community or use some external service's account to access it—the term is also used to describe the more amorphous communities that develop around a given interest or topic, such as "the online community of Battlestar Galactica fans," in which case community interactions take place across a variety of platforms. Online communities are significantly older than modern SNS, having begun in the 1980s with Bulletin Board Systems and email lists.

online victimization: incidences in which users, especially children and adolescents, encounter intimidating and inappropriate sexual content, solicitation, or harassment.

open-source software: Software for which the source code is made freely available. Examples of open-source software include the BNU-Linus operating system, the Mozilla Firefox internet browser, the statistical and graphing language R, and the programming language Python.

operating system (OS): a specialized program that manages a computer's functions.

operating system shell: a user interface used to access and control the functions of an operating system.

operation: One of a set of functions with special syntax and semantics that can be used to construct an expression.

optical storage: storage of data by creating marks in a medium that can be read with the aid of a laser or other light source.

optical touchscreens: touchscreens that use optical sensors to locate the point where the user touches before physical contact with the screen has been made.

optics: the study of light, including all systems for gathering, concentrating, and manipulating light, such as mirrors, spectacles, telescopes, microscopes, cameras, spectroscopes, lasers, fiber optic communications, and optical data storage and retrieval.

packet filters: filters that allow data packets to enter a network or block them on an individual basis.

packet forwarding: the transfer of a packet, or unit of data, from one network node to another until it reaches its destination.

packet sniffers: a program that can intercept data or information as it moves through a network.

packet switching: a method of transmitting data over a network by breaking it up into units called packets, which are sent from node to node along the network until they reach their destination and are reassembled.

paradigm: A fundamental style of computer programming to which the design of a programming language typically has to cater, such as imperative programming, declarative programming, or, on a finer level, functional programming, logic programming or object-oriented programming.

parameter: a measurable element of a system that affects the relationships between variables in the system.

parallel processing: the division of a task among several processors working simultaneously, so that the task is completed more quickly.

PATRIOT Act: a 2001 law that expanded the powers of federal agencies to conduct surveillance and intercept digital information for the purpose of investigating or preventing terrorism.

pattern recognition: A field of study concerned with identifying patterns within any type of data, from mathematical models to photographs and auditory information. Applied pattern recognition aims to create machines capable of independently identifying patterns and using patterns to perform tasks or make decisions.

pedagogy: a philosophy of teaching that addresses the purpose of instruction and the methods by which it can be achieved.

peer-to-peer (P2P) network: a network in which all computers participate equally and share coordination of network operations, as opposed to a client-server network, in which only certain computers coordinate network operations.

pen/trap: short for pen register or trap-and-trace device, devices used to record either all numbers called from a particular telephone (pen register) or all numbers making incoming calls to that phone (trap and trace); also refers to the court order that permits the use of such devices.

peripheral: a device that is connected to a computer and used by the computer but is not part of the computer, such as a printer, scanner, external storage device, and so forth.

personal area network (PAN): a network generated for personal use that allows several devices to connect to one another and, in some cases, to other networks or to the internet.

personally identifiable information (PII): information that can be used to identify a specific individual.

phased software development: an approach to software development in which most testing occurs after the system requirements have been implemented.

phishing: the use of online communications in order to trick a person into sharing sensitive personal information, such as credit card numbers or social security numbers.

Phonebloks: a concept devised by Dutch designer Dave Hakkens for a modular mobile phone intended to reduce electronic waste.

pipelined architecture: a computer design where different processing elements are connected in a series, with the output of one operation being the input of the next.

piracy: in the digital context, unauthorized reproduction or use of copyrighted media in digital form.

PL: programming language.

planned obsolescence: a design concept in which consumer products are given an artificially limited lifespan, therefore creating a perpetual market.

platform: the specific hardware or software infrastructure that underlies a computer system; often refers to an operating system, such as Windows, Mac OS, or Linux.

platform as a service: a category of cloud computing that provides a virtual machine for users to develop, run, and manage web applications.

plug-in: an application that is easily installed (plugged in) to add a function to a computer system.

polarity: The existence of two opposite characteristics, such as the north and south poles of a magnet or the positive and negative poles of a battery.

port scanning: the use of software to probe a computer server to see if any of its communication ports have been left open or vulnerable to an unauthorized connection that could be used to gain control of the computer.

portlet: an independently developed software component that can be plugged into a website to generate and link to external content.

postproduction: the period after a model has been designed and an image has been rendered, when the architect may manipulate the created image by adding effects or making other aesthetic changes.

preemptive multitasking: an implementation of multitasking in which the operating system will initiate a context switch while a process is running, usually on a schedule so that switches between tasks occur at precise time intervals.

Pretty Good Privacy: a data encryption program created in 1991 that provides both encryption and authentication.

principle of least privilege: a philosophy of computer security that mandates users of a computer or network be given, by default, the lowest level of privileges that will allow them to perform their jobs. This way, if a user's account is compromised, only a limited amount of data will be vulnerable.

printable characters: characters that can be written, printed, or displayed in a manner that can be read by a human.

printed circuit board: a flat copper sheet shielded by fiberglass insulation in which numerous lines have been etched and holes have been punched, allowing various electronic components to be connected and to communicate with one another and with external components via the exposed copper traces.

prisoner's dilemma: a famous problem in game theory, in which two participants must each choose one of two possible outcomes. It is most often described by the following type of story: two criminals are interrogated separately concerning a crime. Each can confess or not confess, and the length of their sentence depends not only on their own behavior, but also on that of the other participant (and they cannot collaborate with each other, or otherwise influence the other's decision).

Privacy Incorporated Software Agents (PISA): a project that sought to identify and resolve privacy problems related to intelligent software agents.

procedure: a subroutine or function coded to perform a specific task.

process: the execution of instructions in a computer program.

processor coupling: the linking of multiple processors within a computer so that they can work together to perform calculations more rapidly. This can be characterized as loose or tight, depending on the degree to which processors rely on one another.

processor symmetry: multiple processors sharing access to input and output devices on an equal basis and being controlled by a single operating system.

program: a software application, or a collection of software applications, designed to perform a specific task.

programming languages: sets of terms and rules of syntax used by computer programmers to create instructions for computers to follow. This code is then compiled into binary instructions for a computer to execute.

projected capacitive touch: technology that uses layers of glass etched with a grid of conductive material that allows for the distortion of voltage flowing through the grid when the user touches the surface; this distortion is measured and used to determine the location of the touch.

proprietary software: software owned by an individual or company that places certain restrictions on its use, study, modification, or distribution and typically withholds its source code.

prototype: a piece of software that requires more work before it is finished, but is complete enough for the value of the finished product to be evaluated or the current version improved.

proxy: a dedicated computer server that functions as an intermediary between a user and another server.

proxy server: a computer through which all traffic flows before reaching the user's computer.

pseudocode: a combination of a programming language and a spoken language, such as English, that is used to outline a program's code.

public-key cryptography: a system of encryption that uses two keys, one public and one private, to encrypt and decrypt data.

push technology: a communication protocol in which a messaging server notifies the recipient as soon as the server receives a message, instead of waiting for the user to check for new messages.

radio waves: low-frequency electromagnetic radiation, commonly used for communication and navigation.

random access memory (RAM): memory that the computer can access very quickly, without regard to where in the storage media the relevant information is located.

ransomware: malware that encrypts or blocks access to certain files or programs and then asks users to pay to have the encryption or other restrictions removed.

rapid prototyping: the process of creating physical prototype models that are then tested and evaluated.

raster: a means of storing, displaying, and editing image data based on the use of individual pixels.

readiness: a student's entry point relative to a skill or new technology.

read-only memory (ROM): a type of nonvolatile data storage that can be read by the computer system but cannot be modified.

real-time monitoring: a process that grants administrators access to metrics and usage data about a software program or database in real time.

real-time operating system: an operating system that is designed to respond to input within a set amount of time without delays caused by buffering or other processing backlogs.

receiver: a device that reads a particular type of transmission and translates it into audio or video.

recursive: describes a method for problem solving that involves solving multiple smaller instances of the central problem.

remote monitoring: a platform that reviews the activities on software or systems that are located off-site.

render farm: a cluster of powerful computers that combine their efforts to render graphics for animation applications.

rendering: the process of transforming one or more models into a single image; the production of a computer image from a 2-D or 3-D computer model; the process of selecting and displaying glyphs.

resistive touchscreens: touchscreens that can locate the user's touch because they are made of several layers of conductive material separated by small spaces; when the user touches the screen, the layers touch each other and complete a circuit.

resource allocation: a system for dividing computing resources among multiple, competing requests so that each request is eventually fulfilled.

resource distribution: the locations of resources available to a computing system through various software or hardware components or networked computer systems.

resource holding: a situation in which one process is holding at least one resource and is requesting further resources; one of the necessary conditions for deadlock.

reversible data hiding: techniques used to conceal data that allow the original data to be recovered in its exact form with no loss of quality.

RGB: a color model that uses red, green, and blue to form other colors through various combinations.

robotics: an interdisciplinary field concerned with the design, development, operation, and assessment of electromechanical devices used to perform tasks that would otherwise require human action. Robotics has many applications, from performing repetitive tasks in industrial assembly lines to surgery to the operation of advanced military vehicles.

routing: selecting the best path for a data packet to take in order to reach its destination on the network.

run time: the time during which a program is executing, as oppose to the compile time.

Sarbanes-Oxley Act (SOX): a 2002 law that requires all business records, including electronic records and electronic messages, to be retained for a certain period of time.

scareware: malware that attempts to trick users into downloading or purchasing software or applications to address a computer problem.

scientific method: a process for investigating nature by observation and experiment, creating hypotheses to make sense of observations.

Scientific Working Group on Digital Evidence (SWGDE): an American association of various academic and professional organizations interested in the development of digital forensics systems, guidelines, techniques, and standards.

screen-reading program: a computer program that converts text and graphics into a format accessible to visually impaired, blind, learning disabled, or illiterate users.

script: a group of written signs, such as Latin or Chinese characters, used to represent textual information in a writing system.

scrubbing: navigating through an audio recording repeatedly in order to locate a specific cue or word.

search engine optimization (SEO): techniques used to increase the likelihood that a website will appear among the top results in certain search engines.

selection: a statement that chooses between several possible execution paths in a program.

semantics: a branch of linguistics that studies the meanings of words and phrases.

semiconductor: a material that conducts electricity more efficiently than an insulator, but less efficiently than a conductor, useful in constructing diodes, which conduct electricity in only one direction. Common semiconductor materials include silicon, germanium, and selenium. Semiconductors are essential to construction and design of computers and most electronic equipment.

sensor: a device capable of detecting, measuring, or reacting to external physical properties.

separation of concerns: a principle of software engineering in which the designer separates the computer program's functions into discrete elements.

set: A collection of objects, usually of the same type, described either by enumerating the elements or by stating a common property, or by describing rules for constructing items in the set.

shadow RAM: a form of RAM that copies code stored in read-only memory into RAM so that it can be accessed more quickly.

shell: an interface that allows a user to operate a computer or other device.

short message service (SMS): the technology underlying text messaging used on cell phones.

signal-to-noise ratio (SNR): the power ratio between meaningful information, referred to as "signal," and background noise.

silent monitoring: listening to the exchanges between an incoming caller and an employee, such as a customer service agent.

simulation: a computer model executed by a computer system.

smartphone: a mobile telephone that has the capability of running software applications and accessing the internet.

social network: in the social sciences, a structure consisting of a set of individuals, the ties that connect them, and the interactions among them. Social networks are usually informal but may overlap with formal, official social groups; for instance, a social network analysis of a high school class would include a formal group (students enrolled in that class and faculty assigned to it) and many informal groups (various groups of friends, project partners, or study groups, and depending on the scope of the analysis, relevant interactions with individuals outside the class, such as library personnel, parents, friends, or members of the administration). Sometimes social network is used informally as a synonym for social networking service, but they are distinct, albeit related, concepts.

social network analysis: a cross-disciplinary method for analyzing social networks (a set of actors and the relationships that connect them) that integrates techniques from science, social science, mathematics, computer science, communication, and business.

social networking services (SNS): online platforms in which one of the primary functions is to create and maintain social networks that users opt into (by adding one another as friends or following accounts). Often synonymous with social media, but technically social media is a related concept that includes online social services that either do not use or do not require defined social networks.

software as a service: a software service system in which software is stored at a provider's data center and accessed by subscribers.

software: the sets of instructions that a computer follows in order to carry out tasks. Software may be stored on physical media, but the media is not the software.

software-defined antennas: reconfigurable antennas that transmit or receive radio signals according to software instructions.

software patch: an update to software that correct bugs or make other improvements.

solid modeling: the process of creating a 3-D representation of a solid object.

solid-state storage: computer memory that stores information in the form of electronic circuits, without the use of discs or other read/write equipment.

sound card: a peripheral circuit board that enables a computer to accept audio input, convert signals between analog and digital formats, and produce sound.

source code: Human-readable instructions in a programming language, to be transformed into machine instructions by a compiler, interpreter, assembler or other such system.

speaker independent: describes speech software that can be used by any speaker of a given language.

special character: a character such as a symbol, emoji, or control character.

spreadsheet: a table of values arranged in rows and columns in which the values have predefined relationships. Spreadsheet application software allows users to create and manipulate spreadsheets electronically.

spyware: software installed on a computer that allows a third party to gain information about the computer user's activity or the contents of the user's hard drive.

stack: A collection of data items where new items are added and old items retrieved at the same place, so that the last item added is always the first item retrieved, and so on. An important part of compilers, interpreters, processors, and programs.

static random-access memory (SRAM): a form of RAM in which the device's memory does not need to be regularly refreshed but data will still be lost if the device loses power.

statistical process control: A method of quality control in industry in which random samples of an output stream are selected and compared to their design standard, variations from the desired value are determined, and the data accumulated over time are analyzed to determine patterns of variation.

Strava: a social media service available online and by application wherein athletes post activities they participate in, collected usually by wearable GPS devices, and share them with other users who "follow" them. Groups and clubs may form sub-communities within Strava, and users can choose to post as privately (themselves) or publicly as they so desire. GPS data can also be hidden, so users cannot be tracked extensively.

subclass: In object-oriented programming, an object class derived from another class (its superclass) from which it inherits a base set of properties and methods.

subprogram: A piece of code that has been named and can be referred to by that name (called) as many times as is needed. Either a procedure or a function.

subroutine: A section of code that implements a task. While it may be used at more than one point in a program, it need not be.

supercomputer: an extremely powerful computer that far outpaces conventional desktop computers.

surface capacitive technology: a glass screen coated with an electrically conductive film that draws current across the screen when it is touched; the flow of current is measured in order to determine the location of the touch.

symmetric-key cryptography: a system of encryption that uses the same private key to encrypt and decrypt data.

synchronous discussions: online discussions that occur in real-time, meaning participants must be online at the same time to participate. Chat is an example of synchronous discussion.

syntax: a branch of linguistics that studies how words and phrases are arranged in sentences to create meaning.

system: a set of interacting or interdependent component parts that form a complex whole; a computer's combination of hardware and software resources that must be managed by the operating system.

system agility: the ability of a system to respond to changes in its environment or inputs without failing altogether.

system identification: the study of a system's inputs and outputs in order to develop a working model of it.

system software: the basic software that manages the computer's resources for use by hardware and other software.

tableless web design: the use of style sheets rather than HTML tables to control the layout of a web page.

tablet: a mobile computer that is small enough to be held in the hand and that provides access to a wide range of software applications and the internet. A self-contained touch screen and trackpad replace a peripheral monitor, keyboard, and mouse.

telecom equipment: hardware that is intended for use in telecommunications, such as cables, switches, and routers.

telemedicine: health care provided from a distance using communications technology, such as video chats, networked medical equipment, smartphones, and so on.

telemetry: automated communication process that allows a machine to identify its position relative to external environmental cues.

terminal: a set of basic input devices, such as a keyboard, mouse, and monitor, that are used to connect to a computer running a multi-user operating system.

third-party data center: a data center service provided by a separate company that is responsible for maintaining its infrastructure.

thread: the smallest part of a programmed sequence that can be managed by a scheduler in an OS.

tiered activities: a collection of assignments designed at different levels of complexity and depth according to student readiness levels.

time-sharing: a strategy used by multi-user operating systems to work on multiple user requests by switching between tasks in very small intervals of time: the use of a single computing resource by multiple users at the same time, made possible by the computer's ability to switch rapidly between users and their needs.

topology: the way a network is organized, including nodes and the links that connect nodes.

trace impedance: a measure of the inherent resistance to electrical signals passing through the traces etched on a circuit board.

trackbacks: tools that allow bloggers to notify someone when they link to another blogger's blog or to be notified when someone else links to theirs.

transactional database: a database management system that allows a transaction— a sequence of operations to achieve a single, self-contained task—to be undone, or "rolled back," if it fails to complete properly.

transistor: a computing component generally made of silicon that can amplify electronic signals or work as a switch to direct electronic signals within a computer system.

transmedia: literally, across media; more recently, a description of media projects that use multiple platforms (print, film, web, etc.) to communicate an idea, a narrative, or information with greater complexity and dynamic potential than is possible in a single medium.

transmedia play: the engagement of learners in understanding, reconfiguring, creating, collaborating, and communicating various kinds of media content across the conventional barriers that separate learning at school, at home, and in other contexts.

transmission medium: the material through which a signal can travel.

transmitter: a device that sends a signal through a medium to be picked up by a receiver.

transparent monitoring: a system that enables employees to see everything that the managers monitoring them can see.

traveling salesman problem: a classic mathematical problem based in the following premise: Imagine a salesperson that needs to travel to a fixed number of cities. The salesperson wants to begin in his or her hometown, visit every city exactly once, and return to the hometown. In what sequence should the salesperson visit the cities in order to minimize the total amount of traveling time on the road between cities? The significance of the traveling salesman problem (TSP) lies in the fact that many other problems can be translated into a traveling salesman formulation.

tree: a collection of connected objects called nodes with all nodes connected indirectly by precisely one path. An ordered tree has a root and the connections lead from this root to all other nodes. Nodes at the end of the paths are called leaves. The connections are called branches. All computer science trees are drawn upside-down with the root at the top and the leaves at the bottom.

tuning: the process of making minute adjustments to a computer's settings in order to improve its performance.

Turing test: a game proposed by computer scientist and mathematician Alan Turing in 1950 in order to determine whether machines can think.

tweet: a message posted to the social media service Twitter, limited to a maximum of 140 characters.

type: A tag attached to variables and values used in determining what values may be assigned to what variables; A collection of similar objects, See ADT and data type. Objects can be fundamental, pointers, or have their type determined by their class.

typography: the art and technique of arranging type to make language readable and appealing.

ubiquitous computing: an approach to computing in which computing activity is not isolated in a desktop, laptop, or server, but can occur everywhere and at any time through the use of microprocessors embedded in everyday devices.

ultrasound: vibrations or sound waves at a higher frequency than the human ear can detect.

undervolting: reducing the voltage of a computer system's central processing unit to decrease power usage.

unmanned aerial vehicle (UAV): an aircraft that does not have a pilot onboard but typically operates through remote control, automated flight systems, or preprogrammed computer instructions.

user-centered design: design based on a perceived understanding of user preferences, needs, tendencies, and capabilities.

user-generated content: content contributed by users on an online community or SNS, such as uploaded images and videos, text posts/blogs/status updates, or comments. A key development of the internet in the 21st century is the increasing centrality of user-generated content in commercial online spaces, whether the comments sections of newspaper articles or the news feeds of Twitter and Facebook.

utility program: a type of system software that performs one or more routine functions, such as disk partitioning and maintenance, software installation and removal, or virus protection.

variable: a symbol representing a quantity with no fixed value.

video scratching: a technique in which a video sequence is manipulated to match the rhythm of a piece of music.

virtual memory: memory used when a computer configures part of its physical storage (on a hard drive, for example) to be available for use as additional RAM. Information is copied from RAM and moved into virtual memory whenever memory resources are running low.

virtual reality: the use of technology to create a simulated world into which a user may be immersed through visual and auditory input.

virus: a piece of rogue computer code that, when allowed to operate on a computer, causes the computer to malfunction, often leading to the loss or compromising of sensitive electronic data such as banking information or Social Security numbers.

voice over internet protocol (VoIP): a set of parameters that make it possible for telephone calls to be transmitted digitally over the Internet, rather than as analog signals through telephone wires.

volatile memory: memory that stores information in a computer only while the computer has power; when the computer shuts down or power is cut, the information is lost.

wardriving: driving around with a device such as a laptop that can scan for wireless networks that may be vulnerable to hacking.

web application: an application that is downloaded either wholly or in part from the internet each time it is used.

widget: an independently developed segment of code that can be plugged into a website to display information retrieved from other sites.

wiki: a website that allows anyone with access to the site to add or change the content.

word prediction: a software feature that recognizes words that the user has typed previously and offers to automatically complete them each time the user begins typing.

worm: a type of malware that can replicate itself and spread to other computers independently; unlike a computer virus, it does not have to be attached to a specific program.

zombie computer: a computer that is connected to the Internet or a local network and has been compromised such that it can be used to launch malware or virus attacks against other computers on the same network.

TIMELINE OF DIGITAL LITERACY

The timeline below lists technological milestones and cultural events related to the development of digital technologies and artificial intelligence.

3000 BCE The method of writing known as cuneiform begins as pictographs but evolves into more abstract patterns of wedge-shaped marks, usually impressed into wet clay. This system of marks allows record keeping to develop.

ca. 1023-957 BCE Yan Shi presents King Mu of Zhou with mechanical men.

800-700 BCE Greek myths of Hephaestus and Pygmalion incorporated the idea of intelligent robots (Talos) and artificial beings (Galatea and Pandora).

384–322 BCE Aristotle describes the syllogism, a method of formal, mechanical thought.

ca. 300 BCE Archimedes describes simple machines: the lever, the pulley, and the screw. He also creates the scientific method, the first useful set of rules attempting to explain how scientists practice science.

10–70 Heron of Alexandria creates mechanical men and other automatons.

260 Porphyry of Tyros writes *Isagogê*, which categorizes knowledge and logic.

800 Geber develops the Arabic alchemical theory of Takwin, the artificial creation of life in the laboratory, up to and including human life.

815 al-Khwārizmī develops algebra, the mathematics that solves problems by using letters for unknowns (variables) and expressing their relationships with equations.

1034 Movable type made of baked clay is invented in China.

1206 al-Jazari creates a programmable orchestra of mechanical human beings.

1260 Roger Bacon develops rules for explaining how scientists practice science that emphasize empiricism and experimentation over accepted authority.

1439 Johann Gutenberg creates the printing press, which makes learning possible for the masses instead of just the learned. Gutenberg combined a press, oil-based ink, and movable type made from an alloy of lead, zinc, and antimony to create a revolution in printing, allowing mass-produced publications that could be made relatively cheaply and easily disseminated to people.

1485 Leonardo da Vinci designs a parachute, great wings flapped by levers, and a person-carrying machine with wings to be flapped by the person. Although these flying devices were never successfully realized, the designs introduced the modern quest for aeronautical engineering.

1580	Rabbi Judah Loew ben Bezalel of Prague is said to have invented the Golem, a clay man brought to life.
1594	John Napier's logarithms allow the simplification of complex multiplication and division problems.
1637	René Descartes proposes that bodies of animals are nothing more than complex machines (but that mental phenomena are of a different "substance").
1641	Thomas Hobbes publishes *Leviathan* and presents a mechanical, combinatorial theory of cognition.
1642	Eighteen-year-old Blaise Pascal invents the first mechanical calculator, which helps his father, a tax collector, count taxes.
1672	Gottfried Wilhelm Leibniz develops a calculator that can add, subtract, multiply, and divide, as well as the binary system of numbers used by computers today.
1672	Gottfried Leibniz improves his earlier machines, making the Stepped Reckoner to do multiplication and division. He also invents the binary numeral system and envisions a universal calculus of reasoning (alphabet of human thought) by which arguments could be decided mechanically. Leibniz worked on assigning a specific number to each and every object in the world, as a prelude to an algebraic solution to all possible problems.
1738	Jacques de Vaucanson builds cunning, self-operating devices (Flute Player and Digesting Duck automatons) to charm viewers.
1750	Julien Offray de La Mettrie publishes *L'Homme Machine*, which argues that human thought is strictly mechanical.
1763	Thomas Bayes's work *An Essay Towards Solving a Problem in the Doctrine of Chances* is published two years after his death, having been amended and edited by a friend of Bayes, Richard Price. The essay presents work that underpins Bayes theorem.
1796	Aloys Senefelder invents lithography and a process for color lithography in 1826.
1798	Eli Whitney develops an assembly line for muskets using interchangeable parts.
1800	Charles Stanhope invents the first printing press made of iron.
1805	Adrien-Marie Legendre describes the "méthode des moindres carrés," known in English as the least squares method. The least squares method is used widely in data fitting.
1812	Pierre-Simon Laplace publishes *Théorie Analytique des Probabilités*, in which he expands upon the work of Bayes and defines what is now known as Bayes' Theorem.

1818	Joseph Nicéphore Niépce creates the first lasting photographic images.
	Mary Shelley publishes the story of *Frankenstein; or the Modern Prometheus*, a fictional consideration of the ethics of creating sentient beings.
1821	Louis Braille develops a tactile alphabet—a system of raised dots on a surface—that allows the blind to read by touch.
1822	Charles Babbage's difference "engine" is a programmable mechanical device used to calculate the value of a polynomial—a precursor to today's modern computers.
1826	Aloys Senefelder invents color lithography.
1835	Joseph Nicéphore Niépce codevelops photography with Louis-Jacques-Mandé Daguerre.
1837	Electric telegraph is invented. William Fothergill Cooke and Charles Wheatstone devise a system that uses five pointing needles to indicate alphabetic letters.
	The mathematician Bernard Bolzano makes the first modern attempt to formalize semantics.
1839	Improving on the discoveries of Joseph Nicéphore Niépce, Jacques Daguerre develops the first practical photographic process, the Daguerreotype.
1840	Samuel F. B. Morse creates his electrical telegraph. Others had already built telegraph systems, but Morse's system is superior and soon replaced all others.
1841	William Henry Fox Talbot, an English polymath, invents the calotype process, which produces the first photographic negative.
1843	Richard March Hoe creates the rotary printing press. Patented in 1847, the steam-powered rotary press is far faster than the flatbed press.
1854	George Boole set out to "investigate the fundamental laws of those operations of the mind by which reasoning is performed, to give expression to them in the symbolic language of a calculus," inventing Boolean algebra.
1859	Charles Babbage & Ada Lovelace complete a decades-long project to develop mechanical calculating machines.
1860	William Bullock creates the web rotary printing press. Bullock's press has an automatic paper feeder, can print on both sides of the paper, cut the paper into sheets, and fold them.
1861	Thomas Sutton develops the first color photo based on Scottish physicist James Clerk Maxwell's three-color process.

1863	Samuel Butler suggests that Darwinian evolution also applies to machines, and speculates that they will one day become conscious and eventually supplant humanity.
1873	After patenting the first practical typewriter, Christopher Latham Sholes develops the QWERTY keyboard, designed to slow the fastest typists, who otherwise jammed the keys. The basic QWERTY design remains the standard on most computer keyboards.
1876	Alexander Graham Bell and Elisha Gray file for a patent for the telephone the same day. While the case is not clear-cut, and Gray fought with Bell for years over the patent rights, Bell is generally credited with the telephone's invention.
1877	Thomas Alva Edison invents the phonograph—an unexpected outcome of his telephone research.
1878	American inventor Frederic Eugene Ives develops the halftone process for printing photographs.
1884	George Eastman creates the first roll film. It will replace heavy plates, making photography both more accessible and more convenient.
1886	Ottmar Mergenthaler designs the linotype machine. Pressing keys on the machine's keyboard releases letter molds that drop into the current line. The lines are assembled into a page and then filled with molten lead.
1886	The gramophone is invented by Emile Berliner. A major contribution to the music recording industry, Berliner's gramophone uses flat record discs for recording sound. Berliner goes on to produce a helicopter prototype (1906-1923).
1887	A radio transmitter and receiver are created by Heinrich Hertz. Hertz will use these devices to discover radio waves and confirm that they are electromagnetic waves that travel at the speed of light; he also discovers the photoelectric effect.
	Distortionless transmission lines are created by Oliver Heaviside. Heaviside recommends that induction coils be added to telephone and telegraph lines to correct for distortion.
1888	Charles Eastman and William Hall invent the Kodak camera, making photography accessible to the masses.
1889	George Eastman replaces paper film with celluloid.
1892	Thomas Alva Edison completes his Kinetoscope; the first demonstration is held a year later.
	William Seward Burroughs builds the first practical key-operated calculator; it prints entries and results.

1893　　　The first color photography plate is created by Gabriel Jonas Lippmann. It uses interference patterns, rather than various colored dyes, to reproduce authentic color.

1895　　　The Victrola phonograph is created by Eldridge R. Johnson. Johnson develops a spring-driven motor for phonographs that provides the constant record speed necessary for good sound reproduction.

Auguste Lumière's and Louis Lumière's combined motion-picture camera, printer, and projector (called a Cinématographe) helps establish the movie business. Using a very fine-grained silver-halide gelatin emulsion, they cut photographic exposure time down to about one minute.

Aleksandr Stepanovich Popov demonstrates radio reception with a coherer, which he also used as a lightning detector.

1896　　　Guglielmo Marconi is the first to send wireless signals across the Atlantic Ocean, inaugurating a new era of telecommunications.

1900　　　George Eastman introduces the Kodak Brownie camera. It is sold for $1 and the film it uses costs 15 cents. The Brownie made photography an accessible hobby to almost everyone.

1905　　　Albert Einstein announces his theory of special relativity. At the age of twenty-six, Einstein uses the constancy of the speed of light to explain motion, time, and space beyond Newtonian principles. During the same year, he publishes papers describing the photoelectric effect and Brownian motion.

1905　　　French psychologist Alfred Binet devises the first of a series of tests to measure an individual's innate ability to think and reason.

1906　　　Broadcast radio is realized by Reginald Aubrey Fessenden. In broadcast radio, sound wave forms are added to a carrier wave and then broadcast. The carrier wave is subtracted at the receiver leaving only the sound.

1908　　　Lee De Forest invents a vacuum tube used in sound amplification. In 1922, he will develop talking motion pictures, in which the sound track is imprinted on the film with the pictures, instead of on a record to be played with the film, leading to exact synchronization of sound and image.

1910　　　Neon lighting is created by Georges Claude. The glowing tubes revolutionize advertising displays.

1913　　　Bertrand Russell and Alfred North Whitehead published *Principia Mathematica*, which revolutionized formal logic.

1915　　　Albert Einstein refines his 1905 theory of relativity (now called special relativity) to describe the theory that states that uniform accelerations are almost indistinguishable from gravity. Einstein's theory provides the basis for physicists' best understanding of gravity and of the framework of the universe.

1915   Leonardo Torres y Quevedo builds a chess automaton, El Ajedrecista, and publishes speculation about thinking and automata.

1923   Karel apek's play R.U.R. (*Rossum's Universal Robots*) opens in London. This is the first use of the word "robot" in English.

1925   Leitz introduces the first 35-millimeter Leica camera at the Leipzig Spring Fair.

First U.S. television broadcast: Charles Francis Jenkins transmits the silhouette image of a toy windmill.

1927   Philo T. Farnsworth transmits the first all-electronic television image using his newly developed camera vacuum tube, known as the image dissector. Previous systems combined electronics with mechanical scanners.

Vannevar Bush builds the first analogue computer. He is also the first person to describe the idea of hypertext.

1928   The first regularly scheduled television programs in the United States air. They are produced out of a small, experimental station in Wheaton, Maryland.

1928   IBM introduces a new punch card that has rectangular holes and eight columns.

NBC establishes the first coast-to-coast radio network in the United States.

1929   Vladimir Zworykin claims that he, not Philo T. Farnsworth, should be credited with the invention of television.

Harold E. Edgerton's strobe is used as a flash bulb. He pioneers the development of high-speed photography.

1930   Bernhard Voldemar Schmidt's telescope uses a spherical main mirror and a correcting lens at the front of the scope. It can photograph large fields with little distortion.

1931   One of the founders of the field of radio astronomy, Karl G. Jansky detects radio static coming from the Milky Way's center, paving the way for more radio astronomy studies.

Kurt Gödel showed that sufficiently powerful formal systems, if consistent, permit the formulation of true theorems that are unprovable by any theorem-proving machine deriving all possible theorems from the axioms. To do this he had to build a universal, integer-based programming language, which is the reason why he is sometimes called the "father of theoretical computer science."

1933   Semi Joseph Begun builds the first tape recorder, a dictating machine using wire for magnetic recording. He also develops the first steel tape recorder for mobile radio broadcasting and leads research into telecommunications and underwater acoustics.

Alan Dower Blumlein's patent for stereophonic recording is granted.

1935　　　　Edwin H. Armstrong exploits the fact that, since there are no natural sources of frequency modulation (FM), FM broadcasts are static-free.

Leopold Mannes and Leopold Godowsky, Jr. invent Kodachrome, a color film that is easy to use and produces vibrant colors. (With the digital revolution of the late twentieth century, production of Kodachrome is retired in 2009.)

1937　　　　George Stibitz's model K, an early electronic computer, employs Boolean logic.

1938　　　　Alfred J. Gross's portable, two-way radio, called a walkie-talkie, allows the user to move around while sending messages without remaining tied to a bulky transmitter. Gross invents a pager in 1949 and a radio tuner in 1950 that automatically follows the drift in carrier frequency due to movement of a sender or receiver.

George Philbrick builds the Automatic Control Analyzer, which is an electronic analogue computer.

1939　　　　John Vincent Atanasoff and Clifford Berry's Atanasoff-Berry Computer, the world's first electronic digital computer, uses binary numbers and electronic switching, but it is not programmable.

Hewlett-Packard is founded.

1940　　　　Peter Carl Goldmark produces a system for transmitting and receiving color-television images using synchronized rotating filter wheels on the camera and on the receiver set.

William Redington Hewlett invents the audio oscillator, a device that creates one frequency (pure tone) at a time. It is the first successful product of his Hewlett-Packard Company.

1941　　　　Konrad Zuse and his colleagues complete the first general-purpose, programmable computer, the Z3.

1942　　　　In 1926 Enrico Fermi helps develop Fermi-Dirac statistics, which describe the quantum behavior of groups of electrons, protons, or neutrons. He now produces the first sustained nuclear chain reaction.

1943　　　　Warren Sturgis McCulloch and Walter Pitts publish "A Logical Calculus of the Ideas Immanent in Nervous Activity," laying foundations for artificial neural networks.

Arturo Rosenblueth, Norbert Wiener, and Julian Bigelow coin the term "cybernetics." Wiener's popular book by that name is subsequently published in 1948.

1944　　　　The Mark series of electromechanical computers is built, designed by Howard Aiken and Grace Hopper. The U.S. Navy uses it to calculate trajectories for projectiles.

Colossus, the world's first vacuum-tube programmable logic calculator, is built in Britain for the purpose of breaking Nazi codes.

1945   While Alan Mathison Turing's Automatic Computing Engine (ACE) is never fully realized, it is one of the first stored-program computers.

Hugh Le Caine builds the first music synthesizer, coined the Electronic Sackbut, joined by the Special Purpose Tape Recorder in 1954, which could simultaneously change the playback speed of several recording tracks.

John William Mauchly and John Presper Eckert's Electronic Numerical Integrator and Computer, ENIAC, is the first general-purpose, programmable, electronic computer. (The Z3, developed by Konrad Zuse from 1939 to 1941, did not fully exploit electronic components.) Built to calculate artillery firing tables, ENIAC is used in calculations for the hydrogen bomb.

Game theory, which would prove invaluable in the progress of AI, is introduced with the 1944 paper, Theory of Games and Economic Behavior by mathematician John von Neumann and economist Oskar Morgenstern.

Vannevar Bush publishes "As We May Think" (*The Atlantic Monthly*) a prescient vision of the future in which computers assist humans in many activities.

1946   Marvin Camras develops a magnetic tape recording process that will be adapted for use in electronic media, including music and motion-picture sound recording, audio and videocassettes, floppy disks, and credit card magnetic strips. For decades his method is the primary way to record and store sound, video, and digital data.

1947   Hoping to build a solid-state amplifier, the team of John Bardeen, Walter H. Brattain, and William Shockley discover the transistor, which replaces the vacuum tube in electronics. Bardeen is later part of the group that develops theory of superconductivity.

1948   Dennis Gabor publishes his initial results working with holograms in Nature. Holograms became much more spectacular after the invention of the laser.

Peter Carl Goldmark demonstrates the long-playing record (LP), playing the cello with CBS musicians. The musical South Pacific is recorded in LP format and boosts sales, making the LP the dominant form of recorded sound for the next four decades.

Working to make nuclear reactors safer, Roscoe Koontz invents the gamma-ray pinhole camera. The pinhole acts like a lens and form an image of the gamma source.

Edwin Herbert Land develops the simple process to make sheets of polarizing material. He perfects the Polaroid instant camera in 1972.

Les Paul develops multitrack recording.

1949   Magnetic core memory (Jay Wright Forrester) is used from the early 1950's to the early 1970's.

1950   Oregon optometrist George Butterfield develops a lens that is molded to fit the contours of the cornea. It is called the contact lens.

Alan Turing proposes a "learning machine" that could learn and become artificially intelligent. Turing's specific proposal foreshadows genetic algorithms.

Alan Turing proposes the Turing Test as a measure of machine intelligence.

Claude Shannon publishes a detailed analysis of chess playing as search.

Isaac Asimov publishes his Three Laws of Robotics.

1951   John Mauchly and John Presper Eckert invent the Universal Automatic Computer (UNIVAC). UNIVAC is competitor of IBM's products.

Marvin Minsky and Dean Edmonds build the first neural network machine, able to learn, the SNARC.

The first working AI programs are written to run on the Ferranti Mark 1 machine of the University of Manchester: a checkers-playing program written by Christopher Strachey and a chess-playing program written by Dietrich Prinz.

1952   Grace Murray Hopper invents the compiler, an intermediate program that translates English-language instructions into computer language, followed in 1959 by Common Business Oriented Language (COBOL), the first computer programming language to translate commands used by programmers into the machine language the computer understands.

Arthur Samuel joins IBM's Poughkeepsie Laboratory and begins working on some of the very first machine-learning programs, first creating programs that play checkers.

Arthur Samuel (IBM) writes the first game-playing program, for checkers, to achieve sufficient skill to challenge a respectable amateur. His first checkers-playing program is written in 1952, and in 1955 he creates a version that learned to play.

1954   Jerome H. Lemelson's Machine vision allows a computer to move and measure products and to inspect them for quality control.

The first transistor radio is introduced by Texas Instruments.

The IBM 650 computer becomes available. It is considered by IBM to be its first business computer, and it is the first computer installed at Columbia University in New York.

John Warner Backus develops the computer language Fortran, which is an acronym for "formula translation." Fortran allows direct entry of commands into computers with English-like words and algebraic symbols.

1955   Ernst Alexanderson's television RGB system uses three image tubes to scan scenes through colored filters and three electron guns in the picture tube to reconstruct scenes.

Working at the California offices of International Business Machines (IBM), Alan Shugart develops the disk drive, followed by floppy disks to provide a relatively fast way to store programs and data permanently.

An Wang's pulse transfer controlling device allows magnetic core memory to be written or read without mechanical motion and is therefore very rapid.

1956   Narinder S. Kapany, the father of fiber optics, coins the term "fiber optics." In high school, he was told by a teacher that light moves only in a straight line; he wanted to prove the teacher wrong and wound up inventing fiber optics.

Charles P. Ginsburg's video recorder allows programs to be shown later, to provide instant replays in sports, and to make a permanent record of a program.

IBM produces the first computer disk storage system, the 350 RAMAC, which retrieves data from any of fifty spinning disks.

The Dartmouth College summer AI conference is organized by John McCarthy, Marvin Minsky, Nathan Rochester of IBM and Claude Shannon. McCarthy coins the term artificial intelligence for the conference.

The first demonstration of the Logic Theorist (LT) written by Allen Newell, J.C. Shaw and Herbert A. Simon, is often called the first AI program, though Samuel's checkers program also has a strong claim.

1957   Gordon Gould, Charles Hard Townes, Arthur L. Schawlow, Theodore Harold Maiman succeed in building a small optical laser. Gould coins the term "laser," which stands for light amplification by stimulated emission of radiation.

1958   The microchip, independently discovered by Robert Norton Noyce and Jack St. Clair Kilby, proves to be the breakthrough that allows the miniaturization of electronic circuits and paves the way for the digital revolution.

Jean Hoerni develops the first planar process, which improves the integrated circuit.

John McCarthy (Massachusetts Institute of Technology) invents the Lisp programming language.

Herbert Gelernter and Nathan Rochester (IBM) describe a theorem prover in geometry that exploits a semantic model of the domain in the form of diagrams of "typical" cases.

Teddington Conference on the Mechanization of Thought Processes is held in the UK and among the papers presented were John McCarthy's Programs with Common Sense, Oliver Selfridge's Pandemonium, and Marvin Minsky's Some Methods of Heuristic Programming and Artificial Intelligence.

Jack Kilby invents the integrated circuit, an electronic device that allows for complex circuits to be placed upon a single chip.

1959　　　John McCarthy and Marvin Minsky found the MIT AI Lab.

1950s–1960s　　　Margaret Masterman and colleagues at University of Cambridge design semantic nets for machine translation.

1960　　　John R. Pierce worked on the first passive-relay telecommunications satellite, Echo, reflected signals. The signals, received from one point on Earth, "bounce" off the spherical satellite and are reflected back down to another, far distant, point on Earth.

"Man-Computer Symbiosis" written by J.C.R. Licklider.

1961　　　Walt Disney established WED, a research and development unit that developed the inventions he needed for his various enterprises. WED produced the audio-animatronic robotic figures that populated Disneyland, the 1964-1965 New York World's Fair, films, and other attractions. Audio-animatronics enabled robotic characters to speak or sing as well as move.

James Slagle (PhD dissertation, MIT) wrote (in Lisp) the first symbolic integration program, SAINT, which solved calculus problems at the college freshman level.

In "Minds, Machines and Gödel," John Lucas denied the possibility of machine intelligence on logical or philosophical grounds. He referred to Kurt Gödel's result of 1931: sufficiently powerful formal systems are either inconsistent or allow for formulating true theorems unprovable by any theorem-proving AI deriving all provable theorems from the axioms. Since humans are able to "see" the truth of such theorems, machines were deemed inferior.

Unimation's industrial robot Unimate worked on a General Motors automobile assembly line.

1962　　　John R. Pierce's Telstar satellite is the first satellite to rebroadcast signals goes into operation, revolutionizing telecommunications.

The Philips company of the Netherlands releases the first audiocassette tape.

Optical lithography, a process that places intricate patterns onto silicon chips, is first used in semiconductor manufacturing.

1963　　　Seymour Cray's 6600 computer was the first of a long line of Cray supercomputers.

Donald Michie creates a machine consisting of 304 match boxes and beads, which uses reinforcement learning to play Tic-Tac-Toe (also known as noughts and crosses).

Thomas Evans' program, ANALOGY, written as part of his PhD work at MIT, demonstrated that computers can solve the same analogy problems as are given on IQ tests.

Edward Feigenbaum and Julian Feldman published *Computers and Thought*, the first collection of articles about artificial intelligence.

Leonard Uhr and Charles Vossler published "A Pattern Recognition Program That Generates, Evaluates, and Adjusts Its Own Operators," which described one of the first machine-learning programs that could adaptively acquire and modify features and thereby overcome the limitations of simple perceptrons of Frank Rosenblatt.

1964   Emmett Leith and Juris Upatnieks present the first three-dimensional hologram at the Optical Society of America conference. The hologram must be viewed with a reference laser. The hologram of an object can then be viewed from different angles, as if the object were really present.

Robert Moog invents The Moog synthesizer which uses electronics to create and combine musical sounds.

John Kemeny and Thomas Kurtz develop the BASIC computer programming language. BASIC is an acronym for Beginner's All-purpose Symbolic Instruction Code.

Danny Bobrow's dissertation at MIT (technical report #1 from MIT's AI group, Project MAC), shows that computers can understand natural language well enough to solve algebra word problems correctly.

Bertram Raphael's MIT dissertation on the SIR program demonstrates the power of a logical representation of knowledge for question-answering systems.

Ray Solomonoff lays the foundations of a mathematical theory of AI, introducing universal Bayesian methods for inductive inference and prediction.

The computer mouse is invented by American engineer Douglas Engelbart.

1965   Ken Olsen builds perhaps the first true minicomputer, the PDP-8 is released by Digital Equipment Corporation. Founder Olsen makes computers affordable for small businesses.

Gene Roddenberry creates the science fiction television series *Star Trek*. The series inspires several technological advancements along the way, including ear buds, 3D printers, and phasers, and cell phones, among others.

J. Alan Robinson invents a mechanical proof procedure, the Resolution Method, which allowed programs to work efficiently with formal logic as a representation language.

Joseph Weizenbaum (MIT) builds ELIZA, an interactive program that carries on a dialogue in English language on any topic. It becomes a popular toy at AI centers on the ARPANET when a version that "simulated" the dialogue of a psychotherapist was programmed.

Edward Feigenbaum initiates Dendral, a ten-year effort to develop software to deduce the molecular structure of organic compounds using scientific instrument data. It was the first expert system.

1966   While working for Texas Instruments, Jack St. Clair Kilby does for the adding machine what the transistor had done for the radio, inventing a handheld calculator that retails at $150 and becomes an instant commercial success.

Ross Quillian (PhD dissertation, Carnegie Inst. of Technology, now CMU) demonstrates semantic nets.

Machine Intelligence workshop at Edinburgh is the first of an influential annual series organized by Donald Michie and others.

Negative report on machine translation kills much work in natural language processing (NLP) for many years.

1967   The nearest neighbor algorithm is created, which is the start of basic pattern recognition. The algorithm is used to map routes.

Edward Feigenbaum, Joshua Lederberg, Bruce Buchanan, Georgia Sutherland at Stanford University develop the Dendral program and demonstrate how to interpret mass spectra on organic chemical compounds. It is the first successful knowledge-based program for scientific reasoning.

Stanford's SUMEX-AIM resource project, headed by Ed Feigenbaum and Joshua Lederberg, begins. In the 1970s it demonstrates the power of the ARPAnet for scientific collaboration.

1968   James Fergason develops a practical liquid crystal display (LCD) screen that has good visual contrast, is durable, and uses little electricity.

Douglas Engelbart presents the computer mouse, which he had been working on since 1964.

Astronauts on Apollo 7, the first piloted Apollo mission, take photographs and transmit them to the American public on television.

Bolt Beranek and Newman Incorporated win a Defense Advanced Research Projects Agency (DARPA) contract to develop the packet switches called interface message processors (IMPs).

Joel Moses's PhD work at MIT demonstrates the power of symbolic reasoning for integration problems in the Macsyma program. It becomes the first successful knowledge-based program in mathematics.

Richard Greenblatt at MIT builds a knowledge-based chess-playing program, MacHack, that was good enough to achieve a class-C rating in tournament play.

Wallace and Boulton's program, Snob, becomes a model of and tool for unsupervised learning. It uses classifications (clusterings) such as the Bayesian Minimum Message Length criterion, a mathematical realization of Occam's razor.

1969   Willard S. Boyle and George E. Smith develop the charge-coupled device, the basis for digital imaging.

The Advanced Research Projects Agency starts ARPANET, which is the precursor to the internet. UCLA and Stanford University are the first institutions to become networked.

Marvin Minsky and Seymour Papert publish their book *Perceptrons*, describing some of the limitations of perceptrons and neural networks. The interpretation that the book shows that neural networks are fundamentally limited is seen as a hindrance for research into neural networks.

Stanford Research Institute (SRI) develop Shakey the Robot, which demonstrates a combination of animal locomotion, perception and problem solving.

Roger Schank (Stanford) defines conceptual dependency model for natural language understanding. This is later developed (in PhD dissertations at Yale University) for use in story understanding by Robert Wilensky and Wendy Lehnert and for use in understanding memory by Janet Kolodner.

Yorick Wilks (Stanford) develops the semantic coherence view of language called Preference Semantics, embodied in the first semantics-driven machine translation program; this becomes the basis of many PhD dissertations since such as Bran Boguraev and David Carter at Cambridge.

First International Joint Conference on Artificial Intelligence (IJCAI) held at Stanford.

The Advanced Research Projects Agency Network (ARPANET), the first network to use packet switching, is created.

1970   Robert Murer Maurer, joined by Donald Keck, Peter Schultz, and Frank Zimar, produce an optical fiber that can be used for communication.

The compact disc (CD) is invented by James Russell, and revolutionizes the way digital media is stored.

Bell Laboratories' employees Dennis Ritchie and Kenneth Thompson complete the UNIX operating system, which becomes popular among scientists.

The Network Working Group deploys the initial ARPANET host-to-host protocol, called the Network Control Protocol (NCP), establishing connections, break connections, switch connections, and control flow over the ARPANET.

Seppo Linnainmaa publishes the general method for automatic differentiation (AD) of discrete connected networks of nested differentiable functions. This corresponds to the modern version of backpropagation, but is not yet named as such.

Jaime Carbonell (Sr.) develops SCHOLAR, an interactive program for computer assisted instruction based on semantic nets as the representation of knowledge.

Bill Woods describes Augmented Transition Networks (ATN's) as a representation for natural language understanding.

Patrick Winston's PhD program, ARCH, at MIT uses concepts from examples in the world of children's blocks.

1971

Sony begins selling the first videocassette recorder (VCR) to the public.

Ted Hoff invents the microprocessor, which is a computer's central processing unit (CPU) reduced to the size of a postage stamp.

Erna Schneider Hoover invents the electronic switching system for telecommunications. Hoover's system prioritizes telephone calls and fixes an efficient order to answer them.

Intel builds the world's first microprocessor chip.

Sam Hurst's touch screen can detect if it has been touched and where it was touched.

Terry Winograd's PhD thesis (MIT) demonstrates the ability of computers to understand English sentences in a restricted world of children's blocks, in a coupling of his language understanding program, SHRDLU, with a robot arm that carried out instructions typed in English.

Work on the Boyer-Moore theorem prover started in Edinburgh.

Intel releases the first microprocessor, labeled the 4004.

1972

George R. Carruthers builds the Far-Ultraviolet Camera. The Carruthers-designed camera is used on the Apollo 16 mission.

ARPANET system designer Robert Kahn organizes the first public demonstration of the new network technology at the International Conference on Computer Communications in Washington, D.C.

Nolan K. Bushnell and Ted Dabney register the name of their new computer company, Atari, and issue Pong shortly thereafter, marking the rise of the video game industry.

Karen Spärck Jones publishes the concept of TF-IDF, a numerical statistic that is intended to reflect how important a word is to a document in a collection or corpus. 83% of text-based recommender systems in the domain of digital libraries use tf-idf.

Prolog programming language is developed by Alain Colmerauer.

Earl Sacerdoti develops one of the first hierarchical planning programs, ABSTRIPS.

1973

Robert Steven Ledley designs the Automatic computerized transverse axial (ACTA) whole-body CT scanner. Ledley goes on to spend much of his career promoting the use of electronics and computers in biomedical research.

Vinton Gray Cerf and Robert Kahn develop transmission control protocol/internet protocol (TCP/IP), protocols that enable computers to communicate with one another.

Don Wetzel receives a patent for his Automated Teller Machine (ATM). To make it a success, he shows banks how to generate a group of clients who would use the ATM.

Astronauts aboard Skylab, the first U.S. space station, take high-resolution photographs of Earth using photographic remote-sensing systems. The astronauts also take photographs with handheld cameras.

The Assembly Robotics Group at University of Edinburgh builds Freddy Robot, capable of using visual perception to locate and assemble models.

The Lighthill report gives a largely negative verdict on AI research in Great Britain and forms the basis for the decision by the British government to discontinue support for AI research in all but two universities.

1974

Ted Shortliffe's PhD dissertation on the MYCIN program (Stanford) demonstrates a very practical rule-based approach to medical diagnoses, even in the presence of uncertainty. While it borrowed from DENDRAL, its own contributions strongly influenced the future of expert system development, especially commercial systems.

1975

Robert Metcalfe and David Boggs invent the Ethernet, a system of software, protocols, and hardware allowing instantaneous communication between computer terminals in a local area.

Scientists working at Diode Labs develop the first commercial semiconductor laser that will operate continuously at room temperature.

Earl Sacerdoti develops techniques of partial-order planning in his NOAH system, replacing the previous paradigm of search among state space descriptions. NOAH was applied at SRI International to interactively diagnose and repair electromechanical systems.

Austin Tate develops the Nonlin hierarchical planning system able to search a space of partial plans characterized as alternative approaches to the underlying goal structure of the plan.

Marvin Minsky publishes his widely read and influential "A Framework for Representing Knowledge" defining "frames" as a representation of knowledge, in which many ideas about schemas and semantic links are brought together.

The Meta-Dendral learning program produces new results in chemistry (some rules of mass spectrometry) the first scientific discoveries by a computer to be published in a refereed journal.

Barbara Grosz (SRI) establishes limits to traditional AI approaches to discourse modeling. Subsequent work by Grosz, Bonnie Webber and Candace Sidner developed the notion of "centering", used in establishing focus of discourse and anaphoric references in Natural language processing.

David Marr and MIT colleagues describe the "primal sketch" and its role in visual perception.

Altair releases the first computer to use a microprocessor, the Altair 8800.

The VHS (Video Home System) is invented by the Japanese company JVC. Though Sony's competing Betamax system is released around the same time, JVC allowed companies to use their technology for free, thus signaling the end of the Betamax system.

1976

IBM's 3800 Printing System, first laser printer, is released. The ink jet is invented in the same year but does not become prevalent in homes until 1988.

Steve Jobs co-founds Apple Computer with Steve Wozniak.

Steve Wozniak develops the Apple II, the best-selling personal computer of the 1970's and early 1980's. It features a color graphics display, a built-in keyboard, and expandable memory.

Ray Kurzweil develops the Kurzwell Reading Machine, an optical character reader (OCR) able to read most fonts.

Bill Gates, along with Paul Allen, founds software company Microsoft. Gates will remain head of Microsoft for twenty-five years.

Douglas Lenat's AM program (Stanford PhD dissertation) demonstrates the discovery model (loosely guided search for interesting conjectures).

Randall Davis demonstrates the power of meta-level reasoning in his PhD dissertation at Stanford.

1977

Ivan A. Getting launches the Global Positioning System (GPS) satellite. It is designed to pinpoint the location of a radio receiver on Earth's surface.

The first fiber-optic telephone cables are tested.

British physicist Peter Mansfield develops the echo-planar imaging (EPI).

1978   Tom Mitchell, at Stanford, invents the concept of Version spaces for describing the search space of a concept formation program.

Herbert A. Simon wins the Nobel Prize in Economics for his theory of bounded rationality, one of the cornerstones of AI known as "satisficing."

The MOLGEN program, written at Stanford by Mark Stefik and Peter Friedland, demonstrates that an object-oriented programming representation of knowledge can be used to plan gene-cloning experiments.

1979   William Moggridge, of Grid Systems in England, designs the first laptop computer.

The VisiCalc spreadsheet for Apple II is designed by Daniel Bricklin and Bob Frankston. It helps drive sales of the personal computer and becomes its first successful business application.

Tom Truscott, Jim Ellis, and Steve Belovin create USENET, a "poor man's ARPANET," to share information via e-mail and message boards between Duke University and the University of North Carolina, using dial-up telephone lines.

Bill VanMelle's PhD dissertation at Stanford demonstrates the generality of MYCIN's representation of knowledge and style of reasoning in his EMYCIN program, the model for many commercial expert system "shells."

Jack Myers and Harry Pople at University of Pittsburgh develop INTERNIST, a knowledge-based medical diagnosis program based on Dr. Myers' clinical knowledge.

Cordell Green, David Barstow, Elaine Kant and others at Stanford demonstrate the CHI system for automatic programming.

The Stanford Cart, built by Hans Moravec, becomes the first computer-controlled, autonomous vehicle when it successfully traverses a chair-filled room and circumnavigates the Stanford AI Lab.

BKG, a backgammon program written by Hans Berliner at CMU, defeats the reigning world champion (in part via luck).

Drew McDermott, Jon Doyle, and John McCarthy publish work on non-monotonic logics and formal aspects of truth maintenance.

1980s   Neural Networks become widely used with the Backpropagation algorithm (first described by Paul Werbos in 1974).

1980   The U.S. Department of Defense adopts the TCP/IP suite as a standard.

Kunihiko Fukushima first publishes his work on the neocognitron, a type of artificial neural network (ANN). Neocognition later inspires convolutional neural networks (CNNs).

First National Conference of the American Association for Artificial Intelligence (AAAI) is held at Stanford.

Lisp machines are developed and marketed.

1981   The first IBM PC, the IBM 5100, goes on the market with a $1,565 price tag.

Gerald Dejong introduces Explanation Based Learning, where a computer algorithm analyzes data and creates a general rule it can follow and discard unimportant data.

Danny Hillis designs the connection machine, which utilizes Parallel computing to bring new power to AI, and to computation in general. (Later founds Thinking Machines Corporation)

IBM releases a PC based on the Intel 8088 microprocessor, and this computer will become one of the most ubiquitous computers of all time.

1982   Compact discs are sold and start replacing vinyl records.

John Hopfield popularizes Hopfield networks, a type of recurrent neural network that can serve as content-addressable memory systems.

The Fifth Generation Computer Systems project (FGCS), an initiative by Japan's Ministry of International Trade and Industry, begins in 1982, to create a "fifth generation computer" (see history of computing hardware) which was supposed to perform much calculation utilizing massive parallelism.

1983   Martin Cooper develops the cell phone. It becomes the first mobile (wireless) phone. The DynaTAC 8000X, receives approval by the Federal Communications Commission (FCC), heralding an age of wireless communication.

ARPANET, and the networks attached to it, adopt the TCP/IP networking protocol. All networks that use the protocol are known as the internet.

John Laird and Paul Rosenbloom, working with Allen Newell, complete dissertations on the Soar cognitive architecture, which has been widely used to creative cognitive models of human behavior.

James F. Allen invents the interval calculus, the first widely used formalization of temporal events.

1984   Paul Mockapetris and Craig Partridge develop domain name service, which links unique internet protocol (IP) numerical addresses to names with suffixes such as .mil, .com, .org, and .edu.

Apple introduces the Macintosh, a low-cost, plug-and-play personal computer with a user-friendly graphic interface. The machine was based on the Motorola 68000 microprocessor and featured a built-in screen and mouse.

Philips and Sony introduce the CD-ROM (compact disc read-only memory), which has the capacity to store data of more than 450 floppy disks.

Danish veterinarian Steen M. Willadsen clones a lamb from a developing sheep embryo cell.

Bill Gates' Windows operating system is released.

1985

Mark Dean and Dennis Moeller design and patent the standard way of organizing the central part of a computer and its peripherals, Industry Standard Architecture (ISA) bus.

Terry Sejnowski develops a program that learns to pronounce words in the same way as a baby.

The autonomous drawing program, AARON, is created by Harold Cohen, and is demonstrated at the AAAI National Conference (based on more than a decade of work, and with subsequent work showing major developments).

1986

The process of backpropagation, an algorithm used in artificial intelligence, is described by David Rumelhart, Geoff Hinton and Ronald J. Williams.

The team of Ernst Dickmanns at Bundeswehr University of Munich builds the first robot cars, driving up to 55 mph on empty streets.

Barbara Grosz and Candace Sidner creates the first computation model of discourse, establishing the field of research.

1987

French neurosurgeon Alim-Louis Benabid implants a deep-brain electrical-stimulation system into a patient with advanced Parkinson's disease.

Rick Adams forms UUNET and Bill Schrader forms PSINet to provide commercial internet access.

Marvin Minsky publishes *The Society of Mind*, a theoretical description of the mind as a collection of cooperating agents. He had been lecturing on the idea for years before the book was published (c.f. Doyle 1983).

Rodney Brooks introduces subsumption architecture and behavior-based robotics as a more minimalist modular model of natural intelligence; Nouvelle AI.

Commercial launch of generation 2.0 of Alacrity by Alacritous Inc./Allstar Advice Inc. Toronto founders Alistair Davidson and Mary Chung. It is the first commercial strategic and managerial advisory system. A forward-chaining system with 3,000 rules, it also includes a financial expert feature that can interpret financial statements and models. The system's engine was developed by Paul Tarvydas.

Star Trek returns to television with *The Next Generation* series. Among the new concepts popularized there are holograms and adaptive technologies for the blind. The series also features a robot human and considers the ethical considerations of artificial humans.

1988　　　The first transatlantic fiber-optic cable is installed, linking North America and France.

1989　　　Philip Emeagwali receives the Gordon Bell Prize, considered the Nobel Prize for computing, for his method for tracking oil flow underground using a supercomputer. This method demonstrates the possibilities of computer networking.

Tim Berners-Lee and Robert Cailau find a way to join the idea of hypertext and the young internet, leading to the World Wide Web.

The World debuts as the first provider of dial-up internet access for consumers.

Christopher Watkins develops Q-learning, which greatly improves the practicality and feasibility of reinforcement learning.

Axcelis, Inc. releases Evolver, the first software package to commercialize the use of genetic algorithms on personal computers.

Dean Pomerleau creates ALVINN (an autonomous land vehicle in a neural network).

1990s　　　This decade sees major advances in all areas of AI, with significant demonstrations in machine-learning, intelligent tutoring, case-based reasoning, multi-agent planning, scheduling, uncertain reasoning, data mining, natural language understanding and translation, vision, virtual reality, games, and other topics.

1991　　　Quantum Computer Services changes its name to America Online (AOL). Steve Case is named president. AOL offers e-mail, electronic bulletin boards, news, and other information.

Although carbon nanotubes have been seen before, Sumio Iijima's 1991 paper establishes some basic properties and prompts other scientists' interest in studying them.

DART scheduling application is deployed in the first Gulf War. It validates DARPA's investment of 30 years in AI research.

Linus Torvalds releases Linux, a free, open-source operating system that eventually becomes the most popular operating system in the world.

1992　　　Apple introduces Newton, one of the first handheld computers, or personal digital assistants, which has a liquid crystal display operated with a stylus.

Gerald Tesauro develops TD-Gammon, a computer backgammon program that uses an artificial neural network trained using temporal-difference (TD) learning. TD-Gammon is able to rival the abilities of top human backgammon players.

1993   Shuji Nakamura's blue light-emitting diode (LED) makes white LED light possible (a combination of red, blue, and green).

Ian Horswill extends behavior-based robotics by creating Polly, the first robot to navigate using vision and operate at animal-like speeds (1 meter/second).

Rodney Brooks, Lynn Andrea Stein, and Cynthia Breazeal start the widely publicized MIT Cog project with numerous collaborators in an attempt to build a humanoid robot child in just five years.

ISX corporation wins "DARPA contractor of the year" for the Dynamic Analysis and Replanning Tool (DART) which reportedly repaid the US government's entire investment in AI research since the 1950s.

Tim Berners-Lee and Marc Andreessen release the first web browser, Mosaic.

1994   With passengers on board, the twin robot cars VaMP and VITA-2 of Ernst Dickmanns and Daimler-Benz drive more than one thousand kilometers on a Paris three-lane highway in standard heavy traffic at speeds up to 130 km/h. They demonstrate autonomous driving in free lanes, convoy driving, and lane changes left and right with autonomous passing of other cars.

English draughts (checkers) world champion Tinsley resigns a match against computer program Chinook. Chinook defeats second-highest rated player, Lafferty. Chinook won the USA National Tournament by the widest margin ever.

Web crawlers and other AI-based information extraction programs become essential in widespread use of the World Wide Web. Webcrawler, said to be the first, debuts in 1994.

1995   Dean Kamen invents iBOT, a super wheelchair that climbs stairs and helps its passenger to stand.

Ivan A. Getting's Global Positioning System (GPS) becomes fully operational.

Valerie L. Thomas creates an image that appears to be three-dimensional. Thomas' system, the Illusion transmitter, uses a concave mirror at the camera and another one at the television receiver.

Tin Kam Ho publishes a paper describing random decision forests.

Corinna Cortes and Vladimir Vapnik publish their work on support vector machines.

A semi-autonomous car drives coast-to-coast across the United States with computer-controlled steering for 2,797 miles (4,501 km) of the 2,849 miles (4,585 km). Throttle and brakes are controlled by a human driver.

One of Ernst Dickmanns' robot cars (with robot-controlled throttle and brakes) drives more than 1000 miles from Munich to Copenhagen and back, in traffic, at up to 120 mph, occasionally executing maneuvers to pass other cars (only in a few critical situations a safety driver took over). Active vision is used to deal with rapidly changing street scenes.

Microsoft releases Windows 95, a major update to the Windows operating system that features a new graphical interface that approximates the highly successful Macintosh GUI.

1996   The first computerized excimer laser (LASIK), is designed to correct the refractive error myopia, is approved for use in the United States.

Scottish scientist, Ian Wilmut, clones the first mammal, a Finn Dorset ewe named Dolly, from differentiated adult mammary cells.

The first DVD is released, allowing for the storage and playback of high-quality video content.

1997   Swedish appliance company Electrolux is the first to create a prototype of a robotic vacuum cleaner.

Sepp Hochreiter and Jürgen Schmidhuber invent long short-term memory (LSTM) recurrent neural networks, greatly improving the efficiency and practicality of recurrent neural networks.

The Deep Blue chess machine (IBM) defeats world chess champion Garry Kasparov.

First official RoboCup football (soccer) match featuring table-top matches with 40 teams of interacting robots and over 5000 spectators.

Computer Othello program Logistello defeats world champion Takeshi Murakami with a score of 6–0.

A demonstration of an intelligent room and emotional agents occurs at MIT's AI Lab.

The initiation of work on the Oxygen architecture, which connects mobile and stationary computers in an adaptive network, begins.

Netflix media-streaming and video-rental company is founded in 1997 by Americans Reed Hastings and Marc Randolph.

1998   College dropout Shawn Fanning creates Napster, an extremely popular peer-to-peer file-sharing platform that allows users to download music for free. In 2001 the free site will be shut down because it encouraged illegal sharing of copyrighted properties. The site will later become available by paid subscription.

Larry Page, a cofounder of Google, along with Sergey Brin, devise PageRank, the count of web pages linked to a given page and a measure of how valuable people find that page.

A team led by Yann LeCun releases the MNIST database, a dataset comprising a mix of handwritten digits from American Census Bureau employees and American high school students. The MNIST database will become come a benchmark for evaluating handwriting recognition.

Tiger Electronics' toy, Furby, is released, and becomes the first successful attempt at producing a type of AI to reach a domestic environment.

Tim Berners-Lee publishes "Semantic Web Road Map" paper.

Leslie P. Kaelbling, Michael Littman, and Anthony Cassandra introduce the first method for solving POMDPs offline, jumpstarting widespread use in robotics and automated planning and scheduling

Google is founded by Larry Page and Sergey Brin, two Stanford University students. It is named after the mathematical large number googol, which is 10 to the 100th power, or 1 followed by one hundred zeroes.

1999   The Palm VII organizer appears on the market. It is a handheld computer with 2 megabytes of RAM and a port for a wireless phone.

A wireless handheld device that began as a two-way pager, the BlackBerry, is introduced; it is also a cell phone that supports Web browsing, e-mail, text messaging, and faxing—in effect, the world's first smart phone.

Sony introduces an improved domestic robot similar to a Furby. The AIBO becomes one of the first artificially intelligent "pets" that is also autonomous.

2000   Japanese scientists clone a bull from a cloned bull.

The Library of Congress initiates a prototype system called Minerva (Mapping the Internet Electronic Resources Virtual Archives) to collect and preserve open-access Web resources.

The ASCI White supercomputer at the Lawrence Livermore National Laboratory in California is operational. It can hold six times the information stored in the 29 million books in the Library of Congress.

Interactive robopets ("smart toys") become commercially available, realizing the vision of the 18th century novelty toy makers.

Cynthia Breazeal at MIT publishes her dissertation on Sociable machines, describing Kismet, arobot with a face that expresses emotions.

The Nomad robot explores remote regions of Antarctica looking for meteorite samples.

2001   XM Radio initiates the first U.S. digital satellite radio service in Dallas-Ft. Worth and San Diego.

Scientists at Advanced Cell Technology in Massachusetts clone human embryos for the first time.

Dean Kamen introduces his personal transport device, a self-balancing, electric-powered pedestrian scooter called the Segway PT.

Apple releases the iPod, a portable media player that allows users to store and play music. Created by Tony Fadell, it becomes one of the most popular consumer electronics devices of all time.

2002   Torch, a software library for machine-learning, is first released.

iRobot's Roomba autonomously vacuums the floor while navigating and avoiding obstacles.

The Microsoft Xbox is released, a video game console that goes on to become one of the most popular gaming platforms.

Blu-ray discs, an optical disc storage medium mainly used for the storage of high-definition video and data, vastly improves upon DVD technology. It is created by a group of individuals from the fields of electronics, computers, and motion pictures, and is known as the Blu-Ray Disc Association.

2003   Lofti Belkhir introduces the Kirtas BookScan 1200, the first automatic page-turning scanner for the conversion of bound volumes to the first digital books.

Human Genome Project is completed. After thirteen years, the 25,000 genes of the human genome are identified and the sequences of the 3 million chemical-base pairs that make up human DNA are determined.

Mark Zuckerberg establishes Facebook, a social networking website that eventually becomes one of the largest websites in the world.

2004   The world's first embryonic stem cell bank opens in England.

NASA supercomputer Columbia, named for those who lost their lives in the 2003 explosion of the space shuttle *Columbia*, is built by Silicon Graphics and Intel. It achieves sustained performance of 42.7 trillion calculations per second and is considered the fastest supercomputer in the world.

NASA's robotic exploration rovers Spirit and Opportunity autonomously navigate the surface of Mars.

Google launches Gmail, a free email service that will eventually become one of the most popular email services in the world.

2005   The National Nuclear Security Administration's BlueGene/L supercomputer, built by IBM, performs at 280.6 trillion operations per second and is now the world's fastest supercomputer.

Honda's ASIMO robot, an artificially intelligent humanoid robot, is able to walk as fast as a human, delivering trays to customers in restaurant settings.

Recommendation technology based on tracking web activity or media usage brings AI to marketing.

Blue Brain—a project to simulate the brain at the molecular level—is born.

YouTube is founded by three former PayPal employees. The company becomes the world's largest video-sharing website.

2006   By this time, digital cameras almost completely replace film cameras. The *New York Times* reports that 92 percent of cameras being sold are digital.

Nintendo releases the Wii gaming system, which is the first to incorporate motion-sensing controls into gameplay.

2007   Hitachi Global Storage Technologies announces that it has created the first one-terabyte hard disk drive.

Apple introduces the iPhone, a combined cell phone, portable media player, camera phone, internet client (supporting e-mail and web browsing), and text messaging device, to an enthusiastic market.

Philosophical Transactions of the Royal Society, B—Biology, one of the world's oldest scientific journals, puts out a special issue, *Models of Natural Action Selection*, on using AI to increase understanding of biological intelligence.

Checkers game is solved by a program developed by a team of researchers at the University of Alberta.

DARPA launches the Urban Challenge for autonomous cars to obey traffic rules and operate in an urban environment.

2008   The Roadrunner supercomputer is built by IBM and Los Alamos National Laboratory. It can process more than 1.026 quadrillion calculations per second and works more than twice as fast as the Blue Gene/L supercomputer. It is housed at Los Alamos in New Mexico.

Scientists sequence the woolly mammoth genome, the first of an extinct animal.

Anne Wojcicki develops the first retail DNA test. Wojcicki is the wife of Google founder Sergey Brin. Her test is an affordable DNA saliva test and is named 23andMe.

The test determines one's genetic markers for ninety traits. The product heralds what *Time Magazine* dubs a "personal-genomics revolution."

Google releases Android, a freeware operating system for smartphones.

2009   The Large Hadron Collider (LHC) becomes the world's highest energy particle accelerator.

ImageNet is created. ImageNet is a large visual database envisioned by Fei-Fei Li from Stanford University, who realizes that the best machine-learning algorithms wouldn't work well if the data doesn't reflect the real world. For many, ImageNet becomes the catalyst for the AI boom of the 21st century.

Google builds a fully autonomous car.

Satoshi Nakamoto creates Bitcoin, a decentralized digital currency that can be used to buy and sell goods and services. It is the first cryptocurrency.

2010   The Oak Ridge National Laboratory in Tennessee is home to Jaguar, the world's fastest supercomputer, with a peak speed of 2.33 quadrillion floating point operations per second.

Kaggle, a website that serves as a platform for machine-learning competitions, is launched.

Microsoft launches Kinect for Xbox 360, the first gaming device to track human body movement using just a 3D camera and infra-red detection, enabling users to play their Xbox 360 wirelessly. The award-winning machine is developed by the Computer Vision group at Microsoft Research, Cambridge.

Apple introduces the iPad, a tablet computer that features a large touch screen and access to the internet, email, and other applications.

2011   Using a combination of machine-learning, natural language-processing, and information retrieval techniques, IBM's Watson beats two human champions (Rutter and Jennings) in a *Jeopardy!* competition.

Apple's Siri uses natural language to answer questions, make recommendations, and perform actions.

2012   The Google Brain team, led by Andrew Ng and Jeff Dean, creates a neural network that learns to recognize cats by watching unlabeled images taken from frames of YouTube videos.

2013   Robot HRP-2 built by SCHAFT Inc of Japan, a subsidiary of Google, defeats 15 teams to win DARPA's Robotics Challenge Trials. Tasks include driving a vehicle, walking over debris, climbing a ladder, removing debris, walking through doors, cutting through a wall, closing valves and connecting a hose.

NEIL, the Never Ending Image Learner, is released at Carnegie Mellon University to constantly compare and analyze relationships between different images.

Former NSA contractor Edward Snowden reveals the existence of a secret government surveillance program that collects Americans' phone records and internet data. The revelations spark a debate about privacy and security.

2014

Facebook researchers publish their work on DeepFace, a system that uses neural networks that identifies faces with 97.35% accuracy. The results are an improvement of more than 27% over previous systems and rival human performance of facial recognition.

Researchers from Google detail their work on Sibyl, a proprietary platform for massively parallel machine-learning used internally by Google to make predictions about user behavior and provide recommendations.

2015

An open letter to ban development and use of autonomous weapons is signed by Hawking, Musk, Wozniak and 3,000 researchers in AI and robotics.

Google DeepMind's AlphaGo (version: Fan) defeats three-time European Go champion 2 dan professional Fan Hui by 5 games to 0.

2016

Google's AlphaGo program becomes the first Computer Go program to beat an unhandicapped professional human player using a combination of machine-learning and tree-search techniques.

Google DeepMind's AlphaGo (version: Lee) defeats Lee Sedol 4–1. Lee Sedol is a 9 dan professional Korean Go champion who won 27 major tournaments from 2002 to 2016.

2017

Asilomar Conference on Beneficial AI is held to discuss AI ethics and how to bring about beneficial AI while avoiding the existential risk from artificial general intelligence.

Poker AI Libratus individually defeats each of its four human opponents—among the best players in the world—at an exceptionally high aggregated win rate, over a statistically significant sample.

An Open AI-machine played at The International 2017 Dota 2 tournament in August 2017. It won during a 1-versus-1 demonstration game against professional Dota 2 player Dendi.

Google DeepMind reveals that AlphaGo Zero—an improved version of AlphaGo—displays significant performance gains. Unlike previous versions, which learned the game by observing millions of human moves, AlphaGo Zero learns by playing only against itself. AlphaZero masters chess in 4 hours, and defeats the best chess engine, StockFish 8; AlphaZero wins 28 out of 100 games, and the remaining 72 games end in a draw.

The first self-driving car is created by Waymo.

2018   Alibaba language processing AI outscores top humans at a Stanford University reading and comprehension test, scoring 82.44 against 82.304 on a set of 100,000 questions.

The European Lab for Learning and Intelligent Systems (aka Ellis) is proposed as a pan-European competitor to American AI efforts, with the aim of staving off a brain drain of talent, along the lines of CERN after World War II.

Announcement of Google Duplex, a service to allow an AI assistant to book appointments over the phone. The *LA Times* judges the AI's voice to be a "nearly flawless" imitation of human-sounding speech.

2019   The latest generation of wireless technology, 5G, is introduced.

2020   Oculus Rift, the most successful virtual reality headset to date, is released.

2021   The OrCam, which uses computer vision and artificial intelligence to read any written document out loud, is introduced; it can instantly speak any document after users point a laser at it.

2021   QuantumScape invents a successful lithium-metal battery that can potentially increase the range of an electric vehicle by 80% and can be rapidly recharged at stations.

—Laura Nicosia and James F. Nicosia,

updating previous timelines developed by

Charles W. Rogers and the editors of Salem Press.

ORGANIZATIONS AND WEBSITES

American Library Association/American Libraries
225 N. Michigan Avenue, Suite 1300
Chicago, IL 60601
1-800-545-2433
americanlibrariesmagazine.org/tag/digital-literacy/

Center for Media Literacy
22603 Pacific Coast Highway, #549
Malibu, CA 90265
310-804-3985
medialit.org

EdTech Center for World Education
Boston, MA
617-482-9485
Worlded.org
edtech.worlded.org/
    seven-elements-of-digital-literacy-for-adult-
    learners/

**International Society for Technology in Education
    (ISTE)**
2111 Wilson Boulevard, Suite 300
Arlington, VA 22201
iste.org/explore/category/digital-and-media-literacy

**The Literacy Information and Communication
    System (LINCS)**
community.lincs.ed.gov
lincs.ed.gov/about

Media Smarts (Canada)
205 Catherine Street, Suite 100
Ottawa, ON
Canada, K2P 1C3
613-224-7721 or 1-800-896-3342
mediasmarts.ca

**National Association for Media Literacy Education
    (NAMLE)**
P.O. Box 343
New York, NY 10024
namle.net

National Council of Teachers of English
Hall of the States
444 North Capitol Street, NW
Suite 382A
Washington, DC 20001
ncte.org/blog/2021/12/will-internet-literacy/

National Digital Inclusion Alliance (NDIA)
3000 East Main Street
Columbus, OH 43209
digitalinclusion.org

National Science Teaching Association (NSTA)
1840 Wilson Boulevard
Arlington, VA 22201
703-243-7177
nsta.org/science-and-children/science-and-
    children-mayjune-2021/digital-literacy

Office of Educational Technology
400 Maryland Avenue SW
Washington, DC 20202
202-245-7468
tech.ed.gov/team/

The Patterson Foundation
2 North Tamiami Trail
Suite 206
Sarasota, FL 34236
941-952-1413
thepattersonfoundation.org/digital-access-for-all.html

The Tech Edvocate
5322 Markel Road
Richmond, VA 23230
601-630-5238
thetechedvocate.org

UNESCO: Media and Information Literacy
U.S. Department of State
2401 E Street NW Room #L 409
Washington, DC 20037
202-663-2407
unesco.org/en/communication-information/
    media-information-literacy
tate.gov/p/io/unesco/

BIBLIOGRAPHY

"8 Lessons from the Rise of Douyin (Tik Tok)." *Technode,* 15 June 2018, technode. com/2018/06/15/8-lessons-douyin/.

"17.6 Million U.S. Residents Experienced Identity Theft in 2014." *Bureau of Justice Statistics,* 27 Sept. 2015, www.bjs.gov/content/pub/press/vit14pr.cfm.

"2007 Internet Crime Report." *The National White Collar Crime Center.* Bureau of Justice Assistance, Federal Bureau of Investigation, www.ic3.gov/media/annualreports.aspx.

"2012 Internet Crime Report Released: More Than 280,000 Complaints of Online Criminal Activity Reported in 2012." *Federal Bureau of Investigation,* 14 May 2013, www.fbi.gov/sandiego/ press-releases/2013/2012-internet-crime-report-released.

"2018 Data Breach Investigations Report." *Verizon,* verizonenterprise.com.

"31 Privacy and Civil Liberties Organizations Urge Google to Suspend Gmail." *Privacy Rights Clearinghouse,* www.privacyrights.org/ar/GmailLetter.htm.

Abagnale, Frank W. *Stealing Your Life: The Ultimate Identity Theft Prevention Plan.* Broadway Books, 2008.

Abascal, J., and C. Nicolle. "Moving Towards Inclusive Design Guidelines for Socially and Ethically Aware HCI." *Interacting with Computers,* vol. 17, 2005, pp. 484–505.

Ablon, Lillian, Martin C. Libicki, and Andrea A. Golay. *Markets for Cybercrime Tools and Stolen Data.* RAND Corporation, 2014. www.rand.org/pubs/research_reports/RR610.html.

"About." *Reddit,* www.redditinc.com/.

"About Additive Manufacturing." *Additive Manufacturing Research Group,* 2021, www.lboro.ac.uk/research/ amrg/about/.

"About CC Licenses." *Creative Commons,* 2021, creativecommons.org/about/cclicenses.

"About Firewalls." *Indiana University Knowledge Base,* 15 Feb. 2019, kb.iu.edu/d/aoru.

"About Spotify." *Spotify,* newsroom.spotify.com/companyinfo/.

"About Us." *MIT Initiative on the Digital Economy,* ide.mit.edu/about-us.

Abramovich, Sergei, editor. *Computers in Education.* 2 vols. Nova Science, 2012.

Abrams, Abigail. "Here's What We Know So Far about Russia's 2016 Meddling." *Time,* 18 Apr. 2019, time. com/5565991/russia-influence-2016-election/.

Adams, Andrew A., Kiyoshi Murata, and Yohko Orito. "The Japanese Sense of Information Privacy." *AI & Society,* vol. 24, no. 4, 2009, pp. 327–41.

Adams, Richard. "Reddit.com." *The Guardian.* The Guardian News and Media, 7 Dec. 2005, www.the-guardian.com/technology/2005/dec/08/innovations.guardianweeklytechnologysection1.

Adams, Susan. "LinkedIn Still Rules as the Top Job Search Technology Tool, Survey Says." *Forbes,* 12 Aug. 2013.

Adams, Tim. "Sherry Turkle: 'I Am Not Anti-Technology. I Am Pro-Conversation.'" *The Guardian,* the-guardian.com/science/2015/oct/18/sherry-turkle-not-anti-technology-pro-conversation.

Adobe Photoshop: Quick Guide and Quick Reference. CreativeCloud Publications, 2020.

The Adventure of Jasper Woodbury. Peabody.vanderbilt.edu.

Afari, E., J. Aldridge, B. Fraser, et al. "Students' Perceptions of the Learning Environment and Attitudes in Game-Based Mathematics Classrooms." *Learning Environments Research,* vol. 16, no. 1, 2013, pp. 131–50.

Ahmad, Irfan. "The Timeline of #Snapchat—#infographic." *Digital Information World,* 26 Sept. 2014, www. digitalinformationworld.com/2014/09/the-history-of-snapchat-infographic.html.

Airasian, P. "The Impact of the Taxonomy on Testing and Evaluation." *Bloom's Taxonomy: A Forty-Year Retrospective,* edited by L. W. Anderson and L. A. Sosniak, U of Chicago P, 1994, pp. 1–8.

Akta , Calalettin. *The Evolution and Emergence of QR Codes.* Cambridge Scholars, 2017.

Al-Busaidi, K. A., and H. Al-Shihi. "Key Factors to Instructors' Satisfaction of Learning Management Systems in Blended Learning." *Journal of Computing in Higher Education,* vol. 24, no. 1, 2012, pp. 18–39.

Alden, William. "With Reddit Deal, Snoop Dogg Moonlights as a Tech Investor." *The New York Times*, 1 Oct. 2014, dealbook.nytimes.com/2014/10/01/with-reddit-deal-snoop-dogg-moonlights-as-a-tech-investor/.

Alejandro Arzate, Hector. "Cyberbullying Is on the Rise among Teenagers, National Survey Finds." *Education Week*, 15 July 2019, /blogs.edweek.org/edweek/District_Dossier/2019/07/cyberbullying_is_on_the_rise_a.html.

Alexander, Bryan. *The New Digital Storytelling: Creating Narratives with New Media*. ABC-CLIO, 2011.

Alexander, H. A. "A View from Somewhere: Explaining the Paradigms of Educational Research." *Journal of Philosophy of Education*, vol. 40, 2006, pp. 205–21.

Al-Huneidi, A. M., and J. Schreurs. "Constructivism Based Blended Learning in Higher Education." *International Journal of Emerging Technologies in Learning*, vol. 7, 2012, pp. 4–9.

Al-Jumaily, A., and R. A. Olivares. "Bio-Driven System-Based Virtual Reality for Prosthetic and Rehabilitation Systems." *Signal, Image and Video Processing*, vol. 6, no. 1, 2012, pp. 71–84.

Al-Khatib, A., and J. A. T. da Silva. "Stings, Hoaxes and Irony Breach the Trust Inherent in Scientific Publishing." *Publishing Research Quarterly*, vol. 32, no. 3, 2016, pp. 208–19.

Allen, I. E., and J. Seaman. *Making the Grade: Online Learning in the United States, 2006*. The Sloan Consortium. 2006.

Almasy, Steve. "Thailand Baby Killing: Facebook Removes Video." *CNN.com*, 26 Apr. 2017, www.cnn.com/2017/04/25/asia/thailand-baby-killed-facebook-live-trnd/.

Alnahdi, G. "Assistive Technology in Special Education and the Universal Design for Learning." *Turkish Online Journal of Educational Technology*, vol. 13, 2014, pp. 18–23.

Alpaydin, Ethem. *Introduction to Machine Learning*. 4th ed., MIT Press, 2020.

Alper, S., and S. Raharinirina. "Assistive Technology for Individuals with Disabilities: A Review and Synthesis of the Literature." *Journal of Special Education Technology*, vol. 21, 2006, pp. 47–64.

"Alphabetical and Chronological Lists of Countries with FOIA Regimes." *Freedominfo.org*, 28 Sept. 2017.

Altavilla, Dave. "Apple Further Legitimizes Augmented Reality Tech with Acquisition of Metaio." *Forbes*. Forbes.com, LLC, 30 May 2015, www.forbes.com/sites/davealtavilla/2015/05/30/apple-further-legitimizes-augmented-reality-tech-with-acquistion-of-metaio/.

Alton, Larry. "How CAD Software and 3D Printing Are Allowing Customized Products at Scale." *Inc.*, 1 Feb. 2020, www.inc.com/larry-alton/how-cad-software-3d-printing-are-allowing-customized-products-at-scale.html.

Alvermann, Donna E., and Margaret C. Hagood. "Critical Media Literacy: Research, Theory, and Practice in 'New Times.'" *Journal of Educational Research*, vol. 93, no. 3, 2000, pp. 193–205.

Amadeo, Ron. "The (Updated) History of Android." *Ars Technica*, 31 Oct. 2016, arstechnica.com/gadgets/2016/10/building-android-a-40000-word-history-of-googles-mobile-os/.

American University. *Web Site of the Collaboration on Government Secrecy*, edited by Professor Daniel J. Metcalfe, Washington College of Law, 2014, www.wcl.american.edu/lawandgov/cgs/.

Amoroso, Edward. *Cyber Security*. Silicon Press, 2006.

Anders, George. "How LinkedIn Has Turned Your Resume into a Cash Machine." *Forbes*. Forbes.com, 27 June 2012.

___. "LinkedIn Reprices Premium Services, Hoping Users Won't Turn Furious." *Forbes*. Forbes.com, 6 Jan. 2015.

Anderson, J. "Fighting to Bridge the Digital Divide." *Social Policy*, vol. 44, 2014, pp. 56–57, search.ebscohost.com/login.aspx?direct=true&db=sih&AN=95858812&site=ehost-live&scope=site.

Anderson, L. W. "Research on Teaching and Teacher Education." *Bloom's Taxonomy: A Forty-Year Retrospective*, edited by L. W. Anderson and L. A. Sosniak, U of Chicago P, 1994, pp. 9–19.

Anderson, L. W., and L. A. Sosniak, editors. *Bloom's Taxonomy: A Forty-Year Retrospective*. U of Chicago P, 1994.

Anderson, Lindsey, and Irving Wladawsky-Berger. "The 4 Things It Takes to Succeed in the Digital Economy." *Harvard Business Review*, 24 Mar. 2016, hbr.org/2016/03/the-4-things-it-takes-to-succeed-in-the-digital-economy.

Anderson, Monica. "A Majority of Teens Have Experienced Some Form of Cyberbullying." *Pew Research Center*, 27 Sept. 2018, www.pewinternet.
org/2018/09/27/a-majority-of-teens-have-experienced-some-form-of-cyberbullying/.

Anderson, Monica, and Madhumitha Kumar. "Digital Divide Persists Even as Lower-Income Americans Make Gains in Tech Adoption." *Pew Research Center*, 7 May 2019, www.pewresearch.org/fact-tank/2019/05/07/digital-divide-persists-even-as-lower-income-americans-make-gains-in-tech-adoption/.

Anderson, Nate. *The Internet Police: How Crime Went Online—and the Cops Followed*. Norton, 2013.

___. "It's Official: America a Land of Young, Casual Pirates." *Ars Technica*. Condé Nast, 16 Nov. 2011, arstechnica.com/tech-policy/2011/11/its-official-america-a-land-of-young-casual-pirates/.

___. "Report: Piracy a 'Global Pricing Problem' with Only One Solution." *Ars Technica*. Condé Nast, 14 Mar. 2011, arstechnica.com/tech-policy/2011/03/
report-piracy-a-global-pricing-problem-with-only-one-solution/.

Andrew, Levshon. *Reformatted: Code, Networks, and the Transformation of the Music Industry*. Oxford UP, 2014.

Andrews, M. "Decoding MySpace." *U.S. News & World Report*, 18 Sept. 2006, pp. 46–60.

Angwin, Julia. *Stealing MySpace: The Battle to Control the Most Popular Website in America*. Random, 2009.

"Anonymity." *Electronic Frontier Foundation*, www.eff.org/issues/anonymity.

Ansari, S., and E. R. Sykes. "Towards Smarter Intelligent Tutoring Systems: A Proposal for the Inclusion of Enthymemes in Their Design." *Technology, Instruction, Cognition & Learning*, vol. 9, no. 1/2, 2012, pp. 9–29.

Appel, H., J. Crusius, and A. L. Gerlach. "Social Comparison, Envy, and Depression on Facebook: A Study Looking at the Effects of High Comparison Standards on Depressed Individuals." *Journal of Social and Clinical Psychology*, vol. 34, no. 4, 2015, pp. 277–89.

Arditi, David. *Streaming Culture: Subscription Services and the Unending Consumption of Culture*. Emerald Group, 2021.

Aronin, S., and K. Floyd. "Using an iPad in Inclusive Preschool Classrooms to Introduce STEM Concepts." *Teaching Exceptional Children*, vol. 45, no. 4, 2013, pp. 34–39.

Arquilla, John. "In Defense of PRISM." *Foreign Policy*. Graham Holdings Company, 7 June 2013, foreignpolicy.com/2013/06/07/in-defense-of-prism/.

Artero, Juan P. "Online Video Business Models: YouTube vs. Hulu." *Palabra Clave*, vol. 13, no. 1, 201, pp. 111–23, search.ebscohost.com/login.Aspx?direct=true&db=a9h&AN=52258649&site=ehost-live.

Asarch, Steven. "What Is Twitch? Understanding the Explosive Live-Streaming Service." *Newsweek*, 3 May 2018, www.newsweek.com/2018/05/11/twitch-909594.html.

Ashuri, T. "When Online News Was New." *Journalism Studies*, vol. 17, no. 3, 2016, pp. 301–18.

Aslam, Salman. "81 LinkedIn Statistics You Need to Know in 2022." *Omnicore*, 4 Jan. 2022, omnicoreagency.com/LinkedIn-statistics/.

___. "Instagram by the Numbers: Stats, Demographics & Fun Facts." *Omnicore*, 21 June 2017, www.omnicoreagency.com/instagram-statistics/.

Asperl, Andreas. "How to Teach CAD." *Computer-Aided Design & Applications*, vol. 2, no. 1-4, 2005, pp. 459–68.

Assante, Mike. *CyberSkills Task Force Report Fall 2012*. Department of Homeland Security, 2012.

Asselin, M., and M. Moayeri. "The Participatory Classroom: Web 2.0 In the Classroom." *Australian Journal of Language & Literacy*, vol. 34, 2011, p. 45.

Assistive Technology Act of 2004. Public Law 108-364. Frwebgate.access.gpo.gov.

"Assistive Technology, Accommodations, and the Americans with Disabilities Act." *Assistive Technology Partners*. Assistive Technology Partners, U of Colorado, 2011, www.ucdenver.edu/academics/colleges/medicalschool/programs/atp/Documents/ATAccommodationsandtheAmericanwithDisabilitiesAct.pdf.

"Augmented Reality." *Webopedia*. Quinstreet Enterprise, 13 Aug. 2015, www.webopedia.com/TERM/A/Augmented_Reality.html.

Austin, Dennis. "Beginnings of PowerPoint: A Personal Technical Story." *Computer History Museum*, archive.computerhistory.org/resources/access/text/2012/06/102745695-01-acc.pdf.

Austin, Dennis, Tom Rudkin, and Robert Gaskins. "Presenter Specification—May 22, 1986." *Robert Gaskins Home Page*, www.robertgaskins.com/powerpoint-history/documents/austin-rudkin-gaskins-powerpoint-spec-1986-may-22.pdf.

Aycock, John Daniel. *Spyware and Adware.* Springer, 2011.

Bächtold, M. "What Do Students 'Construct' According to Constructivism in Science Education?" *Research in Science Education*, vol. 43, 2013, pp. 2477–96.

Bagwell, Karen. "Teaching, Not Technology, Needed to Enforce Internet Rules." *Education Daily*, vol. 40, no. 212, 2007, p. 2.

Bailey, Jonathan. "What Is Creative Commons Anyway?" *Plagiarism.org*, 24 July 2018, www.plagiarism.org/blog/2018/07/24/what-is-creative-commons-anyway.

Bajarin, Tim. "Google Is at a Major Crossroads with Android and Chrome OS." *PCMag*, 21 Dec. 2015, www.pcmag.com/opinions/google-is-at-a-major-crossroads-with-android-and-chrome-os.

Baker, L. R., and D. L. Oswald. "Shyness and Online Social Networking Services." *Journal of Social and Personal Relationships*, vol. 27, no. 7, 2010, pp. 873–89, search.ebscohost.com/login.aspx?direct=true&db=ufh&an=55209473&site=ehost-live.

Banister, S. "Integrating the iPod Touch in K-12 Education: Visions and Vices." *Computers in the Schools*, vol. 27, no. 2, 2010, pp. 121–31.

Barber, N. W. "A Right to Privacy?" *Human Rights and Private Law: Privacy as Autonomy*, edited by Katja S. Ziegler, Hart, 2007.

Barfield, Woodrow. *Fundamentals of Wearable Computers and Augmented Reality.* 2nd ed., Rowman and Littlefield, 2015.

Barker, V. "Older Adolescents' Motivations for Use of Social Networking Sites: The Influence of Group Identity and Collective Self-Esteem." *Conference Papers—International Communication Association 2008 Annual Meeting*, pp. 1–39, search.ebscohost.com/login.aspx?direct=true&db=ufh&an=36956224&site=ehost-live.

Barlow, Aaron. *The DVD Revolution: Movies, Culture, and Technology.* Praeger, 2005.

Barone, D. "Exploring Home and School Involvement of Young Children with Web 2.0 and Social Media." *Research in the Schools*, vol. 19, 2012, pp. 1–11.

Barone, D., and T. E. Wright. "Literacy Instruction with Digital and Media Technologies." *The Reading Teacher*, vol. 62, 2008, pp. 292–302.

Barr, Jeremy. "SEC Filing Gives Clues to Price Time Inc. Paid for MySpace Parent Viant." *Advertising Age*, 9 May 2016, adage.com/article/media/time-s-purchase-price-myspace-parent-87-million/303898.

Barrett Lidsky, Lyrissa. "Silencing John Doe: Defamation and Discourse in Cyberspace." *Duke Law Journal*, vol. 49, no. 4, 2000, pp. 855–946.

Bartos, J. *What Is the Role of Technology in Education?* Greenhaven Press, 2013.

Bartow, S. M. "Teaching with Social Media: Disrupting Present Day Public Education." *Educational Studies: Journal of the American Educational Studies Association*, vol. 50, no. 1, 2014, pp. 36–64.

Basham, J. D., and M. T. Marino. "Understanding STEM Education and Supporting Students Through Universal Design for Learning." *Teaching Exceptional Children*, vol. 45, 2013, pp. 8–15.

Basl, John. "The Ethics of Creating Artificial Consciousness." *American Philosophical Association Newsletters: Philosophy and Computers*, vol. 13., no. 1, 2013, pp. 25–30.

Bass, Len, Paul Clements, and Rick Kazman. *Software Architecture in Practice.* 3rd ed., Addison-Wesley Professional, 2012.

"Battling the Online Bullies." *BBCNews.* 27 June 2008, news.bbc.co.uk/2/hi/programmes/click&#x005F;online/7477008.stm.

Baudrillard, J. *Simulations.* Semiotext(e), 1983.

Bauer, S., L. J. Elsaesser, M. Scherer, et al. "Promoting a Standard for Assistive Technology Service Delivery." *Technology and Disability*, vol. 26, 2014, pp. 39–48.

Baym, N., and D. Boyd. "Socially Mediated Publicness: An Introduction." *Journal of Broadcasting & Electronic Media*, vol. 56, no. 3, 2012, pp. 320–29, search.ebscohost.com/login.aspx?direct=true&db=ufh&an=79830 560&site=ehost-live.

BBC News. "Video Games 'Stimulate Learning.'" *News.bbc.co.uk*, 18 Mar. 2002.

___. "Video Games 'Valid Learning Tools.'" *News.bbc.co.uk*, 29 Apr. 2000.

Beales, J. Howard. *Legislative Efforts to Combat Spam: Joint Hearing before . . . 108th Congress, 1st Session, July 9, 2003*. US Government Printing Office, 2003.

Beard, Keith W. "Internet Addiction: A Review of Current Assessment Techniques and Potential Assessment Questions." *Cyberpsychology and Behavior*, vol. 8, no. 1, 2007, pp. 7–14.

Beck, U. *Power in the Global Age: A New Global Political Economy*. Polity Press, 2006.

Beer, Jeff. "What It Really Means That Spotify Has Lost Its Second Top Marketing Executive in a Week." *Fast Company*, 18 Sept. 2018, www.fastcompany.com/90238502/ what-it-really-means-that-spotify-has-lost-its-second-top-marketing-executive-in-a-week.

Behrmann, M., and J. Schaff. "Assisting Educators with Assistive Technology: Enabling Children to Achieve Independence in Living and Learning." *Children and Families*, vol. 42, 2001, pp. 24–28.

Bejan, V., M. Hickman, W. S. Parkin, and V. F. Pozo. "Primed for Death: Law Enforcement-Citizen Homicides, Social Media, and Retaliatory Violence." *PLOS One*, vol. 13, no. 1, 2018, pp. 1–23.

Bell, Mary Ann, Mary Ann Berry, and James L. Van Roekel. *Internet and Personal Computing Fads*. Haworth Press, 2004.

Bell, Mary Ann, and Bobby Ezell. *Cybersins and Digital Good Deeds: A Book about Technology and Ethics*. Haworth Press, 2007.

Bellanca, J. *21st Century Skills: Rethinking How Students Learn*. Leading Edge, 2010.

Belsey, Bill. "Cyberbullying: An Emerging Threat to the 'Always On' Generation." *Bullying.org*, 2004, cyberbullying.ca/pdf/Cyberbullying_Article_by_Bill_Belsey.pdf.

Bembenik, Robert, et al., editors. *Intelligent Tools for Building a Scientific Information Platform: Advanced Architectures and Solutions*. Springer-Verlag Berlin Heidelberg, 2013.

Beningo, Jacob. *Reusable Firmware Development: A Practical Approach to APIs, HALs and Drivers*. Apress, 2017.

Benkoil, Dorian. "Tumblr CEO David Karp's Wild Ride from 14-Year-Old Intern to Multimillionaire." *MediaShift*. PBS, 22 May 2013, mediashift.org/2013/05/ tumblr-ceo-david-karps-wild-ride-from-14-year-old-intern-to-multimillionaire/.

Bennett, Colin J. *The Privacy Advocates: Resisting the Spread of Surveillance*. MIT Press, 2008.

Bennett, Colin J., and Rebecca Grant, editors. *Visions of Privacy: Policy Choices for the Digital Age*. U of Toronto P, 1999.

Bennett, James, and Tom Brown, editors. *Film and Television After DVD*. Routledge, 2008.

Bennett, Sue, and K. Maton. "Beyond the 'Digital Natives' Debate: Towards a More Nuanced Understanding of Students' Technology Experiences." *Journal of Computer Assisted Learning*, vol. 26, no. 5, 2010, pp. 321–31.

Benwell, B., and E. Stokoe. *Discourse & identity*. Edinburgh UP, 2006.

Bercovici, Jeff. "Tumblr: David Karp's $800 Million Art Project." *Forbes*. Forbes.com, 2 Jan. 2013, forbes.com/ sites/jeffbercovici/2013/01/02/tumblr-david-karps-800-million-art-project/?sh=556afdaa43f6.

Berg, Madeline. "The Highest-Paid YouTube Stars 2016: PewDiePie Remains No. 1 with $15 Million." *Forbes*, 5 Dec. 2016, www.forbes.com/sites/maddieberg/2016/12/05/ the-highest-paid-youtube-stars-2016-pewdiepie-remains-no-1-with-15-million/#31d1dbfc7713.

Berlatsky, Noah. *Artificial Intelligence*. Greenhaven Press, 2011.

Berman, F., V. G. Cerf, N. Horton, L., et al. "Technologies Do Have Ethics." *Communications of the ACM*, vol. 60, no. 6, 2017, pp. 8–9.

Bernal, Paul. *Internet Privacy Rights: Rights to Protect Autonomy*. Cambridge UP, 2014.

Berners-Lee, Tim. *Weaving the Web: The Original Design and Ultimate Destiny of the World Wide Web by Its Inventor*. Harper, 1999.

Digital Literacy: Skills & Strategies

Bernescu, Laura. "When Is a Hack Not a Hack: Addressing the CFAA's Applicability to the Internet Service Context." *University of Chicago Legal Forum*, 2013, p. 633.

Bernier, Samuel N., Bertier Luyt, Tatiana Reinhard, and Carl Bass. *Design for 3D Printing: Scanning, Creating, Editing, Remixing, and Making in Three Dimensions.* Maker Media, 2014.

Bernstein, Larry. "What Is Computer-Aided Design (CAD) and Why It's Important." *Jobsite*, 11 Oct. 2021, www.procore.com/jobsite/what-is-computer-aided-design-cad-and-why-its-important.

Bernstein, Michael S., et al. "4chan and /b/: An Analysis of Anonymity and Ephemerality in a Large Online Community." *Proceedings of the Fifth International Conference on Weblogs and Social Media, AAAI Press, 2011.* Association for the Advancement of Artificial Intelligence, www.aaai.org/ocs/index.php/ICWSM/ICWSM11/paper/view/2873.

Berry, M. "Computing in the National Curriculum: A Guide for Primary Teachers." *Computingatschool.org*, www.computingatschool.org.

Bers, M. *Designing Digital Experiences for Positive Youth Development: From Playpen to Playground.* Oxford UP, 2012.

Bersin, Josh, and Marc Zao-Sanders. "Boost Your Team's Data Literacy." *Harvard Business Review*, 12 Feb. 2020, hbr.org/2020/02/boost-your-teams-data-literacy.

Beshears, M. "Effectiveness of Police Social Media Use." *American Journal of Criminal Justice*, vol. 42, no. 3, 2017, pp. 489–501. search.ebscohost.com/login.aspx?direct=true&db=sxi&an=124485166&site=e host-live.

Bessette, Chanelle. "Top Peer-to-Peer Payment Apps: Pros, Cons and How to Use them." *Nerdwallet*, 1 Apr. 2021, nerdwallet.com/article/banking/peer-to-peer-p2p-money-transfers.

Bettany, Andrew, and Mike Halsey. *Windows Virus and Malware Troubleshooting.* Apress, 2017.

Betz, David J., and Timothy C. Stevens. *Cyberspace and the State: Towards a Strategy for Cyberpower.* Routledge, 2012.

Bevan, Kate. "Instagram Is Debasing Real Photography." *The Guardian,* 19 July 2012, www.theguardian.com/technology/2012/jul/19/instagram-debasing-real-photography

Biesdorf, S., D. Court, and P. Willmott. "Big Data: What's Your Plan?" *Mckinsey Quarterly*, vol. 2, 2013, pp. 40–51.

"Binary Representation and Computer Arithmetic." *Australian National University*, courses.cecs.anu.edu.au/courses/ENGN3213/Documents/PROJECT_READING_MATERIAL/Binary%20Representation%20and%20Computer%20Arithmetic.pdf.

BinDhim, Nasser F., and Lyndal Trevena. "Health-Related Smartphone Apps: Regulations, Safety, Privacy and Quality." *BMJ Innovations* 1, no. 2, 2015, pp. 43–45.

Bishop, J. "The Internet for Educating Individuals with Social Impairments." *Journal of Computer Assisted Learning vol. 19*, 2013, pp. 546–56.

Bitonti, Francis. *3D Printing Design: Additive Manufacturing and the Materials Revolution.* Bloomsbury, 2019.

Bittman, Michael, Leonie Rutherford, Jude Brown, and Lens Unsworth. "Digital Natives? New and Old Media and Children's Outcomes." *Australian Journal of Education*, vol. 55, no. 2, 2011, pp. 161–75.

Black, P. "Use of Blogs in Legal Education." *James Cook University Law Review*, vol. 13, 2006, pp. 8–29.

Blackhurst, A. E., and D. L. Edyburn. "A Brief History of Special Education Technology." *Special Education Technology Practice*, vol. 2, 2000, pp. 21–36.

Blackmore, Paul. *Intranets: A Guide to Their Design, Implementation and Management.* Aslib-IMI, 2001.

Blanche, Pierre-Alexandre. *Optical Holography: Materials, Theory and Applications.* Elsevier, 2019.

Blanco, Octavio. "The Truth About Those Peer-To-Peer Payment Apps." *Consumer Reports*, May 2022, p. 48.

Blank, Andrew G. *TCP/IP Foundations.* SYBEX, 2004.

Blodget, Henry. "LinkedIn's CEO Jeff Weiner Reveals the Importance of Body Language, Mistakes Made Out of Fear, and One Time He Really Doubted Himself." *Business Insider*, 22 Sept. 2014.

Bloom, B. S. "Reflections on the Development and Use of the Taxonomy." *Bloom's Taxonomy: A Forty-Year Retrospective*, edited by L. W. Anderson and L. A. Sosniak, U of Chicago P, 1994, pp. 1–8.

Bloom, B.S., M. D. Englelhart, E. J. Furst, et al. *Taxonomy of Educational Objectives: The Classification of Educational Goals. Handbook I: Cognitive Domain.* Longman, 1954.

Bloom, Kristen, and Kelly Marie Johnston. "Digging into YouTube Videos: Using Media Literacy and Participatory Culture to Promote Cross-Cultural Understanding." *Journal of Media Literacy Education*, vol. 2, no. 2, 2013, p. 3.

Boatman, Kim. "Beware the Rise of Ransomware." *Symantec Corporation*, ca.norton.com/yoursecurityresource/detail.jsp?aid=rise_in_ransomware.

Bober, M. J., and V. P. Dennen. "Intersubjectivity: Facilitating Knowledge Construction in Online Environments." *Education Media International*, vol. 38, 2001, pp. 241–50.

Bocij, Paul. *Cyberstalking: Harassment in the internet Age and How to Protect Your Family*. Praeger, 2004.

Boellstorff, T. *Coming of Age in Second Life: An Anthropologist Explores the Virtually Human*. Princeton UP, 2015.

Bonaci, T., and H. Chizack. "Privacy by Design in Brain-Computer Interfaces." *U of Washington*. Department of EE, www.ee.washington.edu/ techsite/papers/documents/UWEETR-2013–0001.

Bond, M. "Friends in High-Tech Places." *New Scientist*, vol. 222, no. 2970, 2014, pp. 40–43.

Bond, M. Aaron, and Barbara B. Lockee. *Building Virtual Communities of Practice for Distance Educators*. Springer, 2014.

Bonebright, Marcy. "Thanksgiving vs. Black Friday vs. Cyber Monday: What to Buy Each Day." *The Christian Science Monitor*, 7 Nov. 2015, www.csmonitor.com/Business/Saving-Money/2015/1107/Thanksgiving-vs.-Black-Friday-vs.-Cyber-Monday-what-to-buy-each-day.

Boone, R., and K. Higgins. "New Directions in Research: The Role of Instructional Design in Assistive Technology Research and Development." *Reading Research Quarterly*, vol. 42, 2007, pp. 135–40.

Borja, K., and S. Dieringer. "Streaming or Stealing? The Complementary Features between Music Streaming and Music Piracy." *Journal of Retailing & Consumer Services*, vol. 32, 2016, pp. 86–95, doi:10.1016/j.jretconser.2016.06.007.

Borja, K., S. Dieringer, and J. Daw. "The Effect of Music Streaming Services on Music Piracy among College Students." *Computers in Human Behavior*, vol. 45, 2015, pp. 69–76, doi:10.1016/j.chb.2014.11.088.

Bostrom, Nick. "Ethical Issues in Advanced Artificial Intelligence." *NickBostrom.com*, 2003, nickbostrom.com/ethics/ai.html.

Bostrom, Nick, and Eliezer Yudkowsky. "The Ethics of Artificial Intelligence." *The Cambridge Handbook of Artificial Intelligence*, edited by Keith Frankish and William M. Ramsay, Cambridge UP, 2014, pp. 316–34.

Bottge, B. A., M. Heinrichs, Z. Mehta, et al. "Teaching Mathematical Problem Solving to Middle School Students in Math, Technology Education, and Special Education Classrooms." *Research in Middle Level Education*, vol. 27, 2004, p. 17.

Bottge, B. A., E. Rueda, P. T. Laroque, et al. "Integrating Reform-Oriented Math Instruction in Special Education Settings." *Learning Disabilities Research and Practice*, vol. 22, 2007, pp. 96–109.

Bouchrika, Imed. "50 Online Education Statistics: 2021/2022 Data on Higher Learning & Corporate Training." *Research.com*, 30 June 2020, research.com/education/online-education-statistics.

___. "66 Elearning Statistics: 2021/2022 Data, Analysis & Predictions." *Research.com*, 23 June 2020, research.com/education/elearning-statistics#k-12.

___. "Digital Storytelling: Benefits, Examples, Tools & Tips." *Research.com*, research.com/education/digital-storytelling.

Bouck, E. C. "A National Snapshot of Assistive Technology for Students with Disabilities." *Journal of Special Education Technology*, vol. 31, no. 1, 2016, pp. 4–13.

___. *Assistive Technology*. SAGE Publications, 2017.

Bouck, E. C., S. Flanagan, B. Miller, et al. "Rethinking Everyday Technology as Assistive Technology to Meet Students' IEP Goals." *Journal of Special Education Technology*, vol. 27, 2012, pp. 47–57.

Boudreaux, Ryan. "HTML 5 Trends and What They Mean for Developers. *Web Designer*, 9 Feb. 2012, www.techrepublic.com/blog/web-designer/html-5-trends-and-what-they-mean-for-developers/.

Bourdieu, P. "The Forms of Capital." *Handbook of Theory and Research in the Sociology of Education*, edited by J. C. Richardson, Greenwood Press, 1986, pp. 241–58.

Bourgonjon, J., F. De Grove, C. De Smet, et al. "Acceptance of Game-Based Learning by Secondary School Teachers." *Computers & Education*, vol. 67, 2013, pp. 21–35.

Boyd, Danah. *It's Complicated: The Social Lives of Networked Teens.* Yale UP, 2014.

Boyd D., E. Hargittai, J. Schultz, and J. Palfrey J. "Why Parents Help Their Children Lie to Facebook about Age: Unintended Consequences of the 'Children's Online Privacy Protection Act.'" *First Monday*, vol. 16, no. 11, 2011.

Boyd, D. M., and N. B. Ellison. "Social Network Sites: Definition, History, and Scholarship." *Journal of Computer-Mediated Communication*, vol. 13, no. 1, 2007, pp. 210–30, search.ebscohost.com/login.aspx?direct=true&db=ufh&an=27940595&site=ehost-live.

Boyle, Justin. "11 Tips for Students to Manage their Digital Footprints." *TeachThought*, 8 Mar. 2014. www.teachthought.com/technology/11-tips-for-students-tomanage-their-digital-footprints/.

Bradbury, David. "When Borders Collide: Legislating Against Cybercrime." *Computer Fraud and Security*, vol. 2, 2012, pp. 11–15.

Bradford, Alina. "Everything You Need to Master Instagram Stories." *CNet*, 24 Apr. 2018, www.cnet.com/how-to/how-to-use-instagram-stories/.

___. "What Is Science?" *LiveScience*, 2017, www.livescience.com/20896-science-scientific-method.html.

Brailovskaia, J., and J. Margraf. "Comparing Facebook Users and Facebook Non-Users: Relationship Between Personality Traits and Mental Health Variables—An Exploratory Study." *PLOS One*, vol. 11, no. 12, 2016, pp. 1–17, doi:10.1371/journal.pone.0166999.

Brandom, Russell. "Google Survey Finds More than Five Million Users Infected with Adware." *Verge*, 6 May 2015, www.theverge.com/2015/5/6/8557843/google-adware-survey-ad-injectors-security-malware.

___. "There Are Now 2.5 Billion Active Android Devices." *Verge*, 7 May 2019, www.theverge.com/2019/5/7/18528297/google-io-2019-android-devices-play-store-total-number-statistic-keynote.

Brandon, John. "Making the Internet Safe for Kids." *Fox News*. Fox News Network, 14 May 2011.

Brannon, Valerie C. *Free Speech and the Regulation of Social Media Content.* Congressional Research Service, 27 Mar. 2019, fas.org/sgp/crs/misc/R45650.pdf.

Brenner, Joel. *America the Vulnerable: Inside the New Threat Matrix of Digital Espionage, Crime, and Warfare.* Penguin, 2011.

"Bridging the Digital Divide for All Americans." *Federal Communications Commission*, www.fcc.gov/about-fcc/fcc-initiatives/bridging-digital-divide-all-americans.

"*Brief History of Computer-Assisted Instruction at the Institute for Mathematical Studies in the Social Sciences.* Stanford UP, 1963, eric.ed.gov/?id=ED034420.

"A Brief SGML Tutorial." *W3C*, 11 Aug. 2015, www.w3.org/TR/WD-html40-970708/intro/sgmltut.html.

Britz, Marjie T. *Computer Forensics and Cyber Crime: An Introduction.* 2nd ed., Prentice, 2008.

Brockotter, Robin. "Key Design Considerations for 3D Printing." *HUBS*, www.hubs.com/knowledge-base/key-design-considerations-3d-printing/.

Brogan, Jacob. "What's the Deal with Algorithms?" *Slate*, 2 Feb. 2016, slate.com/technology/2016/02/whats-the-deal-with-algorithms.html.

Brooks-Young, S., and International Society for Technology in Education. *Digital-Age Literacy for Teachers: Applying Technology Standards to Everyday Practice.* International Society for Technology in Education, 2007.

Brown, Abram. "Discord Was Once the Alt-Right's Favorite Chat App: Now It's Gone Mainstream and Scored a New $3.5 Billion Valuation." *Forbes*, 30 June 2020, www.forbes.com/sites/abrambrown/2020/06/30/discord-was-once-the-alt-rights-favorite-chat-app-now-its-gone-mainstream-and-scored-a-new-35-billion-valuation/#67cef99b6b2e.

Brown, Adrian. "Graphics File Formats." *National Archives*, Aug. 2008, www.nationalarchives.gov.uk/documents/information-management/graphic-file-formats.pdf.

Brown, Eric. "True Physics." *Game Developer*, vol. 17, no. 5, 2010, pp. 13–18.

Brown, G. R. "The Blue Line on Thin Ice: Police Use of Force Modifications in the Era of Cameraphones and YouTube." *British Journal of Criminology*, vol. 56, no. 2, 2016, pp. 293–312, search.ebscohost.com/login.aspx?direct=true&db=sxi&an=113170632&site=ehost-live.

Brown, Michael. "Microsoft Windows Is 30: A Short History of One of the Most Iconic Tech Products Ever." *International Business Times*, 20 Nov. 2015, www.ibtimes.com/microsoft-windows-30-short-history-one-most-iconic-tech-products-ever-2194091.

Brown, T. H. "Beyond Constructivism: Exploring Future Learning Paradigms." *Education Today*, vol. 2, 2005, pp. 14–30.

Brown, William Christopher. "An Effective AutoCAD Curriculum for the High School Student." *CSUSB ScholarWorks*, 1999, scholarworks.lib.csusb.edu/etd-project/1791/.

Bruner, J. *Acts of Meaning*. Harvard UP, 1990.

Brunskill, D. "The Dangers of Social Media for the Psyche." *Journal of Current Issues in Media and Telecommunications*, vol. 6, no. 4, 2014, pp. 391–415, search.Ebscohost.Com/Login.Aspx?Direct=True&Db=Ufh&AN=108921776&Site=Ehost-Live.

Brusoni, S., and A. Vaccaro. "Ethics, Technology and Organizational Innovation." *Journal of Business Ethics*, vol. 143, no. 2, 2017, pp. 223–26.

Bryant, P., A. Coombs, and M. Pazio. "Are We Having Fun Yet? Institutional Resistance and the Introduction of Play and Experimentation into Learning Innovation Through Social Media." *Journal of Interactive Media in Education*, vol. 2, 2014, pp. 32–39.

Bryfonski, Dedria. *The Global Impact of Social Media*. Greenhaven, 2012.

Buckingham, David. *The Media Literacy of Children and Young People: A Review of the Research Literature on Behalf of Ofcom*. Ofcom, 2005.

Budra, P. V., and C. Burnham. *From Text to Txting: New Media in the Classroom*. Indiana UP, 2012.

Bułat, R., and A. Zep. "Posthumanism, Androids and Artificial Intelligence: An Aspect Cultural, Biological and Ethical." *International Academic Conference on Social Sciences*, 2017, pp. 36–41.

"Bullying Laws across America." *Cyberbullying Research Center*, cyberbullying.org/bullying-laws.

Buncombe, Andrew. "Family of Sunil Tripathi—Missing Student Wrongly Linked to Boston Marathon Bombing—Thank Well-Wishers for Messages of Support." *Independent*. Independent Digital News and Media, 26 Apr. 2013, www.independent.co.uk/news/world/americas/family-of-sunil-tripathi-missing-student-wrongly-linked-to-boston-marathon-bombing-thank-well-8586850.html.

Burns, Monica. *Deeper Learning with QR Codes and Augmented Reality: A Scannable Solution for Your Classroom*. Corwin Press, 2016.

Burns, Nicholas, Jonathon Price, and Joseph S. Nye, Jr. *Securing Cyberspace: A New Domain for National Security*. Aspen Institute, 2012.

Bush, V. "As We May Think." *The Atlantic Monthly*, July 1945, theatlantic.com.

Bygrave, Lee A. *Data Privacy Law, an International Perspective*. Oxford UP, 2014.

___. "The Place of Privacy in Data Protection Laws." *University of New South Wales Law Journal*, vol. 24, no. 1, 2001, pp. 277–83.

Bynum, Terrell. "Computer and Information Ethics." *Stanford Encyclopedia of Philosophy*, 2008, meinong.stanford.edu/entries/ethics-computer/index.html.

Bynum, Terrell Ward. "A Very Short History of Computer Ethics." *APA Newsletter on Philosophy and Computers*. Research Center on Computing & Society, 2008, web.archive.org/web/20080418122849/http://www.southernct.edu/organizations/rccs/resources/research/introduction/bynum_shrt_hist.html.

Cabaj, Krzysztof, and Wojciech Mazurczyk. "Using Software-Defined Networking for Ransomware Mitigation: The Case of CryptoWall." *IEEE Network*, vol. 30, no. 6, Nov.-Dec. 2016, pp. 14–20.

Cailliau, Robert, and Helen Ashman. "Hypertext in the Web: A History." *ACM Computing Surveys*, vol. 31, Dec. 1999, pp. 1–6.

Calhoun, Karen. *Exploring Digital Libraries: Foundations, Practice, Prospects*. Facet. June 2018.

Calore, Michael. "A History of Microsoft Windows." *Wired*, 10 Dec. 2008, www.wired.com/2008/12/wiredphotos31/.

"Canadians' Mental-Health Info Routinely Shared with FBI, US Customs." *CBC News*. CBC/Radio-Canada, 14 Apr. 2014, www.cbc.ca/news/canada/windsor/canadians-mental-health-info-routinely-shared-with-fbi-u-s-customs-1.2609159.

Cantù, D. Antonio. "Initiatives to Close the Digital Divide Must Last beyond the COVID-19 Pandemic to Work." *The Conversation*, 27 Oct. 2020, theconversation.com/ initiatives-to-close-the-digital-divide-must-last-beyond-the-covid-19-pandemic-to-work-146663.

Cardellini, L. "The Foundations of Radical Constructivism: An Interview with Ernst Von Glasersfeld." *Foundations of Chemistry*, vol. 8, 2006, pp. 177–87.

Cardoza, Nate, Cindy Cohn, Parker Higgins, et al. *Who Has Your Back?: Protecting Your Data from Government Requests*. Electronic Frontier Foundation, 15 May 2014.

Carlin, John P. *Dawn of the Code War: America's Battle Against Russia, China, and the Rising Global Cyber Threat*. Hachette, 2018.

Carlton, Jim. *Apple: The Inside Story of Intrigue, Egomania, and Business Blunders*. HarperBusiness, 1998.

Cartelli, A. *Current Trends and Future Practices for Digital Literacy and Competence*. Information Science Reference, 2012.

Casey, Eoghan. *Digital Evidence and Computer Crime: Forensic Science, Computers, and the Internet*. 3rd ed., Academic, 2011.

Caspi, Avner, and Paul Gorsky. "Online Deception: Prevalence, Motivation, and Emotion." *CyberPsychology & Behavior*, vol. 9, no 1, 2006, pp. 54–59.

Cassidy, K. "To Blog or not to Blog: That Is Not the Question." *Connect Magazine*, vol. 21, 2008, pp. 1–3.

Castells, M. *The Internet Galaxy: Reflections on the Internet, Business and Society*. Oxford UP, 2001.

Cate, Fred. "The Changing Face of Privacy Protections in the European Union and the United States." *Indiana Law Review*, vol. 33, 1999, pp. 173–232.

Cates, W. M. "Instructional Technology: The Design Debate." *Clearing House*, vol. 66, 1993.

Cavazos-Rehg, P. A., M. J. Krauss, S. Sowles, et al. "A Content Analysis of Depression-Related Tweets." *Computers in Human Behavior*, vol. 54, 2016, pp. 351–57.

Caverly, D. C., and A. Ward. "Techtalk: Wikis and Collaborative Knowledge Construction." *Journal of Developmental Education*, vol. 32, 2008, pp. 36–37.

Cellan-Jones, R. "A Computing Revolution in Schools." *BBC Online*. www.Bbc.com.

Cellan-Jones, Rory. "Deepfake Videos 'Double in Nine Months.'" *BBC News*, 7 Oct. 2019, www.bbc.com/ news/technology-49961089.

Cena, M. E., and J. P. Mitchell. "Anchored Instruction: A Model for Integrating the Language Arts Through Content Area Study." *Journal of Adolescent and Adult Literacy*, vol. 41, 1998, p. 559.

Ceniza-Levine, Caroline. "10 Ways to Use Social Media to Supercharge Your Job Search." Time, 4 Apr. 2016, time.com/money/4278588/10-ways-to-use-social-media-to-supercharge-your-job-search.

Center for Applied Special Technology (CAST), 2007, cast.org.

Center for Universal Design. *The Principles of Universal Design, Version 2.0*. NC State UP, 1997, design.ncsu.edu.

Cervantes, Humberto, and Rick Kazman. *Designing Software Architectures: A Practical Approach*. Addison-Wesley Professional, 2016.

Chadha, Peter. "The Return of the Intranet: Old-School Tech Complements the Cloud." *Tech Radar*. Future US, 27 Feb. 2015.

Chadwick, Paul. "How Many People Had Their Data Harvested by Cambridge Analytica?" *The Guardian*, 16 Apr. 2018. www.theguardian.com/commentisfree/2018/apr/16/ how-many-people-data-cambridge-analytica-facebook.

Chafkin, Max, and Sarah Frier. "How Snapchat Built a Business by Confusing the Olds." *Bloomberg*, 3 Mar. 2016, www.bloomberg.com/features/2016-how-snapchat-built-a-business/.

Chak, Katherine M., and Louis Leung. "Shyness and Locus of Control as Predictors of Internet Addiction and Internet Use." *Cyberpsychology and Behavior*, vol. 7, no. 5, 2004, pp. 559–70.

Chambers, D. *Social Media and Personal Relationships: Online Intimacies and Networked Friendships*. Palgrave Macmillan, 2013.

Chan, Melanie. *Virtual Reality: Representations in Contemporary Media*. Bloomsbury, 2014.

Chander, Anupam. *Securing Privacy in the Internet Age*. Stanford Law Books, 2008.

Chandra, A. "Social Networking Sites and Digital Identity: The Utility of Provider-Adolescent Communication." *Brown University Child and Adolescent Behavior Letter*, vol. 32, no. 3, 2016, pp. 1–7.

Chang, Alexandra. "The Most Important LinkedIn Page You've Never Seen." *Wired*. Condé Nast, 15 Apr. 2013.

Cheever, Erik. "Representation of Numbers." *Swarthmore College*, www.swarthmore.edu/NatSci/echeeve1/Ref/BinaryMath/NumSys.html.

Chen, Angela. "Three Threats Posed by Deepfakes that Technology Won't Solve." *MIT Technology Review*, 2 Oct. 2019, www.technologyreview.com/s/614446/deepfake-technology-detection-disinformation-harassment-revenge-porn-law/.

Chen, Chih-Ping. "Exploring Personal Branding on YouTube." *Journal of Internet Commerce*, vol. 12, no. 4, 2013, pp. 332–47.

Chen, I. *Technology and Learning Environment: An Electronic Textbook*. Viking.coe.uh.edu.

Chen, W. "The Implications of Social Capital for the Digital Divides in America." *Information Society*, vol. 29, 2013, pp. 13–25, search.ebscohost.com/login.aspx?direct=true&db=sih&AN=84917786.

Cheong, P. H., P. Fischer-Nielsen, S. Gelfgren, et al., editors. *Digital Religion, Social Media, and Culture: Perspectives, Practices, and Futures*. Peter Lang, 2012.

Chevalier, R. D. "When Did ADDIE Become Addie?" *Performance Improvement*, vol. 50, 2011, pp. 10–14.

Chi, Nan. *LED-Based Visible Light Communications*. Springer-Verlag Berlin Heidelberg, 2018.

Chia-Yi, Mba, and Feng-Yang Kuo. "A Study of Internet Addiction through the Lens of the Interpersonal Theory." *Cyberpsychology and Behavior*, vol. 10, no. 6, 2007, pp. 799–804.

Chigrinov, Vladimir G., Vladimir M. Kozenkov, and Hoi-Sing Kwok. *Photoalignment of Liquid Crystalline Materials*. John Wiley & Sons, 2008.

Chiu, Shao-I, Jie-Zhi Lee, and Der-Hsiang Huang. "Video Game Addiction in Children and Teenagers in Taiwan." *Cyberpsychology and Behavior*, vol. 7, 2004, pp. 571–81.

Chokshi, Niraj. "Facebook Helped Drive a Voter Registration Surge, Election Officials Say." *The New York Times*, 12 Oct. 2016, www.nytimes.com/2016/10/13/us/politics/facebook-helped-drive-a-voter-registration-surge-election-officials-say.html.

Choudhury, Saheli Roy and Arjun Kharpal. "Beyond the Valley: A Look Inside the Mysteries of the Dark Web." *CNBC*, 6 Sept. 2018, www.cnbc.com/2018/09/06/beyond-the-valley-understanding-the-mysteries-of-the-dark-web.html.

Chowdhry, Amit. "Facebook Is Going to Suppress 'Click-Bait' Articles." *Forbes*, 26 Aug. 2014, www.forbes.com/sites/amitchowdhry/2014/08/26/facebook-is-going-to-suppress-click-bait-articles/#51f7bf8b47b0.

Christie, N. V. "An Interpersonal Skills Learning Taxonomy for Program Evaluation Instructors." *Journal of Public Affairs Education*, vol. 18, 2012, pp. 739–56.

Ciampa, M., E. H. Thrasher, and M. A. Revel. "Social Media Use in Academics: Undergraduate Perceptions and Practices." *Journal of Educational Technology*, vol. 12, no. 4, 2016, pp. 10–19.

Ciesla, Robert. *Encryption for Organizations and Individuals: Basics of Contemporary and Quantum Cryptography*. Apress, 2020.

Cilli, Claudio. "Identity Theft: A New Frontier for Hackers and Cybercrime." *Information Systems Control Journal*, vol. 6, 2005, pp. 1–4.

Citron, Danielle Keats. *Hate Crimes in Cyberspace*. Harvard UP, 2014.

Clark, J., and R. Smith. "Firm Action Needed on Predatory Journals." *BMJ* 350, 2015, p. h210.

Clark, Josh. *Creating Keynote Slideshows: The Mini Missing Manual*. O'Reilly Media Inc., 2010.

___. *Sharing Keynote Slideshows: The Mini Missing Manual*. O'Reilly Media Inc., 2010.

Clement, J. "Google Play: Number of Available Apps 2009-2020." *Statista*, 17 June 2020, www.statista.com/statistics/266210/number-of-available-applications-in-the-google-play-store/.

___. "Number of Apps Available in Leading App Stores 2020." *Statista*, 4 May 2020, www.statista.com/statistics/276623/number-of-apps-available-in-leading-app-stores/.

Cleveland, Gary. "Digital Libraries: Definitions, Issues and Challenges." *IFLA Core Programme*, Mar. 1998, archive.ifla.org/VI/5/op/udtop8/udt-op8.pdf.

Clifford, Ralph D., editor. *Cybercrime: The Investigation, Prosecution, and Defense of a Computer-Related Crime.* Carolina Academic Press, 2001.

Cloherty, Jack, and Pierre Thomas. "'Trojan Horse' Bug Lurking in Vital US Computers since 2011." *ABC News.* ABC News Internet Ventures, 6 Nov. 2014.

Closs, Wyatt. "Calling Them 'Girls' Was Their First Mistake: What Happened Next Is a Great Moment in Fierceness." *Upworthy,* 11 July 2013, www.upworthy.com/ calling-them-girls-was-their-first-mistake-what-happens-next-is-a-great-moment-in-fierceness.

Cloud, John. "Bullied to Death?" *Time,* 18 Oct. 2010, pp. 60–63.

Cobb, P. "Where Is the Mind? A Coordination of Sociocultural and Cognitive Constructivist Perspectives." *Constructivism: Theory, Perspectives, and Practice,* edited by C. T. Fosnot, Teachers College Press, 1996, pp. 72–89.

Cohen, D. J., and T. Scheinfeldt. *Hacking the Academy: New Approaches to Scholarship and Teaching from Digital Humanities.* U of Michigan P, 2013.

Coiro, J. *Handbook of Research on New Literacies.* Lawrence Erlbaum Associates/Taylor and Francis, 2008.

Colao, J. J. "Snapchat: The Biggest No-Revenue Mobile App since Instagram." *Forbes,* 27 Nov. 2012.

Colarik, Andrew Michael. *Cyber Terrorism: Political and Economic Implications.* IGI Global, 2006.

Coleman, E. Gabriella. *Coding Freedom: The Ethics and Aesthetics of Hacking.* Princeton UP, 2013.

Collin, Barry. "The Future of Cyberterrorism." *Crime and Justice International,* vol. 13, no. 2, 1997, pp. 15–18.

Collings, Peter J., and Michael Hird. *Introduction to Liquid Crystals.* CRC Press, 2017.

Collins, A., and R. Halverson. *Rethinking Education in The Age of Technology: The Digital Revolution and Schooling in America.* McGraw, 2009.

Collins, Allan, and Richard Halverson. *Rethinking Education in the Age of Technology: The Digital Revolution and Schooling in America.* 2nd ed., Teachers College Press, 2018.

Collins, Ben. "Facebook to Restrict Livestream Feature after Christchurch Attack." *NBC News,* 14 May 2019, www.nbcnews.com/tech/tech-news/ facebook-restrict-livestream-feature-after-christchurch-attack-n1005741.

Collins, Lauren, and Scott Ellis, editors. *Mobile Devices: Tools and Technologies.* CRC Press, 2015.

Collins, Mike. *Pro Tools 11: Music Production, Recording, Editing, and Mixing.* Focal Press, 2014.

Coman, I. A., and M. Coman. "Religion, Popular Culture and Social Media: The Construction of a Religious Leader Image on Facebook." *Essachess,* vol. 10, no. 2, 2017, pp. 129–43, search.ebscohost.com/login.aspx? direct=true&db=sxi&an=126979138&site=Ehost-live.

Comer, Douglas. *Computer Networks and internets.* 6th ed., Pearson, 2015.

"Company Overview of Spotify Technology S.A." *Bloomberg,* 7 Nov. 2018, www.bloomberg.com/research/ stocks/private/snapshot.asp?privcapId=225595077.

"Computer-Aided Design (CAD) and Computer-Aided Manufacturing (CAM)." *Inc.,* 6 Feb. 2020, www.inc. com/encyclopedia/computer-aided-design-cad-and-computer-aided-cam.html.

"Computer Fraud." *Computer Hope,* www.computerhope.com/jargon/c/computer-fraud.htm.

"Computer Internet Fraud." *Cornell U,* July 2017, www.law.cornell.edu/wex/computer_and_internet_fraud.

Conroy, Kevin. "Collaboration in the New Age of Intranets." *CMS Wire.* Simpler Media Group, 2 Apr. 2015.

___. "The New Age of Intranets: Planning & Corporate Communications." *CMS Wire.* Simpler Media Group, 30 Jan. 2015.

Constine, Josh. "Instagram Plans June 20th Launch Event for Long-Form Video Hub." *TechCrunch,* 11 June 2018, techcrunch.com/2018/06/11/instagram-long-form-video/.

Constine, Josh, and Kim-Mai Cutler. "Facebook Buys Instagram for $1 Billion, Turns Budding Rival into Its Standalone Photo App." *TechCrunch.* AOL, 9 Apr. 2012, techcrunch.com/2012/04/09/ facebook-to-acquire-instagram-for-1-billion/.

"Consumer Generated and Controlled Health Data." *Federal Trade Commission,* 7 May 2014, www.ftc.gov/ system/files/documents/public_events/195411/consumer-health-data-webcast-slides.pdf.

"Consumer Watchdog Calls California 'Apps' Privacy Agreement a Step Forward, but Says Do Not Track Legislation Is Necessary to Protect Consumers." *Marketing Weekly News,* 10 Mar. 2012.

Contentwatch. *Netnanny.com.*

Conway, Maura. "Against Cyberterrorism." *Communications of the ACM*, vol. 54, no. 2, 2011, pp. 26–28.

Cook, A. M., and S. Hussey. *Assistive Technologies: Principles and Practice.* 2nd ed., Elsevier/Mosby, 2001.

Cook, Sam. "Cyberbullying Facts and Statistics for 2018-2022." *Comparitech*, 29 Jan. 2022, comparitech.com/internet-providers/cyberbullying-statistics/.

Copes, Heith, and Lynne M. Vieraitis. *Identity Thieves: Motives and Methods.* Northeastern UP, 2012.

Corley, Courtney D., et al. "Text and Structural Data Mining of Influenza Mentions in Web and Social Media." *International Journal of Environmental Research and Public Health*, vol. 7, no. 2, 2010, pp. 596–615.

Cormen, Thomas H. *Algorithms Unlocked.* MIT Press, 2013.

Costello, Sam. "The History of iOS, from Version 1.0 to 13.0." *Lifewire*, 11 Mar. 2020, www.lifewire.com/ios-versions-4147730.

Costello, Vic, Susan Youngblood, and Norman E. Youngblood. *Multimedia Foundations: Core Concepts for Digital Design.* 2nd ed., Routledge, 2017.

Coulthard, Charissa. "Self-Portraits and Social Media: The Rise of the 'Selfie.'" *BBC News.* BBC, 7 June 2013, www.bbc.com/news/magazine-22511650.

Council of Europe. *Journalism at Risk: Threats, Challenges and Perspectives.* Council of Europe, 2015.

Cox, D. "Developing and Raising Awareness of the Zine Collections at the British Library." *Art Libraries Journal*, vol. 43, no. 2, 2018, pp. 77–81.

Craig, Alan B., William R. Sherman, and Jeffrey D. Will. *Developing Virtual Reality Applications. Foundations of Effective Design.* Morgan Kaufmann, 2009.

Crandall, Robert W. *Competition and Chaos: U.S. Telecommunications Since the 1996 Telecom Act.* Brookings Institution Press, 2005.

Crash Override Network. "So You've Been Doxed: A Guide to Best Practices." Crashoverridenetwork.com, crashoverridenetwork.com/soyouvebeendoxed.html.

Crews, T., G. Biswas, S. Goldman, and J. Bransford. "Anchored Interactive Learning Environments." *International Journal of AI in Education*, vol. 8, 1997, pp. 142–78.

The Criminal Spam Act of 2003: Report (to Accompany S. 1293). US Government Printing Office, 2003.

Cross, Mark. *Audio Post Production for Film and Television.* Berklee Press, 2013.

Crossley, N., and J. Roberts. *After Habermas: New Perspectives on the Public Sphere.* Blackwell, 2004.

Crouch, C. *Post-Democracy.* Polity Press, 2004.

Crow, G. "Social Networks and Social Exclusion: An Overview of the Debate." *Social Networks and Social Exclusion: Sociological and Policy Perspectives*, edited by C. Phillipson, G. Allan, and D. Morgan, Routledge, 2017, pp. 7–19.

Crump, Catherine. "Data Retention: Privacy, Anonymity, and Accountability Online." *Stanford Law Review*, vol. 56, no. 1, 2003, p. 191.

CTELL—Case Technologies to Enhance Literacy Learning. Ctell.uconn.edu.

CTGV. "Anchored Instruction and Its Relationship to Situated Cognition." *Educational Researcher*, vol. 19, 1990, pp. 2–10.

___. *Anchored Instruction in Science and Mathematics: Theoretical Basis, Developmental Projects, and Initial Research Findings.* SUNY P, 1992.

___. "The Jasper Series as an Example of Anchored Instruction: Theory, Program Description, and Assessment Data." *Educational Psychologist*, vol. 27, 1992, pp. 291–315.

Curtis, Craig R., Michael C. Gizzi, and Michael J. Kittleson. "Using Technology the Founders Never Dreamed Of: Cell Phones as Tracking Devices and the Fourth Amendment." *University of Denver Criminal Law Review*, vol. 4, no. 61, 2014, pp. 61–101.

Curtis, George E. *The Law of Cybercrimes and Their Investigations.* CRC Press, 2012.

Curwen, Peter, and Jason Whalley. *Mobile Telecommunications Networks: Restructuring as a Response to a Challenging Environment.* Edward Elgar, 2014.

Cyberbullying and Hate Speech." *Ditch the Label | Brandwatch*, 2016, www.ditchthelabel.org/wp-content/uploads/2016/11/Cyberbullying-and-hate-speech.pdf. "Cyberbullying: What Is It and How to Stop It." UNICEF, www.unicef.org/end-violence/how-to-stop-cyberbullying.

"Cyberbullying: Definition." *Pacer's National Bullying Prevention Center.* Pacer Center, 2020, www.pacer.org/bullying/resources/cyberbullying/.

Cybersmart Education Company. "About Us."

Cyberstalking, a New Challenge for Law Enforcement and Industry a Report from the Attorney General to the Vice President. Department of Justice, 1999.

D'Costa, Krystal. "Catfishing: The Truth about Deception Online.*" Scientific American.* Nature America, 25 Apr. 2014.

D'Onfro, Jillian. "Snapchat Now Has Nearly 100 Million Daily Users." *Business Insider,* 26 May 2015, www.businessinsider.com/snapchat-daily-active-users-2015-5.

Daine, K., K. Hawton, V. Singaravelu, et al. "The Power of the Web: A Systematic Review of Studies of the Influence of the Internet on Self-Harm and Suicide in Young People. *PLOS One,* vol. 8, no. 10, 2013, pp. 1–6.

Dale, Nell, and John Lewis. *Computer Science Illuminated.* 6th ed., Jones & Bartlett Learning, 2016.

Dastbaz, Mohammad, Colin Pattinson, and Bakbak Akhgar, editors. *Green Information Technology: A Sustainable Approach.* Elsevier, 2015.

Data Literacy Project, 2021, thedataliteracyproject.org.

Davies, P. L., C. L. Schelly, C. L. Spooner, et al. "Measuring the Effectiveness of Universal Design for Learning Intervention in Postsecondary Education." *Journal of Postsecondary Education & Disability,* vol. 26, 2013, pp. 195–220.

Davis, Amanda. "Three Life-Changing Technologies at the 2017 Assistive Technology Conference." *The Institute.* IEEE, 10 Mar. 2017, theinstitute.ieee.org/ieee-roundup/blogs/blog/three-lifechanging-technologies-at-the-2017-assistive-technology-conference.

Davis, J. J. "Marketing to Children Online: A Manager's Guide to the Children's Online Privacy Protection Act." *S.A.M. Advanced Management Journal,* vol. 67, no. 4, 2002, pp. 11–21.

Dean, Brian. "DuckDuckGo: Usage Stats for 2022." *Backlinko,* Apr. 2022, backlinko.com/duckduckgo-stats#key-duckduckgo-stats.

___. "Instagram Demographic Statistics: How Many Users Use Instagram in 2022?" *Backlinko,* 5 January 2022, backlinko.com/instagram-users.

___. "Snapchat Demographic Stats: How Many People Use Snapchat in 2022." *Backlinko,* backlinko.com/snapchat-users.

DeAngelis, Stephen F. "Artificial Intelligence: How Algorithms Make Systems Smart." *Wired,* Sept. 2014, www.wired.com/insights/2014/09/artificial-intelligence-algorithms-2.

"A Deep Dive on End-to-End Encryption: How Do Public Key Encryption Systems Work*?" Surveillance Self-Defense,* 29 Nov. 2018, ssd.eff.org/en/module/deep-dive-end-end-encryption-how-do-public-key-encryption-systems-work.

"Definition of: XML." *PC Mag.* Ziff Davis, LLC, PCMag Digital Group, 13 Aug. 2015, www.pcmag.com/encyclopedia/term/55048/xml.

Deibert, Ronald. "Black Code: Surveillance, Privacy, and the Dark Side of the Internet." *Internet Law & Policy,* edited by Janine Hiller and Ronnie Cohen, Prentice Hall, 2002.

Delaney, E. "The Children's Online Privacy Protection Act and Rule: An Overview." *Journal of Civil Rights and Economic Development,* vol. 16, no. 3, 2012, pp. 641–48.

Delepierre, Gabriel, et al. "Green Backlighting for TV Liquid Crystal Display Using Carbon Nanotubes." *Journal of Applied Physics,* vol. 108, no. 4, 2010.

Delfino, Devon. "What is Discord? Everything You Need to Know About the Popular Group-Chatting Platform." *Business Insider,* 26 Mar. 2020, www.businessinsider.com/what-is-discord#:~:text=Discord%20is%20a%20group%2Dchatting,for%20all%20sorts%20of%20communities.&text=Discord%20also%20allows%20users%20to,other%20programs%20from%20their%20computers.

Delfs, Hans, and Helmut Knebl. *Introduction to Cryptography: Principles and Applications.* 3rd ed., Springer-Verlag Berlin Heidelberg, 2015.

Delo, Cotton. "Tumblr Announces First Foray into Paid Advertising." *Ad Age.* Crain Communications, 18 Apr. 2012, adage.com/article/special-report-digital-conference/social-media-tumblr-announces-foray-paid-ads/234214.

Demirer, V., and I. Sahin. "Effect of Blended Learning Environment on Transfer of Learning: An Experimental Study." *Journal of Computer Assisted Learning,* vol. 29, no. 6, 2013, pp. 518–29.

Denham, Hannah. "These Are the Platforms That Have Banned Trump and His Allies." *The Washington Post,* 14 Jan. 2021, www.washingtonpost.com/technology/2021/01/11/trump-banned-social-media.

Denning, Dorothy. "A View of Cyberterrorism Five Years Later." *Internet Security: Hacking, Counterhacking, and Society,* edited by Kenneth Elinor Himma, Jones, 2007.

"Department of Justice Guide to the Freedom of Information Act." *US Department of Justice,* 2009, www.justice.gov/oip/doj-guide-freedom-information-act-0\.

Derene, Glenn. "Samsung, LG, and Vizio Smart TVs Are Recording—and Sharing Data about—Everything You Watch." *Consumer Reports,* 27 Feb. 2015, www.consumerreports.org/cro/news/2015/02/samsung-lg-vizio-smart-tvs-watch-everything-you-watch/index.htm.

"Development History." *W3C,* 13 Aug. 2015, www.w3.org/XML/hist2002.

DiBona, Chris. *Open Sources Voices from the Open Source Revolution.* O'Reilly, 1999.

Dice, Pete. *Quick Boot: A Guide for Embedded Firmware Developers.* 2nd ed., Walter de Gruyter, 2018.

Dieny, Bernard, Ronald B. Goldfarb, and Kyung-Jin Lee. *Introduction to Magnetic Random-Access Memory.* IEEE Press/John Wiley & Sons, 2017.

"Digital Accessibility." *Partnership on Employment & Accessible Technology,* www.peatworks.org/futureofwork/a11y.

Dingli, Alexiei, and Dylan Seychell. *The New Digital Natives: Cutting the Chord.* Springer, 2015.

"Discord Safety Center." *Discord,* 2019, discord.com/safety.

Disessa, A. A. *Changing Minds: Computers, Learning, and Literacy.* MIT Press, 2011.

"Distributed Denial of Service Attacks." *Imperva Capsula,* www.incapsula.com/ddos/denial-of-service.html.

Dixon, Rod. *Open Source Software Law.* Artech House, 2004.

Dodd, Annabel Z. *The Essential Guide to Telecommunications.* 6th ed., Pearson, 2019.

Donegan, Richard. "Bullying and Cyberbullying: History, Statistics, Law, Prevention and Analysis." *Elon Journal of Undergraduate Research in Communications,* vol. 3, no. 1, 2012, pp. 34–36.

Dorman, S. "Internet Safety for Schools, Teachers, And Parents." *Journal of School Health,* vol. 67, 1997, p. 355.

Dormehl, Luke. *The Apple Revolution: Steve Jobs, the Counterculture and How the Crazy Ones Took Over the World.* Virgin Books, 2012.

___. "Assistive Tech Is Progressing Faster Than Ever, and These 7 Devices Prove It." *Digital Trends,* 6 Apr. 2018, www.digitaltrends.com/cool-tech/assistive-tech-examples.

Dotson, Chris. *Practical Cloud Security: A Guide for Secure Design and Deployment.* O'Reilly Media, 2019.

Dotterer, G., A. Hedges, and H. Parker. "Fostering Digital Citizenship in the Classroom." *Education Digest,* vol. 82, no. 3, 2016, pp. 58–63.

Douglas, C. "Religion and Fake News: Faith-Based Alternative Information Ecosystems in the US and Europe." *Review of Faith & International Affairs,* vol. 16, no. 1, 2018, pp. 61–73, doi:10.1080/15570274.2018.1433522.

Douglas, David M. "Doxing: A Conceptual Analysis." *Ethics and Information Technology,* vol. 18, no. 3, 2016, pp. 199–210.

Doyle, Charles. *Cybercrime: An Overview of the Federal Computer Fraud and Abuse Statute and Related Federal Criminal Laws.* Congressional Research Service, 2010.

"Dr. Stephen Hawking: A Case Study on Using Technology to Communicate with the World." *DO-IT Knowledge Base,* U of Washington, 2013. www.washington.edu/doit/articles?370.

Dreamson, Neal. *Critical Understandings of Digital Technology in Education.* Routledge, 2020.

Dredge, S. "Coding at School: A Parents' Guide to England's New Computing Curriculum." *The Guardian*, www.theguardian.com.

Drnevich, P. L., and D. C. Croson. "Information Technology and Business-Level Strategy: Toward an Integrated Theoretical Perspective." *MIS Quarterly*, vol. 37, no. 2, 2013, pp. 483–509.

Drucker, Jesse, and Simon Bowers. "After a Tax Crackdown, Apple Found a New Shelter for Its Profits." *The New York Times*, 6 Nov. 2017, www.nytimes.com/2017/11/06/world/apple-taxes-jersey.html.

Drummond, Caitlin, and Fischoff, Baruch. "Individuals with Greater Science Literacy and Education Have More Polarized Beliefs on Controversial Science Topics." *PNAS*, 2017, www.pnas.org/content/114/36/9587.

Ducate, L. C., and L. L. Lomicka. "Adventures in the Blogosphere: From Blog Readers to Blog Writers." *Computer Assisted Language Learning*, vol. 21, 2008, pp. 9–28.

Duelm, Brian Lee. "Computer Aided Design in the Classroom." *LearnTechLib*, Dec. 1986, files.eric.ed.gov/fulltext/ED276885.pdf.

Duffy, Jill. "The Best Online Collaboration Software of 2017." *PCMag*, 3 Aug. 2017, www.pcmag.com/article2/0,2817,2489110,00.asp.

___. "LinkedIn." *PC*. Ziff Davis, 27 Nov. 2013.

Duggan, M. "Online Harassment 2017." *Pew Research Center*, 11 July 2017, www.pewinternet.org/2017/07/11/online-harassment-2017/.

Dummett, Paul, Helen Stephenson, and Lewis Lansford. *Keynote 4*. Cengage Learning, 2020.

Dunn Cavelty, Myriam. "Breaking the Cyber-Security Dilemma: Aligning Security Needs and Removing Vulnerabilities." *Science & Engineering Ethics*, vol. 20, no. 3, 2014, pp. 701–15.

___. *Cyber-Security and Threat Politics: U.S. Efforts to Secure the Information Age*. Routledge, 2008.

Dupont, B. "Bots, Cops, and Corporations: On the Limits of Enforcement and the Promise of Polycentric Regulation as a Way to Control Large-Scale Cybercrime." *Crime, Law and Social Change*, vol. 67, no. 1, 2017, pp. 97–116, search.ebscohost.com/login.aspx?direct=true&db=sxi&an=120927470&site=ehost-live&scope=site.

Durflinger, D. "Balancing Student Empowerment with Online Safety." *School Administrator*, vol. 72, no. 10, 2015, p. 11.

Dutson, Phil. *Creating QR and Tag Codes*. Sams Publishing, 2013.

___. *Responsive Mobile Design: Designing for Every Device*. Addison-Wesley, 2015.

Dwight, Ken. *Bug-Free Computing: Stop Viruses, Squash Worms, and Smash Trojan Horses*. TeleProcessors, 2006.

Dwoskin, Elizabeth, and Craig Timberg. "Facebook Wanted 'Visceral' Live Video. It's Getting Live-Streaming Killers and Suicides." *The Washington Post*, 17 Apr. 2017, www.washingtonpost.com/business/technology/facebook-wanted-visceral-live-video-its-getting-suicides-and-live-streaming-killers/2017/04/17/a6705662-239c-11e7-a1b3-faff0034e2de_story.html.

Dyson, M. P., L. Hartling, J. Shulhan, et al. "A Systematic Review of Social Media Use to Discuss and View Deliberate Self-Harm Acts." *PLOS One*, vol. 11, no. 5, 2016, pp. 1–15.

Easttom, Chuck. *Computer Security Fundamentals*. 4th ed., Pearson, 2019.

Eckert, P., and J. McConnell-Ginet. "Communities of Practice: Where Language, Gender, and Power All Live." *Readings in Language and Gender*, edited by Jennifer Coates, Blackwell, 1992, pp. 573–82.

"Economic News Release: Job Openings and Labor Turnover Summary." *BLS*. US Bureau of Labor Statistics, 8 May 2018, www.bls.gov/news.release/jolts.nr0.htm.

Edwards, Benj. "The Little-Known Apple Lisa: Five Quirks and Oddities." *Macworld*, 30 Jan. 2013, www.macworld.com/article/2026544/the-little-known-apple-lisa-five-quirks-and-oddities.html.

Edwards, Jim. "Proof That Android Really Is for the Poor." *Business Insider*, 27 June 2014, www.businessinsider.in/Proof-That-Android-Really-Is-For-The-Poor/articleshow/37328668.cms.

Edyburn, D., K. Higgins, and R. Boone, editors. *Handbook of Special Education Technology Research and Practice*. Knowledge by Design, 2006.

Efrati, Amir. "Google's Data-Trove Dance." *The Wall Street Journal*, 30 July 2013, www.wsj.com/articles/SB10001424127887324170004578635812623154242.

Eisenberg, M., C. A. Lowe, K. L. Spitzer, et al. *Information literacy: Essential Skills for the Information Age.* Libraries Unlimited, 2004.

Electronic Privacy Information Center. *Ben Joffe v. Google, Inc.*, epic.org/amicus/google-street-view/.

Elenkov, Nikolay. *Android Security Internals: An In-Depth Guide to Android's Security Architecture.* No Starch Press, 2015.

Elkind, D. "Response to Objectivism and Education." *Educational Forum*, vol. 69, 2005, pp. 328–34.

Else, Liz. "Sherry Turkle. Living Online: I'll Have to Ask My Friends." *New Scientist,* no. 2569, 20 Sept. 2006, newscientist.com/article/mg19125691.600.

"The Employment Situation—April 2018." *BLS.* US Bureau of Labor Statistics, 4 May 2018, www.bls.gov/news.release/pdf/empsit.pdf.

Engdahl, Sylvia. *Mobile Apps.* Greenhaven Press, 2014.

English, Cameron. "Social Media Use Causes Depression and Suicide? It's a Surprisingly Difficult Question to Answer. "*American Council on Science and Health*, 24 June 2021, acsh.org/news/2021/06/24/social-media-use-causes-depression-and-suicide-its-surprisingly-difficult-question-answer-15628.

"Enough Is Enough: Internet Safety 101: Educate, Equip, Empower." *Internetsafety101.org.*

Ensslin, A. *The Language of Gaming.* Palgrave, 2012.

Ensslin, A. I., and I. Balteiro. "Locating Videogames in Medium-Specific, Multilingual Discourse Analysis." *Approaches to Videogame Discourse.* Bloomsbury Academic, 2019, pp. 1–10.

"Ensuring BotNets Are Not 'Too Big to Investigate." *US Department of Justice*, 22 Nov. 2016, www.justice.gov/archives/opa/blog/ensuring-botnets-are-not-too-big-investigate.

Entous, Adam, Ellen Nakashima, and Greg Miller. "Secret CIA Assessment Says Russia Was Trying to Help Trump Win White House." *The Washington Post*, 9 Dec. 2016, www.washingtonpost.com/world/national-security/obama-orders-review-of-russian-hacking-during-presidential-campaign/2016/12/09/31d6b300-be2a-11e6-94ac-3d324840106c_story.html.

Epstein, D., E. C. Nisbet, and T. Gillespie. "Who's Responsible for the Digital Divide? Public Perceptions and Policy Implications." *Information Society*, vol. 27, 2011, pp. 92–104, search.ebscohost.com/login.aspx?direct=true&db=sih&AN=59132055.

Erbschloe, Michael. *Trojans, Worms, and Spyware: A Computer Security Professional's Guide to Malicious Code.* Elsevier Butterworth Heinemann, 2005.

Erramilli, Vijay. "The Tussle around Online Privacy." *IEEE Internet Computing*, vol. 16, no. 4, 2012, pp. 69–71.

Ertmer, P. A., and T. J. Newby. "Behaviorism, Cognitivism, Constructivism: Comparing Critical Features from an Instructional Design Perspective." *Performance Improvement Quarterly*, vol. 26, 2013, pp. 43–71.

Etherington, Darrell. "People Now Watch 1 Billion Hours of YouTube Per Day." *Tech Crunch*, 28 Feb. 2017, techcrunch.com/2017/02/28/people-now-watch-1-billion-hours-of-youtube-per-day.

"EU Prepares to Launch First Cybercrime Centre." *Euractive*, 29 Mar. 2012, www.euractiv.com/infosociety/eu-prepares-launch-cybercrime-ce-news-511823.

Evans, Alan, Kendall Martin, and Mary Anne Poatsy. *Technology in Action.* 16th ed., Pearson, 2020.

Evans, E. *Transmedia Television: Audiences, New Media, and Daily Life.* Routledge, 2011.

"Explained: What Is Twitch?" *WebWise*, 2020, www.webwise.ie/parents/explained-what-is-twitch/.

"Extensible Markup Language (XML)." *W3C*, 13 Aug. 2015, www.w3.org/XML/.

Ezmailzadeh, Riaz. *Broadband Telecommunications Technologies and Management.* John Wiley & Sons, 2016.

"Facebook Reports Second Quarter 2020 Results." *Facebook*, 30 July 2020, s21.q4cdn.com/399680738/files/doc_financials/2020/q2/Q2'20-FB-Financial-Results-Press-Release.pdf.

"Facebook Reports Third Quarter 2021 Results." *Facebook Investor Relations*, 25 Oct. 2021, investor.fb.com/investor-news/press-release-details/2021/Facebook-Reports-Third-Quarter-2021-Results/.

Faculty Spotlight: John Bransford. Depts.washington.edu/coe/news/facand#x005f;spotlight/bransford.html.

Falloon, G. "What's the Difference? Learning Collaboratively Using iPads in Conventional Classrooms." *Computers & Education*, vol. 84, 2015.

Family Online Safety Institute. "About ICRA." *Fosi.org.*

Farber, Dan. "The Next Big Thing in Tech: Augmented Reality." *CNET*. CBS Interactive Inc., 7 June 2013, www.cnet.com/news/the-next-big-thing-in-tech-augmented-reality/.

Farber, M. "Coding Across the Curriculum." *Edutopic.org*, www.edutopia.org.

"Features." *Google*. Google, Inc., www.gmail.com/intl/en_us/mail/help/features.html.

Federal Bureau of Investigation. "Cybercrime: Computer Intrusions." *Federal Bureau of Investigation*, 2012, www.fbi.gov/about-us/investigate/cyber/computer-intrusions.

___. "A Parent's Guide to Internet Safety." *Fbi.gov*.

Federal Communications Commission. "Children's Internet Protection Act." *Fcc.gov*.

Federal Trade Commission. "Children's Privacy." *Business.ftc.gov*.

Feiler, Bruce. "For the Love of Being 'Liked': For Some Social-Media Users, an Anxiety from Approval Seeking." *The New York Times*, 9 May 2014.

Feiner, Lauren, and Salvador Rodriguez. "FTC Slaps Facebook with Record $5 Billion Fine, Orders Privacy Oversight." *CNBC*, 24 July 2019, www.cnbc.com/2019/07/24/facebook-to-pay-5-billion-for-privacy-lapses-ftc-announces.html.

Feinstein, B., V. Bhatia, J. Latack, et al. "Social Networking and Depression." *The Wiley Handbook of Psychology, Technology, and Society*, edited by L. D. Rosen, N. A. Cheevery, and L. M. Carrier, Wiley Blackwell, 2015, pp. 273–86.

Feinstein, Ken. *Fight Spam, Viruses, Pop-Ups and Spyware (How to Do Everything)*. McGraw-Hill, 2004.

Feldman, Brian. "Even If Facebook Stops Aggressively Collecting Data, Developers Will Still Supply It." *New York Magazine*, 22 Feb. 2019, nymag.com/intelligencer/2019/02/why-facebooks-data-collection-practice-is-so-messy.html.

Feller, Joseph. *Perspectives on Free and Open Source Software*. MIT Press, 2005.

Felvégi, E., and K. I. Matthew. "Ebooks and Literacy in K-12 Schools." *Computers in the Schools*, vol. 29, no. 1/2, 2012, pp. 40–52.

Ferguson, J., and J. Oigara. "iPads in the Classroom: What Do Teachers Think?" *International Journal of Information & Communication Technology Education*, vol. 13, no. 4, 2017.

Ferguson, R. Stuart. *Practical Algorithms for 3D Computer Graphics*. 2nd ed., AK Peters/CRC Press, 2013.

Fernheimer, J. W., and J. T. Nelson. "Bridging the Composition Divide: Blog Pedagogy and the Potential for Agonistic Classrooms." *Currents in Electronic Literacy*, vol. 9, 2005, www.currents.cwrl.utexas.edu.

Fibbe, George H. "Screen-Scraping and Harmful Cyber-trespass after Intel." *Mercer Law Review*, vol. 55, no. 1011, 2004.

Finn, J. C., R. Peet, S. Mollett, and J. Lauermann. "Reclaiming Value from Academic Labor: Commentary by the Editors of Human Geography." *Fennia-International Journal of Geography*, vol. 195, no. 2, 2017, pp. 182–84.

Fischetti, M. "The Networked Primate." *Scientific American*, vol. 311, no, 3, pp. 82–85.

Fisher, D., and N. Frey. "Access to the Core Curriculum." *Remedial & Special Education*, vol. 22, 2001, pp. 148–57.

Fisher, M. "Digital Learning Strategies: How Do I Assign and Assess 21st Century Work?" *ASCD*, 2013.

Fisk, Nathan W. *Understanding Online Piracy: The Truth about Illegal File Sharing*. ABC-CLIO, 2009.

Fitter, Hetal N., Akash B. Pandey, Divyang D. Patel, and Jitendra M. Mistry. "A Review on Approaches for Handling Bezier Curves in CAD for Manufacturing." *Procedia Engineering*, vol. 97, 2014, pp. 1155–66.

Fitzpatrick, Eileen. "DVD POV: Perspective on a Deep-Pocketed Market." *Billboard*, 27 May 2000, p. 129.

Flanagan, M., and H. Nissenbaum. *Values at Play in Digital Games*. MIT Press, 2014.

Folger, Tim. "Revealed World." *National Geographic*. National Geographic Society, ngm.nationalgeographic.com/big-idea/14/augmented-reality.

Forest, Amanda L., and Joanne V. Wood. "When Social Networking Is Not Working: Individuals with Low Self-Esteem Recognize but Do Not Reap the Benefits of Self-Disclosure on Facebook." *Psychological Science*, vol. 23, no. 3, 2012, pp. 295–302.

Foroohar, Rana. "Money, Money, Money: Silicon Valley Speculation Recalls Dotcom Mania." *Financial Times*, 17 July 2017, www.ft.com/content/968f2022-6878-11e7-9a66-93fb352ba1fe.

Foster, C. "Anchored Instruction. (Hoffman, B.)" *Encyclopaedia of Educational Technology.* Coe.sdsu.edu.

Fostnot, C. T. *Constructivism: Theory, Perspectives, and Practice.* Teachers College Press, 1996.

Foundations of Information Ethics, edited by John T. F. Burgess and Emily J. M. Knox, ALA Neal-Schuman, 2019.

Fox, Kara. "Instagram World Social Media App for Young People's Mental Health." *CNN.com,* 19 May 2017, www.cnn.com/2017/05/19/health/instagram-worst-social-network-app-young-people-mental-health/index.html.

Frampton, Ben. "Clickbait: The Changing Face of Online Journalism." *BBC News,* 14 Sept. 2015, www.bbc.com/news/uk-wales-34213693.

Francalanci, C., and V. Piuri. "Designing Information Technology Architectures: A Cost-Oriented Methodology." *Journal of Information Technology,* vol. 14, no. 2, 1999, pp. 181–92.

Franceschi-Bicchierai, Lorenzo. "Love Bug: The Virus That Hit 50 Million People Turns 15." *Motherboard,* 4 May 2015, www.vice.com/en_us/article/d73jnk/love-bug-the-virus-that-hit-50-million-people-turns-15.

Francis, Ryan. "The History of Ransomware." *CSO Online,* 20 July 2016, www.csoonline.com/article/3095956/data-breach/the-history-of-ransomware.html#slide10.

Franklin, M. *Digital Dilemmas: Power, Resistance, and the Internet.* Oxford UP, 2013.

Frazel, Midge. *Digital Storytelling Guide for Educators.* ISTE, 2010.

Frazier, M., and D. Hearrington. *The Technology Coordinator's Handbook.* International Society for Technology in Education, 2017.

Freeman, Michael. *Digital Image Editing & Special Effects: Quickly Master the Key Techniques of Photoshop & Lightroom.* Focal Press, 2013.

Freeman, Will. "A Parents' Guide to Twitch." *Ask About Games,* 17 Aug. 2018, www.askaboutgames.com/a-parents-guide-to-twitch.

Freitas, D. *The Happiness Effect: How Social Media Is Driving a Generation to Appear Perfect at Any Cost.* Oxford UP, 2017.

Frenzel, Louis E., Jr. *Principles of Electronic Communication Systems.* 4th ed., McGraw-Hill, 2016.

"Frequently Asked Questions." *Reddit,* n.d., 23 Jan. 2016, www.reddit.com/wiki/faq#Whatdoesthenameredditmean.

Friedewald, Michael, and Ronald J. Pohoryles, editors. *Privacy and Security in the Digital Age.* Routledge, 2014.

Friend, Tad. "Letter from California: Hollywood and Vine." *The New Yorker.* Condé Nast, 15 Dec. 2014, www.newyorker.com/magazine/2014/12/15/hollywood-vine.

Froehlich, Thomas. "A Brief History of Information Ethics." *Biblioteconomia i Documentació Universitat de Barcelona,* 2004, bid.ub.edu/13froael2.htm.

"FTC Report Raises Privacy Concerns on Mobile Apps for Children." *Entertainment Close-Up,* 26 Feb. 2012.

"FTP Protocol (File Transfer Protocol)." *CCM Benchmark Group,* 16 Oct. 2008, ccm.net/contents/272-ftp-protocol-file-transfer-protocol.

Fuchs, Christian. *Social Media: A Critical Introduction.* Sage, 2014.

Fulle, Ronald G. *Telecommunications History and Policy into the Twenty-first Century.* RIT Press, 2010.

Fullerton, T. *Game Design Workshop: A Playcentric Approach to Creating Innovative Games.* CRC Press, 2014.

Fung, B. "Comcast Is Expanding Its $10-A-Month Internet Program for the Poor." *The Washington Post,* 4 Aug. 2014, www.washingtonpost.com/blogs/the-switch/wp/2014/08/04/comcast-is-expanding-its-10-a-month-internet-program-for-the-poor/.

Furst, E. J. "Bloom's Taxonomy: Philosophical and Educational Issues." *Bloom's Taxonomy: A Forty-Year Retrospective,* edited by L. W. Anderson and L. A. Sosniak, U of Chicago P, 1994, pp. 28–40.

Gada, Kosha. "The Digital Economy in 5 Minutes." *Forbes,* 16 June 2016, www.forbes.com/sites/koshagada/2016/06/16/what-is-the-digital-economy/#14397bc37628.

Gaget, Lucie. "How to Learn CAD in Schools: Top 15 of the Best Educational Software." *Sculpteo,* 26 Dec. 2017, www.sculpteo.com/blog/2017/12/26/how-to-learn-cad-in-schools-top-15-of-the-best-educational-software/.

Gagné, Robert M., Leslie Briggs, and Walter W. Wager. *Principles of Instructional Design.* 4th ed., Harcourt Brace Jovanovich College Publishers, 1992.

Galer, Mark, and Philip Andrews. *Photoshop CC Essential Skills: A Guide to Creative Image Editing.* Focal Press, 2014.

Gallagher, Sean. "'Locky' Crypto-Ransomware Rides in on Malicious Word Document Macro." *Ars Technica,* 17 Feb. 2016, arstechnica.com/information-technology/2016/02/locky-crypto-ransomware-rides-in-on-malicious-word-document-macro/.

Gallardo-Camacho, Jorge. "The Low Interaction of Viewers of Video Clips on the Internet: The Case Study of YouTube Spain." *Revista Latina de Comunicación de Social,* vol. 13, no. 65, 2010, pp. 1-14, search.ebscohost.com/login.Aspx?direct=true&db=a9h&AN=60167086&site=ehost-live.

Gancarz, Mike. *The UNIX Philosophy.* Butterworth-Heinemann, 1995.

Ganis, Matt, and Avinash Kohirkar. *Social Media Analytics: Techniques and Insights for Extracting Business Value Out of Social Media.* IBM, 2016.

Garcés-Conejos Blitvich, P. "The Status Quo and Quo-Vadis of Impoliteness Research." *Intercultural Pragmatics,* vol. 7, no. 4, 2010, pp. 535–59.

Garcés-Conejos Blitvich, P., and M. Sifianou. "Im/politeness in Discursive Pragmatics." *Quo Vadis Pragmatics? Recent Developments in the Field of Pragmatics,* edited by Michael Haugh and Marina Terkourafi, Special Issue of *Journal of Pragmatics,* vol. 145, 2019, pp. 91–101.

Gardiner, B. "Adding Coding to the Curriculum." *The New York Times.* www.nytimes.com.

Garfinkel, Simson, and Gene Spafford. *Web Security, Privacy & Commerce.* 2nd ed., O'Reilly Media, 2011.

Garrison, D. R., and N.D. Vaughan. *Blended Learning in Higher Education: Framework, Principles, and Guidelines.* Jossey-Bass, 2018.

Gashi, L., and K. Knautz, K. "Somebody That I Used to Know—Unfriending and Becoming Unfriended on Facebook." *Proceedings of the European Conference on E-Learning,* 2015, pp. 583–90.

Gaskins, Robert. "Sample Product Proposal: Presentation Graphics for Overhead Projection." *Robert Gaskins Home Page,* www.robertgaskins.com/powerpoint-history/documents/gaskins-powerpoint-original-proposal-1984-aug-14.pdf.

___. "Viewpoint: How PowerPoint Changed Microsoft and My Life." *BBC,* 31 July 2012, www.bbc.com/news/technology-19042236.

Gecer, A. "Lecturer-Student Communication in Blended Learning Environments." *Educational Sciences: Theory and Practice,* vol. 13, no. 1, 2013, pp. 362–67.

Geçer, A., and F. Da . "A Blended Learning Experience." *Educational Sciences: Theory and Practice,* vol. 12, no. 1, 2012, pp. 438–42.

Geddes, James. "The Short History of Cyber Monday Is Still Being Written." *Tech Times,* 30 Nov. 2015, www.techtimes.com/articles/111779/20151130/the-short-history-of-cyber-monday-is-still-being-written.htm.

Gee, James Paul. *Unified Discourse Analysis: Language, Reality, Virtual Worlds, and Video Games.* Routledge, 2015.

Gee, James Paul, and Elisabeth R. Hayes. *How to Do Discourse Analysis: A Toolkit.* 2nd ed., Routledge, 2014.

___. *Introducing Discourse Analysis: From Grammar to Society.* Routledge, 2017.

___. *An Introduction to Discourse Analysis: Theory and Method.* 4th ed., Routledge, 2014.

___. *Language and Learning in the Digital Age.* Routledge, 2011.

___. *Literacy and Education.* Routledge, 2015.

___. *Social Linguistics and Literacies: Ideology in Discourses.* Routledge, 2014.

___. *What Is a Human?: Language, Mind, and Culture.* Springer Nature, 2020.

___. *What Video Games Have to Teach Us About Learning and Literacy.* 2nd ed., Macmillan, 2014.

Geekwire.com, www.geekwire.com/2014/geekwire-radiobraincomputer-interfaces-future-personal-privacy.

Gehl, Robert W. *Weaving the Dark Web: Legitimacy on Freenet, Tor, and I2P.* (The Information Society Series). MIT Press, 2018.

Gelman, Robert B., and Stanton McCandlish. *Protecting Yourself Online: The Definitive Resource on Safety, Freedom, and Privacy in Cyberspace.* HarperEdge, 1998.

Gentile, Douglas A. "Pathological Video-Game Use among Youths Ages 8 to 18: A National Study." *Psychological Science,* vol. 20, 2009, pp. 594–602.

Gentile, Douglas A., et al. "Pathological Video-Game Use among Youths: A Two-Year Longitudinal Study." *Pediatrics,* vol. 127, 2011, pp. 319–29.

Gershbein, J. D. "LinkedIn Publishing: A New Era of Social Influence." *The Huffington Post.* HuffingtonPost. com, 28 Apr. 2014.

Gershgorn, Dave. "A California Law Now Means Chatbots Have to Disclose They're Not Human." *BotLaw. Quartz, 3* Oct. 2018, qz.com/1409350/a-new-law-means-californias-bots-have-to-disclose-theyre-not-human/.

Giambene, Giovanni. *Queuing Theory and Telecommunications: Networks and Applications.* 2nd ed., Springer, 2014.

Gibbs, Samuel. "From Windows 1 to Windows 10: 29 Years of Windows Evolution." *The Guardian,* 2 Oct. 2014, www.theguardian.com/technology/2014/oct/02/ from-windows-1-to-windows-10-29-years-of-windows-evolution.

Gillett, Rachel. "How the Most Successful Brands Dominate Instagram, and You Can Too." *Fast Company.* Mansueto Ventures, 22 Apr. 2014, www.fastcompany.com/3029395/ how-the-most-successful-brands-dominate-instagram-and-you-can-too.

Gillispie, M. *From Notepad to iPad: Using Applications and Web Tools to Engage a New Generation of Students.* Taylor and Francis, 2013.

Gladstone, Julia Alpert. "Data Mines and Battlefields: Looking at Financial Aggregators to Understand the Legal Boundaries and Ownership Rights in the Use of Personal Data." *Journal of Marshall Computer and Information Law,* vol. 19, no. 313, 2001.

Glaser, Anton. *History of Binary and Other Nondecimal Numeration.* Rev. ed., Tomash, 1981.

Glaser, C. W., H. J. Rieth, C. K. Kinzer, et al. "A Description of the Impact of Multimedia Anchored Instruction on Classroom Interactions." *Journal of Special Education Technology,* vol. 14, 1999, pp. 27–43.

Glazer, Eliot. "Assessing Second-Tier Social-Media Sites." *New York Times Magazine,* 16 Feb. 2014, p. 9.

Glazer, F. S. *Blended Learning: Across the Disciplines, Across the Academy.* Stylus, 2012.

"Gmail." *Google.* Google, Inc., www.gmail.com/intl/en_us/mail/help/about.html.

Goel, Vindu. "LinkedIn Wants to Be Your Soapbox, Not Just Your Résumé." *The New York Times,* 19 Feb. 2014.

Goelker, Klaus. *Gimp 2.8 for Photographers: Image Editing with* Open Source *Software.* Rocky Nook, 2013.

Goggin, G., and Mark McLelland, editors. *The Routledge Companion to Global Internet Histories.* Routledge, 2017.

Gogolin, Greg. *Digital Forensics Explained.* CRC Press, 2013.

Golden, T. P., and A. Karpur. "Translating Knowledge Through Blended Learning: A Comparative Analysis of Face-To-Face and Blended Learning Methods." *Rehabilitation Research, Policy, and Education,* vol. 26, no. 4, 2012, pp. 305–14.

Goldman, S. R., K. Lawless, J. Pellegrino, et al. "A Technology for Assessing Multiple Source Comprehension: An Essential Skill of the 21st Century." *Technology-based Assessments for 21st Century Skills: Theoretical and Practical Implications from Modern Research,* edited by M. C. Mayrath, J. Clarke-Midura, D. H. Robinson, G. Schraw, Information Age Publishing, 2012, pp. 173–209.

Goldsmith, A. "Disgracebook Policing: Social Media and the Rise of Police Indiscretion." *Policing & Society,* vol. 25, no. 3, 2015, pp. 249–67, rsearch.ebscohost.com/login.aspx?direct=true&db=sxi&an=101347947& site=ehost-live.

Goldstein, Emmanuel. *Best of 2600: A Hacker Odyssey.* Wiley, 2008.

Goldstein, Phil. "How Cities Are Forging Partnerships to Close the Digital Divide." *StateTech,* 10 Dec. 2020, statetechmagazine.com/article/2020/12/how-cities-are-forging-partnerships-close-digital-divide.

___. "How Computer-Aided Design Is Used in Government." *FedTech,* 24 June 2020, fedtechmagazine.com/ article/2020/06/how-computer-aided-design-used-government-perfcon.

Gong, Y., J. E. Beck, and N. T. Heffernan. "How to Construct More Accurate Student Models: Comparing and Optimizing Knowledge Tracing and Performance Factor Analysis." *International Journal of Artificial Intelligence in Education*, vol. 21, no. 1/2, 2011, pp. 27–46.

Good, James. "What Is Twitch? A Beginner's Guide to Live Streaming." *GameQuitters*, 9 Nov. 2019, gamequitters.com/what-is-twitch.

Goodale, Gloria. "Privacy Concerns? What Google Now Says It Can Do with Your Data." *The Christian Science Monitor*, 16 Apr. 2014, www.csmonitor.com/ USA/2014/0416/ Privacy-concerns-What-Google-nowsays-it-can-do-with-your-data-video.

Goodman, Ryan, et al. "Incitement Timeline: Year of Trump's Actions Leading to the Attack on the Capitol." *Just Security*, 11 Jan. 2021, www.justsecurity.org/74138/ incitement-timeline-year-of-trumps-actions-leading-to-the-attack-on-the-capitol.

Goodman, Shalom. "Neil Young, Joe Rogan Podcast and Spotify: What to Know." *The Wall Street Journal*, 2 Feb. 2022, www.wsj.com/articles/joe-rogan-podcast-neil-young-spotify-what-to-know-11643663216.

"Google Gets the Message, Launches Gmail." *Google*. Google, Inc., 1 Apr. 2004, googlepress.blogspot.com/2004/04/google-gets-message-launches-gmail.html. Accessed 28 Aug. 2015.

"Google Unveils Smartphone with 3D Sensors." *BBC News: Technology*. BBC, 20 Feb. 2014. wn.com/computer_accessibility/bbc.

Gordon, Sherri Mabry. *Downloading Copyrighted Stuff from the Internet: Stealing or Fair Use?* Enslow, 2005.

Gordon, Steve. *The Future of the Music Business: How to Succeed with the New Digital Technologies*. Hal Leonard, 2011.

Govindjee, S. "Internal Representation of Numbers." *University of California Berkeley*, 2013, faculty.ce.berkeley.edu/sanjay/e7/numbers.pdf.

Graham, S. "Impoliteness and the Moral Order in Online Gaming." *Internet Pragmatics*, vol. 1, no. 2, 2018, pp. 303–28.

___. "Interaction and Conflict in Digital Communication." *Routledge Handbook of Language in Conflict*, edited by M. Evans, L. Jeffries, and J. O'Driscoll, Routledge, 2019, pp. 310–28.

Graham, S., and C. Hardaker. "(Im)Politeness in Digital Communication." *The Palgrave Handbook of Linguistic (Im)Politeness*, edited by J. Culpeper, M. Haugh, and D. Z. Kádár, Palgrave Macmillan, 2017, pp. 785–814.

Gralla, Preston. *How the Internet Works*. 4th ed., Que Publishing, 1998.

Grant, Maria, and Lapp, Diane. "Teaching Science Literacy." *Educational Leadership*, 2011, www.ascd.org/publications/educational-leadership/mar11/vol68/num06/Teaching-Science-Literacy.aspx.

Granville, Kevin. "Facebook and Cambridge Analytica: What You Need to Know as Fallout Widens." *The New York Times*, 19 Mar. 2018, www.nytimes.com/2018/03/19/technology/facebook-cambridge-analytica-explained.html.

"Graphical User Interface (GUI)." *Techopedia*, 13 Jan. 2017, www.techopedia.com/definition/5435/graphical-user-interface-gui.

Gray, Leon. *How Does a Touchscreen Work?* Rosen, 2013.

Gray, Tony. *Projected Capacitive Touch: A Practical Guide for Engineers*. Springer International, 2019.

Graziani, Thomas. "How Douyin Became China's Top Short-Video App in 500 Days." *Walk the Chat*, walkthechat.com/douyin-became-chinas-top-short-video-app-500-days/.

Grebenshchikova, E. "NBIC-Convergence and Technoethics: Common Ethical Perspective." *International Journal of Technoethics*, vol. 7, no. 1, 2016, pp. 77–84.

Green, Jason. "The Promise, Progress and Pain of Collaboration Software." *TechCrunch*, 24 May 2014, techcrunch.com/2014/05/24/the-promise-the-progress-and-the-pain-of-collaboration-software/.

Green, Joan L. *Assistive Technology in Special Education: Resources for Education, Intervention, and Rehabilitation*. Prufrock Press, 2014.

Green, M. *3-2-1 Code It*. Cengage, 2011.

Greenberg, Andy. *Sandworm: A New Era of Cyberwar and the Hunt for the Kremlin's Most Dangerous Hackers*. Doubleday. 2019

Greenemeier, Larry. "5 Mobile Technologies Help Level the Playing Field for People with Disabilities." *Scientific American*, 5 Aug. 2015, www.scientificamerican.com/article/5-mobile-technologies-help-level-the-playing-field-for-people-with-disabilities-video.

Greenstein, L. *Assessing 21st Century Skills: A Guide to Evaluating Mastery and Authentic Learning*. Corwin, 2012

Greenstein, Shane M., and Feng Zhu. *Collective Intelligence and Neutral Point of View: The Case of Wikipedia*. National Bureau of Economic Research, 2012.

Gregory, Sam, and Eric French. "How Do We Work Together to Detect AI-Manipulated Media?" *Witness Media Lab*, 2019, lab.witness.org/projects/osint-digital-forensics/.

Greifner, L. "Students from U.S., Europe Collaborate on Internet Safety." *Education Week*, vol. 26, 2017, p. 9.

Grey, K. L. "Intersecting Oppressions and Online Communities: Examining the Experiences of Women of Color in Xbox Live." *Information, Communication and Society*, vol. 15, no. 3, 2012, pp. 411–28.

Griffin, Andrew. "Facebook Live: Site Adds Huge New Update to Feature That Lets People Stream in Their Timeline." *The Independent*, 6 Apr. 2016, www.independent.co.uk/life-style/gadgets-and-tech/news/facebook-live-site-adds-huge-new-update-to-feature-that-lets-people-stream-in-their-timeline-a6971566.html.

Griffiths, Devin C. *Virtual Ascendance: Video Games and the Remaking of Reality*. Rowman, 2013.

Gross, Benjamin. *The TVs of Tomorrow: How RCA's Flat-Screen Dreams Led to the First LCDs*. U of Chicago P, 2018.

Gross, Ralph, and Alessandro Acquisti. "Information Revelation and Privacy in Online Social Networks." *WPES '05: Proceedings of the 2005 ACM Workshop on Privacy in the Electronic Society; November 7, 2005, Alexandria, Virginia, USA (Co-located with CCS 2005)*, edited by Sabrina De Capitani di Vimercati and Roger Dingledine, ACM Press, 2005, pp. 71–80.

___. "Information Revelation and Privacy in Online Social Networks: The Facebook Case." *Heinz.cmu.edu*, 2005.

"Groupware." *Inc.*, www.inc.com/encyclopedia/groupware.html.

"Groupware." *Techopedia*, www.techopedia.com/definition/7481/groupware.

Gruba, P., and D. Hinkleman. *Blending Technologies in Second Language Classrooms*. Palgrave Macmillan, 2012.

Gundecha, Pritam, and Huan Liu. "Mining Social Media: A Brief Introduction." *INFORMS Tutorials in Operations Research*. INFORMS, 14 Oct. 2014.

Gustafson, Krystina. "Cyber Monday Sales Top $3 Billion, Beat Forecast." *CNBC*, 1 Dec. 2015, www.cnbc.com/2015/12/01/cyber-monday-sales-top-3-billion-beat-forecast.html.

Gutierrez, Peter. "Every Platform Tells a Story." *School Library Journal*, vol. 58, no. 6, 2012, pp. 32–34.

Habermas, J. *The Structural Transformation of the Public Sphere*. MIT Press, 1991.

Hacker, Scot. "Tutorial: FTP Made Simple." *UC Berkeley Graduate School of Journalism*, 2014, multimedia.journalism.berkeley.edu/tutorials/ftp/.

Hadley, G., and M. Mars. "Postgraduate Medical Education in Paediatric Surgery: Videoconferencing—A Possible Solution for Africa?" *Pediatric Surgery International*, vol. 24, 2008, pp. 223–26.

Hagen, A. N. "The Metaphors We Stream By: Making Sense of Music Streaming." *First Monday*, vol. 21, no. 3, 2016, p. 8, doi:10.5210/fm.v21i3.6005.

___. "The Playlist Experience: Personal Playlists in Music Streaming Services." *Popular Music & Society*, vol. 38, no. 5, 2015, pp. 625–45, doi:10.1080/03007766.2015.1021174.

Hajek, A., and H. H. König. "The Association Between Use of Online Social Network Sites and Perceived Social Isolation Among Individuals in the Second Half of Life: Results Based on a Nationally Representative Sample in Germany." *BMC Public Health*, vol. 19, no. 1, 2019, pp. 1–7.

Hall, Ryan. "The History and Evolution of Intranet Software." *Intranet Connections*. Intranet Connections, 12 Sept. 2013.

Hallanan, Lauren. "Is Douyin the Right Social Video Platform for Luxury Brands?" *Jing Daily*, 11 Mar. 2018, jingdaily.com/douyin-luxury-brands/.

Hamari, J., and J. Koivisto. "Social Motivations to Use Gamification: An Empirical Study of Gamifying Exercise." *Proceedings of the 21st European Conference on Information Systems, Utrecht, Netherlands, June 5-8, 2013*.

Hamblin, James. "It's Everywhere, the Clickbait." *The Atlantic,* 11 Nov. 2014, www.theatlantic.com/entertainment/archive/2014/11/clickbait-what-is/382545/.

Hamburger, Ellis. "Instagram's New Editing Features Could Make It Your Only Photo App." *The Verge.* Vox Media, 3 June 2014, www.theverge.com/2014/6/3/5771860/instagram-new-editing-features-could-make-it-your-only-photo-app-vsco-cam-afterlight.

Hamedy, Saba. "Report: Online Piracy Remains Multi-Hundred-Million-Dollar Business." *Los Angeles Times,* 19 May 2015.

Hammitt, Harry A., et al., editors. *Litigation under the Federal Open Government Laws.* Electronic Privacy Information Center, 2010, epic.org/ bookstore/foia2010/.

Hampton-Sosa, W. "The Impact of Creativity and Community Facilitation on Music Streaming Adoption and Digital Piracy." *Computers in Human Behavior,* vol. 69, 2017, pp. 444–53, doi:10.1016/j.chb.2016.11.055.

Harcourt, Bernard E. *Exposed: Desire and Disobedience in the Digital Age.* Harvard UP, 2015.

Hariharan, P. *Basics of Holography.* Cambridge UP, 2010.

Harkinson, Josh. "Here's How Twitter Can Track You on All of Your Devices." *Mother Jones,* 24 Sept. 2013.

Harlow, S., R. Cummings, and S. Aberasturi. "Karl Popper and Jean Piaget: A Rationale for Constructivism." *Educational Forum,* vol. 71, 2006, pp. 41–48.

Harpur, P., and N. Suzor. "The Paradigm Shift in Realising the Right to Read: How Ebook Libraries Are Enabling in the University Sector." *Disability & Society,* vol. 29, no. 10, 2014, pp. 1658–71.

Harrington, K. "From Tablet to Tablet, from Mesopotamia to Galway." *Adult Learner,* 2014, pp. 94–102.

Harris, Patricia. *What Are Binary and Hexadecimal Numbers?* Rosen Publishing Group, 2018.

Hart, Archibald D., and Sylvia Hart Frejd. *The Digital Invasion: How Technology Is Shaping You and Your Relationships.* Baker, 2013.

Hartley, John, and Kelly McWilliam, editors. *Story Circle: Digital Storytelling around the World.* Blackwell, 2009.

Harwell, D. "Facebook Acknowledges Pelosi Video Is Faked but Declines to Delete It." *The Washington Post,* 24 May 2019, www.washingtonpost.com/technology/2019/05/24/facebook-acknowledges-pelosi-video-is-faked-declines-delete-it/.

Hastings, Glen, and Richard Marcus. *Identity Theft, Inc.: A Wild Ride with the World's #1 Identity Thief.* The Disinformation Company, 2006.

Hatmaker, Taylor. "Instagram Adds Shopping Tags Directly into Stories." *TechCrunch,* 12 June 2018, techcrunch.com/2018/06/12/instagram-adds-shopping-tags-directly-into-stories/.

Hausman, Kalani Kirk, and Susan L. Cook. *IT Architecture for Dummies.* John Wiley & Sons, 2010.

Hawi, Nazir S., and Maya Samaha. "The Relations Among Social Media Addiction, Self-Esteem, and Life Satisfaction in University Students." *Social Science Computer Review,* vol. 35, no. 5, 2017, pp. 576–86.

Hawkins, Andrew J. "Uber Has Resumed Testing Its Self-Driving Cars in San Francisco." *Verge,* 10 Mar. 2020, www.theverge.com/2020/3/10/21172213/uber-self-driving-car-resume-testing-san-francisco-crash.

Heater, Brian. "Why Spotify Is Betting Big on Podcasting." *TechCrunch,* Verizon Media, 6 Feb. 2019, techcrunch.com/2019/02/06/why-spotify-is-betting-big-on-podcasting/.

Heath, N. "FBI Cybercrime Chief on Botnets, Web Terror and the Social Network Threat." *Management. silicon.com,* 16 Apr. 2008, www.fbi.gov/about-us/investigate/cyber/computer-intrusions.

Heaven, Will Douglas. "Predictive Policing Algorithms Are Racist: They Need to Be Dismantled." *MIT Technology Review,* 17 July 2020, www.technologyreview.com/2020/07/17/1005396/predictive-policing-algorithms-racist-dismantled-machine-learning-bias-criminal-justice.

Heisler, Yoni. "The History and Evolution of iOS, from the Original iPhone to iOS 9." *BGR,* 12 Feb. 2016, bgr.com/2016/02/12/ios-history-iphone-features-evolution/.

Held, Gilbert. *Introduction to Light Emitting Diode Technology and Applications.* Auerbach, 2019.

Helland, P. "If You Have Too Much Data, then 'Good Enough' Is Good Enough." *Communications of the ACM,* vol. 54, no. 6, 2011, pp. 40–47.

Heller, P. B. "Technoethics: The Dilemma of Doing the Right Moral Thing in Technology Applications." *International Journal of Technoethics,* vol. 3 no. 1, 2012, pp. 14–27.

Henderson, Harry. *Encyclopedia of Computer Science and Technology.* Facts On File, 2003.

Henrie, C. R., L. R. Halverson, and C. R. Graham. "Measuring Student Engagement in Technology-Mediated Learning: A Review." *Computers & Education*, vol. 90, 2015, pp. 36–53.

Henry, G. B. "Are Social Media Changing Religion?" *USA Today*, 21 June 2010, search.ebscohost.com/login.aspx?direct=true&db=asn&an=j0e230620908010&site=ehost-live.

Henson, K. T. *Curriculum Planning: Integrating Multiculturalism, Constructivism, and Education Reform.* Waveland Press, 2015.

Herbert, Lin. "A Virtual Necessity: Some Modest Steps toward Greater Cybersecurity." *Bulletin of the Atomic Scientists*, vol. 68, no. 5, 2012, pp. 75–87.

Hern, Alex. "Ask.fm's New Owners Vow to Crack Down on Bullying or Shut the Site." *The Guardian*, 19 Aug. 2014, www.theguardian.com/technology/2014/aug/19/askfm-askcom-bullying.

___. "Mark Zuckerberg's Letter Annotated: What He Said and What He Didn't." *The Guardian*, 17 Feb. 2017, www.theguardian.com/technology/ng-interactive/2017/feb/17/mark-zuckerberg-facebook-letter-annotated-what-he-said-what-he-didnt.

Herring, S. "A Faceted Classification Scheme for Computer-Mediated Discourse." *Language@Internet*, vol. 4, 2007, Urn:Nbn:De:0009-7-7611.

Herrman, John. "What Happens When Facebook Goes the Way of Myspace?" *The New York Times*, 12 Dec. 2018, www.nytimes.com/2018/12/12/magazine/what-happens-when-facebook-goes-the-way-of-myspace.html.

Herr-Stephenson, B., Alper, M., Reilly, E., & Jenkins, H. "T Is for Transmedia: Learning Through Transmedia Play." *USC Annenberg Innovation Lab and the Joan Ganz Cooney Center at Sesame Workshop*, annenberglab.com.

Herzog, David. *Data Literacy: A User's Guide.* Sage, 2015.

Hey, Tony, and Gyuri Pápay. *The Computing Universe: A Journey Through a Revolution.* Cambridge UP, 2015.

Heyd, T. "Email Hoaxes." *Pragmatics of Computer-Mediated Communication*, edited by S. Herring, Mouton Degruyter, 2013, pp. 387–410.

HHS Cybersecurity Program. "Ransomware Trends 2021." *US Department of Health and Human Services*, hhs.gov/sites/default/files/ransomware-trends-2021.pdf.

Highfield, Tim. *Social Media and Everyday Politics.* Polity, 2016.

Hill, Kashmir. "Facebook's Mark Zuckerberg: 'We've Made a Bunch of Mistakes.'" *Forbes*, 29 Nov. 2011, www.forbes.com/sites/kashmirhill/2011/11/29/facebooks-mark-zuckerberg-weve-made-a-bunch-of-mistakes/.

Himma, Kenneth Einar. *The Handbook of Information and Computer Ethics.* Wiley, 2008.

Hinduja, Sameer. *Music Piracy and Crime Theory.* LFB, 2005.

Hinduja, Sameer, and Justin W. Patchin. *Cyberbullying Prevention and Response: Expert Perspectives.* Routledge, 2012.

Hintz, Arne, Lina Dencik, and Karin Wahl-Jorgensen. *Digital Citizenship in a Datafied Society.* Polity Press, 2019.

Hirschey, Jeffrey Kenneth. "Symbiotic Relationships: Pragmatic Acceptance of Data Scraping." *Berkeley Technical Law Journal*, vol. 29, no. 897, 2014.

"History and Timeline." *Open Group*, www.unix.org/what_is_unix/history_timeline.html.

"The History of Design, Model Making and CAD." *Creative Mechanisms*, 14 Dec. 2015, www.creativemechanisms.com/blog/the-history-of-design-model-making-and-cad.

"The History of HTML." *Ironspider*, www.ironspider.ca/webdesign101/htmlhistory.htm.

"The History of HTML." *Landofcode.com*, landofcode.com/html-tutorials/html-history.php.

"History of Microsoft Excel." *Haresoftware*, www.haresoftware.com/ExcelHistory.htm.

"A History of Microsoft Windows." *Microsoft*, Oct. 2015, windows.microsoft.com/en-US/windows/history#T1=era0.

"A History of Windows." *Windows.* Microsoft, windows.microsoft.com/en-us/windows/history#T1=era0.

"History, Data, and Success in the Digital Economy." *SAPInsider*, 19 Oct. 2017, sapinsider.wispubs.com/Assets/Blogs/2017/October/SAP-Database-and-Data-Management.

Hitchcock, C., and S. Stahl. "Assistive Technology, Universal Design, Universal Design for Learning: Improved Learning Opportunities." *Journal of Special Education Technology*, vol. 18, 2003, pp. 45–52.

Hoadley, Christopher. "What Is a Community of Practice and How Can We Support It?" *Theoretical Foundations of Learning Environments*, edited by David H. Jonasson and Susan M. Land, 2nd ed., Routledge, 2012, pp. 287–300.

Hockenson, Lauren, and Rani Molla. "Facebook Grows Daily Active Users by 25 Percent, Mobile Users by 45 Percent." *Gigaom.com*, 13 Oct. 2013.

Hoffman, Jan. "Online Bullies Pull Schools into the Fray." *The New York Times*, 27 June 2010, www.nytimes.com/2010/06/28/style/28bully.html.

Hofmann, Chris, Marcia Knous, and John V. Hedke. *Firefox and Thunderbird Garage*. Prentice Hall Professional Technical Reference, 2005.

Hohpe, Gregor. *The Software Architect Elevator*. O'Reilly Media, 2020.

Holcombe, Jane, and Charles Holcombe. *Survey of Operating Systems*. 6th ed., McGraw-Hill Education, 2020.

Hollander, Dave, and C. M. Sperberg-McQueen. "Happy Birthday, XML!" *W3C*, 13 Aug. 2015, www.w3.org/2003/02/xml-at-5.html.

Hollander, P. "Popular Culture, the New York Times and the New Republic." *Society*, vol. 51, 2014, pp. 288–96, search.ebscohost.com/login.aspx?direct=true&db=sih&AN=96203565&site=ehost-live&scope=site.

Hollows, Joanne. *Media Studies: A Complete Introduction*. Hodder & Stoughton, 2016.

Holt, Thomas J., Adam M. Bossler, and Kathryn C. Seigfried-Spellar. *Cybercrime and Digital Forensics: An Introduction*, 2nd ed., Routledge, 2017.

Holtzman, David H. *Privacy Lost: How Technology Is Endangering Your Privacy*. Jossey-Bass, 2006.

Hong, Jason. "The State of Phishing Attacks." *Communications of the ACM*, vol. 55, no. 1, 2012, pp. 74–81, search.ebscohost.com/login.aspx?direct=true&db=a9h&AN=71678156.

Hoofnagle, Chris Jay. "Identity Theft: Making the Known Unknowns Known." *Harvard Journal of Law and Technology*, vol. 21, no. 1, 2007, pp. 97–122.

Hormes, Julia M., Brianna Kearns, and C. Alix Timko. "Craving Facebook? Behavioral Addiction to Online Social Networking and Its Association with Emotion Regulation Deficits." *Addiction*, vol. 109, no. 12, 2014, pp. 2079–88.

Hornshaw, Phil. "What Is Discord?" *Digital Trends*, 1 Sept. 2020, www.digitaltrends.com/gaming/what-is-discord/.

Horowitz, M., D. M. Bollinger, and American Association of School Administrators. *Cyberbullying in Social Media within Educational Institutions: Featuring Student, Employee, and Parent Information*. Rowman & Littlefield, 2014.

Horrigan, J. "Home Broadband Adoption 2008." *Pew Internet & American Life Project*, pewinternet.org/PPF/r/257/report%5fdisplay.asp.

Horton, Sarah, and Whitney Quesenbery. *A Web for Everyone: Designing Accessible User Experiences*. Rosenfeld Media, 2014.

Horvath, Joan. *Mastering 3D Printing: Modeling, Printing, and Prototyping with Reprap-Style 3D Printers*. Apress, 2014.

Hoskins, Stephen. *3D Printing for Artists, Designers and Makers*. Bloomsbury, 2013.

Hou, H., K. Chang, and Y. Sung. "An Analysis of Peer Assessment Online Discussions within a Course That Uses Project-Based Learning." *Interactive Learning Environments*, vol. 15, 2007, pp. 237–51.

Hovious, A. "Inanimate Alice." *Teacher Librarian*, vol. 42, no. 2, 2014, pp. 42–46.

Hovious, A. S. *Transmedia Storytelling: The Librarian's Guide*. Libraries Unlimited, 2016.

"How Firewalls Work." *Boston University Information Services and Technology*, www.bu.edu/tech/about/security-resources/host-based/intro/. Accessed 28 June 2020.

"How Snaps Are Stored and Deleted." *Snapchat Blog*, 9 May 2013.

"How Speech-Recognition Software Got So Good." *Economist*, 22 Apr. 2014, www.economist.com/the-economist-explains/2014/04/22/how-speech-recognition-software-got-so-good.

"How to Protect Yourself While on the Internet." *Computer Hope*, 15 Sept. 2017, www.computerhope.com/issues/ch000507.htm.

"How to Recognize Phishing Email Messages, Links, or Phone Calls." *Microsoft*, www.microsoft.com/en-us/safety/online-privacy/phishing-symptoms.aspx.

Howard, Alex. "A Conversation with MIT's Sherry Turkle About Conscious Consumption of Tech." *Tech Republic*, 11 Apr. 2016, techrepublic.com/article/a-conversation-with-mits-sherry-turkle-about-conscious-consumption-of-tech/.McCorduck, Pamela. "Sex, Lies and Avatars: Sherry Turkle knows what role-playing in Cyberspace Really Means. A Profile." 1 Apr. 1996. *Wired*. www.wired.com/1996/04/turkle/.

Howard, J., P. Vu, and L. Vu. "How Do Undergraduate Students Use Their iPad?" *Journal of Technology Integration in the Classroom*, vol. 4, no. 3, 2012, pp. 5–12.

Hoy, Matthew B. "Alexa, Siri, Cortana, and More: An Introduction to Voice Assistants." *Medical Reference Services Quarterly*, vol. 37, no. 1, 2018, pp. 81–88.

Hrynyshyn, Derek. "The Outrage of Networks: Social Media and Contemporary Authoritarian Populism." *Democratic Communiqué*, vol. 28, no. 1, 2019, pp. 27–45, search.ebscohost.com/login.aspx?direct=true&db=ufh&an=135902018&site=ehost-live.

"HTML Basics." *MediaCollege.com*, www.mediacollege.com/internet/html/html-basics.html.

"HTML Introduction." *W3Schools.com*. W3 Schools, www.w3schools.com/html/html_intro.asp.

"HTML Tutorial." *Refsnes Data*, www.w3schools.com/html/default.asp.

Hu, Jane C. "The Whitney Houston of the 3D Hologram Tour Will Be Neither 3D nor a Hologram." *Slate*, 22 May 2019. slate.com/technology/2019/05/whitney-houston-3d-hologram-tour-technology.html.

Huang, Ronghuai, J. Michael Spector, and Junfeng Yang. *Educational Technology: A Primer for the 21st Century*. Springer Singapore, 2019.

Hudak, Heather C. *Cybercrime*. Abdo, 2020.

Huddleston, Rob. *HTML, XHTML, and CSS: Your visual Blueprint for Designing Effective Web Pages*. John Wiley & Sons, 2009.

Hudson, David L., Jr. "Free Speech or Censorship? Social Media Litigation Is a Hot Legal Battleground." *ABA Journal*, 1 Apr. 2019, www.abajournal.com/magazine/article/social-clashes-digital-free-speech.

Humphreys, Ashlee. *Social Media: Enduring Principles*. Oxford UP, 2016.

Humphries, Matthew. "Internet Eyes Will Pay You to Watch Security Camera Feeds." *Geek.com*, Ziff Davis, 6 Oct. 2010, www.geek.com/news/internet-eyes-will-pay-you-to-watch-security-camera-feeds-1288416/.

Hunter, Philip. "Cyber Security's New Hard Line." *Engineering & Technology*, vol. 8, no. 8, 2013, pp. 68–71.

Husak, Douglas. *Overcriminalization: The Limits of the Criminal Law*. Oxford UP, 2008.

Hutchinson, Lee. "Home 3D Printers Take Us on a Maddening Journey into Another Dimension." *Ars Technica*, 27 Aug. 2013, arstechnica.com/gadgets/2013/08/home-3d-printers-take-us-on-a-maddening-journey-into-another-dimension/.

Hutchison, Tom, Paul Allen, and Amy Macy. *Record Label Marketing*. Taylor & Francis, 2012.

Huth, Alexa, and James Cebula. "The Basics of Cloud Computing." *US-CERT*, 2011, www.us-cert.gov/sites/default/files/publications/CloudComputingHuthCebula.pdf.

"The ICT Development Index (IDI): Conceptual Framework and Methodology." *International Telecommunication Union*, www.itu.int/en/ITU-D/Statistics/Pages/publications/mis/methodology.aspx. Accessed 29 June 2020.

"An Illustrated History of Mac OS X." *Tower*, 12 Jan. 2016, www.git-tower.com/blog/history-of-osx/.

"The Impact of Recent Cyberstalking and Cyberharassment Cases: Leading Lawyers on Navigating Privacy Guidelines and the Legal Ramifications of Online Behavior." *Cyberstalking and Cyberbullying*, edited by Samuel C. McQuade and Sarah Gentry, Chelsea House, 2012.

Individuals with Disabilities Education Act Amendments of 1997, 20 U.S.C. §1415 *Et Seq*.

Individuals with Disabilities Education Improvement Act of 2004, P.L. 108-446, 20 U.S.C. §1400 *Et Seq*.

"Information and Technical Assistance on the Americans with Disabilities Act." *ADA.gov*. US Department of Justice, Civil Rights Division, www.ada.gov/ada_intro.htm.

Information Resources Management Association, editor. *Assistive Technologies: Concepts, Methodologies, Tools, and Applications.* Vol. 1. Information Science Reference, 2014.

Ingram, Mathew. "Facebook Killing Another Example of Live Video Feature's Dark Side." *Fortune*, 17 Apr. 2017, fortune.com/2017/04/17/facebook-killing/.

"Instagram 2022—What You Need to Know!" *Lounge Lizard*, 8 Feb. 2022, loungelizard.com/blog/instagram-2022-what-you-need-to-know/.

International Council of E-Commerce Consultants. *Computer Forensics: Investigating File and Operating Systems, Wireless Networks, and Storage.* 4 vols. 2nd ed., Cengage, 2016.

Internet Crime Complaint Center. "2016 Internet Crime Report." *Federal Bureau of Investigation*, pdf.ic3.gov/2016_ic3report.pdf.

"Internet Porn 'Increasing Child Abuse.'" *The Guardian*, 12 Jan. 2004, www.guardian.co.uk/technology/2004/jan/12/childprotection.childrensservices.

"Introduction to Image Files Tutorial." *Boston University Information Services and Technology*, www.bu.edu/tech/support/research/training-consulting/online-tutorials/imagefiles/.

"The Invention of the Internet." *History.com*, www.history.com/topics/inventions/invention-of-the-internet.

"iOS." *AppleInsider*, 27 June 2020, appleinsider.com/inside/ios.

"iOS 14." *AppleInsider*, 25 June 2020, appleinsider.com/inside/ios-14.

"iOS: A Visual History." *Verge*, 16 Sept. 2013, www.theverge.com/2011/12/13/2612736/ios-history-iphone-ipad.

Iqbal, Monsoor. "LinkedIn Usage and Revenue Statistics: 2022." *BusinessofApps*, www.businessofapps.com.

Isaac, Mike. "Facebook Renames Itself Meta." *The New York Times*, 28 Oct. 2021, www.nytimes.com/2021/10/28/technology/facebook-meta-name-change.html.

___. "Instagram May Change Your Feed, Personalizing It with an Algorithm." *The New York Times*, 15 Mar. 2016, www.nytimes.com/2016/03/16/technology/instagram-feed.html.

Isaacson, Walter. *Steve Jobs.* Simon & Schuster, 2011.

Isaranon, Y. "The Role of Facebook Affirmation Towards Ideal Self-Image and Self-Esteem." *International Journal of Behavioral Science*, vol. 14, no. 1, 2019, pp. 46–62.

Israelashvili, Moshe, et al. "Adolescents' Over-Use of the Cyber World: Internet Addiction or Identity Exploration?" *Journal of Adolescence*, vol. 35, no. 2, 2012, pp. 417–24.

Ito, Mizuko, et al. *Hanging Out, Messing Around, and Geeking Out: Kids Living and Learning with New Media.* MIT Press, 2010.

"iTunes." *Apple Inc.*, www.apple.com/itunes.

Jacko, Julie A., editor. *The Human-Computer Interaction Handbook: Fundamentals, Evolving Technologies, and Emerging Applications.* 3rd ed., CRC Press, 2012.

Jackson, Wallace. *Digital Audio Editing Fundamentals.* Apress, 2015.

Jacobs, Bruce. "Cyberbullying a Growing Concern." *HTRNews.com.* HTR Media, 5 Dec. 2014.

Jaishankar, K. "Cyber Criminology: Evolving a Novel Discipline with a New Journal." *International Journal of Cyber Criminology*, vol. 1, 2007, www.geocities.com/cybercrimejournal/editorialijcc.pdf.

Jakobsson, Markus, and Steven Myers, editors. *Phishing and Countermeasures: Understanding the Increasing Problem of Electronic Identity Theft.* John Wiley & Sons, 2007.

James, Jeffrey. "The ICT Development Index and the Digital Divide: How Are They Related?" *Technological Forecasting and Social Change*, vol. 79, no. 3, 2012, 587–94, doi.org/10.1016/j.techfore.2011.08.010.

James, Lance. *Phishing Exposed.* Syngress Publishing, 2005.

Jargon, Julie. "The Dark Side of Discord, Your Teen's Favorite Chat App." *The Wall Street Journal*, 11 June 2019, www.wsj.com/articles/discord-where-teens-rule-and-parents-fear-to-tread-11560245402.

Jarnow, Jesse. "Apple's iTunes Is Alienating Its Most Music-Obsessed Users." *Wired*, 17 Nov. 2015, www.wired.com/2015/11/itunes-alternatives.

Jasper, Margaret C. *The Law of Obscenity and Pornography.* 2nd ed., Oceana, 2009.

Jelenchick, L., J. Eickhoff, and M. Moreno. "Facebook Depression?: Social Networking Site Use and Depression in Older Adolescents." *Journal of Adolescent Health*, vol. 52, 2013, pp. 128–30.

Jenkins, Henry. *Comics and Stuff.* NYU P, 2020.

___. *Confronting the Challenges of Participatory Culture: Media Education in the 21st Century.* MIT Press, 2009.

___. *Convergence Culture: Where Old and New Media Collide.* NYU P, 2008.

___. *Sam Ford and Joshua Green. Spreadable Media: Creating Value and Meaning in Networked Culture.* NYU P, 2018.

___. "Searching for the Origami Unicorn: The Matrix and Transmedia Storytelling." *Convergence Culture: Where Old and New Media Collide,* NYU P, 2006, pp. 93–130.

___. *Textual Poachers. Television Fans and Participatory Culture.* Updated 20th Anniversary ed., Routledge, 2013.

___. "Transmedia Storytelling and Entertainment: An Annotated Syllabus." *Continuum: Journal of Media & Cultural Studies,* vol. 24, no. 6, 2010, pp. 943–58.

Jenkins, Henry, Mizuko Ito, and Danah Boyd. *Participatory Culture in a Networked Era: A Conversation on Youth.* John Wiley & Sons, 2015.

Jenkins, Simms. *The Truth about Email Marketing.* FT Press, 2009.

Jeon, Myounghoon, editor. *Emotions and Affect in Human Factors and Human-Computer Interaction.* Academic Press, 2017.

Jimenez, Jorge, et al. "Destroy All Jaggies." *Game Developer,* vol. 18, no. 6, 2011, pp. 13–20.

Jimoyiannis, A., P. Tsiotakis, D. Roussinos, et al. "Preparing Teachers to Integrate Web 2.0 in School Practice: Toward a Framework for Pedagogy 2.0." *Australasian Journal of Educational Technology,* vol. 29, 2013, pp. 248–67.

"Jobvite Recruiter Nation Report 2016: The Annual Social Recruiting Survey." *Jobvite,* July 2016, www.jobvite.com/wp-content/uploads/2016/09/RecruiterNation2016.pdf.

Johns, Adrian. *Piracy: The Intellectual Property Wars from Gutenberg to Gates.* U of Chicago P, 2009.

Johnson, D. *The Classroom Teacher's Technology Survival Guide.* Jossey-Bass, 2012.

Johnson, Jeff. *Designing with the Mind in Mind.* 2nd ed., Morgan Kaufmann, 2014.

Johnston, C. "Brave New World or Virtual Pedophile Paradise? Second Life Falls Foul of Law." *The Age,* 10 May 2007, acrime/2007/05/09/1178390390098.html.

Johnston, Sean F. "Absorbing New Subjects: Holography as an Analog of Photography." *Physics in Perspective,* vol. 8, no. 2, 2006, pp. 164–88.

Joiner, Richard, et al. "Comparing First and Second Generation Digital Natives' Internet Use, Internet Anxiety, and Internet Identification." *CyberPsychology, Behavior & Social Networking,* vol. 16, no. 7, 2013, pp. 549–52.

Jokinen, Jussi P. P. "Emotional User Experience: Traits, Events, and States." *International Journal of Human-Computer Studies,* vol. 76, 2015, pp. 67–77.

Jones, Chris. "A New Generation of Learners? The Net Generation and Digital Natives." *Learning, Media & Technology,* vol. 35, no. 4, 2010, pp. 365–68.

Jones, M. J. "Shady Trick or Legitimate Tactic—Can Law Enforcement Officials Use Fictitious Social Media Accounts to Interact with Suspects?" *American Journal of Trial Advocacy,* vol. 40, no. 1, 2016, pp. 69–81.

Jones, Nicola. "How to Stop Data Centres from Gobbling Up the World's Electricity." *Nature,* 13 Sept. 2018, www.nature.com/articles/d41586-018-06610-y.

Jones, V. L., and L. J. Hinesmon-Matthews. "Effective Assistive Technology Consideration and Implications for Diverse Students." *Computers in the Schools,* vol. 31, 2014, pp. 220–32.

Joosten, T. *Social Media for Educators: Strategies and Best Practices.* Jossey-Bass, 2012.

Joseph, L. "Keeping Safe in Cyberspace." *Multimedia & Internet@Schools,* vol. 14, 2007, pp. 17–20.

Jost, M. B., and B. F. Mosley. "Where IT's AT? Teachers, Assistive Technology, and Instructional Technology." *Journal of Technology Integration in the Classroom,* vol. 3, 2011, pp. 5–16.

Junco, R. *Engaging Students Through Social Media: Evidence Based Practices for Use in Student Affairs.* Jossey-Bass, 2014.

Jung, Timothy, and M. Claudia tom Dieck, editors. *Augmented Reality and Virtual Reality: Empowering Human, Place and Business.* Springer International, 2018.

K, Toly. *Keynote Survival Guide: Step-by-Step User Guide for Apple Keynote: Getting Started, Managing Presentations, Formatting Slides and Playing a Slideshow.* MobileReference, 2012.

Kahraman, H., S. Sagiroglu, and I. Colak. "A Novel Model for Web-Based Adaptive Educational Hypermedia Systems: SAHM (Supervised Adaptive Hypermedia Model)." *Computer Applications in Engineering Education*, vol. 21, 2013, pp. 60–74.

Kale, Vivek. *Guide to Cloud Computing for Business and Technology Managers*. CRC Press, 2015.

Kane, Yukari Iwatani. *Haunted Empire: Apple after Steve Jobs*. HarperBusiness, 2014.

Kardell, Nicole. "FTC Will Propose Broader Children's Online Privacy Safeguards." *Natlawreview.com*, 2 Dec. 2011.

Kariuki, M., and M. Duran. "Using Anchored Instruction to Teach Preservice Teachers to Integrate Technology in the Curriculum." *Journal of Technology and Teacher Education*, vol. 12, 2004, pp. 431–45.

Karlin, S. "Futurist Liebowitz Looks at Tomorrow's Schools Today." *American School Board Journal*, vol. 194, 2007, p. 36.

Kato, Hiroki, Keng T. Tan, and Douglas Chai. *Barcodes for Mobile Devices*. Cambridge UP, 2010.

Katz, Adrienne, and Aiman El Asam. "Look at Me: Teens, Sexting, and Risks." *Internet Matters.org*, 2020. internetmatters.org/about-us/sexting-report-look-at-me/.

Katz, J. "The Three Block Model of Universal Design for Learning (UDL): Engaging Students in Inclusive Education." *Canadian Journal of Education*, vol. 36, 2013, pp. 153–94.

Kaul, Ankit. "History of Microsoft Excel 1978–2013 (Infographic)." *Excel Trick*, www.exceltrick.com/others/history-of-excel/.

Kavanagh, Paul. *Open Source Software Implementation and Management*. Elsevier Digital Press, 2004.

Kävrestad, Joakim. *Fundamentals of Digital Forensics: Theory, Methods, and Real-Life Applications*. Springer International, 2018.

Kay, Russell. "How-To: Phishing." *Computerworld*, 19 Jan. 2004.

Keamy, R. "Of Waves and Storms: Supporting Colleagues Adopting Blended Approaches in Their Teaching." *Transformative Dialogues: Teaching and Learning Journal*, vol. 10, no. 3, 2017.

Kearns, Michael. "How to Build an Ethical Algorithm." Interview by Dan Costa. *PCMag*, 27 Feb. 2020, www.pcmag.com/news/how-to-build-an-ethical-algorithm.

Kearns, Michael, and Aaron Roth. "Ethical Algorithm Design Should Guide Technology Regulation." *Brookings*, 13 Jan. 2020, www.brookings.edu/research/ethical-algorithm-design-should-guide-technology-regulation.

___. "Who Is Responsible for Biased and Intrusive Algorithms?" *Knowledge@Wharton*. University of Pennsylvania, 2 Dec. 2019, knowledge.wharton.upenn.edu/article/who-is-responsible-for-biased-and-intrusive-algorithms.

Kelly, Heather. "Why Gmail and Other E-mail Services Aren't Really Free." *Cable News Network*. Turner Broadcasting System, Inc., 1 Apr. 2014, www.cnn.com/2014/03/31/tech/web/gmail-privacy-problems/.

Kemp, Simon. "WhatsApp Is the World's Favorite Social Platform (and Other Facts)." *Hootsuite*, 22 Apr. 2021, blog.hootsuite.com/simon-kemp-social-media/.

Kendal, Simon, and Malcolm Creen. *An Introduction to Knowledge Engineering*. Springer-Verlag, 2007.

Kennedy, Helen. *Post, Mine, Repeat: Social Media Data Mining Becomes Ordinary*. Palgrave Macmillan, 2016.

Kenton, Will. "Copyright." *Investopedia*, 13 Sept. 2020, www.investopedia.com/terms/c/copyright.asp.

Kern, Kirsten, and Naticia Chetty. "Peer-to-Peer Payments in the Fintech Revolution." *Fintech Weekly*, 5 Jan. 2022, fintechweekly.com/magazine/articles/peer-to-peer-payments-in-the-fintech-revolution.

Kernighan, Brian W. *UNIX: A History and a Memoir*. Kernighan, 2019.

Kerr, Orin S. "Cybercrime's Scope: Interpreting 'Access' and 'Authorization' in Computer Misuse Statutes." *New York University Law Review*, vol. 78, 2003, p. 1596.

___. "Vagueness Challenges to the Computer Fraud and Abuse Act." *Minnesota Law Review*, vol. 94, 2010, p. 1561.

Ketelaar, P. E., R. Konig, E. G. Smit, et al. "In Ads We Trust: Religiousness as a Predictor of Advertising Trustworthiness and Avoidance." *Journal of Consumer Marketing*, vol. 32, no. 3, 2015, pp. 190–98, search.ebscohost.com/login.aspx?direct=true&db=bsu&an=102992949&site=ehost-live.

Khalid, S., O. Jurisic, H. S. Kristensen, et al. "Exploring the Use of iPads in Danish Schools." *Proceedings of the European Conference on E-Learning*, 2014, pp. 264–72.

Khan, Gul N., and Krzysztof Iniewski, editors. *Embedded and Networking Systems: Design, Software, and Implementation.* CRC Press, 2014.

Kharaz, Amin, et. al. "UNVEIL: A Large-Scale, Automated Approach to Detecting Ransomware." *USENIX: The Advanced Computing Systems Association*, 2016, www.usenix.org/system/files/conference/usenixsecurity16/sec16_paper_kharraz.pdf.

Kharchenko, Vyacheslav, Yuriy Kondratenko, and Janusz Kacprzyk, editors. *Green IT Engineering: Social, Business and Industrial Applications.* Springer Nature Switzerland, 2019.

Kilgore, D. "The Medium Is the Message: Online Technology and Knowledge Construction in Adult Graduate Education." *Adult Learning*, vol. 15, no. 3/4, 2004, pp. 12–15.

Kim, A. "DVDs Poised to Become Future Teaching Tool." *T H E Journal*, vol. 30, 2002, pp. 2–3.

Kim, J., C. Nam, and M. H. Ryu. "What Do Consumers Prefer for Music Streaming Services?: A Comparative Study between Korea and US." *Telecommunications Policy*, vol. 41, no. 4, 2017, pp. 263–72, doi:10.1016/j.telpol.2017.01.008.

Kirkpatrick, David. *The Facebook Effect: The Inside Story of the Company That Is Connecting the World.* Simon, 2011.

Kirshenbaum, Sheril. "What Is Scientific Literacy?" *Discover Magazine*, www.discovermagazine.com/the-sciences/what-is-scientific-literacy-02.

Kisselburgh, L., and S. Matei. "The Role of Media Use, Social Interaction, and Spatial Behavior in Community Belonging." *Conference Papers—International Communication Association 2007 Annual Meeting*, 2007, pp. 1–50, search.Ebscohost.Com/Login.Aspx?Direct=True&Db=Ufh&AN=26951131&Site=Ehost-Live.

Kitai, Adrian, editor. *Materials for Solid State Lighting and Displays.* John Wiley & Sons, 2017.

Kittle, Peter. "Online Literacy and Communities of Practice." 11 Sept. 2010, www.thecurrent.educatorinnovator.org/resource/online-literacy-and-communities-of-practice.

Kizza, Joseph Migga. *Guide to Computer Network Security.* 5th ed., Springer Nature Switzerland, 2020.

Klaus, C. L., and T. S. Hartshorne. "Ethical Implications of Trends in Technology." *The Journal of Individual Psychology*, vol. 71, no. 2 2015, pp. 195–204.

Klein, A. "As NCLB Waivers Take Hold, Revision of Law Remains Up in Air." *Education Week*, vol. 32, 2013, p. 25.

Klein, André. "A Brief History of Peer-to-Peer Networks." *Learnoutlive*, 20 Oct. 2020, learnoutlive.com/a-brief-history-of-peer-to-peer-networks/.

Klein, Ezra. "Mark Zuckerberg on Facebook's Hardest Year, and What Comes Next." *Vox*, 2 Apr. 2018, www.vox.com/2018/4/2/17185052/mark-zuckerberg-facebook-interview-fake-news-bots-cambridge.

Kleymenov, Alexey, and Amr Thabet. *Mastering Malware Analysis.* Packt, 2019.

Klinger, Lauren, and Kelly McBride. "Stop Calling Every News Article Clickbait." *Poynter*, 22 Feb. 2016, www.poynter.org/2016/clickbait/397841/.

Knight, Michelle. "What Is Data Literacy?" *Dataversity*, 14 Oct. 2020, www.dataversity.net/what-is-data-literacy/.

Knudson, Julie. "What Can an Intranet Do for Your Small Business?" *Small Business Computing.com*. QuinStreet, 31 July 2014.

Koble, Nicole. "TikTok is Changing Music as You Know It." *GQ*, 28 Oct. 2019, www.gq-magazine.co.uk/culture/article/what-is-tiktok.

Kofman, Ava. "Dueling Realities." *The Atlantic.* The Atlantic Monthly Group, 9 June 2015, www.theatlantic.com/technology/archive/2015/06/dueling-realities/395126/.

Kong, S. C. "A Curriculum Framework for Implementing Information Technology in School Education to Foster Information Literacy." *Computers & Education*, vol. 51, 2008, pp. 129–41.

Konijn, Elly A., et al. "YouTube as Research Tool—Three Approaches." *CyberPsychology, Behavior & Social Networking*, vol. 16, no. 5, 2013, pp. 1–7.

Koops, Bert-Jaap. "The Trouble with European Data Protection Law." *International Data Privacy Law*, vol. 4, no. 4, 2014, pp. 250–61.

Kopacz, Maria A. "Rating the YouTube Indian: Viewer Ratings of Native American Portrayals on a Viral Video Site." *American Indian Quarterly*, vol. 35, no. 2, 2011, pp. 241–57, search.ebscohost.com/login.Aspx?direct=true&db=a9h&AN=59422220&site=ehost-live.

Kostopoulos, George K. *Cyberspace and Cybersecurity.* CRC Press, 2013.

Kowalkiewicz, Marek. "How Did We Get Here? The Story of Algorithms." *Towards Data Science*, 10 Oct. 2019, towardsdatascience.com/how-did-we-get-here-the-story-of-algorithms-9ee186ba2a07.

Krahmer, Shawn M., Ginette McManus, and Rajneesh Sharma. "Ensuring Instructional Continuity in a Potential Pandemic." *Inside Higher Ed*, 4 Mar. 2020, www.insidehighered.com/advice/2020/03/04/preparing-instructional-continuity-advent-covid-19-pandemic-opinion.

Krathwohl, D. R. "A Revision of Bloom's Taxonomy: An Overview." *Theory into Practice*, 2002, pp. 212–18.

Krebs, Brian. "Shadowy Russian Firm Seen as Conduit for Cybercrime." *The Washington Post*, 13 Oct. 2007, www.washingtonpost.com/wp-dyn/content/article/2007/10/12/AR2007101202461.html.

Kreimer, Seth F. "Sex, Laws, and Videophones: The Problem of Juvenile Sexting Prosecutions." *Children, Sexuality, and the Law*, edited by Sacha M. Coupet and Ellen Marrus, New York UP, 2015, pp. 133–62.

Kreitzer, A. E., and G. F. Madaus. "Empirical Investigations of the Hierarchical Structure of the Taxonomy." *Bloom's Taxonomy: A Forty-Year Retrospective*, edited by L. W. Anderson and L. A. Sosniak, U of Chicago P, 1994, pp. 28–40.

Kross, E., P. Verduyn, E. Demiralp, et al. "Facebook Use Predicts Declines in Subjective Well-Being in Young Adults." *PLOS One*, vol. 8, no. 8, 2013, pp. 1–6.

Krotoski, Aleks. "WikiLeaks and the New, Transparent World Order." *Political Quarterly*, vol. 82, no. 4, 2011, pp. 526–30, search.ebscohost.com/login.aspx?direct=true&db=a9h&AN=66793319&site=ehost-live.

Kruk, Robert. "Public, Private and Hybrid Clouds: What's the Difference?" *Techopedia*, vol. 22 Feb. 2017, www.techopedia.com/2/28575/trends/cloud-computing/public-private-and-hybrid-clouds-whats-the-difference.

Ktoridou, D., N. Eteokleous, and A. Zahariadou. "Exploring Parents' and Children's Awareness on Internet Threats in Relation to Internet Safety." *Campus-Wide Information Systems*, vol. 29, 2012, pp. 133–43.

Kuehnl, Eric, Andrew Haak, and Frank D. Cook. *Ableton Live 101: An Introduction to Ableton Live 10.* Rowman & Littlefield, 2019.

Kumar, Arun. "History & Evolution of Microsoft Office Software." *The Windows Club*, 28 Jan. 2013, www.thewindowsclub.com/history-evolution-microsoft-office-software.

Kurz, T. L., and I. Batarelo. "Using Anchored Instruction to Evaluate Mathematical Growth and Understanding." *Journal of Educational Technology Systems*, vol. 33, 2004, pp. 421–36.

La Counte, Scott. *The Ridiculously Simple Guide to Surfing the Internet with Google Chrome.* GOLGOTHAPressNC, 2020.

Laalaoui, Yacine, and Nizar Bouguila, editors. *Artificial Intelligence Applications in Information and Communication Technologies.* Springer International, 2015.

Lackey, Ella Deon, et al. "Introduction to Public-Key Cryptography." *Mozilla Developer Network*, 21 Nov. 2019, developer.mozilla.org/en-US/docs/Archive/Security/Introduction_to_Public-Key_Cryptography.

LaCounte, Scott. *The Ridiculously Simple Guide to Google Slides: A Practical Guide to Cloud-Based Presentations.* Ridiculously Simple Books, 2019.

Lacy, Sarah. *Once You're Lucky, Twice You're Good: The Rebirth of Silicon Valley and the Rise of Web 2.0.* Gotham Books, 2008.

Laidlaw, L., and J. O'Mara. "Rethinking Difference in the Iworld: Possibilities, Challenges and 'Unexpected Consequences' of Digital Tools in Literacy Education." *Language & Literacy: A Canadian Educational E-Journal*, vol. 17, no. 2, 2015, pp. 59–74.

Lakier, Genevieve. "The Great Free-Speech Reversal." *The Atlantic*, 27 Jan. 2021, www.theatlantic.com/ideas/archive/2021/01/first-amendment-regulation/617827.

Lam, Lawrence T., et al. "Factors Associated with Internet Addiction among Adolescents." *Cyberpsychology and Behavior*, vol. 12, no. 5, 2009, pp. 551–55.

Lambert, Jeffrey A. "How to Erase Your Digital Footprint." *MaximumPC.* Future US, Inc., 10 Nov. 2011, www.maximumpc.com/article/features/how_erase_your_digital_footprint.

Lambert, Joe. *Digital Storytelling: Capturing Lives, Creating Community.* 4th ed., Routledge, 2013.

Lanagan, James and Alan Smeaton. "Video Digital Libraries: Contributive and Decentralized." *International Journal on Digital Libraries*, vol. 12, no. 4, 2012, pp. 159–78.

Lande, Daniel R. "Development of the Binary Number System and the Foundations of Computer Science." *Mathematics Enthusiast*, 2014, pp. 513–40.

Lange, A., M. McPhillips, G. Mulhern, et al. "Assistive Software Tools for Secondary-Level Students with Literacy Difficulties." *Journal of Special Education Technology*, vol. 21, 2006, pp. 13–22.

Langmia, K., T. C. M. Tyree, P. O'Brien, et al. *Social Media: Pedagogy and Practice.* University Press of America, 2014.

Langone, J., D. M. Malone, and G. N. Clinton. "The Effects of Technology-Enhanced Anchored Instruction on the Knowledge of Preservice Special Educators." *Teacher Education and Special Education*, vol. 22, 1999, pp. 85–96.

Lankshear, Colin, and Michele Knobel, editors. *Digital Literacies: Concepts, Policies and Practices.* Peter Lang, 2008.

Lapowsky, Issie. "David Karp: Why I Sold Tumblr." *Inc.* Mansueto Ventures, 31 May 2013, inc.com/issie-lapowsky/david-karp-why-i-sold-tumblr-yahoo.html.

Lapsley, Phil. *Exploding the Phone: The Untold Story of the Teenagers and Outlaws who Hacked Ma Bell.* Grove Press, 2013.

Larson, E. "Coding the Curriculum: How High Schools Are Reprogramming Their Classes. Mashable Online." *Mashable, Inc.*, mashable.com.

Lash, S., and J. Urry. *Economies of Signs and Space.* SAGE, 1994.

Lashinsky, Adam. *Inside Apple: How America's Most Admired—and Secretive—Company Really Works.* Business Plus, 2012.

Lathi, B. P., and Zhi Ding. *Modern Digital and Analog Communication.* 5th ed., Oxford UP, 2018.

Lau, L. "A Postcolonial Framing of Indian Commercial Surrogacy: Issues, Representations, and Orientalisms." *Gender, Place and Culture: A Journal of Feminist Geography*, vol. 25, no. 5, 2018, pp. 666–85.

Lavaveshkul, Liz. "How to Achieve 15 Minutes (or More) of Fame through YouTube." *Journal of International Commercial Law & Technology*, vol. 7, no. 4, 2012, pp. 370–85.

Lavé, Jean, and Etienne Wenger. *Situated Learning: Legitimate Peripheral Participation.* Cambridge UP, 1991.

Layton, Julia, and Jonathan Strickland. "How iTunes Works." *HowStuffWorks.com*, 20 Mar. 2006, electronics.howstuffworks.com/itunes.htm.

Le Khac, Nhien An, and Kim-Kwang Raymond Choo, editors. *Cyber and Digital Forensic Investigations: A Law Enforcement Practitioner's Perspective.* Springer International, 2020.

Lea, M. "Computer Conferencing and Assessment: New Ways of Writing in Higher Education." *Studies in Higher Education*, vol. 26, 2001, pp. 163–81.

"LED Lighting." *Energy.gov*, www.energy.gov/energysaver/save-electricity-and-fuel/lighting-choices-save-you-money/led-lighting.

Lee, Cheng-Chung, editor. *The Current Trends of Optics and Photonics.* Springer Netherlands, 2015.

Lee, H.-R., H. E. Lee, J. Choi, et al. "Social Media Use, Body Image, and Psychological Well-Being: A Cross-Cultural Comparison of Korea and the United States." *Journal of Health Communication*, vol. 19, no. 12, 2014, pp. 1343–58, search.ebscohost.com/login.aspx?direct=true&db=ufh&an=99907281&site=ehost-live.

Lee, Justin. "Prolexic Study Offers E-Commerce Website Strategies to Combat Holiday DDoS Attacks." *The Whir.* Penton, 29 Oct. 2012, www.thewhir.com/web-hosting-news/prolexic-study-offers-e-commerce-website-strategies-to-combat-holiday-ddos-attacks.

Lee, M. *Anchored Instruction in a Situated Learning Environment.* Association for the Advancement of Computing in Education (AACE), 2002. (ERIC Document Reproduction Service No. ED477052).

Lee, Newton. *Counterterrorism and Cybersecurity: Total Information Awareness.* Springer, 2013.

___. *Facebook Nation: Total Information Awareness.* 2nd ed., Springer Science + Business Media, 2014.

Lee, W., C. Chen, J. Huang, and J. Liang. "A Smartphone-based Activity-aware System for Music Streaming Recommendation." *Knowledge-Based Systems*, vol. 131, 2017, pp. 70–82, doi:10.1016/j.knosys.2017.06.002.

Legon, Jeordan. "'Phishing Scams Reel in Your Identity." *CNN*. Cable News Network, 26 Jan. 2004.

LeJeune, Urban A., and Jeff Duntemann. *Netscape and HTML Explorer*. Coriolis Group Books, 1995.

Lenhart, A. "Cyberbullying And Online Teens." *Pew Internet and American Life Project*, 27 June 2007, www.cyberlaw.pro/docs/pewcyberbullying.pdf.

Lentzner, Rémy. *Getting Started with Keynote: Professional Training*. Editions Rémylent, 2022.

___. *Google Slides Online: Professional Training*. Editions Rémylent, 2021.

Leonard, Tom. "Instacash: The Nerds Who Made a Billion in 551 Days from Camera App." *Daily Mail Online*, 11 Apr. 2012, www.dailymail.co.uk/sciencetech/article-2128518/Instagram-The-nerds-billion-551-days-camera-app.html.

Lerner, Joshua, and Mark Schankerman. *The Comingled Code: Open Source and Economic Development*. MIT Press, 2010.

Leskin, Paige. "Trump's Push to Ban TikTok in the US, Explained in 30 Seconds." *Business Insider*, 8 Aug. 2020, www.businessinsider.com/donald-trump-tiktok-ban-us-china-explained-in-30-seconds-2020-8.

Leung, K. Ming. "History of Microsoft Excel?" *K. Ming Leung*. New York University Polytechnic School of Engineering, cis.poly.edu/~mleung/CS394/f06/week01/Excel_history.html.

Levi, M. "Assessing the Trends, Scale and Nature of Economic Cybercrimes: Overview and Issues." *Crime, Law and Social Change*, vol. 67, no. 1, 2017, pp. 3–20, search.ebscohost.com/login.aspx?direct=true&db=sxi&AN=120927472&site=ehost-live&scope=site.

Levin, Avner, and Mary Jo Nicholson. "Privacy Law in the United States, the EU, and Canada: The Allure of the Middle Ground." *University of Ottawa Law & Technology Journal*, vol. 2, no. 2, 2005, pp. 357–95.

Levin, B., and L. Schrum. *Leading Technology-Rich Schools: Award-Winning Models for Success*. Teachers College Press, 2012.

Levine, Robert. "Billboard Cover: Spotify CEO Daniel Ek on Taylor Swift, His 'Freemium' Business Model and Why He's Saving the Music Industry." *Billboard*, 5 June 2015, www.billboard.com/articles/business/6590101/daniel-ek-spotify-ceo-streaming-feature-tidal-apple-record-labels-taylor-swift.

___. "Billboard Power 100's New No. 1: Spotify Streaming Pioneer Daniel Ek." *Billboard*, 9 Feb. 2017, www.billboard.com/articles/business/7685308/no-1-power-100-daniel-ek-spotify.

Levy, Nicole. "Once the Web's Fastest Growing Aggregator, Upworthy Pivots." *Politico*, 17 June 2015, www.politico.com/media/story/2015/06/once-the-webs-fastest-growing-aggregator-upworthy-pivots-003881.

Levy, Steven. "Apple Is Defying History with Its Pricey iPhone X." *Wired*, 12 Sept. 2017, www.wired.com/story/apple-is-defying-history-with-its-pricey-iphone-x/.

___. *Hackers: Heroes of the Computer Revolution—25th Anniversary Edition*. O'Reilly Media, 2010.

Lewis, James A., Denise E. Zheng, and William A. Carter. *The Effect of Encryption on Lawful Access to Communications and Data*. Center for Strategic & International Studies/Rowman & Littlefield, 2017.

Li, Austen, and Jacqueline Sussman. "Bridging the Digital Divide." *Wharton School of the University of Pennsylvania Public Policy Initiative*, 10 Apr. 2018, publicpolicy.wharton.upenn.edu/live/news/2420-bridging-the-digital-divide/for-students/blog/news.

Li, Jinyu, et al. *Robust Automatic Speech Recognition*. Academic Press, 2016.

Li, Lisa Bei. "Data Privacy in the Cyber Age: Recommendations for Regulating Doxing and Swatting." *Federal Communications Law Journal*, vol. 70, no. 3, 2018, pp. 317–28.

Libby, Kristina. "This Bill Hader Deepfake Video Is Amazing. It's Also Terrifying for Our Future." *Popular Mechanics*, 13 Aug. 2019, www.popularmechanics.com/technology/security/a28691128/deepfake-technology/.

Liebowitz, M. "Online Bullying Rampant Among Teens, Survey Finds." *Security News Daily*, 9 Nov. 2011, www.technewsdaily.com/3396-online-bullying-teens-facebook.html.

Liebowitz, Stan. "Word Processors." *University of Texas at Dallas*, www.utdallas.edu/~liebowit/book/wordprocessor/word.html.

Lien, Tracey. "Virtual Reality Isn't Just for Video Games." *Los Angeles Times*, 8 Jan. 2015.

Lih, Andrew. *The Wikipedia Revolution: How a Bunch of Nobodies Created the World's Greatest Encyclopedia*. Hyperion, 2009.

Lin, L., J. E. Sidani, A. Shensa, et al. "Association between Social Media Use and Depression among U.S. Young Adults." *Depression and Anxiety*, vol. 33, no. 4, 2016, pp. 323–31.

Lincoln, Sian, and Brady Robards. "10 Years of Facebook." *New Media & Society*, vol. 16, no. 7, 2014, pp. 1047–50, doi:10.1177/1461444814543994.

Lininger, Rachael, and Russell Dean Vines. *Phishing: Cutting the Identity Theft Line*. Wiley, 2005.

Linksy, Dorian. "Is Daniel Ek, Spotify Founder, Going to Save the Music Industry...or Destroy It?" *The Guardian*, 10 Nov. 2013, www.theguardian.com/technology/2013/nov/10/daniel-ek-spotify-streaming-music.

Linzmayer, Owen W. *Apple Confidential 2.0: The Definitive History of the World's Most Colorful Company*. Rev. 2nd ed., No Starch Press, 2004.

Lipson, Hod, and Melba Kurman. *Fabricated: The New World of 3D Printing*. Wiley, 2013.

Liska, Allan, and Timothy Gallo. *Ransomware: Defending Against Digital Extortion*. O'Reilly Media, 2016.

Liu, Aaron. "The History of Social Networking." *Digital Trends*. Designtechnica, 5 Aug. 2014.

Locher, M., B. Bolander, and N. Höhn. "Introducing Relational Work in Facebook and Discussion Boards." *Pragmatics*, vol. 25, no. 1, 2015, pp. 1–21.

Locke, John L. *The De-Voicing of Society: Why We Don't Talk to Each Other Anymore*. Simon & Schuster, 1998.

Logue, D., and M. Edwards. "Across the Digital Divide." *Stanford Social Innovation Review*, vol. 11, 2013, pp. 66–71, search.ebscohost.com/login.aspx?direct=true&db=sih&AN=91718527&site=ehost-live&scope=site.

Lombrozo, Tania. "Scientific Literacy: It's Not (Just) About the Facts." *NPR*, 2015, www.npr.org/sections/13.7/2015/09/14/440213603/scientific-literacy-it-s-not-just-about-the-facts.

Lonbere, Philip. *A History of Communication Technology*. Routledge, 2021.

Long, K., B. Judd, J. O'Mara, et al. "Orientations Toward Communication, Computer Anxiety, and the Development of Personal and Professional Relationships Face-to-Face and Online: Conference Papers–International Communication Association." *International Communication Association, 2006 Annual Meeting*, pp. 1–4.

Long, Simon. *An Introduction to C & GUI Programming*. Raspberry Pi Press, 2019.

Lorenz, Taylor. "How an App for Gamers Went Mainstream." *The Atlantic*, 12 Mar. 2019, www.theatlantic.com/technology/archive/2019/03/how-discord-went-mainstream-influencers/584671/.

"Lotus Notes." *PCMag*, www.pcmag.com/encyclopedia/term/46341/lotus-notes.

Love, M. S. "Multimodality of Learning Through Anchored Instruction." *Journal of Adolescent and Adult Literacy*, vol. 48, 2004, pp. 300–310.

Lovink, Geert. *Networks without a Cause: A Critique of Social Media*. Polity, 2011.

Luber, B., C. Fisher, P. S. Appelbaum, et al. "Non-invasive Brain Stimulation in the Detection of Deception: Scientific Challenges and Ethical Consequences." *Behavioral Sciences & the Law*, vol. 27, no. 2, 2009, pp. 191–208.

Luce-Kapler, R. "Radical Change and Wikis: Teaching New Literacies." *Journal of Adolescent and Adult Literacy*, vol. 51, 2007, pp. 214–23.

Luebke, S., and J. Lorié. "Use of Bloom's Taxonomy in Developing Reading Comprehension Specifications." *Journal of Applied Testing Technology*, vol. 14, 2013, pp. 1–27.

Luke, Carmen. "As Seen on TV or Was That My Phone? *New Media* Literacy." *Policy Futures in Education*, vol. 5, no. 1, 2007, pp. 50–58.

___. "Cyberpedagogy." *The International Handbook of Virtual Learning Environments*, edited by Joel Weiss, Jason Nolan, Jeremy Hunsinger, and Peter Pericles, Springer, 2006, pp. 269–77.

Lunden, Ingrid. "Tumblr Overtakes Instagram as Fastest-Growing Social Platform, Snapchat Is the Fastest-Growing App." *Tech Crunch*. AOL, 25 Nov. 2014, techcrunch.com/2014/11/25/tumblr-overtakes-instagram-as-fastest-growing-social-platform-snapchat-is-the-fastest-growing-app/.

Luther, J., F. Farmer, and S. Parks. "Special Issue Editors' Introduction: The Past, Present, and Future of Self-Publishing: Voices, Genres, Publics." *Community Literacy Journal*, vol. 12, 2017, pp. 1–4.

Macaulay, M. "Status Update: Celebrity, Publicity, and Branding in the Social Media Age." *Canadian Journal of Communication*, vol. 40, no. 1, 2015, pp. 143–46, search.ebscohost.com/login.aspx?direct=true&db=ufh &an=101106489&site=ehost-live.

Maccallum-Stewart, E. *Online Games, Social Narratives*. Routledge, 2014.

MacCormick, John. *Nine Algorithms That Changed the Future: The Ingenious Ideas That Drive Today's Computers*. Princeton UP, 2012.

Mackey, T. P., and T. Jacobson. *Using Technology to Teach Information Literacy*. Neal-Schuman, 2008.

Mackie, M. "Proven Practices for Content Management." *KM World*, vol. 22, no. 7, 2013, pp. S3–S4.

Madden, M., S. Cortesi, U. Gasser, A. Lenhart, and M. Duggan. *Parents, Teens, and Online Privacy*. Pew Internet & American Life Project, 2012.

Madden, Mary, et al. "Teens and Technology 2013." *Pew Research Center*. Pew Research Center, 13 Mar. 2013.

Madigan, D. "Statistics and the War on Spam." *Statistics: A Guide to the Unknown*. 4th ed., Thompson Higher Education, 2006.

Madrigal, Alexis. "How Tumblr Hired Its 3rd Employee, or, the Luckiest Cold 'Call' Ever." *The Atlantic*. Atlantic Monthly Group, 23 Oct. 2011, theatlantic.com/technology/archive/2011/10/ how-tumblr-hired-its-3rd-employee-or-the-luckiest-cold-call-ever/247226/.

"The Magic of the Internet." *IMGUR*, imgurinc.com.

Magliaro, S., B. Lockez, and J. Burton. "Direct Instruction Revisited: A Key Model for Instructional Technology." *Educational Technology Research & Development*, vol. 53, 2005, pp. 41–55.

Mahdawi, Arwa. "Melania Trump Rails against Cyberbullying—But She Is Using Social Media to Gaslight the World." *The Guardian*, 21 Aug. 2018, www.theguardian.com/commentisfree/2018/aug/21/ melania-trump-rails-against-cyberbullying-social-media-gaslight-world.

Maheshwari, S. "YouTube Is Improperly Collecting Children's Data, Consumer Groups Say." *The New York Times*, 9 Apr. 1028, www.nytimes.com/2018/04/09/business/media/youtube-kids-ftc-complaint.html.

Mak, J. "Coding in the Elementary School Classroom." *Learning & Leading with Technology*, vol. 41, no. 6, 2014, pp. 26–28.

Makarov, Andrew. "10 Augmented Reality Trends of 2022: A Vision of the Future." *MobiDev*, 1 Jan. 2022, mobidev.biz/blog/augmented-reality-trends-future-ar-technologies.

"Making Communication and Information Accessible." *National Association of the Deaf*. National Association of the Deaf, 2014, nad.org/issues/technology.

Mandinach, Ellen B., and Edith S. Gummer. *Data Literacy for Educators: Making It Count in Teacher Preparation and Practice*. Teachers College P/West Ed, 2016.

Manishin, Glenn B. *Complying with the CAN-SPAM Act and Other Critical Business Issues: Staying Out of Trouble*. Practicing Law Institute, 2004.

Mantlero, Alessandro. "The EU Proposal for a General Data Protection Regulation and the Roots of the 'Right to Be Forgotten.'" *Computer Law & Security Review*, vol. 29, no. 3, June 2013, pp. 229–35.

Maras, Marie-Helen. *Computer Forensics: Cybercriminals, Laws and Evidence*. Jones and Bartlett, 2015.

Marchand, D. A., and J. Peppard. "Why IT Fumbles Analytics." *Harvard Business Review*, vol. 91, no. 1, 2013, pp. 104–12.

Marcum, C., G. Higgins, T. Freiburger, et al. "Exploration of the Cyberbullying Victim/Offender Overlap by Sex." *American Journal of Criminal Justice*, vol. 39, 2014, pp. 538–48, search.ebscohost.com/login.aspx?direc t=true&db=sih&an=97320502.

Markelo, Steve. *Microsoft Edge: A Beginner's Guide to the Widows 10 Browser*. Conceptual Kings, 2015.

Marken, J., and G. Morrison. "Objectives Over Time: A Look at Four Decades of Objectives in the Educational Research Literature." *Contemporary Educational Technology*, vol. 4, 2013, pp. 1–14.

Markowitz, Eric. "How Instagram Grew from Foursquare Knock-Off to $1 Billion Photo Empire." *Inc.* Mansueto Ventures, 10 Apr. 2012, www.inc.com/eric-markowitz/life-and-times-of-instagram-the-complete-original-story.html.

Marlin-Bennett, Renée. *Knowledge Power: Intellectual Property, Information, and Privacy*. Lynne Rienner, 2004.

Marschner, Steve, et al. *Fundamentals of Computer Graphics*. 4th ed., CRC Press, 2016.

Martin, A. M., and K. R. Roberts. "Digital Native ≠ Digital Literacy." *Principal*, vol. 94, no. 3, 2015, pp. 18–21.

Martindale, Jon. "Cortana vs. Siri vs. Google Assistant vs. Alexa." *Digital Trends*, 17 June 2020, www.digitaltrends.com/computing/cortana-vs-siri-vs-google-now/.

Martínez-Pérez, Borja, Isabel De La Torre-Díez, and Miguel López-Coronado. "Privacy and Security in Mobile Health Apps: A Review and Recommendations." *Journal of Medical Systems* 39, no. 1, 2014, p. 181.

Martinovic, Ivan, Doug Davies, Mario Frank, et al. "On the Feasibility of Side-Channel Attacks with Brain-Computer Interfaces." *The Proceedings of the 21st USENIX Security Symposium.* USENIX, 2012.

Marwick, A. E., and D. Boyd. "Networked Privacy: How Teenagers Negotiate Context in Social Media." *New Media and Society*, vol. 16, no. 7, 2014, pp. 1051–67, search.ebscohost.com/login.aspx?direct=true&db=ufh&an=98993397&site=ehost-live.

Marx, Gary T. "What's in a Name? Some Reflections on the Sociology of Anonymity." *Information Society*, vol. 15, no. 2, 1999, pp. 99–112, search.ebscohost.com/login.aspx?direct=true&db=a9h&AN=2030997&site=ehost-live.

Marzano, R. J. "Targets, Objectives, Standards: How Do They Fit?" *Educational Leadership*, vol. 70, 2013, pp. 82–83.

Marzolf, Julie Schwab. *Online Privacy.* Gareth Stevens, 2013.

Masic, I., and E. Suljevic. "An Overview of E-Health Implementation in Countries, Members of the European Union." *Acta Informatica Medica*, vol. 15, 2007, pp. 242–45, search.ebscohost.com/login.aspx?direct=true&db=a9h&AN=27747476&site=ehost-live.

Masunaga, Samantha. "Cyber Monday Sales on Record Pace to Crack $3 Billion." *Los Angeles Times*, 30 Nov. 2015, www.latimes.com/business/la-fi-cyber-monday-numbers-20151130-htmlstory.html.

Matineau, Paris. "What Is a Bot?" *Wired*, 16 Nov. 2018, www.wired.com/story/the-know-it-alls-what-is-a-bot/.

Matney, Lucas. "YouTube Has 1.5 Billion Logged-In Monthly Users Watching a Ton of Mobile Video." *Tech Crunch*, 22 June 2017, techcrunch.com/2017/06/22/youtube-has-1-5-billion-logged-in-monthly-users-watching-a-ton-of-mobile-video.

Matulka, Rebecca, and Matty Greene. "How 3D Printers Work." *Energy.gov*, 19 June 2014, www.energy.gov/articles/how-3d-printers-work.

Matusitz, J., and G. M. Breen. "E-health: A New Kind of Telemedicine." *Social Work in Public Health*, vol. 23, 2007, pp. 95–113, search.ebscohost.com/login.aspx?direct=true&db=sih&AN=30012503&site=ehost-live.

Matusitz, Jonathan. "Cyberterrorism: Postmodern State of Chaos." *Information Security Journal: A Global Perspective*, vol. 17, no. 4, 2008, pp. 179–87.

McAlister, Matthew. "How Social Media Helps Your Job Search." *Career Glider*, 7 Jan. 2015.

McBride, Sarah, and Alexei Oreskovic. "Snapchat Breach Exposes Flawed Premise, Security Challenge." *Reuters*, 14 Oct. 2014.

McCarthy, Ellen. "What Is Catfishing? A Brief (and Sordid) History." *The Washington Post*, 9 Jan. 2016.

McCloskey, W., S. Iwanicki, D. Lauterbach, et al. "Are Facebook 'Friends' Helpful? Development of a Facebook-Based Measure of Social Support and Examination of Relationships among Depression, Quality of Life, and Social Support." *Cyberpsychology, Behavior and Social Networking*, vol. 18, no. 9, 2015, pp. 499–505.

McClure, Charles R., and Paul T. Jaeger. *Public Libraries and Internet Service Roles: Measuring and Maximizing Internet Services.* American Library Association, 2009.

McCormick, Kristen. "The Six Biggest, Baddest, Most Popular Social Media Platforms of 2022." *WordStream*, www.wordstream.com/blog/ws/2022/01/11/most-popular-social-media-platforms.

McCracken, Harry. "How Gmail Happened: The Inside Story of Its Launch 10 Years Ago." *Time*. Time, Inc., 1 Apr. 2014, time.com/43263/gmail-10th-anniversary/.

McDaniel, Adam. *HTML 5: Your Visual Blueprint for Designing Rich Web Pages and Applications.* John Wiley & Sons, 2011.

McDaniel, B., S. Coyne, and E. Holmes. "New Mothers and Media Use: Associations between Blogging, Social Networking, and Maternal Well-Being." *Maternal and Child Health Journal*, vol. 16, no. 7, 2012, pp. 1509–17.

McDonald, Paul. *Video and DVD Industries.* British Film Institute, 2008.

McDonald, R., and J. Parker. "When a Story Is More Than a Paper." *Young Adult Library Services*, vol. 11, no. 4, 2013, pp. 27–32.

McElhearn, Kirk. "15 Years of iTunes: A Look at Apple's Media App and Its Influence on an Industry." *Macworld*, 9 Jan. 2016, www.macworld.com/article/3019878/software/15-years-of-itunes-a-look-at-apples-media-app-and-its-influence-on-an-industry.html.

McEwan, B. "Managing Boundaries in the Web 2.0 Classroom." *New Directions for Teaching & Learning*, 2012, pp. 15–28.

McFarland, Matt. "Dear CNN: Please Be Careful about Copying Our Headlines. Sincerely, Upworthy." *The Washington Post*, 5 Feb. 2014, www.washingtonpost.com/news/innovations/wp/2014/02/05/dear-cnn-please-be-careful-about-copying-our-headlines-sincerely-upworthy/?utm_term=.7a2ebcd38cbe.

McGarry, Caitlin. "Hands On with the New Spotify: Still the Streaming Service to Beat." *Macworld*, vol. 32, no. 7, 2015, pp. 112–14.

___. "How Apple Plans to Make iCloud, Siri, and iTunes Better." *Macworld*, 6 Oct. 2016, www.macworld.com/article/3128754/software/how-apple-plans-to-make-icloud-siri-and-itunes-better.html.

McGonigal, J. *Reality Is Broken.* Jonathan Cape, 2011.

Mcguire, J. M., S. S. Scott, and S. F. Shaw. "Universal Design and Its Applications in Educational Environments." *Remedial & Special Education*, vol. 27, 2006, pp. 166–75.

McHenry, David. *Drawing the Line: Technical Hand Drafting for Film and Television.* Routledge, 2018.

McKalin, Vamien. "Augmented Reality vs. Virtual Reality: What Are the Differences and Similarities?" *TechTimes.com.* TechTimes.com, 6 Apr. 2014, techtimes.com/articles/5078/20140406/augmented-reality-vs-virtual-reality-what-are-the-differences-and-similarities.htm.

McKenna, Katelyn Y. A., and John A. Bargh. "Plan 9 from Cyberspace: The Implications of the Internet for Personality and Social Psychology." *Personality and Social Psychology Review*, vol. 4, no. 1, 2000, pp. 57–75, search.ebscohost.com/login.aspx?direct=true&db=a9h&AN=3176644&site=ehost-live.

Mckenna, M. C., and S. Walpole. "Assistive Technology in the Reading Clinic: Its Emerging Potential." *Reading Research Quarterly*, vol. 42, 2007, pp. 140–45.

McLaurin, Joshua. "Making Cyberspace Safe for Democracy: The Challenge Posed by Denial-of-Service Attacks." *Yale Law and Policy Review*, vol. 30, no. 1, 2011, p. 11.

McLellan, Charles. "The History of Windows: A Timeline." *ZDNet*, 14 Apr. 2014, www.zdnet.com/article/the-history-of-windows-a-timeline/.

Mcleod, S., and C. Lehmann. *What School Leaders Need to Know About Digital Technologies and Social Media.* Jossey-Bass, 2012.

McLoughlin, Ian. *Computer Systems: An Embedded Approach.* McGraw-Hill, 2018.

McLuhan, M. *The Gutenberg Galaxy: The Making of Typographic Man.* U of Toronto P, 1962.

McNally, Megan. *Identity Theft in Today's World.* Praeger, 2012.

"Media Ethics." *Purdue Online Writing Lab*, owl.purdue.edu/owl/subject_specific_writing/journalism_and_journalistic_writing/media_ethics.html.

"Media Literacy: A Definition and More." *Medialit.org.* Center for Media Literacy, n.d.

Mehta, Prateek. *Creating Google Chrome Extensions.* Springer Science + Business Media, 2016.

Meinders, Erwin R., et al. *Optical Data Storage: Phase-Change Media and Recording.* Springer Netherlands, 2011.

Melgosa, A., and Scott, R. "School Internet Safety: More Than 'Block It to Stop It.'" *Education Digest*, vol. 79, 2013, pp. 46–49.

Melson, Brent. "Protecting Privacy and Security in Software and Mobile Apps: How to Take Precautions to Keep Your Data Secure." *Wireless Design & Development*, 1 July 2015.

Mendoza, Menchie. "Facebook Popularity Drops among Teens as Tumblr, Pinterest, Snapchat Gain Steam." *Tech Times*, 1 Dec. 2014, techtimes.com/articles/45159/20150409/teens-still-prefer-facebook-instagram-snapchat-among-social-media-platforms.htm.

Menn, Joseph. "US and Russian Experts Turn Up Volume on Cybersecurity Alarms." *Chicago Tribune.* Tribune Media, 27 Sept. 2012.

Metcalfe, Daniel J. "Amending the FOIA: Is It Time for a Real Exemption 10?" *Administrative and Regulatory Law News*, vol. 37, no. 16, Summer 2012, www.wcl.american.edu/faculty/metcalfe/ABA.article.2012.pdf.

___. "Hillary's E-Mail Defense Is Laughable." *POLITICO Magazine*, 16 Mar. 2015, www.politico.com/magazine/story/2015/03/hillaryclinton-email-scandal-defense-laughable-foia-116116. html#.VXw6lvlViko.

___. "The History of Transparency." *Research Handbook on Transparency*, edited by Padideh Ala'i and Robert G. Vaughn, Edward Elgar, 2014.

___. *"The Nature of Government Secrecy."* *Government Information Quarterly*, vol. 26, no. 305, 2009, www.wcl. american.edu/faculty/metcalfe/nature.pdf.

Meyer, A., and D. H. Rose. *Learning to Read in the Computer Age*. Brookline, 1998.

Meyer, Robinson. "The New Terminology of Snapchat." *The Atlantic*, 2 May 2014.

Mezrich, Ben. *The Accidental Billionaires: The Founding of Facebook, a Tale of Sex, Money, Genius and Betrayal*. Doubleday, 2009.

Militello, M., and J. I. Friend. *Principal 2.0: Technology and Educational Leadership*. Information Age, 2013.

Miller, C., and A. H. Doering, editors. *The New Landscape of Mobile Learning: Redesigning Education in an App-based World*. Routledge, 2014.

Miller, Carolyn Handler. *Digital Storytelling: A Creator's Guide to Interactive Entertainment*. 3rd ed., Focal, 2014.

Miller, Claire C. "YouTube to Serve Niche Tastes by Adding Channels." *The New York Times*, 7 Oct. 2012, www. nytimes.com/2012/10/08/business/media/YouTube-to-serve-niche-tastes-by-adding-channels.html.

Miller, James. "Spotify Controversy: What You Need to Know." *The Siskiyou*, 23 Feb. 2022, siskiyou.sou. edu/2022/02/23/spotify-controversy-what-you-need-to-know/.

Miller, Lisa C. *Make Me a Story: Teaching Writing through Digital Storytelling*. Stenhouse, 2010.

Miller, Michael. *Cloud Computing: Web-Based Applications That Change the Way You Work and Collaborate*. Que Publishing, 2009.

Miller, Michelle D. *Minds Online: Teaching Effectively with Technology*. Harvard UP, 2014.

Miller, Philip. "File Transfer Protocols." *TCP/IP: The Ultimate Protocol Guide*, Vol. 2. Brown Walker Press, 2009, pp. 607–38.

Minor, Jordan. "What Is Discord and How Do You Use It?" *PC Mag*, 11 May 2020, www.pcmag.com/how-to/what-is-discord-and-how-do-you-use-it.

Minsky, Marvin, and Seymour A. Papert. *Perceptrons: An Introduction to Computational Geometry*. Reissue ed., MIT Press, 2017.

Mistrik, Ivan, et al., editors. *Software Architecture for Big Data and the Cloud*. Morgan Kaufmann, 2017.

Mitchell, Bradley. "FTP—File Transfer Protocol." *Lifewire*, 19 Oct. 2016, www.lifewire.com/file-transfer-protocol-817943.

Mitchem, S. Y. "Editorial: Technologies of Religions." *Cross Currents*, vol. 65, no. 4, 2015, pp. 408–9, search. ebscohost.com/login.aspx?direct=true&db=asn&an=112708103&site=ehost-live.

Mitnick, Kevin. *Ghost in the Wires: My Adventures as the World's Most Wanted Hacker*. Little, Brown and Company, 2011.

Mitra, Tilak. *Practical Software Architecture: Moving from System Context to Deployment*. IBM Press, 2015.

Mitroff, Sarah. "Everything You Need to Know About YouTube Red." *CNET*. CBS Interactive, 28 Oct. 2015, www.cnet.com/how-to/youtube-red-details/.

Moallem, Abbas. *Human-Computer Interaction and Cybersecurity Handbook*. CRC Press, 2019.

Mobbs, Richard. "HTML Developments." *University of Leicester*, Oct. 2009, www.le.ac.uk/oerresources/bdra/html/page_04.htm.

"Mobile Operating System Market Share Worldwide." *Statcounter*, May 2020, gs.statcounter.com/os-market-share/mobile/worldwide.

Moe, Wendy, and David A. Schweidel. *Social Media Intelligence*. Cambridge UP, 2014.

Moford, J. "Perspectives Constructivism: Implications for Postsecondary Music Education and Beyond." *Journal of Music Teacher Education*, vol. 16, 2007, pp. 75–83.

Mohapatra, Manas, Andrew Hasty, et al. "Mobile Apps for Kids Current Privacy Disclosures Are Disappointing." *Federal Trade Commission*, 1 Feb. 2012.

Molla, Rani. "Posting Less, Posting More, and Tired of It All: How the Pandemic Has Changed Social Media." *Recode*, Vox Media, 1 Mar. 2021, www.vox.com/recode/22295131/social-media-use-pandemic-covid-19-instagram-tiktok.

Monckton, Paul. "Instagram Makes Biggest Ever Photo Changes." *Forbes*, 27 Aug. 2015, www.forbes.com/sites/paulmonckton/2015/08/27/instagram-makes-biggest-ever-photo-changes/.

Montalvo, G. "Online Design Elements: Improving Student Success and Minimizing Instructor Load." *Mid-Western Educational Researcher*, vol. 19, 2006, pp. 35–39.

Moore, Adam, editor. *Information Ethics: Privacy, Property, and Power*. U of Washington P, 2005.

Moos, D. "Examining Hypermedia Learning: The Role of Cognitive Load and Self-Regulated Learning." *Journal of Educational Multimedia & Hypermedia*, 22, 2013, pp. 39–61.

Moreno, M., D. Christakis, K. Egan, et al. "A Pilot Evaluation of Associations between Displayed Depression References on Facebook and Self-Reported Depression Using a Clinical Scale." *Journal of Behavioral Health Services and Research*, vol. 39, no. 3, 2012, pp. 295–304.

Moretti, Marcus. "Before Mac OS X, There Was OS 1 Through 9: A History of Apple's Operating System." *Business Insider*, 10 July 2012, www.businessinsider.com/mac-os-i-through-x-2012-7?op=1.

Morgan, B., and R. D. Smith. "A Wiki for Classroom Writing." *The Reading Teacher*, vol. 62, 2008, pp. 80–82.

Morozov, Evgeny. *The Net Delusion: The Dark Side of internet Freedom*. PublicAffairs, 2012.

___. "WikiLeaks' Relationship with the Media." *The New York Times*. Room for Debate, 11 Dec. 2010, www.nytimes.com/roomfordebate/2010/12/09/what-has-wikileaks-started/wikileaks-relationship-with-the-media.

Morreale, Joanne. "From Homemade to Store Bought: Annoying Orange and the Professionalization of YouTube." *Journal of Consumer Culture*, vol. 14, no. 1, 2014, pp. 113–128, search.ebscohost.com/login.aspx?direct=true&db=a9h&AN=94776861.

Morris, H. "Europe Cracks Down on Cybercrime." *International New York Times*, 12 Mar. 2012, rendezvous.blogs.nytimes.com/2012/03/29/europe-cracks-down-on-cybercrime,

Morris, Jeremy Wade. *Selling Digital Music, Formatting Culture*. U of California P, 2015.

Morris, Mary. *HTML for Fun and Profit*. SunSoft Press, 1995.

Morris, R. R., S. M. Schueller, and R. W. Picard. "Efficacy of a Web-Based, Crowdsourced Peer-to-Peer Cognitive Reappraisal Platform for Depression: Randomized Controlled Trial." *Journal of Medical Internet Research*, vol. 17, no. 3, 2015, p. e72.

Morris, Tee. *Twitch for Dummies*. Wiley, 2019.

Morrison, Kimberlee. "Snapchat Is the Fastest Growing Social Network." *Adweek*, 28 July 2015, www.adweek.com/digital/snapchat-is-the-fastest-growing-social-network-infographic/.

Morrow, Jordan. *Be Data Literate: The Data Literacy Skills Everyone Needs to Succeed*. Kogan Page, 2021.

Moscaritolo, Angela, and Chloe Albanesius. "Zuckerberg's Vision for Facebook: A Global Community Backed by AI." *PC Magazine*, 16 Feb. 2017, www.pcmag.com/news/351809/zuckerbergs-vision-for-facebook-a-global-community-backed.

Moss, Caroline. "Strangers Have Been Using This Woman's Photos to Catfish People Online for Ten Years." *Business Insider*, 21 Jan. 2015.

"The Most Popular Social Networking Sites in 2022." *BroadbandSearch.net*, www.broadbandsearch.net/blog/most-popular-social-networking-sites.

Mottier, Patrick, editor. *LEDs for Lighting Applications*. John Wiley & Sons, 2009.

Mourey, J. A., J. G. Olson, and C. Yoon. "Products as Pals: Engaging with Anthropomorphic Products Mitigates the Effects of Social Exclusion." *Journal of Consumer Research*, vol. 44, no. 2, 2017, pp. 414–31, Search.Ebscohost.Com/Login.Aspx?Direct=True&Db=Ufh&AN=124308268&Site=Ehost-Live.

Mowery, David C., and Timothy Simcoe. "Is the Internet a U.S. Invention? An Economic and Technological History of Computer Networking." *Research Policy*, vol. 31, Dec. 2002, pp. 1369–87.

Moynihan, Tim. "Tumblr Finally Adds a GIF-Maker to Its iPhone App." *Wired*. Condé Nast, 17 Nov. 2015, wired.com/2015/11/tumblr-adds-gif-making-tools-to-its-iphone-app/.

___. "Tumblr's New Messanger Is Chat for the Cool Kids." *Wired.* Condé Nast, 10 Nov. 2015, wired. com/2015/11/tumblr-gets-its-very-own-messaging-app/.

Muise, Amy M., Emily Christofides, and Serge Desmarais. "More Information Than You Ever Wanted: Does Facebook Bring Out the Green-Eyed Monster of Jealousy?" *Cyberpsychology and Behavior,* vol. 12, no. 4, 2009, pp. 441–44.

Muller, Vincent C. "Ethics of Artificial Intelligence and Robotics." *Stanford Encyclopedia of Philosophy*, 30 Apr. 2020, plato.stanford.edu/entries/ethics-ai/.

Murphy, D., R. Walker, and G. Webb. *Online Learning and Teaching with Technology: Case Studies, Experience and Practice.* Taylor and Francis, 2013.

Murray, Brian H. *Defending the Brand: Aggressive Strategies for Protecting Your Brand in the Online Arena.* AMACOM, 2004.

Murray, Ryan Patrick. "Myspace-ing Is Not a Crime: Why Breaching Terms of Service Agreements Should Not Implicate the Computer Fraud and Abuse Act Written February 2, 2009." *Loyola of Los Angeles Entertainment Law Review,* vol. 29, no. 3, June 2009, p. 475.

Musa, Sarhan M. *Network Security and Cryptography.* Mercury Learning and Information, 2018.

Musciano, Chuck, and Bill Kennedy. *HTML and XHTML: The Definitive Guide.* 4th ed., O'Reilly, 2000.

Mutikani, Lucia. "U.S. Job Openings Jump to 11 Million; Fewer Workers Voluntarily Quitting." *Reuters,* 8 Dec. 2021, reuters.com/business/us-job-openings-jump-11-million-october-2021-12-08/.

"Myth-Busting: The Court of Justice of the EU and the 'Right to be Forgotten.'" *European Commission,* ec.europa.eu/justice/data-protection/files/factsheets/factsheet_rtbf_mythbusting_en.pdf.

Nackerud, S., and K. Scaletta. "Blogging In the Academy." *New Directions for Student Services,* Winter 2008, pp. 71–87.

Nagelhout, Ryan. *Digital Era Encryption and Decryption.* Rosen, 2017.

Naone, Erica. "When Social Media Mining Gets It Wrong." *MIT Technology Review,* 9 Aug. 2011.

National Association for Media Literacy Education. "Core Principles of Media Literacy Education in the United States." *NAMLE.net.* NAMLE, n.d.

National Center for Education Statistics. "Fast Facts: Access to the Internet." *US Department of Education,* 2021, nces.ed.gov/fastfacts/display.asp?id=46.

___. "In Brief: Computer and Internet Access in Private Schools and Classrooms: 1995 and 1998." *US Department of Education,* Feb. 2000, nces.ed.gov.

___. *US Department of Education,* nces.ed.gov.

"National Economies Threatened by Cybercrime, according to EU Information Security Agency." *AVG Anti-Virus and Internet Security,* 9 June 2008, www.grisoft.com.

National Instructional Materials Accessibility Standard (2003). *NIMAS Report Executive Summary: National Instructional Materials Accessibility Standard Report–Version 1.0. NIMAS,* nimas.cast.org.

National Research Council, et al. *Computers at Risk: Safe Computing in the Information Age.* National Academy, 1991.

Neal, D. R. *Social Media for Academics: A Practical Guide.* Chandos, 2012.

Neal, M. R. *Writing Assessment and the Revolution in Digital Texts and Technologies.* Teachers College Press, 2011.

Nester, Gilbert. "Number of Active Gmail Users 2022/2023: Statistics, Demographics, & Usage." *Finances Online,* financesonline.com/number-of-active-gmail-users/.

Neuburg, Matt. *Programming iOS 13: Dive Deep into Views, View Controllers, and Frameworks.* O'Reilly Media, 2019.

Neumann, C. "Teaching Digital Natives: Promoting Information Literacy and Addressing Instructional Challenges." *Reading Improvement,* vol. 53, no. 3, 2016, pp. 101–6.

"The New Digital Economy and Development." *United Nations Conference on Trade and Development,* Oct. 2017, unctad.org/en/PublicationsLibrary/tn_unctad_ict4d08_en.pdf.

Newitz, Annalee. "Facebook Fires Human Editors, Algorithm Immediately Posts Fake News." *Ars Technica,* 29 Aug. 2016, arstechnica.com/business/2016/08/ facebook-fires-human-editors-algorithm-immediately-posts-fake-news/.

Newman, Jared. "Android Laptops: The $200 Price Is Right, but the OS May Not Be." *PCWorld*, 26 Apr. 2013, www.pcworld.com/article/2036451/android-laptops-the-200-price-is-right-but-the-os-may-not-be.html.

___. "With Android Lollipop, Mobile Multitasking Takes a Great Leap Forward." *Fast Company*, 6 Nov. 2014, www.fastcompany.com/3038213/with-android-lollipop-mobile-multitasking-takes-a-great-leap-forward.

Newon, L. "Online Multiplayer Games." *Routledge Handbook of Language and Digital Communication*, edited by A. Georgakopoulou and T. Spillioti, Routledge, 2015.

"News Values and Principles." *Associated Press*, 2021, www.ap.org/about/news-values-and-principles/.

Ng, Cindy. "5 Things Privacy Experts Want You to Know About Wearables." *Varonis Blog*, 17 July 2014, blog.varonis.com/5-things-privacy-experts-want-youto-know-about-wearables/.

Nhan, Johnny. *Policing Cyberspace: A Structural and Cultural Analysis*. LFB, 2010.

Nicas Jack. "Apple Is Worth $1,000,000,000: Two Decades Ago, It Was Almost Bankrupt." *The New York Times*, 2 Aug. 2018, www.nytimes.com/2018/08/02/technology/apple-stock-1-trillion-market-cap.html.

Nichols, Robin. *Mastering Adobe Photoshop Elements*. Packt, 2019.

Nick, E. A., D. A. Cole, S. J. Cho, et al. "The Online Social Support Scale: Measure Development and Validation." *Psychological Assessment*, vol. 30, no. 9, 2018, pp. 1127–43, doi:10.1037/pas0000558.

Nicolson, M., L. Murphy, and M. Southgate. *Language Teaching in Blended Contexts*. Dunedin Academic P, 2011.

Nicosia, Laura. *Educators Online: Preparing Today's Teachers for Tomorrow's Digital Literacies*. Peter Lang, 2013.

Nielsen. "An Era of Growth: The Cross-Platform Report Q4 2013." *Nielsen*. Nielsen, 5 Mar. 2014.

Nielsen, Jakob. *Multimedia and Hypertext: The Internet and Beyond*. SunSoft Press, 1995.

No Child Left Behind Act of 2001, P.L. 107-110, 107th Congress, 1st Session. Ed.gov.

Noor, A. D. H. S., and J. A. Hendricks. *Social Media: Usage and Impact*. Lexington Books, 2012.

Nortey, Justin. "More Houses of Worship Are Returning to Normal Operations, But In-Person Attendance Is Unchanged Since Fall." *PEW Research Center*, 22 Mar. 2022, pewresearch.org/fact-tank/2022/03/22/more-houses-of-worship-are-returning-to-normal-operations-but-in-person-attendance-is-unchanged-since-fall/.

North, Anna. "The Double-Edged Sword of Online Anonymity." *The New York Times*. Taking Note, 15 May 2015, takingnote.blogs.nytimes.com/2015/05/15/the-double-edged-sword-of-online-anonymity/.

Null, J. W. "Is Constructivism Traditional? Historical and Practical Perspectives on a Popular Advocacy." *Educational Forum*, vol. 68, 2004, pp. 180–88.

Nusca, Andrew. "Myspace Acquired by Time Inc, Fortune's Publisher." *Fortune*, 11 Feb. 2016, fortune.com/2016/02/11/myspace-acquired-time-inc/.

Nyholm, Sven, and Jilles Smids. "The Ethics of Accident-Algorithms for Self-Driving Cars: An Applied Trolley Problem?" *Ethical Theory & Moral Practice*, vol. 19, no. 5, 2016, pp. 1275–89.

O'Dea, S. "U.S. Smartphone Subscriber Share by Operating Platform 2012-2019, by Month." *Statista*, 28 Feb. 2020, www.statista.com/statistics/266572/market-share-held-by-smartphone-platforms-in-the-united-states/.

O'Keeffe, G. S., and K. Clarke-Pearson. "Clinical Report—The Impact of Social Media on Children, Adolescents, and Families." *Pediatrics*, vol. 127, no. 4, 2011, pp. 800–804.

O'Leary, Timothy, Linda O'Leary, and Daniel O'Leary. *Computing Essentials 2021*. McGraw-Hill, 2020.

O'Neill, Megan." Video Infographic Reveals the Most Impressive YouTube Statistics of 2012." *SocialTimes*, 10 Sept. 2012, socialtimes.com/video-YouTube-statistics-2012%5Fb104480.

Obendorf, Hartmut. *Minimalism: Designing Simplicity*. Springer Science + Business Media, 2009.

Ohler, Jason B. *Digital Storytelling in the Classroom: New Media Pathways to Literacy, Learning, and Creativity*. 2nd ed., Sage, 2013.

Olivenbaum, Joseph M. "Ctrl-Alt-Delete: Rethinking Federal Computer Crime Legislation." *Seton Hall Law Review*, vol. 27, 1997, p. 574.

Oliver, K. M., and D. T. Stallings. "Preparing Teachers for Emerging Blended Learning Environments." *Journal of Technology and Teacher Education*, vol. 22, no. 1, 2014, pp. 57–81.

Olson, Parmy. "Facebook Wants Users to Help It Weed Out Fake News." *Forbes*, 6 Dec. 2016, www.forbes. com/sites/parmyolson/2016/12/06/facebook-users-fake-news/.

___. *We Are Anonymous: Inside the Hacker World of LulzSec, Anonymous, and the Global Cyber Insurgency*. Little, Brown and Company, 2012.

Omernick, Eli, and Sara Owsley Sood. "The Impact of Anonymity in Online Communities." *2013 International Conference on Social Computing (SocialCom 2013)*. IEEE, pp. 526–35.

"On Reddit, Unlike Other Social Sites, It's About the Topic, Not the Brand." *PR News*. Access Intelligence, 28 Oct. 2013, www.prnewsonline.com/topics/social-media/2013/10/28/ on-reddit-unlike-other-social-sites-its-about-the-topic-not-the-brand/.

"Online Anonymity and Identity." *American Civil Liberties Union*, 10 Apr. 2017, www.aclu.org/issues/free-speech/internet-speech/online-anonymity-and-identity.

"Operating System Market Share Worldwide." *Statcounter*, May 2020, gs.statcounter.com/os-market-share/ all/worldwide/2019.

Oppliger, Rolf. *Internet and Intranet Security*. 2nd ed., Artech House, 2002.

"Optical Storage." *Computer History Museum*, 2020, www.computerhistory.org/revolution/ memory-storage/8/262.

Oral, A. E., and E. B. Güzelo lu. "Zines as an Alternative Media: An Analysis on Female Zinsters in Turkey." *Communication & Media Researches*, vol. 219, 2017.

Ordoñez, Franco. "In Wake of Pipeline Hack, Biden Signs Executive Order on Cybersecurity." *NPR*, 12 May 2021, www.npr.org/2021/05/12/996355601/ in-wake-of-pipeline-hack-biden-signs-executive-order-on-cybersecurity.

Oreskovic, Alexei, and Jennifer Saba. "Yahoo Buying Tumblr for $1.1 Billion, Vows Not to Screw It Up." *Reuters*. Thomson, 20 May 2013, reuters.com/article/us-tumblr-yahoo-idUSBRE94I0C120130520.

Orr, Emily S., et al. "The Influence of Shyness on the Use of Facebook in an Undergraduate Sample." *Cyberpsychology and Behavior*, vol. 12, no. 3, 2009, pp. 337–40.

Orsmond, Paul, Stephen Merry, and Arthur Callaghan. "Communities of Practice and Ways to Learning: Charting the Progress of Biology Undergraduates." *Studies in Higher Education*, vol. 38, no. 66, 2013, pp. 890–906.

Osnos, Evan. "Can Mark Zuckerberg Fix Facebook Before It Breaks Democracy?" *The New Yorker*, 17 Sept. 2018, www.newyorker.com/magazine/2018/09/17/ can-mark-zuckerberg-fix-facebook-before-it-breaks-democracy.

Ostrowsky, O. *Engineering Drawing with CAD Applications*. Routledge, 2019.

Oswald, Vanessa. *Indie Rock: Finding an Independent Voice*. Greenhaven Publishing LLC, 2018.

Ott, K. "Hacking the System." *Journal of Feminist Studies in Religion*, vol. 31, no. 2, 2015, pp. 140–44, search. ebscohost.com/login.aspx?direct=true&Db=asn&an=110195289&site=ehost-live.

Owen, S. "Monitoring Social Media and Protest Movements: Ensuring Political Order Through Surveillance and Surveillance Discourse." *Social Identities*, vol. 23, no. 6, 2017, pp. 688–700, search.ebscohost.com/ login.aspx?direct=true&db=sxi&AN=125909013&site=ehost-live.

Pacansky-Brock, M., and S. S. Ko. *Best Practices for Teaching with Emerging Technologies*. Routledge, 2013.

Palma, Paul. *Computers in Society 09/10*. 15th ed., McGraw-Hill Irwin, 2010.

Panetta, Kasey. "Champion Data Literacy and Teach Data as a Second Language to Enable Data-Driven Business." *Gartner*, 6 Feb. 2019, www.gartner.com/ smarterwithgartner/a-data-and-analytics-leaders-guide-to-data-literacy/.

Papacharissi, Z. *Affective Publics: Sentiment, Technology, and Politics*. Oxford UP, 2015.

Parahakaran, S. "An Analysis of Theories Related to Experiential Learning for Practical Ethics in Science and Technology." *Universal Journal of Educational Research*, vol. 5, no. 6, 2017, pp. 1014–20.

Paratii. "A Brief History of P2P Content Distribution, in 10 Major Steps." *Paratii*, 25 Oct. 2017, medium. com/paratii/a-brief-history-of-p2p-content-distribution-in-10-major-steps-6d6733d25122.

"Parents: Cyber Bullying Led to Teen's Suicide." *ABC News*, 19 Nov. 2007, abcnews.go.com/GMA/ story?id=3882520.

Parisi, Tony. *Learning Virtual Reality: Developing Immersive Experiences and Applications for Desktop, Web, and Mobile.* O'Reilly, 2015.

Park, Jane. "What Is Creative Commons and Why Does It Matter?" *Common Sense Education*, 4 May 2016, www.commonsense.org/education/articles/what-is-creative-commons-and-why-does-it-matter.

Park, S. "The Potential of Web 2.0 Tools to Promote Reading Engagement in a General Education Course." *Techtrends: Linking Research & Practice to Improve Learning*, vol. 57, 2013, pp. 46–53.

Parker, Matt. *Things to Make and Do in the Fourth Dimension: A Mathematician's Journey through Narcissistic Numbers, Optimal Dating Algorithms, at Least Two Kinds of Infinity, and More.* Farrar, 2014.

Parks, Bob. "Death to PowerPoint!" *Bloomberg Business.* Bloomberg L.P., 30 Aug. 2012, www.bloomberg.com/bw/articles/2012-08-30/death-to-powerpoint.

Passey, D. *Inclusive Technology Enhanced Learning: Overcoming Cognitive, Physical, Emotional, and Geographic Challenges.* Routledge, 2014.

Patrignani, N., and D. Whitehouse. "Slow Tech: Bridging Computer Ethics and Business Ethics. " *Information Technology and People*, vol. 28, no. 4, 2015, pp. 775–89.

Patterson, Dan. "Dark Web: A Cheat Sheet for Business Professionals." *TechRepublic*, 26 Oct. 2017, www.techrepublic.com/article/dark-web-the-smart-persons-guide/.

Patterson, Kelsey T. "Narrowing It Down to One Narrow View: Clarifying and Limiting the Computer Fraud and Abuse Act." *Charleston Law Review*, vol. 7, no. 3, Mar. 2013, p. 489.

Pavone, V., and L. Martinelli. "Cisgenics as Emerging Bio-Objects: Bio-Objectification and Bio-Identification in Agrobiotech Innovation." *New Genetics and Society*, vol. 34 no. 1, 2015, pp. 52–71.

Paynter, Robert T. *Introductory Electronic Devices and Circuits: Conventional Flow Version.* 7th ed., Prentice Hall, 2006.

Payton, Theresa, and Theodore Claypoole. *Privacy in the Age of Big Data: Recognizing Threats, Defending Your Rights, and Protecting Your Family.* Rowman & Littlefield, 2014.

Paz, V., M. Moore, and T. Creel. "Academic Integrity in an Online Business Communication Environment." *Journal of Multidisciplinary Research*, vol. 9, no. 2, 2017, pp. 57–72.

Pearl, Cathy. *Designing Voice User Interfaces.* O'Reilly Media, 2017.

Pengue, Maria. "Reddit Statistics: Traffic, Subreddits, Demographics, and More." *Writers Block Live*, 16 June 2021, writersblocklive.com/blog/reddit-statistics/.

Penrod, Diane. *Using Blogs to Enhance Literacy: The Next Powerful Step in 21st-Century Learning.* Rowman & Littlefield, 2007.

Pentland, Alex. "The Data-Driven Society." *Scientific American*, vol. 309, no. 4, 2013, pp. 78–83.

Penttinen, Jyrki T. J. *The Telecommunications Handbook: Engineering Guidelines for Fixed, Mobile, and Satellite Systems.* John Wiley & Sons, 2015.

Pepitone, Julianne, and David Goldman. "The Evolution of iTunes." *CNN Money*, 26 Apr. 2013, money.cnn.com/gallery/technology/2013/04/25/itunes-history.

Peratello, Gabriela. "What Are Peer-to-Peer (P2P) Payments?" *Wise*, 10 Apr. 2022, wise.com/us/blog/p2p-payments.

Percival, Lynn C., and Poyner Spruill. "New Children's Online Privacy Protection Act (COPPA) Rule Now in Effect." *Natlawreview.com*, 1 July 2013.

Perez, Sarah. "The NFL Joins TikTok in Multi-Year Partnership." *TechCrunch*, 3 Sept. 2019, techcrunch.com/2019/09/03/the-nfl-joins-tiktok-in-multi-year-partnership/.

___. "Redesigned Version of iTunes Launches with iCloud Music Glitches." *Tech Crunch*, 13 Sept. 2016, techcrunch.com/2016/09/13/redesigned-version-of-itunes-launches-with-icloud-music-glitches.

___. "TikTok Surpassed Facebook, Instagram, Snapchat & Youtube in Downloads Last Month." *TechCrunch*, 2 Nov. 2018, techcrunch.com/2018/11/02/tiktok-surpassed-facebook-instagram-snapchat-youtube-in-downloads-last-month/.

Perloff, R. M. "Mass Communication Research at the Crossroads: Definitional Issues and Theoretical Directions for Mass and Political Communication Scholarship in an Age of Online Media." *Mass Communication and Society*, vol. 18, no. 5, 2015, pp. 531–56.

Perrin, Andrew, and Erica Turner. "Smartphones Help Blacks, Hispanics Bridge Some—But Not All—Digital Gaps with Whites." *Pew Research Center*, 20 Aug. 2019, www.pewresearch.org/fact-tank/2019/08/20/smartphones-help-blacks-hispanics-bridge-some-but-not-all-digital-gaps-with-whites/.

Peterson, T. F., and Institute Historian. *Nightwork: A History of Hacks and Pranks at MIT*. Updated ed., MIT Press, 2011.

Pew Research Center. "The Future of Free Speech, Trolls, Anonymity, and Fake News Online, 2017." Elon. elon.edu/docs/e-web/imagining/surveys/2016_survey/Pew%20and%20Elon%20University%20Trolls%20Fake%20News%20Report%20Future%20of%20internet%203.29.17.pdf.

Phillips, Bill, et al. *Android Programming: The Big Nerd Ranch Guide*. 4th ed., Big Nerd Ranch Guides, 2019.

Phillips, Matt, and Taylor Lorenz. "'Dumb Money' Is on GameStop, and It's Beating Wall Street at Its Own Game." *The New York Times*, 25 Feb. 2021, www.nytimes.com/2021/01/27/business/gamestop-wall-street-bets.html.

Phirangee, K. "Beyond the Elementary Classroom Walls: Exploring the Ways Participation within Web 2.0 Spaces Are Reshaping Pedagogy." *Journal of Educational Multimedia & Hypermedia*, vol. 22, 2013, pp. 299–316.

"Phishing." *Computer Hope*, 11 Oct. 2017, www.computerhope.com/jargon/p/phishing.htm.

"Phishing." *OnGuardOnline*. US Federal Trade Commission, Sept. 2011, www.consumer.ftc.gov/articles/0003-phishing.

Picciano, A. G., and J. Seaman. "K-12 Online Learning: A Survey of U.S. School District Administrators." *The Sloan Consortium*, 2007, sloan-c.org.

Pick, J. B., and R. Azari. "Global Digital Divide: Influence of Socioeconomic, Governmental, and Accessibility Factors on Information Technology." *Information Technology for Development*, vol. 14, 2008, pp. 91–115, search.ebscohost.com/login.aspx?direct=true&db=a9h&AN=31581293&site=ehost-live.

Pinch, T. J., and Karin Bijsterveld, editors. *The Oxford Handbook of Sound Studies*. Oxford UP, 2013.

Pinkston, G. "Forward 50, Teaching Coding to Ages 4-12: Programming in the Elementary School." *Annual International Conference on Education & E-Learning*, 2015, pp. 34–39.

Pinola, Melanie. "Speech Recognition through the Decades: How We Ended Up with Siri." *PCWorld*, 3 Nov. 2011, www.computerworld.com/article/2499980/speech-recognition-through-the-decades--how-we-ended-up-with-siri.html.

———. "What Is Groupware?" *Lifewire*, 22 Aug. 2017, www.lifewire.com/what-is-groupware-2377429.

Pisani, Bob. "Spotify's IPO Disrupted Wall Street. What Lies Ahead Now for Unicorns Looking to Go Public." *CNBC Disruptor/50*, 22 May 2018, www.cnbc.com/2018/05/22/spotifys-ipo-disrupted-wall-street-what-lies-ahead-now-for-unicorns-looking-to-go-public.html.

Pitcan, M., A. E. Marwick, and D. Boyd. "Performing a Vanilla Self: Respectability Politics, Social Class, and the Digital World." *Journal of Computer-Mediated Communication*, vol. 23, no. 3, 2018, pp, 163–79, search.ebscohost.com/login.aspx?direct=true&db=ufh&an=129489443&site=ehost-live.

Plantenberg, Kirstie. *Engineering Graphics Essentials with AutoCAD 2022 Instruction*. SDC Publications, 2021.

Pless, Vera. *Introduction to the Theory of Error-Correcting Codes*. John Wiley & Sons, 2011.

Poggenpohl, Sharon, and Keiichi Sato. *Design Integration: Research and Collaboration*. Intellect, 2009.

Pokin, S. "'My Space' Hoax Ends with Suicide of Dardenne Prairie Teen." *Suburban Journals*, 11 Nov. 2007, suburbanjournals.stltoday.com/articles/2007/11/13/news/sj2tn20071110-1111stc&#X005f.

Polanin, Joshua R., et al. "A Meta-analysis of School-Based Bullying Prevention Programs' Effects on Bystander Intervention Behavior." *School Psychology Review*, vol. 41, no. 1, 2012, pp. 47–65.

Pollard, Barry *HTTP/2 in Action*. Simon & Schuster, 2019.

Pollitt, Mark. "A History of Digital Forensics." *Advances in Digital Forensics VI*. Edited by Kam-Pui Chow and Sujeet Shenoi. Springer Berlin Heidelberg New York, 2010, pp. 3–15.

Pongnumkul, S., and K. Motohashi. "A Bipartite Fitness Model for Online Music Streaming Services." *Physica A*, vol. 490, 2018, pp. 1125–37, doi:10.1016/j.physa.2017.08.108.

Poon, Ting-Chung, and Jung-Ping Liu. *Introduction to Modern Digital Holography: With MATLAB*. Cambridge UP, 2014.

Porolli, Matias. "Cybercime Black Markets: Dark Web Services and Their Prices." *welivesecurity by eset*, 31 Jan. 2019, welivesecurity.com/2019/01/31/cybercrime-black-markets-dark-web-services-and-prices/.

Porup, J. M. "How and Why Deepfake Videos Work–And What Is at Risk." *CSO*, 10 Apr. 2019, www.csoonline. com/article/3293002/deepfake-videos-how-and-why-they-work.html.

Potter, James W. "Review of Literature on Media Literacy." *Sociology Compass*, vol. 7, no. 6, 2013, pp. 417–35.

Poulsen, Kevin. *Kingpin: How One Hacker Took Over the Billion-Dollar Cybercrime Underground*. Broadway, 2011.

Power, D. J. "A Brief History of Spreadsheets." *Museum of User Interfaces*. Department of Computer Science, University of Maryland, www.cs.umd.edu/class/spring2002/cmsc434-0101/MUIseum/applications/spreadsheethistory1.html.

"PowerPoint." *Office*. Microsoft, products.office.com/en-US/powerpoint?legRedir=true&CorrelationId=1e 6f9d59-6693-4d10-aff3-e1ce0ae02d22.

Pozin, Ilya. "200 Million Users? LinkedIn Is Just Getting Started." *Forbes*. Forbes.com, 18 Apr. 2013.

Prado, M. M., and R. S. Gravoso. "Improving High School Students' Statistical Reasoning Skills: A Case of Applying Anchored Instruction." *Asia-Pacific Education Researcher (De La Salle University Manila)*, vol. 20, 2011, pp. 61–72.

Pressman, Aaron. "What Really Happens When the FCC's Online Privacy Rules Are Cancelled." *Fortune*, 3 Apr. 2017, fortune.com/2017/04/03/fcc-online-privacy-faq/.

Prichard, J., P. Watters, T. Krone, et al. "Social Media Sentiment Analysis: A New Empirical Tool for Assessing Public Opinion on Crime?" *Current Issues in Criminal Justice*, vol. 27, no. 2, 2015, pp. 217–36, search. ebscohost.com/login.aspx?direct=true&db=sxi&an=111395844&site=ehost-live.

Primack, A., A. Shensa, J. E. Sidani, et al. "Social Media Use and Perceived Social Isolation in the U.S." *American Journal of Preventive Medicine*, vol. 53, no. 1, 2017, pp. 1–8.

"The Printed World." *Economist*, 10 Feb. 2011, www.economist.com/briefing/2011/02/10/the-printed-world.

Pritchard, Sara B., and Carl A. Zimring. *Technology and the Environment in History*. Johns Hopkins UP, 2020.

"The Problem with PowerPoint." *BBC News Magazine*. BBC, 19 Aug. 2009, news.bbc.co.uk/2/hi/uk_news/magazine/8207849.stm.

Prouix, J. "Constructivism: A Re-Equilibration and Clarification of Concepts, and Some Potential Implications for Teaching and Pedagogy." *Radical Pedagogy*, vol. 7, 2006, p. 5.

Pruitt, Sarah. "What's the Real History of Black Friday?" *History*. A+E Networks, 24 Nov. 2015, www.history. com/news/whats-the-real-history-of-black-friday.

Prust, Z. A., and Peggy B. Deal. *Graphic Communications: Digital Design and Print Essentials*. 6th ed., Goodheart-Willcox, 2019.

Pstatz. "FTP for Beginners." *Wired*, 15 Feb. 2010, www.wired.com/2010/02/ftp_for_beginners/.

Purchase, Helen C. *Experimental Human-Computer Interaction: A Practical Guide with Visual Examples*. Cambridge UP, 2012.

Purtill, Corinne. "Sherry Turkle's Plugged-in Year." *The New Yorker*, 23 Mar. 2021, newyorker.com/culture/persons-of-interest/sherry-turkles-plugged-in-year.

"Q2 2020 Letter to Shareholders." *Twitter*, 2020, s22.q4cdn.com/826641620/files/doc_financials/2020/q2/Q2-2020-Shareholder-Letter.pdf.

Qualman, Erik. *Socialnomics: How Social Media Transforms the Way We Live and Do Business*. Wiley, 2010.

Quinn, Michael J. *Ethics for the Information Age*. Pearson, 2016.

Rahman, N. "Refreshing Data Warehouses with Near Real-Time Updates." *Journal of Computer Information Systems*, vol. 47, no. 3, 2007, pp. 71–80.

Rainer, R. Kelly, Brad Prince, and Hugh J. Watson. *Management Information Systems: Moving Business Forward*. 4th ed., John Wiley & Sons, 2016.

Rainie, Lee, and Janna Anderson. "Code-Dependent: Pros and Cons of the Algorithm Age." *Pew Research Center*, 8 Feb. 2017, www.pewresearch.org/internet/2017/02/08/code-dependent-pros-and-cons-of-the-algorithm-age.

Rains, S. A. "Health at High Speed: Broadband Internet Access, Health Communication, and the Digital Divide." *Communication Research*, vol. 35, 2008, pp. 283–97, search.ebscohost.com/login.aspx?direct=true &db=a9h&AN=31987928&site=ehost-live.

Rains, Tim. *Cybersecurity Threats, Malware Trends, and Strategies*. Packt, 2020.

Rakower, Lauren. "Blurred Line: Zooming in on Google Street View and the Global Right to Privacy." *Brooklyn Journal of International Law*, vol. 37, no. 1, 2011, pp. 317–47.

Ralston, Anthony, Edwin D. Reilly, and David Hemmendinger, editors. *Encyclopedia of Computer Science*. 4th ed., Nature Publishing Group, 2000.

Ramachandran, Muthu, and Zaigham Mahmood, editors. *Software Engineering in the Era of Cloud Computing*. Springer International, 2020.

Ramasubramanian, S. "Racial/Ethnic Identity, Community-Oriented Media Initiatives, and Transmedia Storytelling." *Information Society*, vol. 32, no. 5, 2016, pp. 333–42.

Ranmuthugala, Geetha, et al. "How and Why Are Communities of Practice Established in the Healthcare Sector? A Systematic Review of the Literature." *BMC Health Services Research*, vol. 11 supp. 1, 2011, pp. 273–88.

Ransdell, Sarah, Brianna Kent, Sandrine Gaillard-Kenney, and John Long. "Digital Immigrants Fare Better than Digital Natives Due to Social Reliance." *British Journal of Educational Technology*, vol. 42, no. 6, 2011, pp. 931–38.

"Ransomware and Businesses 2016." *Symantec Corporation*, 2016, www.symantec.com/content/en/us/ enterprise/media/security_response/whitepapers/ISTR2016_Ransomware_and_Businesses.pdf.

"Ransomware Facts." *Microsoft Corporation*, 2016, www.microsoft.com/en-us/security/portal/mmpc/shared/ ransomware.aspx.

Rao, Leena. "Cyber Monday Is the Biggest Online Sales Day Ever." *Fortune*, 1 Dec. 2015, fortune. com/2015/11/30/record-cyber-monday/.

Raphael, J. R. "Android Versions: A Living History from 1.0 to 11." *Computerworld*, 26 June 2020, www. computerworld.com/article/3235946/android-versions-a-living-history-from-1-0-to-today.html.

Rappolt-Schlichtmann, G., S. G. Daley, L. Seoin, et al. "Universal Design for Learning and Elementary School Science: Exploring the Efficacy, Use, and Perceptions of a Web-Based Science Notebook." *Journal of Educational Psychology*, vol. 105, 2013, pp. 1210–25.

Ratan, R. A., J. E. Chung, C. Shen, at al. "Schmoozing and Smiting: Trust, Social Institutions, and Communication Patterns in an MMOG." *Journal of Computer-Mediated Communication*, vol. 16, no. 1, 2010, pp. 93–114.

Ratcliff, A. J., J. Mccarty, and M. Ritter. "Religion and New Media: A Uses and Gratifications Approach." *Journal of Media & Religion*, vol. 16, no. 1, 2017, pp. 15–26, search.ebscohost.com/Login.Aspx?Direct=Tru e&Db=Asn&AN=121290536&Site=Ehost-live.

Rathnappulige, Sasikala, and Lisa Daniel. "Creating Value through Social Processes: An Exploration of Knowledge Dynamics in Expert Communities of Practice." *International Journal of Technology Management*, vol. 63, no. 3-4, 2013, pp. 169–84.

Raval, Vasant. "Information Ethics: Information Ethics in the Mid-21st Century." *ISACA Journal*, vol. 6, 2016.

Ray, Deborah, and Eric Ray. *Unix and Linux*. 5th ed., Peachpit Press, 2015.

Raymond, Eric S. *The Art of UNIX Programming*. Addison-Wesley, 2008.

Rayome, Alison DeNisco. "10 Most-Downloaded Apps of the 2010s: Facebook Dominates the Decade." *CNET*, 16 Dec. 2019, www.cnet.com/ news/10-most-downloaded-apps-of-the-decade-facebook-dominated-2010-2019/.

Razeghi, Manijeh. *Fundamentals of Solid State Engineering*. 4th ed., Springer International, 2019.

Rea, J., A. Behnke, N. Huff, et al. "The Role of Online Communication in the Lives of Military Spouses." *International Journal*, vol. 37, no. 3, 2015, pp. 329–39.

Reagle, Joseph Michael. *Good Faith Collaboration: The Culture of Wikipedia*. MIT Press, 2010.

"Reddit.com." *SimilarWeb*, n.d., www.similarweb.com/website/reddit.com#referrals.

Reduction in Distribution of Spam Act of 2003: Hearing before the Subcommittee on Crime, Terrorism, and Homeland Security of the Committee on the Judiciary, House of Representatives, One Hundred Eighth Congress, First Session, on H.R. 2214, July 8, 2003. US Government Printing Office, 2003.

Reimer, Jeremy. "A History of the GUI." *Ars Technica*, 5 May 2005, arstechnica.com/features/2005/05/gui/.

"Research and Analysis: Online Copyright Infringement Tracker Survey (10th Wave) Executive Summary." *Intellectual Property Office*, gov.uk/government/publications/online-copyright-infringement-tracker-survey-10th-wave/online-copyright-infringement-tracker-survey-10th-wave-executive-summary.

"A Research Synthesis of the Literature on Multimedia Anchored Instruction in Preservice Teacher Education." *Journal of Special Education Technology*, vol. 26, 2011, pp. 1–22.

"Researchers Develop Nanoparticle Films for High-Density Data Storage." *OSA: The Optical Society*, 3 Apr. 2018. www.osa.org/en-us/about_osa/newsroom/news_releases/2018/researchers_develop_nanoparticle_films_for_high-de/.

Retzkin, Sion. *Hands-On Dark Web Analysis: Learn What Goes on in the Dark Web, and How to Work with It.* Packt Publishing, 2018.

Reyns, Bradford W. *The Anti-social Network: Cyberstalking Victimization among College Students.* LFB Scholarly Publishing, 2012.

Ribble, Mike. *Digital Citizenship in Schools: Nine Elements All Students Should Know.* International Society for Technology in Education, 2015.

Ribble, Mike, and Marty Park. *The Digital Citizenship Handbook for School Leaders: Fostering Positive Interactions Online.* International Society for Technology in Education, 2019.

Richards, J., L. Stebbins, and K. Moellering. "Games for a Digital Age: K-12 Market Map and Investment Analysis." 2013, joanganzcooneycenter.org.

Richards, Mark, and Neal Ford. *Fundamentals of Software Architecture: An Engineering Approach.* O'Reilly, 2020.

Richardson, Martin J., and John D. Wiltshire. *The Hologram: Principles and Techniques.* John Wiley & Sons, 2017.

Rideout, Victoria J., Ulla G. Foehr, and Donald F. Roberts. "'Generation M2': Media in the Lives of 8- to 18-Year-Olds—A Kaiser Family Foundation Study." *Kaiser Family Foundation*, Jan. 2010.

Rieth, H. J., D. P. Bryant, C. K. Kinzer, et al. "An Analysis of the Impact of Anchored Instruction on Teaching and Learning Activities in Two Ninth-Grade Language Arts Classes." *Remedial and Special Education*, vol. 24, 2003, p. 173.

Rifkin, Adam. "Tumblr Is Not What You Think." *Tech Crunch*. AOL, 18 Feb. 2013, techcrunch.com/2013/02/18/tumblr-is-not-what-you-think/.

Riley, Gail Blasser. *Internet Piracy.* Cavendish, 2010.

Riselvato, John. *Bandcamp for Artists and Music Labels: Marketing Tips to Sell More Music and Merch.* Amazon Digital Services LLC, 2020.

Rizzo, Albert "Skipp," and Stéphane Bouchard, editors. *Virtual Reality for Psychological and Neurocognitive Interventions.* Springer-Verlag New York, 2019.

Roberts, Barrie. *Step-by-Step Guide to Google Slides.* Independently published, 2020.

Roberts, Eric. "The Ethics (or Not) of Massive Government Surveillance." *Stanford Computer Science Department.* Stanford University, cs.stanford.edu/people/eroberts/cs181/projects/ethics-of-surveillance/ethics.html.

Robertson, James. *Essential Intranets: Inspiring Sites That Deliver Business Value.* Step Two Designs, 2013.

Robinson, Matthew. "Myspace Apologizes after Losing 12 Years' Worth of Music." *CNN*, 18 Mar. 2019, www.cnn.com/2019/03/18/us/myspace-lost-12-years-music-uploads-apology-intl-scli/index.html.

Roblyer, M. D., and Aaron H. Doering. *Integrating Educational Technology into Teaching.* 6th ed., Pearson, 2013.

Rocha, Álvaro, Ana Maria Correa, Tom Wilson, and Karl A. Stroetmann. *Advances in Information Systems and Technologies.* Springer, 2013.

Rodrigues, P., and J. Bidarra. "Transmedia Storytelling and the Creation of a Converging Space of Educational Practices." *International Journal of Emerging Technologies in Learning*, vol. 9, no. 6, 2014, pp. 42–44.

Roesner, Franziska, Brian T. Gill, and Tadayoshi Kohno. "Sex, Lies, or Kittens? Investigating the Use of Snapchat's Self-Destructing Messages." *Financial Cryptography and Data Security, Lecture Notes in Computer Science*, vol. 8437, 9 Nov. 2014, pp. 64–76.

Rogers, Scott. *Swipe This!: The Guide to Great Touchscreen Game Design.* Wiley, 2012.

Rogers-Whitehead, Carrie. *Digital Citizenship: Teaching Strategies and Practice from the Field.* Rowman & Littlefield, 2019.

Rogow, Geoffrey. "In Social Media Mining, Some Go Slow." *The Wall Street Journal: Money Beat.* Dow Jones, 1 Dec. 2014.

Rohwer, W. D., and K. Sloane. "Psychological Perspectives." *Bloom's Taxonomy: A Forty-Year Retrospective*, edited by L. W. Anderson and L. A. Sosniak, U of Chicago P, 1994, pp. 41–63.

Rolston, Clyde Philip, Amy Macy, Tom Hutchison and Paul Allen. *Record Label Marketing: How Music Companies Brand and Market Artists in the Digital Era.* CRC Press, 2015.

Romano, Aja. "Kicking People Off Social Media Isn't about Free Speech." *Vox*, 21 Jan. 2021, www.vox.com/culture/22230847/deplatforming-free-speech-controversy-trump.

Romm, Tony. "Millions of Low-Income Americans Will Receive Internet Access Rebates under New $7 Billion Broadband Stimulus Plan." *The Washington Post*, 22 Dec. 2020, www.washingtonpost.com/technology/2020/12/22/internet-rebate-coronavirus-stimulus.

Rose, D. H., and A. Meyer, editors. *A Practical Reader in Universal Design for Learning.* Harvard Education P, 2006.

___. *Teaching Every Student in the Digital Age: Universal Design for Learning*, 2002.

Rose, Damon. "Smartphone Cameras Bring Independence to Blind People." *BBC News: Technology.* BBC, 12 July 2012.

Rosen, David J. "Limiting Employee Liability under the CFAA: A Code-Based Approach to 'Exceeds Authorized Access.'" *Berkeley Technology Law Journal*, vol. 27, 2012, p. 737.

Rosen, L. D., K. Whaling, S. Rab, et al. "Is Facebook Creating Idisorders"? The Link between Clinical Symptoms of Psychiatric Disorders and Technology Use, Attitudes and Anxiety." *Computers in Human Behavior*, vol. 29, no. 3, 2013, pp. 1243–54.

Rosen, Larry D. *iDisorder: Understanding Our Dependency on Technology and Overcoming Our Addiction.* Palgrave, 2012.

Rosenbaum, Steven. "YouTube Reveals a Curated Future." *Forbes*, 10 Oct. 2012, www.forbes.com/sites/stevenrosenbaum/2012/10/10/YouTube-reveals-a-curated-future-2/.

Rosenberg, Matthew, and Sheera Frenkel. "Facebook's Role in Data Misuse Sets of Storms on Two Continents." *The New York Times*, 18 Mar. 2018, www.nytimes.com/2018/03/18/us/cambridge-analytica-facebook-privacy-data.html.

Rosenthal, S. R., S. Buka, B. D. L. Marshall, et al. "Negative Experiences on Facebook and Depressive Symptoms among Young Adults." *Journal of Adolescent Health*, vol. 59, no. 5, 2016, pp. 570–76.

Rossing, J., W. Miller, A. Cecil, et al. "Ilearning: The Future of Higher Education? Student Perspectives on Learning with Mobile Tablets." *Journal of the Scholarship of Teaching and Learning*, vol. 12, no. 2, 2012, pp. 1–26.

Rossington, Richard. "Is It Safe to Use Google Docs?" *CEO Today*, 9 Oct. 2019, ceotodaymagazine.com/2019/10/is-it-safe-to-use-google-docs/.

Rountree, Derrick, and Ileana Castrillo. *The Basics of Cloud Computing.* Elsevier, 2014.

Rouse, Margaret. "Digital Economy." *TechTarget*, Sept. 2017, searchcio.techtarget.com/definition/digital-economy.

___. "Microsoft Exchange Server." *TechTarget*, searchwindowsserver.techtarget.com/definition/Microsoft-Exchange-Server.

___. "XML (Extensible Markup Language) Definition." *TechTarget*, 13 Aug. 2015, searchsoa.techtarget.com/definition/XML.

Rowan, L., and C. Bigum, editors. *Transformative Approaches to New Technologies and Student Diversity in Futures Oriented Classrooms: Future Proofing Education.* Springer, 2012.

Rowsell, J. *Working with Multimodality: Rethinking Literacy in the Digital Age.* Routledge, 2013.

Rubin, Aaron. "How Website Operators Use CFAA to Combat Data-Scraping." *Law360,* www.law360.com/articles/569325?utm_source=rss&utm_medium=rss&utm_campaign=articles_search.

Rubin, Victoria L. "Deception Detection and Rumor Debunking for Social Media." *The SAGE Handbook of Social Media Research Methods,* edited by Luke Sloan and Anabel Quan-Haase, Sage Publications, 2017, pp. 342–64.

Rumelhart, David E., James L. McClelland, and the PDP Research Group. *Parallel Distributed Processing: Explorations in the Microstructure of Cognition.* 2 vols. 1986. MIT Press, 1989.

Russell, Stuart, and Peter Norvig. *Artificial Intelligence: A Modern Approach.* 4th ed., Pearson, 2020.

Ryan, Dan. *History of Computer Graphics: DLR Associates Series.* AuthorHouse, 2011.

Ryder, M. "Instructional Design Models: Instructional Technology Connections." www.carbon.cudenver.edu.

Sacharoff, Laurent. "Do Bots Have First Amendment Rights?" *Politico,* 27 Nov. 2018, www.politico.com/magazine/story/2018/11/27/bots-first-amendment-rights-222689

Sachowski, Jason. *Digital Forensics and Investigations: People, Process, and Technologies to Defend the Enterprise.* CRC Press, 2018.

Sadun, Erica. *The Advanced iOS 6 Developer's Cookbook.* Addison-Wesley, 2013.

Safesurf. "The Safesurf Internet Rating Standard." *Safesurf.com.*

Salguero, Ricardo A. Tejeiro, and Rosa M. Bersabe Moran. "Measuring Problem Video Game Playing in Adolescents." *Addiction,* vol. 97, 2002, pp. 1601–6.

Salter, A., and B. Blodgett. *Toxic Geek Masculinity in Media: Sexism, Trolling, and Identity Policing.* Palgrave Macmillan, 2017.

Salter, M. "From Geek Masculinity to Gamergate: The Technical Rationality of Online Abuse." *Crime Media Culture,* vol. 14, no. 20, 2018, pp. 247–64.

Saltzman, Steven. *Music Editing for Film and Television: The Art and the Process.* Focal Press, 2015.

Samani, Raj. "'McAfee Labs Threats Report' Spotlights Innovative Attack Techniques, Cryptocurrency Mining, Multisector Attacks." *McAfee,* 26 June 2018, securingtomorrow.mcafee.com/other-blogs/mcafee-labs/mcafee-labs-threats-report-spotlights-innovative-attack-techniques-cryptocurrency-mining-multisector-attacks/.

Samuelson, Pamela. "Privacy as Intellectual Property?" *First Amendment Handbook,* edited by James L. Swanson, C. Boardman, 2002.

Sandars, J., M. Homer, K. Walsh, and A. Rutherford. "Don't Forget the Learner: An Essential Aspect for Developing Effective Hypermedia Online Learning in Continuing Medical Education." *Education for Primary Care,* vol. 23, 2012, pp. 90–94.

Sander, Peter J. *What Would Steve Jobs Do? How the Steve Jobs Way Can Inspire Anyone to Think Differently and Win.* McGraw-Hill, 2012.

Sanders, James, and Conner Forrest. "Hybrid Cloud: What It Is, Why It Matters." *ZDNet,* 1 July 2014, www.zdnet.com/article/hybrid-cloud-what-it-is-why-it-matters/.

Sanger, David E., et al. "Cyberattack Forces a Shutdown of a Top U.S. Pipeline." *The New York Times,* 8 May 2021, www.nytimes.com/2021/05/08/us/politics/cyberattack-colonial-pipeline.html.

Sanz, E., and G. Turlea. "Downloading Inclusion: A Statistical Analysis of Young People's Digital Communication Inequalities." *Innovation: The European Journal of Social Sciences,* vol. 25, 2012, pp. 337–53, search.ebscohost.com/login.aspx?direct=true&db=sih&AN=83467960&site=ehost-live&scope=site.

Sarkar, Jayanta. *Computer Aided Design: A Conceptual Approach.* CRC Press, 2017.

Sarker, Samit. "YouTube Gaming Launches Aug. 26 with Website and Mobile Apps." *Yahoo.* YAHOO/ABC News Network, 25 Aug. 2015, www.polygon.com/2015/8/25/9208245/youtube-gaming-launch-date-web-android-ios#:~:text=Google%20will%20launch%20YouTube%20Gaming,looking%20for%20gaming%20video%20content..

Sarpu, Bridget A. "Google: The Endemic Threat to Privacy." *Journal of High Technology Law,* vol. 15, no. 1, 2014, pp. 97–134.

Saul, Roger. "KevJumba and the Adolescence of YouTube." *Educational Studies*, vol. 46, no. 5, 2010, pp. 457–77, search.ebscohost.com/login.Aspx?direct=true&db=a9h&AN=54166670&site=ehost-live.

Saxby, Graham, and Stanislovas Zacharovas. *Practical Holography*. 4th ed., CRC Press, 2016.

Scandura, J. M. "Comments on Ansari & Sykes and Gogus, and Suggestions for Future Research." *Technology, Instruction, Cognition & Learning*, vol. 9, no. 1/2, 2012, pp. 51–56.

Schalk, Gerwin, and Brendan Z. Allison. *Neuromodulation: Comprehensive Textbook of Principles, Technologies, and Therapies*. 2nd ed., Academic Press, 2018.

Schapire, Robert E., and Yoav Freund. *Boosting: Foundations and Algorithms*. MIT Press, 2012.

Schechner, Sam. "Facebook Privacy Controls Face Scrutiny in Europe." *The Wall Street Journal*, 2 Apr. 2015, www.wsj.com/articles/facebook-confronts-european-probes-1427975994.

Scheff, Sue. "Online Safety: What Does It Mean to You?" *The Huffington Post*. TheHuffingtonPost.com, 21 Nov. 2014.

Schell, Bernadette H., and Clemens Martin. *Cybercrime: A Reference Handbook*. ABC-CLIO, 2004.

Schieck, Glenn R. "Undercutting Employee Mobility: The Computer Fraud and Abuse Act in the Trade Secret Context." *Brooklyn Law Review*, vol. 79, no. 2, 2014, p. 831.

Schmitt, Michael N. "The Law of Cyber Warfare: Quo Vadis?" *Stanford Law & Policy Review*, vol. 25, no. 2, 2014, pp. 269–99.

Schneider, C. J., and D. Trottier. "The 2011 Vancouver Riot and the Role of Facebook in Crowd-Sourced Policing." *BC Studies*, vol. 175, 2012, pp. 57–72.

Schneider, Shari Kessel, et al. "Cyberbullying, School Bullying, and Psychological Distress: A Regional Census of High School Students." *American Journal of Public Health*, vol. 102, no. 1, 2012, p. 171.

Schneps, M., J. Ruel, G. Sonnert, et al. "Conceptualizing Astronomical Scale: Virtual Simulations on Hand-held Tablet Computers Reverse Misconceptions." *Computers and Education*, vol. 70, 2014, pp. 269–80.

Schrader, D. E. "Constructivism and Learning in the Age of Social Media: Changing Minds and Learning Communities." *New Directions for Teaching and Learning*, vol. 144, 2015, pp. 23–35.

Schulman, Miriam. "Little Brother Is Watching You." *Markkula Center for Applied Ethics*. Santa Clara University, www.scu.edu/ethics/publications/iie/v9n2/brother.html.

Schwabach, Aaron. *Internet and the Law: Technology, Society, and Compromises*. ABC-CLIO, 2006.

Schwartz, John. "Two German Killers Demanding Anonymity Sue Wikipedia's Parent." *The New York Times*, 12 Nov. 2009.

"Scientific Literacy." *Literacynet*, www.literacynet.org/science/scientificliteracy.html.

"Scientific Literacy: Definition and Examples." *Study.com*, 2020, study.com/academy/lesson/scientific-literacy-definition-examples.html.

Scott, A. O. "The World Where You Aren't What You Post." *The New York Times*, 16 Sept. 2010.

Seabrook, John. "Revenue Streams." *The New Yorker*, 24 Nov. 2014. www.newyorker.com/magazine/2014/11/24/revenue-streams.

Segall, Ken. *Insanely Simple: The Obsession That Drives Apple's Success*. Portfolio/Penguin, 2012.

Segura, Diana. "13 Best CAD Programs for Kids." *3DPrinterChat.com*, 8 Feb. 2020, 3dprinterchat.com/13-best-cad-programs-for-kids/.

Sen, Soumya, Anjan Dutta, and Nilanjan Dey. *Audio Processing and Speech Recognition*. Springer Singapore, 2019.

"Senate Considers Internet Safety." *American Libraries*, vol. 38, 2007, pp. 23–24.

Senn, J. A. *Information Technology: Principles, Practices, Opportunities*. 3rd ed., Pearson, 2004.

Senn, James. *Information Technology: Principles, Practices, and Opportunities*. 3rd ed., Prentice Hall, 2004.

Seo, K. K. J. *Using Social Media Effectively in the Classroom: Blogs, Wikis, Twitter, and More*. Routledge, 2012.

Serafino, K., and T. Cicchelli. "Cognitive Theories, Prior Knowledge, and Anchored Instruction on Mathematical Problem Solving and Transfer." *Education and Urban Society*, vol. 36, 2003, pp. 79–93.

Sessink, O., H. Beeftink, J. Tramper, et al. "Proteus: A Lecturer-Friendly Adaptive Tutoring System." *Journal of Interactive Learning Research*, vol. 18, 2007, pp. 533–54.

Shah, H., K. Warwick, J. Vallverdú, and D. Wu. "Can Machines Talk? Comparison of Eliza with Modern Dialogue Systems." *Computers in Human Behavior,* vol. 58, 2016, pp. 278–95.

Shand, K., and S. Farrelly. "Using Blended Teaching to Teach Blended Learning: Lessons Learned from Pre-Service Teachers in an Instructional Methods Course." *Journal of Online Learning Research*, vol. 3, no. 1, 2017.

Shao, Grace. "What 'Deepfakes' Are and How They May Be Dangerous." *CNBC,* 13 Oct. 2019, www.cnbc.com/2019/10/14/what-is-deepfake-and-how-it-might-be-dangerous.html.

Share, Jeff. *Media Literacy Is Elementary: Teaching Youth to Critically Read and Create Media.* Lang, 2009.

Sharp, Helen, Jennifer Preece, and Yvonne Rogers. *Interaction Design: Beyond Human-Computer Interaction.* 5th ed., John Wiley & Sons, 2019.

Shaw, A. "Do You Identify as a Gamer? Gender, Race, Sexuality and Gamer Identity." *New Media and Society,* vol. 14, no. 1, 2011, pp. 28–44.

Shema, Mike. "Browser & Privacy Attacks." *Hacking Web Apps: Detecting and Preventing Web Application Security Problems.* Syngress, 2012.

Sherman, William R., and Alan B. Craig. *Understanding Virtual Reality: Interface, Application and Design.* 2nd ed., Morgan Kaufmann, 2018.

Shibley, I., K. E. Amaral, J. D. Shank, et al. "Designing a Blended Course: Using ADDIE to Guide Instructional Design." *Journal of College Science Teaching,* vol. 40, 2011, pp. 80–85.

Shirky, Clay. *Here Comes Everybody: The Power of Organizing without Organizations.* Penguin, 2009.

Shneiderman, Ben, et al. *Designing the User Interface: Strategies for Effective Human-Computer Interaction.* 6th ed., Pearson Education, 2018.

Shoenberger, Allen. "Privacy Wars." *Indiana International & Comparative Law Review,* vol. 17, 2007, pp. 355–93.

Shontell, Alyson. "Snap Is a Lot Bigger Than People Realize and It Could be Nearing 200 Million Active Users." *Business Insider,* 3 Jan. 2015.

"A Short History of FTP with Resources." *WhoIsHostingThis.com,* www.whoishostingthis.com/resources/ftp/.

"A Short History of HTML." *W3C-HTML.com,* W3C Foundation, w3c-html.com/html-history.html.

Shotton, Margaret A. *Computer Addiction? A Study of Computer Dependency.* Taylor, 1989.

___. "The Costs and Benefits of 'Computer Addiction.' " *Behaviour and Information Technology,* vol. 10, 1991, pp. 219–30.

Shreekumar, Advik. "Rise of the YouTube Star." *Harvard Political Review,* vol. 41, no. 1, 2014, p. 16, search.ebscohost.com/login.aspx?direct=true&db=pwh&AN=95604237&site=pov-live.

Shustek, Len. "Microsoft Word for Windows Version 1.1a Source Code." *Computer History Museum,* www.computerhistory.org/atchm/microsoft-word-for-windows-1-1a-source-code/.

Shyu, H.-Y. "Effects of Media Attributes in Anchored Instruction." *Journal of Educational Computing Research,* vol. 21, 199, pp. 119–39.

Sickels, Robert C. *The Business of Entertainment.* 3 vols. ABC-CLIO, 2009.

Siddiqi, Muzaffer A. *Dynamic RAM: Technology Advancements.* CRC Press, 2013.

Siegel, Lee. "The Kids Aren't Alright." *Newsweek,* 15 Oct. 2012, pp. 18–20.

Silberschatz, Abraham, Peter Baer Galvin, and Greg Gagne. *Operating System Concepts.* 10th ed., John Wiley & Sons, 2018.

Silva, Alberto J. Cerda. "Enforcing Intellectual Property Rights by Diminishing Privacy: How the Anti-Counterfeiting Trade Agreement Jeopardizes the Right to Privacy." *American University International Law Review,* vol. 26, no. 3, 2011, pp. 601–43.

Simmons, C. "Losses Rise in Internet-Related Scams." *CIO Today,* 7 Apr. 2008, www.newsfactor.com"xlink:type="simple">http://www.newsfactor.com.

Simmons, Colin H., Dennis E. Maguire, and Neil Phelps. *Manual of Engineering Drawing: British and International Standards.* Butterworth-Heinemann, 2020.

Simonite, Tom. "Prepare for the Deepfake Era of Web Video." *Wired,* 6 Oct. 2019, www.wired.com/story/prepare-deepfake-era-web-video/.

Simons, M. "Dutch Say a Sex Ring Used Infants on Internet." *The New York Times,* 19 July 1998, query. nytimes.com/gst/fullpage.html?res=990de3da1330f93aa25754c0a96e958260&scp=1&sq=dutch+sex+ring &st=nyt.

Sinacole, Patricia Hunt. "Use Social Media Wisely When Job Hunting." *Boston Globe.* Boston Globe Media Partners, 26 Oct. 2014.

Sinclair, G., and J. Tinson. "Psychological Ownership and Music Streaming Consumption." *Journal of Business Research*, vol. 71, 2017, pp. 1–9, doi:10.1016/j.jbusres.2016.10.002.

Singel, Ryan. "Feds Charge Activist as Hacker for Downloading Millions of Academic Articles." *Wired.* Condé Nast, 19 July 2011, www.wired.com/2011/07/swartz-arrest/.

Singer, Natasha. "Ways to Make Your Online Tracks Harder to Follow." *The New York Times.* Arthur Ochs Sulzberger, Jr., 19 June 2013, bits.blogs.nytimes.com/2013/06/19/ ways-to-make-your-online-tracks-harder-to-follow-2/?_php=true&_type=blogs&_r=0.

Singer, P. W., and Allan Friedman. *Cybersecurity and Cyberwar: What Everyone Needs to Know.* Oxford UP, 2014.

Singh, Lakhwinder Pal, and Harwinder Singh. *Engineering Drawing: Principles and Applications.* Cambridge UP, 2021.

Skinner, E. "Building Knowledge and Community Through Online Discussion." *Journal of Geography in Higher Education*, vol. 31, 2007, pp. 381–91.

Slama, M. "Practising Islam Through Social Media in Indonesia." *Indonesia & The Malay World*, vol. 46, no. 134, 2018, pp. 1–4, doi:10.1080/13639811.2018.1416798.

Sluckin, Timothy J., David A. Dunmur, and Horst Stegemeyer. *Crystals That Flow: Classic Papers from the History of Liquid Crystals.* CRC Press, 2004.

Smalheiser, Neil R. *Data Literacy: How to Make Your Experiments Robust and Reproducible.* Academic Press, 2017.

Smith, Aaron, and Maeve Duggan. "Online Dating & Relationships." *Pew Research*, 21 Oct. 2013.

Smith, Bud E. *Green Computing: Tools and Techniques for Saving Energy, Money, and Resources.* CRC Press, 2014.

Smith, Craig. "Eighteen Amazing Gmail Facts and Statistics (January 2018)/By the Numbers." *DMR*, 31 Mar. 2018, expandedramblings.com/index.php/gmail-statistics/.

___. "IMGR Statistics, User Count and Facts: 2022." *DMR Publisher*, expandedramblings.com/index.php/ imgur-statistics/.

Smith, J. K., L. I. Given, H. Julien, et al. "Information Literacy Proficiency: Assessing the Gap in High School Students' Readiness for Undergraduate Academic Work." *Library and Information Science Research*, vol. 35, no. 2, 2013, pp. 88–96.

Smith, Jeremy N. *Breaking and Entering: The Extraordinary Story of a Hacker Called "Alien."* Eamon Dolan/ Houghton Mifflin Harcourt, 2019.

Smith, Marcia S. *"Junk E-mail": An Overview of Issues and Legislation concerning Unsolicited Commercial Electronic Mail ("Spam").* Congressional Research Service, Library of Congress, 2001.

Snart, J. A. *Hybrid Learning: The Perils and Promise of Blending Online and Face-To-Face Instruction in Higher Education.* Praeger, 2010.

Sobers, Rob. "81 Ransomware Statistics, Data, Trends and Facts for 2021." *Inside Out Security.* Varonis Blog, varonis.com/blog/ransomware-statistics-2021.

"Social Engineering Fraud." *Interpol*, www.interpol.int/Crime-areas/Financial-crime/Social-engineering- fraud/Types-of-social-engineering-fraud.

"Social Media and Mental Health." *HelpGuide*, www.healthguide.org/articles/mental-health/social-media- and-mental-health.htm.

"Social Media Fact Sheet." *Pew Research Center*, 12 June 2019, www.pewresearch.org/internet/fact-sheet/ social-media/.

"Social Media Use Increases Depression and Loneliness." *University of Pennsylvania.* PennToday, penntoday. upenn.edu/news.social-media-use-increases-depression-and-loneliness.

Soegaard, Mads, and Rikke Friis Dam, editors. *The Encyclopedia of Human-Computer Interaction.* 2nd ed., Interaction Design Foundation, 2014.

Somani, A., D. Choy, and J. C. Kleewein. "Bringing Together Content and Data Management Systems: Challenges and Opportunities." *IBM Systems Journal*, vol. 41, no. 4, 2002, pp. 686–96.

Sonmez, John Z. *Soft Skills: The Software Developer's Life Manual.* Manning, 2015.

"Sony Cyber-Attack: North Korea Faces New US Sanctions." *BBC News.* BBC, 3 Jan. 2015.

Sosniak, L. A. "The Taxonomy, Curriculum, and Their Relations." *Bloom's Taxonomy: A Forty-Year Retrospective*, edited by L. W. Anderson and L. A. Sosniak, U of Chicago P, 1994, pp. 41–63.

Souk, Jun, et al., editors. *Flat Panel Display Manufacturing.* John Wiley & Sons, 2018.

Spangler, Todd. "Musical.ly Is Going Away: Users to Be Shifted to Bytedance's TikTok Video App." *Variety*, 2 Aug. 2018, variety.com/2018/digital/news/musically-shutdown-tiktok-bytedance-1202893205/.

Spector, J. M. "Philosophical Implications for the Design of Instruction." *Instructional Science*, vol. 29, no. 4/5, 2011, pp. 381–402.

Spizman, R. J., and M. K. Miller. "Plugged-In Policing: Student Perceptions of Law Enforcement's Use of Social Media." *Applied Psychology in Criminal Justice*, vol. 9, no. 2, 2013, pp. 100–123, search.ebscohost.com/login.Aspx?Direct=True&Db=Sxi&AN=95588738&Site=Ehost-live.

Stahl, B. C., J. Timmermans, and C. Flick. "Ethics of Emerging Information and Communication Technologies: On the Implementation of Responsible Research and Innovation." *Science and Public Policy*, vol. 44, no. 3, 2017, pp. 369–81.

Stallings, William, and Lawrie Brown. *Computer Security: Principles and Practice.* 4th ed., Pearson, 2018.

Stamp, Mark. *Information Security: Principles and Practice.* Wiley, 2011.

Stanaland, A. J. S., M. O. Lwin, and S. Leong. "Providing Parents with Online Privacy Information: Approaches in the U.S. and the UK." *Journal of Consumer Affairs*, vol. 43, no. 3, 2009, pp. 474–94.

Stanglin, D., and W. M. Welch. "Sheriff Says He Made Arrests After One Suspect Posted on Facebook That She Didn't Care the Victim Had Died." *USA Today*, 16 Oct. 2013, www.usatoday.com/story/news/nation/2013/10/15/florida-bullying-arrest-lakeland-suicide/2986079.

"State Assistive Technology Programs." *Exceptional Parent*, vol. 41, 2011, pp. 46–48.

Steiner, Christopher. *Automate This: How Algorithms Came to Rule Our World.* Penguin, 2012.

Stephens, G. "Crime in Cyberspace." *Futurist*, vol. 29, 1995, pp. 24–31.

___. "Cybercrime in the Year 2025." *Futurist*, vol. 42, 2008, pp. 32–36, retrisearch.ebscohost.com/login.aspx?direct=true&db=aph&an=32526239&site=ehost-live.

Stephenson, Brad. "Twitch: Everything You Need to Know." *Lifewire*, 9 Sept. 2019, www.lifewire.com/what-is-twitch-4143337.

Stergioulas, L., and H. Drenoyianni. *Pursuing Digital Literacy in Compulsory Education.* Peter Lang, 2011.

Stevens, M. "Space for All: Middle Level Students in Blended Learning Environments." *Voices from the Middle*, vol. 24, no. 2, 2016, pp. 50–55.

Stevens, Sarah, and Tracy Morris. "College Dating and Social Anxiety: Using the Internet as a Means of Connecting to Others." *Cyberpsychology and Behavior*, vol. 10, no. 5, 2007, pp. 680–88.

Stevens, W. Richard, and Stephen A. Rago. *Advanced Programming in the UNIX Environment.* 3rd ed., Addison-Wesley, 2013.

Stewart, Christian. "The Best Private Search Engines—Alternatives to Google." *Medium*, 8 Feb. 2018, hackernoon.com/untraceable-search-engines-alternatives-to-google-811b09d5a873.

Stinson, Liz. "Facebook Reactions, the Totally Redesigned Like Button, Is Here." *Wired*, 24 Feb. 2016, www.wired.com/2016/02/facebook-reactions-totally-redesigned-like-button/.

Stobing, Chris. "Ransomware Is the New Hot Threat Everyone Is Talking About; What Do You Need to Know?" *Digital Trends*, 6 June 2015, www.digitaltrends.com/computing/what-is-ransomware-and-should-you-be-worried-about-it/.

Stockson, Eric. *Brave Browser: Blockchain Internet Browsing Made Easy.* First Rank, 2019.

STOMP Out Bullying, 2020, www.stompoutbullying.org/.

"The Story of TCO Certified." *TCO*, 2020, tcocertified.com/the-story-of-tco-certified/.

Stott, T. C., A. Maceachron, and N. Gustavsson. "Social Media and Child Welfare: Policy, Training, and the Risks and Benefits from the Administrator's Perspective." *Advances In Social Work*, vol. 17, no. 2, 2016, pp. 221–34, search.ebscohost.com/login.aspx?direct=true&db=sxi&an=121190728&site=ehost-live.

Strassberg, Donald, Ryan K. McKinnon, Michael A. Sustaíta, and Jordan Rullo. "Sexting by High School Students: An Exploratory and Descriptive Study." *Archives of Sexual Behavior*, vol. 42, no. 1, 2012, pp. 15–21.

Sugarman, J., S., M. Shivakumar, J. F. Rook, C. Loring, et al. "Ethical Considerations in the Manufacture, Sale, and Distribution of Genome Editing Technologies." *American Journal of Bioethics*, vol. 18, no. 8, 2018, pp. 3–6.

Suhr, H. Cecilia. *Evaluation and Credentialing in Digital Music Communities: Benefits and Challenges for Learning and Assessment*. MIT Press, 2014.

Suler, John. "The Online Disinhibition Effect." *CyberPsychology & Behavior*, vol. 7, no. 3, 2004, pp. 321–26, Academic Search Complete, search.ebscohost.com/login.aspx?direct=true&db=a9h&AN=13621589&site=ehost-live.

Sulleyman, Aatif. "Facebook Live Killings: Why the Criticism Has Been Harsh." *The Independent*, 27 Apr. 2017, www.independent.co.uk/life-style/gadgets-and-tech/features/facebook-live-killings-ai-artificial-intelligence-not-blame-fatalities-murders-us-steve-stephens-a7706056.html/.

Summers, Danny. *Imgur: 42 Success Secrets–42 Most Asked Questions–Imgur: What You Need to Know*. Emereo Pty Ltd., 2014.

Sun, Jiming, et al. *Embedded Firmware Solutions: Development Best Practices for the Internet of Things*. Apress, 2015.

Sunghee, S. "Ebook Usability in Educational Technology Classes: Teachers and Teacher Candidates' Perception Toward Ebook for Teaching and Learning." *International Journal of Distance Education Technologies*, vol. 12, no. 3, 2014, pp. 62–74.

"Supreme Court Grants Cert. in Case that May Redefine Scope of FOIA Exemption 4…" *Dashboard Insights*, 29 Jan. 2019.

Surianarayanan, Chellammal, and Pethuru Raj. *Essentials of Cloud Computing: A Holistic Perspective*. Springer International, 2019.

Swaine, Jon. "Twitter Admits Far More Russian Bots Posted on Election Than It Had Disclosed." 19 Jan. 2018, www.theguardian.com/technology/2018/jan/19/twitter-admits-far-more-russian-bots-posted-on-election-than-it-had-disclosed.

Swarts, Jason. *Wicked, Incomplete and Uncertain: User Support in the Wild and the Role of Technical Communication*. UP of Colorado, 2018.

Swartz, J. "Online Crime's Impact Spreads." *USA Today*, 11 Apr. 2008.

Sweatt, Brian, Sharon Paradesi, Ilaria Liccardi, Lalana Kagal, and Alex Pentland. "Building Privacy-Preserving Location-Based Apps." *2014 Twelfth Annual International Conference on Privacy, Security and Trust, Toronto, Ontario, Canada, July 23–24, 2014*. IEEE/Wiley, 2014.

Sweeney, Latanya. "k-Anonymity: A Model for Protecting Privacy." *International Journal of Uncertainty, Fuzziness and Knowledge-Based Systems*, vol. 10, no. 5, 2002, pp. 557–70.

Sweeny, Jo Anne. "Sexting and Freedom of Expression: A Comparative Approach." *Kentucky Law Journal*, vol. 102, 2013–2014, pp. 103–46.

Sylvester, Ruth, and Wendy-lou Greenidge. "Digital Storytelling: Extending the Potential for Struggling Writers." *Reading Teacher*, vol. 63, no. 4, 2009, pp. 284–95.

Sysomos, Inc. "Inside Blog Demographics." June 2010, sysomos.com.

Szkutnicka, Basia. *Flats: Technical Drawing for Fashion: A Complete Guide*. Lawrence King, 2017.

Tafoya, William L. "Cyber Terror." *FBI Law Enforcement Bulletin*. FBI, n.d.

Tandoc, Jr., E. C., and J. Jenkins. "The Buzzfeedication of Journalism? How Traditional News Organizations Are Talking About a New Entrant to the Journalistic Field Will Surprise You!" *Journalism*, vol. 18, no. 4, 2017, pp. 482–500.

Tang, Jiliang, Yi Chang, and Huan Liu. "Mining Social Media with Social Theories: A Survey." *ACM SIGKDD Explorations Newsletter*, vol. 15, no. 2, 2013, pp. 20–29.

Tate, Emily. "The Digital Divide Has Narrowed, but 12 Million Students Are Still Disconnected." *EdSurge*, 27 Jan. 2021, www.edsurge.com/news/2021-01-27-the-digital-divide-has-narrowed-but-12-million-students-are-still-disconnected.

Tatnall, Arthur, and Bill Davey, editors. *Reflections on the History of Computers in Education: Early Use of Computers and Teaching about Computing in Schools.* Springer-Verlag Berlin Heidelberg, 2014.

Taylor, Dave. *Learning Unix for OS X.* 2nd ed., O'Reilly Media, 2016.

Taylor, Jim. *Everything You Ever Wanted to Know About DVD: The Official DVD FAQ.* McGraw-Hill, 2004.

Taylor, Jim, et al. *Blu-ray Disc Demystified.* McGraw-Hill, 2009.

Taylor, Jim, Mark R. Johnson, and Charles G. Crawford. *DVD Demystified.* 3rd ed., McGraw-Hill, 2006.

"TEAM—Advancing the Math Skills of Low-Achieving Adolescents in Technology-Rich Learning Environments." 2007, wcer.wisc.edu.

"Tech Support Scams." *Federal Trade Commission*, July 2017, www.consumer.ftc.gov/articles/0346-tech-support-scams.

Technology-Related Assistance for Individuals with Disabilities Act of 1994. Public Laws 100-407 and 103-218. Resna.org.

TED Talk. *Sherry Turkle: Cultural Analyst.* Apr. 2012, ted.com/talks/sherry_turkle_connected_but_alone.

Tehrani, Kiana, and Andrew Michael. "Wearable Technology and Wearable Devices: Everything You Need to Know." *Wearable Devices Magazine*, 26 Mar. 26 2014. www.wearabledevices.com/what-is-a-wearable-device/.

Teo, Timothy. "An Initial Development and Validation of a Digital Natives Assessment Scale (DNAS)." *Computers & Education*, vol. 67, 2013, pp. 51–57.

ThinkProgress. "Post-shut Down, an Ocean of Outrage Greets Interior's Proposed Changes…" *thinkprogress.org*, 30 Jan. 2019.

Thomas, Lauren. "Cyber Monday Becomes Largest Online Shopping Day in US History." *CNBC*, 28 Nov. 2017, www.cnbc.com/2017/11/28/a-record-6-point-59-billion-spent-online-on-cyber-monday-making-us-history.html.

Thompson, Derek. "The Death of Music Sales." *The Atlantic*, 25 Jan. 2015, www.theatlantic.com/business/archive/2015/01/buying-music-is-so-over/384790.

Thompson, Penny. "The Digital Natives as Learners: Technology Use Patterns and Approaches to Learning." *Computers & Education*, vol. 65, 2013, pp. 12–33.

Thomson, S., B. L. J. De, and Australian Council for Educational Research. *Preparing Australian Students for the Digital World: Results from the PISA 2009 Digital Reading Literacy Assessment.* ACER Press, 2012.

Tidwell, Jenifer, Charles Brewer, and Aynne Valencia. *Designing Interfaces: Patterns for Effective Interaction Design.* 3rd ed., O'Reilly Media, 2020.

"Time to Close the Digital Divide." *Financial Times*, 22 May 2020, www.ft.com/content/df6d1cd2-9b6e-11ea-adb1-529f96d8a00b.

Titcomb, James. "Instagram Is Changing Its Iconic Logo—Here's Why." *The Telegraph*, 11 May 2016, www.telegraph.co.uk/technology/2016/05/11/instagram-is-changing-its-iconic-logo–heres-why/.

Tomar, David A. "11 Reasons We're Too Dumb to Resist Clickbait." *The Quad*, The Best Schools, 5 Aug. 2018, thebestschools.org/magazine/why-clickbait-works/.

Toomey, Warren. "The Strange Birth and Long Life of Unix." *IEEE Spectrum*, 28 Nov. 2011, spectrum.ieee.org/tech-history/cyberspace/the-strange-birth-and-long-life-of-unix.

"Top 10 iPhone Apps for People Who Are Deaf or Hard of Hearing." *Accessible Technology Coalition.* AT Coalition, 2014, atcoalition.org/news/top-10-iphone-apps-people-who-are-deaf-or-hard-hearing.

"Top 15 Most Popular Social Networking Sites." *EBizMBA Guide.* EBizMBA, May 2016.

Torr, James D. *Internet Piracy.* Greenhaven, 2004.

Torrisi-Steele, G., and S. Drew. "The Literature Landscape of Blended Learning in Higher Education: The Need for Better Understanding of Academic Blended Practice." *International Journal for Academic Development*, vol. 18, no. 4, 2018, pp. 371–83.

Tran, B. "Machine (Technology) Ethics: The Theoretical and Philosophical Paradigms." *International Journal of Technoethics*, vol. 7, no. 2, 2016, pp. 77–99.

Trepte, Sabine, and Leonard Reinecke, editors. *Privacy Online: Perspectives on Privacy and Self-Disclosure in the Social Web.* Springer, 2011.

Tripathi, Nishith D., and Jeffrey H. Reed. *Cellular Communications: A Comprehensive and Practical Guide.* Wiley-IEEE Press, 2014.

Trivedi, Mayank. "Digital Libraries: Functionality, Usability, Accessibility." *Library Philosophy and Practice,* 2010, digitalcommons.unl.edu/libphilprac/381.

Trotman, Andrew, and Katherine Rushton. "Facebook Mined Private Messages to Advertisers, Lawsuit Claims." *The Telegraph.* The Telegraph Media Group, 2 Jan. 2014, www.telegraph.co.uk/technology/facebook/10548196/Facebook-mined-private-messages-to-advertisers-lawsuit-claims.html.

Trottier, D. "Coming to Terms with Social Media Monitoring: Uptake and Early Assessment." *Crime, Media, Culture,* vol. 11, no. 3, 2015, pp. 317–33, search.ebscohost.com/login.aspx?direct=true&db=sxi&an=111190330&site=ehost-live.

Troussas, C. C., and M. M. Virvou. "Information Theoretic Clustering for an Intelligent Multilingual Tutoring System." *International Journal of Emerging Technologies in Learning,* vol. 8, 2013, pp. 55–61.

Tryon, C. "Writing and Citizenship: Using Blogs to Teach First-Year Composition." *Pedagogy,* vol. 6, 2006, pp. 128–32.

Tucker, C. "Creating A Safe Digital Space." *Educational Leadership,* vol. 73, no. 2, 2015, pp. 82–83.

Tucker, C. R., T. Wycoff, T., and J. T. Green. *Blended Learning in Action: A Practical Guide Toward Sustainable Change.* Corwin, 2017.

Tufekci, Zeynep. "Can You See Me Now? Audience and Disclosure Regulation in Online Social Network Sites." *Bulletin of Science, Technology & Society,* vol. 28, no. 1, 2008, pp. 20–36, doi:10.1177/0270467607311484.

"Tumblr Statistics, User, Demographics and Facts for 2021." *Saas Scout.org,* saasscout.com/statistics/tumblr-statistics/#Tumblr_Statistics_User_Demographics_And_Facts_For_2021.

Turkle, Sherry. *Alone Together: Why We Expect More from Technology and Less from Each Other.* Basic Books, 2017.

___. "Whither Psychoanalysis in Computer Culture." *Psychoanalytic Psychology,* vol. 21, no. 1, 2004, pp. 16–30.

"Turkle, Sherry." *MIT,* sherryturkle.mit.edu.

Tuten, Tracy L., and Michael R, Solomon. *Social Media Marketing.* Pearson, 2013.

"A Tutorial on Data Representation: Integers, Floating-Point Numbers, and Characters." *Nanyang Technological University Singapore,* Jan. 2014, www3.ntu.edu.sg/home/ehchua/programming/java/datarepresentation.html.

Tynes, B. "Internet Safety Gone Wild? Sacrificing The Educational and Psychosocial Benefits of Online Social Environments." *Journal of Adolescent Research,* vol. 22, 2007, pp. 575–84.

"The Ultimate List of Cyber Security Statistics for 2019." *PurpleSec,* 2019, purplesec.us/resources/cyber-security-statistics/.

"U.S. Charges Five Chinese Military Hackers for Cyber Espionage Against U.S. Corporations and a Labor Organization for Commercial Advantage." *US Department of Justice,* 19 May 2014, www.justice.gov/opa/pr/us-charges-five-chinese-military-hackers-cyber-espionage-against-us-corporations-and-labor.

Ucciferri, Frannie. "Parents' Ultimate Guide to Discord." *Common Sense Media,* 1 Mar. 2020, www.common-sensemedia.org/blog/parents-ultimate-guide-to-discord.

University of Wisconsin-Milwaukee. "Does Facebook Make You Lonely?" *ScienceDaily,* 9 Oct. 2014.

Upadhyay, P. "Climate Change as Ecological Colonialism: Dilemma of Innocent Victims. " *Himalayan Journal of Sociology and Anthropology,* vol. 7, 2016, pp. 111–40.

US Census Bureau. "The 2007 Statistical Abstract: 1143—Households with Computers and Internet Access: 1998 and 2003." *US Census Bureau,* 2007, census.gov.

US Department of Education, Office of Special Education and Rehabilitation Services. *A New Era: Revitalizing Special Education for Children and Their Families.* US Department of Education, 2002.

US Department of Homeland Security. "Digital Footprint: Assessing Risk & Impact." *US Department of Homeland Security,* 18 Feb. 2014, www.urmc.rochester.edu/MediaLibraries/URMCMedia/flrtc/documents/IT-20140218_Digital-Footprint.pdf.

US Department of Justice. "OIP Gives FOIA Implementation Advice to Other Nations." *FOIA Post*, 12 Dec. 2002, www.justice.gov/archive/ oip/foiapost/2002foiapost30.htm.

___. *1999 Report on Cyberstalking: A New Challenge for Law Enforcement & Industry*. DOJ, 1999.

"User Interface Design Basics." *Usability.gov*, www.usability.gov/what-and-why/user-interface-design.html.

"Using Technology to Support Education Reform—September 1993." 2001, ed.gov.

V., Carlotta. "What Is the Current State of Microscale 3D Printing?" *3DNatives*, 16 Apr. 2020, www.3dnatives. com/en/what-is-the-current-state-of-microscale-3d-printing/.

Vacca, John R., editor. *Cloud Computing Security: Foundations and Challenges*. CRC Press, 2017.

___. *Network and System Security*. 2nd ed., Elsevier, 2014.

Vaidhyanathan, Siva. *The Googlization of Everything (And Why We Should Worry)*. U of California P, 2011.

Valiant, Leslie. *Probably Approximately Correct: Nature's Algorithms for Learning and Prospering in a Complex World*. Basic, 2013.

Valkenberg, Patti M., and Jessica Taylor Piotrowski. *Plugged In: How Media Attract and Affect Youth*. Yale UP, 2017.

Vanacker, Bastiaan, and Don Heider. *Ethics for a Digital Age*. Peter Lang, 2016.

Vanhemert, Kyle. "Leap Motion's Augmented-Reality Computing Looks Stupid Cool." *Wired*. Condé Nast, 7 July 2015, www.wired.com/2015/07/ leap-motion-glimpse-at-the-augmented-reality-desktop-of-the-future/.

Vanlehn, K. "The Relative Effectiveness of Human Tutoring, Intelligent Tutoring Systems, and Other Tutoring Systems." *Educational Psychologist*, vol. 46, 2011, pp. 197–221.

Varghese, M. E., and M. C. Pistole. "College Student Cyberbullying: Self-Esteem, Depression, Loneliness, And Attachment." *Journal of College Counseling*, vol. 20, no. 1, 2017, pp. 7–21, doi:10.1002/jocc.12055.

Varnelis, Kazys, editor. *Networked Publics*. MIT Press, 2008.

"Victims of Identity Theft, 2016." *Bureau of Justice Statistics*. bjs.gov, 2019, www.bjs.gov/index. cfm?ty=pbdetail&iid=6467.

Vigil, T. T., and H. D. Wu. "Facebook Users' Engagement and Perceived Life Satisfaction." *Media and Communication*, vol. 3, no. 1, 2015, pp. 5–16, search.ebscohost.com/login.aspx?direct=true&db=cms&an= 111212352&site=ehost-live.

Vince, John. *Introduction to Virtual Reality*. Springer-Verlag London, 2004.

Vogels, Emily A., et al. "53% of Americans Say the Internet Has Been Essential during the COVID-19 Outbreak." *Pew Research Center*, 30 Apr. 2020, www.pewresearch.org/ internet/2020/04/30/53-of-americans-say-the-internet-has-been-essential-during-the-covid-19-outbreak/.

Von Glasersfeld, E. "Introduction: Aspects of Constructivism." *Constructivism: Theory, Perspectives, and Practice*, edited by C. T. Fosnot, Teachers College Press, 1996.

"VR Futures: Where Will Virtual Reality Take You?" *EandT*, 15 Mar. 2016, eandt.theiet.org/content/articles/2016/03/vr-futures-where-will-virtual-reality-take-you/.

Vromen, Ariadne. *Digital Citizenship and Political Engagement*. Palgrave Macmillan, 2017.

Wacholtz, Larry. *Monetizing Entertainment: An Insider's Handbook for Careers in the Entertainment and Music Industry*. CRC Press, 2016.

Wager, Karen A., Frances W. Lee, and John P. Glaser. *Health Care Information Systems: A Practical Approach for Health Care Management*. 4th ed., Jossey-Bass, 2017.

Wakabayashi, Daisuke. "Legal Shield for Social Media Is Targeted by Lawmakers." *The New York Times*, 28 May 2020, www.nytimes.com/2020/05/28/business/section-230-internet-speech.html.

Wall, D. *Cybercrime: The Transformation of Crime in the Information Age*. Polity, 2007.

Wall, D. S., and M. L. Williams. "Policing Cybercrime: Networked and Social Media Technologies and the Challenges for Policing." *Policing and Society*, vol. 23, 2013, pp. 409–12, search.ebscohost.com/login.aspx? direct=true&db=sih&an=91557437.

Wall, David. *Cybercrimes: The Transformation of Crime in the Information Age*. Polity, 2007.

Wang, Yongtian, Qingmin Huang, and Yuxin Peng, editors. *Image and Graphics Technologies and Applications*. Springer Singapore, 2019.

Wankel, C., and P. Blessinger. *Increasing Student Engagement and Retention in E-Learning Environments: Web 2.0 and Blended Learning Technologies.* Emerald, 2013.

Ward, Tom. "The Biggest Gamer in the World Breaks Down Twitch for Us." *Forbes*, 1 May 2018, www.forbes.com/sites/tomward/2018/05/01/the-biggest-gamer-in-the-world-breaks-down-twitch-for-us/#36132d0d5bb5.

Wardley, L. L., and C. Mang. "Student Observations: Introducing iPads into University Classrooms." *Education & Information Technologies*, vol. 21, no. 6, 2016, pp. 1715–32.

Warren, Christina. "The Evolution of Mac OS, From 1984 to Mountain Lion." *Mashable*, 17 Feb. 2012, mashable.com/2012/02/17/mac-os-timeline/#KKsyA8f26qqR.

Warren, Tom. "Windows Turns 30: A Visual History." *Verge*, 19 Nov. 2015, www.theverge.com/2015/11/19/9759874/microsoft-windows-visual-history-30-years.

Waterman, C. "Online Safety Still Not Good Enough but Who Cares Enough to Act?" *Education Journal*, 2014, pp. 17–18.

Watson, J. A., and L. L. Pecchioni. "Digital Natives and Digital Media in the College Classroom: Assignment Design and Impacts on Student Learning." *Educational Media International*, vol. 48, no. 4, 2011, pp. 307–20.

Wayne L., A., and L. A. Johnson. "Current United States Presidential Views on Cyber Security and Computer Crime with Corresponding Department of Justice Enforcement Guidelines." *Journal of International Diversity*, 2011, pp. 116–19, search.ebscohost.com/login.aspx?direct=true&db=sih&an=72324633.

Weber, Thomas E. "How Microsoft Excel Changed the World." *Business Insider.* Business Insider, Inc., 28 Dec. 2010, www.businessinsider.com/how-microsoft-excel-changed-the-world-2010-12.

Wehmeyer, M. L. "Universal Design for Learning, Access to the General Education Curriculum, and Students with Mild Mental Retardation." *Exceptionality*, vol. 14, 2006, pp. 225–35.

Wei, L., and D. Hindman. "Does the Digital Divide Matter More? Comparing the Effects of New Media and Old Media Use on the Education-Based Knowledge Gap." *Mass Communication & Society*, vol. 14, 2011, pp. 216–35, search.ebscohost.com/login.aspx?direct=true&db=sih&AN=59131821.

Weis, Robert, and Brittany C. Cerankosky. "Effects of Video-Game Ownership on Young Boys' Academic and Behavioral Functioning: A Randomized, Controlled Study." *Psychological Science*, vol. 21, 2010, pp. 463–70.

Weisburg, H. K. "Knowledge in Bloom." *School Librarian's Workshop*, vol. 33, 2012, p. 19.

Weiss, Daniel. "Cyber And Online Harassment." *Myrocktoday.org*, 11 Apr. 2007.

Weiss, Patrice L. (Tamar), Emily A. Keshner, and Mindy F. Levin, editors. *Virtual Reality for Physical and Motor Rehabilitation.* Springer-Verlag New York, 2014.

Weizenbaum, J. *Computer Power and Human Reason: From Judgement to Calculation.* W. H. Freeman, 1976.

Wells, Chris. *The Civic Organization and the Digital Citizen: Communicating Engagement in a Networked Age.* Oxford UP, 2015.

Wells, J., and M. Lewis. *Internet Access in U.S. Public Schools and Classrooms: 1994–2005.* US Department of Education, 2006.

Wenger, Etienne. *Communities of Practice: Learning, Meaning, and Identity.* Cambridge UP, 1998.

Wenger, Etienne, Richard A. McDermott, and William Snyder. *Cultivating Communities of Practice: A Guide to Managing Knowledge.* Harvard Business School, 2002.

Werbach, K., and D. Hunter. *For the Win: How Game Thinking Can Revolutionize Your Business.* Wharton Digital Press, 2012.

Werner, A. "Moving Forward: A Feminist Analysis of Mobile Music Streaming." *Culture Unbound: Journal of Current Cultural Research*, vol. 7, 2015, pp. 197–213.

Weyers, Benjamin, et al., editors. *The Handbook of Formal Methods in Human-Computer Interaction.* Springer International, 2017.

"What Is Copyright?" *Copyright.gov*, 2021, www.copyright.gov/what-is-copyright.

"What Is Creative Commons?" *Smartcopying*, 2021, smartcopying.edu.au/what-is-creative-commons.

"What Is a Creative Commons License?" *Copyright Alliance*, 2021, copyrightalliance.org/faqs/what-is-creative-commons-license.

"What Is Cyberbullying." *StopBullying.gov*, 21 July 2020. www.stopbullying.gov/cyberbullying/what-is-it.

"What Is a Deepfake?" *The Economist*, 7 Aug. 2019, www.economist.com/the-economist-explains/2019/08/07/what-is-a-deepfake.

"What Is Digital Economy?" *Deloitte*, www2.deloitte.com/mt/en/pages/technology/articles/mt-what-is-digital-economy.html.

"What Is Digital Libraries?" *IGI Global*, igi-global.com/dictionary/fol-learning-knowledge-discovery-documents/7657.

"What Is Discord?" *Discord*, discord.com/safety/360044149331-What-is-Discord.

"What Is the History of Microsoft Windows?" *Indiana University Knowledge Base*, 18 Jan. 2018, kb.iu.edu/d/abwa.

"What Is Intellectual Property?" *Ohio University*, www.ohio.edu/people/tl303308/intellectual-property1.html.

"What Is Pharming?" *Kaspersky Lab*, usa.kaspersky.com/internet-security-center/definitions/pharming#.WDXNKLIrJQI.

What Is a Screen Scraper? wiseGEEK, www.wisegeek.com/what-is-a-screen-scraper.htm.

"What Is Unix?" *Indiana University Knowledge Base*, 28 Nov. 2018, test.kb.iu.edu/kmssc-snd/d/agat.

"What Should Parents Know About Twitch?" *Common Sense Media*, 2020, www.commonsensemedia.org/social-media/what-should-parents-know-about-twitch.

"What We Do." *Creative Commons*, 2021, creativecommons.org/about.

"What's New in Excel 2013." *Office*. Microsoft, support.office.com/en-us/article/What-s-new-in-Excel-2013-1cbc42cd-bfaf-43d7-9031-5688ef1392fd?CorrelationId=e75af659-e5a8-4d3c-a810-9a8017781cf5&ui=en-US&rs=en-US&ad=US.

White, Michele. *Touch Screen Theory: Digital Devices and Feelings*. MIT Press, 2022.

Whitman, James Q. "Two Western Cultures of Privacy: Dignity versus Liberty." *Yale Law Journal*, vol. 113, no. 6, Apr. 2004, pp. 1151–221.

Whitt, Phillip. *Beginning Pixlr Editor: Learn How to Edit Digital Photos Using This Free Web-Based App*. Apress, 2017.

Whittaker, Z. "At Hearing, Facebook's Zuckerberg Rejects Law to Protect Privacy of Children." *ZDNet*, 10 Apr. 2018, www.zdnet.com/article/at-hearing-zuckerberg-rejects-law-to-protect-the-privacy-of-children/.

Whittaker, Zack. "Atlanta, Hit by Ransomware Attack, Also Fell Victim to Leaked NSA Exploits." *ZDNet*, 27 Mar. 2018, www.zdnet.com/article/atlanta-hit-by-ransomware-attack-also-fell-victim-to-leaked-nsa-exploits/.

Wiburg, K. M. "An Historical Perspective on Instructional Design: Is It Time to Exchange Skinner's Teaching Machine for Dewey's Toolbox?" *Internettime.com*.

Wierzel, Kimberly L. "If You Can't Beat Them, Join Them: Data Aggregators and Financial Institutions." *North Carolina Banking Institute*, vol. 5, no. 457, 2001.

Wiesinger, S., and R. Beliveau. *Digital Literacy: A Primer on Media, Identity, and the Evolution of Technology*. Peter Lang, 2016.

Wijekumar, K. "Implementing Web-Based Intelligent Tutoring Systems in K-12 Settings: A Case Study on Approach and Challenges." *Journal of Educational Technology Systems*, vol. 35, 2006, pp. 193–208.

Williams, Joe. *Entertainment on the Net*. Que, 1995.

Williams, M. L., A. Edwards, A. Housley, et al. "Policing Cyber-Neighbourhoods: Tension Monitoring and Social Media Networks." *Policing & Society*, vol. 23, no. 4, 2013, pp. 461–81, search.ebscohost.com/login.aspx?direct=true&db=sxi&AN=91557440&site=ehost-live.

Williams, Rhiannon. "Apple iOS: A Brief History." *Telegraph*, 17 Sept. 2015, www.telegraph.co.uk/technology/apple/11068420/Apple-iOS-a-brief-history.html.

Wilson, B. "Innovators Ignite Revolution in Desktop Publishing and Scholastic Media." *Communication: Journalism Education Today*, vol. 47, no. 4, 2014, pp. 3–17.

Wilton, Paul, and Jeremy McPeak. *Beginning JavaScript*. 4th ed., John Wiley & Sons, 2011.

"Windows 10 Privacy Settings: How to Stop Microsoft from Spying on You." *The Star*, 16 Feb. 2019.

Winer, L. R., and M. A. Carrère. "Qualitative Information System for Data Management." *Qualitative Sociology*, vol. 14, no. 3, 1991, pp. 245–62.

Winter, Mick. *Scan Me—Everybody's Guide to the Magical World of QR Codes*. Westsong, 2011.

Wise, Donny. *Using Apple Keynote for the Classroom*. Lulu.com, 2015.

Wohn, D. Y., C. T. Carr, and R. A. Hayes. "How Affective Is A 'Like'? The Effect of Paralinguistic Digital Affordances on Perceived Social Support." *CyberPsychology Behavior and Social Networking*, vol. 19, no. 9, 2016, pp. 562–66, doi:10.1089/cyber.2016.0162.

Wolak, J., D. Finkelhor, K. J. Mitchell, et al. "Online 'Predators' and Their Victims: Myths, Realities, and Implications for Prevention and Treatment." *American Psychologist*, vol. 63, 2008, pp. 111–28.

Wolverton, Troy. "Snapchat Users Hate the Redesign So Much, It Could Have Turned Away Millions of Users." *Business Insider*, 1 May 2018, www.businessinsider.com/snaps-daily-active-users-flatlined-then-fell-in-the-first-quarter-2018-5.

Wood, David. *Interface Design: An Introduction to Visual Communication in UI Design*. Fairchild Books, 2014.

Wood, M., H. Center, and S. C. Parenteau. "Social Media Addiction and Psychological Adjustment: Religiosity and Spirituality in the Age of Social Media." *Mental Health, Religion & Culture*, vol. 19, no. 9, 2016, pp. 972–83, doi:10.1080/13674676.2017.1300791.

Woollaston, Victoria. "WannaCry Ransomware: What Is It and How to Protect Yourself." *Wired*, 22 May 2017, www.wired.co.uk/article/wannacry-ransomware-virus-patch.

"Word: Write On." *Office*. Microsoft, 15 July 2015, products.office.com/en-US/word?legRedir=true&CorrelationId=2a80dbed-2adc-4646-bcf2-439ad39b8911.

"World Summit on the Information Society." *WSIS Stocktaking*, 2005, www.itu.int/wsis/docs2/tunis/off/5.pdf.

"Worldwide Spending on Augmented and Virtual Reality Expected to Reach $18.8 Billion in 2020, According to IDC." *IDC*, 27 Nov. 2019, www.idc.com/getdoc.jsp?containerId=prUS45679219.

Wroot, Jonathan, and Andy Willis. *DVD, Blu-ray & Beyond: Navigating Formats and Platforms within Media Consumption*. Palgrave MacMillan, 2017.

Wu, Jinsong, Sundeep Rangan, and Honggang Zhang, editors. *Green Communications: Theoretical Fundamentals, Algorithms and Applications*. CRC Press, 2013.

Wuerthele, Mike. "Apple Unveils iPadOS, Adding Features Specifically to iPad." *AppleInsider*, 2 June 2019, appleinsider.com/articles/19/06/03/apple-supplements-ios-13-with-new-tablet-specific-ipad-os-branch.

"XML Tutorial." *W3Schools*, 13 Aug. 2015, www.w3schools.com/xml/.

Xu, Duanyi. *Multi-Dimensional Optical Storage*. Springer Singapore, 2016.

Yam, Caleb. "'Deplatformed': Trump's Social Media Suspension." *The Science Survey*, 21 Mar. 2021, the-sciencesurvey.com/editorial/2021/03/21/deplatformed-trumps-social-media-suspension/.

Yao, Jiewen, and Vincent Zimmer. *Building Secure Firmware: Armoring the Foundation of the Platform*. Apress, 2020.

Yar, Majid. *Cybercrime and Society*. SAGE, 2006.

Yates, S. "Oral and Literate Aspects of Computer Conferencing." *Computer-Mediated Communication: Linguistic, Social, and Cross-Cultural Perspectives*, edited by S. Herring, John Benjamins Press, 1996, pp. 29–46.

Ybarra, Michele L., and Kimberly J, Mitchell. "How Risky Are Social Networking Sites? A Comparison of Places Online Where Youth Sexual Solicitation and Harassment Occurs." *Pediatrics*, vol. 121, no. 2, 2008, pp. e350–e357.

Yeung, Ken. "LinkedIn Now Has 400M Users, but Only 25% of Them Use It Monthly." *VentureBeat*, 29 Oct. 2015.

Young, A., A. Young, and H. Fullwood. "Adolescent Online Victimization." *Prevention Researcher*, vol. 14, 2007, pp. 8–9.

Young-Joo Lee, and Ji-Young Park. "Identification of Future Signal Based on the Quantitative and Qualitative Text Mining: A Case Study on Ethical Issues in Artificial Intelligence." *Quality and Quantity*, vol. 52, no. 2, 2018, pp. 653–67.

"Your Rights under Section 504 of the Rehabilitation Act." *Fact Sheet*. US Department of Health and Human Services Office for Civil Rights, 2006, www.hhs.gov/ocr/civilrights/resources/factsheets/504.pdf.

Youth Risk Behavior Surveillance—United States, 2017. *Centers for Disease Control and Prevention*. US Department of Health and Human Services, 15 June 2018, www.cdc.gov/healthyyouth/data/yrbs/pdf/2017/ss6708.pdf.

Yurieff, Kaya. "TikTok Is the Latest Social Network Sensation." *CNN*, 21 Nov. 2018, edition.cnn.com/2018/11/21/tech/tiktok-app/index.html.

Zafarani, Reza, and Mohammad Ali Abbasi. *Social Media Mining: An Introduction*. Cambridge UP, 2014.

Zager, Michael. *Music Production: A Manual for Producers, Composers, Arrangers, and Students*. Rowman & Littlefield, 2021.

Zajácz, Rita. "WikiLeaks and the Problem of Anonymity: A Network Control Perspective." *Media, Culture & Society*, vol. 35, no. 4, 2013, pp. 487–503, doi:10.1177/016344371348379.

Zala, Paul. *How to Make Great Music Mashups*. Routledge, 2018.

Zdziarski, J. *Ending Spam: Bayesian Content Filtering and the Art of Statistical Language Classification*. No Starch Press, 2005.

Zen, E-an. "Science Literacy and Why It Is Important." *Journal of Geological Education*, 2018, www.tandfonline.com/doi/abs/10.5408/0022-1368-38.5.463?journalCode=ujge19.

Zetlin, Minda. "Want to Make Facebook Stop Tracking Your Location When Not in Use? Here's How." *Inc.*, 22 Feb. 2019.

Zetter, Kim. *Countdown to Zero Day: Stuxnet and the Launch of the World's First Digital Weapon*. Broadway, 2014.

Zhao, Pengfei, et al., editors. *Advanced Graphic Communications and Media Technologies*. Springer Singapore, 2017.

Ziden, Azidah Abu, Fatariah Zakaria, and Ahmad Nizam Othman. "Effectiveness of AutoCAD 3D Software as a Learning Support Tool." *International Journal of Emerging Technologies in Learning (iJET)*, vol. 7, no. 2, 2012, pp. 57–60.

Ziobro, Paul, and Jeff Horwitz. "Facebook Suspends Donald Trump for at Least Two Years." *The Wall Street Journal*, 4 June 2021, www.wsj.com/articles/facebook-suspends-donald-trump-for-two-years-11622825480.

Zittrain, Jonathan. "What the Publisher Can Teach the Patient: Intellectual Property and Privacy in an Era of Trusted Privication." (Symposium: Cyberspace and Privacy: A New Legal Paradigm?) *Stanford Law Review*, vol. 52, no. 5, May 2000, pp. 1201–50.

Zuckerberg, Mark. "Building Global Community." *Facebook*, 16 Feb. 2017, www.facebook.com/notes/mark-zuckerberg/building-global-community/10103508221158471/.

Zydney, J., B. A. Mannheimer, and T. Hasselbring. "Finding the Optimal Guidance for Enhancing Anchored Instruction." *Interactive Learning Environments*, vol. 22, no. 5, 2014.

INDEX

U

V